D1605319

5/4/90

To Dr. and Linda Diamond,
With your talents, the luck of the Irish, and
the grace of God, hopefully we will be needing the
Apgar scoring proceduce for our newborn infant!
Virginia Apgar is one of the many notable
women whos biography appears in the book.
Enjoy the book.

Fondly,
Linda Quinn

# Past and Promise

## Lives of New Jersey Women

## Editor-in-Chief

Joan N. Burstyn

## Introduction

Suzanne Lebsock

## Associate Editors

Delight Wing Dodyk      Carolyn DeSwarte Gifford      Carmela Ascolese Karnoutsos

## Managing Editors

Caroline Wheeler Jacobus      Gayle Samuels

**Bibliographic Editor**                                                    **Copy Editor**

Patricia Smith Butcher                                                      Lois Krieger

## Photographic Editors

Doris Friedensohn      Ferris Olin      Barbara Rubin

## Book Design and Layout

Linda C. Quinn

# Past and Promise

## Lives of New Jersey Women

## THE WOMEN'S PROJECT OF NEW JERSEY INC.

The Scarecrow Press, Inc.    Metuchen, N.J., & London    1990

British Library Cataloguing-in-Publication data available

**Library of Congress Cataloging-in-Publication Data**

Past and promise : lives of New Jersey women / compiled by the Women's
   Project of New Jersey, Inc. ; Joan Burstyn, editor-in-chief.
       p.   cm.
   Includes bibliographies and index.
   ISBN 0-8108-2201-6
   1. Women—New Jersey—History.   2. Women—New Jersey—
   Biography.
   I. Burstyn, Joan N.   II. Women's Project of New Jersey.
   HQ1438.N5P37     1990
   305.4'09749—dc20                       89-34946
                                                 CIP

# CONTENTS

# KEY TO ABBREVIATIONS

*Books and Journals*

| | |
|---|---|
| *DAB* | Johnson, Allen, ed. *Dictionary of American Biography.* 20 vols. New York: Charles Scribner's Sons, 1928–37. *Supplement.* 7 vols. New York: Charles Scribner's Sons, 1944–81. |
| *LCR* | American Association of University Women. New Jersey Division. *Ladies at the Crossroads: Eighteenth-Century Women of New Jersey.* Morristown, NJ: Compton Press, 1978. |
| *NAW* | James, Edward T., ed. *Notable American Women, 1607–1950: A Biographical Dictionary.* 3 vols. Cambridge, MA: Harvard University Press, 1971. |
| *NAW-MP* | Sicherman, Barbara, and Carol Hurd Green, eds. *Notable American Women: The Modern Period.* Cambridge, MA: Harvard University Press, 1980. |
| *NJHSP* | *New Jersey Historical Society. Proceedings.* |
| *WOTC* | Willard, Frances E., and Mary A. Livermore, eds. *A Woman of the Century.* Buffalo, NY: C. W. Moulton, 1893. |

*Locations*

| | |
|---|---|
| C-YU | Beinecke Rare Book and Manuscript Library, Yale University, New Haven, CT |
| DC-LC | Library of Congress, Washington, D.C. |
| M-SC | Sophia Smith Collection, Smith College, Northampton, MA |
| M-SL | Arthur and Elizabeth Schlesinger Library on the History of Women in America, Radcliffe College, Cambridge, MA |
| NJ-BCL | Burlington County Library, Mount Holly, NJ |
| NJ-BHS | Bordentown Historical Society, Bordentown, NJ |
| NJ-BPL | Bloomfield Public Library, Bloomfield, NJ |
| NJ-CPL | Cranford Public Library, Cranford, NJ |
| NJ-DC | Mabel Smith Douglass Library, Douglass College, New Brunswick, NJ |
| NJ-DU | United Methodist Church Archives, Drew University, Madison, NJ |
| NJ-EOPL | East Orange Public Library, East Orange, NJ |
| NJ-EPL | Elizabeth Public Library, Elizabeth, NJ |

| | |
|---|---|
| NJ-GCHS | Gloucester County Historical Society, Woodbury, NJ |
| NJ-GSC | Savitz Library, Glassboro State College, Glassboro, NJ |
| NJ-HS | New Jersey Historical Society, Newark, NJ |
| NJ-IPL | Irvington Public Library, Irvington, NJ |
| NJ-JCPL | Jersey City Public Library, Jersey City, NJ |
| NJ-KC | Kean College of New Jersey, Union, NJ |
| NJ-MadPL | Madison Public Library, Madison, NJ |
| NJ-MaPL | Maplewood Memorial Library, Maplewood, NJ |
| NJ-MCL | Morris County Free Library, Whippany, NJ |
| NJ-MO | Joint Free Public Library of Morristown and Morris Township, Morristown, NJ |
| NJ-MoCHA | Monmouth County Historical Association, Freehold, NJ |
| NJ-MPL | Montclair Free Public Library, Montclair, NJ |
| NJ-NJSL | New Jersey State Library, Trenton, NJ |
| NJ-NPL | Newark Public Library, Newark, NJ |
| NJ-PCHS | Passaic County Historical Society, Paterson, NJ |
| NJ-PHS | Historical Society of Princeton, Princeton, NJ |
| NJ-PPL | Plainfield Free Public Library, Plainfield, NJ |
| NJ-PTS | Speer Library, Princeton Theological Seminary, Princeton, NJ |
| NJ-PU | Special Collections, Firestone Library, Princeton University, Princeton, NJ |
| NJ-RU | Special Collections and Archives, Alexander Library, Rutgers University, New Brunswick, NJ |
| NJ-SCHS | Salem County Historical Society, Salem, NJ |
| NJ-UMDNJ | G. F. Smith Library, University of Medicine and Dentistry of New Jersey, Newark, NJ |
| NJ-UTPL | Union Township Public Library, Union, NJ |
| NY-CU | Butler Library, Columbia University, New York, NY |
| NY-HS | New York Historical Society, New York, NY |
| NY-PL | New York Public Library, New York, NY |
| NYPL-LC | Performing Arts Research Center, New York Public Library, Lincoln Center, New York, NY |
| NYPL-SC | Schomburg Center for Research in Black Culture, New York Public Library, New York, NY |
| NY-VC | Library, Vassar College, Poughkeepsie, NY |
| P-FLP | Free Library of Philadelphia, Philadelphia, PA |
| P-HC | James P. Magill Library, Haverford College, Haverford, PA |
| P-HSP | Historical Society of Pennsylvania, Philadelphia, PA |
| P-SC | Friends Historical Library, Swarthmore College, Swarthmore, PA |
| V-HS | Vermont Historical Society, Montpellier, VT |

# FOREWORD

IN 1984 A NEW STATEWIDE effort was launched. The Women's Project of New Jersey was initiated to increase awareness of the role of women in the history and culture of our state. That desire propelled our original project, the creation of this first comprehensive reference volume on the history of women in New Jersey, and inspired our traveling photographic exhibit also titled, "Past and Promise: Lives of New Jersey Women."

The idea for this book was introduced by Barbara Little Lombardi when she brought *Our Hidden Heritage: Pennsylvania Women in History* to the attention of several colleagues. Diana Simon, director of the Mendham Free Public Library, recognized the need for a similar book on New Jersey women, offered the support of the library, and asked me to recruit and head a committee which would produce such a work. In November 1984, the New Jersey Women's Project was created. Historians, editors, educators, writers, fund raisers, librarians, archivists, and women's studies faculty were attracted to the project which met at Drew University. Work on developing a list of candidates for inclusion in the book began and suggestions were solicited from a variety of sources. The magnitude of the task that lay ahead, however, became obvious very soon; it was beyond the staff and budget of a small local library. So with gratitude for its birth place, the New Jersey Women's Project severed ties with the Mendham Free Public Library and, in July 1985, became a self-sustaining tax-exempt corporation called the Women's Project of New Jersey, Inc. (WPNJ).

Having conceptualized the reference volume, the original board (now the Board of Trustees) created an Editorial Board, headed by Joan Burstyn, to refine and execute the book. Work began on subject selection and we simultaneously sought writers to produce the biographies. The task of recruiting and organizing these volunteer writers/researchers was undertaken primarily by Caroline Jacobus. This force of 248 women and men became the heart of the Women's Project, frequently traveling great distances and spending enormous amounts of time to gather the data required to produce their biographical entries. Like the Board of Trustees and the Editorial Board, the writers were drawn from both the community and the academy.

Thus, individuals who had not previously been involved in writing history worked along with experienced historians in every phase of this project. All WPNJ writers were given a set of guidelines, developed by Jacobus and others, which specified the style and content of the biographies we were seeking. Many writers also attended one of the orientation workshops we offered in the summer and fall of 1985. In the process of exploring the writing of history, we made friends we will long treasure.

After the subject selection and writer recruitment processes were in place, we joined in another venture. The WPNJ participated with Drew University in a state-funded lecture/panel series which brought six nationally known scholars in the field of women's biography to Drew University in the fall of 1985 and offered twelve panels of WPNJ writers to various New Jersey audiences in the spring of 1986. The brainchild of Wendy Kolmar, director of Women's Studies, Drew University, working with Delight Dodyk of the Drew History Department and the WPNJ, the series offered our writers an opportunity to meet with and discuss the problems of biography with well-known biographers. In addition to disseminating our research, the panel programs provided a format and a speakers pool for numerous other WPNJ presentations.

In doing a state-based history we were confronted with several problems. Who is a New Jersey woman? How should we select our subjects from the more than 1,000 women brought to our attention? How should we organize the volume? And how should we define the time span of our research?

Our decisions were informed by two major concerns: first, would a subject enhance our understanding of what it has meant to be a New Jersey woman during the past four centuries and second, was enough information available to produce a biographical essay? To fully explore the diverse experience of New Jersey women, the editors chose to include those subjects whose lives illustrated the role of women in the more private domains of family, community, and religious life, along with those who made outstanding contributions in the public spheres of science, medicine, letters, sports, government, business, education, and the arts. Our goal was to be inclusive rather than exclusive. We interpreted "New Jersey" broadly and decided that a woman need not be born here to be considered, but rather she had to have had an impact on New Jersey or New Jersey had to have had an impact on her. We easily agreed to reach as far back as written and archaeological data would permit. Selecting a closing date was more difficult. We chose 1923 because living subjects born by that date would be at a point in their lives when some evaluation of their careers or contributions could be made. Furthermore, 1923 was the year that Alice Paul, a New Jersey suffragist, wrote the Equal Rights Amendment, an event of significance to our state, nation, and sex.

We did not attempt the exhaustive research effort required to locate every outstanding New Jersey woman. We did, however, contact all of the local historical societies in the state, numerous women's organizations, institutions and experts in the many fields covered in this volume in addition to combing secondary sources. Where we felt more information was needed to help us in the selection process, we sought expert advice. Every subject brought to our attention, even if not included in this volume, is mentioned in our archive at Rutgers, The State University of New Jersey, in New Brunswick.

We divided the book chronologically into four periods so that readers could examine each subject in her historical context. We found it particularly exciting to discover, in this way, the scope and longevity of women's networking. The introduction and the overview essays which precede each period create a unifying narrative framework, provide historical context, and simply tell the story another way. In defining the four eras, we chose dates of significance to both women's history and New Jersey history. Within each period we chose an alphabetical arrangement for easy access.

It took hours and hours of hard work by all to complete this volume and our exhibit in four and one-half years. Certain individuals, however, deserve particular praise for their contributions. Our first funding came from the New Jersey Division on Women through the efforts of former staff member Barbara Irvine. To Irvine and to Valerie Peed of the Geraldine R. Dodge Foundation, who both believed in our vision, we owe particular thanks. To our attorney, Anne E. Aronovitch, of Schenck, Price, Smith & King, who gave us her wisdom along with her legal skills, many thanks. Also, we are most appreciative of the services rendered by our accounting firm, Britton & Eaton Assoc. and specifically by Robert J. DiQuollo and Ellen Adesso, who made an alphabet soup of forms tolerable. To our genealogist, Katherine P. Randall, who guided many of our writers through the complicated web of family genealogies and to Barbara Sicherman, editor of *Notable American Women: The Modern Period,* who was generous in sharing both her time and her expertise, many thanks. We are very grateful to Irene Rich for her copyediting of the pre-liminary drafts of this manuscript and our very special thanks go to Marcia Zweig for her generous help with publicity. We are grateful to Tom Ferguson and Henry Luce of Thomas G. Ferguson Associates for their extraordinary support of our exhibit. Syracuse University has been particularly generous and we especially want to thank Barbara Pauley and Barbara DiPiazza of the School of Education for all of their work in assisting our Editor-in-Chief with the preparation of this manuscript. Countless librarians and historical society archivists have provided invaluable assistance in this effort. In particular we want to thank Frances Osborne and Barbara Smith Irwin, who combed the collections of the New Jersey Historical Society for information on potential subjects, and Virginia Blacketter, who organized some of the preliminary volunteer research. Our thanks also to Victoria Schmidt for our title and to Drew University for providing our meeting space.

We are grateful for the outstanding support provided by the foundations, state agencies, and corporations listed below as well as the many individuals who gave so generously. We also thank our fund-raising committee and particularly the following people who played a special role in our fundraising efforts: Governor and Mrs. Thomas H. Kean, Noreen G. Bodman, Vivian Bull, Barbara M. Caspersen, Barbara Friedland, Margaret Hayes, and Christine T. Whitman.

Having worked on the initial research myself, I know the countless hours that were spent. The following individuals gave generously of their time: Ruth Brucato, Margaret Burdge, Helen Fenske, Janet Fickeissen, Elena Goodman, Lee Hagen, Susan Hanna, Suzanne Head, Sheila Hellman, Caroline Jacobus, Barbara Lombardi, Carolyn Manthey, Robert Meade, Sid Olson, Ann Pason, Edna Reiners, Judith Rousseau, Dorothy Ryan, Jennifer Samuels, Joanne Schwartz, Shirley Stake, Lisa Vincenzi, and Judith Willaman.

We are also grateful to the following individuals who served on our Advisory Board: Gloria Harper Dickinson, Elsalyn P. Drucker, Barbara Little Lombardi, Katharine P. Randall, Catharine R. Stimpson, Diana Simon, and Joan Meyers Weimer.

When Alice Paul was 89 she observed: "I have never doubted equal rights was the right direction. Most reforms, most problems are complicated. But to me there is nothing complicated about ordinary equality. . . ." This work was made possible by the dedication and skill of our writers, by the vision and talent of our Editorial Board, and by the extraordinary commitment of our Board of Trustees. The tie that binds us all is our shared belief in the value of "ordinary equality."

GAYLE SAMUELS
President
WPNJ Board of Trustees

# FOREWORD

# INTRODUCTION

"SOMETHING DREW ME to the state of New Jersey." So said CLARA BARTON of her decision to locate in the Garden State, where in 1852 she began an illustrious humanitarian career. Barton's New Jersey years were dedicated to a crusade to establish free public schools. Later an uncommonly resourceful Civil War nurse, and later still the founder of the American Red Cross, Barton was a heroine in her own time. In our time, she is one of the few women from the American past whose name is widely known.

There should be dozens more. For a very long time, however, most American history—and most New Jersey history, too—was written as though women had never existed. There were two main reasons for this. One was the consensus among historians on what mattered in history: warfare mattered; formal politics mattered; public policy mattered. Because women were for the most part excluded from these things—they were not allowed to serve in the military, vote, or hold office—it made a certain kind of sense to leave them out of history. There was also a second, and less sensible, reason why women were left out, and that was a double standard in the writing of history. Even when the documentary evidence made it clear that women had engaged in politics or had shaped public policy, the typical historian still left them out. If a woman did it, the assumption went, it must have been unimportant by definition. Thus were countless women forgotten.

This book aims to restore some of those women to present memory, to resurrect the life stories of women who by any standard should have been in the textbooks all along. At the same time, and perhaps more important, this book is designed to help us rethink what is significant in history.

From this project's beginnings, the editors proceeded from the conviction that ordinary people are important, that their experience and their contributions are legitimate and intriguing subjects for historical investigation. For this reason, not all the women selected for inclusion were women of unusual achievement. Some, rather, were selected because they were typical or somehow peculiarly illustrative of women's situation. ELIZABETH DAVIS BRICK WORTHINGTON DUNLAP, for example, became momen-

tarily famous when she fled her marriage in 1742. Her husband took out a newspaper ad to warn merchants he would not be responsible for her debts; she responded in kind, claiming she had left to end "the threats and abuses for several years repeatedly offered and done to her." Their war of words signified several facts of married life in Colonial America: that all economic powers were vested in the husband, that the wife was extremely vulnerable if a marriage went wrong, that divorce was well nigh impossible.

Because the Dunlaps took their conflict to the newspapers, we are able to reconstruct a good part of ELIZABETH DUNLAP's story. Every so often some other woman would write an autobiography or keep a diary, in the process opening parts of her world to later generations. SILVIA DUBOIS's autobiography, *Silvia Dubois (Now 116 Years Old): A Biografy of the Slav Who Whipt Her Mistress and Gand Her Fredom*, has given us a remarkable account of the life of a slave who escaped her bondage, was several times a mother, and worked at multiple occupations; at various times she was a domestic, an innkeeper, a hog farmer, and a ferryboat pilot. The labors of farm women, meanwhile, were sometimes sketched in diaries. ABBIE ELIZA MAGEE cleaned, washed, ironed, sewed, churned, gardened, canned, plucked chickens, butchered hogs, and in harvest season cooked massive meals to feed the crews who brought in the crops. "Threshers came," she wrote in 1905. "Seventeen in family."

The inclusion of women like MAGEE in this volume is evidence of a new sensibility in the writing of history that no longer takes women's nonstop labor for granted. To the politics and warfare that once were at the center of historical writing we add childbearing, the building of human relationships, and all the varieties of women's characteristic work—in homes, on farms, in the silk mills, in offices and stores. All of these activities have histories of their own. All of them were central to the development of New Jersey.

At the same time, the majority of women in this book are here because they did something unusual. (Not that this typically freed them from women's work.) The sweep of their achievements is impressive. In these pages there are athletes, politicians, and tycoons. There are pioneers in every profession and artists of every description. There is the occasional felon. There are philanthropists, missionaries, and numerous reformers. One New Jersey woman founded a new religious denomination. Another developed the cultivated blueberry. Still another was the first woman to drive an automobile from coast to coast, this in 1909 when there were no road maps and in some places no roads. One of the purposes of women's history is to awaken in people living today an expanded sense of what women can be and do. New Jersey's past provides ample inspiration.

This is not to say that women all along, if they had sufficient pluck, could do whatever they aspired to do. It was possible, after a fight, for MARY PHILBROOK to be admitted to the New Jersey Bar in 1895; she was the first female attorney to be so admitted. SARAH MOORE GRIMKÉ, born nearly a century earlier, wanted with all her heart to be an attorney. But nowhere in the United States was that as yet possible. The sketches in this book, while they compile a striking record of achievement, also make clear that there were innumerable barriers. Some of these could be overcome by a woman of exceptional gifts and ambition. Others could not be overcome under any circumstances.

It was in large part because of the barriers that relatively few New Jersey women registered their achievements in the arenas that historians have traditionally identified as central. There were exceptions, of course, from the Revolutionary War legend Molly Pitcher (MARY LUDWIG HAYS MCCAULEY), who stood behind the guns at the Battle of Monmouth, to Congresswoman MARY TERESA NORTON, an architect of the pivotal labor legislation enacted during the New Deal. "I'm no lady," Norton once proclaimed. "I'm a member of Congress." These exceptions—warriors and politicians—were especially rare before the 20th century.

And yet scores of New Jersey women were active in public life and they did make a difference. How, then, do we characterize women's contributions? We are back to the proposition that women's history gives us an opportunity to rethink what matters in history. We propose that women who fought for women's rights were engaged in activity of signal importance, comparable to all the other great democratic movements of recent centuries. From the inception of American feminism in the 1830s, New Jersey was home to a glittering constellation of women's rights leaders. Among them were SARAH MOORE GRIMKÉ and ANGELINA EMILY GRIMKÉ, southern expatriates who were the first to take the moral lessons of the antislavery movement and fashion them into arresting arguments for the rights of women. ANTOINETTE LOUISA BROWN BLACKWELL, a prominent spokeswoman for feminism and the first woman in the nation to be ordained a minister, lived most of her adult life in New Jersey. ELIZABETH CADY STANTON, for decades the intellectual powerhouse behind the women's movement, based her operations in New Jersey for seventeen years. LUCY STONE was the guiding force behind the American Woman Suffrage Association; she, too, spent a good deal of her career in New Jersey. After the vote was achieved it was ALICE STOKES PAUL, a New Jersey native, who introduced the Equal Rights Amendment in 1923 and who championed it against insuperable odds for the next 50 years.

These national figures were supported and inspired by scores of locally notable women who challenged convention on almost every front. There were dress reformers, who refused to wear the bone corsets and heavy, confining skirts dictated by 19th-century fashion. MARY E. TILLOTSON, who campaigned "for womanhood with power of choice," once spent the night in a Jersey City jail, only to be released when her jailers learned there was no law against a woman wearing pants. Others sought to eliminate women's legal disabilities. In the 1870s, for instance, ANN HORA CONNELLY led the campaign to give mothers equal guardianship rights over their children, thus overturning a centuries-old doctrine that preferred the father, no matter what the circumstances.

Battles for access to education and employment were perpetual and had to be fought over and over again. In education, New Jersey lagged behind much of the rest of the nation; the "something" that drew CLARA BARTON to New Jersey, in fact, was its relative backwardness in publicly supported education, especially for female students. The first continuous four-year college for women was not opened until 1899, when MOTHER MARY XAVIER MEHEGAN and the Sisters of Charity founded the College of St. Elizabeth. Not until 1918, when the redoubtable MABEL SMITH DOUGLASS led the New Jersey Federation of Women's Clubs in founding the New Jersey College for Women (now Douglass College), was there a state-supported four-year college for women. Undergraduate programs at New Jersey's most prestigious institutions of higher learning—Princeton University and Rutgers College—remained steadfastly male until 1969 and 1972 respectively.

As for gainful employment, it took action by numerous daring individuals to pry open the gates to occupations traditionally reserved for men. Medicine is one good example. From about 1880 to the 1920s women made more progress in medicine than in any other male-dominated profession—an advance documented by the impressive number of physicians whose lives are sketched in this book. Each step in each community, however, required at least one woman who would brave being the first—the first to practice in her town, the first to apply for membership in her local medical society, the first to receive staff privileges at the local hospital. As time went on, medicine itself became increasingly professionalized, and new generations of women doctors, like their predecessors, had to risk being first—the first women to practice the new 20th-century specialties, like radiology or endocrinology.

Many of the women in this book are here because they pioneered and distinguished themselves in the male-dominant professions. Equally important were the women who fought to make the women's professions more professional, that is, to increase the training required, to enhance the dignity and rewards of the work, and to inspire greater public confidence in their expertise. ELIZABETH ALMIRA ALLEN, for instance, led the battle for pensions for New Jersey's public school teachers, and social work, nursing, and librarianship all had their champions as well. African-American women, meanwhile, took up the added challenge of making the women's professions more inclusive. The story of NELLIE KATHERINE MORROW PARKER, who in 1922 was appointed Bergen County's first black teacher, makes clear just how difficult that could be, even in the profession that had traditionally offered the greatest opportunities to black women. Among New Jersey's women of achievement, those who challenged racial and ethnic discrimination deserve a special, honorable place.

One of the most remarkable qualities of these working women was their striking tendency to volunteer—to find missions that took them beyond their paid work. MARY PHILBROOK, the first woman admitted to the New Jersey Bar, was the founder of legal aid in New Jersey. HETTY GOLDMAN, the first woman appointed to Princeton's world-renowned Institute for Advanced Study, left her archaeological dig in war-torn Greece to serve as a nurse in a hospital. As World War II approached she sponsored Jewish refugees in flight from the Nazis. These examples are multiplied many times in this book, and they are of course testimony to the high energy of exceptional women.

But there is greater significance in this pattern—and here is another place where the history of women encourages us to think differently about what matters in history. Excluded for the most part from real or even formal power in conventional politics, women—homemakers as well as the gainfully employed—created a public life of their own, mainly through voluntary associations. They sponsored countless causes, and on some issues different women's groups conflicted sharply with one another. And yet there were highly significant trends that historians are just now beginning to identify.

First, from the beginning of the 19th century, organized women's groups sought either explicitly or implicitly to enlarge women's sphere. Even a woman like JENNIE TUTTLE HOBART, who in the early 20th century was a leader in the movement that opposed the vote for women, still lived a life of intense activism on behalf of numerous reform and charitable causes. Second, organized women sought to remake their world into a place where women, and children, could flourish. This was not just a matter of

giving women access to privileges already given to men; in many instances it meant inventing agencies or policies that were totally outside the male political tradition. New Jersey's first birth control clinic, launched by CORA LOUISE HARTSHORN in 1928, is a good example.

Third, many women's organizations went beyond the interests peculiar to women and children to encompass a larger vision of social justice—one that emphasized the interdependence of human beings and the need for concerted action to solve pressing problems. After about 1880, especially, these groups looked more and more to government as the center for that action, sometimes working in coalition with men who shared similar visions. Examples, once again, are legion, from ALICE LAKEY's campaign for pure food legislation, to EDITH ELMER WOOD's drive for low-cost housing, to EDITH ELIZABETH LOWRY's ministry to migrant workers. Their efforts seem especially noteworthy when we recall the context in which they worked, for these women and their backers were challenging both the American tradition of minimal government and the reigning ethic of competitive individualism. It can in fact be argued that organized women sought nothing less than to change the meaning of American democracy.

Conscious as we all are of the strains experienced by today's "superwomen," we might well ask how they did it, where they found the energy and the time, how they managed families. It is only for the 20th century—when we can interview the subjects themselves or people who were close to them—that we can arrive at adequate answers to these questions. A substantial proportion of New Jersey's activist women remained single; this was particularly true at the turn of this century when women with career ambitions ordinarily were made to feel that they had to choose between career and marriage. Another high proportion of our 20th-century women had help: they hired housekeepers and child minders; they lived in extended families with mother or mother-in-law to run households; or they drew strength and routine help with chores from devoted female friends. In all these cases, the daily labor of other women—sometimes uncompensated, often poorly compensated—freed our subjects to achieve. Men, of course, received such services as a matter of custom and right, services that their biographers have ignored with supreme consistency. In this book, we try to make the proper acknowledgments.

It also helped to be rich. Many of these women came from relatively well-to-do families and some married into other well-to-do families, a position of strength in more ways than one. Once higher education became available to women, these women were in the best position to take advantage of it. A high income, obviously, permitted the hiring of household help. And there were less tangible factors as well, like the self-confidence that could come from belonging to a "good" family with an unshakable local reputation. None of this is surprising: studies of American men have shown that the surest way to become a wealthy and prominent man was to begin life in a wealthy and prominent family. It is possible that for achieving women, initial advantages of birth were even more important. In any case, the importance of class privilege in the lives of so many of our subjects underscores the achievement of other women who began with relatively little.

Altogether, it seems clear that the history of New Jersey women, once it is written, is going to look different from that of New Jersey's men. What is less clear is whether the history of women in New Jersey is going to look different from the history of women in the rest of the country. Does New Jersey have a distinctive history of women? It is still much too early to say. Neither for New Jersey nor for other states has the requisite research been done, and comparison is therefore not yet possible. But we can point out some features of New Jersey's past that might make for an especially interesting history of women.

One is ethnic diversity. This was a central factor in New Jersey's history, beginning in the 17th century, when the native LENNI LENAPE first encountered strange invaders from Sweden, Holland, England, and Africa. From the mid-19th century to the 1920s there was a second great migration of Europeans—Germans and Irish at first, later to be replaced by peoples from southern and eastern Europe. In the early 20th century New Jersey's African-American population was swelled by new arrivals from the American South. In the 1960s Congress once again opened the doors to massive immigration from abroad, and the result has been another great influx, not only of Europeans, but also of Hispanics and Asians of many nationalities. In our own time, as in the past, New Jersey is a laboratory for the study of cultural accommodation and conflict. What this has meant for women has yet to be fully discovered.

Closely related to New Jersey's ethnic diversity is its heritage of religious diversity. The migrations of the 19th and early 20th century meant that, for the first time, significant numbers of New Jerseyans would be Catholic or Jewish. Each group imported distinctive ideas about the roles of women. So did the Quakers, prominent in New Jersey affairs since Colonial times. Quaker women could be ministers, and they took care of their own business through women's meetings. That tradition of empowerment was manifested in many ways; in this book it shows in the numbers of Quaker women who took leading parts in feminism and reform.

Third, New Jersey experienced early and rapid industrialization. We know that women were essential to industrialization—as paid workers, as housewives who sustained laboring husbands and children, and as the people who literally produced each subsequent generation of workers. We are coming to understand better the relation-

ships between these working-class women and women of the upper and middle classes. Higher-income women benefited from the class system both directly—as employers of domestic workers—and indirectly, for those high incomes were drawn from profits generated in large part by a poorly paid working class. At the same time, wealthier women were instrumental in attempts to ease the plight of the working class, especially of working-class women. The fate of the "radium girls," traced here in two biographies, makes vivid some of the major themes. There was KATHERINE SCHAUB, a watch dial painter whose work resulted in her death from radium poisoning in 1933. And there was CARYE-BELLE HENLE, who demonstrated decisively (and much too late to save Schaub) the toxic effects of radium. This was a landmark case in occupational safety—the sort of dubious honor that comes often to a state like New Jersey, placed as it has been in the vanguard of industrial innovation, with all its rewards and risks.

Other themes have yet to be explored in depth, such as the struggles of workers to enlarge their share of New Jersey's abundance through unions, and women's struggle to receive their due within the unions. And what of women's roles as consumers? This is clearly a central theme for women of all classes, especially with the growth of our 20th-century consumer culture. In close mesh with industrial growth, meanwhile, and largely as a result of it, came the classic cycle of modern urban development. Again, New Jersey was in the vanguard, first of explosive urban growth, then of progressive central city decay, of mushrooming suburbs, and most recently of attempts at urban revitalization. Here, too, is a set of frontiers whose meaning for women would make an intriguing study.

Finally, New Jersey is a cosmopolitan place, and has been ever since Philadelphia and New York first laid claim to big-city glitter. New Jersey has paid the price for its proximity to two of the country's premier cities, as demonstrated by the unending stream of New Jersey jokes perpetrated chiefly by denizens of New York City's five boroughs. But this book also documents one of the enormous blessings of New Jersey's location: its uncommonly rich aggregation of artists, performers, and authors. On farms, in towns, or down the shore—creative people have time and again found homes in New Jersey that allowed them easy access to metropolitan galleries, concert halls, broadcast studios, and publishers.

What all this may mean for women as a group, and for women of different groups, we cannot yet see. The biographies generated by this project, however, provide hundreds of leads for future research. In the meantime, there is much to enjoy in the sheer individuality of some of the women sketched here. One of them was HETTY HOWLAND ROBINSON GREEN, a financier believed to have been the richest woman of her time, who dressed in shabby clothes and begged grocers for food that would otherwise have been tossed in the garbage bins. Another is VIRGINIA APGAR, famous for the Apgar score for newborns, who routinely carried a pocketknife in case someone needed an emergency tracheotomy. She claimed to have used it sixteen times. "Nobody, but nobody," she said, "is going to stop breathing on me."

The land of the turnpike and the truck farm is also a land with a fascinating history of women. Someday that history will be reconstructed in full, and it will change the way we think about New Jersey's history as a whole. When that happens, we can thank the instigators of this project for helping to bring it about. Perhaps the appearance of this book will itself stand as a landmark in the history of New Jersey women—and as testimony to the continuing power of female voluntarism.

*Suzanne Lebsock*

The home of Tempe Wick, still standing near Morristown, was the scene of her patriotic resistance to mutinous soldiers in December 1780. *Photo credit: George Goodwin.*

# HISTORICAL OVERVIEW: 1600-1807

THE WOMEN OF COLONIAL NEW JERSEY contributed to founding a society of scattered settlements and towns between the Delaware and Hudson rivers. From the early decades of the 17th century, with their male counterparts, women emigrated from Holland, Sweden, England, Germany, Ireland, and Scotland, envisioning opportunities of prosperity and well-being in the New World.

New Jersey's territory offered natural resources and potential commercial development. Through the years its good farmland and trade facilities also attracted settlers from neighboring colonies. In time a heterogeneous population engaged in an array of trades from agriculture to glassmaking took their place in the economy of the colony.

In 1664 a successful naval maneuver on the Hudson River gave England control over the Dutch-claimed region on both sides of the Hudson River. John Lord Berkeley and Sir George Carteret were made proprietors of the colony of New Jersey. The promise of generous land grants, religious freedom, and representative self-government brought new settlers, including Quakers, members of the Society of Friends, looking for freedom of conscience.

From the earliest English settlement, landholders or freeholders were defined as persons worth £50, opening proprietorship to both men and women. In "The Concessions and Agreements of the Lords Proprietors" of 1664–65, the terms *freeman*, *freewoman*, *master*, and *mistress* were used for landholders. Accordingly, female settlers not only became property owners but were also entitled to land grants for the recruitment of new settlers specified in the Agreements. In 1669, after the English takeover of the colony, Carteret honored the gift of 2,260 acres to SARAH KIERSTED, a settler of New Amsterdam, from the Lenni Lenape chief Oratam.

Prior to white settlement of New Jersey territory, American Indians known as the LENNI LENAPE lived in the region. They developed a matrilineal society in which kinship was established through the female members and ancestry traced through one's mother. Lenape women were responsible for farming, harvesting of crops, meal preparation, manufacture of clothes, and child care, while men attended to hunting and fishing and controlled political leadership. Women also performed the sewing, weav-ing, and tanning of skins. The importance of tanning increased as a result of the white settlers' desire to obtain animal skins in exchange for European trinkets and utensils.

In 1676 New Jersey's proprietors, Carteret and Berkeley, divided the colony, forming East Jersey and West Jersey; they later individually sold their divisions to Quaker subproprietors. LADY ELIZABETH CARTERET was proprietor of East Jersey after the death of her husband in 1680, and as executor of his estate she attended to the sale of the land. The proprietors surrendered their governing rights to the crown in 1702, and the colony was reunited with a population of approximately 15,000.

Women were a vital part of the developing Colonial society in New Jersey. Their activities varied according to the wealth and social standing of their families. Agriculture dominated the life-style of most of the population, who toiled as independent farmers. The soil was suited to a variety of grain crops (wheat, corn, rye, oats, barley, buckwheat, flax), as well as dairy farming, fruit orchards, lumbering, and mining of iron and coal. Some settlers also worked at fishing and as merchants, artisans, and laborers. Supply routes by either river or road brought New Jersey produce to markets in New York and Philadelphia.

The life of women in the colony reflected Colonial society at large combined with the particular features of the New Jersey settlement. Women's existence was family-centered. They labored as worker-companions with their spouses and followed a sexual division of labor conventional in an agricultural economy. All women, white or black, free, slave, redemptioner, or indentured servant, contributed to households, essentially economically self-sufficient and responsible for what would be considered consumer goods today.

Slave women in the colony attended to the needs of both their masters' family and their own. While no data on the number of female slaves exist, the combined total of male and female slaves in Colonial New Jersey was 3,981 in 1737, 4,606 in 1747, and 11,423 by 1790. The demand for cheap labor for farming and mining was responsible for a steady growth rate of approximately 7.5 to 8.5 percent during these years. Antislavery sentiments of some

Quakers in the colony brought few results during the Colonial era. In 1804, however, the New Jersey legislature passed the Gradual Abolition Act. According to its provision, female offspring of slave mothers were to be freed at age 21 and males at age 25.

A shortage of labor throughout the Colonial period required that women labor in the fields during planting and harvest seasons. Women assumed the economic responsibility of running family trades, shops, and businesses in the absence or death of their husbands. They ran general stores, taverns, mills, and shops of many kinds. Colonial newspapers carried advertisements for the goods and services of women, especially those of widows and single women regarded as heads of households. MARY SPRATT PROVOOST ALEXANDER ran an importing business in European goods out of New Jersey and New York. CATHARINE ANDERSON of Rahway and EUNICE FOSTER HORTON of Madison worked as partners with their husbands operating taverns. ESTHER EDWARDS BURR, wife of the Rev. Aaron Burr, became an extension of her husband's ministry, visiting parishioners and attending to other aspects of his clerical service.

More than today, Colonial women provided most family health care services. They maintained herb gardens for the preparation of special concoctions and recorded home remedies in "household receipt books." (Cowen, *Medicine*, 3) Until the 1760s male physicians did not attend childbirth. It was primarily a female concern, and the role of the midwife was regarded as vital to the community. Like many women of her time, MARGARET VLIET WARNE worked as a midwife. She traveled throughout Warren County during the crisis of the Revolutionary War and for many years thereafter.

Women performed gender-defined tasks essential to the survival of the settlement and their families. They were responsible for cooking, food preservation, laundering, herb and vegetable gardens, tending small animals such as chickens for eggs, weaving, and spinning, as well as religious instruction of children. Female children and unmarried sisters, or spinsters, assisted in domestic responsibilities.

Nonetheless, married women held inferior legal status in the society. Furthermore, the omission of women's names on deeds, mortgages, and tax schedules and the substitution of the Latin term *uxor* for the wife's name thwart the accurate reconstruction of women's role in the public life of the colony.

As in other English colonies, the legal and property rights of women in New Jersey came under English common law, which was codified by Sir William Blackstone in his *Commentaries on the Laws of England* (1765) and brought to America by English settlers. A married woman, known as *feme covert* or a woman "covered" by her husband's status, forfeited all personal property and surrendered control of real property to her husband. Wages earned by a married woman legally belonged to her husband. She could not vote, sue or be sued, draft wills, make contracts, or buy and sell land. Her welfare, interests, and rights were regarded as "one with her husband's."

ANNETJE VAN WAGENEN PLUME inherited property from her father and uncle, which passed into her husband's control when she married him. She regained ownership and control of the property, according to her husband's will, when she became a widow. When SYBILLA RIGHTON MASTERS traveled to London to obtain patents for her inventions—a process for stamping rather than grinding corn meal (1715) and another for working straw for hats (1716)—they were issued in her husband's name.

In New Jersey, as in a few other colonies, a somewhat liberal atmosphere prevailed concerning family matters. A wife's consent was required in the sale of property or the "putting out" of children for apprenticeship. Prenuptial agreements provided alternate spousal property rights from those found in common law. Elizabeth Smith Lawrence (LADY ELIZABETH CARTERET) entered a prenuptial contract upon her marriage to Philip Carteret, the first Colonial governor of New Jersey, to secure the inheritance of her seven children from her previous marriage. MARY SPRATT PROVOOST ALEXANDER entered a prenuptial agreement drawn up by her uncles when she married her second husband, James Alexander.

Single women and widows, known as *femes soles* under common law, worked in trades and other occupations out of necessity. Unmarried women were permitted to own property, form businesses, and enter contractual arrangements for trade in an attempt to be self-supporting. The status of *feme sole*, however, was not considered an enviable one. Rather, widows and single women were objects of pity. RACHEL BRADFORD BOUDINOT did not marry until age 34 and performed nursing and household tasks for friends and relatives while single.

As *femes soles*, women had the right to own property, sue and be sued, and enter into contracts. Widow ELIZABETH RAY CLARK BODLY managed her late husband's estate, later named Port Elizabeth in her honor. Two widowed sisters, RACHEL LOVELL WELLS and PATIENCE LOVELL WRIGHT from Crosswick, made wax figures to support themselves and exhibited them professionally.

The settlement of Quakers in the colony is generally regarded as the main contributor to the liberal tradition of early New Jersey. Quakers profess a belief in the "equality of the souls," granting to Quaker women a unique role in their communities. They traveled as ministers "preaching the word." In 1767, 25 female Quaker ministers were listed in the records of Burlington County. HANNAH DENT COOPER of the Haddonfield Friends Meeting traveled to Barbados and Boston as a Quaker minister. Women participated on committees through a structure of autonomous women's meetings that engaged women in social activism ranging from family life counseling and education of children to welfare of Indians. ELIZABETH HADDON, proprietor of Haddonfield, served as clerk of her local Women's Meeting for 50 years.

The Revolutionary War worked severe hardships on women as well as men in New Jersey. New Jersey's location between New York and Philadelphia made it the "cockpit" of the Revolution as the military struggled to occupy the two cities. General George Washington moved his army across New Jersey four times during the war years. The encampment of British and Hessian forces, and of the Continental army, brought fear and misery to Jersey residents. During the numerous military engagements, family life and businesses were disrupted, consumer goods were scarce and expensive, and disease took its toll among the civilian as well as military population. Diarist JEMIMA CONDICT HARRISON wrote of the epidemic conditions bringing sickness and death as well as the task of spinning once again necessitated by the boycott of English manufactured cloth. During a smallpox epidemic in 1777, THEODOSIA JOHNES FORD of Morristown lost her daughter and in-laws, and EUNICE FOSTER HORTON, her son and husband.

New Jersey women represented the full political spectrum of public sentiment during the war, sometimes differing with members of their own families. CORNELIA BELL PATERSON, a patriot and wife of William Paterson, corresponded throughout the war with her brother Andrew Bell, a Loyalist in the British army. The family of SARAH LIVINGSTON ALEXANDER, "Lady Stirling," also experienced the rancor of divided allegiances.

Notable patriot women include "TEMPE" WICK, who refused her horse to mutinous New Jersey soldiers headed for Pennsylvania. MARY LUDWIG HAYS MCCAULEY, known as "Molly Pitcher," was a camp follower like other wives of Continental soldiers who cooked, cleaned, mended, and nursed the wounded for half-rations. She reportedly took over her injured husband's cannon at the Battle of Monmouth. HANNAH OGDEN CALDWELL was shot and killed in her home in Connecticut Farms (now Union) as a result of the patriot activism of her minister husband, the Rev. James Caldwell. Widow THEODOSIA JOHNES FORD opened her home and grounds in Morristown to General Washington and his officers during the winter of 1779–80. ANNIS BOUDINOT STOCKTON expressed her patriotism in her poetry commemorating the Battles of Trenton and Princeton. The Stockton estate, Morven, was ransacked and occupied by British troops during the Battle of Princeton.

ELIZABETH DOWNES FRANKLIN sided with her Tory husband, William Franklin, the last royal governor of New Jersey. He was placed under arrest in 1776, and she died thirteen months later without seeing him again. Quaker MARGARET HILL MORRIS, a pacifist, hid a Tory minister for whom the patriot soldiers were searching. Quaker ANN COOPER WHITALL made no retaliatory efforts when a cannonball, fired during the Battle of Red Bank in 1777, entered the side of her home and disturbed her spinning. While opposed to the sufferings and hostilities of the war, both Morris and Whitall nursed soldiers after battles near their homes.

With the onset of the Revolution, New Jersey adopted its first state constitution on July 2, 1776. It gave "all inhabitants . . . worth fifty pounds proclamation money" the right to vote. The omission of the term *male* gave New Jersey women of property the franchise and made them the only women in the nation eligible to vote. Additional legislation that passed in 1790 and 1797, credited to Quaker influence in the legislature, further accentuated women's access to the polls by referring to voters as "he or she." The provisions, maintaining New Jersey's liberal view on freeholding, meant that widows and unmarried women, white or black, who paid taxes were entitled to vote in New Jersey elections. At first the practice of open voting and use of taverns as polling places discouraged women's participation, but increased voter turnout by women over the years between 1790 and 1807 has been documented in certain New Jersey communities.

In 1807 a special election in Elizabeth and Newark over the location of a new courthouse for Essex County drew attention to voting practices in the state. An investigation after the election brought charges of fraudulent voting by persons not worth £50, married women, black slaves, servants, underage men, aliens, and even Philadelphians. On November 16, 1807, the New Jersey legislature passed a law for "the enfranchisement of all free, white, male citizens" with a taxpayer requirement.

Whether true or not, the main objection to women's voting was that they voted the way they were told to vote by the men who invariably escorted them to the polls to vote. Women, it was claimed, had no separate political views and did not need the vote. Both public and private sentiments of women regarding the war and independence contradict that assumption. The elimination of the franchise for women met no resistance, however, reflecting compliance with the general societal views on women at the time.

While the American Revolution changed the complexion of American society, it did not immediately improve the status of women. After 1807 New Jersey women found themselves with no political rights under the state constitution, except in the case of single women and widows, who retained their legal business rights. Women, therefore, gained few of the legal freedoms for which the Revolution had been fought.

*Carmela Ascolese Karnoutsos*

## Selected References

Blackstone, William. *Commentaries on the Laws of England.* New York, 1877.

Boyd, Julian P. *Fundamental Laws and Constitution of New Jersey.* Princeton, NJ, 1964.

Cowen, David L. *Medicine and Health in New Jersey.* Princeton, NJ, 1964.

Kraft, Herbett C. *The Lenape: Archeology, History and Ethnography.* Newark, NJ, 1986.

McCormick, Richard P. *The History of Voting in New Jersey.* New Brunswick, NJ, 1953.

Philbrook, Mary. "Woman's Suffrage in New Jersey Prior to 1807." In *NJHSP* 57 (1939).

Pole, J. R. "The Suffrage in New Jersey, 1790–1807." In *NJHSP* 71 (1953).

Weiss, Henry Bischoff. *Life in Early New Jersey.* Princeton, NJ, 1964.

## MARY SPRATT PROVOOST ALEXANDER, 1693–1760

Mary (Spratt) Provoost Alexander was the quintessential working mother, whose New York-based importing company was a major mercantile firm of the Colonial era. She was one of the most successful New York retail merchants of her generation, when women were generally considered unsuited for business.

Alexander was born April 17, 1693, the third child and younger of two daughters of John and Maria (DePeyster) Schrick Spratt of New York City. Born in Glasgow, Scotland, her father was a merchant and alderman in New York. Her mother was a descendant of prominent Dutch goldsmiths and merchants. Married at age seventeen to Samuel Provoost, a thriving merchant and younger brother of her mother's third husband, she was widowed in 1719. After her husband's death, Alexander assumed control of the business and also reared sons John (b. 1714) and David (b. 1715). Her daughter Maria (b. 1712) had died in infancy. Alexander attracted the carriage trade by having a flagstone walk, the first in New York City, built before her business establishment. Scarcely a ship came into port that did not bring large consignments of goods to her business.

In 1721 she married James Alexander of Perth Amboy, NJ, and New York City, a distinguished lawyer, politician, and surveyor who had arrived in America from Scotland in 1715. Alexander's Dutch uncles drew up prenuptial agreements for the couple. Alexander provided offices for her husband, who later built an imposing brick mansion, surrounded by a large yard, at the corners of Broad and Beaver streets in New York City, where the Provoost sons and five Alexander children were raised. The children included son William Alexander (b. 1725) and daughters Mary (b. 1721), Elizabeth (b. 1726), Catharine (b. 1727), and Susannah (b. 1737), all of whom married socially prominent men. Two other children, James (1723–31) and Anna (1731–46), died from smallpox.

Upon the birth of daughter Mary in October 1721, James Alexander wrote a glowing account of his wife to his brother, stating that within a few hours of delivering the child she was in her shop and sold more than £30 of merchandise.

Alexander provided her husband with funds for his political and financial endeavors from "the Emporium," her establishment. Noted for her intelligence and business acumen, she took full advantage of the colonies' prosperity to amass a fortune. The store was the leading distributor for dry goods, fine imported fabrics, Indian blankets, and European luxuries such as china, silver, glass, and wines.

Described as having robust health, fine features, and a keen eye, Alexander dressed without elegance, in a commonplace frilled cap, folded kerchief, and close sleeves. However, she spent her money freely. She is said, at one

period, to have been the only person in New York, except for the governor, who kept a coach. Her opulent life-style greatly influenced her son William Alexander. Renowned by all for her vivacity, which matched the Scottish wit and repartee of her husband, Alexander was also the recognized leader of the English set at Trinity Church, New York City. (She had left the Lutheran Dutch Congregation, and her husband the Presbyterian, to join the Anglican church.)

A friend of the Manhattan Island Indians, Alexander learned their medicinal talents. She was known as the "Medicine Woman" for her curative recipes using herbs from her proper Dutch garden. She devised a salve for burns, herbal teas, and a special brand of tobacco for use in her home.

Once, in the early 1730s, Alexander sailed secretly to Perth Amboy in her private yacht and traveled to Philadelphia to obtain the services of barrister Andrew Hamilton to assist her husband, who, with another member of the New York Bar, William Smith, had been disbarred from practice because they tried to defend printer John Peter Zenger. He had been charged with libel by Governor William Cosby for printing in the *New York Weekly Journal* their criticism of the governor for firing Chief Justice Lewis Morris. Tradition states that the necessary documents were carried to Philadelphia quilted in Alexander's best silk petticoat. Hamilton was successful in reinstating Alexander and Smith, thus clearing Zenger. Anxious about her husband's health and many political interests, Alexander purchased land in New Jersey in 1739 and had a large house built in Perth Amboy for his use when meeting with the Provincial Council.

By 1743 the Alexander fortune was estimated at £100,000. In 1744, in addition to property and land he already owned at Basking Ridge, James Alexander purchased 10,000 acres in Hunterdon County from the West New Jersey Society. This included Round Valley and surrounding mountains, bordered by Lebanon, Bray's Hill, and Whitehouse. A generation later patriotic members of the Alexander, Livingston, Rutherfurd, and Stevens families, when hard pressed by British enemies, sought refuge at their estates, built in the area as a family compound. Alexandria Township was named in honor of James Alexander.

Alexander's son William, as a young boy, helped his mother in the Emporium and developed an early love for commerce. She took him into partnership in the business when he was 23, and it was he who was responsible for expanding his mother's operations outside the New York area, into New England, New Jersey, and Philadelphia. From 1748 to 1750, in partnership with John Stevens of Hoboken, a sea captain and merchant who married Elizabeth Alexander in 1748, William Alexander dealt in slaves, traded into the colonies from the African coast.

Prices ranged from £40 to £48 per boy to £43 to £48 per girl. This trade was provided for the New York and New Jersey colonies, with Stevens conducting the Alexander business in New Jersey. At the same time, the New York store became more and more prosperous, in both wholesale and retail trade.

In the early 1750s the senior Alexanders moved to their Perth Amboy home. To their son William, who had married SARAH LIVINGSTON in 1748, they gave the Broad Street mansion, for which he forfeited £5,000 of his cash inheritance. James Alexander was a member of the King's Council of New Jersey as well as New York, a dual citizenship allowed by the authorities since he claimed homes in both colonies. He suffered a sudden attack of gout in 1756 and died on April 2, at age 65. Alexander became his executor. She made a new will, in which she changed her husband's wish to leave one-third of the estate to their son William and made arrangements for an equal share of one-fifth for each child. After her husband's death, Alexander continued to conduct the family's business with William until he became an aide to General William Shirley, after which she ran the business alone. Alexander's estate holdings in New Jersey included the tract at Canoe Brook; 6,000 acres of East Jersey lands; 1,000 acres near Basking Ridge; an equal amount on the Rockaway River; more than 1,300 acres at Roxciticus, the great Mine Mountain tract; 500 acres near the New York–New Jersey line; and 10,000 acres in Hunterdon County. This estate was in litigation during her final years.

Alexander never saw her son again after he sailed for Europe with General Shirley to claim, unsuccessfully, the earldom of Stirling. She died of pleurisy on April 18, 1760, at age 67, in the old family home on Broad Street, New York City, surrounded by her daughters and grandchildren. She was buried beside her husband in the family vault at Trinity Church, New York City, with the governors of New York and New Jersey as pallbearers. Her stock of goods was sold off at auction in December 1760.

As well as providing handsomely for her children by James Alexander, Alexander's will provided for the surviving Provoost son, John (David died in 1741), and several slaves. She was the grandmother of Samuel Provoost, who became the first Protestant Episcopal bishop of the diocese of New York; and through her daughter Elizabeth Alexander Stevens, Alexander was the great-great-great-great-grandmother of MILLICENT FENWICK, noted New Jersey legislator.

An account of Alexander's life and business activities appears in May Van Rensselaer, *The Goede Vrouw of Mana-ha-ta* (1898). Sketches of her appear in *NAW* and in *DAB*, vol. 1 (1955).

*June O. Kennedy*

## SARAH LIVINGSTON ALEXANDER, 1725–1804

Sarah (Livingston) Alexander, also known as "Lady Stirling," was prominent in New Jersey and New York social circles. She acted as hostess to General Nathanael Greene at Basking Ridge during the Revolution and accompanied her husband, William Alexander, to General George Washington's camp at Valley Forge.

Born in Albany, NY, and baptized on November 7, 1725, she was the ninth child and oldest surviving daughter of Philip Livingston (1686–1749), second lord and proprietor of Livingston Manor, and Catrina (Van Brugh) Livingston (1689–1756). Like many elite women of the period, Alexander was educated at home. She received religious and moral instruction and basic training in accounting, reading and writing in both English and Dutch, and the traditional female occupations of cooking and needlework from her mother. She became proficient enough in accounting for her husband to appoint her his attorney in 1777, with the power to recover rents from his tenants. Brought up in the Dutch Reformed Church, Alexander remained a devout member until her death.

In 1748, at age 23, she married William Alexander (1725–1783), the self-proclaimed "Lord Stirling," son of James Alexander, a wealthy Scot, prominent in Colonial New York and New Jersey society, and MARY SPRATT PROVOOST ALEXANDER, a highly successful New York merchant. William Alexander was well educated in private schools in New York and trained by his parents in mathematics and astronomy. At the time of his marriage, he was associated with his mother in the family business, which traded in dry goods and imported slaves from the West Indies. Sarah and William Alexander had two daughters, Mary (b. 1749) and Catherine (b. 1755). The Alexanders resided on Broad Street in New York City during the 1750s.

William Alexander, then aide and secretary to Massachusetts Governor William Shirley, accompanied Shirley to England in September 1756 when the latter was recalled. During this visit Alexander attempted to assert his claim as sixth earl of Stirling, a title forfeited by his father, who had been exiled from Scotland because of his role in the 1715 Jacobite rebellion. On his return to America in October 1761, the Alexanders assumed the titles of earl and countess of Stirling, which they continued to use even after the House of Lords rejected his claim to the title in 1762.

The Alexanders built a country seat at Somerset Hills, near Basking Ridge in northern New Jersey. With her husband, between 1761 and 1767 Alexander presided over the construction and furnishing of "the Buildings," as Somerset people referred to the estate. She also managed a staff of domestic slaves brought from New York and trained British indentured servants who served as domestics, coachmen, gardeners, smiths, and seamstresses.

"Lord and Lady Stirling" entertained a stream of prominent guests at the Buildings, which became the couple's principal residence after 1762. Guests included members of her own family, the Livingstons of New York and New Jersey, the Morrises of New Jersey, the Jays of New York, and close friends such as General George and Martha Washington of Virginia. Elias Boudinot, later president of the Continental Congress, and his daughter Susan were frequent visitors.

At the center of Colonial society and the later revolutionary community, "Lady Stirling" and her daughters, "Lady" Mary and "Lady" Kitty, were noted for their wit, elegance, and cultivation. General Nathanael Greene was their guest during January and February 1777, when Greene's division of the Continental Army was located at Basking Ridge. Greene clearly appreciated his hostesses' character and hospitality, for he described Alexander and her daughters to his wife as "of distinguished merit, sensible, polite and easy." (Schumacher, *Major-General the Earl of Stirling*, 29–31)

Alexander's political loyalties were nevertheless strained by the exigencies of the Revolution. Within the family circle, there was Robert Watts, the husband of her eldest daughter, Mary, and son of a prosperous Loyalist family. The Wattses moved to New York City after their marriage in February 1775. Alexander visited her daughter in August 1778 and tried without success to persuade her to leave. Sympathetic to her daughter's position, Alexander noted that "duty to her husband" compelled her to remain in New York. (Valentine, *Lord Stirling*, 236) William Alexander, however, may never have forgiven his daughter for her decision, making no mention of her in his will. Denied permission by General Washington to cross enemy lines and enter New Jersey, Mary was unable to attend the wedding in July 1779 of her sister, Kitty, to Colonel William Duer. Mary remained in New York City throughout the British occupation.

In 1777 Alexander attempted to intervene a second time on behalf of a Loyalist relative. Her brother-in-law, Walter Rutherfurd, had been arrested in early 1777 by her brother, New Jersey Governor William Livingston. Rutherfurd had been charged with participation in a Loyalist plot. Alexander's appeals to the governor for clemency were unsuccessful, and Rutherfurd remained in custody at Morristown for some time.

In the spring of 1778 Alexander left Basking Ridge to join her husband, who had recently been promoted to major general at Washington's camp in Valley Forge, PA. General Washington and Martha Washington, William and Sarah Alexander, and General and Mrs. Nathanael Greene attended a military festival of thanksgiving proclaimed at Valley Forge on May 7, 1778, in celebration of France's treaty of alliance with the United States.

From 1780 on the fortunes of the Alexander family seem to have declined. On January 15, 1783, William Alexander died in Albany of a combination of gout and pneumonia, leaving an estate heavily encumbered by debt. Washington, who had esteemed him highly as a friend and military adviser, sent a letter of tribute to his widow.

At the same time Alexander's brother, William Livingston, informed her that although he realized she would be "exposed to many inconveniences" as a widow, he would not be able to assist her financially. (Prince and Lustig, *The Papers of William Livingston*, vol. 4) Livingston's prediction of his sister's financial embarrassment was accurate. Biographer William Duer described William Alexander's legacy to his wife: "he left nothing but the certificates issued by the State of New Jersey, for the depreciation of his pay, which . . . he delivered to his wife, for her future support. Even the bounty land promised by Congress to those officers who served during the war was denied to his widow" on technical grounds. (Duer, quoted in Valentine, 142–43) Virtually nothing of worth was left to Alexander for her support.

She outlived her husband by 21 years. After his death it is likely that she went to live with her daughter Kitty Duer and son-in-law William, a founder of the Bank of New York and in 1789 assistant secretary of the Treasury under Hamilton. At Washington's Inauguration Ball, given at the Assembly Rooms on Broadway in 1789, it was noted that "among the most distinguished women present were Lady Stirling and her two daughters Lady Mary Watts and Lady Kitty Duer." (Griswold, *The Republican Court*, 154–56) In 1791 "Lady Stirling" and "Lady" Kitty appeared on the list of civic hostesses prominent at New York City's reception of Martha Washington.

Little is known of Alexander's last years. Elizabeth Ellet, a 19th-century historian of women, has left a brief character sketch of Alexander shortly before her death in 1804 at age 82: "Possessed naturally of a strong mind, she preserved her mental faculties unimpaired to the last and found in her religious faith consolation for the reverses of fortune she had experienced in her later years." (Ellet, *The Women of the American Revolution*, 384–85)

Letters and documents written to and by Lady Stirling, are available at the NY-HS. Some of her writings appear in Carl Prince, Dennis Ryan, and Mary Lou Lustig, eds., *The Papers of William Livingston*, 5 vols. (1979–in press). Biographical references to Lady Stirling are found in Alan Valentine, *Lord Stirling* (1969); Elizabeth Ellet, *The Women of the American Revolution*, vol. 3 (1850); Ludwig Schumacher, *Major-General the Earl of Stirling* (1897); and Rufus Wilmot Griswold, *The Republican Court, or American Society in the Days of Washington* (1855).

*Claire McCurdy*

## CATHARINE ANDERSON, 1749–1806

Catharine Anderson was born in 1749. There are no records to confirm the place of her birth, the names of her parents, or if she had any siblings.

She married John Anderson, tavernkeeper of what is today Merchants and Drovers Tavern. This building, located on St. George Avenue in Rahway (Union County), NJ, was probably first known as Rahway Community House. It was the first stop for most coaches after they left Elizabethtown, NJ, in the morning. Three times each week, express riders carried mail through to Rahway. After the Andersons made this building home, John Mecerau's "Flying Machine" traveled here twice each week from Paulus Hook to Philadelphia over the King's Highway, now called St. George Avenue. Local residents referred to it as the road to Bridgetown (Rahway). This road was broadened in the early 1700s, when it was linked with the road from Amboy Ferry to Elizabethtown and to Newark via Broad Street. The only "thoroughfare" in New Jersey to connect the Dutch on Manhattan Island with the settlers living along the Delaware River, it stretched from Elizabethtown Point to Indian's Ferry (New Brunswick), then above Trenton to the Delaware River.

At the Andersons' tavern, passengers came aboard and horses were changed. The Andersons allowed peddlers to sell their wares in the tavern. As tavern owners, who were highly respected citizens in this era, the Andersons had ready access to funds and granted a number of loans, thus serving as a kind of bank. Circuit court judges held court sessions in the tavern's public rooms, which also served as polling places for farmers and tradesmen to vote for members of the provincial assembly and other officials.

When she was 42 or 43 Anderson had a daughter, Phebe (b. 1792), who married David Steward Craig who later had ownership of the tavern. Anderson may have also borne a son, James (ca. 1775–80), but information is sketchy.

As was true of Colonial tavern owners of her day, Anderson was responsible for the food, amenities, and cleanliness of her business. She most probably attended to other details necessary for operating such an establishment. It was well known that Merchants and Drovers Tavern was a thriving establishment that grew in size from two to four stories, and Anderson's role as proprietor, with her husband, was the reason for its acclaimed prosperity.

Anderson died on May 16, 1806, in Rahway.

An interview on Sept. 17, 1985, with Vincent Parlapiano, president of the Rahway Historical Society (Rahway, NJ), provided information about Anderson's tavern. The Rahway Historical Society maintains papers describing the building and its furnishings. Useful background books are: Robert Hoffman, *The Revolutionary Scene in New Jersey* (1942), and Walter Von Hoesen, *Early Taverns and Stagecoach Days in New Jersey* (1976).

*Betty Olson*

## ELIZABETH RAY CLARK BODLY, 1737–1815

Elizabeth (Ray) Clark Bodly, founder and benefactor of Port Elizabeth in Cumberland County, was born in Pilesgrove Township (Salem County), NJ, in 1737, the daughter of John Ray. She married Cornelius Clark, a native of Burlington, and moved to Cumberland County in 1757. Four children were born to the Clarks: Joel, John, Susan, and Elizabeth. On August 19, 1771, Cornelius and Elizabeth Clark purchased a large tract of land (213 acres) at the mouth of Manumuskin Creek in Cumberland County from John Bell for £260 sterling. This land later became the site of Port Elizabeth. Although a few settlers were reportedly in the area as early as 1750, the land was virtually a pine wilderness, and the Clarks set about clearing meadows and reclaiming the lowlands from the tides. When Cornelius Clark died shortly thereafter, his widow continued to manage the estate. Exceptionally tall, with dark eyes and hair, she soon married John Bodly. She bore two more children, Sarah and Mary Bodly. John Bodly died young, leaving his widow to manage a sizable estate and care for six children.

Meanwhile, the settlement that came to be known later as Port Elizabeth, in honor of Elizabeth Bodly, was beginning to thrive. Originally called "the Dam," and later "the Store," the area boasted successful wood and bog iron industries. Prior to 1785 Bodly hired surveyors Eli Elmer and Nathan Hand to plot the future Port Elizabeth. The main portion, called a 30-rod square, was bounded on the north by Broadway, east by Second Street, south by Lombard or Quaker Street, and west by Front Street. The first lot was deeded by Bodly, a Quaker, to the Methodist Episcopal Church on October 1, 1785, for a nominal sum of five shillings "for the purpose of building a preaching-house on and a burying-yard, and to build a school-house for the use of the neighborhood after the said meeting-house is built." (Quoted in *History of Gloucester, Salem, and Cumberland*, 718–19) The church was built the following year. The fate of the school is unknown, but on June 30, 1798, Bodly deeded another lot to the trustees of the Federal School, the site of which continued to be used for educating Port Elizabeth's youngsters well into the 20th century. (It is currently the location of a senior citizens' center.) Bodly was known as a woman of great charity, regularly dispensing food and clothing to anyone who came to her door in need.

Port Elizabeth reached its zenith in the half century or so following an act of the U.S. Congress that established the port as a center for the collection of duties on imports in 1789. Established as an official port of delivery, it became a bustling center for direct trade with the West Indies. The town was also an important glass manufacturing center until 1884.

Today, Port Elizabeth is a quiet village that more

closely resembles the town Bodly founded in 1785 than the busy trade and industrial center it became in her later years and during the half century following her death.

Bodly survived all but two of her six children. Joel Clark died a year after his marriage to Ann Dallas. John Clark died of camp fever after enlisting in the army during the Whiskey Rebellion. Susan Clark died a few months after marrying Jonathan Dallas, brother of Ann. Jonathan Dallas then married Elizabeth Clark, his first wife's sister, and they had five children. Mary Bodly married Maurice Beasley; they had one son, Theophilus Elmer Beasley, who became a prominent Salem physician. Sarah Bodly died during childhood.

Bodly died at Port Elizabeth on November 25, 1815, but her contributions to Port Elizabeth have not been forgotten. In 1985 a marble stone commemorating her as "Founder and Benefactor of Port Elizabeth" was placed on her grave in the Friends' burial ground on the banks of Manumuskin Creek.

Bodly is first mentioned biographically in John W. Barber and Henry Howe, *Historical Collections of the State of New Jersey* (1844). Books providing information on her and Port Elizabeth are: Thomas Cushing and Charles Sheppard, *History of the Counties of Gloucester, Salem, and Cumberland, New Jersey* (1883); F. W. Bowen, *History of Port Elizabeth* (1885); and Henry C. Beck, *Forgotten Towns of Southern New Jersey* (1936).

*Jean Graham*

## RACHEL BRADFORD BOUDINOT, 1764–1805

Rachel (Bradford) Boudinot, philanthropist, correspondent, skilled nurse, and property manager, was born in Philadelphia, PA, in 1764, one of the younger of six children (three girls and three boys) of William Bradford of Philadelphia and New York, "the Patriot (newspaper) Printer of 1776" and Rachel (Budd) Bradford of a prosperous family from Burlington County, N.J.

Family finances of the patrician Bradford newspaper dynasty were reduced by the family's support of the American Revolution but Boudinot was taught to read and write at an early age: she became both a proficient and a prolific correspondent within the Bradford-Boudinot-Stockton families and their powerful and wealthy circle of friends. Her manuscript letters illuminate the world of an educated woman of the upper-class in the last quarter of the eighteenth century.

By 1789, when she was 25, Boudinot, an ardent Presbyterian and an industrious person, was living with her beloved brother William Bradford and sister-in-law Susan Vergereau (Boudinot) Bradford. In her role as household manager, Boudinot received a letter, on April 23, 1789, from Elias Boudinot, her brother's father-in-law, request-

ing her to buy a plough for the newly purchased farm, Rose Hill, near Philadelphia "in consequence of your lately commencing the double character of Master & Mistress within your little domestic seignory." (Stimson Boudinot Collection) This letter from Elias Boudinot reveals Boudinot's character and multiple roles at this time, as he teased: "Do not look grave & make a serious speech of what am I come to, that I must turn Farmer, as well as Lawyer & Gardner, &, &, &; I'll repay you." (Stimson Boudinot Collection)

Boudinot's domestic circle at Rose Hill was shattered by her brother's death from yellow fever in August 1795, a year after he had been appointed attorney general by President George Washington. Boudinot had been his chief nurse and witnessed his death. She immediately wrote to Samuel Bayard, formerly her husband's law partner, on August 27, 1795: "My friend, my guide, my counsellor, my protector, my companion, my idol, my earthly all—oh gracious Heaven have you suffered me to live to say it, my brother, my all is gone . . . (who) . . . for 20 years he has been my soul's centre, the Alpha and Omega of every plan." (Bradford Papers)

From William Bradford's death and Boudinot's witness of it, there emerged a bitter family dispute between physician Benjamin Rush and statesman Elias Boudinot. During the remaining years of her life, she wrote many letters and prepared for numerous appearances in court regarding her brother's death.

In 1797, Catherine Peartree (Smith) Boudinot, wife of Elisha Boudinot, brother of Elias, died from yellow fever, and the following year Elisha himself was stricken in Trenton. Boudinot, a skilled nurse, healed him, to the relief and gratitude of both families. (Boyd, *Elias Boudinot, Patriot and Statesman*, 236) On October 22, 1798, Elias wrote to her from Newark, NJ: "The appearance of a recovery in our Brother has given . . .joy throughout this village. . . .We are exceedingly obliged by your constant & faithful account of my brother's illness—I am anxious to know how you are; do take prudent care of yourself." (Stimson Boudinot Collection)

On December 22, 1798, Rachel Bradford and Elisha Boudinot were married. There had been a prenuptial agreement, "a certain Deed of trust and settlement . . . to certain Trustees" between this 35-year-old woman and her 58-year-old husband, father of six surviving children. (*New Jersey Archives, Wills*, vol. 3448B) The children were Anna Maria, Catherine, Susan, Julia, Elias E., and Eliza Pintard Boudinot.

Boudinot lived at Elisha's newly rebuilt mansion (an earlier house had burned in 1797) at 74 Park Place, Newark, from 1799 to 1805. During these six years she took her duties as wife, hostess, and stepmother seriously, executing them with characteristic skill and sensitivity. Writing to her husband in Burlington on February 26, 1799,

Boudinot hoped he would be "getting a pair of over shoes to preserve your feet . . . and are well cloathed in that cold Court House." (Stimson Boudinot Collection) While in Burlington on April 1, 1799, she wrote to him in Newark: "Kiss my dear children for a parent, that loves them with a love that hope will show itself through Eternity." (Stimson Boudinot Collection) On September 2, 1800, Boudinot reported with pride that all the children were well and that she was pleased with (son) Elias's devotion to his drawing: "I am glad however that a passion so harmless acts so powerfully as to overcome idleness, and keep him out of the society of Boys that would perhaps injure & corrupt him." (Stimson Boudinot Collection) In another letter, written on September 4, 1800, she gloried in the chance to serve her husband's guests oysters and recounted how much it pleased him to offer his guests a fine table. (Stimson Boudinot Collection) She sought roots for rare annuals for her house garden, found the best pickling cucumber, prepared sweetmeats, and requested that her quilt patterns be returned from a relative.

Boudinot pondered, read and wrote about the role of African-Americans in the new republic. In a letter to Samuel Bayard dated August 13, 1796, she recounted "two late curiosities of that city (Philadelphia)" one of which was a "Black swan turned white." In this letter—really an extraordinary essay—she reviewed the plethora of theories of what this "curiosity" might mean for African-American. "Some politicians may say it is a striking prof [sic] that all men *shall* be *equal*, seeing the Doctrine of Equality is so advocated that others more moderate may use it [as] an argument in favour of Negro emancipation only," she wrote. "Our friend Doct [Samuel Stanhope] Smith I find is much pleased with the fact, as tending to strenthen his Hypothesis—and Good Doct [Benjamin] Rush who has long been of opinion that the dye of the Negroes skin is the effect of an hereditary Leprosey and so accounts for it, upon Natural Principles—is delighted to find even a single case to prove his position." (Bradford Papers) Boudinot was referring to Benjamin Rush's essay "Observations intended to favour a supposition that the Black Color (as it is called) of the Negroes is derived from the leprosy," which was read at the American Philosophical Society in 1792 and published in 1799.

She wrote to her husband about a Boudinot slave in May 1800: "This morning I parted with Jack. Had I have known how many tears and what pains it would have cost me to sell him, I should I believe have recalled my word—yet, when I consider the dreadful example from which he is removed, and the advantage under which he is placed I cannot regret the step I have taken as I hope he will be filled for time, and instructed for eternity." (Stimson Boudinot Collection) She lost money on this sale, her letter continued, "but I readily gave up the £5 to secure five years freedom to the poor little fellow" (who was to be freed at 25 years old). (Stimson Boudinot Collection)

In her will, drawn up on June 29, 1802, Boudinot stipulated that the interest on $250 "be paid to our black Woman Phebe, if she shall remain in my service at the time of my death, during her life." (*New Jersey Archives, Wills*)

Boudinot's values of Christian charity and concern for the ills of society found expression in the establishment of the "Female Society for the Relief of Poor and Distressed Persons in the Village of Newark." This private welfare agency was founded in response to a challenge from the pulpit of the First Presbyterian Church. On Monday, January 31, 1803, Boudinot met with Newark women in her house at 74 Park Place and was unanimously chosen moderator and chaired the first meeting, at which her stepdaughters Anna-Maria, Julia, and Susan were in attendance.

Organizing other women into officers and managers, Boudinot, the first directress, helped establish criteria for distributing help to the poor, in kind, never in cash. Each member paid one dollar annual dues. Each manager, in turn, was responsible for finding schools for children, paid jobs for adults who met certain criteria of what was then called "character" but which were in reality tests of lifestyle and morality. The motto "To Help the Poor to Help Themselves" explained the purpose of the Society in a town which numbered 4,500 by 1805. (*Record of the Newark Society,* 127)

The Female Charitable Society for the relief of the poor and distressed persons, renamed the Newark Female Charitable Society, celebrated its centennial in 1903, wrote its own history, and continues to serve the Newark populace today as the Newark Day Center for Older People, which operates at the building erected on Hill and Halsey streets in 1887.

On May 11, 1803, Boudinot wrote to her husband of her own tenuous health: she would attend to a garden as long as she was able "but how long that will be the Author & Giver of Life alone knows if the Pain in my Breast continues." (Stimson Boudinot Collection) Boudinot had complained of severe colds, which lasted for months, possibly caught as a result of her almost constant nursing duties for members of the extended family. Her will was drawn up June 29, 1802, possibly after one of these bouts of illness. It was probated on July 18, 1808. Besides her husband, her will named exclusively female beneficiaries: her female friends, her sisters and their children, her slave Phebe, and "the female children of my husband Elisha." (*New Jersey Archives, Wills*)

Boudinot died in Newark on June 6, 1805. She was buried in the Boudinot family plot in the Presbyterian Churchyard in Newark, NJ.

Excerpts from the manuscript letters of Boudinot published by permission of NJ-PU in the Stimson Boudinot, the Thorne

Boudinot, and the Bradford collections. NJ-HS holds documents relating to the founding of the Newark Female Charitable Society, including the *Record of the Newark Society*. For additional information on Boudinot's work with the society, see Mrs. A.R.F. Martin, *A Century of Benevolence, 1803–1903* (1903). References to Boudinot appear in George Adams Boyd, *Elias Boudinot, Patriot and Statesman* (1952); and Barbara L. Clark, *E.B.: The Story of Elias Boudinot IV, His Family, His Friends, and His Country* (1977). Her will appears in the *New Jersey Archives*.

*Constance Killian Escher*
*Clare E. Meyer*

## ESTHER EDWARDS BURR, 1732–1758

Esther (Edwards) Burr was the wife of the second president of the College of New Jersey (now Princeton University) and mother of the third vice-president of the United States. Born February 13, 1732, she was the third of eleven children (third daughter) born to the Rev. Jonathan Edwards, pastor of the Congregational church at Northampton, MA, and Sarah (Pierpont) Edwards. On both sides, a lineage of local gentry and distinguished ministers stretched back to New England's founders.

Jonathan Edwards was famous as the intellectual leader of an evangelical resurgence within the Congregational and Presbyterian churches of the northeastern colonies. When Burr was eighteen, her father was dismissed by his church in a dispute over the rules for admission to the church. In 1752 the family was exiled to the dangerous frontier settlement at Stockbridge, MA, where Edwards preached to an Indian mission.

We know little of Burr's childhood. At home she received an unusually good education for a girl of her times: letters she wrote later show variable phonetic spelling (common in that era) but also familiarity with advanced levels of religious and literary culture. Her youthful personality was remembered by a ministerial student who had lived with the family as demonstrating a "lively, sprightly imagination . . . [and] penetrating thought. . . . She knew how to be pleasant and facetious without trespassing on the bonds of gravity, or strict and serious religion." (Hopkins, *Life and Character of Jonathan Edwards*, 104)

On June 29, 1752, she married the Rev. Aaron Burr, member of a notable Connecticut family and pastor of the Presbyterian church at Newark, NJ. The bride's transition to her new home and role was eased by her familiarity with the duties of life in the home of an evangelical pastor who was thoroughly enmeshed in the politics of congregations and ministerial associations. Despite the seventeen-year difference in their ages, husband and wife shared a deep spiritual commitment and freely expressed their affection for each other in letters to friends.

This marriage, which produced two children—Sarah, known as Sally (b. 1754), and Aaron, Jr. (b. February 6, 1756)—was subjected to the strain of Aaron Burr's almost constant travels as well as his duties as president of the College of New Jersey, which moved from Newark to Princeton in 1756. Burr's role in all of these events was not that of a direct actor, but her maintenance of the minister's household was an indispensable part of his public career. Although the cultural ideology of the time mandated that women devote themselves to housework and child rearing, a college president's wife found that her "housework" included feeding and conversing with the leading men of the region, housing a number of the college students, and lodging an inexhaustible stream of wayfaring clergymen and gentry. In addition, the pastor's wife had to visit parishioners on all occasions of birth, sickness, and death and to receive calls whenever her neighbors had important business or leisure time.

Characteristic entries in Burr's diary are: "For about a Month past there has not been above 4 or 5 nights except on the Sabbath but I have had Travellers to Lodge." (April 23, 1756) And: "All the Women in Princeton to see me and my Sister[;] hurried a preparing for Company that is to come tomorrow to the synod." And the next day: "Sundry Minnisters to dine and a Whole Room full to Tea and three to Lodge." (May 16 and 17, 1757; Karlsen and Crumpacker, eds., *Journal*, 198, 260) Burr's children needed constant supervision, and they were frequently sick, as was their mother. Although her husband's relatively high income and her essentially urban residence enabled Burr to avoid much household drudgery by buying some clothing and foodstuffs, hers was not a "ladylike" existence of gentility and leisure. Rather, she had the exhausting responsibility of managing the complex household of a community leader in provincial America.

Burr complained in her journal that she "could not get one vacant moment for my Life" (*Journal*, 209), by which she probably meant her personal thoughts, religious meditations, and the psychologically sustaining writings that are the major surviving record of her life. Her "journal" is actually a series of letters, beginning in late 1754 and containing almost daily entries, mailed periodically to Sarah Prince of Boston. Despite physical separation, Burr and Prince maintained an intensely close friendship that encompassed practical advice, sharing news of friends and kin, discussing new books (for example, Samuel Richardson's *Pamela* and *Clarissa*), philosophical discussions of the role of women in their culture, and shared spiritual confessions and convictions.

It is through this journal, recently published for the first time, that Burr claims her greatest historical importance. Detailed records of the daily lives of women in pre-Revolutionary America are rare, and even rarer is the record of a woman's thoughts and feelings. Unfortunately, Burr's diary ends abruptly in September 1757, just before the death of her husband. Jonathan Edwards succeeded his son-in-law as president of the College of New Jersey; he then died of a smallpox inoculation in March 1758, a month after his arrival in Princeton.

Burr contracted a fever and died, at age 26, on April 7, 1758; she is buried in Princeton near her husband and father. The sad journey of Burr's mother, Sarah (Pierpont) Edwards, from Stockbridge to Princeton to gather up her two orphaned grandchildren also ended in tragedy: she died of dysentery in October 1758.

Until recently, Burr's major claim to historians' attention was her role as the mother of Sarah Burr, who married Tapping Reeve of Litchfield, CT, founder of America's first law school, and of Aaron Burr, Jr., who became the third vice-president of the United States in 1800. But now, through the survival of the letters she wrote to Sarah Prince, Burr is historically important in her own right, an individual who articulated a unique perspective on cultural life in 18th-century America.

The most important source of information on Burr is Carol F. Karlsen and Laurie Crumpacker, eds., *The Journal of Esther Edwards Burr, 1754–1757* (1984). The original of the journal is at C-YU. Details of Burr's childhood and family life appear in Samuel Hopkins, *The Life and Character of the Late Reverend, Learned and Pious Mr. Jonathan Edwards* (1799).

*Patricia J. Tracy*

## HANNAH OGDEN CALDWELL, unknown–1780

Hannah (Ogden) Caldwell, minister's wife and American Revolutionary War victim, was the daughter of John Ogden, an attorney living in Newark (Essex County), NJ. She was the wife of the Rev. James Caldwell, known as "the Fighting Parson," a Presbyterian minister and chaplain to the American army stationed in Jockey Hollow, near Morristown. Caldwell was not the only innocent victim of the British army, but her position of respect as a minister's wife and mother of nine, plus her husband's fame, made her murder a focus of outrage.

When the war began, Caldwell was living with her husband and children in Elizabethtown, where the Rev. Caldwell was a clergyman in the First Presbyterian Church. The town's proximity to New York, with its British garrison, led the Rev. Caldwell to move his family farther west to the rural village of Connecticut Farms (now the town of Union). As pastor of the Connecticut Farms Church, he lived with his family in the parsonage behind the church.

In 1780, the year she died, Caldwell was mother to nine children, aged two to sixteen. Because of her husband's prolonged absences with the army she had shouldered the day-to-day responsibilities of this large family since the war's beginning. It was a difficult task, compli-

cated by frequent evacuations whenever enemy forces threatened the area. For the most part, these evacuations had proved unnecessary, and Caldwell was determined not to subject her family to more of them. She was confident in the protection of her God and the mannerly conduct of the British.

On June 7, 1780, General Baron Wilhelm von Knyphausen, commander of the Hessian troops in the British army of occupation, first ventured into the hills of New Jersey, with 2,500 men. He marched toward Springfield, where he met American resistance. Like the British before him, he had underestimated the Americans and found it necessary to withdraw to plan a new strategy. Furious at this turn of events, he left behind a company of soldiers with instructions to burn Connecticut Farms.

Earlier that day Caldwell's neighbors had encouraged her to evacuate to Bottle Hill, but she refused. She had been up most of the night with her sick daughter and felt the trip might do the baby harm. Moreover, her seven oldest children were away visiting her sister, and they were not in danger. She remained at home with her two youngest children, her housekeeper, Constance Benward, and a young girl named Abigail Lennington.

As soon as enemy soldiers were seen entering the village, Caldwell and the others went to a back room, which was considered secure, with stone walls on three sides and one window on the north side. Caldwell sat on a bed with Benward, who held the baby. Caldwell's four-year-old son stood by her and Lennington stood at the side of the window. According to Lennington's later deposition, a short, thick man wearing a red coat came around the end of the house and stood opposite the window. He raised his gun and fired at Caldwell, who fell back and died immediately. According to Benward, soldiers then broke into the house and plundered it before setting it on fire. It was only through the intervention of other villagers that Caldwell's body was saved from the flames. The soldiers burned nine other homes, as well as the schoolhouse, barns, and shops, before leaving the village.

According to General (Marquis de) Lafayette, who recounted the story while visiting Hannah Caldwell's monument in 1824, the Rev. Caldwell was in a tent at Jockey Hollow chatting with Lafayette when a messenger arrived with news of his wife's death. Another source states that the Rev. Caldwell was in Short Hills when he heard two soldiers discussing the death of his wife.

Although the British maintained that Caldwell had been killed by a random bullet, the Rev. Caldwell believed she had been murdered in retaliation for his association with the American army. Three months after his wife's death, the Rev. Caldwell published a pamphlet containing depositions from several witnesses supporting his position. This pamphlet was widely circulated and effectively strengthened the patriot cause.

The Rev. Caldwell's accusations were given further credence by his own death a year later. While meeting a passenger at Elizabethtown wharf, he was shot point-blank by an American soldier named James Morgan. Even though the prosecution was unable to prove at Morgan's trial that he had been hired by the British, the belief still persisted.

Caldwell and her husband were buried in Elizabethtown, NJ, near the site of the First Presbyterian Church where he had once been minister. The grave is marked by a monument that reads: "Sacred to the memory of the Rev. James Caldwell and Hannah, his wife, who fell victims to their country's cause in the years 1780–1781."

James Caldwell's pamphlet *Certain Facts Relating to the Tragic Death of Hannah Caldwell, Wife of Rev. James Caldwell* (1780) contains depositions of neighbors and witnesses and appears in the *Union County Historical Society. Proceedings* 2 (1923–24):10–15. "Sketch of the Rev. James Caldwell," in Isaac Van Arsdale Brown, *Memoirs of the Rev. Robert Finley, D.D.* (1819), contains background information on James Caldwell. Robert Hoffman, *The Revolutionary Scene in New Jersey* (1942), presents a dramatized account of the deaths of Hannah and James Caldwell; and Linda Grant DePauw, *Fortunes of War: New Jersey Women and the American Revolution* (1975), places the murder of Hannah Caldwell in the context of other female victims of the war.

*Sally Stone Forester*

Elizabeth Carteret, oil portrait by Sir Peter Lely. An English woman from the Isle of Jersey, Carteret succeeded her husband as Colonial proprietor of East Jersey from 1680 to 1682. *Courtesy, Free Public Library of Elizabeth, NJ.*

## ELIZABETH CARTERET, 1615–1696

Elizabeth Carteret, briefly proprietor of East Jersey, was born in 1615 at Castle Elizabeth, Isle of Jersey, the youngest of four surviving children of Philip and Anne (Dowse) Carteret. In 1640 Carteret married her first cousin George Carteret, who succeeded his father-in-law as bailiff and governor of the Isle of Jersey in 1643. He held a number of other important posts, including a vice-admiralship in the navy, and became first proprietor of New Jersey when Charles II gave this acquired territory to him and to John Lord Berkeley in 1669. Berkeley sold his rights to a company of Quakers in 1674, and two years later New Jersey was divided into East Jersey and West Jersey. East Jersey remained under the proprietorship of the Carterets until 1682, when it was sold to Pennsylvania Quakers. Eventually, the two Jerseys were reunited as one colony in 1702 by Queen Anne.

Sir George and Lady Carteret never came to New Jersey themselves, but appointed Philip Carteret, their fourth cousin, to be the first governor of East Jersey. When Philip arrived in the colony in 1665, he found a small settlement, which he named Elizabeth Towne, in honor of his cousin. Lady Carteret was thereby immortalized in the colony, and the later state of New Jersey.

It is believed that George and Elizabeth Carteret were the parents of eight children, three boys and five girls, although inadequate documentation makes it impossible to verify this. *The Diary of Samuel Pepys,* however, provides insight into the family life of the Carterets and into the character of Elizabeth Carteret.

According to Pepys, the Carteret family was a happy and a warm one. The Carteret home in Deptford, England, was the scene of music, merriment, fine suppers, and friendship. Pepys was first received by Carteret in 1662. Thereafter, he was a regular visitor to the Carteret manor house and a good friend of the family. Every reference of his to Carteret contains the most extravagant praise, and he describes her as a most kind and excellent woman. Carteret bestowed hospitality as graciously to a commoner, such as Pepys, as she did to English royalty.

Carteret's likeness was celebrated in a famous painting by Sir Peter Lely, who captured the gentle and kind qualities Pepys wrote about. In the painting, she wears a maize silk gown. Her hair is classically coiffed, arranged in corkscrew curls at each side with tiny ringlets at the hairline. Her throat is encircled by a strand of exceptional pearls, thought to be a gift from Sir George.

Carteret's significant relationship to the colony of New Jersey developed after her husband's death in 1680. In George Carteret's will his wife was designated not only as his heir, but also as proprietor of East Jersey. This action reflected both the love and respect of a husband for his wife and the business partnership they shared. Such responsibility was not uncommon for a 17th-century wife, who often worked her husband's lands or took care of his business ventures in his absence or after his death. Under English common law the status of an independent woman, or *feme sole*, as was accorded to Carteret, allowed her to exercise all the privileges of an independent person, including the buying and selling of land.

Carteret, as proprietor of East Jersey, had theoretically almost limitless authority and answered only to the crown—although to ignore the Provincial Assembly would not have been a wise political action. Thus, aspects of the ancient feudal basis for holding the title of proprietor of East Jersey had to give way to the changing reality of Colonial government. Carteret's role as East Jersey proprietor and sole executor of her husband's will placed her, however, in a unique position to exercise ultimate authority in the affairs of the colony.

In 1682 Carteret and the designated trustees of the Carteret estate decided to sell East Jersey to Quaker followers of William Penn, thereby ending her tenure as proprietor of East Jersey.

Carteret's brief place in the history of New Jersey is significant: few women in the 17th century were granted such authority either in fact or in name. She is, however, noted more for the status she held and the authority she possessed than for her accomplishments as proprietor of the Colonial province of East Jersey during her short tenure of office. Carteret died, at age 81, in 1696 of natural causes and was buried next to her husband in the Carteret chapel at Hawnes Manor, Deptford, England.

*The Diary of Samuel Pepys*, 2 vols. (1951), edited by Henry B. Wheatley, provides historical perspective into the lives of Elizabeth and George Carteret. G. R. Balleine, *All for the King: The Life Story of Sir George Carteret* (1976), is a secondary source on the Carteret family and their political activities. Sophie H. Drinker, "The Two Elizabeth Carterets," *NJHSP* 79 (1961):95–110, is an informative article that correctly differentiates the two Elizabeth Carterets, one the wife of Sir George and the other the wife of Philip Carteret. An article by Charles Lee Meyers, "Lady Elizabeth, Wife of Sir George Carteret, and Her Portrait," *NJHSP* 11 (1926):145–51, at one point confuses her with the wife of Philip Carteret.

*Dorothy Prisco*

## HANNAH DENT COOPER, unknown–d. 1754

Hannah (Dent) Cooper, memorialized in early Colonial religious history as a minister of the Society of Friends, was born in Wensleydale, Yorkshire, England, the daughter of Robert Dent. Raised in a devout Quaker family, she early demonstrated a calling for the ministry because of her talent as a speaker at the Friends Monthly Meeting in Richmond, England. In the Society of Friends, ministers were not appointed; anyone, man or woman, could work at a ministry.

Early in 1732 the Richmond Monthly Meeting sent Cooper to visit meetings in the American colonies. She sailed to Philadelphia with her sister, Ann, who married shortly after their arrival. Accompanied by another minister, Mary Nicholls of Philadelphia, Cooper visited and spoke at meetings in Maryland, Virginia, and North Carolina, where they were warmly received.

In 1734 she and another Philadelphia minister, Elizabeth Widdifield, visited meetings in the eastern colonies. At one of these, Cooper met Joseph W. Cooper, Jr., a widower, an elder of the Newton (Camden, NJ) Meeting, and a prominent member of the New Jersey Assembly under the first Colonial governor, Lewis Morris. They were married on May 1, 1735, at the Arch Street Meeting House in Philadelphia.

Although the Coopers had no children, they cared for three grandchildren when Cooper's stepdaughter died. They lived in the three-story brick house Joseph Cooper had built for his first family. He was a wealthy man and undoubtedly his wife had servants to help her with housekeeping and entertaining her husband's friends and associates and the many traveling Quaker ministers who visited them. They were known to be friends with Benjamin Franklin, who did printing work for Joseph Cooper.

Soon Cooper became active in the Haddonfield Friends Meeting, which had been established by ELIZABETH HADDON in 1724. The minutes of the Haddonfield Friends Meeting record that in 1736, a year after her marriage, Cooper was transferred from the Yearly Meeting in London to the Haddonfield Meeting. At this time she was deeply involved in her ministry and traveled extensively. In 1739 she went to Barbados, the easternmost island of the West Indies, with Mary Foulke, and the following year she sailed to Boston to visit New England. Their visit helped strengthen Boston Quakers, persecuted under the Cart and Whip Act of 1661.

After she returned, her health broke down, and she no longer traveled. Throughout her ministry, Cooper gained a reputation for wisdom and piety. Her ministry included not only the spreading of the "Truth," as a speaker at Friends meetings, but also the duties prescribed for women in the early years of Quaker work in London: "to visit the sick and to search out the necessities of the poor, weak, widows and aged." In addition to the labors of her ministry, Cooper maintained her position as the wife of an important political figure, winning many friends among her husband's associates.

When she died, on February 11, 1754, after being widowed for five years, her Monthly Meeting described Cooper as a "living minister, an humble, tender-hearted Friend, a true sympathizer with those in affliction," and as a "nursing mother to those that were young in the service of the ministry."

[Information on Cooper appears in the Cooper *Family Register* (1679); Willard C. Heiss, ed., *Quaker Biographical Sketches of Ministers and Elders* (1972); and Arnold Lloyd, *Quaker Social History, 1669–1738* (1950).

*Joan L. Aiken*
*Sheila Cowing*

## ELIZABETH CROOK, ca. 1718–unknown

Elizabeth Crook enters New Jersey's Colonial history with a brief entry on page 162 in the fading manuscript court proceedings for Salem County. It was the morning of Tuesday, November 30, 1732, and Elizabeth Crook was charged with petty larceny. The offense was the theft of some object probably worth less than one shilling (a twentieth of a pound). The case has attracted the attention of local historians for over 150 years because of Crook's knowledge of English common law, which forced the judge, Josiah Fithian, to call a second jury of twelve women to determine if Crook's punishment would be inflicted immediately or be postponed because of her pregnancy. No other personal information is currently available on Crook.

After pleading not guilty to the petty larceny charge, Crook used the device of diplomatic language to address the judge and the grand jury of sixteen men. She is recorded as saying: "Because she will not Contest with Our Lord the King she retracts her plea of not guilty, and pleads Guilty and puts herself in favor of the Court." (*Minutes*, 162) The judge, and the grand jury, imposed a brutal sentence: "twenty lashes well laid on her bare back at the common whipping post and committed till pays fees." Crook, we suspect, was astonished at the severe punishment. A reading through the *Minutes* of Salem County court proceedings for this time (1727–42) shows the punishments given to other defendants (men) who used the formula of asking for mercy when changing their plea to guilty. In such cases, the same court officials imposed sentences ranging from a fine of ten shillings to five lashes of the whip. Five months prior to Crook's trial, Richard Crook (there is no evidence of a relationship between the two) received the ten-shilling fine for an unspecified crime and was ordered to be committed to the custody of the sheriff until the fine and the court fees were paid. (*Minutes*, 139) In the afternoon immediately following Elizabeth Crook's hearing, Charles Crook, also charged with petty larceny, submitted "himself to the favour of the Bench" (*Minutes*, 162) and was given a sentence of five lashes.

Hearing her punishment, Crook asked for a delay in the whipping because she was "quick with Child." (*Minutes*, 162) In formal terms, this was the common law writ *de ventre inspiciendo*—to inspect the body of a woman for pregnancy—a postponement of the death penalty because the convicted woman was pregnant. It required the court to impanel a jury of twelve discreet women or matrons (a married woman or an elderly woman) to verify that the pregnancy was at least in the fourth month of gestation. It was essential that the jury be able to detect fetal movement. The law made a distinction between being just with child (the punishment, even death, was inflicted) and being quick with child (punishment was postponed until the baby was delivered).

In this Salem County case, twelve women were summoned to jury duty: Susannah Goodwin, Sarah Hunt, Ann Grant, Mary Grey, Elizabeth Hackett, Sarah Loft, Elizabeth Hall, Phoebe Saterthwaite, Ann Woodnot, Elizabeth Huddy, Elizabeth Axford, and Sarah Fithian. Being duly qualified according to the law, the jury of women returned their verdict that the defendant was "quick with a living Child." (*Minutes*, 162) The court records continue with the attorney general moving that Crook be committed into the custody of the sheriff, George Trencher, until she delivered her child, and then the sentence of 20 lashes was to be given.

With that, Crook disappears from the public eye and there is no further record about her. We suspect that in the intervening months she and her family were encouraged to leave the county. Even in the 1720s the sheriffs of Salem County had difficulty in keeping prisoners in the jail. It would seem an economic move to allow indigent troublemakers to escape while still maintaining the facade of law enforcement. Historians of the American Colonial period help us deduce a little more about this incident. Crook was a white woman—because she was not described otherwise; she was married—because she was not described as being unmarried and pregnant with a bastard child; and she was caught in some mischief involving an article probably worth less than a shilling. The theft of a small amount of food, clothing, or household utensils seems likely. The stolen item was definitely worth less than 20 shillings (one pound), which was considered larceny and was punishable by up to 39 lashes, according to a 1739 law. We assume that the definition of larceny would have been commonly accepted throughout the decade of the 1730s. Crook was probably over the age of fourteen and under the age of 50 because of her verified pregnancy. If she did stay in Salem County, or in New Jersey, her descendants have not been anxious to include references to her sojourn in the Salem County jail in their genealogies. So today we know only a few facts from the court records and surmise a little more: Crook was a married white woman of childbearing age—a woman of strong character who learned what she needed to know about the legal system in order to use it to her best advantage.

The primary source for material on Crook is *Minutes, Quarter Sessions, 1727–1742, Salem County*, available at the Office of the

Salem County Clerk. References to Crook appear in Robert Gibbon Johnson, *An Historical Account of the First Settlement of Salem, in West Jersey . . .* (1839); and in Joseph Sickler, *The History of Salem County, New Jersey . . .* (1937).

*Mary Alice Quigley*

## ELIZABETH DAVIS BRICK WORTHINGTON DUNLAP, ca. 1705–1761

Elizabeth Davis (Brick) Worthington Dunlap, an 18th-century Salem County woman who was able to extricate herself from an unhappy and probably abusive marriage, was born into the Quaker family of John and Hannah (Davis) Brick. John Brick and Hannah Davis were married about 1703, but only one birth date (1705) of their four sons and no birth date of their two daughters is recorded. Elizabeth Brick's birthplace and date can only be inferred to have been Salem County ca. 1703–6.

As early settlers and large landowners in Salem County, the Brick family became involved in farming, lumbering, milling, and tavern keeping. John Brick's civic activities included service as overseer of the poor and representative to the General Assembly from 1730 to 1733. John Brick first proposed the creation of Cumberland County out of what was Salem County, but it was not until his son John Brick, Jr., served in the assembly (1745–51) that Cumberland County actually separated in 1748.

Little is known about Dunlap's first husband, Ephraim Worthington, a yeoman of Pilesgrove (Salem County). He, too, was evidently a Quaker. The records of Salem Friends Meeting indicate that the Worthingtons were married September 26, 1722, when Elizabeth was somewhere between sixteen and nineteen years old. Two sons, John and Ephraim, were born to them, although their birth dates are not known. Ephraim Worthington died in 1727.

As his widow, Dunlap was named administrator of his personal estate, which included farm animals, implements, and household goods. The will was signed with her mark, a crude backward letter *E*, indicating that she may have been illiterate at that time. By March 1728 she had settled all her husband's debts. Her father, John Brick, and uncle, Malachi Davis, were fellow bondsmen of the will.

On March 29, 1731, she married, as his second wife, Captain James Dunlap (d. 1758), of Penn's Neck (Salem County), who had settled in that area as a large land purchaser in about 1715. His family had come from Delaware and was supposedly of Irish descent. Virtually nothing is known of his first wife except that her given name was Bathsheba and that her baptism and that of her infant son James (1725–73) took place in the First Presbyterian Church of Philadelphia on February 6, 1727. Two other sons, whose birth dates are unknown, were born: John (d.

1767) and Thomas (d. 1775). Presumably Bathsheba Dunlap died prior to March 1731.

With their marriage the Dunlaps merged two already established families, which included her two sons and his three sons. There is almost no documentation of the next decade in their lives. James Dunlap probably persuaded his wife to his Presbyterian leanings because both she and Ephraim Worthington, her son, were baptized at Pilesgrove on October 22, 1740. Together James and Elizabeth Dunlap joined with 47 others on April 30, 1741, to found the Pilesgrove Presbyterian Church, with David Evans as pastor.

The next year was cataclysmic in the Dunlaps' marriage. James Dunlap published a notice in the March 18–25, 1742, issue of the *American Weekly Mercury* and the *Pennsylvania Gazette*, which warned the public that his wife had "eloped" and that he would no longer be responsible for her debts. She denied the accusation on April 8, 1742, contending instead that she had fled to her father's home for "the safety of her life" to escape "the threats and abuses for several years repeatedly offered and done to her." (*N.J. Archives*, 12:120–21, 130–31, 142–43) In addition, she warned she would not accede to any sale of land to which she claimed a third by right of dower. The *American Weekly Mercury* of June 10–17, 1742, published her rebuttal. James Dunlap published his own rebuttal during the week of August 5–12, 1742, essentially denying her charges. The Presbyterian Church at Pilesgrove had censured them on June 12, 1742, and had debarred both of them from communion for "breaking their marriage" and "unchristian behavior in words and actions." (Turner, *Presbyterian Historical Society Journal*, 69) With the fiery disintegration of her marriage, Dunlap numbered herself among six of the 134 "eloped" wives during the 50-year period from 1730 to 1780 who publicly declared maltreatment by their husbands.

Dunlap presumably relied on her family network for refuge and support in her decision to separate from her husband. Indeed, when her father died in 1753 he made special provision for her for the duration of her life and for her two children, John and Ephraim Worthington. The Worthington children were, in fact, the only grandchildren he named in his will.

The 1758 will of James Dunlap left his estate to a daughter, Mary Ann, raising the slim possibility that Elizabeth and James had had a daughter during their marriage.

Dunlap died in April 1761 in Salem County. The exact date, cause of her death, and place of burial are unrecorded. Her personal estate amounted to nearly £450, to be divided among John, David, Hannah, Rachel, and Sarah Worthington, her five grandchildren. She further declared that her two mulatto servants, a boy named Ned and his mother, be freed at ages 21 and 30 years, respectively. No mention is made of a daughter. Dunlap signed her own name to her will, a fitting gesture of her success at extricating herself from a contentious marriage.

Microfilmed copies of the wills of Elizabeth Dunlap, James Dunlap, John Brick, and Ephraim Worthington are available at NJ-NJSL. *New Jersey Archives*, 1st series, 12 (1895):120–21, 130–31, and 142–43, reprinted the 1742 newspaper notices between Dunlap and her husband. An invaluable published source is Rev. Joseph Brown Turner, "The Vital Records of the Pilesgrove Presbyterian Church, 1740–1768," *Presbyterian Historical Society Journal* 9 (1917):65–94. Important genealogical guides are H. Stanley Craig, *Salem County New Jersey Genealogical Data* (1934– ; 1980); and William W. Hinshaw, *Encyclopedia of American Quaker Genealogy* (1969).

*Patricia A. Beaber*

## THEODOSIA JOHNES FORD, 1741–1824

Theodosia (Johnes) Ford, a widow with four children and mistress of the Ford Mansion in Morristown, NJ, was a contributing patriot of the American Revolution who extended the use of her home to General George Washington for his military headquarters when Washington and his staff officers occupied her home from December 1779 to June 1780.

Ford was born September 13, 1741, presumably in Connecticut, the second child of the Rev. Timothy Johnes, the respected pastor of the Presbyterian Church of Morristown, and Elizabeth (Sayre) Johnes. Both her parents were of English ancestry.

From Ford's early life on, she was influenced by her family's religious, social, and political ties. The Rev. Johnes graduated from Yale (1737) as a doctor of divinity and became the undisputed leader of the Morristown community. It was Johnes who greeted General George Washington and his staff at his semiannual communion service in 1777. During the Revolution, he also organized care for military and civilian smallpox victims at his church.

Elizabeth (Sayre) Johnes died on September 19, 1748, just six days after Ford's seventh birthday, leaving Ford and her siblings motherless for over a year. These siblings included an older sister, Phebe (who died at age thirteen), Samuel Stevens, Elizabeth, and Timothy. Ford's father married Keziah (Oldfield) Ludlow, then a childless widow, on November 15, 1749. The Johnes children by this marriage were Anne and William. The extent of Ford's education is unknown. As a young girl, her life focused on family and church, with time spent on the homemaking skills and handiwork of that era.

On January 27, 1762, she married Jacob Ford, Jr., son of Jacob and Hannah (Baldwin) Ford of Morristown. Like his father, Jacob Ford, Jr., was a prominent landowner and successful businessman. He owned an iron mine and 2,000 acres of land in Mount Hope, four miles north of Rocka-

way, and the Middle Forge on Picatinny Peak, now the location of the Picatinny Arsenal.

In 1770 he erected a stone mansion at Mount Hope, where the Fords lived until the birth of their fourth child. At that time the Fords were asked by Jacob Ford, Sr., to return to Morristown to manage the Ford family holdings. Leasing their Mount Hope properties, they moved in with Jacob Ford, Jr.'s parents and his grandmother, Elizabeth Lindsley. In return for their efforts, the Fords were given 200 acres of the estate, on which the "Ford Mansion" construction began in 1772, using the exact floor plan of their home in Mount Hope. By 1774 the Fords had settled into one of the largest and most prestigious homes in the area, although the second floor remained unplastered.

With the onset of the Revolution, Ford's husband received permission from the Provincial Congress to construct a powder mill a short distance from Morristown in which he would manufacture a large quantity of gunpowder for the Continental Army. As an outstanding patriot, he was commissioned colonel of the Eastern Battalion of New Jersey forces and served until he took ill during the New Jersey "Mud Rounds." He died of pneumonia on January 10, 1777, leaving Ford a widow at 36. By order of Washington, he was buried with full military honors.

Ford was bequeathed the house, furniture, cattle, a gray horse with a riding chair, and a gold mourning ring. She also received annual rents from the Mount Hope holdings to raise and educate her five children: Timothy (b. 1762), Gabriel (b. 1765), Elizabeth (b. 1767), Jacob (b. 1772), and Phebe (b. 1775). The house was designated to go to Ford's oldest child upon his reaching the age of 21, with Ford having the privilege of staying on if she remained a widow. With the outbreak of smallpox in Morristown in 1777, Ford lost her in-laws and two-year-old Phebe.

Like her father and husband, Ford believed in the good of the patriotic cause. In 1777 Ford's home accommodated Rodney's Light Infantry troops during their encampment at Morristown. Two years later, on December 1, 1779, Washington and his entourage arrived during a severe snowstorm. In preparation, Ford and her four surviving children moved furniture and objects of value into their two rooms and possibly a storage area, since stealing by the soldiers was a problem. Martha Washington arrived a few days after Christmas 1779, and was the "official hostess" when present. The Washingtons were allowed use of selected furnishings, including a Chippendale mirror with a Phoenix bird ascending from the top. "By 1780, the Phoenix bird motif evolved into the young nation's symbol, the American eagle." (*Ford Mansion*, 5)

Many important guests visited the Ford Mansion during Washington's stay. They included the Marquis de Lafayette, French Minister Chevalier de la Luzerne, and

Spanish Ambassador Don Juan de Miralles, who unfortunately took ill and died while there. Another guest at the mansion was Washington's aide Alexander Hamilton, who courted Betsy Schuyler of Morristown during his stay. It is believed that Ford was not involved with any of the Washingtons' entertaining.

Ford and her family endured harsh inconvenience during the winter of 1779 to 1780, considered the worst of the 18th century. Washington described the conditions in his letter to General Nathanael Greene: "Eighteen of my family and all of Mrs. Ford's are crowded together in her kitchen, and scarce one of them able to speak for the colds they have caught." (Jan. 22, 1780) Food and supplies were scarce. Ford's necessities were purchased separately from the military, requiring her to be extremely watchful of her finances. Her family no longer enjoyed the privacy and comfort they were accustomed to, for Ford and her children ate, slept, and entertained in their two rooms. They were expected not to interfere with any military business in the rest of the house.

The Ford family frequently experienced unnerving alarms that brought bodyguards charging into their home, at any time, to thwart attempts on the life of Washington from spies in the area.

Washington was especially considerate of his hostess and her children during his stay. He had a log structure built for use as his kitchen and another building for an office, to ease the crowding. Before his departure, Washington inquired if all Ford's silver had been returned. "All but one silver table-spoon," was her reply. A few days later a spoon engraved with the initials "G.W." arrived at the mansion. (Lossing, *The Pictorial Field-Book of the Revolution*, 1:314) Washington also paid Ford the rent agreed upon, replaced the china chipped during his use, had the mansion cleaned and replastered, and left a "large camp chest" as a gift to Ford. (*Ford Mansion*, 4)

As the war continued, Ford remained at the house. Her eldest son, Timothy, who appeared to be a favorite of Washington's, joined the army as a volunteer, wearing his father's sword. "My beloved mother girded it on my thigh," he later said. (Diary of Timothy Ford, 1785–86) Wounded in the Battle of Connecticut Farms, Timothy returned home and later, after graduating from Princeton, moved to South Carolina.

Ford's second child, Gabriel, became a lawyer, handled his mother's interests, and filed her petition for widow's pay from the Revolutionary Claims Court. He later became a New Jersey Supreme Court judge. In 1805 he purchased the mansion from his siblings. Ford's daughter, Elizabeth, eventually married Henry William DeSaussure and moved to South Carolina with him. Jacob Ford III also followed his brother and sister to South Carolina.

Ford never remarried, remaining at the Morristown mansion until her death there on August 31, 1824, at age

83. She is buried in Morristown. Among her possessions found at the time of her death were her husband's silver-mounted sword, the Phoenix mirror, the camp chest, a Quarto Bible, other religious volumes, and a history of Greenland.

Business papers indicated that she owned shares in the Morris Turnpike Co., incorporated by her son Gabriel, as well as various bonds, notes, and stock certificates of the United States. Ford's home eventually became a historic site operated by the National Park Service. Her sacrifice was recognized as a significant contribution to New Jersey, a strategic state hard hit by the Revolutionary struggle.

[The *Ford Family Papers, 1738–1904*, are available at the Ford Mansion Library (Morristown, NJ). A biographical sketch of Ford appears in *LCR*. The NJ-MO maintains an extensive collection of material on the Ford and Johnes families. Her son's diary appears in "The Diary of Timothy Ford, with Notes by Joseph Barnwell," *South Carolina Historical and Genealogy Magazine* 13 (1912):132–47. Washington's comments about his stay with the Fords appear in John C. Fitzpatrick, ed., *The Writings of George Washington*, 39 vols. (1931–44; 1970). Material on the Ford Mansion appears in the National Park Service, *The Ford Mansion: Washington Headquarters, 1779–1780*; James Elliott Lindsley, *A Certain Splendid House* (1974); and Vera Craig and Ralph Lewis, *Furnishing Plan for the Ford Mansion, 1779–1780* (1976); Bension J. Lossing, *The Pictorial Field-Book of the Revolution*, vol. 1 (1851; reprint, 1969).

*Patricia Conroy Gray*

## ELIZABETH DOWNES FRANKLIN, 1728–1777

Born on September 8, 1728, in St. Thomas Parish, Barbados, Elizabeth (Downes) Franklin was a member of the rich sugar plantation society and daughter-in-law of Benjamin Franklin. Her parents, John and Elizabeth (Parsons) Downes, following the custom of the day, sent their daughter to family in England for her education and social debut. She was the wife of William Franklin, the last royal governor of New Jersey.

She met William Franklin in 1760 when he was visiting England with his father, Benjamin Franklin. In contrast to his father, William Franklin preferred to socialize with the English upper class, not only for pleasure but also because he saw political advantages for himself. He met his future wife in the endless social round they both seemed to enjoy so much. By the spring of 1761 she was known to his friends as "his old flame from St. James' Street." (Lopez and Herbert, *The Private Franklin*, 93) William Franklin, now contemplating marriage, was maneuvering at the English court and in the government for an important Colonial post in the Americas, such as governor of Barbados or royal representative in the Carolinas. His father tried to interfere by taking his son away on a series of travels, and later he did not even stay for the wedding.

Elizabeth Downes, at 34 considered old for a first marriage, married William Franklin at St. George's Church, Hanover Square, London, on September 4, 1762. Within a week, William Franklin was appointed royal governor of New Jersey by George III, and after a brief honeymoon, the newlyweds set sail for New Jersey.

Since she came from an aristocratic plantation family, it is not surprising that Franklin fell in easily with her husband's Tory inclinations and quickly adapted to a social round based in Burlington, Perth Amboy, and Philadelphia. William Franklin was sworn in as New Jersey's last royal governor early in 1763 and decided to settle in Burlington, the western capital of New Jersey, close to his family in Philadelphia. Franklin established a congenial relationship with her sister-in-law, Sally Franklin (later Bache); visits between the two were frequent. Franklin delighted in decorating her houses with the finest furnishings that could be found, ordering luxury goods directly from London. Some of her decorating schemes were so elaborate that it was said the silk damask bed used for visitors was such that the guest "could hardly find himself in the morning!" (Mariboe, *The Life of William Franklin*, 148)

This pleasant life of entertaining, races, parties, and balls was threatened by the political instability of the relationship between England and the colonies. Over the years the Franklins had found themselves coming increasingly closer to the society of the East Jersey Proprietors—the Colonial aristocrats of the region. The decision to move into Proprietary House in Perth Amboy, which was provided for the Franklins by the Proprietors, was symbolic as well as personal. Proximity to New York City, with its core of Tory sympathizers, provided a surer channel of communications with London, as well as access to society and merchants. Franklin was, as usual, engrossed with the domestic details—packing up the old establishment and supervising the decorating of the new. Many of the resources for refurbishing the old house in Perth Amboy came from the Colonial Proprietors themselves, and the shops and merchants in New York were used heavily.

Franklin welcomed another member of the Franklin family as they settled into the new home in Perth Amboy; William Temple Franklin, her husband's illegitimate son, had been brought to America by his grandfather, who insisted that the boy attend school in Philadelphia but allowed him to spend his vacations with his father in Perth Amboy. Franklin seems to have greeted him cordially; she never had any children of her own. Later, after her husband's arrest, she came to rely on Temple Franklin, as he was known, and kept up correspondence with him. In one letter she briefly and almost superficially recorded the last meeting between her husband and his father, Benjamin Franklin, before the Revolution broke out, dividing the family so dramatically.

Franklin soon found her life seriously disrupted by fast-moving political events in which she took little part and

over which she had absolutely no control. On January 2, 1776, the Continental Congress passed a resolution to put a stop to the activities of the Loyalists. William Alexander—no friend to the royal governor—had seized the governor's latest dispatches to the government in London and immediately took the opportunity to harass the Franklins. Three days later, at 2:00 A.M., Alexander's militia broke into Proprietary House to ensure that the governor did not escape to New York City. The effect of this intrusion on Franklin was devastating. Two weeks later, she was still so nervous that "the least sudden Noise almost throws her into Hysterics. . . . Another Alarm of the like Nature will put an End to her Life." (Lopez and Herbert, 207)

In spite of suffering badly from nerves and asthma, a condition certainly aggravated by stress, Franklin resolutely refused to leave her husband, who, realizing the dangerous situation they were in, had urged her to return to London or Barbados. She did, however, manage to maintain some correspondence with her sister-in-law, Sally Franklin, complaining of the changed circumstances of her life: "instead of those joyous, social evenings we used to pass with each other, we only meet now to condole together over our wretched situation. But I will stop my pen lest I should infest you with vapors and dejection of spirits." (Lopez and Herbert, 207)

Worse was yet to come. When her husband was placed under house arrest in June 1776, Franklin's health deteriorated. No visitors, not even her "beloved doctor" or her friends, were admitted. Elizabeth and William Franklin parted on June 21, 1776, not realizing that it was the last time that they would see each other—he to his hearing in Burlington and she to the upper floors of her mansion.

Alone in Perth Amboy and alarmed by the occupation of the town by English troops who "have terrified me almost out of my senses" (Lopez and Herbert, 211), she turned to Temple Franklin for help. He offered to deliver letters to his father, then imprisoned in Connecticut, far from Loyalist territory, but this plan was vetoed immediately by Benjamin Franklin, who was keeping a close watch on Perth Amboy. Temple Franklin, however, did what he could for Franklin, acting as courier to the family in Philadelphia, running her errands, and buying her asthmatic elixir and tooth powder. But family ties turned sour; in spite of her precarious situation, Franklin pleaded for her husband. On August 6, 1776, she wrote to her father-in-law: "I will not distress you by enumerating all my Afflictions, but allow me, dear Sir, to mention that it is greatly in your Power to relieve them. Suppose that Mr. Franklin would sign a Parole not dishonorable to himself and satisfactory to Governor Trumbull, why may he not be permitted to return to this Province and to his Family?" (Lopez and Herbert, 212) Out of fear, she added: "if I have said or done anything wrong, I beg to be forgiven." Finding herself alone, Franklin retreated like a frightened child to a few upper rooms in the mansion where she had once reigned as First Lady of New Jersey and watched the British take possession of the rest of the house.

For the next few months events seemed to be at a standstill for Franklin; she could make no headway with Benjamin Franklin, and she was not allowed to write to her husband. Under the influence of his grandfather, Temple Franklin became less reliable. Then a change in English policy resulted in the evacuation of Perth Amboy to New York City. She found herself packing up her household for what was to be the last time. William Franklin's books and papers went into barrels, household furnishings crammed into crates, and all were stored in an old sugar warehouse in New York City, which later burned, thus destroying their private papers. Franklin moved to the city and found herself lodgings with a Loyalist family.

Stressed by the move and distracted by the uncertainty of her husband's future and her own situation, Franklin's health, never robust, began to fail. Her doctor managed to visit her briefly and, seeing the seriousness of her condition, sent word to her husband that she was dying. William Franklin at once applied for parole to visit his dying wife. Reluctant to take responsibility for this, General George Washington sent the request to the Second Continental Congress. By the time Congress's *denial* for parole reached William Franklin, his wife was dead.

Franklin died on July 28, 1777. She was given a funeral and burial at Trinity Church, New York City, attended by "influential and respectable people." (Randall, *A Little Revenge*, 449) Years later, from the safety of his home in England, her husband ordered a memorial plaque placed in Trinity Church recalling her "affectionate tenderness and constant performance of all the duties of a good wife."

Franklin, a gracious lady who was pampered, sheltered, and accustomed to the easy life of a planter's daughter and the comfortable Georgian life-style of the English upper classes, died virtually alone—ignored by her in-laws and isolated from her husband, to whom she had given her unswerving love and support.

For details of Franklin's genealogy, see *Barbados Records. Baptisms, 1637–1800; Marriages, 1643–1800; Wills, 1639–1725* (1984). Additional biographical information, including some of Franklin's correspondence, appears in Claude-Anne Lopez and Eugenia Herbert, *The Private Franklin: The Man and His Family* (1975); Willard Sterne Randall, *A Little Revenge: Benjamin Franklin and His Son* (1984); William H. Mariboe, "The Life of William Franklin" (Ph.D. diss., University of Pennsylvania, 1962); and Larry Gerlach, *William Franklin, New Jersey's Last Royal Governor* (1975).

*Marylin A. Hulme*

## ELIZABETH HADDON, ca. 1680–1762

Elizabeth (Haddon) Estaugh, Quaker leader, was born on July 5, 1680, in Bermondsey, London, England, the second daughter and third child of John and Elizabeth (Clarke) Haddon. Of eight children, only she and her sister, Sarah, who was born December 9, 1687, survived to adulthood.

Haddon's whole life was dedicated to the Religious Society of Friends (also known as Quakers). Because of the persecution of Quakers in England, her father had twice been fined for voicing his religious views. Seeking freedom of worship, he bought hundreds of acres of land in West Jersey in the New World. He signed an agreement with Thomas Willis in November 1701 to settle land in Newton Township, Gloucester County, West Jersey, within six months.

When he signed that agreement, Quakers were not allowed to become officers in English firms because they would not take oaths. Shortly after the agreement was signed, however, intensive negotiations were entered into by John Haddon and several of his colleagues to secure admittance to official positions in companies by affirmation. John Haddon then took an important post with the London Lead Company and subsequently the Pennsylvania Land Company, while continuing at his previous work as a blacksmith. Having achieved his goals as an officer of two companies, he hesitated to leave and settle the land he bought. Therefore, Haddon, his nineteen-year-old daughter, sailed alone to the New World to fulfill the land settlement contract with the expectation, never realized, that the rest of her family would join her. She had full power to transact business in her father's name by a power of attorney from him dated June 4, 1701, which mentioned it was given her because of natural love and affection. It was sealed with a coat of arms.

Her Newton Township home in West Jersey was probably a log cabin. While living there she became reacquainted with John Estaugh, a Quaker preacher, who was born in Kelvedon, England. He had preached in her home parish of Bermondsey several times. Their courtship was detailed in "Elizabeth," the only story of Henry Wadsworth Longfellow's *Tales of a Wayside Inn* set outside New England. Longfellow's source for the story was the writer Lydia Maria Child. She had heard of Haddon through the Quaker family of Isaac Hopper, former residents of West Jersey with whom she boarded in New York. Child wrote abolitionist pamphlets, cookbooks, and articles and edited magazines. She also wrote the legend of Elizabeth Haddon Estaugh, "The Youthful Emigrant," which she later included in her book *Fact and Fiction*.

Haddon married John Estaugh at a Quaker ceremony at her home on the banks of the Cooper's Creek, Newton Township, on December 1, 1702. Four years later her sister, Sarah, married Benjamin Hopkins on August 29, 1706, at the Horsleydown Meeting in Bermondsey, England. Sarah Hopkins never traveled to West Jersey, but since Haddon was childless she persuaded Sarah's daughter, also named Sarah, to live with her in the New World for several years. Little Sarah returned to England with her aunt, and in 1723 Ebenezer Hopkins, Sarah's brother, returned with Haddon and her husband to West Jersey. He became the progenitor of a large family in the New World.

The Estaughs had a large brick home built in West Jersey in 1713 while on one of their trips to England. The site, about a mile from their previous residence, was in the center of the tract John Haddon had purchased from Richard Mathews. It was a fitting setting for a couple who were regarded with the greatest affection and respect by their friends and neighbors. The house featured extensive gardens, a brew house that is still standing, and elegant furniture. Perhaps Haddon's special pride was an eight-foot cherry wood grandfather's clock made by Marmaduke Storr in London, since it was one of the few pieces of furniture she mentioned in her extensive will. She also willed to John Estaugh Hopkins, son of her deceased nephew, a beautiful walnut slant-top secretary with curved drawers and well-designed feet. It was on this that she wrote the minutes of the women's Quaker meeting for 50 years.

The family was noted for its gracious hospitality. Haddon's many guests must have appreciated a walnut chest of drawers with drop design handles and early William and Mary pattern moldings sent by her father on July 17, 1714, from England. Also in walnut was a Queen Anne side chair where Haddon probably sat while she used a mahogany tilt-top tea table with a "bird's nest" to pour tea for her notable guests. Many were leading Quakers of the day, such as SYBILLA RIGHTON MASTERS, who obtained the first two patents in the colonies; Esther Palmer and Susanna Freeman, who rode over 5,000 miles on horseback preaching the Quaker way of life; Hannah Logan, daughter of James Logan, the provincial governor of Pennsylvania, who often came with John Smith, a Burlington merchant, whom she married after a long courtship; John Woolman, the writer and tailor; and several diarists, among whom were Mary Pace Weston, Edmund Peckover, and Thomas Chalkley.

According to Gerald McDonald in *Notable American Women*, Elizabeth Haddon was considered the founder of Haddonfield, NJ. The land where her home was located, however, was originally part of Newton Colony, or the Irish Tenth, and was settled in 1681 by a group of Irish Quakers from Ireland and England. In October 1682 Francis Collins had 500 acres in Newton surveyed and built a home there called "Mountwell." In 1720 a Friends Meeting House was built and it was necessary to distinguish it from other such places of worship. Since it was on John Haddon's land in a great Indian field, the name Haddon's

Field was chosen. In 1722 the first indication of the use of the name seems to be in the Salem Friends Meeting, where it was written "Haddus fealds." The September 11, 1735, minutes of the Religious Society of Friends first mention the name Haddonfield when announcing a special town meeting held to raise money for the poor.

Haddon also was said to have a knowledge of medicine. Esther Palmer's diary recorded visits to her home during short illnesses. Haddon stayed with Sarah Woolman, a local tailor who had smallpox, and she witnessed Woolman's will, along with the local doctor, just prior to her death.

John Estaugh, Haddon's husband, became an agent of the Pennsylvania Land Company in West Jersey, of which his father-in-law was an officer. He also took many religious ministry trips. He died in 1742 while on one such trip in the British West Indies, several days after their 42nd wedding anniversary. He was buried on the small island of Tortola beside John Cadwallader and Thomas Chalkley, two other Quaker preachers.

Haddon had worked with her husband for the Pennsylvania Land Company and upon his death continued writing business letters for the company with help from her great-nephew John Estaugh Hopkins, who officially was named the agent.

Haddon was ill the last several months of her life and died at her Haddonfield home, at age 82, on March 30, 1762. She was buried in an unmarked grave in the cemetery of the Haddonfield Religious Society of Friends. During her third and last trip to England she had obtained the deed from her father for an acre of land on which to construct the Friends Meeting House, with the cemetery adjoining it. There is a brass plaque near where her grave is probably located. Although happily married to John Estaugh for 42 years, she is referred to by her maiden name, which is part of several municipalities, a school, municipal streets, and businesses.

Sources of material on Haddon are Hannah J. Sturge, *Fragmentary memorials of John and Elizabeth Estaugh* (1881); Rebecca Nicholson, *Contributions to the Biography of Elizabeth Estaugh* (1894); Lydia Maria Child, "The Youthful Emigrant," in *Fact and Fiction: A Collection of Stories* (1846); Henry Wadsworth Longfellow, "Elizabeth," in *Tales of a Wayside Inn* (1874); and John Clement, *Sketches of the First Emigrant Settlers in Newton Township, Old Gloucester County* (1887). A sketch of Haddon appears in *NAW*. Discrepancies in the exact date of birth, marriage, and death of Haddon have arisen in the past from the problem of translating dates from the Quaker dating system which was in effect from the time of George Fox until 1752. Fox chose March 25 as New Year's Day, which created a three-month difference in the dates recorded.

*Elizabeth A. Lyons*

## JEMIMA CONDICT HARRISON, 1755–1779

Jemima (Condict) Harrison, Colonial diarist, was born on August 24, 1755, the third of eight children born to Ruth (Harrison) and Daniel Condit, a farmer on Second Mountain near Pleasantdale (Essex County), NJ. The Condit family were members of the Mountain Society, a group of independent and intermarried settlers living simply in the Newark Mountains. Their social and spiritual lives centered around the two-story stone Mountain Society Meeting House, where Daniel Condit occasionally preached.

Harrison, who spelled her family name differently than her parents (not unusual for that time), began her diary in 1772, when she was seventeen, and continued it until 1779, when she married. In her matter-of-fact, often appealing record, she reflects the concerns of ordinary New Jersey women during the American Revolution.

Between 1773 and 1777 many mountain colonists died in epidemics of dysentery, smallpox, and throat distemper, and Harrison's major concern is the illness and death of friends and acquaintances. Only one doctor was available for miles around. In one section of the diary, between October 1772 and March 1774, Harrison's only entry is a list of deaths. Her writing is filled with scriptural quotations and extracts from preachers' sermons that give both warning and comfort.

Harrison's diary is also interesting for what she omitted. Seldom does she mention what she did all day. Days must have been extremely busy with cooking, milking, haying. She mentions weaving in the shop but never writes about the shop. She mentions that she loves to write: "for I don't know how to content myself without writing something." (Condict, *Her Book*, late 1774)

She mentions unusual "daily" events. When she needed a tooth pulled, the dentist, her cousin and the physician brought in to help cope with mountain epidemics, readied his "cold iron," and he and Harrison argued and laughed about the pain, "for its true I believe I want so fraid as I pretended to be" [*sic*]. (Condict, *Her Book*, Feb. 1775) She doesn't write how the extraction felt, but the next few days she had a terrible "cold" in her face.

Harrison never writes about her brothers and sisters at home and her parents are seldom mentioned. Her friends and her grown sisters, however, meant a great deal to her. There are several references to visiting and, occasionally, to a party: "a great sing . . . at my sister Ogden's." (Condict, *Her Book*, Feb. 7, 1775)

The most interesting omission from Harrison's diary is the establishment of the new nation. Late in 1774 she expressed concern: "It seems we have troublesome times a coming for there is great disturbance abroad in the earth and they say it is tea that caused it. So then if they will quarrel about such a trifling thing as that, what must we expect but war and I think or at least fear it will be so."

(Condict, *Her Book*, Oct. 1, 1774)

But Harrison could not be excited about war or very interested in expelling British rulers. War would only make a difficult life harder. Her friends and family were dying in epidemics and farm accidents. She was more concerned about human misery in her own community than she was about British taxes or the establishment of the United States.

Harrison rode down to watch the men train for battle with muskets, rifles, tomahawks, and pitchforks. After war erupted near Boston, she wrote that 30 men were killed. But her entry for July 23, 1776, never mentions the Declaration of Independence. In September 1776 she wrote of the deaths of neighbors in the army at Montague, one killed by Indians, others dying of the "camp disorder." (Condict, *Her Book*, Sept. 1776)

Although several incidents of the war took place near the Mountain Society's burying ground, Harrison doesn't write of them. She records the skirmish at Wardesson (now Watsessing), about four miles from her home. Three British detachments marched through Newark to the Second River region, where the New Jersey militia attacked. The British who escaped took "all the cattle they could" (Condict, *Her Book*, Sept. 12, 1977)—400 sheep, horses, oxen, and cows.

In the diary there is no excitement about victories over the British rulers. Ordinary women were anxious and angry about the war being fought in their village streets. They could not understand its significance. Every family was involved. Harrison's father, brother, uncles, and cousins were in the Continental "Jersey Line" and the New Jersey militia.

Harrison belittled herself in writing, but she was a young woman with a mind of her own. Relatives, friends, and suitors asked her repeatedly when she would marry. She replied that she was in no hurry. She discouraged a suitor, saying that she was a "cross, ill-contrived piece of stuff." (Condict, *Her Book*, Thursday, Oct. 1774) In reality, she was struggling with her desire to marry her mother's nephew, a union between first cousins, which, although common among the mountain people, was cause for concern. When she did marry Aaron Harrison, a private in the militia, early in 1779, she was 24, older than most brides of the time.

During her first (and only) pregnancy, she wrote a letter to her parents and favorite sister asking their forgiveness "for all I have done amiss while in your service," and asking for prayers. "I am going where I shall have no father to pray night and morning," she wrote. (Condict, *Her Book*, 1779)

Harrison died on November 14, 1779, shortly after giving birth to a son, Ira. She was buried in the Mountain Society's burying ground, now cared for by the First Presbyterian Church in Orange.

Her diary was published with the title *Jemina Condict, Her Book, 1772–1779* (1930). An excerpt appears in Elizabeth Evans, *Weathering the Storm: Women of the American Revolution* (1975).

*Sheila Cowing*

## EUNICE FOSTER HORTON, 1722–1778

Eunice (Foster) Horton, wife and mother, farmer and shopkeeper, was one of the most prominent and hard-working citizens of 18th-century Madison (Morris County), NJ. She was born in 1722 in Shinnecock, Long Island, NY, where she met and married the Rev. Azariah Horton in 1742. Rev. Horton, a Presbyterian minister, was born in Southold, Long Island, in 1715 and graduated from Yale in 1735. Upon completion of his theological studies and ordination, he became the first American foreign missionary to the Shinnecock Indians of Long Island (now Southampton area). After the Hortons married they shared the Rev. Horton's next assignment to the Delawares of Wyoming, PA. In 1751 they moved to Bottle Hill (now Madison) in New Jersey for the final phase of Rev. Horton's ministry.

While the Bottle Hill ministry was a period of relative ease and civility for Horton and her husband, her considerable energy and resourcefulness were fully employed in the raising of their seven children—daughters Mary (married Jacob Morrel), Hannah (married Lewis Woodruff), Charlotte and Eunice (married Mr. Tuttle), and sons Azariah, Foster, and Johnathan.

According to contemporary accounts, Horton was a well-educated woman. Although there is no documentary evidence specifying the nature of that education, her activity on behalf of the education of others reveals her understanding and appreciation of such endeavors.

The Bottle Hill post provided Rev. Horton with a salary of only £70 per year, so the income from Horton's general store at the corner of Kings Road and Green Village Road and the revenue from a small farm in Madison were necessary for the day-to-day support of their family. Later the funds from Horton's enterprises provided means not only for educating their own children but also for helping to support the church-related school for classical studies, which the couple founded and which advanced several young Morris County men for their degrees from Princeton and Yale.

Horton knew the anxiety of waiting and the pain of loss endured by families during the American Revolution, when her son Foster was captured by the British during the Battle of Long Island, on August 27, 1776. In late December of that year—after months of imprisonment, first in an abandoned Flatbush church and later aboard a British ship—Foster was released with minimal provisions near South Amboy, NJ, to make his way home. His health broken, he eventually moved to Chatham, opened a store opposite the town's Liberty Pole, and married Sally Low of New York City.

In 1777, during the smallpox epidemic that decimated the Continental Army in Morris County, the Rev. Horton left retirement to join his son Johnathan, a doctor, in ministering to the stricken soldiers. He contracted the disease and died on March 27, 1777, followed soon after by his son. Horton survived her husband and son a brief time and died at age 56 on August 18, 1778.

Material on Horton appears in Barbara Parker and Viola Shaw, *Madison, New Jersey Presbyterian Church: Vital Records 1747–1900* (1982); and William P. Tuttle, *Bottle Hill and Madison: Glimpses and Reminiscences from Its Earliest Settlement to the Civil War* (1917).

*Jane M. Rainis*

## SARAH VAN BRUGH LIVINGSTON JAY, 1756–1802

Sarah Van Brugh (Livingston) Jay was born in New York City on August 2, 1756. She was the fifth child and fourth surviving daughter of William Livingston (1723–90), governor of New Jersey during the Revolution, and Susannah (French) Livingston (1723–89), daughter of wealthy landowner Philip French of New Brunswick, NJ.

Vivacious, intelligent, and an ardent patriot, Jay accompanied her husband, John Jay, to Europe on his peacemaking mission of 1779. She also acted as his hostess during his appointment as secretary of Foreign Affairs from 1784 to 1789. Her personal account of experiences during these years makes her letters a useful source for political and social historians.

The Livingstons were a close-knit family of landowners and politicians active in Colonial New York affairs. In the decades prior to the Revolution, Jay's father formed the "New York Triumvirate" with John Morin Scott and William Smith, Jr. These lawyers "kept the New York political kettle aboil by their opposition to crown measures." (Morris, *Jay Papers,* 1:123)

After the decline of the family's prominence in New York, Jay, aged fourteen, and her family moved to Elizabethtown, NJ, in 1770. Liberty Hall, the family home, became the center of William Livingston's revitalized New Jersey career and of Elizabethtown social life.

Jay and her sisters seem to have received an unusually rigorous, albeit informal, education. Familiar with their father's satirical political writings and fluent with their pens, they corresponded with their father and each other on the political and social affairs of the day. Jay's education probably included accounting, for she later acted as business manager and estate overseer in her husband's absence.

On April 28, 1774, at Liberty Hall, she married the lawyer John Jay (1745–1829). A member of a prominent New York Huguenot mercantile family and a 1764 graduate of King's College (later Columbia University), John Jay had been in legal partnership with his wife's uncle Robert Livingston, Jr., from 1768 to 1771. Their early years of marriage were marked by separations imposed by John Jay's public career, especially his activities as a member of the New York Provincial Congress between 1774 and 1777, as a delegate to the First and Second Continental Congress, and as chief justice of the New York State Court of Judicature.

Jay spent most of her time with her parents at Liberty Hall in Elizabethtown or at her in-laws' home in Rye, NY. Her letters of this period express both deep affection for her husband and loneliness in his absence, the latter eased somewhat by the birth on January 4, 1776, of Peter Augustus, the Jays' first son. After John Jay's election as president of the Continental Congress in 1779, Jay joined him in Philadelphia with their son and Kitty Livingston, her sister. The group remained there for the summer.

This period of domestic tranquility was brief. John Jay, elected minister plenipotentiary to Spain, embarked for Spain on October 20, 1779, with orders to obtain financial assistance and a treaty of alliance with Spain. To the distress of her parents, Jay decided to accompany her husband and to leave their son in his grandparents' care during the trip.

The Jay family's voyage to Spain onboard the frigate *Confederacy* nearly ended in disaster. Jay's letters to her mother and sister Kitty describe the disabling of the vessel in a gale and later narrow escape from capture by a fleet of English ships. (Sarah Livingston Jay, *Letterbook*, 43–44; Ellet, *Queens of American Society*, 48) The *Confederacy*, driven completely off course, sought shelter and repairs in St. Pierre, Martinique, on December 18, 1779. The Jay party reembarked for Toulon aboard the French frigate *Aurora* on December 28, 1779, arriving in Cadiz on January 22, 1780. In the second week of March the party set out for Madrid, a trip particularly arduous for Jay, who was pregnant with her second child. The Jays arrived in Madrid on April 4, 1780.

The Jays' stay in Madrid was marked in part by isolation and grief. Because Spain refused to recognize John Jay as the official representative of a sovereign nation, the Jays were cut off from Spanish society. Moreover, they were grief-stricken at the death of their daughter Susan on August 4, 1780, less than a month after her birth. Nevertheless, Jay began to study Spanish and attempted to keep up a cheerful family correspondence. (Morris, 1:697) The birth of Maria, a second daughter, on January 31, 1782, provided Jay some consolation for the loss of Susan.

At the orders of Congress, the Jays set out for Paris on May 21, 1782. After a journey during which both Jay and her daughter were frequently ill, the family arrived in Paris on June 23 and moved into the Hotel d'Orléans, rue des Petits Augustines, where the peace commissioners frequently assembled.

The Jays quickly entered into an active social life. Their circle included a small group of expatriate Americans and those French officers who were veterans of the war in America. Jay established an intimate friendship with the Marquise de LaFayette, who had been among the first to offer "tender homage" to the Jays on their arrival in Paris. (Morris, 2:455; Ellet, 61)

The preliminary articles of peace were signed on January 20, 1783. On the following day, Jay wrote to congratulate her husband on his achievements: "I long, my dear, to embrace you now as a deliverer of our country, as well as an affectionate and tender husband." (Prince and Lustig, *The Papers of William Livingston*, vol. 3; Ellet, 59)

The Jays moved to Benjamin Franklin's house at Passy in the summer of 1783, where their daughter Anne was born on August 13. In November the Jays took a house at Chaillot. Jay's letters from Chaillot in late 1783 to her husband concern her decision to have the children inoculated, the ascension of a balloon designed by the Montgolfier brothers, and the procession in Paris when the Declaration of Peace was proclaimed.

The Jays left Paris on May 16, 1784, arriving in New York on July 24, after an absence of four and a half years. When John Jay was appointed to the position of secretary of Foreign Affairs in 1784, Jay acted as his hostess. Her "Dinner List of 1787/8" included distinguished European visitors, prominent statesmen and politicians of New York and New Jersey, and members of the bar, churchmen, and physicians. The Jays' New York residence on lower Broadway also became the center of New York social life prior to the inauguration of the new federal government in 1789.

Jay was again separated from her husband for long periods—in 1789, when he was appointed chief justice of the Supreme Court, and in the spring of 1794, when he was made special ambassador to England to negotiate what became known as the Jay Treaty. While John Jay was in England between 1794 and 1795, Jay acted as his business manager, "collecting money on his notes and bonds, investing it in bank shares, and sending him minute market reports and calculations of profits she had already made in a rising market." (Monaghan, *John Jay*, 384) Her letters report on her sales of Jay lands and on the progress of the mill and dam then being built at the Jay estate at Bedford, NY. Jay also reported that she had decided to permit their daughter Maria, then eleven, to attend the Moravian Seminary for Young Ladies in Bethlehem, PA, for the formal education she herself had never received.

John Jay returned to America in May 1795 to learn that he had been elected governor of New York State during his absence. When the state government moved from New York City to Albany in 1797, Jay and her five children, including William (b. 1789) and Sarah Louisa (b. 1792), joined John Jay in Albany, where they remained until the end of his second term in 1801.

Jay, seriously ill, stayed with her sister Kitty Livingston at Oak Hill, near Hudson, while her husband retired to Bedford, NY, in May 1801 to superintend the building of a family homestead. When the buildings were completed in October, she moved to Bedford, but her enjoyment of the estate and comfort of her family's presence was brief, for her health continued to fail. Jay lived less than a year after her arrival; she died on May 28, 1802, aged 45, surrounded by her husband and children. According to Jay family tradition, her remains, buried in the Jay family vault at the Church of St. Marks-in-the-Bouwerie in New York, now lie in the Jay Cemetery in Rye, NY.

Jay's letter book (1779–81) is contained within the Papers of John Jay, NY-CU. The John Jay Homestead (Rye, NY) owns a facsimile of the letter book, *Letters from Mrs. Jay to Her Friends in America* (1784). Selections from her correspondence appear in Richard B. Morris, *John Jay: The Making of a Revolutionary* (1975); in Carl E. Prince, Dennis P. Ryan, and Mary Lou Lustig, eds., *The Papers of William Livingston*, 5 vols. (1979-in press); and in Frank Monaghan, *John Jay: Defender of Liberty* (1935). Her social activities in Europe, New Jersey, and New York appear in Elizabeth Ellet, *The Queens of American Society* (1867); and in Susan Mary Alsop, *Yankees at the Court: The First Americans in Paris* (1982). Education for women in the Livingston and Jay families is discussed in Cynthia Kierner, "From Entrepreneurs to Ornaments: The Livingston Women, 1679–1790," and in Claire McCurdy, "Domestic Politics and Inheritance Patterns: The Family Papers of William Livingston," both in Richard T. Wiles, ed., *The Livingston Legacy: Three Centuries of American History* (1987).

*Claire McCurdy*

## SARAH KIERSTED, 17th century

Very little has been recorded concerning the life of Sarah Kiersted, one of the more remarkable 17th-century Dutch women of New Netherland. As confidante and interpreter of the great Lenape Chief Oratam, she figured prominently in the adjudication of disputes and in treaty negotiations during the turbulent years of the Dutch invasion and settlement of the Manhattan region.

Kiersted's mother was Annake Jans, of Trinity Church property. Upon the death of her husband, Annake Jans married Domine Bogardus, the first settled minister of New Amsterdam, and Kiersted was raised in the Bogardus household. In 1642 she married Dr. Hans Kiersted. Her life, like that of most New Netherland matrons, is obscure, for there was no status attached to being a "housevrou" in New Netherland. Why Kiersted took the extraordinary step of learning the Lenape language, and the circum-

In the 17th century Sarah Kiersted, a Dutch housewife, learned the language of the Lenapes and served as interpreter for Chief Oratam. Depicted here in a modern tapestry, Kiersted was honored with a large grant of land by Oratam in 1666. *Courtesy, Anna C. Scott School, Leonia, NJ. Photo credit: Carol Kitman.*

stances that enabled her to serve Chief Oratam and his followers, have also gone unrecorded.

Oratam, a respected man of peace, was a moderating voice in these times of highly charged emotions. Europeans and American Indians enlisted him to arbitrate disputes and negotiate treaties of peace and amity. He witnessed the early trade contacts and settlement, and observed the growing hostilities that culminated in Governor Willem Kieft's unjustifiable massacre of the Lenape at Pavonia (now Jersey City, NJ) and Corler's Hook in 1643, and the wars that followed.

In these endeavors Oratam depended on the wisdom and integrity of Kiersted, for, like most American Indians of that time, he could neither read nor write; moreover, he was not proficient in the Dutch language and could not fully comprehend the intricacies of European jurisprudence. It is uncertain how many years Kiersted devoted to the cause of the Lenapes, but in 1666, one year before he died, Oratam presented her with 2,260 acres of land extending from the Hackensack River to Overpeck Creek (formerly Tantaqua), an area now encompassing all of Ridgefield Park and parts of Bogota and Teaneck.

So magnanimous a land grant demonstrates Oratam's esteem for this Dutch woman who had honored the Lenapes by learning their language and serving their interests. In 1664 the English captured New Netherland, and though unbound by prior Dutch/American Indian arrangements, Governor George Carteret, in 1669, confirmed the claim of Kiersted's gift from Oratam.

Kiersted is mentioned in Geraldine Huston, *Oratam of the Hackensacks* (1950); Frances Westervelt, *The Indians of Bergen County* (1923); Dorothy Cross, *New Jersey's Indians* (1965); and Samuel Smith, *The History of the Colony of Nova Caesaria, or New Jersey* (1877).

*Herbert C. Kraft*

## MARY LEWIS KINNAN, 1763–1848

Mary (Lewis) Kinnan, who lived as a captive of Delaware Indians for three years and later published an account of her experience, was born on August 22, 1763, near Basking Ridge (Somerset County), NJ. She was one of the six children of Ann (Doty) Lewis, a descendant of Edward Doughty, a passenger on the *Mayflower*, and Zephaniah Lewis, whose grandfather came to Basking Ridge from Wales. Zephaniah Lewis died of "camp fever" after serving in the Revolutionary Army.

On January 8, 1778, Kinnan, age fifteen, married Joseph Kinnan, about whom little is known except that he was born on October 15, 1755, enlisted as a private in the Somerset County militia in 1776, was promoted to sergeant in 1777, and served intermittently throughout the Revolutionary War. The Kinnans lived in Somerset County until 1787, when they moved to Tygart Valley, near the Allegheny Mountains in Randolph County, western Virginia. At this time, they had three children: Lewis (b. 1779), Joseph (b. 1781), and Mary, whose date of birth is not known.

The Kinnans lived in Virginia until May 13, 1791, when three armed Indians entered their cabin. This was the first attack in the area by Indians in four years. Also present in the cabin were Mary Kinnan's older brother, Jacob Lewis, who had come to work with the family a year earlier; two neighbors; and two children of another neighbor. Kinnan was outside at the time of the attack. In her account of the episode, she wrote, "I saw the flash of the musket!—I heard the groan of my husband!" (Kinnan, *True Narrative*, 4) Joseph Kinnan was killed after speaking to the Indians. Jacob Lewis, the two Kinnan sons, and two of the visitors managed to escape. Kinnan, who hid her baby behind a bush and ran for safety, did not. She later recorded, "I scarcely touched the ground as I coursed over

the plain, when the cry of my child, supplicating me for help, arrested my ear. The yearnings of maternal affection extinguished my prudence; forgetting my imbecility, I flew to assist her, and was taken." (Kinnan, *True Narrative*, 4).

After being knocked to the ground with a tomahawk, Kinnan was carried inside the cabin, where she saw her scalped daughter and husband. The next day the neighbors found the bodies of Joseph Kinnan, his daughter, and one of the neighbor's children.

After gathering many of the family's possessions, the Indians made a hurried escape with Kinnan. They fled all night without rest; Kinnan was given no food until the third day. Exhausted, she was beaten to keep up with them. Then, fortunately for Kinnan, one of her captors was bitten by a snake and the group stopped for nineteen days while he recovered. They continued their journey toward the Ohio River, which they crossed on a raft. On June 29 they neared settlements of Shawnee Indians. Here her captors painted Kinnan and themselves and began "the scalp-whoop." Each person struck her violently, according to Kinnan's account, "till I could not see, and till I finally dropt down senseless." The Indians then explained, according to Kinnan, "that all the abuse which had been so liberally bestowed upon me, was to welcome me amongst them." (Kinnan, *True Narrative*, 7–8) Throughout her travels with the Indians, whenever Kinnan appeared unhappy, her companions would try to cheer her by presenting her daughter's scalp, which one of the Indians wore on his belt.

Living with the sister of one of her captors, Kinnan was made to chop and carry wood until the Indians noticed her skill at sewing. Then, on July 3, 1791, Kinnan was sold to a Delaware squaw "and by her was put to the most menial and laborious offices." (Kinnan, *True Narrative*, 8).

Kinnan claimed that while she lived with the Indians she kept a careful record of the date and observed holidays important to her. She was able to learn the Indians' language. In addition, she wrote: "One of the principle objects of my attention, whilst I lived among the Indians, was the humiliating condition of their women." (Kinnan, *True Narrative*, 8) She observed that Delaware women, rather than improving the men's manners, were as ferocious and rough as the men. Kinnan remained with the squaw until the Indians' defeat of General Arthur St. Clair, governor of the Northwest Territory, in 1792.

In January 1793, ready for an end to the war, the Shawnees sent three men and a trader named Robert Wilson to General Anthony Wayne, who insisted that all prisoners must be surrendered in order for a peace settlement to occur. However, just before the prisoners, including Kinnan, were to depart for Fort Jefferson, a British agent persuaded the Indians that the United States would ambush and kill them while they were delivering the hostages. So the war continued and, according to Kinnan, "we were again dismissed to our laborious occupations." (Kinnan, *True Narrative*, 10) Kinnan soon gave up all her hopes of freedom: "I yielded myself up entirely to despondency, and endeavored to stifle the few scattered rays of hope. . . . In consequence of these impressions, I fell dangerously ill of a fever." (Kinnan, *True Narrative*, 11)

In the meantime she had related the story of her capture to a trader named Robert Albert, who wrote a letter to her friends in Basking Ridge, NJ. The letter was delayed, and the people of Basking Ridge did not receive news of Kinnan until the fall of 1793. A collection was immediately taken up by the Basking Ridge Presbyterian Church to finance an expedition for her rescue. Her sons were living with her brothers in Basking Ridge at the time; the family had abandoned the farm in Virginia because of its dangerous location. Jacob Lewis, chosen for the trip because he was Kinnan's only unmarried brother, set out from Basking Ridge on November 1, 1793. By means of a trader, Kinnan received a letter from her brother soon after he reached Detroit on February 3, 1794. Lewis had traveled through western New York, to the mouth of the Genesee River, on to Niagara, and then through British territory to Detroit, where he was given a permit to remain. Lewis now had to proceed cautiously so the Indians would not move his sister to another camp. Lewis met Robert Albert and Israel Rulin, both of whom knew Kinnan. After an unsuccessful attempt by Rulin to buy Kinnan from the Indians, Lewis found work as a timber cutter near Fort Maumee in northern Ohio. Living approximately 140 miles apart, Kinnan and Lewis corresponded for six months.

With the approach of General Anthony Wayne's army in August 1794, the Indians fled for the rapids of the Miami River. Kinnan planned to escape on August 10, during the journey, but cut her foot on a tent pole and had to be carried by horseback for the rest of the eighteen-mile journey.

Jacob Lewis and Thomas Matthews, his companion, visited the new campsite of the Indians. Lewis hoped to look for his sister and, according to Kinnan, "As he was passing through the camp I accidentally saw him . . . my joy was so great that I involuntarily gave a scream of pleasure." (Kinnan, *True Narrative*, 13) So as not to arouse suspicion, she quickly stuck her finger with the needle she was using to sew a moccasin, giving this sewing "accident" as explanation for her cry. After the sighting, Kinnan and Lewis arranged a secret meeting at night. Once they met, they fled by ship to Niagara and then to the mouth of the Genesee River, where Lewis had left his horse.

Kinnan and Lewis reached New Jersey in October 1794. She was 32 years old when she returned home and had lived with the Indians for three years. After her return, she worked as a nurse and also spent time writing an account of those three years that was published in Elizabeth-

town in 1795. On March 12, 1848, at age 84, Kinnan died in Basking Ridge. She was buried there next to Joseph Kinnan, her son, in the cemetery of the Presbyterian church.

The best account of Mary Kinnan's adventure is her own, *A True Narrative of the Sufferings of Mary Kinnan, Who Was Taken Prisoner by the Shawanee Nation of Indians on the Thirteenth Day of May, 1791, and Remained with Them Till the Sixteenth of August, 1794* (1795). Also informative is the biography of Jacob Lewis, Kinnan's brother and rescuer, in *A History and Biographical Cyclopaedia of Butler County, Ohio* (1881). Another source is the account of Oscar M. Voorhees, "'Aunt Polly' Kinnan: An Indian Tragedy of the Eighteenth Century," *Somerset County Historical Quarterly* 1 (1912):179–90. Although Voorhees did not have access to Kinnan's own account, his article adds material gleaned from interviews with Kinnan's descendants. Discrepancies exist between these sources, most notably about the number of Kinnan's children and the identity of her captors, who may have been either Shawnee or Delaware Indians.

*Julia P. Cowing*

## THE WOMEN OF LENAPEHOKING

Lenape women were the first New Jersey women about whom we have substantial information. Lenapehoking, the "Land of the Lenape," which included New Jersey, southeastern New York, eastern Pennsylvania, and northern Delaware, was occupied by American Indians for more than 12,000 years. The historic Lenape Indians were living in the area when European settlers arrived in the 17th century. Lenape means "common" or "ordinary people," but early in the 17th century the English introduced the name "Delaware Indians," because so many of these people lived near the Delaware Bay and River.

Like all eastern woodland American Indians, the Lenape subsisted by hunting, fishing, gathering, and gardening. Their simple society offered no alternative ways of life. From early childhood, a girl learned by observation and imitation, helping the women of the tribe to gather wild roots, berries, seeds, nuts, birds' eggs, and shellfish, which made up more than half of the tribe's diet even after the introduction of horticulture. By participation a girl discovered what was beneficial and what was harmful, how and when to harvest certain foods and medicinal herbs, how to select and prepare the raw materials needed to make clay pots, and which reeds and plants were best for plaiting mats and baskets. Women and girls collected firewood, cleaned and tanned hides, sewed garments, cultivated garden crops, dried and preserved surplus foods, made hominy, milled corn into meal and flour, cooked meals, and attended to the children.

There was always work to be done, but the common perception among European settlers of the women as "squaws" or drudges would have surprised most Lenape

Indians. Their culture respected women, who often achieved high social status. Theirs was an egalitarian system of shared responsibilities and mutual support in which descent passed through the female line. Residence was usually matrilocal, and possessions, including the house, were owned by the women.

Clothes were simple. In mild weather, women and girls wore a short wraparound skirt extending from a belt at the waist to a little below the knees. In colder weather, soft-soled moccasins, leggings, and a fur mantle made of bear, beaver, or deer hide were added. Some women made beautiful mantles from turkeys' iridescent breast feathers, which were fastened to a netted backing. To enhance their appearance, women wore necklaces and pendants of bone, shell, or seeds, and ear ornaments. They also painted themselves with red ocher or the juice of bloodroot. The usual beauty mark was a round spot on each cheek. It was also acceptable to redden the eyelids, forehead, rims of ears, and temples in moderation. Black circles drawn around the eyes were another favorite decoration. Lenape women occasionally had themselves tattooed with designs pricked into the skin with needles or the sharp teeth of fish. Soot, or burnt poplar bark finely ground, was rubbed into the puncture wounds to achieve permanent stains or slightly raised scars.

Lenape women commonly allowed their hair to hang loose, sometimes reaching to the knees. Hair might be tied with a snakeskin or dyed deer-hair ring, or gathered and wrapped at the back of the head. A single braid extending from the crown of the head was another alternative. Both women and men anointed their hair with clarified bear's grease to make it shine.

The onset of menstruation signaled a girl's physical maturity. It also indicated her marriageability, which might now be declared by wearing a headpiece or modestly covering her face in public. Virginity was not prized, and a girl might have numerous sexual experiences before marriage. But a girl who was too promiscuous was admonished and derided.

In the 18th century marriages were sometimes preceded by courtship and negotiation in which the expectant bridegroom's mother or a close friend acted as go-between. In other cases a simple agreement to live together sufficed. In 1770 John Heckewelder, a Moravian missionary, heard one Lenape explain how a marital union might be arranged (note that since the Lenape had no gender pronouns in their language there is a peculiar use of *he* or *him* instead of *she* or *her*): "Indian when he see industrious Squaw, which he like, he go to *him*, place his two forefingers close aside each other, make two look like one—look Squaw in the face—see *him* smile—which is all one *he* say, Yes! so he take *him* home." (Heckewelder, *History, Manners and Customs*, 162)

The Lenape lived in extended families, and it was not unusual for five or more related families to occupy a single bark longhouse. Because the Lenapes were a matrilineal society, all the females in any given household were related from grandmother to mother, to married daughters and their children. When a boy came of age and married, he usually moved into the house of his wife or he started a household of his own. Rules of exogamy required a woman to marry a man from a different lineage. As an outsider unrelated to the other women, the husband was often regarded as a guest in the household dominated by his wife's relatives. The children he fathered became identified with his wife's lineage.

Either spouse could easily break the union for reasons of adultery or other incompatibility. When children were involved, marriages tended to be more stable, but in the event of a dissolution, children remained with the mother.

During pregnancy and menstruation, women secluded themselves in a special hut at the edge of the settlement. At such times they were considered to be polluting. In fact, a woman preparing a meal at the onset of menstruation would leave it unfinished and go directly to the menstrual hut because it was believed that anyone eating food prepared under such circumstances would develop stomach cramps. The custom of menstrual separation allowed women several days of rest each month, but certain taboos had to be observed. Some foods, such as liver, could not be eaten, and meats could not be touched with the fingers. Sticks or bone skewers had to be used. Women who were menstruating also had to use sticks to scratch themselves.

The menstrual hut was also used during childbearing, and similar food and personal proscriptions were observed by the pregnant woman. When it was time to give birth the prospective mother was secluded and other women, who had gone through childbirth themselves, assisted in the delivery. Birth was accomplished in a squatting position, or by having the mother-to-be pull on a rope or hang onto an overhead pole. Once delivered, the child was washed, diapered with moss or other soft vegetable fluff, and tied to a flat cradle board described by William Penn as "a little more than the length and breadth of the Child . . . and thus they carry them on their backs." (Penn, *Own Account*, 26) The umbilical cord was not casually discarded because it was believed that should it come into the wrong hands, danger might befall the child. Some accounts indicate that a girl's umbilical cord, and probably the placenta, were buried near the house to help ensure a lifelong attachment to womanly occupations; a boy's were buried in the woods so that he might develop a liking for the forest and hunting.

A Lenape mother generally nursed her infant for two or more years. During this time the father was denied sexual intercourse, for it was thought to spoil the breast milk. Because of this prohibition a husband sometimes cohabited with co-wives or concubines, although not in the wife's house. This kind of extramarital relationship was tolerated. A married woman might sleep with another man, provided she had her husband's permission. Such a courtesy might be extended to a visiting friend.

Life expectancy among American Indians up to the 19th century was not high. Women often died in childbirth, and many illnesses were fatal because of lack of medication or surgery. There was no way to treat acute appendicitis, gall bladder infection, pneumonia, tuberculosis, arthritis, and other serious ailments. Most Lenape seem to have died before age 35. Gray-haired people were revered as especially favored by supernatural beings, for it was believed that they must be very wise and prudent to have attained so great an age.

Visions received from the spirit world were considered very auspicious and attested to the help and protection of supernatural beings. Not all women received a vision, but those who experienced an apparition in a dream or when dangerously ill were considered highly favored. Medicines prepared and administered by these visionaries were thought to be efficacious. Visionaries were also granted the privilege of reciting their revelations in sacred ceremonies.

When European explorers, traders, and settlers began to arrive in Lenapehoking in the 17th century, their contact profoundly affected the Lenapes' way of life. Beaver, otter, and other animal furs, which had little value to the Lenape, were suddenly in great demand by European markets. In exchange for pelts the explorers and traders brought iron hoes, axes, knives, glass beads, mirrors, brass kettles, cloth, and other useful and desirable objects.

As the desire for European trade items increased, the Lenape were forced to hunt fur-bearing animals relentlessly, and women had to devote more time to the preparation and tanning of skins. The fur-bearing animals in New Jersey were decimated in a few decades, thereby forcing the Lenape trappers to move into remote western forests. This inevitably resulted in hostile encounters with stronger tribes who were anxious to protect the fur trade for themselves. Unable to get pelts, the Lenape were deprived of the European luxuries, tools, and weapons on which they had grown dependent. The traditional matrilineal social order was also compromised as a result of the European presence. Dutch, Swedish, and English traders and land purchasers, accustomed to holding their own women in subservience, were reluctant to deal with independent Lenape women. Instead, the Europeans appointed males as sachems or "chiefs" to act on behalf of the American Indian bands.

The health and well-being of the Lenape deteriorated quickly as Europeans unwittingly introduced deadly epidemic diseases. Smallpox, diphtheria, measles, malaria, and venereal diseases annihilated entire families and reduced some communities by 90 percent. Rum and other intoxicants also did much harm, for the Lenape had no tolerance for alcohol. Warfare, resulting from land disputes and a general European intolerance of different religious beliefs and customs, further reduced the native populations.

Unable to live harmoniously with the ever-increasing European settlers, the Lenape gradually abandoned Lenapehoking. After the Treaty of Easton in 1758, a majority of the Lenape moved westward into Pennsylvania, then into Ohio, Indiana, Kansas, and ultimately into Oklahoma and Ontario, Canada. Some Lenape converts to Christianity continued to live on or near the Brotherton Reservation in Indian Mills, Burlington County. But economic and political circumstances, and continual harassment by neighboring white settlers, made their life increasingly precarious. In 1801 the Brotherton group sold their reservation and moved west to join relatives and friends.

The 1980 census has identified only about 100 American Indians of Delaware or Lenape heritage living in New Jersey. Scarcely a dozen Lenape can still speak the language. The Big House religion and other ceremonies were discontinued after 1924, and it seems unlikely that the ancient rituals and customs will ever be revived.

For additional information, see Albert Cook Myers, ed., *William Penn's Own Account of the Lenni Lenape or Delaware Indians* (1970); John Heckewelder, *History, Manners and Customs of the Indian Nations Who Once Inhabited Pennsylvania and the Neighboring States* (1876); Nora Thompson Dean, "Delaware Indian Reminiscences," *Bulletin of the Archaeological Society of New Jersey*, no. 35 (1978):1–17; and Herbert C. Kraft, *Lenape: Archaeology, History, and Ethnography* (1987).

*Herbert C. Kraft*

## SYBILLA RIGHTON MASTERS, d. 1720

Sybilla (Righton) Masters, inventor, was the second of seven children born to William and Sarah Righton. Her father was a Quaker merchant who owned a plantation in Burlington Township, NJ, on the Delaware River. In the 1690s she married Thomas Masters, a prominent Philadelphia merchant. Thomas Masters, also a Quaker, was successively a Philadelphia judge, alderman, mayor, and provincial councilor. One of their four children, William Masters, unsuccessfully sought the hand of one of William Penn's daughters.

About 1712 Masters went to London. In 1715 she obtained, under her husband's name, a British patent on a method of reducing corn into cornmeal by stamping, instead of the usual process of grinding. There was no Patent Office in Colonial America, and this was probably the first patent issued to an American colonist. The patent drawings show that Masters envisioned a small mill using horsepower and a larger mill using waterpower. Thomas Masters may have purchased the Governor's Mill in 1714 in order to produce this cornmeal in large quantities. As "Tuscarora Rice" it was sold in Philadelphia as a cure for consumption.

In 1716 Masters secured another British patent, this one for a method of working straw for hats and bonnets. With a monopoly on importing palmetto leaf, she opened a hat shop in London, but soon left it to return to Philadelphia. She died in 1720.

A sketch of Masters appears in *NAW*.

*Joseph P. Sullivan*

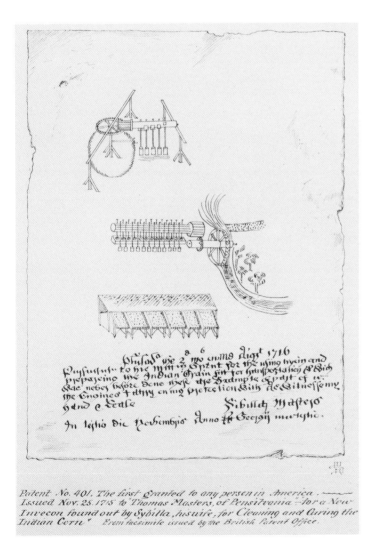

*Patent No. 401. The first granted to any person in America. Issued Nov. 25, 1715 to Thomas Masters, of Pensilvania — for a New Invecon found out by Sybilla, his wife, for Cleaning and Curing the Indian Corn. From facsimile issued by the British Patent Office.*

These patent drawings detail a new method of reducing corn to cornmeal developed by Sybilla Righton Masters of Burlington Township and patented in her husband's name in England in 1715. This patent was probably the first issued to an American colonist. *Reprinted with permission, Samuel H. Needles, "The Gover-*

*nor's Mill, and the Globe Mills, Philadelphia." Pennsylvania Magazine of History and Biography 8, no. 3 (1884):286.*

## MARY LUDWIG HAYS McCAULEY, ca. 1754–1832

Mary (Ludwig) Hays McCauley, who became famous as the American Revolutionary War heroine "Molly Pitcher," was probably born on October 13, 1754, at her father's dairy farm near Trenton, in Mercer County, NJ. John George Ludwig, her father, had emigrated with his wife from the Palatinate, Germany, in 1730.

There are no existing descriptions of McCauley as a girl, but in later life she was described as being of average height, muscular, strong and heavyset, with a florid complexion and one defective eye. She was always talkative and became more so with age.

At fifteen she worked as a domestic in the home of Dr. William Irvine in Carlisle, PA. Although her given name was Mary, she seems to have been generally known in Carlisle by the nickname "Molly." Here she met John Casper Hays, a barber, whom she married on July 24, 1769. When Hays enlisted in the First Pennsylvania Regiment of Artillery in December 1775, his wife returned to the Irvines' employ. A year later Hays transferred to the Seventh Pennsylvania Regiment, an infantry company stationed near Trenton, and his wife joined him there. As was the custom then, many wives would travel with the troops, laundering, mending, cooking, or nursing the soldiers in exchange for rations.

The battle at Monmouth, NJ, fought on the morning of June 28, 1778, began when the Americans caught up with the British army near Freehold. Forced out of Philadelphia, the British were marching toward New York, with the Continental Army in hot pursuit. Inexplicably, while the Americans were gaining ground, General Charles Lee ordered a retreat, an act for which he was later dismissed from the army.

Fifty soldiers reportedly died of thirst that day, one of the hottest of the year, with as many soldiers falling from heat exhaustion as from gunfire. Amidst the noise, heat, and smoke, McCauley carried water from a nearby spring to the thirsty soldiers. Throughout the battle, from eleven in the morning until the late afternoon, she was on the battlefield, tending the wounded.

McCauley also watched for her husband, who had been detailed from the infantry to the artillery to replace a casualty. When Hays was wounded by British gunfire, there were not enough soldiers to operate the cannon, and the crew was ordered to take the gun behind the lines to prevent it from falling into enemy hands. But before the crew could act, McCauley, who had appeared to tend her husband, took up the rammer staff, then loaded and fired the gun as she had seen her husband do. She kept the gun in action while General George Washington rallied the troops and fought the British to a standstill.

Private Joseph Plumb Martin, a witness to her action that day, described it this way: "While in the act of reaching a cartridge and having one of her feet as far before the other as she could step, a cannon shot from the enemy passed directly between her legs without doing any other damage than carrying away all the lower part of her petticoat. Looking at it with apparent unconcern, she observed that it was lucky it did not pass a little higher for in that case it might have carried away something else, and continued her occupation." (Somerville, *Women and the Revolution*, 10) It was said afterward, but never authenticated, that Washington himself complimented McCauley on her bravery at Monmouth.

After the battle, McCauley and her husband returned to Carlisle, where he recovered from his wound. He died a few years after the war. They had a son, John Ludwig Hays.

In 1792 she married John McCauley (also known, variously, as George McAuley or M'Kolly), another veteran and a comrade of her first husband. He was not a good provider, so she supported herself as a laundress and nursemaid. He died in 1814.

Residents of Carlisle remembered McCauley for her battle stories and her acts of kindness. On February 21, 1822, the legislature of Pennsylvania granted her, by special act, an annuity for her services during the Revolutionary War.

McCauley died, at age 78, on January 22, 1832, in the home of her son. She was buried in the Old Graveyard in Carlisle, PA, where in 1876 local citizens erected a headstone, marked by a cannon and flagstaff.

Some historians maintain that "Molly Pitcher" was a generic name used to describe the many women who worked on the Revolutionary War battlefields, carrying water to cool heated cannons and parched throats, tending the wounded, and probably loading and firing weapons when the need arose. This may well be the case. But it is also true that McCauley distinguished herself at the Battle of Monmouth and became immortalized as the representative, if not the only, "Molly Pitcher."

Accounts of McCauley's life appear in John B. Landis, "Investigation into American Tradition of Woman Known as 'Molly Pitcher,'" *Journal of American History* 5 (1911):83–96; J. C. Pumpelly, "Molly Pitcher," *Americana* 10 (1915):818–24; and Mollie Somerville, *Women and the American Revolution* (1974). A sketch of her appears in *NAW*. Linda Grant DePauw, *Fortunes of War: New Jersey Women and the American Revolution* (1975), considers the term "Molly Pitcher" a generic one for camp followers.

*Sally Stone Forester*

## MARGARET HILL MORRIS, 1737–1816

Margaret (Hill) Morris, diarist, correspondent, and lay medical practitioner, was born into the Quaker family of Deborah (Moore) and Richard Hill, a physician who later became a merchant, in September 1737, in South River, MD. In a large family of twelve siblings, Morris was the eighth daughter and tenth child. When she was only two years old, the family was separated because of her father's financial difficulties. For many years Morris and several siblings were left in Philadelphia in the care of an older sister and brother-in-law, Hannah and Samuel Preston Moore, a physician like her father. Her parents and other siblings settled in Funchal on the island of Madeira, where they eventually regained financial prosperity in the wine trade. Affectionate family ties were maintained through frequent letters. It is not known whether Morris received any formal education, but she must at least have had careful tutoring at home, since she enjoyed writing descriptive, articulate letters and diaries throughout her long life. Indeed, one of the many solicitous letters from her father to Hannah Moore shows great concern that his children be encouraged to read and write and to keep a spelling book and dictionary close at hand.

In 1758 she married William Morris, a moderately successful merchant. Their marriage was happy but cut short by William Morris's sudden death in 1766. They had six children: twins Richard and John (b. 1759; Richard died at age one), Deborah (b. 1760), Richard Hill (b. 1762), Mary (b. 1764; died in infancy), and Gulielma Mary (b. 1766), who was born a few weeks after her father's death. Morris never remarried but supported herself and her children through the care of her invalid sister, some rents, and inheritances from her father and from her husband.

In 1770 Morris and her family moved to Burlington, NJ, where she lived for the rest of her life except for the period between 1784 and 1797, when she lived in Philadelphia. During the years in Burlington Morris kept a diary for her sister Milcah Martha Moore (from December 6, 1776, to June 11, 1777), one of the relatively few civilian diaries of the American Revolution written by a woman. Her lively descriptions of the confusion, rumors, and suffering of war at the critical period of the Battles of Trenton and Princeton have merited several reprintings. Faithful to her Quaker principles of peacemaking, Morris deplored the suffering and killing of war and did not take sides. Indeed, she helped both Tory and patriot alike and longed for an end to the hostilities. To her brother Henry Hill she lamented, "Oh, that the cruel contest was over and the present distinctions amongst us at an end; that friendship might extend her kindly influence to either party alike and all be friends again." (Letter to Henry Hill, Oct. 12, 1777) In her diary and letters she grieved for everyone who fell in battle, for all the sick and wounded. She tried unsuccessfully to convince a young neighbor not to go to war and then bemoaned, "When I see so many pretty hopeful young men going out to be slain—I feel what I can't express." (Letter to M. M. Moore, Jan. 7, 1777) She brought food to hungry American soldiers quartered next door and ministered to the sick. Her acts of kindness are corroborated in the diary of one of the soldiers she fed, Sergeant William Young.

Likewise her quick thinking and gentle humor made possible the escape of her Tory friend and physician Dr. Jonathan Odell. Now remembered as a Loyalist poet and Anglican minister, Odell fled to Morris's home to escape patriots who were hunting down Tories. While Odell was hiding in a secret chamber in Morris's house and patriots were pounding on her front door, Morris cleverly stalled for time by turning the key in the keyhole several times and then luring the patriots to a neighboring house. Odell gained time to hide and ultimately to find haven in New Brunswick, Canada. The patriots had been attracted to Morris's house because her teenaged son Richard had been observed using a spyglass to watch the fleet on the Delaware River. Suspecting the boy might be a spy, the patriots hurried to investigate. In order to convince the patriots that her son was simply curious, Morris allowed her sister to give the spyglass to the American commander. The commander was mollified, but Morris couldn't help regretting the loss of her spyglass.

Another incident described in the diary is important to a long controversy concerning the loyalty of Adjutant General Joseph Reed, one of Washington's close advisers. In a single paragraph (June 14, 1777), Morris describes a conversation between Reed and John Cox, both of whom were considering going over to the British until they heard the news of the American victory at Trenton and resolved to remain with the patriots. The conversation was relayed to Morris by a friend and Morris considered telling the two that their disloyal talk had been overheard, but decided not to mention it when she saw Cox and Reed later. The issue of Joseph Reed's loyalty to the patriot cause is still controversial.

Although Morris was certainly a very active lay medical practitioner, she never served an apprenticeship under a trained medical doctor, nor did she assume the title of doctor. It is unlikely she would have been comfortable with assertions that she was Burlington County's first woman physician. But as the daughter of a physician-merchant, reared by a sister whose husband was a physician, mother of a physician, and close friend of Jonathan Odell, her family doctor, she had ample opportunity to observe the practice of medicine. Her recipe book intermingled home cures with a New Year's cake recipe, and her correspondence with physicians frequently requested and traded medical advice for treatments of various illnesses. Shortly after her arrival in Burlington she is known to have provided medicines to sick neighbors and for a short time in 1780 to have sold various medicines from her own apothecary shop there. Several entries in the Revolutionary War diary made reference to successfully treating sick and wounded soldiers. While she was living in Philadelphia (1784–1797) she recorded the ravages of yellow fever epidemics in 1793 and again in 1797. Indeed, both her son John, a physician, and his wife died of yellow fever during the 1793 epidemic and left Morris with their five orphaned children to rear.

When she returned to Burlington in 1797, Morris cared for her sister Hannah Moore, an invalid, until Moore's death in 1799, and devoted her energy and resources to the rearing of her orphaned grandchildren. Morris's two other sisters, Milcah Martha Moore and Sarah Dillwyn, and Dillwyn's husband, George Dillwyn, provided a warm, supportive Quaker family network in Burlington to assist Morris during this final period of her life.

Morris herself suffered from chronic illness from young adulthood and in later years reported frequent and severe bouts of fevers and rheumatism. Despite these illnesses and the death of her husband, three children, and several grandchildren, Morris remained a positive and optimistic person. As late as 1811 she was still overseeing her gardens and providing people with medical advice. In 1813 she suffered a stroke. A courageous, pious, resourceful woman, Morris died, at age 79, in Burlington on October 10, 1816, probably the victim of a massive stroke. She is buried in the Burlington Friends' Cemetery, directly behind the Friends meetinghouse on High Street in Burlington.

The manuscript diaries, letters, recipe books, and miscellaneous papers of Morris are available at P-HC. Published sources, mainly her Revolutionary War diary, include: *Private Journal, Kept During a Portion of the Revolutionary War* (1969); *Margaret Morris, Her Journal* (1949); "The Revolutionary Journal," *Friends Historical Society of Philadelphia Bulletin* 9 (1919):2–14, 65–75, 103–14; and *Letters of Doctor Richard Hill and His Children* (1854; 1969), which contains an invaluable genealogy of the Hill-Morris family. Other useful materials are: John Jay Smith, *Recollections* (1892); and the "Journal of Sergeant William Young," *Pennsylvania Magazine of History and Biography* 8 (1884):255–78.

*Patricia A. Beaber*

## CORNELIA BELL PATERSON, 1755–1783

Cornelia (Bell) Paterson was a mother, a faithful and talented correspondent, the mediator in a family of opposing political allegiances, and a model of courage and independence during the American Revolution. Paterson was the first child and only daughter of a New Jersey landowner, John Bell, formerly of Withern, Essex, England. He came to America in the 1740s, settling initially in Philadelphia, where Paterson was born in 1755 and her only brother, Andrew Bell, in 1757. Although most sources have referred to "Mrs. Bell" as the mother of his children, Bell's 1769 will asserts that it was Hannah Smith, of Philadelphia, rather than his wife, Anna (Myer Tilden) Bell; letters between the two siblings make the distinction between "Mrs. B." and their beloved mother in Philadelphia. In 1769 John Bell purchased an estate of 50 acres in Bridgewater (Somerset County), NJ, which he named "Bellfield." There the family resided until the outbreak of the Revolutionary conflict.

The Revolution separated the Bell family first physically and later philosophically, which proved very difficult for Paterson throughout her short lifetime. At the time of the outbreak, her brother, Andrew Bell, who had been studying law, espoused the Loyalist cause. Appointed a confidential clerk in the office of the British commander-in-chief in New York City, he remained in that service until the end of the war. Their father, also a Tory, remained at Bellfield with his wife, Anna, until his death in 1778.

Paterson apparently was anxious about the British troops entering their region. In the remarkable collection of letters between the two siblings that has been preserved, we find that Paterson expected the troops not to "be very desirable visitors, as they mark their own way with ruin and devastation. . . . I think their proceedings in that way all very impolitic, as they make [for] themselves many enemies who would otherwise have been their friends." (*Proceedings* 15:511) In April 1777 she wrote to her brother: "we have nothing to expect from them but the utmost harshness and severity. . . . I don't know whether to go or stay at their approach, but I think I cannot be safer anywhere then with Papa. I hope he will be able to protect me." (*Proceedings* 15:514) Within four months of this writing, she left Bellfield. Intending only to stay for two months at the home of their neighbor, Judge Anthony White, at Union Farms, she remained for nearly two years, writing to her brother that it seemed more like home than the one she had left, and that "between company, cards, reading, work and musick, the weeks slide away pleasingly, and not quite uselessly." (*Proceedings* 15:517)

During the seven years of her brother's military service (1776–83) Paterson maintained an intimate and illegal correspondence with him across enemy borders. Her letters from these years reveal affection, determination, and independence. Contrary to her father's and brother's Loyalist sentiments, she believed firmly in the American cause. She never tried to influence their views, yet she never concealed her own. Letters to Andrew Bell chiefly concerned their mutual safety and the tragedies of the conflict in general. Her interests were not outside politics, however, as the following excerpt reveals: "I'll not trouble you with any more of my politics; they are so disagreeable to you. Every

rational creature, you know, has a right to think, and every one cannot be of the same opinion. I am not a politician . . . but we must say something, if it is nonsense." (*Proceedings* 15:513)

While living at Union Farms in Hunterdon County, she met William Paterson, a prominent patriot and New Jersey's attorney-general. William Paterson was a member of the Constitutional Convention; later in his career he served in the U.S. Senate (1789–90), became governor of New Jersey (1790–93), and served on the Supreme Court (1793–1806). During most of their courtship, William Paterson's responsibilities kept him away from home. Following more than a year of writing letters, they married on February 9, 1779, in a private ceremony at Union Farms performed by the Rev. Samuel Blair. The couple remained at Anthony White's home until April 1779, at which time William Paterson purchased a valuable estate, "the Raritan Plantation," which was forfeited by a fleeing Loyalist attorney, Bernardus LaGrange.

William Paterson's great esteem and affection for his wife, "the sweetest pattern of female excellence," were expressed time and again in his letters. She returned his sentiments, conveying to her brother: "We are united by indissoluble ties, those of affection, tenderness, sentiment, delicacy—an union of hearts." And: "Our happiness increases with each new day, and we experience what you so kindly wish us, domestic felicity, untainted, uninterrupted!" (*Proceedings* 16:60)

Given their deep affection, it is not surprising that William Paterson's leave-taking for political reasons grieved them both greatly. During the long periods of separation from her husband, Paterson wrote of "the many tedious hours I pass alone" and looked forward to her mother's visit to Raritan, "for surely no one ever required the presence of a Mother more than I do, being frequently indisposed and entirely alone." (*Proceedings* 16:63) The couple longed for the coming of peace, which would mean that William Paterson could finally make up for the months he had been forced to write to his wife from far away that "this absence is tormenting." (*Proceedings* 16:56)

From Paterson's letters we see that she struggled with her position as a sensitive and passionate woman attached, as a result of family ties, to opposite sides of the Revolution. Since her father disapproved of her connection to so active a patriot, it was extremely important to her that her brother, with whom she was very close, was not opposed to her marriage as well. Likewise, she obtained assurance from her husband that he would not stand between his wife and her Tory brother. As she wrote to Andrew Bell, "his arms will always be ready to receive the beloved brother of his Cornelia." (*Proceedings* 16:59) Indeed, such a posture must have been awkward for William Paterson himself, since he was responsible for upholding New Jersey's laws against Loyalists, including the law requiring confiscation and sale of all Loyalist properties. When his wife's father died, Andrew Bell, her Loyalist brother, became the owner of the family's property. Thus, William Paterson had no choice but to bring indictment against his brother-in-law. This situation, potentially catastrophic for Andrew Bell, was alleviated somewhat by William Paterson, who helped by assessing the value of the estate and its furnishings so that Bell could address the king for compensation. William Paterson also aided his wife by transporting communications and goods to her brother via friends with military passes.

Little is known of Paterson's organized patriot activities during the war, but an effort to form a Women's Relief Society included her name. A broadside from the society, dated July 4, 1780, and published in the New Jersey *Gazette* on July 12, 1780, lists the many prominent women in New Jersey who gave their time and talent to the cause of providing financial assistance to the Continental Army.

The war took its toll on Paterson as she bore many responsibilities at home alone. Her first child, Cornelia, was born in 1780. Her second daughter, Frances, born in January 1782, died in June 1783, soon after peace was made and William Paterson was coming home to stay. Paterson, at the time expecting another baby in the fall, took the loss very hard. A three-day reunion in July with her brother, after seven years of separation and many thwarted attempts to meet, briefly lifted her spirits. But in October she apparently became ill. Bell wrote on October 11 that he was greatly alarmed by his sister's indisposition. In a few weeks, on November 9, 1783, William Bell Paterson was born. Presumably the strain of childbirth on her already weakened condition was too much for Paterson. She died four days later, on November 13, 1783, at age 28, in New Brunswick—a tragic ending to the couple's long-awaited hopes for a life together. She was buried at the First Presbyterian Church in New Brunswick, which William Paterson was said to have attended for the rest of his life.

Biographical information on Paterson appears in John E. O'Connor, *William Paterson: Lawyer and Statesman* (1979). Letters between Paterson and her brother and husband reveal the most authentic portrait of the woman; see the three-part article by J. Lawrence Boggs, "The Cornelia (Bell) Paterson Letters," *NJHSP* 15 (1930):508–17; 16 (1931):56–67, 186–201.

*Ann Copeland*

## ANNETJE VAN WAGENEN PLUME, 1752–1816

Annetje (Van Wagenen) Plume, described at her death as the richest woman in Newark, was born on October 30, 1752, and known as Ann. She became the second wife of Isaac Plume and lived with him in his ancestral home at what is now the corner of State and Broad streets in New-

ark, NJ. The land on which the house sat was originally deeded to Isaac Plume's grandfather, Samuel Plum, as part of the original partition of land in this area in May 1673.

Plume came to the marriage a wealthy woman, having inherited several properties in New York State, reportedly from both her father and her English uncle, General Garret Visscher. However, in accordance with the laws of the time, which did not allow married women to own property, all of Plume's holdings became her husband's on their wedding day.

She spent the rest of her life at the Broad Street house, caring for her stepchildren and bearing five children—John Isaac, Joseph, Garret, Mary, and Nelly—keeping the house and helping to manage the farm on which they lived. This seemingly peaceful life became difficult and dangerous during the years of the Revolutionary War, when Newark was occupied by the enemy more than once. The Plumes were American patriots and Isaac Plume was a first lieutenant in the Regiment of Grenadiers during the winter of 1777, when the Continental Army was forced to retreat to Newark after being defeated at the Battle of Long Island. Several days later the Americans were forced to retreat farther west to Morristown, leaving Newark to General Charles Cornwallis's troops of Redcoats and Hessians.

According to local legend, the Plume farm, which was on the outskirts of the town, attracted the notice of a troop of Hessians, who demanded food for their horses and made themselves at home in the parlor. They went too far, though, when they began chopping firewood on Plume's spotless floor. She scolded them fiercely and demanded that they stop. The Hessian leader threatened her, saying, "If you say another word I'll shoot you." But instead of backing down, Plume, a staunch Presbyterian and a gentlewoman born and raised, summoned up the coarsest phrase she knew and replied, "Ram's horn if I die for it!" This reportedly startled the Hessian so much that he laughed and ordered his men to chop wood outside.

The legend does not end here, for the Hessians remained on the property several days and Plume eventually had her revenge. One morning while walking to the barn she saw a Hessian soldier enter the dairy to help himself to fresh milk. She quickly shut the dairy door and bolted it from the outside. The dairy walls were two feet thick and effectively muffled the soldier's shouts, and his comrades did not notice his absence when they marched away the next morning. Several hours later a company of New Jersey Blues marched by, and Plume stopped them and turned over her prisoner. The soldiers gave her his steel helmet, which she later had made into a knocker for the front door. Reportedly the knocker was still on the door when the house was sold to the House of Prayer in 1850.

Isaac Plume died in 1799 and in his will left his wife the house they lived in and all of the property that she had owned before marriage. The rest of his estate was divided among his children. As a widow, Plume could legally own property, and as a landowner she had the right to vote, at least until 1807, when the women of New Jersey lost the franchise. Plume managed her properties well and at the time of her death, in 1816, her estate was valued at $106,985.36. The house was left to her youngest son, John Isaac Plume, and the rest of the property to her children and grandchildren and the Second Presbyterian Church in Newark. Her property included four slaves, one of whom, Sukey, was to be freed at Plume's death. An interesting bequest was a tract of land in Saratoga County, NY, "containing 92 acres, in trust, they paying rents and profits therof to my daughter, Nelly, for life (not subject to any control of her husband)."

Plume died on February 19, 1816, in Newark.

An abstract of Plume's will appears in *New Jersey Post-Revolutionary Documents, Calendar of Wills* (1814–17):334–35. A detailed account of Plume's encounter with the Hessians appears in an anonymously written pamphlet, *The Plume Family in New Jersey, 1668–1849*, available at the NJ-HS. A sketch of Plume appears in *LCR*.

*Sally Stone Forester*

Annis Boudinot Stockton, the mistress of "Morven" in Princeton, was a poet and patriot during the Revolutionary Era. *Anonymous American artist, courtesy, Art Museum, Princeton University.*

## ANNIS BOUDINOT STOCKTON, 1736–1801

The poet Annis (Boudinot) Stockton, one of the most cultured, literary, and patriotic women of the Revolutionary period, was born July 1, 1736, in Darby, PA. Stockton was the oldest child and only daughter of Elias Boudinot, a goldsmith of French Huguenot descent, and Catherine (Williams) Boudinot. Her brother Elias was born in Philadelphia in 1740 and Elisha, in 1749.

Few records of Stockton's childhood exist. From her writings there is reason to believe that as a girl she read widely and with discrimination, being especially well versed in the popular literature of the day. She apparently received more education than most girls of her time. Her extant manuscripts, correspondence, and the Stockton records provide considerable material on her adult life.

Her first poetry was written before her marriage to Richard Stockton—a notable New Jersey lawyer, landowner, and, later, signer of the Declaration of Independence—and some of the poems celebrate their courtship. "I find on earth no charms for me / But what's connected with the thought of thee!" (Butterfield, "Morven," 12) In the romantic fashion of the day, many loving letters passed between her and her husband. He called her by her poetic name, Emilia. She called him Lucius. Richard Stockton encouraged her work, and eventually her audience embraced more than just her family.

No record of their wedding has been found, but the Stocktons were probably married around 1757, in spite of alleged family disapproval. Annis Stockton wrote in "The Dream. An Ode": "I found thee all my own in spite of those whose cold unfeeling minds would bid us part." (Cowell, *Women Poets*, 87)

Richard Stockton was devoted to his wife and impatient to return when he traveled any distance from her. His confidence in her is obvious in his letters concerning public and business affairs. He wrote, "I have left my letters to the Governor open, that you may see their contents." (Quoted in Ellet, *Women of the American Revolution*, 18)

When her husband visited England for sixteen months in 1766 through 1767, Stockton refused to go with him, choosing to stay with their four children: Julia (b. 1759), twins Mary and Susan (b. 1761), and Richard (b. 1764). The Stocktons later had two more children, Lucius Horatio (b. 1768) and Abigail (b. 1773). Stockton's daughter Julia married Benjamin Rush, a famous physician who cared for the wounded at the Battle of Princeton; Susan married Alexander Cuthbert of Canada; Mary married the Rev. Dr. Andrew Hunter; Richard became a leading national lawyer and a member of both the House of Representatives and the Senate; Lucius also became a lawyer; and Abigail married Robert Field of Burlington, NJ.

Stockton wanted to make her home beautiful and the gardens a work of art. She named her estate near Princeton

"Morven," after the imaginary land of Ossian's (James Macpherson's) Fingal, and made it the center of culture and influence for the Princeton area, a tradition that has continued for 200 years.

Encouraged by her husband's admiration, Stockton wrote a large collection of poems. In 1985 a manuscript volume of Stockton's poetry was donated to the New Jersey Historical Society by a direct descendant of the poet. Dissemination and critical evaluation of this volume will allow redefinition of her role in American history and her importance in American literature. Using the pseudonym "Emelia" (sometimes spelled "Amelia"), Stockton occasionally published poems in Colonial periodicals. Elizabeth Graeme Fergusson, with whom Stockton corresponded, was the "Laura" in her writing. Stockton's first known publication appeared in the *New York Mercury* on January 9, 1758. ESTHER EDWARDS BURR, a close friend, included two of Stockton's poems in her private journal.

Stockton's writing reflects themes of life, courtship, marriage, nature, friendship, patriotism, old age, and grief. She was uncertain about the appropriateness of women publishing their works. On May 1, 1789, she wrote to her brother Elias, "If you think it will only add one sprig to the wreath the country twines to bind the brows of my hero, I will run the risk of being sneered at by those who criticize female productions of all kinds." (Quoted in Cowell, 89) Her need to write is felt in this 1781 confidence to Elias: "Pardon this fragment, but when the fit is on me, I must jingle." (Quoted in Cowell, 89)

Her quiet, secure world of family, friends, and poetry exploded with the Revolutionary War. Committed to the cause of American freedom, Stockton and her husband found themselves completely engulfed in the military as well as the political war. They gave both time and money to the patriotic cause. She wrote to her brother, "Though a female, I was born a patriot." (Quoted in Hoyt, *A House Called Morven*, 53)

Their estate was directly along the route of the British army, and during the Battle of Princeton (December 1776), Morven was occupied by the British. The house was pillaged, animals driven away, furniture turned to firewood, wine drunk, and valuable papers and books burned. Some of her early poems disappeared. Fortunately, Stockton had hidden many papers and valuables, as well as the records of the American Whig Society. Because of this deed, Stockton was later named an honorary member of the Whigs, the only woman so honored.

Before the British captured the house, the family had fled. Nonetheless Richard Stockton was captured and thrown in jail. Upon the family's return to the ransacked house, Stockton set upon the task of restoring it and in the process found letters her husband had written her.

During the war there could not but be a political awareness in her work. She wrote themes for Colonel Philip

Schuyler upon his return to New Jersey, on the death of General Joseph Warren at Bunker Hill, as well as several for General George Washington after the Battles of Trenton and Princeton and the surrender of Lord Charles Cornwallis and the British army. Washington's warm acknowledgment shows his appreciation of her work.

Richard Stockton was released in 1777, but the poor treatment he received hastened his death. His health deteriorated until he died on February 28, 1781.

Stockton, who was named one of the executors of her husband's will, took over management of the large estate at the age of 45. She continued to entertain, using Morven as a social center. Retaining her position in society, her sense of humor, and her vigor of mind and body, she continued to care for house and family, garden, fields, and orchards. She lived at Morven until age 60, when she felt she could no longer be useful. Stockton then moved in with Abigail, her youngest daughter, at Whitehill in Burlington County, where she died, at age 64, on February 6, 1801. Neither the cause of her death nor her place of burial are known.

Letters and papers of Stockton, including a manuscript volume of thirteen of her poems, are available at NJ-PU. Other pertinent materials are available at the P-HSP, in the Washington Papers Collection at DC-LC, and in the Esther Burr journal held at the C-YU. Useful books on Stockton are: Elizabeth Ellet, *The Women of the American Revolution*, 3 vols. (1848–50); Pattie Cowell, *Women Poets in Pre-Revolutionary America, 1650–1775* (1981); and Thomas Coates Stockton, *The Stockton Family of New Jersey, and Other Stocktons* (1911). Information on Stockton's poetry appears in Lyman Butterfield, "Morven: A Colonial Outpost of Sensibility. With Some Hitherto Unpublished Poems by Annis Boudinot Stockton," *Princeton University Library Chronicle* 6 (1944):1–16, and in his "Annis and the General: Mrs. Stockton's Poetic Eulogies of George Washington," *Princeton University Library Chronicle* 7 (1945):19–39. Alfred Hoyt, *A House Called Morven* (1954), contains details on the Stockton home in Princeton.

*Wendy Pfeffer*

## MARGARET VLIET WARNE, 1751–1840

Margaret (Vliet) Warne, a midwife during the Revolutionary era, was born on October 1, 1751, the only daughter and fourth of eight children of Daniel and Gertruitje (Springsteen) Vliet, both of Dutch descent, at Six Mile Run (Somerset County), NJ. She was baptized at the Six Mile Run Dutch Reformed Church in Franklin Township on October 26, 1754. Daniel Vliet, a farmer, served as captain in a Revolutionary War regiment. Five of Warne's brothers, including General Garret Vliet, also served as soldiers in the War of Independence. The Vliet family moved to a larger farm in Hunterdon County before Warne's marriage.

In her early twenties she married Joseph Warne, the

grandson of Thomas Warne, one of the lord proprietors of East Jersey. They lived on a farm near the town of Broadway (Warren County) that her husband had bought from two of his brothers, Elijah and Elisha. There the Warnes raised nine children, six girls and three boys: Ann, Abigail, Charity, Margaret, Elijah, Abrahm, Elisha Spring, Rhoda, and Frances.

Known as "Aunt Peggy," Warne attended to the sick and to women giving birth at a time when many male physicians were traveling with the armies of the American Revolution. She continued her midwife duties in the years to follow. In his description of the early 18th-century medical profession in Warren County, James Snell says of Warne: "She not only practiced in her own neighborhood, but kept a horse ready night and day and rode into the surrounding country, through Warren and Hunterdon Counties, undeterred by rain, hail, or drifting snow." (Snell, *History of Warren and Sussex Counties*, 504)

Warne's husband died in 1798, and she later married his brother Elijah, who died in 1844. She reportedly died in 1840 at age 89. Her grave, and those of both her husbands, are at Old Mansfield Cemetery, Washington, NJ. A boulder and bronze marker were placed at the burial site by the Peggy Warne Chapter of the Daughters of the American Revolution in 1915. The Peggy and Joseph Warne Homestead Farm is preserved in Franklin Township, NJ.

There is conflicting data concerning birth and death dates for Warne. Useful genealogical references appear in *Somerset County Historical Quarterly* 7 (1918):152–55, and 8 (1919):123–28. Also helpful is James Snell, *History of Warren and Sussex Counties* (1881).

*Cynthia Scott Amerman*
*Carmela Ascolese Karnoutsos*

## RACHEL LOVELL WELLS, ca. 1735–ca. 1796

Rachel (Lovell) Wells, wax sculptor, entrepreneur, patriot, and sister of PATIENCE LOVELL WRIGHT, was born about 1735 in Crosswicks (Burlington County), NJ. John and Patience (Townsend) Lovell, her parents, were of English descent and married ca. 1713 at Oyster Bay, Long Island. John Lovell was a farmer and miller, and Patience (Townsend) Lovell was a Quaker and homemaker. They had ten children, nine girls and one boy; Wells was the youngest. The Lovells sold their Oyster Bay land in 1729 and moved south to Crosswicks in West Jersey. Both Lovells signed the deed of sale, in line with the Quaker philosophy of the full equality of women and men in the management of affairs.

Wells's father was reportedly a rich and honest man who owned large tracts of land and raised "every kind of living thing." (Quoted in Sellers, *Patience Wright*, 17) The family practiced a type of Quakerism set forth by Thomas Tryon that espoused complete vegetarianism, not even allowing use of leather, the by-product of slaughtered animals.

The family dressed entirely in white and wore wooden shoes and straw hats. The Lovells' nine daughters, who were "instructed in the Arts of the Dairy, and Agriculture . . . as tended to make them good wives," were so sheltered that they went veiled in public from the age of seven. (Quoted in Sellers, 14)

Rachel Lovell married James Wells, a shipwright, on October 23, 1750, and moved to Philadelphia. There is no record of her having children prior to her husband's death, which occurred between 1762 and 1769.

Reportedly, as children, Wells and her sisters began to make images in bread dough and clay and then used natural dyes to color them. In later years, Wells had advanced to working in wax. When PATIENCE LOVELL WRIGHT was widowed in 1769 Wells taught her to work in wax to support herself and her five children. By 1770 the two widows were in business.

The women found a new use for wax by creating contemporary pieces. Both Wells and Wright sculpted figures; Wells's figures were usually biblical while Wright's were contemporary. Wells is noted for her full-length figure of Great Awakening Minister George Whitefield. Although wax is light and portable compared to other sculpting media, it requires warmth and is fragile. So the sisters moved south in the winter as far as Charleston, SC, and north again in the spring. As the wax collection grew, they established two fixed exhibitions: Wells kept one at her home in Philadelphia and Wright kept one in New York City. There is evidence to suggest that the sisters left others in charge of the exhibits at times and continued to travel.

On June 3, 1771, a fire started in the New York waxworks. The *New York Gazette* or the *Weekly Post-Boy* reported the fire on June 10, stating that it started while Wright was away and only the children were home. There was "little Damage to the House; but, tho' most of the Wax-Work was destroy'd, together with some new pieces which Mrs. Wells had lately brought from Charlestown: the whole amounting it is said to the Value of several Hundred Pounds."

The news of the fire was reported also in the *Pennsylvania Chronicle* of June 10–17 and the *Boston News-Letter* of June 20 (cited in Kelly, *Notes on American Artists*, 9–10), proving that the sisters were newsworthy and that people would recognize their names. On August 5, 1771, an article reported that the sisters had repaired the damage and produced some new pieces that were better because the artists were more experienced.

In September 1771 the sisters traveled to Boston. It was here they became friends with Jane Franklin Mecom,

Benjamin Franklin's widowed sister. Mecom gave Wright a letter of introduction to present to her brother when Wright traveled to London in spring 1772.

Before the ship sailed, Wright made a will. In it she stated that Aunt Rachel Wells, whenever she might come to New York, was to be honored and obeyed as having been "the means under God to permote my wellfare and instruct me in waxwork to enable me to maintain my family and I order Betsy Wright to keep a regualor book of all profits that arise from my waxwork And to pay a quarter part to her aunt Wells after the rent is paid." (Quoted in Sellers, 42).

Many secondary sources stated that Wells and Wright had a system for spying on the British. No hard evidence can be found to support these claims. In 1773–74 Wells appears to have received from Wright, who was in London, a wax head of Lord Chatham with dispatches inside for the Continental Congress at Philadelphia. Other information may have been smuggled past the British in this fashion, but surviving material tends to cast doubt on the importance of the information or its timely arrival.

John Adams visited Wells's waxwork in Philadelphia and described it in a letter to his wife, Abigail Adams, dated May 10, 1777. He observed the two "chambers" filled with pieces. Wells returned to Bordentown after the British took over Philadelphia in 1778. She appears on the 1778 and 1780 census reports and on the tax ratables as a householder with a house and a small lot.

On November 15, 1785, Wells entered the first of three petitions before the New Jersey General Assembly. In it she stated that she "had loaned considerable sum of moneys" to the state to fight the war, that she had been robbed of "2,000 pounds and more," and that she struggled to survive. The New Jersey Assembly ruled that Wells's 1783 move to Philadelphia deprived her of her claim to the interest on the money she lent to the state. Wells then applied to Pennsylvania, which declared her a New Jersey resident.

Wells entered her second New Jersey petition on October 30, 1786. She explained that she had moved to Philadelphia so she could make a living, which was not possible in Bordentown. After the New Jersey Assembly ruled against her for the second time, Wells petitioned the Congress on May 18, 1786, claiming she was owed £300 and that "one of our Chaplens to our army I believe has Robed me of one hundred & Eighty Six pounds." She also claimed a loss of £2,805 "hard cash" damage by the British. (Quoted in Kerber, *Women of the Republic*, 87n)

On October 26, 1787, Wells entered her third New Jersey petition, suggesting that an exception be made to "widows and orphans" on the residency rule. The outcome of Wells's case is not known, but she may have been repaid since a similar case was made good in 1787.

In the summer of 1785 Wells was asked by her sister Patience Wright, now also in financial difficulty and wanting to come home from Europe, to make requests about a piece of land. Wright assumed that, because of her attempts to pass information back from Europe, she might be entitled to a grant, as were some Colonial soldiers.

Wells, ill and aging, wrote a confusing letter to Benjamin Franklin in December 1785. She left the letter unsigned but hinted that the idea for it came from a member of Congress. In the letter she inquires "if aney thing has bin don for Mrs. Wright." Wells then states that "her [Wright's] inteligence was the best. We Recevd them by the hand of her sister wells who found them in ye wax heads." Wells also states that she was "advanced in years and have bin Confind to my Rum Ever sence your arivell." She also made a reference to a Colonel Carbright, who had made "Sister Rachel wells a Present of a Lott in Bordentown to build her a Museum on a few months Past." (Quoted in Sellers, 218–19)

The colonel referred to by Wells was Joseph Kirkbride, who owned a large estate in Bordentown. Nothing has been discovered regarding the building of a museum, but an article in the *New Jersey Gazette* of Trenton, dated July 17, 1786, states that Wells had opened an exhibition room nearby.

Wells wrote her will on September 17, 1795. It states that she lived in Bordentown, Burlington County. She left 33 wax figures to her brother John Lovell, "to be set up when he thinks proper," along with a spinet and a guitar. Her estate included furniture, clothing, dividends in "the Townsend estate" (inherited from her mother's sister Deborah Townsend), and a house and three acres of land in Germantown. The date or cause of her death and the location of her burial are unknown. Her will was probated in Burlington County on March 23, 1796. (*N.J. Archives*, 38:403–5).

Biographical information on Wells appears in the *New Jersey Archives*. The *Minutes of the General Assembly* for Nov. 15, 1785, Oct. 29, Oct. 31, Nov. 1, and Nov. 6, 1787, contain responses to her petitions. The *New Jersey Gazette*, July 17, 1786, carries a notice of the opening of her waxworks. Useful secondary sources of information are Charles Coleman Sellers, *Patience Wright: American Artist and Spy in George III's London* (1976); James Magee, *Bordentown, 1682–1932* (1932); Linda Kerber, *Women of the Republic: Intellect and Ideology in Revolutionary America* (1980); William Dunlap, *History of the Rise and Progress of the Arts of Design in the United States* (1834); and William Kelby, *Notes on American Artists: With Lists of Portraits and Sculpture in the Collection of the New York Historical Society 1754–1820* (1922).

*Virginia M. Lyttle*

## ANN COOPER WHITALL, 1716–1797

Ann (Cooper) Whitall, Quaker diarist and Revolutionary War heroine, was born April 23, 1716, in Woodbury

(Gloucester County), NJ, the second daughter of John and Ann (Clark) Cooper. She spent the whole of her life in Woodbury with one goal in mind: to uphold the teachings of the Society of Friends and to perfect in herself Christ's admonition to "love one another." The keeper of a lengthy spiritual diary, Whitall gained historical note as a result of her actions during the Battle of Red Bank in the Revolutionary War.

Her grandfather, William Cooper, a Quaker clergyman, arrived in America from England in 1682, settling in Pyne Poynte, now part of Camden, NJ. Her maternal grandfather, Benjamin Clark, was the publisher of Friends' books in London, England.

As a child, Whitall was raised to be obedient to her parents, to be industrious and cheerful, and to avoid idleness, gossip, vanity, and mischief. Like other girls of her day, Whitall received training in the arts of housekeeping and spinning and she developed a passion for reading and writing. She also gathered leaves, herbs, and roots for brewing into medicinal teas, a skill she learned from her mother. This interest developed from her desire to be of service to others, which she viewed as being of service to God.

On September 23, 1739, at age 23, she married James Whitall, the only son of Job and Jane (Sidon) Whitall. He had inherited a 96-acre farm on the east bank of the Delaware River. The couple raised six sons and three daughters there, attempting to instill in them the same Christian principles they had been taught. Life, for the most part, was quiet, simple, and busy, centering around family, work, and the Society of Friends' weekly "meetings."

In February 1760, at age 44, Whitall began to keep her diary of daily activities and spiritual insights, or "Medditations," as she deemed her writings. Out of her busy schedule she found time to record how well she, her family, and friends were faring as disciples of Christ in the world. She would often berate herself for failing to be the person she knew her Lord would want her to be. Of particular concern, as well, was the fact that her husband and sons rarely attended Meeting.

"It makes me sick sometimes," she wrote, "to see such doings, year after year. Now, we have been married about thirty years and he so cold about religion and the children grown men. This is the greatest trouble I meet with." (Diary, July 3, 1768)

Throughout her writings we see Whitall's unceasing efforts to expand her spiritual horizons, to grow in her faith and in her love for others. When a thief broke into her home one day she calmly but firmly shoved him outside with a broom, lecturing him on the Seventh Commandment.

The external world and its rumblings of war finally burst in on Whitall's private drama on October 22, 1777, when 1,500 Hessian soldiers advanced into the American zone and British ships occupied the waters of the Delaware. The contingent of American troops was small, numbering only about 400. One of them, Whitall's son Benjamin, was a captain of artillery. John Cooper, her brother, was also among their ranks, as a member of the Provincial and Continental Congress. For the most part, however, the Society of Friends, as pacifists, refused to bear arms, even in the cause of liberty.

As the fighting drew closer to rural Woodbury, residents were urged to leave their homes for safer ground. Believing God had a purpose for her there, Whitall refused. If the Lord called her, she said, He would find her at home. Concerned for her safety, Whitall's husband and eldest son, Job, begged her to take shelter at the nearest neighbor's. "The Lord is strong and mighty," she replied calmly, "and He will protect me. I may do good by staying." (Quoted in McGeorge, "The Heroine of Red Bank," 5) After putting her house in order, she set about occupying herself with something useful—her spinning wheel. Suddenly, as the guns of the British ships *Augusta* and *Merlin* were heard firing at close range, a cannonball burst through the room in which she was sitting and fell to the floor. Whitall decided to descend into the cellar with her wheel and continue spinning until the battle was over, recalling that "Providence favors those who aid themselves." (Quoted in McGeorge, 5) Forty-five minutes later, the outnumbered Americans had routed their invaders.

In the evening the wounded and dying—all of them Hessian soldiers—were brought in. But to Whitall, the word *enemy* did not exist. The Lord was the Lord of all and the spirit of love was to be extended without prejudice. Though her house was filled to the attic rafters, she set about tirelessly bandaging and ministering to those in need, brewing herbal medicines, and speaking softly of God's grace to those breathing their last. Impressed by her courage in the midst of danger and her unfailing charity to hostile troops, historians from that time on dubbed her "the Heroine of Red Bank."

On September 23, 1797, at age 82, Whitall succumbed to a yellow fever epidemic that also claimed the lives of two sons and two grandchildren. She was buried on the summit of Woodbury Hill, the Friends' burial ground, and as is the custom, her grave is unmarked except by a small, eight-by-two-inch marble slab. Her diary was tucked away in an attic until the early 1900s, when it was discovered.

Material on Ann Whitall, including a typescript copy of her diary, is available in the Frank H. Stewart Collection of the Savitz Library at NJ-GSC. The best source of information on her is a biography by daughter Hannah Whitall Smith, *John M. Whitall: The Story of His Life* (1879), which includes extracts from John Whitall's diary and letters.

Additional information on Whitall appears in a paper read before the NJ-GCHS by Isabella McGeorge, "Ann Whitall, the

Heroine of Red Bank" (1917); and in a seminar paper given at NJ-GSC by Tressie Pamela Davis, "Ann Cooper Whitall: A Woman of the American Revolution" (1962); and in *LCR*.

*Kristen McLaughlin*

## TEMPERANCE WICK, Revolutionary era

Temperance Wick, known as "Tempe," was a Revolutionary War heroine of the Morristown (Morris County), NJ, area and her story, although undocumented, has been handed down from generation to generation. She was the daughter of a farmer named Henry Wick, who lived in Wick House in Jockey Hollow, near Morristown. Henry Wick was a patriot who served in the Morris County cavalry as a captain. He also allowed Washington's army to winter on his land, where during the winter of 1780–81 the First Pennsylvania Brigade under General "Mad Anthony" Wayne was camped.

During the army's winter at Morristown, supplies for the large force put severe burdens on the small community. The troops were poorly fed and clothed, many forced to go barefoot in the snow. One field north of the Wick House is the burial site of at least 100 soldiers who died that winter in the brigade hospital, a dirt-floored wooden hut.

The troops had not been paid for a year and had no hope of being paid in the near future, despite many pleas to the Second Continental Congress. It is not surprising that many deserted. The crisis came in December 1780, when the soldiers organized a mutiny, planning to march to Philadelphia to demand their pay and discharges. In preparation for the march, soldiers spent several days foraging through the countryside and commandeering any horse they could find.

It was a difficult winter for the Wick family as well. On December 21, 1780, Henry Wick died, leaving Wick alone with her mother, who had been ill. Within a few days Wick's mother's illness worsened and it became obvious that a doctor was needed at once. Wick bundled up her mother and carried her to the cellar for safety, then saddled her horse and rode to fetch William Leddell, the family physician, who lived about a mile away, in the direction of Mendham. After leaving her message at Dr. Leddell's, Wick turned for home, when two or three soldiers suddenly appeared. One of them seized her horse's bridle, demanding she dismount and give them her horse. Wick pretended to acquiesce, prompting the soldier to release the bridle to help her dismount. She then whipped her horse and dashed between the soldiers toward home. A patriot like her father, Wick was prepared to do what she could to keep the soldiers from leaving New Jersey defenseless.

As she neared home, Wick must have realized that her horse was still not safe, for she was a familiar sight to the soldiers and they would surely follow her and search the property until the horse was found. In desperation, she led the horse into the house, through the kitchen and parlor into the small back bedroom that was kept for guests. She closed the shutter over the window, tied the horse to a ring-bolt fastened to the wall, and put a featherbed under his hooves to muffle his movements. She then brought her mother upstairs again. The soldiers arrived soon after and searched the barn and outbuildings and the woods around the house, but they left empty-handed. Legend has it that Wick kept her horse in the bedroom until New Year's Day, when the mutineers marched south toward Princeton.

The Wick House still stands, part of Jockey Hollow National Historical Park, and visitors may see the spare bedroom where Wick hid her horse. There is, however, no documentation of her life or death.

Wick's story and information on Wick House are found in Andrew M. Sherman, *Historic Morristown* (1905). An account of the incident appears in Linda Grant DePauw, *Fortunes of War: New Jersey Women and the American Revolution* (1975). Fictionalized versions of the adventure appear in Frank Stockton, *Stories of New Jersey* (1896), and in two books for young people: Patricia Edwards Clyne, *Patriots in Petticoats* (1976); and Patricia Lee Gauch, *This Time, Tempe Wick?* (1974).

*Sally Stone Forester*

## PATIENCE LOVELL WRIGHT, 1725–1786

Patience (Lovell) Wright, sculptor in wax and self-appointed Revolutionary War spy, elevated waxworking into fine art and, other than woodcarvers and carvers of tombstones, was America's first professional sculptor. Wright was probably born at Oyster Bay, Long Island, NY, in 1725. She was one of ten children (the fifth of nine girls), of farmer John Lovell and his wife, Patience (Townsend) Lovell. When she was four, the Lovells sold their Oyster Bay farm and settled on a farm in or near Bordentown (Burlington County), NJ, where her frugal father eventually accumulated large landholdings.

John Lovell practiced an eccentric form of Quakerism set forth a century earlier in the writings of Thomas Tryon, and he made his whole family follow its strict tenets. As children, Wright and her sisters, including RACHEL LOVELL WELLS, modeled figures in dough or clay, colored them with natural dyes, and dressed them in clothing.

Wright's first disobedience, she later said, was her flight, in her early twenties, to Philadelphia, where she hoped to enter a wider art world. Little is known of her stay there, but evidently she did not meet with artistic success. On March 20, 1748, she married Joseph Wright, a man she later reportedly described as having "nothing but

Late eighteenth-century wax sculpture of a young woman by Patience Lovell Wright. *Courtesy, Bordentown Historical Society.*

Elizabeth, Joseph, and Phoebe until they reached the age of 21 or married. By these terms, perhaps Joseph Wright hoped to tie his wife to Bordentown, where family would watch over her and the children. Instead, he propelled her into a career that would take her far from Bordentown.

Wright found the means to support herself and her children through her sister RACHEL LOVELL WELLS, also widowed by 1769. Wells had continued their childhood pastime of modeling but had also moved on to sculpting in wax. She taught Wright the technique and together they formed a waxwork show, which they then took on tour. The exhibit earned them commissions for portraits and tokens of appreciation from those invited to view the show. Generally, their private portrait commissions were for busts, but figures for the exhibit were full-length.

Previous wax exhibits had shown historical or allegorical subjects, but there had been no attempt at contemporary portraiture. Wright, however, specialized in realistic, life-size wax sculptures of well-known living subjects, while Wells favored biblical subjects. Wright is reported to have received encouragement from her Bordentown neighbor Francis Hopkinson, an artist-lawyer and future signer of the Declaration of Independence, who had been to London, England, and undoubtedly had seen the wax exhibits there.

Because wax needs to be kept warm in order to be pliable, Wright molded the hollow heads of wax on her lap under her apron. After the molding, the wax heads and hands of the figures were finished in minute detail: textured or wrinkled skin; veins introduced under the skin; glass eyes with lids, lashes, and brows; even fine hair on male hands; and real hair wigs. Head and hands were then mounted on wood and cardboard bodies and dressed in the subject's own clothing.

Within two years the women had a large enough collection of waxes for Wright to establish a fixed exhibit in New York City, and Wells one in Philadelphia. They each contributed work to the other's exhibit by making duplicates, and they continued to travel for more subjects and commissions.

Wright had given her baby Sarah into the care of her sister Rezine, who was married to Ephraim Anderson of Trenton (Mercer County), NJ, but Elizabeth, Joseph, and Phoebe, then between the ages of about 10 and 20, lived with their mother in New York. The children apparently had charge of the exhibit when Wright traveled. On June 3, 1771, during her absence, a fire started in the waxworks. The children were unhurt and there was little damage to the house, but many waxes were destroyed; a few important pieces were spared. Wright was sufficiently famous that the fire was reported in various newspapers, as was the news two months later that the waxworks had reopened with new and better pieces. RACHEL LOVELL WELLS had hastened to help her sister restock the exhibit, and indeed

*Age* and *Money* to *recommend* himself to her Favour." (Quoted in Sellers, *Patience Wright*, 23) Joseph Wright, a Quaker, was a native of Burlington County and a cooper by trade.

After their marriage the Wrights bought a brick house, which still stands in the center of Bordentown at the corner of Farnsworth Avenue and Park Street. Some 20 years later Wright and her children still lived there, but her husband lived in Philadelphia. Joseph Wright died in Philadelphia in May 1769, leaving his 44-year-old wife with five children: Mary, by then married to Benjamin Van Cleve; Elizabeth; Joseph (b. 1756); Phoebe (b. 1761); and Sarah, born after her father's death. Apparently, Joseph Wright, Sr., was unaware of the unborn child: he made no provision for her in his will. He left the four oldest children the proceeds from lands he owned, but he left his wife no income. Wright was to have the Bordentown house and its contents on the condition that she raise and provide for by September the two women were off to Boston with still another exhibit.

In Boston they met Jane Mecom, who, when she heard Wright was thinking of going to London to seek new subjects for portraiture, offered a letter of introduction to her brother Benjamin Franklin. Wright sailed for London in February 1772, leaving her daughter Elizabeth to run the waxworks and care for young Phoebe, while Joseph was in school in Philadelphia. The sculptor evidently planned to return to New York with her likenesses of Britain's great, but her rapid success in London exceeded perhaps even her own expectations, and eventually the three children joined her there.

Benjamin Franklin, in London as an official agent for several colonies, including New Jersey, introduced Wright to distinguished Londoners and allowed her to make his own portrait in wax. Soon her rooms in fashionable Westminster were filled with full-scale wax portraits of London's nobility, political leaders, and scholars. Members of English society marveled at the realism of her work, and many humorous tales were told of the wax figures being taken for real persons. But the Londoners were struck even more by how the portraits went beyond mere replication of physical features and revealed character. They began even to imagine Wright a prophet and called her the American Sibyl.

In London, as in New York, patrons were attracted to Wright's exhibit almost as much by her colorful personality as by her modeling skill. She was warm, hearty, intuitive, uninhibited, and outspoken, and Londoners loved her for it. She fitted the idealized 18th-century European vision of the child of nature: pure genius emerged from the uncorrupted wilderness of America. While rising in London society she displayed Quaker egalitarianism. When she was commissioned to sculpt busts of the king and queen, she addressed them bluntly as "George" and "Charlotte," and just as bluntly gave the king advice on Colonial policy. Although warmly attached to England, Wright was an American patriot and a fervent advocate of rights and liberties. She found a hero in William Pitt, Earl of Chatham, who advocated making the colonies free and equal partners with Britain.

Prominent Britons and Americans frequented the waxworks, and Wright by her manner—talkative, irreverent, and inquisitive—invited incaution in her interlocutors. Thus, when relations worsened between England and her American colonies, Chatham turned to Wright among others for information. This led her to assume the role of informant for the colonies and their friends in England. She delighted in the intrigue and soon was sending apparently unsolicited information and surely unsolicited advice to American leaders. It is thought that Wright sent information to Congress hidden in the wax heads she periodically shipped to the Philadelphia exhibit of her sister. Undoubt-

edly her letters were read. However, gossip culled from even Wright's prominent clientele and tips from opposition leaders were seldom important, correct, or timely enough to be of much use. In fact, the British may have intentionally fed her misinformation.

Because they found her amusing, eminent Britons continued to come to the waxworks even though she did not hide her sympathy for the American cause. After the spring of 1776, however, Wright received no more acclaim in the British press. Wright agitated for the release of American prisoners of war in Britain, and one of them, Ebenezer Platt, married her daughter Elizabeth upon his release in March 1778. The couple returned to America.

The Earl of Chatham died in May 1778, and Wright was commissioned to make a wax effigy to be placed in Westminster Abbey. There it remains, widely acclaimed, and the only undisputed example of Wright's work to have survived to the present. Thereafter, Wright's popularity in England waned, due in part to the war with America and in part to a fad for cheaper small wax profiles. But the waxworks remained a gathering place for artists, radicals, and opposition leaders.

In 1780 Phoebe Wright, who had posed for American artist Benjamin West, married the British portraitist John Hoppner, and Joseph Wright made his debut at the Royal Academy's exhibition with a painting of his mother. He showed her modeling a wax head of Charles I (beheaded in 1649 for his denial of his subjects' constitutional rights) while casting a meaningful glance at the heads of George III and Queen Charlotte.

During the ensuing uproar Patience Wright hurried off to Paris, where she hoped to repeat the success of her early days in London. Although she made another bust of Franklin and one of the Duchess of Chartres, she did not find her niche in France: the French did not always understand her forthright manner. Her son, Joseph, came to Paris in December 1781, after the American victory, to paint a portrait of Franklin, and then he returned to America to paint other national heroes.

In the summer of 1782 Wright returned to London, but her heyday was over. Instead of a sibyl, the Londoners now regarded her as either mad or romantic. In 1785, when she was 60, she longed to return to America and wrote to her sister RACHEL LOVELL WELLS asking her to see if she might be granted a little land, as was being given to soldiers, in return for her role as an informant. Wright died in London on February 25, 1786, as the result of a fall after a visit to the American embassy. Her place of burial is not known.

The most complete biography of Wright is Charles Coleman Sellers, *Patience Wright: American Artist and Spy in George III's London* (1976). (In this biography, Sellers corrected Wright's death date and other data on Wright from earlier writings, see p. 220.)

An earlier biography was Parker Lesley, "Patience Lovell Wright: America's First Sculptor," *Art in America* 24 (Oct. 1936):148–57. Her New Jersey connections are stressed in J. C. Long, "Patience Wright of Bordentown," *NJHSP* 79 (1961):118–23. A profile of her appears in *NAW*.

*Maggie Sullivan*
*M. M. Pernot*

SCENES FROM THE BATTLE-FIELD AT GETTYSBURG, PA.

SECOND CORPS HOSPITAL.

Christian Commission Tents in the foreground.  This Hospital contains 2500 wounded.

F. GUTEKUNST, Photographer, 704 and 706 Arch St., PHILADELPHIA.

Cornelia Hancock, of Hancock's Bridge, served as a nurse in the Civil War. She is said to be one of the nurses in this photograph of the 2nd Army Corps hospital at the Gettysburg battlefield (*standing by tent, left of center*). *Courtesy, Historical Society of Pennsylvania Photograph Collections.*

# HISTORICAL OVERVIEW: 1808-1865

IN THE EARLY 1800S New Jersey was still primarily rural and the majority of its women lived on farms. Farm wives, daughters, unmarried female relatives in the household, servants, and in some instances slaves labored at a variety of tasks necessary to maintain the family farm as a productive economic unit. SARAH STAATS BAYLES, who lived on a farm in Somerset County, described a daily round of household chores in a diary she kept from 1835 to 1851. Often she was needed outside in the barnyard as well as indoors; one diary entry recorded: "Cow had calf. Put house aside."

During the 19th century, women often combined work with socializing as female members of a farm household came together with kin and neighbors to share tasks. Diarist ELIZABETH MULFORD CRANE, a farm wife in Berkeley Heights, wrote that neighborhood women helped one another with sewing and weaving, picking over wool, and dipping candles, and enjoyed quilting and apple-cutting bees.

Women not only shared work; they took turns nursing among neighboring families, assisting at sickbeds and with childbirths. Midwife MARTHA AUSTIN REEVES helped to deliver over 1,000 babies in Shiloh and Hopewell townships during the first several decades of the 19th century. The entries she kept in her *Record Book of Births* (1801–31) show that Reeves also functioned as a lay medical practitioner, dispensing homemade medications to the many patients she treated over her 40-year career.

At the turn of the century, when scientific agricultural methods had not yet caught on in the state and crop yields were poor, the gardens kept by farmers' wives often provided half of the support for farm families. (Fleming, *New Jersey*, 97) By the 1820s improved farming practices increased productivity and New Jersey's steadily growing population provided larger markets for farmers' crops. Some women, such as former slaves ELIZABETH SUTLIFF DULFER and SILVIA DUBOIS, ran their own farms. In 1847 Dulfer purchased 87 acres of land on the west bank of the Hackensack River, where she raised cash crops and worked clay beds, selling clay to nearby potteries. After many years in a succession of occupations, including household domestic, ferryboat pilot, and tavern owner,

Dubois raised prize hogs on her farm near Cedar Summit.

A fast-developing transportation system made it possible to deliver farm goods to the entire state, as well as New York City and Philadelphia. Besides providing easier access to diverse markets for farm produce, the growth of a transportation infrastructure made travel faster and more convenient for New Jerseyans. During the first several decades of the 19th century, waterways were the fastest means of transport as newly invented steamships moved up and down the Jersey coast, linking the state's ports with cities in other states and with European trade centers. ANNE MARGUERITE HYDE DE NEUVILLE, one of New Jersey's early artists, portrayed this popular mode of transportation, painting the earliest known representation of a steamboat on its run between New York City and New Brunswick, NJ, in 1809.

By the 1830s a railway network had replaced the canal system, crisscrossing the state and connecting it with the nation's interior. Produce traveled to market by rail, and coal from Pennsylvania was supplied by rail to fuel the infant industries springing up in New Jersey's cities. Besides carrying goods, the railroads transported passengers, making travel less onerous than it had been by wagon and stagecoach. In 1854 the commuter line from Jersey City to New Brunswick advertised a "Ladies Car" on all through trains for "the exclusive use of ladies and their companions" (Wilson, *Outline History*, 66), hinting at the growing importance of woman's role as a consumer of goods and services during the antebellum period.

Like their sisters elsewhere in the Northeast, the tasks of many middle- and upper-class New Jersey women changed, as America began to industrialize in the first half of the 19th century and items formerly produced by members of individual household economic units were made in factories. These women became home managers responsible for creating and maintaining a harmonious domestic environment for husbands who spent much of their time in the urban workplace. Women presided over the domestic sphere while men took charge of commerce and government. Part of woman's task was to acquire manufactured products that would enhance her home, choosing from among a variety of goods now offered for sale. For example, rather than weaving and dyeing fabric themselves as their farm counterparts still did, more affluent, urban women bought velvet made in Newark and silk manufactured in Paterson; instead of whitewashing or stenciling walls, they purchased wallpaper from companies in New Brunswick.

As household managers, women often directed the work of hired help and trained daughters in the art of household management. The correspondence of ELIZABETH MILLER KEASBEY, a young Morristown woman, recounts her many chores, including caring for younger children, nursing, sewing, picking and preserving fruit. Although she grew up in a house with a staff of servants, Keasbey's time was circumscribed by how often her mother could "spare" her from household duties. As the middle class grew larger toward midcentury, its need for and ability to pay wages of servants meant that domestic service became a way of earning a living for many women—native-born whites and African-Americans, as well as newly arrived Irish immigrants such as BRIDGET DERGAN, from County Sligo, Ireland, who worked as a "hired girl" in the home of a doctor in New Market.

Growing numbers of factories also meant jobs for New Jersey women in the burgeoning manufacturing cities of Newark, Paterson, Jersey City, Trenton, Camden, Elizabeth, and New Brunswick. As in other areas of the industrializing Northeast, female operatives were needed for positions in a work force where tasks were sex-segregated and women received lower wages than men. Although organized worker response to bad working conditions and poor pay was slow to develop in the first half of the century, one of the country's earliest known "turnouts" (strikes) of women workers took place in 1828 in a Paterson, NJ, cotton mill to protest management's arbitrary shift of the lunch hour from noon to one o'clock. (Clinton, *Other Civil War*, 26)

As a small but increasing number of women entered factory work during the first half of the century, others became schoolteachers, an expansion into the public realm of woman's role as "republican mother," the moral and intellectual educator of the young. Both private and public school systems developed in New Jersey during the period. Academies such as the New Brunswick Female Institute, founded in the late 1830s by HANNAH HOYT, were established to educate the children of well-to-do families. These academies were either denominationally supported or funded by groups of a town's leading citizens.

The state legislature was slow to vote the funds necessary for a public school system; thus many New Jersey children could not attend school during the first half of the 19th century. Education for African-American children depended largely on individual initiative like that of BETSEY STOCKTON, who organized a public school for black children in Princeton by the late 1830s. The lack of free public education for New Jersey children disturbed young schoolteacher CLARA BARTON when she arrived in the state in 1851. She persuaded the Bordentown School Committee to open the town's first public school in 1852 and served without pay as its principal. By 1855 a normal school for teacher training was established in Trenton, after successful lobbying by the New Jersey State Teachers' Association.

Church activities were further avenues for extending the middle-class woman's sphere beyond the home as many women joined church-based benevolent and charitable societies during the early decades of the century. Typical of such women was LOUISA SANDERSON MACCULLOCH of Morristown, a founding member of the Female Charitable Society, which was composed of members of the local Presbyterian church. Societies such as these functioned in nearly every community as a private welfare system responding to the needs of the poor, ill, orphans, and elderly within a town. Marriage to a clergyman was another route to a leadership role in the church for some 19th-century women, such as AGNES MORGAN REEVES APPLETON of Haddonfield, who married a Baptist minister in 1865.

For a very small number of women religion provided more new roles as missionaries and preachers. Before BETSEY STOCKTON became a schoolteacher she had participated for a time as a member of a mission to Hawaii, and JARENA LEE from Cape May County was one of several New Jersey African-American women evangelists who traveled the Mid-Atlantic region preaching at the revivals and camp meetings popular during the first half of the century. Countless women were instrumental in establishing churches in their areas and in raising funds for ministers' salaries and upkeep of church buildings. Many were content with such auxiliary roles in religious life, but a few sought recognition by church hierarchies through ordination.

The right of women to vote in New Jersey was a concern of the first ordained woman minister in the United States, the Rev. ANTOINETTE LOUISA BROWN BLACKWELL. In 1858 Blackwell moved from New York, where she had briefly pastored a Congregational church, to a farm near Millburn, NJ, and turned her attention from the struggle for the right to be ordained to broader women's rights reform. That same year Blackwell's sister-in-law, LUCY STONE, protested New Jersey women's lack of voting privileges by refusing to pay real estate taxes on her house in East Orange. In 1844, when the state held a constitutional referendum, women apparently launched no significant push to reinstate the voting rights taken away from them in 1807. They did, however, make scattered, sporadic attempts to vote during the next two decades. By 1867 the New Jersey Woman Suffrage Association was organized.

The fight for women's rights was only one of a number

of reforms New Jersey women, together with their sisters in other areas of the country, participated in from the 1820s on. The state received nationwide attention through the campaign of DOROTHEA LYNDE DIX to galvanize the legislature into funding a hospital for the mentally ill. Dix toured jails and almshouses documenting the deplorable conditions in which the insane were kept and pressured reluctant politicians to act. Her almost single-handed efforts resulted in the establishment of the New Jersey State Lunatic Asylum near Trenton in 1848, which Dix helped design.

Dorothea Lynde Dix, c. 1840. Dix convinced the New Jersey legislature of the need for humane care for the insane, and in 1848, as a result of her work, the state's first hospital offering this care was opened at Trenton. *Courtesy, Trenton Psychiatric Hospital.*

Some 19th-century American reformers' dreams of alternatives to the prevailing socioeconomic system led to the founding of experimental utopian communities such as the North American Phalanx near Red Bank, where MARY PAUL lived during the early 1850s until the group disbanded. She and the other members of the community set up an egalitarian mode of living emphasizing equal credit for the labor of both sexes. Paul wrote to her father: "Both men and women have the *same* pay for the same work." (Woloch, *Women,* 189)

REBECCA BUFFUM SPRING and her husband, Marcus, were chief stockholders in the Phalanx and became leaders of another utopian community, the Raritan Bay Union, founded in 1853 near Perth Amboy. The focus of this community was progressive education and the Springs invited ANGELINA GRIMKÉ WELD and SARAH MOORE GRIMKÉ, nationally known abolitionists, to teach in the union's coeducational and interracial school. Both the Springs and the Grimké sisters shared a deep commitment to the antislavery cause, an unpopular reform in New Jersey, which had strong commercial ties to the South.

Nevertheless, abolition sentiment grew during the 1840s and 1850s, particularly among south Jersey Quakers who helped operate several Underground Railroad stations. ABIGAIL GOODWIN, a Quaker from Salem, hid escaped slaves in her house and raised money for abolition societies, working closely with leaders from the Philadelphia antislavery movement such as William Still, "the father of the Underground Railroad." Early in the century his mother, CHARITY STILL, had made a daring escape from slavery in Maryland to freedom in New Jersey's Pine Barrens, a feat repeated by hundreds of other African-Americans before the Civil War.

The war was a watershed event for New Jersey, as it was for the rest of the nation. Though it was a border state and never enthusiastic about forcing abolition on the South (it was the only northern state that did not challenge the Fugitive Slave Law), New Jersey responded to Lincoln's call to save the Union, mobilizing troops and voting funds to finance its share of the war. New Jersey women such as CORNELIA HANCOCK of Hancock's Bridge also aided the war effort, organizing relief shipments and volunteering to serve as nurses with the Union army. Along with other northern women, Hancock went South after the war to teach African-American children in schools sponsored by the Freedmen's Aid societies.

As women enlarged their sphere of activity over the first two-thirds of the 19th century, more occupations opened up for them outside the home. During this period women also began to be taken seriously in previously male-dominated professions such as art. In the early 1820s the artistic talent of CHARLOTTE BONAPARTE was sufficiently recognized that she was invited to exhibit her sketches of northern New Jersey scenes at the Pennsylvania Academy of the Fine Arts; yet she did not think of herself as a professional artist. By midcentury SUSAN MOORE WATERS of Bordentown was making a living for herself and her ailing husband by painting portraits and still lifes, selling two paintings at the 1876 Centennial Exposition in Philadelphia. LILLY MARTIN SPENCER, one of the most popular midcentury American painters, purposely set out to become an artist, with the support of her husband and the prominent Newark art patron Marcus L. Ward, who invited her to move to that city in 1858 and establish herself as a painter.

The biographies of these three New Jersey women artists show a progression from talented amateur status to the necessity of earning money by painting to the pursuit of a career, a progression that reveals the professionalization of women's activities over the course of the century. One can trace a similar trend toward professionalization in the biographies of writers such as ELIZABETH CLEMENTINE DODGE STEDMAN KINNEY, who began to submit poetry to popular periodicals during the 1830s and published her collected poems to critical acclaim by the 1860s. By the final third of the century New Jersey women, like women in other areas of the nation, were entering many professions in slowly increasing numbers, illustrating by their lives the gradual widening of woman's sphere during the 19th century.

*Carolyn DeSwarte Gifford*

## Selected References

Clinton, Catherine. *The Other Civil War: American Women in the Nineteenth Century*. New York, 1984.

Cott, Nancy F. *The Bonds of Womanhood: "Woman's Sphere" in New England, 1780–1835*. New Haven, CT, 1977.

Du Bois, Ellen Carol. *Feminism and Suffrage: The Emergence of an Independent Women's Movement in America, 1848–1869*. Ithaca, NY, 1978.
1978.

Fleming, Thomas. *New Jersey: A History*. New York, 1984.

Price, Clement Alexander, ed. *Freedom Not Far Distant: A Documentary History of Afro-Americans in New Jersey*. Newark, 1980.

Ruether, Rosemary Radford, and Rosemary Skinner Keller, eds. *Women and Religion in America: The Nineteenth Century*. New York, 1981.

Smith-Rosenberg, Carroll. *Disorderly Conduct: Visions of Gender in Victorian America*. New York, 1985.

Welter, Barbara. *Dimity Convictions: The American Woman in the Nineteenth Century*. Athens, OH, 1976.

Wilson, Harold F. et al., eds. *Outline History of New Jersey*. New Brunswick, NJ, 1950.

Woloch, Nancy. *Women and the American Experience*. New York, 1984.

## AGNES MORGAN REEVES APPLETON, 1839–unknown

Agnes Morgan (Reeves) Appleton, diarist, was born in 1839 in Haddonfield, NJ, the youngest of at least seven children of Hannah (Hopkins) and Samuel Morgan Reeves. Her sisters were from three to 20 years older than she. Her only known brother, Samuel, died in 1845 at the age of thirteen, when Appleton was six.

Appleton's parents were both born in New Jersey. They moved to Haddonfield and built a spacious brick home on Main Street in 1818, shortly after their marriage. Her father was a prosperous farmer and merchant.

If it were not for the existence of two volumes of her diary (Sept. 21, 1856–June 26, 1857, and Sept. 25, 1859–Oct. 23, 1864) little would be known about Appleton. Although not very introspective, Appleton reveals much about her character in the diary. The earlier volume covers a period when she was a student at the Moravian Seminary for Young Ladies in Bethlehem, PA. The later volume was written while she was at home in Haddonfield.

Her childhood was apparently happy. Exceedingly homesick while a student at the Moravian Seminary, she wrote lovingly of her family. She found the studies at school rigorous and the discipline more so. A teacher, reprimanding her and other students for making noise in their dormitory room, "proceeded with a long lecture on the evilness of Woman Kind in general." (Mar. 28, 1857) Although full of normal adolescent self-doubt—"I think I am the most wicked girl in the whole world, for I am always forgetting and sinning against my kind heavenly Father" (Feb. 1, 1857)—she did not agree with her teacher's views on women. In one entry about two of her classmates, she wrote, "Rexie had an arguement [sic] with Clara Lindsley about the women. Rex said that she thought the whole sex a deceitful, fickle, & what not persons. Clara tried to defend her sex. And as she had the best side of the question succeeded pretty well." (Apr. 14, 1857)

At school she made friends, attended social events, went to dances with young gentlemen, and looked forward to marrying someday. Returning from the marriage of one of her teachers, she had "a piece of their wedding cake to dream on." (Jan. 8, 1857)

After leaving school, she returned to Haddonfield. She pursued no profession and her life was seemingly ordinary for a young, unmarried woman of her era. Much of her time was spent calling on friends and relatives, and in turn being visited by them, attending church and church-related activities. Although she was a member of religious and civic groups such as the Ladies Society at church and the Haddonfield Soldiers Aid Society, she was not a leader in any of these organizations.

Her visits took her to many parts of southern New Jersey, to Philadelphia, and at least once to New York City. Despite her travels, her view of the world was provincial. She wrote about the Civil War only when it affected someone she knew. After a visit to a Dr. Howell, she indicated that "there had been a battle near Richmond in which some of the Jersey Regiments were engaged and many of our brave men were slain. Among them a young man not eighteen years, Captain Thomas Howell, a nephew of Dr. Howell. They had just gotten the news last week and all seemed very sad about it. Father in Heaven preserve our Country and prevent the shedding of blood. Thou and Thou alone canst save us. Oh save us speedily." (July 7, 1862)

Even more typical of her thinking, on hearing that a friend had lost part of a finger in a mowing machine, she "felt badly whenever I thought of it. I have read of the soldier's sufferings, without feelling [sic] so very badly. But this seemed more real, when it concerned one with whom I am acquainted." (July 9, 1862)

Appleton was a deeply religious woman. Her background on her father's side was Quaker, but in 1857 she joined the Haddonfield Baptist Church. Typical of many of her contemporaries, her life was dominated by her religious attitudes. She referred to Sunday as the "day of all the week the best." (Feb. 17, 1860) She would often attend services twice on Sunday, frequently worshiping at the Episcopal or another church, in addition to the Baptist Church. But her ecumenical spirit was not universal. Reflecting the sentiments of most Protestants of her time, especially those from small towns, Appleton wrote that she had gone to Philadelphia "to see the new Catholic Cathedral a magnificent building at 18th and Vine St. God grant that all idolatrous forms very soon be done away with and He be alone worshipped in simplicity and truth." (Nov. 4, 1863)

Christian salvation was a theme that ran through her life. She was deeply affected by the death of her cousin Rebecca Hopkins in 1857, followed closely by the death of a young classmate at the Moravian Seminary. It became important to her that "we be prepared when the summons comes for us." (Apr. 5, 1862) She was most thankful above all for a "Father and a Savior in the better land to which we trust we are hastening . . . oh, how our hearts should kindle at the thought." (Nov. 27, 1862) When Appleton learned that a friend had become a mother similar thoughts were evoked in her, for she wrote, "God bless her and help her to feel her responsibility and train her [son] for Heaven." (Jan. 22, 1863)

She worried constantly about friends and family who were not yet saved: "Clement Reeves was up. We went to church in the eve. I felt as if I could not rest unless he gave his heart to Jesus. Oh God my Father have mercy on his soul now!" (Jan. 24, 1864)

On May 9, 1865, she married the Rev. James H. Appleton of Philadelphia. She left New Jersey, and her membership in the Haddonfield Baptist Church was transferred on May 25, 1865, to Point Pleasant, PA. Nothing more is known about her life after this. It is believed that she died in 1901.

The Appleton diary is available on microfilm at NJ-RU. Small bits of genealogical information about her and her family appear in the records of the Haddonfield Baptist Church and in materials at NJ-GCHS. Haviland F. Reves, *The Reves Family* (1951), provides apparently correct information about Appleton's parents and ancestors, but is not accurate about her.

*Douglas B. Rauschenberger*

Clara Barton, founder of the American Red Cross, established Bordentown's first free school in 1852. *Courtesy, Bordentown Historical Society.*

## CLARA BARTON, 1821–1912

An American heroine, teacher, humanitarian, Civil War nurse, lecturer, founder of the American Red Cross, and author, Clarissa Harlowe Barton was born on December 25, 1821, in North Oxford, MA. She was the youngest of five children born to Stephen E. and Sarah (Stone) Barton. The Barton family was of English ancestry and Stephen Barton's kin were some of the first settlers of Massachusetts.

In her memoirs, published in 1907, Barton wrote of herself: "being the youngest by a dozen or so years of a family of two brothers and two sisters . . . each one manifested an increasing personal interest in the newcomer, and as soon as developments permitted, set about instructing her in the various directions most in accord with the tastes and pursuits of each." (Barton, *The Story of My Childhood*, 12–17) Indeed, the template for her life achievements was the attention and instruction given by her family. Captain Stephen E. Barton, a farmer, was of a gentle disposition, military spirit, and philanthropic bent. War stories of his service under General "Mad Anthony" Wayne engaged young Barton in the large family sitting room. (W. Barton, *Life of Clara Barton*, 1:17) Her mother was of the "good old New England sort looking well to the ways of her household and eating not the bread of idleness." (W. Barton, 1:17) Compassionate, sensible, and forgiving, she sought to give her daughter a level head. Of Barton's siblings, David taught her horsemanship; Stephen was a noted mathematician and "inducted me into the mystery of figures" (Barton, *Story of My Childhood*, 18); and her sisters, Sarah and Dorothea, established a kind of school at home and practiced on their younger sister.

By 20th-century standards young Clara Barton would be judged to be intellectually gifted. Reading at age three, her intellectual achievements continued throughout her schooling. She was self-critical, persistent, curious, enthusiastic about learning, outstanding in her range of interests, and had a strength of character that soon became grounded in a pervasive sense of social responsibility. She was sensitive and retiring to the extreme as a child, and her inner tensions found a creative outlet through writing verse. Like many women of this period, Barton believed that people are spiritual beings. She was a Universalist, but not within a church: nothing in ritual appealed to her.

Her formal schooling was extensive for a woman of the early 19th century: she attended common school from age three to seven, Richard Stone's Select Academy from eight to eleven, and Lucien Burleigh's School from fifteen to sixteen. She received her teaching certificate in 1839 and prepared for her first assignment (1840) in Oxford, School District no. 9, teaching 40 pupils, age four to fourteen. (Williams, *Clara Barton*, 29–38)

An important interruption in her schooling occurred

when she was eleven. Her brother David, seriously injured during a fall, lay bedridden for two years. Compelled to care for him, Barton remained near his side from the first days and nights of illness. During this time she learned to take all directions for care and medications from his physician. "I was the accepted and acknowledged nurse of a man almost too ill to recover." (Barton, *Story of My Childhood*, 83) As with all her education, each lesson served her well in her lifetime; early experiences as her brother's nurse provided her with the skills to administer to wounded and dying Union and Confederate soldiers.

In 1850, after teaching in various schools for ten years, she enrolled at Clinton Institute in Oneida County, NY, a seminary for boys and girls, to complete her education. Her success at the institute was palled by the death of her beloved mother. Barton never again returned to her home in Oxford. Instead, she accompanied her friend Mary Norton to her home in Hightstown, NJ, where, prompted by Norton, she took a teaching position at Cedar Swamp School in 1851. "Something drew me to the state of New Jersey. I was a teacher dyed in the wool and soon discovered that this good state had no public school, that a part of its children were in private schools, the remainder in the streets. . . . I considered this state of things and decided to take upon me the opening of public schools generally in that state as well as the eyes of the people." (Epler, *Life of Clara Barton*, 22)

After visiting Bordentown, NJ, and finding 200 children in school and 400 on the street, Barton met with Peter Suydam, chairman of the School Committee. Although the committee doubted the ability of a woman to teach the renegade youngsters, Barton was permitted to undertake the experiment, without salary, and in late May 1852 opened the town's first free school in the "Old Schoolhouse" on Crosswicks Street. Six boys, age ten to fourteen, attended the first day. Attendance doubled on the second day, and by the end of the year grew to 600 pupils. The school was such a success that Barton sent for an assistant, Frances Childs, of Oxford, MA. Supported by the prejudices of that period, which held that a large organization, though created by a woman, must be headed by a man, Barton was replaced as principal of the new school. Barton stepped down from her position of control unwillingly, feeling resentment and hurt. After informing her brother of her intent to resign, he replied, "You have done much to establish the system of free schools in [Bordentown] and in so doing have done an infinite amount of good to the rising generation." (Williams, 52) Suffering from emotional strain and physical exhaustion, Barton left her work in Bordentown, and her career as a teacher, in early 1854 and traveled to Washington, D.C., to recuperate.

During this period Barton faced the choice between the separate spheres of career and family imposed upon 19th-century women. Though courted by several suitors, she could never be the submissive wife required by social custom, and thus never married. As she later remarked, "[I] had been more useful to the world by being free from matrimonial ties." (W. Barton, 77) Instead, she accepted an appointment as clerk in the Patent Office at the request of Colonel Alexander DeWitt, the representative in Congress from her home district. Barton was one of the first women to hold a regular position in a federal department with wages and responsibilities equal to that of a man.

Residing in Washington, D.C., when Civil War was declared, Barton began service by sitting in the vice-president's chair in the Senate chamber reading to a group of Union soldiers. At first "she roamed the hills where the men tented around Washington." (Ross, *Angel of the Battlefield*, 29) Later that year (1861) she cooked and hand-fed the men, bandaged wounds, wrote letters to mothers and wives, escorted the sick to hospitals, and distributed clothing, liquors, and supplies of all kinds. She overcame the resistance and prejudice that barred women from the battlefield, considered an unsuitable place for them. Using her small apartment on Seventh Street as a storehouse for donated goods, and demonstrating the practicability of getting to the front early by "following the cannon," Barton brought relief to thousands of wounded and dying Union and Confederate troops. As she described her experience, "My post the open field between the bullet and the hospital." And at Antietam: "On the ground before the first gun was fired and did not leave until the last wounded man had been cared for." (W. Barton, 1:247, 199) The combined armies suffered 22,000 casualties. Her ministrations touched the soldiers at the Battles of Bull Run, Chantilly, Fredericksburg, Harper's Ferry, and many others.

During the war her distinctive contribution was the organization and distribution of relief to those with the greatest need at the place of greatest danger. At war's end she labored four years searching for missing soldiers and was responsible for informing the government and families of the names and fate of more than 20,000 who otherwise might never have been identified.

After dismissing the notion of writing a book, the now well-known and admired Barton toured the country, giving over 300 lectures, at $100 per night, recounting her wartime activities. In 1869, at age 47, shortly after the close of the one-year lecture circuit, she suffered a nervous collapse similar to that of 1854, lost the use of her voice, and was ordered by her physicians to retire to Europe for three years of complete rest. During this fateful sojourn she learned of the activities of the Red Cross and embarked on a life's journey that would command her public and private attention and identity.

Barton admired the work of the Red Cross, and in 1871, at the request of Dr. Louis Appia, an important member of the International Committee of Geneva, she agreed to participate in relief efforts in the Franco-Prussian

War. Prudently, deliberately, and for no remuneration, she administered relief without regard to political disposition. She received 27 decorations of honor for service, including honors from Spain, Turkey, and Russia, the Official Medal of the International Red Cross, and the Iron Cross of Germany, conferred by Emperor William I and Empress Augusta.

Resolving to introduce the Red Cross to the United States, she returned home in 1873 to begin a long and lonely struggle against seemingly unreasonable opposition. She became the first president of the American Red Cross in 1881 at age 60. During the first two decades of its existence, the Red Cross society remained a personal creation of Barton. Completely in charge, she directed all activities, managed funds, and took over most of the field relief work, aiding victims of the 1881 Michigan forest fire, 1882 Ohio flood, 1888 Florida yellow fever epidemic, the Johnstown flood, and other disasters.

Relinquishing her Red Cross presidency in 1904, she retired to her home in Glen Echo, MD, to manage her household affairs, tend her garden, correspond with family and friends, and continue a journal she had unfailingly maintained since she began teaching. During the rigor of the winter of 1911–12 she contracted double pneumonia and grew progressively weaker. Barton died, at age 90, on April 12, 1912. The medical verdict was that she had "succumbed to old age." (Ross, 267) A few days before her death she requested that the main funeral service be held in Oxford and the chief speakers be her friend the Rev. Percy Epler and her cousin the Rev. William E. Barton. She was buried, along with generations of Bartons, in the North Oxford Cemetery, MA, her childhood home.

Barton's autobiography, *The Story of My Childhood* (1907), covers her life up to her first teaching assignment. Biographies of her are: Elizabeth Brown Pryor, *Clara Barton: Professional Angel* (1987); William Barton, *The Life of Clara Barton: Founder of the American Red Cross*, 2 vols. (1922); Blanche Colton Williams, *Clara Barton, Daughter of Destiny* (1941); Percy Epler, *The Life of Clara Barton* (1915); and Ishbel Ross, *Angel of the Battlefield: The Life of Clara Barton* (1956). Archival material on Barton is kept at DC-LC, the Library of the American Red Cross (Washington, D.C.), and NJ-BHS. She is profiled in *NAW*.

*Ellen Giarelli*

## SARAH STAATS BAYLES, 1787–1870

Sarah (Staats) Bayles was born on March 15, 1787, at her parents' farmhouse in what is now South Bound Brook (Somerset County), NJ. She was the sixth of seven daughters and one son of Abraham and Margaret (DuBois) Staats. From 1835 to 1851 Bayles kept a daybook or diary, jotting down domestic activities and the social events of her family and community, including births, marriages, and deaths.

Bayles's paternal grandfather, John Staats, moved from Long Island, purchased a large tract of land in the Raritan Valley in the early 1730s, and farmed successfully enough to leave a farm of over 200 acres in the bend of the Raritan River in Franklin Township (now South Bound Brook) to Bayles's father. Other parcels of land passed to John Staats's other sons in what is now Hillsborough and Montgomery townships. The Staats men, as well as Abraham DuBois, Bayles's maternal grandfather, are listed as "free holders" in the Eastern Precinct (Bound Brook area) and Hillsborough Township in the "List of Officers and Free Holders, April 24, 1790."

On May 10, 1814, she left this prosperous family to marry William Bayles of North Branch, son of John Bayles, a miller, and Teuntje Van Dyke (Bergen) Bayles. Their one child, Margaret Ann Bayles, was born in North Branch on June 24, 1815. The marriage was brief; on September 16, 1817, Bayles left her husband and returned with her daughter to her family home. Family history records that William Bayles was an alcoholic. At a time when women were expected to stay in a marriage, Bayles took the unusual step of leaving her husband and, moreover, of taking her daughter with her. She must have had considerable support and help from her family in making this uncommon move; her father's will (dated 1819, two years later) stipulated that she have part-share of the family homestead and equal right with other unmarried daughters "provided she remain separate from her husband Wm. Bayles." (*Genealogical Magazine of New Jersey*, 29) She also received a legacy that was to be held in trust for her during the lifetime of her husband (deceased 1853), presumably to protect her from any attempts on William Bayles's part to control her income. Bayles remained on the farm for the rest of her life, helping her father and, then, her brother to run it. She eventually inherited it and left it to her daughter.

From 1839 to 1850 Bayles kept a diary or, more accurately, a daybook recording the everyday events of her life. It is incomplete; pages forming a signature have been torn out of a small notebook, and there are other scraps attached to it. It maintains no particular format; what remains on the fragile paper written in brown ink form inconsistent entries. Sometimes entries are written consecutively every day, as in January 1839, and sometimes a whole year is recorded on one page. The writing is legible, but occasionally crowded and small, with extra lines between the entries. This diary fragment records the day-to-day events in Bayles's community: births and deaths, marriages and membership in the church, meetings of the church society, and life on the farm.

The entries for January 1839 depict a busy, energetic, and efficient homemaker; on Monday, January 14, Bayles "ran bredths for Comfortable"; on Wednesday she was quilting. She made "candals," finished a frock for "Deyan, our coloured Woman," darned the carpet, baked and mended. She also helped in the farmyard: "Thursday. Cow had a calf. Put house aside." Her grandson, Charles Olmstead Bayles, was left with her for almost a month to be weaned.

Most of the entries are very brief, recording visits, the names of the different preachers she has heard, and where the church society has met. Bayles does not elaborate, not even to record what was discussed at the society, or the cause of death for those noted in her diary. The entry for September 10, 1837, records: "Margaret Ann's little son was born. Mr. Pollock preached at Boundbrook." She does not record the death of her grandson in August 1849. Even for those close to her, members of her immediate family, the entries are short, stark, and without elaboration. Her daughter's husband died suddenly, when her daughter was pregnant with their second child, and this event is simply recorded: "Dr. Bayles died suddenly between four and Five o'clock in the afternoon of Wednesday. Thursday Margaret Ann . . . came home . . . Doctor Bayles buried on Friday 5th April 1839. Mr Comfort preached." Family history attributes the death to Dr. Bayles accidentally shooting himself while cleaning his gun. Bayles took her daughter into her home, much as she herself had gone home 22 years earlier.

A devoted and regular churchgoer, Bayles attended Bound Brook Presbyterian Church, where she recorded the texts of the sermons by the Rev. Rodgers between 1835 and 1839. He seems to have been a favorite of hers, although she does not comment on the content of his sermons. Perhaps he spoke clearly; Bayles may have had some trouble with her hearing. On May 28, 1837, she "went to the Presbyterian church in New Brunswick. Heard nothing." She also recorded in some detail the new members of the church, whether they came recommended from another church, by certificate, or as Maria Brokaw and Cynthia Onderdonk did, "on profession of their faith." Bayles was also active in raising money for the Presbyterian Education Society and involved herself in the meetings of the church society, hosting some at her farmhouse. Unfortunately she has told us nothing of their meetings or activities.

Included with the daybook are several loose leaves with notes on home remedies, such as a cure for a felon: "A strong lye of hickory ashes, add a pint of beer and thicken with wheat bran, then grease the poultice with lard and apply"—probably a kill or cure for the finger. And: "Linseed, Sugar, licorice and lemon juice, added to a little rum, is an excellent remedy for a cough." These few notes also contain references to servants or slaves; Bayles did not clarify their status. Both Hannah Staats and Deyan (also spelled Dian) were described by Bayles as "our Coloured Woman," whose deaths were listed on the same fragment as Old Harry's, and those of the Williams family. Old Har-

ry and Hannah were both listed in the inventory of the personal estate of Bayles's father, Abraham Staats, as being worth $75 each. It seems that Hannah, Harry, and probably Deyan, for whom Bayles made clothes, were slaves; and that James Williams and his wife, Phillis, were servants.

Bayles died on February 2, 1870, where she had been born, in the family farmhouse by the Raritan. She was buried in the family plot on the farm beside her parents and her sister. The graves were later moved to the Staats–La Tourette plot in Bound Brook Cemetery.

Bayles's incomplete diary, or daybook, accompanied by some loose leaves, is available at NJ-RU. Genealogical information on the Staats, DuBois, and Bayles families appears in the *Genealogical Magazine of New Jersey* 33 (1925):25–32. Abraham Messler's *First Things in Somerset* (1899) and *Forty Years at Raritan* (1873) contain additional details about the families and the area.

*Marylin A. Hulme*

## ANTOINETTE LOUISA BROWN BLACKWELL, 1825–1921

Antoinette Louisa (Brown) Blackwell, the first ordained woman minister in the United States and a reformer, lecturer, and writer, was born on May 20, 1825, in Henrietta, NY. She was the fourth of seven daughters and the seventh of ten children born to farming parents Joseph and Abby (Morse) Brown. Both parents were descendants of English colonists, her mother of Puritan leader Samuel Morse.

The Browns lived in upstate New York, which was an area of religious ferment during her youth. When Blackwell was six, her parents and older brothers and sisters experienced conversion as a result of the preaching of Charles Grandison Finney. At the age of nine, she made a precocious declaration of faith and was accepted as a member by her local Congregational church.

Blackwell began her education at the local district school when she was three. Subsequently, she attended Monroe Academy, a secondary school, and then taught for several years. In 1846 she entered Oberlin College's Ladies Literary Course. With advanced standing, she received her diploma in 1847. While at Oberlin, Blackwell began a lifelong friendship with LUCY STONE, the abolitionist and feminist.

Her family encouraged her college studies and helped pay some of her expenses, but they opposed her subsequent decision to study for the ministry. The Oberlin faculty reluctantly allowed her to attend courses offered by the theological department. While a student, Blackwell published an essay, "Exegesis of I Corinthians, XIV, 34, 35 and I Timothy, II, 11, 12," in the *Oberlin Quarterly Review* (July 1849). In it she argued that biblical passages requiring women to keep silent in church, if correctly translated, forbade idle, disruptive chatter or arrogant pronouncements, not serious, public religious teaching.

Although the Lorain County Congregational Association customarily granted preaching licenses to Oberlin students in the final year of theology, they refused Blackwell and informed her she must preach or be silent on her own authority. She completed her work in 1850 but was not allowed to graduate with the male theological students; in 1878 Oberlin granted her an honorary A.M. and in 1908, an honorary D.D. (doctor of divinity).

Despite her family's objections, Blackwell lectured for women's rights, antislavery, and temperance and served as guest preacher in New England, New York, Pennsylvania, and Ohio. She also regularly attended women's rights meetings, where she excited controversy with arguments that the Bible, correctly interpreted, supported the woman's cause. Though an accredited delegate to the 1853 World's Temperance Convention, Blackwell was shouted down on two successive days by a tumultuous audience that disapproved of public speaking by women. That same year Blackwell was invited to become pastor of the Congregational church in South Butler, NY. On September 15, 1853, she was ordained for the service of that congregation—the first woman known to have been formally ordained in the United States. Her controversial ordination was widely denounced.

Within a year of ordination, Blackwell experienced a spiritual crisis while in the process of rejecting the stern, judgmental image of God still prevalent in orthodox Calvinist Christianity. Troubling questions about infant damnation arose when she presided at the funeral of an illegitimate baby. And, in a separate incident, she was disturbed when a female parishioner asked her to terrify the woman's dying son into conversion with visions of hell fire. (She refused.) Physically exhausted and emotionally upset, Blackwell resigned her pastorate in July 1854, after which she worked on behalf of immigrants, the poor, the disabled, and the imprisoned in New York City. Her essays on these experiences appeared in the *New York Tribune*.

On January 24, 1856, she married Samuel C. Blackwell, a member of a famous family of reformers. (His brother Henry had already married LUCY STONE.) At various times, Samuel Blackwell participated in a family hardware business, worked as a bookkeeper, and invested in real estate. Throughout their long marriage, Samuel firmly supported his wife's intellectual and social reform activities and shared domestic duties in an extraordinary fashion for a 19th-century husband. Florence Brown Blackwell, their first child, was born in November 1856. (Each of their children received the double name Brown Blackwell.) After the baby's birth, the Blackwells moved to Newark, NJ.

Mabel, a second daughter, was born in April 1858; she died a few months later. About this time the Blackwells moved to a farm near Millburn, NJ. During these early married years, Blackwell continued to lecture, took part in reform meetings, and preached, in addition to attending to her family responsibilities.

After the birth of daughter Edith in December 1860, Blackwell cut back sharply on her public activities. However, she combined homemaking with serious intellectual study, devoting at least three hours a day to research and writing about religion, philosophy, and science. Blackwell bore Grace in July 1863, suffered the stillbirth of her only male child in 1865, and gave birth to Agnes in 1866. When Samuel Blackwell became ill, the family sold their Millburn home, lived briefly in New York State, and then moved to Somerville, NJ.

In 1869 Blackwell helped to found the American Woman Suffrage Association and was elected vice-president from New Jersey. She wrote for the association's paper, *Woman's Journal*, and was also vice-president of the New Jersey Woman Suffrage Association.

Blackwell bore Ethel, her final child, in 1869 and published *Studies in General Science*. In this work, and in *The Physical Basis of Immortality* (1876), Blackwell struggled with one of the major intellectual challenges of her time—reconciling science and religion. Both these books strove to clarify humanity's place in a natural, moral, and religious order ordained by the infinite mind of a rational, beneficent designer. In *Physical Basis* Blackwell sought to offer "scientific" evidence for personal immortality. She published further metaphysical reflections on the implications of scientific thought in *The Philosophy of Individuality, or the One and the Many* (1893).

In *Sexes Throughout Nature* (1875), Blackwell sought to refute both Charles Darwin's and Herbert Spencer's claims that woman contributed less to human evolution than man; she argued that the sexes of every species were equal, although not identical. Blackwell believed that women's equality with men could eventually be established by scientific, quantitative methods. She challenged physiologists who claimed that rigorous education jeopardized women's reproductive capacities. Blackwell also wrote a novel, *The Island Neighbors* (1871), and a book of poems, *Sea Drift or Tribute to the Ocean* (1902).

During the 1870s the Blackwells moved from Somerville to Elmora (now a part of Elizabeth). In 1878 Blackwell applied to the Unitarian Association for official acknowledgment of her ministerial credentials and was recognized. Pressured by financial problems, she unsuccessfully sought a permanent pulpit and briefly resumed lecturing and preaching.

She was elected a member of the American Association for the Advancement of Science in 1881. In addition, she served as vice-president of the Association for the Advancement of Women (AAW), and she worked with the astronomer Maria Mitchell on the AAW's project to encourage women to study science. Blackwell also acted as first vice-president of the New Jersey State Federation of Women's Clubs.

From 1896 to 1901 the Blackwells lived in New York City. After her husband died in 1901, Blackwell returned to Elizabeth, NJ, where she helped to found All Souls Unitarian Church. While serving as pastor emeritus, she preached there until 1917.

Blackwell published *The Making of the Universe* in 1914 and *The Social Side of Mind and Action*, her last book, in 1915. She lived to rejoice in the passage of the woman suffrage amendment, but by 1920 Blackwell was blind and in ill health. There is conflicting information about whether she was able to vote in the presidential election.

Through her struggles for theological training and ordination, Blackwell opened up the ministry as a recognized vocation for women in the United States. During a span of more than 40 years, she combined family responsibilities, intellectual tasks, and efforts to improve local, state, and national life. She explored the moral and religious implications of scientific discoveries, and encouraged other women to pursue scientific knowledge. Blackwell continued writing and preaching into her nineties, thus providing a role model for older women.

Blackwell died on November 5, 1921, at age 96, in the home of her daughter Agnes (Mrs. Samuel T. Jones) in Elizabeth, NJ. Her body was cremated and her ashes taken to Martha's Vineyard.

The most significant collection of Blackwell's papers, including a typescript copy of her "Memoirs" (1909), is found in the Blackwell Family Papers at M-SL. Other important manuscripts on Blackwell are found at DC-LC, M-SC, and at the Bird Library, Syracuse University (Syracuse, NY). A scholarly biography of Blackwell is Elizabeth Cazden, *Antoinette Brown Blackwell: A Biography* (1983). For correspondence between Blackwell and her sister-in-law, Lucy Stone, see Carol Lasser and Marlene Deahl Merrill, eds., *Friends and Sisters* (1987). Biographical sketches of her appear in *NAW*, *DAB*, vol. 2 (1929), and *WOTC*. Obituaries appeared in the *New York Times*, Nov. 6, 1921; the *Newark Evening News*, Nov. 5, 1921; and the *Elizabeth* (NJ) *Daily Journal*, Nov. 5, 1921.

*Barbara Hilkert Andolsen*

## CHARLOTTE BONAPARTE, 1802–1839

Charlotte Bonaparte, artist and proud member of the Bonaparte family, was born in Mortefontaine, France on October 31, 1802, the second surviving child (both girls) of Joseph and Julie (Clary) Bonaparte. Bonaparte also had two half-sisters, Pauline and Caroline, born of a liaison between her father and Annette Savage while he lived in Bordentown, NJ. Her father, the elder brother of

Napoleon Bonaparte, was born in Corsica; her mother was the daughter of a wealthy merchant of Marseilles, France. Bonaparte grew up at her father's country estate in Mortefontaine and in Paris.

Except for three months spent in Naples, Italy, in 1808, Bonaparte, her sister, Zénaïde, and their mother remained in France during the time Joseph Bonaparte was king of Naples and all the years he was king of Spain. He fled Spain in 1813 and took the title Count of Survilliers. In 1815, after Napoleon Bonaparte's defeat at Waterloo, Joseph Bonaparte escaped to exile in the United States. Julie, Zénaïde, and Charlotte Bonaparte remained in Paris until forced into exile in May 1816. They then went to Frankfurt, Germany, and later to Brussels, Belgium. Bonaparte received instruction in drawing from an early age. In exile in Brussels, she took lessons from Jacques Louis David, former official painter for Napoleon.

In America, Joseph Bonaparte settled first in Philadelphia. Then, in July 1816, he bought a 211-acre estate called "Point Breeze" on the Delaware River in Bordentown, NJ. Here he built a large mansion and later extended his property to over 1700 acres. His wife never joined him in America.

Bonaparte herself arrived in Philadelphia in December 1821. She lived with her father at Point Breeze and at his house in Philadelphia for almost three years. During that time she went by the title Countess of Survilliers.

In the summers Joseph Bonaparte took his daughter to the best resorts and most scenic spots in New Jersey and New York. They visited Long Branch, NJ, and twice went to Schooley's Mountain (Morris County), NJ. Bonaparte sketched views of Point Breeze and scenes on their trips in a formal, romantic style. Some of these sketches were later lithographed, including one of Point Breeze, several of Passaic Falls, NJ, and one of Lebanon (Hunterdon County), NJ. She made drawings in sepia, crayon, oil, and watercolor. In 1822 she painted a watercolor portrait of Cora Monges, daughter of Joseph Bonaparte's physician in Philadelphia.

In May 1822 Bonaparte exhibited a drawing in Philadelphia at the Pennsylvania Academy of the Fine Arts. The following spring the academy exhibited ten of Bonaparte's drawings, including landscapes, portraits, and flower studies, and in 1824 two of her landscapes.

Napoleon Bonaparte, who died in May 1821, had specified in his will that his nieces and nephews should marry among themselves in order to consolidate the Bonaparte family power. Thus, Zénaïde Bonaparte married her cousin Charles Lucien Bonaparte, and they too came to live at Point Breeze. Like her sister, Charlotte Bonaparte was expected to marry one of her cousins. Bonaparte was petite, with large dark eyes, an intelligent face, and great vivacity. She was said to be capricious and sometimes brutally frank, but her father was rich, and many suitors called at Point

Breeze. Joseph Bonaparte rejected them all, however, in favor of Napoleon-Louis Bonaparte, elder son of his brother Louis, and a marriage contract was signed.

Bonaparte left the United States in August 1824 and in July 1826 married Napoleon-Louis Bonaparte in Florence, Italy. The young couple lived in Florence with Louis Bonaparte and spent their winters in Rome, where Bonaparte took drawing lessons from the French painter Leopold Robert. In February 1831 Napoleon-Louis Bonaparte and his younger brother Louis-Napoleon, the future Napoleon III of France, joined Italian insurgents fighting to unify Italy. During the campaign Napoleon-Louis Bonaparte died, probably of measles.

After the death of her husband, Bonaparte lived with her mother in Florence. Among the visitors they received there was a Polish count whose lover Bonaparte is said to have become. In late 1838, finding herself pregnant, she went to Rome and then headed for Genoa. On the way she began to hemorrhage, and at Sarzana she underwent a cesarean section. The baby, however, was already dead and soon after, on March 2, 1839, Bonaparte herself died from loss of blood. She was entombed in the Church of Santa Croce in Florence, Italy. Her mother had inscribed on her tomb: "Here lies / Charlotte Napoleon Bonaparte / Worthy of her name / 1839."

Biographical material on Charlotte Bonaparte is found mainly in biographies of her father, Joseph, foremost of which is the one by A. du Casse, *Mémoires et correspondance politique et militaire du Roi Joseph*, 10 vols. (1853–54). Additional material appears in: Gabriel Girod de l'Ain, *Joseph Bonaparte* (1970); George Bertin, *Joseph Bonaparte en Amerique* (1893); and Diego Angeli, *I Buonaparti a Roma* (1938). The only modern work in English is Owen Connelly, *The Gentle Bonaparte* (1968). The Bordentown Area Bicentennial Committee, *Bordentown, 1682–1976* (1977), contains material on the Bonaparte era in that town. Mary Bartlett Cowdry, "Charlotte Bonaparte: Draftsman," *NJHSP* 81 (1963):47–49, describes Bonaparte's New Jersey drawings. *Vues pittoresques de l'Amerique dessinées par la Comtess Charlotte de Survillier* (1824), a rare album of lithographs from Bonaparte's drawings, is in NYPL, Prints Division.

*Maggie Sullivan*

## ELIZABETH MULFORD CRANE, 1775–1828

Elizabeth (Mulford) Crane, diarist and farm wife, was born on January 27, 1775, in what is now known as Berkeley Heights (Union County), NJ. Captain Jonathan Mulford, her grandfather, bought a piece of property there in 1740. One of eight children born to John and Deborah (Ludlow) Mulford, Crane was known then as Betsey. Little is known of Crane's girlhood, except that she was probably educated locally at a school in Berkeley Heights. Evidences of some basic schooling are her clear, fine handwriting and her references to books, such as the novel

*Pamela* and a volume of poetry she loaned to a friend.

She married her neighbor, John Crane, on September 23, 1792, and the couple had ten children. Jonathan (b. 1793), Elias (b. 1795), Hulda (b. 1797), Orpha (b. 1800), Deborah (b. 1802), Sylvester (b. 1805), Mary (b. 1807), Daniel (b. 1810), Harriet (b. 1812), and Elizabeth (b. 1815).

The family lived in a farmhouse two doors away from Crane's childhood home on Springfield Avenue, where they raised domestic animals and various crops. John Crane crafted wagons, furniture, houses, and coffins when he filled in as the local undertaker. He and his sons delivered the *Jersey Journal* newspaper throughout the Long Hill and Passaic Valley area.

Between May 1824, when she was 49, and January 1828, Crane kept a diary that was a compendium of daily notations on the weather and happenings at home and in the community. Although her record of events betrays little of her emotions or opinions, it recounts daily experiences and the shared work of dyeing, weaving, sewing clothing, making carpets, quilts, gloves, bonnets, and binding shoes.

Crane was at the center of her family's life. Her older daughters Hulda, Orpha, and Deborah were married and living nearby. She visited neighbors and relatives and they visited her; she went to the homes of the sick, and they in turn came to her when she was bedridden. Her diary, which tells of neighborhood women helping each other with sewing and weaving, picking over wool and making candles, was consulted by family and neighbors to determine when someone visited last, or when a relative was married, or how much flax was harvested the previous year. Crane attended local "frolics," quilting and apple-cutting bees, vendues, "infairs," and church events.

In 1806, during a major religious ferment, Crane had joined the Methodist church in New Providence (then known as Turkey). Daniel Mulford, her brother, attending Yale at the time, was shocked that Crane should join this new religious group and wrote of his concern to his brother David in Morristown. But Crane soon wrote to her brother telling him the Methodists were "very numerous here and they are still increasing, and I hope some of them are quite rational beings." (Day, "Methodism in New Providence," 7)

Crane and her husband became active Methodists. She attended two meetings on Sundays, to hear various preachers, one in New Providence and one in Union Village. At times poor health and bad weather kept her from attending meetings, and at other times it seems she would stay away if she did not care for the preacher who was to speak. In her diary, Crane named those "struck under conviction" or converted to Methodism, and she told of her daughter Harriet becoming "somewhat convicted."

She and her family kept the meetinghouse clean and

comfortable with handmade carpets and curtains. She attended camp meetings held on Long Hill in Gillette, on Stoney Hill in Murray Hill, and on Wolf Hill in Warren. The camp meetings were great events; the meeting at Stoney Hill in 1824 was reported to have attracted 4,000 people. Although she had no say in the proceedings, Crane also accompanied her husband to Methodist quarterly conferences.

In the last few pages of her diary, Crane's daily notations become shorter and show signs of her increasing ill health. Her weight, which had been 102 pounds the year before, declined to 85 pounds. She died at age 53, barely a month after the last entry in her book, on March 9, 1828. From her brief notations of pain and other symptoms, and the specific treatments she underwent, we can surmise that she died of tuberculosis of the lungs. She was buried in the United Methodist Churchyard on Springfield Avenue in New Providence.

A typescript of Elizabeth Crane's diary, as well as a microfilm copy of her brother Daniel Mulford's diary for the years 1801–8, are available at NJ-RU. Information on the family of Elizabeth Crane, as well as most of the nearly 200 families mentioned in her diary, appears in John Littell, *Genealogies of the First Settlers of the Passaic Valley* (1852). A paper written by Crane descendant Stephen S. Day, "Methodism in New Providence" (1898), is available at NJ-RU.

*Ingeborg Rist Lincoln*

## BRIDGET DERGAN, 1844–1867

Bridget Dergan, also known as Durgan or Deignan, an Irish servant who arrived in this country in 1864, was memorable to no one until, on February 25, 1867, she was accused of murdering Mary Ellen Coriell, her employer's wife. Even after she was arrested, her former employers could think of nothing good or bad to say about Dergan. This "ordinary-looking Irish girl, with plain features" (*New York Times*, May 21, 1867, 1) was born in Clough, County Sligo, Ireland, in 1844, the fourth of five children. Patrick Dergan, her father, had owned a grocery store, and Hannah Dergan, her mother, kept a dairy. The family was "in good circumstances," according to one of the several "confessions" the illiterate Dergan was said to have made. ("Confession to Messrs. Randolph and Jefferies," 105)

It was not poverty that caused Dergan to come to America, but rather a friend who coaxed her to emigrate after Dergan's father broke up her romance with a young man deemed unsuitable for her. Dergan stole £20 from her father and made the trip in the winter of 1864. She was one among thousands of Irish to arrive that year—the young women, for the most part, to scrub and clean and serve in the households of middle-class families.

Dergan worked as a servant in Brooklyn and then in Manhattan. Through a Manhattan domestic employment agency, she met a man named Mr. Dayton who offered to give her a position at his home in Middlesex County, NJ. She spent a year with the Dayton family, and then moved around the county, rarely spending more than a month or two at any house. In her "confessions," she could recall the names of seven men who employed her.

One of these employers was William Coriell, a 40-year-old physician who lived in New Market and treated Dergan for "sore eyes" and "the complaint called by him Epilepsy." Dergan was prone to epileptic seizures—"slumbers," as she called them—that lasted from five minutes to "hours," and that in her last months came upon her with great frequency. (Jones, *Women Who Kill*, 197)

Coriell was intrigued with Dergan's medical problems and enticed her to leave her employer and work for him. The household was small—Coriell; his 31-year-old wife, Mary Ellen; and their only living child, a two-year-old girl named Mamie. (Mary Ellen Coriell had lost a number of babies over the years.) But Dergan's seizures began to occur with such regularity that often Dr. Coriell had to hire someone to watch over her at night. Frequently she was not able to work. She had been in their employ for four months when she was asked to leave.

On Monday, February 25, 1867, Dergan washed her clothes in preparation for her departure the next morning. That night, after Dr. Coriell left to see a patient in Piscataway, Dergan attacked Mary Ellen Coriell with such ferocity that the list of wounds she inflicted took up half a column in the newspaper—26 gashes, some to the bone, scratches, jagged tearing wounds, teeth marks, hair torn in clumps from the scalp—all attesting to a long, fierce struggle. She set rags and paper on fire and then, grabbing the Coriells' child, ran barefoot through the snow to a neighbor's house to report that two burglars were at the house, that they had set it on fire and could very well be murdering Mary Ellen Coriell at that moment.

Dergan denied responsibility for the crime, though the details of her alibi changed often. The burglars came at 7:30 A.M., or at 8:30 P.M.; they were strangers; they were men she knew named Doyle and Hunt; they were not men at all, but rather another servant named Anne Linen; it was not Anne Linen, it was Mary Gilroy.

While she waited for trial at the Middlesex County jail, curiosity seekers were allowed to gawk at her. Each day, 50 to 100 would wait by her cell. Her jailers testified that she had seizures all the time, and that she would fall over and remain unconscious for hours and that blood and froth ran from her mouth. But in the newspapers she was described as being a beast, a morally idiotic creature. The poet and novelist Elizabeth Oakes Smith reported that Dergan's "human intelligence" was "on the very lowest level." (Jones, 202)

The trial lasted for 20 days, and on June 27, 1867, after

less than an hour of deliberation, the verdict of guilty was handed down, and Dergan was sentenced to hang from the neck until dead. Executions were no longer public events open to all, but rather private showings, and thousands applied for tickets to witness the hanging of Dergan. On August 30, 1867, some 2,000 men and women showed up to see her get what they believed was her due.

"I then turned upon Mrs. Coriell and pushed her back on the bed, and with this white handled knife stabbed her repeatedly." Bridget's Confession.—*Page 35.*

Bridget Dergan, a young Irish servant, gained notoriety in 1867 by murdering her mistress. Her crime and subsequent execution were sensationalized in the popular press. *Courtesy, Special Collections and Archives, Rutgers University Libraries.*

Why did Dergan murder Mary Ellen Coriell? According to the "confession" published after the hanging by her lawyer, Garnet B. Adrain (or Garnett R. Adrain), Dergan said that "Mrs. Coriell was very kind and pleasant to me. . . . I never had any quarrel with her." (Quoted in Cunningham and Sinclair, *Murder Did Pay,* 102) In the "confession" that her jailer, Mr. Randolph, and the recorder, Mr. Jefferies, offered for sale, Dergan reported overhearing the doctor say that he wished Mrs. Coriell was dead or out of the way. "I made myself think from this remark that the doctor liked me, and I did really think that he wanted to get her out of the way, and this so preyed on my mind that I thought I must kill her." (Quoted in Cunningham and Sinclair, 108) But feminist historian Ann Jones, in her book *Women Who Kill,* writes that "she probably killed Mary Ellen Coriell while suffering what modern medicine calls a seizure of psychomotor or temporal lobe epilepsy—a type of seizure often characterized by rage, physical violence and amnesia." (Jones, 202)

At 5:00 A.M. on the day of her hanging, the sheriff woke Dergan and administered "appropriate stimulants." (Jones, 206) She wore a plain brown dress and white gloves, and on her way to the scaffold, more than likely very drunk, she was supported on the arms of two priests. Concerned that she might have a seizure, the sheriff rushed things along, so that prayers were still being said when the black cap was being fitted over her face. The professional executioner had refused to help with this hanging, because he would not hang a woman, so the device for the hanging had been rigged by amateurs. A weight was released, and Dergan was jerked three feet off the ground and held there while she slowly choked to death. She was buried in a Catholic burying ground in Middlesex County.

Accounts of the murder and Dergan's trial appeared in the *New York Times* on May 18, May 21, May 23, May 28, May 29, June 1, Aug. 25, and Aug. 31, 1867. Her "confessions" appear in Rev. Mr. Brenden, *Life, Crimes, and Confession of Bridget Durgan* (1867), and *The Life and Confession of Bridget Dergan* (which includes "Her Confession to Messrs. Randolph and Jefferies"; 1867). Additional accounts of the crime appear in John T. Cunningham and Donald Sinclair, *Murder Did Pay* (1981); and Anne Jones, *Women Who Kill* (1980).

*Jane Bernstein*

## DOROTHEA LYNDE DIX, 1802–1887

Dorothea Lynde Dix, internationally renowned health care reformer who focused her attentions on humane care for the mentally ill, was born in the rural outpost of Hampden, ME, on April 4, 1802. Little is known about her mother, Mary (Bigelow) Dix, except that she came from a poor family in Sudbury, MA, had no education, was eighteen years older than her husband, and was prone to periods of nervous breakdown that left her unable to attend to the needs of her daughter and two infant sons. Joseph Dix, Dix's father, was born into a wealthy New England family and attended Harvard until his marriage caused his expulsion from college. Attracted to what his mother termed "fanatical Methodism," he became an itinerant preacher and religious tract writer who was absent from home for weeks at a time and seldom earned enough to keep his family fed and clothed.

"I never knew a childhood," Dix wrote to one of her female friends later in her life. (Snyder, *The Lady and the President,* 56) The frequent family moves and her mother's illness often placed on the girl complete responsibility for household tasks and for care of her two younger brothers, Charles and Joseph. Yet even at this early age, Dix had a keen sense of a world with other possibilities. She loved books and attended grammar school classes whenever possible, teaching her brothers to read as well. In the summer she occasionally visited her grandparents in Boston, where she observed the discipline, virtues, and accomplishments that surrounded life in a properly run New England home.

In 1814, at age twelve, Dix ran away from the emotional turmoil of her own home and took up residence with her grandmother, Dorothy Lynde Dix, a widow living in Boston. In temperament, Dix was ready to be shaped by the vigorous discipline imposed by her grandmother, who taught her piety, industry, duty, economy, and thoroughness.

Young Dix, however, was too large a responsibility for the aging woman, so she was sent to live with her cousins in Worcester, MA. There, at age fourteen, she was regarded as competent to earn a small income in the only field acceptable for a girl in her position: teaching. She opened a school in which she taught reading, writing, manners, and sewing to about 20 young children. Testimony from her students showed her to be an effective but unusually strict teacher. In 1819 she returned to Boston, where she furthered her own education by reading assiduously at the Free Public Library, the Athenaeum, and the Academy of Arts and Sciences. Natural science, mathematics, and astronomy were some of her interests. She again opened a school, this time for wealthy young girls, in an unused room in her grandmother's mansion. But Dix's humanitarian conscience was now emerging; she persuaded her grandmother to allot her another room in one of the outbuildings of the property, where she also taught the impoverished waifs of Boston and established a Sunday school for them.

Dix spent long hours reading Scripture, teaching, and studying nature, working late into the night and rising before dawn each day. In a six-year period she published seven books: *Conversations on Common Things* (1824; over 60 reprintings), *Hymns for Children, Selected and Altered* (1825), *Evening Hours* (1825), *Ten Short Stories for Children* (1827–28), *Meditations for Private Hours* (1828), *The Garland of Flora* (1829), and *The Pearl, or Affection's Gift; A Christmas and New Year's Present* (1829). The result of this continual work now surfaced: Dix's health failed for the first of many times. From 1830 until her death, Dix would be plagued by weak, hemorrhaging lungs, nervous collapses, and eventually by malarial fevers. She suspended teaching periodically for several years and finally closed her schools permanently in 1836, after which she traveled to England to convalesce.

The most serious of Dix's marriage proposals came during these early years. While teaching in Worcester, she met her lawyer cousin, Edward Bangs, fourteen years her senior. They became engaged, but during their eight-year friendship Dix could not bring herself to give up her teaching to become the wife of a politician.

The major philosophic influence on Dix's early years was the Boston preacher William Ellery Channing, who espoused the unity and value of all of Divine Creation. Dix quickly accepted Channing's Unitarian approaches and used them as the theoretical basis for all her humanitarian arguments in later years.

The second period of Dix's life began with her return to Boston after regaining her health during a stay in England. Abroad, she had met Quakers and Unitarians who were involved with progressive institutions serving the mentally ill. In March 1841, after teaching a Sunday school class in the East Cambridge jail, Dix saw firsthand the horrible conditions under which several insane women were kept. Her life changed that day. After speaking with Channing and several other prominent Bostonians, Dix saw clearly a lifetime of work ahead of her.

Dix persuaded her philanthropist friend Samuel Howe, husband of Julia Ward Howe, to write a news article in the September 1841 Boston *Advertiser* about conditions under which the insane were being confined. It met with angry denials and protests. Dix was outraged, but with encouragement from her friends, she attacked the problem with a scientific thoroughness that was to be her hallmark throughout her career. For the next year and a half Dix traveled, nearly always alone, on a round of tours that took her to every jail and other establishment in Massachusetts that housed the insane. She kept careful notebooks documenting each instance of mistreatment: "Newburyport almshouse: A door to a closet beneath the staircase was opened, revealing in the imperfect light a female apparently wasted to a skeleton, partially wrapped in blankets, face furrowed by suffering. She poured forth the wailing of despair. 'Why am I consigned to hell?'" (Wilson, *Stranger and Traveler*, 113)

By January 1843 Dix had assembled the evidence she needed to present her case supporting the building of units to house the insane at several state hospitals. Her "Memorial to the Legislature of Massachusetts" was presented by Dr. Howe. Written in clear and dramatic language and documented by the pages of examples from her notebooks, the "Memorial" had an immediate impact. It was called "the first piece of social research ever conducted in America" (Wilson, 124), and the legislation that resulted from it was hailed as the most sensational Massachusetts had seen since the Revolutionary War. It was passed on February 25, 1843.

Encouraged by her success, Dix immediately began similar investigations and legislative proposals in Rhode Island, New York, Kentucky, Pennsylvania, and New Jersey. Her reputation now preceded her, and she found doors opening more easily and other reformers willing to assist with the political entanglements peculiar to each state.

The first opportunity for Dix to fulfill her vision of building a modern hospital offering humane care for the insane occurred in New Jersey. There were no institutions in the state devoted to such care; each community was responsible for its own patients. Dix arrived in New Jersey on November 4, 1844. She spent eight weeks of intensive work touring the jails and county almshouses, visiting the state's more than 600 insane, and documenting what she saw. Then on January 23, 1845, Senator Joseph S. Dodd of Essex County presented her "Memorial" to the legislature. The same procedure that Dix had used successfully in other states was employed. She never spoke on the floors of the all-male legislatures, but for eight weeks met with small groups of senators and impressed them with gentle or dramatic intellectual arguments, and with strong evidence about current confinement practices, or appeals to their humanity and emotions. She wrote newspaper articles and encouraged writing campaigns among her supporters. She wrote to a friend during this time: "You cannot imagine the labor of conversing and convincing. Some evenings I had at once twenty gentlemen for three hours' steady conversation." (Wilson, 147) On March 25, 1845, in a nearly unanimous vote, the "Memorial" was passed. Dix was invited to offer advice on the site selection and blueprints for the design of the new hospital. In Ewing Township, near Trenton, she chose a hill with a view of fields, groves of trees, and the river. The architects were told to include columns, a portico, a dome, and in the interior, large, airy rooms for the patients. The New Jersey State Lunatic Asylum at Trenton was opened in May 1848. Dix's dream had been fulfilled, and from this point on, she often referred to the New Jersey hospital as "her first-born child." (Herrmann, *Dorothea Dix*, 29)

Dix never slowed her efforts. She went from state to state, eventually visiting every one east of the Rockies. Her only major defeat in these crusading years occurred with the federal government. For six years, from 1848 to 1854, Dix lobbied in the U.S. Congress for passage of a bill that would set aside federal land funds for use by the insane poor. When Congress finally passed the measure in 1854, President Franklin Pierce vetoed it, dashing all hopes for a nationwide system of humane health care institutions.

Dix's spirits and health were now broken. She again turned to England and Europe for respite, but was drawn, even there, to her favorite work. In her two-year stay, she visited fourteen countries and hundreds of mental health institutions.

The third stage of Dix's life centered on a different kind of social work. When the Civil War broke out, Dix offered her services to the government. Although she had no direct medical knowledge, her organizational skills earned her the position of superintendent of women nurses in the Union army, the highest office held by any woman during the war. Many of her actions in this job, though, were controversial. In order to create a nursing corps she considered professional and whose motives were above moral reproach, she refused to accept as a nurse any woman under 30, any married women, any woman who was not plain-looking, or even nuns who were already qualified nurses.

Following the war, Dix returned to her campaigns for the mentally ill. Her ability to change the face of America came not from any physical strength or supporting environment. She was ill much of her life and spent most of her time alone. She once wrote to a friend, "I am no enthusiast; what I have done is only from a determined will, and because I think it is my duty." (Wilson, 278)

Although Dix was generally viewed as a charismatic personality, she wrote all her life of her sense of personal inadequacy. She avoided public appearances and formal social gatherings, even declining White House invitations. In her last years, when she had become internationally famous, she received many requests for biographical information, but she always declined to offer even small amounts of information, saying that she wished her works to be the record of her life.

As a reformer, Dix believed she was only working for what she knew to be the rights of every human. In her view, industrialized societies had created unlimited opportunities for people to advance, but had also thereby created the stress to achieve. When this stress produced breakdowns, as it inevitably would, society had to assume responsibility for treating its mentally ill with modern therapeutic methods and humane custodial care. As she wrote in her New Jersey "Memorial," "I come to ask *justice* . . . for those who, in the providence of God, are incapable of pleading their own cause." (Quoted in Herrmann, 3)

Dix was responsible for founding or enlarging 32 mental institutions in the United States and abroad. When she collapsed in Trenton in 1881, she was given a suite of her hospital's rooms for her personal use. For the final six years of her life, she lived in the only "home" in which she had ever spent so much time. She died on July 18, 1887, at age 85, and was buried in Cambridge, MA.

Two biographies of Dix are Helen Marshall, *Dorothea Dix: Forgotten Samaritan* (1937) and Dorothy Clarke Wilson, *Stranger and Traveler: The Story of Dorothy Dix, American Reformer* (1975). Charles Synder, *The Lady and the President* (1975), contains the correspondence between Dix and Millard Fillmore from 1850 to 1869. Frederick Herrmann, *Dorothea L. Dix and the Politics of Institutional Reform* (1980), emphasizes Dix's New Jersey activities. Sketches of Dix appear in *NAW* and *DAB*, vol. 5 (1930).

*Sara Beekey Pfaffenroth*

## SILVIA DUBOIS, 1768–1888

Silvia Dubois, an African-American slave who sought and gained her freedom and who lived to be 120, was a household domestic, a ferryboat pilot, a hog breeder, a tavern owner and keeper, and a mother of five daughters and a son. Dubois's mother was Dorcas Compton, slave of Richard Compton, and her father was Cuffie Bard, slave of John Bard. Dubois was born at Compton's tavern near Rock Mills in the Sourland Mountains of Hunterdon County, NJ, on March 5, 1768. Her surname was that of her mother's second master, Dominicus Dubois. Dubois's date of birth was substantiated by her biographer, Cornelius W. Larison, who examined the family records of the Compton family. (*A Biografy*, 88ff.)

Dubois's 1883 oral narrative, transcribed and appended by Larison, a physician, schoolteacher, and neighbor of Dubois, provides a rare first-person account by a slave woman who could neither read nor write.

Dorcas Compton, Dubois's mother, was serving Richard Compton, Sr., as a domestic and farm worker at Compton's Rock Mill tavern when Dubois was born. "Ambitious to be free" (*A Biografy*, 45), she tried to buy her freedom from several successive masters by mortgaging herself against a loan pledged by a third party. Although Harry Compton, Dorcas Compton's father, had gained manumission through this practice, Compton herself failed to earn enough cash for repayment of the loan. Therefore, after Richard Compton, she became the property in turn of Dominicus Dubois, William Bard, and Wills Smith, on whose farm, probably in New Brunswick, she died and was buried around 1838, still a slave.

Cuffie Bard, Dubois's father, was reputedly a fifer for the Minute Men of Hunterdon County in the Battles of Trenton and Princeton. Bard seems to have been absent from Dubois's life after she was about ten or eleven.

Dubois and her mother were separated because of their service to different masters. In 1772, when Dubois was five, Dominicus Dubois moved to Flagtown, possibly from Neshanic, his previous farm site. In 1782 Dubois, then fourteen, accompanied the household, driving two cows on a northwestern trek across the Delaware River at Easton, PA, through "the Beech Woods" of the Pocono Mountains to the village of Great Bend on the Susquehanna River, south of present-day Binghamton, NY. In 1785, or shortly thereafter, Dubois watched her master build a new frame house, the first one in that growing trading post and settlement. The house became a tavern and a ferry stop for drivers, traders, and western settlers on the border of Pennsylvania and New York states. Dubois learned to operate the ferry and its accompanying skiff from her master and "stole" customers from their competitor, a Captain Hatch. She earned "many a shilling" and her master's appreciation: "When I was about, folks didn't have to wait [for the ferry] . . . that's why my master liked me [to do it]." (*A Biografy*, 52) She learned to row the smaller skiff and won all river races with male challengers.

At Great Bend, Dubois seems to have learned strategies for surviving the exhausting farm chores. Physically strong and industrious, she was expert at cleaning house, making soap and peach brandy, and surviving on the foodstuffs of black servitude, especially mush and coarse bread. Dubois weighed 200 pounds and stood five feet ten inches tall during her maturity: she assumed traditionally masculine roles and chores that demanded risks and strength.

She recalled a good relationship with her master, Dominicus Dubois, nicknamed Minna, whom Dubois called

Silvia Dubois, *right*, shown here in her old age with her daughter, was born a slave in Hunterdon County but gained her freedom by protesting the brutality of her mistress. Records show she lived to be 120 years old. *Courtesy, Hunterdon County Historical Society Collections, Flemington, NJ.*

"Minical." He allowed her to attend "frolics and balls with other Black folks." (*A Biografy*, 66) She admitted that she was "a little sassy" (*A Biografy*, 59), and thus she suffered continual and brutal beatings from Mistress Dubois, who once broke her skull. Young Dubois recovered and silently vowed revenge: "I made up my mind that when I grew up I'd do it . . . and when I had a good chance, when some of her grand company was around I fixed her. I knocked her down, and blame near killed her." (*A Biografy*, 63)

Dubois fled temporarily, but returned at her master's bidding. And as her mother had done previously, she cited a little-known practice that she incorrectly thought was New Jersey law: if a master and slave did not get along, the slave had the right to find a new master. (*A Biografy*, 45, 65; Bogan and Loewenberg, *Black Women*, 42) Because of her known abuse at the hands of her mistress and her good relationship with her master, "[Dominicus Dubois] told me that, as my mistress and I got along so badly, if I would take my child and go to New Jersey, and stay there, he would give me free." (*A Biografy*, 65)

Dubois then fled from slavery through the "Beech Woods" to Flagtown, NJ, carrying her eighteen-month-old child and a written pass from Dominicus Dubois. The fugitive recalled that a man asked, "Whose nigger are you?" during her flight and she replied, "I'm no man's nigger—I belong to God—I belong to no man." (*A Biografy*, 70) Undaunted, Dubois put down her baby and showed the stranger her fist, but not her pass. She was threatened with arrest but continued her journey.

She traveled from Flagtown to New Brunswick, where she found her mother and paid work, probably as a domestic or a field hand. This hiatus lasted several years, which allowed Dubois a change in status from transient freed slave with a written pass to accepted wage earner with a dependable local relative, her mother.

By the early 1800s she was working in the household of French Huguenot patriarch Louis Tulane. She recalled his son Paul's birth in 1801. (*A Biografy*, 71) She worked for Victor Tulane, another son, during the following years, but her duties and the length of her employment in his household in Princeton remain as yet unclear.

Dubois returned to Cedar Summit from Princeton, probably in the mid-1830s, to nurse Harry Compton, her ailing maternal grandfather, at his request. A manumitted slave, "Harry Put" Compton was reputed to be a fifer at the Battle of Princeton, as was her father. He made and sold charcoal to buy his freedom from Richard Compton. (*A Biografy*, 106) Later, Compton bought land and built and ran a substantial tavern near Rock Mills (not to be confused with Richard Compton's tavern). This rural house of revelry was inherited by Dubois "at her father's or her grandfather's death." (*A Biografy*, 71)

Following the common practice of wives or widows to keep taverns as a means of livelihood during these years in New England and the Middle Atlantic states, Dubois owned and kept "Put's Old Tavern" for several years. But a dwindling local clientele reduced her profits even as the virgin forest surrounding the tavern was sold for lumber. (*A Biografy*, 107) In 1840 Dubois's tavern was sacked and burned in her absence. She lost all of the value of her furnishings and real estate, and she could not afford a lawyer's fee to sue the perpetrators.

Afterward Dubois built a primitive house of cedar on the inherited "old homestead," where she lived alone and raised prize hogs until the late 1870s. "Them damned democrats" (*A Biografy*, 71) burned her primitive mountain home a second time, in her absence. As Larison wrote, "Advanced in years, penniless and dismayed, she accepted an invitation to abide with her [youngest] daughter." (*A Biografy*, 113) Although named Elizabeth Alexander in her mother's will, Larison referred to this daughter repeatedly as Elizabeth Dubois. Alexander may be the surname of Elizabeth's father, but this is unsubstantiated.

Details of "Mrs. Silvia Dubois'" family are furnished only by Larison (not Dubois herself), who notes that she bore Moses, Judith, Charlotte, Dorcas, Rachel, and Elizabeth by unknown partners. No mention of any marriage was included in his description. Rachel was said to have lived in Princeton in 1883, although no supporting evidence has surfaced. Elizabeth Alexander, called "Lizi," presumably owned the lot and house near Ringoes (Hunterdon County) in which her mother lived the last 20 years of her life. Elizabeth Alexander was described by Larison as courteous, tall, and stout, well proportioned and active, and was a champion amateur boxer as well as a fortune-teller.

Dubois died at Cedar Summit, NJ, in the rural hut of her daughter Elizabeth Alexander on May 1, 1888. She claimed an affinity with Old Side Presbyterians of her time; she also believed in woodland spirits. Her will names her longtime nurse, her "beloved daughter Elizabeth," as her sole administrator, executor, and inheritor of all personal and real estate. (*New Jersey Archives, Wills*, 15:476) This document shows the scratches penned by Dubois and Elizabeth Alexander in lieu of their signatures.

Dubois was her own woman, in and out of bondage. Amazingly, she was permitted to flee after her attack on her mistress, an act of violence that would normally have resulted in a severe beating or death. Dubois was a survivor: she endured hunger, physical abuse, and abject rural poverty while her family ties and her singular persona remained intact.

The major work on the life of Dubois is Cornelius W. Larison, *Silvia Dubois (Now 116 Years Old). A Biografy of the Slav Who Whipt Her Mistres and Gand Her Fredom* (1883). Ruth Bogin and Bert James Loewenberg, eds., *Black Women in Nineteenth-Century American Life: Their Words, Their Thoughts, Their Feelings* (1976), adds information and footnotes to the Dubois narrative. Silvia Dubois's Huguenot master, Dominicus Dubois, was identified in Emily C. Blackman's *History of Susquehanna County, Pennsylvania* (1873). A special edition of the *Princeton Recollector: A Monthly Journal of Local History* 5 (Winter 1980) provides more details on her life. Her will appears in the *New Jersey Archives*.

*Constance Killian Escher*

## ELIZABETH SUTLIFF DULFER, 1790–1880

Elizabeth Sutliff Dulfer, farmer, purveyor of clay, and real estate investor, was born into slavery in 1790 in Bergen County, NJ. Her only known sibling was a half-sister named Jane Newton. Her mother, Isabel, father, Dickerson, and paternal grandmother were African-Americans. Her paternal grandfather was an American Indian.

Dulfer was owned by William Campbell of New Barbadoes, NJ. William Campbell and Polly (Blanchard)

Campbell had thirteen children and lived along the west bank of the Hackensack River near the site of the Little Ferry toll bridge in Bergen County. Dulfer was a slave in this household until she was 32 years old. She spoke only Jersey Dutch.

On June 17, 1822, Dulfer was manumitted. The deed of manumission provided that "Betty shall & may at all times hereafter, exercise, hold and enjoy all and singular the liberties, rights, privileges and immunities of a free woman full to all intends and purposes, as if she had been born free." (*Bergen County Clerk, Liber A of Manumissions*, 143) It is unknown whether Dulfer purchased her freedom for cash or whether it was granted in consideration of past services rendered.

It is uncertain when Dulfer moved to New York City, where, prior to 1830, she married Alexander Sutliff, an African-American and a teacher who was born on the island of Jamaica. She had no children. The 1820 *New York City Directory* lists an Elizabeth Campbell, seamstress, residing at "Thompson nr. Spring," indicating possible use of her master's surname, but it does not designate her color. (*New York City Directory for 1820*) In 1830 Elizabeth and Alexander Sutliff lived on Spring Street in New York City. She remained in New York City until 1847 and attended the Abyssinian Baptist Church at 44 Anthony Street there.

On April 3, 1847, as a married woman, she purchased in her name alone 87 acres of farm and clay-bearing land along the west bank of the Hackensack River (now Little Ferry). This bold and independent act was unusual for a married woman in the mid-19th century. It took five deeds from a total of 22 persons to give her title to the property. She paid $1,323 for it. One can appreciate her business acumen when one considers the complexity of the transaction as well as the efforts it must have taken to save the necessary funds.

Since Dulfer grew up along the west bank of the Hackensack River, it can be assumed that she was well acquainted with the clay deposits on the land she purchased. In a number of West African cultures clay was used in making pottery, utensils, and ornaments. In the Lenape culture, also, clay was used in making pottery. She knew what she was buying and how the resources could best be used.

William Earle of Carlstadt, NJ, the grandson of Dulfer's former master, stated in an orphans court proceeding held in 1880, "I always took her to be a very smart intelligent woman that is what all my people say she was one of the smartest kind of women." (*Bergen County Surrogate, Record of Cost and Testimony*, 5:6068)

*The Seventh U.S. Census* (1850) did not give credit for the ownership of the farm to Dulfer but rather to her husband. She was listed as "Betsey," living with her husband, Alexander Sutliff. No occupation was listed for Dulfer, whereas her husband was listed as a farmer. The real property was credited to Alexander Sutliff, although title was in Dulfer's name; it was valued at $2,000.

She worked her clay beds and sold clay in huge quantities every year for 20 years, employing numerous persons in this business pursuit. Frances A. Westervelt has noted that Dulfer carried on a large business in the sale of clay, which was sent by boats to potteries in Newark, Jersey City, and other places. (Westervelt, *History of Bergen County*, 9)

Life for Dulfer was hard, and the land desolate. The clay had to be dug out of pits by shovels and loaded into horse-drawn wagons. It was then transported to the loading docks to await shipping. Sloops plied the river, taking clay and clay products to Jersey City, Newark, Boston, and other places.

Alexander Sutliff died sometime between 1851 and 1855. On April 4, 1859, his widow married John Bernardus Conrad Dulfer, a recent settler from Rotterdam, Holland. The year of her marriage Dulfer was 69 years old and her husband 36.

In 1860 the U.S. Census again failed to credit Dulfer with the ownership of the 87 acres. She is incorrectly listed as 60 years old, and as black, female, head of household, and without an occupation. In the same census, John Dulfer was named John Bennet Coonrough Dulfer, age 37, white, male, and a farmer. The value of the real estate was set at $10,000 and personal property at $500, all attributed to John Dulfer.

Not only was Dulfer engaged in the clay business, but she and her husband operated the farm started by her and her first husband. They sold produce at the market as cash crops. The 1860 census reveals that they farmed 50 acres of their property. Their farming implements were valued at $20, and they had one horse, five cattle, and four swine. Their annual output was 450 bushels of Irish potatoes and miscellaneous garden produce, valued at $1,000. They made 100 pounds of butter, produced four tons of hay, and slaughtered animals for meat valued at $50.

In 1864 Dulfer purchased .51 acre in New Barbadoes Township from Paul R. Paulison "et ux" for $100. In 1867, after 20 years, she sold the clay beds property to Herman H. Brunges of Hoboken for $15,200. She purchased a new home nearby and a meadow lot containing 8 acres for $4,500. She also purchased 12.5 acres in New Barbadoes Township from William Winant "et ux" in 1867 for $4,500; 13 acres in Lodi Township from John C. Westervelt in 1868 for $159.37; two lots in New Barbadoes Township from Christian W. Campbell "et ux" for $1,000; 9.12 acres in New Barbadoes Township from the sheriff in 1875, to protect a mortgage loan she had made to Andrew Sears for $6,000; 2.14 acres in Lodi Township from the sheriff in 1878, again to protect a mortgage loan she had made to James H. Thompson for $50; and one lot in the village of Hackensack from David Van Horn "et ux" in

1878, in lieu of a foreclosure on a mortgage loan she had made to Van Horn for $6,188.

Dulfer's keen intellect and business acumen led her to invest her excess funds in high-interest-bearing mortgages on real estate. She loaned a total of $16,300 in five different transactions between 1867 and 1872.

Dulfer lived a robust life. She farmed the land and dug clay with the help of her husband and hired labor. She would walk all the way from Little Ferry to Hoboken to market her garden produce. In later life, however, she was described as squat and weighing 180 pounds. Dulfer suffered in her later years from consumption.

On January 11, 1880, Dulfer died at the age of 90. She was buried in the Sand Hill Cemetery, now known as the Gethsemane Cemetery, in Little Ferry, NJ.

Information on Dulfer appears in Arnold E. Brown, *The Elizabeth Sutliff Dulfer Story: Black Enterprise in the 19th Century* (1986); and Frances A. Westervelt, *History of Bergen County, New Jersey, 1630–1923*, 3 vols. (1923). Public records used to document her property ownership are: *Bergen County Clerk, Liber A of Manumissions*; *New York City Directory* (1820, 1840); *Bergen County Surrogate, Record of Cost and Testimony*, vol. 5; U.S. Bureau of the Census, *Seventh Census: 1850, New Jersey*; and U.S. Bureau of the Census, *Eighth Census: 1860, New Jersey*.

*Arnold E. Brown*

## ABIGAIL GOODWIN, 1793–1867

Abigail Goodwin, abolitionist and humanitarian, was born in Salem County, NJ, on December 1, 1793, the fifth of the six daughters of William and Elizabeth (Woodnutt) Goodwin. Goodwin's father was a modestly prosperous farmer. Both sets of grandparents were Quakers, with New Jersey and Pennsylvania roots from the early decades of the 18th century, which made her a birthright Quaker.

Prior to Goodwin's birth, her father and her Uncle Thomas had manumitted their slaves during the American Revolution, following the practice of most members of the Religious Society of Friends of Salem County. It was in such a humanitarian tradition that the six Goodwin sisters matured.

From her home at 47 Market Street in Salem, Goodwin aided fleeing refugees from southern slavery. From the 1840s to the Civil War, hundreds of runaway slaves traveled to the shores of Cape May, Cumberland, and Salem counties and made it safely northward to New Brunswick on the Raritan River through the efforts of Goodwin and her sister Elizabeth's devotion and the dedication of Quaker friends.

Historical records about Goodwin's formative years are unavailable. From her literary and mathematical skills, however, it may be assumed that she received at least an elementary school education at the Friends' School in Salem.

There are no records of her life from 1793 to 1814; however, the minutes of the Female Benevolent Society of Salem, an association dedicated to the relief of the infirm, aged, widowed with small children, and the unemployed, indicate that Goodwin was among the founders of the society in 1814. She served for many years on the Committee to Visit the Sick.

Not until 1837 did Goodwin emerge as an active abolitionist. For the next 30 years her life was devoted to the abolitionist cause, but not at the expense of other humanitarian activities. Her letter to Mary Grew of the Philadelphia Female Anti-Slavery Society on June 20, 1837, indicated her interest in an active role in the Underground Railroad. She became a correspondent and friend of many leading abolitionists of New England, New Jersey, and Pennsylvania, including Ester Moore, James Miller McKim, and William Still (son of CHARITY STILL). McKim, especially, inspired Goodwin to continue her work despite the great odds she faced outside the Quaker community in Salem.

At her urging, McKim, a former Presbyterian minister and founder of *the Nation* in 1865, came to Salem City on June 21, 1837, to talk to Quaker ladies interested in helping runaway slaves. A second appearance of McKim scheduled at the Salem Court House resulted in a mob of anti-abolitionists burning his effigy. The mob continued its harassment by traveling to Goodwin's residence, where McKim was staying.

The attacks on McKim did not dampen Goodwin's enthusiasm for the abolitionist cause. Exactly when runaway slaves first came to the Goodwin house is unknown; however, a very important document has survived at Salem—the "Diary of a Quaker Farmer" by William Goodwin Woodnutt, a nephew of the Goodwin sisters. In his entry of September 9, 1848, Woodnutt noted that he "had gone to Salem, took butter and apples to Aunts Goodwin" (who had an Underground Railroad Station in Salem). Also, Woodnutt wrote in the December 5, 1852, entry that he had "called at Aunts Goodwin, brought home with us Daniel Drayton, the individual who suffered in jail at Washington a/c [on account] of slaves." (Drayton, a Quaker ship captain caught with some 75 runaway slaves aboard his ship in 1848, was convicted and sentenced to four years in jail. Because of abolitionist pressure, President Millard Fillmore pardoned Drayton, who, within a few weeks, was at Goodwin's house in Salem.)

Because those who broke the law suffered severe penalties under the Fugitive Slave Act of 1850, one can understand the blanks in the record of Goodwin's activities from December 1852 to January 1855. On January 25, 1855, she wrote to Still: "The enclosed ten dollars I have made, earned in two weeks . . . may go for the fugitives, or

Carolina slaves, whichever needs it most. I am sorry the fugitives' treasury is not better supplied." The Carolina slaves mentioned by Goodwin were owned by a southerner who wished to sell them into freedom in the North.

In another letter to Still (May 25, 1855), Goodwin reported that four fugitives had arrived in Salem and that "they had no money, the minister said, but were pretty well off for clothes. I gave him all I had and more, but it seemed very little for four travelers—only a dollar for each—but they will meet with friends and helpers on the way." She expressed great concern about the fugitives who would be leaving the next day: "I am afraid, it's so cold, and one of them had a sore foot; they will not get away—it's dangerous staying here."

Goodwin constantly urged her Quaker friends to contribute to the cause of the Underground Railroad. Increasingly, it was very little, as she reported to Still on July 30, 1856: "I have tried to beg something for them, but have not got much; one of our neighbors, S. W. Acton, gave me three dollars for them; I added enough to make ten, which thee will find inside."

By June 9, 1861, Goodwin was finding it even more difficult to raise money. She told Still that in answer to his "urgent appeal for money to aid our good cause, I send my usual donation and much wish to oblige you by obtaining what I can from others and that I am afraid will be very little. It seems useless to ask any body; money is hard to get, and harder still to give away when they don't want to." In addition, Goodwin told him that New Jersey "had a $100,000 tax to raise, which will make the people poorer than ever."

It was her view at that time that "the war will not interfere with slavery unless it stands in its way of quelling the rebellion." As for President Abraham Lincoln and those in political power in the North, it was her firm belief that they did not "care anything about the poor slaves; if the country could have peace and prosperity with slavery, they would scarcely move a finger to remove it."

In September 1862, at age 69, Goodwin was still involved in her abolitionist activities in Salem. She informed Still on September 23, that "on the 22nd, yesterday, Amy Reckless [a black friend] came here, after I began writing, and wished me to defer sending for a day or two, thinking she could get a few more dollars, and she has just brought some and will try for more and clothing."

In the same letter, she noted that she had read President Lincoln's "proclamation of emancipation, with thankfulness and rejoicing; but upon a little reflection, I did not feel quite satisfied with it; . . . Slavery, I fear will be a long time in dying, after receiving the fatal stroke."

While no letters have been located from and to Goodwin after the ones quoted above, we can assume that she continued her work and took much pleasure in the passage of the Thirteenth Amendment to the U.S. Constitution in 1865, which abolished slavery. She was then 72 years old and time, plus her untiring devotion to the abolitionist movement, had taken its toll. Woodnutt wrote in his diary on February 20, 1866: "Aunt Abby very sick."

Goodwin's long career in humanitarian pursuits did not gain her the fame of Lucretia Mott. Indeed, it would have been out of character for Goodwin to seek applause for what she did. Nevertheless, William Still, with whom Goodwin worked for years, wrote that "she worked for the slave as a mother would work for her children." Today she is noted as a feminist, humanitarian, and proprietor of the most important station in all of southern New Jersey on the Underground Railroad.

Goodwin died at her home on the morning of November 2, 1867, at age 74. Woodnutt reported in his diary on that day that "the poor have lost a friend."

Her death resulted from the complications of advanced years. Even in death Goodwin remembered the poor of Salem, for her will of May 26, 1863, specified: "I give to Sarah Woodnutt and Mary E. Acton the disposal of my household goods, books and clothing, giving most of my clothing to the poor which may be suitable for them." She is buried beside her sisters in the ancient Friends' Cemetery in Salem, NJ.

The best source of material on Goodwin is William Still, *The Underground Railroad: A Record of Facts, Authentic Narratives, Letters* (1872). Valuable material appears in William Goodwin Woodnutt, *The Diary of a Quaker Farmer* (1848), available at the NJ-SCHS. Two articles by Robert W. Harper are "Abigail Goodwin: Abolitionist," *The Way It Used to Be* 1 (1975):4, and "South Jersey's Angel to Runaway Slaves," *Sunday Press* (Atlantic City), June 5, 1975. Goodwin's letters to Mary Grew and William Still are at P-HSP. Two of her letters to McKim are at NY-CU. The *Minutes of the Female Benevolent Society of Salem* are available at NJ-SCHS.

*Robert W. Harper*

## SARAH MOORE GRIMKÉ, 1792–1873
## ANGELINA GRIMKÉ WELD, 1805–1879

Sarah Moore Grimké and Angelina Emily (Grimké) Weld, abolitionists and leaders of the antebellum women's movement, were born in 1792 and 1805, respectively, in Charleston, SC. Their mother, Mary (Smith) Grimké, came from a wealthy Charleston merchant family of Irish and Puritan ancestry; their father, John Faucheraud Grimké, also came from a leading family of Charleston merchants and property owners, of Huguenot ancestry. He served successively as an American lieutenant colonel in the Revolutionary War, as representative and Speaker of the South Carolina House of Representatives, and as the senior associate judge of South Carolina.

Sarah was the sixth and Angelina the last of fourteen children born to the Grimkés. Three of the children died in infancy. While two of her elder brothers studied Latin, Greek, philosophy, and law, first at home and eventually at Yale, Sarah received the standard education of women of fashionable families, including lessons in French, drawing, and music. Sarah nevertheless shared her brothers' intellectual abilities, studying their lessons on her own, participating in family debates, and pleading unsuccessfully for the opportunity to be tutored in Latin and law.

The male-dominated intellectual atmosphere that characterized Sarah's early family life was less important in the education of Angelina, thirteen years her junior. As a young girl Angelina attended a private Charleston seminary. By the time she reached her mid-teens, her father had died, and most of her siblings, including Sarah, had left the house. Later, at 26, when she herself had left home, Angelina planned to attend Catharine Beecher's Hartford Female Seminary, but disapproval from her Quaker friends of the time and from her then suitor, Edward Bettle, dissuaded her. Neither sister enjoyed any other formal schooling.

However, the sisters were highly educated, as their antislavery and women's rights arguments reveal. Both women were brought up in the Episcopal church. Their mother reinforced the importance of their religious education, leading daily family prayers and seeing that her daughters taught Bible classes, often in a "colored school." The sisters also were influenced by the evangelical fervor of the late 1810s and the 1820s. Sarah experienced an adult conversion under the preaching of a Presbyterian minister, and Angelina rejected Episcopalianism for membership in a Charleston Presbyterian church in 1826. Eventually, their religious quest led them both away from their family and the South, and into Quakerism, the North, and the abolitionist cause.

That their lives became permanently intertwined through this sense of mission owes something to the role of godmother and surrogate parent that Sarah played in Angelina's childhood. From 1819 to 1827, however, the sisters lived quite separate lives, and it was not until 1837, when they made their famous tour as abolitionist agents, that they earned a joint biography. For Sarah, the route to those events began with her trip north to nurse her dying father, who sought medical treatment in Philadelphia and passed away in her companionship in August 1819, in Long Branch, NJ. In addition to bearing this loss alone, Sarah encountered Quakerism on this trip. Back in South Carolina, she studied Quaker thought and began attending Quaker meeting. In 1821 she moved to Philadelphia, joining the Quakers officially in 1823, and residing primarily with Quaker Catherine Morris until 1836.

Sarah's conversion to Quakerism became Angelina's route to a new life as well. In October 1827 Sarah returned home for what became a six-month visit, preached Quakerism to Angelina, and brought the latter's church commitments again into doubt. Angelina then suffered a year-long ordeal of withdrawal from her deep involvement in the Presbyterian church and from the minister who had been instrumental in her conversion experience. The ordeal culminated in her formal Presbyterian church trial in May 1829, her move to Philadelphia in November of that year, and her official acceptance as a member of the Philadelphia Quakers in 1831.

These months of decision for Angelina also appear to mark the germination of her antislavery sentiments. The Quakers forbade ownership or trading of slaves by Friends. The Grimkés were plantation and slave owners, and Angelina made the Quaker arguments against slaveholding an issue within her family. To reject ownership of slaves for oneself and one's family was not the same, however, as working for abolition of the slavery system itself. This conversion from Quakerism to abolitionism awaited Angelina's encounter with antislavery arguments in the North.

The action that first earned Angelina repute as an antislavery advocate was the publication in 1835 of her letter from Shrewsbury, NJ, to William Lloyd Garrison, applauding his defiance of mob violence against antislavery leaders. Owing partly to the prominence of the Grimké family in the South, the letter was reprinted widely. Angelina joined the Philadelphia Female Anti-Slavery Society that same year. Such activity did not accord with the interpretation of Quakerism held by the Philadelphia Friends with whom the Grimkés were associated, however. In the summer and fall of 1836 Angelina sealed her identity as an abolitionist, and her break with the Philadelphia Friends, by writing (also in Shrewsbury) her *Appeal to the Christian Women of the Southern States*, and by accepting the invitation of the American Anti-Slavery Society to serve as one of its speakers and agents.

She spoke to tens of thousands of people in New York, New Jersey, and New England from the winter of 1836–37 through the spring of 1838. In doing so she tested the claims to the moral and political agency of women that lay behind her *Appeal*. But it was Sarah who most fully articulated these latent feminist issues.

At first Sarah shared the Philadelphia Friends' disapproval of Angelina's abolitionist activities, but in August 1836 she was publicly silenced at the Quakers' Philadelphia Yearly Meeting, an experience that solidified her own disaffection from their society and made her more open to Angelina's position. In November she accompanied Angelina to a convention in New York where Theodore Weld, a leader of the abolitionist network, initiated 40 new recruits as antislavery agents. Thoroughly converted to the cause through this initiation, Sarah wrote her own *Epistle to the Clergy of the Southern States* (1836), while Angelina issued a second treatise, *Appeal to the Christian Women of the Nominally Free States* (1836). The two then formed a team of the first female antislavery agents in the country.

The deployment of new agents by the American Anti-Slavery Society in 1836–37 was part of a drive to present antislavery petitions to state legislatures and to the U.S. Congress. Women as well as men could supply petition signatures. At first the sisters appeared before all-female audiences in churches and homes. Angelina, less self-conscious than Sarah, did most of the speaking and by all accounts was a compelling orator. Soon the sisters started generating wide publicity, attracting larger audiences of men as well as women, and threatening the equanimity of the congregations and ministers in whose churches they appeared. In the spring of 1837 the doors of many Massachusetts churches closed to them. Their presumption as women to lecture publicly to "promiscuous audiences" and to enlist other women in the cause became a focus of opposition to their activity. This experience clarified the Grimké sisters' views regarding women's rights.

The sisters' writing on this subject took the form of epistles or letters, which were published in the press and reissued as pamphlets or tracts. Both the Grimkés argued that women and men were equal before God, that their rights and responsibilities derived from this equality as moral beings.

From this position Sarah developed an account of how, despite this fundamental moral equality, women everywhere found themselves in a condition of subjection. Questioning the very legitimacy of ecclesiastical and civil institutions, she aligned herself with the radical wing of the Anti-Slavery Society, led by Garrison, and brought the Grimkés into the center of a controversy that by 1840 had split the abolition movement. Angelina echoed and cited her sister's arguments in her last Beecher letters, but was somewhat less radical than Sarah. Nevertheless, as the more politically potent of the Grimké team, she bore the brunt of criticism from more moderate abolitionists such as John Greenleaf Whittier and Theodore Weld, who argued that Angelina would better serve women if she showed that she would not be diverted from the greater cause of abolishing slavery. Angelina chafed at these remarks, but her response to Weld had a strange result. Theodore Weld wrote back declaring his love for her, and the two were married on May 14, 1838.

In the meantime, Angelina did withdraw from further public debate on women's rights and made the most significant speeches of her career on abolition. First she presented the Massachusetts petitions collected by the Grimkés in an unprecedented speaking appearance by a woman before a committee of the state legislature in February 1838. Because the crowd was so large, Angelina delivered the last of three addresses from the Speaker's chair in the House chamber. In March and April the Grimkés gave a series of lectures, Sarah delivering the first, and An-

gelina the remaining four, in Boston's largest meeting hall, the Odeon. Finally, two days after her wedding to Weld in Philadelphia in May, Angelina gave an opening day address at the Anti-Slavery Convention of American Women in that city. As anti-abolitionists rioted just outside Pennsylvania Hall (which they burned down on the third day of the convention), Angelina urged upon her audience the same courage and dedication in the face of opposition as she had commended in Garrison with her first fateful letter to him in 1835.

This proved to be Angelina's last public appearance until the 1860s. With the close of the convention, the Welds and Sarah moved to New Jersey, where they resided for the next 25 years, first in Fort Lee (to 1840), then in Belleville (to 1854), and finally in Perth Amboy (to 1863). Sarah, who had always been more comfortable with the pen than behind the podium, gave one more speech, to the Philadelphia Female Anti-Slavery Society in 1839. Theodore Weld had virtually retired from his prodigious speaking career in 1836, after leading the convention at which the Grimkés had been inducted into abolitionist work. Angelina's public retirement was abetted by a difficult pregnancy in 1839, which resulted in the birth of Charles Stuart Weld on December 14, but also in a protracted illness for her. With their move to New Jersey, their establishment of a home and family, and the fragmentation of the abolitionist organization, the Weld-Grimkés redirected their energies in ways that built on their abolitionist commitments, but gave a different focus to their lives.

First the three collaborated on a major research and writing project. The Grimkés' effectiveness as antislavery agents had been greatly strengthened by their ability to appeal to their own experience with southern slavery. *American Slavery as It Is* recognized and exploited the power of this appeal, presenting testimony to the evils of slavery collected from southern sources, including thousands of southern newspapers that the Grimké sisters spent months reading and clipping. The book, published in 1839, sold over 100,000 copies in its first year.

With the completion of this project, Sarah and Angelina began hosting a stream of visitors and temporary lodgers—American and British abolition and reform leaders, antislavery agents, missionaries, and freed slaves. Thus the Weld-Grimké residence became an important junction of the abolitionist network at the same time as the movement decentralized organizationally. In time, the maintenance of the household in this network developed into second careers for Theodore Weld and the sisters. The three bought and moved to a farm in Belleville in 1840, and Angelina bore, with a miscarriage in between, two more children: Theodore Weld II (b. 1841) and Sarah Grimké Weld (b. 1844). Already educating their own children at home, the Welds took on two additional students in 1848, and by 1851 had established a small boarding school of 20 pupils in Belleville. Many of their students came from the families of their abolitionist friends, including the Henry Stantons, the Gerrit Smiths, and the James Birneys. Angelina taught history and Sarah, French, and the two sisters did all the cooking, washing, and cleaning for the school.

Seeking more favorable conditions for expanding this new work, the Weld-Grimkés accepted in 1852 an invitation to join abolitionists Marcus and REBECCA BUFFUM SPRING in founding the Raritan Bay Union, an Associationist community just outside Perth Amboy, NJ. As part of the union's Associationist plan, the threesome were to establish and operate the community's school. Unlike the school at Belleville, the Raritan Bay school was communally supported. Laundry services, farming, and dining room were managed as distinct enterprises of the union. A large main building was erected with the aid of personal capital from the Springs, who also provided 270 acres of land for the community. In accepting the invitation, the Weld-Grimkés purchased shares in the joint stock company that constituted the union, and Angelina assumed the position of secretary to the Board of Directors. In the summer of 1854 the family moved to Eagleswood and prepared for the October opening of what came to be called the Eagleswood School.

The school operated on manual labor principles, with students participating in farming and housekeeping duties, making the "practical arts" an essential component of the curriculum in addition to traditional academic subjects. Like the Belleville school, Eagleswood enrolled a number of students from abolitionist families. In response to appeals made by Sarah and Angelina, Gerrit Smith also paid the tuition of some students who could not otherwise afford it. The school was interracial and coeducational, and the antislavery cause was freely promoted there, with students involved in efforts such as providing relief for antislavery victims of the Wakarusa War in Kansas. Students provided the impetus and focus for nature walks and excursions, Saturday evening dances, and Sunday Lyceum lectures, which in turn attracted the participation of many visitors. As at Belleville, students of both sexes participated extensively in physical activities, including rowing, swimming, diving, and gymnastics. Dramatic productions were also a feature of Eagleswood life, as Theodore Weld's teaching specialty was Shakespeare. Angelina and Sarah again taught history and French, respectively.

During these years the sisters sustained avid interests in the social and political issues that directed their early careers. In the wake of cases prosecuted under the fugitive slave law and of the passage of the Kansas Nebraska Bill, for instance, Angelina addressed an incisive political commentary to Gerrit Smith, begging him to reconsider his decision to resign from Congress. Both sisters made written contributions to the women's rights conventions of the early 1850s, and Angelina attended the 1851 Rochester

convention. Sarah continued to be more particularly engaged by women's issues than Angelina, however. Her unfinished manuscripts include a study of state laws pertaining to women and a history of marriage and divorce. Woman, she wrote, must be allowed to "draw from the yet unworked mine of her intellect a wealth of which the world is now defrauded and which is yet destined to elevate and bless mankind." (S. Grimké to Sarah Wattles, Dec. 27, 1856) Sarah believed strongly in increasing educational opportunities for women.

The relative success and fame of the Eagleswood School never provided the Weld-Grimkés with a good income. They blamed this, at least in part, on unfairly high rent charged them by the Springs after the association disbanded in 1856. It was chiefly due to the school and the visitors it drew, they reasoned, that any of the other, now private, enterprises at Eagleswood—such as the laundry and boardinghouse—enjoyed any business. Making these and other arguments, Angelina formally complained in 1861 to Marcus Spring and requested that the rates be lowered. It is not known whether any adjustment was offered, but this financial situation, together with the serious illness of the Welds' second son, contributed substantially to the decision to close the school in July 1861, at which time Marcus Spring established a military academy in the facilities at Eagleswood. The Weld-Grimkés resided temporarily in a private home in Perth Amboy and as boarders in West Newton, MA, before settling on a house in Hyde Park, near Boston, in 1864.

Although steeped in the pacifist tradition of their Quaker and Garrisonian pasts, Angelina and Sarah had come to the conclusion in the mid-1850s that the national issue of slavery would not be resolved peaceably. Once the passage of the Emancipation Proclamation in 1862 assuaged their remaining objections, they made their support of the North active. While Theodore Weld temporarily resumed his career as a touring abolitionist speaker, the sisters worked through the Women's Central Committee, a steering organization of the women's rights movement. At the 1863 women's convention Angelina at last spoke publicly again, and again urged women to join in supporting the abolitionist cause. Both sisters then returned to their work as collectors of petition signatures, this time promoting an abolition amendment to the constitution; and both contributed tracts and letters to the press about the war on slavery.

After the war, the Weld-Grimkés taught again for two years, at a female seminary in Lexington, MA. In 1868 the sisters discovered the existence of three nephews, all former slaves and illegitimate sons of one of their brothers. With the elder two, Francis James and Archibald Henry Grimké, who were pursuing their education in the North, the sisters established warm relations, welcoming them into their home and contributing to their support. Both became public figures in their own right, Francis particularly in academic circles, and Archibald as a leader of the National Association for the Advancement of Colored People (NAACP). Through the lives of these nephews and through activity in the Massachusetts Woman Suffrage Association, the Grimké sisters spent their final years working toward the reality that they dreamed of in their youth. Both women died in Hyde Park: Sarah on December 23, 1873, at age 81, of uncertain illness, and Angelina on October 26, 1879, at age 74, after several strokes. They were buried in Mt. Hope Cemetery in Boston, MA.

Published Grimké works include: Angelina Emily Grimké, *Appeal to the Christian Women of the Southern States* (1836) and *Letters to Catherine E. Beecher* (1838); and Sarah Moore Grimké, *Letters on the Equality of the Sexes and the Condition of Woman* (1838). For a full bibliography of primary Grimké materials, see Gerda Lerner, *The Grimké Sisters from South Carolina* (1967). The sisters are profiled in *NAW*. For the period in which the Grimkés resided in New Jersey, primary sources include Sarah Grimké's correspondence from Eagleswood, 1856–61, in the Weld-Grimké Papers, Clements Library, University of Michigan (Ann Arbor); and correspondence in the Gerrit Smith Papers, George Arents Research Library, Syracuse University (Syracuse, NY). Materials on the Raritan Bay Union, the Eagleswood School, and the Grimkés' involvement in them are available at NJ-HS and the Perth Amboy Free Public Library. Articles include: Maud Honeyman Greene, "Raritan Bay Union, Eagleswood, New Jersey," *NJHSP* 68 (1950):1–20; Jayme Sokolow, "Culture and Utopia: The Raritan Bay Union," *New Jersey History* 94 (1976):89–100; and George Kirchmann, "Unsettled Utopias: The North American Phalanx and the Raritan Bay Union," *New Jersey History* 97 (1979):25–36.

*Nancy Beadie*

## CORNELIA HANCOCK, 1840–1927

Cornelia Hancock was a Union army volunteer nurse, the founder of a school for African-Americans in South Carolina during Reconstruction, and a social reformer in the poor southwest section of Philadelphia. Born February 8, 1840, at Hancock's Bridge (Salem County), NJ, to Thomas Yorke and Rachel (Nicholson) Hancock, she was the fourth child and third daughter in this old Quaker family. Her younger brother, Tom, drowned during childhood.

Hancock's family, descendants of Richard Hancock, an original settler of Hancock's Bridge in 1675, and of Judge William Hancock, a victim of a British massacre in 1778, lived in the fishing village, a few miles south of Salem. Runaway slaves ("contraband") were both hunted and protected in this border area where many residents were strong abolitionists. Hancock's father fished every day and gave away the extra fish the family did not eat.

After attending the common school at Hancock's Bridge, Hancock went to the Friends' School in Salem through the financial assistance of her cousins Sarah Hancock Gibbon and Henrietta Hancock, who were upset by the family's apparent neglect of the girl's education. After this schooling, Hancock engaged for a short time in the only profession open to her: teaching at Hancock's Bridge. The children were unruly and unwilling to learn. She later recalled, "I never suffered in my life as I did then." (Letter to her mother, May 27, [1866?])

Hancock's sister Ellen (Hancock) Child, the wife of Dr. Henry T. Child, lived in Philadelphia, where during her frequent visits Hancock met feminists Lucretia Mott, Susan B. Anthony, and LUCY STONE and learned of Henry Child's antislavery work. The Battle of Gettysburg gave Hancock the opportunity she longed for—a chance to participate in the effort to free the slaves and to preserve the Union. Her brother had gone to war, and she wanted to help. Doctors and nurses were desperately needed at Gettysburg to care for the wounded, so Dr. Child took Hancock with him, despite the opposition of DOROTHEA DIX, superintendent of nurses. Dix wanted only older women and considered Hancock unsuitable because she was young, small, and pretty; but Hancock, independent and resourceful, simply got on the train while her case was being argued. Once at Gettysburg, there was such an overwhelming need for workers that Hancock's competence was no longer questioned. She later obtained an agreement that the surgeons-in-charge of field hospitals could appoint whomever they wished to work under them "irrespective of *age, size,* or *looks.*" This agreement made it possible to get around Dix's authority. (Jaquette, *South After Gettysburg,* 33)

Compassionate and energetic, Hancock's character was well suited to meet the challenges she faced at Gettysburg. In the hot summer air there was the stench of hundreds of wounded who lay unattended while amputations were performed continuously under trees or on tables in the open air. It took 300 surgeons five days and nights to complete all the needed amputations. Hancock also found food and water for Confederate soldiers when she could and took time to write letters for all the men. She enjoyed an unusual degree of energy and well-being in spite of the long hours of constant work.

She wrote often to her family and friends back in Salem County and Philadelphia, asking for food, clothing, bandages, sheets, and blankets, which they gladly supplied to supplement the stores of the U.S. Sanitary Commission. Thus, Hancock's wounded were often better cared for than those in the general issue. In gratitude, her patients presented her with a silver medal, engraved with these words: "Miss Cornelia Hancock, presented by the wounded soldiers 3rd Division 2nd Army Corps. Testimonial of regard for ministrations of mercy to the wounded soldiers at Gettysburg, Pa.—July 1863." (Quoted in Jaquette, 12)

After Gettysburg, Hancock turned to work among the black refugees crowding into Washington, where there were almost no facilities to provide them with food, clothing, and shelter. Smallpox was epidemic. Some refugees were without feet because of amputations suffered when their limbs were frozen or broken. Faced with the impossibility of providing sufficient help to these desperate people, Hancock wrote, "Where are the people who have been professing such strong abolition proclivity for the last thirty years?—certainly not in Washington." (Quoted in Jaquette, 40) She was convinced that the greatest need was to enable blacks to work and survive on their own.

In February 1864 volunteer Hancock again gained permission to return to the battlefield and followed the 3rd Division 2nd Army Corps until Richmond was taken in April 1865. Highly valued as an administrator and organizer, she supervised huge kitchens and hundreds of wounded and ill soldiers. Her friends were the doctors under whom she worked, especially Dr. Frederick Dudley, with whom she had a romantic involvement. She said, however, "He is down on the coloreds but always does his duty by his patients." (Quoted in Jaquette, 56) Hancock ended her relationship with Dudley after the war. Unlike Hancock, he was apparently not an abolitionist, but Hancock never explained why their romance ended.

Supplies of clothing, blankets, or whatever Hancock asked for continued to flow from Salem County, although disapproval was expressed because she lived alone among men at the field hospitals. She defended her unconventional way of life vigorously and courteously, saying that she would "do nothing rash or romantic." The culmination of her army duty came as she stood on the reviewing stand in Washington to watch Sherman's victory parade.

She returned to her sister's home in Philadelphia after the war. Then the Philadelphia Friends Association for the Aid and Elevation of the Freedmen sent her to South Carolina, where she founded a school (later known as the Laing School) at Mt. Pleasant. At the school 50 barefoot, ragged children began learning with no materials other than charcoal picked up from the fire, which they used to write on the white pillars of a bullet-riddled church. In the evening she taught the adults sewing and other practical arts such as reading, writing, and arithmetic. She begged family, government agencies, and the Friends Association back in Philadelphia for books, seeds, tools, cloth, and money. Finally, 200 children were enrolled at the school. These children, in contrast to Hancock's pupils back home, were eager to learn and a delight to teach.

Hancock and her coworkers were not welcome among the white southerners, who gladly would have run them out of town. Called "nigger teacher" and "Yankee," they were openly threatened. The blacks' virtual reenslavement came about when their former owners, who refused to work their farms themselves, hired the former slaves for very low wages. Hancock wrote bitterly, "All the negroes have gained is liberty to starve." (Letter to her brother, May 24, 1868)

When General Winfield Scott was appointed by President Andrew Johnson to administer the government's Freedmen's Bureau in Mt. Pleasant in place of Brigadier General Rufus Saxton, who had commanded a regiment of freed slaves in the war, Hancock feared the work of Reconstruction would be seriously undermined. She said, "Have we won the war only to lose it? Do we free the slaves only to abandon them?" (Quoted in McConnell, *Cornelia*, 162) She and her supporters and coworkers were not stopped, however, for she remained at Mt. Pleasant as principal of the Laing School until 1875.

Suffering from dyspepsia, headaches, and hemorrhages, Hancock left the Laing School and returned to Philadelphia in 1875. A short rest seemed to renew her energy, and she was soon off to England to study philanthropic social work. Upon her return to Philadelphia, she helped to found the Society for Organizing Charity in 1878 (later the Family Society of Philadelphia) and the Children's Aid Society of Pennsylvania. Since the port city's large population of immigrants needed to learn English and find work, Hancock managed a corps of volunteers to meet these needs through the charitable societies.

In 1884 Hancock and her friend Edith Wright led a movement to prove that good management could create a healthful, as well as profitable, community in Wrightsville, a squalid neighborhood in southwest Philadelphia. The streets were not paved; animals wandered about freely; sanitation, police protection, and doctors were unknown. The school was a disgrace, and there was no library. Hancock and Wright made rules for the residents, repaired buildings, pressured city bureaus for paved streets and police protection, enforced rules of cleanliness and order, placed an effective principal in the school, and even initiated the opening of a public library with books in both English and German. In addition, the venture made a small profit. By 1914 all the residents of Wrightsville were home owners, a triumph of the crusade.

During her last years, Hancock lived with a niece in Atlantic City, NJ, where she died of nephritis on December 31, 1927, at the age of 87. Her ashes are buried at what is now known as Cedar Hills Friends' Cemetery in Harmersville, NJ, near her birthplace.

Hancock's letters are available at the Clements Library, University of Michigan (Ann Arbor, MI), and at P-SC. A selection from her letters appears in Henrietta Jaquette, *South After Gettysburg, Letters of Cornelia Hancock, 1863–1868* (1956). Jane McConnell, *Cornelia: The Story of a Civil War Nurse* (1959), is a children's biography. A sketch of her appears in *NAW*. A chapter in John T. Cunningham, *The New Jersey Sampler* (1964), recounts Hancock's Civil War experiences. An issue of the *Laing School Visitor* 20 (1913) recounts the history of the school Hancock founded. The Wrightsville reform is detailed in an anonymously written pamphlet, *Record of Wrightsville: An Experiment in the Care of Property* (1889).

*Doris B. Armstrong*

## HANNAH HOYT, 1805–1871

Hannah Hoyt, founder and principal of the New Brunswick Female Institute, also known as Miss Hoyt's Seminary, the Young Ladies' School, and the Female Academy, was born in Connecticut on June 10, 1805, the third and youngest child and only daughter of Salmon and Hannah (Husted) Hoyt. (One brother, James Hervey, was born in 1798; the other brother, Amos, was born in 1801.) The family was descended from John Hoyt, an early settler of Salisbury, MA. Hoyt's father died on November 21, 1809, and her mother remained a widow until 1820, when she married Benjamin Weed. As a result of that marriage, Hannah Hoyt acquired a stepsister, Rebecca, and then a half-brother, Benjamin.

Before coming to New Brunswick, NJ, from Connecticut in the mid-1830s, Hoyt had been the principal of the North Stamford Academy, a school that "prepared young men for college and business life." (Hoyt, *A Genealogical History*, 467) After a few shaky years and an offer of "a flattering position" from a seminary in Sing Sing (later Ossining), NY, Hoyt settled into New Brunswick life. She was given an annual salary of $800 by some of the leading men of New Brunswick. In September 1839 she became a communicant of the Presbyterian church; by the time of her death, she was considered a prominent member and attended church every Sabbath with the students who boarded at her school. By 1847 she was able to purchase a house on George and Paterson streets in which she ran her school until her death.

Little is known about Hoyt's own upbringing and education, but one contemporary noted that "she must have been reared in the old school of thorough womanhood." She was known to be a strict but beloved disciplinarian. She was described as both "severe" and "scholarly." As a teacher, Hoyt was particularly interested in the classics and was reputed to be the first woman to teach a class in Sophocles. Apparently, she was also skilled at teaching arithmetic. Although she was neat in appearance, she was unconcerned with dress and wore the same clothes year after year.

Hoyt was hailed by her contemporaries, and especially by graduates of her school, as one of the outstanding women educators of her time. Her school was widely known and attracted boarding students from every part of the country. Lady Randolph Churchill was at one time a pupil at the Hoyt school. Hoyt emphasized academic subjects such as geography, philosophy, astronomy, English (including Shakespeare, Cooper, and Milton), French, Latin,

Greek, mathematics, and physiology, in addition to the Bible. Her school was much more than a finishing school. Her students faced public examinations by Rutgers professors before they could graduate.

Hoyt's influence on her students is attested to by the fact that in 1898, almost 30 years after her death, the graduates of her school and their daughters formed the Hannah Hoyt Association to recognize "what an important factor the discipline and teachings of Hannah Hoyt had been in the lives of her students."

In addition to honoring Hoyt's memory, the association aimed "to encourage advanced education for women." It contributed $500 to the New Jersey College for Women (later Douglass College) at the opening of the college, and $500 on the occasion of the silver jubilee of the Hannah Hoyt Association, for a permanent Hannah Hoyt Mathematics Prize at the New Jersey College for Women.

When Hoyt, who never married, died, at age 66, in New Brunswick on November 7, 1871, her school closed. It was her wish that at her death all of her property except her books, but including the building that housed her school, be sold and that an income be paid to her mother, who was still living in Connecticut. Her books were left to her half-brother, Benjamin.

Hoyt's school was just one of several "notable schools for girls" in New Brunswick's history. Miss Sophia Hay ran an academy for girls that opened after the Revolution and offered its students, among other subjects, French, music, and dancing. In the 19th century other schools were opened and operated by women, including Miss Croe's in 1856, Miss Beck's, Miss Ten Broeck's, Miss Bever's, the Misses Bucknall's, all in 1871, and Miss Bell's, Miss McDede's, Miss McLaughlin's, and the Misses Anables. The Misses Anables' School, run by five sisters, was opened in 1883 and operated until 1918 in the tradition of Miss Hoyt's School.

Family information is found in David Hoyt, *A Genealogical History of the Hoyt, Haight and Hight Families* (1871). A scrapbook and materials on Hoyt and her school are available at NJ-RU. See also Mary Demarest, "Some Early New Brunswick Schools for Girls," *NJHSP* 53 (1935):163–85.

*Ellen F. Mappen*

## ANNE HYDE DE NEUVILLE, unknown–1849

Anne Marguerite Josephine Henriette (Rouillé de Marigny) Hyde de Neuville, artist and devoted wife of a political activist and diplomat, was born in France, but her exact birthplace and date are not known. Both 1749 and 1779 have been suggested as the year she was born, but there is evidence that neither is correct and an intermediate date is most likely. She was enough older than her husband, born in 1776, to disguise him as her son when he was a fugitive. Furthermore, she remembered the festivities accompanying the birth of Princess Marie Thérèse in 1778. Hyde de Neuville was the only daughter and probably the only child of Monsieur Rouillé de Marigny, but nothing is known of her mother; she was raised by one of her father's sisters. Her paternal grandmother was a wealthy and distinguished Parisian.

Anne Hyde de Neuville, a well-to-do French woman who lived on a farm on the Raritan River outside New Brunswick in the 1810s, made many sketches depicting early 19th-century New Jersey countryside and life. *Self-portrait, the New-York Historical Society.*

Hyde de Neuville grew up in Fleury and Paris, but at the outbreak of the French Revolution in 1789 she and her father fled Paris to Sancerre. Like other privileged young women of her day, she probably had some instruction in drawing. In 1794 she married Guillaume Jean Hyde de Neuville, an eighteen-year-old fervent Royalist from the town of La Charité. They had no children. An active agent of the exiled Bourbons, her husband was often under threat of arrest and forced to live in hiding. As his wife, Hyde de Neuville was drawn into eleven years of danger and persecution, first by the revolutionaries and later by Napoleon, for her husband's refusal to betray the royal cause. Twice when the police failed to capture her husband they arrested and imprisoned her instead, but she was not held long. Finally, in 1805, after a direct appeal from Hyde de Neuville, Napoleon agreed to permit her and her husband exile in the United States.

The Hyde de Neuvilles sailed for America from Spain, arriving in New York in June 1807. They remained in exile in the United States for seven years. Throughout these years, as during all her travels, Hyde de Neuville recorded what she saw in delicate pencil and watercolor sketches. Her first American drawing was of New Jersey's Sandy Hook lighthouse, sketched as her ship entered New York Harbor. Drawings she made are among the earliest depictions of Utica and Geneva, NY; New Haven, CT; New York City; and Washington, D.C. Much of her drawings' charm comes from their lack of artistic pretense and their wealth of detail. In them, men, women, children, and domestic animals pursuing normal activities give a sense of the industriousness and optimism of early America. She also sketched the country estates of her friends and made portraits of people from all walks of life.

In the summer of 1807 the Hyde de Neuvilles traveled through upstate New York, where she sketched the farms and towns recently carved out of the wilderness. She recorded the appearance of New York's Iroquois Indians with such fidelity and detail that her drawings now have great historical and ethnological importance.

Hyde de Neuville and her husband established a residence in New York City. They probably first came to New Jersey in 1809; her New Jersey drawings *Passaic Bridge, Totowa; Saint Peter's Church, Perth Amboy;* and *Vue d'Amboy et du Steam-Boat* date from this year. The last is the earliest known representation of a steamboat in New York waters. The steamboat was Fulton's *Raritan* on a run between New York City and New Brunswick, NJ. *Ram, Bachelor Hall, NJ; Young Lady, Bachelor Hall, NJ;* and *Cottage at Amboy* were all sketched in 1810.

In 1811 the Hyde de Neuvilles bought a 101-acre farm overlooking the Raritan River on the Easton Avenue Turnpike in Somerset County, just outside of New Brunswick. Here they raised Merino sheep and lived the simple life that Hyde de Neuville preferred. New Brunswick was close to New York City, where they had helped to found a school for French refugees and where they continued to live in the winter.

Two Hyde de Neuville sketches from 1811 and 1812 inscribed *La Bergerie* (The Sheep Farm) are undoubtedly of their New Brunswick farm, which she later recalled as "our modest retreat . . . where we spent so many calm and happy hours." (*Hyde de Neuville*, 1890, 2:196) Their farm is also depicted in her 1813 watercolor *Le Cottage.* They lived either in this cottage or in another house, which a letter of 1818 says was on the property.

In October 1813 Hyde de Neuville visited Princeton, NJ, where she made a watercolor drawing of a church under construction. The Presbyterian Meeting House there had burned down; its replacement, which she saw being built, was completed in 1814, but it burned in 1835 and was replaced by a third structure. Hyde de Neuville's drawing is the only evidence remaining that the second structure, with its pointed window arches, was probably the first Gothic Revival Presbyterian church built in this country.

In anticipation of Napoleon's fall, the Hyde de Neu-villes ended their exile in spring 1814. Back in France, un-der the restored Bourbon monarchy, Guillaume Hyde de Neuville was elected to the Chamber of Deputies. Louis XVIII appointed him minister plenipotentiary to the Unit-ed States in January 1816. Either this appointment or a later one, in 1821, brought him, ex officio, the title of bar-on. He feared that for his wife the new appointment, "so contrary to her simple tastes, would be the greatest trial." But she maintained, "If it is our duty, we cannot hesitate." (*Hyde de Neuville*, 1913, 2:73) The first ordeal she had to undergo was presentation at court before their departure.

The Hyde de Neuvilles arrived in the United States in June 1816 and hastened to their New Jersey farm. Looking to the months ahead, Hyde de Neuville lamented, "My happy homelife will soon be over, for I must spend the winter in Washington in great state." (*Hyde de Neuville*, 1913, 2:77)

Despite her reluctance, Hyde de Neuville performed her duties in Washington with grace and kindness. John Quincy Adams described her in his diary as "a woman of excellent temper, amiable disposition, unexceptional pro-priety of demeanor, profuse charity, yet of judicious econ-omy and sound discretion." (*Memoirs of John Quincy Adams*, 5:137)

The Hyde de Neuvilles retreated to their New Jersey farm in the summer of 1817 and did not return to Wash-ington until December. In the fall of 1818 they sold the farm in anticipation of their return to France, which finally occurred in July 1820.

Hyde de Neuville joined her husband on further diplo-matic missions to Washington (1821–22) and to Portugal (1823–24). With the French Revolution of 1830 Guillaume Hyde de Neuville withdrew from political life, and the Hyde de Neuvilles retired to their country estate, "Lestang," although they continued to spend a part of each winter in Paris.

Hyde de Neuville died at Lestang on September 12, 1849. Her drawings remained in the possession of the Hyde de Neuville family until the 20th century. The most important collections of her works now in the United States are 88 drawings owned by the New York Historical Society and six drawings in the Stokes Collection at the New York Public Library.

The autobiography of her husband, *Mémoires et souvenirs du Baron Hyde de Neuville*, 3 vols. (1888–92), is the best source of bio-graphical information on Anne Hyde de Neuville; a translated and abridged version by Frances Johnson is titled *Memoirs of Bar-on Hyde de Neuville: Outlaw, Exile, Ambassador*, 2 vols. (1913). *Memoirs of John Quincy Adams*, edited by Charles Francis Adams, vols. 5, 6 (1875), contains anecdotes and descriptions of the baroness. Her American visits are detailed in Wayne Andrews, "The Baroness Was Never Bored," *New York Historical Society Quarterly* 38 (1954):105–17. Some papers and letters related to

the couple's New Brunswick days are available at NJ-RU. Her artwork is described in William Fenton, "The Hyde de Neuville Portraits of New York Savages in 1807–1808," *New York Histor-ical Society Quarterly* 38 (1954):119–37; and William Sturtevant, "Patagonian Giants and Baroness Hyde de Neuville's Iroquois Drawings," *Ethnohistory* 27 (1980):331–48.

*Maggie Sullivan*

## ELIZABETH MILLER KEASBEY, 1828–1852

Elizabeth (Miller) Keasbey, a diarist, lived within the scope of her home and family. She died shortly before her 24th birthday, yet she left a lengthy and detailed corre-spondence with her then fiancé, Anthony Q. Keasbey, which gives a vivid record of her times and social class, her feelings and prospects, and her short life.

Born on September 18, 1828, in Morristown (Morris County), NJ, Keasbey was the second oldest of nine chil-dren in the prestigious Miller family. Her parents were Jacob Welch Miller, the last Whig senator to the U.S. Con-gress from New Jersey, and Mary Louisa (Macculloch) Mil-ler.

Keasbey's correspondence consists of more than 100 letters, written to or by Anthony, during their extended betrothal from May 1847 to October 1848—while he waited for her to reach her 20th birthday. The correspon-dence includes a number of related letters from family members and friends, which provide insight into the ex-traordinary contacts and experiences of her family and the concerns and details of ordinary domestic life for a young, educated woman of the mid-19th century.

Keasbey was raised in Macculloch Hall, the home of her maternal grandparents, George Perrott Macculloch and LOUISA SANDERSON MACCULLOCH, in Morristown. Community leaders, the Macullochs were surrogate par-ents for Keasbey and her brothers and sisters as congres-sional duty called Senator Miller and his wife to Trenton and Washington, D.C., for long periods. George Mac-culloch, a Scotsman educated at Edinburgh University, presided over the children's primary education. Keasbey then attended Mme. Chegaray's Boarding School in New York City, the same school where her mother was edu-cated. She confessed to her fiancé that she would have liked to go to college, but that was unheard of for women of her day, and it was her brothers who had that privilege. Still, her letters show that she was very well educated: she was literate and graceful in her self-expression, and her spelling and construction were perfect. She read Dickens and Longfellow, as well as philosophical and religious tracts.

Keasbey's correspondence is brimming with lively ac-counts of the activities of her social milieu, with the letters depicting outings by wagon and carriage to natural sites, long rides to enjoy beautiful sunsets and walks in the moonlight. The letters recount gatherings in the parlor to play games such as jackstraws and long talks by firelight. Several hint at private moments together, of kisses and embraces exchanged in an era noted for circumspect lives.

The letters also tell of travel by a variety of means in the "cars" (trains), by horseback, steamboat, and carriage. One letter describes the plush interior of a new steamship and gives the names of fellow travelers who, as in much of the correspondence, included important political personages of the day. Some letters include accounts of meetings with and opinions on such people as Henry Clay, Daniel Webster, and Dolley Madison. Finally, the letters discuss every decision, every choice, and every step in the construction of the young couple's new home, including the colors and patterns of carpets, style of furniture, and fireplace mantels. They detail where these were purchased, how they were shipped, and what they cost.

The letters grow in interest as they document Keasbey's gradual acceptance and then embrace of the idea of a new life in her husband's hometown of Salem (Salem County), NJ, where he had begun to practice law.

Though Keasbey wrote of being poor in relation to wealthier friends, she grew up in a family comfortable enough to retain servants. But life was duty, and in addition to religious and charitable works there were chores for all, including caring for the younger children, nursing the sick, sewing, picking produce and fruit, and putting up preserves. Although accorded time to travel with a friend's family as far as Boston and Northampton, MA, the summer before her wedding, Keasbey was only free as long as her mother could "spare" her.

Keasbey's correspondence speaks tellingly of the lack of autonomy in her life. She had no privacy; she could only write to her fiancé when neither father nor grandfather was disposed to use "the office." She often wrote of being "sent to bed"—even at the age of nineteen—before finishing a letter. On her 20th birthday, just one month before she was to be married, she was not "allowed" to stay at home for a private moment to write to Anthony, but was "obliged" to accompany the family on a social call. Anthony's personal letters to her were usually addressed to her father, on the line above her name.

The family was religious, and Keasbey was evidently considered especially good and beloved, being referred to often as "our dear Lizzie." In 1847 she wrote to Anthony that she had intended to be a spinster so as to devote herself to good works. At this early point in their sixteen-month courtship there began a theme that persisted throughout the letters: her anxiety about love and marriage. "I believe it was as you told me," she wrote in June of that year. "I unconsciously reasoned myself away from loving you because I persuaded myself it was better that I should not, my 'old maid's education' had unfitted me for

it." This comment shows her torn between her feelings for Anthony, which clearly confused and upset her, and her concern over where her destiny lay. She felt disloyal to her family, to a sister who was also in love with Anthony, and worried about her duty, both to her family and to her God. She resolved this dilemma by deciding that to marry Anthony *was* her duty.

During this period she felt foreboding, which is typical of a 19th-century woman's concern with the dangers implicit in marriage and childbirth. Keasbey's letters reflect a growth from fearful, reluctant fiancée, embarrassed by her feelings and keeping her ardent suitor away for months at a time, to a confident and happy bride-to-be. But traces of reticence recurred: she suggested putting the wedding off again, within three weeks of the date.

The Keasbeys were married on October 18, 1848, in St. Peter's Church in Morristown. Her first child, Edward Quinton, was born in 1849, and she was pregnant during most of the last four years of her life. The children who followed were George Macculloch and Elizabeth Miller (b. June 1852).

Little else is known of those years, except what Keasbey stated in one stained, unfinished letter written eight days after her marriage in which she comments sadly to a friend on how "strange" her new life is.

She died in Salem on August 14, 1852, two months after the birth of her daughter, and was taken back to be buried at St. Peter's Church in Morristown. The entry in the church record book for August 16 reads: "Mrs. Anthony Q. Keasbey, daughter of the Hon. J. W. & Mary L. Miller, was this day buried in the Cemetary [*sic*]. She died at Salem, N.J. on the 14th inst. Aged 24 yrs. in Sept. next."

The Keasbey correspondence is in the Archives of Macculloch Hall Museum (Morristown, NJ). The family's history is covered in John Langstaff, *New Jersey Generations: Macculloch Hall, Morristown* (1964), and in a booklet by the Junior League of Morristown, *Macculloch Hall: A Family Album* (1980).

*Jane B. Rawlings*

## ELIZABETH CLEMENTINE DODGE STEDMAN KINNEY, 1810–1889

The product of two notable literary families, Elizabeth Clementine (Dodge) Stedman Kinney, poet and essayist, was born in New York City on December 18, 1810. Kinney was the sixth of seven children of David Low Dodge, a prominent merchant and renowned Presbyterian author of theological works, and Sarah (Cleveland) Dodge, daughter of the Rev. Aaron Cleveland, a poet of the Colonial period. Through her mother, Kinney was also related to President Grover Cleveland and Colonel Thomas Wentworth Higginson, a literary critic and writer who was a friend and mentor of Emily Dickinson. Kinney's brother William Earl Dodge became a merchant and, like his father, a well-known religious philanthropist.

Although educated in New York City, Kinney resided in Connecticut for part of her childhood because her father supervised mercantile interests there. During these early years, she was already honing her creative powers through poetry. In 1830, at age nineteen, she married Colonel Edmund Burke Stedman of Hartford, a lumber merchant and major in the Governor's Foot Guard for many years. The couple had a daughter, Julia Clementine, who died in infancy, and two sons, Edmund C. Stedman, who later became a poet and literary critic, and Charles F. Stedman. The family lived in Hartford until Colonel Stedman's death at sea in 1835.

After Stedman's death Kinney and her boys moved to "Cedar Brook," her father's country home near Plainfield, NJ. The rural atmosphere reawakened her lifelong love of nature, and she began to contribute verse to the *Knickerbocker* under the name of Mrs. E. C. Stedman. *Graham's Periodical*, *Sartain's*, and *Blackwood's Magazine* also published her work.

Such exposure not only won her a reading public, but also so intrigued William Burnet Kinney that he sought her acquaintance. As a result, in 1841 the young widow married Kinney, who had given up his law studies to pursue a career in journalism and was founder and editor of the *Newark Daily Advertiser*.

During the first ten years of their marriage, the couple resided in Newark, NJ, where Kinney bore two daughters, Elizabeth Clementine and Mary Burnet. She also submitted poems and critical essays to her husband's paper and to other periodicals.

In 1850 William Kinney was appointed U.S. chargé d'affaires to Sardinia. The couple resided in Turin, Italy, until 1853, during which time Kinney's liveliness and wit ensured her popularity at the court of King Victor Emmanuel II. When the mission at Sardinia ended the couple moved to Florence, where they lived for the next twelve years. Because of her artistic and social reputation, Kinney welcomed such eminent figures as Elizabeth Barrett and Robert Browning, Charles and Frederick Tennyson, Anthony and Frances Trollope, Mary Somerville, Hiram Powers, Buchanan Read, and the young Bulwer Lytton to her literary receptions in the Casa del Bello. With such associates it is not surprising that her own creative work increased during this period. *Felicita: A Metrical Romance*, presumably based on a true incident in which a miserly man sells his daughter into slavery, was published in 1855. *Bianca Cappello: A Tragedy*, a second romance in verse, involves a protagonist caught between her obsession with power and her passions; it was published in 1873. Both works illustrate Kinney's love of adventure, color, and action. These two romances, as well as her short verse, great-

ly conformed to the popular taste of the time. One of her most reprinted short poems is "To an Italian Beggar Boy," which her son Edmund included in his *Library of American Literature*. The ready compassion expressed toward the child's lot—

Thine is the famished cry
Of a young heart unfed
Thy hollow spirit's sigh
For something more than bread. (stanza 5)

could not fail to appeal to her readers' sentimental side. Nature poems, such as "To an Eagle," reflect an aesthetic eagerness that many of her contemporary critics found pleasing and unaffected.

Kinney also was a regular correspondent for her husband's Newark newspaper, reporting on art and manners in Italy. She kept a journal recounting her impressions of the country and the people with whom she associated, and these efforts were particularly significant, for they extended her reputation for provocative observations and gentle wit. In fact, her travel pieces proved so estimable that they were reprinted in London and Edinburgh journals. Modern readers will find these works of special interest because of her keen insight into cultural differences and her appreciation of 19th-century European manners.

Of interest, also, are her revelatory accounts of the relationship between the Brownings and her husband and herself. Although her first impression of Elizabeth Barrett Browning was disappointment, the popular poet became her intimate friend. Kinney found Robert Browning entertaining and unsentimental, but she agreed with the popular Victorian view of his poetry as "obscure." Her unfinished manuscript "Personal Reminiscences" is filled with such anecdotes as a lively dispute between herself and the Brownings over George Sand's lifestyle and an attempt by Kinney and Elizabeth Barrett Browning to disguise themselves as male students to gain entrance to a monastery and view its art. The cholera epidemic of 1856, the obsequious behavior of the young Bulwer Lytton toward Robert Browning, a seance attended by the Kinneys at the home of Frances Trollope, and Elizabeth Barrett Browning's death in 1861—all are described in concise yet vivid detail. Her writing shows a devotion to accuracy and to understanding her friends and her experiences through retrospection.

When she and her husband returned to Newark in 1865, Kinney tried to collect her prolific verse into one volume. An edition entitled *Poems* was published in 1867. Because her work was so widely disseminated to various periodicals and newspapers from the 1830s to the 1850s, however, there were many omissions. *Poems* was well received by the critics and the public. In her later years, Kinney worked on a manuscript she called "Personal Reminiscences," which she planned to publish as part of her autobiography. But when William Kinney died in 1880, she took up residence with her daughter, Julia Easton, in Summit and never finished the project. She spent her final years peacefully, submitting pieces to magazines occasionally. She died at her daughter's home on November 19, 1889, shortly before her 79th birthday, and was buried in Woodlawn Cemetery in New York.

Manuscript copies of Kinney's unpublished journal and "Personal Reminiscences" are kept at NY-CU. A biographical sketch of her appears in *DAB* 10 (1933) and an assessment of her writing appears in *American Women Writers* 2 (1980). Her obituary appeared in the *Newark Daily Advertiser*, Nov. 20, 1889, and in the *New York Times*, Nov. 21, 1889.

*Laura M. Gabrielsen*

## JARENA LEE, 1783–unknown

Jarena Lee, the first known woman preacher in the African Methodist Episcopal Church (AMEC), was born to free African-American parents in Cape May (Cape May County), NJ, on February 11, 1783. Her birth name and the names of her parents are unknown. She had at least one sister. At age seven, she was sent 60 miles from Cape May to be a house servant.

In 1804, when Lee was 21, she experienced a spiritual awakening during a Presbyterian service in a Cape May schoolroom. Deeply convinced of her sinful nature, Lee felt driven by Satan to commit suicide, but believed that "the unseen arm of God . . . saved me from self murder." (Andrews, *Sisters of the Spirit*, 28) Wishing to learn more about the Christian faith, she began to read the Bible and visit churches of various denominations. About 1805, when she was employed as a house servant in Philadelphia, she attended a service at Bethel Church, the center of African-American Methodism in the United States. There she heard a sermon by the Rev. Richard Allen, a leader of the black Methodist movement, and was moved by his preaching to join the Methodist denomination.

Three weeks later she had a dramatic conversion experience during which she testified before the entire congregation to her conviction that "God, for Christ's sake, had pardoned the sins of my soul." (Andrews, 29) Lee's conversion was typical of the religious experience of early 19th-century American revivalism, when thousands of persons were converted in an atmosphere of intense emotionalism, often accompanied by visions, dreams, and temporary debility or illness. In the Methodist tradition, both women and men were expected to testify in public, describing their conversion experiences and urging other sinners to repent and be saved. Thus Methodist women were accustomed to speaking in church, despite biblical and traditional injunctions against women speaking during public worship.

from Lith by A Hoffy.                                          Printed by PSDuv

## MRS JARENA LEE.

*Preacher of the A. M, E, Church .*

*Aged 60 years on the 11th day of the 2nd month 1844.*

Jarena Lee, in 1843, at the age of 60. Lee was the first known woman preacher in the African Methodist Episcopal Church. *Courtesy, the Library Company of Philadelphia.*

For the next several years, Lee struggled with doubts about her faith and felt herself tempted by the devil to abandon her beliefs. At times she became nearly overwhelmed by the knowledge of her sinfulness and her inability to feel the saving grace of Christ, although she understood the concept intellectually. Finally, after praying, studying Scripture, and seeking counsel from pastors and friends, Lee was baptized.

A short time after her baptism (probably in 1807), Lee met William Scott, a pious Methodist layman who introduced her to the idea of sanctification, which John Wesley, the founder of Methodism, had preached. Scott explained that Methodists recognized three stages of an individual's spiritual journey: conviction that one was a sinner; the faith that one was saved from sin by Christ's atoning death (justification); and the certainty that one's soul was entirely consecrated to God (sanctification). Confident that she had experienced the first two stages of her spiritual journey, Lee earnestly prayed that she might be sanctified.

After another period of intense spiritual struggle, Lee suddenly felt herself sanctified: "That very instant, as if lightning had darted through me, I sprang to my feet and cried, 'The Lord has sanctified my soul!' There was none to hear this but the angels who stood around to witness my joy—and Satan, whose malice raged the more. . . . I now ran into the house and told them what had happened to me, when, as it were, a new rush of the same ecstasy came upon me, and caused me to feel as if I were in an ocean of light and bliss. During this, I stood perfectly still, the tears rolling in a flood from my eyes. So great was the joy, that it is past description." (Andrews, 34)

About four years after Lee experienced sanctification (probably 1811), she felt called by God to preach. Overcoming her initial reluctance, she went to Rev. Richard Allen and told him of her call. He replied that there was a precedent for Methodist women to lead prayer meetings and exhort (speak briefly after the sermon at the invitation of the preacher, calling listeners to repentance), but that the denomination did not allow women to preach. Lee was momentarily relieved to hear this since it meant that she would not have to defy prejudices against women preaching. But almost immediately she experienced great internal pressure to preach, which continued during the next eight years.

In 1811 Lee married Joseph Lee (also spelled Lea), the pastor of a black Methodist church in Snow Hill (now Lawnside), NJ, six miles from Philadelphia. Lonely and unhappy in her new home, Lee tried to persuade her husband to move to Philadelphia. But God appeared to her in a dream, indicating that her husband's congregation needed his ministry, and Lee was content to stay in Snow Hill.

Over the next six years, Lee buried five members of her family, one of them her husband, reported dead by 1818. She was left with two small children to support, a two-year-old and an infant of six months. Her sense of God's abiding presence gave her strength, and she provided for her children by teaching school.

Sometime between 1811 and 1819 Lee had obtained permission to be an exhorter from Allen, now a bishop in the African Methodist Episcopal Church. (By 1816 the AMEC had become a black denomination, officially separated from the Methodist Episcopal Church.) But Lee only rarely received invitations by preachers to exhort during their services. By 1821 she was allowed to lead prayer meetings in a house she rented for that purpose. According to her autobiography, Lee was a powerful and popular prayer meeting leader whose gatherings were well attended. But the roles of exhorter and prayer leader did not satisfy Lee, who still strongly desired to preach.

One Sunday during a sermon at Bethel Church, Lee interrupted the preacher, jumping up and exhorting the congregation without his invitation. She spoke movingly of her call to preach, explaining that she had waited many years for the opportunity. She described the response to her exhortation: "I now sat down, scarcely knowing what I had done, being frightened. I imagined that for this indecorum, as I feared it might be called, I should be expelled from the church. But instead of this . . . Bishop [Allen] rose up in the assembly, and related that I had called upon him eight years before, asking to be permitted to preach, and that he had put me off; but that he now as much believed that I was called to that work, as any of the preachers present." (Andrews, 44–45)

This moving public endorsement of Lee's preaching ability by the acknowledged leader of the AME denomination launched her on an evangelistic career lasting over three decades. Like many other 19th-century evangelical revival preachers—black and white, female and male—Lee traveled thousands of miles from Canada to the Mid-Atlantic states and on to the frontier in western New York and Ohio. She often preached several times a day, moving from church to church wherever people gathered to hear her. By her simple yet dramatic preaching style she gained many converts and thus many invitations to lead revival meetings.

Lee described her preaching career in her autobiography, which she paid to have published in 1836 and distributed at camp meetings. An expanded version of her autobiography appeared in 1849. These volumes document many preaching engagements in New Jersey towns, including Trenton, Princeton, Burlington, Salem, Woodstock, and Snow Hill. She was able to return to see her parents in Cape May several times, combining visits with preaching in nearby churches. For a time her mother looked after Lee's young, ailing son while she continued her preaching mission.

No records of Lee's life after 1849 have been discovered and the date of her death is unknown. According to local legend, Lee and her husband, Joseph, were buried in unmarked graves near the present Mt. Pisgah AME Church at Lawnside (formerly Snow Hill).

Like many other 19th-century AMEC women preachers, Lee was not granted a license to preach and thus was not officially recognized by the denomination as a minister. But along with several other AMEC women evangelists active during the century in New Jersey—among them Rachel Evans, Margaret Wilson, Emily Calkins Stevens, and world-renowned revivalist Amanda Berry Smith—Lee, the first known woman preacher in the AME tradition, helped to open the way for a larger role for women within the denomination.

Jarena Lee's first autobiographical account, *The Life and Religious Experience of Jarena Lee . . .* (1836), is reprinted in William L. Andrews, ed., *Sisters of the Spirit* (1986). An expanded version of the autobiography, *Religious Experience and Journal of Mrs. Jarena Lee . . .* (1849), is available in the American Theological Librarians Association Microfiche Series, *Women and the Church.* Additional information on Lee appears in Hilah Thomas and Rosemary Skinner Keller, eds., *Women in New Worlds: Historical Perspectives on the Wesleyan Tradition*, vol. 1 (1981). Jean B. Williams, "Jarena Lee Was First Woman Preacher in A.M.E. Church," *Philadelphia Tribune*, Feb. 15, 1977, summarizes Lee's career.

*Constance Killian Escher*
*Carolyn DeSwarte Gifford*

## LOUISA SANDERSON MACCULLOCH, 1785–1863

Louisa Martha Edwina (Sanderson) Macculloch was a woman of obscure origins who became the leader of two early women's benevolent associations in Morristown (Morris County), NJ. She is believed to have been born in England in 1785, but nothing is known directly of her parents or her early life. Her letters show that she had some education.

A family tradition suggests she was an actress when she met George Perrott Macculloch, whom she married on August 17, 1804, at St. Luke's, Finsbury, in London. In 1806 her husband retired from business on the continent, and the couple settled in the United States with their two children, Francis Law Macculloch, said to have been baptized in Clerkenwell Parish on October 18, 1801, and Mary Louisa, said to have been born on May 20, 1804. After a brief stay in New York City, they built a large home in Morristown called Macculloch Hall. Here they settled in 1809 and established a family that became active in the leadership of local, statewide, and national affairs for five generations.

Macculloch and her husband raised their own children and nine grandchildren in their home, a large Georgian house on a farmstead that produced many of the family's provisions. Family letters speak of Macculloch supervising servants and cooperating in domestic chores, picking fruits, canning and sewing, and cutting up a side of beef. She also helped her husband run the Macculloch Hall Academy for boys from 1815 to its demise in 1830, while pursuing her own activities within the community. She was a religious woman, who set high religious and moral standards for her family by instruction and example. Since there was no Anglican church in Morristown at the time, she attended the Presbyterian church, occasionally taking her children to New York City to attend services. She is credited with the founding of several churches that held services at Macculloch Hall.

This zeal encouraged Macculloch, like many other women of her time, to join in organizing such groups as the Female Charitable Society (1813) and the Fragment Society (1829). Though relatively prosperous during the economic upheavals of the post–Revolutionary War period, Morristown had poor people among its population. The founders of the Female Charitable Society might well have wished to spare them the humiliation imposed by the poor relief laws of the time of wearing a pauper badge (a large red or blue *P*) on the shoulder.

Macculloch's leadership of the Female Charitable Society had far-reaching implications. When she became its "second directress" (or vice-president) in 1819, a businesslike approach already characterized every aspect of the society, which was one of dozens of similar organizations founded to meet community needs in the first decades of the 19th century. The founders of the Morristown Society, all members of the Presbyterian Church, had first met in the home of their minister and his wife. They elected a first and second directress to head the society and provided for recorded meetings, dues, rules for participation, and a plan for the society's activities. They raised funds through dues and individual donations, charity sermons, collections at church services, and benefit theater performances at the Morristown Academy.

Following the pattern of the earlier Newark Society, the Female Charitable Society of Morristown appointed volunteer "managers." These were women like Macculloch, drawn from the membership to identify "the aged, the lame, the sickly dependent on aged parents, the widow with children, the widow not able to work," and to minister to them for the society. The managers purchased staple foods, meals, fuel, household items, or clothing for their charges. Later they provided cloth or raw materials such as cotton or "linsey-woolsey" to be spun and woven into cloth. They offered relief to some by employing them in spinning or weaving cloth to be provided for others. In Macculloch's 1820 annual report as second directress the society had "relieved seventy persons," distributed 131 yards of cloth paid for with $98.36 in subscription, dues, donations, and the proceeds of spinning "shoe thread," sewing thread, and carpet yarn. By 1838, under Macculloch's direction, the society owned sheets, pillowcases, nightgowns, and caps, and the minutes note the loan of a "comfortable" to "Biddy at Mr. Collins'."

Macculloch became first directress of the society in 1830 and held this post for the next 33 years. During that time Morristown—the county seat at the center of a growing area with a well-balanced economy—grew steadily, and with it the Female Charitable Society's role. In early years the records had noted relief to named individuals, mostly widows with children, including whites and freed blacks. Later the list included unnamed Irish families, reflecting the increasing numbers of immigrants to small American cities during the middle of the century.

The Female Charitable Society continued in its basic pattern throughout the 19th century. Over the last 90 years it has evolved to become a fully professional organization, known today as the Family Service of Morris County. Macculloch's strong and consistent leadership prepared the society to carry on into the 20th century.

During her years with the Female Charitable Society, Macculloch was also the directress of the Fragment Society, a little-known benevolent society that she helped organize in August 1829 to produce, from fragments of leftover cloth, "articles to be sold at a fair once a year." The proceeds were donated toward the construction of Presbyterian churches in nearby towns and toward projects connected with Morristown church and civic causes. Macculloch was still the directress in 1835, when the records of the organization stop.

Macculloch died suddenly on December 28, 1863, after years of community service. She had been reelected first directress of the Female Charitable Society that November. The society's records hold a poignant tribute: "the recent sudden death of our much lamented 1st Directress Mrs. McCulloch [sic], the Managers had no meeting—We mourn our loss—Mrs. McCulloch had been our 1st Directress for 33 years." She was buried in the churchyard at St. Peter's Church, Morristown, which she had helped organize in Macculloch Hall many years before.

Much of the biographical information on Macculloch comes from John Langstaff, *New Jersey Generations: Macculloch Hall, Morristown* (1964). Other useful sources are the Junior League of Morristown, *Macculloch Hall: A Family Album* (1980), and *A History of Morris County* (1914). Manuscript collections on the Macculloch family are available at NJ-MO, Macculloch Hall, and the NY-PL. Information on Macculloch's social welfare activities appears in the *Minutes of the Female Charitable Society*, available at the NJ-MO; and in Edwin Be, *Family Service of Morris County, New Jersey: A Historical Case Study* (1963).

*Jane B. Rawlings*

## MARY PAUL, 1830–unknown

Mary Stiles (Paul) Guild was born on January 26, 1830, to Bela and Mary (Briggs) Paul in Barnard, VT. From 1854 to 1855 Paul was one of the few single female members of the North American Phalanx, a utopian community in Monmouth County, NJ.

She lived away from home from the time she was fifteen. Her mother died when she was ten, leaving herself, her father, and three brothers (two older and one younger). Paul first worked as a domestic servant in a neighboring town, but disagreement with her employer led her to seek employment in the textile mills in Lowell, MA, where she lived at a company boardinghouse run by her future mother-in-law. On and off for the next four years she worked in the textile mills, returning to her father's home in Claremont, NH, in 1850. Two years later she was residing in Brattleboro, VT, working as a seamstress to support herself.

Her correspondence with her father over a seventeen-year period documents both her connections to her family and her efforts to provide for herself and to "work where I can get more pay." Her letters clearly indicate that as an independent, unmarried young woman in antebellum America, she felt both the pull of family and the need to assert her independence. Her continuing quest for self-reliance brought her to New Jersey in 1854.

That year, an invitation from friends she met while working in Lowell brought her to New Jersey to reside at the North American Phalanx, a utopian community near Red Bank based on the teachings of Charles Fourier. The Phalanx was founded in 1843 by a group of Albany Associationists. By 1844 they purchased a farm in Atlantic Township, and about seven families took up residence. The community was in its waning years when Paul became a member, even though it had survived from 1843 to 1855, longer than other Fourierist communities.

For single women like Paul the community offered security, food, shelter, and an opportunity to work. Shortly after her arrival, in May 1854, she began to work in the kitchen and dining room and to do some sewing. By October she was working as a seamstress, sewing men's stocks that were sold at the Phalanx store in New York City. She worked an average of six hours a day and figured that at the North American Phalanx she could do as well as or better than she could do in the outside economy.

Fourierist or Associationist communities were organized as joint-stock, cooperative ventures. (See REBECCA BUFFUM SPRING) Each member invested in the stock of the community and was supplied with food, clothing, and shelter. Because Paul joined the community late in its existence, she was most likely a probationary member when the community disbanded and therefore may not have purchased stock. Housing was supplied communally. Each family received an apartment and single individuals were allotted dormitory space in the Phalanstery, a large residential building that included communal dining and recreational areas in addition to sleeping space.

The central philosophy of the Phalanx lay in the division of work. Work was organized according to groups and series. Ideally individuals, male or female, had free choice among the different work groups. At the North American Phalanx, some of the major work groups were manufacturing, agriculture, domestic, and festal. Paul was one of the few female members of the manufacturing work group. According to Fourier's plan, members would have to work only about four hours each day and could vary their tasks from one work group to another, based on their interests.

The remainder of the time could be devoted to intellectual or artistic improvement or recreational activities. Financial profits from the community were distributed according to a member's stock holdings. In theory, the community was designed to free women from the drudgery of housekeeping and child rearing by making these tasks communal responsibilities, thus opening their intellectual and artistic talents to society.

Only about seven single women over the age of sixteen resided at the Phalanx. The total population in the community at its peak was a little greater than 100 individuals. Criticism from the outside, especially from some conservative members of the religious community who equated communal living with sexual permissiveness, may have been a deterrent to some. The accepted female role of wife, mother, and spiritual center of the nuclear family came into question in the communal setting, prompting editorials and magazine articles condemning the communities. Young women themselves wrote articles cautioning their counterparts to avoid joining communal ventures. Notwithstanding the difficulties of finding adequate employment as a single woman, cultural pressures to conform to the accepted female role most likely reduced the number of single women who applied for membership.

The community suffered the loss of many of its manufacturing and agricultural buildings in a fire late in 1854 and consequently had to disband. Within a year's time, the land was sold and the membership dispersed. Paul was forced to leave and found work as a housekeeper in New Hampshire. By that time, however, she had become a true Associationist and promoted the Fourierist plan in her correspondence to her father.

She married Isaac Orr Guild, the son of her boardinghouse keeper from Lowell, on October 7, 1857, and lived in Lynn, MA, where her husband was a marble worker. She bore two sons, Irving Tracy (b. 1860) and Sydney Paul (b. 1862). The family remained in Lynn until 1894, when it moved to Cambridge, MA. Whether Paul was still alive when this move was made is not known. No record of her death has been found.

The letters of Mary Paul are located at V-HS. For material on the North American Phalanx, see Dolores Hayden, *Seven American Utopias* (1976); and Herman Belz, "The North American Phalanx: Experiment of Socialism," *NJHSP* 81 (1963):215–46. For a resident's account of the Phalanx, see Charles Sears, *The North American Phalanx* (1886). The *Proceedings of the North American Phalanx* are available at NJ-MoCHA and contain information about daily life in the community.

*Dorothy White Hartman*

## MARTHA AUSTIN REEVES, 1760–1832

Midwife Martha (Austin) Reeves was born April 9, 1760, the daughter of Cornelius and Ruhama (Sheppard) Austin. Married on or shortly after November 19, 1777, to John Reeves of Hopewell Township (Cumberland County), NJ, Martha gave birth to six children who lived to adulthood: Cornelius, David, Hannah, Ruth, Mary, and John. Reeves very likely began her midwifery work in her thirties, for by her fortieth birthday she had attended close to 200 childbirths, mostly in and around the townships of Shiloh and Hopewell in Cumberland County. Hers was a lifelong calling, begun while she still had children to care for at home and continuing long after she was widowed, at age 51, and left to care for her chronically ill daughter Mary.

Little is known about the private life of midwife Reeves. In the sparse record she left behind, she resembles most other American midwives, indeed most other women in America. The midwifery and nursing work she did during nearly her entire adult life was rarely publicly recognized as wage or career work likely to be included in a town history. Thus, though women such as Reeves might be well-known and highly regarded members of communities even into the 20th century in America, they were rarely acknowledged as valued community servants as were others doing comparable work, such as physicians. Midwives' work and life histories are consequently unlikely to be recorded in the various public records kept by towns and municipalities—town histories, newspaper reports, and extended obituaries. We learn about them when private sources such as diaries or family letters come to light; from these sources, combined with whatever traces can be found in public records such as wills and death certificates, we can piece together the contours of their life and work.

Midwife Reeves left behind a *Record Book of Births*, which she kept as a Cumberland County midwife, a record that has proven very useful to amateur and professional genealogists. In it she included the names of those whose births she attended along with one of their parents' names, as well as a few recipes for preparations used for the ills she was frequently called upon to treat—colds, fevers, and "the bloody flux." Reeves also listed the services she rendered from 1801 to 1832 and the fees she presumably collected. Her usual fee for attending a birth was $2.00, although she occasionally charged $2.50 or $3.00, average fees among town and rural midwives of the period. Also typical of 19th-century midwives' practices were Reeves's nursing duties. Many of her *Record Book* entries indicate that she was called to bring her homemade ointments, pills, and syrups along in her nursing visits to the community's men, women, and children. For most of the remedies she offered, Reeves charged from 12 to 36 cents. For a nursing visit, she usually charged 25 or 50 cents.

During her 40-year career, Reeves averaged close to 30 childbirths a year. By the time of her death in August 1832, at age 72, she had attended over a thousand births and had nursed a comparable number of Cumberland County's sick and ailing.

Reeves' *Record Book of Births* is reprinted as "Martha Reeves Record Book of Births, 1801–1831," *Vineland Historical Magazine* 24 (1939):247–52; 264–67; 25 (1940):27–35, 57–63, 90–103.

*Janet Carlisle Bogdan*
*Linda Holmes*

## LILLY MARTIN SPENCER, 1822–1902

Lilly (Martin) Spencer, one of the most popular American painters of the mid-19th century, was born Angelique Marie Martin on November 26, 1822, in Exeter, England. Her parents, Gilles Marie and Angelique Perrine (Le Petit) Martin, were natives of Brittany, France. Both were teachers of French and emigrated to England, where her father taught at the famous Exeter Boys' Academy. With the idea of establishing a utopian colony according to the precepts of the French social critic Charles Fourier, they sailed for America in 1830, taking with them their eldest daughter, nicknamed "Lilly" (also spelled "Lily" and "Lilli"), and their two sons, Henri Gilles and Charles François. Another daughter, Marie Henriette, was born in December 1831, soon after their arrival.

In New York, Spencer's father resumed his teaching, but in 1831 an outbreak of cholera induced the Martins to seek a healthier climate in the West. They settled in Marietta, OH, where Spencer's father doubled as a farmer and a professor. The farmhouse was five miles out of town, and Spencer was educated at home. The Martins had an extensive library containing the works of Shakespeare and other classics, which later became sources of inspiration for Spencer's paintings and drawings. The intellectual atmosphere that permeated her early years was fostered by her parents' active involvement in abolitionism, the temperance movement, and women's rights. Although the Martins did not found a utopian community, their home, which was free from stifling conventions, served as a springboard for Spencer's artistic career.

Spencer's artistic beginnings are steeped in legend. One account relates that her decoration of the plaster walls of her family's farmhouse with charcoal drawings became something of a tourist attraction. These murals were brought to the attention of the local press and Spencer's career was launched.

In the summer of 1841 an exhibition in Marietta of Spencer's work attracted the attention of Nicholas Longworth, a patron of contemporary American artists. Spencer declined both his offer to send her to Boston to study with Washington Allston and his subsequent offer to send her abroad to study. This was, however, the beginning of a lifelong friendship.

In November 1841, accompanied by her father, Spencer went to Cincinnati, a leading art center. There she met with Longworth, whose private collections included Dutch works, sculptures, and a large painting by Benjamin West. Confident that his daughter could establish herself in the metropolis, Gilles Martin returned to Marietta. At a time when the prevailing social conventions made it difficult for women to make professional commitments of any kind, Spencer was a rare example of an independent woman.

After a period of financial hardship, Spencer became a successful portrait painter. Within three years of her arrival in Cincinnati she married Benjamin Rush Spencer. A husband and a helpmate, Benjamin Spencer prepared her canvases, managed her business affairs, and shared in the housework and care of their thirteen children, seven of whom lived to maturity.

Within two years of her marriage, Spencer was recognized as one of the finest artists in Cincinnati. By the late summer of 1848 she felt ready to take on New York, a mecca for many mid-19th-century artists.

In April 1858, when Spencer was 35 years old, she and her family moved to 461 High Street in Newark, NJ, where the growing family sought to supplement their income by raising chickens and planting a garden. Another compelling reason for choosing to live in Newark was the interest of Nicholas Longworth, who had recognized Spencer's genius when she was a girl of seventeen. Longworth was a relative of Marcus L. Ward, a prominent New Jersey patron of American artists and later the governor of New Jersey (1866–69), who rented the High Street property to the Spencers. Ward commissioned portraits of his children, and these paintings established Spencer's reputation as a mature and serious artist. Two years later the Spencers moved to 294 High Street, Newark, where they lived for the next nineteen years.

The Ward portraits remain examples of Spencer at her best and are significant examples of 19th-century art. In 1939 the group portrait *Children of Marcus L. Ward* (Newark Museum Collection) was included in the Metropolitan Museum of Art's retrospective exhibition of 300 years of American art. It was considered important enough to be illustrated in the exhibition catalog, but was erroneously attributed to Thomas R. Read. The portrait *Nicholas Longworth Ward* (Newark Museum Collection), another son who was named after Ward's uncle, is an equally accomplished painting. The posthumous nature of the portrait is indicated by the dead flowers in the beautifully painted silver vase, inscribed with the subject's name.

Without the knowledge of these works by Spencer, scholars and critics of 19th-century art have considered Spencer solely a genre painter. Her genre paintings, in which she used her own family as models for domestic scenes, reflected 19th-century tastes and Spencer's eco-

Artist Lilly Martin Spencer lived for many years in Newark, where she rendered this accomplished oil portrait of the children of Marcus L. Ward in 1858. *Courtesy, Collection of the Newark Museum.*

nomic need to cater to these tastes. But two paintings of the New Jersey experience, both of which stress the reporting of events, illustrate her genius in transcending the sentimentality of the Victorian age. *The War Spirit at Home: Celebrating the Victory of Vicksburg* (Newark Museum Collection) contrasts the unreality of war as seen through the eyes of children, who turn it into a game, with the sober reflection of the mother and the housemaid, who, at battle's end, remain fully aware of the horrors of war. *The Picnic or the Fourth of July: A Day to Be Remembered* (Library of Congress Collection), like many other paintings by Spencer, was reproduced as hand-tinted lithographs. Family tradition reports that its setting was near Newark, possibly a Passaic River locale.

With her departure from New Jersey for New York City in 1870, Spencer's artistic career began to fade when it seemed at its brightest. She had just completed *Truth Unveiling Falsehood* (private collection), a large allegorical painting that was exhibited in France. But changes in popular aesthetic tastes forced her career into eclipse. The American Civil War shattered the sense of optimism that had created a demand for her paintings, works that illustrated reassuring moments of family life. By this time Spencer had already produced a large enough body of work to assure her a place in the history of American art. The Ward portraits have earned her a niche among the best American portrait painters.

Spencer was widowed in 1890 and spent her last days in New York City. She estimated that she had painted over a thousand canvases. When she died at age 79 on May 22, 1902, she was living at 910 Columbus Avenue and working at her easel. Spencer is buried in Highland, NY.

For information on Spencer, see Robin Bolton-Smith and William Truettner, *Lily Martin Spencer, 1822–1902: The Joys of Sentiment* (1973); Ann Byrd Schumer, "Lilly Martin Spencer: American Painter of the Nineteenth Century" (M.A. diss., Ohio State University, 1959); and Schumer's "Aspects of Lilly Martin Spencer's Career in Newark, New Jersey," *NJHSP* 77 (1959):244–55. A sketch of Spencer appears in *NAW*.

*Victor Gualano*

## REBECCA BUFFUM SPRING, 1811–1911

Rebecca (Buffum) Spring, Quaker abolitionist and educational reformer, was a sponsor of New Jersey's two most celebrated antebellum communitarian ventures. Born in Providence, RI, on June 8, 1811, she was the fourth of seven children born to Arnold Buffum of Smithfield, RI, and Rebecca (Gould) Buffum of Newport, RI. All four of her grandparents, William and Lydia (Arnold) Buffum and John and Sarah (Coggeshall) Gould, were from New England.

Spring belonged to a politically active family. Her father, a merchant, inventor, and sheep raiser, was the first president of the New England Anti-Slavery Society. Her sister Elizabeth Buffum Chace, active in prison reform, pacifism, and abolition, was an officer of the American Woman Suffrage Association and founder of the Rhode Island Suffrage Association.

Spring spent her childhood in Smithfield and Pomfret, RI, and Fall River, MA. Educated at the Quaker-run Smithfield Academy, she and her sisters organized the Smithfield Female Mutual Improvement Society, a literary club. Two concerns dominated her youth: education and abolition.

She taught at factory schools for mill children in Fall River and Uxbridge, MA, and later in Philadelphia, where the family moved in 1834. At 23, according to her sister, Spring's letters were "throbbing with tender sympathy" for the cause of the slave, and her involvement in integrated Philadelphia schools attested to her growing antislavery sentiments. In 1840 she participated in a Women's Anti-Slavery Convention in Philadelphia, where she met such luminaries as William Lloyd Garrison, Theodore and AN-GELINA GRIMKÉ WELD, and Maria Chapman.

Spring's passion for abolition was shared by Marcus Spring. A dry goods merchant, he was the son of Adolphus and Lydia (Taft) Spring of Uxbridge, MA, where he was born on October 21, 1810. The Springs were married on October 26, 1836, in Philadelphia. They had three children: Edward (b. 1837), Jeanie (b. 1843), and Herbert (b. 1848).

The Springs' collected letters suggest a companionate, egalitarian marriage and a mutuality of interests. Spring worked with her husband on social and political projects, often conducting his business affairs during his absence. Her New York City home soon became a favorite gathering spot for the cultural, political, and literary intelligentsia, and her circle of friends included Christian leaders of various faiths.

Noteworthy was her relationship with Margaret Fuller, who, despite their close friendship, chided Spring for her conventional femininity. In one especially revealing letter, Fuller strongly challenged Spring's conviction that "it is still better to give the world [a] living soul, than a part of [one's] life in a book." (Spring, "Auld Acquaintance," 87) The Springs were accompanied by Fuller on a European tour in 1845, which rekindled Spring's interest in the establishment of a community where, in the words of her granddaughter, "people could live in cleanliness and plenty within a spiritual environment." (Borchardt, "Lady of Utopia," 45) This concern was first awakened during a girlhood spent among factory workers in Fall River. In the early years of her marriage she had hoped to establish a cooperative colony for slum dwellers to foster appreciation of art, music, and the classics. Her husband's eagerness to improve living standards among the urban poor resulted in their sharing the common ideals of two utopian communities, which placed New Jersey in the vanguard of antebellum America's fascination with social reform. These two communities were the North American Phalanx in Red Bank (1843–55) and the Raritan Bay Union in Perth Amboy (1853–59). Although inspired by the French socialist Charles Fourier, the Springs' motivations were primarily philanthropic, entrepreneurial, and religious. Spring's conception of socialism was simplistic. Her decision to become a socialist was made "because the Bible teaches socialism," yet she was convinced that personal property was fundamental to organized society and always remained opposed to communal living.

Although the Springs were the chief stockholders in the Phalanx, Spring resisted moving to the colony. A staunch individualist, she feared too much regimentation. Her sensitivity to women's needs also played a role, for her sister-in-law Lydia Arnold, who supervised the Phalanx's domestic work, was tired and disillusioned by the demands of community life. Women's lot seemed not so different in utopia than in the larger society, for she confided to Rebecca: "We work harder than ever, and I cannot see the advantages in cooperative living." (Borchardt, 48)

The main reason for Spring's distaste for Phalanx life was religious. She seems to have mistaken the Phalanx's climate of religious tolerance and pluralism for irreligion, since she believed that the community lacked sufficient religious spirit. Factionalism over the place of institutionalized religion became so acute that in 1853 a group of dissidents, clustered around the Springs, seceded to form the Raritan Bay Union, located at Eagleswood, an estate in nearby Perth Amboy. The Springs moved to a private residence in the colony.

According to Spring, the Union's central focus was education. Eagleswood School, the progressive, coeducational boarding school established by the Springs, hosted some of the most renowned intellectuals of the day—Thoreau, Emerson, Greeley, Bronson Alcott—who came to the school as visiting lecturers. A remarkable group of women teachers—SARAH MOORE GRIMKÉ and ANGELINA GRIMKÉ WELD, Catharine Ireland, Mary Mann, Elizabeth Palmer Peabody—served as role models for students. The school provided a supportive environment highly conducive to female achievement, with girls encouraged to "speak up" at public gatherings, act in plays, and excel in athletics.

Despite the novelty that surrounded her, Spring persisted in relatively traditional roles; she served as hostess at Sunday evening colloquia and taught in the school. Abolition remained her primary concern. An 1852 trip to Cuba and South Carolina left her revolted by the conditions under which slaves lived and worked. An avid supporter of the new Republican party, she established a station of the "underground railroad" at Eagleswood. Her most celebrated activity was a missionary visit to insurrectionist John Brown after his attack on the federal arsenal at Harpers Ferry, VA, in 1859. Comforting Brown in his last hours, she promised to bury Absolom C. Haslett and Aaron Dwight Stevens, two of his raiders, in free soil. Despite heated local resistance, the burial was conducted at Eagleswood as promised. Thereafter, Eagleswood became a meeting place for Brown sympathizers, and Spring opened her home to Brown's wife.

During the Civil War, Spring and her husband supported a school for slave children in Norfolk, VA. They also financed a soup kitchen to aid the increasing number of fugitives and refugees traveling north in the wake of the Emancipation Proclamation. Eagleswood School was then converted into a military academy. Although Spring had to reconcile herself to the "un-Quakerish" idea of training young boys for military duty, she believed the move was necessary to serve the cause of freedom. She personally supervised the strict codes of religious and moral discipline enforced at the school and played hostess to the continual flow of visitors. Fulfilling her lifelong cultural interests, she was instrumental in creating an art colony on the premises from 1863 to 1867, which hosted such celebrated figures as William Page, George Inness, Louis Tiffany, and James Steele MacKaye.

By the late 1860s the Springs grew tired of caring for the large estate and closed the military academy at the end of 1868. After this Spring busied herself with family and cultural pursuits. She helped her son Edward open his Chautauqua School for Sculpture and Modeling in New York and supported her son Herbert in his venture to offer lessons in singing and terpsichore. After her husband's death on August 21, 1874, she moved to California at the urging of daughter Jeanie, who had made her home there. The experiments in New Jersey, however, were never far from her thoughts. "Poor, dear Eagleswood," she lamented frequently during her last years, " . . . that sacred spot. How we planted and built and spent money there! A noble company gathered to develop a society that would create harmony, love, and usefulness. Now I sit on the grave of great hopes. . . . I look back to see a light that went out from it—small, but bright and pure and true. I believe some holy work is yet to be done through our Eagleswood." (Spring, letter to J. L. Kearney, Oct. 25, 1897)

In California, Spring pursued her literary interests by joining the Los Angeles Friday Morning Club, a women's club organized by her friend Caroline Severance in 1891. She wrote "Auld Acquaintance," her autobiography, at 89, and died in Los Angeles on February 8, 1911, four months short of her 100th birthday.

The Raritan Bay Union Collection at the NJ-HS contains correspondence as well as fragments of her diary and autobiography. The Huntington Library (San Marino, CA) holds the remainder of her papers, as well as the original manuscript of her unpublished autobiography, "Auld Acquaintance" (1900). Her granddaughter, Beatrice Borchardt, wrote "Lady of Utopia" (1970), an unpublished biography available at both NJ-HS and the Huntington Library (San Marino, CA). Contemporary recollections of the Springs appear in niece Little Buffum Chace Wyman's *American Chivalry* (1873) and *Elizabeth Buffum Chace*, 2 vols. (1914); and in Fredrika Bremer, *Homes of the New World* (1853).

*Marie Marmo Mullaney*

## CHARITY STILL, ca. 1775–1857

Charity Still, born Sidney, runaway slave, family and community builder, was born in slavery about 1775. There is no known record of her family name. Still, along with at least three sisters, was raised by her mother on a plantation on the Eastern Shore of Chesapeake Bay in Maryland. When she was a young girl, she watched as her father was shot through the head and killed by a drunken slave master. She vowed then that she would not meet a similar fate; she would not die a slave, but rather would become free. Should she someday have children of her own, they too would live as free men and women.

During the last decade of the 18th century, she married Levin Still, a man who shared her passion for freedom. Her husband's ancestors had arrived in south Jersey, from Guinea, Africa, on a Dutch slave ship during the mid-1600s. Oral and written histories tell how her husband's family developed their own community while yet in slavery and were among the original settlers of Lawnside, NJ, one of the oldest incorporated all-black communities in the country. At some point after the family's arrival in south Jersey several of them were sold south to the Eastern Shore. Thus, according to oral history, some 200 years later, when Still met her husband, included among the remnants of his remembered heritage were the name of a place, New Jersey, and the name of his family, Still. Today, of the thousands of Still descendants who reside in the middle-class suburban community of Lawnside and in the south Jersey area, many share the direct lineage of Charity and Levin Still.

In 1804, when New Jersey passed an abolition bill, Still and her husband vowed to make their way to south Jersey so that their dreams of freedom for themselves and their children could come true. According to oral tradition, news of the New Jersey law had been passed along the underground grapevine.

Declaring to the slave master that "I will die before I submit to the yoke" (W. Still, *Underground Railroad*, 37), Still's husband tried to buy freedom for himself and his family but was unsuccessful. He was allowed to buy his own free papers, but Still was told that she and the children must remain in slavery.

Undaunted, Still pretended to be resolved to the imminent separation of her family. But unknown to the slave master, while her husband worked odd jobs and extra hours to save enough money to purchase his freedom, Still helped lay the groundwork for her own escape. She vowed that as soon as her husband was safely away and established in New Jersey, she would run away to join him and bring the children with her. At the time Still's oldest child, Levin, Jr., was seven, and her younger son Peter was five, her older daughter Mahalia was three, and her younger daughter Kiturah was little more than an infant. In spite of the impossible odds against a woman and four small children making a successful escape, within weeks of Levin's departure Still made her own "bold strike for freedom." (W. Still, 37)

Watching by day and traveling by night, Still trusted in God, as she half led, half carried her children to safety. Pushing on through river and wilderness, and in spite of fatigue, bad weather, and hunger, they arrived at a bordertown haven located near Greenwich, NJ, where she and the children were reunited with Levin. But the reunion was short-lived. Within months, their new home was raided by slave hunters, and Still and her children were shackled and returned to the Eastern Shore and slavery.

Still had so greatly angered the slave master by running away that he ordered her to be kept locked up until he felt she was cured of her foolish notion regarding escape. But the old childhood promise she had made to herself had been reinforced by having lived free, for however short a time, and she was now more determined than ever to escape from her life of bondage. And so, turning to God, as she was to do time and again throughout her life, she began to pray. Only this time she prayed loudly and imploringly, and she sang aloud the master's favorite Methodist hymns. So convincing was she of her state of contrition that the master believed her to be "cured" and released her from her imprisonment. As soon as opportunity presented itself, she exchanged word along the "underground" with her husband and once again set off to the North and freedom.

Still knew that because this was her second escape, the search for her would be even more intense, and running away to a location close to the state line would not protect her and her children. She also understood that under such circumstances she could take no more than two of the children with her if she were to survive. She believed that the boys would be relatively safe until her husband could come back and steal them away, so she left them under such limited protection as her mother could provide. Still's knowledge of the special vulnerability of women and girls in slavery was further reason to take her daughters with her.

During her second escape attempt she stopped using her given name, Sidney. Because Sidney is an unusual name for a woman, she hoped that using a different name would make it harder for the slave hunters to find her. From that time on she was known as Charity.

The long, arduous journey took its toll and before they could reach their destination, little Kiturah became too sick to travel. Still had to leave her with a family who had assisted them along the way. Later Still's husband came back for Kiturah and brought her safely to her mother. The exhausted woman with one frightened little girl in tow finally made her way to Levin in the Pine Barrens of Burlington County, NJ. Charity Still and two of her children were free.

For Peter and Levin, Jr., the escape proved to be a disaster. The plan for Levin's return to steal them away had to be abandoned. Upon discovering Still's second deception, the slave master, in a fit of rage, sold the two little boys. For 40 years Still grieved and prayed, believing her boys had been lost to her forever. Indeed, she never did see Levin, Jr., again, for while he was still a young man Levin found his own route to freedom from oppression—in death.

In 1850 newspapers in the North and Canada told the story of another ex-slave, who with the help of two Jewish brothers bought his own freedom. The man traveled from Alabama to Connecticut, before going to the office of the Vigilance Committee of Philadelphia, where he told the story of his search for his mother, whom he thought he might be able to find because her first name was Sidney. The stunned young man to whom the story was told was William Still, the youngest free-born son of Still and her husband. The ex-slave who told the story was Peter, the younger of Still's two "lost" sons.

Charity Still had 18 children, among them William Still, an abolitionist, philanthropist, and millionaire who was called by some the "Father of the Underground Railroad"; Dr. James Still, a homeopathic physician and philosopher, known as "the Black Doctor of the Pines"; and Peter Still, headlined in newspapers of his day as "the Man Who Bought Himself."

Among Still's grandchildren was Caroline Still Anderson, a graduate of Oberlin College and the Woman's Medical College of Philadelphia (now the Medical College of Philadelphia), who was one of Philadelphia's first black women physicians. Another of Still's grandchildren was James Thomas Still, who graduated from Harvard Medical School in 1871 and pursued a successful career in medicine and public service.

In 1987 more than 300 of Still's descendants came together in historic Lawnside, NJ, to celebrate the 118th Still family reunion. On that occasion her descendants proposed a toast to "the woman whose courage and determination to find freedom for herself and her children helped strengthen the bloodline of our great family. Endowed with her tenacious spirit, our forefathers helped to shape history. Because of her example, among us here to-

day, disproportionate to the odds, are scientists, teachers, models, musicians, sports figures, doctors, military heroes, air pilots, lawyers, and business men and women representing the generations of our great family matriarch Charity (Sidney) Still, runaway slave and family and community builder."

Information on Still was gathered from the Still family oral history and from books authored by her sons: William Still, *The Underground Railroad* (1879); James Still, *The Life and Recollections of Dr. James Still* (1877); and Kate E. Pickard, as told by Peter Still, *The Kidnapped and the Ransomed* (1856).

*Gloria Tuggle Still*

Betsey Stockton, a freed slave from Princeton, served as a missionary teacher and nurse in Hawaii between 1823 and 1825. This photograph was taken around 1863, long after she had returned and established herself as a schoolteacher and important member of the Princeton community. *Courtesy, Hawaiian Mission Children's Society, Honolulu, HI.*

## BETSEY STOCKTON, 1798–1865

Betsey Stockton, a freed slave, was a Presbyterian missionary who was also a founder of the first English school for common people in Hawaii, a schoolteacher, principal, nurse, cook, seamstress, and matriarch of the black community of Princeton (Mercer County), NJ.

Stockton is presumed to have been born in 1798. Her mother, whose name is unknown, was a slave in the household of Robert Stockton of "Constitution Hill," Princeton. The identity of her father, who was probably white, is unknown. Stockton was given by Robert Stockton to his daughter Elizabeth, first wife of Ashbel Green, later president of the College of New Jersey (now Princeton University). Emeline Brazier, Stockton's niece, and a cousin named Flora were her only sure relatives, although other Stocktons of African-American descent were members of the Witherspoon Street Church in the 1840s.

Stockton became a well-trained domestic nurse, cook, and seamstress in the Green household in Philadelphia and Princeton. A friend remembered her as a nervous and excitable child, but she enjoyed a special status in the Green home. Though Stockton served as a domestic, she was taught to read by Green's son James and was permitted the use of the Rev. Green's library. She studied on her own and attended Bible classes at Princeton Theological Seminary; she continued personal study until her death, reading *Caesar's Commentaries on the Gallic Wars* in Latin in her later years.

During Ashbel Green's college presidency (1812–22), Stockton was caught up in one of the spiritual revivals that were common in the Presbyterian church in the late 1700s and early 1800s. Stockton, who joined the (First) Presbyterian Church on September 20, 1816, was listed in the session minutes not as a servant, but as "Betsey Stockton— a coloured woman living in the family of the Rev. Dr. Green." ("Session Records") She was freed by the Greens in 1818, when she was about 20, but continued to live with them as a hired domestic.

Charles Samuel Stewart, a candidate for the ministry at Princeton Theological Seminary, was a frequent visitor to the Green household, where Stewart (and later his bride, Harriet) became Stockton's adopted family. With Ashbel Green's blessing and help, Stockton joined the Stewarts as a missionary to the Sandwich Islands (Hawaii). They sailed from New Haven, CT, on November 19, 1822, on the *Thames*, a British whaler. Stockton's contract with the American Board of Commissioners for Foreign Missions, dated October 24, 1822, at Princeton, reveals her multiple duties and privileges. Stockton was a missionary under the control of the board, but was "to be regarded neither as an equal nor as a servant but as an humble christian friend" within the missionary family of nineteen people headed for the Sandwich Islands. ("Contract," 1) She was not to do more than an equal share of menial duties, which might "prevent her being employed as a teacher of a school, for which it is hoped that she will be found qualified." ("Contract," 2)

The originals of her letters and journal, written aboard

the *Thames* and at Lahaina, Hawaii, have been lost. But Stockton sent substantial parts of both to friend and mentor Ashbel Green by means of passing whalers. Green proudly published them in the *Christian Advocate* between 1822 and 1825 in Philadelphia.

Stockton wrote in December 1822: "I am happy to tell you that since I left home, in all the storms and dangers I have been called to witness, I have never lost my self-possession. This I consider as a fulfillment of the promise that as my day is, so my strength shall be." (Stockton, "Letter," 424)

The missionaries landed in Lahaina, their assigned station, an important whaling port on the island of Maui, in late May 1823. Within days of her arrival, Stockton began teaching children in the mission house, which she shared with the Stewarts. She conducted the equivalent of a New England dame school, teaching both native Hawaiian and English children.

In addition, on September 20, 1824, the Lahaina plantation farmers asked the missionaries for school materials and a teacher for themselves. Stockton, by then familiar with the Hawaiian language, was placed in charge of a class of 30 adults. She kept this adult school every afternoon in the mission chapel.

Stockton's competency as a medical nurse proved critical to frail Harriet Stewart, who bore a son and a daughter in Hawaii. Stockton probably functioned as midwife, and certainly shouldered most of the child-care duties for the Stewart children. In turn, the Stewart family nursed Stockton through bouts of illness, some related to chest congestion, and included her on nearly every family outing. Stockton operated a home clinic, saving the life of at least two Hawaiian children. Stockton and the Stewart family left Hawaii in the fall of 1825 because of Harriet Stewart's poor health.

On August 18, 1826, Stockton and the Stewarts arrived at New York City by way of London, England, on the ship *Fawn*. The following year Stockton is reported to have taught at "an infant school for children of color" in Philadelphia. In 1828 she lived in Cooperstown, NY, with the Stewarts. In 1829 she reportedly went to Canada, where she organized schools for American Indians, under unknown sponsorship. But in 1830 she was back at Cooperstown, where Harriet Stewart was now an invalid. For five years after Harriet Stewart's death, while Charles Stewart held a navy chaplaincy, Stockton assumed the role of surrogate mother to the Stewart children. It was Stockton who brought the children to Princeton in 1833, where she enrolled Charles in the Edgehill (High) School.

After 1835, when the Stewart children left Princeton and her care, Stockton assisted in founding several institutions that helped to stabilize and enrich the free black community in Princeton. A fire damaged the racially integrated First Presbyterian Church on Nassau Street that year, and its black members began to worship separately elsewhere. By 1840 a church had been built on Witherspoon Street for the black congregation by the First Church trustees, responding to the growing controversy over abolition at the time. At the same time, Stockton's name was first on the list of 92 black members who wished to leave the First Church and form the First Presbyterian Church of Colour of Princeton (today called the Witherspoon Street Church) and who did so at a formal meeting on March 10, 1846. Records of the Morning Sabbath School of this church show a series of white male superintendents from the college and female teachers from the black community, including "Miss Betsey Stockton (Aunt Betsey) of Quarry Street." ("Records," 3) (She lived in her own two-story, four-room house on the northwest corner of Witherspoon Street and Quarry Street.) Stockton taught infant boys, among others, from 1835 to 1865. Her method was silent and oral reading of the Bible during her lessons.

By 1837 Stockton was teaching black children in a public or common school in Princeton. In 1847 she was registered as the only teacher of the single public school for black children, District School No. 6, in Princeton Township. Her wooden school building housed an average of 40 students, who learned spelling, reading, grammar, geography, and arithmetic under a system of "parental" discipline. Her salary for one year was $36, while a Miss Lockwood, who taught the school for white children in the same district, earned $42 for the same period. Stockton was licensed annually to teach by various Princeton township superintendents for at least the next ten years. All of them noted in their district register the stability and excellence of her school and her students' progress.

At Stockton's request, Lewis W. Mudge started a night school for young women and men at 110 Witherspoon Street, later the Presbyterian Church parsonage. Stockton persuaded teachers at the College of New Jersey and Princeton Theological Seminary to donate their time and skills to teach young black adults history, English literature, algebra, and Latin. This night school prepared a number of students who became college graduates.

Stockton's central role in establishing these three schools and the Witherspoon Street Church was recognized in a memorial published, more than 40 years after her death, in the *Princeton Press* on April 7, 1906. Written by her lifelong friends Lewis Mudge and Alfred A. Woodhull, the article described the dedication of a bronze memorial plaque in Stockton's honor in the Witherspoon Street Church in 1906. "Among her own people she moved [like] a queen, and her word was law," eulogized Mudge. He recalled her portrait photograph, taken around 1863, which revealed her turbaned head, placid face, and portly form. Her former students also donated a stained glass window in honor of "Elizabeth Stockton," the only known usage of that name, in the same church.

Stockton's manuscript letters reveal the depth of her courage in the face of ill health and poverty. The major achievement of her life was her ability to inspire lasting friendships of trust, respect, and affection that overcame racial and sexist prejudice. These friendships within the black and white communities of Princeton buttressed Stockton's own prodigious efforts in religion and education for nearly five decades.

Stockton died on October 24, 1865, at age 67, in Princeton, NJ, after suffering failing health for several years. She was buried in the Stewart family plot, Lakewood Cemetery, Cooperstown, NY, as she requested.

Portions of Stockton's letters and "Journal" appeared in *The Christian Advocate* (1823–25). A holograph copy of Stockton's 1822 contract with the American Board of Commissioners for Foreign Missions is at the Hawaiian Mission Children's Society (Honolulu). The "Town Superintendent's Common School Register of the Township of Princeton, County of Mercer, New Jersey, April 20, 1847–1858" documents Stockton's founding of black public education in Princeton and is published by permission of NJ-PHS. Her role in religious education is documented in "Records of the Morning Sabbath School of the Presbyterian Church (Colored) in Witherspoon Street, Princeton, NJ, 1835–1866," published by permission of NJ-PU. A list of the black members of the First Presbyterian Church appears in "Session Records, 1822–1847," available at NJ-PTS. A. A. Woodhull and Lewis Mudge, "Betsey Stockton," *Princeton Press*, Apr. 7, 1906, is a useful biographical sketch. Obituaries appeared in the *Freeman's Journal* (Cooperstown, NY), Nov. 3, 1865.

*Constance Killian Escher*

## LUCY STONE, 1818–1893

Lucy Stone, feminist, abolitionist, lecturer, 19th-century pioneer in the American women's rights movement, was born August 13, 1818, in Coy's Hill near West Brookfield, MA, the third daughter and eighth of nine children born to Hannah (Matthews) and Francis Stone. Stone's forefathers were staunch, courageous men who fought for their convictions. In 1635 an ancestor, Gregory Stone, came to America from England in search of religious liberty. A great-grandfather, Jonathan Stone, died fighting in the French and Indian Wars, and her paternal grandfather, Francis Stone, fought as a captain in the American Revolution. Her mother's people, the Forbush and Bowman families, were also spirited defenders of the public weal.

When Stone was growing up, women had few rights and were treated as inferior citizens. A woman couldn't vote, make a will, file a lawsuit, or own property in her own name. If she married, her husband owned the very clothes on her back; if he wanted to give away their children he could, and she had no right to object. Stone became aware of these and other injustices at an early age.

Her father, a well-to-do farmer and a tanner by trade, was a strong-willed person who, although not deliberately unkind, believed it was a husband's divine right to rule over his wife and daughters. Stone recalled years later, "There was only one will in our home, and that was my father's!" (Blackwell, *Lucy Stone*, 9) Distressed by her father's domineering treatment of her mother and herself, and indignant over the way the law treated women, Stone had found her purpose in life: to speak out against injustice toward women and to fight for their rights.

It was not until she had taught school for several years, attended Mt. Holyoke Female Seminary, and graduated from Oberlin College (1847)—the first Massachusetts woman to receive a college degree—that she was able to begin her work. Then, with great zeal, she started lecturing on equal rights for women, as well as another one of her great concerns, the injustice of slavery. Her first speech was at her brother Bowman's church in Gardner, MA. Afterward, she was hired as a lecturer by the American Anti-Slavery Society. Even during her lectures against slavery, however, she spoke out for the rights of women.

She was a success from the first. A natural speaker who knew how to hold her audience, she had a musical voice. A small person, she had expressive gray eyes, thick brown hair that she wore collar length, and a rosy complexion. All this, combined with her driving passion for woman's rights and strong feelings against slavery, helped to stir whatever group she spoke to.

Her audience was not always receptive to what she had to say, however. Frequently she was the target of jeers, threats, and brickbats. Sometimes the hecklers turned into an ugly mob. They would tear down posters advertising her lectures, throw prayer books at her, burn pepper during her talks to make her sneeze, and even drench her with water. Newspapers were cruel, too. One paper called her a hyena and warned her away.

Undaunted, she worked even harder. Recognized as a driving force in the women's rights movement, she drew huge crowds to her lectures. Many came just to see what the "hellcat" looked like. Sometimes, Stone wore a bloomer costume as a symbol of women's emancipation.

In addition to her speaking tours, she helped organize the first national Women's Rights Convention, held October 1850, in Worcester, MA, and produced a printed report of the proceedings, at her own expense, which she later sold at her lectures. She also made a speech during the convention, judged one of the best of her career, which so moved Susan B. Anthony when she read a newspaper version of it later that she joined the cause.

Then Lucy Stone's life took a strange twist. To her own surprise, she met and married Henry Blackwell, a hardware salesman and prominent antislavery advocate from Cincinnati, OH. Stone had vowed she would never marry. She knew she could not give up her individuality, nor bend to a man's will. But Blackwell was a sensitive, loving man who understood Stone's feelings, and after a gentle courtship, he finally won her. Nevertheless, at their wedding, which took place in Coy's Hill on May 1, 1855, Stone expressed her intent to love and honor her husband, but *not* obey him. The two read a protest of women's inequality that they had written together. Stone also insisted on keeping her maiden name.

In April 1857 Blackwell took a position with a New York book firm, and the couple purchased their first house, a small cottage on Cone Street in Orange, NJ. Stone loved this little country house, which she called, "this dear little home of our own, which is simple and unpretending, and where our friends are welcome." (Blackwell, 193) She was pregnant then and although, to her disappointment, her husband had to make frequent business trips out West, she was perfectly content to stay home and keep house. Her inactivity disturbed those of her friends active in the women's rights cause. When she wrote Susan B. Anthony that she was unable to attend a forthcoming convention because she was soon to be a mother, Anthony angrily replied, "Lucy, *neither* of us have *time* . . . for much *personal* matters." (Wheeler, *Loving Warriors*, 169)

On September 14, 1857, while Henry Blackwell was on a visit home, Stone gave birth to a daughter. The baby was first named Sarah, but a short time later her name was changed to Alice. The biggest problem, however, was what the child's surname should be: Stone, after her mother, or Blackwell, after her father? Henry Blackwell was willing to give his daughter his wife's surname, but Stone felt it would be unjust to Henry. The couple came to a decision satisfactory to both of them: Alice would have the surname Blackwell with Stone as her middle name. Anxious to give her baby the best possible care, Stone stayed at home and curtailed her women's rights work until after the Civil War. But she never lost her dedication to it.

During one of her husband's business trips, the taxes came due on the house, which was in Stone's name. As a protest against taxation without representation, she refused to pay them. In retaliation, the tax collector ordered an auction held to sell enough of the household goods to cover the taxes. On the day of the sale, January 22, 1858, several tables, two steel engravings, and according to tradition, baby Alice's cradle were sold. Fortunately, a neighbor purchased the possessions and returned them to Stone. Newspapers throughout the country had a field day with the event, and Stone's name was on the lips of men and women across the country. In 1915 a bronze tablet was placed on the Stone-Blackwell cottage in honor of Stone's defiant act, and a thousand suffragists crowded into the yard to see the unveiling. The plaque bore these words: "In 1858, Lucy Stone, a noble pioneer in the emancipation of women, here first protested against their taxation without representation in New Jersey." (Blackwell, 196)

In 1858 Lucy Stone refused to pay the taxes on her East Orange home because she could not vote and would not be taxed without representation. *Courtesy, Sophia Smith Collection, Smith College, Northampton, MA.*

In the summer of 1859 Henry left the book publishing company and went into real estate, opening offices in Orange and New York. Stone took charge of the Orange office while her husband was in New York and frequently showed property to the customers. In 1862 the Stone-Blackwells sold their home in Orange and lived for a few years on a farm in West Bloomfield (now Montclair), where Stone raised and sold vegetables and fruit for added income. Then in 1865, after spending two winters in New York (summering in the country), they moved to the

Roseville section of Newark, where they lived for seven years. One election day, Stone and her mother-in-law went to the Roseville polls and attempted to vote without success.

After the Civil War, when Alice was old enough to be left with others, Stone once again threw herself into suffrage work. She helped organize the American Equal Rights Association, which was designed to work for Negro and woman suffrage; appealed, in vain, to Congress and the New Jersey State Legislature for woman suffrage; served as president of the New Jersey Woman Suffrage Association (NJWSA); took part in the unsuccessful Kansas and New York campaigns for state woman suffrage amendments; and assisted in founding the New England Woman Suffrage Association, with Julia Ward Howe as president. She also wrote a pamphlet entitled *Reasons Why the Women of New Jersey Should Vote.* The last page carried the endorsement of the Executive Committee of the NJWSA, Vineland. In addition, she maintained a full lecture schedule.

In 1869, at the urging of Massachusetts women's rights leaders, the Stone-Blackwells reluctantly left New Jersey and moved to the Boston area, where Stone, as always supported by her husband, led the New England women's rights movement.

She also was greatly involved, on a national level, in the fight for woman suffrage, becoming in 1869 a leader of the American Woman Suffrage Association (AWSA), the more conservative of the two large national woman suffrage organizations. She founded and financed the *Woman's Journal,* the weekly newspaper of the AWSA, which throughout its 47 years of publication (Alice Blackwell took over the editorship after her parents) was recognized as a major influence in the woman suffrage movement.

In her later years Stone's voice began to fail, and although she still had an amazing ability to sway her audience, she was forced to limit her speaking engagements after 1887. Her last lectures were given at the Chicago World's Fair in early 1893. She was also suffering from stomach trouble, diagnosed in September 1893 as a cancerous tumor. Stone returned home to Dorcester (near Boston), where her health failed rapidly. She died on October 18, 1893, at age 75. Her last intelligible words, whispered to her daughter, were: "Make the world better." (Blackwell, 282)

Stone is profiled in *NAW.* Biographies of her are: Alice Stone Blackwell, *Lucy Stone* (1930); and Elinor Rice Hays, *Morning Star: A Biography of Lucy Stone, 1818–1893* (1961). Correspondence between Stone and her husband appears in Leslie Wheeler, ed., *Loving Warriors* (1981); and between Stone and her sister-in-law, Antoinette Brown Blackwell, in Carol Lasser and Marlene Deahl Merrill, eds., *Friends and Sisters* (1987).

*Dorothy A. Voss*

## SUSAN CATHERINE MOORE WATERS, 1823–1900

Susan Catherine (Moore) Waters, itinerant portrait painter, painter of still lifes and animals, and advocate of feminist and Quaker causes, was born on May 18, 1823, in Binghamton, NY. She was one of six children of Lark Moore, a farmer and cooper, and Sally Moore. Much of her youth was spent in the small Quaker community of Friendsville, PA, near the New York border. She almost certainly attended the Friendsville Boarding School for Females in 1838, when she was fifteen, and paid the tuition for her sister Amelia and herself by painting copies of specimens for the natural history class.

She married William Church Waters, also of Friendsville, on June 27, 1841. He was born in Providence, PA, and was five years her senior. Although he was plagued by ill health for much of their married life, William Waters was reportedly cheerful and active in religious and civic causes. Waters had his encouragement for her artistic and intellectual pursuits throughout 52 years of marriage. They had no children.

Waters's career as an itinerant portrait painter began in the early 1840s, soon after her marriage. She traveled to small communities in northern Pennsylvania and in southern New York state. In her portraits the faces and postures of her subjects are stylized, whereas the costumes and settings are often elaborately detailed. Although there is no record of Waters having received formal training in art, her paintings have survived without pronounced cracking, proving she knew her craft well.

Waters painted at least 28 portraits between 1843 and 1845, but demand for painted portraits decreased steadily in the 1840s and 1850s with the introduction in America of photography (daguerreotypes, ambrotypes, and a rapid series of improvements). This and her husband's failing health probably caused Waters to turn to photography. She and her husband worked as photographers for at least ten years.

In the early 1850s Waters and her husband lived briefly in Bordentown, NJ, and built a house at 38 Mary Street. They left Bordentown for more than a decade, but returned and settled permanently in the house on Mary Street in 1866. Waters's parents also moved to Bordentown that year. After her return, she lived for 33 years in this Delaware River town, which had a strong Quaker tradition and was home to many artists.

Waters and her husband were quickly integrated into the community. They became received members of the Chesterfield Friends' Meeting. Waters was active in the New Jersey Woman Suffrage Association, and when she was elected the association's recording secretary at the February 15, 1871, meeting, she spoke to members about the depressing influence of subjection upon a woman's moral character. Later that year she lectured at the Temperance Hall in White Hill (now Fieldsboro), NJ, on "Woman's Work and Sphere."

During the 19th century a schism developed in the Society of Friends between Orthodox Quakers, who gave primacy to the authority of the Bible, and the Hicksites (followers of Elias Hicks), who gave primacy to the concept of Inner Light, the direct relationship between souls and the Creator. Waters, a Hicksite like her husband, wrote three articles for the *Bordentown Register* disputing the divine inspiration of the Bible. Her first article appeared on January 10, 1870, and four days later the *Register* published the opposing views of one Jacob Ford. Thus began a newspaper debate that ended in March 1870 with Ford's withdrawal. Twenty-two years later Waters was still an active Quaker: at age 69 she served as representative from the Chesterfield Friends' Meeting to the Mount Holly Quarterly Meeting.

Waters was especially successful as an artist during her Bordentown years. She returned to painting, but she rarely did portraits, turning instead to still lifes and animal paintings. Her fame grew with the sale of at least two of her paintings at the 1876 Centennial Exposition in Philadelphia, and her work was much in demand. Fifty of the known Waters works date from her years in Bordentown, and it is thought that she produced many more.

Waters excelled in painting cows and sheep: almost a third of her known paintings are of sheep, and at one time she kept a pen of them to sketch. A meadow at Samuel E. Burr's farm along Thorntown Creek in Bordentown was the setting for many of her paintings. Several area farmers, including Anthony Bullock of Chesterfield, had her document their prize-winning herds. Waters's love of animals and her gentle sense of humor are evident in *Mischief*, an oil on canvas she painted in the 1870s that is now in the Fine Arts Collection of the New Jersey State Museum in Trenton. It features two squirrels munching on the delicious blossoms of someone's carefully tended potted plants.

On November 21, 1893, William Waters died. For six years Waters continued to live in Bordentown and paint. In 1899 she moved to a Quaker nursing home in Trenton, NJ.

Waters died in Trenton of hepatitis on July 7, 1900. She was eulogized by several Friends at funeral services held at the Trenton Meetinghouse. Waters was buried beside her husband and her parents in the family plot in the Bordentown Cemetery on July 10, 1900. The *Bordentown Register* biography published a few weeks later read, in part, "She needs no eulogy in Bordentown. Here she was well known as a lady of refinement, modest and unassuming. . . . Her character was as beautiful as her paintings."

The most authoritative account of Waters and her work is Colleen Cowles Heslip, *Mrs. Susan C. Waters: 19th Century Itinerant Painter* (1979). Heslip also wrote "Susan C. Waters," *Antiques* 115 (Apr. 1979):769–77. A memorial biography of Waters appeared in the *Bordentown Register*, July 27, 1900, and her obituary appeared in that paper, July 13, 1900.

*Elizabeth G. Carpenter*
*Maggie Sullivan*

Young women working at "picking" in a Paterson silk mill, c. 1914. Thousands of women, mostly immigrants and the daughters of immigrants, worked at skilled and unskilled jobs in the heyday of the Paterson silk industry. *Courtesy, The Paterson Museum.*

# HISTORICAL OVERVIEW: 1866-1920

DURING THE 55 YEARS FROM 1865 TO 1920, the number and diversity of New Jersey women increased dramatically. In 1860 the total population of the state was 672,035; by 1920 it had more than quadrupled to 3,155,900.* While in 1875 more than half the state's population still lived on farms or in very small towns, the urban areas were growing the fastest. By 1900 72 percent of the population was urban.* For New Jersey women, city and town life was quickly becoming the more common experience, especially in the densely populated corridor between New York City and Philadelphia.

New Jersey's economic growth and proximity to the ports of New York and Philadelphia made it a natural destination for thousands of the immigrants flowing into the United States in the late 19th and early 20th century. Continuing a process that had begun in earnest with the Irish in the 1840s, thousands of new immigrants, families as well as single women and men, syphoned through the ferry and railroad terminal in Jersey City (now Liberty State Park) to other parts of the state. As a result, the New Jersey female population, which already included women from Great Britain, Ireland, Germany, Scandinavia, the Netherlands, and Switzerland, as well as women of African and American Indian heritage, quickly came to include women of an even wider variety of national, religious, and racial backgrounds: Poles, Jews from the Pale of Settlement, Hungarians, Estonians, Finns, Rumanians, Bulgarians, Turks, Greeks, Italians, Spanish, Portuguese, Chinese. By 1920 only about two-fifths of New Jersey's population claimed American-born parents of at least two generations.

New Jersey's rapidly expanding industrial economy offered many opportunities. Managerial and business jobs, professional practice, skilled and unskilled manufacturing and domestic service, as well as increasingly commercialized farming attracted women and men from other sec-

tions of the country and from abroad. Using the state's well-developed railway system, one of the densest in the country by the late 19th century, some New Jerseyans commuted into New York City and Philadelphia for work and social life. New Jersey also became a summer and leisure haven when seashore locations were linked by rail to population centers and people discovered the tranquility of hills and lakes in the northwestern part of the state.

Girls and women were directly involved as workers in the industries that came to distinguish New Jersey's economy in this period. In addition to farm work and domestic service, which still continued to employ thousands of women, manufacturing provided an increasing proportion of women's employment. Many of the new goods and services enjoyed by New Jersey women were produced by women. Women worked in the garment and shirtwaist shops, in commercial laundries, in silk, cotton, and woolen textile mills, in retail stores, as shoemakers, hat trimmers, rubber garment makers, cigar makers, "tailoresses," and pottery decorators; they made electrical machinery, jewelry, leather goods, musical instruments, patent medicines, soap, surgical items. They were increasingly employed as secretaries and clerks in business and offices, especially after the typewriter was introduced in the 1890s; and they were hired as operators in the new Bell Telephone Company. By 1910 over 25 percent of New Jersey's adult wage earners were women.

Most working women were young, single immigrants or daughters of immigrants. In order to curb the employment of young children the New Jersey legislature voted in 1883 to set a fourteen-year minimum work age for girls and a twelve-year age for boys. Young women such as CLARA LOUISE MAASS and HANNAH SILVERMAN were typical of female workers in the late 19th and early 20th century. Maass, who later became a celebrated nurse, was the daughter of German immigrants; she went to work at fifteen, in 1891, at the Newark Orphan Asylum and contributed half of her meager wage to her family. Silverman was the daughter of German and Polish Jews and, at seventeen, was already a seasoned weaver when she joined striking silk workers in Paterson in 1913.

---

*Statistics on New Jersey population are drawn from New Jersey Department of State, *Compendium of Censuses, 1726–1905* (Trenton, 1906), 41; U.S. Department of Commerce and Labor, Bureau of the Census, *Thirteenth Census of the United States, 1910* (Washington, D.C., 1913), 57; and H. F. Wilson *Outline History of New Jersey* (New Brunswick, 1950), 152.

Married women also worked for wages, especially in urban centers where work opportunities were more diverse. In Paterson by World War I, for example, over 15 percent of the working women were married. A high percentage of employed married women were foreign-born themselves or the daughters of the foreign-born, or they were African-American. MARIA BOTTO, for example, was an immigrant Italian textile worker in West Hoboken in her early married years; later she supplemented her family's income by taking in boarders and doing piecework at home.

MARION HARLAND

Mary Virginia Hawes Terhune of Newark and Pompton Lakes, c. 1906. Terhune was known as "Marion Harland" by the thousands of American women who read her household advice books, cookbooks, and syndicated columns. *Courtesy, Collections of the Passaic County Historical Society, Paterson, NJ.*

Working women in New Jersey participated in the developing union movement of the late 19th century. In the 1880s in particular several thousand women joined trade unions and local assemblies of the Knights of Labor, a union that encouraged women's participation. Hat trimmers in Millburn, laundry workers in Belleville, jute and silk workers in Paterson, and pottery decorators in Trenton were among those who became "lady Knights," supporting each other during strikes and pooling funds for sick benefits and funeral costs. When the influence of the Knights of Labor waned, skilled women in lesser numbers joined trade unions and some, like HANNAH SILVERMAN, joined the radical Industrial Workers of the World in the 1910s.

While New Jersey was quickly becoming industrialized, its agricultural interests remained a major part of the state's economy and involved large numbers of women and girls as farm workers and farm wives. With the increased economic importance of commercial crops, farmers looked for new and improved varieties. ELIZABETH COLEMAN WHITE, who grew up in the Pine Barrens, was instrumental in developing an important commercial crop, the cultivated blueberry, in 1916.

Despite the growing numbers of women wage workers, most women in the late 19th century, whether white or black, native-born or immigrant, expected to marry and devote their mature lives to the nurture and care of their families and homes. The laborious nature of traditional housework, however, was slowly changing in the late 19th and early 20th century as the fruits of industrialization began to reach into the home and standards of cleanliness improved. Writers MARY VIRGINIA HAWES TERHUNE ("Marion Harland") and her daughter CHRISTINE TERHUNE HERRICK developed careers advising women through the popular media about housekeeping techniques and the use of new equipment. In her highly successful book *Common Sense in the Household* (1871), Terhune recommended to her readers such laborsaving devices as the manual eggbeater, raisin seeder, applecorer, and clothes wringer. By 1926, when Herrick revised her mother's 1871 book, a virtual household revolution had taken place, and Herrick was extolling the virtues of the electric vacuum cleaner.

At first only affluent women living in the cities could enjoy the benefits of the many technical advances changing domestic life in New Jersey. Late 19th-century innovations in power sources such as natural gas and then electricity revolutionized housekeeping, as did the building of municipal water and sewerage systems. Between 1890 and 1920 innovations such as indoor plumbing and running water, ready-to-wear clothing, prepared foods, electrified household appliances, and commercial laundries became more widely available to New Jersey homemakers. A measure of the new availability of manufactured consumer goods and household improvements was the success of L. Bamberger

& Company, Newark's first department store, opened in 1893. CAROLINE BAMBERGER FULD, later known for her philanthropy, became a partner in the company.

Educational opportunities for women began to expand after the Civil War. Access to basic schooling was improved when, in 1871, local public schools were made tuition free by the state legislature. Schooling was not mandatory, however, until 1909, and most young women did not have a high school education. Private schools and seminaries for women continued to educate the daughters of affluent families, and parochial schools, both Roman Catholic and Protestant, were an important resource of the immigrant community. Schools for specialized training proliferated in the late 19th century. Coleman Business College, directed by EMMA COLEMAN of Newark, helped young women gain the skills needed to enter the business world as clerks and secretaries. Nursing schools, such as that at Orange Memorial Hospital, trained young women in the relatively new field of professional nursing.

For middle-class women, both white and black, school-teaching continued to be the most widely accepted occupation. Normal school training prepared young women such as GRACE BAXTER FENDERSON and ELIZABETH ALMIRA ALLEN to teach until they married, or it provided them with a lifetime career. Fenderson, a founder of the Newark chapter for the National Association for the Advancement of Colored People in 1914, was a strong advocate for the hiring of black school principals and vice-principals. Allen became concerned with the financial straits of retired women schoolteachers and was instrumental in getting the New Jersey legislature to pass legislation protecting teacher tenure and providing retirement benefits (1896).

While teacher education was available and attracted increasingly more women than men, higher education for women in New Jersey lagged behind that in other northeastern states. By 1893 there were only seventeen public high schools in the state accredited to send students to the state normal school in Trenton to train as teachers. If New Jersey women wanted more than normal school training they had to go elsewhere for four-year college education. Not until 1899 did New Jersey have a four-year college that would educate women. In that year St. Elizabeth's College was opened in Convent Station by the Roman Catholic Sisters of Charity under the leadership of MOTHER MARY XAVIER MEHEGAN, an Irish immigrant nun. Nearly 20 years later, after concerted effort and pressure by women like MABEL SMITH DOUGLASS, the New Jersey College for Women (now Douglass College) was opened in 1918 at Rutgers College (now Rutgers, the State University of New Jersey).

Nevertheless, horizons for women were expanding in the late 19th century. The avenues for satisfying work outside marriage were increasingly varied, and though the early pioneers in many fields had to struggle against restric-

Mabel Smith Douglass, shown here with her daughter, led the effort to found New Jersey College for Women (now Douglass College). She was its first dean from 1918 to 1933. *Courtesy, Archives, Mabel Smith Douglass Library, Rutgers, the State University of New Jersey.*

tion, negative public opinion, and wages inferior to men's, change was taking place.

Traditionally, single women like diarist ABBIE ELIZA MAGEE often lived with relatives and found a place helping with housework and sewing. But opportunities improved for single women, who previously had few alternatives for paid work or independence. In the decades after the Civil War it became more common for single women to devote their lives to public roles in community institutions and social service. MARGARET BANCROFT founded (1883) and devoted her life to administering the Bancroft Training School for the multiply disabled in Haddonfield; CORNELIA FOSTER BRADFORD founded (1894) and directed the Whittier House social settlement in New Jersey City; LYDIA YOUNG HAYES organized (1910) and directed the New Jersey Commission for the Blind. BEATRICE WINSER and SARAH BYRD ASKEW both made significant careers for themselves as librarians.

New Jersey women pushed against professional barriers and gradually gained entry to the scientific, medical, and legal professions. MARY LUA ADELIA DAVIS TREAT of Vineland, for example, was a pioneer entomologist and botanist who supported herself by writing on science for popular journals in the 1870s. EMMA WARD EDWARDS, who had a medical practice in Newark, was one of the first doctors trained at Elizabeth Blackwell's Women's Medical College in Manhattan. Early women physicians found that after getting medical training they were not welcomed into the male-dominated medical profession. SOPHIA PRESLEY graduated from the Woman's Medical College of Pennsylvania in 1879 and was instructor of surgery there for three years before opening a practice in Camden. Despite her credentials, the Camden Medical Society denied her membership for seven years, until it finally relented in 1890. Similar barriers faced women wishing to practice law. MARY PHILBROOK, the first woman admitted to the New Jersey Bar, had to secure a special enabling act from the New Jersey legislature before she was admitted to the bar in 1895.

During this period women were also becoming visible in new ways in organized religion, one area in which traditionally women's lay participation had been encouraged. Ordination was a possibility for a few, such as PHEBE COFFIN HANAFORD, Universalist minister in Jersey City in the 1870s and 1880s, and FLORENCE SPEARING RANDOLPH, ordained in the African Methodist Episcopal Zion church in 1903. MARY JONES BENNETT became a national leader in the powerful Woman's Board of Home Missions of the Presbyterian church in 1894. ALMA BRIDWELL WHITE founded her own church, the Pillar of Fire, in 1901 and became a bishop of the church in 1918.

After the 1860s an organizational enthusiasm seemed to stir women to new forms of activity, altering the widely held dictum that women's energies should be directed solely to home, family, and church. In noting the increase in community activity by women in the late 19th century, historians have suggested that women were extending their traditional domestic caretaking roles into the larger community as "municipal housekeepers." This interpretation seems particularly apt for New Jersey women. As some working women in the same period began to organize on their own behalf in the workplace, so middle-class women began to respond with increased vigor to the social needs of the state's mushrooming cities and towns. The ready availability of low-paid household servants, as well as improvements in transportation, enabled many middle- and upper-class women to devote time to community activities. They established libraries, clinics, schools, and day nurseries for workers' children; they pushed for improved housing and working conditions, reform of prisons and facilities for the mentally ill. Women in immigrant neighborhoods worked through churches and lodge auxiliaries to provide services and stable social networks within their ethnic communities.

Women's cultural, professional, and reform organizations sprang up throughout the state. Some groups were independent educational clubs like Jersey City's "Daugh-

ters of Aesthetics," founded in the late 1870s by ethnologist ERMINNIE ADELE PLATT SMITH. Others like the New Jersey State Nurses' Association, founded in 1901, linked professional women together across the state and pressed for reforms. By the end of the 19th century many local groups were combined into state and even national networks. The career of SARAH JANE CORSON DOWNS in the Woman's Christian Temperance Union (WCTU) illustrates the growth of such organizational networks. Downs joined the local Pennington branch of the WCTU when it was organized in the mid-1870s. When she became president of the state organization (NJWTCU) in 1881 there were 26 chapters; during the ten years she was in office, the organization grew to 208 chapters and over 8,000 women and became part of an extensive international organization.

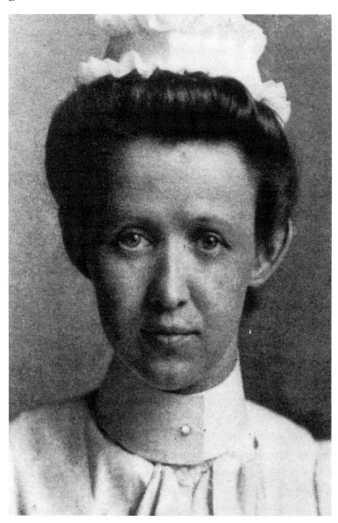

Irene Taylor Fallon was the first president of the New Jersey State Nurses' Association (NJSNA). Fallon was born on November 25, 1866, and graduated in 1894 from the Cooper Hospital School of Nursing in Camden. She never married and worked all her life in nursing.

When the NJSNA was founded at Newark City Hospital on

December 4, 1901, Fallon was one of 175 graduate nurses attending the meeting. The association was one of four such state nursing associations founded that year, the earliest in the nation. During Fallon's term as president (1901–03), she and the association lobbied vigorously for a New Jersey nurse registration law. This goal was achieved in 1903 with the passage of a bill requiring two years of training for nurses. In 1912 NJSNA-backed legislation created the Board of Nurse Examiners.

The NJSNA continued to be concerned with health and health care issues. In 1907 its members signed a petition calling for the ban of cigarette sales to boys, and in 1908 it surveyed health conditions in almshouses and called for reform. During these years Fallon was working as night supervisor at Cooper Hospital and then as a district nurse in Millburn.

In 1909 Fallon took a job in New York state and then in 1919 at the Chestnut Hill Home for Consumptives in Philadelphia, where she lived and worked the rest of her life. She died on September 1, 1952, at the age of 85 and was buried in the Mt. Moriah Cemetery in Philadelphia.

Information on Fallon and the early NJSNA is found in Bullough, Church, and Stein, *American Nursing: A Biographical Dictionary* (1988); and Janet L. Fickeissen, "Lobbying for Registration Laws: Letters from the Past," *Journal of Nursing History* 1 (Apr. 1986):12–19. *Photo courtesy, New Jersey State Nurses' Association.*

The women's clubs formed a particularly popular and powerful middle-class women's organization. The first club formed in New Jersey was the Women's Club of Orange (1871), which counted among its members CHARLOTTE EMERSON BROWN, a founder and first president of the National Federation of Women's Clubs in 1890, and MARGARET TUFTS SWAN YARDLEY, who became the first president of the New Jersey Federation of Women's Clubs when it was organized in 1894. African-American women's clubs organized independently into the New Jersey Federation of Colored Women's Clubs in 1915 with FLORENCE SPEARING RANDOLPH as their first president. The proliferation of women's organizations led one frustrated suffrage advocate to complain: "New Jersey has so many associations of women that they have acted as a bar against the formation of suffrage clubs, women feeling that they had already too many meetings to attend." (Anthony, *History*, 4:834)

The broadened dimensions of late 19th-century women's lives was also reflected in the world of the arts, literature, and entertainment. Women such as CAROLINE PEDDLE BALL, sculptor, EMILIE KOEHLER GREENOUGH, stained glass artist, MARY MAPES DODGE, author and editor of children's literature, and CAROLYN WELLS, humorist, not only had ready markets for their work but were increasingly able to support themselves and sometimes their families through their art.

Many women became more active physically during this period. Vineland dress reformers MARY E. TILLOTSON and SUSAN PECKER FOWLER lectured and wrote in the 1870s urging a freer and more healthful style of dress for women, better suited for an active life. German immigrants advocated gymnastics for young people and organized gym clubs or *turnvereins* for girls as well as boys in many communities. MINNIE RADCLIFFE DOUGLASS, who took up the new sport of roller skating as a child in the 1880s, soon became a performer and toured widely to great acclaim during her short public career. ELISABETH HOLMES MOORE of Ridgewood rose to national women's singles lawn-tennis champion in 1896, 1901, 1903, and 1905. ALICE HUYLER RAMSEY of Hackensack, an expert driver in the early days of the automobile, drove her green Maxwell to San Francisco in 1909 over largely unpaved roads, the first woman to make such a trip.

Annie Oakley was born Phoebe Ann Moses in Darke County, OH, on August 13, 1860. She became an expert sharpshooter as a girl, helping to support her family by selling wild game she had shot. After her marriage in 1876 to Frank Butler she began a vaudeville shooting act with him. Her fame soared after she joined Buffalo Bill's Wild West Show in 1885. She performed for Queen Victoria of England and Kaiser William I of Germany and toured in France, Spain, Italy, Germany, and England with the Wild West Show.

In the 1890s, following the European tour, Oakley and her husband lived for ten winters in Nutley, NJ. In 1894 Oakley and others from the Wild West Show met in West Orange with Thomas A. Edison, who made a kinescope of their performance.

Oakley was seriously injured in 1901 in a train crash while on tour. Thereafter her career was limited largely to acting performances and shooting demonstrations and lessons at resort hotels. She suffered further serious injury in an automobile accident in 1922 that left her partially paralyzed. She died on November 3, 1926, in Greenville, OH, near her birthplace.

A biographical sketch of Oakley appears in *NAW*. *Photo courtesy, the Nutley Historical Society Collection, Nutley, NJ.*

Despite the expanding economic and social participation of women in New Jersey, changes in state law affecting women's legal and economic status did not keep pace, and shortly after the Civil War aspects of the law came into serious question by women. In 1871 ANN HORA CONNELLY of Rahway prompted the state legislature to pass a law giving mothers and fathers equal rights to custody of children in a divorce. Other rights were gained by married women in 1874, considerably later than in some industrializing states, when New Jersey law was amended to guarantee married women the right to their personal property and inheritance. In 1895 married women gained the right to contract and to sue and be sued for property and then in 1896 were granted the legal right to their earnings and wages as separate property.

Women's right to vote became an issue among New Jersey women shortly after the Civil War. Spurred by debate over the 14th Amendment to the U.S. Constitution, which granted the vote to black men, and critical of the prohibition of woman suffrage in the 1844 state constitution, some women in scattered communities in the 1860s challenged the law against female suffrage. Women in Vineland and Orange took direct action against the system by voting in protest and tallying their votes in spite of opposition by polling officials. LUCY STONE organized the first statewide woman suffrage society in 1867, and suffrage reform activity continued in New Jersey until 1920. Women were able to secure the vote in local school board elections in 1887, only to have the right struck down by the courts in 1894 and defeated at the polls in 1897. But that brief encounter invigorated the suffragists, who had reorganized in 1890; they stayed with the issue until suffrage became a broad-based movement in the 1910s. Then thousands of women joined the New Jersey Woman Suffrage Association led by LILLIAN FORD FEIKERT. Others joined the National Woman's Party (founded by ALICE STOKES PAUL of Moorestown) through its New Jersey branch, which was led by ALISON TURNBULL HOPKINS.

Suffrage was not a universally accepted goal of New Jersey women, however. Thousands of women also joined antisuffrage organizations, and though they could not prevent the final passage of the federal amendment, they did contribute to the defeat of a suffrage amendment to the state constitution in 1915.

Many activist women on both sides of the suffrage issue put aside their political and social concerns when the United States entered World War I in 1917. They joined the war effort by organizing for the Red Cross, the Women's Land Army, and various foreign relief projects. Resistance in the U.S. Congress to the woman suffrage amendment softened after the Armistice in 1918, however, so the full influence of New Jersey suffrage organizations was brought to bear for the New Jersey legislature's ratification of the 19th Amendment, which granted women the right to vote; the state's ratification occurred on February 10, 1920. By that time the lives of New Jersey women had become substantially different from those of their mothers and grandmothers.

*Delight Wing Dodyk*

## Selected References

Anthony, Susan B., and Ida Husted Harper. *History of Woman Suffrage.* Vol. 4, 1883–1900. Rochester, NY, 1902.

Fleming, Thomas. *New Jersey: A History.* New York, 1984.

Gordon, Felice. *After Winning: The Legacy of the New Jersey Suffragists, 1920–1947.* New Brunswick, 1986.

New Jersey Board of Education. *Annual Report of the Board of Education and the Superintendent of Public Instruction of New Jersey, for Year Ending June 30, 1893.* Trenton, 1894.

New Jersey Bureau of Statistics of Labor and Industries. *Tenth Annual Report.* Somerville, 1888.

New Jersey Commissioner of Education. *New Jersey School Laws.* Trenton, 1911.

New Jersey Department of State. *Compendium of Censuses, 1726–1905.* Trenton, 1906.

Strasser, Susan. *Never Done: A History of American Housework.* New York, 1982.

Vecoli, Rudolph J. *The People of New Jersey.* Princeton, 1965.

Wilson, H. F. *Outline History of New Jersey.* New Brunswick, 1950.

## ELIZABETH ALMIRA ALLEN, 1854-1919

Elizabeth Almira Allen, expert teacher and teachers' rights advocate, was the first woman president of the New Jersey Education Association. Little is known of her childhood other than that she was the eldest of five children born to James and Sarah J. (Smith) Allen on February 27, 1854, in Joliet, IL. Her father, who fought in the Civil War, was a descendant of Ira Allen, brother of Ethan Allen, and a founder of the University of Vermont.

The family lived for brief periods in Massachusetts and Pennsylvania before settling in New Jersey in a house loaned to them by Allen's maternal grandfather. Allen attended grade school in Mendham and in 1867, at the age of thirteen, entered the Model School of Trenton, a teaching adjunct to the New Jersey State Normal School, now Trenton State College. Graduating from the State Normal School two years later, Allen secured a teaching appointment in Atlantic City. In 1871 Allen began her long career in the public schools of Hoboken. For 48 years she served first as teacher, then principal at the elementary school and Hoboken High School, and finally supervised the education of teachers at the Hoboken Normal and Training School.

At age 28, she was named vice-president of the New Jersey Teachers' Association (NJTA), later the New Jersey Education Association (NJEA). But it was her pioneering work for a teachers' retirement fund and later for teachers' tenure that kept her in the public eye and often at the center of controversy from 1890 until her death in 1919. Allen chronicled her work for the pension movement in an 1897 article, "Teachers' Pensions: The Story of a Woman's Campaign." In it she told of how, seven years earlier, meeting by chance on a Hoboken street corner, she and two other public school teachers discussed the case of a fourth, retired, who was "doomed for the poorhouse." (Allen, "Teachers' Pensions," 700) With that conversation, the teachers' pension movement was born.

In the next year, 1891, the three women arranged to have the first of many pension bills introduced into the New Jersey State Legislature. It was to be a six-year battle, but in 1893 the cause of Allen and her cohorts was considerably strengthened when the NJTA appointed a committee on teachers' pensions by congressional district. What Allen had originally conceived of as a pension system for New Jersey's urban teachers was now envisioned as a statewide plan for all teachers.

As Allen writes in her spirited article: "Here and there among the statesmen we found a cordial, frank, if not aggressive supporter; but there was a deep rooted aversion to the word 'pensions.' Some talked 'socialism,' while others stood behind the word 'paternalism' as a solid rock of defense." (Allen, "Teachers' Pensions," 700) Allen was fighting for a progressive cause on two fronts—against the prej-

udice of an oligarchy that saw any form of welfare legislation as a free handout, and against the entrenched sexism that denied women the vote along with so much else. She good-humoredly persisted in the face of slander and ignorance, pointing out the bias against a woman schoolteacher, which kept her ill paid as well as "practically debarred from marriage under peril of losing her position." (Allen, "Teachers' Pensions," 702)

Finally, in 1896, Senator John B. Vreeland of Morristown introduced a new bill; it provided that a half-pay annuity be granted to teachers with 20 years of service who were no longer able to teach, the fund to be financed by a one percent pay stoppage from the monthly salary of all those who elected to come under the law. The bill passed, becoming the first statewide teacher retirement law in America; but Allen found that the real struggle had just begun. Since membership in the plan was voluntary, and the legislature had allowed a mere three months for teachers to enroll, Allen and her friends were forced to mount an energetic enlistment drive. Many of the leading male educators were against it. They called it unconstitutional, actuarially unsound, and "the work of a lot of old maids." (Allen, "Teachers' Pensions," 704) Only to this last did Allen assent, though she admitted there were some "old bachelors" in on it, too. Through speeches, flyers, and a letter-writing campaign to the state's newspapers, Allen and her friends prevailed: at the end of three months, more than half of New Jersey's teachers had enrolled. Allen nonetheless continued to urge mandatory enrollment in a secure retirement system.

The NJTA had backed Allen's work for pension legislation, but there were some in the organization who felt threatened by her efforts to expand membership and guarantee wider representation in the association's governance for women and the rank-and-file teacher. In 1900, after a bitter two-year struggle, Allen and her supporters won their points, and she was made secretary of the Teachers' Retirement Fund. That year Allen spoke at the annual convention, and the objectives she set forth have remained a major doctrine for the association to this day. She urged the assembled teachers to bear responsibility for one another's conduct and welfare, saying that the association should be a forum in which teachers could be heard on all matters that touched them. "The highest ambition should be to make our annual meeting controversial." (Johnson, NJEA, 61)

For nine years Allen and the association, under her leadership, campaigned for the Tenure of Office Act. When the law passed, it remained for the association to ensure legal redress for teachers unfairly deprived of their jobs. In 1911 Allen was instrumental in forming a grievance committee. In a speech to the convention that year, she said: "It is [the association's] *duty*, it ought to be its *joy*, to fight the just battles of its members." (Johnson, 71)

In 1913, with extraordinary achievements to her credit, Allen became the first woman president of the NJTA. She considered her election both a vindication of her past efforts and a vote of confidence to continue. Yet for a number of reasons the Teachers' Retirement Fund, which she continued to manage almost as her own personal fiefdom, was looked on by many as financially unsound. Controversy over her leadership grew, until in 1918 Allen's forces in the association lost control of the pension reform process. Allen cooperated in the state-mandated actuarial investigation, and though by this time tired and ill, she compiled an exhaustive catalog of teachers' retirement systems in use around the country in an effort to educate her fellow teachers. When Governor Walter E. Edge signed an amended annuity bill, she was too ill to know it.

Allen's private interests and accomplishments also deserve notice. A gifted writer on the concerns of teachers, she found time to write poetry as well, and her first published work was a book of poems on the deeds of famous people, *Golden Nails to Hang Memories On* (1890). Though Allen held no college degree, she was a diligent student of history and literature, and spoke French and German fluently, as well as some Russian and Italian. On one occasion, while traveling alone in Russia, she joined up with a party of wealthy people from Massachusetts and became their guide.

Allen traveled widely, crossing the Atlantic 54 times despite her limited means. She had a genius for friendship and took pride and delight in the people she knew on both sides of the Atlantic. She went to Central America, Algiers, the Canadian Rockies, and Alaska. Her last journey abroad was in 1915 at the start of World War I, when for a time she was stranded in Naples and assisted the U.S. vice-consul there in getting Americans home.

Allen died on May 3, 1919, less than a month after the amended NJ teachers' annuity bill was signed into law, of congestive heart failure at the River Lawn Sanitorium in Paterson. She was buried in Boonton, NJ. After her death she was made an honorary president of the NJTA *in perpetuum.*

Allen's work is chronicled in her "Teachers' Pensions: The Story of a Woman's Campaign," *Review of Reviews* 16 (1897):700–711. Ida E. Housman, *The Life of Elizabeth Alvira Allen* (1944), is a biography written by a friend. Allen's work is cited in Lawrence Johnson, *NJEA: The Story of an Organization* (1953).

*Cynthia Robinson*
*Blair T. Birmelin*

## SARAH BYRD ASKEW, 1877–1942

Sarah Byrd Askew, librarian, was born on February 15, 1877, in Dayton, AL, the youngest of three daughters of Thyrza (Pickering) and Samuel Horton Askew, an accountant and bank manager. Her mother died in 1879, and her father later married Kittie Reeves. The number of children resulting from their marriage cannot be documented. Askew's family was Presbyterian. She attended Dayton Academy until she was thirteen. After her family moved to Atlanta, GA, she graduated from high school and attended a business school there. She then worked as a stenographer.

While visiting a sister in Cleveland, OH, she met William H. Brett, the librarian of the Cleveland Public Library. His enthusiasm for library work struck a responsive chord in Askew. She found librarianship could provide her with an opportunity to combine her love of reading with a way to help others, so she accepted Brett's offer of a temporary position at the Cleveland library. In 1903 Askew attended Pratt Institute (Brooklyn, NY), where she studied library science. Upon completing her studies in 1904, she returned to the Cleveland Public Library. In January 1905 she accepted a position as "organizer" for the New Jersey Public Library Commission. Her assignment was to develop and organize libraries in the state, a task she made her life's work.

Askew believed that her first job was "to convince the public of the value and use of books to earn, to save, to learn, to enjoy," then to convince the public that libraries were the most economical and efficient method to make books available. (*Twenty-second Annual Report of the Public Library Commission of New Jersey*, 1921) She became the driving force for organizing and implementing a statewide program to bring library service to all residents of New Jersey. When she arrived, there were only 66 free public libraries in New Jersey; when she died in 1942, there were over 300 public libraries and 12 county libraries.

Askew was an innovator, entrepreneur, and politician. She used these skills to develop effective library services in many rural areas and to improve the quality of library services. One of her original assignments was to organize the "traveling libraries," general collections of 300 or so books, which were housed in sturdy wooden cases that could be shipped to stations in local community buildings. She soon began customizing some of these collections to meet the social and economic needs of those being served. By 1913 she began supplying specifically requested titles from the commission's collection or from larger libraries in New Jersey, New York City, and Philadelphia. This was the forerunner of the current interlibrary loan system. She speeded the delivery of books through the use of parcel post. In the 1920s she created an early book truck by modifying a Model-T truck to carry books and library service to areas without such service.

Askew realized that many small towns and villages could never support libraries on their own. She decided that a regionalized approach to library service was needed.

By 1920 she had succeeded in getting a county library law passed, and the first county library was voted in Burlington County the same year. Askew envisioned a county library in all but one or two urban counties within ten to fifteen years. She was well on the way to reaching this goal when the Depression of the 1930s slowed progress and World War II stopped it.

Finally, Askew believed that good library service could only be provided by trained librarians and workers. One of her first projects was to develop a summer school in 1906, a four- to six-week course of basic library skills for workers in small libraries without trained librarians. She continued her involvement even after it became part of the program at New Jersey State Teachers College at Trenton. She also began regional institutes to bring special lecturers and new library techniques to those who could not come to the summer school.

Askew was a tireless worker who traveled the state, first by horse and buggy and later by automobile, to speak before groups on behalf of reading and libraries. Her annual reports contain vivid descriptions of drives through desolate pinelands and snow storms to reach her audiences. During World War I, she organized a "Books for Camp Libraries" drive in order to provide reading material for the nation's armed services. In its first year, the people of New Jersey donated almost 300,000 books, which were placed in New Jersey military camps, hospitals, and on ships. Several of these collections developed into support collections for training centers and vocational rehabilitation hospitals. With the outbreak of World War II, Askew started a "Books for Victory" campaign and again began providing library materials for military installations.

Askew was a consummate politician. She knew that she needed broad popular support as well as the active support of the library community if she was to accomplish her goals. To further her objectives, she became a member of many state and local organizations and supported their activities. In return, she gained their support for her causes. Typically, she included in her annual reports a section acknowledging those who had backed the commission's library programs that year.

Askew was also a super salesperson. A small redhead with an outgoing personality enhanced by wit and southern charm, she was an excellent speaker who attracted and held audiences of all ages. She was a natural storyteller and was known for her renditions of the B'rer Rabbit stories. Her pamphlet *The Place, the Man and the Book* (1916) is a lively first-person story of how she got a library for a remote New Jersey coast town.

Askew traveled widely, presenting New Jersey's library program and her philosophy to library and educational organizations. In her later years, she became very active in educational activities and associations. She was president of the New Jersey Library Association (1913–14, 1939–40), vice-president of the American Library Association (1938–39), a member of the Trenton Board of Education (1923–33), and chair of the Children's Reading Committee of the National Congress of Parents and Teachers (1924–29). During this period, Askew wrote numerous articles for education and library journals. In 1930 the New Jersey College for Women (now Douglass College, Rutgers, the State University) conferred upon her the honorary degree of doctor of library science.

Askew died on October 20, 1942, in Trenton, NJ, of bronchial pneumonia, a complication of cancer. She was buried in a family plot in Atlanta, GA.

Askew's book is *The Place, the Man and the Book* (1916). Her work is cited in *Twenty-second Annual Report of the Public Library Commission of New Jersey* (1921). She is profiled in *NAW*. Obituaries appeared in the *Trenton Evening Times* and the *Newark Evening News*, Oct. 21, 1942.

*Susan B. Roumfort*

## CAROLINE CHEEVER PEDDLE BALL, 1869–1938

Caroline Cheever (Peddle) Ball, sculptor of figurines, fountains, and bas-reliefs, was born on November 11, 1869, in Terre Haute, IN. There she grew up and graduated from high school in 1887. She was the third of six children and first of four daughters of Charles Rugan and Mary Elizabeth (Ball) Peddle. Her father was general purchasing agent for the Vandalia Railroad Company.

Although in the mid-1800s several American women had made their mark as sculptors, it was a common belief that women did not have the mechanical ability or strength to do the heavy work of sculpting. In the 1870s and 1880s, however, modeling classes opened for women in New York and Chicago, and by 1900 more women were establishing reputations as major sculptors. The acceptance of women sculptors was speeded by the great demand in late 19th- and early 20th-century America for public sculpture in the form of Civil War monuments and sculptural decoration on public buildings. Furthermore, the American world's fairs, beginning with that in Philadelphia in 1876, were lavishly embellished with sculpture and provided exhibition opportunities for artists of all kinds.

Ball, known also as "Carrie," first studied art at the Rose Polytechnic Institute in Terre Haute. She left Indiana and went to Philadelphia, where in 1889 she studied briefly at the Pennsylvania Academy of the Fine Arts. The spotty early records of the Philadelphia School of Design for Women leave it unclear whether or not Ball also attended classes there, as is sometimes reported, before moving to New York City. In New York she studied drawing with Kenyon Cox at the Art Students' League, then located on 23rd Street, above a stable. Later, she said, the smell of a stable always recalled student days.

In 1890 Ball joined the league's modeling class for women, then in its twelfth year. The following year Augustus Saint-Gaudens became master of the class, and it was he, one of America's foremost sculptors of the period, who had the greatest and most lasting effect on Ball the artist. Her work's immediacy and realism are derived from Saint-Gaudens, and she was later considered "one of the best sculptors in low relief" (Lonergan, "America's Woman Sculptors," 361), a form at which Saint-Gaudens excelled.

Ball's life-size figure *Young Virgin*, made for Tiffany and Company, was included in the fine arts exhibit at the Chicago World's Columbian Exhibition in 1893 and was exhibited at the Society of American Artists the same year. She was commissioned to design the Queen Isabella commemorative coin for the Columbian Exhibition. Later, she resigned the commission in a dispute with the Mint over control of the design.

In 1894 she made a memorial fountain for Flushing, Long Island, NY. She exhibited at the Annual Exhibition of the Architectural League of New York in 1894 and in 1895, when her entry was a bronze andiron in the figure of a laughing boy, arms stretched out to warm his hands by the fire.

Ball spent the winter of 1895 in Florence, Italy, studying the Renaissance masters. After a year or two back in New York City, where she exhibited again at the Architectural League in 1897, she returned to Europe. For three years she lived and had a studio in Paris, France.

Saint-Gaudens recommended Ball to A. Phimister Proctor, a renowned American animal sculptor, to design the figure of Victory for Proctor's quadriga (a chariot drawn by four horses abreast, often with Victory at the reins) on the U.S. Pavilion at the Universal Paris Exposition in 1900. Ball won honorable mention for her statue. The quadriga was on exhibit the following year at the Pan American Exposition in Buffalo, NY.

On October 14, 1902, she married Bertrand Emery Ball of Mount Kisco, NY. Soon afterward they moved to Westfield, NJ, where they lived for about 20 years. They had one child, a daughter, Mary Aseneth.

At the height of her career in Westfield, Ball produced a variety of works and preferred not to be thought a specialist. She made a memorial fountain for Auburn, NY, the SPCA Memorial Fountain for Westfield, NJ, and corbels (supporting brackets) for Grace Church, Brooklyn, NY. She also produced sundials, mantels, medallions, bas-reliefs, and figurines in bronze.

Early in Ball's career her statue *Young Virgin* demonstrated her understanding of innocence. She continued to explore this theme and became known for her modern sensitivity to the psychology of childhood. Done in the late 1890s, her bas-relief *The Candle Child*, a small child gazing in wonder at a candle, was very popular, and numerous copies were made. This plaque, like many of her others,

especially those of children, was inscribed with a verse, apparently composed by the artist herself. Another bas-relief by Ball, made sometime before 1906 and entitled *Gravitation*, features a young child in a high chair, leaning over pondering the toy horse she has let fall to the floor. It is inscribed:

Lying there so far below me
While there's no one near at hand to show me
How to make my dear horse fall up high
Like birds and smoke that rise into the sky.

Although not one of the top few women sculptors nationally, Ball was mentioned, between 1895 and 1911, in magazine and journal articles on the women achieving success as sculptors. Two art journals published articles devoted to Ball: the *Scrip* in 1906 and *Arts and Decoration* in 1911. Both focused on her as an interpreter of childhood. William H. Gerdts, Jr., has written that in New Jersey "probably the best known of the women sculptors of the period was Caroline Peddle Ball." (Gerdts, *Painting and Sculpture in New Jersey*, 191)

Ball exhibited yearly at the Pennsylvania Academy of the Fine Arts in Philadelphia from 1905 through 1910, and again in 1913 and 1914. Two of her figurines shown there received popular and critical attention: *Bashful Boy* and *Child with a Picture Book*, sometimes also called *The Student*, which was exhibited in both 1906 and 1907. *Bashful Boy* was also shown at the Newark (NJ) Museum in 1913 and bought by the museum the next year. Ball exhibited at the National Academy of Design in 1909 and the Architectural League in 1910.

In 1911 the Balls built a new house in Westfield, with a studio for Ball. A visitor to the studio in 1916 described it as extending the width of the house, rising to the roof rafters, and full of the great variety of sculpture for which Ball was known. She made decorations for the new house, including a mantel for the living room and one featuring elves for the nursery. Behind the house was a garden in which Ball apparently took great delight. For her entry in *Woman's Who's Who of America* (1914–15), she listed gardening and propagating dwarf fruit trees as her recreations. She also expressed herself in favor of woman suffrage in that entry.

Around 1923 Ball moved to Harwinton, CT, where she devoted much time to gardening. One of her projects in her last years, when she was a widow, was bringing to publication her mother's account, written for her children and grandchildren, of her family's migration from New York State to the wilderness of Indiana. Ball wrote the introduction to the book, but she did not live to see it published (in 1939). Her family dedicated the book to her memory.

After several months of failing health, Ball died on October 1, 1938, in Charlotte Hungerford Hospital in Torrington, CT.

Articles about Ball and her work are: "The Work of Caroline Peddle Ball," *The Scrip: Notes on Art* 1 (July 1906):310–12; Mira Edson, "Caroline Peddle Ball: An Interpreter of Childhood," *Arts and Decoration* 1 (Oct. 1911): 484–85; and Elizabeth Lonergan, "America's Woman Sculptors," *Harpers Bazar* 45 (Aug. 1911):360–61. Ball is mentioned in William H. Gerdts, Jr., *Painting and Sculpture in New Jersey* (1964); and in Chris Petteys, *Dictionary of Women Artists* (1985). Obituaries appeared in the *New York Times*, Oct. 3, 1938, and the *Westfield* (NJ) *Leader*, Oct. 6, 1938.

*Maggie Sullivan*
*Maryanne M. Garbowsky*

## MARGARET BANCROFT, 1854–1912

Margaret Bancroft, educator and founder of the Bancroft Training School in Haddonfield, NJ, was born June 28, 1854, in Philadelphia, PA, the fourth of five children of Harvey and Rebecca (Haines) Bancroft. Her father, after emigrating to the United States from Garthgannon, Wales, built up a successful mercantile business. The family was Quaker and lived in the Germantown section of Philadelphia.

As a young woman, Bancroft studied at the Philadelphia Normal School and became a fifth-grade teacher in the Philadelphia public schools. When her father's business suffered financial reverses and failed, she became the primary support of her parents.

Bancroft's fervor and diligence as a teacher brought her to the attention of a school board member, Dr. W. W. Keen, a noted surgeon and professor of surgery at Jefferson Medical College. She frequently conferred with Keen about pupils with problems. Of particular interest to her were students who could not study successfully, and she began to classify the reasons for their academic problems, finding that some had poor vision, defective hearing, or were what she termed "mentally deficient."

Bancroft devoted much of her time and thought to these special children, adjusting her program to suit their individual needs and becoming known in the school system for her work. She consulted with Keen and Dr. S. Weir Mitchell, a noted neurologist who had worked with Keen as a surgeon during the Civil War. Eventually Keen suggested she devote full time to her special students by starting a school of her own. Denied leave from her teaching to try the plan, Bancroft resigned her teaching post and started what turned out to be her life's work.

Bancroft selected rural Haddonfield as the site for her school because her brother lived there and because of its proximity to Philadelphia, where she could continue to consult with the two doctors. She acquired a house with her parents and there in 1883 the Haddonfield School for the Mentally Deficient and Peculiarly Backward was opened, with its first pupils referred by Keen.

Using her drive, intelligence, experience, and determination, and perhaps most of all, her imagination, Bancroft evolved innovative ways of educating developmentally disabled children. At the time, little, if any, training was given such children. Most were institutionalized and, at best, given custodial care. The societal stigma was such that families were careful about hiding disabilities. Even Bancroft's private school protected the identities of its residents by not using students' surnames.

Bancroft created a specialized program for each student's physical, mental, and spiritual growth. Proper nutrition, personal hygiene, exercise and physiotherapy, daily prayers, lessons suited to mental age, tasks and projects for sensory and artistic development, as well as recreation and visits to circuses, theaters, concerts, and museums were all part of the program. Bancroft claimed that no student admitted to the school was hopeless. Sometimes she kept a child with her night and day for months on end to accomplish the progress she felt was possible. The school buildings and grounds were homelike and attractive.

Bancroft added to her staff teachers of physical culture and gymnastics, manual training, speech, and kindergarten skills, and soon the school's growth necessitated a move to a larger house on Chestnut Street. In 1888 Bancroft brought Jean Cox, an experienced kindergarten teacher, into the management of the school.

A major setback to Bancroft's work occurred in March 1892 when a fire caused by a defective chimney flue destroyed the house. The school family stayed in Atlantic City for several weeks while the search for new quarters went on. Ultimately Charles Lippincott of Philadelphia helped Bancroft purchase "the Lindens," a small estate in Haddonfield, in exchange for the lifetime care of his handicapped daughter.

In the early years of the school Bancroft sent her students home during the summer, but she later decided that their slow, painstaking progress should not be interrupted. In 1903 she took the financial risk of buying an old hotel in Owl's Head on the coast of Maine, and in the summer of 1904 the school family took its first trek to the summer quarters, a practice followed ever since. In 1904 the trip took a day and a half and involved traveling by ship and railroad.

In the same year that the summer program was initiated, Bancroft had the school formally chartered as the Bancroft-Cox Training School. Very soon, however, she and Jean Cox had a major falling out and Cox resigned, taking some of the school's students with her. The school was renamed the Bancroft Training School. In 1907 Bancroft hired Dr. Ernest A. Farrington as resident physician and psychologist, and he soon became her trusted coadministrator.

In addition to her life at the school, Bancroft participated in community life in Haddonfield. In 1894, with twelve friends, she organized the Haddon Fortnightly, a women's club that promoted its members' educational, literary, and social interests and is still active today.

Bancroft was widely known in her field and was active between 1892 and 1909, delivering her message to such groups as the Association of Medical Officers for American Institutions for Idiotic and Feebleminded Persons, the National Congress of Mothers, the National Conference of Charities and Corrections, the American Academy of Medicine, the Woman's Medical College of Philadelphia, and the National Education Department.

In an article written in 1904 Bancroft described her view of her students' disabilities: "I am with those who believe that which we commonly call 'the mind' is the soul-light working through and utilizing the bodily organs of sense. In a normal person the motor and sensory nervous systems act as the windows of the individual personality. . . . The broken, many-stained and pictorial windows through which the light is struggling under disadvantages to harmonize itself with the physical world at large are found in three classes of persons—the mentally deficient, the morally deficient, and the insane. In these, the light is there, but the images, as in a broken cathedral window, are more or less shattered and confused." (Bancroft, *Collected Papers*, 60–61)

In her other writings Bancroft advocated abandoning the use of terms with derogatory connotations such as "idiot" and "imbecile," preferring instead "mentally deficient" and later "mentally subnormal." She pleaded for awakening public awareness and understanding of special children, and she suggested the restructuring of public institutions giving specific guidelines for grouping children.

Bancroft died, at age 57, on January 3, 1912, of cerebral thrombosis. She was buried beside her parents in Laurel Hill Cemetery, Philadelphia. Her will held detailed instructions for the perpetuation of her school, which today is a significant nonprofit institution with residential and day care, and an evaluation and treatment center. Owl's Head is now a year-round residential center.

The Bancroft School (Haddonfield, NJ) maintains material on Bancroft, including *Collected Papers of Margaret Bancroft on Mental Subnormality . . .* (n.d.). Emma Lewis, *Pioneer Women of Historic Haddonfield* (1973), has a brief biography of Bancroft. Claire Griese, director of Special Services at Bancroft School, was interviewed for this article.

*Shirley M. Montgomery*

## MARY KATHARINE JONES BENNETT, 1864–1950

Mary Katharine (Jones) Bennett, born in Englewood (Bergen County), NJ, on November 28, 1864, lived during the most crucial years in the advancement of the role of women in the Presbyterian Church, USA, a crusade to which she gave untiring leadership as a churchwoman and a spokeswoman for home mission and interdenominational work. The younger of two daughters born to Henry Jones, a builder, and Winifred (Davies) Jones, both natives of northern Wales, Bennett (who was known as Katharine) grew up in comfortable circumstances and was well educated, attending the Dwight School in Englewood and the Bordentown (NJ) Academy. She entered Elmira College in 1881, where she was an excellent student, and graduated with an A.B. in 1885.

After graduation, she returned home to teach for several years in both public and private schools in Englewood. But what was to become a lifelong zeal for social and religious work led her, in 1894, to take a position as national secretary of young people's work for the Woman's Board of Home Missions of the Presbyterian Church, whose antecedent board, the Woman's Executive Committee, was the first national woman's organization in the Presbyterian Church, U.S.A. Thus was launched a career in the church that began in one century and ended in another.

The context in which Bennett established the new direction of her life work was a post-Civil War commitment by American Protestant women to organize national and regional denominational societies to send money, supplies, and personnel to foreign and domestic mission fields. Churchwomen were concerned with women and children in need, such as prostitutes, widows, orphans, paupers, and the unchurched of the U.S. frontier and overseas, believing that "Christianity had awarded them favor and freedom compared to women of other lands and to the non-Christian of America, and they felt a responsibility to share this with others." (Boyd and Brackenridge, *Presbyterian Women in America*, 15) So, although Presbyterian women of the late 19th and early 20th centuries were barred from the pulpit and the halls of church government, they exerted a powerful influence through their mission boards. Bennett, reflecting on this influence, called "woman's work for women and children a vital asset in nation-building." ("The Past a Promise for the Future," *Home Mission Monthly*, March 1924, 106)

She was married on July 20, 1898, to Fred Smith Bennett, a resident of Englewood and a prosperous New York manufacturer and merchant. They had no children, and her husband was supportive of her religious work, so her career continued relatively uninterrupted by her marriage. She resigned from her paid employment with the Woman's Board, however, after her marriage, but she was elected a member of that board soon afterward. In 1909 she was chosen its third president and served in that office until the board's 1923 merger with the Presbyterian Board of National Missions.

During Bennett's almost 30-year association with the Woman's Board, she led it to develop a structure that raised over $16 million for the mission of the church and to create an awareness of the contributions of women that set the stage for the ordination of women to the ministry.

Bennett's election to the presidency of the Woman's Board of Home Missions was one of the most significant events in the history of the church, according to one writer: "A woman of unique abilities, Katharine Bennett was to leave her mark, not only on the Woman's Board, which she guided through the rest of its life as a separate organization, but also on the status of women in the Presbyterian Church." (Verdesi, *In But Still Out*, 65) Although a volunteer, she exercised the capabilities of an executive throughout her term of office. She was an able administrator, fund raiser, public speaker, and writer. She administered the board's seventeen committees and its over $1 million annual budget, and under her leadership standing rules were developed that led in 1915 to the board's incorporation (it had previously existed under the authority of the all-male Board of Home Missions). From that year on, it could receive and administer its own funds and receive legacies in its own name. In May 1916 in Atlantic City, NJ, Bennett became the first woman to speak as a board president to the General Assembly, the national governing body of the church. As reported by the press: "And talk she did— brightly, sprightly, and wittily, much to the point and entirely to the delight of the 900 men who made up her audience."

From 1916 until 1923 the Woman's Board of Home Missions flourished under her leadership. Times were changing in the church and the nation, and Bennett was a woman who understood the need for flexibility. She wrote that young women in the 1920s were "a generation looking with unafraid eyes at all institutions, even ecclesiastical— and asking 'why?' of many accepted customs." (*Presbyterian Magazine*, Dec. 1929) She helped reconcile the women of the church to a new structure as the Woman's Board was merged with the new Board of National Missions. At the final meeting of the Woman's Board, she was cited for her "executive ability, her beautiful spirit, and her fineness of leadership—a pilot who has steered her ship with no uncertainty." (*Home Missions Monthly*, June 1923, 182) A week later, she was elected vice-president of the Board of National Missions and served until 1941.

Bennett also served her denomination as a corresponding member of the General Council from 1924 to 1932. She traveled widely in the interest of mission at home and abroad. Interested in the ecumenical movement, she represented the Presbyterian church at the founding of the interdenominational Council of Women for Home Missions in 1908 and was its second president from 1916 to 1924. She was the first president of the interchurch Board of Christian Work in Santo Domingo (1920–36) and

served on several committees of the Federal Council of the Churches of Christ (FCC) in America, including the famous Commission on the Steel Strike of 1919, which contributed to the elimination of the twelve-hour workday in the steel industry. She also represented her denomination at the worldwide Life and Work Conference of the FCC in Oxford, England, in 1937. Near the end of her career with the church, she devoted special attention to work with migrants and American Indians.

Bennett also found time to devote to civic affairs in her hometown. She was the first president of the Englewood Civic League (1901–11), president of the Woman's Club (1902–6), and founder of the Englewood Forum (1916). She was chair of the local Woman's Council of National Defense (1917) and organized a Girls' Patriotic League on a countywide basis. In 1920 she served as historian of the celebration of Englewood's 50th anniversary.

To those who knew her, Bennett "combined a brilliant mind and the ability to write and speak effectively with personal charm and wit." (Brackenridge and Boyd, 66) She wrote numerous articles in *Home Mission Monthly* and *Women and Mission*, and authored several pamphlets, including *Home Missions and the Social Questions* (1914), *Causes of Unrest among Women of the Church* (1927), and *How It Grew: The Story of Woman's Organization in the Presbyterian Church in the United States of America* (1942). In the final years of her life, she wrote a book, *The Emergence of Interdenominational Organizations among Protestant Church Women* (1944).

In the church of the late 1800s and early 1900s, the only path open to her was that of volunteer churchwoman. In that capacity, for half a century Bennett advocated for women in her church as a full-time volunteer churchwoman who led the church in its far-reaching national mission. Although not known as a feminist, she was educated in women's schools, worked outside her home before and after her marriage, and strove toward the goal of equal recognition for women. In her own words, "Woman asks to be considered in the light of her ability and not her sex." (Bennett, *Causes of Unrest*, 27)

A widow at the end of her life, Bennett died at Englewood Hospital, Englewood, NJ, on April 11, 1950, at age 86, from a fractured hip and hypertensive cardiovascular disease. She was buried in the Jones family plot at Brookside Cemetery in Englewood.

Archival material on Bennett, including her publications, some correspondence, and unpublished speeches, is available at the Presbyterian Church, USA, Presbyterian Historical Society (Philadelphia). Her work is noted in Lois A. Boyd and R. Douglas Brackenridge, *Presbyterian Women in America* (1983); and Elizabeth Howell Verdesi, *In But Still Out: Women in the Church* (1975). Bennett is profiled in *NAW*. Obituaries appeared in the *New York Times*, Apr. 12, 1950, and in the *Press Journal* (Englewood, NJ), Apr. 13, 1950.

*Barbara A. Chaapel*

Marietta Boggio Botto, c. 1910, *standing top center*, on the front porch of her Haledon home with her husband, *top left*, two daughters, and visiting neighbors. Botto's home became a meeting place for striking Paterson silk workers in 1913. *Courtesy, Botto Family Collection, Botto House National Landmark.*

## MARIA BOTTO, 1870–1915

Marietta (Boggio) Botto, immigrant silk worker and homemaker whose home was a meeting place for striking workers during the Paterson silk strike of 1913, was born on March 14, 1870, in Biella, Piedmonte, Italy, a region at the foothills of the Alps known for its production of linen and wool. She was the daughter of Joseph Boggio and his wife, whose name is unknown. Little is known of Botto's family in Piedmonte, except that they are said to have owned a chocolate-making business.

In 1885, at the age of fifteen, Maria (as she came to be known) married Pietro Botto, a young man of 21 from a nearby village. Their daughter Albina was born in 1889, before they decided to emigrate to the United States. In 1892 the Bottos arrived in West Hoboken, NJ, where both Maria and Pietro found work as silk weavers. They lived in West Hoboken for fifteen years and had three more daughters: Adelia (b. 1894), Eva (b. 1895), and Olga (b. 1899).

The Bottos saved their money until they could afford to build their own home in Haledon, a community on the streetcar line north of Paterson, where many of their countryfolk from Biella had already settled. In 1908 the family moved into their new twelve-room Norwood Street home, which included two three-room units on the second floor that were rented for additional income. Pietro Botto and the couple's daughters worked as weavers in the local silk mills.

Like other women in her neighborhood who had previously worked in silk mills, Botto did "outwork" for the local mills. As a skilled "picker" who cleaned and snipped imperfections from finished bolts of silk, she worked at a special frame in her dining room on bolts of fabric brought to her from the mill by her daughters. Botto was paid a small sum per yard for this work.

Botto ran a large household and, like many immigrant women, used her domestic skills to bring added income to the family. The kitchen and dining room were the focal point of her work. In addition to renting the apartments on the second floor, she took in boarders, serving noonday meals to working men in her dining room.

Since the Botto home was situated on a country hillside near the trolley line, it was a convenient location for their Sunday business, hosting fellow silk workers and Piedmontese neighbors looking for recreation and sociability. The attractions were their bocce court, the card tables, shady grape arbor, and Botto's northern Italian cooking. Their home became a popular meeting place and the recreational attractions provided them with valuable extra income. The bulk of work for this enterprise was Botto's since she, with help from her daughters, was responsible for all kitchen and serving duties.

Botto might have lived out her life in relative anonymity had it not been for the role her home played as an important meeting place for striking workers during the Paterson silk strike of 1913.

During that long and unsuccessful labor protest, nearly 25,000 Paterson area silk workers, assisted by local socialists and national organizers for the Industrial Workers of the World, picketed the mills and demanded improved wages and working conditions. When the mayor of Paterson denied the strikers freedom of assembly, the socialist mayor of Haledon invited them to meet in his town.

The Botto residence, with its surrounding fields, was an ideal focal point for the strike rallies. The second-floor balcony over the front door served as a speakers' platform for such notables as William (Big Bill) Haywood, Elizabeth Gurley Flynn, and John Reed, who addressed thousands of strikers and their families on Sundays. Botto's Sunday business mushroomed out of all proportion, and during the week she provided room and board for strike leaders—often unremunerated during the last days of the protest, when strikers' resources diminished.

During this period Botto was not well, although she was still relatively young. In 1910 she had begun to suffer from dropsy, and though she continued to work, her condition gradually worsened. She died of exophthalmic goi-ter at the age of 45 on November 11, 1915, two years after the silk strike. She was buried in Laurel Grove Cemetery in Paterson. Her home is now a national historic landmark.

The archives of the American Labor Museum (Haledon, NJ) contain the principal records and sources of information on Botto. An interview with Bunny Kuiken, Botto's granddaughter, took place in March 1986. A detailed account of Botto's contributions is John A. Herbst, "A Slice of the Earth," *New Jersey History* 99 (1981):33–48.

*Janet Gibbs-Albanesius*

## CORNELIA FOSTER BRADFORD, 1847–1935

Cornelia Foster Bradford, founder and head worker of the Whittier House social settlement of Jersey City, was born in the northern Finger Lakes region of New York State on December 4, 1847. Her father, Benjamin Franklin Bradford, a descendant of Governor William Bradford of Plymouth, was a Methodist minister who later opted to serve the Congregational church and held pastorates in several small towns in the Finger Lakes region. Often at odds with his parishioners over slavery, Benjamin Bradford was an abolitionist whose residences were stops on the Underground Railroad. He was also an advocate of Prohibition and women's rights. He and his wife, Mary Amory (Howe) Bradford, were the parents of Amory, born in 1846, who later became a noted Congregational minister based for over 40 years in Montclair, NJ; Cornelia, called Nellie for many years; and Mary.

Bradford graduated from Houghton Seminary in Clinton, NY, and attended Olivet College in Michigan for several years beginning in 1867. Residence in Chester, NJ (1872–75), provided Bradford with firsthand knowledge of the growing momentum of industrialization, for her three years there coincided with an iron mining boom in the town. Housing was rapidly thrown together for immigrants and native-born workers, with railroads hastily assembled to cart away the iron to market. Bradford and her sister, Mary, taught Sunday school at the Chester Congregational Church, where their father served as pastor.

For nearly 20 years thereafter, following her sister's marriage and her mother's death, Bradford searched for meaningful activity. She taught and delivered lectures on history, literature, and travel, drawing upon her experiences in Europe, attending universities and visiting England's newly conceived settlement houses. By 1893 she had visited Toynbee Hall, the first settlement initiated in East London in 1884 by university students determined to help the poor by means other than alms. Bradford stayed longer in Mansfield House, Cannington, East London, where its head worker, Percy Alden, became a personal friend. J. Ramsey MacDonald, another English friend, visited Bradford in America on trips in 1897 and 1898, long before he became prime minister.

When Bradford returned to the United States, she became an associate of Jane Addams at the famous Chicago settlement Hull House, before founding her own settlement in Jersey City. After she arrived in Jersey City on December 20, 1893, Bradford began by initiating service programs at the People's Palace on Grand Street, headed by Dr. J. L. Scudder, a clergyman. Quarters for a permanent settlement were established at another location on Grand Street four months later under the name Whittier House, in honor of the recently deceased Quaker poet John Greenleaf Whittier. Bradford had met Whittier on his 75th birthday, and so the poet's lines, "He serves Thee best who loveth most / His brothers and Thy own," became the new settlement's motto. Bradford's sympathies were undoubtedly influenced by her father's example and by the reforming ardor engendered by the Civil War and Reconstruction. She always believed people were their brothers' and sisters' keepers.

Whittier House, New Jersey's first settlement house, quickly became a success despite its opening during the depths of a major depression. Financial assistance was at first supplemented by Bradford's brother Amory, who was also the first president of the board. The settlement rapidly added activities and new sources of income. A variety of classes were taught and numerous clubs were started, including the first free kindergarten and the first women's club in Jersey City. An important innovation was legal aid, originally described as the poor man's lawyer, after English models. Residents at the settlement helped Bradford, who was designated head worker.

The settlement aided immigrants attracted to Jersey City because of its proximity to Ellis Island. Immigrants outnumbered the native-born in Jersey City before the end of the 19th century, with Slavs, Scandinavians, Italians, English, Irish, and Scots predominating. The factories and ferries employed these men, women, and children, who crowded into the First Ward near Whittier House.

When Whittier House opened the first playground in Jersey City, it was a small but welcome antidote to the city's slums. Annual summer outings for the children, sponsored by Amory Bradford's First Congregational Church in Montclair, became pleasant diversions from hot city streets. The settlement also supplemented the minimal local health facilities.

The achievements of Whittier House under Bradford's direction extended far beyond the immediate neighborhood, however. Bradford and her settlement workers made significant advances in state, county, and city reforms. By 1900 Bradford had provided the impetus for JULIET CLANNON CUSHING's organization, the Consumers' League of New Jersey. Cushing and Bradford helped lead New Jersey to major reforms, particularly in child labor law. In the summer of 1904 Bradford and Secretary Dale of the Consumers' League visited glass factories and homes of glass blowers in southern New Jersey. The investigation led to the formation of the Child Protective League, as well as an attempt to pass a comprehensive child labor bill and the formation of a watchdog child labor agency. In much the same way, Whittier House and its residents played a key role in helping to pass a state tenement house code.

Bradford helped create a state settlement house group, the New Jersey Association of Neighborhood Workers, in March 1905. The group, modeled on the New York City Association, in which Bradford was a charter member, became a clearinghouse for lobbyists in numerous causes, such as the ten-hour workday for women, the juvenile court, and woman suffrage.

The settlement sponsored the 1906 meeting that created the Hudson County Tuberculosis Association, acted as a "mother" to the Society for Prevention of Cruelty to Children, the North American Civic League, the New Jersey State Bureau of Immigration, and also became a member of the State Board of Charities and Correction.

Then, in 1912, Mayor H. Otto Wittpenn appointed Bradford to Jersey City's Board of Education. She became vice-president of the National Federation of Settlements and had an elementary school in the First Ward named after her. Bradford was honored at celebrations in 1914 and 1919 marking the 20th and 25th anniversaries of Whittier House. Bradford always insisted that the purpose of her effort, and of Whittier House, was democracy. On the 29th anniversary of Whittier House, she said, "Its aim, too, after all these years, is still democracy, because this was the basic stone, and also because its religious beliefs are reciprocity, social and economical, and that as all are simply human, the strong should bear the infirmities of the weak." (Whittier House scrapbook, no. 3) The New Jersey College for Women (now Douglass College) awarded her an honorary M.A. in 1923.

Bradford combined religious faith and common sense to combat the problems created by industrialism and mass immigration. She was a pioneering social worker of the Progressive Era and for 32 years her name was connected with efforts to bring about reform.

Characteristically, as the Great Depression deepened, Bradford returned 10 percent of her pension to Whittier House. Nine years after retiring from Whittier House, Bradford died on January 15, 1935, at 88, of myocardial degeneration, at the Montclair home of her niece, STELLA STEVENS BRADFORD, with whom she made her home in the last years of her life. Interment was in the family plot in Rosedale Cemetery in Orange, NJ.

For documents pertaining to Bradford, see Whittier House Social Settlement Papers, NJ-HS. For her assessment of her work, see the *Annual Reports* of Whittier House, beginning in 1894, as well as her articles "The Association of Neighborhood Workers of New Jersey," *New Jersey Review of Charities and Correction* 4 (1905):128–29; "For Jersey City's Social Uplift: Life at Whittier House," *Commons* 10 (1905):101–6; and "The Settlement Movement in New Jersey," *New Jersey Review of Charities and Correction* 10 (1912):23–28. Additional information on her appears in Ella Handen, "In Liberty's Shadow: Cornelia Bradford and Whittier House," *New Jersey History* 100 (1982):49–69, and in *NAW*.

*Ella Handen*

## STELLA STEVENS BRADFORD, 1871–1959

Stella Stevens Bradford, renowned physician and pioneer in the use of physical therapy to rehabilitate physically handicapped children and adults, was born on June 27, 1871, in Montclair (Essex County), NJ, the eldest child of the Rev. Dr. Amory Howe Bradford and Julia (Stevens) Bradford. Her father, born in 1846 in Grandby, NY, the son of the Rev. Benjamin Franklin Bradford and Mary (Howe) Bradford, was descended on his father's side from William Bradford, first governor of the *Mayflower* settlers in Plymouth Colony, MA, and on his mother's side from Abraham Howe, a founder of Marlborough, MA. Bradford's mother, born in 1846 in Little Falls, NY, married in 1870 and had four children: Stella, Arthur, Cornelia, and Clara. Stella Bradford was the niece of CORNELIA FOSTER BRADFORD, noted social worker.

Bradford grew up in the Congregational church parsonage in Montclair, where she described her home life as "hospitable without calculation." Her parents welcomed into their household those who were temporarily without home or work. Bradford attended Montclair public schools and went on to graduate with a B.A. from Smith College in 1893. While at Smith, she was president of the Association of Christian Work. She did postgraduate study for a year in Italy and Germany and then returned to the United States and took sociology courses at New York University. She taught for a few years in a private school, at Montclair High School, and at Smith College. When Bradford decided to become a physician she entered Cornell University Medical College. She graduated in 1902 and served a year's internship at Worcester Memorial Hospital in Massachusetts, where she developed an interest in orthopedics.

In the fall of 1903, Bradford started her medical practice in Montclair. She served as a school medical inspector there and as a clinical assistant in the outpatient department of Gouverneur Hospital in New York City. At Gouverneur Hospital she and another physician established a tuberculosis clinic, the first of its kind in any New York City hospital.

In 1905 she returned to Smith College for a year as the school physician, and she traveled in Europe again the following summer. In 1907 she returned to Montclair as the resident physician at Ramapo Hills Sanitarium. During this period Bradford was active in developing health care for tuberculosis patients in Montclair. She helped establish the Montclair Tuberculosis Committee, which employed a nurse to visit tuberculosis patients in their homes, a service that evolved into the Montclair Public Health Nursing Service. She also organized and was the medical director of the first Fresh Air School in her area.

In 1910 Bradford became medical superintendent of Adams Place in Pompton Lakes, NJ. By this time she had become interested in the work of W. Curtis Adams, who had developed a method of physical exercises to retrain muscles of handicapped people. Bradford published a paper on his methods and later, in 1913, took a course in physical therapy at Boston City Hospital. The use of therapeutic exercises to retrain the muscles of children and adults who had been crippled by diseases such as rheumatic fever, polio, and arthritis became her specialty for the rest of her medical career.

In the summer of 1929 Bradford went to Denmark to study the methods of Nils Bukh at the Nils Bukh Folk High School of Physical Training. The following year she presented a paper on Bukh's work before the New York Electrotherapeutic Society, which was reprinted in the *Medical Times*.

During her long practice in Montclair Bradford was associated with Mountainside Hospital. In 1932 she was appointed director of the Physical Therapy Department at the hospital, but she retired from this position in 1936 to devote full time to her private practice. Called back in 1950 to head the newly organized Physical Medicine and Rehabilitation Department, she served as acting director until a permanent director could be found. She left this position in 1953 after the department had doubled in size. Bradford then helped the hospital develop an employee health service and served as its first director.

During her career in physical therapy, Bradford enlarged the public and medical understanding of the specialty through lectures and published papers. In tribute at her retirement, Mary Arny, a friend, wrote: "Because of her, many people who were hopeless have gained hope. She has seen the real meaning of her calling. She has known that to heal the body without consideration of healing the spirit is a useless and empty gesture." (*Montclair Times*, Apr. 12, 1956)

Bradford expressed her philosophy of healing in letters written to her patients. To one patient she wrote: "I know you are ill, weak, low, wretched, but cannot see why you should not advance a step, say every few days, until you reach a height from which the beauty and a little of the plan of this wild and confusing world can be seen." (Bradford, *Letters*, 6–7) Bradford described her philosophy of health in another letter: "There is no such thing as 'perfect health,' but if one learns how to use the portion allotted to him wisely, and in so doing steadily increases that portion, all is well." (*Letters*, 11)

Despite a busy medical practice, Bradford found time for community and professional organizations at the local, state, and national level. She was a lifetime member of the First Congregational Church in Montclair and an active member of the College Women's Club. She was a member of the Town Improvement and Health Prevention Association, which established the first social worker service in the city. She also taught in the Adult Education School and was president of the Montclair Business and Professional Women's Club and of the Service Clubs Council of Montclair. Because of her contributions she was chosen for the Outstanding Woman of Essex County Award by the Executive Council of Women's Service Clubs of Essex County in 1950. On April 28, 1957, the Medical Society of New Jersey honored Bradford for 50 years of medical practice with its Golden Merit Award.

Bradford died of natural causes on January 20, 1959, at age 88, in the Mary Manning Walsh Home in New York City. She was buried in Rosedale Cemetery in Montclair.

A booklet of Bradford's letters to her patients, *Letters of a Physician*, provides insight into Bradford's personality; a copy belongs to her niece, Jean Chesterman. Clipping files on Bradford are available at Mountainside Hospital and NJ-MPL. Personal interviews with Dr. Roger Lochhead, Bradford's personal physician and friend, and with another friend, Mary Arny, provided additional insights into Bradford's life. Bradford's tribute to her father appeared in the *Montclair Times*, Apr. 5, 1945, and gives insights into her family life. Bradford's obituary appeared in the *Montclair Times*, Jan. 22, 1959.

*Constance B. Schuyler*

Charlotte Emerson Brown, an organizer of the General Federation of Women's Clubs, was the organization's first president from 1890 to 1894. *Reprinted with permission, from* A History of the New Jersey State Federation of Women's Clubs.

## CHARLOTTE EMERSON BROWN, 1838–1895

Charlotte (Emerson) Brown, an organizer and first president of the General Federation of Women's Clubs, was born on April 21, 1838, in Andover, MA, the youngest of nine children (six boys and three girls) of Ralph and Eliza (Rockwell) Emerson. Brown's father, a Yale graduate, Congregational clergyman, and professor of ecclesiastical history at Andover Seminary, was a cousin of Ralph Waldo Emerson.

Brown grew up in a family that valued education and intellectual achievement, and she amply fulfilled their expectations. She and her older sister Elizabeth were educated at Abbot Female Academy in Andover. She had an able mind and became accomplished in modern languages and music. After her graduation in 1857, Brown traveled for two years with her brother Joseph in Europe, where she studied modern Greek. Upon returning from Europe, she taught for a while at Miss Hannah Lyman's School in Montreal, Canada. She then studied briefly at a business school in Chicago and settled in Rockford, IL, where her parents had moved. Brown became secretary to her brother Ralph, a Rockford merchant and manufacturer of agricultural implements.

In 1865 Brown assumed a teaching job at Rockford Female Seminary, filling a position her sister Elizabeth had held before she married. Members of her family were well-known supporters of Rockford; Brown's brother Joseph had been a founder of the seminary and president of its Board of Trustees for many years, and her brother Ralph was an early benefactor of the school. Brown taught English literature, history, French, and German at Rockford off and on until 1880, but her tenure there was apparently punctuated by study and travel in Europe, especially in Italy and Germany. Rockford was a small school at the time, with a faculty of twelve women who lived and took meals with the students. From 1877 to 1880 Brown taught French and German exclusively and counted among her students the young Jane Addams, who became one of Rockford's most illustrious alumnae.

At the end of the school year in 1880, on July 27, Brown married the Rev. Dr. William Bryant Brown, a Congregational clergyman 21 years her senior and a widower with one son. William Brown had been a clergyman in Andover during the years she was studying at Abbot and was the brother of ANTOINETTE BROWN BLACKWELL, the first woman to be ordained in a recognized denomination (Congregational). He was the minister emeritus of the Congregational church in Newark, NJ, where he had served for 33 years. After their marriage Brown and her husband traveled abroad for three years, visiting the major European cities as well as Egypt and Syria. It was said that she was so fluent in languages that she could pass for a native in several European countries.

When Brown returned from her extended wedding trip, she settled into her new home on Chestnut Street in East Orange, NJ, and quickly became involved in women's activities there. While she had been living in Rockford, she had organized a club for the study of French and another, called Euterpe, for the study of music. Such clubs were popular in the post–Civil War period, when women in many towns organized for literary and educational purposes. In East Orange Brown soon joined the Fortnightly Club and the Women's Club of Orange.

Brown's erudition and leadership ability were quickly acknowledged and by 1888 she was made president of the Woman's Club of Orange. As one of the pioneer women's clubs in the state (founded in 1872), the Orange club was one of only three New Jersey groups (the others being the El Mora Ladies Literary and Social Club of Elizabeth and the Monday Afternoon Club of Plainfield) invited by Jane Croly to send representatives to New York City in 1889 to celebrate the 21st birthday of Sorosis, the noted club she had organized in the 1860s. Brown represented the Orange club at the celebration, where the idea of a national organization of women's clubs was put forward. Brown was made a member of the advisory board, which worked throughout the following year to design and organize the founding convention of the new organization.

When the General Federation of Women's Clubs was founded at the New York City convention in April 1890, Brown was elected its first president. She believed deeply in the value of the club movement and the mission of clubwomen. During her presidency she wrote: "Our club women must be the synonyms of light, life and love. They must stand for all that is good and against all forms of evil." (Wells, *Unity in Diversity,* 54) She also understood the value of women's organizations as training grounds for women in larger society. She wrote in January 1894 in the federation magazine, the *New Cycle*: "Young ladies clubs are training schools for young ladies to graduate from into women's clubs of larger experience where profounder work and where greater responsibilities are to be assumed." (Wells, 260)

Brown's crucial task as the federation's first president was uniting and coordinating the diverse and far-flung clubs, establishing lasting organizational forms and procedures. A strong leader, she traveled widely and corresponded voluminously to create links among member clubs and to spur the formation of new groups. To assure proper business organization she led the federation to obtain its charter in New Jersey in 1893. Brown presided over the first two biennial conventions of the federation, in Chicago in 1892 and in Philadelphia in 1894. By the end of her term the membership of the federation had grown from 51 charter member clubs to 350. Brown had succeeded in establishing the solid organizational structure on which the federation could develop.

After her two terms as president were completed, Brown served as chair of the Foreign Correspondence Committee and was asked to write the history of the federation, a task she could not complete. On February 4, 1895, she died of pneumonia at age 57 in her East Orange home. Friends in the club movement felt her death had been hastened by the intense pace she had set for herself as federation president. She was buried at Mt. Pleasant Cemetery in Newark.

Materials on Brown are contained in the archives of Phillips Academy (Andover, MA) and Rockford College (Rockford, IL). For additional information on Brown and her activities, see Robert McHenry, ed., *Liberty's Women* (1980); Mildred W. Wells, *Unity in Diversity: The History of the General Federation of Women's Clubs* (1953); and Jane C. Croly, *The History of the Woman's Club Movement in America* (1898).

*Delight Wing Dodyk*

## EMMA COLEMAN, 1864–1935

Emma B. (Holman) Coleman, educator and business college administrator, was born in Poughkeepsie, NY, on August 14, 1864, to Edward and Margaret (Middlemass) Holman. Her father was born in the United States and her mother in Scotland. Little is known of Coleman' early life, except that she had a sister, Mary Alice. On February 19, 1892, at age 28, she married Henry Coleman, age 53, an Irish immigrant who had been the owner and president of the Coleman Business College in Newark, NJ, since 1880. It is likely that Coleman met her husband in Poughkeepsie, NY, at the Eastman Business College. There Henry Coleman had served seventeen years as a faculty member, gaining the experience necessary to take over the ailing Newark school in the Bryant and Stratton business college chain. Coleman was 25 years younger than her husband, who had two children by a prior marriage. The age difference between Coleman and her husband ensured special longevity of family control of the Coleman Business College.

In 1880, when Coleman's husband took it over, the Coleman Business College was one of 130 such business colleges nationwide training a new type of person for the expanding administrative work of corporate America. At that time, females constituted from 10 to 30 percent of the 23,000 students enrolled nationally. Many such schools created a "Ladies Department," which made explicit overtures to "daughters of wealth." "With the care of an estate resting upon her shoulders," a Coleman Business College promotion ran, "how many a woman has for the first time seen the value of a knowledge of business affairs?" However, realistically such schools trained women to be cashiers, bookkeepers, and correspondents, situations business college leaders felt preferable to that of saleswomen, seamstresses, or factory laborers.

During the last decades of the 19th century three-quarters of business college enrollments represented day students, who ideally attended for three months and studied commercial law, business customs and habits, practical penmanship, arithmetic, spelling, bookkeeping, and practical grammar. In its early years the Coleman Business College publicly welcomed students from ages 12 to 50 and offered free instruction in their Preparatory Department for those without common school education. At that time, the cost of study for a residential student for three months—tuition, books, room and board—ranged from $95 to $105, roughly one-quarter of the average annual salary of nonfarm employees in those years. Colleges such as the Coleman Business College were clearly opportunities for a new urban middle class that commanded steady work (that is, not unskilled laborers) in an unsteady economy. Newark in these years boasted in excess of 1,300 manufacturing establishments and a population of 150,000.

In the early years of their marriage, Coleman and her husband had three daughters—Henrietta, Margaret, and Evelyn. During this period Coleman also began her long involvement in the school and her effort to adapt the school's resources to the 20th century. At the time Coleman Business College advertised as "the oldest, largest, cheapest and best business college in the United States." In addition to its core programs, the school promoted its instruction in German, Spanish, Latin, French, and, of course, English. It also featured typewriting skills, ornamental penmanship, mechanical drawing, and telegraphy. By the time of Henry Coleman's death on December 6, 1903, tuition at Coleman Business College had dropped substantially, from $40 20 years before to $20 for three months of instruction. The costs of one year's instruction now became $75, approximately 15 percent of the annual salary for nonfarm employees. In part a function of competition from other business schools and commercial courses in large public high schools, the reduced tuition effectively eliminated the business college from serious competition with four-year academic colleges and their more advantaged clientele. Instead, the business college became an established part of its own regional, industrial community; it cultivated ambitious young men and women for whom an academic college was "not practical."

Coleman presided over the fortunes of Coleman Business College from her husband's death in 1903 to her own in 1935. The heart of the school's instruction was its practical orientation. In the central course of study students were issued "Coleman money," sufficient funds to begin an actual dry goods and marketing business. If they succeeded over a period in all the steps of commerce—buying, selling, borrowing, investing, and more—the student received promotion through a gauntlet of other enterprises: a post office, railroading, brokering, insurance agent, advertising agent, real estate agent, wholesale house, and finally, featured as the epitome, the Coleman National Business College Bank. Instruction went well beyond lectures alone. Students were immersed in practical situations in which their ingenuity, precision, and honesty were thought to be tested and refined. The success of these methods received testimonials from prominent Newark businessmen and also from the nationwide network the school had fashioned.

Coleman continued to adapt the school's offerings. Later features included shorthand of several varieties (the Gregg, Benn Pitman, and Isaac Pitman systems) and a new spelling reform "approved by President [Theodore] Roosevelt." This latter innovation involved the "simplification" of English words: *abridgment* for *abridgement*, *arbor* for *arbour*, *domicil* for *domicile*, *fantasy* for *phantasy*, for example. The school published its own textbook, *The Coleman Business Speller*. Its instructional program advertised its "personal" instruction, which meant not only close supervision but also entry into classroom instruction on any day of the week. The Coleman Business College boasted "no vacations" and 52 graduations a year. Instead of traditional "classes" and "programs of study," the school tailored itself to its clientele rather than to new professional standards of commercial education emerging at the turn of the century. There is no evidence that Coleman or her husband participated in the national or New Jersey state conventions of teachers. They devoted themselves to local, civic, and religious organizations, such as the First Methodist Episcopal Church, and to the redesign of their special school building on the corner of Academy and Halsey streets in Newark's central business district.

Coleman's school explicitly stated the central truth of her own life: a woman working outside the home "requires a certain knowledge of business matters which ladies are not apt to possess, though our experience warrants the assertion that they are very *apt* in acquiring it, if allowed the opportunity." Fixed in the routines of the city's business life, the business college provided an important economic and social service. Coleman's singular contribution lay not only in her own representation of this ideal but in her successful institutionalization of it in a large urban complex.

Coleman died of a heart ailment, shortly before her 71st birthday, on July 21, 1935, at the Maplewood, NJ, home of her daughter Henrietta Helthall and was buried in nearby Fairmount Cemetery.

The NJ-HS holds materials on the Coleman Business College. Other useful references are: Alice Kessler-Harris, *Out to Work* (1982); and Barbara Solomon, *In the Company of Educated Women* (1985). Coleman's obituary appeared in the *New York Times*, July 23, 1935.

*Paul H. Mattingly*

## ANN HORA CONNELLY, 1824–1880

Ann (Hora) Connelly, a New Jersey teacher, initiated a reform of New Jersey law in 1871 making the rights of women equal to those of men in the custody of their children. Very little is known about Connelly's early life. She was born in New Jersey in 1824, the fourth of five daughters of Mary and James Hora, a prosperous Irish-born farmer in Rahway (Union County), NJ. Her mother died when Connelly was in her teens and as a young woman in her twenties Connelly lived in Rahway with her father and older sister Mary; her other sisters had married.

Sometime between 1850 and 1861 she married a man named Connelly and moved to Georgia. In 1861 in Georgia her only child, a daughter, Mary H. Connelly, was born. Reportedly unhappily married, Connelly was not compelled by economic circumstances to remain with her husband. She and her daughter returned to New Jersey to live with one of her older sisters, Jane (Hora) Jackson, on Railroad Avenue (later Broad) in Rahway. In the 1870s the Jackson household also included Jackson's son, John H. Jackson, a lawyer, and another sister, Mary Hora. With a small income from teaching in a Rahway public school and as owner of a substantial amount of real estate, Connelly could afford to act in accordance with her own wishes.

Desirous of seeking a divorce from her husband, Connelly nonetheless kept from taking legal action for fear of losing custody of her daughter. New Jersey courts at the time applied common-law doctrine, holding the father as head of the household, entitled to custody and control of his children in preference to the mother. The courts preferred the father in custody disputes even where he engaged in gross misconduct. As the sole parent with legal ownership rights to the children, the father without the consent of the mother could apprentice out their children as laborers and appoint in his will a legal guardian for the children other than their mother, his living wife.

Custody law was considerably changed in New Jersey in 1860 by a law that established a "tender years" doctrine, providing that children under the age of seven years should be in custody of the mother. This law, however, did not change the primary right of the father to the ultimate custody of the child, nor was it based on any recognition of women's rights. Instead it was based on the popular cultural belief in the nurturing capacities of the mother. As the mother of a nine-year-old, Connelly would not have qualified for the limited benefits offered by the 1860 statute.

Thus Connelly began a campaign in 1870 to petition the New Jersey State Legislature to grant equal legal rights of custody to both parents and to make the best interests of the child the priority. She was aided in her efforts by influential citizens who signed petitions and by her nephew John H. Jackson, who as a new junior partner of Rahway lawyer Garrett Berry in October 1870 drafted the bills regarding the rights of mothers. The bills were presented to the legislature in 1871 by Essex County senator John W. Taylor.

Connelly's campaign was carried out, in part, through the press. In August and September of 1870 letters appeared in the *National Democrat*, the Rahway weekly newspaper, signed "J," "Equity," and "Justice." It is highly probable that John H. Jackson authored the "J" letter since its focus, the cruelly oppressive and unjust nature of New Jersey law with regard to mothers and their children, and its content and style directly parallel the bill he subsequently drafted on the subject. Given Connelly's employment as a teacher and her reputation as an intelligent and respected citizen, her association with her nephew, and her recognized role in the effort, it is likely that she alone or in conjunction with her nephew drafted the other letters. The editor of the *Democrat* supported the reform but was cautious in the scope of his endorsement. In a September 8, 1870, editorial that promoted the effort to improve women's rights to custody, he carefully confined his support to the context of mothers' concerns and declared "we do not favor 'woman's rights' in the full acceptation of the term."

The letters and petitions aroused sufficient public clamor and support, resulting in the enactment on February 21, 1871, of laws (*Laws of New Jersey*, 1871, 15–16) that established the rights of parents as equal with respect to custody and that modified the father's right to appoint legal guardians in his will and to apprentice children as contingent on the mother's consent.

Upon the enactment of the 1871 statute, which represented the first time New Jersey law deemed men and women equals with respect to custody, Connelly was applauded for her efforts by Cornelia Collins Hussey, secretary of the Essex County Woman Suffrage Society, who sent a resolution of thanks from that group. Connelly reportedly replied, "This unexpected and distinguishing recognition of my imperfect, but earnest, efforts for justice is inexpressibly gratifying." (Stanton, *History of Woman Suffrage*, 483)

Connelly did not personally avail herself of the potential benefits of the law. Her husband's death sometime in the 1870s would have made a claim unnecessary. Nev-

ertheless, while Connelly may not have personally benefited, the 1871 statute created extraordinary precedent and a sharp departure from common law. The statute was based on a recognition of a legal right and not premised, as was its 1860 predecessor, on cultural claims regarding a mother's nurturing capacities. Moreover, Connelly's statute espoused the preferable standard of the best interests of the child in determining custody rather than the culturally bound "tender years" doctrine. This standard is almost uniformly accepted by the courts today as the primary concern in determining questions of custody. Significantly, the language of today's custody law, NJSA 9:2–4, almost exactly duplicates the 1871 act.

Later in the 1870s Connelly was reported to be "strongly interested in suffrage." (Stanton, 483) She was in poor health, however, and after a brief illness, she died of pneumonia on January 2, 1880, at her sister's home in Rahway. Her place of burial is not known for certain, although her death certificate cites Hazelwood Cemetery in Rahway; other members of her family are buried in Rahway Public Cemetery.

Connelly's contributions to the legal status of New Jersey women are noted in Elizabeth Cady Stanton, Susan B. Anthony, and Matilda Joslyn Gage, eds., *History of Woman Suffrage* 3 (1886). Newspaper references to her campaign appeared in the *National Democrat* (Rahway, NJ), Aug. 11, Aug. 25, Sept. 8, Dec. 8, 1870, and Feb. 16 and Mar. 16, 1871. The 1871 statute for which Connelly is noted appears in *Laws of New Jersey* (1871):15–16.

*Audrey Wolfson Latourette*

## MARGARET ANNA CUSACK, 1829–1899

Margaret Anna Cusack, a writer and the founder of the Sisters of Peace, a religious congregation of women that began its work in New Jersey one year after its founding in England, was born in Dublin, Ireland, on May 6, 1829, to Dr. Samuel Cusack and Sarah (Stoney) Cusack, both of Anglo-Irish aristocratic families. Cusack and her only sibling, a younger brother named Samuel, were christened in the Church of Ireland (Anglican). In a household that provided necessities but no luxuries, Cusack's mother kept the home while her father gave over his medical practice to serving the poor.

Apparently inspired by her father, Cusack later stated that her devotion to ameliorating the life of the poor was her desire from childhood. Her early education, unusual for a girl in those times, began with tutors in languages, mathematics, and music. For reasons that remain unclear, her parents separated, and she left Ireland at the age of thirteen or fourteen with her mother, brother, and great-aunt for Exeter, England, to live with other relatives. She continued her education at a boarding school near there.

At the time the Oxford Movement was in full flower. Promoted within the Anglican church (Episcopal) by the Revs. John Henry Newman, John Keble, and Edward B. Pusey, the movement brought its members in ritual and belief close to Catholicism and thereby caused tension within the Anglican church. Cusack was attracted to this movement. She wrote later: "Young, eager minds like my own were looking on, and taking part in all this religious fray, with an intensity of purpose which would scarcely be imagined today." (Cusack, *Story of My Life*, 40) She read social and political philosophers such as John Locke and Thomas Carlyle, whose works helped shape her own convictions. She became engaged to a friend of her brother, but while she was in Ireland to share this happy news with her father, her fiancé died of fever. Overcome by depression, she became absorbed in the reading of religious books. She wrote: "Keble's 'Christian Year,' together with Manning's and Newman's sermons, became my constant companion. Gradually, through this reading, I began to grasp the idea of a visible church, and to long for certainty of belief." (Cusack, *Story of My Life*, 11).

Although surrounded by a loving family, only Pusey was able to comfort her: "I have rarely met with a man so intensely sympathetic and capable of entering into the feelings of others." (Cusack, *Nun of Kenmare*, 12) On his advice, she entered a sisterhood in London and there acquired "a very thorough knowledge of the London poor and their surroundings." (Cusack, *Nun of Kenmare*, 16) But change in the administration of this Anglican convent, coupled with religious doubts, led Cusack to renew her interest in Catholicism.

She left the sisterhood and was subsequently received into the Catholic church on July 2, 1858. "My principal reason [for entering the Roman Catholic Church] was the strong assurance which that church gives that it has always taught and always will teach the same doctrine." (Cusack, *Nun of Kenmare*, 16–17)

Following her conversion, she decided to join a Catholic sisterhood, and after a short trial in an English convent she joined the Poor Clares in Ireland. Encouraged to continue her literary efforts, Cusack, now known as Sister Mary Frances Clare, became a well-known, prolific author. Moved by the terrible poverty in Ireland, she organized a famine relief fund in 1879 and addressed the issue of land reform as a structural cure for the famine in articles and letters to the press. Irish emigrants spread her fame, but a letter posted anonymously from London threatened her with assassination if she continued her writing and assistance to the poor.

She therefore transferred her efforts to a twofold project to assist women: an industrial training school to prepare them for emigration, and a religious congregation whose rule would be directed to this purpose. The first part of the project failed because of misunderstandings and public criticism; the second part met with success, for several young women joined her efforts.

Cusack's works were founded on a conviction that there could be no peace without justice. This justice was denied the poor, especially women. "I assert that the first, and fundamental right of every woman," she wrote, "is to be allowed the free exercise of her own belief; and that free exercise is not allowed when she is in any way restrained, either morally or intellectually." (Cusack, *Woman's Work in Modern Society*, 279)

In December 1883 she was referred to Bishop Edward Bagshawe of Nottingham, England, who gave official approval to her plans for the poor. She went immediately to the Vatican "to obtain permission from the Pope [Leo XIII] to found a new religious Order, to be called the Sisters of Peace." (Cusack, *Story of My Life*, 338) Her visit was highly successful: she was released from her vows as a Poor Clare and received permission to establish the new congregation of the Sisters of Peace.

Only a few months later she came to the United States to establish residences for immigrants. The church authorities of New York, Archbishop McCloskey and, later, Archbishop Michael A. Corrigan, refused to allow her to begin work within the diocese, and so she turned to Winand Michael Wigger, the bishop of Newark, NJ, who gladly welcomed her and her Sisters of Peace. Within three months, the sisters rented space for a working women's residence and employment agency in Jersey City and a summer home in Orange Valley. In September 1885 the sisters purchased property at 78 Grand Street, Jersey City, as a home for working girls and orphaned children. In the following spring they opened another home on the Palisades in Englewood Cliffs. Cusack's aim was to establish a chain of residences for immigrant girls where they might find help in getting jobs and protection from exploitation and unhealthy living conditions. She also proposed setting up a training school for the blind and began traveling the eastern seaboard to solicit funds.

Having already published more than three dozen books—some translated into several languages—as well as music, newspaper articles, and letters, she now wrote to describe the sisters' work among the immigrants in the *Dove*, a newsletter the Sisters of Peace published six times a year. (Under various names, including *St. Joseph Messenger and Advocate of the Blind*, it has continued publication to the present day.) She also wrote a play and several articles for journals and New York newspapers, notably the *Sun*. In response to requests for a commentary on the land theory of Henry George, a mayoral candidate in New

York City in 1886, Cusack (as Sister Frances Clare) brought out a pamphlet entitled *The Question of Today: Anti-Poverty and Progress*. To it she attached a critique of the case of the Rev. Edward McGlynn, a staunch supporter of Henry George, who was disciplined by the Vatican for his political activity. This critique provoked a decisive encounter between Cusack and church authorities. She came to see herself as an obstacle to the growth of the congregation she had founded, and so she left it. Despite personal failure, she retained confidence in her vision and in the women who had joined her: "I believe, however, that it [my mission here] will be an immense success for I leave it in the hands of Sisters who are capable of making it such. And I hope the interest which will be revived when the injustice with which I have been treated is known will help to establish the Sisters firmly in their great work." (Cusack, *Nun of Kenmare*, 382)

Cusack had guided her congregation to incorporation in New Jersey, where the members continue to serve, and she also founded a Union of Peace and Prayer to draw together laity and religious in a system of spiritual support. Her educational theories, innovative in her day, are practical now. Her ethical demands on public policy make her contemporary today. Her concern for women's rights finds its place with those who, yesterday and today, seek justice for women.

In 1891 Cusack returned to England. In 1899, cut off from the sisters and alone, she turned to friends who welcomed her back to the Anglican church. After many years of heart trouble and complications, she died on June 5, 1899, at age 70, in Leamington, England, and was buried there in the Anglican cemetery.

Cusack's autobiographies are *The Nun of Kenmare* (1888) and *The Story of My Life* (1893). A biography of her is Irene Ffrench Eagar, *Margaret Anna Cusack* (1970; 1979). Sister Dorothy Vidulich, *Peace Pays a Price* (1975), profiles Cusack and lists her publications. The provincial archives of the Sisters of St. Joseph of Peace (Englewood Cliffs, NJ) maintains a collection of her writings. *An Index to Published Writings of Margaret Anna Cusack* (1987) was funded by the N.J. Historical Commission and the SSJP.

*Rosalie McQuaide, csjp*
*Janet Davis Richardson, csjp*

## JULIET CLANNON CUSHING, 1845–1934

Juliet (Clannon) Cushing, organizer and president for 30 years of the Consumers' League of New Jersey, was a reformer of the Progressive Era. Born on September 17, 1845, at Broadway and White Street in New York City, she was the daughter and, possibly, the only child of Simon and Sarah (Olmstead) Clannon. Her father, born in County Roscommon, Ireland, and graduated from Trinity College, Dublin, at a time when Trinity was reserved for Protestants, came to the United States in 1820. Her mother, whose ancestors included Jonathan Gilbert, an early member of the Massachusetts General Assembly, claimed descent from Sir Humphrey Gilbert.

Cushing's childhood was passed in lower Manhattan, where Battery Park was her playground. She was educated at local private schools and Miss Wadleigh's department of the Twelfth Street School, then an institution for young women's higher education. After graduation from the Twelfth Street School, she became a member of its faculty and, at the time of her resignation, was assistant principal.

Her resignation was occasioned by her marriage in East Orange, NJ, on October 14, 1875, to George Wade Brooks Cushing, a son of Prentice and Eleanor (Taintor) Cushing of Massachusetts, and an officer of the Delaware, Lackawanna and Western Railroad. Between 1876 and 1889, five children were born to the Cushings: Helen Childs, Laura Sherwood, Edna, Prentice, and Eliot Olmstead. After her husband's death in 1888, Cushing continued to live in the family home on South Munn Avenue, East Orange. Church work was her first outlet from family responsibilities. She presided over the Missionary Society of the Munn Avenue Presbyterian Church in East Orange and the Presbyterial and Synodical societies of New Jersey, becoming an honorary president of the Presbyterian Society of Morris and Orange in later years. She spent 35 years as president of the Orange branch of the McAll Mission in France and served on the Advisory Council of the Federation of Women's Church Organizations of East Orange.

Cushing was a founder and president of the Travelers' Club of East Orange, a member of the Woman's Club of Orange, and its president from 1896 to 1898. But her most spectacular work in welfare and club work was as founder and president for 30 years of the Consumers' League of New Jersey. Credit for launching the league in 1899 goes to CORNELIA FOSTER BRADFORD of the Whittier House social settlement in Jersey City, who held meetings to explain the need for a New Jersey Consumers' League. Actual formation of the league came on March 1, 1900, when a group of 38 met at Cushing's home, where she was elected president.

Cushing described the league's aims as "to teach us to want right things, rightly made," and to better the conditions under which women and children worked. The league inspected factories that applied for the National Consumers' League label, made careful analyses of the conditions of employment for very young children in the glass district and for child migrant workers, and investigated stores, sweatshops, and factories.

In 1904 hopes for a league-sponsored bill limiting all child labor were dashed when the Swayze Bill passed, restricting only the employment of the youngest factory workers. A comprehensive school attendance law in the next decade covered children employed in areas other than farming. Thereafter the league continued its attempts to add school requirements for migratory farm working children. To supervise the ongoing effort, the league organized the New Jersey Child Labor Committee in 1904. Cushing chaired the committee, later renamed the New Jersey Child Labor and Welfare Committee.

Cushing was largely responsible for the initiation of state factory inspection and the reorganization of the state's Department of Labor in 1904, but her attempts to obtain state supervision for store clerks ran into difficulties. The Consumers' League had to mount a special campaign before the state interceded. Cushing wanted consumers to shop early in the day, especially on Saturdays, so that sales people would not have to stand fourteen hours a day, six days a week. By 1911 the state legislature approved a league-sponsored bill to require seats in stores, and individual towns began to comply with the Saturday half-holiday concept.

A major breakthrough came in 1912, when the league successfully supported New Jersey State Senator Walter E. Edge's "Ten Hour Law" to limit the workday of women. Though questioned by some women's rights advocates today, the law was hailed in its time, and Cushing was instrumental in enacting it. She had called a meeting of delegates from many statewide organizations to form a "central council," which circulated 11,000 appeals. A doctors' questionnaire brought numerous replies, one of which stated: "long hours of toil menaced the health of the next generation." (Consumers' League of New Jersey, *Fiftieth Anniversary Booklet*) After the law's enactment, Cushing became a factory inspector and visited factories, stores, and laundries.

World War I brought Cushing's appointment as chair of the Committee on Women in Industry of the Advisory Commission of the Council of National Defense in New Jersey. As war industries applied to the state's Department of Labor for permission to employ women workers, Cushing was one of three who determined whether required conditions for women were being met. Her achievement contributed to her appointment in the later war years as assistant commissioner for New Jersey of the U.S. Employment Service. Cushing developed procedures to determine whether labor standards in manufacturing plants

were being maintained. She also supervised the state's employment offices, which she used to visit incognito to apply for positions, in order to evaluate their reception of applicants.

Under her leadership, the Consumers' League discovered what came to be known as the "powder puff" scandal. New York factories were sending supplies to New Jersey for the manufacture of "sanitary" puffs, which were produced under unsatisfactory conditions. Young slum children from slum families in the Orange area were discovered producing the puffs on the streets and in dirty homes. A careful survey persuaded the state legislature in 1917 to pass a league-approved industrial home work bill.

Another effort of the league during Cushing's presidency was to reduce occupational diseases. Katherine Wiley, executive secretary of the league in the 1920s, investigated the tragic radium poisoning cases—then called "radium necrosis"—which killed young women factory workers at the United States Radium Corporation's operation in Orange. Beginning in World War I and continuing into the 1920s, the workers had been trained to wet their radium-encrusted brushes on their tongue in order to make a finer point for painting the luminous dial of a clock or watch. The Cushing-led league also sponsored a bill to provide Workman's Compensation for this "unlisted" disease. After this experience, the league determined that the list method of qualifying for Workman's Compensation was faulty, and that all occupational diseases, not just those identified on an official list, should be compensable under the Workman's Compensation Act.

The New Jersey College for Women (now Douglass College) paid tribute to Cushing's achievements by awarding her an honorary master of philanthropy degree in 1928. She left the office of president in April 1930, but continued to battle for the league's goals in her new position as honorary president.

Cushing, who died at age 88 in Short Hills, NJ, on September 6, 1934, lived at her South Munn Avenue residence until nine months before her death, when she moved into the home of her daughter, Edna Weathers. Funeral services were held at her longtime church, the Munn Avenue Presbyterian Church in East Orange, with burial in Greenwood Cemetery, Brooklyn, NY.

For information on Cushing see entries for her in the *National Cyclopaedia of American Biography* (1934), in *Scannell's New Jersey's First Citizens and State Guide* 1 (1917–18), and her obituary in the *East Orange Record*, Sept. 7, 1934. Material on her association with the Consumers' League of New Jersey is available in the Consumers' League Papers at NJ-RU.

*Ella Handen*

## MARY FENN ROBINSON DAVIS, 1824–1886

Mary Fenn (Robinson) Davis, spiritualist and feminist lecturer and writer, was born July 17, 1824, in Clarendon, NY, to Chauncey and Damaris (Fenn) Robinson, farmers and members of the Baptist church. Chauncey Robinson was a fervent temperance advocate and apparently made a comfortable living, since he was able to send his daughter to the local village school at Holley until she turned sixteen, and then to LeRoy Female Seminary in LeRoy, NY. Davis graduated with honors from LeRoy in 1846.

Soon after her graduation she married Samuel G. Love, a teacher in Buffalo, NY. The couple had two children, Frances and Charles, and were later reported to have lived happily together for the first five years of marriage. By the 1850s, however, problems had arisen between them. During these troubled years they became interested in spiritualism. Beginning in 1848 in upstate New York, women and men had reported that they could communicate with spirits of the dead in seances. Since women during the early 19th century were considered more emotional and ethereal than men, they were seen as naturally suited for the vocation of medium. The prominence of women in spiritualism ensured that spiritual expression would be given to feminine concerns. Marriage, central to women's lives, received a lot of discussion and criticism in spiritualist circles. Davis and her husband took spirit advice seriously as their marriage ran into problems.

In 1854 the Loves attended a lecture by Andrew Jackson Davis (1826–1910), who had begun offering his own brand of spiritual revelations in the mid-1840s. Davis was soon corresponding with him about her marital problems and found the spiritualist philosopher sympathetic and helpful. By later that year, when she went to Indiana to obtain a divorce under that state's more liberal divorce laws, she and Andrew Davis had come to the conclusion that they were spiritual affinities and destined to be united for all eternity. After her divorce, she returned to her parents' home in Clarendon, NY. Although her parents viewed Andrew Davis as a home wrecker, Davis and he were able to convince them to accept the match by the time of their marriage on May 15, 1855. For the next several years Davis's children remained with their father, Samuel Love.

The Davises lectured throughout the northern and midwestern states from 1855 to 1858 to promote the "harmonial philosophy," Andrew Davis's version of spiritual truth. The key element in harmonialism was the development of the individual so that spirit would prevail in his or her life and allow the person continual communion with the spiritual sphere. Spiritual development included consequences for the material world. Harmonialists looked forward to a time when fully developed individuals would restructure society, eliminating ill health, poverty, crime,

and injustice. With the growth of feminism by the late 1840s, and with the large number of female mediums, no person claiming spiritual insight could ignore the condition of women; virtually all seers demanded that women be given full legal equality to match their spiritual equality. "If a woman be a human being," Davis told an audience in Rutland, VT, "then she is entitled to consideration as an absolute entity—an individual, responsible, immortal being." (*Proceedings of the Free Convention*, 119)

By the late 1850s the Davises settled in Orange, NJ, and focused their work in the New York City area. Davis wrote articles and poems for the *Herald of Progress*, a paper edited by her husband. Her writing, like her lectures, applied spiritualist principles to social issues. In 1863 the Davises founded the Children's Progressive Lyceum, which was devoted to giving children proper training for individual development. Both of the Davises served as officers of the New Jersey Woman Suffrage Association when it was formed in the late 1860s. Davis became active in the Orange Woman Suffrage Club and was a member of Sorosis, a woman's club that began meeting at Delmonico's in New York City in 1868. In 1869 she helped found the Woman's Parliament, a movement that sought to advance the interests of women and children, and to bring the influence of women to bear on society.

Although Davis's continued persistence in the cause of reform earned her the praise of suffrage leaders, by the late 1850s her activities were limited by household demands. An important reason for the Davises' move to Orange in 1859 was to provide a home for the family members under their care. These included Andrew Davis's father and sister, and his sister's two sons. In 1865 Davis's children, Frances and Charles, came to live with her. Frances was already old enough to begin teaching in the public schools, which she continued until her marriage in 1871. Charles soon secured government work in Washington, D.C.

In 1876 Davis's daughter, Frances (Love) Baldwin, died. The sorrow that Davis felt seems to have inspired renewed reflections on the promises of spiritualism. She firmly repudiated the Christian view of death, declaring that it tended "to belittle, debase, and disgrace humanity." She believed, rather, that "we should aim to arise into that harmonious state—that oneness with the Divine nature which would make *communion* with the departed possible." (Davis, *Death in the Light*, iv, 14) She felt communion with her daughter in spite of the veil of death. After Frances's death Davis took her four grandchildren into her house and cared for them for the next ten years.

By the 1870s the tensions between harmonial philosophy and popular spiritualism became more pronounced, especially in regard to the "esoteric wisdom" then being publicized. In distinction to harmonialists, who ignored traditional occult language, the new seers embraced the writings of the ancients and claimed continuity with eastern religions. Andrew Davis attacked the new movement as a degeneration, and Davis aided the cause with a pamphlet, *Danger Signals*. The goal of spiritualism, she wrote, was to individualize people, thereby freeing them from superstition, creeds, and materialism. Religious knowledge was progressing, she asserted, implying that "ancient wisdom" was the wrong direction to look for truth.

The Davis marriage had been a profitable partnership for both of them, providing Davis encouragement and opportunity for a public career, and Andrew Davis the stability of home life. In harmonialist terms, their central temperaments were united. Andrew Davis, however, seems to have drifted away from his wife. After graduating from the United States Medical College in 1883, he moved to Watertown, MA, while Davis remained in Orange. In 1884 he claimed that spiritual insight revealed that Davis was not his eternal affinity and that their marriage should be ended. Although she was grieved by the decision, she agreed to a divorce. The marriage was annulled by an 1885 New York Supreme Court decision. Andrew Davis soon remarried.

Davis took her mother's maiden name, Fenn, and moved into the home of her son-in-law, Frank W. Baldwin. Her health had been poor for many years and the divorce seems to have shaken her greatly. In 1885 symptoms of cancer appeared. On July 18, 1886, at age 62, she died at the Baldwin home, in Orange, and was buried in that city's Rosedale Cemetery.

Davis authored two books: *Danger Signals* (1875) and *Death in the Light of the Harmonial Philosophy* (1876). *Proceedings of the Free Convention, Held at Rutland, VT* (1858) contains her speeches. Andrew Jackson Davis, *The Magic Staff* (1857) and *Beyond the Valley* (1885), are major sources of information about the couple's life and beliefs. She is profiled in *NAW*. Her obituary, probably written by her son-in-law, Frank W. Baldwin, appeared in the *Orange* (NJ) *Chronicle*, July 24, 1886.

*John C. Spurlock*
*Cheryl Day LuSane*

## REBECCA HARDING DAVIS, 1831–1910

Rebecca Blaine (Harding) Davis, author and pioneer in the literature of social protest, was born in Washington County, PA, on June 24, 1831, to Rachel Leet (Wilson) and Richard W. Harding, an English immigrant from Ireland. The eldest of five children (three boys and two girls), she spent her early years in Alabama, but was reared in

Wheeling, WV, where her father was in insurance and city affairs. She is claimed as a New Jersey writer because she spent her summers in Point Pleasant, from 1864 until her death in 1910.

Davis was prepared for formal schooling by private tutors, but was largely self-educated through the reading of Bunyon, Scott, Dickens, and Hawthorne. A book called *Moral Tales*, containing three stories by Hawthorne, opened a world to her "where the commonplace folk and things I saw took on a sudden mystery and charm," she wrote in later life. (Langford, *Richard Harding Davis Years*, 6) Her observations of ordinary people and their activities, immigrant families in native costume in Conestoga wagons going West, workers in the iron mills, and great vans, heavy with bales of cotton, prepared her to become one of the earliest authors of naturalistic writing.

In 1845, at age fourteen, she entered Washington Female Seminary in Pennsylvania and lived with an aunt during her three years of schooling. After graduation, she returned to help her mother at home. She read widely and studied subjects that her brother William was studying at Washington College. During the decade that preceded the Civil War, she kept within the confines of her own family but keenly followed the activities of Horace Greeley, Francis Le Moyne (the radical abolitionist), and John Brown. In 1861 she wrote to Nathaniel Hawthorne to tell him of her admiration for him. He replied to her letter and met with her the following year, after the publication of her first literary work.

*Life in the Iron-Mills*, a novella published anonymously (at her request) by the *Atlantic Monthly*, made her reputation. It appeared in the magazine in April 1861 and later in book form. It is considered one of the revolutionary documents in American literature. This grimly descriptive story of a furnace tender in a western Virginia steel mill was compared at that time to the realistic works of the Russian school of writing. In an era of sentimental and flowery writing, this marked a new genre of American literature.

Davis became a pioneer in presenting life from firsthand observation. The same year, in the fall of 1861, her serialized novel *A Story of Today* (later published in book form as *Margaret Howth*) appeared in the *Atlantic Monthly* in six installments. Again Davis wished to be anonymous. The novel portrayed the life of a young woman bookkeeper in a woolen mill and illustrated the effect of industrialism on the human personality. Once again, her realistic descriptions of surroundings and feelings captured the thinking and behavior of the working class.

On March 5, 1863, at age 32, she married L. Clarke Davis, a lawyer involved in journalism as well as the law. The couple had three children, but Richard Harding Davis, their first child, born in 1864, was her favorite. He became celebrated for his writings as a war correspondent, and his literary and personal glamor made him a prominent, much-admired figure among the young people of America in the late 19th and early 20th century. Davis believed that he was her greatest achievement. Belmont Davis, her second son, was born in 1866, and Nora, her daughter, was born in 1872.

The Davis family settled in Philadelphia, and during the summers following the birth of their first child they lived in Point Pleasant on the Jersey shore. The first year they boarded along with another family or two in a rambling old farmhouse. They became so devoted to this seaside retreat that several years later they purchased a cottage in Point Pleasant where they could be with friends they had met during their summer sojourns.

Davis continued writing after her marriage and the birth of her children, but later short stories and novels never achieved the success of her first work. In 1868 *Waiting for the Verdict*, her melodramatic study of the problems of a mulatto surgeon in Philadelphia, brought uncomplimentary reviews because of its awkward rendering of dialect and unconvincing characterization.

Nevertheless, in 1869 Davis became a contributing editor for the *New York Tribune*, writing articles and editorials on topics of the day. She dealt with problems of the untrained woman who had to make her own living. She published children's stories and essays in the *Youth's Companion* and *St. Nicholas Magazine* and sold gothic thrillers to *Peterson's Magazine*.

Undeterred by the criticism of *Waiting for the Verdict*, Davis wrote several novels after its publication, but she was never to achieve the artistry of *Life in the Iron-Mills*. She became best known for her journalistic observations and wrote travel literature and fictional stories based on legends and characters of the New Jersey coast.

In middle and later life, she wrote in opposition to woman suffrage and a woman's right to enter professions dominated by men. She believed that women were not as capable of sustained and continuous mental exertion as men and expressed her ideas in *Pro Aris et Focis*, a book of essays published in England in 1869 and in the United States in 1870.

After her husband's death in 1904, Davis devoted her life to the concerns of her son Richard and his illustrious career. Her two final works were *Bits of Gossip* (1904) and a short story that appeared in *Scribner's* in 1909.

Davis died, at age 79, from edema of the lungs while visiting her son Richard at his home in Mount Kisco, NY, on September 29, 1910. Her ashes were buried in Leverington Cemetery in Philadelphia.

Davis's autobiography is *Bits of Gossip* (1904). For additional information on her, see Gerald Langford, *The Richard Harding Davis Years: A Biography of a Mother and Son* (1961). Davis is profiled in *NAW* and *DAB*, vol. 5 (1930). Her obituary appeared in the *New York Times*, Sept. 30, 1910.

*Helene T. Svihra*

## MARY MAPES DODGE, 1830–1905

Mary Elizabeth (Mapes) Dodge, author of the classic *Hans Brinker: or, The Silver Skates*, poet, and editor of *Saint Nicholas* magazine, transformed 19th-century children's literature and influenced generations of English-speaking writers. She was born in New York City on January 26, 1830, to Sophia (Furman), an amateur artist and musician, and James Jay Mapes, a scholar, inventor, and agrarian scientist of wide renown. Both parents came from wealthy, socially prominent Long Island and New York families of English ancestry. "Lizzie," as Dodge was known, joined a sister, Louise, and was followed a year later by Sophie, and then by Charlie and Kate. Though the family moved often, each time to a less affluent setting, the children thrived in the comfortable and stimulating Mapes home, where some of the most influential figures of the day were frequent visitors.

Dodge was deeply influenced by her father, whom she resembled both in looks and temperament. She shared his curiosity about the natural world, his love of literature, and his belief that reading was the key to education. The Mapes children were taught at home and allowed free run of the large library. Shunning the dull, moralistic literature then thought appropriate for children, Dodge's imagination was fired by history and the classic tales of King Arthur, the Arabian Nights, Perrault's fairy tales, and *Robinson Crusoe*. From the age of eight, she helped her father document his agrarian experiments and edit his publications.

The city-bred Dodge first experienced country life in 1846, at age 16, when James Mapes, with the help of New York lawyer William Dodge III, bought "Mapleridge," a run-down farm in Waverly (Essex County), NJ (now part of Newark). New Jersey's farms, then failing because of soil depletion, provided a proving ground for James Mapes's theories on the restoration of land through chemical fertilization. The family moved to the clapboard mansion in 1848 and it quickly became a meeting place for Newark artists, writers, and scientists. Dodge became the primary writer and editor of her father's new magazine, the *Working Farmer*, and spent many of her leisure hours with William Dodge III, fifteen years her senior.

She married William Dodge III on September 13, 1851, and joined the extended Dodge family in New York City. Within four years she bore two sons, James (b. 1852) and Harrington (b. 1855). The young family led a happy life until the 1857 economic downturn hit William Dodge. Encumbered by the numerous mortgages that had supported his father-in-law's financial maneuverings and distraught by the grave illness of his son James, the 43-year-old lawyer disappeared on the night of October 28, 1858, and was presumed drowned, leaving Dodge, at 28, a widow with two small children and a legacy of debts.

Following this tragedy, Dodge returned to the family home in New Jersey with Harrington and the convalescing James. Struggling to pay back the tangle of mortgages and loans her father and husband had incurred, she turned her childhood ambition of writing into a reality.

Encouraged by her father, in 1861 Dodge became sole editor and author of all but the agricultural side of the now expanded *Working Farmer*. In the opening issue Dodge gave this advice on the liberation of women: "Depend upon it, your home will become happier and better regulated should the lady of the house have some independence of her own . . . bid her think for herself. It may be a risk, especially for those who have married dolls instead of women . . . this time risk something in the hope of becoming happier." (Wright, *Lady of the Silver Skates*, 24) Two 1862 articles were entitled "A Law Against Obtaining Husbands" (Feb., 40) and "How to Avoid a Bad Husband." (July, 160)

Writing every morning in the solitude of a converted cottage on the farm and devoting afternoons to hiking, skating, or fishing with her sons, Dodge was prolific, selling stories to *Harper's* and other magazines beginning in 1863 and publishing the *Irvington Stories*, based on family and historic incidents, in 1864. Her pieces for both adults and children were immediately successful. Urged by her sons to write a story about the new European craze of skating, she published *Hans Brinker: or, the Silver Skates* in 1865. It was a lively and instructive tale of Dutch life based on the recollections of family friends and painstaking research. *Hans Brinker* became an instant best-seller, went through more than 100 printings in several languages during Dodge's life (it is still a best-seller today), and was awarded the Prix Monthyon by the French Academy in 1869. When she visited Holland for the first time, in 1873, her son asked a bookseller for the best book on Dutch life. He was handed a copy of *Hans Brinker*.

With her father's death in 1866, just weeks after the success of *Hans Brinker*, Dodge became the breadwinner and practical head of a three-generation extended family. While her mother and sisters shared child care duties, Dodge was introduced through her friend the reformer Robert Dale Owen into New York literary circles. She forged lifelong relationships with such prominent figures as Louisa May Alcott, Frances Hodgson Burnett, and her greatest friend, Lucia Gilbert Calhoun Runkle, the first woman on the editorial staff of the *New York Times*.

In 1868 Dodge published her adult game book, *A Few Friends and How They Amused Themselves,* and became an associate editor, under Harriet Beecher Stowe and Donald G. Mitchell, of *Hearth and Home*, a position in which she thrived. She continually produced articles on all kinds of subjects, feeling equally at home with domestic, literary, artistic, and scientific topics. But her first concern remained her children. She was their teacher, friend, adviser,

and companion. She commuted daily between Waverly and New York, fitting her heavy editorial and writing deadlines to the responsibilities of a single parent.

In 1872, at age 42, Dodge was simultaneously offered two head editorships—that of *Hearth and Home* and of Scribner's new magazine for children. Faced with the possibility of effecting a larger change in children's literature through the creation of a high-quality magazine, she subordinated her own writing career to the new monthly magazine, which she christened the *St. Nicholas Magazine for Girls and Boys*. Dodge had complete control over the recruiting of authors and illustrators, over all management and content, with no expense spared. Like her books, the magazine was an instant success.

Founded on James Mapes's theory that children instinctively like good reading if they are fortunate enough to find it, *St. Nicholas* was a new literary force that ministered to the thoughts, interests, and aspirations of children. Dodge strove for a magazine that was "stronger, truer, bolder, more uncompromising" than adult periodicals. ("Editing for the Young," *Scribner's Magazine*, July 1873) "It must mean freshness and heartiness, life and joy," she continued. She wanted no "condescending editorial babble . . . no sermonizing either, no wearisome spinning out of facts, nor rattling of the dry bones of history." In her first issue, Dodge set forth a nine-point policy from which she never deviated in the 32 years of her editorship. She sought first to give fun, inspire an appreciation of art, cultivate the imagination, foster high ideals, and prepare children through realistic role models for living in the world. Her goals, like the magazine content, were imbued with the forward-looking optimism of the era.

The high standards she set soon attracted the leading authors of the day, including: Henry Wadsworth Longfellow, Alfred Lord Tennyson, John Greenleaf Whittier, Louise May Alcott, Mark Twain, R. L. Stevenson, Frank Stockton, Theodore Roosevelt, George Macdonald, Laura Ingalls Wilder, and Frances Hodgson Burnett. Leading illustrators such as Reginald Birch, Howard Pyle, and N. C. Wyeth were also recruited. Dodge encouraged reader involvement, promoting new talent. Writers such as E. B. White, Edna St. Vincent Millay, and Eudora Welty first published as children in the famous "St. Nicholas League." When Rudyard Kipling, already a world famous adult writer, first met Dodge, he asked, "Aren't you going to ask me to write for *St. Nicholas?*" "Do you think you are equal to it?" was her quick reply. (Yost, "Mary Mapes Dodge," 99–100; *Famous Women of America*, 161) He was; the result was the classic *Jungle Books* and *Just So Stories*.

During her editorship of the magazine Dodge also published numerous volumes of her own poetry and prose for children and adults that were immensely popular.

A "stout, corseted, desk-bound sociable grandmother who played 'Pok-ah' with her colleagues" (Wright, 156),

Dodge was the center of a distinguished group of artists, writers, and notable figures in Newark, at her New York apartment, and at her summer cottage, "Yarrow," at Onteora Park in the Catskills.

Through the years, Dodge faced and overcame one tragedy after another, the greatest being the death of her adored son Harrington in 1881. Overburdened with nursing, running *St. Nicholas*, paying back her father's still lingering debts, and helping her many friends and relations, she was often exhausted. Yet she was to her friends "that live spark of a woman" (Wright, 155) whose popularity only grew with the years. Her brother wrote in 1876: "Lizzie deserves it all and more if possible for she has bravely fought her battle and kept her courage when the present was not pleasant and the future far from promising. Lizzie is a trump—and no wonder she has won the hearts of thousands of youngsters." (Wright, 99)

Dodge died of cancer, at the age of 75, at "Yarrow" on August 21, 1905, and was buried at Evergreen Cemetery near Elizabeth, NJ. At Onteora Park the children formed a spontaneous procession at her funeral. She had loved them, understood them, and opened up the world of literature to them.

Catharine Morris Wright, *Lady of the Silver Skates* (1969), is a biography of Dodge and contains a complete bibliography of her writings. See also: Edna Yost, *Famous American Pioneering Women* (1961); and Lucia Gilbert Runkle, *Our Famous Women* (1884). She is profiled in *NAW* and *DAB*, vol. 5 (1930). Her obituary appeared in the *New York Times*, Aug. 22, 1905.

*Caroline Wheeler Jacobus*

## AMANDA MINNIE DOUGLAS, 1831–1916

Amanda Minnie Douglas, prolific author of books for girls and historical novels, was born in New York City on July 14, 1831, the second child of John Nelson and Elizabeth (Horton) Douglas. She had an older brother, Oscar, who became a newspaperman, a younger brother, Charles, who became an Episcopal minister, and a younger sister, Annie. After many moves, including one pleasant interlude on a farm in Poughkeepsie, NY, the family settled in New Jersey in 1850, living first in Belleville and three years later taking up residence in Newark.

At an early age Douglas demonstrated her storytelling ability by creating and narrating long, imaginative tales to groups of neighborhood children. She was educated at the City Institute of New York and was so interested in art that, at the age of eighteen, she planned to attend the Cooper Institute to study engraving and design. But like many young women of the 19th century, Douglas placed the needs of her loved ones above her own interests; when illness in the family forced her to abandon her plans to study art, she redirected her energies toward writing,

something she could do at home between her nursing duties. She also studied English and American literature with a private tutor and was an avid reader who delighted in the wide variety of literature available to her. Known as "Aunt Minnie" to the family, Douglas used the earnings from her writing to support her sick father, her mother, and her sister, Annie, who had a congenital heart defect and was often ill.

Douglas's first literary efforts were contributions to the *New York Ledger*, *Saturday Evening Post*, *Ladies' Friend*, *Paterson's Monthly*, and *Godey's Lady's Book*. Her first novel, *In Trust*, was published in 1866. This was followed steadily by one or more books each year until the end of her life. She even illustrated some of her own early works; but she is best known for the girls' books she wrote in various series: the Kathie series, beginning with *Kathie's Stories* (1871); the Sherburne series, beginning with *Sherburne House* (1892); the Little Girl series, beginning with *A Little Girl in Old New York* (1896); and the Helen Grant series for older girls, beginning with *Helen Grant's Schooldays* (1903). Her last books, *Red House Children's Year* (1915) and *Red House Children Growing Up* (1916), were part of another series. All these books were entertaining and commercially successful, but Douglas also used them to foster the character development of her readers.

Although most of her novels were written for girls, the story of *Larry* (1893) was written primarily for boys and brought her a $2,000 prize offered by *The Youth's Companion* for the year's best fiction work for young people. This was reportedly the most money paid outright to a woman author for a story at that time.

Douglas's ancestors were members of a small group of Huguenots who settled in New Rochelle and were involved in the Revolutionary War. This fueled her interest in history and led her to trace her genealogy. Her historical novels, such as *Heroes of the Crusades* (1890), which was illustrated by the famous French artist Louis Auguste Doré, reflect her concern for accuracy and thorough research. This was also apparent in the Little Girl series, with its detailed and accurate historical background of such cities as New York, Boston, and Philadelphia.

The themes of Douglas's works are clear and simple, for virtue always triumphs. Although Douglas herself never married or had children, her books depict family life lovingly and home as a haven of warmth and stability—the sort of background lacking in her own early life with its frequent moves. Her later life (1873 on) was also characterized by frequent changes of address, in direct contrast to the stability and security she portrayed. Douglas wrote mainly about the world she knew, and, in an idealized way, about the world spinsterhood denied her: the daily life of a Victorian household; the good and bad aspects of life with children; the virtues of cheerful industry, patience, and humor; the moral improvement afforded by suffering life's "burdens." She also believed that single women should be respected for their independence and that marriage was not the only worthwhile "career" for a woman. She believed in suffrage for women, but thought only educated men and women should have the right to vote.

Her innate storytelling ability and her style of writing, characterized by warmth and vitality, help raise her somewhat repetitive work above the merely mundane and didactic. A love of nature is evident in many of her books, most notably in *A Modern Adam and Eve in a Garden* (1889), written after a failed attempt to run a chicken farm in Belleville (1885–87). The novels were extremely popular, and because the author dealt conservatively with many different topics, her books were also popular additions to Sunday school libraries.

Douglas wrote rapidly and neatly, most often in pen and ink. "I did try to learn to use the typewriter," she said, "but the clicking noise distracted me—I never could compose on the thing. Very soon I went back to my pen." (*Newark Sunday Call*, May 23, 1915) After thinking each story through very carefully, she sat down, wrote it out, and claimed to mail the first draft to the publisher with almost no corrections.

Less than five feet tall, with a fragile, gentle, and dignified appearance, Douglas spoke in a soft monotone that belied her often self-deprecating sense of humor. She showed her individuality through dress: she sewed her own clothes and usually disregarded the prevailing fashion. Her general creativity was also evident in her invention of a folding frame for supporting mosquito netting over a bed, for which she held a patent.

Douglas was vice-president of the New Jersey Women's Press Club, a forerunner of the present-day New Jersey Press Women. She was also a member of the Ray Palmer Club, the oldest women's literary organization in the area, which was associated with the Second Presbyterian Church and named after a well-known Newark minister and author.

On February 16, 1899, Mary Fisher, a retired schoolteacher who had started a retirement home in Brooklyn, NY, met in Newark with representatives of New Jersey Women's Clubs and some professional people to explore the possibility of opening a retirement home in the country for "tired brain workers" such as authors, artists, and teachers. "There and then they organized the Mary Fisher Home Association of NJ." It seems very likely that Douglas was at that meeting, for when the Mary Fisher Home opened later that year in Tenafly, NJ, Douglas became a member of the Board of Managers, a group of volunteers who performed helpful tasks for the residents, such as hanging curtains, mending linen, and writing letters. "In the beginning, the Managers and their friends gave recitals, teas and held Authors' Matinees and Harvest Home Festivals in order to raise funds to run the Home." This group was distinct from the officers and trustees, who took care of the finances of the home and the residents. (Mary Fisher Home Archives)

Douglas was friendly with a number of literary figures of her day, including MARY VIRGINIA HAWES TERHUNE (who wrote under the pen name "Marion Harland"), an early supporter and first vice-president of the Mary Fisher Home. She was also friends with Louise Chandler Moulton, William Taylor Adams (Oliver Optic), and Louisa May Alcott, though no primary evidence of this last relationship has been found. Douglas, the successful author, was always willing to give advice and help to struggling young writers who approached her. For example: "Don't waste time and strength on short stories. If you can write books, do it!" (*Newark Sunday Call*, May 25, 1915)

Throughout her life Douglas was generous to family members and others and provided unstintingly for her sister until Annie's death in 1913. Douglas died in Newark, at age 85, on July 18, 1916, after several months of failing health. She left a legacy of 92 published books. She is buried in Mt. Pleasant Cemetery, Newark, and shares a single gravestone with the sister for whom she had so faithfully cared.

Frank Polkington, "A Biographical Sketch of Amanda Minnie Douglas" (1969), is an unpublished profile available at NJ-HS. The NJ-NPL maintains a clipping file on Douglas. See also "Author of Seventy Books for Girls a Newark Resident," *Newark Sunday Call*, May 23, 1915. Material on her founding of the home for aged professionals is available at the Mary Fisher Home (Tenafly, NJ). Douglas is profiled in *American Women Writers* 1 (1979). Obituaries appeared in the *Newark Evening News*, July 18, 1916, and the *New York Times*, July 19, 1916.

*Helen Kuryllo*
*Kirsten Jensen Cais*

## MABEL SMITH DOUGLASS, 1877–1933

Mabel (Smith) Douglass, a leader in the movement to establish the New Jersey College for Women (now Douglass College) and its first dean, was born on February 11, 1877, in Jersey City (Hudson County), NJ, the elder of two daughters of James Weaver and Wilhelmine Joanne (Midlige) Smith. Her father was a merchant, the descendant of Dutch burghers who had come to New Amsterdam and settled in Berge, later a part of Jersey City. Douglass graduated from Dickinson High School in Jersey City and went on to Barnard College, from which she graduated in 1899. At Barnard, she made the difficult choice of college studies over continuing her musical studies.

Following her graduation, Douglass taught for three years in the New York public schools. During that period she met William Shipman Douglass, a New York commission merchant, whom she married in 1903. For the next decade she lived a conventional life as the wife of a businessman and the mother of two children, Edith (b. 1905) and William (b. 1907). She was active in the College Club of Jersey City, one of whose projects was to familiarize high school girls in Jersey City with opportunities in higher education, almost all of which lay outside New Jersey. By her own account, her involvement in the campaign to establish the College for Women came by accident. In 1911 Douglass, then president of the College Club, was invited to attend a district meeting of the New Jersey State Federation of Women's Clubs, an organization whose goals she did not find entirely compatible with those of the College Club. However, at that meeting, Mrs. John V. Cowling, chairman of education, proposed the "speedy admission" of women to all-male Rutgers College, the land-grant college for New Jersey, on the grounds that since Rutgers College was supported by federal and state funds it should "provide higher education for the youth of the State, irrespective of sex." (Quoted in Douglass, *Early History*, 5) An enthusiastic Douglass quickly persuaded the College Club of Jersey City to join the federation in the campaign for higher education for women in New Jersey. She agreed to serve as chair of a subcommittee on the state college, formed to explore the subject.

Douglass embarked on the campaign with the "incessant and unselfish zeal" (Demarest, "Tribute") that characterized her later career. She began with exhaustive research, gathering statistics on the status of women at state universities, the number of girls attending New Jersey high schools and future projections, and the number of girls going out of state to attend college. In addition, she explored the history of and made visits to coeducational institutions and separate colleges for women. To gather support for the project she met with numerous public officials, including President Woodrow Wilson, and launched a one-dollar subscription campaign in the hope of raising $150,000 as a way of persuading the trustees of Rutgers College and the state to "take more kindly to the project." (Douglass, *Early History*, 10) She sought endorsements from a wide range of organizations, including the Grange and the New Jersey Teachers Association. In an address to the latter organization in 1914, she set forth the arguments for the establishment of a college for women, a mixture of the pragmatic and the idealistic. At a modest estimate, she pointed out, New Jersey lost about a half million dollars annually because of the 800 New Jersey girls who went to college outside the state. Further, all of the 355 college graduates employed in the public high schools of New Jersey that year had come from other states because high school teachers were required to hold a four-year college degree. "Why," she asked, "give away all our best paid positions to those trained elsewhere?" But the most important argument was simple justice: "New Jersey offers a woman one chance, to be trained [in a normal school] as a

teacher. Be she ever so fine in another subject, the State offers no other opportunities. They give a boy a chance to be an engineer, an agriculturalist, a doctor or a lawyer, but for the girls, there is only one opportunity." (Mss, Douglass Collection)

In January 1915 the stress of the vigorous three-year campaign, coupled with family problems, took its toll on Douglass's health. She suffered a nervous breakdown and withdrew from the campaign. Though she soon recovered her health, family crises continued to absorb her energies. The death of her mother and the illness and death of her husband in 1917 kept her occupied. She took over her husband's business in New York, an enterprise she sold in 1918. During this period, others had carried forward the campaign for the establishment of a college for women, though in the absence of Douglass it lost some of its momentum. But as the result of a happy conjunction of circumstances—passage of the Smith-Hughes Bill, which provided funding for teaching home economics at land-grant schools, and the coming onto the market of a property suitable for the establishment of a college for women—the trustees of Rutgers College passed a resolution in April 1918 to establish a college for women as a department of the state university and took a three-year lease on the Carpender estate.

Shortly thereafter, William C. Demarest, president of Rutgers, invited Douglass to become the first dean of the college. Despite the temptation to rest rather than to accept the "call to larger service" (Douglass, *Early History*, 14), Douglass accepted the appointment in May 1918. The same energy and administrative skill that had impelled her throughout the three-year campaign for the establishment of the college served her in her new capacity as dean. Sitting at a desk in the corner of the Summer Session Office of Rutgers College, she organized a college for the young women who would enroll in September of that year. Her tasks included fund raising; supervising workmen renovating the Carpender house, which would become College Hall; hiring essential staff; and organizing a curriculum that would provide a sound liberal arts education as well as vocational courses in home economics. What carried her forward through that frantic summer was the great incentive she saw for every applicant to the college "really to create something. Here was a place where nothing was crystallized. There were no traditions, no customs, no college songs. . . . There were no rules and regulations. All would have to be thought of, planned, built up, created—what a magnificent opportunity!" (Douglass, *Early History*, 20) She made the most of that opportunity.

The New Jersey College for Women opened in September 1918 with 54 students. During that first year Douglass literally lived with her work, making her home in her College Hall office. She endured a flu epidemic that began two weeks after the college opened and a faulty heating system that remained faulty throughout the winter. She made endless visits to women's clubs and high schools and frequently went to Trenton to lobby the governor and the legislature. At the same time, she made an effort to know each student personally and to draw both students and staff into the formulation of college policy. In those early years her ingenuity became legendary. During the second year in the life of the college, since she lacked funds to construct a new building, she instead built a gymnasium out of packing boxes originally intended to ship airplane engines to Europe during World War I. She assiduously cultivated members of the Board of Managers of the College and other potential friends of the college. By the time of her formal retirement in 1933, the New Jersey College for Women, which had opened in 1918 with 54 students, two buildings, and a faculty of eighteen had become one of the largest women's colleges in the East, with 1,071 students and a faculty of 115.

Douglass received many honors. In 1931 she became the first woman ever to receive the Columbia University Medal, and in 1932 she was made an Officier d'Academie by the French government in appreciation of her influence in the teaching of French. She received a doctor of laws degree from Rutgers in 1924 and from Russell Sage in 1932. What seemed important to her, however, was not just what she had achieved but how she had achieved it. A woman who put a great premium on charm and good manners, she noted with particular satisfaction in her 1929 memoir that those who created the college had lived up to the ideals of the early days, "never to cause Rutgers College any worry as to our finances or our behavior." (Douglass, *Early History*, 45)

Her public achievements, however, came at great personal cost. In a 1922 letter to President Demarest she remarked without rancor that "all of us who have done this work have had practically no life of our own, no chance to go out among the people of the town or into New York for relief from the strain of being constantly surrounded by students both at meal times and in the evenings." More tragically, her son died of a self-inflicted gunshot wound in 1923, an event to which she does not allude in her memoirs. Inevitably the personal tensions and the pressures created by the continuing controversy over the relation of the New Jersey College for Women to Rutgers and the state wore her down. In June 1932 she was granted a leave of absence for reasons of health, and she withdrew from the New Jersey College for Women, as she had withdrawn from the campaign to establish it in 1915. This time, however, she failed to regain her strength and officially resigned on July 1, 1933. Her resignation occasioned an outpouring of tributes to her achievement that went far beyond conventional regrets, reflecting rather a deep sense of personal loss at her departure. Douglass, still seeking to recover her strength, retired to her summer cot-

tage on Lake Placid. On September 21, as was her custom, she went for a row on the lake after lunch. The boat she had taken was found empty late that afternoon. It was not until three decades later that skindivers came upon her well-preserved body in the depths of the lake. In September 1963 a coroner ruled her death accidental, though she had almost certainly committed suicide, and she was buried in the family plot in Brooklyn.

In an address at the memorial service held for Douglass on October 29, 1933, Dr. Demarest, then retired, paid tribute to her. He recounted all of her achievements, both in the campaign for the New Jersey College for Women and its creation, but he noted that what was most memorable about Mabel Smith Douglass was her personality, "the uprightness and vigor of physical carriage, . . . the directness and zest of the spoken word, . . . the liveness of her spirit." In April 1954 the Trustees Committee of the New Jersey College for Women recommended that the name of the institution be changed to Douglass College. That change was proclaimed officially on Founder's Day, April 16, 1955.

NJ-DC holds materials relating to the history of the college, including manuscripts and correspondence of Douglass. Also useful are: Mabel Smith Douglass, *The Early History of New Jersey College for Women: Personal Recollections by Dean Douglass* (1929); Rosemary Moxon and Mabel Peabody, *Twenty-five Years: Two Anniversary Sketches of New Jersey College for Women* (1943); George Schmidt, *Douglass College: A History* (1968); and William Demarest, "A Tribute to Mabel Smith Douglass," *Alumnae Bulletin of New Jersey College for Women* 9 (Nov. 1933):1–2. For an account of her death, see George Ortloff, *A Lady in the Lake* (1985). Douglass is profiled in *NAW*.

*Louise Duus*

## MINNIE RADCLIFFE DOUGLASS, 1877–1955

Minnie Radcliffe Douglass, champion roller-skater, dancer, choreographer, and businesswoman, was born March 23, 1877, in Paterson (Passaic County), NJ. She was the only child of Edward and Anna (Hill) Douglass. Her father, a prosperous blacksmith in the city at a time when this occupation was evolving into tool-and-die making for the burgeoning machine industries, had left his native England as a young boy to come to Paterson to serve an apprenticeship with the blacksmithing firm of Radcliffe and Stansfield.

Family photographs reveal that Douglass inherited her graceful beauty from her mother, and that she grew from a frail, pretty child into a beautiful young woman. Considered a sickly child at the age of six, Douglass took up the newly popular sport of roller-skating as a restorative. Within six months, she was giving exhibitions at the Union Rink located on Broadway in Paterson.

Douglass began her formal roller-skating career on May

In the 1880s Minnie Radcliffe Douglass of Paterson had an illustrious career as a child roller-skating star, performing throughout the United States. *Courtesy, Collection of the Paterson Museum.*

Her act consisted of tricks and dances such as the hornpipe and skilled imitations of other famous skaters. She skated forward and backward, on heels and toes, weaving among a dozen burning torches placed eighteen inches apart. At the Steel Pier, Coney Island, NY, she defeated three of the top female skaters in the country to win the Sporting World's Medal. Her open challenge to any skater under fifteen years of age to compete for a prize of $250 was never taken up.

In February 1885, just before her eighth birthday, Douglass joined with champion cyclist Warren Wood, champion skater A. F. Smith, and stilt-skater Frank Geraghty to form the Great Western Rink Combination. On September 30, 1885, she became part of the new team, known as Douglass-Wood-Atkinson. By December 25, 1885, Douglass and Wood had formed their own partnership. They gave exhibitions until Douglass retired on March 9, 1886, after nearly 400 performances in 123 different U.S. cities.

After her short but illustrious skating career, Douglass returned home to Paterson and was graduated in 1894 from St. Aloysius Academy, a Paterson girls' school operated by the Roman Catholic order of the Sisters of Charity. At the academy, she was involved in class plays and received prizes for her painting.

In her second public career, which centered around dancing, Douglass excelled as both instructor and performer. As a child, she had received dance training in New York, and she attended the Empire Theater Ballet School in London as a young woman. During the years 1897–1916, Douglass operated a dance school for young children and high school students in Paterson. Her "Lilliputians," or young minstrel students, were a favorite with local audiences. During a student recital of *The Great Republic* in 1897, Douglass's own dance performance was described by the press as "most beautifully executed, critics not having seen it surpassed in grace of movement by the most noted dancers of the day." (Scrapbook, Douglass Collection) Douglass organized fund-raising shows for local charities using her students as performers, and during World War I her Red Cross dance classes raised enough money to purchase three ambulances for the war effort.

Douglass was a vital member of several local opera companies in Paterson. She was largely responsible for the success of St. Joseph's (Roman Catholic) Opera Society's productions of *Runaway Girl* and *Floradora* in their 1911 and 1912 seasons, and was described as "the talented dancing mistress of this city" by the local press in a preview of *Floradora.* Douglass also assumed directorial responsibilities for the productions of the Paterson Amateur Opera Association, the first amateur opera company in New Jersey, which was active between 1893 and 1914. This group depended on the multitalented Douglass for all choreography, staging, and lighting.

1, 1884, at age seven, at the Union Rink. For nine months, she toured many cities in the United States, earning $15 per show, plus expenses for herself and her mother, who was her constant traveling companion. Newspaper clippings dating between 1884 and 1886 give her rave reviews for her performances. Phrases such as "graceful," "well poised," "pretty," "dazzling," "astonishing capabilities," "a marvel," "champion," "undoubtedly the best," and "finest skatist in the land" leave little room for doubt that young Douglass was gifted. Because of this press coverage and the great public demand for her exhibitions, she commanded $150 for a three-day show at Newport, NY, in November 1885. She toured as far west as Nebraska, Kansas, and Missouri, where Frank James (of the infamous Jesse James gang) is said to have attended one of her shows.

A preview of the association's 1911 production of *The Girl from Paris* states that the opera was Douglass's one annual public performance and that "upon these occasions, her dance and dancing [had] to a large extent been responsible for the good opinion expressed after each performance." The opera association, which had halted its productions in 1914, was revived in 1920 mainly through the efforts of Douglass.

Douglass married George S. Curtis, an amateur athlete and assistant superintendent of the Public Service Electric Corporation, on June 3, 1903. The couple resided with Douglass's parents in Paterson, enjoyed prominent social status, entertained friends and associates at the Douglass summer home in Longwood (Jefferson Township), Morris County, NJ, and had their own automobiles, a privilege not enjoyed by many people in pre–World War I days. There were no children in this marriage, and Douglass continued with her dancing classes and her involvement with local opera productions.

Several major events occurred in Douglass's life between 1913 and 1918: her father died suddenly in 1913 and her mother married Warren Wood, Douglass's former professional partner. In July 1915 George S. Curtis left Douglass, and by 1916 she had assumed the proprietorship of her late father's hammer-forging business in Paterson.

On July 16, 1917, she filed a petition with the New Jersey Superior Court to end her marriage and to allow her to resume using her family name. The marriage had been rather one-sided, since George Curtis, by his own admission, was unwilling to give up his bachelor ways. Douglass, who had received little monetary or emotional support from her husband during their married life, was granted an uncontested divorce on grounds of desertion on May 13, 1918. No settlement, monetary or otherwise, was involved in the legal proceedings. Several months later, on August 2, 1918, Douglass's mother died after a brief illness.

From 1916 to 1924 Douglass operated the family business, the Douglass Forge, on Spring Street in Paterson. By 1925 she had established a millinery shop known as the Band Box on Hamilton Street in Paterson. In 1936 the clothing business was moved to her home at 77 Ward Street and became known as Minnie R. Douglass, Women's Clothing. Douglass remained in the clothing business until her death in 1955. In the later years of her life, she devoted her time to painting and a deep involvement with the affairs of the First Presbyterian Church of Paterson.

Douglass died in Paterson, at age 78, on October 14, 1955, from cerebral thrombosis. She was buried in the Douglass family plot in Cedar Lawn Cemetery in Paterson. The *Paterson Morning Call* eulogized Douglass in a front-page article the day after her death, calling her a famous child roller-skater and a prominent dancer, artist, and businesswoman in the city.

Memorabilia on Douglass, including photographs, clippings, and scrapbooks, is available at the Paterson Museum (Paterson, NJ).

*Jessica E. Peters*
*Gordon Cameron*

## SARAH JANE CORSON DOWNS, 1822–1891

One of the most influential temperance leaders of 19th-century New Jersey, Sarah Jane (Corson) Downs joined the organized dry reform only later in life. Born to a Philadelphia family of old American stock, Downs was the youngest of four children (she had two brothers, Thomas and John, and a sister, Elizabeth). Her mother, Ann Somers (Addis) Corson (1782–1867), was the daughter of a Revolutionary War veteran, and her father, James Corson (1784–1827), was descended from some of New Jersey's earliest Dutch colonists. The Corsons moved to Addisville, PA, the seat of her mother's family, when Downs was an infant. Her father died when she was five, and in the 1830s, after raising the children alone, her mother moved with Downs to Pennington, NJ (into the home of Downs's married sister, Elizabeth Phillips). Downs attended Pennington Female Institute, a Methodist school. At seventeen, she professed a conversion experience and led her mother, sister, and brother-in-law to a Methodist baptism (the family had been Dutch Reformed). Evangelical Methodism remained the central force in her life. Teaching school briefly in Pennington and Milford, NJ, she found a stable position in New Egypt, NJ, where she taught for seven years. There she met the Rev. Charles S. Downs, a Methodist circuit minister, and she left her teaching career to marry him in 1850.

For almost two decades Downs was the helpmate of a country parson. Her husband had ridden Methodist circuits since 1838, and Downs followed him from New Egypt through three other southern New Jersey districts: Allowaystown (1851–53), Cape May (1853–55), and Millville (1855–57). She played hostess at church functions, accompanied her husband on church business, taught Sunday school, and was mother to two stepsons and a daughter and son of her own (John and Sara Louise; two other children died as toddlers). In 1860 failing health forced Rev. Downs from the ministry and the family moved to Tuckerton. To make ends meet, Downs returned to teaching and wrote local news articles for the *New Jersey Courier* of Toms River. The death of Downs's husband left the family in precarious economic circumstances, and while Downs effectively managed her limited resources, the experience left the future reformer acutely aware of the financial difficulties of single women and their children. All the while, she remained active in local Methodist affairs, headed her congregation's Ladies Aid Society, and raised funds for a new church. In 1874 she returned to Pennington as principal of the public school, and after supporting the education of her children, she moved into a modest home in the Methodist seashore community of Ocean Grove. By this time she had won considerable recognition for her educational and church work.

Since her teenaged conversion, Downs had shared her denomination's sympathy for the dry cause. In New Egypt, she was a member of the local Daughters of Temperance (an affiliate of the larger Sons of Temperance), and in Tuckerton she joined the Good Templars. Both groups were fraternal and neither was especially militant; but they had chapters across the nation and did help keep the temperance issue alive during the movement's doldrums after the Civil War. Militancy, however, returned in 1873 and 1874. As part of the so-called Women's War—a virtually spontaneous revolt of women across America against the liquor traffic—women in several New Jersey towns organized a series of public protests. They marched and prayed and proclaimed against the threats that drunkenness posed to their homes and children. Although Downs took no part in these activities, the protection of hearth and home was a subject dear to her, and the evangelical appeal of the crusade fit neatly into her church-oriented outlook. Thus, while still principal in Pennington, she had joined the local chapter of the Woman's Christian Temperance Union (WCTU), the organized successor (in New Jersey and nationally) to the informal crusade of 1873–74. For the first time, leadership in a major national reform movement had passed into women's hands.

After her move to Ocean Grove, Downs devoted virtually all her time to the New Jersey WCTU and she rose steadily in its ranks. Her forte was the ability to inspire and organize others. A physically large woman (she remarked early in life that others would love her for her spiritual qualities, not her appearance) with a quick wit and determination in debate, Downs was imposing on the platform. She generally spoke without notes and frequently without preparation, which brought a spontaneous and sincere quality to her presentations. Contemporaries, including opponents, credited her with real eloquence and she became a sought-after speaker on the New Jersey reform circuit. Frances Willard, president of the national WCTU, later commented that had Downs been a male, the New Jersey reformer could well have emerged a Methodist bishop. Thus there was little surprise when, in 1881, a state WCTU convention almost unanimously selected Downs to replace an ailing Mary R. Denman as president.

Downs led the state union for a decade, and during that time she built the group into an effective force in state politics. With Downs herself leading the organizational drive, membership in local New Jersey unions increased from 517 women in 26 chapters in 1881 to over 8,000 women in 208 chapters ten years later. She became a familiar figure to legislators, speaking often and forcefully in favor of prohibitory laws, and she kept antiliquor activity constantly in the public eye. Her platform was simple— "the entire extirpation and annihilation of the liquor traffic"—and wets (antiprohibition supporters) fully conceded that she was a dangerous foe. While wets frustrated efforts to ban liquor sales during the 1880s, there were some important reform victories. The WCTU led a successful campaign to require "scientific temperance instruction" in the public schools (for which the drys supplied the curriculum), and Downs worked strenuously to promote woman suffrage, the election of women to local school boards (the only electoral posts legally open to them), and the right of women to play wider roles in church affairs. In a state with a growing and generally wet immigrant population, and with a powerful liquor lobby, Downs had done as much as anyone to make the WCTU a force to reckon with.

Downs ultimately became a figure of some importance in the national affairs of the WCTU. As state president, she was a member of the national union's Executive Committee, where she was a staunch Willard loyalist. Brooking no opposition to the national president, whom she adored, Downs became a trusted lieutenant and Willard relied on her to carry debate on policy questions and to enforce discipline. She was, as Willard phrased it, "the Andrew Jackson of the Executive Committee." Downs stood by Willard in one of the bitterest disputes within union ranks. A significant WCTU faction had never accepted Willard's attempts to broaden the union's reform agenda beyond temperance issues, and they objected in particular to Willard's prosuffrage stance. Losing the debate, the conservatives finally seceded to form the separate Nonpartisan WCTU. Downs helped to keep most of the Executive Committee with Willard and, at the state level, assured that the breakaway group never received any important New Jersey support.

While she was loyal to Willard, however, Downs was not in the vanguard of temperance thinkers. She was a good soldier, an ideal mid-level commander of the reform legion who worked within parameters others established. To the end, the chief interests of "Mother Downs" (as her admirers called her) were prohibition and "home protection," with "gospel temperance"—the dry message wrapped in evangelical Christianity—her normal motif. Her support for suffrage, for example, came only after the strong remonstrances of other New Jersey union women; she supported the ballot, she explained, as a means for women to better protect their homes and children. Still, she seemed to understand that extending the vote to women would inevitably broaden their roles in society. Participation in WCTU activities had opened the way for many women to exert their talents and influence beyond the home, and once raised, expectations of greater access to public life were inherent in the thinking of many union members. To her credit, Downs came to accept these changes, even if she only cautiously endorsed them.

Downs died on November 10, 1891, in East Orange, at the home of her married daughter. It was indicative of her character that she died virtually in harness. A flu-like ailment, probably pneumonia, had confined her to bed for the previous week; but she insisted on keeping up with WCTU affairs and on following a state legislative campaign involving Prohibition party candidates. Early on November 10, she read the election results, announced that she was pleased with the dry vote, and then went into a rapid decline. She died in the evening, surrounded by family, who quickly sent word to the WCTU. The announcement reached the initial session of the World's WCTU Convention the next day, casting a pall over the event. Dry leaders from around the nation, led by Frances Willard, quickly sent regrets and tributes. They had lost one of their most stalwart comrades.

Shortly after Downs's death, a memorial to her, containing a biographical sketch, was edited by Rev. J. B. Graw: *Life of Mrs. S.J.C. Downs . . .* (1892). References to Downs appeared in issues of the WCTU's *Union Signal* during the 1880s; her death was noted in the *Union Signal*, Nov. 19, 1891.

*Mark Edward Lender*

## FLORENCE PESHINE EAGLETON, 1870–1953

Florence (Peshine) Eagleton, a major leader for woman suffrage and for women's higher education in New Jersey, was born in Newark on April 16, 1870, to Elizabeth M. (Jelliff) and Francis Strafford Peshine, a family combining English and French ancestry. Edward Ball, one of her ancestors, was related to Mary Ball, mother of George Washington. He was also one of the twelve proprietors of the town of Newark and held office there as early as 1666.

Eagleton's French ancestry went back to Pierre Abraham Péchin, who settled at Middletown Point about 1763 and whose residence was looted and burned to the ground by the Hessians after the Battle of Monmouth. John Jelliff, her maternal grandfather, was an outstanding cabinetmaker and a noted civic leader of Newark.

Because of her younger sister's illness, Eagleton's parents sent her to live with her cousin Clarence E. le Massena and his family, during which time she attended private girls' schools in Newark. When her sister died as a teenager, Eagleton continued living with her cousin's family until her marriage at 22.

Eagleton's first marriage, in 1892, was arranged by her parents to Henry Benjamin Riggs, a widower more than twice her age, with a son only two years younger than she. Riggs regarded her as the daughter he never had, but it was a loveless marriage for her. She and Riggs had a son,

Strafford ("Teddy") Peshine Riggs, in 1899. Her sense of loss at the lack of love prompted a divorce. The divorce was amicable, and Riggs, in an unusual move, named her, along with his sons, heir to his estate. As a result of her divorce, however, Eagleton's family and immediate society regarded her as a fallen woman. According to her cousin Virginia le Massena Brownell only one relative supported her decision.

In 1913 she married Wells Phillips Eagleton, M.D., a 48-year-old bachelor, already well established in Newark as a specialist in brain, eye, and ear surgery, whom she had known for years as her son's physician. This marriage was the love match she had longed for and provided the mutual support needed by both for what became a lifelong devotion to each other, family, work, and community.

Eagleton was identified with many of Newark's philanthropic, social, and educational movements and had a special interest in improving the lives of women. She was a trustee of the Newark YWCA, president of the Newark Visiting Nurse Association, director of the New Jersey Consumers' League, an organizer of the New Jersey Birth Control League, and a member of Newark's Maternal Health Center. A supporter of many cultural institutions, she was a trustee of the Newark Museum, the Newark Music Foundation, the Art Club of Newark, a life member of the New Jersey Historical Society, and a member of the Browning Society of New York. Other positions she held were vice-president of the Travelers Aid Society and honorary vice-president of the League of Nations Non-Partisan Association.

Eagleton was a leader in the long struggle for woman suffrage, serving as president of the Women's Political Union (WPU) and first vice-president of the New Jersey Woman Suffrage Association. These efforts culminated on January 27, 1920, when petitions containing over 125,000 names were presented in Trenton urging the legislature to ratify the federal suffrage amendment. These signatures were secured when the Newark WPU, under Eagleton's leadership, organized squads of women to canvass the wards and districts of Newark. In an interview prior to ratification, Eagleton reported that "the majority of women were eager or willing to sign. Hesitation was usually found to be the result of ignorance." (*N.J. Archives,* League of Woman Voters, box 3)

Soon after the legislature ratified the amendment, Eagleton presided over the final meeting of the WPU on May 4, 1920, during which all of its assets were voted to the new Newark League of Women Voters (LWV). A resolution passed at that meeting commended the "enthusiastic and faithful leadership of Mrs. Wells P. Eagleton." (N.J. Archives, LWV, box 3) After organizing the Newark LWV, Eagleton became its first president and later served the state LWV in many capacities.

A pioneer in the campaign for higher education for

women in the state, Eagleton was a member of the original Board of Managers of the New Jersey College for Women (now Douglass College); she was one of the first women to serve as a Rutgers University trustee and became trustee emeritus in 1946. Her generosity to the college and contributions to the scholarship fund and the Student Center drive were noted when the Class of '33 made her an honorary member.

Combining her interest in women's political participation and women's education, Eagleton left a bequest to the college of more than a million dollars to provide education in the techniques of practical politics for the young women of New Jersey. The result was the Wells Phillips Eagleton and Florence Peshine Eagleton Foundation to promote "the advancement of learning in the field of practical political affairs and . . . actual . . . governmental processes . . . through the education of young women and men in democratic government." (*Bulletin of the League of Women Voters of New Jersey*, Jan. 1954) Since 1956 the Eagleton Foundation (now the Eagleton Institute of Politics) has been housed at Wood Lawn on the Douglass campus of Rutgers, the State University.

Eagleton was a towering woman, standing almost six feet tall, with an aristocratic, matriarchal bearing. Despite her vigorous support for women's progress in the public sphere, she was still a product of the Victorian age. According to her cousin Virginia Brownell, Eagleton envisioned a traditional role for women—in the home, not on soapboxes. She expected women's lives to be circumscribed by their homes and families. To her, women should be educated and involved in public affairs, but not career oriented. She saw no inconsistency between her espousal of women's traditional role and her strenuous efforts to broaden educational opportunity and political rights.

Eagleton died, at age 83, in Newark on November 22, 1953. Her son (d. 1943) and husband (d. 1946) had predeceased her.

Documents pertaining to Eagleton are found at NJ-RU and NJ-DC. Information on Eagleton was provided by a personal interview with Virginia le Massena Brownell, a cousin, in November 1985. *Scannell's New Jersey's First Citizens and State Guide*, vol 2 (1919–20), contains a biographical sketch. Obituaries appeared in the *New York Times*, the *New York Herald Tribune*, and the *Newark Evening News*, Nov. 24, 1953.

*Rebecca L. Lubetkin*

## EMMA WARD EDWARDS, 1845–1896

Emma Cornelia (Ward) Edwards, one of the leading women doctors in Newark and the state of New Jersey of her time, was among the first generation of women to be

trained and inspired by the great 19th-century women pioneers of medicine, Drs. Elizabeth and Emily Blackwell. The first of seven children, four of whom reached adulthood, Edwards was born in Newark on June 5, 1845, to Deidamia (Bowles) and Caleb S. Ward. Her father was a grocer by trade and a member of the prominent Ward family, associated with Newark since its founding. His business at 498 Broad Street probably catered to the fine homes around nearby Washington Park, where his residence at 11 Washington Street stood on old family property. He counted among his neighbors, and most likely his customers as well, his brother Joseph Ward, president of the Essex County National Bank, and his more distant relative Marcus Ward, philanthropist and governor of New Jersey from 1866 to 1869.

Edwards attended local private schools for her early education. An illness at seventeen, requiring several years of medical care, reputedly influenced her determination to become a physician, as did probably the tragic deaths of three siblings in their infancy and childhood. By age 21 she had persuaded several local doctors to let her study under them. At the time, medical schools were virtually closed to women. However, in 1868 a serendipitous breakthrough occurred. The Women's Medical College of the New York Infirmary, the first medical college run for and by women, was founded by the Blackwell sisters; it was only a short ride away in lower Manhattan. Edwards successfully passed the entrance exam, immediately enrolled, and apparently excelled in the rigorous course of study, which was equal to and even more progressive than that of most 19th-century American medical schools.

In 1870 Edwards graduated as the valedictorian of the college's first class and she remained associated with the school through 1871 in multiple capacities: as clinical assistant for the Medical Clinic of the Faculty of Medicine, dispensary physician, and instructor in "practice." During this postgraduate year she is said to have further expanded the breadth of her knowledge by working for Dr. Edward Loring of New York, an esteemed ophthalmologist and perfector of the ophthalmoscope.

With her excellent training behind her, Edwards pursued private practice, the preferred avenue of medicine in the 19th century. In the 1871 Newark City Directory she advertised her services as an allopathic (regular medical) physician at her family home at 11 Washington Street. Despite the rarity of women in the medical profession at the time, and the opposition to them, Edwards is said to have met with unusual success. Initially, the high standing of the Ward family name may have assisted in her acceptance by the community. In time, however, her demonstrated skills must have been the determining factor.

On April 13, 1872, she married Arthur Mead Edwards, a professor of theoretical and practical chemistry (1870–73) and microscopy (1872-73) at the Women's College of the New York Infirmary, and withdrew from active practice. They chose to make their home in Newark, which was a rapidly growing city in need of doctors, and by 1873 Arthur Mead Edwards had opened a general practice. Edwards apparently devoted herself to her duties as a young wife and a mother of two daughters, Harriet Smith (b. 1873) and Eleanor Pierrepont (b. 1875).

Whether this hiatus in Edwards's career was meant to be permanent is not known. In 1877 Arthur Mead Edwards accepted an appointment to teach chemistry at the University of Tokyo, newly established in 1868, and he launched his young family on the difficult first leg of the journey to Japan, by way of California. The exact cause remains obscure, but in Berkeley (or San Francisco) he fell ill and lost his memory to the extent that he felt compelled to refuse his academic post. He is then said to have practiced medicine in Berkeley for two years.

In 1879 the family returned to Newark by train, shipping their belongings around Cape Horn for the second time, and joined Edwards's parents and siblings at 11 Washington Street. Exhibiting great resilience, Edwards reestablished her services as a doctor by the end of the year. Her husband apparently soon withdrew from active medical practice and until his death in 1914 concentrated on field work, research, and publishing in the burgeoning young field of microbiology.

Edwards excelled at clinical work. Once again her general practice became large and thriving. Any lingering resistance to her as a woman physician was removed by her proven medical abilities, energy, conscientious attitude, and kind and tactful manner. Evidence of the range of Edwards's expertise and compassionate spirit is seen in the letter she wrote to the editor of the widely read *Medical Record* of New York in 1879 advocating the use of an ingenious rawhide jacket for sufferers of tuberculosis of the spine in place of heavier, less comfortable ones of plaster or metal. Noting that she hoped that the deforming disease would soon be recognized and cured, she ended the letter: "The physical suffering saved will be enormous, but who can estimate the mental stress prevented?" (*Medical Record,* 407) The high regard in which Edwards's fellow professionals held her is attested to by her acceptance in 1880 to both the Essex County and the New Jersey medical societies, through a process of competitive exams and elections, at a time when medical societies were only beginning to open their memberships to women.

In 1885 Edwards was joined in her offices at 11 Washington Street by a young fellow graduate of the Women's Medical College of the New York Infirmary, Dr. Sarah R. Mead. This loyal alliance lasted for more than ten years, and following Edwards's death, Mead continued her practice in the same area of the city and carried on some of her partner's charity work. Alice Hamilton Ward, Edwards' youngest sibling, born in 1865, was likely influenced by her sister's example to attend the Women's Medical College. Graduating in 1890, she briefly shared a practice with Edwards and Mead before working on her own as a physician.

Emma Ward Edwards, a 19th-century Newark physician and reformer, was valedictorian in 1870 of the first class graduated by Elizabeth Blackwell's Woman's Medical College. *Courtesy, private collection.*

As with most Victorian women physicians, the middle class probably formed the backbone of Edwards's practice. The Newark City Health Department Delivery Records for 1887–92 reveal that she frequently assisted at the births of children of blue- and white-collar workers of the community: die cutters, iron workers, printers, merchants, diamond brokers, clerks, bankers, and lawyers. The financial security thus afforded her and her family enabled her to devote countless hours, probably largely in a volunteer capacity, to serving the indigent and poor. Soon after her return to Newark, she began to work on the medical staffs of the Society for the Relief of Respectable Aged Women, the Home for Incurables and Convalescents and the Working Girls Club boardinghouse, both run by the

YWCA. She also was one of the attending physicians of the Newark City Dispensary, which provided drugs, small-pox vaccines, and programs on child hygiene and other health concerns at little or no cost.

Edwards found still more time to be involved in efforts for social reform as well as her own self-renewal and en-richment. Dr. Elizabeth Blackwell had strongly exhorted her students to focus particularly on the health and welfare of children, and Edwards apparently was long aware of the high incidence of child neglect and mortality in Newark. (Her medical college thesis in 1870 had been on infan-ticide.) From 1882 to 1896 she fought to improve the lives of victims of child abuse, which numbered 5,000 annually in Newark alone, as a physician and director for the Chil-dren's Aid Society for the Prevention of Cruelty to the Children of Essex County. She also promoted the free kin-dergarten movement in her city. Still at the center of de-bate over its efficacy in 1896, proponents such as Edwards touted the wide benefits of early education, particularly for the poor and working classes. Her daughter Harriet Ed-wards shared her belief in this progressive form of educa-tion and ran a kindergarten in her home from the year of Edwards's death in 1896 until 1900.

For Edwards's own self-improvement and the oppor-tunity to socialize with women friends, she turned to the Ray Palmer Club, a reading association encouraged by and named for a well-loved Belleville, NJ, preacher, poet, and hymn writer. Bimonthly topics included literature, history, art, music, philanthropy, science, the home, and current events and helped link Edwards to the world outside of the demands of her work and family life.

In early March 1896 Edwards, tired and suffering from what was thought to be a slight ailment, took her usual trip to Florida for a brief respite. Within a week she showed signs of what may have been a recurrent malarial fever and that probably lowered her resistance to what was reported varyingly as typhoid fever or dysentery. Any of these dis-eases could have been contracted by her in Newark, where they were widespread. On March 28, 1896, with Dr. Sarah R. Mead in attendance, she died in Clearwater, FL. She was buried in Newark's Mount Pleasant Cemetery in the fam-ily plot.

Tributes ran for days in the Newark papers, and her devoted friend and noted Newark art educator Sarah A. Fawcett donated a new central altar to the House of Prayer in her memory.

Edwards authored two articles: "The Raw-hide Jacket for Spinal Disease," *Medical Record* 16 (1879):406; and "Undeveloped Uterus with Apparent Absence of Ovaries," *Medical Record* 20 (1881):653. Obituaries appeared in *Transactions of the Medical Society of New Jersey* (1896):359–60; *Medical Record* 49 (1896):852; the *Newark Daily Advertiser*, Mar. 30, 1896; *Newark Evening News*, Mar. 30, 1896; and the *Women's Journal* (Boston) 27 (May 9, 1896).

*Susan Newberry*

## ELIZABETH HARKER ELMER, 1832–1915

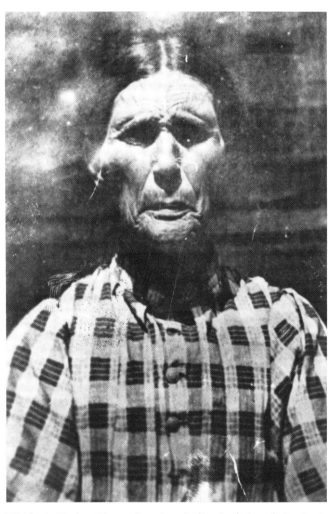

Elizabeth Harker Elmer, American Indian herbal medicine heal-er, was born on July 28, 1832, in Monmouth County, the daugh-ter of Elizabeth (Pierce) and William Harker. She married James Henry Elmer in 1853 and lived on a farm near Neptune, where over the next 20 years she had twelve children.

Elmer had a knowledge of plant lore and the use of herbs and roots to help cure minor illness. She taught her skills to her youn-gest daughter, Minnie, who in turn passed them on. Elmer's exact recipes were not recorded, but the types of cures she used were preserved in the memories of her descendants. She used a salve made from linden or basswood flowers and tallow to heal cuts, beeswax to fill dental cavities, a syrup cooked from onions and honey for sore throats, and a powder from dried puffball mush-rooms for nose bleeds.

Elmer was widowed in 1903 and died October 2, 1915, in Neptune. *Courtesy, Margaret Ann Burdge.*

## LILLIAN FORD FEICKERT, 1877–1945

Lillian (Ford) Feickert, suffragist and political leader, was born on July 20, 1877, in Brooklyn, NY, one of four children (two boys and two girls) of Emeline Margaretta (Kirkland) and Herbert Lord Ford. Her parents were Episcopalians, of English, Irish, and Scottish descent. Her father, a lawyer, was born in New York State; her mother, a homemaker, was born in the West Indies. The Fords' home at South Elliott Place in the Fort Greene section of Brooklyn had a view of lower Manhattan across the East River.

Little is known about Feickert's education and upbringing. In public statements as an adult she often referred to her family in one context only—noting that her direct ancestors could be traced back to 1622, when Martha Ford, a widow with two young children, ventured across the Atlantic to America on the ship *Fortune*. Her plucky female ancestor was clearly an important role model.

She married Edward Foster Feickert, a 28-year-old banker from New York, on December 6, 1902. She was 25 years old. The couple moved immediately to Plainfield, NJ, where Edward joined the newly organized Plainfield Trust Company as assistant secretary. Over the next eight years Feickert led a relatively quiet suburban life, tending her home and garden, which was her pride, as her husband moved up in the banking world. The Feickerts suffered a personal tragedy when their child died in infancy, an event they never mentioned in later years. They had no more children. Within a short time Edward Feickert became treasurer of the Plainfield Trust Company. In 1910 he organized and assumed the vice-presidency of what was to become a much larger institution: the State Trust Company. The Feickerts moved to a large property at the foothills of the Watchung Mountains in North Plainfield Township in 1908.

Even in this period Feickert exhibited some of the organizational talents and boundless energy that would fully emerge in the next decade. She organized and led local, and then statewide, mission study classes for Grace Episcopal Church of Plainfield. She also joined a number of women's organizations, among them the Woman's Christian Temperance Union, the Daughters of the American Revolution, and the New Jersey Woman Suffrage Association (NJWSA). When Clara Laddey, NJWSA president, appointed her enrollment chairman of the association in late 1910, Feickert became a public figure for the first time.

She proved to be an ideal choice for the post. The NJWSA, like other suffrage organizations throughout the nation, was entering a period of renewed activity, and Feickert had definite ideas about increasing membership. Borrowing methods from the political parties, she supervised house-to-house canvasses in the wards of large cities,

conducted indoor and outdoor meetings, and oversaw mass distribution of suffrage literature. When Feickert assumed the presidency of the NJWSA in 1912, the association's membership had grown from a few hundred in 1910 to 1,200.

As president of the NJWSA from 1912 to 1920, Feickert became the leading figure of the New Jersey suffrage movement, and she was at the association's helm when the vote was finally won. By then the membership had grown to 120,000. She honed her political skills by presiding over the unsuccessful fight to win male voter approval of the state suffrage amendment in October 1915, countering the efforts of the substantial body of New Jersey antisuffragists, opposing the militant tactics of suffragists in the New Jersey state branch of the National Woman's Party, and guiding the NJWSA as it gained new adherents from both men and women during the war years. In July 1919 Feickert was chosen to head the formal effort of several organizations to convince the state legislature to ratify the federal suffrage amendment. The legislature finally voted to ratify it on February 10, 1920.

With the winning of the vote Feickert had become supremely confident of women's abilities to achieve their postsuffrage objectives—either to elect candidates to office or to secure passage of favored legislation. Indeed, events in the early 1920s bore out her initial optimism. Early in 1920 the state Republican party, respecting Feickert's achievements as New Jersey's leading suffragist, named her vice-chairman of the Republican State Committee and assigned her the task of organizing the Republican women in the state. (The party also created a Woman's Division of the State Committee, to which it appointed a number of other suffragist leaders.) Simultaneously elected treasurer of the newly formed New Jersey League of Women Voters (NJLWV), Feickert parted ways with the NJLWV in mid-1921, rejecting the organization's nonpartisan direction. "Now that we have the vote," she wrote in a letter to the league's board, "we should become political workers. I, for my part, am through with creating sympathy in favor of industrial laws, etc. I want to see the women well organized in both parties, so that we can work for the measures we believe in by the direct method instead of the indirect method." (Feickert to the directors of the NJLWV, Jan. 17, 1921, NJLWV Papers, box 3) By severing her ties to the league when her term ended that April, Feickert chose to focus her energies as president of the New Jersey Women's Republican Club (NJWRC). The club soon had a reported membership of 100,000, with some financial backing from the state Republican organization.

In later years Feickert asserted that her acceptance of the vice-chairmanship of the State Committee was part of a bargain she had struck with Edward C. Stokes, Republican chairman and former governor. By May 1921 this "bargain" resulted in the passage by the Republican-dominated legislature of several bills that advanced women's political and legal status. "I was not willing to accept the vice-chairmanship without making a bargain," she related. "I laid my terms before the men who offered it to me. These were that all political committees should be composed of an equal number of men and women; that there be women on all juries; and that at least two members of the State Board of Education and the Department of Health should be women." (*New York Times*, Apr. 15, 1928)

Feickert and organized Republican women had a few other successes. Most notable of these was a favored Consumers' League–supported bill passed in March 1923—known as the Night Work Bill—which prohibited women from working at night, between 10:00 P.M. and 6:00 A.M., in manufacturing and mercantile establishments, laundries, and bakeries.

The supportive attitude of the Republican party organization toward the NJWRC gradually changed, however. By late 1923 Feickert's demands for strict party support of Prohibition and her insistence on legislative passage of women's bills had brought her (and the NJWRC) into disfavor with Republican party leaders. In 1925, with open party concurrence, she was defeated in her quest for re-election to the State Committee, thereby losing her position as vice-chairman.

The ensuing years brought both personal and political disappointment for Feickert. In 1925, after 23 years of marriage, Edward Feickert sued for divorce, stating that his wife's nonstop political activities had caused him extreme suffering. Although he, too, had been an active suffragist, he could not accept the fact that his wife had chosen to continue in public life after 1920. Six weeks after the divorce he married Iva Dayton, his secretary. At the same time the "independent" NJWRC was becoming increasingly isolated as sentiment grew in New Jersey for complete repeal or modification of Prohibition laws (allowing beer or wine). The NJWRC was gradually supplanted by "regular" Republican women's organizations and was formally replaced in November 1929 by the Women's State Republican Club of New Jersey. Unlike the NJWRC, the new women's Republican organization put party loyalty first. It did not write party platforms, nor did it seek to extract political pledges from the party leadership. The party now had what it wanted: women on whose loyalty it could depend. In late 1930 Feickert established the State Council of Republican Women as a rival organization, but it did not survive.

Feickert moved briefly into the public limelight when she ran unsuccessfully as a pro-Prohibition candidate for the U.S. Senate in 1928. Her public role ended finally in the early 1930s with the defeat of Prohibition and the demise of the State Council.

She then returned to private life, spending her time remodeling her new home with antiques; devoting time to her garden, which was reputed to be a showplace; reading history and biographies; and traveling widely. Following a brief illness, Feickert, 67, died in Saint Vincent's Hospital in New York City on January 21, 1945, of a cerebral hemorrhage. Her body was cremated in Fresh Pond, NY.

Material on Feickert's suffrage activities is contained in the New Jersey League of Women Voters Papers at NJ-RU. See also Ida Husted Harper, ed., *History of Woman Suffrage, 1900–1920* 6 (1922); and Felice Gordon, *After Winning: The Legacy of the New Jersey Suffragists, 1920–1947* (1986). Two interviews with Feickert appeared in the *New York Times*, May 27, 1923, and Apr. 15, 1928. Obituaries appeared in the *New York Times* and the *Plainfield Courier-News*, Jan. 22, 1945.

*Felice D. Gordon*

## GRACE BAXTER FENDERSON, 1882–1962

Grace (Baxter) Fenderson, an activist for the advancement of African-Americans, was born November 2, 1882, in Newark (Essex County), NJ. A lifelong resident of the city, she was the third child of James Miller and Pauline (Mars) Baxter. She had one sister, Elizabeth, and three brothers: Le Roy, Louis E., and Ernest S.

Education was emphasized in Fenderson's childhood home. Her father was a graduate of Philadelphia's Institute for Colored Youth, a forerunner of Cheyney State College, which was founded by the Quakers in 1837 to train black teachers. At the invitation of the Board of Education, he came to Newark from Philadelphia in 1864 to teach black elementary children and later became the city's first black principal. On his retirement in 1909, after 45 years of teaching, the "colored school" was discontinued by action of the Board of Education.

After graduating from the "colored school" (1896) and Newark High School (1901), Fenderson entered Newark Normal and Training School, a predecessor of Kean College, in 1904 and graduated in 1906. She began her teaching career in her father's school and subsequently became one of the first regular African-American teachers in the Newark public school system. She retired from the Monmouth Street School in 1948, after 42 years of teaching. A founder and first president of Monmouth's Parent-Teacher Association, she was made a life member after her retirement.

In 1917 she married Walter E. Fenderson, a purchasing agent for the New York (City) Century Club. They had no children. From the outset she and her husband shared a commitment to full integration of black Americans. For more than half a century both were undaunted in their efforts against race discrimination.

Fenderson was a founder in 1914 of the Newark chapter of the National Association for the Advancement of

Colored People (NAACP), which she served in later years as president and chairperson of its Executive Committee. The parent body of the NAACP had been organized in 1909 to oppose the segregation and oppression of black Americans. She was also a vice-president and longtime member of the organization's national board. Fenderson was a leader in the Newark NAACP's campaign for the appointment of African-American principals and vice-principals by the Newark Board of Education. At an NAACP dinner in 1959, she said, "I am determined not to die until I see another Negro principal in Newark." (*Newark Sunday News*, Feb. 2, 1967) She did not live to see her wish fulfilled, but two years after her death in 1962, Dr. E. ALMA FLAGG, an African-American, was appointed principal of Hawkins Street School.

A key figure in the yearly celebrations of the Lincoln-Douglass Memorial Association, Fenderson served in the 1940s as president of that organization, which held memorial programs for over 40 years. The association was started in 1912 by a group of black and white citizens of Newark who held public meetings to commemorate the life and work of Abraham Lincoln. Five years later, the members agreed to include Frederick Douglass, the black abolitionist, in the yearly tributes. Fenderson was also a member and historian of the black St. Phillips Episcopal Church, which was founded in Newark in 1848.

Among other civic and educational pursuits, Fenderson served on the Board of Directors of the Sojourner Truth Branch, the black branch of the Newark YWCA, which operated until the 1950s, and the New Jersey Mental Hygiene Association. She was a member of the Schoolwomen's Club of Newark, an organization of Newark teachers whose civic activities benefited the community and its own members, and the New Jersey Education Association. She was active in the Republican party.

An award she especially valued was a written tribute in the *New Jersey Herald News*, January 5, 1940, given by E. Frederick Morrow, a columnist for the paper, who cited fellow New Jerseyans for their contributions to the cultural progress and civic advancement of African-Americans. It read: "Mrs. Grace B. Fenderson, Newark. School teacher, club woman, member national board of the N.A.A.C.P. For many years a tireless worker in the interest of race advancement and interracial respect. Gives time, money and active support to any endeavor of consequence. . . . She inherited [her father's] indomitable pioneering spirit, and has used it with courage. She speaks out against injustice anywhere, without compromise or fear."

Fenderson died of a cerebral hemorrhage on March 19, 1962, at age 79, in Philadelphia, PA, and was buried in Evergreen Cemetery in Hillside, NJ. Her eulogy was read into the *Congressional Record* by New Jersey Representative Hugh Addonizio, who cited her far-reaching influence for good and her "notable contribution to the great cause of education and of civil rights." (*Congressional Record* 108: 5740)

Family papers and photographs of Fenderson are in the possession of her nieces, Louise Baxter Fields and Julia Baxter Bates. See also *Newark Sunday News*, Feb. 12, 1962, and the *Congressional Record*, Apr. 2, 1962.

*Mildred L. Lipscombe*

### SUSAN PECKER FOWLER, 1823–1911

Susan Pecker Fowler, Vineland, suffragist, tax protester, and dress reformer, was born on May 31, 1823, in Amesbury, MA. Her mother was Mary (Pecker) Fowler and her father's given name is unknown. By her own account she suffered impaired health in childhood "by the scourge of scarlet fever with maltreatment, hence . . . had little vitality." (Tillotson, *Woman's Way Out*, 31)

Although little is known about Fowler's formal training, her expressive use of language in letters and her rhetoric and logic suggest a foundation of study. Her background was sufficient to permit her to become a teacher, though she found her energy depleted after each day's work. Often her written appeals are passionate calls for action. Fowler's words suggest a woman of brisk and businesslike nature.

At age 28, on reading an account of short skirts and Turkish pants in a newspaper, Fowler fashioned a suit that, she wrote, gave her "the sense of a bird uncaged." She called the dress she wore the "American costume," the term used by Harriet Austin and James Jackson in the *Laws of Life*, a health reform newspaper. She testified that the mobility thus gained made it possible to carry out her strenuous vocations of teacher, merchant, and farmer. Her costume was similar to a mandarin coat, buttoned down the front, lightly tailored to the torso, and flared from the waist to about calf length. Beneath the coat she wore tapered trousers and sometimes a simple white blouse.

Fowler did not marry. She probably settled in Vineland in the mid-1860s shortly after it was founded by Charles K. Landis in 1861 as a planned agricultural community. Early Vineland was akin to a pioneer town, welcoming settlers no matter what their ideas. The town had an active intellectual life and its Plum Street Hall served as a center for lectures by visiting speakers, the exchange of ideas, and social gatherings. Fowler played an active role in the social and political life of the community, where she was a farmer of blueberries, secretary of the Grange, and acting secretary of the New Jersey Association of Spiritualists and Friends of Progress. When the local dress reform society sponsored an Anti-Fashion Convention in 1874, she served as vice-president.

She was committed to equal rights for women. In a tes-

Susan Pecker Fowler in reform dress. A suffragist and tax protester who settled in Vineland in the 1860s, she was an early advocate of dress reform for women. She said the costume she adopted gave her "the sense of a bird uncaged." *Courtesy, Vineland Historical and Antiquarian Society.*

timonial letter she wrote for *Women's Way Out*, a book by her friend MARY E. TILLOTSON, she stated: "Through all opposition the personal benefits of the reform [dress] have compensated; but had it been mainly sacrifice, the thought of working for the amelioration of women and the elevation of humanity would still have been the beacon-star guiding me on amid all discouragements." (Tillotson, 31)

Fowler worked both locally and nationally for woman suffrage. She and others circulated a petition for equal rights in 1867 and gathered 678 signatures in Vineland. The petition was presented to the Republican State Convention at Trenton and called for the convention "to organize a campaign for Impartial Suffrage, irregardless of Sex

and Color." She and 171 other determined Vineland women, including TILLOTSON, voted in the election of November 3, 1868. Their humble ballot box, fashioned of two blueberry cartons and covered with green fabric, still remains in the Vineland Historical Society and is a memorial to those disenfranchised women.

By 1872 Fowler seemed to abandon hope for equality in existing political parties. She traveled widely and sent an open letter from Fernandina, FL, to editors throughout the South urging citizens to join women of the North to form a new political party. The *Key-West Guardian* (April 6, 1872) printed her letter on the front page: "The intelligent women of the North will be ignored no longer. They are demanding the right of the ballot. . . . There are many widespread and rapidly growing parties outside the women suffragists. The working men, the Internationalist, the Temperance party, the Spiritualists and all the new educational forces are working toward a union."

Like many financially independent women of the period, Fowler resented being taxed while she was denied the vote. She protested payment of taxes each year by a letter to the *Vineland Evening News*. On December 16, 1907, she wrote: "As a Tax-Paying Citizen of the United States I am entitled to a voice in Governmental affairs. . . . Having paid this *unlawful Tax under written Protest* for forty years, I am entitled to receive from the Treasury of 'Uncle Sam' the full amount of both Principal and Interest."

Fowler died at her home in Vineland, at age 87, on April 30, 1911, of gangrene of the legs. She was buried at Oak Hill Cemetery.

A profile of Fowler appears in Mary Tillotson, *Woman's Way Out* (1876). Additional information on Fowler's work for equal rights and dress reform is available at the Vineland Historical and Antiquarian Society (Vineland, NJ).

*Charlotte Perry-Dickerson*
*Joyce Bator-Rabinoff*

## MARY E. WILKINS FREEMAN, 1852–1930

Mary E. (Wilkins) Freeman (baptized Mary Ella Wilkins), noted author, was born on October 31, 1852, in Randolph, MA, a rural New England town fourteen miles south of Boston, to Eleanor (Lothrop) and Warren Edward Wilkins. Of four Wilkins children, only Freeman and her younger sister, Anna, survived infancy. Her father was a housewright and carpenter who traced his ancestors to the earliest settlers in Salem, MA; the Lothrops and Holbrooks, her mother's family, had lived in the Randolph area since 1645.

Freeman's childhood, in a Congregational family, was secure and loving. Characterized as imaginative but withdrawn and shy, the blue-eyed child with reddish-gold hair

Mary Wilkins Freeman, *front right*, noted author, was a guest at a December 1905 dinner party at Delmonico's in New York City in honor of Mark Twain's 70th birthday. *Courtesy, Library of Congress.*

was pampered by relatives who excused her from household chores. In grammar school, Freeman remained aloof from the other children, who called her that stuck-up "little dolly-pinky-rosy." The nickname "Dolly" stayed with her throughout her life. Freeman avidly read fairy tales and adventure stories and played at the farmhouse of Mary Elizabeth Wales, who became her informal business manager and lifelong friend.

In 1867 the Wilkins family moved to Brattleboro, VT, where Freeman's father opened a dry goods business. Freeman graduated from Brattleboro High School, attended Mt. Holyoke Seminary for one year, and concluded her formal education with a year at Mrs. Hosford's Glenwood Seminary in West Brattleboro.

With Evelyn Sawyer, her best friend, she read Charles Dickens, Edgar Allen Poe, Nathaniel Hawthorne, Leo Tolstoy, and William Makepeace Thackeray, and contem-

porary female writers such as Sarah Orne Jewett and Harriet Beecher Stowe. Freeman and Sawyer also shared their own stories. The staples of Freeman's stories were her New England characters of village gossips, and the strife between husband and wife and parent and child.

In 1873, when Warren Wilkins's dry goods business failed, the family moved back to Randolph, where Freeman's sister died at age seventeen. Three years later, when her mother died, Freeman changed her middle name to Eleanor, in memory of her mother. Forced to seek employment, she tried teaching at a local academy, a job she hated and soon quit.

Freeman then began to write religious poetry, which was never published, and children's verse. In 1881 *Wide Wake* published "The Beggar King," a ballad poem for children. In the same year the *Boston Sunday Budget* featured "A Shadow Family," her first published adult story, and paid her $50. In 1882 a major break came for Freeman when *Harper's Bazar* accepted "Two Old Lovers" for publication.

Freeman's father died suddenly of a fever in 1883 and left his daughter without any immediate family and an estate of $973. Following his death, Freeman moved into the north wing of her friend Mary Wales's family house, where she supported herself by writing.

Freeman believed in writing about those subjects she knew thoroughly. Michele Clark, a modern feminist critic, discusses Freeman's great respect for the strength of women as rearers, earners, survivors, and maintainers, but notes that with few exceptions Freeman's male characters are meek, dominated, gentle souls. Clark believes that "what distinguishes [her] women from others in both British and American literature is that theirs is a world in which women's primary relationships are to each other rather than to men." (Clark in Freeman, *The Revolt of Mother and Other Stories*, 195)

Edward Foster, her biographer, has said, "technically, the most striking characteristic of the [Freeman] story is its pace and directness: the short and wiry sentence; the short paragraph; concision in narrative, expository, and descriptive elements; boldness in moving fast to the scene developed in dialogue." (Foster, *Mary E. Wilkins Freeman*, 68)

Often compared to Chekhov, Tolstoy, Jewett, and Maupassant, Freeman became exceedingly popular for her adult and juvenile short stories, poetry for children, and novels. Her letters reveal her shrewd price negotiations and her ability to pit one publisher against another. She was very skillful in working with editors who were also close personal friends, such as Eliza Anna Farman Pratt, MARY MAPES DODGE, Kate Upson Clark, and Mary Louise Booth, who offered her steady criticism and a continual place to publish her stories. It was Mary Louise Booth who persuaded Henry Mills Alden to publish several Freeman short stories in *Harper's Bazar* and *Harper's Monthly*.

Throughout her career Freeman consulted with literary advisers and even employed literary agents. In the mid-1880s, fearful that her public might become tired of short stories, she wrote to a friend: "I wonder if there is such a thing as working a vein so long, that the gold ceases to be gold." (Kendrick, *The Infant Sphinx*, 61) She considered alternatives and began to write serialized novels as well as short stories. Her novels often had elaborate, amateurish plots, but were successful with the public. Modern critics consider *Pembroke* her most significant novel.

During a visit to Metuchen, NJ, in 1892 Freeman was introduced to Dr. Charles Manning Freeman, seven years her junior and a nonpracticing medical doctor who ran his father's coal and lumber business. Charles Freeman, who came from a prominent New Jersey family with roots in Colonial America, was a bachelor, heavy drinker, and womanizer—the antithesis of Freeman's male characters.

"I am wondering," Freeman wrote to a friend, "if I will make a good wife and my husband will be happy. I shall try, but it is dealing with unknown quantities and sometimes I feel afraid." (Kendrick, 256) Finally, after years of courtship and postponements, the Freemans were married in Metuchen on January 1, 1902. Freeman wrote to *Harper's* at the time: "I wish my full name—Mary E. Wilkins Freeman—to be used with all my work." (Kendrick, 299)

The couple, who built a new home in Metuchen, hosted receptions, teas, luncheons, recitals, and bridge parties there. Freeman established a new circle of women friends: her husband's mother, four unmarried sisters, and Henry Mills Alden's three unmarried daughters.

Freeman was regarded in Metuchen as a local celebrity, even though in her novels *The Debtor*, "*Doc*" *Gordon*, and *The Butterfly House* she used Metuchen for the setting and satirized local manners and the idiosyncrasies of life in a small New Jersey village. Despite her many jabs at Metuchen villagers, she also wrote: "Yes, indeed, if I'd been born in Metuchen I'd have found just as quaint and romantic people to write about here in New Jersey as ever stepped through the pages of a New England story book. For people are all alike, especially if they happen to be women, whether they live in Massachusetts or Metuchen." (Kendrick, 274)

Despite domestic responsibilities, chronic insomnia, and increasing deafness, Freeman wrote eleven other volumes, collaborated on a motion picture, and wrote many short stories during her 28 years in Metuchen.

By 1920 her husband, who had become an alcoholic and a drug addict (sleeping powders), had to be committed to the N.J. State Hospital for the Insane at Trenton. Freeman obtained a legal separation from him in 1921. When he died in 1923, leaving the bulk of his estate to his young chauffeur and only one dollar to Freeman, she and his sisters contested the will in one of the most famous court cases in Middlesex County history.

Freeman published little during the 1920s but continued to be active in securing reprints and copyrights for her works. In 1925 the American Academy of Arts and Letters awarded her the first William Dean Howells Medal for distinguished work in fiction. In 1926 she and Edith Wharton were among the first women elected to the National Institute of Arts and Letters.

Freeman died in Metuchen on March 15, 1930, at age 77, of a heart attack and was buried in the Hillside Cemetery in Plainfield, NJ. She was honored posthumously in 1938 when the American Academy of Arts and Letters in New York City installed new bronze doors at its entrance with the inscription "Dedicated to the Memory of Mary E. Wilkins Freeman and the Women Writers of America."

Freeman's short stories, particularly "A New England Nun" and "The Revolt of 'Mother,'" are widely anthologized today. Critics have become increasingly aware of Freeman's willingness to experiment with genre, her innovative exploration of topics such as homosexuality in *The Shoulders of Atlas*, and her ability to portray women as strong-willed individuals. Perhaps her own words are her most fitting legacy: "aside from the financial aspect, [there] is more: the life of my work. I feel that is all I came into the world for, and have failed dismally if it is not a success." (Kendrick, 424)

The most authoritative biography of Freeman is Edward Foster, *Mary E. Wilkins Freeman* (1956). An analysis of her writing appears in Perry Westbrook, *Mary Wilkins Freeman* (1967). Her correspondence is published in Brent Kendrick, ed., *The Infant Sphinx: Collected Letters of Mary E. Wilkins Freeman* (1985). Michele Clark provides a feminist assessment of Freeman's work in her introduction to Freeman's *The Revolt of Mother and Other Stories* (1974). A sketch of Freeman appears in *NAW*. Her obituary appeared in the *New York Times*, Mar. 15, 1930.

*Sondra Fishinger*

## CAROLINE BAMBERGER FRANK FULD, 1864–1944

Caroline (Bamberger) Frank Fuld, nicknamed Carrie, businesswoman and philanthropist, was born on March 16, 1864, to Jewish parents in Baltimore, MD. She was the fifth of six children, two boys and four girls. Her mother, Theresa (Hutzler) Bamberger, grew up in Baltimore, where her father owned a large department store. Elkan Bamberger, Fuld's father, emigrated from Bavaria in 1840 and worked in the wholesale notions business. Fuld and her brother Louis entered the dry goods business and later became millionaires as co-owners of L. Bamberger & Co. Both were prominent philanthropists; their most notable philanthropy was founding the Institute for Advanced Study at Princeton, NJ.

Fuld spent her childhood in Baltimore. Always close to her brother Louis, she accompanied him when he moved to Philadelphia, in 1883. In Philadelphia she met and married Louis Meyer Frank, a native of Lewiston, PA, who later became a business partner of Louis. Frank died in 1910, and three years later, on February 20, 1913, his widow married Felix Fuld, her brother's other partner. Neither marriage produced children.

In 1892 Louis Bamberger, Louis Frank, and Felix Fuld bought out the bankrupt firm of Hill and Craig in Newark, NJ. After selling out the stock, they organized the firm of L. Bamberger & Co., opening a department store in the two-story building on the corner of Market and Halsey streets in Newark on February 1, 1893. Carrie Fuld and the three men worked in the store to make it prosper, developing new methods of retail advertising and selling; the business grew from two to five floors.

Fifteen years later they built a new $2 million building and employed 2,500 people. When Louis Frank died in 1910 his interest was purchased by Louis Bamberger and Felix Fuld. The business soon became one of the largest mercantile companies in the United States, with annual sales of $35 million by 1928. After the death of her second husband on January 20, 1929, Fuld lived with her brother in South Orange, NJ. In 1929 Fuld and her brother decided to sell L. Bamberger & Co. to R. H. Macy & Co. in order to "devote their time and their fortunes to the welfare of others." (Woolf, *Community of Scholars*, ix) They sold their interest in the business to Macy in June 1929, just weeks before the stock market crash.

Fuld gave generously of her fortune throughout her life. She contributed jointly to many causes with her second husband, Felix Fuld. They gave $500,000 to the building fund for Newark's Beth Israel Hospital, as well as substantial sums to the Jewish Relief Committee, Community Chest, and Boy Scouts, and they assisted the Negro Welfare League of New Jersey (later the Urban League). Both were interested in the arts and contributed generously to the Newark Museum and to several music societies of Newark and New York City. After her husband's death, Fuld continued her gifts to Jewish service organizations, among them the Jewish Nursery and Neighborhood House of Newark, Hadassah, and the Woman's Zionist Organization of America. As reported in her obituary, "she and her husband disliked public mention of their gifts to philanthropy." In keeping with Jewish tradition, "whenever possible" they "obtained anonymity in making their benefactions." (*New York Times*, July 19, 1944)

After selling their business in 1929, Fuld and her brother decided to contribute a large sum of money to benefit not only New Jersey, but all of humankind. During their search, they heard of Dr. Abraham Flexner, who had written of his desire for an American institute "where everyone—faculty and members—took for granted what was known and published, and in their individual ways endeavored to advance the frontiers of knowledge." (Flexner, *I Remember*, 356) After several meetings with Flexner, Fuld and Bamberger agreed to endow the Institute for Advanced Study, to be located in Princeton, NJ. Their only condition was that Flexner should undertake its organization, which he agreed to do. Fuld and Bamberger contributed $5 million in 1930 for the initial endowment of the institute and approximately $18 million in all for its development. It was incorporated under the laws of New Jersey as the Institute for Advanced Study—Louis Bamberger and Mrs. Felix Fuld Foundation. Bamberger became president and Fuld vice-president until the institute was formally established in 1933, when they became life trustees.

The institute's objectives were described in a letter written by Fuld and Bamberger: "The primary purpose is the pursuit of advanced learning and exploration in fields of pure science and high scholarship to the utmost degree that the facilities of the institution and the ability of the faculty and students will permit." (Letter, June 6, 1930) The institute, the first of its kind in the United States, attracted scholars from all over the world. "It operated . . . on the premise that science and learning transcend national boundaries and that scholars and scientists are members of one republic of the spirit." (Woolf, xi)

They drew no class, race, or religious lines, as indicated in a letter Fuld and Bamberger wrote to the trustees of the institute: "It is fundamental in our purpose, and our express desire, that in the appointments to the staff and faculty, as well as in the admission of workers and students, no account shall be taken, directly or indirectly, of race, religion or sex." (Letter, June 6, 1930)

The first academic appointments of the institute were Albert Einstein, whose theory of relativity had made him world renowned, and Oswald Veblen, another noted mathematician. From its earliest years, the institute was internationally recognized as one of the world's leading centers of research, and Einstein's presence was a factor that attracted others from outside his field.

Fuld maintained her commitment to service organizations, in addition to her support of the Institute for Advanced Studies. In 1931 she was elected national director of the National Council of Jewish Women, where her special interest was vocational guidance and employment programs. She was also active on the Child Welfare Committee of America. She was a quiet, unpretentious woman whose concern for the welfare of others was demonstrated through her immense generosity in philanthropic work.

After suffering a long illness, Fuld died, at age 80, of a cerebral vascular hemorrhage on July 18, 1944, at her summer home in Lake Placid, NY. She was buried beside her brother and husbands in B'nai Jeshurun Cemetery in Elizabeth, NJ, on July 21, 1944. After bequests to relatives, friends, and employees, Fuld left the remainder of her fortune to the Institute for Advanced Study and to public health, welfare, and cultural institutions in Newark.

Historical documents on Fuld and her family are kept at NJ-NPL and at NJ-RU. Fuld's involvement with the Institute of Advanced Study is detailed in Abraham Flexner, *I Remember* (1940), and in Harry Woolf, *A Community of Scholars: The Institute for Advanced Study* (1980). The trustees of the Newark Museum published *Louis Bamberger: A Tribute to His Memory* (1944), which describes the generosity of Fuld and her husband. A sketch of Fuld appears in *NAW*. Her obituary appeared in the *Newark Evening News*, July 18, 1944, and in the *New York Times*, July 19, 1944.

*Constance B. Schuyler*

## LUCY MCKIM GARRISON, 1842–1877

Born on October 30, 1842, Lucy (McKim) Garrison, a musicologist who transcribed slave songs, was the first child of James Miller and Sarah Allibone (Speakman) McKim. Charles Follen McKim, her brother (the noted architect of the Boston Public Library and other public buildings), was born on August 24, 1847. The McKim family lived at Hilltop in Germantown and was distinguished in Philadelphia abolitionist circles. Garrison's maternal grandfather, a Chester County Quaker, had been extremely active in the Underground Railroad. Her father, originally a Presbyterian minister, was converted by the writings of William Lloyd Garrison to such violent abolitionism that he left the ministry to become an antislavery lecturer and was one of the founders of the Pennsylvania Anti-Slavery Society, of which he was a leader for many years. Thus began the friendship between the McKim and Garrison families that was to culminate in the marriage of Lucy McKim to Wendell Phillips Garrison.

James Miller McKim's abolitionist work brought him into active involvement with the Hicksite Quaker faction of Philadelphia abolitionists dominated by Lucretia Mott and her husband, James Mott. Within this circle the Motts, ANGELINA (GRIMKÉ) WELD, her husband, Theodore Weld, and her sister, SARAH MOORE GRIMKÉ, became close friends of the McKim and Garrison families, bound by moral and intellectual sympathies as well as by affection. This provided a setting for young Garrison in which she was continually exposed to liberal abolitionist and suffragist ideals. Although she lacked the fire of her father's commitment, her liberal sympathies combined with her education to create in her a concern for preserving the threatened culture of the emancipated slaves.

She was educated in Philadelphia until 1856 or 1857, at which time she began attending the Eagleswood School in Perth Amboy, NJ, which was run by Theodore Weld and the GRIMKÉ sisters. By 1856 the school was operated under the sole auspices of Theodore Weld, the Raritan Bay Union (a Fourierist colony that had originally sponsored the school) having officially dissolved. The coeducational school attracted about 50 students, some from as far away as California, and was visited by such notables as Henry David Thoreau. The curriculum reflected Weld's belief that life and study should work together, offering "woodwork, agriculture, household skills and bookkeeping" (Lerner, *Grimké Sisters*, 329) as well as academic subjects. Students were encouraged to progress by love, personal example, and individual attention rather than by rote learning and corporal discipline, which was practiced by most schools of the time. Attending Eagleswood at the same time was Garrison's close friend since childhood, her future sister-in-law Ellen Wright, Lucretia Mott's niece. In addition to its progressive nature, Eagleswood remained an intellectual center for the abolitionists. The children of the school were involved in raising funds to aid the Kansas free-soil settlers, and there was speculation that the school may have been an Underground Railroad station.

Garrison taught piano for a short time in Philadelphia in 1857 but returned to her friends at Eagleswood to teach and study further. In 1859 she had to forego a visit to the Garrison household because William Garrison was suffering from a mild form of smallpox. At William Lloyd Garrison, Sr.'s suggestion, the news was given to her by her future husband, then a student at Harvard. Presumably, when she left Eagleswood in 1861, she knew that the school was closing. Her separation from Eagleswood at this time allowed her to travel with her father to the Sea Islands of South Carolina in June 1862, where she was to initiate a significant work of musicology. James Miller McKim, then secretary for the Port Royal Relief Committee, was engaged in aiding newly freed slaves in the Sea Islands.

In her three weeks in the islands, Garrison became interested in the songs of the freedmen and became one of the first musicians to reduce the songs to musical notation. Hoping to publish as a series "Songs of the Freedman of Port Royal," she issued "Roll Jordan Roll" and "Poor Rosy" separately, and wrote in the November 8, 1862, issue of *Dwight's Musical Journal* of the difficulty of capturing in manuscript "the entire character of the Negro ballads. . . . The odd turns made in the throat, and the various rhythmic effects produced by single voices chiming in at different irregular intervals." (Garrison, *Slave Songs*, vi)

She was acutely aware of the need to transcribe the songs before their character was irrevocably changed by the new forms of African-American life outside the bonds of slavery. The public was not receptive to her work at that time, however, and the project was put aside.

In 1864 she and Wendell Phillips Garrison, William Lloyd Garrison's third son, became engaged. Both families were delighted. William Lloyd Garrison wrote of his future daughter-in-law that she was "comely in person with large self respect, great purity of character, a high standard of goodness and affectionate character." (Merrill, *Letters*, 5:217) The genuine astonishment of William Lloyd Garrison, who was an interested parent, suggests that the couple may have deliberately kept their attachment secret until the formal engagement.

After her marriage on December 6, 1865, Garrison was occupied writing reviews and helping with editorial work at the *Nation*, of which her husband was part founder and literary editor. In 1866 the couple set up joint housekeeping with her parents at Llewellyn Park in Orange, NJ. The birth of her first son, Lloyd, was followed by a lengthy and difficult recovery in 1867, but in the same year, in collaboration with William Francis Allen and Charles Pickard Ware, she produced the volume *Slave Songs of the United States*. Last reprinted in 1951, the book is widely recog-

nized as the best existing source of slave songs. Garrison's first two published manuscripts, "Roll Jordan Roll" and "Poor Rosy," appear in the book as numbers one and nine.

The births of Garrison's son Phillip in 1869 and her daughter, Katherine, in 1873 were also followed by long and difficult recoveries. Nonetheless, she was able to be at her father's bedside when he died in June 1874. Later that summer she suffered from a "rheumatic inflammation" (Merrill, 6:337) for which she sought relief at Watch Hill, a Rhode Island seaside resort. On April 27, 1877, Garrison suffered a paralytic stroke. She died at Llewellyn Park on May 11, 1877, at age 34, attended by her sister-in-law Fanny Garrison Villard. Her grave is in Rosedale Cemetery in Orange, NJ.

Garrison's *Slave Songs of the United States* (1867) offers, in addition to the musical text, an exposition of her views on the songs she transcribed. A discussion of her musical accomplishments is Dena Epstein, "Lucy McKim Garrison, American Musician," *Bulletin of the New York Public Library* 67 (Oct. 1963):529–46. Gerda Lerner, *The Grimké Sisters from South Carolina* (1967), gives details of life at the Eagleswood School. Walter Merrill, ed., *The Letters of William Lloyd Garrison*, 6 vols. (1971–81), provides insights into her life and temperament. She is profiled in *NAW*.

*Phebe E. Davidson*

## MARY EXTON GASTON, 1855–1956

Mary Exton Gaston, Somerville's first woman physician and a major force in the borough's development, lived for more than 100 years. A native and lifelong resident of Somerville (Somerset County), NJ, she was born on November 24, 1855, the third of seven children (five girls and two boys). She did not marry and lived most of her life in her family's home at 18 West High Street.

The Gastons were prominent in civic activities. Her father, Hugh M. Gaston, was an attorney and her mother, Frances (Malet-Prevost), was descended from a French family that had settled in Frenchtown.

An avid student all her life, Gaston first aspired to be a teacher. She attended Vassar Preparatory School in Poughkeepsie, NY, in 1873–74. The following year she was a freshman at Vassar College, but she did not continue there after 1875 because of financial difficulties at home.

Gaston became interested in the medical field, and although her mother raised strong objections, Gaston persevered. Thirteen years later, in 1888, she obtained her medical degree from the Woman's Medical College in Philadelphia (now the Medical College of Pennsylvania). Gaston was one of 27 graduates in 1888, but the "blizzard of '88" prevented her family from attending her commencement. She is said to have later interned at a Boston hospital before beginning practice in Somerville.

In search of additional medical training, Gaston traveled to Germany for further study in 1894. She was accompanied by her mother, then in her seventies, to whom she was devoted. They made two more trips to Europe in subsequent years. Family members indicate that Gaston pursued a career in medicine because this profession allowed her to continue living at home.

There was no community-supported medical facility in Somerville in the 1890s, when Gaston began her practice. She responded to calls throughout the borough from her office in the family home. It is said that her father gave her a pistol to carry on night calls, but that she carried it only a few times. She claimed to have less fear of a threatening encounter than of the pistol itself. Gaston often walked to all parts of the borough on night calls, saving time by not rousing the stable man to harness the horse and carriage her father made available to her.

When there was a major outbreak of influenza in the early 1890s, Gaston enlisted the aid of other women to establish a small emergency hospital where the illness could be treated. This hospital soon closed for lack of funding, but after the tragic accidental death of a young laborer in 1898, the citizens of Somerville were motivated to support a permanent borough hospital incorporated in 1899.

Gaston and three male physicians formed the initial full-time staff of the Somerville Hospital (now the Somerset Medical Center). The first location for the hospital was the John Lord house, purchased in 1900. It stood on the corner of what is now Gaston Avenue and Main Street.

Gaston's emergency hospital is credited with donating many of the supplies and equipment for the operating room. During its first full year of operation in 1901, Gaston and the hospital staff treated 46 patients for ailments such as appendicitis, cancer, crushed limbs, and bullet wounds. The hospital's caseload and its facility grew each year, and Gaston remained on the staff until 1905, when she went into private practice. In 1908, at age 53, she suffered a serious heart attack, which forced her to retire.

Although retired from her work as a physician, Gaston became an active civic booster. She also traveled extensively. Known as "Dr. Mary," she was the moving force behind many civic endeavors. In the years just prior to World War I, she helped organize the Somerville Public Library. She founded the Somerville-Raritan chapter of the Red Cross in 1917 and the Somerset County Anti-Tuberculosis League and the Somerville Civic League in 1918.

The Civic League celebrated its 20th anniversary in 1938 by honoring Gaston, "the Mother of Clubs," as she was known in the area. A portrait of Gaston by Edmund McGrath was unveiled at the celebration and still hangs in the Somerville Public Library, next to the portrait of her brother Hugh. McGrath's work shows an erect, graceful woman with a strong, gentle face. White-haired and in her eighties at the time, Gaston's vitality is evident in the portrait.

Gaston was an invalid during the last years of her life because of a broken hip. She died in Bridgewater Township on April 19, 1956, at age 100, and is buried in Somerville's New Cemetery.

Much of her estate was left to the Somerset Medical Center, the Somerville Public Library, the Somerville Civic League, the First Unitarian Society of Plainfield, and the Woman's Medical College of Philadelphia.

The clipping files of the Vassar College Alumnae Association (Poughkeepsie, NY) and the *Messenger Gazette* (Somerset, NJ) provided useful information on Gaston. Interviews with her grandnieces, Mrs. C. Stewart Hoagland of Bernardsville (NJ) and Mrs. Robert Thompson (Somerville, NJ), provided additional details.

*Barbara Tune Griswold*

## HETTY HOWLAND ROBINSON GREEN, 1834–1916

Hetty Howland (Robinson) Green, financier and builder of a vast fortune, was born in New Bedford, MA, on November 21, 1834, the only daughter of Edward Mott and Abby Slocum (Howland) Robinson. Her father, born of a prominent Quaker family in Providence, RI, became a partner in the firm of Isaac Howland, Jr. and Co., the major fleet of whaling ships and China traders out of New Bedford. Because her mother was in poor health, she spent most of her time in bed, and Green's aunt, Sylvia Howland, supervised the girl's upbringing. Her only brother died in infancy, and thus it was Green who spent time during her childhood accompanying her father to his warehouses, observing his total dedication to making money, and reading the financial pages to her maternal grandfather, who was active in the business until his death in 1847.

The Quaker values of simplicity of life-style, frugality and industry dominated Green's family life, making business the main focus. Her father was a man of strong will who treated his workers without compassion and cared more that the job get done than for human life. He sometimes punished his daughter by forcing her to remain silent for 24 hours. She was sent to the strict Quaker boarding school of Eliza Wing in Sandwich, MA, at a young age, and then to finishing school in Boston.

Green's mother died in 1860, leaving a bequest of $8,000 to her daughter. This, plus a gift of $20,000 from her Aunt Sylvia, was the beginning of the Hetty Green fortune.

Her father, anticipating that kerosene would displace whale oil, sold the New Bedford business in 1861 and

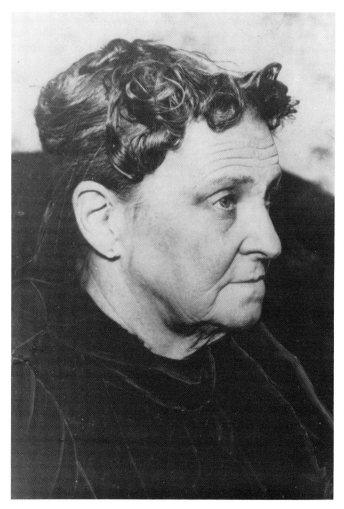

Hetty Howland Robinson Green amassed a vast fortune but chose to live a penurious life, residing in Hoboken flats in the 1910s. *Wide World Photos.*

moved to New York, where he became a partner in Wm. T. Coleman and Co. (shipping merchants). Introduced to society through relatives in the Grinnell family, Green was a striking young woman admired in social circles for her healthy complexion, beautiful hair, and stately carriage. But she found the social whirl uninteresting.

As she told a reporter much later, "Don't you think it is a great deal better for me to live simply, as I do, than to spend my time playing bridge and drinking champagne, as they do in society? . . . I am a Quaker, and I am trying to live up to the tenets of that faith. That is why I dress plainly and live quietly." (*New York Times*, July 5, 1916)

Her father died suddenly on June 14, 1865, leaving her $1 million outright and some $4 million in a trust fund. Two weeks later her Aunt Sylvia died, leaving half of her estate to charity, the other half to establish a trust fund for Green, to whom $65,000 of the income was to be paid annually.

Financially she was well provided for, but she was alone

in the world. Through her father she had met Edward Henry Green, who had returned from eighteen years as a silk trader in Manila. He was 46 and she was 32. They were married July 11, 1867, in the New York home of Henry Grinnell.

Meanwhile, dissatisfied with the probated will of Sylvia Howland, she brought suit, claiming the total estate on the basis of a will in her own handwriting, purportedly dictated and signed by her aunt. Thus began the famous Howland will trial, which involved many eminent authorities of the day, including Harvard professors Oliver Wendell Holmes, Louis Agassiz, and Benjamin Pierce. Litigation continued for five years, including a countersuit for perjury brought against Green, until final settlement was reached, awarding her $660,000 accrued in the trust fund but maintaining the charitable bequest.

In 1867 the Greens moved to London, England. Edward Green served as director of several banks; Hetty Green speculated in U.S. greenbacks, profiting when U.S. currency was not devalued after the Civil War, as expected. A son, Edward Henry Robinson Green, was born August 22, 1868, and a daughter, Hetty Sylvia Ann Howland Green, on January 7, 1871.

The family returned to the United States in 1873, living for some time in Bellows Falls, VT. Green continued to build her fortune, investing in government bonds, railroad stocks, and widespread urban real estate holdings acquired largely through mortgage foreclosures. She never made industrial investments, but with her shrewd sense of timing, she managed always to have cash at times of panic so that she could buy at bottom prices and finance overcommitted investors at high rates of interest. Edward Green, overcommitted at the time of the crash of 1885, went into bankruptcy. In accord with their prenuptual agreement of financial independence, his wife took no responsibility either for him or his debts. They separated, and except for some vacations together in Bellows Falls, they never lived together again. She moved with the children into tenements or boardinghouses in Brooklyn and Hoboken, where rents were cheap, and he moved into bachelor's quarters.

Green is famous for amassing a great fortune and for carrying thrift and abhorrence of waste to extremes. People were fascinated that one so rich chose to wear clothes until they were near rags, dressed her children in secondhand clothes, and begged for food that might otherwise be thrown out by grocers. She distrusted lawyers and doctors and felt that, being rich, she was always overcharged for professional services.

She had a few friends in New York and in Bellows Falls where the family often went in the summer and for winter holidays. One friend, Annie Leary of New York, a papal countess, persuaded Green to send her children to parochial schools: Sylvia to Sacred Heart Academy and Edward

(Ned) to Fordham College. Leary also tried to give the children some social opportunities, taking Sylvia to her villa in Newport in 1891; but Sylvia was miserable and returned to her mother as soon as possible, happy to cook and keep house.

Annie Leary did persuade Green to provide a debut for Sylvia in Morristown, NJ, on December 7, 1892. Mother and daughter lived for a while that year in Mrs. Hunter's on Washington Street in Morristown, a fashionable boardinghouse near the home of a cousin, Nina Howland, a member of Morristown society. They then moved back to a Hoboken flat from which Green could walk to the ferry to downtown New York.

When Ned Green injured his leg in a sledding accident while vacationing in Bellows Falls, his mother refused to take him to a private doctor for the infection that developed, instead bringing him to a clinic at New York University Medical School. He was treated by a professor of orthopedics and presented to medical students until it was discovered who his mother was, and free treatment was suspended. Finally, after further injury, the leg had to be amputated.

Green was particularly well positioned at the time of the crash of 1907. She became prominent on Wall Street, and after Russell Sage died in 1906 she became the recognized "ready money" lender on a large scale. She also continued to figure in large real estate transactions. By 1910 her financial interests had grown so extensive that she established two holding companies in which she owned all the stock. Her son took over much of the management. Toward the end of her life she moved again to Hoboken to evade payment of New York personal property taxes.

Her son attests to her generosity to her family and to employees of the family, but her charity was very private. She kept few possessions and moved constantly through tenements, boardinghouses, and small hotels, often under assumed names so that she could not be traced by tax collectors and those seeking to beg or borrow. Raised largely in a man's world, Hetty Green, with all the vigor and skill of the shrewdest investor, stewarded her inheritance into the largest fortune held by a woman in her time. She suffered a stroke in April 1916 and died of another stroke on July 3, 1916, in New York. She is buried in the churchyard of Immanuel Episcopal Church, Bellows Falls, VT, with her husband and two children.

The best biography of Green is Boyden Sparkes and Samuel T. Moore, *Hetty Green: A Woman Who Loved Money* (1930), later reprinted as *The Witch of Wall Street: Hetty Green* (1935). The dissolution of the Green estate is detailed in Arthur Lewis, *The Day They Shook the Plum Tree* (1963). A sketch of Green appears in *NAW*. The *New York Times* carried numerous articles about Green, including her obituary, July 4, 1916; an editorial, July 5, 1916; and a piece in the magazine section of the paper, July 9, 1916.

*Phyllis Smith*

## EMILIE KOEHLER GREENOUGH, 1863–1955

Emilie (Koehler) Greenough, known as "Millie," was a stained-glass artist and a successful portrait and landscape painter at a time when gaining artistic recognition was particularly difficult for women. Greenough was born on April 14, 1863, in Sharpsburg, PA. Her father, Herman Koehler, a graduate of the University of Berlin, had come to the United States in 1854. With a German colleague, he built an oil refinery called "the Vesta" on the Susquehanna River in Sharpsburg. He played the flute, and the family surmised that a love of music first drew him to Greenough's mother, Emilie Henrietta Lewis, a gifted pianist with a good contralto voice. Together, they provided a loving, musical, and culturally rich environment for Greenough and her three brothers and one sister.

When the Vesta was destroyed by fire in 1876, Herman Koehler took a position with the Standard Oil Company, to become, eventually, its "expert chemist" in New York City. The family moved to Ravenswood, Long Island, into a house on the bank of the East River.

Shortly after they moved, Greenough, age sixteen, won a poster contest sponsored by a local baker. Her design was used as an advertisement on the backs of trolley cars. For first prize, she received a full scholarship to the Philadelphia School of Design. She completed her program there and continued her art studies at Cooper Union in New York City, receiving certificates for successful completion of first- and second-year drawing courses in 1883 and 1884.

Greenough then took a position as a designer in the stained glass studio of John LaFarge in New York City. There she met and worked with an artist named Walter Conant Greenough. Walter Greenough's family was not pleased with his choice of career, for he had given up promising architectural studies against their wishes. Therefore, when the couple married in 1885, they were financially on their own. Using a small inheritance from a great-aunt, they spent their first year together studying art in Germany and Italy.

When they returned, they lived with Greenough's family on Long Island. Both pursued artistic careers, she as a portrait painter and teacher and he as a painter and illustrator. Both worked for the LaFarge Studio, creating windows that would grace the Church of the Ascension on Fifth Avenue and 10th Street in New York City, the Swedish Lutheran Church at E. 22nd Street, also in New York, the Russian Cathedral in Hoboken, NJ, and the Stock Exchange Building in Chicago.

Two children, Walter Herman and Emilie Charlotte, were born during this period. Shortly after Emilie's birth in 1890, Greenough and her family moved to Montclair, NJ, to become part of the Montclair Art Colony, a group of artists wishing to raise their families in a country setting while maintaining contact with dealers and studios in New York City. The Greenoughs became active in the cultural pursuits of their community—concerts, tableaux, and pageants—sometimes to raise money for causes but often just to provide entertainment. Greenough, who had trained as a portrait painter, became interested in landscape painting. Both she and her husband painted the lovely scenery around their community, stimulated in part by the work of George Inness.

The Greenoughs had two more children, Margaret Julie and Kathryn, while living in Montclair. Their delight in their children was clearly visible to all.

By 1898 the Greenoughs felt financially secure enough to build a large Tudor home in Upper Montclair with an art studio that doubled as a stage for skits and musical recitals. Four months after the family moved into their new home, Walter Greenough contracted pneumonia. He died suddenly on December 27, 1898.

When her husband died, Greenough was left with $5,000 in life insurance, a large mortgage, and four young children. She was also left with a sense of commitment to the home, interests, and values that she and her husband had shared. So, although she dressed in mourning for ten years after his death, an atmosphere of mourning was not present in the household. What was present was an appreciation and enjoyment of art, music, theater, and nature—an enjoyment of life.

To support her family, Greenough brought in income from her art whenever and however she could. She continued her work for John LaFarge until the studio closed its doors. Because she specialized in the painting of fleshtone glass for stained-glass windows, she arranged for the glass faces, hands, and feet to be brought to Montclair from New York City. These she painted in her home studio.

Greenough also taught and exhibited in her studio, selling what she could, even seaweed greeting cards made with the children during stays at her family's Rhode Island summer cottage. Especially important were the commission of portraits, full-size in oil on canvas and small miniatures on enamel. She sometimes traded paintings for necessary medical and dental care.

Love of her art never diminished, and throughout her long life Greenough sketched and painted tirelessly. She experimented with colored monoprint techniques and became one of the first women members of the American Watercolor Society.

The Greenough children appeared never to have sensed how desperately their mother struggled to make ends meet until Emilie was in her teens and her mother confessed her great relief that their father's family had finally offered financial assistance on an ongoing basis. The children benefited from their culturally stimulating home life. All four pursued an art, either vocationally or for pleasure.

By age 64, Greenough's rheumatism was so severe she needed a cane to walk. She was a short, plump woman, still dressed frequently in black, whose eyes sparkled with love for her family and her art. Her children would drive her into the country, settle her under a large tree to paint or sketch while they walked and hiked nearby. Greenough was prolific, frequently inscribing these landscapes as gifts for her family.

Though she never received wide celebration as an artist, Greenough was well known and admired. She died, at age 92, on October 10, 1955, of uremia and is buried at Mount Hebron Cemetery in Montclair.

Greenough's family history and letters of are in the possession of Nancy Stehli Knoerzer of Montclair, NJ. Additional information appears in Lolita Flockhart, *Art and Artists in New Jersey* (1938).

*Donna Walling*
*Sheila Cowing*

## PHEBE ANN COFFIN HANAFORD, 1829–1921

One of the first ordained women ministers in the United States and the third Universalist woman minister, Phebe Ann (Coffin) Hanaford entered the ministry in 1868 at the age of 38 while the mother of two teenage children. She served parishes in Hingham, MA (1868–70), New Haven, CT (1870–74 and 1884–91), with her longest pastorate in Jersey City, NJ (1874–84). Throughout her career and her retirement Hanaford was active in the women's and the temperance movements, lecturing, writing, and serving in church and civic leadership positions.

Hanaford was born in 1829 in Siasconset on Nantucket Island, MA. Her mother, Phebe Ann (Barnard) Coffin, died shortly after Hanaford's birth and she was raised by her father, Captain George W. Coffin, and then her stepmother, Emmeline (Barnard) Cartwright. Hanaford had an older stepbrother and seven younger half brothers and sisters. Captain Coffin, whose English ancestors had founded the first settlement on Nantucket in 1659, was a ship owner and merchant. Hanaford's mother was a shopkeeper and a descendant of Gregory Priest, pilot of the *Mayflower*, and Peter Folger, grandfather of Benjamin Franklin. Hanaford herself was the cousin of Lucretia Mott and Maria Mitchell.

An exceptionally gifted child, Hanaford attended schools in Nantucket until she was needed to care for an ailing grandmother. Though she did not graduate from high school, she studied mathematics, Latin, and theology under the tutelage of the Rev. Ethan Allen of St. Paul's Church (Episcopal) in Nantucket. She began teaching school on Nantucket at age sixteen. On December 2, 1849, she married Dr. Joseph Hibbard Hanaford, a homeopathic physician, teacher, and writer whom she met while he was also teaching on Nantucket. They had two children: Howard (b. 1851) and Florence (b. 1854).

Raised in the Society of Friends (Quakers), Hanaford joined her husband's Baptist tradition when she married. But she began attending Friends' meetings, at first secretly. In 1857 she helped establish the First Nantucket Female Praying Circle, an ecumenical group that met for theological discussion and community service. Sometime around 1864 Hanaford began reading about Universalism. As she recorded in her diary, her religious persuasions contributed to tensions in her marriage.

Financial as well as religious difficulties plagued the Hanafords, who moved from Nantucket in 1857 to Beverly, MA, and then again to Reading, MA, in 1864. Apparently Joseph Hanaford had trouble supporting his family. Hanaford took to writing to supplement the family income, publishing numerous speeches, editorials, stories, poems, sketches, and a total of fourteen books before she died.

While still affiliated with the Baptist church, Hanaford joined the Reading Universalist Church in 1864. On a visit home to Nantucket she preached a Universalist-inspired sermon in front of a congregation of family and friends. Her Baptist pastor was appalled and accused her of attending Universalist meetings and of publicly advocating Universalism. Hanaford formalized her Universalist faith and in so doing also achieved financial stability. For an annual salary of $600, she accepted the position of editor of the *Ladies Repository* (1866–68), a monthly Universalist magazine, and the *Myrtle* (1866–68), a Universalist Sunday school paper.

Hanaford's editorial position brought her into contact with Universalist leaders, including Olympia Brown, the first regularly ordained woman minister in the United States, who encouraged her to enter the ministry. On February 19, 1868, Hanaford was ordained to the Universalist ministry and installed as minister of the First Universalist Church of Hingham, MA. Julia Ward Howe played the organ at the service and Howe's daughter, Maude, sang an ordination hymn written by her mother. Olympia Brown delivered the Right Hand of Fellowship at the morning's ordination service and the sermon at the afternoon installation. Brown addressed Hanaford: "It will be yours, as a woman to sympathize with and aid suffering woman, who needs the sympathies of her sex. It will be yours to strengthen those who suffer from the evil influence of intoxicating drinks. Give them the hand of helping and lift them up out of their sad estate." (*Services at the Ordination and Installation of Rev. Phebe A. Hanaford*, 30)

After ministering in Hingham and New Haven, CT, and serving as the first woman chaplain in a state legislature (Connecticut), Hanaford came to the Church of the Good Shepherd (Universalist) in Jersey City in 1874. By this time she was no longer living with her husband, who had stayed in Reading when she went to New Haven in

1870. Hanaford now had a constant companion in Ellen E. Miles, an unmarried hymnist. Hanaford and Miles's friendship lasted 44 years, until Miles's death in 1914.

In the first three years of Hanaford's pastorate the membership of her church doubled in size. Miles, a member of the church, ran the Sunday school. But during this same time dissent grew in the congregation over women's rights and Miles's character. In 1879 a congregational vote of 45 to 42 demanded that unless Miles left the Hanaford household, another minister would be hired. Miles offered to leave, but Hanaford would not allow it. A schism in the church followed.

Less than two months after the congregational vote, the Second Universalist Church of Jersey City was established, with Hanaford as its minister. Services were held in the Library Hall next door to the Church of the Good Shepherd. Despite the fact that the Second Universalist Church of Jersey City flourished, the General Universalist Congress in 1877 refused to accept the new church's delegates at the state Universalist convention. Without the sanction of the congress, the church was unable to claim membership in the national Universalist convention, and it therefore became an unrecognized affiliate. Hanaford remained minister of the Second Universalist Church for five years.

Before she entered the ministry and throughout her pastorates Hanaford was active in many reform movements. She was a leader of the American Woman Suffrage Association, organized in 1869 as a more moderate rival to the National Woman Suffrage Association. In 1874, a year after it was organized, Hanaford served as one of the vice-presidents of the Association for the Advancement of Women. She was also an officer of the Daughters of Temperance and women's auxiliary lodges of the Good Templars. In 1870 she was vice-president of the Women's Peace Convention, which had been called by Julia Ward Howe in New York City. In 1888 she served as chaplain of the International Council of Women, which met in Washington, D.C. Her extensive involvement in women's advancement is reflected in her being asked to conduct the funeral services of her co-workers in the suffrage movement, Susan B. Anthony and ELIZABETH CADY STANTON.

After the death of Ellen Miles, Hanaford lived with her granddaughter, Dionis Werner Santee, in Basom and later in Rochester, NY. She died there on June 2, 1921, at age 92, of endocarditis and hardening of the arteries and was buried in Orleans, NY. Hanaford lived long enough to celebrate the passage of the 19th Amendment and to cast her vote in the 1920 presidential election.

The Phebe Ann Hanaford Papers, including scrapbooks, diaries, and speeches, are kept at the Peter Folger Museum (Nantucket, MA). Her works *From Shore to Shore* (1871) and *Daughters of America; or Women of the Century* (1882) contain biographical information. Her welcome into the ministry appears in *Services at the Ordination and Installation of Rev. Phebe A. Hanaford* (1870).

Her work is noted in Catherine Hitchings, *Universalist and Unitarian Women Ministers* (1985); and Russell Miller, *The Larger Hope: The First Century of the Universalist Church in America, 1770–1870* (1978). She is profiled in *NAW* and *DAB*, vol. 8 (1932).

*Marta Morris Flanagan*

## LYDIA YOUNG HAYES, 1871–1943

Lydia Young Hayes, the first director of the New Jersey Commission for the Blind, was born in Hutchinson, MN, on September 11, 1871. Her mother's name is not known; her father was Charles W. Hayes. Her parents were farmers, and it was on the family farm that, at the age of eight, Hayes suffered an injury from a charging bull that resulted in total loss of sight. Her parents, anxious for her welfare and determined that she would grow in body and mind, sent her to her uncle in Massachusetts so she could attend Perkins Institution, also known as the Massachusetts School for the Blind.

Following her graduation from Perkins, Hayes studied at the Boston Kindergarten Normal School and for two years conducted a private nursery for sighted children. She also volunteered as a home teacher for the adult blind and later served as a private tutor in Ohio. In 1900, when Massachusetts gave official sanction to a plan for teaching the adult blind at home, Hayes was recalled to the commonwealth to become one of the two pioneer home teachers.

In 1909 Hayes was selected to organize the New Jersey Commission for the Blind and in 1910 was appointed by Governor Woodrow Wilson as its first chief executive officer. An exceptional person for such a post, both because of her blindness and her sex, she continued in the position (except for a two-year hiatus) until 1937, when she became the commission's education and research consultant, a role she filled until her full retirement in 1942.

Hayes established the first headquarters for the commission in downtown Newark, NJ, then the shopping and business center of the state. The facility was set up in a ten-room house at 14 James Street, which was provided rent-free by a friend. It housed a men's workshop, social rooms, offices, classrooms, and rooms for making and selling handicrafts. A blind man and his sighted wife served as caretakers. One of the commission's first tasks was the compilation of a registry of the blind residents of the state, and within its first year it had registered 750 people.

As the commission's first executive, Hayes set the policy and direction of its early programs, which had a long-term impact on the course of New Jersey services for the blind. Hayes was a strong advocate of the rights of the blind, believing that the blind had a right to "health, to an education, to work, and to an opportunity to serve." (Ryan, "Lydia Y. Hayes," 62) She emphasized the obligations of the blind to society and was opposed to the segregation of the blind into separate educational institutions. She also gave strong emphasis to the prevention of blindness.

Largely because of Hayes's influence, New Jersey did not maintain a state residential school for the blind, a practice followed in other states, but instead provided state support and supervision of braille classes in the public schools. In 1910 Hayes and another teacher set up the first integrated classes for the blind and sighted in Newark's public schools, classes that were recognized as an innovative model throughout the country. Hayes believed that "education concerning the blind should be two-fold: the education of the individual regarding his responsibility to the community and the education of the community to promote understanding of the capabilities of the individual." (New Jersey Department of Human Services, *A History*, ii)

Hayes's belief in the blind person's right to work led in 1915 to a commission program that opened industrial jobs to the blind and that took advantage of labor shortages during World War I to increase their employment opportunities. The commission also established a Home Teaching Service Program to provide home instruction in braille, typewriting, and the production of salable items. The commission's Home Industries Program marketed products made by the blind.

Though she worked in the city, Hayes preferred the country and lived in rural Far Hills. Forthright in expressing her views, she was a strict but caring disciplinarian. She never married and felt it was inappropriate for two blind people to marry.

Upon her retirement in 1942 Hayes moved back to Minnesota to the home of a nephew and his blind wife, and it was there in Bemidji, MN, that she died of nephritis at age 72 on February 8, 1943. She was buried in Bemidji.

A biographical sketch of Hayes appears in Stetson Ryan, "Lydia Y. Hayes, an Appreciation," *Outlook for the Blind* 37 (Mar. 1943):61–63. For additional information on her work, see New Jersey Department of Human Services, *A History of the New Jersey Commission for the Blind and Visually Impaired* (1985); and Helen McGrath, "An Historical Survey of the New Jersey State Commission for the Blind, 1909–1949" (M.S.W. thesis, Fordham University, 1950).

*Marion Mann Roberts*

## CHRISTINE TERHUNE HERRICK, 1859–1944

Christine (Terhune) Herrick, a versatile writer on child rearing, household duties, and personal growth for women, was born on June 13, 1859, in Newark (Essex County), NJ. She was the eldest daughter and the second of six children (three of whom survived childhood) of the Rev. Edward Payson Terhune, a Presbyterian minister of Dutch descent whose ancestry could be traced back to the Revolutionary War, and MARY VIRGINIA (HAWES) TERHUNE, a writer of novels and household advice books who used the pen-name "Marion Harland." Herrick's mother could trace her ancestry to a solid Virginia family.

Herrick's early childhood was spent with tutors in private lessons at home. She was an eager student who took full advantage of her father's theological library. Balancing this studious side with her outgoing personality, Herrick spent summers rowing, fishing, and riding at the family home, "Sunnybank," in Pompton, NJ, later made famous through the books of her brother, Albert Payson Terhune.

In 1876, when Herrick was fifteen, her mother contracted tuberculosis. The family went abroad for her treatment. They spent the first winter in Rome and the second in Geneva. Herrick became fluent in Italian and French. The family returned to the United States in 1878, and later that year Herrick made her debut in Richmond, VA. When Herrick was nineteen her family settled in Springfield, MA. She improved her education, especially in English literature and philology, and eventually taught a class for girls.

She married James Frederick Herrick, an editor for the *Springfield Republican*, on April 23, 1884. She became an Episcopalian. Herrick's first child died at birth. In 1886 James Herrick accepted a newspaper editorship in Brooklyn, NY. Later that year a daughter was born (who died at age three), followed by two sons, Horace (b. 1887) and James Frederick (b. 1890). Summers were spent at the family's country home, "Outlook," in Pompton, NJ.

Herrick gained success when she began to write about household subjects, with which her mother had made her so comfortable. Her first published article was in the inaugural issue of *Good Housekeeping*, May 1885. Over the next two years Herrick's magazine articles on subjects ranging from field hockey and "Some Books for the Days of Leisure" to "Do Women Want the Vote?" appeared regularly in *Harper's Bazar, Ladies Home Journal, Demorest Monthly, Outlook, Era, Woman's Home Companion*, and the *Delineator*. In 1888 her first book, *Housekeeping Made Easy*, was published. After that her books appeared in print almost every year. Other early titles were *Cradle and Nursery* (1889), *Liberal Living upon Narrow Means* (1890), and *What to Eat and How to Serve It* (1891).

In 1893 Herrick's husband died, but her strong convictions on household responsibilities and her energy helped her through the loss. She took on the dual roles of homemaker and wage earner. Her writing success gave her the financial security needed to educate both of her sons at private preparatory schools and at college. How she coped is preserved in the endearing book *My Boy and I* (1913). Her comments seem timeless: "It is cowardly to be rude to those who have no right to answer back. I had seen and heard too much insolence to employees on the part of spoiled children to tolerate anything of that sort in my own home" (p. 45).

Herrick continued to publish regularly: *The Letters of the Duke of Wellington to Miss J* (1894); *The Chafing Dish Supper* (1897); *First Aid to the Young Housekeeper* (1900); *In City Tents* (1902); *The Expert Maid Servant* (1904); *Sunday Night Supper* (1907); and *The ABC of Housekeeping* (1915). With her mother (under the name of Marion Harland) as coauthor, Herrick wrote: *The Cottage Kitchen* (1895); *The National Cookbook* (1896); and *The Helping Hand Cookbook* (1912).

*In City Tents* contains chapters on decorations, suitable clothes, and business acquaintances that reveal Herrick's emphasis on propriety. A chapter called "How to Be Happy with the Janitor" suggests avoidance of familiarity. "How to Manage a Small Home on Slender Means" and "What to Do Without" show Herrick's sensitivity to the personal touches that make up a home.

Herrick had a weight problem, and this prompted her to write, anonymously, *Lose Weight and Be Well* (1917). In her book *The New Common Sense in the Household* (1926) she revised her mother's popular *Common Sense in the Household* to reflect the new electric technology in the home.

Herrick was an articulate speaker and an active member of the Sorosis Club of New York, an influential women's club. She was also a member of the National Society of Colonial Dames of America and the Washington Club. In 1928 she moved to Washington, D.C., to be near her son Horace.

Herrick died on December 2, 1944, at age 85, in the Emergency Hospital in Washington, D.C., twelve days after fracturing her thigh in a fall in her residence at the Hotel Chastleton in Washington. The burial was held at the Pompton Reformed Cemetery in Pompton Lakes, NJ.

Biographical sketches of Herrick appear in *WOTC, NAW*, and in *Who Was Who in America* (1950). Her obituary appeared in the *New York Times*, Dec. 3, 1944.

*Ann J. Pason*

### JENNIE TUTTLE HOBART, 1849–1941

Jennie (Tuttle) Hobart, philanthropist, Paterson community leader, prominent New Jersey antisuffragist, and Second Lady of the nation during the first administration of William McKinley, was born in Paterson (Passaic County), NJ, on April 30, 1849. Though her given name was Esther Jane, she was known throughout her life as Jennie. She was the only child of Socrates and Jane (Winters) Tuttle, whose brief marriage ended with Jane Tuttle's death shortly after her daughter's birth. When Hobart was two and a half, Socrates Tuttle married again, to Mary Dickey of Paterson, and it was in the household of her father's second family that Hobart was raised.

Hobart was married in July 1869 to Garret Augustus Hobart, the son of a boyhood friend of her father. Garret Hobart, an 1863 Rutgers graduate, had read law in Socrates Tuttle's law offices and was a practicing attorney in Paterson. For the next 27 years the Hobarts made their home in Paterson. As a prominent Paterson matron, Hobart gained a reputation as a woman of warm wit and hospitality. She was an exemplar of late 19th-century womanhood, devoted to home, husband, and benevolence. During this period, Garret Hobart built a highly successful career as a corporation attorney and rose in Republican party politics from Paterson city solicitor in 1871 to a member of the New Jersey Assembly in 1872, becoming speaker in 1874, and then in 1876 to a member of the New Jersey Senate, becoming its president in the sessions of 1881 and 1882.

The Hobarts had four children, only one of whom survived them. Fannie Beckwith was born in 1871. Elizabeth was born in 1875, only to die before her first birthday. In 1884 Garret Augustus, Jr., was born, and in 1886 Katherine Gray, who died at the age of two weeks. In 1895 Fannie, 23, died of diphtheria in Bellagio, Italy, while the family was on a European trip.

Jennie Tuttle Hobart as a very young girl in an anonymous oil portrait of the early 1850s. Hobart became a prominent philanthropist and community activist in Paterson and was the Second Lady of the nation from 1897 to 1899. *Courtesy, Collection of the Passaic County Historical Society, Paterson, NJ.*

Hobart's community service began with her support of the Paterson Orphan Asylum and the Old Ladies Home (now known as the Westmont Home), both important private social service facilities during a time when Paterson's population was growing, before the development of municipal services. Hobart was president of the Old Ladies Home from 1883 to 1922. She also involved herself with Presbyterian church affairs, becoming active in Paterson's Church of the Redeemer when the parish was organized in 1886.

It was through the city missionary auxiliary of the Church of the Redeemer that Hobart was instrumental in establishing the Children's Day Nursery of Paterson in 1887, one of the state's earliest day-care centers. Known today as the Memorial Day Nursery, the center was established to serve the children of Paterson's mill workers. Hobart was vice-president of the nursery for 50 years, until 1937, when she was made honorary president. She became a major benefactor of the nursery in 1901 when she donated land on Grand and Hamilton streets, a large bequest for a new building, and a sizable operating endowment in memory of her daughter Fannie, who had been active in the day nursery.

The Hobarts' life in Paterson was interrupted in 1896 when Garret, a strong gold standard supporter, was nominated and elected vice-president on the Republican ticket of William McKinley of Ohio. In March 1897 the Hobarts moved to 21 Lafayette Square in Washington, D.C., with Garret, Jr., their only remaining child.

The Hobarts and the McKinleys became close personal friends. This, coupled with Mrs. McKinley's poor health, led Hobart to be called upon frequently to act as official hostess for the White House. Many observers commented on her intelligence, ease of conversation, and keen sense of humor. In Washington, as in Paterson, she enjoyed a reputation as an accomplished hostess whose hospitality attracted people of varied interests. She relished her role as Second Lady and later in her life recounted in two slim volumes, privately published in 1930 and 1933, her recollections of the Washington social scene.

Unfortunately, Hobart's services as Washington hostess were short-lived. The increasing ill health of Garret Hobart forced him to give up his official duties in the fall of 1899, and the family returned to Paterson, where he died of heart disease at home in November.

Residing once again in Paterson, Hobart began a new chapter of her life. Left a wealthy and prominent widow at the age of 50, she redevoted her energies to various philanthropic and community activities. She lent her support to local churches and social agencies and became a champion of traditional values in the Paterson community during the 1910s, a period in the city's history marked by rapid change and labor unrest. She was a financial backer of the Rev. Billy Sunday, whose evangelistic campaign was held in Paterson during the spring of 1915. But her support went beyond funding. She chaired the Women's General Committee for the campaign, headed the child-care facility set up for the meetings, and personally entertained Billy and "Ma" Sunday in her home.

In 1914 Hobart lent her prestige to the antisuffrage cause. She organized the Paterson branch of the New Jersey Association Opposed to Woman Suffrage (NJAOWS) and immediately the group began holding public meetings in Paterson. Hobart also served on the state board of the NJAOWS as a vice-president from 1914 to 1916. During 1915, when New Jersey was debating and voting on a woman suffrage amendment to the state constitution, Hobart was outspoken against the measure. She characterized woman suffrage as a "great injustice" and a "grave menace to our state" in an October 16, 1915, letter to the *New York Herald*. The New Jersey amendment was defeated in a special election that fall.

Hobart undertook extensive relief work to benefit France and Belgium during World War I. Following the lead of other branches of the NJAOWS, she turned the energies of the Paterson branch to the war effort. A sizable sewing project was organized in Carroll Hall, her home, and by 1915 thousands of garments and dollars were collected in Paterson for Belgian war relief. She helped organize Paterson chapters of the American Red Cross in 1917 and encouraged further war relief work by Paterson residents under Red Cross auspices. In 1932 King Albert of Belgium conferred on her the Chevalier de l'Ordre de Leopold for this service. In addition, Hobart served on the advisory council of the New Jersey division of the Women's Land Army during 1918.

In the 1920s and 1930s Hobart's interests extended to the development of a county park system and the establishment of the Passaic County Park Commission, which her son, Garret Hobart, Jr., chaired from 1931 until his death in 1941. She was a supporter of the Passaic County Historical Society and endorsed the establishment of its museum and headquarters at the county-owned Lambert Castle in Garret Mountain Park. With the hope of fostering cultural interests in Paterson, she donated the family's painting collection to the Danforth Memorial Library in 1925. This collection of 26 canvases included works by Ralph Albert Blakelock, William Merritt Chase, and Eastman Johnson.

Hobart received statewide recognition for her public-spiritedness in June 1933 when she was awarded the honorary doctor of philanthropy degree by Rutgers University and was cited as one who had taken a "living interest in social enterprises."

She maintained a close relationship with her son and in later years, when her health was failing, lived with his family at Ailsa Farms in Haledon. She died there of bronchial pneumonia, at age 91, on January 8, 1941, and was buried at the Cedar Lawn Cemetery in Paterson.

A scrapbook of clippings and memorabilia on Hobart is kept at NJ-PCHS. Hobart's experiences in Washington, D.C., are detailed in her *Memoirs* (1930) and *Second Lady* (1933). R. P. Brooks, "Jennie Tuttle Hobart: Benefactor," *Bulletin of the Passaic County Historical Society* 4 (Dec. 1955):21–28, describes her civic activities in Passaic.

*Delight Wing Dodyk*

## ALISON LOW TURNBULL HOPKINS, 1880–1951

Alison Low (Turnbull) Hopkins, New Jersey suffragist and leader in the National Women's Party, was born on May 20, 1880, in Morristown (Morris County), NJ. Her father, Lt. Commander Frank Turnbull, was a naval officer and Annapolis graduate. Her mother, Marion Louise (Bates) Turnbull, was a descendant of William Bradford, governor of Plymouth Colony, and was the widow of Edwin Lord when she married Frank Turnbull in 1877.

Hopkins's socially prominent family lived at "Featherleigh Farms," the Morristown estate Hopkins's father had purchased in 1877 when he retired from the navy. Hopkins was the eldest of three children and was educated privately by tutors. She made her social debut in the 1901 season and on October 11, 1901, married John Appleton Haven Hopkins, a New York insurance executive.

Hopkins and her husband lived on Tenth Street in New York City from 1901 to 1908. Their three children—John Milton, Marion Louise, and Douglas Turnbull—were born during this period. Then in 1908 they took up permanent residence at Featherleigh Farms while still spending some of the winter months in New York City.

During the early years of her marriage, Hopkins was active in social and charitable affairs in Morristown. She served as president of Morristown's "Summer Shelter" and was active in the Speedwell Society, the Women's Town Improvement Committee, the Morristown Field Club, and the Morris County corn-growing and industrial contests. She was an Executive Committee member of the Morris County branch of the State Charities Aid Society. John Hopkins was also active in public affairs and in 1912 was chairman of the Progressive party of New Jersey.

By 1914 Hopkins had become active in the suffrage movement. She claimed that her civic and charitable work had "taught her that only through political power could women secure the reforms they wished for in our government and in our labor laws." (Scannell, *First Citizen's and State Guide*, 41) When the Congressional Committee of the National American Woman Suffrage Association (NAWSA) split off from its mother organization to become the independent and more militant Congressional

Union for Woman Suffrage (CU), Hopkins was elected a member of its Executive Committee. Unlike the NAWSA, which had a well-established state organization in New Jersey, the CU, led by New Jerseyan ALICE PAUL, was a smaller, Washington-based group devoted solely to lobbying and pressuring for a woman suffrage amendment to the U.S. Constitution.

Hopkins's work with the CU, however, did not keep her from working for suffrage at the state level. She was involved in the 1915 campaigns in both New Jersey and New York for passage of referenda on woman suffrage amendments to both state constitutions. When these state referenda and similar referenda in Massachusetts and Pennsylvania were defeated at the polls in late 1915, it became clear to Hopkins, as to most suffragists, that work for the federal amendment was the key strategy for winning the vote. Early in 1916 she became the president of the newly formed New Jersey branch of the CU.

Hopkins's leadership of the NJCU suggests that the New Jersey branch did not participate to any extent in the general CU strategy adopted during the 1916 presidential election. This strategy, initiated by ALICE PAUL and based on English suffragist policy, held the political party in power, in this case the Democrats, responsible for the failure of Congress to pass a woman suffrage amendment and intended to work for their defeat at the polls. This CU policy was opposed by the NAWSA, the larger, broad-based suffrage association, and was particularly problematic in New Jersey. Democratic President Woodrow Wilson, running for reelection, was a New Jerseyan, and though he had not yet supported suffrage nationally, he had advocated the passage of the 1915 New Jersey referendum, endearing himself to New Jersey suffragists. In addition, Hopkins's husband, a strong supporter of her suffrage activities, had switched his allegiance to the Democratic party and was head of Wilson's reelection campaign in New Jersey. The Hopkinses were social friends of the Wilsons.

Nevertheless, Hopkins participated fully in CU actions after Wilson's reelection. When the CU merged with the Woman's Party to become the National Woman's Party (NWP), Hopkins was elected to the NWP Executive Board, and in January 1917 the NJCU became the New Jersey branch of the NWP. Hopkins was part of the NWP inner circle in January 1917, when the NWP began the tactic of picketing the White House in Washington on behalf of the suffrage cause.

By March Hopkins herself was participating in the picketing. Then in July she and her friend Julia Hurlbut, also of Morristown, went to Washington to participate in the picketing planned for July 14, Bastille Day. Armed with banners that read "Liberty, Equality, Fraternity" and "How Long Must Women Wait for Liberty," a sedate throng of women walked two by two to the White House gates. When they refused to move on as directed by police,

the sixteen leaders were arrested on charges of unlawful assembly.

Hopkins and Hurlbut were among those arrested and sentenced to 60 days in prison. On July 17 they were carted off to the infamous Occoquan Workhouse in Maryland, where they were dressed in prison uniform and housed with the other women prisoners. Hopkins was visited in jail by her husband, who was appalled at prison conditions and went directly to protest to President Wilson, convincing him to issue a pardon for Hopkins and Hurlbut. Released after three days in jail, Hopkins used her arrest to draw further attention to the suffrage cause. She wrote a strong letter to the president stating that his unexplained pardon had deprived her of legal redress in her unjust arrest; and she charged him with acting solely to save himself political embarrassment. She then went to the White House again, alone, and stood by the gates with a sign that read, "We ask not pardon for ourselves but justice for all American women." She was not arrested again.

Hopkins continued to work for suffrage until the 19th Amendment passed both houses of Congress. Then she spearheaded NWP lobbying efforts on behalf of ratification by the New Jersey State Legislature. In February 1920 New Jersey was the 26th state to ratify the amendment.

Little is known of Hopkins's life after the winning of suffrage. She lived at Featherleigh Farms until the house was destroyed by fire in 1925. Her husband continued in politics, making an unsuccessful bid for the U.S. Senate from New Jersey in 1926. Hopkins and her husband were divorced in 1927, when she presumably moved to New York City.

Hopkins was a member of Heterodoxy, a unique New York luncheon club that met in Greenwich Village from 1912 to the early 1940s. Composed of feminist women in public life, reform, and the arts, the club celebrated the activities and achievements of its diverse membership, which included such women as Elizabeth Gurley Flynn, Charlotte Perkins Gilman, Agnes deMille, and Fannie Hurst. Hopkins and ALICE DUER MILLER were two notable New Jersey members of the group.

Hopkins died, at age 70, of a heart attack at her home on E. 53rd Street in New York City on March 18, 1951. Her death certificate lists her occupation as "saleslady."

Information on the Hopkins family is available in the files of the NJ-MO. Biographical information on Hopkins appears in *Scannell's New Jersey's First Citizens and State Guide*, vol. 2 (1919–20). Her arrest was detailed in the *New York Times*, July 15, 1917. Her obituary appeared in the *New York Times*, Mar. 20, 1951.

*Janet Gibbs-Albanesius*

## MARTHA BROOKES HUTCHESON, 1871–1959

Martha Brookes (Brown) Hutcheson, one of the first professional women landscape architects in the United States, was born on October 2, 1871, in New York City, the second of five children born to Joseph Henry and Ellen Douglas (Brookes) Brown. Her parents' ancestors had lived in Burlington, VT, for generations and were of English ancestry.

From her earliest years Hutcheson's temperament and interests set her apart from her older brother, Douglas, and her younger siblings, Herbert, Eliot, and Elsie. They attended school in New York City, but the entire family spent summers in Vermont, where young Hutcheson, according to family records, showed an early love of gardening by digging and changing plant material and working in her mother's garden from the age of ten.

Her education as a young woman reflected her creative interests. She attended the School of Applied Design for Women for two years, studying mechanical drawing and fabric design. She also took lessons in watercolor painting of flowers and studied native trees and shrubs at the University of Vermont. Travels abroad exposed her to the classic traditions of horticultural design in the gardens of England, France, and Italy.

Landscape architecture came of age in the United States around the turn of the century. In 1900 the Massachusetts Institute of Technology (MIT), bowing to growing interest in the design of public and private grounds, introduced the first courses in landscape architecture ever given in the United States. Despite family disapproval, Hutcheson enrolled in the course from 1900 to 1903, using a small bequest for the tuition. She was the second woman to take formal academic training in the field.

MIT was a turning point in Hutcheson's life, a time when her goals were clarified. Garden work had always claimed her creative energies. Now, armed with impressive credentials, she could compete on a professional level in the field of landscape architecture. Besides, she was proud of her unique academic achievement. Although not a feminist, she was aware of her education's historic significance for other women.

Independent, even rebellious, she blithely ignored prejudice against well-bred women working, and by 1903 was designing gardens in the Boston area. To her parents' dismay, she even circulated a brochure to clients listing her professional methods and charges. By 1906 she had proven herself in the field and moved back to New York. Her clients now ranged from Massachusetts to Long Island and New Jersey.

In 1910, at age 39, she married William Anderson Hutcheson at Fern Hill, Burlington, VT. Her husband, born in Greenock on the Clyde, Scotland, came to New York in 1899 and became actuary of the Mutual Life Insur-

ance Company. Distinguished, friendly, humorous, he complemented his wife's frank and forceful temperament. The marriage became a long and happy alliance. Their only child, Martha, was born in 1911.

The couple wanted an outlet for their mutual love of plants, birds, and woods. A country place in New Jersey was the answer. In 1911, for $800, they bought a 100-acre working farm in Morris County near the village of Gladstone. It became home for the rest of their lives. The property had been settled by Huguenot refugees in 1710 and last occupied by sharecroppers. Renamed "Merchiston Farm," in honor of William Hutcheson's boyhood school in Edinburgh, Scotland, the farm challenged Hutcheson's professional skills and her husband's administrative abilities. She tamed the open fields near the old farmhouse into classical gardens using English and Italian concepts of pools, stone walls, and vistas. He supervised the farm operation beyond the gardens, overseeing the plantings, crops, and animals. The entire setting expressed her philosophy that the "natural scene should blend with the cultivated."

They divided their time between family life on the farm and their careers in New York. During the World War I years Hutcheson branched out into lecturing and writing on landscape architecture and horticulture. Always concerned and energetic, she helped organize the Women's Land Army, the forerunner of World War II Victory Gardens, in New York, and spoke extensively at garden club fund raisers for the war effort.

Her ability in the drafting, designing, and execution of commissions won her election to the prestigious American Society of Landscape Architects in 1920. In barely 20 years she proved that a woman could succeed in this field. In 1935 she was advanced to fellow in the society.

Merchiston Farm inspired her book *The Spirit of the Garden* (1923). In this substantial work, typical of the era, Hutcheson stressed practical garden concepts, many of which are still applicable today. Her New Jersey country home exemplified her belief that a garden involved more than plants. "The garden," she poetically noted in her book, "was not only the exquisite playground of the house, but a place of inspiration, promise, and tranquility." (Hutcheson, *Spirit*, 3)

Her excellent standing in landscape architecture brought requests to design important gardens along the northeastern seaboard ranging from city courtyards to seaside estates. Secure in her success, she now took only jobs she liked. Also, her concept of landscape architecture had broadened. Horticultural design was not limited to the gardens of the wealthy. It played a vital role in the progress of cities and towns. Lecturing throughout the United States and England, she pressed for better general landscape planning through use of plants for cities, trees for schoolyards, better front door yard treatments for rural towns, and the education of citizens for these beautification efforts.

But her greatest satisfaction was Merchiston Farm. From May to November family summers in the country were combined with writing and studying. Visiting artists and bagpipe recitals in the rambling farmhouse were pleasant diversions, but her greatest pleasure was developing new designs in her gardens. "Look-throughs" were her specialty. With her particular talent for line and form, she created appealing views through hedgerows and arbor paths that remain major attractions of Merchiston Farm today.

The farm became the Hutchesons' permanent home with William Hutcheson's retirement in 1940. After her husband's death in 1942 Hutcheson stayed on and continued her professional practice. To the end she was a distinctive presence, a tall woman with upswept hair who disdained long dresses, wearing corduroys for her working attire.

Hutcheson died at Merchiston Farm on July 23, 1959, at age 87. She is buried in Gladstone, NJ. In 1974 her daughter, Martha Hutcheson Norton, gave the property to the Morris County Park Commission in memory of her parents. Renamed after the stream that runs through the farm, the Bamboo Brook Outdoor Education Center is maintained today as a significant example of an early 20th-century New Jersey garden and is visited by over 4,000 people annually. Undeniably Hutcheson was an important role model for all women in landscape architecture. Her passion and enthusiasm for gardening is now shared with the public at Bamboo Brook, her greatest contribution to New Jersey.

Hutcheson's book is *The Spirit of the Garden* (1923). Records of her family, as well as details of her educational and professional background, are in the possession of her daughter, Mrs. C. McKim Norton, Princeton, NJ. Interviews with Norton and Benjamin Blackburn, Hutcheson's longtime neighbor, on Oct. 15, 1985, provided insights into her professional and personal life. Her obituary appeared in the *New York Times*, July 25, 1959.

*Sharon M. Doremus*

## WOMEN IN NEW JERSEY'S JEWISH FARM COMMUNITIES

Jewish farming efforts in America can be traced back to the late 18th century. These early communities, scattered all over the United States and generally communal in nature, were short-lived. The first successful and enduring settlements were established in south Jersey at the end of the 19th century. Vineland, Alliance, Carmel, Rosenhayn, and Woodbine were all founded between 1882 and 1891. In the 20th century, Jewish farm communities could be found all over New Jersey. Jewish immigrants, without previous farm experience, planted crops, bred cattle, ran

In the late 1800s and early 1900s a small number of Jewish immigrant women and men settled with their families in southern New Jersey farming communities such as Alliance and Farmingdale. Their descendants, like Minnie Meltzer and her granddaughter, photographed here in the 1950s, continued to farm well into the 20th century. *From the Farmingdale Collection, courtesy of Gertrude Dubrovsky.*

dairy farms, and pioneered in poultry farming, making it a major branch of United States agriculture. The community of Farmingdale in central New Jersey became one of the largest egg-producing communities in the country. In the 1940s New Jersey was called "the egg basket of America" and the "cradle of the Jewish farm movement," even as it became the white leghorn capital of the world.

The typical Jewish farmers at the end of the 19th century and the early years of the 20th century emigrated to America from Eastern Europe, had little or no experience in farming, did not know the manners or language of rural America, and were generally poor. They came to their farms with little money, great dreams, young families, and youthful energies. Their early years of hard work were often frustrating and disappointing, in spite of their backbreaking labor in clearing woods, digging fields by hand, and constructing their homes. Yet they persevered, learned farming by trial and error, and ultimately succeeded.

The life of the early days in Alliance (founded in 1882) is captured in a sketch by Elizabeth (Rudnick) Levin, a daughter of one of the original settlers, who appreciated the hard life and heroic efforts made by the immigrant pioneer women. She writes:

"Clearly can I picture women like Mrs. Rothman, Mrs. Bakerman, Mrs. Helig and my mother, wearing, in Old World fashion, a three-cornered scarf over their heads, bending low to the ground, slowly following their husbands along the long rows of corn or sweet potatoes.

"Only the poorest of memories can forget the . . . strawberry season in our small community! Children trudging along with their mothers, going from one farm to another to crawl along the rows of strawberries, each picker competing with his or her associates, to see who could fill up more quarts. . . . I can see those same mothers and children with stockings drawn over their arms as a protection from the thorns, plucking blackberries. . . . I remember these wearied families, when the day's work was over, hurrying to take a swim in the clear, cool, shallow waters of the Maurice River. . . .

". . . Many of those pioneer womenfolk, in the fall of the year, . . . walked miles to pick cranberries, while others went far from home to work in the canning factories near Bridgeton . . . spurred on by the realization that this was one's last opportunity to earn something before the lean months of winter would prevent any work! . . .

"The only recreation that those tired bodies really enjoyed were the Saturday morning services at the synagogues. . . . Well do I recall the yearly contribution they made toward beautifying the interiors of the 'shule.' To them, it meant their only haven of pleasure and relaxation." (Levin, "Pioneer Women of the Colonies," in *Yoral*, 30–31)

At first, some of the area schools attempted to segregate Jewish children, although this effort was abandoned as uneconomical. Sending children to high school in town involved significant sacrifice. Nevertheless, two pioneer women in Alliance, Mrs. Rudnick and Mrs. Bailey, were the first to decide that their daughters would receive the benefits of a high school education. By both Old and New World standards, and especially in rural areas, this was a radical venture. Neighbors tried unsuccessfully to dissuade them. Elizabeth (Rudnick) Levin describes the mothers' determination and their ultimate success: "In the Old World, a grammar school education was deemed sufficient for the girls. Consider, then, the consternation created when mothers like mine crashed through traditional restriction and insisted that their daughters continue their education by attending high school in Vineland. . . . The miracle of it all was that those mothers of ours, hardly able to read or write, early saw the value of an educated mind, and found the means to send us away from home to procure the necessary instruction." (Levin, 32–33) Mrs. Bailey walked the two girls more than two miles each day to the railroad station in Norma. Then she opened a small store in Vineland to make it possible for her daughter to attend high school there. Eventually her daughter became a physician, and Elizabeth Rudnick a teacher.

Farm work was hard for the Jewish women of south Jersey agricultural settlements, and life was often lonely. Nevertheless, rural America was a far better place for many Jewish immigrants than the cities. Forming alien enclaves within the larger Christian communities, the Jewish farmers of the early settlements "huddled together like chicks under the brooder stove" (Sokol, Interview, Oct. 7, 1973), in the words of a Farmingdale settler, and created the institutions they needed to live a Jewish life.

Husbands and wives worked side by side in forging their futures, but it was the men rather than the women who received recognition as community builders. For example, Benjamin Peskin's efforts in 1919 to attract more Jewish settlers to the infant Farmingdale community in central New Jersey has resulted in his being called its "founder" or the "father." The impetus, however, came from his wife, Rose, who threatened to leave him and return to the city with their children if more Jewish people did not settle there.

Mary (Peskin) Weisgold, the younger of the two Peskin daughters, who came to the farm as a child, remembers her mother's unhappiness at her isolated life and her very hard work: "Being the only Jewish woman in the community for several years was very lonely and isolating for her, as well as for us. She had absolutely no one to talk to. Even if she did feel comfortable with the English of her Christian neighbors, she had no common experience or background to share. . . . And she worked very hard. I remember her taking water out of the well in the wintertime, and her fingers sticking on the chain." (Weisgold, Interview, May 4, 1976)

Benjamin Peskin knew that if the family was going to stay on the farm he loved, he would have to work hard encouraging Jews to settle. He obtained a real estate license and was in constant communication with the Jewish Agricultural Society to send prospective customers to him. He met them at the railroad station, housed them free of charge in his own home, and showed them farms. Once the new farmers settled, he instructed and helped them.

Increasing numbers of Jewish people made life more tolerable for Rose Peskin, but her work grew more burdensome. In the summer, her husband tried to augment the family income by renting out rooms to paying guests, a practice later followed by other Jewish farmers. For Jewish immigrants living in New York City, the farm offered an inexpensive vacation, wholesome food, and contact with nature, which they sorely missed. For Benjamin Peskin, whose inexperience in farming produced one failure after another, the summer boarders represented his first successful "crop."

He converted his barn into sleeping quarters and his

home into a gigantic dining room; his wife cooked all the meals herself and the children waited on the tables. Within two years, the business grew until the farm accommodated as many as 60 people. But Rose Peskin could not keep up with the work and suffered complete exhaustion, forcing the boarding business into early retirement. However, the summer guests helped spread the word of the Jewish farming community of Farmingdale, and some of those early guests later returned with their families to become chicken farmers.

On the produce and the poultry farms of New Jersey, the women worked alongside their husbands. Putting on overalls and rubber boots, they planted fields, cleaned out chicken coops, helped prepare the outdoor ranges for the chickens, milked cows, made cheese and butter, and did the myriad other day-to-day chores a farm demands. A casual observer, seeing a husband and wife working together, might sometimes have had trouble distinguishing one from the other.

Although the physical work was shared, the leadership roles in the community were not. "The men were expected to be on the board of the center, to go to meetings, to take care of the community. The women were left with the drudgery," said one woman recalling her farm experience in Farmingdale. (Morgan, Interview, Sept. 2, 1975) Unlike Elizabeth (Rudnick) Levin, who remembered Alliance pioneer farm women as heroines, Amour Morgan's impression of the early Farmingdale women was different: "These European women always seemed to me to be old. Old and plodding. They were neither interesting nor interested. They served the coffee and cake to the men, who sat around figuring out how to save the world."

By the middle of the century, changing farm conditions made survival increasingly difficult for the small family farmer. Women and men both began preparing themselves for other jobs and professions, fully aware that a way of life was passing. In spite of the difficulties they experienced, few regret the years they spent on their farms, or the labors they expended. It was a challenge they met successfully. In summing up their experiences, the women invariably agree with one early East European woman settler who, when asked what life on the farm was like, said in Yiddish: "We worked very hard on the farm. But we were free. It was a nice life, a beautiful life. I wish I had it now." (Wishnick, Interview, May 10, 1973)

For a discussion of the early south Jersey farm communities, see Joseph Brandes, *Immigrants to Freedom* (1971); Gabriel Davidson, *Our Jewish Farmers* (1943); and Sidney Bailey, ed., *Yoval: A Symposium Upon the First 50 Years of the Jewish Farming Colonies of Alliance, Norma and Brotmanville, NJ* (1932). Interviews with Harry Sokol, Oct. 7, 1973; Mary Weisgold, May 4, 1976; Amour Morgan, Sept. 2, 1975; and Hilda Wishnick, May 10, 1973, are part of the Farmingdale Collection assembled by Dr. Gertrude Dubrovsky and in her possession.

*Gertrude W. Dubrovsky*
*Joseph Brandes*

## SARAH E. JONES

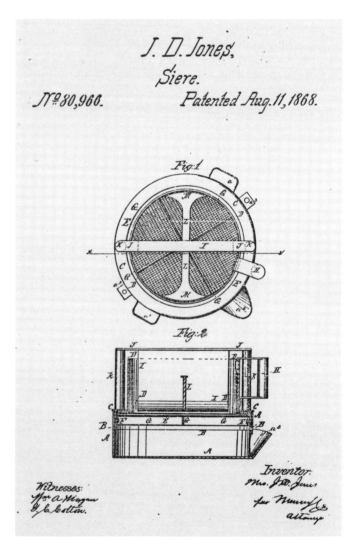

An 1868 patent drawing for an improved sieve for straining hot food invented by Sarah E. La Salle Jones. Jones was born in Pennsylvania about 1829. She married John D. Jones of Jersey City, a boot and shoe merchant. During the early 1860s he had a store in the commercial sector of Jersey City and a house in another part of the city.

In 1868 Jones was issued a patent for an improved sieve for straining hot food. She envisioned using a larger version of her invention for the factory production of jellies, jams, and catsups. Her patent was filed by Munn and Company, the largest firm of patent solicitors in the United States and publishers of *Scientific American*.

Jones's husband died in 1879 or 1880. She lived in her own home until about 1883, when she shared a house with Charlotte E. Jones, a teacher. She died on June 14, 1884.

Information on Jones appears in the *Jersey City Directory* (1854–85).

By Joseph P. Sullivan. *Drawing courtesy, U.S. Department of Commerce, Patent and Trademark Office.*

## JULIA HART BEERS KEMPSON, 1834–1913

Julia (Hart) Beers Kempson, one of the nation's first women landscape painters and a longtime resident of Metuchen, NJ, was born on December 28, 1834, in Pittsfield, MA. She was the tenth child and sixth daughter of James Hart, probably a woolen mill worker, and Marion (Robertson) Hart. Both parents were originally from Paisley, Scotland. Kempson's six older brothers and sisters were born in Paisley, and the next three were born in Kilmarnock, Scotland. In 1831 the Harts and their nine children sailed from Liverpool, England, to Boston, MA, settling in Pittsfield. In 1835, a year after Kempson's birth, the family moved to a home on Water Street in Albany, NY.

Kempson was the youngest sister, and a pupil, of the well-known Hudson River school landscape painters William (1823–94) and James MacDougal Hart (1828–1901). Both brothers began their careers as apprentices to carriage makers; they traveled abroad to further their artistic education, particularly in landscape painting, and eventually opened studios in New York City, where Kempson received her training and was heavily influenced by their approach to painting nature. The brothers showed the reverence for America's still untouched wilderness typical of members of the Hudson River school, and they often painted views outdoors, directly from nature. Kempson often went on sketching trips, and her concern for every aspect of nature is apparent in her work. Indeed, throughout her career she was continually influenced by her brothers' example. She shared a studio with James for many years in New York City and lived with William and his family from 1860 to 1876.

At age eighteen, Kempson met George Washington Beers (1829–60), her first husband, who was a well-known journalist with the *Albany Evening Journal*. They were married in the State Street Baptist Church in Albany on January 13, 1853. The couple had two children, Marion ("Minnie") Robertson (b. 1853), who in previous biographical dictionaries has been described as the husband of Kempson (rather than her daughter), and Kathryn ("Kitty") Schreiber (b. 1856). In 1860 George Washington Beers died, and Kempson, along with her two daughters and her mother, moved to the Brooklyn, NY, home of William Hart.

It was in Brooklyn, beginning in 1860, that Kempson began a serious career as a painter. She and her daughter

Marion, also an artist, were instrumental in the development of the artistic education of other women. Indeed, for several years, until 1876, they accompanied James and William Hart, as well as parties of young women, on sketching trips throughout Vermont and the Adirondack Mountains.

In December 1863 Kempson (as Julia H. Beers) exhibited her first work at the Brooklyn Art Association, a painting titled *A River Bank*. Until 1884 she showed at least one painting each year at this gallery. Her work came to include still lifes as well as landscapes. In 1867 Kempson exhibited a work titled *Autumn Flowers* at the Boston Athenaeum, and in the same year she began to exhibit landscapes at the National Academy of Design in New York.

In addition, records at the Pennsylvania Academy of the Fine Arts indicate that she exhibited *A View Near Bethel, Maine* in their 1868 exhibition. An extant work of 1871, *Landscape with Cattle*, depicts an idyllic and reverential view of nature and the rural environment framed by trees, all typical elements in Hudson River school painting. New Jersey scenes such as *Near Metuchen, New Jersey*, which she exhibited at the Brooklyn Art Association in 1880, were also popular subjects.

In 1876, more than sixteen years after her first husband died, Kempson married Dr. Peter Tertius Kempson (1814–90), a physician from Metuchen. He was a native of England and an 1843 graduate of the Royal College of Surgeons. After her marriage, Kempson moved with her two daughters to Peter Kempson's home, "Fir Tree Cottage," in Metuchen. Kempson maintained a studio there and continued to paint, teach, and exhibit her work. Winters were regularly spent in St. Augustine, FL.

After the death of her second husband in 1890, Kempson and her daughter Kathryn continued to live in Metuchen. In 1903 they decided to move to Mount Vernon, NY, apparently to be near Marion, who had married Dr. Edward Fletcher Brush in 1877. Ten years later, on June 1, 1913, Kathryn, who had lived with her mother all her life, died. This event had a devastating effect on Kempson, who just two months later, on August 13, 1913, at age 78, died of the effects of a gastric ulcer while visiting relatives in Trenton, NJ. She was buried in the Presbyterian Cemetery, Metuchen.

Paintings by Kempson can be found in several private and public collections, including those in the Allen Memorial Museum at Oberlin College and the Newark Museum, owner of *Heigh Ho! Daisies and Buttercups*.

Information on Kempson appears in *Who Was Who in American Art* (1985) and in *Dictionary of Women Artists* (1985). Obituaries appeared in the *Trenton State Gazette*, Aug. 16, 1913; the *New York Times*, Aug. 15, 1913; and the *American Art Annual* 11 (1914). Interviews with Robert Fuld, of the Mount Vernon (NY) Public Library, and Mrs. W. Carlton Brush, wife of Kempson's grandson, provided information on the Brush and Hart families.

*Barbara J. Mitnick*

## ELIZABETH SARAH KITE, 1864–1954

Elizabeth Sarah Kite, author and social scientist of the New Jersey Pine Barrens, was born December 4, 1864, in Philadelphia, PA, the youngest of three children of James and Mary Anna (Bonwill) Kite. Her family moved to a farm in Chester Hill, OH, when she was three, and there she was raised in a strict Quaker household with its disciplines of frequent worship and recitation. Memorizing and reciting poetry and Bible verses followed her family tradition as well as religious expectation.

Volumes in her father's library such as Boswell's *Life of Johnson*, Rollins's *Ancient History*, and Daubigny's *History of the Reformation* sparked an early curiosity in her, later to be fanned to an ardent love of history. Farm life gave her a freedom to explore and be active. As a girl, she developed a wildflower garden that began a lifelong interest in botany, and she was taught by her brother, John Alban, to ride horseback by the age of five.

Kite's social conscience was awakened by her mother's sister, Huldah Bonwill, who in 1868 had been sent to Indian territory west of the Mississippi by the Committee on Indian Affairs of the Philadelphia Yearly Meeting of Friends to work with American Indians and African-Americans after the Civil War.

As a child, Kite was educated at home by her parents and a governess. Then, at eleven, in 1876, she was sent to Westtown Boarding School, where most Kite family members had been educated. Adjustment to life at Westtown was difficult for her, although she impressed teachers with her recitation ability. She attended the school for only a couple of years before returning to Chester Hill to study at home with her sister, Anna Huldah.

When Kite was in her late teens her brother assumed a medical practice on Nantucket. Her aunt, Huldah Bonwill, bought a house there and the family summered on Nantucket.

In 1886 Kite became a teacher in a cousin's Quaker school in Philadelphia, and in 1888 she was made principal of a new Quaker school. The next few years, however, brought Kite striking losses. Her mother died in 1888, followed a few weeks later by her sister, Anna, and then in 1891 by her brother, John.

Accompanied by Huldah Bonwill, Kite traveled to the West in 1892 and while there pursued her interest in botany in a summer course at State College at Colorado Springs. After meeting there a young married man to whom she was attracted, she resolved to let reason rather than emotion govern her life. Kite consciously decided

that marriage was not to be an option for her, feeling it was God's will for her to lead a single life. "There were a thousand ways open to pass a free and useful life and I felt a distinct sense of purpose that could not be taken away." (Kite, "The Beggar Maid and the King," 120)

While in Colorado, Kite was advised to study French and German so she would be able to read the best botanical writing of the day. From 1895 to 1897 she studied at the University of Goettingen in Germany and the Sorbonne in Paris. In her memoirs she writes: "My whole heart and mind and soul were now set in France, cradle of my mother's ancestors, in love of which country I had always been brought up." (Kite, "Beggar Maid," 190)

While Kite was in Europe, both her sister's husband and her brother's wife died, leaving her responsible for five nieces and nephews. Over the next few years, between her own studying and teaching, she saw to the raising and educating of these children.

Kite took one of her nieces to England to be educated in 1904, while she studied in Paris and London. In 1905 she received the Diplome d'Instruction, Primaire-Superieure, from the Sorbonne. Studying history at the University of London with Dr. Emil Reich, she was challenged to begin writing on the importance of French aid to America during the Revolutionary War, a subject that commanded her attention for the rest of her life.

While living in London Kite was aware of a growing "spiritual hunger," and her experiences in Catholic France and in Algiers during a trip with friends led to her conversion to Roman Catholicism in 1906. She was a devout Catholic for the rest of her life.

From 1909 to 1918 Kite worked as a member of the research laboratory staff of the Training School at Vineland, NJ, performing investigative research under the direction of Professor E. R. Johnstone and Dr. Herbert H. Goddard, director of research. She performed fieldwork tracing the family background of the residents of the Vineland school, including that of the so-called Kallikak family. Kite went on to investigate the factors of isolated living and the resultant inbreeding in many families in the Pine Barrens, an area that covers one-fourth of New Jersey and that contributed many of the retarded members of the school at that time. From her work she concluded that retardation was inherited.

Little was known about genetics in the early years of this century and the conclusion drawn by Kite as a result of her research, that mental retardation is inherited, is not supported by current knowledge. But her research in the Pine Barrens and her advocacy of the families she worked with led to improvements in the state's response to the mentally disabled.

During her work in the Pine Barrens, Kite came to know ELIZABETH WHITE, a commercial farmer of blueberries and cranberries who was impressed by Kite's friendliness toward the families she studied and her willingness to aid them when she could. Kite wrote a number of papers reporting the results of her research. In one she wrote: "this work of science carried with it no power to act. Its aim was first, to ascertain the source of mental defect; second, through publicity, to influence both legislation and public sentiment so that laws dealing with the situation might be enacted and subsequently enforced." (Kite, "Research Work in New Jersey," 9)

As a result of her efforts, the New Jersey State Legislature appropriated money for research, the first such appropriation made by any state legislature. The commissioner of charities and corrections hired Kite to continue the study in the Pine Barrens as an agent of the department, giving her the power to act as emissary of the state. A direct result of her work was the Colony at New Lisbon, organized in the early 1920s as a private institution for mentally retarded boys. The Colony was later taken over by the state.

Because of her fluency in French, Kite collaborated with Herbert Goddard in producing the 1916 U.S. editions of Alfred Binet and Theodore Simon's works on human intelligence, *The Development of Intelligence in Children* and *The Intelligence of the Feebleminded*. Kite translated the works and Goddard edited them.

Although Kite is known in New Jersey for her research on the residents of the Pine Barrens, she had another distinct career, her scholarship on the role played by France in the American Revolution. Between 1918 and 1949 she published eight historical works, including books on the Marquis de Lafayette and Pierre L'Enfant. In 1926, when the Institut Français de Washington was established, Kite was a founding member and was elected to the first Board of Trustees. In 1933 the French government awarded her the Cross of the Chevalier de la Legion d'Honneur. That same year she was awarded an honorary doctorate at Villanova University, the first woman to receive such an honor at that institution. From 1932 to 1949 she was archivist of the American Catholic Historical Society of Philadelphia.

Kite died of heart disease, at age 89, in Wilmington, DE, on January 6, 1954. A requiem mass was celebrated for her and she was buried at the Friends Burial Ground in Philadelphia.

The Elizabeth S. Kite Collection at NJ-RU includes her unpublished autobiography, "The Beggar Maid and the King," research notes, correspondence, copies of her published articles, newspaper clippings, and obituaries. Kite authored *Research Work in New Jersey* (1913).

*Shirley M. Montgomery*

## ALICE LAKEY, 1857–1935

Alice Lakey, activist in the pure food movement and advocate of insurance, was born on October 14, 1857, in Shaneville, OH, the only child of Methodist minister Charles D. Lakey and his English-born wife, Ruth (Jacques) Lakey. Ruth Lakey died in 1863 when her daughter was six years old, and the following year Charles Lakey married Emily Jane Jackson, a painter. Ill health forced him to resign from the ministry, and he entered the insurance business, first in Cleveland, OH, and later in Chicago, IL.

Lakey was educated in public schools in Chicago until she was fourteen. Then the family moved to New York City, and she attended St. Mary's Hall in Burlington (Burlington County), NJ, from 1872 to 1874. When she was in her early twenties she and her stepmother went to Europe, Emily Lakey to paint and Alice Lakey to study voice. For about eight years Lakey, a mezzo-soprano, studied in Florence, Paris, and London. She received favorable reviews when she sang onstage in London, where she also taught voice. She returned to the United States in 1888, intending to pursue a career in opera, but she became ill and remained an invalid for seven years.

In 1896 the Lakeys moved to Cranford (Union County), NJ, a quiet town where Lakey could continue her recovery. Soon she was teaching voice in Cranford and in New York City. In October 1896 Emily Lakey died, and Alice Lakey took over as housekeeper for her father. Because he was fussy about food, she became interested in the pure food movement. As president of the Cranford Village Improvement Association (VIA), Lakey, in 1903, invited Dr. Harvey W. Wiley to speak to the group about food adulteration. Since 1880 nearly 100 bills to regulate interstate traffic in food and drugs had been introduced in Congress, but none had passed both houses. Wiley, chief of the Bureau of Chemistry of the Department of Agriculture since 1883, traveled throughout the country to educate the public about candy containing toxic colorings or narcotics, food artificially colored to conceal the filth and decomposed matter it contained, and poisonous preservatives. He found in Lakey an immediate and zealous convert to the movement for pure food legislation, and she collected over 200 signatures on a petition Wiley drafted to the New Jersey members of Congress.

Lakey began to organize women in support of a federal pure food law. In 1904 she secured the New Jersey State Federation of Women's Clubs' passage of a resolution calling for federal legislation. She brought the issue to the attention of the General Federation of Women's Clubs (GFWC) by distributing 1,000 circulars at their 1904 convention in St. Louis, MO, and she persuaded them to form a pure food committee. In 1905 she became chairman of the National Consumers' League's newly formed Food Committee, a post she held until 1913.

As a leading advocate of pure food legislation Lakey was one of six, including Wiley, who visited President Theodore Roosevelt in February 1905 to make a direct appeal for his support. In December 1905, in his annual message to Congress, he called for a pure food law.

The Food and Drugs Act passed the Senate in February 1906, but food industry lobbyists had stepped up their opposition, and hopes for passage in the House of Representatives were dim. That month, however, public alarm rose with the publication of *The Jungle*, Upton Sinclair's exposé of the meatpacking industry. (One of Lakey's prized possessions was an autographed copy of Sinclair's book.) Urged on by Lakey and other activists, citizens flooded Congress with over one million letters in support of the law. At this point the food industry realized that government regulation was the only way to regain consumers' confidence. The Food and Drugs Act passed the House and, with a Meat Inspection Act, was signed into law by President Roosevelt on June 30, 1906.

For Lakey and other reformers, however, the fight was not over. The federal law prohibited interstate commerce in adulterated, mislabeled, or poisonous foods, but it did not stop their manufacture or sale within individual states. State legislation was needed. Tuberculous milk and meat were other serious problems that had to be addressed on a state and local level. Lakey was the only female charter member of the New York Milk Committee, formed in 1906 to promote a clean milk supply for the city. In 1907, as chair of the Pure Food Committee of the New Jersey State Federation of Women's Clubs, she mobilized women to write to state legislators in support of a food bill and a meat and slaughterhouse inspection bill. In a letter to the editor of the *Newark Evening News* she urged that meat inspection not be left out of the pending state legislation. Lakey organized a Food Convention in Cranford in 1907 with speakers on safe, clean milk and meat, and on detecting food adulteration.

Under this pressure, bit by bit the New Jersey State Legislature enacted food and drug laws: in 1907 covering adulteration and mislabeling, with amendments added in 1908; in 1909 regulating sanitation in food establishments; and finally in 1910 instituting licensing and inspection of slaughterhouses. All the while, Lakey continued to address the topic of the federal law, lecturing for the New York Board of Education, the Woman's Christian Temperance Union, and other groups on what the federal law had accomplished. She warned the public that reforms were still needed: foods contaminated with disease or with naturally occurring poisons were not covered in the law. With a traveling exhibit of adulterated foods, assembled for the National Consumers' League in 1910, she taught the public to recognize illegal products, such as those preserved with borax, that were still on the market.

Lakey kept up a correspondence with Wiley, asking him for accurate, up-to-date data and apprising him of her activities for the cause. Complaining about the revival of lobbying, she wrote to Wiley in 1908: "'Special interests' never die they only sleep." (National Archives, Nov. 9, 1908) During the administration of President William Howard Taft (1909–13) food lobbyists obtained many concessions that weakened the Food and Drugs Act of 1906, and late in 1910 Lakey spoke to the New York and Connecticut State Federations of Women's Clubs on "the Betrayal of the Pure Food Law." She told her audiences: "There is nothing that cannot be accomplished by the women if we unite in action. We worked to place the law on the statute books—let us work to save it." (National Archives) She drew up two resolutions concerning the adulteration and mislabeling of malt liquors and whiskey that were subsequently passed by the Food Committee of the National Consumers' League, the Cranford VIA, and the New York State Federation of Women's Clubs. In 1912 Lakey's work with the National Consumers' League helped secure passage of a Compulsory Weight Branding Bill as an amendment to the Food and Drugs Act. Woodrow Wilson's inauguration as president raised Lakey's hopes for stricter enforcement of the 1906 law.

Lakey sought to intensify the activity of the Food Committee of the National Consumers' League by transforming it into a separate organization called the American Pure Food League in 1914, but the new group eventually collapsed for lack of funds. By 1914 she had been made a member of the National Institute of Social Sciences in recognition of her work for the pure food movement, and she became pure food editor for *Osteopathic Magazine*. She chaired the Committee of Women's Organizations for Women's Day at the 1918 and 1919 National Milk Expositions in New York.

In 1919 Lakey, age 62, embraced another cause when her father died and she took over as owner-manager of his magazine, *Insurance*. She undertook to educate the public on the importance of life insurance for a family's financial security and insurance as a way to save for children's education. She became an insurance specialist for the GFWC and spoke about insurance to women's clubs and on the radio in the 1920s. So persuasive was she on the topic that her article "If I Had Only Known," in the April 1924 *Woman's Home Companion*, generated over 600 letters from readers. That year Secretary of Commerce Herbert Hoover appointed Lakey a member of the Insurance Division of the Street and Highway Safety Conferences in Washington, D.C.

Besides her many state and national interests, Lakey was involved in civic affairs in Cranford. She helped found the local Visiting Nurse Association and the Needlework Guild, which made clothing for the needy. She was part of a pioneering effort to provide school lunches. She served many times as president of the Cranford VIA and for seven years as president of the parish circle at Trinity Episcopal Church. In 1910 Lakey spoke out in the local newspaper about Cranford's water supply, and some 250 citizens showed up for a meeting dealing with the water pollution. She also helped clean up the local milk supply. She started Cranford's PTA, and in 1933, at age 74, led the fight to clean up the town's streets. In her later years, heart disease often kept Lakey bedridden for months at a time, but she continued to arrange speakers and write letters for her causes.

From 1904 on a housekeeper and companion, Bella Jordan, lived with Lakey. The two women spent summers vacationing and entertaining guests in Melvin Village, NH.

Lakey died of heart disease, at age 77, on June 18, 1935, in Cranford. Following a funeral at Trinity Episcopal Church she was buried in Fairview Cemetery in Westfield (Union County), NJ. Mayor George E. Osterheldt of Cranford declared an official ten-day period of mourning.

Lakey's rallying of the powerful network of women's clubs in support of pure food legislation and its enforcement was a decisive factor in the achievement of real reform. In 1976 the U.S. Department of Agriculture honored her for her contribution to the 1906 Food and Drugs Act.

Information on Lakey's work are part of the Records of the Food and Drug Administration and Bureau of Agricultural and Industrial Chemistry in the National Archives (Washington, D.C.). The NJ-CPL maintains a clipping file on Lakey. She is profiled in *NAW*. Obituaries appeared in the *New York Times*, June 19, 1935, and in the *Cranford* (NJ) *Citizen and Chronicle*, June 20, 1935.

*Fran Moffett*
*Maggie Sullivan*

## ELLA CONDIE LAMB, 1862–1936

Ella (Condie) Lamb, a painter, muralist, mosaic artist, and designer of stained glass windows, was born in New York City in 1862, the daughter of James and Ellen (Harrison) Condie, whom Lamb herself described as "an accurate, determined Scotch father [and] a beauty-loving, sensitive English mother." (Edgerton, "Home in a Pasture Lot," 290)

Lamb entered the National Academy of Design in New York City when she was sixteen and a year later took the academy's first prize in a woman's life drawing class. In 1880, at eighteen, she began study at the Art Students' League, also in New York City, and remained there for several years as "one of its most promising and active members." (Fraser, "The Advent Angel," 318) She left there to study at a newly established art school in Bushey, England, but finding that atmosphere uncongenial she moved to Paris for private study.

Shortly after her return to the United States, Ella Condie married Charles Rollison Lamb, an artist and architect. As their family grew, eventually including five children—Richard, Karl, Katharine, Donald, and Joseph—they moved to Cresskill (Bergen County), NJ. There they began, in 1901, to build a home designed to blend with the natural beauty of the pasture land. The family of Frederick Lamb, Charles's brother, was living on adjoining property. The home, called "The Fold," was located in an area where the Lamb brothers had spent time as children. In a 1907 interview Lamb said of her New Jersey home: "We had to have a garden. . . . The children needed it to grow in, I needed it to work off city nerves, and as for Mr. Lamb—well, every artist should have a flower garden. . . . the house . . . was to grow up out of the earth, just as inevitably as the garden would." (Edgerton, 282)

Much of Lamb's work was done in collaboration with her husband, who, Lamb said, "believed I could do things in the art world and who never has permitted me to shut up the studio for the nursery and the kitchen." (Edgerton, 290) He designed buildings and she designed the stained glass windows, mosaics, or murals that went into them. Her best-known work is their collaborative effort, the Henry W. Sage Memorial Chapel at Cornell University, for which she designed windows titled *The Arts* and *The Sciences*.

She also designed a three-panel stained glass window for Wells College in Aurora, NY, in which three female figures represent science, art, and literature. Her paintings include a number of portraits, among them one of her husband, and a large painting, *The Advent Angel*, done while she still was in her twenties, of a winged woman in Lamb's characteristic detailed drapery. *The Christ Child*, in the Conrad Memorial at St. Mary's Church, in Wayne, PA, and four panels for the Lakewood Memorial Chapel in Minneapolis, each with a human figure representing a quality such as hope or memory, are examples of her mosaic work.

Much of Lamb's work was associated with the J. and R. Lamb Studios, which designed and produced stained glass windows, primarily for churches. Run by Charles and Frederick Lamb, the studios had been founded by Joseph and Richard Lamb, their father and uncle, in 1857.

Lamb's son Karl became president of Lamb Studios in 1926 and moved the business from Manhattan to Tenafly (Bergen County), NJ, in 1935. Lamb's daughter, Katharine, a stained glass designer, mosaic artist, and an illustrator, also worked for the studios.

Among Lamb's more interesting murals are those in the Flower Memorial, which was donated to Watertown, NY, by Emma Flower Taylor. Lamb used Taylor's and her own children as models for the murals. The larger mural shows a woman with an open book and a child on her lap, and four other children surrounding her, with Greek-style drapery and contemporary hairstyles. *The Open Book*, like

Lamb's other work, is classical and full of reserve and charm.

Lamb won a number of awards: the Dodge Prize, given by the National Academy of Design in 1889, when she was 27; an award in the American Fine Arts section of the Columbian Exposition in Chicago in 1893; a gold medal at the Atlanta Exposition in 1895; and medals at both the Pan-American and the Buffalo expositions in 1901. She was a life member of both the Art Students' League and the National Art Club and was a member of the Women's Art Club. She was one of the first two women elected to the National Society of Mural Painting.

Lamb died of "acute dilation of the heart," at age 73, at her home, "The Fold," on January 23, 1936. The woman whose work is found in so many public memorials had a private funeral and was buried in Brookside Cemetery in Englewood, NJ.

Two articles detail Lamb's life and work: Giles Edgerton, "Home in a Pasture Lot: Artists Who Live There," *Craftsman* 13 (1907):280–92; and W. Lewis Fraser, "The Advent Angel: Reproduction with Discussion," *Century Illustrated Monthly* 47 (1893):185, 318. Sketches of her appear in *Who Was Who in America* 3 (1960) and in *Dictionary of Women Artists* (1985). Her obituary appeared in the *New York Times*, Jan. 25, 1936.

*Martha C. Merrill*

## MARIE LOUISE LEFORT, 1874–1951

Marie Louise Lefort, the first woman appointed a district physician for the city of Newark (1898), was born on September 23, 1874, in an old mansion on Washington Street in Newark (Essex County), NJ. Her parents, Henry and Adalina (Klamere) Lefort, lived comfortably due to Henry Lefort's success as a manufacturer of high-quality watchcase parts. This business, which he inherited from his father, also enabled his daughter to attend the Barringer High School and, later, the Woman's Medical College of the New York Infirmary, where she graduated in 1897 with a medical degree.

After graduation from medical school, Lefort served the Newark community from 1898 until 1902 as district physician. During her tenure as the Board of Health–appointed physician, Lefort saw Newark's previously high death rate drop significantly. The census report in 1910 attributed this change to the "advanced policy of the Board of Health along the line of preventive measures." Since the 1890 census, which listed Newark as having the highest death rate of all American cities with a population of 100,000 or more, preventive medicine techniques had been introduced by the practicing physicians of Newark. Working to overcome crowded, unsanitary living conditions of the city's poor residents, the city's doctors pres-sured the Board of Trade to upgrade occupational conditions throughout the city, which the physicians hoped would thwart the spread of contagious diseases. Newark physicians also concentrated on curbing infant mortality, which had accounted for 50 percent of the deaths in Newark in 1870. Newark experienced its drop to sixth among cities with the lowest death rate by 1910, due, in part, to the implementation of preventive medicine techniques.

Beginning in 1902 Lefort conducted a private medical practice in New York City at 43 E. 28th Street. After practicing for sixteen years, she left New York City in 1918 for the battlefields of France. Until the end of World War I Lefort headed a medical unit that cared for soldiers gassed during the war. Immediately after the war, Lefort became the director of the Temporary Hospital at Rheims, the first hospital to treat civilians in the devastated area surrounding the city. Lefort continued as the director of the Temporary Hospital until November 1924, when it was closed and replaced by the newly opened American Memorial Hospital.

Lefort became the first director of the new hospital and continued in that post until 1939. In 1936 a new wing of the hospital was named for Lefort in honor of her work as director. On March 26, 1939, Lefort was awarded an officership in the French Legion of Honor for her dedication to the hospital and the distinction with which she served the French community. Just after receiving this award, Lefort returned to the United States and retired to Maplewood, NJ, where she remained until her death, at age 76, on August 6, 1951.

Information on Lefort appeared in obituaries in the *Newark Evening News*, Aug. 7, 1951, and the *New York Times*, Aug. 8, 1951.

*Jennifer E. Samuels*

## ANNA LINDNER, 1845–1922

Watercolorist Anna Lindner was one of many women artists of the 19th century to remain largely unrecognized during their lifetime. She was born in Germany on May 13, 1845, and was brought to New York City around 1850 by her parents, Emily D. and George Hermann Lindner. Her father was a carpenter by trade.

Lindner, crippled by polio before she was a year old, was unable to walk without the aid of braces and crutches. Essentially confined to her home, her artistic development is both unique and revealing. Though there are no accounts of her early life, it is believed that she had no formal artistic training. It is evident, however, that the deft hand that rendered her brightly colored watercolors was influenced by outside sources. It was very likely she was affected by several German books, which were left among her few prized possessions. One, a fairy tale reader dated 1856 with "Anna" written on the cover, is profusely illustrated with charming engravings. The other, with "Anna Lindner, 1846" written on the cover, is a spelling book published in 1843 that translates from German into French and English; it contains brightly hand-colored engravings. There are also two leather-bound volumes titled *Dresdener Gallerie*, with the name "H. Lindner" embossed in gold on the covers. These beautiful German books contain high-quality engravings depicting the works of many artists, including Caravaggio, Veronese, Claude Lorraine, Rubens, Rembrandt, and the Dutch Masters. One may assume, therefore, that Lindner's love for art was reinforced by books that were readily available to her. Indeed, her drawings use the delicate crosshatched line so often found in the etchings and book illustrations she apparently admired. It is her use of line in this manner that achieves the nuances of shading in her paintings, whereas her color is applied in a more summary manner, which can be compared to the book illustrations or fashion plates that were prevalent during the 19th century.

Lindner's life has been compared to that of Emily Dickinson, but in contrast, she did not withdraw from the outside world to an inner refuge. Lindner's restricted world of her family and immediate surroundings was the *only* world she knew. She depicted this world with happiness and exactitude, for it represented everything that was available to her.

In 1892 Lindner moved to Bayonne, NJ, to "Tanglewood," the estate of her brother, Frank, a successful New York lithographer, and his wife, Pauline (Seuss) Lindner. Three years later, in 1895, Lindner began a diary, which offers a glimpse into her life and alludes to the sources of inspiration for her artistic observations.

Lindner's first entry in her diary, dated February 19, 1895, marked the birth of her niece Emilie Pauline, named after the child's two grandmothers. Lindner wrote, "This is a journal kept for Emilie to note her progress and study her character."

Thus, Lindner's diary records every detail of raising her beloved niece. Each feeding, crying spell, or outing is dutifully noted. Lindner records Emilie's growth into adolescence with deliberate objectivity of the daily routine, including visitors to the house as well as brief mentions of family birthdays and holidays. The diaries come to life only through the pencil and pen-and-ink drawings that illustrate the pages. Carefully drawn portraits of the sleeping baby reveal the affection and devotion Lindner felt for Emilie. A small sketch of a dogwood bough or a tiny vase of flowers reveals the beauty to which Lindner's thoughts were attracted. As in her finished watercolors, her diaries depict the family scenes and surroundings of her brother's Bayonne estate overlooking Newark Bay. Cats and dogs romping playfully on the front porch, Emilie reading

quietly in a large chair, or small kitchen utensils such as salt and pepper shakers or dishes are drawn with equal dexterity. Lindner's watercolors, including *Tanglewood at Bayonne, A New Jersey Summer, 1901*, and *Caught in the Act*, depict similar scenes from everyday life centered around the Lindner household. The backyard and the front porch are frequent settings for children and pets at play. Another favorite subject for Lindner was the Christmas holiday scene, decorating the house and the tree. Lindner was also fond of birds and floral painting, again rendering every detail with delicacy and accuracy.

In 1908 the Lindners moved to Willard Avenue in Bloomfield, NJ, in order to take Emilie away from the sea air, which was thought to be detrimental to her health. Lindner continued to paint until 1914, when her eyesight began to fail. In the diary of 1908, Emilie has written her own entry and draws small pictures of a doll, flag, Christmas tree, and a cup at the bottom of the page. Lindner had previously mentioned trying to get Emilie to finish a painting for her father before Christmas, perhaps indicating that Lindner wanted to encourage her niece to love drawing as much as she did.

On July 31, 1908, Lindner wrote her last entry and revealed her personal sentiments for the first time: "For this book which I kept for Emilie, I will hereafter write occasionally as Emilie is growing so much away from me. She often seems like a stranger." Lindner felt her role as favorite aunt and "playmate" was gradually slipping away as Emilie became involved with her school activities and friends.

Over 600 of Lindner's watercolors, drawings, and paintings are now in the collection of the New Jersey Historical Society. The majority of these were executed during the period from 1892 to 1908 when Lindner resided at "Tanglewood." The earliest is a pear dated 1863 and the last is a bouquet with goldenrod painted in 1914. The New York Historical Society owns an oil painting by Lindner titled *In the Neighborhood of East 65th Street* (ca. 1870), which was donated by Mrs. L. H. Lindner in 1925. The only known exhibit of her work during her lifetime was *Study of Fruit, 1869*, shown at the National Academy in New York in 1869. Not until 1975 did the New Jersey Historical Society in Newark exhibit Lindner's paintings, which were donated by Emilie (Lindner) Westerdahl. Lindner's works have since been reproduced on note cards and seasonal posters by the Port Authority of New York and New Jersey.

Lindner died of arterial sclerosis on May 26, 1922, at age 77, in Bloomfield, NJ. She was cremated at Linden Cemetery. Her death was not noted publicly, nor were her artistic achievements. Her work has provided a vivid record of middle-class Victorian life as well as a testament to the artistic expression of a woman whose life was restricted but not devastated by her physical constraints.

Lindner's diaries and artworks are kept at the NJ-HS. Several articles about her, many of which contain discrepancies, are: "The Small Bright World of Anna Lindner," *American Heritage* 28 (Dec. 1975):4–10; Jack Sheehan, "Anna Lindner, 1845–1922," *New Jersey History* 96 (Spring-Summer 1978):69; and the *New York Times*, May 4, 1975.

*Lynn Harris Heft*

Clara Louise Maass, a young New Jersey nurse who lost her life in Cuba in 1901 in the battle to eradicate yellow fever, was honored in 1976 by a commemorative postage stamp issued on the centennial of her birth. *Courtesy, U.S. Postal Service.*

## CLARA LOUISE MAASS, 1876–1901

Clara Louise Maass was a heroic nurse who lost her life in the battle to eradicate yellow fever. Born on June 28, 1876, in East Orange (Essex County), NJ, she was the eldest child of Robert E. and Hedwig A. Maass. As young adults Maass's parents emigrated from Germany and settled in New Jersey, where they married and had nine children, six girls and three boys, between 1876 and 1898.

From early childhood, Maass's life in East Orange was full of hard work. She assisted with housework in the care of her siblings and, while still of grade-school age, was boarded with another family as a "mother's helper" to clean and mind their children. She had a short respite when her family moved to a farm in Livingston, NJ, when she was eleven. She attended school in Livingston, but her family soon moved back to East Orange and she again became a mother's helper. Continuing this work, she was able to complete three years of East Orange High School. At fifteen, she left school to work full time in the Newark Orphan Asylum for $10 a month. Half of her pay from this

job was sent home.

In 1893, at age seventeen, Maass became one of the first students to enter the Newark German Hospital School of Nursing. She graduated in 1895 and worked at the hospital, becoming a head nurse early in 1898. Later that year, after the outbreak of the Spanish-American War, Maass applied to be a "contract nurse" in the U.S. Army. She was accepted and served under her first contract in field hospitals in the Seventh Army Corps in Jacksonville, FL, Savannah, GA, and Santiago, Cuba. Most of the soldiers at that time were ill from tropical diseases such as malaria, typhoid fever, and dysentery. Her first army contract ended on February 5, 1899.

When insurrection occurred in the Philippines a short time later, American troops were again placed in tropical surroundings. Late in 1899 Maass applied a second time as a contract nurse and was sent to the Philippines in November. She served at the First Reserve Hospital in Manila until May 1900, caring for soldiers suffering from tropical diseases such as yellow fever, to which they succumbed in great numbers since they did not have the acquired immunity of the natives. While there, Maass saw the terrible ravages of yellow fever and developed a deep interest in its eradication. Maass did not contract yellow fever herself while in the Philippines, but her stay there was cut short by another tropical disease, dengue fever. She was so debilitated by this disease that she was sent back to the United States to recover in May 1900.

Yellow fever had been the scourge of tropical countries for centuries, but after the United States' conquest of Cuba in the Spanish-American War, Major William Gorgas was sent to Havana as chief sanitary officer to wipe out the disease. Gorgas believed that yellow fever was caused by poor sanitation, and therefore in 1898 he carried out a massive campaign to clean up Havana. But the situation became so desperate that by 1900 the U.S. surgeon general established a Yellow Fever Commission, with Major Walter Reed as chair, to investigate the cause of the disease.

After several experiments, the Yellow Fever Commission learned three things: the disease was spread from person to person by the bite of a female Stegomyia mosquito that had sucked the blood of a yellow fever patient within the first three days of the onset of the disease; after biting the patient, the mosquito could infect someone else only after twelve to twenty days had elapsed. Blood taken from a yellow fever patient during the first and second day of the disease and injected into a nonimmune person could also cause yellow fever. And an attack of yellow fever produced by the bite of the mosquito, if survived, conferred on the person immunity against a subsequent injection of blood of a yellow fever patient.

Reed left Cuba early in 1901, having accomplished his mission. He left Gorgas the work of clearing the mosquitoes out of Havana. Gorgas, however, thought that vaccination might be the best measure to prevent the spread of the disease, and Las Animas Hospital, the yellow fever hospital of Havana, was chosen as the site of the program. Dr. John Guiteras took charge of the vaccination work.

By the fall of 1900 Clara Maass had recovered from the dengue fever contracted in the Philippines. She heard of the Yellow Fever Commission and again volunteered to nurse yellow fever patients, this time in Cuba. Maass went to Havana that fall and met with Yellow Fever Commission members. Witnessing their experiments, she was impressed by the commission's efforts to solve the yellow fever problem.

In 1901 Maass learned of Gorgas's and Guiteras's plans to immunize people against yellow fever. They were going to have volunteers submit to infectious mosquito bites to cause mild cases of yellow fever, which would then create immunity. On June 24, 1901, Maass volunteered to be bitten by an infected mosquito. She contracted a mild case, which doctors felt was insufficient to achieve immunity. On August 14, 1901, she again volunteered to be bitten. This time she developed a fatal case of yellow fever. Before she died, Maass wrote to her mother: "Goodby, Mother. Don't worry. God will care for me in the yellow fever hospital the same as if I were at home." (Quoted in Cunningham, *Clara Maass*, 44) During the last ten days of her life, Maass suffered the anguish of yellow fever.

She died, at age 25, on August 24, 1901. A few years later, Gorgas testified: "While [Maass's] case was not directly connected with the experimentation of the army board, it had much more effect in the city of Havana in convincing the physicians and people generally that yellow fever was conveyed by the mosquito than did the army board." (Guinter, "A Nurse among the Heroes of the Yellow Fever Conquest," 175) Gorgas's wife later wrote: "The fact that one of the deaths was that of Miss Maass . . . cast a gloom over the whole proceeding. Inoculation was evidently too dangerous a method of fighting yellow fever, and was accordingly abandoned. It was now apparent that the only possible cure lay . . . in the destruction of mosquitos." (M. Gorgas, *William C. Gorgas*, 116–17)

Clara Maass was buried in Cuba the day after she died. The *New York Journal* ran a story on her on its front page on August 26, and the *New York Times* ran an editorial on the nobleness of her sacrifice. On February 20, 1902, the army brought her coffin back to New Jersey and buried her in Fairmont Cemetery, in Newark, with military honors. The army also granted Maass's mother a pension of $12 a month in recognition of her daughter's sacrifice. Other acknowledgments were made to her by Newark German Hospital and nursing historians.

Then, for a time, Maass seemed to be forgotten. While Leopoldine Guinter was superintendent of nursing at German Hospital in 1927 she noticed a column in the paper headlined "25 Years Ago Today," which told of Maass's burial with military honors. This item spurred Guinter to search out the history of Maass, which brought her into contact with Maass's mother and also took her to Cuba twice to document Maass's story. She then raised funds to erect a new headstone over Maass's weed-strewn grave. The new gravestone displayed a bronze profile of Maass with the engraved epitaph "Greater love hath no man than this."

Other groups and individuals worked to renew public interest in Cuba and the United States in Maass's work. In Newark, the Rev. Arthur Herbert publicized her life and worked to have a commemorative stamp printed in her honor. Eventually, both Cuba and the United States printed a Clara Maass stamp.

Newark German Hospital was renamed Clara Maass Memorial Hospital, and later a son of one of its original founders gave $1 million to build a new Clara Maass Memorial Hospital. Today Maass is honored, along with fourteen other nursing pioneers, in the Nursing Hall of Fame.

Material on Maass is at NJ-HS and NJ-NPL. Biographies are John Cunningham, *Clara Maass: A Nurse, a Hospital, a Spirit* (1968); and Mildred Tengbom, *No Greater Love: The Gripping Story of Clara Maass* (1978), written for younger readers. Her story appears in Marie Gorgas, *William Gorgas: His Life and Work* (1924); and in Leopoldine Guinter, "A Nurse among the Heroes of the Yellow Fever Conquest," *American Journal of Nursing* 32 (1932): 173–76.

*Constance B. Schuyler*

## MARY WILLIAMSON MACFADDEN, 1892–1969

Mary (Williamson) Macfadden, once acclaimed as "Great Britain's Perfect Woman," was born in Oldham, England, on July 13, 1892, to Sarah Ann (Hudson) and Robert Williamson, a mechanical engineer. Because she was sickly, her parents enrolled her in swimming lessons at the Battison Road School, Halifax, and as her health and vigor improved, Macfadden gained recognition in swimming meets. She earned the Award of Merit from the Royal Lifesaving Society when she was fifteen, the youngest girl in England to receive this honor. By the age of nineteen, she had won more than 60 prizes and was acknowledged as one of the swimming champions of England.

While working at a Yorkshire carpet mill, Macfadden was urged to enter a contest for "Great Britain's Perfect Woman," sponsored by Bernarr Macfadden, American physical culturist and publisher. She won the contest, and Bernarr Macfadden as well. They toured England—promoting his physical culture theories through gymnastic performances—and were married in London on March 5, 1913.

She was nineteen and he was 45. His theories, highly controversial at the time, stressed fresh air, exercise, a meatless diet based on nuts and carrots, and an avoidance of alcohol, coffee, and tobacco. He was opposed to doctors and drugs, believing that natural methods were the only cures for illness.

In 1919 the Macfaddens returned to the United States, and he inaugurated *True Story*, a magazine devoted to personal narratives of plain people, their problems, and how they solved them. Mary Macfadden was instrumental in its conception and editing. With no pretension to literary standards, by 1926 it had become the most widely circulated 25-cent monthly in the world.

In support of her husband's doctrines, Macfadden agreed to raise the first "physical culture family." She later said of his philosophy: "It appeared to me that the children I was to have would be looked upon by Bernarr as the beginning of a new race of human beings uncontaminated by the things that had put civilization where he thought it was." (Macfadden, *Dumbbells*, 55) Even at this stage, there were stirrings of her husband's political ambitions. Macfadden faithfully followed a regimen of exercise, diet, and natural childbirth. Deliveries were performed without anesthetics by midwives. She described these experiences in agonizing detail in her biography of her husband, *Dumbbells and Carrot Strips*. After she bore him four daughters, Macfadden participated in his sex-determination experiments. Based on his theory of conception at certain times of the month, she produced three sons. The first died a year after birth. At her husband's insistence, each child's name started with the letter B, forming initials that matched his own.

Financial success increased for Macfadden publications, and the growing family moved to an estate in Englewood, NJ. The Englewood grounds were transformed into a fresh air gymnasium. "People who knew them . . . in Englewood believe that the Macfaddens' domestic life was probably the most energetic on record. His children grew up to be splendid physical specimens, though not as showily muscular as he had hoped." (Taylor, "Physical Culture," 48) Macfadden's sons inherited her swimming abilities: Bruce broke the relay swimming record at Yale and Berwyn was swimming champion of the New York Athletic Club.

Although Macfadden could accept her husband's physical culture theories, she could not support his growing political ambitions. "The man I fell in love with and married in England . . . probably would have continued to be my husband if he had never met his two 'king makers,' who filled him with the idea that he could do in America what a paper-hanger had accomplished in Germany." (Macfadden, *Dumbbells*, 306) One of the "king makers" was Fulton Ousler, an editor for Macfadden publications, who encouraged Macfadden's presidential visions.

Bernarr Macfadden had the notion that his physical fitness theories would resolve the nation's ills and problems. When Mussolini invited him to Italy in 1930 to establish a military training program, he told his wife during the trip: "Woman, you are no longer necessary to my success." (Macfadden, *Dumbbells*, 405) Disillusioned with her husband's expanding ego and erratic demands, she returned to the United States. He later became a Republican nominee for president, but his costly campaigns angered stockholders, who claimed he was using corporate funds for personal use. His wife's comment on his obsession was hardly flattering: "I will attempt to draw few morals or conclusions of a social aspect from the tragic situation that was to develop from all this and to be headlined from coast to coast, including even my hometown paper in Yorkshire. In the middle of it, I was often to wish I was back dreaming at my loom in the carpet mill." (Macfadden, *Dumbbells*, 308) The Macfaddens separated in 1933 and, after protracted legal proceedings, were divorced in 1946.

Macfadden continued to live in the Englewood mansion. Always a strong proponent of swimming, she urged the initiation of compulsory swimming training for members of the armed services after the drowning of six marines. Her correspondence was cited in the *Congressional Record* of the 84th Congress, and in 1958 she had an entry in *Who's Who of American Women*. In an interview a year before her death, she said: "I truly believe that, next to walking, swimming is the best possible exercise for a woman." (*Bergen County Record*, Jan. 24, 1968)

Described by former friends and neighbors as a lovely and lonely woman, Macfadden died, at age 77, in Englewood of a heart ailment on November 26, 1969, and was buried in the Woodlawn Cemetery, Bronx, NY.

Macfadden's biography of her husband, *Dumbbells and Carrot Strips* (1955), contains insights into her own life. Telephone interviews with friends and neighbors of the Macfaddens—Julia Lamb, Englewood, NJ; and Campbell Noorsgaard, Lakeville, CT—provided useful insights. See also: "Macfadden Family Lived Today's Fitness Program," *Record* (Hackensack, NJ), Jan. 24, 1968; and Robert Lewis Taylor, "Profiles: Physical Culture," *New Yorker* 26 (Oct. 28, 1950):37–51. Her obituary appeared in the *New York Times*, Nov. 27, 1969.

*Elizabeth Keill*

## ABBIE ELIZA MAGEE, 1847–1909

Abbie Eliza Magee, born on August 19, 1847, in Marlboro Township (Monmouth County), NJ, was a farm woman and diarist. Her father, a farmer, James J. R. Magee, and her mother, Sarah Jane (Cahill) Magee, both New Jersey natives, were the parents of seven daughters, all born between 1837 and 1851. The household also included an invalid grandmother.

Two of Magee's sisters, Margaret and Jane, died within

months of each other, in early childhood. Two other sisters died as young wives. Eleanor and Lydia both married and raised families, and Abbie remained at home to care for her parents.

There is no record of Magee's formal education, even though her grandfather was founder and head of the Magee school district in Marlboro Township. In 1865 Magee's sister Angeline Magee Kipp died, leaving two small children, Charles H. and Mary Kate. Two years later, when Magee was 20, her mother died. Magee kept house for her father and her sister's two small children on the Magee family farm in the Union Hill school section of Marlboro. It was with Mary Kate Kipp McElvaine (known as Kate in the diary) that she eventually made her home.

Abbie Eliza Magee left a detailed record of the life of a rural New Jersey woman in the diary she carefully kept during 1905. *Courtesy, Lydia Stillwell Wikoff.*

After her father's death in 1882, Magee supported herself by living and working in the homes of others. She lived in a close-knit community made up of her sisters and their husbands and children, aunts, uncles, hired hands, church and neighborhood friends, and her pastor, the Rev. F. R. Symmes of the historic Old Tennent Church in Tennent, NJ. In her diary, she recorded the daily life of a single woman on a turn-of-the-century New Jersey farm, focusing on her family and friends.

"Aunt Abbie," as she was known to the young children of the area, was a special favorite. She was remembered as "quite tall with brown eyes. She wore her hair in the style of the day, taken up and wrapped in a knot on top of her head. She was so much fun for the children and would give us cookies whenever she came." (Marion Symmes, Interview, Sept. 15, 1985)

Magee's extant diary begins on January 1, 1905, with a simple penciled notation: "Here we are started on another

year. I went to Church and stopped on the corner. I do wonder what will happen this year." Of particular interest is the initial *K* on the entry, denoting her primary residence at the home of her niece Kate. When Magee went to the homes of family members or people from the community who needed her, she marked her diary with the first initial of the name of the lady of the house. Thus we find her diary marked with an *L* on January 8, when she went to help her sister Lydia Magee Stillwell. Over the course of the year she lived and worked in six households.

While she was at these homes she did a variety of chores: washing and cleaning the cellar, where the milk was stored; cleaning the out-kitchen; washing clothes on a Monday and ironing on a Tuesday; churning butter and tending the kitchen garden. Her diary shows that between January 9 and 12 she and Lydia killed and cut up hogs, producing 128 pounds of sausage.

Magee was paid for the chores she performed and recorded a partial list of accounts at the end of her diary: "For cutting potatoes [for planting] - $1.50; for cleaning house - $2.00; for keeping house while Lydia had her operation - $5.00; for canning - $5.00; for Christmas - $10.00." Her largest source of income—and most frequently mentioned activity—was sewing and dressmaking. Her diary lists income from "dressmaking - $5.00; making curtains - $10.00; for making Wilbur's [Kate's five-year-old son] dresses - $1.00." Her diary recounts numerous occasions on which she stayed at the homes of others for the express purpose of refurbishing their wardrobes. On February 17 and 18 she wrote: "Olive and Tennent [her niece and nephew] came for me at night. I sewed on Aunt Ellen's old dress." On February 23 she was again at Ellen's and "made two blankets." She sewed for Lydia and Kate that winter. By June she found time to make herself a lawn dress and the next day she sewed again "all day making skirts shorter." Through prudent management, Magee accumulated an estate of $2,000, which at her death was shared in three parts by her sisters Eleanor and Lydia, with the remaining part divided between her niece and nephew Kate and Charles.

Magee's August 1905 entries describe the local celebration of Harvest Home, a community feast of the harvest that kept the womenfolk busy for weeks. August 4: "Kate started to solicit for the Harvest Home." On August 8, Magee took her turn and "went soliciting in the morning and to give in report in the afternoon - tomatoes, peaches and corn." Working for Harvest Home meant not only soliciting the foods but preparing them as well. Chickens, for instance, were donated live. The women would then kill, singe, pluck, dress, and finally cook them.

The fall of the year found the farm women besieged by threshers and pressers. On November 22 Magee wrote: "Threshers came. Seventeen in family." Threshers and pressers, who went from farm to farm, worked with farm families to bring in the crops. The women were responsible for feeding these large groups. On November 25 Magee wrote: "Pressers here. Feel tough and overworked." Then on December 12: "Hurrah, Threshing sounds like hell-a-balu." Finally on December 15, after the crops were in, she wrote: ". . . cold and snow. I made Lydia a wrapper to keep her warm."

The year brought its share of troubles to Magee's circle. On March 27, 1905, a terrible accident occurred. "Staats' [Lydia's oldest son] man sawed his hand off." In order to reach a hospital, Staats Stillwell had to take his hired man by wagon to Freehold, where they boarded a train for Trenton. Two months later Magee was to be upset by another event. She wrote on May 25: "Kate just told me that Charles [the nephew she had raised] is gone to smoking. I cryed [*sic*] to beat the band. What next."

Magee describes a life filled with hard work and close relationships. People shared frequent visits over tea and supper. They relished newly ripened raspberries and the first ice cream. Magee shared in the care of families and their homes. Her diary portrays a life of selfless and devoted service to others. Her company and cheerful ways were sought after as much as her dressmaking and sewing skills. Each Sunday found this community at prayer in Old Tennent Church. On December 31 Magee closed her diary as it had begun: "Went to Church and stopped on my way home. . . . This ends another year."

Magee died on February 11, 1909, at the age of 63, at the home of her sister Lydia, of an "aggravated form of jaundice." Deeply mourned by family and community, she was eulogized by her friend the Rev. Symmes and buried in the Magee family plot in the Old Tennent Churchyard. Her tombstone gives testimony to a life well lived. It reads: "She is missed."

The Magee diary is available at NJ-RU. Genealogical information appears in F. R. Symmes, *History of Old Tennent Church* (1904). Further information about Magee and the events of 1905 came from interviews with her grandniece, Lydia Stillwell Wikoff, on Sept. 14, 1985, and from a telephone interview with Marion Symmes, daughter of the Rev. F. R. Symmes, on Sept. 15, 1985. The eulogy preached by the Rev. Symmes at Magee's funeral is in Wikoff's personal collection, and records regarding the disposition of Magee's estate are in the Monmouth County Surrogates' Office.

*Margaret Dooley Nitka*

## MOTHER MARY XAVIER MEHEGAN, 1825–1915

Mother Mary Xavier Mehegan, religious, educator, and founder of the Sisters of Charity of New Jersey, was born in Skibbereen, County Cork, Ireland, on February 19, 1825. Christened Catherine Josephine Mehegan, she was the youngest of nine children of Patrick and Joanne

Mother Mary Xavier Mehegan, an Irish immigrant, founded the Sisters of Charity of New Jersey as well as the College of Saint Elizabeth, the first college for women in New Jersey. This portrait was probably taken in 1897 in honor of her 50 years as a religious. *Courtesy, College of Saint Elizabeth.*

(Miles) Mehegan. Little is known about the early years of her life, except that her parents were farmers of modest circumstances. Her father, to whom she was devoted, died while she was still young.

Her life was influenced by currents of thought and social forces barely understood at that time. For a Catholic child of the 1820s and 1830s, Ireland offered many disadvantages, and a future that, at best, was bleak. Until the system of national education was founded in 1831, education was only for Protestants and those Roman Catholics willing to participate in Protestant religious instruction. Many Catholic children, therefore, were taught at home by their parents.

Emigration became a way of escaping poverty and gaining the right to earn a living. What inspired Mother Xavier to leave home for America is not known for certain. In 1842, without her mother's knowledge, she coaxed money from her brother Edward and persuaded her sister Margaret, who was three years her senior, to join her on the journey.

No facts are available concerning the date or circumstances of the two girls' arrival in America, nor is it possible to say where they lived in New York or how they supported themselves during these first months. However, since both girls were skilled seamstresses, it is possible that they were employed in dressmaking.

During this time Timothy, the eldest Mehegan child, was dispatched by his mother to bring his sisters back to Ireland since she feared for their safety. Instead of fulfilling that charge, Timothy Mehegan settled in New York and made a home for his sisters on Greenwich Street. Timothy was married in 1844, and in 1847 he and his wife moved to Chicago. Three years later, he moved to St. Paul, MN, where he died in 1854. Despite the strong affection between Timothy and his sister Catherine, he never communicated with her after he left New York.

When her sister Margaret married and moved to Australia, Mother Xavier was left alone. Motivated by the pressing needs of Catholics in New York, especially children, she applied for admission to the New York Sisters of Charity. Shortly before her 22nd birthday on February 16, 1847, she became the first of three postulants received by Mother Elizabeth Boyle of the Sisters of Charity of New York.

She made her profession of vows as Sister Mary Xavier and spent twelve years as a Sister of Charity of New York, serving at first in the newly opened Saint Vincent Hospital in New York City. In time, she transferred from hospital work to orphanages and was sent to Jersey City, NJ, for that purpose. She later returned to New York, to the Industrial School in Brooklyn, and then to Saint Lawrence Academy, Yorkville, before she was sent to New Jersey to succeed Sister M. Borgia, at Saint Joseph's Parish in Newark, in 1857.

In 1859 she was one of two sisters loaned for three years by the New York Sisters of Charity to direct the work and religious life of five novices in the diocese of Newark. One year later their Newark facilities were no longer adequate and the sisters purchased 43 acres in Madison, NJ, from Seton Hall, the diocesan seminary. The move to the new motherhouse, named Saint Elizabeth, took place on July 2, 1860. The members of the new community worked in Newark, Jersey City, and Paterson.

Though the two New York religious were to return to New York at the end of three years, both of them elected to remain with the New Jersey community. James Roosevelt Bayley, bishop of the diocese of Newark, had always looked upon Sister Mary Xavier as the "mother" of the community, and after 1863 this designation was generally accepted. At 38, she was a small, physically frail figure who was humble and self-effacing. But she possessed a shrewd mind and a fearless spirit.

These characteristics served her well, for during the next fifteen years, she successfully amassed 225 acres of

land for her growing community. She had it incorporated in 1864 and arranged for the location of a railroad station on the grounds by agreeing to pay the salary of the first stationmaster for the Lackawanna Railroad. A new convent and academy were erected at Convent Station in 1880. By that year the New Jersey community of the Sisters of Charity owned and managed seven academies, one orphanage, one hospital, and 42 missions, including missions in Massachusetts and Connecticut.

Her early experience in orphanages and a hospital prompted Mother Xavier's continued efforts to serve the sick and the needy, especially the children. She opened seven hospitals, along with nurses' training schools, orphanages, homes for the aged, and a residence for working women. Five of the hospitals, all opened between 1867 and 1913, were located in New Jersey. They were Saint Joseph's, in Paterson; Saint Mary's, in Passaic; Saint Vincent's, in Montclair; Saint Elizabeth's, in Elizabeth; and All Souls, in Morristown.

Perhaps Mother Xavier's most far-reaching decision was her grant of permission for the opening of a Catholic college for women. On September 8, 1899, the College of Saint Elizabeth at Convent Station welcomed its first college class and became the first continuous four-year college for women in New Jersey and one of the first Catholic colleges for women in the United States. Xavier Hall, a new building named in honor of Mother Xavier Mehegan, was completed in 1900.

By 1900 Mother Xavier had begun to feel the weight of her advancing years and had relinquished first one, then another duty. In the early months of 1915 her health steadily declined. On June 24, 1915, at age 90, Mother Xavier died of cardiac arrest at the motherhouse of the Sisters of Charity of Saint Elizabeth at Convent Station. She was buried in the cemetery of the motherhouse on June 28, 1915. She had exercised authority over her community for 56 years and had spent 64 years as a religious. She left behind a community of 1,200 sisters and 94 missions.

The archives of the Sisters of Charity of Saint Elizabeth (Convent Station, NJ) contain some of Mother Mary Xavier Mehegan's personal papers and correspondence. Sister Blanche Marie McEniry, *Woman of Decision* (1953), is Mother Xavier's biography and Sister Mary Agnes Sharkey, *The New Jersey Sisters of Charity*, 3 vols. (1933), describes her founding of the community.

*Sister Blanche Marie McEniry*

## ALICE DUER MILLER, 1874–1942

Alice Maude (Duer) Miller, novelist, poet, and screenwriter, was born on July 28, 1874, on Staten Island, NY, to Elizabeth Wilson (Meads) and James Gore King Duer, a banker, whose distinguished lineage included SARAH LIVINGSTON ALEXANDER and William Alexander, as well as William Alexander Duer, president of Columbia College from 1829 to 1842.

Miller had two older sisters, Caroline King (b. 1865), author and editor of *Vogue* for several years, and Eleanor Theodora (b. 1870). Soon after Miller's birth, financial difficulties forced the Duers to move to Hauxhurst, the estate of Denning Duer, her paternal grandfather, in Weehawken, NJ, on the cliffs of the Palisades half a mile north of the present entrance to the Lincoln Tunnel.

Miller's first ten years were spent at Hauxhurst, where she was surrounded by her immediate family, her grandfather, two maiden aunts, at least twelve servants, and a host of visitors. She became an expert horsewoman and an avid reader, devouring Victorian novels as well as texts on astronomy and mathematics. In 1884 her maternal grandfather died and left enough money for the family to move back to New York into a small house at 127 East 25th Street. In New York her formal education began at Miss Ballou's School on East 22nd Street. Miller graduated in 1896, was presented to society, and much to the shock of her social set decided to go to college and pursue the study of mathematics.

She started at Barnard College in 1896, completed her studies in three years, graduating in 1899, and received the Kohn Mathematical Prize for excellence in mathematics. While at college she helped pay her expenses by writing stories, poems, and essays for *Harper's* and *Scribner's*. Her first published work was the book *Poems,* which she wrote with her sister Caroline in 1896.

Upon graduation she was offered a post as head of the mathematics department of the Brearley School; instead, on October 5, 1899, she married Henry Wise Miller at his home in Morristown, NJ, now known as Macculloch Hall. Henry Miller, a Harvard graduate, was born in 1877 in Nice, France, where his father was serving with the U.S. Navy. He was the brother of DOROTHEA MILLER POST.

The Millers sailed for Costa Rica ten days after they wed. Henry Miller was in charge of a rubber plantation under the sponsorship of the General Electric Company. The couple lived in Costa Rica for three years, and on a brief trip home to New York in September 1901 Denning Duer Miller, their only child, was born. It was in Costa Rica, with her husband off to the fields every day, that Miller "developed her day-in-day-out capacity for work which was the basis of her success as an author." (Miller, *All Our Lives,* 50) *The Modern Obstacle* (1903), her first novel, was written there.

Fever and fiscal difficulties forced the Millers to return to New York in 1903. From 1903 to 1907 they struggled financially, but by 1907 Henry Miller had worked his way up to a trading desk on the New York Stock Exchange, and Miller could write in earnest.

During the 1910s Miller became involved with the woman suffrage movement. From 1914 to 1917 she contributed a weekly column titled "Are Women People?" to the *Sunday New York Tribune.* The heavily ironic and humorous poems included in the column poked fun at the hypocritical nature of antisuffrage arguments. Miller was active in the New York State suffrage campaigns and spoke throughout the state.

Real success and popularity came to Miller in 1915, after fifteen years of steady writing and the publication of seven novels. When her serial *Come Out of the Kitchen* appeared in *Harper's Bazar,* it brought her immediate recognition. It soon became a best-selling novel, then a Broadway play and a motion picture.

Other successful novels followed—almost at the rate of one a year—including the best-sellers *The Charm School* (1919) and *Gowns by Robert* (1933). This latter novel became the Jerome Kern musical *Roberta* and the source for two movies: *Roberta* and *Lovely to Look At.*

Most of Miller's stories and novels were romantic love stories. She had once hoped to be considered a "literary genius" but soon reconciled herself to the ready market and easy money of her romances. In fact, during the 43 years of her writing career she had only three stories rejected. Her frothy narratives did not go unnoticed by the critics. A profile by Harvey O'Higgins in a February 1927 issue of the *New Yorker* states: "She is an inspiring popular success but the pundits of literature do not seriously appraise her. She is the sort of author who sells magazines for editors, books for publishers and plays and films for producers but none of the doctors seem to recognize that this vitality derives from the very blood of art." (O'Higgins, 27)

Since several of her novels were made into movies, Miller went frequently to Hollywood for the Goldwyn and Paramount studios to write scenarios, advise the producers, and in one case to take a part as a spoiled daughter of a millionaire in the movie *Soak the Rich* (1935). Her writing for the movies served as an introduction into a circle of friends that included Alexander Woolcott, Noel Coward, Robert Benchley, Heywood Hayle Broun, Irving Berlin, Edna Ferber and Dorothy Parker. She often traveled to Europe with friends drawn from the celebrity circle. Miller was also a member of Heterodoxy, a New York luncheon group composed of women in public life and which included another noted New Jersey woman, ALISON LOW TURNBULL HOPKINS.

Although Miller's poetry is considered inferior to her prose, she is best remembered for *The White Cliffs* (1940), a serious narrative poem about an American girl who marries an Englishman, loses him in World War I, bears his son and finds herself facing the peril of sending this son off to another war. The poem, which critics considered childish and singsongy, enjoyed an extraordinary success and was read twice on NBC by Lynn Fontanne for the British War

Relief. It was subsequently made into a phonograph record and a film.

Miller was a devoted trustee of Barnard College, her alma mater, from 1922 until her death. Columbia University awarded her the University Medal in 1933 and made her an honorary Doctor of Letters in 1942.

Miller died of cancer in New York City, at age 68, on August 22, 1942, after an eight-month battle with the illness. She was buried in Evergreen Cemetery in Morristown.

A collection of material on Miller is available at the Wollman Library, Barnard College (New York, NY). Her husband's biography of her is *All Our Lives* (1945). Sketches of her appeared in the *New Yorker*, Feb. 19, 1942, and in *NAW*. Her obituary appeared in the *New York Times*, Aug. 23, 1942.

*Judith Heaney Rousseau*

Elisabeth "Bessie" Holmes Moore of Ridgewood was four-time winner of the U.S. Women's Singles Championship in lawn tennis beginning in in 1896. *Collections of the International Tennis Hall of Fame, Newport, RI.*

## ELISABETH "BESSIE" HOLMES MOORE, 1876–1959

Skillful at lawn tennis from early youth, Elisabeth "Bessie" Holmes Moore was the first to win the United States Women's Singles Championship four times (1896, 1901, 1903, and 1905), a total exceeded only by four others, and was elected posthumously to the National Lawn Tennis Hall of Fame in 1971.

Born on March 5, 1876, in Brooklyn, NY, and named for her maternal grandmother, Moore was the younger daughter of George Edward Moore (1840–1911), an affluent cotton broker born in London, Ontario (Canada), of parents from Ireland, and Sarah Z. (Orr) Moore (1857–1942) from New Baltimore, NY, whose father also was born in London, Ontario, of parents from Ireland. Raised and schooled at Ridgewood (Bergen County), NJ, Moore rode her white pony on local trails and roads and, at age twelve, learned to play lawn tennis.

Lawn tennis, partly derived from the ancient game of tennis, spread into America from England during the mid-1870s and flourished as a sport for both men and women during the 1880s. By 1890 a dozen New Jersey clubs belonged to the United States National Lawn Tennis Association and had developed competitors like Ann Burdett (1873–1947) of Englewood (Bergen County), a Vassar College student and U.S. Women's Doubles Champion; Emma (Leavitt) Morgan (1865–1956) of Short Hills (Essex County), already a mother and society matron, the first left-handed woman titleholder; and Lida Voorhees of Bergen Point (Hudson County), who won the 1889 U.S. Women's Singles All-Comers Tournament, but lost in the challenge round to the previous year's tournament winner.

Moore surpassed these players. Encouraged by her father, the president of the Hohokus Valley Tennis Club in the 1890s, she won the club's Women's Singles Championship in 1890. Her first important tournament was at the Ladies Club for Outdoor Sports on Staten Island, NY, in September 1891, where the fifteen-year-old almost won a set before succumbing to Ellen Roosevelt, the 1890 national champion (and first cousin of Franklin Delano Roosevelt). A New Jerseyite did take first prize, however: Burdett defeated Roosevelt in the final.

Moore became the sensation of the National Women's Championships in Philadelphia in June 1892. Quiet, modest, well mannered, good humored, with a ready smile—and clearly the spectators' favorite—she won the all-comers and challenged Mabel Cahill, the stand-out champion. Moore evened the best-of-five-sets match by winning the fourth set decisively from an obviously tired Cahill and appeared the likely winner—but lost.

Clarence Hobart, in "Hobart Talks of Tennis" (June 1896, newspaper unidentified), wrote: "she might have won if she had not then made the common mistake of waiting about outdoors after the fourth set without any extra covering while her opponent retired to the clubhouse for a longer rest than she was entitled to under the rules. Through this carelessness Miss Moore was utterly unable to do herself justice in the fifth set." Thus vanished the opportunity to become the youngest U.S. Singles Champion ever at sixteen years, three months, and eighteen days (which would have made her five months younger than Tracy Austin, when she won in 1979). In succeeding championship matches, Moore lost an 1893 semifinal to Aline Terry, missed the 1894 meeting because of illness, lost the 1895 final to Juliette Atkinson, and then won the 1896 tournament handily, defeating Atkinson in the challenge round.

Not as quick, fast of foot, or hard hitting as her chief rivals, the short, slightly stocky Moore played a slow-paced, all-court style, relying on tireless court coverage, anticipation, accuracy of shot, and sound tactical judgment. Her backhands and forehands were stroked with equal expertise, a rarity among women players of that period. Usually she returned any balls reached, outsteadied baseliners, and thwarted net attackers with passing placements and lobs. An early Ridgewood opponent remembered Moore playing equally well left- and right-handed, but she was solely a right-hander in important tournaments.

As stand-out champion in 1897, she lost a five-set challenge from Atkinson. The first prominent American woman player to compete in Europe, Moore entered the 1898 Irish Championships at Dublin, where she lost. Then ill health sidelined her until 1901.

Moore said, "In 1901 I got my breath back enough to make a comeback." She regained her championship by vanquishing Atkinson and winning exhausting five-setters from Marion Jones and Myrtle McAteer. Moore fainted during the 1902 challenge round, could not continue, and defaulted to Jones, but won her title back in 1903. From 1892 through 1901 the best-of-five-set final and challenge rounds rules maintained, but then the length was shortened to best of three sets, despite objections from Moore and other women. Moore protested publicly: "I do not think any such change should have been made without first canvassing the wishes of the women players. . . . Lawn tennis is a game not alone of skill but of endurance as well, and I fail to see why such a radical change should be made to satisfy a few players, who do not take the time or have the inclination to get themselves in proper condition for playing."

May Sutton routed her in 1904 but Moore won again in 1905. Her three triumphs in 1901, 1903, and 1905 permanently retired the second U.S. Women's Challenge Cup (Atkinson secured the first after three wins in 1898). With this accomplished, she never again played in the National Outdoor Singles. She did, however, win the 1896 U.S. Doubles Championships with Atkinson, the 1903 crown

with Carrie Neely, and the U.S. mixed doubles of 1902 and 1904 with Wylie Grant.

Moore moved to New York, NY, and wintered at the family home in Melrose, FL. She also traveled abroad and played frequently in her favorite European tournament at Hamburg, Germany. She won the first U.S. Indoor Women's Singles Championship in 1907 and the first such doubles title with Helena (Hellwig) Pouch the next year. Thereafter Moore competed mostly in doubles but as late as 1919 reached singles finals in two leading eastern tournaments.

She died, at age 82, from congestive heart failure on January 22, 1959, at Starke, FL. Her death certificate indicated a history of emphysema, probably the illness that plagued her youth.

Moore's tennis career is traceable through issues of the *New York Times*, the *New York Herald*, and the *Philadelphia Inquirer*, as well as in the *Official Lawn Tennis Bulletin* and *American Lawn Tennis*. Her article "Seventeen Years of Woman's Tennis" appeared in *Fifty Years of Lawn Tennis in the United States* (1931) and her letter "Against Shorter Matches for Women" was published in *Lawn Tennis* 2 (1902): 116. Biographical information appeared in "A Coming Tennis Champion," *Harper's Young People* (Aug. 9, 1892):683–84, and in her obituary in the *Ridgewood Herald-News*, Jan. 25, 1959.

*Frank Van Rensselaer Phelps*

## MARY NIMMO MORAN, 1842–1899

Mary Nimmo Moran was one of the first women to achieve recognition in the American painter-etcher movement during the last decades of the 19th century. Born in Strathaven, Lanarkshire, near Glasgow, Scotland, on May 16, 1842, she was the younger child and only daughter of Archibald and Mary (Scott) Nimmo. Her father brought the five-year-old Mary and her brother, Archibald, Jr., to America in 1847, after her mother's death. They settled in Crescentville, PA, a suburb of Philadelphia, where Archibald Nimmo was probably a weaver by trade.

As a young woman Moran was attractive and still retained the burr of her native Scotland when she spoke. Her small frame was accentuated by dark, wide-set eyes and dark curls that reached to her shoulders. She developed an affinity for her young neighbor Thomas Moran, whose family had emigrated from the textile center of Lancashire, England, to Philadelphia in 1858. Thomas Moran was an illustrator at the threshold of a promising career.

The couple married in 1862 after a long engagement. Like many women artists of the 19th century whose careers were inspired by their husbands or other male family members, Mary Moran's love of art was the result of her husband's influence and instruction. Soon after their marriage Moran began to study drawing and painting with him. Subsequently she wrote: "from him came all my first impressions of art and of nature as applied to art. Up to that time I had never thought of using the brush or pencil. We were married in 1862 and from that time on, I may say I have always been my husband's pupil." (Moran, manuscript) She began working in watercolors and was later encouraged to introduce oils. Thomas Moran recognized her talent, which had an originality and a vitality all its own. Moran's early watercolors and oils were exhibited at the Pennsylvania Academy. As her competence increased, she became her husband's trusted critic. Their artistic relationship was mutually beneficial, and they encouraged each other with sympathy and understanding.

The Morans traveled in Europe in 1866 to draw and study the "old masters," and took their first child, Paul Nimmo (b. 1864), with them. Upon returning to Philadelphia, Moran gave birth to a daughter, Mary Scott, in 1868, and a second daughter, Ruth Bedford, in 1870. Domestic responsibilities began to curtail the time she could devote to artistic endeavors. When Thomas Moran was commissioned to produce artwork for *Scribner's Monthly* magazine, the family moved closer to New York City, to a house at 61 Sherman Street in Newark, NJ. Though Newark itself held little attraction for them, the surrounding countryside was reminiscent of the French landscape they had admired in 1866. The meadowlands of the Hackensack and Passaic rivers and the views from the Communipaw in Jersey City, or west to the Watchung Mountains and Scotch Plains, provided inspiration similar to that of the pastoral scenes of the French Barbizon. Moran continued working in New Jersey periodically until 1879 and exhibited her paintings at the Pennsylvania Academy.

In 1872 the Morans purchased another house in Newark, at 9 Thomas Street, which became the gathering place for many notables in the art, literary, and publishing worlds. The revival in the interest in etching and the establishment of the New York Etching Club in 1870 prompted Thomas Moran to renew his own work in the medium. He prepared six plates for his wife to etch while he was away on a western expedition in 1879. Since she was reluctant to use the fresh plates for her first attempt at the medium, she waxed the back of her copper calling card plate and drew a scene on it of the St. John's River. A short time later, while vacationing in Easton, PA, she took a plate and, leading her daughter Ruth by the hand, went outdoors and enthusiastically made a small sketch of a bridge across the Bushkill. Thus Moran began work in a medium that well suited her talents and style; for the next twenty years she was one of America's foremost etchers.

In 1879 Thomas Moran chose four of her etchings to submit to the New York Etching Club. They were signed M. Nimmo and were assumed to be the work of a man. No one suspected that the vigorous and bold lines were done by a woman's hand. The next year the same four etchings were sent to the Royal Society of Painter-Etchers in London, where they were instantly admired. On the strength of these, Moran became the first woman to be admitted to that society.

Two of the prints she submitted depicted New Jersey scenes: *Newark, NJ from the Passaic* and *Hayrides - Newark Meadows*. The vitality of Moran's etching can be attributed to her direct impressions from nature. Sylvestor Rosa Koehler, the first curator of prints at the Boston Museum of Fine Arts, described her etching technique as "nervous, vigorous, rapid and bitten in with a thorough appreciation of the relations of the needle and acid, preferring robustness of line to extreme delicacy." (Koehler, "Works of the American Etchers," 183–84) Her work was clearly the epitome of the painterly quality in etching. Her achievement in nonreproductive printmaking reflects the spontaneity of her observations, as well as her technical control of the medium. While her initial prints were of rustic scenes drawn from locations she had sketched earlier near her New Jersey residence and in Pennsylvania, her final work was done in East Hampton, Long Island, where the landscape, with its inlets and ponds, provided a constant source of inspiration. Her etchings also depicted the romantic ruins and countryside of Scotland and Wales, which she had sketched during a family trip in 1882.

Moran's etchings were included in the exhibition "American Etchings" at the Boston Museum in 1881. The innovative exhibit in 1887 of "The Work of the Women Etchers of America," also at the Boston Museum, included 54 of her etchings. A year later the Union League Club of New York expanded the exhibit and Moran's *Twilight* appeared as the frontispiece of the catalog. She received a medal and diploma for her work at the Chicago Exposition in 1893, yet it wasn't until 1950 that the Smithsonian Institution in Washington, D.C., exhibited a retrospective of her work.

Moran died in East Hampton, Long Island, at age 57, on September 25, 1899, of enterocolitis, after nursing her daughter Ruth through typhoid fever. She was buried in East Hampton opposite the old windmill that was so often seen in her paintings and etchings.

Moran's manuscripts and correspondence are part of the Thomas Moran Biographical Art Collection, East Hampton (NY) Free Library. Articles on her life and work are: Sylvestor Rosa Koehler, "Works of the American Etchers XX, Mary Nimmo Moran," *American Art Review* 2 (1881):183–84; and Marilyn Francis, "Mary Nimmo Moran: Painter-Etcher," *Women's Art Journal* (Winter 1983–84):14–19. She is profiled in *NAW*.

*Lynn Harris Heft*

## MARY STANAHAN HART PATTISON, 1869–1951

Mary Stanahan (Hart) Pattison (known as "Molly"), "domestic engineer," was born on September 7, 1869, in Brooklyn, NY. The only child of Diantha Fitch (Bunnell) and George William Hart, Pattison claimed French and English heritage reaching back to John Hart, a signer of the Declaration of Independence, and to various other early New England colonists. Shortly after her birth, Pattison's parents moved to New Brunswick, NJ, where George Hart was employed as a Custom House officer, and soon after to Metuchen, where Pattison received her education through private tutors, public schools, the Marshall Private School, and the Jackson Seminary.

On June 6, 1893, she wed Frank Ambler Pattison, also of Metuchen, at St. Ignatius Episcopal Church in New York City. Frank Pattison, a Rutgers University graduate, and his brother had formed their own mechanical and electrical engineering consulting firm, which was responsible for the planning of the electrical, mechanical, heating, and ventilating systems for such prominent buildings as the Museum of New York, the Dix Building, and the old New York Stock Exchange. The first years of the Pattisons' marriage were spent in New York, where their two children were born—a daughter, Diantha, in 1896, and a son, Maynicke, in 1905. In 1908 the Pattisons returned to New Jersey, settling in Colonia, a small, predominantly wealthy community near Metuchen.

Frank and Mary Pattison shared a common outlook on life as defined in the early 20th century by the Progressive party. This meant supporting a general improvement in living conditions for the poor, better working conditions and fewer work hours for laborers, prison reform, abolition of child labor, more direct participation in government, woman suffrage, and foreign policy that would lead to world peace. Pattison's husband followed the path traditional for males by participating in the electoral campaigns of such Progressive party presidential candidates as Robert LaFollette, Sr. She followed the path traditional for females by becoming involved initially in such projects as Metuchen's antilittering campaign, which resulted in the founding of the Borough Improvement League, and later by joining the New Jersey State Federation of Women's Clubs (NJFWC), a branch of the General Federation of Women's Clubs, a massive organization of middle- and upper-class women who supported the same general issues as the Progressives did.

In 1909 Pattison was elected president of the NJFWC and by 1911 was the New Jersey secretary for the national organization. In 1912 she joined the State Committee of the Progressive party and in 1913 chaired the Women's Campaign Committee for a local candidate. At the time, New Jersey women did not yet have the vote. At the same time, Pattison served as secretary of the New Jersey branch of the Congressional Union, the militant arm of the woman suffrage movement, and also served as district chair of the New Jersey Woman's Peace Party (WPP), a local chapter of the National WPP, formed in 1915 to encourage U.S. mediation of the European war.

Pattison's chief motivation for her political work was her belief that women's true calling was homemaking, but that the role of homemaker had to be made more socially responsible, efficient, interesting, and creative in order to appeal to the many college educated and middle-class women being attracted away from the home by new career choices. To this end, she concentrated her efforts on the field of "domestic engineering." On June 9, 1910, under the auspices of the NJFWC, Pattison opened a State Housekeeping Experiment Station at her Colonia home. Her hope was to solve three major problems of the day: the high cost of living; the servant shortage caused by the movement of domestic workers into other higher-paying, less time-consuming positions; and "to eliminate drudgery." (Fuller, *A History*, 31)

In her book *The Principles of Domestic Engineering* (1914), Pattison described both the ideology and experiments completed during the year of the station's existence. She acknowledged that her plan required that people have money. Although they need not be wealthy, they did need "proper training, culture, and a broad-minded attitude" to understand what needed to be done. (Pattison, *Principles*, 35) Most of the experiments involved the use of the latest household devices. Denatured alcohol, coal, gas, and electricity were all studied to determine which energy source was best suited to household use. The latest ovens and other cooking and cleaning devices were tried and tested, and of particular fascination was an electric motor that powered everything from a coffee grinder to a vacuum cleaner to a dishwasher.

Another focus of the experiment station was the concept of time-motion study, making Pattison a pioneer in the movement led by Frederich W. Taylor and Harrington Emerson that revolutionized industrial management. Whether scraping a dinner plate or folding a bed sheet, the objective was to perform a task with the least amount of labor in the shortest time possible.

A third and equally important element of the experiment station was the promotion of the aesthetic values of the work environment. Each room was designed to provide ample work space in comfortable, pleasing, and safe surroundings. The walls, curtains, carpets, and furnishings of each room were coordinated to complement each other aesthetically in order to enhance the work environment. Oriental rugs in the kitchen and broadloom in the laundry room were but two of the extravagances proposed to achieve a pleasant effect.

Pattison and the Federation of Women's Clubs were

very much ahead of their time. The experiment station and *The Principles of Domestic Economy* served not only as a consumer's guide to manufactured goods but also as a time-management consultant. Furthermore, Pattison believed that the state should become involved in the training of "domestic engineers" through home economics courses in order "to bring the masculine and feminine mind more closely together in the industry of home-making by raising housework . . . to the plan of Scientific Engineering . . . to the end that the Home may develop progressively more and more as the efficient unit of the state." The final result would be healthy, peaceful communities based on cooperation, collective decision making, and enlightened populations committed to world peace. (Pattison, *Principles*, 1)

Pattison remained politically active all her life. In 1949, at age 80, she wrote *Colonia Yesterday*, one of the earliest town histories ever written. The writing, both humorous and folksy, describes the wealthy nature of the town and her own life there. Pattison's husband, Frank, died in September 1946. She died in her home on June 28, 1951, at age 81, and is buried in the family plot in Mountain Grove Cemetery, Bridgeport, CT.

Pattison's two books are *The Principles of Domestic Engineering* (1914) and *Colonia Yesterday* (1949). She also wrote "Domestic Engineering: The Housekeeping Experiment Station at Colonia, New Jersey," *Scientific American* 106 (Apr. 13, 1912):330–31. Articles describing the experiment station are: "Experiment Station to Solve Housekeeper's Problems," *New York Times*, Mar. 26, 1911; and "Making the Home Efficient," *New York Times*, July 25, 1915. Also helpful is Ada Fuller, *A History of the New Jersey State Federation of Women's Clubs, 1894–1927* (1927). Her obituary appeared in the *New York Times*, June 29, 1951.

*Harriet Hyman Alonso*
*Janet Crawford*

## ALICE STOKES PAUL, 1885–1977

Alice Stokes Paul, who wrote the Equal Rights Amendment (ERA) and led the first nationwide nonviolent civil disobedience campaign for woman suffrage as well as an international movement for women's equality, was born near Moorestown (Burlington County), NJ, on January 11, 1885, the oldest child of William Mickle Paul, a prosperous farmer and banker, and Tacie (Parry) Paul, a member of a Quaker family steeped in the tradition of activism in education and public service. Paul's maternal grandfather, Judge William Parry, president of Rutgers University, helped establish Swarthmore College, where Paul's mother was one of the first students. Her great-grandfather, Charles Stokes, was a Jacksonian legislator and supported the founders of the Hicksite (liberal) branch of the Society of Friends, the Quakers.

As a child Paul learned the Quaker belief in equality,

but also its conflicting traditions of nonviolent civil disobedience and "Quietism," or withdrawal from the world in the interest of piety. She learned to live simply and use the words *thee* and *thou*, to attend long, silent services two or three times a week, "centering down" to her own conscience, the Inner Light. She read voraciously, devouring Charles Dickens, histories, biographies, and journals of reformers and traveling Quaker ministers. At her Hicksite school, she attended small coeducational classes taught by well-educated teachers. With the Quaker assumption of women's equality, Paul's mother took her to suffrage meetings at a neighbor's house.

When she was sixteen, Paul began Swarthmore College on a scholarship. Friendly but shy and inner-directed, she pursued sports, took a wide variety of courses, and became attracted to economics and political science. In 1905 she graduated Phi Beta Kappa. After graduation, she trained as a social worker in the College Settlement on New York's Lower East Side, earning a certificate from the New York School of Philanthropy (Columbia University). A year later, in 1907, Paul received a masters degree in economics and sociology from the University of Pennsylvania.

Although convinced that social work "was not doing much good in the world," Paul remained a social worker during the two years of graduate work in England that would change her life. (Paul, Oral history, 20) A student in the Quakers' Woodbrook Institute in Birmingham and later the London School of Economics, she joined the militant suffragettes of the Women's Social and Political Union (WSPU), led by Emmeline Pankhurst. One of Pankhurst's trusted organizers, Paul was imprisoned three times, during which she undertook hunger strikes and was force-fed. When she sailed for home in December 1909, she feared that the Moorestown Quakers would disown her. However, at a meeting of 500 townspeople at the Moorestown Town Hall, Paul defended the WSPU's strategies and her own involvement to the applause of most of the audience.

Working on her doctorate in Philadelphia, Paul introduced the city to street corner speeches and suffrage parades. After she received her degree in 1912 from the University of Pennsylvania, Paul became co-chair, with Lucy Burns, of the Congressional Committee of the National American Woman Suffrage Association (NAWSA). They were to lobby for a woman suffrage constitutional amendment.

On March 3, 1913, the day before Woodrow's Wilson's inauguration, they staged a parade of 7,000 suffragists, including men and blacks, in Washington, D.C. Crowds taunted and attacked them and federal troops were called. Publicity and the subsequent investigation brought suffrage into the limelight and made Paul a national figure. Paul was unusual: a nationally prominent leader, she remained shy and quiet-spoken, but her intensely blue eyes and intellectual clarity were what people noticed.

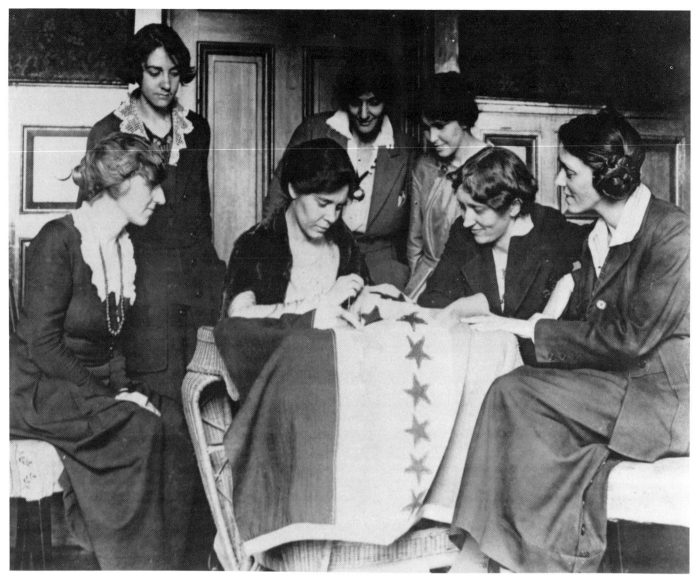

Alice Stokes Paul, woman suffrage leader from Moorestown, NJ, in 1920 with other suffragists, sewing a star on a banner to indicate that another state had ratified the woman suffrage amendment to the U.S. Constitution. *Courtesy, the Schlesinger Library, Radcliffe College.*

In 1914 Paul's fast-moving and often autonomous style led to her separation from NAWSA (which was pushing for individual state referenda). Paul's Congressional Union later became the National Woman's Party (NWP), a national organization to educate congressmen's home districts about suffrage and keep the suffrage issue in the national conscience. In New Jersey, ALISON TURNBULL HOPKINS, an activist during Woodrow Wilson's gubernatorial term, became state chair and organized delegations to the White House. Her husband, J.A.H. Hopkins, helped organize men for suffrage and provided limousine service for street corner speakers. Rose Campbell, MARY PHILBROOK, and Mary Dubrow were loyal workers.

When, in 1917, the possibility of war threatened to dwarf the suffrage issue, Paul sent "silent sentinels" to the White House carrying purple, gold, and white banners insisting that the democracy of Wilson's war phrases did not apply to women. Mobs attacked the demonstrators. Hundreds of women from all over the United States joined the new nonviolent civil disobedience, were imprisoned, began hunger strikes, and were force-fed. Paul herself was imprisoned three times, once in a psychiatric ward, where a doctor released her saying she had "a spirit . . . like Joan of Arc's, and it is useless to try to change it." (Irwin, *Alice Paul*, 294)

At last, immediately before the 1918 elections, Wilson called on Congress to pass the suffrage amendment. The next Congress did so, and with the states already organized, ratification was completed in just fifteen months, on August 26, 1920.

The NWP reorganized to use women's vote to pursue full equal rights. Abandoning her militant strategy, Paul proceeded toward educating women and building a network among their organizations to support full equality. In 1922 she also earned a bachelor's degree from the Washington, D.C., College of Law; in 1927 her master of law degree; and in 1928 her doctor of law degree from American University in Washington, D.C.

Meanwhile, under Paul's direction, the NWP drafted equal rights laws for the States. Paul wrote an amendment for the federal Constitution, which was submitted to Congress in 1923. It stated simply: "Men and women shall have equal rights throughout the United States and the territories under its jurisdiction."

But before a congressional committee in early 1924, the amendment was opposed by the League of Women Voters, the National Consumers' League, the Women's Bureau in the Department of Labor. Throughout the next five decades these groups held that the Supreme Court would use the ERA to strike down special industrial protections for women. Paul did not accept that women as a class were biologically fragile, the rationale courts used in the affirmation of protective labor laws for women. If the Supreme Court wanted to strike down such laws, she thought, it was already empowered to do so through the suffrage amendment. Furthermore, she reasoned, women's protections could be extended equally to men.

Paul led her fight for equal rights on three fronts. She formed alliances for the ERA with national women's organizations such as business and professional women's clubs. Large councils of government employees, industrial workers, and other occupational groups formed within the NWP. The strength of these coalitions steadily increased and they defeated many of the discriminatory New Deal National Recovery Administration codes. In the process, more women became ERA supporters.

Paul's second front for equal rights was on the state level. She and an NWP research committee of twelve attorneys identified discriminatory laws in each state and recommended reform legislation. By 1929 NWP had introduced nearly 600 bills to state legislatures; almost half passed.

Paul also worked for international women's rights. In 1929 she led the NWP in founding the Inter-American Commission for Women in the Pan American Union. In 1933 their Equal Nationality Treaty was signed by all member nations, and Paul's sweeping Equal Rights Treaty was signed by three. Throughout the thirties at the League of Nations in Geneva her association of women's groups from many countries achieved official League of Nation status for their Study Committee on the Status of Women. Then (as she had done earlier for the United States and for

nationality laws of Western Hemisphere countries) she headed a league Committee of Experts that produced multivolume surveys of legal codes pertaining to women in each member nation—a tremendous undertaking for which she is little known.

In 1938 Paul, opposed by U.S. labor interests, founded the World Women's Party (WWP). From its Geneva headquarters, she and the WWP opposed the discriminatory codes that the International Labor Office submitted and lobbied for three goals: equality in nationality laws, more women members in league delegations, and passage of the Equal Rights Treaty (ERT). League committees sent the ERT to the floor of the league assembly just as war broke out.

The WWP villa in Geneva became a refugee center for prominent liberal and feminist leaders stranded there. Paul, while writing hundreds of letters and cablegrams to resettle them, continued to call WWP meetings for postwar plans, but when the war intensified, she returned to Washington.

Between 1941 and the "new wave" of feminism in the 1960s, Paul continued to work for women's equality. In 1943 she rewrote the ERA to read: "Equality of rights under the law shall not be denied or abridged by the United States or by any State on account of sex." In 1946 the ERA lost its first Senate floor vote by only three votes.

Paul haunted United Nations meetings. She led the WWP in the successful struggle to include the wording of sex equality in the UN Preamble and several sections of the charter and later in the UN Universal Declaration of Human Rights, which would be a model for the constitutions of many emerging nations.

Another major victory for Paul came in 1964, when Congress, pressed by diverse interest groups that she organized and led, added the word *sex* to the equality clauses in Title VII of the Civil Rights Act.

When the National Organization for Women (NOW) accepted the ERA as its first priority, Paul convinced them to adopt her version because of the long list of sponsors by organizations and members of Congress. In 1972 Congress passed the ERA to the states, but Paul foresaw that the seven-year ratification time limit plus the section giving Congress, rather than the states, the right to enforce it, would spell defeat. Nevertheless, from her Ridgefield, CT, cottage, Paul, then 87, lobbied by telephone.

In 1974 a slight stroke sent her first to a nursing home in Ridgefield, then to the Quaker Greenleaf Nursing home in Moorestown, NJ, her childhood home. She died there on July 9, 1977, at age 92, of heart failure.

A collection of Paul's papers, including diaries, letters, books, and pamphlets, is available at M-SL. *Conversations with Alice Paul: Woman Suffrage and the Equal Rights Amendment* (1976), an oral interview by Amelia R. Fry of the Regional Oral History Office, Bancroft Library, University of California, Berkeley, is available in many research libraries. Some works that discuss Paul and her political activities are: Amelia Fry, "Alice Paul and the ERA," in Joan Hoff-Wilson, ed., *Rights of Passage: The Past and Future of the ERA* (1986); Amelia Fry, "Alice Paul and the Divine Discontent," in Mary Murrin, ed., *Women in New Jersey History* (1985); "Alice Paul," in Carol and John Stoneburner, eds., *The Influence of Quaker Women on American History: Biographical Studies* (1986); and Doris Stevens, *Jailed for Freedom: The Story of the Militant American Suffragist Movement* (1920; 1976). Paul's obituary appeared in the *New York Times*, July 10, 1977.

*Amelia Fry*
*Sheila Cowing*

In 1895 Mary Philbrook became the first woman admitted to the New Jersey Bar, a right she won only after lobbying the legislature to pass special enabling legislation. *New Jersey Law Journal,* 1904. *Photo courtesy, Carol Kitman.*

## MARY PHILBROOK, 1872–1958

Mary Philbrook, the first woman to be admitted to the bar in New Jersey, was born in Washington, D.C., on August 6, 1872, the second oldest of five children of Harry and Rebecca (Stearns) Philbrook.

In 1878 the family moved to Jersey City (Hudson County), NJ, where Philbrook attended School No. 11 at Bergen Square and Jersey City High School. A course in stenography at Drake's Business School completed her formal schooling. Her first job was as a secretary in the law office of Russ and Oppenheimer in Hoboken. Two years later she became secretary to Henry Gaede, who was a law partner with James Minturn, corporation counsel for Hoboken. Minturn (who later became a justice of the New Jersey Supreme Court) encouraged her ambition to become a lawyer, and sponsored her petition to the court to be allowed to take the bar exam.

Philbrook's lack of college or law school degrees was no obstacle to her admission to the bar at that time when, according to a New Jersey statute, any citizen (after "reading" the law in the office of an attorney) could apply for admission. A real obstacle was the fact that no woman in New Jersey had ever sought admission to the bar, and it was on this ground alone (lack of precedent) that, in June 1894, the New Jersey Supreme Court refused Philbrook's petition. Although she had not previously seen herself as, in her words, a "crusader for women's rights," but simply an ambitious woman seeking a good way to make a living, this rejection by the court was a critical factor in determining Philbrook's future course. Supported by the membership of the New Jersey Woman Suffrage Association, Philbrook lobbied in the New Jersey legislature for a law (passed in 1895) specifically enabling women to become lawyers, which made it possible for her to be admitted to the bar in June 1895.

Philbrook began her practice in Jersey City with the firm of Bacot and Record, and then opened an office of her own. While still a struggling young lawyer, she volunteered her services as the counsel for the Legal Aid Society at Whittier House, a social settlement founded in downtown Jersey City in 1894 by CORNELIA BRADFORD. Philbrook met her at the Jersey City Woman's Club, where BRADFORD, Florence Howe Hall (head of the New Jersey suffragists), and Philbrook were charter members. Suffragists like Philbrook and Hall were often the activists in broad-based organizations such as the Jersey City Woman's Club. Through club activities they were able to draw the support of middle-class, reform-minded women to their cause. Philbrook delivered many educational lectures to club women around the state about women's legal rights. She also campaigned with MABEL SMITH DOUGLASS of the Jersey City Woman's Club for the establishment of a public college for women.

In 1902 Philbrook moved her law practice to Newark, where she organized the first statewide Legal Aid Association. She became active in the State Charities Aid Association, a coalition of public and private charitable institutions, which had a sweeping program for judicial and penal reform. Appointed the first female probation officer for Essex County in 1902, she organized the juvenile court system in Newark and served on the commission headed by CAROLINE ALEXANDER WITTPENN, which spearheaded the drive to establish the New Jersey Reformatory for Women. Appointed undercover investigator for the United States Immigration Committee, which conducted an inquiry into white slavery (the importation of immigrant women for the purpose of prostitution), she traveled across the country, gathering evidence and preparing the report that was submitted to Congress in 1910 and resulted in the passage of the Mann Act.

While Philbrook worked tirelessly for many of the reforms supported by the woman's movement in the Progressive Era, she did not neglect her career. Because of the public attention attracted by her legal aid and penal reform work, she drew many clients and built a prosperous practice in Newark. She was the first woman appointed to practice before the U.S. Supreme Court in 1906 based on the constitutional claim of New Jersey women to vote. (The first state constitution of 1776 had granted women the franchise.) As expected, the court ruled against her, but Philbrook's cogent brief attracted the attention of constitutional experts around the country.

In 1914 ill health forced Philbrook to retire from public life for three years. When she recovered, women were mobilizing themselves for World War I. She served as a Red Cross lawyer in France before the Armistice and, on her return to Washington in 1918, assisted Mabel Boardman, the guiding light of the Red Cross, to assemble her memoirs. While in Washington in 1919, Philbrook participated in some of the militant demonstrations of the National Woman's Party (NWP), which, under the leadership of ALICE STOKES PAUL, was bringing pressure on the Wilson administration for the passage of the 19th Amendment.

With suffrage won, Philbrook returned to New Jersey, where she organized support for the removal of discriminatory laws and for an equal rights amendment to the state constitution. But her position was too radical for her former allies in the suffrage movement, some of whom had worked hard in the Progressive Era for protective legislation for women, legislation that equality-minded women like Philbrook perceived as restrictive. In 1929 Philbrook's demand for equal working conditions cost her the position of counsel for the city of Newark.

During the 1930s, with feminism dormant in the United States, many feminists focused on the international and historical aspects of the movement. Philbrook and ALICE STOKES PAUL worked at the Geneva conferences of the League of Nations to include an equal rights clause in the covenant. Philbrook catalogued the papers of the NWP at its Blair House headquarters and helped to organize the New Jersey chapter of the Women's Archives, established by historian Mary Beard.

In the 1940s Philbrook renewed her campaign for an equal rights amendment to the state constitution. At the 1947 Constitutional Convention, Philbrook (then 75 years old) organized a coalition of women's groups to lobby for an equal rights provision in the new constitution. Though opposed by many powerful organizations, such as the League of Women Voters, Philbrook's delegation was able to secure changes in the language of the constitution (i.e., *person* for *he*) that, though little noted at the time, were cited by the New Jersey Supreme Court in 1979 as grounds to rule that sex discrimination was constitutionally prohibited in New Jersey.

Philbrook died, at age 86, of arteriosclerosis on September 2, 1958, in Point Pleasant, NJ. Her remains were cremated at the Rose Hill Crematory in Linden, NJ.

The Mary Philbrook Papers, including her memoirs, correspondence, clippings, and documents relating to the equal rights movement, are available at NJ-HS. For a fuller discussion of Philbrook's work, see Barbara Petrick, *Mary Philbrook: The Radical Feminist in New Jersey* (1981).

*Barbara Burns Petrick*

## DOROTHEA MILLER POST, 1878–1947

Dorothea (Miller) Post, organizer of the Morris County branch of the Woman's Land Army during World War I, was born on July 16, 1878, the second of four children and eldest daughter of Katherine (Wise) and Commodore Jacob William Miller. Her father, an Annapolis graduate, supervised the building of the Cape Cod Canal and was a founder of the New York State Naval Reserve. Post was born in Morristown (Morris County), NJ, after her father had retired from the navy to become involved with the management of railroad and steamship companies. Post's older brother, Henry, married novelist and poet ALICE DUER MILLER.

Post married James Otis Post, a socially prominent New York architect, on September 20, 1906, and for a while lived with her husband in New York City and with her in-laws in Bernardsville, NJ. The family subsequently moved to Macculloch Hall in Morristown, a large home built by her paternal great-grandfather in 1810. Between 1907 and 1914 Post and her husband had three sons: James Otis, Edward Everett, and Richard Oliver.

Devoted to music and her garden, Post also followed a family tradition of civic service. A year before the United States' entry into World War I, Post became active in the

Movement for National Preparedness and became the first president of the Women's Section of the Morris County branch in March 1916. In April the group's name was changed to the League for Patriotic Service, its aim the coordination of Morris County's civilian preparedness in the event of war.

Dorothea Miller Post, a Morristown socialite and amateur musician, worked with the Woman's Land Army during World War I. *Courtesy, private collection.*

As a result of her concern with preparedness, Post became active in another organization serving the war effort, the Woman's Land Army of America (WLA). In February 1918 the New Jersey division of the WLA was organized and Post became chair of the Morris County unit, which covered Morristown, Boonton, and Schooley's Mountain. Known as the "Farmerettes," the Land Army was a voluntary organization designed to help increase agricultural production during the war by recruiting and organizing female labor for farmers whose male workers were in military service. Unemployed seasonal workers, immigrant women, students, and teachers were recruited to work in groups for designated farmers; sometimes housing, meals, chaperones, and child care were provided by the organization. The WLA was active in New Jersey for one growing season before the Armistice was signed in November.

After the war Post turned her attentions back to cultural affairs. She was an accomplished violinist and Macculloch Hall was a center for musical activities. In 1920 Post was a founder of the Morristown Orchestral Society, and in 1925 she was a founder of the Morris County Choral Society. She also was active in the New Jersey Orchestra, the Fortnightly Choral Club, and the Friday Evening Club of Morristown, as well as the Morristown Woman's Club and the Morristown Garden Club. She was an adviser for the project to build a reflecting pool and cenotaph as a World War I memorial in Morristown.

Post died of a cerebral hemorrhage, at age 69, on November 15, 1947, in Morristown. She was buried in Woodland Cemetery in New York City.

Material on Post and her work with the New Jersey Division of the Woman's Land Army is found in the archives of Macculloch Hall (Morristown, NJ). See also Sally Fairchild Foy and Linda Winterberg, *Macculloch Hall: A Family Album* (1980).

*Joan Barbato*

## SOPHIA PRESLEY, 1834–1909

Sophia Presley, an Irish immigrant, was the first woman physician to gain admission to the Medical Society of Camden County, NJ. Born in Drumcrin, County Fermanagh, Ireland, in 1834, Presley, her sister, Jane Alice, and her brother, William, were raised in Steubenville, OH. No records survive to identify her parents, but her father appears to have been a glasspacker with adequate funds and incentive to insure an enlightened education for Presley.

In the years after her arrival from Ireland, Presley equipped herself with impressive credentials. Graduating from the Granville Female Seminary in Ohio in 1860, she entered the Woman's Medical College of Pennsylvania and graduated in 1879. She successfully completed her internship at the Woman's Hospital in Philadelphia.

Her medical ability and teaching skills must have been of superior quality, for she was appointed instructor of surgery at the Woman's Hospital for a three-year term in 1880, followed by a year there as clinic physician. In 1894 Presley was given full charge of the Gynecological Department of the Camden City Dispensary.

Despite her education and experience, the governing board of the Camden County Medical Society, to whom Presley had applied for membership in November 1882, refused to admit her. No reason for the refusal was noted, but by tradition the members of the medical society were all male. The board rejected her application for seven successive years, the necessary two-thirds majority vote not being reached until the meeting of May 13, 1890. At that time, Presley became the first woman doctor to be granted full privileges in the association. Her full acceptance by the medical society that had long rejected her was shown by her election as secretary in 1894 and 1895.

The seven years of rejection did not blunt Presley's drive to serve the sick. During these years, in addition to her clinic work, Presley was the physician to the West Jersey Orphanage for Destitute Colored Children in Camden. She also served as second vice-president on its Board of Managers in 1894. In addition to this charitable work, she was, by 1890, one of the five medical attendants for the Methodist Episcopal Home in Collingswood. Presley was also involved with the Young Women's Christian Association.

Though her work as a public physician came to be applauded, as a private physician she may have found it more difficult to be accepted. Presley's nine relocations in the 25 years of her private practice may indicate lack of community approval. This view is suggested by a notation in the Camden County Medical Society records after Presley's death. In their encomium, the Resolutions Committee wrote that "by her earnest zeal and ability, she soon had the confidence of many of our prominent families, and secured a large clientele under adverse circumstances." (Teffeau, "Sophia Presley," 41)

While functioning successfully as a public and private physician, Presley also undertook research studies. In her medical school thesis she investigated acquired syphilis. At a December 1891 meeting of the Camden Medical Society, Presley read her treatise on "rectal polypi"; in May 1892 she reported on her work on "puerperal fever." In 1905 she spoke as one of three physicians from the society's Pathology Section.

Presley never married. In her later years she had a close friendship with Amelia H. Lee, who shared her home and to whom she left in her will $2,000, referring to her as the person who "made it possible for me to have and enjoy a home of my own in my old age." (Teffeau, 43)

Presley's influence as a woman and a physician extended well beyond the bounds of her practice. Prominent for 49 years as a public physician and 25 years as a private physician, she served as a role model for aspiring women doctors. When she died in 1909 her four honorary pallbearers were all women physicians from Camden: Jennie B. Sharp, Emma M. Richardson, Beulah Hollinshed, and Lettie Allen Ward. Presley had paved the way for their professional acceptance by the quality of her own work as a physician. Besides the Camden County Medical Society, Presley was a member of the Camden City Medical and Surgical Society, the Camden City Medical Society, and the American Medical Association.

Upon her death the county medical society, which for seven years had rejected her request for membership, prepared a memorial resolution. The powerful influence of their first woman physician is clearly demonstrated in the

preface to the resolution: "It is with sincere sorrow and regret that Camden County Medical Society has learned of the death of one of its most useful members, Dr. Sophia Presley." (Teffeau, 44)

Presley preferred a less dramatic remembrance of her courage and determination. When she died of a heart attack on November 28, 1909, at age 75, the simple grave marker in Harleigh Cemetery in Camden was inscribed according to the exact specification of her will: "Sophia Presley, M.D. / Born in Crumcrin / Beside Lough Erne, / County Fermanagh Ireland. / Died November 28, 1909."

The best source of information on Presley is Cleora Teffeau, "Sophia Presley, M.D. The Spinster Who Struggled Seven Years Against the Bias of Male Doctors," *Bulletin of the Camden County Historical Society* 28 (1975):36–45. An account of Presley's medical career appears in Christine E. Haycock, "Women Physicians of New Jersey: The Early Era," *Journal of the Medical Society of New Jersey* 81 (1984):773–77. Additional information on her appears in Ruth Abram, *Send Us a Lady Physician: Women Doctors in America, 1835–1920* (1985).

*Jennifer Pearce-Lowell*

Asphalt roads were a rarity and repairs frequent during the pioneer cross-county drive of Alice Huyler Ramsey in 1909. Shown here changing a tire on her green Maxwell, Ramsey was a 22-year-old resident of Hackensack when she made the 3,800-mile transcontinental trip. *Courtesy, Elizabeth Elliott.*

## ALICE HUYLER RAMSEY, 1886–1983

Alice (Huyler) Ramsey, a pioneer endurance driver named by the American Automobile Association "Woman Motorist of the Century," was the first female to drive across the United States (1909). She was born on November 11, 1886, in Hackensack (Bergen County), NJ, the second child of John Edwin and Ada Mumford (Farr) Huyler. Her father, of Dutch descent, was a lumber and then a coal dealer and later became a fire chief. Her mother, of English origin, was a homemaker and an expert quilter.

Ramsey attended Union Street Elementary School and, like her father, was mechanically minded; she took a shop course at Hackensack High School, from which she graduated in June 1903. After attending Vassar College for two years, she left to marry John Rathbone Ramsey, an attorney and county clerk more than twice her age. She was his second wife. Her son, John Rathbone Ramsey, Jr., was born in Hackensack, where the Ramseys lived, on February 13, 1907.

After an episode with a runaway horse and rig convinced Ramsey's husband she might be safer with an automobile, he decided to surprise her with a red Maxwell roadster, which she learned to drive in two lessons. When she entered the 150-mile Montauk Point Run, after driving for only six months, she was awarded a perfect score.

Ramsey organized and became president of the Women's Motoring Club of New York. She was challenged by Carl Kelsey to make the first transcontinental drive by a woman in a Maxwell. Before taking up the challenge, she first tested her skill at the Philadelphia Midwinter Run, where she won the Benjamin Briscoe Trophy.

Although he never learned to drive, John Ramsey gave his consent for the 3,800-mile transcontinental trip through partial wilderness. On June 9, 1909, 22-year-old Alice Ramsey sat in the driver's seat of a green Maxwell especially fitted with a 20-gallon tank for the rugged trip across the country. The three passengers were Margaret Atwood and Nettie Powell, her two sisters-in-law, and Hermine Jahns, a friend.

She gave the crank a whirl, retarded the throttle, kissed her husband, and climbed into the driver's seat as she set off from the Maxwell-Briscoe Company salesroom on Broadway in New York City with the slogan "From Hell Gate to Golden Gate!" The only other asphalt roads they crossed were in Chicago and San Francisco; elsewhere the roads deteriorated from gravel to sand to cow paths and dry riverbeds. They took the northern route following the Hudson River, where the 110-pound Ramsey did better than the average chauffeur in grinding valves and changing spark plugs and tires. John Murphy, the advance agent whom they met in Albany, preceded the party in Pullmans, making promotion arrangements since cars and women drivers were a curiosity at the time. A broken coil on the way to Buffalo, a blowout on the bumpy road to Cleveland, and a broken axle as they neared Chicago did not stop them. They added a towing rope, block and tackle, and a shovel to their equipment as they left Chicago.

The Maxwell covered from 4 to 198 miles daily. The worst ordeal was the torrential rains in Iowa, where they found Weasel Creek swollen and were forced to spend a night in the car. The narrow, smooth tires of the Maxwell doubled in size from the mud, so chains were of little help.

The three women passengers took the train and met Ramsey again in Omaha. But John Murphy accompanied her through the worst part as she maneuvered on Danger Hill, towing a Mitchel that was stuck halfway up the hill. Later, the Maxwell got hung up in a chuckhole filled with water. Finally, they detoured to the higher grounds of Sioux City, but it took thirteen days to cross Iowa.

They had no road maps, but east of the Mississippi River, they used Blue Books that provided landmarks for directions. In the western states, pilot cars escorted Ramsey and her three companions out of town and often endangered themselves by getting stuck. When the car's pedal broke loose in Nevada, Ramsey crawled under the car and repaired it with wire. In Grand Island, the rear axle broke when they hit a chuckhole. In Wyoming, cattle gates and irrigation ditches slowed the Maxwell. At one point, Ramsey maneuvered the car along a three-quarter-mile railroad trestle bumping above a chasm of the Platte River. Goggles guarded their eyes over the shifting sands of Utah. Prairie dog holes broke springs. In Nebraska, a band of Native Americans chasing a jackrabbit with drawn bows and arrows terrified the women.

When the Maxwell overheated during the hard climb to the summit of the Sierras, they used water from animal troughs, filling the radiator countless times. Finally, when they reached California, arriving on the Oakland ferry to San Francisco on August 7, their success was marked by honking horns and flowers. Ramsey had driven all the way from ocean to ocean, making history!

Lonely for her family, she spent only three days in California, returning home by train. Ramsey's daughter, Alice Valleau, was born nine months after the trip, on May 27, 1910.

Ramsey enjoyed projects such as taking apart the crankcase of a Studebaker and reassembling it. She was a prime organizer during World War I of the Red Cross Motor Corps for Camp Merrit in Dumont, which carried wounded from Fort Dix.

In the summer of 1919 she resumed coast-to-coast driving and took her children on visits to national parks along the way to California. She drove cross-country more than 30 times after moving to Covina, CA, in 1948.

Ramsey was an accomplished pianist. She also spent eighteen years as a volunteer translating books into braille. She lectured frequently on her cross-country motor trip and was prompted to write of her adventures when Governor Dewey of New York mistakenly gave credit to Blanche Stewart Scott as the first cross-country female driver (1910). Her book *Veil, Duster and Tire Iron* (1960) verified her claim.

The Automobile Manufacturers Association honored her at Cobo Hall, Detroit, on October 20, 1960—the 50th anniversary of her cross-continental drive—as "First Lady of Automobile Travel." She also received the title of

"Woman Motorist of the Century" from the American Automobile Association.

Other awards and honors included grand marshal of the 1970 Auburn, Cord, Duesenberg Club parade, at age 84; a special citation from the American Federation of Women's Clubs; and a plaque from the Movie World Cars of the Stars in 1974. Vassar honored Ramsey in 1981, at her daughter's 50th reunion, and three antique auto clubs awarded her honorary memberships.

Her last challenge was driving the six passes (completing five of them) through the Alps in Switzerland. A snowstorm closed the road one day before her attempt to drive the sixth pass, and her doctor forbade her from trying again because of her pacemaker.

Shortly before her death Nigel Turner interviewed Ramsey for a book (published by Little Brown and Co.) and a T.V. documentary, both entitled *Automania*. Preparations were well under way for the 75th anniversary of her historic drive, when she died on September 10, 1983, at age 96, of natural causes in Covina, CA. Burial was in the Ramsey family plot in Hackensack, NJ.

Ramsey's papers and memorabilia are deposited at the National Automotive History Collection, Detroit Public Library (Detroit, MI). Her longtime companion, Elizabeth Elliott of California, has a copy of Ramsey's *Veil, Duster, and Tire Iron* (1961). An interview with Ramsey by Charles Kuralt appeared on the CBS Evening News, Aug. 19, 1977, and was printed in Kuralt's book *On the Road with Charles Kuralt* (1985). Her obituary appeared in the *Record* (Hackensack, NJ), Sept. 13, 1983.

*Mary Freericks*

## FLORENCE SPEARING RANDOLPH, 1866–1951

Florence (Spearing) Randolph, African Methodist Episcopal Zion (AMEZ) minister and social activist, was born in Charlestown, SC, on August 9, 1866, the seventh child of John and Anna (Smith) Spearing. Her father was a prosperous cabinetmaker, and both parents were members of old free African-American Charleston families.

Randolph attended local public schools and graduated from Charleston's Avery Normal Institute. At that time, employment options for black women were restricted to domestic work, teaching, music, or dressmaking. Many educated African-Americans, seeking to shield their daughters from the drudgery and physical dangers of domestic work, encouraged the other three options. Randolph chose dressmaking, was apprenticed to Charlotte Robinson, and after two years became an instructor in Robinson's Charleston dressmaking school. In 1885, while visiting her older sisters in New York City and Jersey City, she realized that her dressmaking skills could command at least $1.50 per day (as opposed to the 50 cents per day she was then earning) and she decided to move North. She

returned to Charleston for only a few months before permanently relocating to Jersey City, NJ.

On May 5, 1886, she married Hugh Randolph, a Richmond, VA, native employed as a cook in the dining car service of the Pullman Company. They purchased a home in downtown Jersey City and converted an upper story into a workroom for Randolph's already profitable business, which then employed two dressmakers and five girl assistants. The Randolphs' one child, Leah Viola, was born on February 7, 1887. Hugh Randolph died on February 13, 1913.

Randolph was an ardent and lifelong Christian activist. As an eight-year-old accompanying a blind grandmother on prayer and Scripture reading visits to the sick, she was greatly impressed with the teachings of Christianity. Upon conversion at age thirteen, she became engaged in active service in the Charleston Methodist Episcopal Church. In Jersey City she affiliated with the Monmouth Street AMEZ Church and was appointed a Sunday school teacher and youth class leader. Her avocation led to private study of the Bible with a tutor who was a Yale graduate and a Greek and Hebrew scholar. She later completed a course with the Moody Bible Institute of Chicago, IL, as well as special work at Drew Theological Seminary.

Randolph's early avocational interest in Christianity coincided with the launching of an active public service career. Begun in 1892, when she accepted an invitation to join the Woman's Christian Temperance Union (WCTU) of Jersey City, her lecturing and organizing against the liquor traffic continued until after repeal of the 18th Amendment in 1933. Her WCTU work inspired the organization of a "Kings Daughters Society," which engaged in city missionary work. This led to an invitation to talk at a Gospel Mission, which resulted in more invitations to speak at local churches.

Randolph's religious and community service and her oratorical endeavors fused when in 1897 she sought a license to preach. Although her gender instigated opposition among older AMEZ bishops and ministers, the license was granted. With support from Bishop Alexander Walters (one of the founders of the NAACP), Randolph progressed through the subsequent stages toward ordination. She was admitted to the conference and then appointed conference evangelist. At the May 1900 Atlantic City AMEZ Church Conference she was ordained a deacon. She was ordained an elder (with the right to consecrate the sacraments and serve communion) in 1903.

The 1900 conference selected Randolph as an AMEZ delegate to the 1901 Third Methodist Ecumenical Conference in London. While there, Randolph was invited to preach at the Primitive Methodist Church of Mattison Road. After the conference she toured England, Scotland, Belgium, and France.

Upon her return to the United States, Randolph was

chosen pastor of Newark's Pennington Street (later Clinton) AMEZ Church. During her ministry she pastored five churches in New Jersey and New York, working without salary for the first twelve years. The churches to which she was assigned were small, poor, and struggling, with few members and many debts. Invariably, when through her leadership a little church became solvent, a "nice young man" would be assigned and Randolph would move on to the next problem area.

Randolph is most often associated with the Summit, NJ, church that she organized and built. In 1925 she was appointed by AMEZ Bishop P. A. Wallace as temporary supply pastor in charge of a Summit mission known as Wallace Chapel, whose 35 members worshiped at the Lincoln YMCA. Fund raising began in the fall of 1926, and by 1928 Randolph and the trustees had purchased a modern duplex house on three lots at the corner of Broad and Orchard streets in Summit. Alterations to the first floor provided a 100-seat chapel; the second floor was used as a parsonage. Membership increased, and in September 1936, amid the nationwide Depression, ground was broken for a new red brick colonial-style sanctuary, parsonage, and community center, which were completed by early 1937. In 1946, after serving Wallace Chapel for 21 years, Randolph retired from the active ministry.

Throughout her ministry, Randolph participated in state and national AMEZ connectional activities. Among her highest priorities were foreign missions, particularly those in Africa. Having identified problem areas during her first ten years as president of the New Jersey Women's Foreign Missionary Society, in 1911 she recommended to the national convention of the AMEZ Women's Home and Foreign Missionary Society (WHFMS) the creation of a Bureau of Supplies to coordinate the collection and distribution of all donations to foreign mission fields. The 1912 AMEZ General Conference adopted her recommendation and named her secretary of the bureau. Her 1916–20 term as the fourth president of the missionary society was followed by many years of foreign work primarily inspired by her ongoing travels.

Between 1922 and 1924 Randolph traveled throughout the interior of Liberia and the Gold Coast, journeying by truck, oxcart, canoe, and on the shoulders of native carriers to gain firsthand knowledge of the AMEZ foreign mission field. In addition to preaching, she assessed the educational, health care, and other service needs with which the WHFMS was concerned. When she returned to the United States, she brought with her a young African girl, Charity Zumala, whom she educated at Summit (NJ) High School and Hampton Institute. After returning to her Gold Coast (now Ghana) home, Zumala taught school until her death in 1946.

Randolph organized the New Jersey State Federation of Colored Women's Clubs (NJFCWC) in 1915. That Oc-

tober, black women representing 30 New Jersey WCTU societies had met to consider plans for arousing greater African-American interest in the temperance movement. This initial group of temperance society members was first joined by missionary societies, and later by church, civic, literary, business, and political clubs. By 1917 85 clubs, with a combined membership of 2,616, were affiliated. Randolph served the federation as president for twelve years. Her interest and participation continued throughout her life.

Randolph's work in interracial organizations other than the WCTU dated back to her two years as superintendent of the Negro Work for the Christian Endeavor Society of New Jersey. Her continued Christian Endeavor and temperance work led to active participation in the equal rights movement. She served on the Executive Board of the New Jersey Woman Suffrage Association, and in 1920, shortly after the passage of the 19th Amendment, she was invited by former Governor Edward C. Stokes, then chair of the New Jersey Republican party, to assist LILLIAN FEICKERT, head of the Republican women's division, in Warren G. Harding's presidential campaign.

Randolph's work with African-American, interracial, and church-affiliated organizations was lauded on June 7, 1933, when Livingstone College (Salisbury, NC), the largest college supported by the AMEZ Church, awarded her an honorary doctor of divinity degree. In 1942 the NJFCWC selected Randolph to introduce First Lady Eleanor Roosevelt to the July convention at Bordentown (NJ) Industrial School, and the denomination invited her to offer prayer preceding Mrs. Roosevelt's August address to the AMEZ Youth Council meeting at Livingstone College.

After her 1946 retirement from the pulpit, Randolph made her home in Montclair, NJ, with her widowed daughter, Leah, and her grandson, Dr. J. Randolph Johnson. As pastor emeritus of Wallace Chapel, she continued to attend state and national church meetings. Although feeble, she attended and addressed sessions of the 1951 Winston-Salem, NC, WHFMS Quadrennial Convention. Randolph died, at age 85, at the Jersey City Medical Center.

Randolph's family records and papers are in the possession of her great-grandchildren, Lisa and Mark Randolph Johnson. Her obituary appeared in the *Jersey Journal* (Jersey City, NJ), Dec. 29, 1951.

*Gloria H. Dickinson*
*J. Maurice Hicks*

## RESTELLE ELIZABETH RICHARDSON REVEY, 1866–1939

Restelle Elizabeth (Richardson) Revey, American Indian craftsperson and businesswoman, was born near Eatontown (Monmouth County), NJ, in 1866, the youngest of eight children. Her father, Isaac R. Richardson, of Cherokee and Delaware Indian descent, was a carpenter, builder, and general contractor in the Monmouth County, New Jersey shore area. Her mother, Elizabeth (Reavy) Richardson, was of Delaware Indian and Dutch heritage.

When Revey was eleven, her family moved to Whitesville (since 1879, a section of Neptune, NJ), and built a large Victorian home at the top of Sand Hill, where the Sand Hill Indians met each June to dance, sing, and reminisce. She attended local schools up to the eighth grade and also the Episcopal church, and she listened avidly to her relatives, learning about her Cherokee and Delaware heritage.

Members of Revey's family were expert craftspersons; they made many traditional American Indian articles for their own use and sold others at Asbury Park and the vicinity. Young Revey made colorful bags and dolls with human or horse hair for wigs. She became a skillful seamstress, making shirts and jackets for men and other garments for her family.

In her mid-twenties, she married Johnson Revey, of Delaware Indian descent. The couple had a daughter, who died very young, and later two sons, James and Robert. For a time, Revey helped her husband's family farm their 100 acres in Reveytown, named for Thomas Reavy, their ancestor. During the winter, the couple lived at the old homestead on Sand Hill.

After careful planning, Revey and her husband purchased a large house in Asbury Park which she converted into a hotel. To bring good luck to the house, which she named "the Sneaden" after her grandmother's family, Revey hung a gourd bottle of salt in the kitchen. Many young people coming to the shore for summer jobs stayed at the Sneaden, a clean, safe place where they could enjoy meals cooked by "Aunt Del," as they called Revey. Teachers and others stayed there while seeking a more permanent residence. The business thrived for many years.

During the Depression, the Reveys bought a multifamily dwelling in New York City where they provided living space for family members and others who came to the city looking for a better life. Many could not pay rent, but Revey made them welcome. She and her sister Susan interested New York buyers in their beadwork and other crafts.

Other American Indians in New York heard about "Aunt Del" and "Uncle John," and their home became a weekend retreat for conversation and card playing. Revey believed in tradition and she inspired American Indian

consciousness and pride in her children, grandchildren, and guests. When she died on October 25, 1939, at age 73, in the Bronx, Revey was buried near her oldest son in Mt. Prospect Cemetery in Neptune, NJ.

An interview with James (Lone Bear) Revey at the New Jersey Indian Office, Orange, NJ, provided biographical details.

*Margaret T. Goodrich*
*Sheila Cowing*

Ruth St. Denis, in 1918 in "Siamese Ballet." St. Denis was a central figure in the development of modern American dance. *Courtesy, Dance Collection, the New York Public Library at Lincoln Center, Astor, Lenox and Tilden Foundations.*

## RUTH ST. DENIS, 1879–1968

Ruth St. Denis, a founder of the American modern dance movement, was born Ruth Dennis on January 20, 1879, in Newark (Essex County), NJ, the first child and only daughter of Thomas Laban Dennis and Ruth Emma (Hull) Dennis. Her father, an electrical engineer and amateur inventor, was born in Stourbridge, England, and emigrated with his parents to Boonton, NJ, when he was six. Her mother, whose family emigrated from England in the

1840s, was born in Canandaigua, NY, and graduated from the University of Michigan Medical School in 1872, but was never able to practice medicine due to a nervous disorder.

The circumstances surrounding her parents' marriage and her birth caused confusion over her actual date of birth. Her parents met at the Eagleswood Colony of artists and intellectuals in Perth Amboy, NJ, but Thomas Dennis was already married and had a son, Thomas Dennis, Jr. He subsequently obtained a divorce, gained custody of his son, and married the pregnant Ruth Emma Hull on December 6, 1878, in the studio of artist William Page. A little over a month later St. Denis was born, but no birth certificate or christening record exists.

In 1884 the Dennis family moved to a farm called Pin Oaks, near Somerville, NJ, where Brother (actual name), her brother, was born in 1885. Affectionately called "Buzz" by St. Denis, he was devoted to her and played a prominent role in her life and career. During her childhood on the farm St. Denis acquired the deep love of nature that was later reflected in her natural dance movements. It was also as a child that St. Denis felt the "subtle and indescribable attraction of religion" that was to grow in intensity during her life and infuse her dancing and writing. (St. Denis, *An Unfinished Life*, 5) In times of stress, usually associated with money problems, since her father was a heavy drinker who was often unemployed, her mother would read the Bible with "Ruthie" at her feet. St. Denis's religious persuasion, however, unlike the strict, organized Methodism of her mother, was more akin to transcendentalism, supplemented in later life by her study of Eastern religions and acceptance of Christian Science.

St. Denis attended the Adamsville School in Bridgewater Township and then Somerville High School. Though an avid reader and writer, she hated the discipline and formality of school and often got into trouble because of her outspoken and independent ways. As an escape from the restraints of school and church, and the constant arguing of her parents, she resorted to reading, performing Delsarte exercises, and playacting in front of the summer boarders her mother accepted to ease financial woes.

Enrolled by her mother in Maud Davenport's dancing classes in Somerville, St. Denis received plaudits for "remarkable talent" in her solo during the school's recital. Her mother then took her to Karl Marwig, a dance teacher in New York City, who gave her lessons free of charge, though she sold watercress door to door to pay for carfare. St. Denis, in an interview in 1964, said that she felt ungainly and gangly as a child and didn't know what to do with her hands. Ironically, it was her gracefulness, freer use of the torso, and expressive use of her arms that became the hallmarks of her technical contributions to the dance.

In the fall of 1893 a wealthy aunt paid to send St. Denis to the Dwight L. Moody Seminary in Northfield, MA, in an effort to reestablish a more conventional education. But St. Denis left before Christmas after an argument during which Moody referred to the theater as immoral. She arrived home in time to make her dance debut in her mother's production of *The Old Homestead* at the Old Somerset Hall in Somerville. The review in the *Unionist-Gazette* of December 28, 1893, proclaimed that "Ruthie Dennis was the star performing her skirt dances."

St. Denis's mother then took her daughter to New York City, where in 1894 she got her first job dancing in vaudeville at Worth's Museum. Thus began the first phase of St. Denis's career, featuring dancing and acting roles in several David Belasco plays. It was Belasco who inspired her stage name when he "laughingly" referred to her as "Saint" Dennis because of her "prim deportment." (*New York Times*, July 22, 1968)

In 1896 the Dennis family lost their farm and moved to Brooklyn, NY, a place St. Denis hated. After she had achieved fame and some financial stability, she repurchased part of Pin Oaks Farm, though she never lived there again. St. Denis enrolled in Packer Collegiate Institute in Brooklyn in the fall of 1896 at age seventeen, but left in 1898 to continue her stage career.

The catalyst for the emergence of St. Denis as an innovative solo dancer came when she saw the goddess Isis on a poster for Egyptian Deities cigarettes. She began to explore the dance and culture of Egypt, then discovered the dances of India, which led to her choreographing *Radha*, the dance that brought her fame in 1906. Radha, the symbol of the human soul seeking the divine, epitomizes the focus of her entire life and career. Although some critics labeled her the "Jersey Hindoo," most of the public and press found her dance interesting, with its innovative use of bare feet, bare midriff, and exotic movement. From 1906 to 1909 St. Denis toured Europe with *Radha* and its companion pieces, *Cobra*, *Nautch*, and *Incense*. The Europeans treated her as an artist and seemed to grasp the spiritual content at the core of her dance concepts, as exemplified by the London *Times* critic describing her performance as "dancing that was charged with meaning." (Shelton, *Divine Dancer*, 72)

As a dancer, St. Denis was almost entirely self-taught. Although her dancing was influenced in part by Delsarte movement and by the opulence of the Belasco productions, the primary motivations were her use of nature as a model for movement. She had a strong belief that dance is "the divine impulse of spirit to move rhythmically, proportionately and perpetually." (Shawn, *Ruth St. Denis*, 101)

After her successful European tour, St. Denis returned to the United States and laid the foundations for her dance work, aiming to popularize dance as more than just frivolous entertainment. During her 1909–10 American tour she performed in Plainfield, NJ, where "more than 300

Somerville residents" came to see "the hometown girl who made good." (Shelton, 99) In 1914 Ted Shawn, a young dancer, became her partner, and on August 13, 1914, he also became her husband. Shawn came at a crucial time in her life, offering her the support she had previously received from her mother and brother. Reticent about marriage, St. Denis acquiesced but asserted her independence by having the word *obey* deleted from the vows and by refusing to wear a ring.

In 1915 St. Denis and Shawn founded the Denishawn School in Los Angeles, CA, dedicated to teaching eclectic styles and techniques of dance. The center of the school was moved to New York City in 1920 and Denishawn House was built in 1929. They also formed the Denishawn Dance Troupe, which brought dance to small-town America during the 1920s. Their school and troupe gave birth to such great modern dancers as Martha Graham, Charles Weidman, and Doris Humphrey.

St. Denis often experienced an internal conflict between the need to experiment and the necessity to popularize her art. In 1919 she broke briefly from Denishawn to form her own company, the Ruth St. Denis Concert Dancers. The group performed her interpretive dances based on classical music, called "music visualizations."

During the early 1930s St. Denis experienced difficult times. Denishawn failed; her marriage ended in separation in 1931, although it never became a legal separation or divorce; and in the spring of 1931 her mother, the driving force behind her career and her most severe critic, died. St. Denis's professional career went into temporary eclipse, and her active influence on modern dance ended.

A series of events at the end of the 1930s and the beginning of the 1940s brought St. Denis back into prominence and introduced her to a new generation. She became the founder and director of the dance department of Adelphi College in 1938. She published her autobiography in 1939 and had an acclaimed revival of *Radha* at her husband's dance festival, Jacob's Pillow, in Becket, MA, in 1941. In 1940 she founded, with La Meri, an ethnic dancer and scholar, the Authentic School of Oriental Dancing in New York City. Most of her remaining years were spent in Hollywood, CA, where her brother built a studio with a small theater in 1948 for her "Church of the Divine Dance." She also appeared regularly at Jacob's Pillow from 1949 to 1955, participated in lecture-performances throughout the country, and devoted herself to the Ruth St. Denis Foundation, which was organized in part to assemble, catalog, and record material related to her career.

In 1964 Shawn and St. Denis celebrated their fiftieth wedding anniversary at Jacob's Pillow and performed together for the last time in a dance based on one of her poems, "Siddhas of the Upper Air."

Throughout her life St. Denis wrote constantly, keeping journals, writing poems, some of which were published

in a volume titled *Lotus Lights* (1932). She also composed essays on such topics as the slavery of war, the need for artists to be leaders, and the dangers of a mechanical world. In a personal reminiscence of St. Denis, Martha Graham stressed her integrity to dance as she saw it, her humor, her vanity, and commented that she had "all the mystery, all the magic." (*New York Times*, Aug. 4, 1968)

On July 21, 1968, at age 89, Ruth St. Denis died of a stroke at Hollywood Presbyterian Hospital. She was cremated, and her brother erected a tombstone to her in Forest Lawn Cemetery inscribed with the lines from her poem "Calling," the first four lines of which fittingly capture her life: "The Gods have meant / That I should dance, / And by the Gods / I will!"

The Dance Collection of the NYPL-LC houses the Ruth St. Denis papers, as well as the Ted Shawn Collection, the Denishawn Scrapbooks, and the most complete video collection of St. Denis performing. The Ruth St. Denis Collection at the Library at the University of California, Los Angeles, houses her journals, letters, and other memorabilia. Her published works include her autobiography, *Ruth St. Denis: An Unfinished Life* (1939), and a volume of poetry, *Lotus Lights* (1932). A memoir is: Walter Terry, *Miss Ruth: The "More Living Life" of Ruth St. Denis* (1969). Biographies of her are: Suzanne Shelton, *Divine Dancer: A Biography of Ruth St. Denis* (1981); and Ted Shawn, *Ruth St. Denis: Pioneer and Prophet* (1920). A taped interview with St. Denis in which she discusses her life and dance is available at NJ-MCL. A sketch of her appears in *NAW-MP*. For specific dance information, consult C. L. Schundt, *The Professional Appearances of Ruth St. Denis and Ted Shawn: A Chronology and an Index of Dances, 1906–1932* (1962). Her obituary appeared in the *New York Times*, July 22, 1968.

*Donna L. Singer*

## MARY BUELL SAYLES, 1878–1959

Mary Buell Sayles, social reformer, writer, and educator, was born in Chicago, IL, on January 2, 1878, the daughter of John E. and Julia (Wilson) Sayles, Little information is available on her family or early education, other than that she graduated from Smith College in 1900, and at a remarkably young age her research and writing skills began to have a far-reaching effect on housing conditions and reform legislation throughout New Jersey.

Immediately after graduation from Smith, Sayles moved to Jersey City, NJ, where for two years she was a resident of Whittier House, the famous settlement founded in 1893 by CORNELIA BRADFORD. Whittier House had been established to bring needed services to the poor of Jersey City and, as Sayles's work demonstrates, also to effect social change through legislation.

As part of her duties at Whittier House, Sayles led a club of young women in a program of parties, lectures, and study sessions. But since its members came to the settlement after working at menial jobs "from eight o'clock in the morning until nine in the evening," the club leaders sought primarily to bring some "brightness and laughter" into their lives. (Whittier House Eighth Annual Report, 1902–3, 38)

During her second year as resident of Whittier House, Sayles received the fellowship of the College Settlements Association, under whose aegis she undertook a research project on "Housing Conditions in Jersey City." The study was described as the first "scientific" investigation of the condition of the tenements in the city. She investigated 2,286 apartments in "clearly defined representative districts" (Supplement to *The Annals of the American Academy of Political and Social Science,* January 1903, iii), and her sharp, incisive descriptions had a strong impact. Moreover, her report was published in 1903 by the American Academy of Political and Social Science, an impressive academic achievement for so young an author and one that considerably strengthened the credibility of her research.

Sayles was an effective writer—clear but pointed in her carefully researched and documented report. She urged action, noting that "there is a lack of realization, among the cultivated and wealthy, of the need of reform and a lack of realization among the uneducated and struggling, of the possibility and the means of securing reform." (Report, 54) Detailing and enumerating the flaws of the often overcrowded, dangerous tenements, largely inhabited by foreign-born factory workers and their families, she described "stagnant air wells," windowless bedrooms, locked fire exits or nonexistent fire escapes, lack of privacy, unsanitary conditions, and damp and "unwholesome" cellars and yards with "nauseating odors." Her conclusion in the report was that "only through the rousing of interest can any permanent improvement in conditions be brought about, since without a strong pressure of public opinion, reform legislation cannot be secured or enforced." (Report, 70)

Sayles's study did lead to action. Whittier House immediately organized a public meeting in March 1903, to which elected officials of Jersey City were invited. A blue ribbon committee was formed and within two weeks had been convened in the mayor's office. CORNELIA BRADFORD later wrote that Sayles's report "so astounded" Governor Franklin Murphy "as to the probable living conditions in other cities in New Jersey that he immediately appointed a New Jersey State Tenement House Commission." (Bradford to Albert J. Kennedy, Oct. 2, 1920) The commission's work led to the enactment of a statewide tenement code.

Sayles was made sanitary inspector in New York City in 1904. By 1911 she was working for the Russell Sage Foundation. During World War I she served in France with the Red Cross and in 1921 published a book, *Home Service in Action,* describing Red Cross casework. That same year she returned briefly to New Jersey to serve as executive director of the Central Bureau of Social Service in Morristown. Thereafter, the balance of her career was spent in writing, research, and teaching in New York City.

By 1923 Sayles was involved in an emerging field: the use of psychiatry in dealing with children's problems. She went to work for a division of the Commonwealth Fund, called the Joint Committee on Methods of Preventing Delinquency, which she described as a "fearful name." (*Smith Alumnae Quarterly,* May 1924) Under the fund's auspices, her next two books were published: *The Problem Child in School* (1925) and *The Problem Child at Home: A Study in Parent–Child Relationships* (1928). This last work was awarded honorable mention by *Children: The Parents Magazine* for the best book on child development that year. Both books were "widely read in this country and abroad." (*Smith Alumnae Quarterly,* May 1959) In 1936 another of Sayles's books appeared, *Substitute Parent: A Study of Foster Families,* published by the Commonwealth Fund and Oxford University Press.

Sayles never married. She eventually retired with her college friend, Helen Richards, to a cottage in Meriden, NH, where they had spent many summers. Sayles died, at age 81, in Hanover, NH, on March 9, 1959, from chronic kidney disease. She was buried in Springfield Cemetery, Springfield, MA.

The NJ-HS maintains a collection of material relating to Whittier House, notably the *Annual Reports* for the years Sayles lived there and correspondence from Cornelia Bradford relating to Sayles, including the letter to Arthur J. Kennedy, Oct. 2, 1920. Her activities were noted in the Alumnae Notes section of the *Smith Alumnae Quarterly* 15 (May 1924):340, and her obituary appeared in the *Smith Alumnae Quarterly* 50 (May 1959):191.

*Jeannette D. Kahlenberg*

## HANNAH SILVERMAN, 1896–1960

Hannah (Silverman) Mandell, labor activist, was born January 28, 1896, in New York City. Morris Silverman, her father, was an American-born Jew of German parentage. Sarah (Sarna) Silverman, her mother, was a Polish Jew born in the manufacturing city of Lodz, where her family worked in textiles. There were thirteen children in the Sarna family. Hirsh Sarna, their father, brought his wife, Fannie, and eight or nine children to the United States, where Sarah met and married Morris Silverman. Silverman was the second of their four children.

She became famous in 1913, when only seventeen, for her leading role in the Paterson, NJ, silk strike of 1913. Her life is obscure before 1913, and after 1913 it becomes obscure again. Only in the months during and immediately after the Paterson strike was she a public figure. But in that brief period she became a symbol of what women could do in labor conflicts, if given the opportunity.

Silk was Paterson's biggest industry, and strikes at one or another of the almost 300 silk mills were a common occurrence. The 1913 strike was different because all the mills went out on strike together, and because the strikers invited the radical Industrial Workers of the World (IWW) to help them. When the strike began, late in February 1913, Silverman was working at the Westerhoff silk mill, which she enthusiastically joined in picketing. By April 25, 1913, she had become the captain of the pickets around the mill. So when the police arrived on that day and attempted to disperse the crowd, it was to the seventeen-year-old that they turned. She refused to cooperate, and they arrested her, before arresting 47 of her fellow picketers. She was charged with "unlawful assembly" and spent the night in the city jail. But she was undaunted. Out awaiting trial, she returned to the picket line and was arrested again, and again. In May, she and six other girls were charged with harassing two female strikebreakers. Silverman, in recognition of her growing leadership, was given the stiffest sentence, 60 days in the county jail. Cheered by hundreds along the way to jail, she and the six other girls sang union songs to show that they were unrepentant. A writ was filed on her behalf and she was freed on $5,000 bail after only two days. Not satisfied, Silverman threatened to take the case to the upper courts and to bring suit for false arrest. The charge was quietly dropped. Speaking that Sunday from the balcony of the BOTTO house, in nearby Haledon, to tens of thousands of silkworkers and their relatives and friends, she said she had been to the county jail three times but that the police could not keep her away from the picket lines. Now she was beginning to acquire a reputation as the incarnation of the fierce pride, resilient spirit, and idealistic hopes of the silk strikers.

She came to trial on the original charge of unlawful assembly early in June 1913, while the strike continued. The prosecutor, hammering away on the theme of outside agitators from the IWW stirring up local workers, tried to use her to make his point. He demanded that she tell what the IWW really was and admit that "Big Bill" Haywood, the famous labor agitator, was really the IWW. "Haywood is Haywood," declared the unflappable Silverman. "The workers in the mills are the IWW."

The next day, while waiting for her trial to resume, she was seated in the rear of the courtroom when the judge gave an unusually harsh sentence to another striker. Some accounts say Silverman gasped and others say she hissed, but the judge was furious and slapped her with a 20-day sentence for disorderly conduct. Lawyers secured her release from county jail in time for her to lead the massive New York parade to Madison Square Garden, where the strikers, on June 7, acted out the drama of their strike before an overflow crowd.

"One of the leading lights in the present strike" was the way a Paterson newspaper described the seventeen-year-old. Opinions of Silverman varied according to attitudes held toward the strike. Described by a defense lawyer as a "mere slip of a girl, in fact only a kid," she was denounced as the "little agitator" by an assistant prosecutor and as an "impudent girl" by the judge. Elizabeth Gurley Flynn, the IWW organizer who encouraged Paterson women to come forward and be leaders, called Silverman "the heroine of the strike" and cited her in an article two years later as an example of what women could do in strikes, once given the chance.

But the strike was lost. Silverman was almost certainly blacklisted. It is not clear how she spent the next nine years. In 1922 she married a 39-year old Lithuanian Jew named Harry J. Mandell, who did not come from Paterson. She became a homemaker. The family, which included Robert and Jack, their two children, struggled economically during the Depression. In 1935 they moved from Paterson to Brooklyn, where Harry Mandell tried to make a living running a candy store. After it went bankrupt they were dependent on relief for several years. Eventually, Silverman's husband bought a new store in Paterson, and she worked alongside him. She never spoke of her role in the strike in front of the children, though she and her husband frequently made mention of Haywood, Flynn, and the IWW, and he sometimes teased her about her strike activities.

Silverman's own family reflected the social and political divisions in the Jewish community. Her older sister Bertha married a mill owner who moved his business out of state to escape Paterson's labor militancy. Her younger brother Harold worked as a mill hand in Paterson and continued to denounce the owners. Silverman was particularly kind to him. Always proud of her Jewish heritage, she was never religious. She lived out her life with quiet integrity, but without special excitement or attention, and without an arena for her proven abilities as a speaker and leader.

In the 1967 school board election in Wayne, her son Jack, who was not aware of his mother's activity in the 1913 strike, bravely withstood anti-Semitic attacks and became (like his mother) briefly famous. Silverman herself had died seven years earlier, on July 17, 1960, from a heart attack. She is buried in King Solomon's Cemetery in Clifton, NJ.

Interviews with Silverman's son, Jack Mandell, and his wife, Mona, of Wayne, NJ, on Jan. 4, 1984, provided biographical details. The major source information on Silverman's role in the 1913 strike is Steve Golin, *The Fragile Bridge: Paterson Silk Strike, 1913* (1988).

*Steve Golin*

## ERMINNIE ADELE PLATT SMITH, 1836–1886

Erminnie Adele (Platt) Smith, geologist and ethnologist, was born on April 26, 1836, in Marcellus, NY, the ninth of ten children. Her mother, Ermina (Dodge) Platt, died when Smith was two years old. Joseph Platt, her father, was a farmer whose family was among the earliest settlers in the area. He was also an amateur naturalist and greatly encouraged her interest in the natural sciences. Under his guidance she began a collection of mineral and geological specimens. Pursuing this interest throughout her life, she eventually developed an extensive and valuable private collection.

In 1850, at fourteen, Smith entered Emma Willard's famous school, the Troy Female Seminary, graduating three years later. There she displayed a gift for learning languages, studying French and German. During vacations she was tutored in Latin and Greek by Dr. Arthur, father of President Chester A. Arthur. Within a year after leaving school, she married Simeon H. Smith, a native of Troy. They moved to Chicago, where Simeon Smith was first a commission merchant during the Civil War years and then a banker for the First National Bank of Chicago. She was soon rearing four sons: Simeon, Willard, Carlton, and Eugene.

In 1866 the family moved to Jersey City, NJ, where Simeon Smith was superintendent of the stockyards and held local political office. When the boys were old enough for school, probably in the early 1870s, Smith and her sons went to Europe for four years to travel and study. Smith graduated from a two-year course in mineralogy at the School of Mines in Freiberg. At Strasburg she studied crystallography and at Heidelberg she was tutored in German language and literature. She investigated principles of light polarization and techniques used to cut stones for lenses and scientific purposes at Oberstein. Smith visited the Baltic coast, where she gathered information on the amber industry. After returning to the United States, she presented a paper on amber to the American Association for the Advancement of Science (AAAS) and published an article, "Concerning Amber," in the *American Naturalist.*

By 1876 Smith returned to Jersey City, where she received much local attention as a popular lecturer on scientific and cultural subjects. She devoted considerable effort to a women's society she founded in Jersey City, the Daughters of the Aesthetics. With Smith as its president (until her death), this group held monthly meetings for which members—eventually numbering 500—made a study of music, literature, and the sciences. Lectures were given by such notable guests as Thomas Edison, Matthew Arnold, Oscar Wilde, and John Wesley Powell, the director of the U.S. Geological Survey. Smith prepared many talks herself for these meetings, as well as for other organizations. In 1878 she became a member of Sorosis, a New York women's club, and for several years chaired its Committee on Science. She became an active member of the AAAS, reading a paper on jade in 1879.

Through her involvement with scientific societies and her acquaintance with John Wesley Powell, Smith became interested in ethnographic studies being done on American Indians. In 1879 the Smithsonian's Bureau of Ethnology employed Smith as a scientific explorer, concentrating on the Six Nations (the Onondaga, Tuscarora, Mohawk, Iroquois, Oneida, and Seneca tribes). The Onondaga Reservation was within three miles of her childhood home, and since she was familiar with the area and some of its inhabitants, she selected this as the first location for her fieldwork. With advice and guidance from Lewis Henry Morgan and Major Powell, she traveled during the summers of 1879 to 1884 throughout New York State and Canada, gathering data on language and culture. Recognizing the urgency that fueled her research, she wrote to Morgan: "Whatever is done must be done quickly as the old ideas are nearly gone or sadly intermingled with modern notions." (Letter to Lewis Henry Morgan, undated)

As one of the pioneers in field ethnography, Smith worked with American Indian assistants, compiling thousands of words of the languages of the Six Nations. Her research efforts centered on the production of a dictionary and grammar of the Tuscarora language, a task still uncompleted at the time of her death. J.W.B. Hewitt, a scholar and member of the Tuscarora tribe who had worked with Smith for six years, continued the work. In 1883 her study "Myths of the Iroquois" appeared in the Bureau of American Ethnology's second *Annual Report.* Other manuscripts on Iroquois language and customs were read by Smith at meetings of the AAAS.

As an indication of the high regard in which she was held by the people with whom she worked, the Tuscarora tribe adopted Smith as a sister of the head chief, John Mountpleasant, at whose house she was a guest. Describing this occasion, Smith wrote: "So I have been adopted into the Nation as a member of the Bear Clan. . . . My name is more poetical than appropriate—being translated Beautiful Flower the White Bear of the Tuscaroras!" (Letter to Lewis Henry Morgan, undated)

Smith was the first woman elected a fellow of the New York Academy of Sciences. Elected secretary of the section of anthropology in 1885, she was the first woman ever appointed an officer of the AAAS. In that same year Governor Abbett appointed her commissioner of the Department of Woman's Work, to represent the state of New Jersey at the New Orleans Exposition.

On June 9, 1886, at age 50, Smith died in Jersey City of heart disease and a cerebral embolism. Funeral services were held in the Lafayette Reformed Church. She was interred in the New York Bay Cemetery, Jersey City, next to her son Simeon, who died in 1882. In 1888, on the second anniversary of her death, a group of friends delivered a memorial address at Vassar College and established the Erminnie A. Smith Memorial Fund to award an annual prize to the best student research paper on geology or mineralogy.

Smith's papers are available at the Smithsonian Institution (Washington, D.C.). The NJ-JCPL maintains a collection of material on her. Letters to her are available in the Lewis Henry Morgan and Henry Ward Papers, University of Rochester (Rochester, NY). A complete bibliography of her works appears in James Pilling, *Bibliography of the Iroquoian Languages* (1888). Her papers before the American Association for the Advancement of Science appear in its *Proceedings, 1880–1887*. She is profiled in *NAW*. Her obituary appeared in the *New York Times*, June 10, 1886.

*Patricia Fleming Blacker*
*Pamela P. Grossman*

Elizabeth Cady Stanton, noted women's rights leader, *right*, with her friend and collaborator Susan B. Anthony in a photograph taken around 1870 during the time Stanton lived in Tenafly. *Courtesy, the Schlesinger Library, Radcliffe College.*

## ELIZABETH CADY STANTON, 1815–1902

Elizabeth (Cady) Stanton, women's rights leader and theoretician, was born in Johnstown, NY, on November 12, 1815, the eighth of eleven children of Daniel and Margaret (Livingston) Cady. Of these eleven children, only five—all daughters—lived into adulthood. Her father was a prominent lawyer and wealthy landowner in upstate New York, her mother one of New York's "blue-blooded first families." Although she lived most of her life in New York, Stanton resided in Tenafly, NJ, from 1868 to 1885, some of the most active years of her long and busy life.

Stanton graduated from the Johnstown Academy, a coeducational secondary school, in 1830. Unable to attend Union College with the boys in her class, she wrote years later in her autobiography: "I felt more keenly than ever the humiliation of the distinctions made on the ground of sex." (Stanton, *Eighty Years and More*, 33–34) She graduated from the Troy Female Seminary in 1833.

Formal education, according to Stanton, was less important in the formation of her feminist ideologies than were certain key individuals. Her parents, both strongminded and intelligent, served as role models. The death of Stanton's older brother Eleazer, at age 20, was an event she later cited as one that "changed considerably the current of my life" (Stanton, *Eighty Years and More*, 20) as she tried, without much success, in her early life to become the son her father no longer had.

As a young woman, Stanton often visited the family of Gerrit Smith, her cousin, in Peterboro, NY. Smith, one of the wealthiest and most philanthropic individuals of 19th-century America, was a leading supporter of many reform movements—the abolition of slavery, women's rights, temperance, and prison reform. According to one biographer, "Her visits [to Peterboro] made her receptive to the reform spirit. She was challenged to think about issues that were never discussed in her own home, and she thrived on the arguments and exchange of ideas." (Griffith, *In Her Own Right*, 25)

During a visit to Peterboro in October 1839, she met Henry Brewster Stanton (1805–87), a well-known abolitionist agent and speaker. After a brief romance, they were married in May 1840, against the wishes of her father. Their wedding date was hastened by their determination to attend together the first World Anti-Slavery Convention, to be held the following month in London, where Henry Stanton was an elected delegate.

American abolitionists were split over the proper role of women in their organizations, and Wendell Phillips's motion in London to include the American women delegates as participants in the convention brought this issue to the floor. The overwhelming defeat of Phillips's motion by the male delegates forced Stanton for the first time in her life to confront the issue of women's rights. In London she met Lucretia Mott and they vowed after the convention to hold a meeting in the United States to discuss women's rights.

The meeting, however, was delayed for eight years as Stanton became preoccupied with family responsibilities, particularly childbearing and rearing. Stanton's first three children were born during this period (Daniel, 1842; Henry, 1844; and Gerrit, 1845); at the time, the family lived in Boston, where Henry Stanton worked as a lawyer. In 1847 Stanton's father purchased a house for the Stanton family in Seneca Falls, NY, where, after the intellectually stimulating atmosphere of Boston, Stanton felt increasingly limited in her role as housewife and mother. The following year, as the result of a conversation with Lucretia Mott, and others, about her dissatisfaction, a "Woman's Rights Convention" was called for July 19–20, 1848. This historic meeting, held in the Wesleyan Chapel in Seneca Falls, insured Stanton's place in history and began her lifelong commitment to women's rights. Her ideas, including the radical notion of woman suffrage, were embodied in her composition "A Declaration of Rights and Sentiments," modeled on the Declaration of Independence. The Seneca Falls convention received national newspaper coverage. Despite ridicule in the press, other regional and state conventions on women's rights were organized immediately.

In the years following, Stanton attempted to balance her family responsibilities with her increasing involvement and leadership role in the burgeoning woman's rights movement. Four more children were born in these years (Theodore, 1851; Margaret, 1852; Harriot, 1856; and Robert, 1859). From her home she prepared speeches and articles for women's rights conventions and for the *Lily*, a temperance journal published locally.

Stanton viewed her role as a mother with some ambivalence. In a letter to Susan B. Anthony in the late 1850s, she wrote: "As I contrast Henry's freedom with my bondage and feel that, because of the false position of woman, I have been compelled to hold all my noblest aspirations in abeyance in order to be a wife, a mother, a nurse, a cook, a household drudge, I am fired anew and long to pour forth from my own experience the whole story of woman's wrongs." (Theodore Stanton Collection, Douglass Library, Rutgers University)

Stanton produced resolutions, articles, and speeches on divorce, temperance, rights for blacks, women's property legislation, coeducation, and suffrage. She began to assume the role of the major proponent and theoretician of women's rights issues with help from Amelia Willard and Susan B. Anthony, who allowed Stanton to balance her public and familial commitments. Willard was the housekeeper for the Stantons from 1851 to 1881.

Susan B. Anthony met Stanton in 1851 when Anthony was in Seneca Falls to attend a temperance meeting. She was easily converted to the women's rights cause, and she often delivered speeches that Stanton wrote or watched a baby or even the stew as Stanton "cranked out" resolutions. Stanton and Anthony's famous 50-year friendship and collaboration was one of respect and affection, if not without occasional differences of opinion.

Stanton made speeches before the New York State Senate (1854) and the Assembly (1860) to support the Married Women's Property Act. Her advocacy of divorce split the women's movement between those who agreed with her and those who did not, such as LUCY STONE, ANTOINETTE BROWN BLACKWELL, and William Lloyd Garrison.

When Stanton and Anthony campaigned across Kansas in 1867 to promote a state referendum on the ballot for universal suffrage, they further antagonized their friends in the East by their association and monetary support from George Train, a wealthy, eccentric Democrat who was openly opposed to black suffrage. After the referendum was defeated in Kansas, and with the subsequent passage of the constitutional amendment granting black male suffrage, Stanton's writings on black male suffrage became increasingly vituperative. Stanton and Anthony formed the National Woman Suffrage Association (NWSA); shortly thereafter LUCY STONE organized the American Woman Suffrage Association (AWSA).

Stanton resided in New York City from 1862 to 1868; she and Anthony published their women's right journal, the *Revolution*, for two years at the end of this period. In 1868 Stanton purchased a home in Tenafly, NJ, a "charming colonial dwelling at the crest of the Highwood Avenue hill" (Sisson, *The Story of Tenafly*, 25–27), partly with money she inherited from her father, and partly from her own earnings as a speaker.

While Stanton resided in Tenafly she spent several months of each year away from home, lecturing or visiting Europe. Her child-rearing responsibilities lessened, she dedicated full time to her causes and earned a good income by participating in the lyceum lecture circuit. This undertaking, which involved crossing the continent a few times a year, could have been difficult for someone like Stanton, then in her late fifties and overweight. But by all reports she delivered her speeches—among them, "Home Life," "Marriage and Divorce," "Our Girls," and 'The Bible and Women's Rights"—very ably. She was well received, particularly in the western states.

Her correspondence and writings do not indicate that Stanton ever worked with local New Jersey suffragists, yet Tenafly served as an important base for her. Here she was reunited with her family during Christmas and summers, when she rested from the demanding lecture tours. Three volumes of the *History of Woman Suffrage* were written in Tenafly with Anthony (Matilda Joslyn Gage was a coauthor of the third volume). Stanton's correspondence includes many references to time spent in Tenafly and its importance to her. In 1877 she wrote to Anthony: "As I sit here on the blue hills of Jersey in peace and quiet and think of you started again on one of those perilous journeys, I wish, in my inmost soul, we had a few thousand a year each that we might remain together and write up the record [*The History of Woman Suffrage*] as we long to do." (Theodore Stanton Collection, Douglass Library, Rutgers University)

Stanton caused a great deal of excitement in Tenafly when she attempted to vote in 1880. She was denied the right to do so and, with Susan B. Anthony at her side, left the polls. Later, in a letter to her son Theodore, she said: "We had great fun frightening and muddling these old Dutch inspectors. The whole town is agape with my act." (Theodore Stanton Collection, Douglass Library, Rutgers University)

In 1882 Stanton rented her Tenafly home and went on the first of several trips to Europe. She reopened the house for the last time in 1885 and finished the third volume of the *History* with Anthony and Gage. In 1886 Stanton returned to England. A few months later Henry Stanton died in New York City, where he had lived for the last 20 years, with occasional visits to Tenafly. Stanton remained in Europe and sold the Tenafly house.

She was still an active feminist while in her eighties, although her work and interest in the traditional suffrage organizations had steadily decreased over the years. Stanton continued to support herself by writing pieces for newspapers and periodicals. Her autobiography, *Eighty Years and More*, was published in 1898. She delivered what is considered her best speech on women's need for self-reliance, "The Solitude of Self," before the U.S. Congress in 1892, at age 76.

Stanton's later years were not without controversy. Believing that Christianity was extremely degrading to women, in 1895 she published *The Woman's Bible*, a work organized as a series of commentaries on biblical passages that discuss women. Its publication created a national scandal and resulted in her censure by the National American Woman Suffrage Association (NAWSA) in 1896. Undaunted, she published the second volume of the work in 1898, renouncing the "religious bigotry" of the women who opposed it.

Stanton died of heart failure in New York City on October 26, 1902, at age 87, after failing health and increasing blindness. The previous day she had written a letter to President Theodore Roosevelt urging his support of woman suffrage. She was cremated and buried at Woodlawn Cemetery in New York.

Stanton's correspondence is located at NJ-DC, DC-LC, and NY-VC. Her autobiography, *Eighty Years and More* (1898; 1971), is an important source, as is Ellen DuBois, *Elizabeth Cady Stanton, Susan B. Anthony: Correspondence, Writings, Speeches* (1981). Several biographies of Stanton exist, including Elisabeth Griffith, *In Her Own Right: The Life of Elizabeth Cady Stanton* (1984), and Alma Lutz, *Created Equal* (1940). A sketch of her appears in *NAW*. Eva Sisson, *The Story of Tenafly* (1939), refers to Stanton's residence in the town.

*Amy Dykeman*

## MARY MERCER STEELE, 1849–1936

Mary Mercer Steele was the second woman admitted to the New Jersey Bar. She was born in Somerville (Somerset County), NJ, on July 9, 1849, the first of two children, a girl and a boy, of William Gaston and Mary Elizabeth (Henry) Steele.

Steele's father was the cashier of the Somerset County Bank and a prestigious member of the Somerville community. He was related to the well-known Gaston family, one of the first families to settle in Somerset County (as early as 1699), and served two terms in the U.S. Congress during the Civil War. Steele's mother was a descendant of the old and distinguished Stryker family, which can be traced back in New Jersey to 1777, when Captain John Stryker successfully aided the Revolutionary cause.

Steele's lineage became very important in light of her choice of career. Because she was a member of two of the most distinguished New Jersey families, she was afforded many opportunities and experiences.

Steele was educated in the Somerville public school system as well as in private school. She attended the Oakland Female Institute, located in Norristown, PA. The school, while not exclusive, was for the well-to-do. It offered students a well-rounded, liberal education and expected the women students to achieve success. Its pupils came from all over the States and various foreign countries, including Cuba, Greece, and Scotland. Steele took advantage of her educational experience at Oakland and graduated as the valedictorian of the Class of 1869.

Afterward Steele went on to teach school. Some time later she decided to study law. It is not clear what motivated this decision, but in all likelihood it was family influences. The Gaston family had its share of lawyers, her father was a member of Congress, and her brother was soon to become an attorney. In the 1800s one could read law in the office of an attorney or a judge and then make an application to be admitted to the New Jersey Bar. Steele decided she would study law in the office of Gaston & Bergen in Somerville. She also studied law with the Honorable A. A. Clark of Somerville, with whom her brother had studied law. Studying law for her was easy; the hard part was being admitted to practice in the state. In 1894 the New Jersey Bar was receptive to and yet skeptical of the idea of female attorneys: "If women are really satisfied that it would be good for them to be lawyers, we should not be so ungallant as to say anything against it, nor will it do to seem to fear their competition. It is not a question to be decided lightly." (*New Jersey Law Journal*, Mar. 1894, 93)

In 1894 MARY PHILBROOK, the first female attorney in New Jersey, applied for admission to the bar. The petition was denied and she was not admitted until 1895. Steele pursued her own struggle, and in February 1897 she became the second woman in the state to be admitted to the New Jersey Bar. Her admission to the bar prompted an editorial in the 1897 issue of the *New Jersey Law Journal*, in which she was described as a deserving and well-qualified woman.

Steele became a member of the Somerset County Bar and served as its secretary, working as a court stenographer to hold that office. She set up her law practice in the Gaston Building in Somerville, where she worked for the rest of her life. Evidence indicates that Steele's legal practice was not the typical one of her male counterparts. She probably never argued a case in court. Instead, she involved herself in humanitarian and suffrage issues.

Steele introduced a bill extending the position of commissioner of deeds to women. Because of her persistence, the bill became law after being defeated twice before. Steele was the first woman to serve in that capacity after the bill went into effect. She was a charter member of the Somerset County Hospital and represented the Women's Auxiliary Board in legal matters; she was a prominent member of the Society for the Prevention of Cruelty to Animals (SPCA). An active supporter of the woman suffrage movement throughout her life, she championed women's rights.

The legal community regarded Steele as a highly competent and dignified attorney. Her contemporaries described her as possessing a comprehensive knowledge of the law. Others have described Steele as a woman with determination who was courteous, diligent, courageous, merciful, shrewd, and ambitious. Throughout her professional life she showed great courage and determination. These qualities proved to be those most necessary for her success.

While there is some information on Steele's professional life, there is little on her personal life. The dignified manner in which she conducted herself in her legal work was apparent in her personal dealings as well. One neighbor remembered visiting Steele in her office in the Gaston Building. Then in her eighties, Steele was stylishly dressed in lavender reading her law books through Queen Mary glasses. She made an explicit request in her will not to have her property sold at public auction, but rather to antique dealers. In her will she left a considerable sum of money to the Somerset County Hospital and to two wards of her brother, William Vernon Steele. She also urged her executors to obtain the best prices for her property.

Throughout her life, Steele was aware of the significance of her lineage and believed it important to preserve heirlooms within the family. Therefore those items handed down to her were bequeathed to other family members. The portraits of Major General Peter Stryker and his wife were given to General Stryker's grandson. The pictures of her father and mother were given to her cousin, whom she named as one of the executors of her will. The Mercer family silverware was bequeathed to other members of the family.

Steele never married or had children. She died of asphyxiation by coal, at age 85, on January 21, 1936, and was buried in the New Cemetery in Somerville, NJ. Her obituary in the *New Jersey Law Journal*, January 30, 1936, incorrectly named her as the first female attorney of the state.

Short biographies of Steele appear in Edward Keasbey, *The Courts and Lawyers of New Jersey, 1661–1912* 3 (1912); and in Abraham Van Doren Honeyman, *Northwestern New Jersey* (1927). She is mentioned briefly in the *New Jersey Law Journal* 17 (1894):93, 202–3; 20 (1897):67–68; and 59 (1936):index page 44. An interview with Ruth Fern Kane of Wayne, NJ, provided details about Steele as a friend and neighbor.

*Carrie Pastor*

## SARAH STRICKLAND, 1812–1872

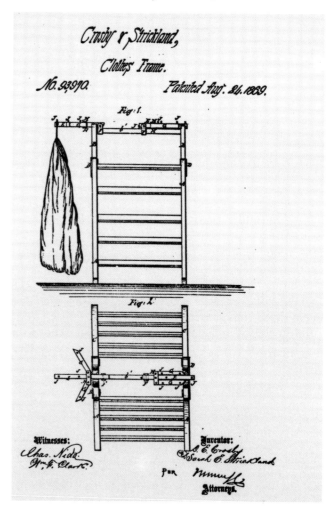

Patent drawing for an improved clothes dryer devised by Sarah E. Strickland. Strickland was born in Massachusetts about 1812 and later moved to Newark, OH. She was a feminist lecturer who spoke on such topics as "The Failing Health of American Women," "Why I Want to Vote," and "What a Woman Can Do."

In 1865 Strickland bought land in Vineland and moved there. In 1870 the value of this real estate was $2,500. She became a farmer, growing fruits and vegetables by her own hands.

In 1869 Strickland and a neighbor, Darwin E. Crosby, were issued a patent for an improved clothes dryer. The purpose of this invention was to dry dresses without wrinkling them. Strickland assigned her rights to this invention to Crosby. Several Vineland women were involved in clothing reform (see SUSAN PECKER FOWLER and MARY E. TILLOTSON), and Strickland's invention may have been related to this movement. Her patent attorney was Munn and Company, the largest firm of patent solicitors in the United States and publishers of *Scientific American*. She died on August 25, 1872, at about age 60.

An article about Strickland appeared in the *Woman's Journal*, Aug. 12, 1871. Her accomplishments as a lecturer are noted in Phebe Hanaford, *Daughters of America* (1882).

By Joseph P. Sullivan. *Drawing courtesy, U.S. Department of Commerce, Patent and Trademark Office.*

## MARY VIRGINIA HAWES TERHUNE, 1830–1922

Mary Virginia (Hawes) Terhune, novelist and authority on domestic life, known to her readers as "Marion Harland," was born on December 21, 1830, in Dennisville, VA, to Samuel Pierce and Judith Anna (Smith) Hawes, both descendants of early Colonial families. She was the second daughter and third of nine children.

Terhune's parents valued books and education, hired tutors to educate their daughters as well as sons, and promoted reading in the home and use of the father's library. When Terhune was thirteen, her father sent the two eldest girls to live with a cousin at Hampden-Sydney College in Prince Edward County, so that they might be educated (by a tutor) "as if they were boys preparing for college." (Terhune, *Autobiography*, 97) The tutor did more; he introduced the girls to a hitherto mostly forbidden fruit: novels, the works of Sir Walter Scott. In 1844 the family moved to Richmond, VA, where Samuel Hawes became a politically active magistrate and his daughters attended what he considered a good Presbyterian girls' school.

The fourteen-year-old Terhune began anonymously to submit stories and essays to a Richmond paper. At sixteen she began her first novel, but kept this a secret from her family: "we had a way of respecting each other's eccentricities." (Terhune, *Autobiography*, 239) After completing her own schooling, she combined writing with a daily four hours of teaching her sisters, and domestic and social duties, thus establishing a disciplined schedule alternating literary and other work that was to endure throughout her life.

In 1853 the *Southern Era* offered a $50 prize for the best serial on a temperance theme. Under the pseudonym "Marion Harland" she submitted "Kate Harper" and won. Encouraged, she began to rewrite the novel begun at sixteen; this time she read it aloud, à la Jane Austen, to her brother and sister. Her mother was said to have been shocked by the idea of a daughter as a professional author, but her father thought her talent "a gift from God" and had the novel *Alone* printed privately after it was rejected by a publisher. It was an immediate success in 1854, and when republished by J. C. Derby of New York in 1856 it sold more than 100,000 copies. Later the same year Derby published her second success, *The Hidden Path*.

On September 2, 1856, she married Edward Payson Terhune, a Presbyterian minister from New Jersey temporarily assigned to Richmond. Terhune thus began a new career in household management that was to make her even more famous than her novels had. By her own account, the housekeeping side of the marriage was a disaster. Her home training had been strong on the educational and social virtues and weak on the practical. The bride's two servants (slaves) seemed to know little more than she. The many books she consulted, especially on the arcane mysteries of cooking, were "written by people who never kept house . . . [or] by a cook who yet doesn't know how to express herself to the enlightenment of others." (Harland, *Common Sense in the Household*, 18) Appliances were few and primitive and the first year an ordeal for this literary lady.

In 1859 the Rev. Terhune was called to the First Reformed Dutch Church in Newark, NJ, which was to be home for the next eighteen years. Six children were born, but only three survived to adulthood. All three—CHRISTINE TERHUNE HERRICK, Virginia (Terhune) Van de Water, and Albert Payson Terhune—became writers and all collaborated, at least once, with their mother.

Terhune continued her writing even while she carried a heavy load of home, parish, and civic responsibilities. She published fourteen novels between 1857 and 1873. She frequently entertained a large circle of friends and colleagues. She taught and superintended Sunday school. She was president of the Women's Christian Association of Newark, for which she raised money, counseled, and found jobs for poor young women. She managed her beloved summer home, "Sunnybank," in Pompton, NJ, which her youngest son was to make famous in his *Lad of Sunnybank* series of books.

In 1873 Terhune was diagnosed as tubercular. Her husband resigned his ministry and took the entire family to Europe for two years. Her health improved rapidly and remained excellent for the rest of her life. Edward Terhune took another parish in Springfield, MA, and then, in 1884, in Brooklyn, NY. Here he revived a failing parish, but the struggle proved exhausting and his health was never robust again. The Terhunes celebrated their golden wedding anniversary at Sunnybank (1906), but Edward Terhune died within the year. "Marion Harland," faithful to the habit of a lifetime, went on writing.

Her productivity was extraordinary. The numerous

novels and three volumes of short stories gratified the taste of her day for romance, sentiment, and piety. Most are set in the antebellum South. Her heroines glorify the traditional feminine role (she took a very dim view of the suffrage movement).

Terhune's ambivalence about the "proper" role for women is reflected in her practical books. In 1871 she decided to make frank use of her own failures and successes as a cook. When her husband questioned why a successful novelist should bother with a cookbook, the confident author replied: "It will do more good than all of them [the novels] put together!" (Quoted in "Common Sense in the Household," *Virginia Cavalcade*, Spring 1955, 29) *Common Sense in the Household* was written in plain English for the beginner. The book was an immediate best-seller and was quickly translated into French, Spanish, German, and Arabic. Many more books on homemaking followed, plus numerous articles, syndicated columns, and lectures.

Terhune's opinions on woman's role in society are set forth most clearly in *Eve's Daughters* (1882). She insists that girls, just as boys, need plenty of air, vigorous exercise, a classical liberal education—through college, if possible—practical command of a profession, and experience in money management. Although she believes that women find their highest fulfillment as wives and mothers, she is firm that these roles should not end active, productive involvement in others. Clearly, her ideal woman is predicated upon herself. She does not consider the problems inherent in pursuit of careers that do not readily combine with the part-time, at-home work conditions of her own career.

She also wrote on travel, biography, and history. *The Story of Mary Washington* (1892) created interest in a monument to the first president's mother. *Some Colonial Homesteads and Their Stories* (1897) dealt with her particular interest in family histories and genealogy. Elected the first woman member of the Virginia Historical Society, she wrote the "Story of Virginia" for a book of state histories and was active in the Daughters of the American Revolution, the Association for the Preservation of Virginia Antiquities, and the Pocahontas Memorial Association. At 70, her writing hand was crippled, so she learned to type. At 89, she lost her vision, so she learned to dictate. She died of natural causes on June 3, 1922, at age 91, in her New York City home. She was buried at Pompton, NJ.

Terhune's autobiography is *Marion Harland's Autobiography* (1910). Two of her notable works are *Common Sense in the Household* (1871) and *Eve's Daughters* (1882). For a complete listing of her writings, see *American Women Writers* 4 (1982). She is profiled in *DAB* 18 (1936) and in *NAW*. Her obituary appeared in the *New York Times*, June 4, 1922.

*Daryl Boylan*
*Ann Pason*

## MARY E. TILLOTSON, 1819–unknown

Mary E. Tillotson, a leading writer on dress reform, was born in Chenango County, NY, in 1819. Nothing is known of her family or parentage, but she lived in Smithville, Chenango County, NY, until she married Chauncey Tillotson in 1850 and moved to the neighboring town of Greene. The Tillotsons had one son.

After a severe illness Tillotson became interested in hydropathic medicine, or "water cure," a health reform movement that extolled the virtues of diet, exercise, and water and criticized establishment medicine for encouraging dependence on medicine and doctors and engaging in interventionist practices.

Through the *Water Cure Journal* Tillotson learned about the reform dress, a short dress and trousers developed as an alternative to the long, cumbersome skirts, heavy petticoats, and tightly laced corsets of the fashionable 19th-century lady. The reform dress found supporters among activists in many reform movements of the day and was greeted with particular enthusiasm by women's rights leaders, who popularized it as the "bloomer costume." Women's rights leaders abandoned the new style when public ridicule of it threatened to eclipse the other social and political changes they were advocating, but a small band of intrepid reformers centered in the water cure movement continued to champion it. Tillotson was an enthusiastic supporter of the reform dress throughout the 1850s, writing ardent letters in support of the cause to the local newspapers as well as to the *Sibyl*, a dress reform and feminist monthly.

In 1864 Mary Tillotson and her son moved to Vineland, NJ. Details of her marriage and separation are not known, but Tillotson made it clear (writing in the reform spelling advocated by the American Filological and Spelling Reform Associations) that she would "never agen accept from the 'best of men' a relashion enslaving my love or making me another's property." (Tillotson, *History*, 28)

In Vineland, Tillotson bought a home, cultivated a garden and small vineyard, participated in the social and political life of the community, and took pride in her self-sufficiency. She wore reform dress at all times, convinced that it gave her the freedom and energy she needed to make a life for herself and her son. "Women," she believed, "hav a right to wear what they like and work as they wil and are hence not less womanly or less worthy." (*Woman's Herald of Industry*, 5) She worked on a variety of women's rights projects with SUSAN PECKER FOWLER, another Vineland dress reformer.

In the early 1870s Tillotson took initiative in revitalizing the dress reform movement, which had languished in the 1860s. She organized a local dress reform society, which sponsored an antifashion convention in 1874, and in 1875 she helped found the American Free Dress League.

She wrote several dress reform pamphlets and contributed regularly to the *Woman's Herald of Industry*, a California-based feminist newspaper.

Tillotson's advocacy of what she began in the 1870s to call the "science" costume was rooted in her commitment to both health reform and "women's liberashun," which she believed to be inextricably related. She counseled women to resist fashion as part of their "rising candidacy for self hood, for womanhood with power of choice." (Tillotson, *History*, 2) She saw the constraining fashions of the 19th century as "badges of bondage" (Tillotson, *Progress*, 15) that reinforced women's powerlessness by emphasizing sexual attractiveness and inhibiting physical activity.

While Tillotson agreed with the women's rights movement of the day that the power relations between women and men needed to be changed, she felt that this could be accomplished only if women challenged these relationships in their daily lives. Her style of reform was that of the individual crusader steadfastly adhering to principles in the face of the harassment of an often hostile world. She berated the leadership of the women's rights movement, whose focus on political change led them to deemphasize personal transformation, and she complained that she was treated badly when she appeared at suffrage conventions in her science costume.

Although Tillotson's style of reform had flourished before the Civil War, it faded in the more conservative climate of the 1870s, and the few lone crusaders who remained were often abused. While in Vineland, Tillotson was somewhat protected from this abuse because the community had attracted reformers of all sorts since its founding as a planned agricultural community in 1861. When she traveled beyond Vineland, however, to attend conventions and speak to women about fashion resistance, she was often harassed and ridiculed. Her writing was full of accounts of persecution, including a night spent in the Jersey City jail before the police were informed that there was no New Jersey law against women wearing pants.

Tillotson continued to write and speak throughout her life about fashion resistance and other reforms that she felt were rational and scientific. She adopted "improved" spelling because of its superior agreement with spoken language and used a dating system that began in 1600, when she believed human beings first began to engage in rational and scientific investigation. No record of her death has been discovered.

Tillotson's books are: *History of the First Thirty-five Years of the Science Costume Movement in the United States of America* (1885); *Progress vs. Fashion* (1874); *Woman's Way Out* (1876); and *Love and Transition* (1878). The Vineland Historical and Antiquarian Society (Vineland, NJ) holds issues of *Woman's Herald of Industry*, the paper Tillotson contributed to, as well as photographs and pamphlets on dress reform.

*Amy Kesselman*

## MARY LUA ADELIA DAVIS TREAT, 1830–1923

Mary Lua Adelia (Davis) Treat, New Jersey's pioneer economic entomologist, botanist, and early supporter of the theory of evolution, was born in Trumansville, NY, on September 7, 1830. She and her sister, Nellie, were the only children of Isaac Davis, an itinerant Methodist minister, and Eliza (English) Davis. In 1839 the Davis family moved to Ohio, where Treat was educated in public schools and briefly attended a private girls' academy.

Treat, according to her friend Anna Lane of Vineland, NJ, possessed a superior intellect and an innate reserve, combining "humility of spirit with the simplicity of a little child." She was a slight woman, only five feet tall with dark hair and eyes.

**Mary Adelia Treat**
*...Worked With Charles Darwin*

Mary Adelia Davis Treat, a resident of Vineland for many years, was a noted scholar of insect and plant life and a supporter of the theory of evolution in the 1870s. *Courtesy, Vineland Historical and Antiquarian Society.*

As a young woman, Mary Davis moved back to New York State and lived with her sister. In 1863 she married Dr. Joseph Burrell Treat, a descendant of a prominent Colonial family. In addition to his medical practice, Joseph

Treat wrote and lectured on such subjects as astronomy, physics, women's rights, atheism, abolitionism, and Transcendentalism. Initially the couple settled in Iowa, but in 1867 they moved to Mays Landing, NJ, and in 1868 to Vineland in order to be part of a new intellectual and agricultural community established by Charles Landis in 1865.

Treat's reputation as a naturalist rests on her research in botany and entomology. Her first scientific article, a note in the *American Entomologist and Botanist*, appeared in 1869, when she was 39. During the next 28 years she authored 81 scientific and popular works, including five books. One of these, *Injurious Insects of the Farm and Field* (1882), was reprinted five times.

After her separation from her husband in 1874, Treat supported herself as a writer of popular science and as a collector of plants and insects used in academic research by such naturalists as Asa Gray, Charles V. Riley, and Sir Joseph Hooker. Earnings from her books and her popular articles on insects, plants, and birds, published in such magazines as *Harper's Monthly* and *Lippincott's*, enabled her to purchase a house in Vineland, travel to Florida, and live comfortably in retirement. As she wrote to Charles Darwin on May 15, 1876, explaining her placement of an article on insectivorous plants, "you may wonder at my selecting a literary magazine rather than a scientific one, but I am wholly dependent upon my own exertions, and must go where they *pay best.*"

In the course of her research, Treat corresponded regularly with well-known naturalists of the time, including Darwin. She also shared scientific information with Charles V. Riley, state entomologist of Missouri and later chief entomologist of the Department of the Interior's U.S. Entomological Commission; Harvard botanist Asa Gray; and European entomologists August Forel and Gustav Mayr. These members of the international scientific community accepted Treat as a naturalist and came to rely on her as a collector of plant and insect species from the New Jersey Pine Barrens and from Florida.

Treat was an early and enthusiastic advocate of the theory of evolution in the United States. In her second letter to Darwin (December 13, 1872) she notes, "Your theory is steadily gaining ground among the masses and thinking people in this country. . . . Nothing brings out a crowd on Sunday like the announcement that Darwinism is to be the theme. Surely the world moves!" In an 1890 lecture Treat delivered to the Brooklyn Ethical Association, she praised the late Asa Gray for his primary role in making Darwin's ideas better understood.

By the time New Jersey's first entomological laboratory, at Rutgers, was founded, in 1888, Treat had already published 22 entomological articles between 1869 and 1882, chiefly in such scientific journals as the *American Entomologist and Botanist*, *The American Naturalist*, and *The Journal of the New York Entomological Society*. Her early entomological publications detailed the life histories, feeding behavior, and methods of control of a variety of insect pests. It was in the field of insect behavior that Treat moved beyond economic entomology and performed her most insightful scientific research. Darwin praised her experiments on controlling the sexes of butterflies as "by far the best, as far as known to me, which have ever been made." (January 5, 1972) Treat's descriptions of the behavior of insects were used by taxonomists in classifying new species. Her own discoveries of new species included an orange aphid, an Ichneumonid fly, two spiders, and an ant named *Aphanogaster treatiae* in her honor.

Some of Treat's most notable research concerned the anatomy and behavior of harvesting ants. She correctly attributed the presence or absence of chewing mandibles to a caste system in which workers had teeth, but the queen and soldiers who performed no work did not. In disagreeing with August Forel's theory that ants with smooth mandibles had worn these down through chewing, Treat redirected entomological thought away from the strictly structural approach used in taxonomy and toward an approach in which anatomical differences were viewed as related to behavioral modification.

Treat and C. V. Riley cooperated extensively in their entomological research endeavors. In addition to sending him specimens and descriptions of suggested new species, she also sent field notes he requested concerning the degree of abundance of insect species and the plants where these were found. Riley published this information under his own name. In return, he sent her drawings of larvae for her article on the carnivorous plant *Utricularia* and allowed her to use sections of his *State of Missouri Entomological Report* for her book *Injurious Insects of the Farm and Garden*.

Treat's studies on injurious insects paralleled her studies of carnivorous plants of the New Jersey Pine Barrens and Florida. Of her 46 articles on Pine Barrens vegetation, "Observations on the Sundew" (1870) and "Is the Valve of *Utricularia* Sensitive?" (1876) are particularly valuable contributions to an understanding of the ecological physiology of carnivorous plants. Treat also discussed her 1874 research on the Venus flytrap, another carnivorous plant, in her book *Home Studies in Nature* (1880).

Treat and Darwin shared their research on the response of the carnivorous *Drosera filiformis* to a variety of substances. Treat added an apple to the inventory of objects "tasted" by the sundew. In noting that the plant's bristles curved inward, "but no glands came in contact with the apple," Treat ascertained the true carnivorous nature of *Drosera*. She also noted that the plant's tentacles did not respond vigorously to small flies. Darwin repeated her experiments, confirmed them, and conjectured that larger insects offered more nutriment to the plant and were more valuable than smaller insects, which might escape through the slowly intermeshing spikes. Darwin acknowledged Treat's contributions in his *Insectivorous Plants* (1875), a book she found so fascinating, as she wrote Darwin on May 15, 1876, "that I sat up nearly all night before I could lay it down."

In their 1875 correspondence on *Utricularia* (bladderwort), Darwin and Treat initially concurred that the plant's trapdoor valve was not irritable, and that insects entered *Utricularia* by, according to Darwin, "forcing their way through the slit-like orifice, their heads serving as a wedge." Treat's 1876 article, however, maintained that the plant's valve was irritable, and that the insect was sucked into the utricle through the valve by means of a partial vacuum. After receiving the article, Darwin wrote to Treat on June 1, 1876: "I have read your article with the greatest interest. It certainly appears from your excellent observations that the valve is sensitive. . . . I cannot understand why I could never with all my pains excite any movement. It is pretty clear I am quite wrong about the head acting like a wedge. The indraught of the living larva is astonishing."

Asa Gray's early communication with Treat (1873–76) was concerned with commissioning her to collect seeds, roots, and bulbs of many Pine Barren plant species. He also encouraged her research.

During the winters of 1874–77 Treat lived in Florida, where she made frequent boat trips along the St. John's River. On one of these trips she discovered a new species of amaryllis, named *Zephyranthus treatiae* in her honor. On another, she rediscovered *Nymphaea lutea*, an aquatic plant with a yellow flower first identified by Lutren and painted by John James Audubon, but lost before it could be described scientifically. Gray, to whom she sent the specimen, was delighted with the find.

During her later years in Vineland, Treat initiated and enthusiastically led a bimonthly botany class for a coterie of Vineland's young women. In 1916 Treat moved to New York State to live with her sister. She died in Pembroke, near Batavia, on April 11, 1923, at age 92, following complications from a fall. The funeral was held in Vineland, where she is buried.

For additional information on Treat, see Nancy Smith, "Mary Treat," *New Jersey Audubon* 9 (Winter 1983):18–20; Harry Gershenowitz, "The Mrs. Treat of Darwin's Scientific World," *Vineland Historical Magazine* 55 (1979):2–7; and Harry B. Weiss, "Mrs. Mary Treat, 1830–1923, Early New Jersey Naturalist," *NJHSP* 73 (1955):258–73, which includes a bibliography of her writings. The Darwin Archive at Cambridge University Library (Cambridge, England) and the Vineland Historical Society (Vineland, NJ) contain correspondence between Treat and Darwin. Brief descriptions of the correspondence appear in Frederick Burkhardt, ed. *A Calendar of the Correspondence of Charles Darwin, 1821–1882* (1985).

*Lorraine Abbiate Caruso*
*Terry Kohn*

## FRANCES BARTLETT TYSON, 1874–1971

Frances Bartlett Tyson, physician and community activist, was born in Vineland (Cumberland County), NJ, on December 26, 1874. She was the oldest of five children of Clara (Buckminister) and Francis Bartlett. Her father, who had been blinded and shell-shocked during the Civil War, was a storekeeper who made and sold harnesses. He was a descendant of Josiah Bartlett, a statesman, physician, and signer of the Declaration of Independence.

At the age of nine Tyson decided to pattern her life after "Dr. Alice," a character in a children's book she had read. After graduating from Vineland High School at age seventeen she tried to enter a nursing school in Philadelphia. Standing before school officials, with her hair in pigtails and ribbons, Tyson resolutely stated her desire to work in medicine as a nurse since she realized that to become a physician at this time would be difficult for a woman.

She was turned away by the interviewers, who told her to return in four or five years. Undaunted by this rejection, she began preparation for a medical career by accepting a part-time job in the drug dispensary of the Philadelphia Woman's Hospital. While employed as a clerk, she enrolled in the Philadelphia College of Pharmacy, graduating in 1896. She became one of the few women to earn a degree as a licensed pharmacist in America during the 1890s.

Tyson also worked in drugstores to earn money for a two-year premedical course at Temple University. She was accepted into Woman's Medical College of Philadelphia, from which she graduated in 1901. Her internship was served at Blockley Hospital (now Philadelphia General Hospital) after it dropped its restrictions against women. Later in life she enjoyed saying with pride, "I used to beat the male interns to the ambulances although the women's quarters were farther away from the ambulance entrance." (*Record*, Jan. 4, 1971)

In 1903, after completing her internship, she was appointed an associate in the surgical unit of the Woman's Hospital of West Philadelphia. During this time she also taught materia medica and therapeutics at the nurses' training school of this hospital. For the next six years she served as gynecologist and head of the clinic at Woman's Hospital.

In 1909, when she married William Tyson, an insurance executive, she promised him she would give up her medical practice. She retired from her profession for nine years. In 1910 Evelyn, her only child, was born. In 1913 the Tysons moved to Leonia, NJ, a town of 5,000 inhabitants, where she busied herself in community work. When four physicians from the town were called into the army in 1918, during World War I, Tyson applied for a New Jersey license to resume her medical practice at the community's request.

This was the beginning of a practice that spanned 42 years. During the flu epidemic in 1918, Tyson almost single-handedly served her community's medical needs when she organized a program of feeding schedules for families with multiple victims of influenza. She contracted the disease herself, losing the hearing in her right ear. In 1919 she joined the staff at Englewood Hospital, where she served in the area of general medicine for 37 years. Tyson also became Leonia school physician in 1918, a post she held until 1955. During World War I as well as World War II she taught for the American Red Cross.

Energetic and resourceful, Tyson was a dedicated community activist. In the early 1920s she organized one of the several Girl Scout troops in Leonia, and for four years the girls conducted their meetings in her home. She then lent her support in the drive to build a headquarters for the Girl Scouts, a building that today is the Leonia senior citizen's center and town hall annex.

After years of continued effort for the betterment of town and state, numerous honors were bestowed upon Tyson. In 1953 she received the Freedom Foundation Award for her help in founding the Youth Museum, a project begun by a group of Leonia citizens that became the nucleus of the Bergen Museum of Arts and Sciences in Paramus. She was instrumental in securing a large donation, given anonymously by one of her patients, toward the foundation of the museum. Tyson received the Cecilia Gaines Holland award of the New Jersey Federation of Women's Clubs (1951) and the "Woman of the Year" award of the New Jersey Medical Women's Association (1957).

Tyson had turned one of the second-floor bedrooms of her home into an office after her husband's death in 1949 and continued to treat private patients until the age of 86. She retired from Englewood Hospital at age 82 and although confined to her home at age 90, Tyson continued a prolific correspondence with friends made during her long years of service to her profession and community. Dr. Albert Schweitzer was one of her favorite correspondents. Although arthritic and almost blind, she spent hours making afghans for the benefit of the Englewood Hospital Auxiliary's fund-raising fairs.

Tyson died, at age 96, on January 3, 1971, in a nursing home in Englewood, NJ. At her request, funeral services were private, and her ashes were scattered over her flower garden in Leonia, NJ.

Information on Tyson was gained from interviews with her daughter, Evelyn Tyson O'Brien (of Leonia, NJ), in June 1985 and with her granddaughter, Frances Holick (of Colorado Springs, CO), in July 1985. A tape-recorded autobiography belongs to Frances Holick. Additional interviews with Dudley Allen, former mayor of Leonia, in Feb. 1986; Ann Beckman, historian of the Leonia Women's Club, in Mar. 1986; Dr. Salina Johnson, on Mar. 24, 1986; and Alyce Freas, Tyson's longtime

secretary, in Wilmington, DE, in Apr. 1986, provided useful details. An article in the *New York Times*, May 18, 1951, supplied information, as did articles in the *Englewood* (NJ) *Press Journal*. A brief profile of Tyson is "Medical Woman of the Year," *Journal of the American Medical Women's Association* 12 (1957):445. Materials on Tyson are available at NJ-UMDNJ. Her obituary appeared in the *Record* (Bergen County, NJ), Jan. 4, 1971.

*Helene T. Svihra*

## JENNIE CAROLYN VAN NESS, ca. 1890–unknown

Jennie Carolyn Van Ness, one of the first two women to be elected to the New Jersey State Legislature, was born in Chicago, IL, and educated in the public and normal schools of that city. During her career in New Jersey state politics, she lived in East Orange (Essex County) with her husband, Frank W. Van Ness, and three daughters, Jane, Dorothy, and Ruth. Before she entered party politics as a Republican candidate for state assembly, Van Ness was an active educator, civic organizer, and suffragist.

As an educator, Van Ness was instrumental in procuring playgrounds in Milwaukee, WI, and Peru, IN, and helped establish a circulating library in Dalton, GA. Before her 1920 bid for a state assembly seat in New Jersey, she was a substitute teacher in the East Orange High School and fought for higher teacher salaries and public playgrounds. Van Ness served as president of the Orange Political Study Club, first vice-president of the Community Club of East Orange, and vice-chair of the Women's Three Minute Speakers Club. She was also active in the New Jersey Woman Suffrage Association (NJWSA), running its citizenship schools throughout the state to educate women's clubs and organizations in the science of government and politics.

In April 1920, when the NJWSA dissolved and reorganized as the New Jersey League of Women Voters, Van Ness became the director of the league's sixth region. She was also made first chair of a board within the league to draw up a state program of legislative issues for study. Under Van Ness, the league continued to run the citizenship schools NJWSA had initiated during the suffrage campaign. The schools operated until the 1924 presidential election.

Van Ness became a candidate for the assembly in September 1920 at the request of leaders in the Essex County Republican League, an organization outside the regular party machine but broadly committed to Republican objectives. Its candidates for the assembly and the county Board of Chosen Freeholders ran on a platform calling for "clean government," continuation of the direct primary system, stringent enforcement of prohibition law, and legislation promoting the role of women in party management and state government. As a campaigner Van Ness "attracted and held audiences by her ability as a rapid fire public speaker." (*Newark Evening News*, Nov. 3, 1920) Like many other suffragists who were then entering party politics for the first time, Van Ness campaigned for "the home and its interests" and for the right of intelligent and active participation by women in public office. In a profile in the *Newark Evening News* announcing her candidacy in the primary, Van Ness defended woman's dual role as homemaker and political activist: "My home is the center, but not the circumference, of my life, . . .just as it is the center but not the circumference of the life of every right-living husband and father." (Sept. 10, 1920)

In the 1920 September primary Van Ness won one of twelve Republican nominations for the assembly with 25,960 votes, or less than 800 votes behind the highest runner on the regular Republican ticket. By early November, 50 percent of women eligible to vote had registered and the returns for the general election were much larger. Among the winners of Essex County's twelve assembly seats, Van Ness ran eleventh. All twelve seats went to Republicans, two of them women. In the 1921 assembly, Van Ness and Margaret B. Laird sat as the first women elected to the legislature.

During her single term in the assembly, Van Ness served on the standing committees for Education and for Unfinished Business, and on the joint committees for the Industrial School for Girls, the School for Feeble Minded Children, and the State Library. In the same period four bills affecting women's political and legal status in the state became law with strong Republican backing. These granted women equal privileges in holding office and in employment; gave women equal representation on municipal, county, and state party committees; granted two positions for women on the State Board of Education and in the Department of Health; and allowed women to serve on juries in civil and criminal cases.

Despite her support for the interests of women and the home, Van Ness's political career suffered when she sponsored a prohibition enforcement bill. The bill had been drawn up in consultation with Anti-Saloon League attorneys and accepted by Republican leaders in the legislature when Van Ness agreed to introduce it. The Van Ness Act, as the bill was named, was intended to supplement the federal Volstead Act. It liberalized search and seizure procedure in the state and defined minor violations of prohibition law as petty offenses resulting in trial by judge and fine or imprisonment.

Passage of the Van Ness Act, which became law over the veto of Democratic governor Edward I. Edwards, ruined Van Ness's chance for a second term in office. In the month before the November 1921 election, the state's Democratic "wets" raised opposition to the act on constitutional and personal liberty grounds. Even "moist" Republicans began to call for modification of the act. At the Octo-

ber state Republican Convention, which Van Ness attended, the party modified its strict position on prohibition enforcement. However, at two subsequent county Republican rallies that opened the fall campaign, the party's slate of candidates openly clashed over the Van Ness Act. Van Ness defended its provisions, while others called for its amendment and complained of the Anti-Saloon League's domination of the party.

Van Ness continued to speak in support of prohibition enforcement, representing the position of many women's organizations in the state. At a meeting of the South Orange Republican Club she responded to critics of the Van Ness Act by defending its trial by judge provision, arguing that "there are forty-four other offenses in New Jersey of a disorderly nature for which a law breaker is tried solely by a judge, and Governor Edwards signed the bills providing for such a trial in the cases of six of these offenses." (*Newark Evening News*, "Republicans Speak in Dry Act's Favor," Oct. 22, 1921)

With the Democratic campaign in Essex County focused on attacks on the Van Ness Act, Van Ness became a target for "wet" propaganda in the November election. Although the Republican party backed the entire ticket, she was the only one of its twelve assembly candidates who failed to be reelected.

In the decade after the election Van Ness continued to work for issues important to many women in the state through her association with the New Jersey Woman's Republican Club. In May 1923 she was one of three featured speakers at the club's annual convention in Atlantic City when the organization met to draft a new legislative program. The new program reasserted, among other issues, two that had been important to Van Ness in her political career. It called for the "selection of honest men and women" in Republican party primaries and for strong law enforcement. Specifically, it recommended opposition to a bill supported by Republican Senator Walter E. Edge that would allow the sale of light beer and wines in the state. In 1926 Van Ness served as the legislative chair for the New Jersey Woman's Republican Club. The following year she summed up the ambiguous feelings of many of the suffragists of her generation who had worked in machine politics. "It's not that we want the political jobs themselves," said Van Ness, " . . . but they seem to be the only language the men understand. We don't really want these $200 a year jobs. But the average man doesn't understand working for a cause." (*Jersey Journal*, Apr. 22, 1927; quoted in Gordon, *After Winning*, 87) After 1931 no reference to Van Ness appears in the public record, and the author has found no further data on her.

A sketch of Van Ness appears in the *Manual of the Legislature of New Jersey* (1921). Her work is noted in Felice Gordon, *After Winning: The Legacy of the New Jersey Suffragists, 1920–1947* (1986). Notable newspaper articles about her appeared in the

*Newark Evening News*: "Home's Claim No Bar to Political Life," Sept. 10, 1920; "Essex Has Pioneers as Assemblywomen," Nov. 3, 1920; "Republicans Speak in Dry Act's Favor," Oct. 22, 1921; "Salmon Seeks Aid for Mrs. Van Ness," Oct. 29, 1921; "Deplores Leniency with Bootleggers," Oct. 31, 1921; and "Republicans Retain Control . . . Mrs. Van Ness Defeated by Essex Wets," Nov. 9, 1921.

*Susan Booker Welsh*
*Gloria S. Dittman*

## GERTRUDE POTTER WARD, 1875–1956

Gertrude Potter Ward, physician and community activist, was born in Bloomfield (Essex County), NJ, on October 16, 1875, the third of five children of Theodore Hastings Ward and Elizabeth (Potter) Ward. As the daughter of one of the community's oldest and most socially prominent families, her civic consciousness was sparked by the example of her father, president of the Bloomfield Savings Bank, who was active in municipal and cultural affairs and one-time chairman of the township council. Another important influence was her aunt, Anna Lydia Ward, a world traveler, lecturer, writer, and community activist in Waterbury, CT. From her aunt, Ward acquired not only a model of female activism and a commitment to social reform on the local level, but an early interest in travel. Aunt Lydia's enthralling tales produced a youthful desire for overseas missionary activity in the young woman that horrified her socially prominent parents. When they quashed her aspirations here, Ward sought another means to perform socially useful work.

After attending college at Wellesley and Columbia, she chose to join her brother, Israel Wilbur Ward (1879–1954), at Cornell Medical School. She graduated in 1900 and opened a practice for women and children in her Bloomfield home. Until 1914 she served as the first school physician ever appointed in Bloomfield, and in 1918 became public health officer for Bloomfield and Glen Ridge, a position she held for several years.

Ward first attracted public attention during a smallpox epidemic that ravaged the state in 1903–4, when her solicitude for Bloomfield victims drew acclaim in the local press. With local hospitals taxed to capacity, quarantine centers or "pesthouses" were rapidly built, but these in turn found themselves stymied by a shortage of doctors able or willing to deal with the crisis. Establishing a facility in the "wilds of Brookdale," Ward went out every day with a horse and buggy to care for the town's sufferers, a pattern she followed until the epidemic had run its course. Although friends avoided her, local papers praised her heroic acts.

Ward is best known for her key role in founding the League for Friendly Service, a social welfare agency in Bloomfield and Glen Ridge considered to have been the first professional social agency in the state's history. Taking New York City's Charity Organization Society as her model, Ward met with community civic and religious leaders in 1910. She envisioned a private, thoroughly professional agency that would maximize private relief efforts by coordinating all charitable and philanthropic resources available to the community. The agency's approach toward its clients was revealed in Ward's first explanation of the league's work. According to her, the league's name expressed its purpose: to give advice and information about where to turn for specific kinds of services and sympathetic personal attention rather than money alone.

Ward chaired the league's Executive Committee for nearly 50 years (until her death in 1956) and initiated important features of the league's work: public health nursing, antituberculosis programs, vocational classes for immigrants, and a home nutrition service. Placing special emphasis on the needs and problems of children, she was instrumental in introducing milk distribution programs, dental clinics, tutoring assistance for the sick, and on-site nursing care into the township's public schools. In 1912, along with Anne Sternberger, she founded a day nursery for the children of working mothers that still continues to serve the community.

Friends remember that throughout her years of league service Ward showed a keen personal interest in every detail, from the need for blotters and extra lamps to the problems of clients. She is said to have had unusual insight into the problems of the young. As a leader, she was both farsighted and flexible, impressing upon the agency the need to adapt to changing times and circumstances. From the start, the organization she founded was composed of both men and women, and of representatives from various religious denominations.

In the 1940s she encouraged the league's day nursery to end its longstanding practice of limiting enrollment to the children of mothers for whom work was an economic necessity. It was wrong, she insisted, for the league to question the motives of working women. In 1944, sensing the civil rights struggle that was to embroil postwar America, she moved the league to develop new interracial programs and to hire additional workers trained to deal with such issues. Increasingly after World War II the league's emphasis shifted to counseling, with a focus no longer limited to the poor alone. This change clearly reflected the original intention of Ward and her cofounders: "to strengthen family life through early intervention."

Ward persisted in her aims and ideals despite occasional local resistance. Early objectors cited the fact that the league gave aid to any needy person, regardless of race, color, creed, or national origin. Moreover, the social climate of the community in the league's early years was hostile to organized charity. Xenophobia also played a role in community tension, with indignant citizens decrying the fact that their dollars were being used to provide medical assistance to foreigners.

Today the League for Friendly Service—renamed the League for Family Service in 1964—continues to serve the residents of Bloomfield and Glen Ridge, taking its place among several hundred family service agencies throughout the United States and Canada. The spirit of its founder continues to be invoked frequently, for Ward awakened her community's conscience and developed an awareness that help and dignity could be attained simultaneously.

She was also a guiding force in other local activities. In 1922 she took over the presidency of the Needlework Guild, the first women's organization in Bloomfield, and served in that capacity for 25 years, followed by 8 years as honorary president (until her death). Founded in Philadelphia in 1885, the guild was a nonsectarian, nonprofit, charitable group of volunteers that collected new garments and household linens and distributed them to the needy. For Ward, the ideals of the Needlework Guild and the League for Friendly Service were complementary. The guild's mission, according to her, was "to keep alive a friendly way of permitting those who have to help others who have not."

Ward also joined in founding the Bloomfield Town Improvement Association, a local beautification committee. A lifelong member of the Bloomfield First Presbyterian Church, she was a charter member of the Bloomfield American Association of University Women and a member of the board of the Bloomfield chapter of the American Red Cross. In the words of a longtime friend: "She served on everything worthwhile in town. She saw the things that needed to be done and she did them."

Ward was never well known outside her local community. She shied away from the limelight, with community, church, and family always remaining her central concerns. Like other female physicians of the day, she was drawn to "feminine" areas of endeavor—public health, the teaching of social hygiene, work with adolescent girls, pediatrics.

Never married, she devoted much time and energy to the care of her parents and to the children of her brother, Israel Wilbur Ward, when he became a widower. She retained an unusual relationship to the League for Friendly Service, the organization she had founded. Although she was never president, she served as chair of the Executive Committee, content to "tell the gentlemen who were Presidents what it might be good to do." Contemporaries considered her reserved, low-key style one of her strengths. While Ward served as an inspirational role model to other achieving women, she never concerned herself with any specifically women's issues, nor was the campaign for suffrage ever one of her interests. Her career demonstrates an important correlation between the emergence of the helping professions and women's professional activity.

After a lifetime of civic involvement, Ward died of cancer on May 20, 1956, at age 80. She was buried in Bloomfield Cemetery, Bloomfield, NJ.

Sources for the study of Ward's life and career are limited. Basic biographical data can be obtained from the archives of the American Medical Association (Chicago). NJ-BPL maintains a clipping file on the Ward family, the Needlework Guild, and the League for Friendly Service. The local press (the *Bloomfield Citizen* and the *Independent Press*) trace the history of the League for Friendly Service (now the League for Family Service).

*Marie Marmo Mullaney*

## CAROLYN WELLS, 1862–1942

Carolyn Wells, humorist, anthologist, and writer, was born on June 18, 1862, in Rahway (Union County), NJ. Wells wrote in her autobiography: "although by all the laws of God and my Colonial gubernatorial ancestors I ought to have been born in New England, an inscrutable decree ordained that I should first see the light in a gay and airy town in middle New Jersey. (Wells, *The Rest of My Life*, 189)

Wells's father, William Edmund Wells, was a prosperous New York City insurance and real estate man who could trace his ancestry back to Thomas Wells, the first treasurer and in 1656 the fourth governor of the colony of Connecticut. Anna (Woodruff) Wells, her mother, was a descendant of Thomas Woodrove, whose English ancestors were among the first settlers in New Jersey. In her autobiography Wells referred affectionately to her parents, her two younger brothers, Walter and Frank, and her younger sister, Allie, and cited only one tragedy that marred what seemed to be an otherwise secure and happy childhood.

When she was six and her sister was three, both children contracted scarlet fever. Allie died, and Carolyn was left with an ever-increasing deafness. Years later, after several painful but unsuccessful operations, Wells wrote, "I cannot agree with Thomas Edison that deafness is a blessing, but I have learned to ignore it and treat it with silent contempt." (Wells, *The Rest of My Life*, 60)

Characterizing herself as a precocious child and "a jack-in-the-box brain surrounded by books," Wells said that she had learned all the letters of her alphabet blocks by age eighteen months, could read fluently at age three, and had written a book at age six. "Writing came by nature, and I should be lost without it." (Wells, *The Rest of My Life*, 30–32)

Wells attended the Rahway public schools and graduated as valedictorian of her Rahway High School class. But she saw school as "waste motion" and decided not to go to college, a decision she said she never regretted. Instead,

Wells sought tutors and friends and learned what she wanted: French, German, history, botany, religions, and natural history.

Under the influence of Mrs. William C. Squier, first president of the Rahway Library Association, who Wells called "my guide, philosopher, and friend in literary matters," Wells became the assistant to the association and later librarian of the Rahway Public Library. "Every book worth having we bought, every periodical worth reading we subscribed to and the librarian sat in the middle and read her way out." (Wells, *The Rest of My Life*, 193)

Wells had been playing word games and writing jingles since childhood, and a neighbor's friend visiting from England encouraged her to send some of her four-line verses to the "little magazines" that were so popular in the 1890s. Wells did so and "woke to find herself not famous, but a successful contributor to the humorous papers of the day." (Wells, *The Rest of My Life*, 121)

Through a lengthy correspondence, Wells gained critical insight from Gelett Burgess, founder and editor of the *Lark*, who taught her to distinguish silliness from nonsense. Oliver Herford, a writer and artist, also admired Wells's work and illustrated a number of the jingles that she contributed to *St. Nicholas*.

Wells had the ability to capture in her humorous verse the fanciful in concrete form; her verse was never caustic or vindictive but characterized by a warmth, wit, and light-heartedness. (Dresner, *Dictionary of Literary Biography*, 559) In addition to the "little magazines," Wells's work also appeared in *Punch*, *Bookman*, *Scribner's*, *Outlook*, *Century*, *Harper's Bazar*, *Harper's Monthly*, *Ladies' Home Journal*, *Life*, *Delineator*, *Good Housekeeping*, *Saturday Evening Post*, *Putnam's*, and *Collier's*.

During three summers at the Sauveur School of Languages, Amherst, MA, Wells studied Shakespeare with William J. Rolfe, a noted literary scholar. Both Wells and Rolfe shared a penchant for charades and puzzles, and together they read William Bellamy's charade books. Wells began to collect locally famous charades, and in 1896 Stone and Kimball published her first anthology—*The Sign of the Sphinx*. It marked the beginning of a writing career that would span more than 40 years and include over 180 works.

By 1902 Wells had published a book of children's jingles, a story for girls, a book of verse for adults, and her best-known single work, *A Nonsense Anthology*, followed in 1904 by *A Parody Anthology* (dedicated to Mrs. Theodore Roosevelt), *A Satire Anthology* in 1905, and *A Whimsey Anthology* in 1906. Although none of these works is distinguished for critical introductions or editing, they are notable as almost unique collections of types of humorous writings.

Wells was considered the chief woman humorist of the first two decades of the 1900s. Her publishers kept asking

for her work and she said that she was too good-natured to refuse. She poked fun at such topics as love and courtship, women's fashions, the ideal woman, the Gibson Girl, the Poster Girl, the Summer Girl, suffragists, fads and faddists, feminine frailties and wiles, romantic and avant-garde poetry, and the popular culture of the day.

As her popularity increased, so too did Wells's circle of famous friends, which included Rudyard Kipling, Mr. and Mrs. Theodore Roosevelt, MARY E. WILKINS FREEMAN, Thomas Edison, and many of the English and American humorists of the period. Wells was so well known that one reviewer stated: "to begin a sentence sharply with 'Carolyn Wells says' is to attract the attention of a whole tableful and silence any spasmodic, needless chatter that may be going on elsewhere around the board." (Dresner, 556)

Wells's literary productivity, however, was not limited just to humorous writing. Beginning in 1900 with *The Story of Betty*, Wells wrote several series of juveniles, focusing on the social conventions of the period, which made her stories popular at the time but also quickly dated them.

During the early 1900s detective stories became popular. Wells, capitalizing on her love of puzzles and her study of Poe, Collins, and Doyle, mastered the formula detective story and began to write such fiction along with her juveniles and humorous books. One of few women writing detective fiction before World War I, she soon became famous for her plots and characterization. Fleming Stone, her sleuth, first appeared in *The Clue* in 1909 and was still solving mysteries 30 years later. Occasionally, in her more than 80 mystery and detective novels, Wells used other sleuths: Kenneth Carlisle, Wise and Zizi, Lorimer Lane, and Alan Ford.

In addition to her many detective novels, Wells also is remembered for her critical study of the writing of mystery stories—*The Technique of the Mystery Story* (1913; revised and enlarged in 1929). This work has been called the most encompassing study of the genre produced up to the time of its publication.

In 1921 Wells wrote a parody of Sinclair Lewis's *Main Street*; she called her novel *Ptomaine Street* and Carol Kennicott became Warble Petticoat. In 1922 she collaborated with her friend Alfred Goldsmith and published *A Concise Bibliography of the Works of Walt Whitman*, a reference guide regarded even today as a major contribution to Whitman scholarship.

For more than 50 years Wells lived in Rahway and commuted often to New York City on the Pennsylvania Railroad. Not until her marriage to Hadwin Houghton, superintendent of a varnish manufacturing company, on April 2, 1918, did she leave Rahway to reside at the Hotel des Artistes in New York City. The marriage ended with Houghton's death, after one year, but Wells continued to live in New York City and to write.

In 1937, succumbing to the pressure of publishers and

friends, she wrote her autobiography, *The Rest of My Life.* However, Wells refused to reveal much about her private life. "Why should a biography always look back and not forward? Why harp on the past when the future beckons?" (Wells, *The Rest of My Life,* 24)

Wells died in New York City on March 26, 1942, at age 79, and was buried in the Wells family plot in the Rahway Cemetery, next to her husband. A rare book enthusiast and collector, Wells bequeathed her Walt Whitman collection to the Library of Congress. The *New York Times* reported that it was one of the most important of its kind, one of the most complete, and contained many rare volumes.

Wells's autobiography is *The Rest of My Life* (1937). A comprehensive list of her work appears in *American Women Writers,* vol. 4 (1982). Her writing is assessed in *Dictionary of Literary Biography, American Humorists,* vol. 11 (1983). She is profiled in *NAW.* Her obituary appeared in the *New York Times,* Mar. 27, 1942. An article about the gift of her Walt Whitman collection appeared in the *New York Times,* Apr. 16, 1942.

*Sondra Fishinger*

## CHARLOTTE FOWLER WELLS, 1814–1901

Charlotte (Fowler) Wells was publisher of the *American Phrenological Journal* with her husband, Samuel Roberts Wells (1820–75). She was born August 14, 1814, in Cohocton (Steuben County), NY, the fourth of eight children of Horace and Martha (Howe) Fowler. Her mother died when Charlotte was five. Her father's family was from New England, and were lineal descendants of William Fowler, of Lincoln, England.

Wells's father, probably a farmer, served as church deacon and a judge. She and all of her sisters and brothers developed inquiring and receptive minds. In the evenings Horace Fowler would read to the children while the girls did their sewing. Wells went to the district school and, for six months (two winters), to the Franklin Academy in Prattsburg, NY. She began teaching, a life-time interest, by the time she was 20.

Wells became interested in phrenology, a popular theory developed by F. J. Gall, an Austrian, who held that character could be determined physiologically by the configuration of the skull. By 1832 there were 29 phrenological societies in Great Britain, and several journals in both Britain and the United States. Americans interpreted Gall's theory to mean that character thus determined by cranial configuration could be changed. Wells and her brothers were early American popularizers of "practical" phrenology. Orson Squire Fowler and Lorenzo Niles Fowler lectured around the country on the subject, applying phrenological concepts to the treatment of the in-

sane, education, marriage, sex, and personal development. In 1835 they established a center for phrenology in New York City, and asked Wells to join them in 1837. By this time the center included a museum, a lecture-booking bureau, and a publishing house. In 1839 they began publishing the *American Phrenological Journal.*

Wells taught the first regular American phrenology class and gave character readings. She was proofreader, writer, business manager, and editor for the family publishing firm, O.S. & L.N. Fowler, and continued working in this field for over 60 years.

On October 13, 1844, she married Samuel Robert Wells. They had no children. Samuel Wells was born in West Hartford, CT, the son of Russell Wells, of Farmington, CT. In 1843 Samuel Wells had begun studying phrenology with the Fowler brothers and he soon became their assistant, traveling with them on lecture tours. In 1844 he became a member of the Fowlers' publishing house. The name of the firm was changed to Fowler & Wells, and it became the main publisher for books and pamphlets on such diverse topics as health, diet, the water cure, sex, marriage, architecture, spiritualism, and mesmerism (hypnosis). When Lorenzo Fowler moved to England in 1855, Charlotte and Samuel Wells became the owners of the firm.

Charlotte and Samuel Wells were instrumental in founding the American Institute of Phrenology in New York City. They continued as leading exponents of phrenology in the United States. Through her husband, Wells became interested in vegetarianism, temperance, shorthand, and advanced agricultural practices.

Wells became sole proprietor of the publishing firm after her husband's death on April 13, 1875. When it was incorporated in 1884, she became president of the new Fowler and Wells Company and from that period to her death she lived in West Orange, NJ.

A proponent of equal rights for women, Wells was an organizer of the New York Medical College for Women and held its organizational meetings in her office. From 1863, when it was founded, to 1901, when she died, she was on its board of trustees. She was connected with many society and professional clubs, including the American Association for the Advancement of Science. She was a charter member of Sorosis in West Orange.

Wells became interested in spiritualism, developed beginning in 1848 by the family of J. D. Fox in Hydesville, NY, which was based on the idea that the spiritual world makes itself known by producing physical effects that can be seen. Spiritualism promised universal social reform because of information that could be gained from other realms of existence. Wells was a medium, or spirit communicator, for the New York Circle.

Described as active, energetic, short and plump, Wells was still reading without glasses at age 80, when she was writing a series of articles for the *Phrenological Journal* about early pioneers of the phrenological movement. She had a bad fall in 1896 that deprived her of the sight of one eye, but she recovered enough to give a series of lectures in 1897–98 at the American Institute of Phrenology in New York.

Wells died on June 4, 1901, at age 86, of "degeneration of the heart" at her home in West Orange. She was buried in Rosedale Cemetery, Orange, NJ.

Wells is profiled in *NAW*. Her obituary appeared in the *Orange (NJ) Chronicle*, June 8, 1901.

*Sherie Fox Schmauder*

## ALMA BRIDWELL WHITE, 1862–1946

(Mollie) Alma (Bridwell) White, founder of the Pillar of Fire church and first woman bishop of a Christian church, was born at Kinniconick (Lewis County), KY, on June 16, 1862. She was the seventh child and fifth daughter of the eleven children born to Mary Ann (Harrison) and William Moncure Bridwell.

White grew up on the family farm and tannery near the Kinniconick River. Because of her large, sturdy build, she was expected to perform physical labor around the household and to care for younger siblings. When these tasks caused her to miss school, her mother tutored her at home.

Three themes from White's childhood continued to predominate throughout her life: diligent labor, conflict with family members, and religious awareness. As a young teen, she was preoccupied with her spiritual condition. It was to her relief that, at age sixteen, she had a conversion experience at a Methodist revival under the preaching of the Rev. W. B. Godbey, an evangelist and author of religious tracts. She felt called to preach, but Godbey advised her to marry a minister and work with him since very few Protestant denominations ordained women.

In 1879, at seventeen, White began teaching school to help her family financially and to earn funds for her own education. The family moved to Millersburg, KY, in 1880, where she studied for a year at Millersburg Female College (which later awarded her an honorary B.A.).

In March 1882, not yet 20, White traveled to her Aunt Eliza Mason's home in the frontier settlement of Bannack, MT. For the next five years White taught school in Bannack and in other Montana and Utah towns. She demonstrated her mettle by traveling alone through the frontier West, keeping discipline in her classrooms, and refusing to yield to frontier mores, which clashed with her religious resolve.

She married Kent White, a Methodist minister from West Virginia, on December 21, 1887, in Denver, CO.

She had met White in 1883 at her aunt's home in Bannack. The couple lived in Denver while Kent White finished his education at the University of Denver. White also took classes at the university and at the Saxton College of Elocution. In 1889 she gave birth to the couple's first child, Arthur Kent. Their second son, Ray Bridwell, was born in 1892, in Morrison, CO, where Kent White served as pastor of the Methodist church.

In Morrison in March 1893 White reported experiencing sanctification or the "second blessing" (which, to her, meant being empowered and endowed with moral perfection by the Holy Spirit). Until this time she had played a supporting role in her husband's ministry—accompanying and leading hymns, occasionally praying in services, and privately criticizing his spirituality and conduct as a minister. After her sanctification, White increasingly acted upon her call to preach. She led revival services that evoked enthusiastic responses from participants but negative reaction from Methodist leaders. The denomination refused to license White or officially recognize her ministry. Her husband was given less desirable parishes as a result of her outspoken preaching and the spirited worship style she encouraged.

White thereafter became more stridently critical of what she regarded as lack of spiritual zeal, piety, and moral rigor among pastors and leaders in the Methodist church and other established denominations. Frustrated also by their refusal to ordain women, White later wrote: "I had to pioneer the way for ecclesiastical recognition of women's ministry, against fierce opposition." (White, *The Story of My Life*, 5:283)

During the next seven years she engaged in interdenominational mission activity, until she decided to found her own religious society. She refused to associate any longer with what she termed hypocrisy and "latter-day apostasy" in other churches, which she called "fallen." On December 29, 1901, White founded the Pentecostal Union church (the name was later changed to Pillar of Fire) with 50 charter members. White was ordained an elder in March 1902, and she was consecrated bishop of the church she had founded in August 1918.

Originally headquartered in Denver, and similar in doctrine and methods to the Salvation Army, the church reflected White's appreciation of John Wesley (the English preacher and founder of Methodism), especially his teachings on sanctification. White's powerful preaching, energetic administration, and strong-minded vision catalyzed church growth and expansion, which she attributed to divine guidance and blessing.

The church headquarters were moved in 1908 to an 81-acre New Jersey farm that White named Zarephath. (The farm was deeded to Pillar of Fire by Carolyn Garretson, who became interested in White's work after reading her *Looking Back from Beulah*. She left New Jersey to study at Pillar of Fire's Denver Bible School.)

White oversaw every phase of the development of this new base of operations, even contracting to pave the road between Zarephath and nearby Bound Brook. During White's lifetime the Zarephath headquarters came to include worship, administrative, publishing, radio broadcasting, and post office facilities. The complex also housed accredited educational facilities from elementary level to a Bible seminary; a children's home (a special interest of White's); plus farming, greenhouse, and nursery operations.

Each year in late summer the church held its annual camp meeting at Zarephath, with White's preaching billed as the main attraction. Revivals were also held in other New Jersey towns, including Plainfield, Morristown, Rahway, Asbury Park, Bound Brook, Newark, and Trenton. The church eventually purchased property in several of these cities.

White pursued an active schedule of preaching (sometimes three to four times a day) and traveled to the church's approximately 50 mission branches throughout the United States and London. She crossed the Atlantic 58 times, visiting Great Britain, France, Germany, and the Middle East. Even World War I could not keep her from her missions in Europe. Meanwhile, she edited up to eight periodicals, collaborated with her son Arthur in publishing five hymnals, and wrote over 35 books.

Always concerned with current events, White was vocal about social causes. She supported women's ministry, publishing the periodical *Woman's Chains* to help women "feel their responsibility in preaching the Gospel, as many of them had been made to believe that it would be unscriptural and out of place for them to do so." (White, *The Story of My Life*, 5:284) She also supported woman suffrage, temperance, dress reform, a homeland for the Jews in Palestine, and "100 percent Americanism." This last emphasis, combined with her opposition to the Roman Catholic church, led to her alliance with the Ku Klux Klan.

White's sons and their wives worked actively in the Pillar of Fire church. She lamented, however, the opposition to her ministry by her mother, several siblings, and her husband, from whom she was estranged during most of the years she actively led the church.

White founded and built a thriving church, which continues to this day. She advocated women's equality in church and state, and exemplified this equality in her own organization and activities, although she denied equality to certain minorities. White died from arteriosclerotic heart disease, at age 84, on June 26, 1946, at Zarephath, NJ. She was buried in Fairmount Cemetery in Denver, CO.

Archival material related to White is available at the Pillar of Fire Church headquarters (Zarephath, NJ). White's autobiographies are *Looking Back from Beulah* (1902) and *The Story of My Life*, 5

vols. (1919–43). Her niece, Gertrude Metlen Wolfram, details White's ministry in *The Widow of Zarephath* (1954). An interview with White's granddaughter, Bishop Arlene White Lawrence, at her home in Belle Mead, NJ, in Sept. 1986 provided additional information. A sketch of White appears in *NAW*.

*Esther Byle Bruland*

The development in the 1910s of the first cultivated blueberry was masterminded by Elizabeth Coleman White, a native of the New Jersey Pine Barrens. White, shown here in 1928, was interested in many New Jersey plants, especially those indigenous to the Pine Barrens. *Courtesy, New Jersey Conservation Foundation.*

## ELIZABETH COLEMAN WHITE, 1871–1954

Elizabeth Coleman White, Pine Barrens resident who masterminded the development of the nation's first cultivated blueberry, was born on October 5, 1871, on her father's cranberry farm in New Lisbon (Burlington County), NJ. She was the oldest of four daughters, the only one to remain unmarried and to pursue the family's agricultural interests.

Both of White's parents were Quakers and members of the landed working gentry. Mary A. (Fenwick) White, her mother, was the daughter of Colonel James A. Fenwick, a pioneer cranberry farmer with 108 acres along Cranberry Run, south of Hanover Furnace. Joseph Josiah ("J.J.") White, her father, an engineer in Camden, inherited 100 acres of promising cranberry land near New Lisbon, which introduced him to cranberry cultivation as well as to Mary A. Fenwick. Following their marriage in 1869, the Whites prepared a book on cranberry culture that became a standard guide in the industry. Later, J. J. White worked as a machinist and an inventor for the H. B. Smith Company in nearby Smithville. Upon his father-in-law's death in 1882, J. J. White became sole executor and manager of the now 600-acre cranberry farm, which he later expanded into a 3,000-acre plantation known as Whitesbog.

As a girl, White often accompanied her father on his weekend visits to Whitesbog. After 1887, when she graduated from the Friends Central School in Philadelphia, she worked in the bogs, helping to supervise the cranberry pickers during the fall harvest. She lived in the farm's small cedar office and was soon deeply involved in the farm's operation, packing and shipping cranberries all over the country.

White's winters were spent in Philadelphia, where she continued her education, taking courses in first aid, photography, dressmaking, and millinery at Drexel University.

Her great love was always the farm at Whitesbog. When, in 1910, the National Child Labor Committee (NCLC) published a pamphlet critical of cranberry growers' treatment of children helpers, she believed the charges to be greatly exaggerated. Families from the Pines and from Philadelphia, mostly of Italian origin, returned year after year to pick in the same bogs, and White knew many families personally, having applied first aid in emergencies. She had watched some children mature.

Reports and magazine articles spread the details nationally. White was an articulate and exacting communicator in the growers' defense. She wrote many letters and spoke widely, arguing that the seven weeks each fall children and their families worked in the bogs trained them "to be self-supporting individuals of a character as near an ideal of American citizenship as possible." (White, *Cranberries*) The controversy, hearings, and correspondence between J. J. White, Elizabeth White, and the NCLC d12continued for four years. At last, the NCLC printed a retraction in the *Trenton Times*. Everett Colby, one of the NCLC's three members, acknowledged White's tireless effort as peacemaker.

At this time, White also championed the research of ELIZABETH KITE from the Vineland Training School, who was investigating intelligence patterns in families living near White's home. Kite's study was widely misinterpreted to have stated that most of the people who lived in the New Jersey Pines—the "Pineys"—were inbred and feeble-minded. White wrote extensively on the issue, refuting misunderstandings and urging establishment of a new training school. She was on the board of the Work-Training School at Four Mile Colony near New Lisbon until she died.

White's deepest involvement with her native Pine Bar-

rens began in 1911 when she read a U.S. Department of Agriculture bulletin describing Frederick Coville's progress in blueberry propagation. Although the soil requirements of blueberries and cranberries are similar and wild blueberries thrive in the swampy Pines, New Jersey farmers believed blueberry cultivation impossible.

White wrote inviting Coville to continue his research at Whitesbog. The J. J. White Company would provide the land and labor needed for the experiments and would keep the proceeds from any crops produced. Coville accepted the offer and the work began a few months later.

During the next five years, White assisted Coville at Whitesbog by locating wild blueberry bushes with desired traits. Tramping through the swampy woods, "Miss Lizzie," as the tall, imposing woman was called, asked woodsmen questions about berry size, vigor, resistance to cold and disease, flavor, texture, productivity, and time of ripening. She enlisted their help in finding the best bushes.

"For each huckleberry picker who was interested I provided a neat little aluminum gauge 16mm or a trifle less than 5/8" in diameter, three 2 oz. jars for samples of the largest berries on a bush and a paper of typewritten directions. . . . The finder was to receive a dollar for marking on any bush the largest berry which would not drop through the gauge, and in addition be liberally paid for the time spent in guiding me to it." (White, *Blueberry Culture*)

White named the new varieties produced from the bushes after their finders. Thousands of cuttings were taken from the more than 100 bushes collected, and their growth and characteristics painstakingly described and documented. While these wild varieties were brought under cultivation, Coville cross-fertilized bushes by hand to create new varieties.

In 1916 their collaboration resulted in the nation's first commercial crop of blueberries. At Whitesbog, the business of blueberry production and bush propagation began.

White was the first to use a cellophane wrapper for protecting and marketing the berries. In 1927 she helped to organize the New Jersey Blueberry Cooperative Association. By 1986 New Jersey's blueberry industry ranked second in the nation, with blueberry bushes derived from early work at Whitesbog .planted extensively in the United States and Canada.

White's horticultural interests extended beyond cranberries and blueberries to include all plants native to the Pine Barrens. Her garden at "Suningive," her home at Whitesbog, received much attention because of its design and its wide diversity of native plants. This garden exemplified White's interest in the district, the rich flora of the Pine Barrens, and the harmonious use of the environment.

Late in life, White widened her interest in native plants by forming Holly Haven, Inc., her own corporation. She was particularly interested in native American holly and was active in rescuing it from obscurity, and so in 1947 she helped to found the Holly Society of America. She propagated and sold many varieties of holly, Pine Barrens plants, and a rare magnolia called Franklinia, which was first discovered in Georgia by John Bartram, an 18th-century botanist.

White was the first woman member of the American Cranberry Association and the first woman to receive the New Jersey Department of Agriculture citation. Horticultural societies from Massachusetts and Pennsylvania awarded her their highest medals. Toward the end of her life, she concentrated on writing and on giving addresses to horticultural clubs and radio audiences. She died of cancer at Whitesbog on November 27, 1954, at age 83. She was cremated at the Ewing Crematory in Ewing Township, NJ, and in accordance with her will, her ashes were distributed by airplane over the headwaters of Whitesbog.

Two of White's papers cited are: "Cranberries and Colony Contributions, or the Appeal of the Colony (Burlington County Training School) to a Dweller in the Pines" (1914) and "Blueberry Culture" (1916). An interview with White taped in 1953 is available at the NJ-BCL.

*Michele S. Byers*
*Sheila Cowing*

## PEARL WHITE, 1889–1938

Pearl White, star of silent films, was born in Greenridge, MO, and began her film career in New Jersey. She was born on March 4, 1889, the youngest of nine children (only four of whom survived beyond infancy). Her father, Edward G. White, was born in Fort Tryon, NY, to wealthy parents of Irish background. His family moved to Greenridge when he was a boy, and it was there that he met and married Elizabeth House. He lived on savings and family money until his later years, when he took up farming out of necessity. Little is known of Elizabeth (House) White's background except that she was of Italian descent and her maiden name had originally been Casa. She died shortly after Pearl White was born.

In her girlhood, White lived with her father, paternal grandmother, sister Grace, and brother Frederick. As a child of six she made her stage debut as "Little Eva" in a local production of *Uncle Tom's Cabin*, and at thirteen she became a bareback rider with a circus. Her relationship with her father was a strained one, and at seventeen she left home to join a stock company.

Originally White wanted to be a singer, but traveling and theatrical work took their toll on her voice, which was damaged during a performance of *Kismet*. Realizing she would have to explore other outlets in the entertainment industry, she looked to the newly developing world of film.

In 1913, when she was 24, she signed her first film contract with the Pathé Film Company in Jersey City, NJ. Her first acting assignments were in westerns. She was athletic enough for the physical work required for such roles, and she was an excellent horsewoman.

While she made many feature films for the William Fox Company in the early 1920s, her most famous role was as "Pauline" in the *Perils of Pauline* serial, which was produced by the Pathé Film Company in Fort Lee, Jersey City, and outdoor locations nearby. *Perils of Pauline* was about the adventures of a young woman who was always being chased by mashers, fortune hunters, conmen, and other villains, thus forcing Pauline into any number of hair-raising situations. Audiences cringed in their seats as they watched the delicate Pauline being chased across train tracks or running across the top of a moving trolley car. She was popular with viewers and became affectionately known as "the lady daredevil."

One stunt of White's, recalled by several historians and by White herself, required "Pauline" to climb into a hot-air balloon while a villain cut the rope and sent her into the unknown. The balloon was anchored at the edge of the Palisades, on the New Jersey side of the Hudson River. Before the scene was shot, an aeronaut had explained to White how to use the rip cord, but she let the balloon drift well over Long Island before navigating it to the ground. Onlookers may have been worried, but White later said that she was having a wonderful time.

Her popularity with audiences made White a powerful figure in the film industry. *Perils of Pauline* was one of the most successful serials in film history. As the first movie serial and first movie to be nationally advertised, it made White one of the first women to become nationally known as a "star." At the height of her career she commanded a $10,000 weekly salary, and within ten years of starting her career she was a millionaire many times over, with several $100,000 contracts to her credit. These kinds of earnings were unprecedented for a woman at that time, but her popularity allowed her to be a tough negotiator at Pathé and Fox.

In addition to being a clever comic actor and a high-spirited athlete, White was outspoken regarding the role of women in society. In the late 1910s and 1920s, some factions of society found movies dangerous to citizens' moral well-being and thought that women who wanted to be friends with men were lowering their standards. White countered these attacks with surprisingly contemporary criticism: "We are not living in the past," White told reporters in 1919, "we don't want to be marble. Besides, there would not be enough pedestals to go around. Why not give our men the same comradeship that many of them never find outside their clubs?" And in 1920 she told the *Cleveland Plain Dealer*: "The tragic thing in the lives of many women is that they settle down; get into a groove;

the thinking and enjoying faculties in them shrivel, enthusiasm dies, the champagne bubbles escape from their lives and they find life stable, flat and unprofitable." She believed that all American women and girls should know how to ride a horse and shoot a gun. She maintained that women should be required by law to have hobbies and interests outside the home so that their minds would remain active.

There are no confirmed dates of White's two marriages. The first was to Victor Sutherland, an actor. They were divorced in 1914, due to Sutherland's infidelity. Her second marriage was to Major Wallace McCutcheon, also an actor. They were divorced in 1921 in Rhode Island. White had no children.

White moved to France in 1924 and made her last film in 1925. She lived the rest of her life in Paris, dying of a liver ailment, at age 49, on August 4, 1938.

White's autobiography is *Just Me* (1919). The major source of information on her is the Pearl White file at NYPL-LC, which contains clippings, film notes, original photos, and other primary source materials. She is profiled in *NAW*. Her obituary appeared in the *New York Times*, Aug. 5, 1938.

*Karen Kelly*

## EMILY HORNBLOWER WILLIAMSON, 1869–1909

Emily (Hornblower) Williamson, social activist and pioneer reformer, was the daughter of Eustace F. and Emily Newport (Reade) Hornblower. She was a direct descendant of Jonathan Hornblower, a well-known English engineer, and on her mother's side was descended from Christopher Newport of Newport News. Her mother was also the cousin of Charles Reade, the novelist.

While records indicate that she was born in England, the exact day and month of her birth are not known. She was educated by tutors and wide reading, first in her father's library and later in her husband's. She had one sibling, an older brother, Josiah M. Hornblower.

She married Benjamin Williamson, a lawyer who was the eldest son of Chancellor Benjamin Williamson and grandson of Governor Isaac H. Williamson of New Jersey. The Williamsons resided in his family mansion in Old Elizabeth, NJ. The couple had no children.

Williamson became deeply involved in charitable work after her husband's death, on March 12, 1900, but even before that time she was active in the field. With her rhetorical and organizational skills, she created new pathways in social welfare for indigent children. As a *Charm Magazine* article, "Modern Pioneers of New Jersey" (July 1927), pointed out: "Sixteen thousand children are cared for today, comfortably and happily, in private homes but as public wards who would otherwise be the flotsam and jetsam washed hither and yon on the waves of human maladjust-

ment. Before Emily Williamson blazed her trail, there was no state agency to help them."

Williamson began her charitable work as a member of the Episcopal church in Elizabeth, which already had a charitable program from the 1850s. An active supporter of a home for aged women and a day nursery, she also founded and was secretary of the State Charities Aid Association (SCAA) and in 1888 became secretary of the Home for the Care and Training of Feeble-Minded Women at Vineland, now the Vineland Development Center.

She contended that she was interested in the practical aspects of charity and believed that every man or woman should be required to contribute enough labor for self-support. The SCAA inspected almshouses in order to keep out lazy people who could help themselves and to find relatives who might take over the care of inmates.

The more exposure she had to conditions in almshouses and other institutions, the less simplistic became her view of charity. She used her rhetorical talents to argue for improved organization of charities, and gradually her interest expanded to include rehabilitation and prevention.

Emily Williamson also became a leading advocate for the cause of children. Her first step was to publicize the dreadful conditions at Snake Hill, the Hudson County almshouse. She protested the treatment of children housed there as well as the system of indenturing young children without any real followup on their treatment. By calling these conditions to the attention of the press, in particular the *Herald*, she was able to win popular statewide support. So strong was her support that she convinced lawmakers to create a legislative investigating commission; she became a member of this commission, which discovered, after studying 48 almshouses, that 400 to 500 children were housed in almshouses because there was no other place for them. The commission's report also cited specific instances in which children who were indentured from the almshouses as apprentices in various trades were never located again and in which no attempt was made to investigate conditions under which they were forced to live. The children who remained in the almshouses fared no better. Education was nominal, with adults and children housed together. In addition, the almshouses were dirty, and the food scarce and of poor quality.

Williamson was determined to save these children, and she decided that home life for dependent children was the only answer, so she went to the New Jersey State Legislature. Because she was intelligent, highly verbal, and aggressive, she was able to speak before the assembly, which few, if any, women had done previously.

As a result of her efforts, a law was passed that created the State Board of Children's Guardians in 1899. The board became the legal parent for the children who were placed with private families at the expense of the county or town from which they came. The state paid the costs of administration of the program by the board, but the board was responsible for vigilantly guarding the children's welfare. Constant visitation and supervision safeguarded their moral and physical well-being.

Before state money was actually allocated, Williamson used more than $10,000 of her own money as an advance to the board. She also convinced other wealthy individuals to donate to the cause. By espousing this plan and convincing legislators to pass the law creating the board, Williamson revealed herself to be a woman of great vision; in fact, with some modification, the system of foster homes in use today is a direct result of her efforts.

After the death of her husband in 1900, Williamson devoted even more time and energy to her charitable work. She paid for a full-time executive for the SCAA and worked with him. In 1902 she was the first New Jersey woman of wealth and position to take a full-time job in social service as a probation officer for Union County. In 1902 she also organized the State Association of Probation Officers and served as president of the first state conference of charities and corrections. She was active in the national conference as well. As a result, President Theodore Roosevelt named her a delegate to the International Prison Association, which met in Budapest in 1904.

To a large extent, she was the founder of probation in New Jersey. She lobbied for the law to establish probation and also saw the plan enacted. Her chief aim was to better the conditions of people in penal and charitable institutions throughout the state. It was largely because of her efforts that Rahway State Prison was founded.

She visited almost every prison and almshouse in the state, and so was able to speak for her cause with more conviction since she had personally observed the conditions described to lawmakers and philanthropists. Reputed to have been a beautiful woman, her oratorical skills were aided by a splendid voice. Jerome Allen, dean of the School of Pedagogy, said of her: "Mrs. Williamson is a fluent and inspiring speaker." (Ricord, *History*, 208)

In addition to her other interests, Williamson was a member of the Woman's Advisory Committee of New York University (NYU); she was supportive, in particular, of the School of Pedagogy. She was president of the New Jersey State Federation of Women's Clubs (1899–1901) and a director until 1905. When she resigned, she held a gala reception at the Williamson mansion for 500 women.

Williamson's energy, enthusiasm, and brilliance were used to the fullest to support reform and centralization of New Jersey's institutions. Through her strong connection with the State Federation of Women's Clubs, she was in an excellent position to influence club women to support reform, in particular for women and children in schools, hospitals, probation and labor conditions.

As a pioneer in social reform, Williamson has earned her place in New Jersey history. Her visionary methods and ideas helped to improve life for thousands of indigent children and prisoners. In addition, she was probably the first female lobbyist, championing the cause of the poor and helpless, to exert both direct and indirect pressure on legislators to influence social legislation.

Williamson died of apoplexy, at age 60, on September 13, 1909, at her home in Elizabeth, NJ. She was buried in Evergreen Cemetery in Elizabeth.

James Leiby, *Charity and Corrections in New Jersey* (1967), provides a detailed description of Williamson's contributions to social reform. Frederick Ricord, *History of Union County, New Jersey* (1897), cites her contributions. See also Beatrice Stern, "Modern Pioneers of New Jersey: Emily Williamson," *Charm* (July 1927):38–39, 87. Her obituary appeared in the *New York Times*, July 14, 1909.

*Maria Gillan*

## BEATRICE WINSER, 1869–1947

Beatrice Winser, director of the Newark Public Library and the Newark Museum, was born in Woodside (Essex County), NJ (now part of Newark), on March 11, 1869, the eldest of three children of Henry Jacob and Edith (Cox) Winser. A strong believer in women's rights, she made distinguished contributions to civic affairs in New Jersey and in education and, by supporting an early effort to establish a world archive center for women's history, presaged the modern women's studies movement.

Her father was a journalist who served as correspondent for the *New York Times* during the Civil War and reported the fall of Fort Sumter for that paper. He left his post as city editor when on April 16, 1869, President Grant appointed him consul-general to the court of Saxe-Coburg, where he served until 1881. Later he had a career as assistant editor of the New York *Commercial Advertiser*, and he was city editor of the *Newark Daily Advertiser* at the time of his death.

Winser's mother, Edith (Cox) Winser, fulfilled her duties of hostess as wife of a consul-general and mother of three children. Her intellectual vitality is expressed in her memoirs of Saxe-Coburg. She wrote a variety of essays on Martin Luther, "Newark in Colonial Days," "Jeanne d'Arc: The Maid of Orleans," "Historic Castles of Thuringen," and an essay on eastern New Jersey.

Winser learned fluent French and German during her childhood years in Saxe-Coburg. She received a liberal education from governesses and tutors and developed an interest in art and books.

Winser attended Columbia University Library School from 1888 to 1889 and then joined the Newark Public Library staff as German and French cataloger. In 1894 she became assistant librarian to Frank P. Hill and then in 1902 to John Cotton Dana when he was appointed librarian. Winser advocated the open-stack system along with Dana. She applied ideas of community outreach by offering books to public school classes without school libraries, by opening libraries in union halls, and by making the library responsive to the needs of citizens. A prime interest for Winser was encouragement of schoolchildren's development of individual interests at the library and the Newark Museum. Dana depended on Winser's competent administrative ability and broad knowledge of culture during his extended absences and illnesses. Upon Dana's death in 1929, Winser succeeded him as librarian, a post she held for thirteen years.

Winser also became deeply involved with the Newark Museum, founded by Dana in 1909. In 1915 she became assistant director and secretary, and in 1916 a member of its Board of Trustees. She succeeded Dana as director and secretary of the museum after his death, even though Dana had expressed dismay that a man was not being trained for the job. Under her leadership, the museum mounted major exhibitions and presented public cultural programs during the Depression years.

Winser was the first woman in Newark's history to become a member of a governing body when she was appointed to the Newark Board of Education in 1915. Believing in the effectiveness of strong professional leadership, she presented a proposal to reduce school board authority and centralize responsibility for administration in the superintendent of schools. This plan was defeated, and she resigned from the board on principle when her opponent became its president. In 1918 Winser was made a member of the Women's Committee for the New Jersey College for Women (now Douglass College).

Her commitment to professionalism was borne out in her own career by involvement in several professional associations. She was a charter member of the New Jersey Library Association, founded in 1890, and was its president in 1907–8 and 1921–22. She was also a member of the American Library Association Council of Fifty from 1909 to 1913 and was reelected in 1930, serving as second vice-president in 1931.

During World War I, Winser successfully challenged the policy of excluding women librarians from employment in military libraries. And though she was a member of the Essex County Committee Against Peacetime Conscription, she was quick to establish the Victory Book Committee to send books to soldiers when World War II began.

In 1923 Winser publicly joined the debate over protective labor legislation for women in New Jersey by siding with many other professional women to oppose legislation that restricted night work for women. "Personally I object strenuously to a law which abridges on account of sex my personal liberty. . . . A more insulting and insolent bill it has never been my lot to read," she commented. (*Newark*

*Sunday Call*, Apr. 11, 1923)

During the Depression, Winser was chair (1935) of the New Jersey Art Division of the Work Projects Administration (WPA), a committee charged with selection of artists to execute commissions on public building projects. Later she was named chair of the advisory committee to assist the work of the WPA writers' project in New Jersey. Winser opposed federal aid to libraries, fearing political control, and in 1930 joined with 500 other educators to petition Congress to abolish the law permitting customs officers to censor books from foreign countries.

On June 21, 1936, in Newark, a group of prominent New Jersey women, including Winser, MARY PHILBROOK, and FLORENCE P. EAGLETON, met with historian and feminist Mary Ritter Beard to set up a New Jersey branch of the World Center for Women's Archives (NJWCWA). This was the first state branch of the WCWA established. Winser served as archivist. The purpose of the NJWCWA was to collect and preserve historical records relating to women in a central archive. Neither Winser nor Beard saw this enterprise realized, but their work was a legacy for future women's archives collections. Beard and Winser shared the knowledge and understanding of the archives movement as historian and librarian. The NJWCWA continued for a short period as the New Jersey Center for Women's Archives after the national organization was dissolved in 1940.

Winser resigned as head of the Newark Public Library in 1942, after a 53-year association with the institution, contending that the trustees interfered with the administration of the institution. In her long association with the Newark Public Library, the circulation of volumes increased from 332,078 in 1890 to 2,024,088 in 1942. Winser continued in her unsalaried post as director of the Newark Museum until a few months before her death.

Winser died of heart disease, at age 78, on September 14, 1947, at her home in Newark. Funeral services were held in Trinity Cathedral (Episcopal) in Newark, and she was buried in the Greenwood Cemetery in Brooklyn, NY.

Information on Winser is available in the files of the NJ-HS and the NJ-NPL. A sketch of her appears in *NAW*.

*Charlotte Perry-Dickerson*

## CAROLINE STEVENS ALEXANDER WITTPENN, 1859–1932

Caroline Bayard (Stevens) Alexander Wittpenn, penal reformer, social service worker, and philanthropist, was born November 21, 1859, in Hoboken (Hudson County), NJ, at "Castle Point," the beautiful family home overlooking the Hudson River. The third of seven children born to Martha Bayard (Dod) and Edwin Augustus Stevens, she had two older brothers, one younger sister, and three younger brothers. Her mother, Martha (Dod) Stevens, the daughter of a Princeton professor, was a pious and cultured person known for her sympathy and love of needy people. She founded Holy Innocents Church (Episcopal) in Hoboken, now part of All Saints Parish, in memory of her daughter Juliana, who died at age seven. Wittpenn's father was a manager of the family fortune, head of the Union Line of steamboats and horse coaches, an inventor, treasurer of the Camden and Amboy Railroad, and founder of Stevens Institute of Technology in Hoboken.

Wittpenn's family history covers more than a century of "dreaming and daring," and includes the beginnings of American steamship lines and railroads. The Stevens family abundantly shared both their means and energies with the people of their church, city, state, and country. Because they lived so long in the same place—Hoboken—a sense of the family's tradition was able to be transmitted to Wittpenn. She carried on their religious feeling, culture, and sense of social obligation throughout her life. Wittpenn was educated by tutors and at a private school on the Isle of Wight. Her father, considerably older than her mother, was 60 when Wittpenn was born. She was very close to her mother, whose piety and well-known sympathy for the needy greatly influenced Wittpenn. While still a young woman, Wittpenn was initiated into social service work by her mother through involvement with working women in Hoboken and New York. As a result, the Industrial School for Manual Training and the Memorial Day Nursery of Hoboken became her lifelong interests.

In 1879, when she was nineteen, Wittpenn married Archibald Alexander of Princeton, and in 1880 their son, Archibald, was born. Her marriage to Alexander reportedly ended in a painful separation in 1895, and it was at this time that Wittpenn became more active in public life. Through contacts with various groups and institutions, such as the State Charities Aid Association, she became even more aware of the problems of the underprivileged. Contributing financially and administratively to better the lot of orphans, paupers, the disabled, and prisoners, Wittpenn became associated with nearly 100 social service organizations and many state institutions. She served as manager of the New Jersey State Institution for Feeble-Minded Girls and Women in Vineland in 1897; manager of the New Jersey State Village for Epileptics in 1902; and president of the New Jersey State Board of Children's Guardians in 1913.

Wittpenn is best known for her work in penal reform. Concerned with the treatment of female prisoners, she was appointed by Governor Franklin Murphy in 1902 to a commission to study the creation of a separate prison for females and to make recommendations to the legislature. Shortly thereafter she was also appointed assistant probation officer for Hudson County, a position she held until

her death. Through her efforts on the study commission, a proposal was made to the state prompting her son, Archibald Alexander, then a member of the legislature, to introduce a bill providing for the separate women's institution. Wittpenn became the first president of the Board of Managers of Clinton Farms Reformatory for Women when it opened in 1913. Her son's death from typhoid in 1912 led Wittpenn to donate the Chapel of the Good Shepherd at Clinton Farms in his memory.

Wittpenn was married a second time in January 1915 to H. Otto Wittpenn, whom she had supported as reform mayor of Jersey City. Otto Wittpenn gave up elective politics after conflict with Frank Hague and an unsuccessful gubernatorial bid in 1916, and then devoted himself to the family's business interests. The Wittpenns' marriage lasted until his death in July 1931.

In addition to her work in penal reform, Wittpenn distinguished herself as an accomplished public servant at both the state and national levels. In 1910 she was appointed the U.S. representative to the International Congress of Family Education in Brussels, Belgium. During this period she was also consulted by Governor Woodrow Wilson on New Jersey welfare problems. During Wilson's presidency she served as New Jersey's first National Democratic committeewoman. She was later appointed to the New Jersey Board of Control of Institutions and Agencies by Governors Walter E. Edge (1917–19) and Morgan F. Larson (1929–32). In 1931 President Herbert Hoover appointed Wittpenn the U.S. representative to the International Prison Commission in Switzerland.

Wittpenn received an honorary doctor of laws degree in 1922 at the first commencement of the New Jersey College for Women (now Douglass College) and served as a trustee of Stevens Institute of Technology for several years. She was a devout Episcopalian and in her private life at her estate in Bernardsville was fond of gardening, pets, and fox hunting.

On November 24, 1932, Wittpenn was honored at a public celebration of her 73rd birthday. Two weeks later she contracted pneumonia and suffered a heart attack. She died on December 4, 1932, at Castle Point in Hoboken. More than a thousand people attended her funeral. She was buried in accordance with Stevens family custom in a wicker basket in Hoboken Cemetery, North Bergen, NJ.

Wittpenn is profiled in *NAW*. Obituaries appeared in the *New York Times*, Dec. 5, 1932; the *Jersey Journal* (Jersey City, NJ), Dec. 5, 1932; and the *Newark Evening News*, Dec. 6, 1932.

*Anna D. Kane*

## MARIETTA HUNTOON CRANE WOODRUFF, 1837–1912

Marietta Huntoon (Crane) Woodruff, homeopathic physician and the first woman to practice medicine in Morris County, was born in May 1837, in Pine Brook (Morris County), NJ, the first of two daughters of Judge Benjamin Crane and his second wife, Barbara (Parlaman) Bowlsby Crane. Her ancestors were of English and German descent but had been in North America for seven generations. Woodruff attended the district school and the Pennington Collegiate Institute. In 1861 she married Christopher Denman Woodruff, a native of Rahway who moved to Morris County to teach school but spent most of his adult working life as a buyer and inspector for a local railroad. Their first child, Benjamin Crane Woodruff (b. 1862), died in infancy. Their second child, Flora Crane Woodruff, was born in 1864, and Franklin Crane Woodruff in 1865. In 1878 the Woodruffs adopted another daughter, Eleanor.

In 1871, at age of 34, Woodruff matriculated at the New York Medical College for Women. Established in 1863 by Clemence Lozier, an activist in the antebellum feminist and popular health movements, the New York Medical College for Women emphasized the study of the treatment of women and children and taught the homeopathic system of medicine. Homeopathy was one of several alternative systems of healing that flourished during the mid-19th century. Homeopaths believed that traditional physicians (allopaths) relied too much on large doses of drugs and other "heroic" treatments such as bleeding. Homeopaths adopted the principle of *similia similibus curantur*—treat like with like—and believed that the smaller the dosage of a medicine, the greater its effectiveness. The so-called "sectarian systems" of healing, including homeopathy, won many converts among middle-class women, who were welcomed into reform-oriented and populist circles of sectarian medicine. Woodruff's decision to study medicine after the birth of her third child may have reflected her personal experiences as a wife and mother, but she was also participating in a broad movement by women who believed that scientific education was a key to social reform in the interest of their gender.

In 1874 Woodruff received her M.D. in a class of seven women who had completed a three-year course of lectures. She had already begun acquiring practical experience after her first year of course work as a practitioner in Boonton, NJ. The fact that her mother lived with the Woodruffs and that her sister lived next door was probably essential to her ability as the mother of a seven- and a six-year-old to commute to New York for classes and to practice medicine. In January 1873 Woodruff began keeping a casebook of her obstetrical cases that eventually contained over 600 entries; it provides a fascinating record of part of her medical practice.

For 38 years Woodruff provided medical services to the residents of Boonton and witnessed the transformation of their community from a rural mining enclave into a substantial industrial town with many immigrants. In the 1870s a foreign-born or a Roman Catholic patient was exceptional; by 1900 many of Woodruff's patients were Italians and Slavs, and the Protestant homogeneity of Boonton had given way to the varied religions typical of an industrial region. Woodruff enjoyed considerable success as an obstetrician among all classes of Morris County mothers. As the first well-educated woman to practice medicine in the area, she provided expectant mothers with both feminine sympathy and scientific assistance based on the study of anatomy. Although she had been trained in a homeopathic school, Woodruff administered anesthesia and other drugs when she felt they were needed and occasionally delivered with forceps. Her casebook reveals, however, that her usual practice was to follow the homeopathic dictum that nature is the best healer, and she was willing to wait upon natural labor. In August 1877, for example, Woodruff noted the delivery of a large child by a small mother and that she had been "strongly urged to use instruments [but] was as heartily thanked afterwards that I did not." (Casebook, 58)

Woodruff's casebook is filled with further examples of what it was like to be a woman doctor practicing in the late 19th century and the attitudes she encountered among patients. On one occasion she was dismissed after a difficult but successful delivery and a male physician was employed. (Casebook, 56) Despite occasional misunderstanding ("the placenta adhered in part . . . was obliged to deliver manually. She thought I was killing her"; Casebook, 43) and tragic disappointments ("Child born . . . was limp as a rag . . . had to rub and breath[e] in its mouth to get it to breath[e] . . . the child fainted. I labored for 4 & ½ hours, but it died"; Casebook 2), Woodruff seems to have practiced the title of the poem pasted on the inside cover of her casebook—"resolute Cheerfulness."

Her career provides a well-documented example of the movement of women into the practice of medicine in the middle of the 19th century, largely through networks of social-reform-minded feminists. Participation of women in the medical profession reached a peak of about 6 percent by the first decade of the 20th century, but their numbers dwindled during the next 50 years as the great Victorian crusades for social redemption lost their appeal to new generations of women. By the early 1900s Woodruff's practice began to decline. Her son became a physician, but neither of her daughters became a professional. In 1910 her husband, who "was often seen walking with his wife and carrying her medical bag, or driving the carriage, as she made her round of professional calls," died. (Fowler, "Boonton's First Woman Physician," 8) Woodruff died two years later on November 6, 1912, at age 75, of a bronchial hemorrhage and was buried in Lower Montville Cemetery in Boonton.

Woodruff's casebook and Alex Fowler's unpublished "Boonton's First Woman Physician" are available at NJ-HS. Her obituary appeared in the *Boonton Weekly Bulletin*, Nov. 7, 1912.

*Basia Holub*
*James W. Reed*

## MARGARET TUFTS SWAN YARDLEY, 1844–1928

Margaret Tufts (Swan) Yardley, born in 1844 to Dr. Samuel Swan and Lucretia Green (Staniels) Swan in Auburn, NY, was a pioneer in the women's movement of the late 19th century. As first president of the New Jersey State Federation of Women's Clubs, philanthropist, and civic leader, Yardley "became known as one of the most earnest, energetic and progressive women of the country" for her efforts to enlarge and increase the influence of women in New Jersey. (Whittemore, "Founders and Builders of the Oranges," 454)

Information about her early life is elusive, but it is known that she lived in Wilmington, DE, during the Civil War and cared for the wounded there.

She married Charles B. Yardley (date unknown) and the couple lived in Yonkers, NY, until they moved to East Orange, NJ, in 1876, where she became prominent in the community. Available records state that she had five children—Margaret, Charles B., Jr., Farnham, Samuel, and one whose name is unknown.

In 1893 Yardley served on the Board of Managers at the Columbian Exposition in Chicago, IL, where a collection of writings of New Jersey women compiled by her was exhibited. She received a medal for her efforts. Locally, she served as director and president of the Orange Orphans' Society, helped start the first Homeopathic Hospital of the Oranges, championed the improvement of New Jersey's child labor laws, and remained active in political work in the Fourth District of the Second Ward of East Orange until her eighties.

Yardley's club work began with her membership in the Sorosis Club in New York in 1871. Moving to New Jersey, she joined the Woman's Club of Orange in 1876, the oldest women's club in the state and fourth in the United States, and served as a vice-president. Yardley was one of the founders of the New Jersey State Federation of Women's Clubs and was elected its first president on November 16, 1894. At the first annual meeting in Newark the following year, papers on health culture, forestry, and traveling libraries were read.

With a charter member roster of 36 clubs, and more joining the state federation in satisfactory numbers, Yardley turned her attention to civic action. At her urging, a Literary Day in Trenton took place on March 20, 1896, demonstrating to the legislators women's organized strength on important issues. Papers on preservation of New Jersey's forests and the Palisades, threatened with destruction by commercial enterprise, were presented. This resulted in the formation of a Palisades Study Commission in 1899, the Interstate Park created by New York, and the Palisades Interstate Park Commission, established in 1900. Papers on health, culture, household economics, and "women's place today" were also introduced to the public gathering; the governor was asked to appoint a commission to create state traveling libraries.

"What the legislature of 1896 has done for women" was the main topic of the state federation's second annual convention held in Jersey City on October 29–30, 1896. During Yardley's presidency, the Lily of the Valley was adopted as the federation's state flower and a badge with the colors buff and blue was designed. At the close of her administration, Yardley was named honorary president.

As the great-granddaughter of Major Samuel Swan of the Continental Army, Yardley became a member of the Colonial Dames of America and founded the Essex County (NJ) chapter of the Daughters of the American Revolution (DAR). She briefly served as a regent of the national organization. She was also a member of Nova Caesarea Chapter, DAR, and a charter member of the Charlotte Emerson Brown Club of East Orange founded in 1895.

When the New Jersey College for Women (now Douglass College) honored Yardley with a master of philanthropy degree on June 4, 1927, the citation read in part: "Pioneer leader in the first woman's club in the eastern United States . . . one of the first to discern the potential contribution of women in civic life . . . and one of the wisest in using women's influence for public good." (*A History of New Jersey State Federation of Women's Clubs, 1894–1958*) In 1929, at the state convention of the New Jersey State Federation of Women's Clubs in Atlantic City, the Margaret Yardley Fellowship Fund was established to provide a fellowship for a qualified woman to do graduate work in her field. The first contribution to the fund was $5,000, given by her son Farnham Yardley in his mother's memory in 1930. This fellowship is granted annually to a worthy candidate.

Yardley died September 3, 1928, at age 84, at her summer home at Burke Haven, Lake Sunapee, NH. Although not entirely recovered from pneumonia in the spring, she was in fair health and her death was unexpected. She was buried in Greenwood Cemetery in Brooklyn, NY.

Information on Yardley is scarce. The best collection of material on her is available at NJ-HS. Henry Whittemore, *The Founders and Builders of the Oranges* (1896), contains some details. Also useful is *A History of the New Jersey State Federation of Women's Clubs, 1894–1958* (1958).

*Ruth K. Eames*

All-women jury in Orange, NJ court, 1920. *Courtesy, Newark Public Library.*

# HISTORICAL OVERVIEW: 1921-PRESENT

WOMEN AND MEN IN NEW JERSEY, like their counterparts in other states, have experienced dramatic events since 1921: the stock market crash of 1929 followed by the Great Depression; World War II and postwar adjustment in the forties; economic expansion, the spread of suburban living, and the Korean War in the fifties; the civil rights movement and the Vietnam War in the sixties; the women's movement in the seventies;* and ever since 1945 the struggle to accommodate to a world threatened by nuclear weapons. Women's experience of these events has often been different from men's. Though some women in wartime volunteered for the armed forces, more remained at home assuming the roles of both parents when their spouse went to war, or worked in factories producing war materials. Though some women have joined men each day in the trek to work from suburb to city, more have remained in their suburban homes, creating new community organizations, new friendship patterns, and new professional opportunities for themselves.

In 1920 the 19th Amendment (granting women the vote) provided women new incentive to enter elective politics. New Jersey women took up the challenge at once: Republican JENNIE VAN NESS, elected in 1922 and one of the first two women to enter the New Jersey legislature, introduced the "Van Ness" Prohibition enforcement bill. Women politicians demonstrated their interest in education, other social services, and the work conditions of workers by the legislation they sponsored.

Some women, such as FLORENCE LILLIAN HAINES, a New Jersey assemblywoman before World War II, and MADALINE WORTHY WILLIAMS, a civil rights activist and, in 1958, the state's first black assemblywoman, sponsored legislation to improve child welfare; others worked to develop and maintain special treatment for women workers through protective legislation, believing the value of protection outweighed the dangers of discrimination against women that would arise from such legislation. Those who supported protective legislation for women opposed the federal Equal Rights Amendment proposed in 1923 by another New Jersey woman, ALICE STOKES PAUL, founder of the National Woman's Party.

Other women, less radical than Paul, also pressed for women's social and economic equality: in the 1920s Democratic assemblywoman MAY MARGARET CARTY introduced a successful bill forbidding sex discrimination in the hiring of teachers; assemblywoman GRACE MARGARET FREEMAN was the author of the New Jersey Civil Rights Act of 1949, which outlawed all forms of discrimination in housing, employment, and public accommodation due to race, creed, national origin, or color. Two years before this legislation, in 1947, MARY AUGUSTO, community leader and editor of *La Voce Italiana*, had run unsuccessfully for mayor of Paterson on the Liberal-Progressive ticket, the first woman to run for the mayoralty of a large New Jersey city. Lawyer MARY PHILBROOK was influential in insuring that the Bill of Rights to the new state constitution of 1947 explicitly forbade discrimination because of sex as well as race, color, religion, and national origin. MILLICENT HAMMOND FENWICK and ANN ROSENSWEIG KLEIN supported the renewed effort in the seventies and eighties to pass the Equal Rights Amendment to the U.S. Constitution. Although the state legislature ratified the federal ERA in 1972, a referendum to introduce an ERA amendment to the state constitution was defeated in 1975. Not until 1981, over 60 years after the 19th Amendment was added to the U.S. Constitution, did a woman, JANE GREY BURGIO, a well-known member of the state assembly, hold a senior executive position in state government, as New Jersey's secretary of state.

At the federal level, MARY TERESA HOPKINS NORTON, a Democrat from Hudson County, was elected in 1924 to the first of thirteen terms in the U.S. Congress. As chair of

---

*All the women in this book were born in or before 1923, the year that ALICE STOKES PAUL formulated the Equal Rights Amendment (ERA). Therefore, most women in this period undertook their major work ahead of the second women's movement of the 1970s.

the Labor Committee, she guided the Fair Labor Standards Act of 1938 through the House of Representatives. Although their numbers in any one session of the state legislature or the U.S. Congress did not increase substantially until the late 1970s, New Jersey women throughout the period continued to hold elective political office and, like KATHARINE ELKUS WHITE, U.S. ambassador to Denmark, and ANNE CLARK MARTINDELL, U.S. ambassador to New Zealand, to carry out distinguished work through presidential appointment.

Millicent Hammond Fenwick of Bernardsville in the New Jersey Assembly in the early 1970s. Fenwick became the congresswoman from the Fifth District in 1974 and U.S. ambassador to the United Nations Food and Agriculture Organization in 1982. *Courtesy, private collection.*

During the seven decades since 1920, New Jersey has changed remarkably. It has moved from dense railroad cities to sprawling automobile suburbs; from heavy manufacturing in locally owned firms to light manufacturing in branches of national and international corporations; from ferry boats, dirt roads, and railroad stations to tunnels, interstate highways, and airfields; from telegraph, radio, and telephone to computer, satellite, and fiber optic network. By the end of the 1920s most homes in the state were electrified. Timesaving became the hallmark of new household products, as the belief spread that electricity could reduce the time women had to spend on homemaking. LILLIAN MOLLER GILBRETH's plans for scientific management of the home, therefore, not only guided women on how to exploit new technology but also responded to new demands on women to make time for paid work or volunteer work.

New Jersey, a center for the distribution of goods and people, was among the first states to experience the impact of the automobile. Bridges replaced ferries as links between New Jersey and New York City and Philadelphia. Cars spawned new industries and new service jobs for women as well as men. The federal Highways Act of 1916 at first provided large numbers of jobs for men in road construction, but once the roads were completed, from the 1920s to the 1950s, new factories, stores, restaurants, and later, motels, business plazas, and shopping centers provided women as well as men with work.

At the same time, balloons, airships, and airplanes began to make air travel a reality. Among the pioneer airplane pilots was ANNE MORROW LINDBERGH, who not only flew and navigated planes, but wrote books to describe the work that she and her husband, Charles Lindbergh, did during the 1930s to strengthen the budding airline industry. In the 1930s JEANNETTE RIDLON PICCARD, a scientist, was the first woman to make a balloon flight through the stratosphere. (She made history again in 1974 when she became one of the first group of women ordained by the Episcopal church.)

Lindbergh and Piccard represented the "new woman" of their era, free to become pioneers and to excel in physical activities. Another such woman was ELEANOR EGG, athlete and dance instructor from Paterson, whose exploits as a runner demonstrated a new form of female excellence. No longer hampered by tight corsets and ankle-length dresses, the "new woman" could enjoy not only the healthful experience of strenuous exercise but also the hedonistic pleasures of smoking cigarettes (whose dangers to health were not then understood), dancing to jazz, and freer sexual expression. A new standard of American beauty was publicized in the 1920s through the Miss America pageants held in Atlantic City. LENORA SLAUGHTER, who administered the Miss America pageants for several decades after World War II, developed an educational scholarship program for the prizewinners. However, ELIZABETH HAWES, a designer of clothes for working women, roundly criticized women's continued slavery to fashion.

New forms of entertainment were made possible through the use of electricity and the introduction of radio, film, and the phonograph. Concert singer LUCILLE MANNERS became a radio star in the thirties, and ANNE ELSTNER a popular voice as "Stella Dallas" in a radio serial of the forties. Others who experimented with art forms in diverse settings were BERNARDA BRYSON, artist, writer, and illustrator; JESSIE REDMON FAUSET, one of the most prolific novelists of her day; AGNES SLIGH TURNBULL, whose novels and juvenile books stressed traditional values and the importance of mother-child relationships in the early years; PHYLLIS AYAME WHITNEY, author of romance mysteries; and CARLEEN MALEY HUTCHINS, who has combined scientific knowledge and craft skills to design a new violin family of eight acoustically balanced instruments of graduated sizes.

Anne Matthews Elstner was known as "Stella Dallas" to her millions of radio listeners from 1937 to 1955. *Courtesy, private collection.*

The audience in New Jersey for all forms of artistic entertainment is multiethnic. During World War I heavy industry in New Jersey opened its doors to African-Americans whose relatives migrated north to join them in the following years. In 1920 the black population of the state was just over 117,000; by 1940, it had grown to just under 227,000, all but a couple of thousand of whom were native-born. Employment opportunities for African-American women began to expand slowly; between the wars, for instance, blacks were employed for the first time in Newark as social workers. LENA EDWARDS, a black physician who won the Presidential Medal of Freedom in 1964, worked in private practice from 1925 until 1955 when she joined the faculty at Howard University in obstetrics. She combined her professional work with extensive community activities, as did other women physicians. MYRA LYLE SMITH KEARSE, a civil rights activist, was appointed to the staff of a Newark hospital when World War II created a doctor shortage, but not before. Women such as GLADYS ST. JOHN CHURCHMAN and ANNE LOUISE MCGEE GROOME dedicated their lives to social work among the city workers. Noted for her community spirit was CORA PETERSON SMITH, who, together with her husband, raised over 70 foster children in her home while she worked as a secretary to provide the money for music lessons and other "luxuries" for them. MARGARET CRESWELL, the first woman employed by a police force in New Jersey, spent much of her career between 1924 and 1964 working with female juveniles and with victims of rape.

An early proponent of school desegregation was schoolteacher DOROTHY ALLEN CONLEY, who during the 1940s began to publicize the history of African-Americans, "not only because it is the history of over 19 millions, but American life as a whole cannot be understood without knowing it." (Conley, Interview, 1987) In the same period JEANETTE LAKE CASCONE devised ways to include African and African-American history into the curriculum of the New York City school where she taught. When she retired from teaching school in 1972, Cascone received a joint appointment at Seton Hall University's Center for African-American Studies and the School of Education. OLIVE MAE BOND POLK worked to expand the opportunities for African-American youth in the Girl Scouts, the YWCA, and the public schools. She also helped found New Jersey branches of national organizations for black professionals who provided support for each other in the face of racial discrimination. Black women experienced double discrimination, as African-Americans and as women.

Discrimination sometimes raised complex issues that divided women, as in the twenties over the question of legislation to protect women workers. Such legislation was supported by claims that, because of their special needs, women should have *different* treatment from men, not *equal* treatment with them. Another issue that divided women arose during the Great Depression, when public discussion focused on the need to provide men with a family wage. Although many women did paid work, and sometimes were the sole breadwinner holding together a family of children, the plight of the unemployed *man* was the obsession of society. Women workers were often perceived as taking jobs away from men.

Some workers, like LOUISE DELLING BRANTHWAITE, a silk mill worker in Paterson, felt the conditions under which they worked were reasonable. Others, like KATHERINE SCHAUB, a watch dial painter who died in her

Louise Delling Branthwaite, *standing far left*, at the 1984 reunion of alumnae of the Bryn Mawr Summer School for Women Workers. The Summer School was a central experience in the life of Branthwaite, who was a warp maker in the Paterson silk industry when she attended in 1924 and 1925. *Courtesy, private collection.*

early thirties of radium poisoning, suffered physically and psychologically as a result of their work conditions. (Later, CARYE-BELLE HENLE, another New Jersey woman and a radiologist, was able to document the long-term effects of radium on workers such as Schaub.) Some women became labor organizers, for example, MARY YAMASHITA NAGAO fought for the rights of Japanese workers at Seabrook Farms; MARIANNA FIDONE COSTA was active in the United Textile Workers Union for 20 years after 1933, and AL-BERTA GONZALEZ assisted migrant workers for more than 20 years and in 1980 led the first strike in New Jersey of migrant Puerto Rican workers.

Other women became entrepreneurs and corporate executives. Between 1913 and 1947 SARA SPENCER WASH-INGTON founded a beauty college and her own company for hair care products in Atlantic City; published *Apex News*, a national magazine for beauticians; and worked with organizations to support black businesses. IDA ROSENTHAL, through her Maidenform company, provided women with the brassiere, a new undergarment that gained such popularity in the 1920s and 1930s that it became a conventional part of women's clothing from then on. EMMA LOEHWING CONLON bought a silk dyeing business during the Great Depression and for the next 30 years was a leader of the textile dyeing industry in Paterson. MILDRED FAIRBANKS STONE became the first woman officer of a major American insurance company, and JENNIE E. PRECKER, a lawyer who also worked for the ERA, founded the first women's bank in order to provide women with the special services they needed to finance home mortgages and personal loans.

Throughout the United States in the early 20th century, people concerned about the high level of maternal and infant mortality had focused attention on midwives. (Linda Janet Holmes and Janet Carlisle Bogdan, memorandum to author, 1988) Questions about their training, practices, and effectiveness as birth attendants were asked at a time when their numbers were rising, especially as attendants at immigrant women's childbirths. New Jersey midwives stood up well to this scrutiny, emerging as "probably the best trained and most highly organized state group in the country." (Kobrin, "American Midwife Controversy") Their safety record was consistently as good as, and often better than, that of the physicians who attended the majority of New Jersey births. (White House Conference, 202) Nevertheless, many women used physicians as childbirth attendants and women as well as men physicians were drawn increasingly to the profession of gynecologist and obstetrician. JESSIE D. READ, who served as a major in the U.S. Army from 1943 to 1948, worked in private practice for most of her career and used vaginal smears for diagnostic purposes well before Pap smears became routine. DOROTHY HOPE MARVIN, who delivered more than 3,000 babies during her career, was one of several women involved with setting up birth control clinics in New Jersey.

Other women took up different medical specialties. MARGARET SULLIVAN HERBERMANN, who in 1914 was the first woman appointed to the staff of Jersey City Hospital, pioneered the provision of public education for physically disabled children. VIRGINIA APGAR, director of anesthesiology at Columbia-Presbyterian Medical Center from 1938 to 1949, specialized in the use of anesthesia in childbirth. She gained worldwide renown in the fifties for her Apgar scoring system, still used today in a revised form to identify physical abnormalities in newborns.

With World War II, women were drawn into the military in ways that had not occurred during World War I. A few became senior officers in the women's branches of the armed forces. JOY BRIGHT HANCOCK became director of the Women's Reserve of the U.S. Naval Reserve (WAVES), and RUTH CHENEY STREETER, director of the U.S. Marine Corps Women's Reserve. Other women worked in New Jersey's shipyards and factories turning out war materials. In social service agencies, hospitals, and schools the need to replace men who had gone to war provided women professional jobs previously closed to them.

World War II was not a "conventional" war. Millions of men, women, and children were slaughtered in Nazi concentration camps. Photographs from the camps of bodies and of the emaciated faces of those who were rescued by Allied troops filled the newspapers. Photojournalist MARGARET BOURKE-WHITE reported for *Life* magazine from the battlefield and from Buchenwald concentration camp when it was liberated. MURIEL MORRIS GARDINER, Freudian psychoanalyst and educator, was among several New Jersey women, including physicians, who assisted Jews and political dissidents to escape from the Nazis during the 1930s. In 1945 Gardiner was appointed to supervise an International Rescue Committee aiding prisoners released from concentration camps in Europe.

New Jersey women also have been leaders in the search for peace. AMELIA BERNDT MOORFIELD, a member of the Women's International League for Peace and Freedom (WILPF), helped develop the peace movement in New Jersey between the two world wars. So also did EMILY GREGORY HICKMAN, a professor of history at what is now Douglass College, Rutgers University. One of their colleagues in the peace movement, ESTHER WANNER HYMER, helped found the United Nations at the end of World War II and was the driving force for the establishment of International Women's Year in 1975. DOROTHY DAGGETT ELDRIDGE, a microbiologist, helped found the New Jersey Citizens' Organization for a Sane Nuclear Policy (SANE) and became the state coordinator of the 1980 nuclear freeze campaign in New Jersey.

There was a wave of immigration of Japanese workers to New Jersey during World War II when Japanese families from internment camps in the West came to work at Seabrook Farms. MARY YAMASHITA NAGAO helped other workers adapt to farming at Seabrook and fought for their rights. ELLEN NOGUCHI NAKAMURA served as the only woman on a three-person Relocation Planning Commission for her camp before moving to Seabrook, where she worked with the Housing Corporation and from 1972 to 1973 served as president of the Japanese American Citizens League.

The wartime immigration of Japanese workers came after two decades of many fewer immigrants to New Jersey than during the first years of the 20th century. Nevertheless, immigrant workers, including women, continued to make up a substantial fraction of the work force. In the decades after World War II new immigrant groups came to New Jersey, including Hispanics such as MARIA DE CASTRO BLAKE and CONCEPCÓN VALDÉZ-MUÑOZ, to join the small Hispanic communities that had been founded many years before in Newark and in the cities and towns along the New Jersey shore of the Hudson River.

In the 1950s many men and women turned their attention toward family life partly in reaction to the separation they had experienced in wartime. Yet the model they created of home-centered suburban living was a constrictive one for many women. Readers will find in the biographies

224

Ellen Noguchi Nakamura at the Seabrook School in Seabrook, NJ, April 1944. Nakamura and her two colleagues represented the internees of the Jerome, Arkansas, Relocation Center when they made this visit to Seabrook to assess its suitability for resettling Japanese American families. *Courtesy, private collection.*

## Selected References

Cunningham, John T. *New Jersey: America's Main Road.* New York, 1976.

Haber, Barbara, series ed. *American Women in the Twentieth Century.* Boston, 1982–88. Including Dorothy M. Brown, *Setting a Course: American Women in the 1920s* (1987); Susan Ware, *Holding Their Own: American Women in the 1930s* (1982); Susan M. Hartmann, *The Home Front and Beyond: American Women in the 1940s* (1982); Eugenia Kaledin, *Mothers and More: American Women in the 1950s* (1984); and Winifred D. Wandersee, *On the Move: American Women in the 1970s* (1988).

Kobrin, Frances E. "The American Midwife Controversy: A Crisis of Professionalization." *Bulletin of the History of Medicine* 40 (1966):350–63.

Litoff, Judy Barrett, ed. *The American Midwife Debate: A Sourcebook on Its Modern Origins.* Westport, CN, 1986.

White House Conference on Child Health and Protection. *Obstetric Education: Report of the Subcommittee on Obstetric Teaching and Education.* New York, 1932.

of New Jersey women clues to the reason why Betty Friedan's *Feminine Mystique* became so popular when it was published in 1963, and why the second women's movement became so powerful by the end of the decade. The women's movement had a profound effect, politically and socially, in part because its younger members could learn from and build on the life work of countless older women in private and public life. Among them was PAULA KASSELL, a feminist leader in the 1970s who founded *New Directions for Women*, a national feminist newspaper.

Like women elsewhere in the United States, New Jersey women in this period have not experienced a steady movement toward equal rights with men; there have been setbacks and times when women with professional aspirations have had to fight to maintain their careers. What has occurred in the fourth and last period covered in this book is a democratization of the professional and public service activities undertaken by a privileged few in the earlier periods. Fewer women since 1921 can claim to be the *first* professional or the *first* innovator in any field. Instead, the women included here are representative of many thousands who have made significant contributions to the quality of life in New Jersey. They have faced challenges different from those of women of earlier times, but they have demonstrated by their tenacity and their dedication the same spirit of courage that inspired their foremothers.

*Joan N. Burstyn*

Harriet Stratemeyer Adams with her children, *left to right*, Camilla, Russell, Jr., Patricia, and Edward, 1925. Adams is credited with producing more than 200 of the most popular children's books in America, including the Nancy Drew series. *Courtesy, private collection.*

## HARRIET STRATEMEYER ADAMS, 1892–1982

Harriet (Stratemeyer) Adams, credited with creating more than 200 of the most popular children's books in America, including the *Nancy Drew* series, was born in Newark (Essex County), NJ, on December 11, 1892, the first child of Magdalene (Van Camp) Stratemeyer and the famous author Edward L. Stratemeyer. Her only sister, Edna, was born two and a half years later.

Adams spent her childhood with a father who made up stories instantaneously, for Edward Stratemeyer, who published his first volume of the *Rover Boys* in 1899, had written 150 juvenile books by 1906. Realizing that his imagination generated more stories than he could manage to write, Stratemeyer hired other writers to flesh out his plots, ideas, and fantastic inventions. They received a flat fee, and his Stratemeyer Syndicate collected the royalties. At least 800 books were published by this method, which produced the famous *Tom Swift* and *Rover Boys* series.

Since Edward Stratemeyer was a strict parent, Adams considered her attendance at Wellesley College an important liberating experience. At Wellesley, she studied English literature, creative writing, religion, and music and pursued her great interest in science and archeology. She

took Wellesley's motto, "Not to be ministered unto, but to minister," as her lifelong goal and made this the guiding principle for her main characters, especially Nancy Drew.

After her Wellesley graduation in 1914, Adams was offered jobs with three newspapers. Although her father refused to let her accept a job, Adams's determination and will matched his, and finally he agreed to let her work—but only for him. In the year between graduation and marriage, Adams edited manuscripts that her father brought home from his office. In this way, she learned the formula for his writing success.

After her marriage to Russell Vroom Adams on October 20, 1915, she made her home in Maplewood, NJ. From that time on, whenever Adams asked her father if she could help him, he would advise her to care for her children. So for fifteen years she devoted herself to her husband (a successful stockbroker) and her four children: Russell Vroom, Jr. (b. 1916), Patricia Stratton (b. 1921), Camilla Anne (b. 1923), and Edward Stratemeyer (b. 1925). Adams also taught Sunday school, wrote Sunday school materials, worked with the Red Cross and the Girl Scouts, and was active in civic and other religious projects.

She founded the Maplewood Women's Club magazine and was chair of its literature department. Founder of the New Jersey Wellesley Club, she also served as the college's fund-raising chair. Adams was also a Republican county committeewoman for two years.

When her father died in 1930, he left no provisions for the continuation of his seventeen series, which included *Tom Swift*, the *Bobbsey Twins*, the *Hardy Boys*, and the first three *Nancy Drew* stories. The publishing industry, reeling from the Great Depression, feared financial repercussions if his series ended.

Adams, then 38, and Edna Squier, her sister, inherited the Stratemeyer Syndicate. Although Adams's friends were discouraging, her husband gave his blessing when she hired a nurse to care for the children, then aged four to thirteen, so that she could complete the manuscripts waiting to be edited. When they were finished she began writing and thus began to take over the publishing syndicate.

Some of the pen names she wrote under included: "Carolyn Keene" in the *Nancy Drew* series and the *Dana Girls*; "Franklin W. Dixon" in the *Hardy Boys*; "Laura Lee Hope" in the *Bobbsey Twins*; "Victor Appleton II" in *Tom Swift, Jr.*; "May Hollis Barton" in the *Barton Books for Girls*; "Ann Sheldon" in *Linda Craig*; and "Helen Louise Thorndyke" in *Honey Bunch*. She was still writing and running the Stratemeyer Syndicate full time at the time of her death in 1982, more than half a century later.

Her sister retired after five years, and Adams proved herself to be a fine businesswoman as well as an author. Adams had several partners in the Stratemeyer Syndicate. One of them, Andrew E. Svenson, who had been writing and editing her books for boys since 1947, became a partner in 1961. He was responsible for the *Tollivers*, the first series about a black family, and the *Happy Hollisters* series, as well as most of the *Hardy Boys*. Svenson died on August 21, 1975.

Nancy Axelrad, Lorraine Rickle, and Lieselotte Wuenn, her other partners, were women whom she trained. With the help of these collaborators, she produced four books a year.

Nancy Drew became Adams's favorite character, one she considered a third daughter. Adams's father had written only three *Nancy Drew* books before his death, so she rewrote them, with a less bossy Nancy, and she increased the camaraderie between Nancy, her father, and their housekeeper. Adams was the sole author of the *Nancy Drew* and *Dana Girls* series, but the rest of the series used the syndicate method.

The syndicate's writing formula was simple—and very successful. The first page hooked the reader, the last page of each chapter was a cliff-hanger, and the pages in between contained plenty of suspense, action, and humor. The name of the book was usually chosen first and then a general theme was developed. Adams, or one of her partners, created each plot and developed a detailed outline. Then the text was either dictated, typed, and revised, or assigned to a freelance writer. The completed manuscript was edited and checked for consistency with other books in the series, writing style, and accuracy by at least three people in the syndicate.

Adams was meticulous in researching details of settings, equipment, and techniques. She traveled around the world, collecting foreign locales as settings for her books. She believed that children should not only learn something from each book, but would notice any detail that was not authentic. Her books contained no profanity, lying, or violence on the part of main characters, who used ingenuity to solve mysteries and extricate themselves from hair-raising adventures. Adams held out for clean, wholesome stories, believing that children read for entertainment and should enjoy reading. Although her books were denounced as not literary, or too unrealistic, her refusal to deviate from stories she believed children would like allowed her to achieve a timeless appeal that influenced many young people to read more. By 1980 *Nancy Drew* books had sold 70 million copies in the United States alone, plus hundreds of millions of copies, in eighteen languages, around the world.

In addition to writing and running the syndicate, Adams led a full life as mother, grandmother, world traveler, avid doll collector, and farm owner. Though constantly busy, she always had time for family and friends. She was assisted by a staff of household help, but was always accessible to her children, who were welcome at the office. During their childhood, she saw that the family spent time together by sharing breakfast and dinner each day. Adams also shared a bedtime ritual with her children, which included a nightly story she improvised from topics chosen by each of the three youngest ones.

According to her daughter Camilla, Adams had a passionate concern for education. She felt that all women should be responsible for themselves, not dependent on a husband, and believed that education was the best way to prepare for this.

Widely honored in her lifetime with awards, degrees, and titles (including "1979 Mother of the Year"), her favorite honor came when Wellesley named her "Alumna of the Year" in 1978. Adams recognized Wellesley throughout her life and work; she endowed a chair there for the study of children's literature.

After a disagreement with Grossett & Dunlap, who had published Stratemeyer books for more than 72 years, Adams shocked New York publishing circles in 1979 by granting Simon & Schuster rights to all future titles. The lawsuit that followed became a grueling ordeal for Adams, who, at age 87, was in the courtroom for eleven days. But she won the case.

Though Adams traveled around the world, both her year-round and summer homes were in New Jersey. She had spent childhood summers at a farm in Lebanon, NJ, and from that time on longed to own one. She eventually owned two farms in New Jersey, the first in Colt's Neck and the second in Pottersville. Adams died at age 89, of a heart attack at "Bird Haven Farm" in Pottersville on March 28, 1982. She was buried in the Fairmount Mausoleum on Central Avenue in Newark, NJ.

Accounts of Adams's life and writings appear in *Contemporary Authors* 20 (1976); *Something about the Author* 1 (1971); and *American Women Writers* 1 (1979). The NJ-MaPL and the NJ-HS maintain clipping files on her. Interviews with her daughter, Camilla Witman, of Locust, NJ, and her son, Edward Adams, of Carnegie, PA, supplied useful information and memorabilia. Her obituary appeared in the *New York Times*, Mar. 29, 1982.

*Kathy Bieger Roche*

## VIRGINIA APGAR, 1909–1974

Virginia Apgar, the physician who developed the Apgar score for assessing the physical condition of newborn babies, was born on June 7, 1909, in Westfield (Union County), NJ. She was the youngest child and only daughter of Helen May (Clarke) and Charles Emory Apgar, who also had two sons, Charles, Jr., who died as an infant, and Lawrence.

Apgar's father, a salesman and teacher of salesmanship on Wall Street, had a keen interest in astronomy and music and was known as the "wireless wizard" because of his discovery, using home equipment, of spy transmissions to the Germans from a Sayville, Long Island, base during World

War II. From their father, Apgar and her brother Lawrence developed an interest in music. The family held impromptu concerts in their living room, where Apgar played the violin, which she had studied from the age of six. She also learned skilled woodworking from her father and later put this knowledge to use in crafting her own stringed instruments.

Entering Mount Holyoke College in 1925, Apgar majored in zoology and minored in chemistry. The energy that pervaded the family that "never sat down," as Apgar once called them, became her trademark. At Mount Holyoke, she held several jobs to help pay her tuition, participated in athletics, worked as a reporter on the college newspaper, and performed in dramatic and orchestral productions. Apgar received her A.B. in 1929 and remained a loyal Mount Holyoke alumna throughout her life, serving as alumnae trustee from 1966 to 1971; she returned often to encourage students to enter the field of medicine.

Apgar received her M.D. in 1933 from the College of Physicians and Surgeons at Columbia University and became an intern at Columbia Presbyterian Medical Center in surgery, the fifth woman to do so. After two years, however, Apgar concluded that a woman could not make an independent living as a surgeon at that time, so she turned to the comparatively new field of anesthesiology. Apgar enrolled in nurse-anesthetist instruction at Columbia, followed by study at the University of Wisconsin and Bellevue Hospital in New York City. In 1938, she became the first woman to lead a department at Columbia-Presbyterian Medical Center when she took over as the director of the division of anesthesiology. She served in this post from 1938 to 1949, creating an academic department for anesthesiology and in 1949 becoming Columbia's first professor of anesthesiology and first woman to hold a full professorship.

In 1949 Apgar resigned as department head in order to concentrate on the area of anesthesia in childbirth. She was the creator, in 1952, of the Apgar scoring system for newborns. Administered one minute, and again five minutes, after birth, the Apgar score rates babies on a scale of 0 to 2 on each of five signs: heart rate, respiration, muscle tone, reflexes, and color. Indeed, her name has become an acronym for these signs: *a*ppearance, *p*ulse, *g*rimace or reflex irritability, *a*ctivity, and *r*espiration. Apgar developed the scoring system from observing that after their birth, babies were frequently wrapped in a blanket and not closely examined until they reached the nursery, by which time they could have developed heart and lung problems. The new system permitted trained delivery-room nurses to evaluate the newborn's physical condition and identify any need for emergency care. Use of the Apgar score has become standard procedure in hospitals throughout the world.

Having participated in the births of over 17,000 babies, Apgar decided to take a sabbatical leave in 1959. Citing a desire to learn more about perinatal deaths, she enrolled in the public health program at Johns Hopkins University, receiving her master's degree in 1959 at age 49.

At the conclusion of her study at Johns Hopkins, Apgar was asked by the March of Dimes to head their Division of Congenital Malformations. Intrigued by the need for more information about the cause and prevention of birth defects, she accepted this challenge. Then she embarked on a new career of teaching, traveling, and publicizing the need for further research funds. Travel was a major part of Apgar's life during this period. Frequently the only passenger on board a private plane, Apgar decided to learn to fly so that she could land an airplane in case of emergency. She also held the position of lecturer and later clinical professor of pediatrics at Cornell University Medical College. Apgar returned to Johns Hopkins at the age of 63 to continue her study of medical genetics. She continued her teaching career at Johns Hopkins, where, in 1973, she became a lecturer in medical genetics. In 1972 she coauthored a book with Joan Beck entitled *Is My Baby All Right?* Over the course of her career, Apgar also wrote more than 50 articles for medical journals on the importance of prenatal care in the prevention of birth defects.

Love of learning was obvious throughout Apgar's life, for she would always accept new information or revise her ideas. Integrity and a desire to seek out the truth were her hallmark. These qualities were exemplified by an incident in Apgar's surgical residency in anesthesia, when one of her patients developed postoperative complications and died. Apgar worried that she might have failed to clamp a small but vital artery. Unable to obtain an autopsy permit,

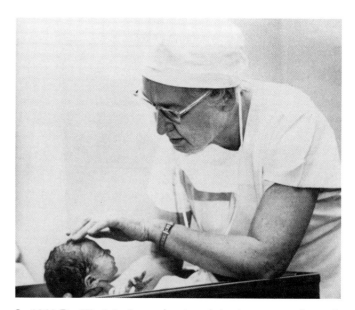

In 1952 Dr. Virginia Apgar developed the Apgar score for evaluating the physical condition of newborn infants. Her system has become a standard procedure in hospitals throughout the world. *Courtesy, Mount Holyoke College Library/Archives.*

she secretly went to the morgue and opened the incision. The artery had been clamped.

As a physician, Apgar's concern and sense of humor inspired trust in her patients. She made it a standard practice to examine and visit any patients she was to anesthetize 24 hours prior to surgery. She practiced what she taught, carrying with her at all times a sharp pocketknife for emergency tracheotomies, an airway tube, a laryngoscope, and Band-Aids. She once said that she had used the airway tube at the site of sixteen auto accidents to resuscitate victims, stating: "Nobody, but nobody, is going to stop breathing on me." (Smith, "In Memoriam," 178)

Apgar received the Gold Medal for Distinguished Achievement in Medicine from the Alumni Association of Columbia College of Physicians and Surgeons; Woman of the Year in Science and Research from the *Ladies' Home Journal*; and the Ralph M. Waters Award of the American Society of Anesthesiologists—all awarded in 1973.

She lived in Tenafly, NJ. An avid gardener, she had a new hybrid orchid named for her in 1961 by the Bergen County March of Dimes. She also belonged to the American Philatelic Society. An accomplished amateur musician, Apgar played in local symphony orchestras and chamber groups and her handcrafted stringed instruments were frequently displayed in local libraries.

There was little Apgar could not do well or did not enjoy. However, she never learned to cook and claimed she never married because "I haven't found a man who can cook." (Waldinger, *Notable American Women*, 28) She also could not speak slowly and was the bane of translators.

Apgar suffered from cirrhosis of the liver in her last years. She died in her sleep at the age of 65 on August 7, 1974, at Columbia Presbyterian Medical Center in New York City, which she had entered for diagnostic tests. She is buried in Fairview Cemetery in Westfield, NJ.

Apgar's personal papers are available at Williston Memorial Library, Mount Holyoke College (South Hadley, MA). She wrote one book, *Is My Baby All Right?* (1972), with Joan Beck, and numerous articles, most notably "A Proposal for a New Method of Evaluation of the Newborn Infant," *Current Researches in Anesthesia and Analgesia* 32 (1953):260–67. Memorials by L. Stanley James, "Fond Memories of Virginia Apgar," *Pediatrics* 55 (1975):1–4; Christina Smith, "In Memoriam," *Mount Holyoke Alumnae Quarterly* (Fall 1974):178–79; and Selma Calmes, "Virginia Apgar: A Woman Physician's Career in a Developing Specialty," *Journal of the American Medical Women's Association* 39 (1984):184–88, provided useful information. Sketches of her appear in *Current Biography* (1968) and in *NAW-MP*. Obituaries appeared in the *New York Times*, Aug. 8, 1974, and the *Westfield* (NJ) *Leader*, Aug. 15, 1974.

*Rebecca Berry Creswell*

Anna Mahala Field Atchison was a gifted and much honored classroom teacher in the Shrewsbury Township public schools for 46 years. *Courtesy, private collection.*

## ANNA MAHALA FIELD ATCHISON, 1904–1985

Anna Mahala (Field) Atchison, educator and church activist, was born on September 25, 1904, in Somerville (Somerset County), NJ, the third of five children, two boys and three girls, of Annie (Pierson) Field and Amos Field, a carpenter who trained himself as a plumber and electrician. He worked as a janitor in the public schools and was well respected in the community.

Atchison grew up in Somerville, attended the public schools there, and graduated, the only black from Somerville High School with the class of 1923. An interesting insight into Atchison is a comment in her yearbook under her nickname "Haily," which reads, "I knew the right and did it."

Atchison enrolled in the teacher education program at Cheyney State Normal School, Cheyney, PA, and graduated in 1925. As a student at Cheyney, Atchison showed her talent in the area of education, for it was she who was sent to a nearby school for difficult students to lay the groundwork for later practice teachers.

Atchison began her teaching career in 1925 in the Port Deposit, MD, school system. In 1927 she returned to New Jersey, where she began teaching in the Shrewsbury Township public school system. Her teaching assignment there in the one-room Pine Brook School lasted for twenty years.

In 1950 she married Wallace William Atchison. Considerably older than she, he was the presiding elder of the Jersey City African Methodist Episcopal Zion District and later presiding elder of the Camden District. Atchison's devotion to her husband and his work was strong: she championed his causes, traveled with him throughout the district, chauffeured him, supported him, and remained his constant companion until his death on November 26, 1968. They had no children.

From 1967 until her retirement in 1973, Atchison taught at the Tinton Falls and Sycamore Avenue schools in Tinton Falls. A year after her retirement, the mayor and Borough Council renamed the Sycamore School for her. During all these productive years she remained in the classroom even though her credentials certified her to supervise or serve as an elementary school principal. During these years she took particular interest in the future of her students and even helped finance several students' education. A strict and demanding teacher, Atchison culled the very best from her students. In addition, she was creative, never using the same lesson plan twice. Her own sense of patriotism inspired a love of democracy in her students.

Atchison displayed equal zeal in her commitment to the church. In 1940 she was appointed by Bishop Cameron Chesterfield Alleyne, presiding bishop of the New Jersey Conference, AME Zion Church, to the office of president of the Camden District, Women's Home and Foreign Missionary Society. She served faithfully in this post until 1983, when she continued her service as district president of the Atlantic City District. These positions involved travel throughout the districts, coordinating programs, soliciting support for churches throughout Africa, and many speaking engagements to increase membership in the mission work in Africa. When she retired from that office in 1984 she was appointed president emeritus. But she soon had to relinquish this office because of illness.

Atchison's church activities were international in scope. At the newly established and recently constructed Janie A. Speaks Hospital in Alfrancho, Ghana, a pediatrics ward was named in her honor in 1983. The naming of the hospital ward was an expression of the deep appreciation of the Ghanaian people for her many financial and spiritual commitments over the years.

In 1973 Atchison, a much honored and revered community leader, retired from teaching after 48 years. Her strong religious faith and commitment brought her recognition by many local and civic organizations, including the New Jersey Organization of Teachers, the Asbury Park

Study Center, Friends of African Missions, and the National Association of Negro Business and Professional Women. All of her awards remain on display in her original schoolhouse, now the Pine Brook Fire Department.

Atchison also was a member of such organizations as the North Shore Section of the National Council of Negro Women (charter member); National Association for the Advancement of Colored People; St. Thomas AME Zion Church, Somerville; and New Jersey and National Retired Educators Association.

Atchison's lifelong career as an educator and church leader was brought to a close by a lengthy battle with cancer. She was mostly confined to her home during the last few years of her life and died on April 19, 1985, at her home in Lincroft, NJ. She was buried in Monmouth Memorial Park, Tinton Falls, NJ.

Material on Atchison, including correspondence, newspaper articles, and personal documents, is in the possession of her niece, Bernice Stratton Van Dunk.

*Joyce C. Payne*

## MARY CRAPELLI AUGUSTO, 1901–1982

Mary (Crapelli) Augusto, journalist, community leader and first woman mayoral candidate in Paterson, NJ, was born April 8, 1901, in Nicastro, Calabria, Italy. Augusto was the youngest child of Filomena (Pugliese) and Vincenzo Gabriele Crapella, farmers who had attended the Analfabeta School. Her father was also a street vendor of small articles, such as combs. Her mother, orphaned at a young age, was raised by the Baroness Nicotera, who taught her to read and write. Filomena instilled the need for education in her youngest daughter, who attended elementary and high school, as well as three years of teacher's college. Just before her nineteenth birthday Augusto emigrated to America, joining three siblings who had emigrated earlier: Angela Curcio, Joseph, and Dominic.

On March 29, 1920, Augusto arrived at Ellis Island. She joined her siblings in their shared home in Paterson and worked in a silk mill where her brother-in-law was a foreman. During the next three years she went to school in Paterson in the evenings, taking the new American course and studying English at the International Institute for Young Women sponsored by the YWCA. She also studied business at the Columbia Shorthand and Business College in Paterson, receiving a degree in shorthand in 1923.

In 1924, at age 23, Augusto went to work as an editor-translator for *I Nuovo Mondo* (The New World), a New York City Italian-language daily newspaper. She worked at the paper for five years, commuting to New York from Paterson, then moving to Brooklyn. In 1928 Mary Augusto became a naturalized citizen; the next year she went back to Italy for about eight months. When she returned economic depression had hit and her newspaper job was gone. After a year working for Brooklyn-based La Rosa macaroni manufacturers as a bookkeeper and typist, she returned to her family in Paterson. In 1931 she opened a neighborhood candy store and taught Italian and English at the Universal Institute in New York City. In 1932 she married Emilio Augusto, an Italian newspaperman she had met while working at *I Nuovo Mondo*, and resumed her newspaper career.

The Augustos set up their home in the Dublin section of Paterson, once an Irish-German neighborhood but by the 1930s the home of a largely Italian population. During the second quarter of the 20th century Paterson was a city in economic decline. By 1932 its once thriving silk and iron industries had largely moved away and the city was left struggling financially.

It was from this base that the Augustos decided to run their own Italian-language newspaper, *La Voce Italiana* (The Italian Voice). Still in publication today, the weekly paper began on the kitchen table of their home, a building leased from the Italian Catholic church across the street. Augusto canvassed the community getting advertisements and subscriptions to support the business, while her husband took over the technical aspects of running the newspaper. They were both involved in its content. It was against the law to publish legal notices in a foreign-language newspaper. Because publishing the notices could be lucrative, the Augustos also printed the English-language *Colonial Sentinel*, which carried legal notices and much the same news as *La Voce*. Since Augusto had become adept in reading and writing English, much of this task fell to her. As time went on other job printing was done on the premises; by 1941 the Augustos were also operating the Paterson Linotype School at the newspaper office.

By the early 1940s *La Voce* was serving a potential market of 75,000 Italian-Americans in the northern New Jersey area, including 42,000 in Paterson alone. Italians constituted the largest foreign-born population in the city by this time. The paper included national, state, and local news, particularly as it related to the Italian community. Letters to the editor and other people's forums were often included in the paper.

Even during these early years photos and articles about distinguished women, often of Italian descent, were featured on the front page, demonstrating Augusto's belief in women's ability to be community leaders while still fulfilling traditional roles at home. Augusto herself had been balancing this dual responsibility since 1939, when her only child, Cesarina, was born.

In the late 1930s and 1940s *La Voce* took an antifacist position, running heated debates, editorials, and columns as World War II ensued. At this time and thereafter Au-

gusto's personal column, "The Parrot," combined political and social commentary. During World War II, in addition to her newspaper responsibilities, Augusto worked the late shift at a nearby Wright Aeronautics defense plant, where she mastered the process of precision grinding and produced plane parts for the war effort. Savings from her work at the Wright plant provided the money to purchase a building for the newspaper in the neighborhood. *La Voce* was published continuously from this location throughout the rest of Augusto's lifetime.

As the representative of the newspaper, Augusto was invited to many social and political functions and frankly commented on them. She often appeared in photos and articles in *La Voce* and other Paterson newspapers. She was a member of 45 women's and neighborhood organizations, Italian-American societies, and the Irish-dominated Republican party.

The latter vantage gave Augusto a view of party politics during the 1940s with which she didn't agree. Paterson's mayor between 1940 and 1948 was William P. Furrey, who under a new charter virtually controlled the entire city through patronage. A deceptively low tax rate was maintained by inflating property assessments, and the school budget ran a deficit. Convinced that change was needed and that the Democrats would continue the same machine politics, in 1947 Augusto threw her hat into the ring as the Liberal-Progressive fusion candidate, the first woman to run for mayor of Paterson. Her platform included school reform, social service, and welfare programs, including day care, housing reform, and fiscal responsibility.

Without a party machine, access to a treasury chest, or monetary tributes from business people or city employees, Augusto conducted a grass-roots campaign based on newspaper publicity, public meetings, and rallies. Her slogan became "Vote with Gusto for Mary Augusto."

During the hotly contested race she was excluded from candidate forums and charged with vote splitting by the Italian-American Democratic candidate. Although Augusto lost the race to the Democrats, gaining only a small percentage of the votes, she was lauded in local newspapers. She is remembered within the community as a courageous, reform-minded woman who demonstrated by her own actions her belief in the ability of women, the working class, and Italian-Americans.

The following year Augusto reentered elective politics at the ward level and won a seat as justice of the peace. She continued through *La Voce* to be an active and vocal supporter of honest city government and strong community services.

In 1955, while continuing her work at *La Voce*, Augusto took a position with Paterson's Department of Public Welfare. Here she was able to use her skill as an Italian interpreter. Later, as the ethnic composition of the city changed, she studied Spanish to help new welfare recipients. In 1959 she engaged in another public controversy through the newspaper and successfully challenged unequal wage increases for male and female welfare workers.

On October 30, 1975, still actively pursuing the newspaper business at age 74, Augusto was mugged in the city, kidnapped, and thrown from her car. She continued to work until her death, but she never fully recovered from this brutal encounter and died on February 13, 1982, survived by her husband. She was buried in Holy Sepulchre Cemetery in Totowa, NJ.

Augusto's personal papers and correspondence belong to her daughter, Cesarina Augusto Earl, of Totowa, NJ. Back issues of *La Voce Italiano* are at NJ-PCHS.

*Jo Ann Cotz*

## CATHERINE HAYES BAILEY, 1921–

Catherine Hayes Bailey, plant scientist and tree fruit plant breeder, was born on May 9, 1921, in New Brunswick (Middlesex County), NJ, the third of five surviving children, two boys and three girls, of H. Gordon and Hettie (Dixon) Bailey. Her father supervised the vegetable research facilities at the New Jersey Agricultural Experiment Station in New Brunswick, where he was employed for 31 years. Her mother, a homemaker, was born and raised on a farm in Pine Brook, NJ.

Bailey was raised and educated in New Brunswick, where she attended the Lord Sterling Elementary School and the New Brunswick High School, graduating in 1932 and 1938, respectively. She went on to earn a B.A. from Douglass College, then the New Jersey College for Women, in 1942, and was awarded her doctorate in plant breeding by Rutgers University in 1957.

During her formative years she lived on the grounds of the New Jersey Agricultural Experiment Station at New Brunswick, where her father was a resident research associate. It was during this period that Bailey developed her interest in plants and science, which was to lead her to a dedicated and productive career in horticulture. As a young girl she often helped her father in the research fields and greenhouses. In 1948 she herself became research assistant to M. A. Blake, noted New Jersey tree fruit breeder, and in 1954 research associate, working under the direction of L. F. Hough.

Upon receiving her doctorate in 1957, Bailey was appointed assistant professor of horticulture and was promoted in 1966 to associate professor in the department of horticulture at Rutgers University. Bailey rose to the position of professor in 1972 and became professor emeritus at Rutgers University in 1980. As a research faculty member Bailey joined forces with L. F. Hough, internationally known tree fruit breeder—a productive relationship that

lasted more than 25 years and produced over 50 new apple, pear, peach, nectarine, and apricot fruit varieties. Many of the tree fruit breeders of today studied under Bailey and Hough during their tenure at Rutgers. Together, Bailey and Hough accumulated a reservoir of tree fruit germ plasm that is used by plant scientists all over the world and has guaranteed a foundation for breeding temperate tree fruit for decades to come. Bailey's accomplishments include introducing the peach varieties that form the mainstay of the peach baby food industry, the cultivars that have resulted in a nectarine fruit industry, and pear and apple varieties that are resistant to disease.

Bailey has traveled and lectured extensively throughout Europe, including the USSR and Eastern European countries, in connection with her fruit breeding research. She was visiting scientist of temperate fruit tree breeding at the University of California, Davis, CA, in 1961, and exchange scientist at the Canada Department of Agriculture, Summerland Fruit Research Station in British Columbia, Canada, in 1966. She is also noted for her work in the field of stone fruit tree breeding.

During her tenure at Rutgers, Bailey authored more than 60 scientific articles on fruit breeding and was the recipient of numerous awards. She received the Gerber Products Agriculture Award for her work on clingstone peaches and the National Peach Council Award for outstanding service to the peach industry. Throughout her professional career she has been an active participant in several prestigious horticultural institutions, including the American and International Societies for Horticultural Science, the American Pomological Society, the Botanical Society of America, and the Torrey Botanical Club.

In addition to her commitment to science and horticulture, Bailey is strongly committed to her Baptist faith and her lifelong hobby of ornithology. During a brief hiatus between her graduate and postgraduate career, she attended the Prairie Bible Institute, Three Hills, Alberta, Canada, where she received a diploma in 1944. She teaches at the First Baptist Church of Jamesburg and serves on the board of deacons. Bailey continues to be an active member of the New Jersey Audubon Society and pursues her hobby of nature photography.

An interview with Bailey in 1986 provided biographical information. She is profiled in *American Men and Women of Science* (1986).

*Paul Eck*

## SYLVIA WOODBRIDGE BEACH, 1887–1962

Sylvia Woodbridge Beach, first publisher of James Joyce's *Ulysses* and proprietor of the most famous English-language bookstore on the mainland of Europe, was born on March 14, 1887, in Baltimore, MD. Her family soon moved to Bridgeton (Cumberland County), NJ, where Beach and her two sisters, Holly and Cyprian, spent their early years and she attended Ivy Hall School. Beach was christened Nancy, but her name was changed to Sylvia before she reached adulthood.

Beach's father, the Rev. Sylvester Woodbridge Beach, D.D., served the First Presbyterian Church of Bridgeton for fourteen years. His mother's family, the Woodbridges, included an unbroken line of nine generations of clergy. Beach's mother, Eleanor Thomazine (Orbison) Beach, descended from the Colonial founder of Bellefonte, PA, was born in Rawalpindi, India, daughter of a medical missionary. She met her husband, a Princeton graduate, while a student at Bellefonte Academy, where he was teaching.

In 1901 Beach went to Paris with her family. While her father ministered at the American Students' Atelier there, Beach and her mother fell in love with Paris. She made a lifelong friendship with Carlotta Welles, whose father represented Western Electric in Paris. During this first sojourn in Europe Beach briefly attended a school in Lausanne, Switzerland; she did not like the strict discipline of the place and so her mother brought her back to Paris. Beach spent much time at the Welleses' country place with Carlotta, whose family had been advised by doctors to suspend her schooling and keep her outdoors.

In 1906 Beach moved to Princeton, NJ, where her father had been called to the pulpit of the First Presbyterian Church. Here Beach became friends with Margaret Sloan, and Annis Stockton, a descendant of Benjamin Franklin and Sarah (Franklin) Bache, while her father ministered to the Grover Clevelands, the James Garfields, and the Woodrow Wilsons. Two of Wilson's daughters were married by the Rev. Beach in White House ceremonies.

Throughout a decade in Princeton, Beach frequently visited France. In 1916 she went to Spain and on to Paris the following year. Her sister Cyprian, an actress, was also there, and the two stayed together briefly. Paris was then under air attack, and the two Beach women "had the choice of catching flu in the wine cellar or enjoying the view from the balcony." (Beach, *Shakespeare and Company*, 11) They chose the latter. That summer Beach worked as a volunteer farmhand; later she joined an American Red Cross aid team in Belgrade for nine months, returning to Paris in July 1919.

Pursuing her interest in contemporary French writing, Beach visited the bookshop La Maison des Amis des Livres and met its proprietor, Adrienne Monnier, who became her mentor, supporter, and closest friend. The two women lived together from 1921 to 1937. With Monnier's help, and her mother's personal savings sent from Princeton, Beach established her own bookshop and lending library, Shakespeare and Company, at 8 rue Dupuytren. At its opening on November 19, 1919, the shop's stock included a number of manuscripts that her aunt, Agnes Orbison,

had rescued from Walt Whitman's wastebasket on a visit to the poet in Camden. French writers such as André Gide and André Maurois, whom Beach had come to know through Monnier, were among her first customers.

One of Beach's first American customers was composer George Antheil, son of the proprietor of the Friendly Shoestore in Trenton, NJ, whose radical music shocked Paris in the 1920s. Beach and Antheil became friends, and he lived for some time with his wife in a two-room apartment above her shop at its second location, 12 rue de l'Odéon, across the street from Monnier's. Beach felt a "bond" between herself and the fellow New Jerseyan.

No expatriate, though a sometime traveler to Europe, William Carlos Williams, the Rutherford, NJ, poet, joined the impressive list of friends of Beach and Shakespeare and Company. Williams visited Paris in 1924 and later reflected that Beach and Monnier "conspired to make that region of Paris . . . a sanctuary for all sorts of writers." (Williams, *Autobiography*, 193)

Beach was described by another friend, Ernest Hemingway, as having "a lively, sharply sculptured face, brown eyes that were as alive as a small animal's and as gay as a young girl's, and wavy brown hair that was brushed back from her fine forehead and cut thick below her ears and at the line of the collar of the brown velvet jacket she wore. She had pretty legs and she was kind, cheerful and interested, and loved to make jokes and gossip. No one I ever knew was nicer to me." (Hemingway, *A Moveable Feast*, 35)

Most prominent among those finding sanctuary at Beach's shop was James Joyce, whose masterpiece, *Ulysses*, was banned in serial form in both the United States and England before the manuscript was completed. In April 1921 Beach offered to take on its publication as her first. The book appeared in February 1922.

Beach's decision to publish *Ulysses* began an intense decade of service to Joyce, in which he frequented her shop almost daily, picking up mail there (as did many other English and American writers), giving her lists of chores, and sometimes literally taking money from the till, originally as loans that he repaid within a day or two, but soon as "advances on *Ulysses*." (Beach, *Shakespeare and Company*, 75) In addition to publishing *Ulysses*, Shakespeare and Company brought out Joyce's *Pomes Pennyeach* (1927) and a collection of essays, *Our Exagmination Round His Factification for Incamination of Work in Progress* (1929), by other writers on Joyce's work then in progress, *Finnegans Wake*.

Beach's business became precarious during the Depression, when the number of Americans living in Paris declined and the demand for English-language books declined also. In 1936 a group of French writers including Gide, Maurois, and Paul Valéry set up "the Friends of Shakespeare and Company" and sold subscriptions to keep the shop going. Contributors included Archibald MacLeish and Helena Rubinstein. All were invited to a series of readings that featured major French and Anglo-American authors of the day, among them T. S. Eliot, Hemingway, and Stephen Spender. In 1938 Beach was decorated with the French Legion d'Honneur for her services to literature.

The efforts of the "Friends" helped keep Shakespeare and Company going well into World War II. But one December day in 1941 a German officer wished to buy *Finnegans Wake*, on display in the window. It was Beach's last copy; she refused. The officer came back two weeks later, threatening to confiscate the contents of the shop if she would not sell him the book. She would not, and after he left her landlady and friends helped her carry everything to an empty apartment upstairs. "Within two hours, not a single thing was to be seen in the shop, and a house painter had painted out the name, Shakespeare and Company, on the front." (Beach, *Shakespeare and Company*, 216) Beach never reopened the store, though she later lived in the apartment the shop's contents had been moved to. First, she spent six months in a German internment camp, and then she lived disguised as a member of a youth hostel. The rest of her life she helped Monnier (who died in 1955), traveled, and wrote her memoirs.

In the spring of 1959 the American embassy in Paris sponsored an exhibition entitled "Les Années Vingt: Les Ecrivains Americans à Paris et leurs amis" (The Twenties: American Writers in Paris and Their Friends). Composed almost entirely of Beach's own photographs, letters, proofs, and first editions, the exhibition clearly indicated her central role in the literary life of the decade. That June she visited the University of Buffalo, to which she donated her collection of Joyce materials, and received the honorary degree of doctor of letters. Also in 1959 her memoir, *Shakespeare and Company*, was published by Harcourt, Brace.

On October 6, 1962, Sylvia Beach's body was discovered in her apartment at 12 rue de l'Odéon, where she had apparently died of a heart attack a few days earlier, at age 75. Her body was cremated and the ashes brought back to Princeton, where they were buried in the cemetery between the graves of her father and her aunt, Agnes Orbison.

Beach's papers are available at NJ-PU. Her memoir is *Shakespeare and Company* (1959); she also wrote an introduction to a book of essays on James Joyce, *Our Exagmination Round His Factification for Incamination of Work in Progress* (1929). See also Noel Riley Fitch, *Sylvia Beach and the Lost Generation* (1983); Ernest Hemingway, *A Moveable Feast* (1964); and William Carlos Williams, *Autobiography* (1951). She is profiled in *NAW-MP* and in *American Women Writers* 1 (1979). Her obituary appeared in the *New York Times*, Oct. 10, 1962.

*William J. Higginson*

## ENID BELL, 1904–

Enid Bell Palanchian, known professionally as Enid Bell, sculptor, was born in London, England, on December 5, 1904, one of three children of Jean (Diack) and Horatio Bell, both of whom were Scottish. Her training in art took place at St. John's Wood School of Art in London and the Glasgow School of Art in Scotland (1920–21). She continued her art studies at the Art Students League, New York City, in 1922–23.

Bell's professional positions have included teaching at Miss Chapin's School, New York City, and at the Newark, NJ, School of Fine and Industrial Art (1944–68), where she headed the sculpture department. In 1932 she and Missak Palanchian, a businessman and artist of Armenian heritage, were married in New York City. John, their son, was born in 1933.

Although Bell is best known as a sculptor and especially as a carver in wood, she says that none of her art training provided instruction in wood carving and that she is virtually self-taught in this area. Her first work in stone was her mother's gravestone; but the artist prefers wood for its warm tone, light weight, and the relative ease of working with it. Bell's artistic career has also included painting theatrical sets, illustrating books, and designing medals, as well as writing about her own work and that of others.

Bell resides in Englewood, NJ, and has long been associated with New Jersey through the many sculptures she created as an artist on the Federal Art Projects of the 1930s. She was awarded commissions by the U.S. Treasury Section of Fine Arts and worked for the more familiar Work Projects Administration (WPA) and its predecessor. She was supervisor for a time of the Sculpture Unit of the New Jersey Arts and Crafts Project of the WPA, which was in operation from 1935 to 1943.

The prestigious commissions she received for art in U.S. Post Offices were awarded on the basis of competitions and were financed by the Department of the Treasury. As a sculptor and as a supervisor in the WPA, she continued her career through marriage and motherhood.

Many of Bell's works are on themes that were typical of the Federal Art Projects and that supported the values of the American way of life so often depicted in the murals of the period: mothers and children, children reading, people studying and working. Although Bell's work respects traditional craftsmanship, most of her pieces are representational, but often carved with sensitivity to cubist formal possibilities.

Several public buildings in New Jersey and elsewhere acquired works by Bell in the late 1930s. New Jersey locations include the former Robert Treat (now Marcus Garvey) School in Newark, U.S. Post Offices in Mount Holly and Boonton, and public libraries in Union City and Hoboken. Bell has been generous in donating work to public libraries of Englewood and Leonia. She has also taken personal responsibility for the conservation of some of her works in situ.

Bell's work has been exhibited at several one-person shows in New York galleries and in museums in Santa Fe, NM; Columbus, GA; and Springfield, IL. She has shared exhibitions with her painter-husband, as well as with other artists. She participated in group exhibits at the 1939 New York World's Fair; the National Academy of Design, New York City; the New Jersey State Museum; the Brooklyn Museum; and the Metropolitan Museum of Art exhibition "Artists for Victory" in 1942.

She has received several prestigious awards and medals for her work, including the Gold Medal Diploma of the Paris Exposition of 1937. She is a former member of the National Sculpture Society and the Associated Artists of New Jersey. She has written a number of articles on sculpture and has been reviewed in such journals as *Art Digest*, *Artnews*, and *New Jersey Music and Arts*.

Bell continues to concern herself with the disposition of her work. A series of renderings depicting salient examples of major world crafts from prehistoric times to the modern age has been used in part by *Encyclopedia Britannica* for a filmstrip.

Materials pertaining to Bell, including letters, clippings, and reviews, are available at NJ-NPL. Her work is discussed in Hildreth York, *New Deal Art: New Jersey* (1980), and in York's "The New Deal Art Projects in New Jersey," *New Jersey History* 98 (1980):132–74. Her work is noted in Jim Collins, *Women Artists in America* (1980).

*Hildreth J. York*

Maria de Castro Blake migrated to the United States from Vieques, Puerto Rico, in 1931, when she was 20. She has been at the forefront of educational programs benefiting Puerto Ricans in New Jersey. *Courtesy, private collection.*

## MARIA DE CASTRO BLAKE, 1911–

Maria (de Castro) Blake is the dean advocate for the educational advancement of Puerto Ricans in New Jersey. A resident of New Jersey since 1946, she has organized many of the struggles that Puerto Ricans have waged in order to gain access to a good education.

Blake was born July 22, 1911, in Vieques, Puerto Rico. Her mother, Clotilde Smaine, was the sole provider for the family of six children. Francisco de Castro, her father, was a fisherman who abandoned the family when Blake was very young. As the oldest girl in the family, Blake was responsible for the care of her brothers and sisters. Her mother's source of income came from cooking for a rich French woman who owned the "big house" in Vieques.

Blake would crawl under the tables at the tobacco factory at an early age and listen to the "lector" read the local newspapers and translated works of philosophers, novelists, and progressive thinkers. She remembered the words and concepts, although she did not understand, and would ask her mother to explain them to satisfy her curious mind.

When Blake learned to read, books became her world. To transcend the limited geographical boundaries of Vieques, she borrowed every book available from her mother's employers and from the public school library. She compensated for her economic poverty by the richness and knowledge she gained from reading.

Her mother died when she was sixteen years old. With her eighteen-year-old brother, Blake became head of the family. They did odd jobs and lived an impoverished life, but Blake would not quit school. She graduated with high honors from Vieques High School in 1929, after completing both the college preparatory and secretarial curriculum.

It took four years for Blake and her brother Valentin to earn the money for her one-way ticket to New York. Blake was 20 years old when she arrived in New York, and the family that shared their apartment with her, who had once been her neighbors in Vieques, she described as "millionaires of the heart."

Blake could understand English: "My eyes could understand things my ears could not." Her attempt at a secretarial career ended the first day, since she had never seen a telephone until her first day on the job. She went to work in a factory in the New York garment district, and these earnings supported her, helped her adoptive family, and brought her sisters and brothers to New York.

Books and learning remained the center of her life. At Columbia University, where she had enrolled for continuing education courses, she met Thomas A. Blake, a young assistant fencing coach. They married in 1942 and Blake wore a rented wedding gown, since she could not afford to buy one.

When the Blakes' first daughter, Clotilde, was born in

1943, they moved to Jersey City, NJ. There they opened a small stationery store and lived in its back room. Their sons, Brian (b. 1946) and Paco (b. 1947), were both born there.

The back room was cold, business was poor, and her husband developed a drinking problem. Aware of Blake's situation, Valentin (her oldest brother), whom she had helped financially while he earned an engineering degree, sent her $1,000 in 1950 for a down payment on a house in East Orange, NJ. Thomas Blake died four years later, leaving his widow a legacy of three small children, bankruptcy, large debts, bittersweet memories, and a 25-year mortgage on a house. She had two tasks: to keep her family alive and to keep her sanity. For survival, she worked to provide child care, food, and money for the mortgage payments. For sanity, she did volunteer work in the Hispanic community.

She needed a connection with the Puerto Rican community and work that was intellectually stimulating and meaningful to others. Her greatest source of pleasure was to teach English to poor Puerto Rican children and their parents at night classes in St. Patrick's Cathedral in downtown Newark.

After several other secretarial jobs, Blake was employed as a secretary at Rutgers University, Newark. However, her volunteer work as a community activist and leader in the Puerto Rican community eventually forced the university to recognize that Blake was more valuable as a community education specialist in the Continuing Education Division. In the civil rights revolution of the 1960s Blake was at the forefront as a leader. Her major weapon in the revolution was education. Her children's favorite comment is: "Mom is a fanatic about education." Blake is quick to point out: "Not only are my children well-educated [they all achieved graduate degrees] but they are all putting their education to work to help the oppressed and the poor."

Blake's volunteer work has included an association with the Newark Board of Education for a bilingual program in the public schools to recruit and train Puerto Rican parents to become involved in the PTA organizations. She was a founding member of the Board of Directors of Aspira, which strives to prevent Puerto Ricans and Hispanics from dropping out of high school; a founding member of the Puerto Rican Congress; founder and president of the Association for the Professional Education of Puerto Ricans; a founding member of the Field Orientation Center for Underprivileged Hispanics (FOCUS) and of Casa de Don Pedro, a nonprofit multiservice agency, both in Newark, NJ; and organizer for the first Black and Puerto Rican Convention of Newark.

Blake led community efforts directed at such institutions as Rutgers, the State Department of Higher Education, the Newark Board of Education, the YWCA-YMCA,

and the Newark Museum to address issues affecting the Hispanic community. She also urged development of new programs to meet the needs of the community. She picketed, typed, mimeographed, and stuffed envelopes for projects that sought the advancement of the Hispanic community in New Jersey. She personally supported these efforts and always answered "Presente" when the community called on her.

In 1980 she retired from Rutgers University, sold her house in East Orange, and moved to New York City, where she currently resides. Now a volunteer teacher at the American Museum of Natural History, she opens the minds of Hispanic schoolchildren to the joys of learning and discovery. For Blake, "being alive means learning and investing in the learning of others. The years of economic struggle are over," she says. "I am a happy and fortunate woman and I can devote full time to the luxury and joy of learning and sharing my learnings with others."

Blake never earned a diploma in higher education, although her efforts made a college education possible for hundreds of Hispanics. For this contribution, the Hispanic community has awarded her the title of dean advocate of higher education.

Information on Blake was obtained from interviews with her in Sept. and Oct. 1986, as well as from personal papers held by Blake.

*Hilda Hidalgo*

## HELEN FRANCESCA FRANZOLIN BOEHM, 1920–

Helen Francesca (Franzolin) Boehm, owner and chair of Boehm International Creators of Porcelain Art, Trenton, NJ, was born in Bensonhurst, NY, on December 26, 1920. She was the third daughter and sixth of seven children of Pietro Franzolin, a cabinetmaker from Florence, Italy, and Francesca (Pizzuto) Franzolin of Sicily. Her parents immigrated to the United States from Genoa in 1911 with their first two children.

Boehm attended public schools and completed elementary school in 1934, a year after her father's death. She continued her education at New Utrecht High School, where she graduated in 1938. Following Boehm's father's death, the whole family worked; her mother embroidered linens and Boehm designed and made dresses for herself and her friends. After graduating from high school she secured a job with an optometrist, attended the Mechanical School of Optics, and was licensed by the Board of Education to become a registered ophthalmic dispenser.

She married Edward Marshall Boehm on October 29, 1944, at St. Mary's Roman Catholic Church in Bensonhurst. The couple had met at the Air Force Base Convalescent Center in Pawling, NY, where Helen Boehm's

Helen Franzolin Boehm with a life-size porcelain sculpture, *Mute Swans*, created by the Trenton porcelain company she chairs, c. 1971. Boehm worked as her artist husband's partner in building the world-renowned enterprise. Her husband's portrait hangs behind her. *Courtesy, Helen F. Boehm.*

second-oldest brother was a patient. Edward Boehm was stationed at the center as a member of the animal husbandry division of the air force. He taught the care of cattle and small animals as therapy for wounded airmen and in his spare hours sculpted horses and cattle in plasticene.

Before World War II Edward Boehm had devoted his life to the breeding of guernseys at a large Maryland farm. After the war he turned to the care of small animals, serving as an assistant to a veterinarian, and spent his leisure hours sculpting. As he became more and more devoted to his sculptures, his wife was determined to find a way for his artistry to become a reality. Their marriage incorporated a close business collaboration and lasted until his death from a heart attack in 1969. They had no children.

Boehm commuted to New York from their home in

Great Neck, Long Island, to work at C. B. Meyerowitz, Inc., a large optical firm. Through her customers she secured financial backing for her husband. He had rented a small studio in Trenton, the recognized porcelain manufacturing center of the United States. There, he learned the secrets of making fine porcelain and finally perfected his formula for the production of superior porcelain pieces.

Boehm, working full time, devoted her lunch hours to selling her husband's work. A Percheron stallion and a Hereford bull, the first major pieces she sold, were purchased by the curator of the American Wing of the Metropolitan Museum of Art. This important recognition gave impetus to the business, which was deeply in debt.

In 1953 the Boehms became sole owners of their company. Because of Helen Boehm's highly effective sales initiatives the company became very profitable. With the purchase in 1954 of a handsome estate in Washington Crossing—where Boehm still resides—the couple became New Jersey residents.

Realizing the need for national recognition of Boehm porcelains, Boehm had an ingenious idea. She offered a porcelain Hereford bull to President and Mrs. Dwight D. Eisenhower in 1954. The Eisenhowers' acceptance of this piece led to a long friendship between the two couples. On the occasion of Queen Elizabeth and Prince Philip's first visit to Washington in 1957, Helen Boehm suggested that the Eisenhowers present the royal couple with the gift of a porcelain mounted polo player. The president accepted the idea, and Edward Boehm's first sculpture of many interlocking parts became internationally recognized and Boehm porcelain became accepted as fitting gifts for heads of state. On his historic visit to China in 1972 President Richard Nixon, following this tradition, presented the Boehm creation of mute swans, entitled Birds of Peace, to Mao Tse-tung. Another rendering of the Birds of Peace sits in the Sistine Chapel, where it was placed by Pope Paul VI after Boehm presented it to the pontiff.

As Boehm traveled around the United States as sales representative, her husband's porcelains were increasingly featured for sale in major stores. Today the company employs 140 people, who enjoy profit-sharing and pensions. Annual sales are more than $10 million.

The porcelain birds, which are almost synonymous with the name Boehm, became well known from Boehm's lectures throughout the country. During the lectures she would present slides showing the studio, their home with its aviaries, and their farm, where prize cattle and race horses were bred. Her spontaneity, friendliness, and natural charm drew many to her and as a consequence, the sales increased dramatically. With Boehm on the road and Edward Boehm in his studio, the Boehms sought someone to handle the business details. They hired Frank J. Cosentino, a Princeton graduate who joined the firm in 1959. He eventually became president of the company and a close personal friend and adviser of Boehm.

Following the death of Edward Boehm in 1969 many feared the decline of Boehm porcelains, but Boehm continued her strong leadership of the company. Trained artisans carried on as though Edward were in the studio. Boehm serves on the design team of the company, which opened a china studio in Malvern, England, in 1971.

Among the many highlights of Boehm's career is the visit of Prince Charles of England to the Malvern studio. A tribute to her vibrant personality, their friendship has continued since that initial meeting. In 1985 the Malvern studio was merged with one that had been opened in 1983 in Llandow, Wales, where objects that combine porcelain with bronze, as well as gold and silver, are made.

Boehm holds honorary degrees from St. Peter's College, Jersey City, NJ, and Jacksonville University, FL. She serves as a board member of the United World College Schools of Montezuma, NM, a trustee of the Institute of Private Enterprise at the University of North Carolina, and is a founding member of the World Wildlife Fund. She sits on the Fine Arts Committee of Blair House, Washington, D.C., on the Council of the Concilium Sodalium of the Vatican, and on the Horatio Alger National Executive Committee. She is a recipient of the Horatio Alger Award and the Star of Italian Solidarity Award. Boehm is also a benefactor of the Scheie Eye Institute of Philadelphia.

*With a Little Luck*, Boehm's autobiography, published in 1985, is an open statement of her love of success, fast horses, polo ponies, and Rolls-Royces. She enjoys a robust participation in the social and financial world.

Boehm's autobiography is *With a Little Luck* (1985). Information on her company appears in Frank Cosentino, *Boehm's Birds: The Porcelain Art of Edward Marshall Boehm* (1960).

*Marion Mann Roberts*

## MARGARET BOURKE-WHITE, 1904–1971

Margaret Bourke-White, industrial photographer, author, and photojournalist, was born on June 14, 1904, in New York City, the second of three children of Joseph and Minnie (Bourke) White. Joseph White, an engineer and inventor of printing press equipment, was born in Rochester, NY, the son of a tailor who had emigrated from Poland. Minnie Bourke, a stenographer who later taught braille, was the daughter of an Irish seaman who became a carpenter, married an English cook, and emigrated to New York. When Bourke-White was 23, she added her mother's maiden name to her surname, and for the rest of her life was known as Margaret Bourke-White.

Soon after Bourke-White was born, her parents moved with her and her older sister, Ruth, to Bound Brook, NJ,

then a rural community, where they fostered their children's interest in nature. Bourke-White credited her childhood experiences in New Jersey with two major influences in her life. The first was her love of natural science, developed on walks with her father. While she listened to his bird calls and observed small meadow and woodland creatures, she learned to distinguish harmless from poisonous snakes. One summer she raised 200 caterpillars under drinking glasses on the dining room windowsill and waited up all night with her mother to see the first butterfly emerge. Although her life took a different direction from the childhood dream of becoming a herpetologist, she never lost her intense interest in natural science. Later in life, while traveling on an icebreaker in the Arctic Ocean, she asked to have the engines stopped while she photographed butterflies emerging from the chrysalises she'd taken aboard.

The second strong influence of Bourke-White's New Jersey childhood was the foundry in Dunellen where her father's printing presses were built. Dazzled by the shining molten metal and rushing sparks, she later sought to capture those images in her first industrial photographs. Her attraction to industrial form and pattern came, she said, from her father, who made her feel comfortable with machinery.

After summer session swimming and dancing courses at Rutgers University, she entered Columbia University in the fall of 1921. As a freshman, she took a course with the great photographer and teacher Clarence H. White, which was her only formal instruction in photography.

Following her father's death, Bourke-White transferred to the University of Michigan, where she studied herpetology. There she met Everett Chapman, a graduate electrical engineering student whom she married in 1924. The next year, Chapman accepted a teaching position at Purdue University, where Bourke-White continued her undergraduate studies. When she and Chapman separated two years later, she attended Case Western Reserve before transferring to Cornell University for her senior year.

To earn money, Bourke-White photographed Cornell scenes in the soft-focus style of Clarence White. Cornell architectural graduates who saw her pictures on the covers of the *Alumni News* encouraged her to consider a career in photography. Deeply influenced by such encouragement, Bourke-White moved to Cleveland after she graduated in 1927 and set up a studio in her apartment.

The first clients for her landscape and architectural photographs were other Cornell alumni. Bourke-White supported herself with their commissions and began to experiment with industrial subjects, photographing giant factories along the Lake Erie shore. Her childhood memory of the fiery New Jersey foundry attracted her to the Otis Steel plant interior. With equipment that she borrowed and the technical help of friends, Bourke-White had a

Margaret Bourke-White on the Chrysler Building scaffolding in New York City in 1930. Bourke-White credited her childhood in New Jersey for her love of natural science and her attraction to industrial form and pattern. *Margaret Bourke-White estate.*

crash course in lighting, paper, and printing. Gone was the soft-focus effect of her first photographs. The finished pictures leaped beyond her primitive equipment and became *The Story of Steel*, a book privately printed for Otis stockholders.

Henry R. Luce, publisher of *Time*, the weekly news magazine, saw the steel plant pictures and called Bourke-White to New York, where he invited her to join the staff of *Fortune*, his newest publication. *Fortune* would celebrate industry by integrating dramatic industrial photographs with text. Bourke-White's pictures of Chicago's meatpacking industry were in the lead story of *Fortune*'s first issue in 1929.

Bourke-White moved to a studio in New York's new Chrysler Building in 1930. There she divided her time between advertising accounts and *Fortune*. Her fascination with industry led to the first of three trips to Russia, a country that she believed had moved directly from feudalism to an industrial society. Her pictures and reports of

Soviet life appeared in newspapers, magazines, and in her books *Eyes on Russia* (1931) and *USSR Photographs* (1934).

For *Fortune*, she covered the 1934 drought in the American Midwest, an assignment that shifted her interest from machines to people. A new concern for humanity emerged in her searing photographic record of the dust bowl and the lives it devastated.

Bourke-White was one of four photographers chosen for the original staff of *Life*, the weekly picture magazine that Luce began in 1936. For the first cover, Luce chose her photograph of Montana's giant Fort Peck Dam. Although her assignment was the mighty engineering project, Bourke-White actually sent back two stories. Her account celebrated both construction of the dam and the lives of the families who came to build it.

In 1938 Bourke-White's full-page photo of Jersey City's Mayor Hague was the highlight of a *Life* story. Bourke-White gathered politically damaging information about Hague while eluding the police who had been assigned to escort her only to those places and events selected by the mayor.

The human quality of the drought and Fort Peck Dam pictures caught the attention of author Erskine Caldwell, who invited Bourke-White to collaborate on a book about rural poverty in America. She gave up her studio and advertising accounts to begin a journey with him in 1936 through the back roads of the Southeast, a journey recorded in their book *You Have Seen Their Faces* (1937). After their marriage in 1939, Bourke-White and Caldwell published *North of the Danube* (1939), a book about life in Czechoslovakia, and *Say, This Is the USA* (1940). *Shooting the Russian War* (1942) recounted the trip she took with Caldwell to Russia during the 1941 German attack.

The marriage ended in 1942 and Bourke-White did not marry again. "Mine is a life into which marriage does not fit very well," she said, citing her need to follow assignments when and where they called. She remained ready to answer the call, subordinating her personal life to her profession. "In the end it is only the work that counts," she said.

Bourke-White was *Life*'s star photographer during World War II. She was accredited as an official U.S. Air Force photographer, but a special arrangement allowed *Life* to use her photographs also. Persistent, flamboyant, and glamorous, she sometimes risked her life for a picture and often scooped her male colleagues. Torpedoed in a troop ship and rescued from a lifeboat in the Atlantic Ocean, she continued to North Africa, where she received long-sought permission to fly a combat mission. A full-length picture of tall, striking Bourke-White with her famous smile and wearing a sheepskin-lined leather flying suit flashed across newsstands as the country followed her wartime reports.

For five months she covered the ground and air war, sometimes under fire, in Italy's Cassino Valley, and she returned home to write *They Called It Purple Heart Valley* (1944). In March 1945 she crossed the Rhine River into Germany with General George C. Patton's Third Army. Her photographs of the Buchenwald concentration camp stunned the world. Reflections on the war's savagery prompted her book *Dear Fatherland: Rest Quietly* (1946).

After World War II, she traveled widely. Photographing the principal characters and events of the time, she retold her adventures on lecture tours in the United States. Assigned to cover the turmoil that preceded Indian independence, she took her famous "Gandhi at His Spinning Wheel" photograph (1946) at their first meeting. She visited the great Indian leader again during the next two years as she followed the struggle for independence. Just hours before his death on January 30, 1948, she interviewed him for the last time. Back in the United States, she wrote *Halfway to Freedom: A Study of the New India* (1949).

Two years later, in South Africa, her photographs of black miners, taken miles below ground in intense heat, produced a visual indictment of the political system of apartheid. Later in 1950 *Life* sent her to cover the Korean War.

On her return from Korea in 1951, she developed physical problems that were later diagnosed as symptoms of Parkinson's disease. The ailment engaged her in a heroic fight against the onset of paralysis, a struggle that rivaled her wartime exploits. She followed an intensive exercise routine and twice submitted to experimental surgical procedures, yet renewed her dedication to work. She spoke to groups of people suffering from Parkinson's disease and offered them hope that they too could overcome its crippling effects. With great difficulty, she continued her photographic assignments until 1957. Association with *Life* continued until 1969, two years before her death.

Her work has been shown in museums and galleries and was included in the 1955 Museum of Modern Art "The Family of Man" exhibition, which celebrated the art and craft of photography. She received an honorary degree from Douglass College in 1948 and from the University of Michigan in 1951. Canada gave her name to a lake and she was listed as one of the ten most outstanding women of the year in 1936, and in 1965 one of the ten notable living women of the century. In 1960 her life and career were highlighted in a television film, *The Margaret Bourke-White Story*.

Her life and career spanned the day of the giant picture magazines, her death came in their twilight. *Look* discontinued publication two months after she died; *Life* stopped publishing a weekly edition the following year.

On August 27, 1971, at age 67, in a hospital near her home in Connecticut, Bourke-White died of the effects of Parkinson's disease. Her remains were cremated.

Bourke-White's autobiography is *Portrait of Myself* (1963). Many of her pictures appear in Sean Callahan, ed., *The Photographs of Margaret Bourke-White* (1972). A well-researched biography is Vicki Goldberg, *Bourke-White* (1986). She is profiled in *NAW-MP*. Her obituary appeared in the *New York Times*, Aug. 28, 1971.

*Catherine Scheader*

## ELIZABETH ROCK BRACKETT, 1892–1974

Elizabeth Rock Brackett, family doctor and public health advocate, was one of several women who practiced medicine with distinction in New Jersey in the mid-20th century. Brackett was born in New York City on October 12, 1892, the first of two children and only daughter of George Frederick and Elizabeth (Rock) Brackett. Brackett's father was educated in Washington, D.C., where he met and married Elizabeth Rock, a native Washingtonian, in 1891. The young couple settled in New York City, but before the turn of the century the family, enlarged by the birth of a son in 1894, moved to the village of Ridgewood in Bergen County, NJ. There Brackett's father prospered as owner of a contracting company that built most of the roads in northern New Jersey. Despite the death of her mother in 1907, the Brackett household remained a close and happy one. Brackett assumed the mother's role. The curiosity and mechanical aptitude for which Brackett was noted throughout her life was exhibited at the age of twelve when she and her father took apart the family automobile. They put it together, with only one bolt left over, and despite the extra piece, had it running again.

Brackett graduated from Ridgewood High School in 1910, after taking a curriculum that included English, French, physics, chemistry, and physiology. Just under six feet tall, Brackett was active in girls' basketball and captained the Ridgewood High School team in 1908-9.

After her father's remarriage in 1912, Brackett moved to New York City to study nursing at the Presbyterian Hospital Training School for Nurses, from which she graduated in 1915. With the entry of the United States into World War I, Brackett joined the Presbyterian Hospital Medical Unit attached to the British Expeditionary Force at Etretat, France. She served there as a member of the U.S. Army Nurse Corps until March 1919. After the war, Brackett was a public health nurse at the Henry Street Settlement in New York City before she enrolled at Teachers College, Columbia University, in 1921. She graduated in June 1925 with a B.S. in education and supervision in public health nursing.

While in France, however, she had decided to become a doctor after observing physicians at the front. Brackett commented to a friend that as a nurse she became tired of taking orders from the young doctors and decided to be-

Elizabeth Rock Brackett, *front row center*, an Army Corps nurse in World War I and for 36 years a physician in Nutley, grew up in Ridgewood, where she captained the girls' high school basketball team. *Courtesy, family collection.*

come a physician so that she could take charge in a medical situation. She entered the College of Physicians and Surgeons of Columbia University in September 1925 and graduated four years later, at age 37, with the Class of 1929. Brackett then interned at Newark City Hospital. After her internship, she took a residency in pediatrics at Babies Hospital in Philadelphia and then at Babies Hospital in Newark.

Brackett started private practice in 1932, in an office over a corner drugstore on Franklin Avenue, in Nutley (Essex County), NJ. Expecting to specialize in pediatrics, she soon found that a general family practice was better suited to the area. She was the town's only woman physician. Nutley in the 1930s was a residential community of slightly over 20,000, which had experienced explosive growth in the previous decade, when its population increased by more than 118 percent. Because Brackett began her practice during the Great Depression, it grew slowly; but she soon moved to a large frame house at 371 Franklin Avenue. With the advent of World War II, Brackett had almost more patients than she could handle, since many male physicians were away on military duty.

For more than 30 years, Brackett held appointments as attending physician at Presbyterian Hospital, Newark, and associate attending physician at Babies Hospital, Newark, St. Barnabas Hospital, and East Orange General Hospital. She was a member of the Council of the Essex County Medical Society, chair of the Committee on Nursing and Nursing Education of the Essex County Medical Society, and president and charter member of the Nutley Public Nursing Association. Brackett's administrative ability was recognized by her election, in 1948–49, as president of the New Jersey Medical Women's Association (NJMWA), and on the national level in the American Medical Women's Association by her appointment to the Finance and Auditing committees in the 1950s, culminating in her selection as national treasurer in 1962.

Brackett presented an imposing but not intimidating figure. Immaculately groomed and well dressed, she was in command of any situation. The elderly found her compassionate and comforting, and children experienced her light, painless touch. She gave unstintingly to her patients, making house calls at any hour of the day or night. By 1962 she had delivered some 2,500 babies and had treated countless patients for minor surgery and diseases.

Brackett remained single, surrounding herself with myriad companions, ranging from Mina Mahony and Isabelle I. Barbier, who made their home with her, to the countless young people she delighted in helping. She enjoyed cooking, working on house repairs, swimming, and horseback riding at her cottage at Fayson Lake.

The NJWMA chose Brackett in 1962 as "Woman of the Year" for the outstanding sense of community welfare she displayed during her career. Two years later, the Nutley branch of the American Association of University Women, of which she was a member, named a fellowship in her honor. Before retiring in 1968, Brackett agreed to serve on the Medical Advisory Board of the Visiting Nurse Service in Nutley. She continued to volunteer her services at local hospitals when she moved to Rossmoor, a retirement community in central New Jersey.

Brackett died of cancer, at age 82, on November 7, 1974, at the Van Dyk Nursing Home in Ridgewood. A devout Episcopalian, her funeral service was held at Christ Church, Ridgewood. She was buried at the Valleau Cemetery in Ridgewood.

Interviews with Warner Windom Brackett, Wyckoff, NJ, and Irene Lamb Howland, Allentown, PA, provided biographical information. Brackett is noted in Christine E. Haycock, "Women Physicians of New Jersey: The Early Era," *Journal of the Medical Society of New Jersey* 81 (1984):773–77. Dorothy Eldridge, one of her patients, was interviewed for this article. Brackett's obituary appeared in the the *Record* (Bergen County, NJ), Nov. 8, 1974.

*Jean L. Willis*

## LOUISE DELLING BRANTHWAITE, 1898–

Louise (Delling) Branthwaite, skilled broadsilk warper, office worker, and student at the Bryn Mawr Summer School for Women Workers in 1924 and 1925, was born on December 9, 1898, in Paterson (Passaic County), NJ, at the home her parents, Max and Minna (Graf) Delling, built within a mile of the "Great Falls" of the Passaic River. Branthwaite was the fourth of five children and the third daughter born to the Dellings, both immigrants from Saxony, Germany, where maternal grandfather Carl Graf operated three woolen looms from his home. Max Delling was a skilled Jacquard broadsilk weaver, a trade he learned in this country. Branthwaite graduated from Paterson's Elementary School No. 5 in 1914. She is the sole sibling to continue her family's textile tradition by going "into the silk" at age sixteen to learn warping. Branthwaite views her years at the warping beam with pride and sense of purpose.

The values and virtues that Branthwaite has manifested throughout her life she learned in a traditional home. Her mother nurtured her family with warmth, encouragement, respect for her children's individualism, and German cooking. Her father inspired fear, through an uncommunicative, stern, exacting manner, and respect owing to his many skills. "I appreciated all my father could do. One time when I was told to throw away a pair of scissors with a broken blade I answered the foreman, 'Oh no, my father can fix them.' Of course they were beyond fixing by anyone." (Branthwaite, Interview, July 7, 1987) The Delling family, which had earlier managed on $9 a week and survived Max Delling's participation in the 1913 Paterson silk strike, also knew many shared pleasures: the garden jointly tended by the parents, the evening card games, picnics, and summer swims in the Passaic River. Branthwaite gets her small features and short stature from her mother, whose generous, optimistic nature she also displays. Branthwaite exhibits her father's artisanal industriousness and perfectionism.

Branthwaite was one of approximately 7,700 female silkworkers in Paterson in 1917. Her father found her an edge-warping position in Holzman's Mill, a job that started her on warping, the skilled, respectably paid work she did continuously until 1931. Branthwaite, a single, teenaged daughter of immigrants who lived with her parents, was representative of young women "in the silk." To the Delling family income she contributed the standard 90 percent of her wages, which ranged in her early years between $12 and $16 a week.

Branthwaite was not all filial obedience. The issue of joining a union engaged her in a complicated power struggle with her father. Branthwaite had absorbed his pragmatic, if not passionate, attitude toward unions. Without consulting him or anyone, she asked to join the newly organized Ladies Horizontal Warpers Union. Her statement of autonomy took her father by surprise. "It was very unusual for someone to ask to join the union. When I got home my father said 'that's just the worst.' What bothered him [was] that I hadn't talked it over with him especially after his friend had got me the job. But there wasn't anything he could do about it." (Branthwaite, Interview, July 8, 1981) In short order, Branthwaite again acted boldly, this time quitting Holzman's for another ribbon-warping position that paid a few dollars more. It was from that job in Maple Mill that she participated in a climactic 1919 industrywide strike, one that brought the eight-hour day to Paterson's silkworkers.

"I just gloried in it," Branthwaite says of the tie-goods warping she did at the Arcola Mill for some ten years between 1921 and 1931. "Especially when there were colors—I loved the stripes and ombres. Each spool of silk had to be in a certain place so the pattern would be right. I didn't want something automatic, I wanted something to think about." Warping of patterned 27- to 36-inch fabric, as opposed to solid-colored 3-inch ribbon, did require thought plus dexterity and an ease with numbers. "To make the warp, the lengthways of the fabric, we put 500 colored threads on at once. The silk came from spools on a creel and then went through reeds of varying widths depending on the pattern. From about 300 to 700 yards went on. It could take up to two days to make just one warp." (Branthwaite, Interview, July 8, 1981)

Branthwaite remembers that warping tie silk at Arcola "went pretty regular." Her eight-hour workday began with two bus rides, first one into downtown Paterson, followed by another out to the Riverside section. Dressed in a smock, called a "bungalow apron," Branthwaite was at her

warping beam from eight to five, five days a week, producing enough piecework to bring her a $28–30 wage. But work was irregular. "When they didn't have orders, they didn't care what happened to you." (Branthwaite, Interview, July 7, 1987) Warpers stood all day to work the beams. Branthwaite's fellow warpers, all women, came from a cross-section of ethnicities in the local silk industry: English, Germans, Swiss, and Italians. Female warpers earned less than male counterparts. Foremen were always males.

One of the greatest steps forward in Branthwaite's long life came in the summers of 1924 and 1925, when she attended the Bryn Mawr Summer School for Women Workers. It was through Elizabeth Stein, a 1922 student at the school and a friend from summers on Lake Hopatcong, that Branthwaite heard of the program. "Since I had only been as high as the eighth grade in school to me it was like a college education." Branthwaite had her confidence enhanced and perspectives broadened through courses in English composition, public speaking, economics, history, psychology, and other electives. The school nurtured cosmopolitan thinking. "I came home with such a different outlook. I remembered hearing that children in Japan, only five or six years old, had to take silk cocoons out of boiling water without a dipper. I always felt sorry for those little children because of their swollen hands." (Branthwaite, Interview, July 7, 1987)

Branthwaite credits the summer school with confirming many of her best instincts: "So many people thought you have to step on people to get ahead. And I didn't think that life should be like that. You have to carry people along with you to something better." (Branthwaite, Interview, July 7, 1987) She also became a copious letter writer and a devoted member of the Industrial Department of the Young Women's Christian Association (YWCA), an agency strongly supportive of the Bryn Mawr Summer School for Women Workers. Branthwaite attracted the notice of at least one YWCA secretary: "Louise, you should be a member of a church. You don't need it, but they need people like you. I guess I was always looking up, rather than in the gutter." (Branthwaite, Interview, July 7, 1987)

With the faltering of the Paterson silk industry in the early 1930s, Branthwaite began a career in office work that spanned her middle years and brought her to retirement. In 1959 romance entered her life when she became a 60-year old first-time bride, marrying George Branthwaite, a Jacquard card cutter. He died in 1976.

At 89 Branthwaite remains engaged with life. She runs her own home in Paterson, has a busy social life based at the local Nutrition Center, crochets, and regularly corresponds with numerous friends, including those she made at the Bryn Mawr Summer School for Women Workers in the 1920s. She also visits and writes to shut-ins as a member of the Shut-In Society.

Branthwaite was interviewed in Paterson, NJ, on July 8, 1981, and July 7, 1987. She was featured in two articles: Stephen Kent, "Father Was a Silk Striker," *Bergen Record*, Dec. 6, 1981; and Anne Rivera, "Memories of Bryn Mawr Summer School for Women Workers," *Labor Unity* (Amalgamated Clothing and Textile Workers Union), Apr. 1981. She appears in two films: *Women in the Silk* (1981) and *The Women of Summer: The Bryn Mawr Summer School for Women Workers, 1921–1938* (1985).

*Rita Rubinstein Heller*

## EVA TOPKINS BRODKIN, 1899–

Eva (Topkins) Brodkin, the first woman dermatologist in New Jersey, was born in Brooklyn, NY, on March 7, 1899, the oldest of four children of Isidore and Theresa (Ashkins) Topkins. Both her parents had emigrated from Europe in their youth. At the time of Brodkin's birth, her father was attending Long Island Medical College. Following his graduation, the family moved to Califon, NJ, where he entered general practice as a country doctor.

Although Theresa (Ashkins) Topkins was a homemaker, she believed that every woman should have a profession and encouraged her only daughter (a younger daughter had died at the age of five) to become a lawyer. But Brodkin adored her father and never thought of becoming anything other than a doctor.

According to a family story, at the age of four Brodkin walked into her father's waiting room and put her ear against a patient's chest to listen to his heartbeat. Later, while she was attending elementary school, her father took her on his house calls in a horse and buggy.

Although she had two uncles who were doctors and an aunt who was the first woman to graduate from the Brooklyn College of Pharmacy, Brodkin did not have a woman doctor as a role model. Some people said she was "crazy" to think of becoming a doctor when she would only marry and "that would be the end of it." (Brodkin, Interview, Mar. 31, 1986) But her determination persisted through her years at High Bridge High School, where she took enough science courses to qualify for a premed program in college.

Although her father approved of a profession for his daughter, he tried to discourage her from studying medicine because he thought a doctor's long hours would be hard on a woman. To that end he took her to visit a woman anesthesiologist, who was "not encouraging." Although she was glad to be a doctor herself, she would not recommend it to Brodkin because women doctors were not readily accepted. When Brodkin could not be dissuaded, her father agreed to support her through medical school, asking her to promise that she would continue to practice even if she married.

After graduating from Cornell University in 1920 with a B.A., Brodkin entered the Woman's Medical College in Philadelphia. Brodkin received her M.D. in 1924 and was accepted as an intern at Muhlenberg Hospital in Plainfield, NJ. The woman who was the hospital superintendent told her that as the first female doctor on the staff she would be "an experiment." Her performance would determine whether other women would be accepted in the future. Brodkin proved herself by "doing everything including carrying stretchers and riding in ambulances." She also heeded her father's advice: "Take care of your work, mind your own business, and never forget that you are a lady and not one of the boys." (Brodkin, Interview, Mar. 31, 1986)

While studying in Philadelphia, she had gone on a blind date with Henry Brodkin, a medical student at Jefferson Medical School. After their respective internships, they were married in Califon on September 6, 1925. Both then went into general practice in Irvington. In 1926 Hyla, their daughter, was born; their son, Richard, was born fifteen months later. Henry Brodkin offered not only moral support but also help with practical chores such as bathing the babies. Brodkin's practice required her to be available at any hour of the day or night to deliver babies, often in her patients' homes. With two young children of their own, she and her husband, who had specialized in thoracic surgery, decided that Brodkin should prepare for an office specialty.

On the day of the stock market crash in 1929, the Brodkins moved into a fifteen-room house in the Weequahic section of Newark. Since they had found a reliable housekeeper and both sets of parents were in the vicinity, Brodkin was able to begin studies in her chosen specialty of dermatology.

For three years, from 1929 through 1931, she traveled each weekday to New York for classes at the Skin and Cancer Hospital (now the New York University Hospital). For seven more years she went there three times a week as a clinical assistant. In 1939 she passed her board examinations and became the first woman dermatologist in New Jersey and the second woman in the state to be certified as a specialist. With an office established in her house, and the freedom to set her own hours, Brodkin had ample time to be at home with her three children (Roger had been born in 1932).

When Brodkin first selected dermatology, she had been advised to spend some time working in a clinic before further study. Therefore, she went to work at the St. Barnabas Medical Center, then in Newark, now located in Livingston. She was named attending dermatologist at St. Barnabas soon after her certification.

At the start of World War II, Henry Brodkin was called into the Army and sent overseas. The war years tested Brodkin's mettle. Not only did she manage a family singlehandedly and keep up her practice, but because of the shortage of civilian male doctors she had to work longer hours.

Nevertheless, she managed to provide leadership in two professional organizations. During the war she was chairman of the Journal Club, a group of women doctors who met informally to share new medical information. The Brodkin cellar also became a collecting area for food and clothing that the group sent to women physicians in Europe who had been displaced by the war.

Brodkin also had been among the first members of the New Jersey Medical Women's Association (NJMWA). During her second consecutive term as president in the war years, the NJMWA worked with the New York branch for passage of legislation to enable women physicians, like their male counterparts, to become commissioned officers when they joined the armed forces. In recognition of her professional service and her efforts to promote the causes of women doctors, the NJWMA named Brodkin Woman of the Year in 1964. Brodkin also was the first, and for some time the only, woman in the New Jersey Dermatological Society. This society elected her president in 1952.

Brodkin remained on the staff at St. Barnabas until her retirement at 65 and she retained her private practice until age 77, when her vision began to fail.

In her 52 years of practice, male patients never refused Brodkin's care, but many women were skeptical. She enjoyed quoting one woman who said: "I might as well tell you I have no use for woman doctors. But since it's only my skin you couldn't do much harm." (Brodkin, Interview, Mar. 31, 1986) A member of her family described her as "a doctor in the old humanistic tradition: so devoted to her patients that she knew all their life histories." (Brodkin, Interview, July 1986)

Marriage to a doctor did not make her life as a woman doctor easier, Brodkin recalled. She did, however, find it an advantage to be married to someone who could understand her work. In 1974, when the Brodkins both received the Golden Merit Award, bestowed on doctors on the 50th anniversary of graduation from medical school, they were the first couple in New Jersey to receive it at the same time.

The Brodkins remained in Newark, where Henry Brodkin was chief thoracic surgeon at Beth Israel Medical Center and Newark City Hospital, until the racial unrest in the late 1960s. Then they established a year-round residency at their summer home in Kinnelon, NJ. They moved to East Orange in 1972. Brodkin was widowed when her husband died in 1985.

At age 87, Brodkin appraised her career: "Women doctors had a tough time, but I don't think I did." She acknowledged that she had been able to accomplish everything she had wanted, and that her only compromise had been to leave her general practice to enter dermatology.

Her greatest satisfaction, along with her family, came from being able to do something that could help people. "I happen to love people," she affirmed.

Interviews with Brodkin in March and June 1986 provided information. Also helpful were telephone interviews with her children, Dr. Roger Brodkin and Dr. Hyla Garlen, and with Dr. Christine Haycock and Dr. Laura Morrow. An interview with Brodkin appeared in the *Evening News* (Newark), Apr. 15, 1964.

*Patricia Malarcher*

## MARGARET CHRISTINA BROWN, 1891–

Margaret Christina Brown, a leader in physical education and president emeritus of Panzer College of Physical Education and Hygiene, was born in Saint Lambert, Quebec, Canada, the second of four children (two daughters and two sons) of James Gentles and Sarah (Gibson) Brown. Her father, an accountant for an engineering firm, was a Scot. Her mother was a well-educated woman and pianist whose parents settled in Montreal after leaving England's Lake District. The Browns enjoyed a middle-class life. James Brown, an avid reader, a musician, and a member of the Board of Education, died in 1907, when Margaret Brown was sixteen.

Brown was an enthusiastic student who distinguished herself in the province of Quebec by placing first in the Latin prose regents exam and second in the ancient history exam. In 1908, at the age of seventeen, she graduated from Saint Lambert Academy in Canada with an associate in arts diploma. The following year she received a normal course diploma from MacDonald College and then taught elementary school for three years for the Montreal Protestant School Board. A pivotal moment in her life was when she saw Ruth Evans teach gymnastics. Determined to do the same, she enrolled for three summers at the School of Physical Education at Chautaqua, NY, Evans's alma mater. In 1912 Brown earned a certificate in physical education. In 1921 she earned another diploma in physical education from the McGill School of Physical Education in Montreal.

Twice she returned to Chautaqua, where she met Henry Panzer, president of the Newark (NJ) Normal School of Physical Education and Hygiene. (The school introduced a four-year course and was renamed Panzer College of Physical Education and Hygiene after it was relocated to East Orange, NJ, in 1926.) Panzer offered Brown a position as his assistant, and eager to progress from public school teaching to teacher education, she accepted.

After her move to the United States, Brown completed her education. She received her B.A. (1930) and M.Ed. (1936) from Rutgers University, and in 1944 she earned a doctorate in education from New York University.

Brown served as the dean of Panzer College from 1921 until 1932 when she was named president of the college.

She acted in that capacity and also served as a professor of education until 1958, when the college was merged with Montclair State College. Brown exercised a strong, progressive, and positive influence over the students at Panzer during her long tenure as president. She stated, "If you want to be a professional educator you have to live it in college." (Interview, Feb. 14, 1986) Classroom theory was integrated with practice through planned professional experiences for students prior to their supervised student teaching in the senior year. A student's training also included summers spent in supervised community service. Appropriate dress for women and jackets and ties for men were the required dress for Panzer College students. Teachers were to be examples of proper adult behavior: they were to help their students grow.

After World War II, with the demand for higher education in business, the arts, and science, normal schools were phased out; curricula in liberal arts and professional studies became the norm. With this trend in teacher education, Panzer College and Montclair State College merged in 1958.

Brown wrote many articles for professional publications, as well as a book (with Betty K. Sommer), *Movement Education: Its Evolution and a Modern Approach*. In her lectures and writings Brown stressed the necessity of guided physical experiences and their implication for the enhancement of human development. She emphasized the belief that scientific, artistic, sociological, and psychological background all factor into the development of human movement. Brown decried the association of physical education with "sweat and scores" and throughout her professional life actively sought to promote the dignity of physical education and its benefits to human health and fellowship.

Brown has held many offices in professional organizations, including the presidency of the New Jersey Association for Health, Physical Education and Recreation from 1947 to 1948, and the presidency of the New Jersey Association of Colleges and Universities in 1950.

Internationally she was a delegate of the U.S. Olympic Gymnastics Committee to the International Federation of Gymnastics and an official at the Olympic Games in Berlin (1936), London (1948), and Helsinki (1952). In 1938 she was a delegate to the World Gymnastic Championship and Sokol Festival at Prague.

Brown is the recipient of many awards in the field of physical education. Among the most prestigious is the William S. Anderson Award presented to her in 1953 by the American Association of Health, Physical Education and Recreation. A room at Montclair State College in the Panzer Center has been dedicated in her honor, and both a scholarship and a senior awards medal at the college bear her name. In 1975 Montclair State College conferred on her an honorary doctor of law degree.

Brown, a resident of the Ward Homestead in Maplewood, she is still keenly interested in the activities of Montclair State College and the progress of her former students.

An interview with Brown on Feb. 14, 1986, provided useful information. Additional details of her life appear in Nancy Jaffer, "Authoress, Educator Approaches 80 with a Progressive Spirit," *Newark Star-Ledger*, Aug. 24, 1971.

*Angeline Giammalvo Long*

## BERNARDA BRYSON, 1903–

Bernarda (Bryson) Shahn (known professionally as Bernarda Bryson), artist, illustrator, and writer, was born on March 7, 1903, in Athens, OH, the younger of two daughters of Lucy Wilkins (Weethee) and Charles Harvey Bryson. Bryson's mother (1876–1937) was of Scottish-English background. A highly educated woman, with a B.A. in liberal arts and an M.A. in biology, she was a professor of Latin at Ohio University. Bryson's father (d. 1945) was a journalist with a B.A. from Ohio University. His family, too, was of Scottish background.

Bryson's interest in art was encouraged by her parents; she studied art and art history throughout her college years. She attended Ohio University for four years, but did not seek a degree; and then took further studies at Ohio State University, Western Reserve, and the Cleveland School of Art, where she studied lithography and etching. Bryson taught these forms of printmaking at the Columbus Museum Art School. (Midtown Galleries, New York City, news release, Aug. 30, 1983)

Bryson's work as a writer for the *Ohio State Journal* took her to New York City in the early 1930s to interview the Mexican muralist Diego Rivera. There she met Ben Shahn, who was working on Rivera's Rockefeller Center mural at the time (1932). She was already aware of Shahn's drawings from his work on the subject of the Sacco and Vanzetti trial. Bryson and Shahn were married in 1936 and had three children: Susanna (b. 1936), Jonathan (b. 1938), and Abigail (b. 1940). Ben Shahn, who also had two children by his first wife, was born in Lithuania in 1898 and had an impressive career until his death in 1969.

When Bryson came to New York she received work assignments in art from the PWAP (Public Works of Art Project, one of the prototypes for the WPA). During the early 1930s her humanitarian and political concerns were expressed in her art, and also in her involvement with the Artists Union in 1933–34. Along with fellow artists, she had participated in protests against PWAP administrators in New York on behalf of needy unemployed artists and for the reform of PWAP hiring practices. (Monroe, "Artists Union," 37–39; and Bryson, Interview, Mar. 24, 1986)

An expert printmaker, Bryson was asked to set up a lithography workshop in Washington for the Resettlement Administration. Many of her own prints of the 1930s concern the plight of the American worker and the decline of the American frontier. (Rubin, "Bernarda Bryson Shahn," 154) Bryson and Shahn took several trips during the years 1935–37 through the South and the Midwest that strongly influenced the content of their work.

In 1937 they moved to Jersey Homesteads (better known as Roosevelt), NJ, a community sponsored by the Resettlement Administration of the federal government in cooperation with garment workers from New York City. Bryson still resides in Roosevelt, the location of one of Ben Shahn's major murals.

Bryson and Shahn were awarded a commission of $7,000 in 1938 by the Section of Fine Arts of the U.S. Treasury to do a mural for the Bronx Central Annex Post Office. The mural, *Industrial and Agricultural Resources of America*, consisted of thirteen large egg-tempera panels and was completed by 1940. ("The Bronx," 26; Park, "City and Country," 37–47)

From the 1940s to the 1970s, Bryson worked as an illustrator and writer. Her illustrations appeared in magazines such as *Fortune, Harpers, Life,* and *Scientific American,* and she is considered one of the most accomplished illustrators in the field. (Bass, "Bernarda Bryson Shahn," 16; Lynes, "Bernarda Bryson: Illustrator," 46–56)

Bryson has also illustrated many books, including *Pride and Prejudice* by Jane Austen (1962) and *The Storyteller's Pack,* a Frank R. Stockton reader (1968). She has been both author and illustrator of *The Zoo of Zeus* (1964) and *Gilgamesh: Man's First Story* (1967).

As a writer, Bryson has also been an important contributor to literature on Ben Shahn. She characterizes her relationship with Ben Shahn as one without professional jealousy and says that life with him was exciting and rewarding. She found her career as an illustrator and writer personally satisfying and financially useful. "All those years," she says, "I accumulated images that I was going to paint." (Bryson, Interview, Mar. 26, 1986)

Bryson returned to painting in the 1970s and had her first solo exhibition at Midtown Gallery, New York City, in 1983. The show was divided into lithographs, etchings, and paintings, with some prints from earlier periods presenting her concerns for the social, economic, and political condition of the country.

Her oil paintings of the 1970s and 1980s are often surreal and enigmatic, with frequent classical references. They include artists' manikins conversing in a landscape; a draped, faceless figure moving silently along a pond's edge; and other unusual and provocative motifs. One reviewer commented: "The use of artists' props, the allusions to Roman art, the free admixtures of academic and modernist traditions, and the oddly compressed or extended space are all reminiscent of *arte metafisica* yet the paintings stand on their own without any need for further explication . . . her images, accomplished with the authority of a seasoned artist, are fixed in reality even as they move toward the world of dreams." (Bass, 16)

In December-January 1985–86, Bryson's work was again exhibited in New York City in a three-person show at Midtown Gallery. Among the paintings shown were several that continue the themes and concerns of the 1983 exhibit. Bryson's paintings of her eighth and ninth decades are informed by art, literature, and her formidable intellect and wit. They are the products of the mind of a writer, as well as the mind and hands of an artist.

An interview with Bryson in March 1986 provided useful information. Critiques of Bryson's work are: Russell Lynes, "Bernarda Bryson: Illustrator," *Print* 10 (Sept.-Oct. 1955):46–56; Ruth Bass, "Bernarda Bryson Shahn," *Arts Magazine* 58 (Dec. 1983):16; and Edward Rubin, "Bernarda Bryson Shahn," *Art News* 83 (Jan. 1984):154. Her mural work is described in "The Bronx—A Typical Treasury Competition," *Art Digest* 12 (June 1938):26; and Marlene Park, "City and Country in the 1930s: A Study of New Deal Murals in New York," *Art Journal* 39 (Fall 1979):37–47. See also Gerald Monroe, "The Artists Union of New York" (Ed.D. diss, New York University, 1971). For additional biographical details, see "News Release," Midtown Gallery (New York, NY), Aug. 30, 1983. Bryson discussed her life and work with Ben Shahn in the *Trenton* (NJ) *Evening Times,* June 6, 1966.

*Hildreth J. York*

## MARY ALLISON BEASLEY BURCH, 1906–

Mary Allison (Beasley) Burch, future "Ma" to 10,000 Newark, NJ, youngsters, was born in Philadelphia, PA, on August 5, 1906, the only child of Charles Henry Beasley, a cabinetmaker from Virginia, and Elsie Amelia (Williams) Beasley, daughter of a middle-class, landowning family from Lewistown, PA. Both her parents were African-American. Charles Beasley's business prospered enough to allow his wife to devote herself full time to the child's care. But in 1918 he died and Elsie Beasley had to find work. She became governess for a Philadelphia family and entrusted her twelve-year-old daughter to the care of her Lewistown family, especially to her proud grandmother, Alice Williams, who took great pleasure in the girl's school success, proclaiming, "Beasie is going to be a teacher." (Burch, Interview, Oct. 25, 1986)

Burch completed elementary and high school in Lewistown's public schools and graduated from Shippensburg University, then a normal school. She and her family understood that career choices for black girls of her time and place were teaching in segregated schools or low-skill domestic and service work; they also knew that even middle-class girls must be prepared to support themselves. The young teacher rejoined her mother in Philadelphia and began a fifteen-year career in segregated elementary schools, principally in Camden, NJ.

On a blind date she met Reynold Edward Burch, a Harlem Hospital intern from Maine, who practiced medicine as a pathologist and surgeon and later as an obstetrician and gynecologist. They were married on November 2, 1942. World War II was a turning point for many African-Americans; suddenly, many previously closed doors were opened. Reynold Burch was assigned to the air corps and was sent to the Air Force School of Aviation Medicine; he then became flight surgeon for the 744th Bomber Group, an elite position in an elite unit. Burch accompanied her husband to his various posts. For the first time in her adult life she was separated from her work with children. Free now to spend her time as she wished, she began to concern herself with needs of the less fortunate.

In 1946 the Burches decided to live and work in Newark, where they made a home on South 14th Street. Here she soon became concerned about the lives and futures, especially the educational futures, of ten neighborhood adolescents. She organized the boys and girls into a group and recruited adult friends to help develop an educational and recreational program. The ten adolescents recruited others, and so began her major work.

The group, incorporated as "The Leaguers" in 1949, has helped more than 25,000 people, particularly Newark's African-American youth. Poets, musicians, artists, scientists, doctors, teachers, public servants—all are represented in the Leaguers' alumni. They have served their city, state, country, and their own community. Today Leaguers' programs include tutoring and volunteer work in hospitals, in addition to their principal efforts in education and recreation.

Not least among Burch's achievements was her introduction of many privileged women to another world: "We learned from the children as they learned from us" has been frequently heard of the organization's work. Its founder also learned that those who might be slow to volunteer for purely altruistic reasons could become involved in other ways—a major fund raiser for Leaguers' scholarships has been the Graduation Cotillion Ball. Singer Dionne Warwick, the most famous alumna (for whom the Leaguers' Performing Arts Auditorium is named), received her first college scholarship at the 1959 cotillion: "If it wasn't for Mrs. Burch and the Leaguers, I don't know where I would be today." (*Star-Ledger*, Nov. 6, 1986) Over the years the Burches became "Ma" Burch and "Pa" Burch to the entire organization. Mary Burch continues to serve on its Board of Trustees as the work has expanded to include the After-School, Life Skills, Tutorial, and Weequahic/Clinton Hill Youth Programs, the Summer Day Camp, the Community Development Project, and the Early Childhood Development Center.

One form of service led to innumerable others, especially in her area of particular concern, the education of children. She was the first black woman appointed to the Newark Board of Education (1951–54). She was delegate to the State Federation of District Boards of Education (1953–54), representative to the Associated Boards of Education of New Jersey (1952–53), secretary of Newark State College (now Kean College) Board of Trustees (1968). She was a member of the Davis Committee, a fact-finding group whose work resulted in establishment of Essex County College, on whose Board of Trustees she sat for more than ten years, taking the chair in 1979. The college's Burch Auditorium is named for her, as is a Kean College dormitory, Mary B. Burch Hall, and Governor Kean has appointed her a member of the New Jersey Citizens Committee for Public Schools.

She also founded the United Women's League of New Jersey (1949), an organization dedicated to the better understanding of parent-child relationships, developing leadership, awakening a sense of citizenship responsibility, and giving volunteer assistance to charities. Active in municipal, county, and state agencies, she found time also to serve on the Executive Boards of the NAACP (1954–57) and the Urban League of New Jersey (1955–58).

Among the many honors, awards, and degrees she has received are those she finds most meaningful: an honorary degree from Seton Hall University (1973), the Brotherhood Award from the National Conference of Christians and Jews (1967), the Afro-American Award (1964), and a plaque from the New Jersey State Federation of Colored Women's Clubs (1964).

Even during their most active years Mary and Reynold Burch found a little time to travel. She particularly remembers a trip to West Africa and "an adult in Nigeria asking us to adopt him," a strange experience for childless Americans. But "we were too busy being there for the children already on earth. My husband was assisting in their birthing, and I in their education." (Burch, Interview, Nov. 22, 1986) Now, in retirement, they have more leisure for traveling, but when at home in Montclair they spend most of their time in Leaguers-generated activities: "We have the family of Leaguers—past, present, and future—and we have the satisfaction of knowing that because all of us believed, we inspired, motivated, and liberated some of the most beautiful people on earth—young, gifted, and black." (Burch, Interview, Nov. 22, 1986)

Interviews with Burch on Oct. 25, 1986, and Nov. 22, 1986, provided useful information. See also Dionne Warwick's tribute to the Leaguers in the *Newark Star-Ledger*, Nov. 6, 1986.

*Georgetta Merritt Campbell*
*Daryl Boylan*

## JANE GREY BURGIO, 1922–

Jane (Grey) Burgio, New Jersey's first woman secretary of state, was born on July 8, 1922, in Nutley (Essex County), NJ, the younger of two daughters of Stephen Grey, a builder, and Bertha Grey, an elementary school teacher. The Greys raised their daughters in an ethical way but without any official religious affiliation.

When Burgio was eight years old, her father died and her mother went back to teaching school to support the family. They moved from their house to an apartment in Nutley. Although the Greys were never poor, the Depression years were hard for them, as they were for so many American families. Burgio grew up fully expecting to work for a living.

As a child, she attended workshops at the Newark Museum, where she developed a lifelong interest in art and even dreamed of becoming an artist one day. She was a superior student, an avid reader who wrote many articles for her high school publications.

After graduating from Nutley High School, she attended the Newark School of Fine and Industrial Art and designed window displays for Kresge's department store. Although she began to feel that she did not have the temperament to be a professional artist, she never lost her love of art and interest in artistic achievement.

In her spare time she joined the Young Republicans and worked for the Republican party. Her first campaign was for Dwight D. Eisenhower. It was at a Republican gathering that she met John Burgio, who was in the tire business. When she married him in 1958, she acquired two stepsons, age six and ten, whom she raised as her own.

For several years Burgio spent most of her time as a homemaker and mother. The family moved to a house in West Caldwell, NJ, where she entertained the children's friends, attended sport events at their schools, joined in community activities, and served as president of the PTA. She held several part-time jobs, one year as census taker. But she continued to be interested in politics and worked diligently for the Republican candidates in her district. Among the candidates she helped elect was Congressman Robert Kean, father of Thomas H. Kean, who later became governor.

From 1963 to 1973 she served as Essex County Republican committee woman, the last two years as vice-chair. In 1967, when Thomas Kean ran for the assembly in her district, she was instrumental in getting him elected. Six years later, when an assembly seat became vacant, Assemblyman Kean encouraged her to try for it. After consulting friends and reassuring her husband and stepsons, Burgio decided to accept the challenge. The first campaign was difficult, but she worked hard and was elected to the assembly seat.

Burgio was the first woman to represent New Jersey's 25th District in the assembly. She attributes her victory in large part to the popularity of Thomas Kean, who, she says, "carried me along with him." But she admits that years of hard work for other Republican candidates were also a strong factor in her election.

She served in the New Jersey Assembly for four terms, from 1973 to 1981. During these years the Republicans were the minority party, so it was difficult to effect major changes. Burgio served on the appropriations committee and considers her role in passing legislation for money to rebuild the historic Paper Mill Playhouse in Millburn, NJ, as one of her major contributions.

An early supporter of Thomas Kean for governor, she worked for his gubernatorial candidacy as a full-time volunteer in 1981. When he became governor, she lobbied for the position of secretary of state. Her involvement with the Bipartisan Coalition for Women's Appointments strengthened her determination to ask for the top position.

Governor Kean appointed her secretary of state in 1981. Burgio accepted this important office at a turning point in its history. The secretary of state had traditionally been the political right hand of the governor, deeply involved in fund raising, but Governor Kean modernized the office and favored the expansion of its activities into cultural areas.

Her record as secretary of state has been outstanding. In addition to the historical responsibilities of the department, which include such diverse activities as maintaining records of commercial loans and of which corporations have state licenses, presiding at ceremonial functions, and running the Division of Elections, Burgio has succeeded in bringing all the cultural agencies of state government into her department. Convinced that these agencies had something in common and would work more effectively together, she negotiated to bring the New Jersey State Council on the Arts, the New Jersey State Museum, the New Jersey State Historical Commission, the Division of Archives and Records, and the Ethnic Advisory Council into the Department of State.

She is particularly proud of her role in promoting and expanding the State Council on the Arts. Burgio, reappointed by Governor Kean in 1986, has become the leading advocate for the arts in state government. She has taken a personal interest in the council, working closely with its members. "It's wonderful," she maintains, "to have art, theater and ballet in New Jersey. So many people can't afford to go to New York." (Burgio, Interview, Feb. 19, 1986) She has also pushed for continued excellence in the State Museum, which has thrived under her leadership.

In the field of history Burgio has supported the New Jersey Historical Commission in expanding their grant-giving program to historians researching New Jersey history and to organizations promoting it. Another important project her department has undertaken is the restoration of Morven, the historic Princeton home of Richard Stockton, signer of the Declaration of Independence. Burgio wants Morven to become the Mount Vernon of New Jersey, a historic restoration attracting visitors from all over the country. She has been chair of the New Jersey Bicentennial Commission to celebrate the 200th anniversary of the U.S. Constitution. Under her leadership both art and history have become important facets of state government. Her most important long-term goal is to see a cultural center built in Newark to serve the people of New Jersey.

Burgio is also an active member of the board of trustees of both Rider College and Caldwell College and serves on the board of Planned Parenthood, a cause to which she is deeply committed.

Burgio's colleagues perceive her as a "perfect lady"—charming, thoughtful, and low-key—but they also recognize her as an astute politician. She is reputed to know what she wants to achieve and is admired for obtaining her goals through quiet, but firm, persuasion. (Celeste Penney, member of the N.J. State Council on the Arts, Interview, Nov. 1, 1986) Burgio believes that the key to success for women is patience and flexibility. "Many women," she explains, "are in a position to take advantage of new opportunities as they come along in a way that is often impossible for men." (Burgio, Interview, Apr. 29, 1986)

Burgio is proud of her accomplishments as secretary of state and would like to be remembered as "someone who managed to forge a step ahead for women." (*Trenton Times*, Mar. 31, 1985)

Interviews with Burgio on Feb. 19, 1986, and Apr. 29, 1986, provided biographical details and personal reflections. Also interviewed was Celeste Penney, a member of the New Jersey State Council on the Arts, on Nov. 1, 1986. See also "Burgio Likes Her Job, Role of 1st Woman," *Trenton Times*, Mar. 31, 1985.

*Frances D. Pingeon*

## MAY MARGARET CARTY, 1882–1958

May Margaret Carty, teacher, lawyer, legislator, and champion of equal rights for women, was born in Jersey City (Hudson County), NJ, on October 13, 1882. Her parents, Thomas Carty, an engineer, and Julia (Tooney) Carty, had emigrated from Ireland. According to her birth certificate and Jersey City population records, she was the youngest of five children. Her brothers were Frank and Thomas; her sisters, Elizabeth and Julia. Carty never married.

After graduating from Dickinson High School and Jersey City Teacher Training School, she began, in 1899, a 20-year teaching career in Jersey City public elementary schools. In 1919 Carty was appointed vice-principal of Jersey City Public School No. 29.

Carty seems to have been one of several women whose political activism was encouraged by Jersey City Mayor Frank Hague in his bid for female support in anticipation of the enfranchisement of women. Though there is no record of her activity within the suffrage movement, Carty immediately took advantage of women's new political role. In 1920 she organized the Jersey City Women's Ninth Ward Democratic Club, which she headed for 28 years. It was disbanded in 1949, following the defeat of Hague's Democratic political "machine."

In November 1923 Carty was elected to the New Jersey State Assembly. She followed two other Hudson County Democratic assemblywomen: Mrs. James A. Brown, elected in 1921; and Mrs. Neil Finn, in 1922. During Carty's seven-term tenure, through 1930, there was an average of seven women in the New Jersey assembly, primarily from urban areas. One news story in 1926 considered it important to note that Carty was the only unmarried female legislator in Trenton at the time. (*Jersey Journal*, Nov. 7, 1925)

During her time in office, Carty was an active member of several standing committees, including Education, Public Health, Judiciary, and Appropriations. In 1925 she was appointed to a special commission to investigate working conditions of New Jersey women, and in 1926 to a commission for the revision of laws restricting Sunday activities, commonly called "Blue Laws." In 1930 she was chosen minority floor leader; according to her male predecessor, Morris E. Barison (who retired to accept a judgeship), she was the first woman in the country to hold that job. (*New York Times*, Jan. 15, 1930)

Social issues and women's progress were Carty's main concerns as a legislator. She was a 1920s feminist who fought against women's second-class citizenship, economic inequalities, and legal and institutional discrimination. She introduced and succeeded in passing a bill to forbid sex discrimination in the hiring of teachers, maintaining that this was the "only equal rights bill to pass the legislature." (*Jersey Journal*, Nov. 7, 1925) She condemned the special commission set up to investigate women's working conditions, claiming that it had never met nor been given an expense appropriation. (*Jersey Journal*, May 11, 1928) It existed, she declared, as a "polite gesture" to appease women and to quiet their demands for effective enforcement of laws that would protect female workers from workplace hazards. On another issue, however, the male lawmakers were forced to concede: they approved a new woman's rest room to accommodate the increased number of women legislators and the female visitors who daily crowded the galleries.

Carty's legislative agenda included various other issues. She pressed for state funding for the Jersey City Normal School (teacher training), declaring that it was disgraceful for public monies to go only to Rutgers University, an all male school. She fought for the elimination of the 1791 Blue Laws, maintaining that the restriction of Sunday activities was hypocritical in the 1920s and only encouraged illegal actions; she also claimed that it was "class legislation," punishing the "shoeshine boy" but not his customer. For similar reasons and in line with Democratic party policy, she advocated repeal of alcohol prohibition. Other items for which she pressed included tenants' rights and divorce laws.

Carty's ability, determination, dedication, and energy were particularly demonstrated during her years in the New Jersey legislature. Several years before Carty entered the assembly, she was offered a scholarship to the New York University Law School, which at that time she was unable to accept; instead she took postgraduate courses in psychology, ethics, English, and Spanish. After one year as a legislator, however, she once again considered legal education as a positive step toward achieving her political and social goals. She entered the New Jersey Law School in Newark: the assembly was part-time, elementary school was over at three o'clock, and her law classes began at four. In addition, she continued her political activities in the Ninth Ward, her contacts and networking with other women, her speeches at women's clubs, and her support for the Democratic party, particularly the 1928 Smith presidential campaign. She passed the bar examination in 1929 and left the state assembly in 1930 (taking a leave of absence from her school) to accept a $5,000 position as law secretary to Jersey City corporation counsel Thomas J. Brogan, who later became chief justice of the New Jersey Supreme Court.

Though she did not return to teaching after 1930, Carty maintained influential connections with educators. She was appointed to the New Jersey State Board of Education, her appointment continuing under several governors. She served eighteen years as a director of the Managing Board of the North Jersey Training School for Girls at Totowa, a vocational facility for retarded girls who were considered "trainable."

In 1937 Carty was elected president of the New Jersey Federation of Business and Professional Women's Clubs (NJFBPWC), which that year voted to support the Equal Rights Amendment. A charter member of the Jersey City club, Carty had previously served as vice-president and as legislative chair of the state group. In contrast to her earlier position in the state legislature ten years before, she was now opposed to legislation that protected women only from workplace hazards. Her change was consistent with that of many other upper-class and professional women during the 1930s: they feared that such protective laws would interfere with their goal of equality with men.

Women remained split on the issue of protective legislation in 1947, the year of the New Jersey Constitutional Convention. They were divided between those groups who supported an equal rights clause for the new constitution, such as the NJFBPWC, and those who feared such a clause would negate women's protective legislation, such as the National Consumers' League and the League of Women Voters. Carty and three other female attorneys representing the NJFBPWC drew up a compromise proposal that satisfied both sides and simultaneously resulted in New Jersey becoming the first state to give equal constitutional rights to women: the word *person* was substituted for *men* in the New Jersey Bill of Rights and, further, the word *person* was explicitly defined as referring to both sexes.

Throughout her life, Carty remained committed to women and their rights. Speaking in 1928 of "Woman in Public Life," she contrasted the current woman's position with the "old days," pointing out that a woman can safeguard her home by going outside the home and taking part in politics. In 1941, after being appointed to a woman's auxiliary committee by Governor Charles Edison, Carty used her influence to arrange a meeting between a reluctant governor and the New Jersey Order of Women Legislators, who urged the appointment of women to boards, commissions, and the judiciary. Carty commented that there was much prejudice against women "but not on election day." (*Jersey Journal*, Dec. 11, 1941) In 1945 she protested that women were ignored for top administrative positions in education.

She was a member of the Women's Division of the Democratic party, the National Council of Catholic Women, Catholic Daughters of America, the Ladies Auxiliary of the Ancient Order of Hibernians, and the national, New Jersey, and Jersey City federations of the Business and Professional Women's Clubs. She also belonged to various education and legal professional groups.

She died January 24, 1958, at age 75, of pneumonia, in St. Francis Hospital in Jersey City and is buried in Holy Name Cemetery there.

NJ-RU holds the collected papers of the NJFBPWC, which provide information on Carty's work for equal rights for women. Articles about her appeared in the *Jersey Journal* (Jersey City, NJ), May 11, 1928, and the *New York Times*, Jan. 15, 1930. Her obituary appeared in the *New York Times*, Jan. 26, 1958.

*Jean Azulay*

## JEANETTE LAKE CASCONE, 1918–

Jeanette (Lake) Wilson Winslow Cascone, teacher and lecturer on African-American history, was born in Gainesville, FL, on August 10, 1918, to Minnie (Chiles) and Thomas Jefferson Lake, a contractor. The second of eight children, Cascone had a comfortable childhood until the age of eight, when her father's sudden death altered the family's situation. Cascone's mother took a job as short order cook with the University of Florida but was unable to support the family entirely through her own efforts. While the oldest sister stayed home with the three surviving younger children, Cascone took her first job washing dishes in a private home for $1.50 a week. She was so short, she recalled later, that she had to stand on a box to reach the sink. In order to make more money, she dropped out of third grade for about a year to work for several white families.

After Cascone's mother remarried in 1929, the family moved to Jacksonville, FL. In 1930 one more child was born before the marriage ended in divorce. Cascone was educated in the Jacksonville public schools, graduating from Davis Street Elementary and Stanton High. A good student, she finished high school in three and a half years but did not consider college because of insufficient funds. Her English teacher, Ruby Oats, recognized her ability, however, and the high school principal found her a full college scholarship; she entered Barber-Scotia Junior College in Concord, NC, in 1937. Two others also influenced this decision—a favorite history teacher, Lucile Horne Butler, and a white woman, Marguerite Coarsey, for whom Cascone had worked as baby-sitter and mother's helper since the sixth grade. Coarsey urged Cascone to continue her education, helped her find her first nondomestic job, and sent her funds at college from time to time. She and Cascone became lifelong friends.

In spite of the sexism and racism prevalent in American society in the thirties, Cascone never doubted that she could reach her goals as an African-American woman in the United States. Feeling limited by the employment available to her in the South, she moved to New York after graduation in 1939. For several years, however, she was forced into low-paying occupations, working as a domestic, practical nurse, hospital attendant, and store clerk.

On October 3, 1942, she married Perry Wilson, a soldier, and subsequently followed him to Washington, D.C., taking a job as a government clerk. She soon found that racial discrimination was not limited to the South or the Northeast but existed in the federal bureaucracy as well. She had to fight for her first promotion, which made her a supervisor.

In Washington she studied at Howard University, graduating magna cum laude in 1945 with a B.A. in history. Returning to New York, she took a job with the Veterans' Administration, began graduate work at New York University (NYU), and in January 1947 started teaching, first as a substitute at Junior High School No. 120 in Harlem and later as a regular teacher at Benjamin Franklin Junior High School in the Bronx (JHS No. 55).

After leaving the army, Wilson joined Cascone and went into business selling real estate and insurance. In 1951 he died suddenly from complications stemming from a blood transfusion during ulcer treatments. Six years later Cascone moved to Englewood, NJ, and married Henry Winslow, from whom she was divorced in 1963.

For 25 years Cascone taught history and social studies in the New York City school system. At Franklin School, which became increasingly African-American and Hispanic, she was particularly concerned that her minority students study not only their own history and culture but also those things important for success in the general society, subjects like French and German, the most common languages of academic research. Cascone modeled what she taught, earning an M.A. in the social sciences from NYU in 1956, doing further graduate work at City College of New York (CCNY) on a fellowship, at Hunter College, and at the University of Maine, and devoting a large part of her personal time to the study of African-American history.

Cascone's interest in history, dating from high school and heightened at Howard, led her in the 1940s to join the Council on African Affairs, where she met and worked with Paul Robeson and W.E.B. DuBois. As a young teacher she devised informal ways of including African and African-American history, not yet part of the prescribed New York City curriculum, in her courses. For several years she kept an "African house" in Englewood, providing African students with a home base and giving them assistance in coping with a foreign culture. In 1960 she requested a leave of absence to teach in Africa. "I had to go because everything about the African-American has its roots in Africa," she said later, "and I wanted to see for myself." She traveled in Ghana and spent a year in Nigeria teaching secondary and college history and training teachers. She also worked for the Ministry of Education to revise the national curriculum, making it Nigerian rather than colonial.

Returning to Franklin School in 1961, Cascone taught there three more years and was named Franklin's "Teacher of the Year" in 1964. Later she was transferred to Harlem's Stitt Junior High. In addition to her regular duties, she taught in-service courses on human rights and African-American history. From 1968 to 1971 she trained new teachers and wrote programs on African-American history, now an official part of the curriculum. She also taught adult education classes in both Manhattan and Englewood.

Meanwhile she met Anthony Cascone, son of Sicilian immigrants, machinist, active member of the steelworkers' union, and father of eleven-year-old Charles. They were married on June 12, 1966, and moved to Roselle, NJ, where they raised Charles and lived until Anthony Cascone's death in 1986.

In addition to her job and the new responsibilities of family life, Cascone continued to share her growing expertise in African-American history through classes at Staten Island Community College and New Brunswick and Edison adult schools; lectures at Columbia, Princeton, CCNY, and New York and New Jersey churches; and consultant work for boards of education throughout New Jersey, as well as for the State Department of Education. In 1971 she became a part-time lecturer in African-American history at Seton Hall University in South Orange. Retiring from the New York City system in 1972, she received a joint appointment to Seton Hall's Center for African-American Studies and School of Education. She remained there until 1984, becoming an assistant professor in 1977. Since her retirement she has continued to teach African-American history to adult education classes, the most recent at the Institute of Study for Older Adults at New York Technical College.

Cascone has belonged to many professional organizations—the Urban League, National Council for the Social Studies, American Academy of Political Science, and New York Society for Experimental Education. Since retirement she has remained active in the African Heritage Association, the National Council on Black Studies, the U.S. Congressional Black Caucus Education and Health Trusts, the Prentice-Hall Publishers Review Board, and the Association for the Study of Afro-American Life and History. She has served the latter in several capacities, including New York chapter president (1964–66), co-founder of a New Jersey branch (1967), and national president (1985).

A lifelong member of the Democratic party, Cascone ran as a peace and civil rights candidate for a state senate seat in the 1965 primary and was a McCarthy delegate to the 1968 Chicago Convention. She has been a district leader in her election district, both in Englewood and Roselle, where she currently lives. She has traveled in the United States, Puerto Rico, Canada, Western Europe, and West Africa, and attended a teachers' seminar in the Soviet Union in 1971 to study the Russian education system. Active for years in the National Association for the Advancement of Colored People (NAACP), she was a delegate to the 1962 convention in Atlanta, participated in hotel desegregation demonstrations, and served as Bergen County president in 1963–64. She is currently a member of the Heard African Methodist Episcopal Church in Roselle and the Board of Directors for the World Fellowship of Faiths. She has served Barber-Scotia College as trustee (1970–77), director of the Alumnae Association, and fund raiser for scholarships, and was named "Outstanding Alumna of the Year" in 1980.

A lifetime of studying, belief in the power of education to help people shape their own lives, and boundless energy have enabled Cascone to serve her community and state throughout her life. Her 35 years of teaching African-American history and culture have brought her awards from the NAACP, the National Council of Negro Women, and the National Association of Negro Business and Professional Women's Clubs. In 1978 she received the latter's Sojourner Truth Award. Governor Thomas Kean appointed her to the New Jersey Historical Commission's Advisory Committee, which gives annual grants for projects in African-American history. In 1984 she attended the White House reception for the annual proclamation of February as Black History Month. In 1987 the New Jersey Association of Black Educators gave her its NIA Award for distinguished leadership in education. (*Nia* is a Swahili word meaning purpose.)

When asked what principle had guided her career, Cascone replied that she had spent her life studying African-American history and culture so that she might try to teach the truth about the past. "We don't want to lose another generation to the false theories of racial and cultural superiority and inferiority. Everyone has a culture, and everyone can contribute to the welfare of society."

A personal interview with Cascone on Sept. 2, 1987, provided information for this profile.

*Ruth T. Penner*
*Vernon E. McClean*

## GLADYS ST. JOHN CHURCHMAN, 1902–1974

Gladys Elizabeth Antoinette (St. John) Churchman, a Newark, NJ, social worker whose dedicated service to community and civic affairs spanned over 40 years, was born October 28, 1902, in Ansonia, CT. She and a younger brother, Joseph Norris, were the children of Clara (Jackson) St. John, a piano teacher, and Joseph St. John.

After her family moved to Newark, NJ, in 1910, Churchman attended Washington Street Elementary School and Central High School, from which she graduated in January 1920. She then enrolled in the State Normal School, Newark (later Kean College), and in January 28, 1922, received the general course certificate, entitling her to teach.

She taught until she married James Enoch Churchman, a Newark funeral director, on November 4, 1923. James Enoch, Jr., their only child, was born on September 1, 1924. The marriage ended in divorce in 1932.

When Friendly Neighborhood House was founded in Newark in 1926, Churchman was persuaded by Stella B. Wright, one of the organizers, to devote some time to working for underprivileged children. A volunteer, she was the first secretary of the center's board of trustees.

The Neighborhood House began in a former saloon at West Kinney and Barclay streets, where hot lunches and a recreational after-school program were provided for children. Relocated in 1929 to a building at 199 Howard Street donated by Louis Bamberger, Friendly Neighborhood House did not move again until its building was razed for urban renewal in 1963. From then on, the Neighborhood House was located on Court Street in the Scudder Homes, a low-rent housing project.

Churchman graduated from volunteer to staff member in February 1931, when Louise B. Shuggard, president of the Friendly Board of Trustees, decided that her five years of free service should be recognized. After service as a group worker and assistant director, she was appointed executive director of the Neighborhood House in 1945. Energetic and enthusiastic, she continued to expand and streamline the services and programs, increasing the number of children of working parents the Neighborhood House could accommodate in its day nursery. She also instituted a full program of after-school and evening activities for children and teenagers. These activities included clubs and craft classes, skating and basketball, a teenage canteen and Scouting.

Churchman became the symbol of the Neighborhood House to generations of children who passed through it, children she watched grow into useful members of society as nurses, teachers, housewives, doctors, and social workers. A close association with the children and their parents, plus a keen interest in their needs, contributed to her success as an executive. Upon her retirement in December 1967, she said, "Young people always need love and guidance, but they need even more of it now. . . . Underprivileged children particularly need the assurance that someone cares about them, and a Neighborhood House often must fill in for parents who are unable to provide this." (*Newark News*, Dec. 3, 1967)

Churchman's work with Scouting began in 1930 when she replaced a leader who was leaving the Neighborhood House. She organized and led Girl Scout Troop 32 until 1945, when she became director of the center. As troop committee chairperson, she also served on the Board of Directors of the Girl Scout Council of Greater Essex County. Years later, a former member of Troop 32 spoke of her as having been as stern as a sergeant, but a sergeant you knew was your friend and to whom you could always turn for help. In May 1965 she was presented the "Thanks" badge, Girl Scouts' highest adult award, "for outstanding contribution to the work of the Council beyond that which is required in the normal performance of duty." (*Newark News*, May 29, 1965)

Mayor Hugh Addonizio appointed Churchman to the Newark Board of Education in May 1966, citing her as a leader of high caliber who would make a real contribution to the improvement of education in Newark. During her two terms, she chaired the board's Instruction Committee.

She lent energetic ability to other civic and social organizations as a member of the Central Ward (Newark) Juvenile Conference Committee, the Robert Treat Council of Boy Scouts of America, the Hill (Central Ward) Social Agencies' Council, Zonta International of Greater Newark, and the Trinity Chapter, Order of Eastern Star,

Prince Hall Affiliation. Churchman was also chair of the Board of Directors of the Newark City Hospital School of Nursing and a member of the Mental Health Board of Essex County.

As a member of St. Phillip's Episcopal Church and, later, Trinity Cathedral, Newark (when the two churches merged), she was active as a member of the Executive Committee of the Cathedral, the Lay Readers' Association, and a secretary of the Girls' Friendly Sponsors.

Over the years, Churchman received a number of honors, including the Annual Fellowship Award, given by the Wesleyan Service Guild of the Philadelphia District, Delaware Conference of the Methodist Church, in April 1961. In March 1959 the F. and M. Shaefer Brewing Company commended her devotion to the improvement of family life in the Central Ward. She received the *New Jersey African-American* newspaper's Honor Roll plaque in October 1956 in celebration of her 25 years as a professional at Friendly Neighborhood House. She was also included in Bamberger's Distinguished Citizens Gallery, a collection of photographs of outstanding New Jersey citizens.

Churchman died, at age 71, of a stroke in Orange Memorial Hospital on January 13, 1974. She is buried in Glendale Cemetery in Bloomfield. In recognition of her leadership, her portrait was hung in the Weequahic High School library in Newark in February 1976, and a collection of black newspapers on microfilm in the library was dedicated to her.

Churchman memorabilia, including clippings from the *Newark News*, program notes, photographs, and letters, is in the collection of her son, James E. Churchman, Jr.

*Mildred Lipscombe*

## DOROTHY ALLEN CONLEY, 1904–

Dorothy Ruth (Allen) Conley Elam, schoolteacher and advocate of African-American studies, was born in Philadelphia on July 23, 1904, the eldest surviving child and only daughter of William A. and Ruth C. (Pannell) Allen. Conley's mother, a Virginian, died when she was three and Conley became devoted to her father and foster mother, Ella Rayside, who were her models of pride, sincerity, and determination. Her father, also a Virginian, was an unschooled but enterprising real estate developer who built a home in Albion, Berlin Township, NJ, in 1907 and became the first black licensed realtor in the area. He used his position to assist other African-Americans in purchasing property in Albion, a predominantly white community.

Conley attended elementary schools in Albion and Clementon and graduated from Haddon Heights High School in 1923. She earned her teaching diploma from the Normal School at Glassboro in 1925.

Dorothy Allen Conley and her students in her West Berlin Elementary School classroom after Berlin Township schools were desegregated in 1952. *Courtesy, private collection.*

On January 7, 1925, in Camden County, she married Harry William Conley, a cook from Virginia. The couple had two sons, Harold (b. 1925) and Nathaniel (b. 1926).

In 1927 Conley began her teaching career at the Berlin Community School, a segregated two-room school for kindergarten through eighth grade. Deeply involved in the community, she visited her students at home, became a leader in the Albion United African Methodist Episcopal Church, and, over the years, spoke out on desegregation at churches and parent-teacher organizations. At the same time she reared two young sons and managed a home, responsibilities that had to be carried alone after her husband's death in 1937.

Since college Conley had pursued an interest in black history and culture. Unable to find what she sought in her college's library, she looked in local libraries and noted that she "read every book about Blacks in Camden County, because there were so few." ("Elam Discusses the History of Blacks," *Voice of the People News*) By 1941 she was working on the Camden County Executive Board of the National Association for the Advancement of Colored People (NAACP). She served on the Black History Committee of the National Sorority of Phi Delta Kappa during the 1940s and promoted radio programs that featured black artists, such as George Arthur of Lawnside, NJ. In 1947 she organized and became president of the Camden

County Inter-Cultural Council, whose primary goal was to foster understanding. She presided over the south Jersey branch of the Association for the Study of Afro-American Life and History until 1980. Under her leadership the branch promoted research, awarded citations to role models, and presented scholarships.

When the public schools of Berlin Township were desegregated in 1952, Conley was transferred to West Berlin Elementary School, where she undertook the integration of a white class. She found the change positive: "Prior to that, children from different schools were always involved in daily incidents of name calling and physical fighting. . . . Integration changed that." (Conley, Interview, Oct. 22, 1987) But an integrated class made her more and more aware of black and white youngsters' ignorance of African-American history.

Conley returned to school and earned her B.S. at Glassboro State College in 1956, while carrying a full teaching load. She then pursued both her scholarly and teaching interests through graduate study at Hampton Institute, Syracuse University, and Rutgers University. She began to develop classroom materials and to write. In 1958 her "Negro History Plan" appeared in the *Negro History Bulletin*. Particularly concerned about the passivity of black pupils about their own history, she developed lesson plans that are models not only of content but of creative ways in which to involve children in curriculum development.

While studying African-American spirituals as part of a music course at Rutgers, she was asked by colleagues about the meaning of some lyrics. She suddenly realized that she did not understand them fully. Although today it is widely known that some of the songs were codes for planned escapes from slavery, in 1961 only a few scholars had studied the subject. Conley began extensive research and wrote a script that was produced as a record in 1968, which today is a collector's item.

In 1964 Conley retired after 38 years of teaching. On March 8, 1967, she married the Rev. Arthur Elam, an active community leader, and returned to the Camden County schools to help develop African-American history units. She also began work on a pilot project for pregnant, unmarried teenagers. Traveling daily by public transportation to Camden, she taught English and counseled the girls, many of whom, despite serious problems, went on to college and productive careers. She also founded Conlam Enterprises to promote distribution of records and poems on the African-American experience. One of her publications was a book of poems (1970) by her grandson, Everet V. Conley.

Conley has received many tributes from students and colleagues, as well as awards from her college (1970), the NAACP (1983, 1984), the New Jersey State Federation of Colored Women's Clubs (1970), the Association for the

Study of Afro-American Life and History (1979), the Association of Business and Professional Women of Camden and Vicinity (1984), and the Tenth Street Baptist Church of Camden (1967). President Jimmy Carter invited her in 1980 to witness his declaration of Black History Month, a project she helped develop.

Today Conley lives alone in Albion, the community her father helped to develop. Her husband, Arthur Elam, died in 1974. Her speech to the Gloucester County Human Relations Council (Oct. 25, 1966) seems as pertinent to her own life as it is to her special subject: "Negro History must be studied, not only because it is the history of over 19 millions, but American life as a whole cannot be understood without knowing it."

An interview with Conley on Oct. 22, 1987, provided biographical information. See also "Mrs. Elam Honored for Work in Black Culture," *Courier-Post* (Camden, NJ), Feb. 23, 1970; and "Elam Discusses the History of Blacks," *Voice of the People News* (Summit, NJ), July 27, 1975.

*Rebecca Batts Butler*

## EMMA LOEHWING CONLON, 1899–

Emma Margaret (Loehwing) Conlon, textile entrepreneur and civic leader, was born on August 16, 1899, in Paterson (Passaic County), NJ. The oldest of three children, Conlon was brought up in a closely knit family. Her father, John H. Loehwing, was the son of German immigrants, and her mother, Elizabeth (Flanders) Loehwing, was a native of Bohemia (now Czechoslovakia) who had come to the United States as a young girl. The owner of a successful billiards supply store, John Loehwing encouraged his children to take advantage of all the educational opportunities that were available to them.

Conlon attended the local public schools, where she was an honors student excelling in mathematics. While growing up, she worked in her father's store, assisting him with the bookkeeping. After graduating from Paterson's Central High School in 1916, she attended the Paterson branch of Pace and Pace Institute of New York City. She interrupted her studies in 1920 to take a job as assistant treasurer with a local business, Apex Piece Dyeing Company. She became purchasing agent in 1929, when this company reorganized and changed its name to Apex Oriental Corporation.

On January 19, 1933, she married Frank T. Conlon, a salesman from Newark. After the marriage, she and her husband resided in Paterson and became deeply involved in business and civic endeavors. Dissatisfied with working conditions at Apex Oriental Corporation, Conlon and three of her male coworkers decided to form their own silk dyeing company. In February 1935 they bought out a bankrupt company, and combining their experience and capital, they formed a new business, Puritan Piece Dye Works in Paterson. Conlon became the treasurer and later the secretary-treasurer of the new concern, while her husband worked as the company's representative in the New York market. Accepting no salary for the first year of operation, the four company founders used their knowledge and skills to make Puritan Piece Dye Works a thriving business.

Conlon went on to become a leader in the textile dyeing industry. She was a trustee of the Insurance Trust of Silk and Rayon Printers and Dyers Association of America (1953–57) and served as a member of the National Production Authority's Textile Finishing and Dyeing Industry Advisory Committee (1952–56). She received national attention in 1954 when President Eisenhower appointed her to the Small Business Administration's National Board of Field Advisors.

In March 1955 Conlon sold her active interest in Puritan Piece Dye Works to her associates in the company. She then became chairman of the Board of Directors of the Colonial Piece Dye Works of North Bergen, a position she held until her retirement in 1964.

Besides her business career, Conlon, like her husband, was also active in community service. After settling in Paterson in 1933, she became involved with the Community Chest, structuring fund raisers for the YMCA and the local hospitals and serving on city-appointed boards.

In 1944 Conlon joined the Zonta Club of Paterson, an organization that was to become an integral part of her life. A women's service club, made up of business executives and professional women who devote themselves to civic and social welfare, it was in Zonta that Conlon felt she accomplished the most. She served the organization in all capacities: Paterson club president (1947–49); district governor (1949–51); second international vice-president (1952–54); first international vice-president (1954–56); and international president (1956–58). She traveled 200,000 miles visiting Zonta Clubs throughout the world. While international president, she initiated a project to form branch service clubs for high school girls and college women. These branches, known as Z Clubs, have become a popular part of the Zonta Organization. In 1961 Zonta International established an Emma Conlon Award to be given annually to the most active Z Club. Between 1958 and 1960 Conlon served as chairman of the Refugee Camp Study Committee, a project that involved six months of research with the United Nations and visits to refugee camps in West Germany. As a result of Conlon's recommendations, Zonta International raised $42,000 to help clear the refugee camps.

While president of the Paterson Zonta Club and with the full support of its members, Conlon campaigned to have women serve on the Board of Directors of the Great-

er Paterson Chamber of Commerce. As a consequence, in January 1948 she was named to fill an unexpired term on this board and for the next three years was involved in the chamber's drive to establish scholarships to help recruit nurses for local hospitals. Paterson's Mayor Michael DeVita appointed her the city's first woman Finance Board commissioner, a post she held between 1949 and 1951; and in 1953 newly elected Mayor Lester Titus appointed her to the Paterson Police and Fire Commission, making her the first woman in New Jersey to hold such a position. Largely as a result of Conlon's efforts at this time, women were being considered for and appointed to positions at all levels of Paterson's city government.

As police and fire commissioner, Conlon lobbied for adequate salary adjustments for the city's police officers. Upon learning that a policewoman, on the force for 26 years, had been repeatedly overlooked for promotion, Conlon sponsored a resolution to rectify the situation, and in July 1953 Sarah Leigh became the first woman to be appointed to the rank of sergeant in the Paterson Police Department. Conlon raised the ire of some local politicians and police personnel when she addressed the issues of police department salaries, morale, dress codes, and work shifts. But she was a popular public figure who had the support of the press, and she was reappointed in 1954 to fill a one-year unexpired term on the Police and Fire Commission. During the next few years, all of her previous recommendations regarding the Police Department were implemented.

In 1955 Conlon began a long involvement with the Memorial Day Nursery of Paterson. Founded in 1887 by the wives of Paterson's silk industrialists (see JENNIE TUTTLE HOBART), the nursery has provided child care for working mothers ever since. As a member of the nursery's Board of Directors for 25 years (1955–80), the last 13 of those years as board president, Conlon instituted a practical system of accounting for the nursery's records and saw to it that all necessary repairs and remodeling of the building were done. In the mid-1970s she insisted that the traditionally all-female Board of Directors combine with the male dominated Advisory Board to form one uniform Board of Directors that would be more responsive to the nursery's needs. Also during this same time Conlon fought against a campaign by the Passaic County government to buy the nursery property for a county parking lot. Although intense pressure was put on the nursery's Board of Directors to move the nursery out of the area, Conlon, as board president, staunchly refused to accept the proposals.

Conlon and her husband retired from their business affairs in 1964, but they both remained active in community functions. Besides continuing her affiliation with the Memorial Day Nursery, Conlon served on the Board of Trustees of the Paterson General Hospital (1966–68) and as a commissioner of the Passaic County Welfare Board

(1968–73). Her strong and mutually supportive marriage ended with Frank Conlon's death in June 1970. She had no children. After her husband's death Conlon moved from Paterson to the nearby community of Hawthorne to live with her brother, George H. Loehwing, D.D.S.

Interviews with Conlon at her home in Hawthorne, NJ, took place on July 18, 1987, and Aug. 8, 1987. Also interviewed were Georgette Hauser, executive director, Memorial Day Nursery (Paterson, NJ), Aug. 7, 1987; and Anna Freund, president, Paterson chapter of Zonta International, Aug. 5, 1987. A biography of Conlon, prepared in 1968, is available at Zonta International (Chicago).

*Jessica E. Peters*

Elizabeth Cooper, "Miss America" in 1937. Cooper, the only New Jersey woman to win the title to date, relinquished it soon after winning. *Courtesy, Miss America Pageant.*

## ELIZABETH COOPER, 1920–

Elizabeth (Cooper) Moore (known as "Bette"), Miss America in 1937, was born on August 11, 1920, in Hackettstown (Warren County), NJ, the second of three children (two girls and a boy) of Le Brun Cooper, an engineer with the New Jersey Highway Department, and his wife. Cooper attended Hackettstown High School for

three years, transferring in 1937 to the Academy at Centenary Collegiate Institute, in Hackettstown, for her senior year.

During the summer of 1937, Cooper went to Bertrand's Island, an amusement park at Lake Hopatcong, NJ. Her friends coaxed and dared her to enter a beauty contest held at the park that night. Cooper, blue-eyed, blond-haired, and five feet six inches tall, won the contest and discovered that she was entitled to compete early that fall in the Miss America Pageant in Atlantic City.

In September Cooper and her family traveled to the shore resort for the contest. On Saturday night, September 11, 1937, Cooper was crowned Miss America. The next day the seventeen-year-old winner could not be found, prompting unfounded rumors that she might have eloped with her official escort. Cooper refused to appear as Miss America, although she did show up a few days later to collect her trophy, a fur coat, and other prizes.

Cooper returned to Hackettstown, graduating in 1938 from the academy and from the two-year college program at Centenary Collegiate Institute in 1940. That summer she worked in radio in Kentucky. She taught kindergarten in 1947–48 at the Edgewood School in Greenwich, CT, and in 1949 attended Columbia University.

Cooper married William F. Moore on April 27, 1951, and had two children, William Gregory (b. 1953) and Cheryl Elizabeth (b. 1955). Her husband died in 1968 and Cooper continues to live in Westport, CT. She was the sole Miss America who did not serve in that role and is the only former Miss America who staunchly refuses to discuss the event, maintaining a very private life through her adult years.

Brief biographical information on Cooper is available from the Alumni Office, Centenary College (Hackettstown, NJ).

*Sheila Lacouture*

## MARIANNA FIDONE COSTA, 1915–

Marianna (Fidone) Costa, labor union activist, was born in Paterson (Passaic County), NJ, on August 15, 1915, the only child of Angela and Pasquale Fidone, who had emigrated from Sicily in 1914. She describes her childhood as happy, though it was not easy. Both parents worked, her father as a hod carrier and assistant mason and her mother as a stringer in a textile plant. As a child Costa learned the value of independence and shared responsibility. "My family was poor," she says. "We had to be self-sufficient to survive." (Costa, Interview, Apr. 1986)

Born with a clubfoot, Costa contracted polio at age five and needed several operations. Yet her physical problems did not defeat her. She credits her mother's courage and support for her ability to cope with her limitations. She recalls her mother as a strong woman and her home as a place where people could come for comfort. Her family was Roman Catholic and Costa was baptized and confirmed.

For a few years she lived with her family in Hackensack, NJ, where she graduated from public elementary school and completed ninth and tenth grade. When she was sixteen, she completed a one-year secretarial training program at Paterson Business College in Paterson.

In 1933, at age eighteen, Costa began working as an assistant shipping clerk at the Arrow Piece and Dye Works in Paterson, where she became a founding member of Dyers Local 1733 of the United Textile Workers (UTW).

That same year, during the textile strike in Paterson, Costa was elected to represent her plant on the strike committee as one of the 200 delegates and shop leaders who met daily to act on the reports of executive officers and various rank-and-file committees. The strike, which lasted for seven weeks and involved most of the local textile industry, launched Costa as a unionist. As a result of the protest, Dyers Local 1733 won its first contract, which included a 40-hour work week, overtime pay, and a guaranteed minimum hourly wage of 57.5 cents for men and 40 cents for women. The men and women, Costa explained, did not do the same work except in isolated cases.

Costa believed that without collective action the workers would never gain strength. She became an activist during the union's stormy, formative years and marched with hundreds of others in Washington to protest the wage codes set under the National Industrial Recovery Act of 1933. Through such efforts, the workers obtained a code for the silk and rayon industries equaling that for the cotton industry, and the organizational seeds of a national textile union were sown. In 1936 Costa attended the First International Convention of the UTW, which voted to join the new Committee of Industrial Organizations, the precursor of the CIO. She subsequently served as a delegate to each national convention until her retirement in 1952.

At the time, the continued involvement of a woman in a leadership role in the UTW was unique. Growing up, Costa had not been treated differently because she was a girl but had been encouraged to participate fully in all aspects of life as an equal to men. She gained the support of fellow workers and unionists through her capacity to see what needed doing, her ability to get things done, and sheer hard work. The only woman officer of Local 1733, she served as assistant secretary-treasurer from 1933 to 1935 and secretary-treasurer from 1935 to 1952. In 1939 her local affiliated with the Textile Workers Union of America, CIO.

For Costa, unionism represents more than bread-and-butter issues. Asked what was unique about Local 1733, she said, "We were a family starting out together with

nothing. We knew we were all in the same boat—and we worked well together." (Costa, Interview, May 1986) The union in many instances functioned as a supportive family unit in an often hostile world. Costa helped union members of Italian descent become citizens, instituting citizenship classes, encouraging them to file their applications, and volunteering to act as their witness. She worked to establish programs to help workers claim Social Security and unemployment benefits and represented members who could not speak English at workmens' compensation informal hearings. She helped organize a members' musical band.

Costa also became politically active on behalf of unionism. In conjunction with the union's Legislative Committee, she led weekly delegations to the New Jersey Assembly to lobby for workmen's compensation and unemployment benefits. Recognized as an articulate union spokesperson, she was drafted in 1936, at age 21, as the insurgent Democratic candidate for the state assembly, but was defeated in the primary. She ran again in 1949, this time as the regular Democratic candidate, losing by a narrow margin.

In 1942 she married Alfred Costa, a carpenter from Haledon. Though deeply committed to her work, Costa left her post in 1952 upon the birth of her son, Joseph. A year later her daughter, Angela, was born. She wanted both a career and a family, however, and nine years later she returned to work. Though marriage and family complicated life for her and there were times when her responsibilities overlapped, her husband gave her his full cooperation.

In 1961, when Costa returned to work as a clerk-typist and payroll clerk at Passaic County's Preakness Hospital, a pattern of unrest was developing among the country's public employees. Although they were the fastest-growing segment of the labor force, public employees had no mechanism for resolving complaints and providing working standards. Costa quickly became involved in organizing an affiliate of the American Federation of State, County and Municipal Workers, and she held in it the offices of president, secretary-treasurer, and grievance chair. By participating in the union's negotiations, she helped to obtain employer recognition, regulate salary increases, develop a grievance procedure, and provide better coverage and job security for all workers.

When Costa was 48, she studied for and earned her high school equivalency. She regrets that she did not have the opportunity to pursue her education. "Maybe I didn't strive hard enough," she says. "I could have been more productive in my life if I had become an attorney. I respect the power of the law." (Costa, Interview, May 1986)

Looking back on her life, Costa remembers serving as a member of the Greeting Committee for Eleanor Roosevelt at the international convention of the Textile Workers' Union of America in 1943, one of the highlights of her life. She is also proud of her role in making the lives of workers easier. "Fifty years ago we fought for more comprehensive Social Security benefits, unemployment compensation, welfare, pensions, paid vacations. Because of union efforts, all workers reap these benefits today." (Costa, Interview, May 1986)

In recent years, Costa has worked for the continuation of a drug plan for union retirees not covered by the state plan, coordinated the social activities of union retirees, and worked part-time as a bookkeeper for the American Labor Museum in Haledon. Still vigorous, she remains a dedicated unionist and serves as secretary-treasurer of the Retirees and Spouses Association of Dyers Local 1733.

Costa retired in August 1980 from her position at the Preakness Hospital. She lives with her husband in the Haledon home they bought in 1960.

Interviews with Costa in Haledon, NJ, in 1986 and 1987 provided useful information.

*Sondra Gash*

## MARGARET CRESWELL, 1899–1978

Margaret (Brier) Creswell Hiawatha (known as "Maggie" Creswell), New Jersey's first policewoman, was born on April 27, 1899, one of three daughters of John and Willie (Ross) Brier of Greenville, SC. Her mother was a homemaker and practical nurse and her father was a contractor; both were of African-American descent. The family was well educated and active in the Republican party.

Like that of many black Roman Catholics of her era, Creswell's religious affiliation was initially inspired by a desire for education. A Mrs. Slattery, an Irish friend of Creswell's grandmother, told Creswell of the St. Francis de Sales School in Rock Castle, VA, a school for black women run by the Sisters of the Blessed Sacrament. The school was one of the 44 schools for blacks founded and funded by Mother Catherine Drexel. After completing Greenville's Union Elementary School and her religious instruction, Creswell went to St. Francis de Sales School. An illness caused her to leave the school before she completed the course, and she graduated from Greenville's Union High School. She then returned to St. Francis de Sales for further education.

In 1917 Creswell married Berned Creswell, a local farmer, in the rectory of St. Mary's Roman Catholic Church in Greenville. They were the first blacks to be married in this white church. Berned Creswell's parents had purchased a 156-acre farm in the area and there the newlyweds built a house, hired sharecroppers to farm the land, and managed the family coal and wood yard.

At the end of World War I, Creswell and her husband moved to Atlantic City, NJ, where her husband had earlier

been employed. The couple sold their farm in South Carolina and Creswell's husband resumed his position as headwaiter at Atlantic City's Craymore Hotel. In 1919 their son, Berned Creswell, Jr., was born.

Creswell's career began in 1921 in the Mays Landing, NJ, sheriff's office. She was one of two black women hired as assistants to one of the clerks. According to Creswell, the position was arranged for her by Republican county leader Enoch L. Johnson as a result of her work for the local Republican party. Similarly, her 1924 appointment to the Atlantic City police force was a political one. After three years, on March 23, 1927, she was sworn in as a permanent member of the force, becoming the first woman on a New Jersey police force. She was active in the Republican party throughout her life.

Creswell was referred to by the press as a "copperette," who "pack[ed] a Colt 38 on her hip." She was given Badge No. 1 and assigned to the predominantly black northside. In 1934 she noted that "the northside is pretty well under control now, and the town's pretty clean. When I first went on the job the children in the colored section were running around just like fillies. The streets were full of them at all hours of the night." (*Atlantic City Press*, Feb. 2, 1934)

Creswell was characterized by colleagues and the press as being more of a social worker than a law enforcement officer. Although she worked all shifts in all weather, visited "cabarets and back-town rendezvous" searching for minors, handled "tough" Vice Squad assignments, and disarmed dangerous criminals, her first love was children. She spent much of her time dealing with what would today be called child welfare issues.

After Berned Creswell's death in an auto accident in 1925, Creswell's sister Clyde came to Atlantic City to be near her, and in 1930 her father sold his South Carolina home and settled in the city. In the mid-1930s Creswell remarried, to St. Clair Hiawatha, an Atlantic City detective and her colleague on the police force.

Creswell's commitment to bettering life for the disadvantaged took many forms. As a police officer she worked tirelessly with female juveniles and rape victims. Privately she collected food and clothing for the needy. Her son and her sister both recalled that family holiday dinners were always late because Creswell refused to come home until she had delivered baskets to the needy.

Creswell was active in many civic organizations. From 1924 she was active in the Elks Ocean Temple Lodge IBPOE of W and held two of the organizations highest honors: Past Grand Daughter Ruler and Lifetime Four-Star General. She was active in the Police Benevolent Association, the Northside Business and Professional Women's Club, the United Sons and Daughters of the British West Indies, and the Atlantic City Chapter of the National Association for the Advancement of Colored People.

When Creswell retired from the Atlantic City police

force in 1964, 500 people honored her at a dinner marking her 40 years of service. On March 14, 1978, at age 77, Creswell died in Atlantic City of a cerebral hemorrhage. During funeral services at St. Nicholas of Tolentine Church, where she was a member, she was eulogized as "a healer, a helper, and a consoler." (*Atlantic City Press*, Mar. 29, 1978) She was buried in the family plot in the Atlantic City Cemetery in Pleasantville, NJ.

Creswell's activities were covered by articles in the *Atlantic City Press*: "First Policewoman in State Appointed Here," Mar. 23, 1927; "Copperette," Feb. 2, 1934; "Well Done, Mrs. Creswell," June 4, 1975; "Maggie Creswell, Country's 1st Black Policewoman," Mar. 25, 1978; and "First Black Policewoman Mourned," Mar. 29, 1978. Interviews with Creswell's son, Berned Creswell, Jr., and with her sister Clyde Walker in Atlantic City, NJ, on Apr. 7, 1978, provided biographical details.

*Gloria H. Dickinson*

## DOROTHY CROSS, 1906–1972

Dorothy (Cross) Jensen, archaeologist and professor of anthropology, was born in Bala Cynwyd, PA, October 21, 1906, to Herbert and Marie Louise Cross. She had one brother, Radley, and a sister, Louise. Little is known of her childhood, which was spent in the Bala Cynwyd area. She earned a B.S. in anthropology from the University of Pennsylvania in 1928.

Cross worked at the University Museum, Philadelphia, from 1930 to 1938. A colleague described her in the early 1930s: "My clearest picture of her is sitting at a desk in the dirty basement of the museum, where we had to work on cataloguing, mending, studying our specimens, steadfastly working, with a cigarette always burning. . . . I admired Dorothy's patience and skill in matching and mending broken pottery." (de Laguna, Personal communication, 1987) The description is a lasting one. Those years coincided with Cross's graduate studies and overlapped with her work at the New Jersey State Museum, where she began in 1929 as archaeologist and continued in 1931 as field supervisor.

In the winter of 1931–32 Cross participated in excavations at Tell Billa and Tepe Gawra, Iraq. "Miss Dorothy Cross assumed the ungrateful task of checking all the catalogue entries and assisting in the revision of proof." (Speiser, *Excavations at Tepe Gawra*, viii) These were typical duties for a woman if she was lucky enough to be invited to join such an expedition in the predominantly male world of archaeology. Cross, however, went beyond her assigned tasks. Her study of pottery provided the only by-lined chapter in Speiser's report. Her Ph.D. in Oriental studies and anthropology was awarded in 1936 by the University of Pennsylvania, and the following year the Ameri-

can Oriental Society published her dissertation. By the time she completed her graduate studies, Cross had made two lasting contributions to Near Eastern archaeology.

On January 26, 1939, she married Paul H. Jensen, a statistical clerk with the New Jersey Board of Education. The marriage lasted until his death of a heart attack on March 4, 1957. A notice from the Archaeological Society of New Jersey at that time identified Jensen as a sustaining member of the society who had been "a helpful co-worker with Dr. Cross in the preparation of archaeological reports and writings for publication." Jensen's helpfulness extended to carrying his full share of household tasks.

Teaching at Rutgers University summer school (1936–40) not only began Cross's professional teaching career, but also was an example of her ability to manage more than one job at a time, combining teaching with the supervision of the Indian Site Survey. The fieldwork for the archaeological sites she oversaw was carried on during the summer.

In 1938 Cross became instructor of anthropology at Hunter College. She moved up through the ranks to full professor in 1961. As chair of the Anthropology Division (1950–57), "she proved to be an excellent administrator and organizer who concentrated on vital matters, could penetrate to the heart of a question, and who remained calm under pressure. She was on good terms with her associates." (Ehrich, *American Antiquity*, 409) At Hunter, she taught fifteen to eighteen hours a week, to which were added the usual teaching support activities and a daily commute from Trenton, NJ (later from Fallsington, PA), to New York City during the academic year. Cross used her married name and was known as "Jense" at Hunter Col-

Dorothy Cross Jensen, *left*, doing archeological field research with a colleague, Eugene Golomshtok, at the Abbott Farm site near Trenton, 1937. *Courtesy, New Jersey State Museum.*

lege, where a generation of students was privileged to learn from her wealth of knowledge and experience.

She was supervisor of the Indian Site Survey, a Work Projects Administration project, from 1936 to 1938. She was named archaeological adviser at the New Jersey State Museum in 1938 and retained that position until her retirement in 1965, after which she continued as consultant. From 1959 to 1967 she was supervisor of the Tocks Island Reservoir Area excavations for the National Park Service.

Under the Indian Site Survey, archaeological sites were surveyed throughout New Jersey, and a number were excavated between 1936 and 1940. Cross published the results in the *Archaeology of New Jersey* 1 (1941). She published the findings of excavating a major site, the Abbott Farm on the Delaware River bluff south of Trenton (1936–41), in the *Archaeology of New Jersey* 2 (1956): "The Abbott Farm." "As a result of her excavations, it was possible to obtain a much clearer picture of the archaeological background of New Jersey." (Ehrich, 408)

Cross continued organizing and supervising archaeological excavations throughout the state. Many of her Hunter College students were invited to do fieldwork at the sites. Thus she gained a work crew and the students gained active experience in the field. The reports of these excavations usually appeared in bulletins of the Archaeological Society of New Jersey.

Cross's activities as a specialist on Delaware Indians and New Jersey archaeology demanded a variety of research and administration skills. She served as the professional spokesperson for these interrelated fields. The archaeological laboratory, a state agency, had to be kept functioning and open to the public. When funds were tight, Cross sought volunteers. Unless detained in New York City, she was at the laboratory for part of each workday, supervising the cleaning, cataloging, storage, analysis, and eventual publication of all excavated materials. She prepared exhibits, gave lectures to local civic groups, and wrote materials such as *The Indians of New Jersey* (1953) to educate the public.

Cross was active in the Archaeological Society of New Jersey, to which she was named an honorary member in 1937. She served on the society's Executive Board from then on, and filled other offices as well. For the Eastern States Archaeological Federation, she was secretary (1938–69), program chairman (1940–60), and assistant editor (1960 on). She was also a member of, and held office in, the New Jersey Academy of Science. She remained active in all these groups until her death in 1972. At various times, she filled chairs for other professional associations to which she belonged.

Despite the work and complicated schedules, Cross was a friendly human being who seldom appeared harried or overworked. She was without a doubt a good, personable administrator who could delegate tasks. She pro-

ceeded with confidence in every undertaking. Physically, her appearance belied her sturdiness. Cross was average height with a tendency toward chubbiness. She dressed appropriately (often in clothes she sewed herself), but comfortably, thanks to her dislike of restricting undergarments. A cigarette completed the picture.

She was not given much to complaining. About her workload she once wrote, "Why can't we have 36 hour days[?] That would be about right." (Personal communication, 1953) She could get upset about those who didn't try to do a job. She could make pithy comments, but didn't cultivate permanent dislikes. She was truly concerned when friends or students had problems, helped as much as possible, but expected the individual to help him or herself as well.

The Jensen home, an old farmhouse in Bucks County, was described as a refuge from her busy career (Ehrich, 410), but more likely, it was itself another career. Besides permanent guests often in residence, almost anyone who needed shelter was welcome. Dig crews, friends, and relatives often filled the house on weekends. Cross loved to cook and accepted help in the kitchen. Meal preparation was a social gathering. She gardened and put up produce. Numerous cats and dogs, mostly outdoors, were looked upon with detached scientific interest, but she also showed concern for their welfare. For several years, rhesus monkeys were housed in floor-to-ceiling cages in the so-called "funeral parlor." The monkeys were informal subjects of primate behavior. But home was still a relaxing change from busy schedules.

Cross died of pneumonia in Trenton, NJ, on February 28, 1972, at age 65. Her health had been deteriorating because she had emphysema, but she was still actively at work at the time of her death. She had lived most of her life in the Delaware Valley and enriched it with her knowledge of its American Indians and the prehistory of New Jersey, while at the same time sharing that interest and knowledge with thousands of college students.

Cross's work is noted briefly in E. A. Speiser, *Excavations at Tepe Gawra* (1935). Correspondence from Frederica de Laguna, a colleague of Cross, on Sept. 9, 1987, provided useful insights. Obituaries of Cross, listing her publications, are: Francis P. Conant, "Dorothy Cross Jensen, 1906–1972," *American Anthropologist* 76 (1974):80–82; and Robert W. Ehrich, "Dorothy Cross Jensen, 1906–1972," *American Antiquity* 38 (1973):407–11.

*Eileen B. Ferguson*

## MARGUERITE LOFFT DE ANGELI, 1889–1987

Marguerite (Lofft) de Angeli, writer and illustrator of children's books, was born in Lapeer, MI, on March 14, 1889, the second of six children (two girls and four boys) of Shadrach George and Ruby Adele (Tuttle) Lofft. By her own account her parents were loving and her childhood happy. Her father was a photographer with a studio where he also drew pastel and crayon portraits. She loved to watch him draw and from an early age often tried it herself, but she was seldom satisfied with the results. She attended the local elementary school and loved books, especially illustrated ones. Shadrach Lofft took a job with a photographic dry plate company when, as photographer in a small town, he was unable to support his large family. He was transferred to Philadelphia, PA, when de Angeli was thirteen.

She entered Girls' High School in Philadelphia in 1904. Among her courses was a drawing class. After school she studied voice and sang in choirs. Eventually her high school studies interfered with her voice lessons, and in 1906 she left high school to dedicate herself to singing.

In 1908 she met John Dailey de Angeli (called "Dai"), a Philadelphian somewhat older than she who had taught violin. They shared a love of music and were immediately attracted to each other. After a six-week courtship they became engaged. Although de Angeli was thrilled the next year at being accepted in an opera company about to go on tour, she quit after the first rehearsal when her parents pointed out that a career in opera would entail many separations from her fiancé. After the de Angelis were married on April 2, 1910, in Toronto, Ontario, Canada (where Dai de Angeli had found a job as a salesman), she was frequently left alone for a week or two at a time while her husband was away on business. When he was home they joined friends for evenings of music, as they would throughout their marriage, with de Angeli singing and her husband playing the violin.

De Angeli bore three children in the first three and a half years of her marriage: John Shadrach (b. 1911), Arthur Craig (b. 1912), and Ruby Catherine (b. 1913). In infancy Catherine suffered from digestive problems and kidney disease. During these years de Angeli studied magazine illustrations and often had the urge to draw, but she believed her household duties did not allow time. She did continue to sing in choirs, however.

In 1914 the de Angelis moved to Collingswood (Camden County), NJ, where her parents were then living. There the de Angelis' daughter Catherine died suddenly in March 1915 of an undetermined infection. The following year they moved again when Dai de Angeli accepted a job in Detroit, MI. In Detroit de Angeli attended art classes; through sketching and oil painting she discovered much about color and her own style.

In 1918 she convinced her husband to move back to New Jersey. They settled in Collingswood, and he got a job at the Philadelphia Naval Base. De Angeli contracted flu in the great epidemic of 1918 and in the midst of her illness delivered their fourth child, a daughter named Nina.

Her career as an illustrator began in 1921 when she met her neighbor, illustrator Maurice Bower. He agreed to critique her work and set her on a program of drawing three scenes over and over for a year. He also advised her to give up choir singing if she was serious about being an artist. It was just the kind of encouragement and discipline de Angeli needed to get started. She set up a studio in her dining room, where she worked whenever she could find time. At the end of the year Maurice Bower sent her to an editor at Westminster Press, who gave her a story to illustrate. Over the next fourteen years she illustrated numerous Sunday school papers, magazines, and children's books.

During these years de Angeli gave birth to a son, Harry Edward, in 1925, and another son, named after her mentor, Maurice Bower, in 1928. She tried to be available to her children even while she worked. Once, when one of them wanted to be with her, she moved his playpen into her studio. When that didn't satisfy him, she put herself and her easel in the playpen and gave him the run of the studio.

When the Depression began in 1929 de Angeli's husband was out of work, and she became the main supporter of the family. In 1932, unable to make payments on the Collingswood house in which they had lived for thirteen years, the de Angelis moved first to Jarrettown, PA, then to Jenkintown, PA. For a while Dai de Angeli's elderly mother and deaf sister lived with them. The strain of intergenerational conflict and too little time for her art led de Angeli to a nervous breakdown, from which it took her a year and a half to recover fully.

Her career took an important turn in 1934 when Helen Ferris of the Junior Literary Guild suggested that she write and illustrate a book for very young children. The artist, eager to write as well as draw, welcomed the encouragement. Doubleday children's book editor Margaret Lesser accepted her book *Ted and Nina Go to the Grocery Store* (1935) and asked for a sequel.

Margaret Lesser, who became de Angeli's longtime editor and friend, next suggested that she write about the Pennsylvania Dutch. That started her writing and illustrating the kinds of books for which she was gifted and that won her many awards. It also made her one of the first to write books for children about minority groups. These include *Henner's Lydia* (1936) and *Yonie Wondernose* (1944), about the Pennsylvania Dutch; *Petite Suzanne* (1937), about French Canadians; *Thee, Hannah!* (1940), about Quakers of Philadelphia; *Elin's Amerika* (1941), about Swedes in colonial Pennsylvania; and *Up the Hill* (1942), about Polish miners in Pennsylvania. Her stories, although set in unfamiliar cultures, are about children with common foibles in happy and loving families; they let children comfortably enter a different world and learn the universality of human feeling. De Angeli's thorough on-site research for each book provided the stories and pictures with authenticity. Cornelius Weygandt, then professor of English at the University of Pennsylvania, wrote to her that upon reading *Henner's Lydia* he "wept because it took him back to his childhood in the Dutch country." (de Angeli, *Butter at the Old Price*, 137)

De Angeli illustrated her early books by the tedious but economic process of making her own color separations. By 1939 her books were selling so well that her publisher allowed her to switch to watercolors and to pencil drawings, which require engraving. Her illustrations won consistent praise for their charm and good composition, and for perfectly reflecting the warmth of her stories. The children in them tend to "have always the same little heart-shaped faces and wistful beauty, but they also have a skipping gaiety which is natural to childhood." (Sutherland and Arbuthnot, *Children and Books* 343)

De Angeli's first significant historical novel, *Skippack School*, about an 18th-century Mennonite schoolmaster, was published in 1939. De Angeli was then 50 years old but still had two children at home. Sometimes, when she regretted that their care kept her from her work, she would remember a happy day in her own childhood and think, "Perhaps *this* will be one of those days my children will remember. I'd better make it a *good* one!" (de Angeli, *Butter at the Old Price,* 163)

As early as 1940 de Angeli had wanted to do a book about a black child in a white community, but Doubleday's Margaret Lesser felt it was too controversial. By 1942 the editor had changed her mind. De Angeli wanted to deal with the memory of slavery, but after talking with many African-Americans she realized she must write of the prejudice they currently suffered. Her *Bright April* (1946) broke literary ground by confronting racial prejudice directly. Although some reviewers felt it made its point too directly, it received generally favorable reviews and was honored at the 1946 *Herald Tribune* Children's Book Festival.

The success of de Angeli's books allowed the de Angelis in 1938 to build a vacation cottage two blocks from the river in Toms River (Ocean County), NJ. Over a period of seventeen years they vacationed there, with their children and grandchildren, and they lived there year-round from 1946 to 1950. During that time de Angeli got the idea for a story set on Money Island, the part of Toms River where they lived. The story, *Jared's Island* (1947), tells of a Scottish boy shipwrecked on the Barnegat shoals in the early 1700s.

*The Door in the Wall* (1949), about a crippled boy in 14th-century England, is generally regarded as de Angeli's finest work. The theme of the story reflects her philosophy that "when you come to a stone wall, if you look far enough, you will always find a door in it." (de Angeli, *But-*

*ter at the Old Price*, 185) *The Door in the Wall* won the prestigious Newbery Medal in 1950.

Although the de Angelis continued to vacation in Toms River until 1955, they moved to Philadelphia in 1950 and later to rural Sumneytown, PA, to be close to their sons. When Dai de Angeli died in 1969, the de Angelis had been married almost 60 years.

De Angeli continued to produce children's books throughout her seventies and eighties. Her autobiography, *Butter at the Old Price*, was published in 1971 when she was 82 years old.

In her later years de Angeli lived in retirement in Philadelphia. She died there, at age 98, on June 16, 1987, and was buried in Red Hill, PA. De Angeli's sympathetic books about minorities, her accomplished historical fiction, and her appealing illustrations have earned her a respected name in children's literature.

De Angeli's autobiography is *Butter at the Old Price* (1971). Clippings and manuscripts are available at the P-FLP and the Kerlan Collection, University of Minnesota. For accounts of her life and work, see *Dictionary of Literary Biography*, vol. 22 (1983); Zena Sutherland and May Hill Arbuthnot, *Children and Books* (1986); and *Something about the Author*, vol. 27 (1982). De Angeli's obituary appeared in the *Philadelphia Inquirer*, June 18, 1987.

*Maggie Sullivan*
*Jill Trask*

## GERALDINE OWEN DELANEY, 1907–

Although she was born in Stonington, IL, Geraldine (Owen) Delaney has spent the last 40 years and the major part of her career as a pioneer in the treatment of alcoholism and drug addiction in New Jersey. She is the only daughter and second surviving child of Jesse Belle and Maureen (Hisel) Owen. Her father was a bank president and owner of several coal mines and lumber mills. Delaney remembers her mother as the town "belle" who sent her daughter to high school in Decatur, IL, because she did not think the school in Stonington was good enough. Delaney later attended Knox College in Galesburg, IL, and then in 1926 transferred to the University of Illinois, where she majored in nutrition. She had to leave school in 1927, however, when her father's business failed. He sold his lumber and mining interests and went to work in the lumberyards to pay off his debts, which he accomplished before his death in the early 1950s.

Delaney went to Chicago and supported herself by working in a hotel and by doing medical editing, which she had begun in college. Through her editorial work she met C. Anderson Aldrich, professor of pediatrics at Northwestern University, whom she credits with having a major influence on her later work in alcoholism treatment by teaching her the value of observation. When Aldrich became the first secretary of the newly founded American Board of Pediatrics in 1934, Delaney became its first part-time employee. By 1937 she worked full-time for the board, which sets standards for the certification of pediatricians in the United States.

Delaney accompanied Aldrich in the early 1940s to the Mayo Clinic to help him with a demonstration project on prenatal care. By that time she had developed a serious problem with alcohol and other drugs but was diagnosed by several psychiatrists as merely overworked and underpaid. When the American Board of Pediatrics moved its offices to Des Moines, IA, Delaney was offered a year's leave of absence with full pay, which she drank up in six months. Out of work, in debt, and in trouble with alcohol and drugs, she realized she had "hit bottom." Her older brother, Oscar, a professor at Rutgers University and a recovered alcoholic himself, brought her to his home in Maplewood, NJ, in 1947. After coming to New Jersey she never drank alcohol again.

Through her contacts on the Board of Pediatrics, Delaney was able to get a job at St. Michael's Hospital in Newark, setting up equipment for cancer patients. She began her work with alcoholics there by persuading hospital officials to let her put in three beds for male alcoholics. In 1948, while still at St. Michael's, she began working with the Essex County Service for the Chronically Ill. There she developed with Marion A. Yaguda an innovative program to provide nonmedical housekeeping assistance for persons with long-term or chronic illness. This Homemaker Service, now called the Home Health Aid Service, served as a model for similar programs in other counties in New Jersey.

In 1949 Delaney was appointed executive director of the Essex County Service, later renamed Chr-Ill; she served in that post until her resignation in 1963. Also in 1949 she married Thomas Francis Delaney, a contractor specializing in underground conduits. She began to work more seriously with alcoholics, and in 1951 she founded the Chr-Ill Council on Alcoholism to provide information about alcoholism and referral for treatment. The Chr-Ill Council became the first New Jersey affiliate of the National Council on Alcoholism. Delaney was especially concerned about the risks of poly-addiction among women. Her own earlier experiences had convinced her of the dangers of prescription and over-the-counter drugs frequently used by women, often in conjunction with alcohol. She brought attention to this fact in her work with the Chr-Ill Council and in her subsequent efforts in alcoholism treatment.

In the late 1950s Delaney became the owner of a fledgling alcoholism treatment facility. According to Delaney, she had provided assistance to the previous owner through unsecured loans, and when the owner suddenly died Delaney was left with the property, a pleasant rural site near

Blairstown, NJ. With the help of her husband until his death in 1969, Delaney turned Little Hill-Alina Lodge into a detoxification and short-term treatment center for alcohol and drug addiction. Later, as more short-term facilities were developed around the country, she shifted the focus of her program toward the "reluctant to recover," persons who had been unable to stay sober through other programs.

Delaney's recovery program is based on a "nonpermissive" approach that involves a strict regimen of rest, regular meals, education on alcoholism and drug addiction, and most important, on how to survive and remain abstinent in a "world oriented to the instant cure." (*Motor Club News*, 3) Her patients are called students, and she requires absolute adherence to all rules of conduct. Although the facility is coed and accepts patients eighteen years and up, fraternization between the sexes is forbidden because it is seen as an impediment to the early stages of recovery. Her program draws heavily on the concepts of Alcoholics Anonymous and its twelve-step plan for developing a sober lifestyle. The minimum stay at Little Hill-Alina Lodge is three months, with students sometimes remaining as much as one year.

In the years since Delaney took over Little Hill-Alina Lodge, she has engineered a number of innovative programs, such as education and counseling for families of alcoholics and drug abusers and treatment for poly-addicted patients. She has lectured before community and professional groups around the country and has served as an instructor at the Rutgers University Summer School of Alcohol Studies. For the past 30 years she has been the trustee and chief executive officer of the Little Hill Foundation, which operates Little Hill-Alina Lodge, and she has donated the land on which the lodge and foundation offices stand to the foundation. Since 1975 she has served by gubernatorial appointment on the New Jersey State Advisory Council on Alcohol Problems, and in 1985 she was appointed to the Advisory Board of the U.S. Alcohol, Drug Abuse and Mental Health Administration. Among the many honors and awards she has received during her long career are the Annual Achievement Award of the New Jersey Task Force on Women and Alcohol (1979), Outstanding Woman of the Year Award from the Business Women's Clubs of Essex County (1979), an honorary doctorate of humane letters from Seton Hall University in 1979, and Citizen of the Year Award from the Carrier Foundation in New Jersey (1980). Shortly after her 80th birthday she was presented with the Distinguished Service Award by the Rutgers University Summer School of Alcohol Studies (1987).

When asked to reflect on the events that most influenced her long and productive career, Delaney credited her father's financial difficulties in the late 1920s. Without that economic incentive, she feels that she might have drifted even further into alcohol and drugs rather than pursuing a career and making the professional contacts that ultimately led to her pioneering work in the treatment of addictions.

Delaney's "Little Hill-Alina Lodge: Nonpermissive Treatment of Alcoholics and Polyaddicts," in Vincent Groupe, ed., *Alcoholism Rehabilitation: Methods and Experiences of Private Rehabilitation Centers* (1978), describes her program. Her work with women alcoholics was detailed in Don Murray, "The Housewife's Secret Sickness," *Saturday Evening Post* 235 (Jan. 27, 1962):80–83. An essay in the Christopher D. Smithers Foundation's *Pioneers We Have Known in the Field of Alcoholism* (1979) covers her career from 1948 to the late 1970s. An interview with Delaney on June 25, 1987, supplied additional details.

*Penny Booth Page*

## ADÈLE DE LEEUW, 1899–1988

Adèle de Leeuw, author of 75 books, primarily for young adults, was born August 12, 1899, in Hamilton, OH. Her father, Adolph Lodewyk de Leeuw (1861–1942), an engineer and inventor with more than 50 patents to his credit, came to the United States from Zwolle, the Netherlands. Her mother, Katherine Caroline (Bender) de Leeuw (1870–1965), a native of Hamilton and a schoolteacher until her marriage, taught her children to read before they started school.

De Leeuw always wanted to be a writer. Her sister, Cateau (b. 1903), always wanted to draw. An artist who studied and maintained studios in New York and Paris, Cateau de Leeuw, encouraged by her sister, became an author in her own right. "We told each other stories beginning at the ages of three and seven. . . . On rainy days we could tell several installments. . . . [It was] pure heaven for . . . the story-teller." (de Leeuw, "The Three Questions," 51) Adele and Cateau collaborated on a number of books, most for children and young adults. Until Cateau's death on June 2, 1975, the sisters were constant companions.

In 1914 the family moved to a Victorian mansion in Plainfield, NJ, the city where de Leeuw lived for the rest of her life. She graduated from Hartridge School for Girls in Plainfield. When her parents gave her the choice of travel with the family or college, de Leeuw picked travel, and she retained vivid memories of that "magical" time. (Kunitz and Haycroft, *Junior Book of Authors*, 99) She learned to speak Dutch, French, German, and Malayan.

Between travels, de Leeuw worked at the Plainfield Public Library as an assistant librarian. She began story hours for children, with her sister drawing pictures on a blackboard to illustrate them. "Some of my happiest memories are of seeing those rows and rows of upturned faces, and of watching them storm downstairs afterwards to get books" with stories like those they'd just heard. (Kunitz, 99)

She took a business course and from 1920 to 1927 worked in Manhattan, for her father, a consulting engineer. He was often away, which gave her the time to write. She did reviews for a theater club, interviews, editorials for the *Herald Tribune* and the *Sun*. When Adolph de Leeuw closed his office, she turned to writing seriously—books, stories, travel articles, and poetry.

The family had visited the Netherlands, her father's birthplace. Her first book, *The Flavor of Holland* (1928), based on their experiences, was so useful to one traveler, an editor at Macmillan's, that de Leeuw was asked to "give a picture of a country but in novel form—for young people." (Kunitz, 99) She did three travel novels for girls and then began a series of "career" novels, each introducing a different profession. The idea for the first, *A Place for Herself* (1937), derived from a clipping about a young girl who turned a discarded trolley car into a shop and from de Leeuw's secret desire to run a bookstore.

She dealt with both contemporary problems and inspiring, historical figures. Her biographies for young people included *Edith Cavell, Nurse, Spy, Heroine* (1968), *Marie Curie* (1969), and *Maria Tallchief* (1970). In *Doctor Ellen*, published in 1943 for teenagers and republished as *A Choice of Angels* for adults, she tried to give young people a positive, affirmative view of what being a doctor is all about. In *Linda Marsh* (1943), written when de Leeuw was doing volunteer work for the Office of Civilian Defense and the Ration Board, a young girl adapts to wartime conditions. She often tackled controversial material. *In the Barred Road* (1952), published before the Supreme Court's decision in Brown v. Board of Education, Topeka, KS, a high school girl takes a stand against discrimination.

She produced two books of poetry: *Berries of the Bittersweet* (1924), which the *Saturday Review* said was "as serene as unused dynamite," and *Life Invited Me* (1936), dedicated to her mother.

She did extensive research before she began to write, producing as many as "100,000 words of notes for a 28,000 word book." (de Leeuw, *Remembered with Love*, 52–53) When she collaborated with her sister, Cateau did the research and Adele wrote. Together, they wrote books for young adults, a cookbook, and an Executive Book Club selection, *Make Your Habits Work for You* (1952). They saw a connection between their father's problem-solving inventions and his use of the subconscious and their own work. "We consciously did all our research . . . ; we told ourselves when we wanted to begin and how long the books should be, and when we wanted to be finished, and then we sat down at our IBM's with a mind clear of everything but the flow from brain to paper, and let ourselves go. . . . We never missed a deadline." (de Leeuw, *Remembered with Love*, 50–51)

Always active in community affairs, de Leeuw inaugurated a three year series of theatrical and musical events, on a subscription basis, called Thursdays at Eight, in the Tri-County Arts Center, a building she owned. She began Words and Music, a group of professional writers and musicians, who still meet regularly after eighteen years to share their work. She wrote columns for a local newspaper, the *Courier News,* and occasionally for the New Jersey section of the *New York Times.*

De Leeuw was on the board of directors of the New Jersey Theatre Forum, chair of the Rutgers University Advisory Council on Children's Literature, president of the Plainfield Symphony Auxiliary, and was a member of several author's organizations, including the Authors League and the Pen and Brush.

A supporter of the Equal Rights Amendment (ERA), she had been a feminist "since I was 10 years old." (Lesher, "80-year-old Author") She felt that "women have been backward in pushing for those rights," noting that "some women don't care about ERA." She believed that women should work for the rights of other women.

After her sister's death in 1975 she produced a memoir, *Remembered with Love: Letters to My Sister,* a recollection of the life they shared and a celebration of her sister and her parents, whose "perfect love story, complete with happy ending . . . a true marriage in every sense of the word . . . was a kind of leitmotif to our own lives." Neither sister married. "We had such a great example before us of what marriage *could* be that we were discouraged from trying to make one like it." (de Leeuw, *Remembered with Love,* 140) Elsewhere she said, "I don't know whether I could have managed marriage and career. Personally I preferred a career. There are no distractions. One problem is that men don't have to choose, but women do." (Lesher)

She was aware of her own good luck. "And [my sister and I] *were* lucky . . . in so many ways of life . . . in our parents, and our trips, and our dogs, and our home life. And above all, in each other." (de Leeuw, *Remembered with Love,* 121) Though her sister found membership in the Unitarian Fellowship useful, de Leeuw attended only occasionally. She found it impossible to believe in a resurrection or an afterlife. "Both of us felt . . . that it was important to live the life we knew to the fullest, enjoying each day . . . , making the most of our talents and our good fortune, rather than to look to some improbable future where we would be rewarded." (de Leeuw, *Remembered with Love,* 114–15)

She remained active in her eighties, working on new books, arranging programs for Words and Music, conferring with the Advisory Committee for Children's Literature, volunteering at the McCutcheon Boarding and Nursing Home in North Plainfield, and in the summers traveling to Cape Cod. She died on June 12, 1988, of cancer of the colon, at age 88, at her home in Plainfield.

Material on de Leeuw appears in Stanley Kunitz and Howard

Haycroft, *Junior Book of Authors* (1951), and in *Something about the Author* (1983). Additional information comes from de Leeuw's *Remembered with Love: Letters to My Sister* (1982); her article "The Three Questions," *Ohioana Quarterly* 2 (1959):50–53; and from a personal interview with de Leeuw on Mar. 11, 1987. Also useful is Tina Lesher, "80-year-old Author Still Very Busy," *Plainfield* (NJ) *Courier News,* Nov. 16, 1979. Her obituary appeared in the *New York Times,* June 14, 1988.

*Marjorie Keyishian*
*Annemarie Kraume Hayles*

## LINI DE VRIES, 1905–1982

Lena (Moerkerk) Fuhr Stoumen (who later in her life used the name Lini de Vries), public health nurse and humanitarian, was born in Paterson (Passaic County), NJ, on July 25, 1905, the oldest of two daughters of Dutch immigrants, Leonard and Elisabeth (de Vries) Moerkerk. Her sister, Elisabeth, was born in 1913. De Vries's father was a furnace stoker and her mother, a Dutch Reform convert from Judaism, was a homemaker. Theirs was a Dutch-speaking household in Prospect Park, a suburb of Paterson that had had substantial Dutch immigration since 1850.

One of de Vries's first memories as the daughter of immigrants was of sitting in the corner of the schoolroom with a dunce cap on her head. Speaking no English, she had been unable to follow the teacher's directions and was punished. Though she yearned to attend high school, she was sent to work in silk mills after she graduated from the sixth grade. Despite this early discouragement, de Vries respected and desired education throughout her life.

De Vries's description of her mill work in her autobiography, *Up from the Cellar,* is a rare printed account by a Paterson silkworker of her work and experience in the mills. Even though she was a young teenager at the time, the legacy of labor militancy exhibited by Paterson's silk labor force influenced her lifelong identification with the working class, for it was in 1919, while she was a mill worker, that Paterson silkworkers won the eight-hour workday. While de Vries struggled with feelings of inferiority as a "mill dolly" and longed to be accepted as a "real American," she developed a heightened sense of herself as a part of history.

Several times, as a girl and later in her life, de Vries visited her relatives in Holland and explored her Dutch and Jewish origins, which she valued deeply. As a young woman she sought to be financially independent so she could leave home and escape the conflict she experienced with her mother, with whom she was bitterly antagonistic. She began working for the telephone company in Paterson in 1921 and then in 1925 entered nurse's training at New Rochelle Hospital School of Nursing in New Rochelle, NY. Becoming a nurse was a proud achievement for de

Vries, and nursing became the basis for her later career in public health.

On June 5, 1928, after graduating from nursing school, de Vries married Wilbur Fuhr of Port Chester, NY, who was in his family's dairy business. Their daughter, Mary Lee, was born in 1930. De Vries was uneasy being part of a privileged social class that looked down on the ethnic poor and she soon became involved with the Port Chester Visiting Nurse Association. She also became interested in the issue of family planning and was affiliated with a birth control clinic in Port Chester that was an extension of the Margaret Sanger Clinic in New York City. When Fuhr died unexpectedly in 1931, de Vries found a way to care for her baby and work part-time as a school nurse while she fulfilled her high school requirements. She graduated from Port Chester High School in 1932.

De Vries went on to study at Teachers College, Columbia University. While in New York City she was absorbed into an intellectual and social community that included strong international and progressive elements. Like many young idealists of the time, she joined the Communist party, an action that was to cast a long shadow over her career.

Led by her idealism, de Vries volunteered as a nurse in the Spanish Civil War, sailing in January 1937 with the first group from the American Medical Committee to Aid Spanish Democracy. After working in a hospital at Costillejo for several months, she was asked to undertake a lecture tour on behalf of the medical unit, and she returned to the United States in May, lecturing for about four months.

From late 1937 until 1949 de Vries's life was punctuated and troubled by frequent moves and job changes within the field of public health nursing. In her autobiography she recounts that during this period she was frequently investigated by the FBI, which was suspicious of her activity during the Spanish Civil War. Seeking meaningful work as well as a beneficial climate for her daughter, who suffered from rheumatic fever, she lived in New Mexico, Puerto Rico, Washington, D.C., Chicago, and finally Los Angeles. She worked in rural health projects, in maternal and infant health care, in venereal disease clinics, and with migrant workers, often as an innovator and organizer of new programs. Between jobs she was able to complete a degree in public health at Teachers College in 1942.

De Vries was married a second time in January 1943 in Chicago to Lou Stouman, a photographer she had met in Puerto Rico. When Stouman went abroad as a war correspondent de Vries moved to Los Angeles, where she organized a health program for *braceros*, or Mexican migrant workers, under the auspices of the Department of Labor. This job she claimed to have liked more than any other she had had. She succeeded in greatly reducing illness and accident rates and in instituting recreational programs and English lessons for the workers.

After the war de Vries was joined by Stouman in San Francisco and her second daughter, Toby, was born in 1946. The marriage foundered, however, and de Vries and Stouman separated in 1947. Then in 1948, when Elizabeth Bentley, the self-styled "spy queen," published her sensational testimony about her activities, she exposed de Vries's membership in the Communist party. A series of jobs lost or compromised by the persistent attentions of the FBI led her to decide to move to Mexico, where other veterans of the Spanish Civil War had sought refuge. In December 1949 she flew to Mexico with her younger daughter to begin a new life.

De Vries lived and worked in Mexico for more than 30 years. Her pioneering work in public health, high in the mountains above Oaxaca, is vividly chronicled in her autobiography. She was involved with public health work undertaken, along with anthropological study, among the indigenous peoples to be displaced by the building of the Pappaloapan Dam. Astride a mule, she ascended mountain trails still largely inaccessible today. Much of her teaching about germ theory, maternity, leprosy, and typhoid was achieved through the medium of lively puppet plays using puppets dressed like the villagers themselves.

In later years de Vries taught and organized educational programs in Mexico for students from the United States. FBI and CIA interest in her activities continued, and trips to the United States were made difficult by problems obtaining visas.

In 1962 de Vries became a citizen of Mexico. During her years there, she lived in Oaxaca, Mexico City, and Jalapa. She was involved in innovative university and community-based programs that sought to give North Americans an understanding of Mexico and Central America. She maintained connections with the artisans and educators of Oaxaca and ran a small shop, or *tiendita*, in her home where she sold the local handicrafts to foreign visitors.

In later years failing health limited de Vries to her home and gardens in Cuernavaca. But the power of her personality and her impulse to bring about connections between people was as undiminished as was her interest in ideas and books.

Lini de Vries returned to northern New Jersey, where her sister lived, for elective surgery in March 1982. She died there, at age 76, at Valley Hospital in Ridgewood on March 27 after a series of strokes following surgery. She was buried in Fair Lawn Memorial Cemetery.

De Vries's papers, including her Spanish Civil War diary, the manuscript of her autobiography, and photographs, are available at M-SL. Her autobiography is *Up from the Cellar* (1979). Her membership in the Communist party was exposed in Elizabeth Bentley, *Out of Bondage* (1951). Taped interviews with De Vries took place between Jan. 6 and Mar. 1, 1982, in Cuernavaca, Mexico. Her obituary appeared in the *New York Times*, Apr. 3, 1982.

*Judy Long*

## GERALDINE ROCKEFELLER DODGE, 1882–1973

Ethel Geraldine (Rockefeller) Dodge, philanthropist, dog breeder, art collector, and founder of the Geraldine R. Dodge Foundation, was born on April 3, 1882, into one of America's most prominent business and philanthropic families. She was the youngest of four surviving children (two daughters, two sons) of William and Almira Geraldine (Goodsell) Rockefeller, and the niece of John D. Rockefeller. Her German and Welsh ancestors emigrated about 1720 and 1673. Her father was president of the Standard Oil Company of New York and an investor. Her mother was dedicated to her family and charities, and was a strict, meticulously well-organized household manager.

Dodge was born at her parents' home on Fifth Avenue and 54th Street in Manhattan. The family had estates in North Tarrytown, NY; Jekyll Island, GA; and the Adirondacks. She attended Miss Spence's School in New York and toured Europe in her own car. Her secretary Mary Jane Ellis and her husband's cousin Grace Mead felt her childhood made her very private and self-sufficient.

On April 18, 1907, she married Marcellus Hartley Dodge, who had inherited part ownership of four companies and was a Phelps Dodge heir. His fortune was estimated at $60 million, hers at more. Marcellus Hartley Dodge, Jr., their son, was born in 1908.

In 1916 Dodge's father bought the couple an estate with a 35-room mansion on Route 24 in Madison, NJ, and Dodge became a meticulous estate manager, supervising a large staff. Giralda Farms, with its wild and domestic animals and large acreage, was a refuge for her.

Feelings of community responsibility led Dodge to donate generously to Madison and area agencies, hospitals, and churches. She gave anonymously to many individuals, and in 1961 she received the Benemerenti Papal Medal for gifts to a Catholic hospital and church. Madison honored her at a dinner in 1950; its Rotary Club named her Citizen of the Year in 1953.

As her son was growing up, Dodge developed a well-maintained kennel at Giralda and entered dog shows. Fiercely competitive, she won more than 180 championships and obedience awards with her dogs and more than 200 Best of Show. She was one of the world's foremost breeders of the shepherd (and about 80 other breeds at her Princeton facility). She was the first woman to judge Best of Show at the Westminster Kennel Club (1933). In praising her, the *New York Herald Tribune* noted critics' doubts that any woman could "remain in command."

Dodge co-founded the Morris and Essex Kennel Club and sponsored 26 famed shows from 1927 to 1957 (war years excepted) for what was the world's largest one-day dog show. In 1939 nearly 50,000 spectators watched as 4,456 dogs were shown.

She founded, in 1939, St. Hubert's Giralda, which developed into an animal shelter and education center. She built the complex on sixteen Giralda acres in 1958. The shelter, which has received several commendations, provides animal warden service for nine communities.

She wrote the book *The English Cocker Spaniel in America* (1942) and coauthored *The German Shepherd Dog in America* (1956). She was named Dogdom's Woman of the Year, and of the Half Century (1949).

Dodge's father coached her on finance; she was an apt pupil. Shocked by her husband's $9–10 million loss when Russian Czar Nicholas II was deposed (1917) and an arms sale to one of her husband's companies was voided, she took over her own finances. She spent Tuesday to Thursday in New York City, dealing with brokers and art dealers, lunching with relatives and friends, seeing operas and movies, and shopping (she favored tailored tweed suits, hats for her closely coiffed hair, and sensible shoes).

When Dodge was away, her husband moved to his nearby, more comfortable family home, Hartley Farms. The Dodges had different interests; the two houses let them pursue these but be together when they wanted to be.

In 1922 Dodge's father died, leaving an estate of over $100 million in trusts. Dodge then built a 35-room mansion and complex at Fifth Avenue and 61st Street. After her brothers died, Dodge became one of four trustees of her father's estate, with definite ideas on how the trusts should be run.

She told her secretary "never forget 60-40," which Ellis said meant 60 percent bonds and 40 percent stocks, or vice versa. She disagreed sometimes with her famous nephews. Her relatives would ask her to contribute to a charity; she would say, "I'll support yours if you'll support mine." (Ellis, Interview, 29) Dodge checked meticulously on the many requests for contributions. She could be very generous but was capable of turning requests down flat. Through careful stewardship, she supported her causes, yet increased her estate to about $85 million.

Like other Rockefellers, she was an avid, eclectic art collector. She frequented New York galleries and auctions. "She was very unhappy if we had nothing to show her each week," said a dealer. (Seiberling, "The Artful Dodge," 49) "So we hustled to find what she liked before Thursday rolled around." When the dealer's business slowed in the Depression, Dodge sent him her collection of salable Remington bronzes, asking only that he turn a good profit for himself.

The Dodges were profoundly affected when a car accident killed their beloved son, Marcellus Hartley, on August 29, 1930. Dodge gave Madison a municipal building, the magnificent Hartley Dodge Memorial, during the peak of the Depression. She checked every detail. She and her husband provided furnishings, art, and a maintenance fund.

Dodge once commented that when she was first married, she loved going out and her husband didn't, but that this reversed. Ellis felt that grief caused Dodge to bury herself in work and see friends quietly, whereas her husband, a warm, kind gentleman, coped by entertaining.

The Dodges were friendly with several American presidents. The Eisenhowers spent weekends at Hartley Farms and viewed Giralda's art. One of the Dodges is rumored to have contacted President Eisenhower (Interior officials were also contacted), opposing a Great Swamp jetport.

As years passed, Dodge rarely left Giralda except for family weddings. The couple increasingly lived apart. They met for meals and church. Dodge found solace in her Episcopal church and a nearby Catholic church.

Dodge's last ten years were characterized by illness and legal battles. In one case, the state supreme court denied Elmira College, which had awarded her a doctorate of humane letters (1960), her art collection.

Dodge died at Giralda Farms on August 13, 1973, ten years after her husband's death. She reportedly turned away relatives and friends in her last years.

Final battles involved her last will's legality and executorship. Her will suggested she wanted a museum built in Madison, but this was not done. St. Hubert's kept a fraction of her animal bronzes, but her other artworks were sold.

The prestigious Sotheby Parke Bernet Galleries of New York ran twelve of the largest, most diverse auctions it ever executed. For five days green-and-white tents enlivened Dodge property; thousands came to glimpse a bygone era and a very private life. "Incredible works of art," jewelry, and coins were reserved for sale at seven New York auctions for a world audience. (Salny)

Her final will established the Geraldine R. Dodge Foundation, which ranks in the top 100 U.S. foundations. The Dodge Foundation had given grants of more than $46 million in 11 years, through December 1987.

Transcripts of interviews for *The Youngest Daughter*, a videotape, are available at NJ-MadPl and include interviews with Mary Jane Ellis, Dodge's secretary and companion; Grace Mead, Mr. Dodge's cousin; Rev. William Nieman, rector of Grace Episcopal Church, Madison, NJ; Ernest Barton, Dodge's butler; and William Rockefeller, her great-nephew. The NJ-MO contains a clipping file on Dodge. See also Valerie Barnes, *Behind the Scenes at Giralda Farms* (1976); Cam Cavanaugh, *Saving the Great Swamp* (1978); Nacie Salny, "Best of Dodge Art Is Yet to Come," *Daily Record* (Morristown, NJ), Oct. 26, 1975; Dorothy Seiberling, "The Artful Dodge," *New York Magazine* 8 (Oct. 13,

1975):46–49; and Ermaline Weiss, "The Dodge Dynasty," *Morris County Magazine* 1 (Autumn 1982):16–19, 44–47. Dodge's obituary appeared in the *New York Times*, Aug. 14, 1973.

*Barbara Shively*

## NELL DOREMUS, 1891–1964

Nell Budlong Doremus, YWCA pioneer, civic leader, and artist, was born in Ridgewood (Bergen County), NJ, on December 26, 1891, the younger of two daughters of Jennie M. (Lake) and Cornelius Doremus, a prominent Ridgewood attorney in the 1920s and later a judge. Doremus's father held memberships in both the New York and the New Jersey bar associations, advised the chancery court in Bergen County, served as counsel to local municipalities, acted as president of three banks, and ran for the gubernatorial nomination in the Republican primary of 1928. Throughout her life, Doremus claimed she was influenced and inspired by her accomplished father.

She graduated from Ridgewood Elementary School in 1904, from Ridgewood High School in 1908, and from Smith College in 1912. In addition, she did postgraduate work in sociology at New York University. Doremus taught in the Ridgewood and Nutley school systems for three years. Her preferred activity, however, was civic work, and she began volunteer work with the national Young Women's Christian Association (YWCA) soon after college. In 1913, together with eight other educated young Ridgewood women, she organized the College Club of Ridgewood and subsequently served as its first president. This prestigious organization still offers scholarships, grants, funds, and loans to qualified young women.

In 1915, after Doremus and other young schoolteachers were inspired by a Billy Sunday crusade in Paterson they had attended "to ridicule," she formed the Girls Patriotic League of Ridgewood, NJ. "God's Pure Lilies," as they were referred to by town boys, began as a Bible study endeavor. During World War I, efforts expanded as the girls worked to aid the war effort, assisted at Camp Merritt, and campaigned for woman suffrage.

In 1920 the Girls Patriotic League applied for and received a charter from the national YWCA, and the YWCA of Ridgewood officially began meeting in the two back rooms of the old Ridgewood Opera House. Doremus wrote of this event: "This was my first experience in this type of organization and my first in trying to translate into corporate action my convictions as a Christian as to a way of life which could mean more abundant living for *all*." (*Courier*, Jan. 1956) Doremus then had the incentive to train professionally at the national YWCA headquarters, and to take a two-year assignment at an army canteen in Bayshore, Long Island. Her work there ultimately led to the formation of the Suffolk County YWCA.

Doremus's permanent career centered in Paterson, NJ. In 1921 she began working as the Girl Reserve secretary for the Paterson YWCA. Six years later she assumed responsibility as executive director and dedicated the next 28 years to the expansion of the facility and its community programs.

Under her authority, the Paterson YWCA exemplified that organization's Christian philosophy as it applied to urban working women. She especially advocated safe, affordable housing, better working conditions, and improved wages for young women in industry. Doremus described her early experience as: "one which awakened me for the first time to the need for minimum wage laws for women, for some regulation of hours to be worked—in fact the whole field of action through legislation which had always seemed dull to me, became intensely alive as the problems became real through knowing YW members who suffered from long hours, poor pay, bad or unsafe working conditions." (*Courier*, Jan. 1956)

Upon her retirement in 1955, Nell Doremus was officially recognized for her service. "Many of us can take a lesson in life itself from this charming, gracious, and considerate woman . . . Miss Paterson YWCA," proclaimed an editorial in the *Paterson News*. (Mar. 4, 1955) Another newspaper editorial affirmed: "Her contribution to Paterson becomes part of the city's history." (*Morning Call*, Mar. 5, 1955) A tribute luncheon to Doremus, complete with a "this is your life program," was held at the Church of the Messiah in Paterson on June 24, 1955. In honor of her services, Doremus was awarded the key to the city of Paterson. On November 12, 1956, a permanent plaque was placed on the door of the all-purpose room of the Paterson YWCA.

Even after her retirement, Doremus continued her community service. She became a leader in the West Side Presbyterian Church of Ridgewood and in its Women's Guild. Always active in the American Association of University Women, Doremus served as president of the Northwest Bergen chapter from 1958 to 1960. In 1963 she was installed as a member of the Board of Directors of the Ridgewood YWCA. On January 24, 1964, during the Ridgewood YWCA's 50th anniversary celebration, Doremus was honored as the recipient of the Essie W. Mayer Award for outstanding service and leadership to the YWCA.

Doremus has been characterized as an artist and nature lover, a loyal friend, and—most of all—an independent career woman. An enthusiastic member of the Ridgewood Art Association after her retirement, Doremus perfected her painting skills, preferring pets and friends as subjects.

From 1949 to 1964 she lived in Ridgewood with two friends and educators, Ruth Johnson and Lulu J. Eisenhauer. For more than 20 years she vacationed on her own island at Lake Winnipesauke in New Hampshire. There, with Binkee, her Welsh terrier, and favored friends, the women became campers, carpenters, canoe-ists, and connoisseurs of nature.

Doremus died of bone marrow cancer in Valley Hospital, Ridgewood, NJ, on June 16, 1964. She is buried in the family plot at Valleau Cemetery, Ridgewood.

An interview with Lulu Eisenhauer, Van Dyke Nursing Home, Ridgewood, NJ, provided personal information about Doremus. Papers at the YWCA's of Paterson and Ridgewood, NJ, contain information on her activities. See also Nell Doremus, "Growing Along with the YWCA," *Courier* (YWCA of Paterson, NJ), Jan. 1956; "Miss Paterson YWCA," *News* (Paterson, NJ), Mar. 4, 1955; and "A Shining Service to Paterson," *Morning Call* (Paterson, NJ), Mar. 5, 1955. Her obituary appeared in the *News* (Paterson, NJ), June 18, 1964.

*Sandra Vander Gaag*

## SISTER HELEN ANGELA DORETY, 1867–1951

Sister Helen Angela Dorety, Roman Catholic religious, teacher, and botanist, was born Alice Dorety on May 4, 1867, in Bath, SC. She was the eldest of two daughters and two sons born to James N. and Ellen (McCallion) Dorety. Dorety's father was born in Boston, MA, and her mother in Ireland. When she was a girl, her family moved to Trenton, NJ, where she received her early education, graduating from the New Jersey State Model High School and later from the New Jersey State Normal School. Dorety also received a certificate from the Philadelphia Academy of Design in 1889. She was proficient in piano and violin, which she studied for five years.

In 1890 Dorety entered the Sisters of Charity of Saint Elizabeth at Convent Station, NJ, where she became known as Sister Helen Angela. She subsequently taught at Chevrus High School in Jamaica Plain, MA, and at St. Peter's High School in New Brunswick, NJ.

After Sister Helen Angela received a B.A. from the College of Saint Elizabeth in 1903, she was sent for graduate study to the University of Chicago, where she received an M.A. in botany in 1907. Considered a gifted botanist by John Coulter, her mentor, Sister Helen Angela remained at the University of Chicago. In 1909 she earned her Ph.D. summa cum laude in botany and was elected to the University of Chicago chapter of Phi Beta Kappa.

In 1910, with her formal studies completed, Sister Helen Angela was appointed head of the botany department at the College of Saint Elizabeth and resumed her career as a teacher. In December 1910 she was elected a fellow of the American Association for the Advancement of Science. Her interests, however, were far broader than her degree in botany might indicate. They included cultural anthropology—which she taught at the college—the history of music, painting and architecture, as well as geology. She studied the early history of New Jersey, particularly of Morris County, and investigated the varied plant life of

Morris County. She also made a geological map of the region of the great terminal moraine upon which the college is situated. She integrated her varied interests into her teaching, becoming a respected professor and influencing generations of Saint Elizabeth students.

As a horticulturalist, Sister Helen Angela created nature study trails and gardens on the campus of the college, where she developed a greenhouse for further experimentation in botany. Between 1925 and 1930 she designed and supervised the development of a Shakespeare garden at the college, modeled on the garden at Stratford-upon-Avon, England, to which she had been asked to contribute plants in 1920. Each plot in the garden represented a play or a poem in which Shakespeare had mentioned particular flowers.

While Sister Helen Angela taught and gave her horticultural skills to the college, she also continued her scholarship. Among other scientific writings, she contributed a paper entitled "Embryo and Seedling of Doon Spinulosum" to the *Botanical Gazette* in 1919. She published *A Syllabus for the Course in General Botany for College Sophomores* and a booklet, *History of Saint Elizabeth Grounds at Convent*, in 1927. Later she published *A Guide to the Shakespeare Garden*.

Sister Helen Angela's long teaching career was ended in 1945 by her failing health. On November 9, 1951, at the age of 84, she died of cardiac arrest at the motherhouse of the Sisters of Charity of Saint Elizabeth at Convent Station. She is buried in the convent cemetery.

Incomplete collections of Dorety's writings, letters, and memorabilia are kept in the Archives of the Sisters of Charity of Saint Elizabeth (Convent Station, NJ) and the Archives of the College of Saint Elizabeth (Convent Station, NJ).

*Sister Blanche Marie McEniry*

## ELSIE DRIGGS, 1898–

Elsie Belknap (Driggs) Gatch (known professionally as Elsie Driggs), a precisionist painter, was born August 5, 1898, in West Hartford, CT, the youngest of three children and second daughter of Louis Labadaie and Roberta (Whiting) Driggs. Her father, an engineer and inventor of French and Dutch descent, was educated at Annapolis. Her mother, of English descent, was a homemaker. Driggs believes her artistic ability is inherited from the women in her family. Her maternal grandfather died when Driggs's mother was nine months old and her grandmother supported herself as an artist, mostly with needlework. Her mother, although artistic, had no opportunity to develop her talents. Driggs had an early desire to be an artist and by the second grade was creating colored chalk murals for special holidays and taking lessons in watercolor, a medium in which she continues to work.

Driggs's father designed a gun for the navy and was subsequently hired as an inspector for navy munitions contracts, which required that the family move from New York City to Sharon, PA, and then to New Rochelle, NY. When Driggs was eight, her family took the night train from Sharon and her parents woke her to see the night sky over Pittsburgh. To Driggs "it was the most glorious inferno. It was terrific, boiling sulphur yellow and orange and red" (Tyler, Interview, Oct. 30, 1985, 4–5), and she promised herself that she would return to paint that scene.

At New Rochelle High School, Driggs took oil painting lessons on Saturdays and later enrolled in the general course at Bradford Junior College, but World War I prevented her from finishing her studies. Her subsequent attempt at nursing was aborted by ill health and the end of the war.

From 1918 to 1923 Driggs attended the Art Students League, where her teachers were George Luks, Maurice Sterne, and John Sloan. Driggs's family, especially her mother, encouraged her studies, and in 1923 she went to study with Maurice Sterne in Rome and the Italian hill town of Anticoli-Corrado for fourteen months.

Upon her return in 1924 a friend, Alanson Hartpence, who was an assistant at the Daniel Gallery in New York City, encouraged her to submit an unsigned piece to the gallery because he was not sure how the owner, Daniel, felt about women artists. Driggs submitted *Cabbage*, painted in Italy and influenced by Cézanne. Daniel liked the painting and included it in a show. When the work was favorably reviewed in all six leading newspapers Driggs's career was launched. She executed a series of watercolors and oils for the Daniel Gallery, while at the same time copying work at the Metropolitan Museum of Art, where she was employed preparing slides for lectures.

In 1926, when Driggs had saved enough money, she announced that she was going to Pittsburgh to paint the night sky. Once again her mother was supportive but her father objected. Upon her arrival, she discovered that the mills had given up the Bessemer process of manufacturing steel and the night sky was no longer fiery red but black. After this initial disappointment, she climbed a cliff near the Jones and Laughlin plant where she could look directly at the imposing forms; she found them beautiful (Tyler, Interview, Oct. 30, 1985, 25), a radical departure from the aesthetic philosophies of the era. She made several drawings and upon her return to New Rochelle painted *Pittsburgh*. When she took it to Daniel, he exclaimed that she was one of the new classicists (the term "precisionist," meaning someone who paints industrial scenes, had not yet been coined). Driggs was apparently one of the first to paint in this style without having had contact with other artists developing a similar approach. Driggs had met Leo Stein, the art writer and connoisseur, by chance while in Italy. From him she learned to admire Piero della

Francesca; she labeled *Pittsburgh* "her Piero della Francesca" because of its static and classical qualities. *Pittsburgh* was exhibited in 1932 at the First Whitney Museum Annual and was purchased for its collection. Georgia O'Keeffe was the only other woman artist represented in the show.

Between 1927 and 1928 she painted four other industrial scenes in the precisionist mode: *Blast Furnace*, *Queensborough Bridge* (owned by the Montclair Museum), *River Rouge*, and *Airplane*, all of which demonstrate an interest in classical proportion of shapes, as well as movement. This is demonstrated in *Pittsburgh* by the steam and smoke, and in *Airplane* by the moving propellers. Driggs refers to these precisionist works as a "loop in my life." Previously, she had worked in a more painterly style, emphasizing fantasy and movement. She never adhered to a strict precisionist style since she introduced movement and some surreal elements in her works; for example, in *Queensborough Bridge* unattached girders cross the work.

In her next work, *Park Avenue* (also known as *St. Bartholmew's*), Driggs experimented with a style other than precisionism. During this period, she painted in watercolors and pastels, depicting figurative scenes with horses, birds, and hippopotami.

Driggs was one of the first artists to participate in the Work Projects Administration (WPA) Federal Art Projects. These were a continuation of programs initiated by the federal government to help artists during the Depression. From 1934 to 1941 she did several murals, including *Animal Cartoons and West African Gold Weights*, Harlem River Housing Project (1934); *La Salle and His Men*, Huntsville Louisiana Post Office (1935); and *History of Fort Tryon*, Fort Tryon, NY (1938; a private commission). For the latter she was given the waiting room of the Lambertville, NJ, railroad station, which she converted into a studio, since the line had changed from a passenger to a freight carrier. For a $23 stipend she was required by the WPA to deliver one painting every month.

In 1935 she received a Yaddo Fellowship to study art in Saratoga Springs, NY, and there met a fellow recipient, Lee Gatch, whom she married later that year. Driggs, 37 at the time, says that when they got married they knew one of their careers would suffer. Because she felt she always had support, and was better known as an artist, she was willing to concentrate on her husband's career.

After living initially in New York City, Driggs and her husband moved to Lambertville, NJ, in 1937. They bought a small house on the side of a hill with one faucet and no hot water, plumbing, or central heating. Gatch had a studio and Driggs painted on the kitchen table. Lacking space, she abandoned painting large-scale works in oils and concentrated on watercolors, influenced by the New Jersey countryside.

A daughter, Merryman Gatch, was born in 1938. Again Driggs compromised: she wanted a child but knew one would slow her career, and in fact for a few years she could only work while Merryman slept. It was from observing her daughter tear and paste paper together that Driggs developed collages.

In the 1940s and 1950s Driggs continued to exhibit, exploring the theme of director for tworkers' unrest. Her watercolors from the 1940s were favorably reviewed. In the 1950s she was in a transitional period between pastel and collages and began drawing figures with a herringbone design. From 1948 to 1949 she taught art at the Hewitt School in New York City.

Driggs was finally able to return to large-scale works and oils in 1961, when a studio was added to the house. These first works were very fluid, with thin washes combined with drawing. In 1968 Lee Gatch died and Driggs, lonely and seeking to rejoin the "real world," returned to New York.

During the last two decades, Driggs has experimented with a variety of styles and her work has become more abstract. In the late seventies she did a series of lucite boxes with shoeforms. From this period is *Cobbles*, a long piece using cobblestones inspired by a "very tough rock" found in Lambertville, which was used in New York City streets. In the 1980s Driggs did graffiti, cartoons, pieces using lettering influenced from billboards, and mixed media constructions combining painting, drawing, photographs, and found objects. She calls her latest works "frames," in which she actually paints a frame with a wide mat on the work. *Dakota Frame* (1986), with an iron fence, a motif from the Dakota building in New York, is an example.

Driggs always sought a balance in what she calls "the quick and the classical," just as she sought to reconcile a love of order with a love of movement. In her art, she has always sought movement and life, and yet she is best known for a small series of paintings that eulogize the static, classical, and industrial.

Besides the Daniel Gallery, Driggs has exhibited with the Rehn Gallery, the J. P. Neuman Gallery, the Artists Gallery, LaBoetie, and the Martin Diamond Gallery, all in New York City. Her works are in many collections, including the New Jersey State Museum (Trenton NJ), the Metropolitan Museum of Art (New York City), and the Whitney Museum of American Art (New York City).

An interview with Driggs on May 7, 1986, in New York City provided useful information. An oral history of Driggs by Francine Tyler, as well as some of her papers, are available at the Archives of American Art (NYC); additional correspondence and documents are at the Whitney Museum (NYC). See also Susan Fillin Yeh, "Elsie Driggs," *Arts Magazine* 53 (May 1980):3; Cindy Lyle, "Return from 30 Years at the Edge of a Ravine," *Women Artists News* (6 May 1980):1,4,6; and J. Loughery, "Blending the Classical and the Modern: The Art of Elsie Driggs," *Women's Art Journal* 7 (Fall-Winter, 1986–87):22–26.

*Françoise S. Puniello*

## FLORENCE PRICE DWYER, 1902–1976

Florence (Price) Dwyer, one of the 20th century's outstanding legislators, was born in Reading, PA, on July 6, 1902. The third of the four children, and the only girl, of Jerry and Mary (Gegenfurtner) Price, she came from an upper-middle-class family. "Flo" Dwyer, as she was known to family, friends, colleagues, and constituents, was warmhearted and outgoing, with a charismatic personality that drew people to her. Gifted with a sense of humor and an excellent memory for detail, she was a superb raconteur.

During her formative years Dwyer developed a close bond with her mother, who educated her to be a gentlewoman. Her father, mechanically talented and a devotee of automobile racing during the sport's infancy, was often away from home helping racers. He later became an executive of the Durant Car Manufacturing Company in Elizabeth.

Dwyer attended elementary school in Reading and graduated from high school in Toledo, OH, where she was a member of the debating team. Relatives remember that she was a student at the University of Toledo after finishing high school. Dwyer left Ohio with her parents when they moved to Elizabeth, NJ.

She was married, on September 27, 1924, to Michael Joseph ("Joe") Dwyer, who had been a football coach and professor at the University of Toledo. The young couple eventually moved to Elizabeth, where their lifetime home was located in the Elmora section. Dwyer's husband became public relations director for the Western Electric Company. He died in 1968.

Although neither of her parents was 'strongly Republican or Democratic, Dwyer and her husband shared a lifelong interest in politics. Concerned about the neighborhood where they would raise their family, Dwyer started visiting schools and city council and county government meetings in an age when this was considered an unusual preoccupation for a woman.

Michael, a son, was born to the Dwyers on August 2, 1933. Dwyer felt strongly about taking part in shaping the world her son would live in, so by the 1930s she was working for local political candidates. By 1944 she was a voting delegate at the Republican national convention. She held offices in civic organizations, crusading for the revision of the New Jersey constitution in the 1940s, and lobbied in Trenton for the New Jersey Federation of Business and Professional Women's Clubs. She also worked for garden clubs and parent-teacher organizations while in Trenton.

In 1947 Dwyer accepted the position of secretary to Joseph L. Brescher, the majority leader of the Assembly who became speaker in 1948. He described Dwyer as "the most remarkable thing that ever hit Trenton" (*Elizabeth Daily Journal*, Mar. 12, 1948), but her introduction to Trenton was not easy. Some of the men she worked with initially would ask her questions for which they had the answers, but Dwyer—who had made a careful study of every bill—answered each one correctly and their respect for her began to grow.

When Brescher retired in 1949 Dwyer agreed to be one of nineteen primary candidates for his Assembly seat. She won the general election in November and was reelected as Twelfth District assemblywoman for three more terms. Dedicated to the well-being of her constituents, Dwyer introduced legislation that promoted the common good. She was extremely skillful in pushing legislation through to passage.

While an assemblywoman she traveled to Albany to plead before the New York Assembly's Excise Committee for a law enforcing a minimum drinking age of 21 for New York residents to correspond with New Jersey's law. Betty Arthur, Dwyer's longtime secretary, remembers that another Dwyer cause, the "Equal Pay for Equal Work" bill (passed by the New Jersey Assembly in 1952), became the model for the federal bill. Throughout her career, Dwyer was not afraid to speak out on sex discrimination.

Dwyer was an early advocate of consumer protection. She used ingenious displays to illustrate how the consumer was endangered. Once, in the Assembly chamber, she set fire to a child's dress to show how flammable the material was.

Always an advocate of good education, Dwyer's bill to establish the first statewide minimum salary scale for teachers was passed by both houses and signed by the governor in 1954. She also fought for increased state aid for public schools.

In 1956 Republican politicians chose Dwyer to run for the House of Representatives, although there was little hope that any Republican could win against the popular Harrison ("Pete") Williams. She astonished everyone by winning, helped along by President Dwight D. Eisenhower's popularity. Dwyer was reelected seven more times, becoming one of the top vote-getters in New Jersey history. She won easily in Democratic cities as well as in Republican suburbs. No amount of redistricting had an impact on the pluralities she was able to obtain. In 1966 she received 73.9 percent of the vote and her Democratic opponent recorded 23.9 percent.

Dwyer again tried to learn all she could about every piece of legislation in Washington, D.C. When the housing and urban development bill was under consideration in 1966, she alone uncovered 52 cases of undebated "pork barreling" that would have rendered the bill useless.

Dwyer persisted in opposing these cases until they were eliminated.

During the course of her sixteen years in the House, Dwyer received 25 pens from four different presidents in recognition for legislation she had sponsored and nurtured to passage. She was an early advocate of mass transportation and was instrumental in establishing the Department of Transportation. Dwyer also sponsored legislation on flood insurance and air pollution. She worked to establish the Department of Environmental Protection. Concerned with consumer rights, she cosponsored a bill to establish a federal agency to protect the consumer.

As a member of a liberal Republican group nicknamed the "Saintly Seven," her leadership and tactical skill brought about agreement to enlarge the Rules Committee. This prevented a coalition of southern Democrats and conservative Republicans from keeping major social legislation in committee.

In 1967, in a fight to establish higher ethical standards for the conduct of members of Congress, she introduced legislation to require public disclosure of all income and its sources. She expanded this to public reports of all spending of appropriated funds, including money spent for salaries and travel. The bill established standards of conduct and penalties for failure to abide by them.

She played a crucial role in the passage of the Fair Credit Reporting Act and introduced legislation to control loan sharking and drug abuse. Dwyer also cast the deciding vote that allowed the Freedom of Information Act to reach the floor of the House. In a courageous act, she was the only House conferee who signed certain provisions, thus providing the needed bipartisan support for passage under unusual parliamentary circumstances.

In 1970, using a rare parliamentary maneuver and with the help of Representative Martha Griffith of Michigan, she garnered enough votes to bring the Equal Rights Amendment, which had been stalled in committee since 1923, to the floor of the House.

Dwyer's legislative courage extended to her personal life, for only her family and a few close friends knew that she was a diabetic who required daily insulin injections and a strict diet. But she never let that make a difference in her activities. When she had to attend a banquet she would dine at home and eat almost nothing at the public dinner. Friends wondered how she survived when she ate so little.

Since she wanted to spend more time with her family, Dwyer decided to retire in 1972. At her retirement she was the ranking member of the House Banking and Currency Committee, senior Republican member of the powerful Government Operations Committee, and one of three members appointed to the Advisory Commission on Intergovernmental Relations.

Dwyer received the honorary degree of doctor of laws from Douglass College at the May 29, 1968, commence-

ment exercises.

In the fall of 1975 failing health necessitated the amputation of her right lower leg. She was fitted for a prosthesis but when winter came her health failed again, and she died of acute myocardial infarction on February 29, 1976, at Elizabeth General Hospital. She is buried in St. Gertrude's Cemetery at Colonia, NJ, a part of Woodbridge Township.

NJ-KC holds Dwyer's papers and correspondence, as well as a replica of her Washington, D.C., office. An article in the *Elizabeth Daily Journal*, Mar. 12, 1948, details her early career. Hope Chamberlin, *A Minority of Members: Women in the U.S. Congress* (1973), summarizes her years in Congress. An interview with Dwyer's niece, Joan Geer, of Fanwood, NJ, provided details of Dwyer's early life. Obituaries appeared in the *New York Times*, the *Elizabeth Daily Journal*, and the *Newark Star-Ledger*, Mar. 1, 1976.

*Katherine S. Allen*

## MARY ANN ROWLEY EAGER, 1904–1984

Mary Ann (Rowley) Eager, a songwriter whose popular works appeared under the name Molly Eager, was born on July 4, 1904, in County Leitrim, in the province of Cannaught, Drumshambro, Ireland. She was the daughter of Thomas and Mary Ann (Reynolds) Rowley. Eager was the fourth of seven children, and her mother always referred to her as "the hinge" because of her family position. Eager's father was a railroad worker and farmer.

Her mother's side of the family was musical, and Eager was taught at a very early age to play the violin. Throughout her life Eager played many instruments, including the piano. She also showed early talent at writing poetry. She attended the National School (similar to American public schools), where inspectors who visited the school to check students' work evaluated her compositions as exceptionally well written.

Because of the constant danger of gunfire due to the conflict between Britain and Ireland (Drumshambro is a border town between northern and southern Ireland), Eager and her two sisters were sent to New York to live with an aunt in 1924. Eager briefly attended Washington Irving High School but never graduated, since she was forced by circumstances to earn her own way.

At first she got a job at Bloomingdales. Then, after losing her Irish brogue through constant practice, she got a job with the telephone company in Manhattan, where she met William Tallis Eager. They were married in New York City on September 16, 1928. Shortly after this they moved to Bloomfield, NJ, where they remained the rest of their lives. Eager became a naturalized citizen in 1929.

The Eagers had two children, Anita Marie (b. ca. 1930) and Arlene Suzanne (b. 1934). The entire family was musi-

Mary Ann Eager, Irish-born songwriter, in her wedding portrait, 1928. *Courtesy, private collection.*

cal. William Eager played the trumpet and collaborated with his wife on the song "Never Let Your Shadow Shade a Sunbeam." Anita received a B.A. in music and was a coloratura soprano. Arlene graduated with a major in voice and later collaborated with her mother on many songs, including "I Wanna Grow Old with Someone I'm Young With," "Mostly Sunny," and "Check the Yellow Pages."

In the late 1930s Eager, who had been penning romantic novels for her own pleasure, joined the Scribblers Club of Montclair and helped edit the *Unicorn*, a poetry journal. Eager was encouraged to "go public" with her poetry and lyric writing and began her professional career in 1942. She was 38 when she wrote and published a ballad inspired by World War II, "When the World Smiles Again." From then on Eager successfully combined home, husband, children, professional career, and community service. Her daughter Arlene described her as a "human dynamo . . . five feet of pure organizational energy" (Interview, Aug. 1986) during these prolific years. During the 40 years of her marriage, Eager served a homemade lunch every day to husband and children, as well as neighborhood friends and children who frequently dropped by to "visit Molly." Ten

minutes after lunch she would place a fresh flower in her lapel and be off on the bus to Manhattan. There she worked as a staff lyric writer for Robbins Music and made the rounds of other publishing houses to plug her pop and choral music.

She encouraged her daughters to pursue their dreams, insisting that although home and family were important, a woman needed an identity for herself, as well as a private income. During the course of Eager's life she had more than 40 songs published. Her poetry appeared in the *New York Times*, as well as in church magazines and various anthologies.

Eager began volunteer work during World War II by selling war bonds and stamps, working for the Community Chest, the United Fund, and the March of Dimes, and by entertaining servicemen at Camp Kilmer, Lyons Hospital, and the Kessler Institute.

Between 1942 and 1953 Eager wrote approximately 23 songs, mostly written in a popular style. In the years after 1953 she concentrated on cantatas and serious choral works. She collaborated on some of her popular tunes with such well-known musical figures as Robert Harry Wilson, Hugo Frey, Peter de Rose, and Marcel Frank, Frank Loesser's arranger. "Blue Eyed Kathleen from Killarney" was written by Eager in collaboration with Morton Downey, the Irish tenor and composer. While on the staff at Robbins Music, she was chosen as lyricist for "The Mother's Theme" in the film *Ben Hur*. The theme was subsequently published in sheet music form. Eager also worked with Geoffrey O'Hara of "K-K-K-Katy" fame and wrote *Painting Piano Pleasures*, a music-teaching book for children, published by Bourne, Inc., as well as the cantatas "Ode to the Hudson" and "Ode to Thomas Moore."

Throughout the 1960s and 1970s Eager was prolific, collaborating on "It's Hard Trying Hard to Forget" and "Stay Around for Awhile" with her daughter Arlene Suzanne Muller. She also contributed poems to anthologies, such as the *Best American Poems* in 1969.

In honor of Bloomfield's sesquicentennial in 1962, Eager was commissioned to compose the melody and lyrics for "Bloomfield, Fair and Free." The official song of Bloomfield's anniversary, it was performed by Eager's daughter Arlene with the Bloomfield Symphony Orchestra. During this period, Eager became a member of the Songwriter's Hall of Fame and was elected to the American Society of Composers, Authors and Publishers (ASCAP).

In 1956 Eager's torch ballad "I Stand Accused" was recorded by Midway Publishers in Chicago and was issued under the Dot label. Other records included "Open Your Eyes" (music) on the Smart label (RCA) and "The Old Rugged Cross" (new lyrics) on the Calvary label. Her song "Hitch a Ride with the Lord" was recorded by the Delta Rhythm Boys.

Eager, a devoted Catholic, often expressed her spirituality through her music. In addition to writing sacred and secular choral music, she penned "Thank God for the New Born Day," "Oh Mary the Mother of Man" (which became the unofficial theme song of Caldwell College, NJ), "Rejoicing in the Risen Lord," and "Pray." She and her husband were founders of St. Thomas the Apostle Church in Bloomfield, and Eager was an active member of the Rosary Society of St. Thomas.

In 1972 Eager was elected to membership in the National League of American Pen Women, the Song Writer's Protective Association, and the International Platform Association. Eager was also a member of Friends of the Library (Bloomfield) and the Bloomfield Historical Society, and she served as a Girl Scout leader for ten years.

Under the auspices of ASCAP, Eager fought to protect the work of artists by extending the term of copyrights. She claimed: "In our beautiful, young, productive and creative America our copyright laws are moldering." To the delight of Eager, Congress did enact legislation in 1976 on behalf of all artists.

When life seemed impossible or a task insurmountable, Eager always counseled, "Create the thought: the goal will be yours." Eager was considered by those who knew her to be truly a renaissance woman.

Eager died at 79, on January 18, 1984, at her home in Bloomfield, of complications caused by breast and bone cancer. She was buried in Immaculate Conception Cemetery in Montclair. She left a husband, two daughters, nine grandchildren, and three sisters, as well as a remarkable body of work that celebrates the human spirit.

ASCAP (New York City) has clippings on Eager, as well as some of her correspondence and music. Material on her can also be found at NJ-BPL. An interview with Eager's daughter, Arlene Suzanne Muller, in August 1986 supplied additional material. Her obituary appeared in the *Independent Press* (Bloomfield, NJ), Jan. 26, 1984.

*Lynn Wenzel*


## LENA FRANCES EDWARDS, 1900–1986

Lena Frances (Edwards) Madison, physician and Presidential Medal of Freedom honoree, was born into a prominent Washington, D.C., family on September 17, 1900. Edwards's father, Dr. Thomas Edwards, taught dentistry at Howard University for many years. A man of strong character whose philosophy of life emphasized social service and civic concern, Thomas Edwards supported his family while acquiring an education. Her mother, Marie (Coakley) Edwards, was a devout Catholic in a cultural environment that was traditionally Protestant. Marie Edwards's father, Gabriel Coakley, had personally petitioned President Abraham Lincoln on behalf of the black Catho-

lics of Washington, D.C., who wanted to sponsor a party on the lawn of the White House to raise money for the building of St. Augustine's Church.

There were three other children in the Edwards household: May, Elmer, and Thomas, who was fifteen years younger than Edwards. Marie Edwards was a loving disciplinarian who raised her children in the Catholic faith, although her husband was not Catholic. When Edwards was twelve her mother was treated for an illness by a friend who happened to be a black female medical doctor. This experience encouraged her to consider medicine as a career choice. As members of the middle-class black community of Washington, the Edwards children had personal contact with many black professionals at a time when the majority of African-Americans did not have access to higher education. Edwards and many of her peers attended Dunbar High School. The principal, Dr. Carter G. Woodson, founder of the Association for the Study of Negro Life and History, took a special interest in her academic development. Because of her association with Woodson and other African-American achievers, Edwards matured with a strong sense of race commitment and pride, which, along with religious faith and a sense of civic responsibility, shaped the course of her life.

Lena Frances Edwards practiced medicine in Jersey City and delivered over 5,000 babies during her 29-year practice. *Courtesy, Jersey Journal.*

In June 1918 Edwards graduated as valedictorian of her high school class. The salutatorian was Sterling Alan Brown, who later became a leading poet of the New Negro Movement. With acceptances at Brown and Howard, she chose to attend Howard University. During her freshman year she pledged Delta Sigma Theta Sorority, a Greek organization founded in the early 1900s on the Howard campus. Edwards was attracted to this sorority because of its devotion to God and neighbor and its "Lift as you climb" philosophy, which encouraged the bringing along of others less fortunate. Having completed all her undergraduate requirements in three years, she entered Howard University Medical School in 1921. Her relationship with Keith Madison of Warrenton, VA, began while they were both medical students. On June 7, 1924, the day after their graduation, they were married. Both completed an internship at Freedman's Hospital and moved to Jersey City, NJ, to establish private practice in July 1925. Edwards decided to retain her family name for professional purposes.

These early years of practice were Edwards's childbearing years. Her first child, Marie, was born in 1925 and her first son, Edward, in 1926. Genevieve Ann was born in 1930, Thomas Alfred in 1933, and John Joseph in 1937. During her sixth and last pregnancy Edwards experienced serious physical problems. In her desperation to save the child, she vowed to attend mass daily for the remainder of her life and, thus, where she lived was always determined by its proximity to a Catholic church. Paul Francis was born prematurely in 1939. Edwards, devoted mother, arranged to spend time enjoying the children and their activities, attending school plays and sports events.

Edwards's practice was primarily among the European immigrants of the Lafayette section of Jersey City. She organized a group, the People's Charitable League, which opened a day nursery where Edwards visited the children regularly to check for contagious diseases and other problems. She also spoke to teenage groups at churches throughout New Jersey. An early promoter of natural childbirth, Edwards battled for years before finally being accepted, at age 44, for a residency in obstetrics and gynecology at Margaret Hague Hospital in Jersey City, where she was on staff.

Many honors were bestowed on her during these years of private practice, but her personal life was altered in 1947 by a permanent separation from her husband. She fortified herself spiritually by joining the Third Order of Franciscans, a religious group started by St. Francis of Assisi for those individuals who wished to live a simple life but because of family obligations could not enter a religious order and take the vows of poverty, chastity, and obedience. Through daily prayers and attendance at the liturgy, Edwards evolved into a deeply religious woman who viewed her choice of profession and strength of character as gifts from God to be used in service to the poor and needy.

After 29 years of private practice and the delivery of over 5,000 babies, Edwards began teaching obstetrics at Howard University Medical School. This career change reflected her desire to pass on to future doctors some of the expertise she had acquired during her years in Jersey City. She continued to fight for the disadvantaged, becoming the medical adviser for the National Association of Colored Women's Clubs, a member of the Board of Directors of the Iona Whipper Home for Unwed Mothers, and chair of the Maternal Welfare Committee of the District of Columbia Urban League. She was a member of the Social Work Advisory Committee of the U.S. Employment Service and an active participant in the Catholic Interracial Council.

In 1960, at age 60, Edwards volunteered her services at St. Joseph's Mission in Hereford, TX, where the Mexican migrant workers were badly in need of prenatal care. While there she used the rent money from her home in Washington as seed money to build a modern maternity hospital for the labor camp. Named after Our Lady of Guadalupe, the hospital was partially supported by fees she earned when she delivered the babies of ranchers' wives and non-Mexicans.

In May 1963 she was elected to Phi Beta Kappa by the Gamma chapter of the District of Columbia. Since she had completed her undergraduate education in three years instead of the usual four, she had missed the opportunity to receive this honor for her outstanding academic achievement. She was also appointed to the Federal Advisory Council on Employment Security. But the greatest national recognition for her contributions to society came in 1964 from President Lyndon B. Johnson when he awarded her the Presidential Medal of Freedom. Her work at the mission ended when a heart attack forced her to return to Washington, where she cared for her elderly mother and worked with Project Head Start.

Edwards returned to Jersey City in 1966 and resumed some of her earlier activities. Her appointment as medical coordinator of Jersey City's preschool antipoverty program and teaching at the St. Peter's College Institute of Industrial Relations satisfied her need to be publicly active. Her free hours were spent sewing and gardening, lifelong pursuits.

Although a recipient of numerous awards, Edwards was most gratified in 1967 when she was given the Poverello Medal. This religious honor is bestowed on those rare individuals whose lives have exemplified the ideals of St. Francis of Assisi. (Edwards had renounced all personal wealth and had established a scholarship trust fund at Howard University Medical School.) In addition to this prestigious award, she was the recipient of more than fourteen honorary doctorates as well as other awards and citations.

Under pressure from her children, Edwards moved in

1972 to Lakewood, NJ, near her daughter Genevieve. She was 72, but she now saw a need for improvement in health care for senior citizens. She also served on the Economic Opportunity Fund for Disadvantaged Students Advisory Board of the Georgian Court College and Ocean County Community College.

On December 3, 1986, she died in her home in Lakewood as she was preparing to move back to Jersey City. Edwards traveled the world and constantly assumed new challenges, yet she said she was never more content than when she was rearing her children, all of whom became successful professionals. A courageous woman of strength and character, Edwards eschewed a life of comfort and material success, but was enriched by the love and gratitude of thousands whose lives she touched and made better.

Edwards's papers are available at the Moorland-Spingarn Research Center at Howard University (Washington, D.C.). An oral interview with Edwards conducted by Dr. Merze Tate is available at M-SL. A biography of her is Sister M. Anthony Scally, *Medicine, Motherhood and Mercy* (1979), and her life is highlighted in Sally Knapp, *Women Doctors Today* (1947). See also "Lady Doctor to Migrant Workers," *Ebony* 17 (Feb. 1962):59–68; and C. W. Thomas, "Three Negroes Receive 1964 Presidential Freedom Medal," *Negro History Bulletin* 28 (Dec. 1964):592–95.

*Cheryl Day LuSane*

## ELEANOR EGG, 1909–

Eleanor Marie (Egg) Krattiger, known as Eleanor Egg, pioneer woman athlete and dance instructor, was born on February 3, 1909, in Wilkes-Barre, PA, the only child of Charles (1887–1950) and Caroline (Schrey) Egg (1888–1985). Her mother, of German descent, was born in Paterson, NJ; her father arrived in Paterson at six months of age with his parents, who emigrated from Switzerland.

Egg's parents, married in 1908, soon became a vaudeville stage duo, entertaining audiences around the country with their balancing and acrobatic routines. Egg became part of her parents' act at age seventeen months. In 1917 the Eggs decided to return to Paterson to stabilize their eight-year-old daughter's life and education, since she had attended thirteen different schools in one year alone. Her father found employment as a sign painter for the Lackawanna Railroad, and her mother worked as a weaver in one of the city's silk mills.

Egg's prowess as an athlete surfaced during the early 1920s. Impressed by her performances at the city championships, local school and recreation officials organized the Paterson Girls' Recreation Association (PGRA) in 1923. They believed that Egg, along with some schoolmates who performed nearly as well, could compete favorably with other female teams in northern New Jersey,

New York City, and Philadelphia. A versatile athlete, Egg emerged as the dominant figure on the PGRA team, competing in nearly every track and field event open to women. From 1923 to 1932 Egg and her Paterson teammates left a legacy of distinguished achievement and world records in women's track and field. Egg herself competed in every national championship tournament held for women during that ten-year period. When she retired from competition, she had collected 227 medals, 22 silver cups, 6 statuettes, and a myriad of other prizes.

Egg entered the athletic arena with her parents' blessing. In fact, Caroline (Schrey) Egg assumed an active role in her daughter's athletic pursuits, serving as frequent chaperone on the PGRA's out-of-town trips and on occasion joining her daughter in competition in the shot put. Egg's father also was a source of inspiration, encouraging her to practice and helping her whenever possible.

Egg competed in track and field when it was unfashionable for women to enter these events. Although her entry into the athletic arena coincided with some of the political and social gains made by women during the 1920s, Egg was not politically motivated, nor did she seek a career built upon her athletic talent. She participated for the fun, excitement, and challenge of the competition.

The climb to stardom began for Egg as a member of the PGRA relay team. She guided the team to an outdoor world record in 1925. The following year she led a hand-picked American relay team to an indoor record-shattering performance over a select Canadian squad. Then, in 1927, she and her PGRA teammates lowered that mark. Her most satisfying experience came in 1930 at the Jersey City Tercentenary, where a bizarre turn of events found her competing for the Canadian relay team. When the Canadians' star sprinter fell victim to appendicitis, the American coach offered Egg as a substitute. Torn between patriotism and her best effort, Egg chose the latter and staked the Canadians to an early lead they never relinquished. As a result of her superb performance, meet officials named her its outstanding athlete.

In addition to her success as a relay runner, Egg excelled at individual events. She won the 1927 broad jump championship at Eureka, CA, and set a world record with a leap of seventeen feet one and three quarters inches. Four years later, at Jersey City, she defeated Stella Walsh, the world record holder and favorite, for the 100-yard dash title.

After these two triumphs, the city of Paterson opened its arms to her. She was honored at testimonial dinners and showered with gifts and benefits. To commemorate her championship run, Paterson commissioned the sculptor Gaetano Federici to capture her form in bronze. The plaque he created was placed in the community's Hinchcliffe Stadium, where it remains today, a lasting tribute to one of Paterson's finest athletes.

This bas-relief of track and field star Eleanor Marie Egg of Paterson was created by sculptor Gaetano Federici in 1932 for Paterson's Hinchcliffe Stadium, *Courtesy, Paterson Museum Collection.*

Blessed with a cheerful outlook, vivacious mannerisms, and a pleasant disposition, Egg captured the hearts of her followers. Her colorful personality and superb athletic skills caused the citizens of Paterson to adopt her as their heroine. Cast in this role, she helped Patersonians cope with the economic disasters of the 1920s and 1930s.

During the mid-1920s Paterson suffered a series of economic crises when nearly two-thirds of its silk mills—the city's major industry—shut down. Some mills moved to other areas in search of greater economic benefit; others simply shut down. Egg, a symbol of success, provided stability and direction to this city in turmoil; her triumphs on the athletic field later soothed the blow of economic despair during the frightening days of the early 1930s. When Egg defeated Stella Walsh for the American sprint championship in 1931, her unexpected victory offered Patersonians the hope that they, too, would overcome the adversity of economic depression.

After retiring from track and field competitions, Egg taught dance at her mother's studio and coached a local track club of adolescent girls. When, in 1935, she married Charles Krattiger (1906–84), who later became supervisor of Public Works in West Milford, NJ, Egg gave up coaching to concentrate on dance, a career that lasted more than 40 years. She taught at four different dance schools before opening her own studio. Carolyn I. Krattiger, her only child, was born in 1939.

The Krattigers moved to West Milford, NJ, in 1945 and lived there until 1979, when they moved to Fort Myers, FL, where Egg and her daughter currently reside.

J. Thomas Jable, "Eleanor Egg: Paterson's Track and Field Heroine," *New Jersey History* 102 (1984):69–84, analyzes Egg's role as Paterson's hometown heroine during the 1920s and 1930s.

*J. Thomas Jable*

## DOROTHY DAGGETT ELDRIDGE, 1903–1986

Dorothy (Daggett) Eldridge, a founder and director of the New Jersey chapter of SANE, a citizen's organization for a sane nuclear policy, was born in San Francisco, CA, on November 8, 1903. She was the first child and only daughter of Josephine (Sharrer) and Royal Bradford Daggett. Eldridge had two brothers, born in 1905 and 1907.

Both Eldridge's parents were of English heritage. Her father, born in Auburn, ME, was descended from the Daggetts who arrived on the *Mayflower*; later descendants served in the Revolutionary and Civil wars. Her mother's birthplace was Bethlehem, PA.

Eldridge's father graduated from Cornell University with a degree in engineering. He held a number of engineering positions, frequently relocating his family throughout Eldridge's early childhood. Consequently, Eldridge attended elementary schools in Berkeley, CA; Newton Center, MA; Narberth, PA; Scarsdale, NY; and White Plains, NY. After this period of constant relocation her father gave up engineering for a career in the insurance field. Her mother, who had a high school education, was a homemaker.

Although her parents' lives did not provide a specific example for Eldridge's antiwar activities, she credited their honesty and responsibility as having a significant effect on her commitment. She believed that "what you do and care about are rooted in what your parents give you." (Interview, Jan. 10, 1986) While she and her father often disagreed on specific issues, his deep concern over political questions and governmental activities taught her the importance of politics. Her mother, a vivacious woman with an exciting personality, taught her enjoyment of life.

After the many relocations of her elementary school years, Eldridge's family settled in White Plains, NY, where she completed high school in 1922. She then earned a B.A. from Mount Holyoke College in 1926, with a major in chemistry and a minor in physiology. Although she hoped to become a physician because, as she wrote later, "I wanted to make myself as useful as possible to the human species" (Warner, "SANE Head to Be Honored," 20), lack of funds prevented her from attending medical school. Later in life, she found another way to fulfill her desire by working for the prevention of nuclear war.

Eldridge was employed after college by the New York City Health Department as a laboratory technician at Bellevue and Harlem hospitals, but she left in 1927 because of low salary to join the Borden Company.

She married Robert W. Eldridge, a chemist, on February 10, 1928. Donald Francis, her first child and only son, was born in 1929; Phyllis Jane in 1930; and Marion Ruth in 1933. Immediately after her marriage, Eldridge lived for brief periods in Queens, NY, and Passaic, NJ. In 1930 she and her husband settled permanently in Nutley, NJ.

Like most women of her generation, Eldridge did not consider continuing her career while she had small children. She felt that society "didn't have facilities" to allow such an option to women. Like her mother, she did not question the then-current pattern of a woman's life: "school, job, marriage, babies." However, even while her children were at home, Eldridge's life included more than homemaking.

During the 1940s, Eldridge served as president of the Nutley chapter of the League of Women Voters, president of the Nutley chapter of the American Association of University Women, and organizer of the Nutley Dumbarton Oaks Committee to support the newly founded United Nations. After World War II, she returned to her scientific career to help support her children through their college years. During these years, she worked as a microbiologist at Hoffmann-LaRoche, a pharmaceutical manufacturer with a facility in Nutley.

In the 1950s Eldridge deepened her involvement in the peace movement with membership in organizations such as the New Jersey Committee for a Peaceful Alternative and the Women's International League for Peace and Freedom. Her long-term involvement with the New Jersey Committee for a Sane Nuclear Policy (SANE), however, turned out to be her most significant contribution. In 1958 Eldridge helped found the New Jersey SANE unit.

Initially hired as a paid staff member of the Essex County chapter, she returned her salary to the organization, with the comment that "although I didn't have a lot of money, I had more than the organization." (Warner, 20) She resigned from her Hoffmann-LaRoche position in 1959 to serve full time without pay as state director for SANE.

Her SANE activities included efforts to stop atmospheric testing of nuclear weapons and to expose what she considered the fallacy of civil defense. From the mid-1960s until the early 1970s, she focused on opposition to military involvement in Vietnam. After the Vietnam War, Eldridge led an effort to transfer expenditures of government funds from weapons to human needs, such as jobs. Eldridge served as state coordinator of the Freeze Campaign (in 1980) for a moratorium on the production, testing, and deployment of nuclear weapons. She helped to organize New Jersey assembly districts to place a "Freeze" referendum on the ballot, an initiative that won by a 66 percent majority.

Often asked whether her years of antiwar work had been wasted because the world still does not have peace, Eldridge continually voiced her confidence that the movement would win, emphasizing that "if we did not have the struggle for peace, we would have eventual nuclear disaster." (Interview, Jan. 10, 1986) Commenting on the personal rewards of her SANE involvement, Eldridge added, "I find it very wonderful to be able to work so consistently for something I feel is so important and so meaningful." Her husband and children shared her commitment through their own volunteer work and financial contributions.

An eightieth birthday celebration for Eldridge at Caldwell College in 1983 produced statements honoring her peace activities. (Jones, "Nuclear Freeze Leader a Warrior against War," 70) At that time a New Jersey State Assembly resolution noted "her great reserve of energy and demonstrated leadership to creating a constituency for peace in New Jersey." In the *Congressional Record* of November 18, 1985, Representative Peter W. Rodino, Jr., of New Jersey claimed that Eldridge "truly deserves the title of 'New Jersey's First Lady for Peace.'" He added: "Her leadership, counsel, and support on many of the most grave problems confronting us as a nation—and indeed all of mankind—

have been invaluable to me."

Eldridge died in Passaic, NJ, at age 82, from a stroke following surgery on July 30, 1986.

An interview with Eldridge on Jan. 10, 1986, provided useful information. For newspaper articles detailing her SANE activities, see Angela Jones, "Nuclear Freeze Leader a Warrior against War," *Sunday Star-Ledger* (Newark), Dec. 4, 1983; and Ray Warner, "SANE Head to Be Honored," *New York Times*, Apr. 16, 1972. Other articles appeared in the *New York Times*, Jan. 13, 1974, and Sept. 16, 1976. Her obituary appeared in the *New York Times*, Aug. 10, 1986.

*Walter Cummins*

## ANNE ELSTNER, 1899–1981

Anne Elizabeth (Elstner) Matthews, known professionally as Anne Elstner, who for eighteen years played the title role in "Stella Dallas," one of radio's earliest and most popular soap operas, was born in Lake Charles, LA, on January 22, 1899. She was the youngest of eight children (four boys and four girls) born to Joseph Casper and Sallie (Kretz) Elstner.

Her family left their rambling southern mansion when Elstner was seven and began a series of moves to Colorado, Arkansas, Illinois, and Texas. Career changes by her father, an accountant who worked with various success as the owner of a wholesale grocery and feed business, insurance salesman, cattle rancher, and land speculator, caused frequent family relocation.

Acting was in Elstner's blood, as demonstrated by her imitations of visitors to her parents' home. Endowed with a vivid imagination and natural stage presence, she rarely failed to perform for family and friends when given the opportunity. She even performed song-and-dance routines between shows at a local movie house when her family resided in Mena, AR. Although her parents supported Elstner's theatrical ambitions, they insisted on a formal education. Her freshman year was spent at Senn High School in Chicago, and then in 1915 her parents sent her to a convent boarding school, Mount de Chantal Visitation Academy in Wheeling, WV, from which her mother had graduated. Elstner maintained her interest in acting at the academy, where she played the lead in *Hamlet* and the Dauphin in *Joan of Arc*. Whenever she was not starring in a school play, she designed costumes and served as a bit player; her senior yearbook praised her dramatic talents and wit.

After graduating in 1918, Elstner moved to New York City to begin her formal acting career, attending classes at the American Academy of Dramatic Arts during 1919. Between the usual rounds of casting offices and auditions she worked at odd jobs, ranging from hosiery sales clerk to secretary for a Wall Street promoter.

Her theatrical career was launched when she was selected as understudy for Eva Le Gallienne in Ferenc Molnar's play *Liliom*. Called to replace the ailing Le Gallienne in Chicago, Elstner was seen by playwright Lula Vollmar, who offered her the starring role of Emmy in the Broadway hit *Sun-Up* in 1923. During the show's run, Elstner made her first radio broadcast to WEAF (New York).

While her acting career was flowering, she became reacquainted with John (Jack) Matthews, Jr. Elstner had first met Matthews when he was stationed in the Seventh and Sixteenth Cavalry near her family's home in San Benito, TX. They were married on December 8, 1924, in the Church of the Transfiguration (Little Church Around the Corner) in Manhattan.

After her marriage, Elstner gave up the lead in *Sun-Up* as the play began its international run and moved to her husband's 500-acre tobacco farm in Maryland. Falling prices for farm products forced them to give up their farming venture, however. Aware that Elstner was still in demand for stage roles, they moved back to New York City, where in 1928 she was immediately given her former lead in a revival of Vollmar's *Sun-Up*.

Elstner's long radio career began when she assumed the role of "Cracker Gaddis," a young hillbilly girl in Lula Vollmar's weekly radio series "Moonshine and Honeysuckle," an early soap opera that ran from 1930 to 1933. During her long radio career, Elstner estimated that she played more than 7,000 roles, with her voice heard on programs such as "Wilderness Road," "The Gibson Family," "Gunsmoke Law," "Maverick Jim," "Hillbilly-Heart Throbs," "Show Boat," "House Beside the Road," "Mr. Keene, Tracer of Lost Persons," and "The Fat Man."

In 1936 Elstner auditioned with 25 others for the leading role in a serial based on Olive Higgins Prouty's celebrated novel *Stella Dallas*. Elstner, who won the part of "Stella," the humble seamstress whose abiding love for her daughter "Lolly-Baby" involved her in a multitude of adventures, enthralled millions of Americans from 1937 to 1956 with the daily fifteen-minute soap opera. The story line centered around mother love and the Golden Rule, as listeners waited to hear Elstner's throaty voice utter the famous, often-repeated line: "Lolly-Baby, I ain't got no time for nothin' but trouble."

In 1940, during a visit to friends living in Stockton, NJ, Elstner and her husband, then an inspector for the Federal Bureau of Investigation, decided to buy an 18th-century stone house in the Jersey countryside. Elstner commuted daily to New York City, either by train or car, from this rustic country retreat. During the eighteen years of "Stella Dallas," she missed only one performance. A busy and popular actress, Elstner enjoyed her life in the small New Jersey town, and in 1953 she and her husband bought a restaurant on the banks of the Delaware River, in nearby Lambertville, NJ. They turned the building, originally an 1835 gristmill, into a popular and elegant dining spot called "River's Edge," which attracted diners in search of well-prepared food as well as "Stella Dallas" fans eager to catch a glimpse of the star. Elstner took an active part in the business. At River's Edge, she supervised the interior decorating, chose the waitresses' costumes, and supplied family recipes for the menu. After a day in New York as "Stella Dallas," Elstner would return home to act as the restaurant's hostess each evening.

"Stella Dallas" ended its run as a radio series in 1955, but Elstner enjoyed an active retirement since she and her husband continued to operate their restaurant until 1973. She also hosted a local radio talk-show broadcast during the 1960s on WBUX (New Hope, PA) from the restaurant and continued to pursue a lifetime interest in game fishing and trapshooting, for which she won numerous prizes.

Although retired, she was not forgotten by fans. In 1976 Elstner received the Fifth National Golden Mike Award from the Golden Radio Buffs of Maryland at a Baltimore ceremony. In 1980 she was inducted into the National Broadcasters' Hall of Fame (Freehold, NJ).

After suffering a stroke at her Stockton home in mid-December 1980, Elstner was taken to Doylestown Hospital (Doylestown, PA), where she died on January 29, 1981. Her only survivor was her husband, who died in 1983. Remembered as one of the early stars of the "golden age of radio," she is buried in Rosemont Cemetery, Rosemont, NJ.

The most complete collection of Elstner memorabilia is held by Carl Cathers of Stockton, NJ. Additional material is at NYPL-LC. The clipping files of the *Trenton Times* and the *Hunterton County Democrat* (Flemington, NJ) contain material on her. Obituaries of Elstner appeared in the *Trenton Times* and in the *Philadelphia Inquirer*, Jan. 30, 1981.

*Patricia Smith Butcher*

## DOROTHY HARRISON EUSTIS, 1886–1946

Dorothy Lieb (Harrison) Wood Eustis, philanthropist and founder of The Seeing Eye, a dog guide school for the blind, was born May 30, 1886, in Philadelphia, PA, to Charles Custis Harrison and Ellen Nixon (Waln) Harrison.

Eustis married Walter Abbott Wood, Jr., in 1906. They had two sons. Widowed in 1915, Eustis married George Morris Eustis in 1923. They lived at Fortunate Fields, her Swiss estate, where Eustis bred German Shepherds for useful public service.

An editor at the *Saturday Evening Post* asked Eustis to write an article on her work in 1927. She focused instead on what the Germans had done with dogs trained as guides for blind veterans in Potsdam, Germany. Morris Frank, a blind young man from Nashville, TN, wrote to Eustis, after reading the article, seeking to establish a dog guide school for the blind in the United States.

The following spring, Frank arrived in Switzerland and met Buddy, his first dog guide. Satisfied that the pair were well trained, Eustis agreed to finance Frank's program to start a school under her tutelage. Initially located in Nashville, TN, The Seeing Eye has been headquartered in Morristown, NJ, since 1930.

The move to Morristown was not without problems. Neighbors were against the school. "They organized meetings and petitioned the local authorities," envisioning their roads and land being overrun with dogs. (Hartwell, *Dogs Against Darkness*, 118) Since that time Morristown residents have grown accustomed to seeing the dog guides and their instructors being trained on town streets.

The campus of The Seeing Eye school is situated on approximately 55 acres. Here the school provides tours for the public, oversees an adoption program for dogs that do not qualify as guides, and works with 4-H club members who raise puppies—usually selected from the school's scientific breeding station in Mendham, NJ—for a year before returning them to the school to be trained. In January 1987 a new Downtown Training Center opened.

Eustis continued as president of The Seeing Eye Corporation until 1940. Along with her interest in The Seeing Eye in America and L'Oeil Qui Voit in Switzerland, Eustis wrote many articles and was active in civic and philanthropic organizations. She was a member of the Colonial Dames of America, and the Daughters of the American Revolution.

She received an honorary degree from the University of Pennsylvania in 1933, and the National Institute of Social Sciences presented her with "its gold medal for distinguished service to humanity" in 1936. (*New York Times*, Sept. 10, 1946)

The Seeing Eye was Eustis's greatest concern until her death. She died on September 8, 1946, from cancer, at her home in New York, NY, at age 60, and was buried in the churchyard of St. David's Church, Wayne, PA.

Eustis wrote *Dogs as Guides for the Blind* (1929) and "The Seeing Eye," *Saturday Evening Post* 200 (Nov. 5, 1927):43–46. Books detailing her life and work are: Dickson Hartwell, *Dogs Against Darkness: The Story of The Seeing Eye* (1942); Morris Frank and Blake Clark, *First Lady of The Seeing Eye* (1957); and Peter Putnam, *Love in the Lead* (1954). Sketches of her appear in *NAW* and in *DAB*, supp. 4 (1950). Her obituary appeared in the *New York Times*, Sept. 10, 1946.

*Dorothy Harnett Ryan*

## MADGE EVANS, 1909–1981

Margherita (Evans) Kingsley (known professionally as Madge Evans), who acted in more than 72 films and in numerous plays on and off Broadway, was born in New York City on July 1, 1909. Her English parents, Arthur John and Maude Mary Evans, had one other child, Thomas.

Evans's career started before she was a year old. She posed as a model for a painter and then, like her mother, modeled for magazines and advertisements. A director who lived in the same apartment building as her family asked her mother if Evans could appear in one of his productions, and by 1914 she was making $150 a week on Broadway as one of the children in *The Highway of Life*, a stage version of *David Copperfield*. She made her film debut that same year in *Sign of the Cross* and appeared in 29 films by the time she was ten, for which she was dubbed "the Shirley Temple of the 1910's" by film historians. (Parish and Bowers, *The MGM Stock Company*, 212) These early films were made in Fort Lee, NJ, which was the world's center of movie making from 1900 to 1920, due to "the inventiveness of Edison's laboratories, New Jersey's varied and spectacular landscapes, and its proximity to New York talent." (Paul C. Spehr, quoted by Shirey, "Fort Lee, the Movie Capital of the World, Almost")

Evans's mother apparently realized how transitory success in the modeling and acting world could be. She not only saved her daughter's earnings, but also allowed Evans's name to be used by a children's hat company, guaranteeing a steady income for her daughter. This thriftiness was farsighted; the child star with the blond curls turned into a tall and somewhat awkward adolescent who acted only sporadically until she was seventeen, when she returned to Broadway as May Phillips in *Daisy Mayne*, one of a number of ingenue roles she would play.

Although she tried to escape the ingenue typecasting by going to Denver in 1928 to work with Elitchs Park, a stock company that had nurtured a number of famous actors, she still was offered "sweet young thing" roles upon her return to New York two years later. In 1931, when she was playing such a part in *Philip Goes Forth*, an executive from MGM noticed her and offered her a term contract. She reentered the world of film, but not without regrets, since the stage remained her real love.

While at MGM, Evans seemed unable to find parts that presented her as a serious dramatic actor. Her roles were more mature—one of three women looking for a man with money in *The Greeks Had a Word for Them* (1932), the mistress of a character played by John Barrymore in *Dinner at Eight* (1933), and the husband-stealing Lady Sybil in *What Every Woman Knows* (1934)—but they were the kinds of roles that caused the *New York Times*, in its film reviews of the period, to call her "pretty," "charming," and "capable," rather than anything more substantial. When her contract with MGM was up in 1937, she made two more films and then returned to the stage, appearing on Broadway in *Here Come the Clowns*. After this, she acted mainly in summer stock and regional theater, going into semiretirement after her marriage to the Pulitzer Prize–winning playwright Sidney Kingsley in 1939. She did return to Broadway in 1943 to appear in Kingsley's *The Patriots* and occasionally worked on radio and television after her marriage.

Her retirement from acting to being a supportive wife, living in Oakland (Bergen County), NJ, and helping her husband do research for his plays was something that was planned, not forced. In an interview in *Photoplay* three years before her marriage, she had stated that whatever she did she wanted to do well, and that she didn't believe she could do well in her career and as a wife simultaneously: "When you marry a person, you begin meddling in his life . . . so far as I'm concerned, I won't put my fingers into anyone's personality until I know I can . . . concentrate all my time and sincerity on the task. I couldn't do that today because I've still another assignment—that of being a *good* actress—to finish first." (Stevens, "Why Madge Evans Has Never Married," 115)

Evans died of cancer, at age 71, on April 26, 1981, at home in the colonial saltbox house in Oakland, NJ, where she had lived for 42 years. In her *New York Times* obituary, Herbert Mitgang called her "a popular actress who frequently portrayed the clean-cut, decent American woman" and noted that her husband "described her as his collaborator in the theater in every sense." Thus at the end of her life she was still involved in the world she had entered at the age of five: the theater.

An overview of Evans's career appears in James R. Parish and Ronald Bower, *The MGM Stock Company* (1973). David L. Shirey, "Fort Lee, the Movie Capital of the World, Almost," appears in the *New York Times Encyclopedia of Film* (1984). Two articles provide interesting profiles of Evans: George Stevens, "Why Madge Evans Has Never Married," *Photoplay* (July 1936): 112–15; and Jean Ludlow, "Madge Evans Kingsley Trades Stardom for Wifedom," *Ridgewood* (NJ) *Herald News*, June 5, 1969. Her obituary appeared in the *New York Times*, Apr. 28, 1981.

*Martha C. Merrill*

## JESSIE REDMON FAUSET, 1882–1961

Among the most prolific African-American novelists of her day, Jessie (Fauset) Harris (known professionally as Jessie Redmon Fauset) was nationally recognized for her contributions to black literature. In addition to four novels, these contributions include poems, reportage, reviews, and translations. Though she is often identified with Philadelphia, where she grew up, and with New York City, where she was a vital force in the cultural awakening known as the Harlem Renaissance, Fauset lived much of her life in her native New Jersey.

Born in Fredericksville, a hamlet in rural Camden County, NJ, Jessie was the seventh child and fifth daughter of Anna (Seamon) and Redmon Fauset. Only three of the children lived to adulthood. Her father, a minister in the African Methodist Episcopal Church, led a congregation in nearby Snow Hill. This all-black settlement, also known as Free Haven, had been founded as a refuge for slaves. Her mother's early death strengthened the bond between Jessie and her father; throughout her life she remained true to the ideals of racial uplift he instilled. Later, the family moved to Philadelphia, where the Rev. Fauset married Belle Huff, a widow with three children. Two sons and a daughter were born of his second marriage.

Jessie Redmon Fauset, a native of Camden County, is widely recognized for her contributions to African-American literature as an editor, writer, and teacher in the 1920s and 1930s. *Courtesy, Prints and Photographs Department, Moorland-Springarn Research Center, Howard University.*

Fauset was a superior student. However, following her graduation from the Philadelphia High School for Girls, she was denied admission to local colleges because of her race. The rejection stung Fauset, although she gained acceptance to Cornell University shortly afterward. Determined to prove her worth, she achieved an outstanding record at Cornell, where she was elected to Phi Beta Kappa in her junior year. She graduated in 1905. Failing to gain a teaching appointment in Philadelphia because of racial barriers, she moved to Baltimore and then to Washington, where she taught high school French and Latin for thirteen years. She continued her own studies at the University of Pennsylvania, where she earned an A.M. in 1919, and at the Sorbonne.

Fauset began contributing reviews and features to the *Crisis* in 1912. Founded by W.E.B. DuBois, the *Crisis* was the official publication of the National Association for the Advancement of Colored People. Fauset was named its literary editor in 1919 and under her direction the *Crisis* gained a reputation for literary excellence that paralleled its eminence in social and political affairs. As literary editor, Fauset was responsible for publication of Langston Hughes's first poems and she also promoted the careers of Countee Cullen and Jean Toomer, all major writers of the Harlem Renaissance. Fauset also solicited most of the material for the *Brownies' Book*, a progressive children's magazine DuBois published in 1920 and 1921. As an editor, Fauset demonstrated sound critical judgment and an appreciation for literary innovation; she also made a particular effort to highlight work by black women.

Fauset's own *Crisis* writings are notable. Her articles covered cultural, historical, and political topics. One of the few women to participate in the 1921 Pan-African Congress, Fauset shared her vivid impressions of that meeting with *Crisis* readers; later she described her travels in Europe and the Middle East during 1925 and 1926. She also reviewed and translated works by French-speaking black writers from Africa and the Caribbean. At the same time, Fauset honed her skills as a poet and fiction writer. She penned her best-known poem, "La Vie C'est la Vie," in 1922 and also wrote several stories for the *Crisis*.

According to one critic, Fauset's *There Is Confusion* (1924) was "the novel the Negro intelligentsia had been clamoring for." Set in Philadelphia, it depicts the struggle of an idealistic young woman to become a professional concert singer without compromising personal and racial pride. *Plum Bun* (1929), generally considered Fauset's best novel, uses the subject of racial "passing" to explore issues of race and gender identity. *Plum Bun* is set mainly in Harlem, but the action of *The Chinaberry Tree* (1931) unfolds in a small New Jersey town. Fictional Red Brook is home to the novel's protagonist, Laurentine, whose obsession with respectability is fueled by shame. She has been ostracized because her mother, though loving and loved by the white man who was her master, was never married. A postslavery woman, Laurentine exults in her own freedom to be virtuous. She finally learns that virtue and morality have more relative meaning than conventional wisdom allows. Fauset's last novel, the ironically titled *Comedy: American Style* (1934), suffers least from the sentimentality to which her fiction was prone. This tragic tale, set in Philadelphia, depicts the effects of self-hatred on a black woman and her family.

In the main, critics have not been impressed by Fauset's novels. Their major complaints are that her plots depend too much on coincidence, the prose is often stilted, and her heroes and heroines are simply too good for credibility. Some revisionist critics argue that Fauset employed the conventions of the sentimental novel deliberately to conceal feminist implications in her work. Such arguments attribute a higher degree of artistic self-consciousness to Fauset than her work seems to support. On the other hand, Fauset has been wrongly accused of simply being an apologist for the black middle class. In truth, her novels—much like her journalism—reveal an effort to explore experience both like and unlike her own.

Regrettably, Fauset published nothing after 1934. After resigning from the *Crisis* in 1926, she returned to teaching. In 1929 she married businessman Herbert Harris; they moved to Montclair in 1939. During the next decade Fauset was active in local cultural affairs. Though she ceased to play a national role, her example continued to inspire. Despite a demanding workload at the *Crisis* and later a full-time teaching job, Fauset had written four novels in ten years. Publishers had not believed an audience existed for her books, but she had proved them wrong. As an editor, she had helped build an audience for other writers. Indeed, as Langston Hughes put it, Fauset was one of those "who midwifed the so-called New Negro literature into being." Following a lengthy illness, this pioneering black woman writer died, at age 79, in Philadelphia on April 30, 1961.

Carolyn W. Sylvander, *Jessie Redmon Fauset: Black American Writer* (1981), is a critical assessment of Fauset's work and provides a complete listing of her writings. Briefer accounts of her life and writings appear in *NAW-MP*, *American Women Writers* 2 (1980), and the *Dictionary of American Negro Biography* (1982). Critical assessments of Fauset's work are: Deborah McDowell, "The Neglected Dimension of Jessie Redmon Fauset," in Marjorie Pryse and Hortense Spillers, eds., *Conjuring: Black Women, Fiction, and Literary Tradition* (1985); and Hiroko Sato, "Under the Harlem Shadow: A Study of Jessie Fauset and Nella Larsen," in Arna Bontemps, ed., *The Harlem Renaissance Remembered* (1972). The NYPL-SC maintains a clipping file on Fauset. Additional information came from an interview with Arthur Huff Fauset. Her obituary appeared in the *New York Times*, May 3, 1961.

*Cheryl A. Wall*

## MILLICENT HAMMOND FENWICK, 1910–

Millicent (Hammond) Fenwick, former U.S. ambassador to the United Nations Food and Agriculture Organizations and former congresswoman from the Fifth District of New Jersey, is the second daughter of Mary Picton (Stevens) and Ogden Haggerty Hammond. She was born February 25, 1910, in New York City. Her childhood was marred by tragedy when her parents sailed for Europe to set up a hospital in France for the wounded in World War I; her mother died on the *Lusitania*, May 7, 1915. Ogden Hammond remarried two years later.

The lives of the Hammond children—Mary, Millicent, and Ogden, Jr.—progressed normally until their father was made ambassador to Spain in 1925. This appointment interrupted Fenwick's formal education at the Foxcroft School in Virginia. However, she began a process of self-education by reading as many of the world's great writers as she could. Coupled with her daily experiences of living in European diplomatic and royal circles, Fenwick emerged highly educated without formal schooling. While living in Spain, Fenwick became fluent in Spanish. She already knew French and later learned Italian.

In 1929 the Hammonds returned to Bernardsville, NJ. Fenwick took courses in philosophy at Columbia University and at the New School for Social Research, where she became friends with an instructor, Bertrand Russell.

At the age of 22, in 1932, she married Hugh Fenwick and lived on a dairy farm in Bernardsville. (*Sunday Star-Ledger*, June 21, 1987) They had two children, Mary (b. 1934) and Hugh (b. 1937). In 1938 Hugh Fenwick left for Europe, and during the following years the marriage dissolved, along with the income from the Hoboken Land and Improvement Company, which she had inherited from her mother. This left Fenwick alone with a string of debts and two small children to raise. When asked why she did not turn to her family for help, she replied, "Why, it just never occurred to me." (Interview, Aug. 19, 1985).

Instead, Fenwick tried to get a job selling stockings at Bonwit Teller's in New York City, but her lack of a high school diploma disqualified her. She tried unsuccessfully to get some of her writing published and, for a short time, modeled for *Harper's Bazaar*. A friend introduced her to Condé Nast, the publisher of *Vogue* magazine, who hired her as a writer. Nast agreed to Fenwick's request that she work in the feature department, where she concentrated on the public service that society women performed rather than on society news and fashion. During World War II Fenwick became the unofficial editor of war news. Fenwick also single-handedly wrote the 648-page *Vogue Book of Etiquette.*

When she began to work, Fenwick's original salary was $40 per week, but increasing raises enabled her to pay off her debts in small installments of $10 and $20 per month, depending on the size of the bill. She even got to know the bill collector who was waiting to meet her every Friday night with "another one" when she came home from her job.

This period of trying times, both worldwide and personal, did not prevent Fenwick from taking part in her family tradition of public service. Horrified by one of Adolph Hitler's speeches, Fenwick immediately joined the National Conference of Christians and Jews. Fenwick says she is a member of the Republican party because "more than any single exploitive tyrannical force, the possibility of what government can do is absolutely terrifying. . . . Way down underneath, I don't trust government." (Lamson, *In the Vanguard*, 8) Concurrent with her career at *Vogue*, Fenwick ran for the Board of Education in Bernardsville, NJ. She served from 1935 through 1941.

In the 1940s the Hoboken Land and Development Company was taken over by a sound real estate firm, gradually restoring Fenwick's finances. As a result, in 1952 she left *Vogue* to stay at home. Not satisfied with gardening and needlework, in 1954 she volunteered to help Senator Clifford Case with his campaign. Fenwick was elected to the Bernardsville Borough Council from 1958 to 1964. Using volunteer work and contributions, she accomplished the building of the Little League Field House and the installation of the community swimming pool.

From 1958 to 1972 Fenwick also served on the N.J. Advisory Committee to the U.S. Commission on Civil Rights. She gained practical experience, visiting and talking with poor blacks and Hispanics, and testified on their behalf concerning living conditions and rent strikes.

Elected to the N.J. General Assembly in 1969, her tenure has been described in the *Almanac of American Politics* as "a distinguished record in a rather undistinguished body." Her bills included migrant labor legislation and consumer issues. One of her more famous causes was the Equal Rights Amendment. When a colleague objected to the amendment because he liked to think of women as "kissable, cuddly and smelling good," Fenwick's often quoted response was: "That's the way I feel about men. I only hope for your sake that you haven't been as disappointed as I have." ("The Very Independent Mrs. Fenwick," 71)

In 1973 Governor William Cahill appointed Fenwick the N.J. Director of Consumer Affairs. The Bureau of Weights and Measures, started by a member of the Stevens family, was part of the Division of Consumer Affairs, and Fenwick took a special interest in it. In fifteen months as Consumer Affairs director, Fenwick implemented over a dozen regulations in the consumer's interest in several different fields.

In 1974 Fenwick ran for U.S. Congress and won by a margin of 83 votes. Discovered by the media, Fenwick was described as a "seventy-one year old, pipe smoking . . .

grandmother." ("The Very Independent Mrs. Fenwick," 71) She became the prototype for Lacey Davenport in the popular "Doonesbury" comic strip by Garry Trudeau. In reality, Fenwick proved herself to be a tough, independent representative, using common sense to assure fair treatment for the individual citizen.

During the administration of President Jimmy Carter, Fenwick's concern for the ordinary citizen was proven by the bills she introduced. Having found that consumers could be protected in bankruptcy cases only through federal legislation, she persuaded a Democratic member of the Judiciary Committee to introduce the necessary amendment. The Debt Practices Bill, also in the interest of consumers, was similarly successful. Both were signed into law. She also persuaded Secretary of Health, Education and Welfare Joseph A. Califano to sign new regulations to allow home health care instead of nursing home care whenever appropriate.

Fenwick's trip to the Soviet Union in August 1975 led to important changes in legislation in connection with the Helsinki Accords. Although she was the most junior member of the visiting delegation, Fenwick went on her own to visit Alexander Turchin, the head of Amnesty International in Moscow. He was in trouble due to his defense of Andrei Sakharov, the famous Soviet dissident who was still in exile. Also Fenwick discovered the plight of Lev Ruitburd, whose wife, Lelia, risked coming to see Fenwick. Ruitburd had been held prisoner ever since he had tried to travel from Odessa to Moscow to see U.S. Senators Jacob Javits and Edward Kennedy. He has since been released and allowed to emigrate. His incarceration, however, was in direct opposition to the Helsinki Accords.

When she returned to Washington, D.C., Fenwick set about creating the Commission on Security and Cooperation in Europe, known as the Helsinki Commission. In September 1975 Bill HR9466 was introduced in the House of Representatives. It provided for a commission of fifteen members: six senators, six congressmen, and one representative each from the Departments of State, Defense, and Commerce. Nothing happened until November, when the same bill was introduced by Clifford Case of New Jersey in the Senate. It was passed by both Houses in May and signed into law by President Gerald Ford on June 6, 1976.

Fenwick also served on the Small Business and Banking Committee, the Foreign Affairs Committee, the Subcommittee on the City, and the Committee on the Official Conduct, known as the Ethics Committee. While serving on this committee, she was involved in the "Koreagate" investigation.

Although a strong advocate of the Equal Rights Amendment (ERA), Fenwick does not think of herself as a feminist. What others call women's rights issues Fenwick calls civil rights and citizenship issues, holding that an elected official is equally responsible to each member of society, not to any special group. On August 17, 1976, as a member of the Republican Women's Task Force at the Republican Convention, Fenwick debated Phyllis Schlafly, the ERA's main opponent, on television.

In 1982 Fenwick lost the race for the U.S. Senate to Frank Lautenberg, a New Jersey businessman. Fenwick then became the U.S. ambassador to the United Nations Food and Agriculture Organizations in Rome, from which she retired in 1987.

Fenwick, referred to as the "conscience of Congress," has been compared to Eleanor Roosevelt because of her integrity and ardent feeling for public service. She strives to put her ideal of furthering justice into action. She has retired from public life to her home in Bernardsville.

An interview with Fenwick on Aug. 19, 1985, provided useful information. Additional material is available from articles such as "Rep. Fenwick: Basics Her Forte," *New York Times*, May 13, 1979; "Millicent Fenwick: Personal Diplomacy," *New York Times*, July 9, 1978; "Fenwick Returns 'Forever' to Where Her 'Roots Are Planted,'" *New York Times*, Mar. 15, 1987; and "Millicent Fenwick Finds Peace at Home," *Newark Star-Ledger*, June 21, 1987. Also helpful were "The Very Independent Mrs. Fenwick," *United Mainline Magazine* (Jan. 1982):48–73; Peggy Lamson, *In the Vanguard: Six American Women in Public Life* (1979); and her profile in *Current Biography* (1977).

*Grace A. Aqualina*

## RITA SAPIRO FINKLER, 1888–1968

Rita (Sapiro) Finkler, M.D., a pioneering endocrinologist, practicing physician, feminist, lecturer, and humanitarian, was the first woman on the senior medical staff at Newark Beth Israel Medical Center, where she founded the department of endocrinology, which she directed from 1939 to 1951. She was born Ricka Sapiro on November 1, 1888, in Kherson, Ukraine, Russia, to Sarah and Woolf Sapiro. Finkler's mother came from a well-educated Jewish family; her father was a miller. She had one brother, who died in early childhood. Her older sister was called Saphira and her younger sister, Rhia. Finkler's mother died of breast cancer when her daughters were very young. Shortly thereafter her father remarried.

As a child, Finkler experienced the political turmoil in Russia at the turn of the century. Her aunts and uncles, ardent revolutionists, were imprisoned for their anticzarist activities. Influenced by their political views, she decided to become a lawyer. An excellent student, she was presented with a gold medal when she graduated from the Latin Male Gymnasium and the Byra Bestow-Gersky College and went on to study law at the University of St. Petersburg. "I had a glorified view of myself as an attorney making speeches in court before an enthralled audience."

(Knapp, *Woman Doctors Today*, 170) But she soon found that the details of studying law bored her.

Although some references mention Finkler's revolutionary activities and subsequent imprisonment, the stories can be traced to a newspaper article in which another woman, Madame Malmberg—a former prisoner in a St. Petersburg fortress—was on the same lecture program with Finkler. Malmberg's imprisonment is mentioned immediately before Finkler is introduced. The article, which is in a collection of Finkler memorabilia held by her daughter, Dr. Sylvia Becker, does not mention the newspaper or the date the story was clipped. Becker, however, is adamant that her mother was never imprisoned and that, in fact, confusion might have been caused by her relatives' revolutionary activities. Having decided to give up her legal studies, Finkler, who intensely disliked her stepmother, ran away with the intention of resettling in New Zealand, a country she viewed as a new land of opportunity. On the way, she stopped in Philadelphia, PA, to visit Dr. Sophie Ostrow, a relative who had recently graduated from the Woman's Medical College of Philadelphia. Ostrow convinced her to remain in the United States and to study medicine.

In 1911 she entered the Woman's Medical College. She earned the money for medical school by working as a waitress and as a seamstress in a factory, the same skills that had earned her passage to the United States. In addition, she became a popular lecturer and a tutor in languages. In her second year at college she won the Robinson-Messner Prize in Anatomy. Finkler graduated in 1915, second in her class.

Between her first and second year at medical school Finkler met Samuel Jacob Finkler, a young chemistry student from the Pennsylvania State University. They were married the following summer (1913) and continued their studies for two more years, seeing each other during semester breaks. They had one daughter, Sylvia (b. 1921). In 1925, Finkler and her husband were divorced.

After graduation Finkler applied for an internship at the Philadelphia Polyclinic Hospital, an institution where the doors were regarded as permanently closed against women doctors. Finkler's appointment seemed doubtful; therefore, she entered the competitive examinations for an appointment to the Philadelphia General, where she scored fifth out of 98 candidates. At about the same time, she was informed of her appointment to the Philadelphia Polyclinic Hospital, which she accepted.

As an intern, Finkler experienced deep-seated opposition to her presence in the hospital; the other interns felt it outrageous that a woman should be numbered among them. Newspaper articles about her caused much discussion among the hospital staff and the general public. Always flamboyant and courageous, Finkler made the news again when she harnessed an ailing horse, "Poor Old Jer-

Rita S. Finkler, c. 1932, in her laboratory at Beth Israel Hospital, Newark, where she performed the first pregnancy tests in New Jersey. *Courtesy, F. G. Smith Library, Special Collections, College of Medicine and Dentistry of New Jersey.*

ry," to a horse-drawn ambulance and rode it around Philadelphia to point out the need for a motor-driven ambulance. From 1916 to 1918 she was director of the Philadelphia Health Center.

She set up a private practice in Newark, NJ, in 1919, when there were fewer than 400 women doctors in the state. Eight years later Finkler, who was fluent in eight languages, studied abroad, concentrating on endocrinology. While she conducted her practice in Newark and developed her specialization in endocrinology, she was on the staff at Newark Beth Israel Hospital. At first, she was in pediatrics; then, she was named associate chief in gynecology. After writing more than 70 papers in the field of endocrinology, she established and headed the first department of endocrinology in New Jersey at Beth Israel Hospital in 1934.

Prior to her admission to the staff of Beth Israel, she had applied and been recommended for a position at St. Vincent's Hospital in New York City. The hospital accepted her, but when she arrived, they were horrified—they had thought Ricka was short for Richard—and refused to have her on their staff. After this incident she changed her name to Rita so no one would mistake her for a man again. While she was on the Beth Israel staff, she opened her first office on High Street, opposite the hospital. After Beth Israel relocated in 1929, she moved her office to Lyons Avenue (1930) so that once again she could be across the street from the hospital. Finally, she moved to Leslie Street in the Clinton Hill section of Newark.

In addition to her work in endocrinology, Finkler, through the N.J. Medical Women's Association, also was active in helping women doctors persecuted by the Nazis prior to World War II to escape and set up practice in the United States. (A colleague, CARYE-BELLE HENLE, was also active in this cause.) After the war, the association mailed more than 6,000 pounds of relief packages to women doctors in France and England. Finkler also was responsible for bringing her younger sister and her sister's children to the United States. After much effort, she traced her older sister, Saphira, also a physician, who had been sent to a labor camp in Siberia. When Saphira contracted breast cancer, the authorities sent her to her hometown, and by the time Finkler located her there, she was too sick to travel to the United States. Later, her sister's daughter also contracted breast cancer and died. Her sister's husband died in the labor camp.

In 1956 Finkler was named Medical Woman of the Year by the American Medical Women's Association (AMWA), branch four, in recognition of her work as national chair of the AMWA's Emergency Committee.

She was a member of the American Medical Association; the AMWA, branch four, NJ; the Endocrine Society; the Pan American Medical Association; and the American Physicians' Committee of the Israel Medical Association. She was also a counselor to the Medical Women's International Association, the American Society for the Study of Fertility, and the International Society of Fertility.

In 1958 Finkler had a stroke. When she recovered she opened an office in Millburn, where she practiced from 1959 until 1968. At the time of her illness she moved into her daughter Sylvia's home in Short Hills, where she lived until her death.

Finkler was an adventurous and courageous woman who traveled extensively, particularly to those countries considered unexplored or unattractive to general tourists. She was a popular and dynamic lecturer who spoke both about her career and her travels.

She died of heart failure on November 8, 1968, at age 80, in New York City, where she was visiting relatives. She was buried in Woodbridge, NJ, at Beth Israel Cemetery.

An interview with Finkler's daughter, Dr. Sylvia Becker, of Verona, NJ, on May 12, 1987, provided biographical details. Finkler's life and career are highlighted in Sally Knapp, *Women*

*Doctors Today* (1947). Papers and materials on Finkler are available at NJ-UMDNJ.

*Maria Gillan*

## E. ALMA FLAGG, 1918–

Eloise Alma (Williams) Flagg, retired educator, present-day lecturer, community activist, and poet, was born on September 16, 1918, in City Point, VA. She was the second of five children of Hannibal Greene Williams, a house painter, and Caroline Ethel (Moody) Williams, a homemaker. When Flagg was very young her family moved to Newark, NJ, where she has lived for most of her life. Hannibal Williams died in 1931 and Flagg's mother worked hard to educate her children.

A 1935 honor graduate of the Newark public schools, Flagg has devoted her life to a personal quest for knowledge and selfless service. She earned her B.S. from Newark State College (Kean College of New Jersey) in 1940, her M.A. from Montclair State College in 1943, and her Ed.D. from Teachers College, Columbia University, in 1955.

On June 24, 1942, she married J. Thomas Flagg, civic leader and now a retired professor of education from Montclair State College, at the First Mount Zion Baptist Church in Newark. They had two children: Thomas Lyle (b. 1949) and Luisa (b. 1952).

Flagg was a devoted fighter for the rights of Newark's black public school teachers and for women's rights. Much of her time was spent obtaining better working conditions, higher standards of living, better educational opportunities, and basic civil rights for the citizens of Newark.

The year Flagg graduated from Newark State College (1940) the Newark Board of Education held no teachers' examination, a prerequisite for employment in Newark's public schools. However, she passed the same type of examination in Washington, D.C., where she taught for two years. In 1943 she was employed as a teacher by the Newark Board of Education, becoming one of sixteen black teachers employed by the board. By that time, Flagg had earned her master's degree and Newark had its first black member of the Board of Education, William R. Jackson.

During a period of 42 years beginning in 1941, Flagg held successively the positions of elementary teacher, principal, citywide administrator of summer elementary reading programs, assistant superintendent of schools, and director of curriculum services. These promotions were not easily obtained because racial and sexual barriers played a dominant role in the employment and promotion policies of the Newark school system.

Flagg and other blacks charged the Newark Board of Education with racial discrimination in 1958, after they took a two-part (written and oral) vice-principals' examination, scored high on the written portion, but faced a subjective oral section that caused the black professionals' overall scores to be reduced dramatically. Charges of racism in hiring procedures were lodged against the board, and these accusations were investigated by several groups. In 1963 Flagg was appointed vice-principal and in 1964 principal, making her the first black woman in Newark to hold that position. Flagg was also responsible for the inclusion of Aerospace Education in the curriculum and for several other innovations.

Flagg is a talented poet. She has published three books of poetry: *Lines and Colors: Twenty-one Poems* (1979), *Feelings, Lines, Colors* (1980), and *Twenty More with Thought and Feeling* (1981). Her poetry demonstrates her deep care for family, friends, students, and her city, and each poem seems to parallel some facet of her life. Flagg also wrote poetry for *Newark, 1967–1977: An Assessment*, edited by Stanley B. Winters. She was a consultant in elementary school mathematics for Harcourt Brace Jovanovich, Inc. (1980–85), and a consultant and author for Houghton Mifflin in elementary school mathematics (1972–88). In addition, Flagg edited curriculum documents for all subjects at all levels for the Newark school system (1967–82).

Many awards and plaques have been bestowed upon Flagg. In recognition of her contributions to education in Newark, the E. Alma Flagg School, located on North Third Street, was named in her honor.

In 1985 Flagg was awarded the Sojourner Truth Award by the North Jersey Business and Professional Women's Club for volunteer work in her city. Scholarships from the E. Alma Flagg Scholarship Fund, Inc., created in her honor by educators and friends of the Flagg family, were presented in 1984 and each year thereafter to qualified graduates of the Newark high schools.

Flagg lives in Newark, where she cared for her mother until her death in November 1987. She still reads poetry for groups and organizations, supervises student teachers, and holds offices in several organizations.

Biographical entries for Flagg appear in *Who's Who Among Black Americans* (1988) and *Who's Who in the East* (1987), *Who's Who in American Education* (1987–88), and *Who's Who of American Women* (1988; since 1966). An account of the racially discriminatory hiring practices of the Newark Board of Education appears in W. M. Philips, *Participation of the Black Community in Selected Aspects of Educational Institutions of Newark, 1958–1972* (1973).

*Esther Vincent Lloyd*

## GRACE MARGARET FREEMAN, 1897–1967

Assemblywoman Grace Margaret Freeman, author of the New Jersey Civil Rights Act (1949), was born April 1, 1897, in Union City (Hudson County), NJ, to Grace E.

(Jones) and Walter H. Freeman, a pioneer of the telephone industry. From all evidence she was an only child and grew up in East Orange, NJ. The family moved from Union City to East Orange in 1905 and eventually lived at 361 North Arlington Avenue. They were active in the Munn Avenue Presbyterian Church in East Orange.

Freeman is said to have attended East Orange public schools, but East Orange High School has no record of her attendance. She attended the New Jersey State Normal School at Montclair (now Montclair State College), graduating at the end of the two-year course in 1918, at the age of 21. Upon completing her work there, she enrolled at Teachers' College, Columbia University, earning a B.S. in 1923, an M.A. in 1926, and a diploma as supervisor in civic education in 1926.

While studying at Teachers' College, Freeman taught civics and history full time in the secondary schools of Caldwell, NJ, and later in Montclair, where her salary was $1500 a year. She stated in her employment application (Montclair, 1920) that she preferred teaching grammar, English literature, U.S. history, general history, and civil government—evidence that at age 22 she already had a strong leaning toward politics.

Her career as a teacher in the Montclair schools came to a dramatic end in 1933, when the closing of the Nishuane School forced a reorganization of the teaching staff. She never took another full-time teaching position, and it is doubtful that she did other salaried work except for teaching social studies and government in adult education classes at Upsala College and the Bloomfield Adult School (1938–39).

During World War II Freeman served on the East Orange Defense Council. When she resigned, the *East Orange Record* (Apr. 15, 1943) account speculated "that [her resignation] was motivated by differences of opinion between Miss Freeman and newly-appointed Defense Chairman Hoyt Lufkin over matters of policy pertaining to the administrative handling of various defense details." The article describes her as "an indefatigable worker" who had "made a full time job of her voluntary post, serving as a sort of liaison officer between the various units of defense, instructor in first aid and motor corps, Defense Council speaker at numerous meetings, handled secretarial duties of various kinds, including the keeping of the minutes of Defense Council meetings, copies of which are sent to the State Defense Council." She was as firmly assertive about matters of policy in 1943 as she had been in 1933, when she resigned from teaching.

After World War II she was elected to the New Jersey Assembly. Her first triumph was the sponsorship of the Civil Rights Act. It passed the legislature and was signed into law on April 5, 1949, by Governor Alfred E. Driscoll. It would be fifteen years before the U.S. Congress passed the Civil Rights Act of 1964. The Freeman bill outlawed all forms of discrimination due to race, creed, national origin, or color in employment, education, housing, public accommodation and recreational facilities such as hotels, bars, restaurants, theaters, beaches and boardwalks, swimming pools, bathhouses, gymnasiums, bowling alleys, and myriad other places.

Freeman was chair of the Education Committee in the House of the General Assembly, where she sponsored such bills as the repeal of the tax on school athletic meets and plays and the outlawing of switchblades. But her most important education-related bill, passed in 1951, established a $15 million bond issue to support building programs at the state teachers' colleges.

Freeman's work in the male-dominated field of politics, she told an interviewer, meant "I learned to be a fighter—but a nice one." (*Newark News*, Apr. 20, 1967) She earned the epithet "the Happy Warrior." On one occasion, an assemblyman said that "school teachers could not do anything but teach school." He bet Freeman could not bake a chocolate cake. After that, she often brought her chocolate cakes to Trenton. (*East Orange Record*, July 5, 1951)

Having served for five years in the assembly, Freeman could not be reelected because of a new four-year limit imposed after the raising of legislators' salary to $3,000 annually. Her bid for nomination to the U.S. Congress on the Republican "clean government" ticket failed, despite strong local support from women's and church organizations.

The long list of clubs and political organizations in which Freeman was active shows that she virtually made a profession of civic responsibility. Some of the groups she served are the Montclair Teachers' Association; the New Jersey branch of the League of Nations Association; the Montclair Women's Club; the League of Women Voters of the Oranges; the Essex County Council of Churches; the Speaker's Bureau of the New Jersey District of the National Conference of Christians and Jews; the New Jersey Council on Japanese-Americans; the Civic Groups Budget Conference for East Orange (the only woman to serve); the Women's Auxiliary of the Essex County Republican party; the Woman's Division of the Chamber of Commerce and Civics of the Oranges and Maplewood; the New Jersey branch of the National Association of Pro-America; the New Jersey branch of the United Nations Association; the American Red Cross; the Civil Rights Commission of East Orange. She held office in all of these organizations. Her sense of responsibility is also reflected in the personal act of providing grants to needy students at Montclair State College.

In 1949 the Department of New Jersey, Ladies Auxiliary of the Jewish War Veterans, USA, presented Freeman with a gold trophy in recognition of her civil rights legislation. In 1950 she received a citation presented by the New Jersey Conference of the National Association for the Advancement of Colored People. On May 12, 1950, she received from the New Jersey State Federation of Women's Clubs the Cecilia Gaines Holland Award for "outstanding service in her community and state." They said of her: "You have made of education a crusade, of civic work a daily occupation and of politics a demonstration of citizenship at its highest level. You have brought to the service of your state clear thinking, wise judgment and noble ideals. Teacher, club member, citizen, lawmaker, New Jersey owes you much." She quietly noted in a 1964 Montclair Alumni Association questionnaire that she had received 37 awards.

Freeman continued her vigorous activity in worthy organizations, adding the national Order of Women Legislators, Delta Kappa Gamma, the National Association of Parliamentarians, the YWCA of Oranges and Maplewood, and New Jersey Council of Churches to her list. Her devotion to the cause of human relations was recognized in 1959 by the New Jersey Region of the National Conference of Christians and Jews. At about that time she was active in a teacher training program in human relations, the Citizenship Institute, at Douglass College of Rutgers University.

As chair of the Montclair State College War Memorial Fund, Freeman was instrumental in the erection of Life Hall, where a reading room is dedicated to her. A girls' dormitory, Grace Freeman Hall, dedicated to her on October 6, 1963, has an oil portrait of her, commissioned by her devoted aunt May Jones.

When president of the Montclair Women's Club, Freeman gave monthly lessons in parliamentary procedure to the club board members. And at business meetings, if a committee had been inactive, the chair was required to say "progress is being made" rather than decline to make a report. Freeman wrote in a rhetorical style that sometimes waxed poetic. One of her favorite sayings, oft repeated, was "Coming together is a beginning. Keeping together is progress. Working together is success." (Personal communication, Hortense J. Felt; and *Quest*, Apr. 1965, 25)

When Freeman died of cancer in East Orange on April 19, 1967, at age 70, her only survivor was her aunt May Jones, who lived with her. Freeman was buried in the Jones family plot in Green-Wood Cemetery in Brooklyn, NY. Her good works did not cease upon her death. In her will she left the North Arlington Avenue residence to be used, after May Jones's death, as a retirement home for Presbyterian ministers and missionaries, their wives and widows. In addition, she left $50,000 to benefit Grace M. Freeman Hall, the dormitory named for her at Montclair State College, providing "niceties, refinements or extras" for the young women there. (*Newark Evening News*, May 6, 1967)

A list of Freeman's education, organizational affiliations, and honors appears in the *Manual of the Legislature of New Jersey* (1948, 1951), and a sketch of her is contained in *Who's Who of American Women* (1958–59). Newspapers such as the *New York Times*, the *Newark News*, the *Montclair Times*, and the *East Orange Record* provide valuable information, especially the *East Orange Record*, Apr. 15, 1943, and July 5, 1951; and the *New York Times*, Mar. 15 and 17, 1949. An especially useful source is *Quest*, the monthly magazine of the Montclair Women's Club, most notably the issues of Oct. 1962, Dec. 1964, Apr. 1965, and May 1966. The file on Freeman in the NJ-EOPL is useful. Additional information on Freeman was provided by an interview with Hortense Felt of the Montclair Women's Club. Freeman's obituary appeared in the *New York Times*, Apr. 21, 1967, and in the *Newark News*, Apr. 20, 1967.

*Doris B. Armstrong*

## WANDA HAZEL GÁG, 1893–1946

Wanda Hazel Gág, artist and author of children's books, was born in New Ulm, MN, on March 11, 1893, the eldest of seven children, to Anton and Elizabeth (Biebl) Gág, Bohemian (Czechoslovakian) immigrants. Although poor and largely uneducated, her parents and her aunts and uncles were aesthetically inclined. Her father was a painter with little formal art training, but dedicated enough to encourage all his offspring toward artistic pursuits. Gág herself remembers that she spent her childhood "in the serene belief that drawing and painting, like eating and sleeping, belonged to the universal and inevitable things of life." (Hearn, "Wanda Gág," 180)

Gág's early life was bittersweet. The family felt alienated from their neighbors because of the Gágs' indifference to organized religion, ignorance of English, and poverty. But as a result of their isolation the young girl was steeped "in an atmosphere of Old World customs and legends, of Bavarian and Bohemian folk songs, of German *Märchen* and *Turneverein* activities." (Hearn, 180)

Gág's father supplied her with contemporary books and magazines featuring the popular illustrations of such artists as Charles Dana Gibson and Jessie Willcox Smith. Unfamiliar with Western masterpieces, Gág found that her taste was largely determined by the commercial artists of her time.

When her father died in 1908, the poverty from which she often escaped through her drawing was more acute, and neighbors began pressuring her to find employment. Such interference made her withdraw even further into her artistic fantasy world, and she became more determined to succeed as an artist. She finally won a one dollar prize from the Minneapolis *Junior Journal*, which afterward accepted other sketches and tales. She also drew greeting cards and painted lampshades in her efforts to provide for her family.

After she graduated from New Ulm High School in

1912, Gág reluctantly became a teacher in a small country school. When two of her sisters found jobs, however, she applied for and won a scholarship to the St. Paul Art School in 1913. In her year's study she found formal training both illuminating and discouraging, but she continued to create in her spare time. She submitted drawings to the University of Minnesota's *Minnehaha* magazine and also illustrated a children's English textbook, *A Child's Book of Folklore*.

She began to attend the Minneapolis Art School in 1914. In 1917 her mother died and Gág moved the remaining family members from New Ulm to Minneapolis. As soon as they were settled comfortably, she secured another scholarship, this time to the Art Students' League in New York in 1917. Having been exposed to unconventional art theory while studying in St. Paul, Gág sought the acquaintance of leftist artists and writers in Greenwich Village. But she never allowed her personal growth or ambitions to blur her first priority, a family that still required economic support. While she waited for a publisher's acceptance of her children's stories, she once again painted lampshades. She also denied herself several opportunities to marry and begin her own family because "I would marry no man unless he would promise to run the house during my drawing moods and would excuse me from scrubbing floors." (Hearn, 181–82)

Such devotion to her art and her pressing need for financial solvency led her to syndicate her illustrated puzzles, "Wanda's Wonderland," in 1925, which appeared in newspapers and the important children's magazine *St. Nicholas*. Her cowriter on this series was a salesman and labor organizer named Earle Marshall Humphreys, whom she married in 1930. The couple had no children.

Nevertheless, Gág's love for children and their world resulted in her design of a board game called "Pick-a-Path" and "Happiwork Story Boxes," cardboard boxes illustrated with different picture stories which Gág believed would be commercially successful. But the venture failed, and she decided to devote her efforts to the graphic arts. She also moved to inexpensive rural Connecticut, determined to escape the complexities of city life and return to a simple existence. The aesthetic outcome was a series of pencil and lithographic prints that the Weyhe Gallery in New York City agreed to exhibit in a one-woman show.

Among Gág's admirers was Ernestine Evans, director of the children's book department at Coward-McCann, who initially asked the artist to illustrate a new edition of a 19th-century juvenile book. When Gág refused, Evans offered to publish an original story with illustrations. The result was the highly acclaimed children's classic *Millions of Cats* (1928), a paradigm of the American picture book, with roots in Gág's own vivid imagination and in Bohemian folklore. The physical structure of the book itself was innovative, with its oblong shape, double-page illustration spreads, and text hand-lettered by Gág's brother, Howard. *Millions of Cats* appeared on the *Nation*'s list of distinguished books, the only work for children included. It was also exhibited at the American Institute of Graphic Arts' annual show and was cited as a Newbery Honor Book.

Published in 1929, the author's second book, *The Funny Thing*, did not achieve as much critical acclaim as her first book, although it was a commercial success. *Millions of Cats* had established an unfortunate precedent. Editors began to demand that all aspects of a book for children—plot, composition, and pictures—be accomplished by one person. Even Gág had difficulty maintaining the high standards of *Cats*.

In 1930 Gág purchased a large farm in the Musconetcong Mountains in northern New Jersey, which she called "All Creation" because "ever since we've been here, whoever comes here seems to want to draw, to write poetry, to paint, even to sew—but to do something!" (Hearn, 186) Gág's aesthetic impulses produced *Snippy and Snappy* (1931), a story derived from Aesop. This work completed what she obviously intended as a trilogy, and the three books were collected together in 1932 under the title *Wanda Gág's Story Book*.

Her next project, *The ABC Bunny* (1932), enabled Gág to ask part of her family to live with her at "All Creation." Her brother Howard again hand-lettered the text of the book, and her sister Flavia composed the lyrics and music of a song appearing at the end of the story. The finished product earned Gág a second Newbery Honor Book citation.

In her New Jersey home Gág found the ideal abode. Surrounded by nature, she had the freedom to work without pressure or restriction. After submitting a drawing of Hansel and Gretel to the *New York Herald-Tribune*, she was inspired to translate the childhood fairy tales that lived so vividly in her imagination. Modern educators, however, proclaimed such fantasies inappropriate and unrealistic for children. Gág strongly disagreed, insisting that youngsters need the "rightful heritage of Fairyland" because "their lives are already over-balanced on the side of steel and stone and machinery—and nowadays, one might well add bombs, gas-masks, and machine-guns." (Hoyle, "Gág, Wanda (Hazel)," 492)

In 1936 her *Tales from Grimm* appeared, containing sixteen of the original stories. Her translations were freely rendered, often relying on secondary sources, and her own taste softened some of the crude details. But the illustrations were diversified, concrete, and clearly defined. Her delight in this project prompted Gág to accept the request of Ann Carroll Moore, a New York librarian dissatisfied with the Disney version, that she rework the Grimms' *Snow White and the Seven Dwarfs*. Interestingly, Gág's text included some violence of the original which Disney had omitted, but her accompanying illustrations failed to re-flect the story's brutalities. "Almost any fairy tale," she remarked, "can be made unterrifying by pictures which are just a little too funny or absurd to be taken seriously." Her *Snow White and the Seven Dwarfs* was published in 1938 and was voted a Caldecott Honor Book in 1939.

In 1940 she edited *Growing Pains: Diaries and Drawings for the Years 1908–1917*, which contained her youthful journals. A second volume never progressed beyond the planning stages. *Nothing at All*, her first picture book in color, appeared in 1941. Her editor at Coward-McCann asked her to write a novel. She resisted, but she did return to her beloved fairy tales, publishing *Three Gay Tales from Grimm* in 1943.

In her final years Gág diversified her output by drawing pictures for juvenile magazines and adapting her books as radio plays. She also continued to translate folktales. Near the end of her life she completed the text for *More Tales from Grimm* (1947), but she had not yet finished the illustrations when she died of lung cancer, at age 53, in New York City on July 27, 1946. Gág's body was cremated and her ashes were scattered on her farm, "All Creation."

Her contemporary appeal is evidenced by the recent publication of three of her translations: *Jorinda and Joringel* (1978), *The Sorcerer's Apprentice* (1979), and *The Six Swans* (1982). But it is her first great success, *Million of Cats*, that earned her acclaim as an expert of the picture book for children. Gág earned two posthumous awards: the Lewis Carroll Shelf Award (1958) and the University of Minnesota Kerlan Award (1977).

Gág's autobiography is *Growing Pains: Diaries and Drawings for the Years 1908–1917* (1940). A biography of her is Alma Scott, *Wanda Gág: The Story of an Artist* (1949), and she is profiled in *NAW*. An assessment of her work is Michael Patrick Hearn, "Wanda Gág," *Dictionary of Literary Biography: American Writers for Children* 22 (1983); and a brief critical overview of her work is Karen Nelson Hoyle, "Gág, Wanda (Hazel)," in *Twentieth Century Children's Writers*, ed. D. L. Kirkpatrick (1978). Her papers, including unpublished diaries and correspondence, as well as a collection of her prints and drawings, are available at the Philadelphia Museum of Art. Her obituary appeared in the *New York Times*, June 28, 1946.

*Laura M. Gabrielsen*

## KATHRYN ELIZABETH GAMBLE, 1915–

Kathryn Elizabeth Gamble, born in Van Wert, OH, on August 19, 1915, served as director of the Montclair Art Museum from 1952 to 1980. During her long tenure, she not only administered the museum, but was largely responsible for building its choice collection, one of the finest small collections of American painting in the United States. When a catalog of the American painting collection of the Montclair Art Museum was published in 1977, 72 percent of the works in it had been acquired under Gamble's direction, including important works by 18th-century painters Charles Willson Peale and John Singleton Copley; 19th-century landscapists Frederick Church and Albert Bierstadt; Thomas Eakins, George Bellows, and many others.

Gamble's maternal grandparents, who were of German stock, lived in the small town of 8000 where she was born. Her mother, May (Cassell) Gamble, worked as a court clerk there before her marriage. She was also a painter, mainly in watercolors—pictures of woodland scenes, which Gamble believes were imagined. Her father, Verne Gorham Gamble, who was of Irish descent, was a real estate salesman. Soon after Gamble's birth, he moved the family to Detroit. Then, in 1921, Gamble's mother died, and the five-year-old Kathryn and her one-and-a-half-year-old brother, Richard Lee, were sent back to Van Wert to live with their grandparents. In 1925 Gamble's father remarried and he and his wife took the children with them to the Detroit suburb of Grosse Point. With the stock market crash of 1929, the family moved back to the old house in Van Wert, and Gamble graduated from high school there.

Gamble's first encounter with art, aside from her mother's watercolors which hung in the Van Wert house, was at the Detroit Art Institute, where she went to earn her Girl Scout service badge. Once, in a part of the museum closed to the public, she glimpsed the great Mexican muralist Diego Rivera at work on his wall for the center court, and she remembers being fascinated to see a work of art in the making.

In 1933 Gamble went to Oberlin College, where she majored in fine arts and biology with the idea of becoming a scientific illustrator. After graduation in 1937 she won an atelier scholarship to the Dayton Art Institute in Dayton, OH. It was while working on weekends in the education department there that she began to think of a museum career. She could not afford to continue her studies at that time, however, and so took a job teaching and supervising art in the public schools of Covington, OH. At the end of three years, she came to New Jersey, to the Newark Museum, where she took the apprenticeship course formulated by the famed museologist John Cotton Dana. Realizing that her background in art history was inadequate as a foundation for a successful museum career, she enrolled at the New York University Institute of Fine Arts and eventually wrote her master's thesis on the mother and child in Egyptian art. Meanwhile, she supported herself by working as a research librarian for the Socony-Vacuum Oil Company (later Mobil) on lower Broadway in New York City. In 1944, still at NYU, she was invited to become an assistant director of the Montclair Art Museum, the beginning of an association that was to last 36 years.

About that time a consensus was reached among the museum's trustees and administrators to use several large bequests, most notably the Lang Acquisition Fund, to establish the Montclair Art Museum as a major collector of American art. The original collection, given by Montclair resident William T. Evans in 1909, consisted mainly of works by his contemporaries, and despite some remarkable gifts made in the years following, almost all the acquisitions work remained to be done. Gamble was in on that effort from the beginning. In 1945, while still assistant director, Gamble acquired Asher B. Durand's *Early Morning at Cold Spring*, one of the masterpieces of the Hudson River School. Until well into the 1950s American art was considered largely the province of antiques collectors and historians, and there was little attempt to judge the aesthetic quality of a work. Gamble had an eye, though, and purchased pieces with aesthetic as well as historical value, including some beautiful anonymous works.

When Gamble was named director in 1952, she was one of the youngest women ever to obtain such a post. Moreover, she was competing in a world that was, and still is, dominated by men. During her directorship, she mounted hundreds of exhibitions and contributed to many documentary catalogs, most notably *George Inness of Montclair*, *The Betty Parsons Retrospective*, and *The American Painting Collection of the Montclair Art Museum*, this last published under her direction with the aid of a grant from the National Endowment for the Arts and support of several private and corporate foundations. She also increased the number of museum programs, everything from gallery talks to art-related community functions. In addition, she was committed to the preservation of the collection in her care, a function she felt was a museum director's particular responsibility.

Gamble was both an astute collector and a determined one. In 1961, in a Manhattan art dealer's office, she saw some untagged photographs of two 18th-century portraits and identified them as being by Charles Willson Peale. It turned out that these were indeed two Peale portraits, one of General Washington and one of General Nathanael Greene, that had originally been sent to England to serve as models for engravings and had been lost since the 18th century. Gamble purchased them for the museum.

In the fine collection of 18th- and 19th-century portraits for which Gamble was almost exclusively responsible, one is struck by the lively quality of the women's portraits. And indeed, in her acquisition of portraits Gamble made a conscious effort to balance between male and female sitters, between the official 18th century as exemplified by Peale's portrait of Washington and the less formal, as in Gilbert Stuart's portrait of Mrs. James Bard, which is delineated with wonderful freshness.

Always an articulate spokeswoman for the Montclair Art Museum, Gamble served several terms as chair of the N.J. Association of Museums. She retired in 1980. In 1983, New Jersey Historical Commission awarded her its prized Pewter Pitcher in recognition of her contribution to the publicizing and preservation of New Jersey's past.

Today Gamble lives in California, close to San Francisco, in a Quaker-sponsored cooperative apartment complex of which she is a financial director. She takes drawing classes and has a studio in which she works; in addition, she is studying Jungian psychology. As she put it, she is doing all the things she never had time for.

A telephone interview with Gamble on Aug. 26, 1987, provided information about her life and work. Information on Gamble's work appears in Robert Carlisle, *A Jewel in the Suburbs: The Montclair Art Museum* (1982).

*Robert J. Koenig*
*Blair T. Birmelin*

Muriel Morris Gardiner was a medical student in Vienna in the 1930s when she became the only American woman in the Austrian antifascist underground. *Courtesy, Trude Fleischmann.*

## MURIEL MORRIS GARDINER, 1901–1985

Muriel (Morris) Gardiner Buttinger, psychoanalyst, educator, and member of the anti-Fascist underground in Austria during the 1930s, was born on November 23, 1901, in Chicago, IL, to Edward and Helen (Swift) Morris. Both parents were from wealthy families who owned meatpacking plants. Her father, son of the founder of Morris and Company, was of Jewish descent. Her mother, daughter of the founder of Swift and Company, was of Protestant ancestry.

Gardiner, the youngest of four children, two brothers and one sister, grew up in great luxury on Chicago's South Side in a mansion with a large staff of servants. Despite her family's wealth, Gardiner was raised in an atmosphere that encouraged and modeled discipline, obedience, and hard work and stressed truthfulness and fairness. She rarely saw her father, who spent much of his time at the stockyards managing his business. She was somewhat afraid of both her parents, although she admired them for their high ethical standards. Gardiner was brought up by her nurse, Mollie, an Irish immigrant who offered her the warmth and comfort she did not feel from her parents. From Mollie and other servants who pointed out the great difference between the wealth of their employers and their own poverty, Gardiner early gained a sense of the injustice that existed in the world, an awareness that would remain with her throughout her life and guide her future actions.

After excellent academic preparation at the exclusive Faulkner School, enhanced by trips to Europe, Gardiner entered Wellesley College in 1918, majoring in English literature. She became a campus leader with a reputation for liberal, even socialist leanings during a time when the United States was becoming more conservative and wary of suspected "Reds." In her junior year at college, Gardiner, with friends from Harvard and Radcliffe, organized a national conference that drew several hundred students to hear well-known liberal and socialist speakers. Gardiner was chosen president of the Intercollegiate Liberal League (later the National Student Forum), which grew out of the 1921 conference. The following year she was elected president of the Wellesley Forum, a group that discussed current political questions. In her work for these two organizations, Gardiner attended many liberal gatherings and became acquainted with leaders such as the eminent socialist Norman Thomas and Roger Baldwin, founder of the American Civil Liberties Union. She arranged for them to speak at Wellesley and remained a lifelong friend and supporter of both.

After graduating from college in 1922, Gardiner spent a year in Rome at the American School of Classical Studies and then attended Oxford University (1923–26), doing graduate work in English literature in preparation for a teaching career. After a brief, unhappy marriage, Gardiner traveled to Vienna in spring 1926 hoping to enter into psychoanalysis with Sigmund Freud. Busy and ill, Freud was not accepting new patients, but referred her to Dr. Ruth Mack Brunswick, his student, with whom Gardiner began a three-year period of psychoanalysis and study.

In 1929, after her analysis was completed, she married Julian Gardiner, a young Englishman studying in Austria. Their daughter, Constance ("Connie"), was born in March 1931. After a separation and eventual divorce, Gardiner resumed analysis with Brunswick and began studying Freudian psychoanalytic theory with several of Freud's circle of students in order to become an analyst. Realizing that she must have a medical degree to practice psychoanalysis in the United States, Gardiner entered the University of Vienna Medical School in 1932.

While Gardiner pursued her psychoanalytic and medical studies, the political situation in Europe grew steadily worse. Hitler had already risen to power in Germany, and during the early 1930s Nazi Fascists within Austria gained strength and threatened to take over the Austrian government. Incidents of anti-Semitism were rapidly increasing, and Gardiner witnessed such incidents at the medical school. By early 1934 she began to think about leaving Vienna and returning to the United States to complete her medical training, but in February 1934 the military forces of the Austrian Fascist government crushed the Socialist Democratic opposition and Gardiner made a commitment to stay in Austria and aid those fighting fascism.

Through friends she made contact with the underground resistance movement then forming and joined a small group whose members she trusted, putting herself and her wealth at their disposal. Choosing "Mary" for her code name, Gardiner became the only American woman in the Austrian anti-Fascist underground. For six years she helped Jews and political dissidents escape from Austria, hiding many in her Vienna apartment and her small cottage in the Vienna Woods. She risked her life to act as a courier delivering messages and false passports to refugees.

With the help of family and friends in the United States, Gardiner obtained hundreds of affidavits guaranteeing the financial support required by the U.S. government before it would allow those fleeing the Nazis to enter the country. She was able to help resettle many refugees. Long after the end of World War II many still remembered Gardiner's help and credited her with saving their lives.

Some refugees noticed the strong resemblance between Gardiner and the heroine of the 1977 film *Julia*, drawn from episodes in Lillian Hellman's book *Pentimento*. Although Hellman repeatedly denied that her heroine was modeled on Gardiner, many persons, including Gardiner herself, were convinced that "Mary" provided the basis for "Julia." The controversy encouraged her to complete the autobiography she had already begun, and *Code Name "Mary"* was published in 1983.

One of the political dissidents whom Gardiner hid in her apartment was Joseph Buttinger, a leader of the Revolutionary Socialists (the underground political party formed after the defeat of the Socialist Democrats). She had worked with "Weiser" (Buttinger's code name), whom she trusted and admired for his honesty. The coworkers became lovers in 1934. As both continued their underground rescue activities, Gardiner kept on with her medical studies. By 1938 conditions in Austria were becoming so dangerous that Gardiner made arrangements for Buttinger and her daughter, Connie, to travel to relative safety in Paris. She joined them there after graduating from medical school in June 1938. In March 1939 she and her daughter returned to the United States, where Gardiner took the New York City medical exams in June. By July she was back in Paris and she and Buttinger were married there on August 1. In November 1939 they sailed for the United States on one of the last ships carrying refugees from Europe prior to World War II.

Gardiner and Buttinger spent the next two years deeply involved in refugee work, finding housing and medical care for newly arrived immigrants. At the same time Gardiner served as a psychiatric consultant in two New York City nursery schools, working under supervision of a child analyst.

In 1940 the couple moved with Connie to Pennington (Mercer County), NJ, while maintaining their New York City apartment. (In 1943 Buttinger adopted Connie after he and she became American citizens.) During the early 1940s Gardiner worked as a psychiatric consultant and did a year-long medical internship in Trenton, finishing in June 1943. Then she served for a year and a half as assistant medical director of the New Jersey Department of Health and field worker in the Bureau of Venereal Disease Control.

In April 1945 Gardiner returned to France as Western European supervisor of the International Rescue Committee, a group she and Buttinger helped to found early in the war, which aided thousands of prisoners being released from German concentration camps. She remained in Europe for six months, setting up a network to maintain relief efforts. When she returned to the United States, Buttinger went to Paris to continue the work his wife had begun.

In 1946 Gardiner did a one-year psychiatric residency at the State Hospital in Marlboro, NJ. After completing her psychoanalytic training at the Institute of the Philadelphia Association for Psychoanalysis, Gardiner was a full-time analyst for nearly six years. She then combined her private clinical work with teaching at the institute and at various social agencies and hospitals, including Trenton State Hospital. In addition, she was an adjunct professor at Rutgers School of Social Work and at Rutgers University Department of Education (1955–59).

For the next fifteen years, Gardiner worked as the chief psychiatric consultant, first, to the Bucks County, PA, public schools (1957–65) and, then, for the Office of Special Education, New Jersey Department of Education (1960–71). She considered her work in the public schools her most satisfying service; not only did she feel she was practicing preventive psychiatry, but she enjoyed the integration of her longtime interests in education and psychoanalysis. She continued this work until her retirement in 1971, at age 70.

Throughout the 1950s and 1960s Gardiner contributed scholarly articles to the *Bulletin* of the Philadelphia Association for Psychoanalysis. In 1971 she edited *The Wolf-Man by the Wolf-Man*, a volume of memoirs by one of Sigmund Freud's most famous patients, whom Gardiner had befriended decades earlier in Vienna and with whom she had maintained contact. Several years later Gardiner wrote *The Deadly Innocents: Portraits of Children Who Kill* (1976). The volume, based on her work as a volunteer psychiatric consultant at several prisons, investigated the connections between child abuse and homicides committed by juveniles and described the dehumanizing treatment of these young offenders in prison.

Gardiner's deep humanitarian concern and her discomfort with her enormous wealth led her to distribute a large portion of her fortune anonymously to needy individuals and to a variety of causes in which she was interested. For her devotion to helping the oppressed, whether victims of the Nazis or of childhood mistreatment, Gardiner received many tributes, including the Cross of Honor from the Austrian government in 1980, recognizing her underground work during the 1930s, and a Wellesley Alumnae Achievement Award for humanitarian efforts (given posthumously in 1985).

Gardiner died of cancer on February 6, 1985, at age 83, in Princeton, NJ. With typical generosity she bequeathed her 500-acre estate in Pennington to an environmental organization. Anna Freud, psychoanalyst and Gardiner's longtime friend, conveyed the significance of Gardiner's life in her foreword to *Code Name "Mary"*: "Two lessons can be learned from [Gardiner's autobiography]: one, that it is possible even for lone individuals to pit their strength successfully against the sinister forces of an unjust regime; and, two, that for every gang of evil-doers who take pleasure in hurting, harming, and destroying, there is always at least one 'just' man or woman ready to help, rescue, and sacrifice his or her own good for fellow-beings." (Gardiner, *Code Name "Mary,"* xiii) Throughout her life Gardiner stood courageously for justice and compassion.

Gardiner's autobiography is *Code Name "Mary": Memoirs of an American Woman in the Austrian Underground* (1983). An article by Linda Witt, "Hellman's Heroine: Fact or Fiction," *Chicago Tribune*, Nov. 25, 1984, details the resemblance between Gardiner and Hellman's "Julia." A videotape, *The Real Julia: The Muriel Gardiner Story* (1987), includes a taped interview with Gardiner. Her obituary appeared in the *New York Times*, Feb. 7, 1985.

*Carolyn DeSwarte*
*Gifford Sheila Cowing*
*Karen G. Howe*

## MARY VIRGINIA GAVER, 1906–

Mary Virginia Gaver, professor of library science, editor, writer, publisher, and a national leader in the development of school libraries, was born on December 10, 1906, in Washington, D.C., the second child and first daughter of Clayton Daniel and Ruth Lydia (Clendening) Gaver, both natives of Hillsboro, VA.

She grew up in Danville, VA, and graduated in 1927 from Randolph Macon Women's College, where she was elected to Phi Beta Kappa. After teaching English for one year at Danville High School, she served as the high school librarian for the next nine years. Meanwhile, she worked toward a B.S. (1932) and M.S. (1938) in library science at Columbia University. She held one of the distinguished Carnegie fellowships for library study in 1937 and took courses at Teachers College, Columbia University, from 1947 to 1950.

Gaver served as technical director of the statewide WPA Library Project of Virginia (1938–39) and as librarian of the Scarsdale (NY) High School (1939–42). From 1942 to 1954 she was librarian and associate professor of library service at the New Jersey State Teachers College in Trenton.

Gaver was a member of the committee established in 1950 to plan the creation of a graduate school of library science at Rutgers, the State University. Her important contributions to that endeavor led to her appointment as one of the six original members of the faculty when the school was opened in 1954. As associate professor (1954–60) and professor (1960–71), she was a respected scholar and teacher and trained hundreds of students. At various times she also taught at the University of Virginia, Emory University in Georgia, and the University of Tehran.

Throughout her professional career, Gaver was best known for her work in the establishment and improvement of libraries in both elementary and high schools. Her primary responsibility at the new Graduate School of Library Science was to develop the program for school librarians. (Letter from Gaver to Dean Lowell Martin, June 26, 1954)

In 1959–60 she directed a research project sponsored by the U.S. Office of Education that led to an influential report titled *Effectiveness of Centralized School Library Services*. She assisted Dr. Frances Henne in preparing *Standards for School Library Programs* and was the chair of a project sponsored by the Council on Library Resources to improve professional leadership among school librarians.

Because of her prominence in the field, she served from 1962 to 1965 as the first chair of the five-year Knapp School Libraries Project. Financed by a $1.13 million grant from the Knapp Foundation to the American Library Association (ALA), this project helped eight school libraries meet ALA standards. "In cooperation with a nearby teachers' college, each library would then be assisted in providing in-service education to show the value of library services provided to the overall school program." (*Current Biographies*, 123) These demonstration libraries were visited by hundreds of people, including school administrators and librarians. As a consequence of this project, several states set up their own demonstration libraries to stimulate the improvement and effective use of school libraries. (*ALA Bulletin*, Oct. 1965, 807–9)

Encyclopedia Britannica, Inc., inaugurated the School Library Awards in 1962 to focus special attention on elementary school libraries, which until that time had received little support in many communities. These awards were given with the assistance of the American Association of School Librarians. Gaver's reports on the applications of the participating elementary schools in 1963, 1965, and 1968 analyzed the development of the libraries and the emergence of media centers. These reports served as a guide and stimulus to many school districts throughout the country.

In 1964 the Library Development Committee of the New Jersey Library Association (NJLA) published a plan for the statewide development of libraries. Gaver, who had served on the committee, coauthored this important report, *Libraries for the People of New Jersey*, with Lowell Martin. As the plan was implemented, specialized and research libraries, area libraries, and local libraries—which included school, college, and community libraries—were linked in a network to minimize duplication and to provide expanded service. State aid to these libraries was tied to standards established for each category of library.

When Title III of the Education Act of 1965 made available state monies that could be used to improve school libraries, *The Elementary School Library Collection*, edited by Mary Gaver, became the "bible" for school librarians setting out to establish or upgrade their elementary school library collections. This book, which she edited through eight printings (1965–73), provided a bibliography for an elementary school library and also served as a catalog for the collection.

Gaver served as president of the NJLA, the American Association of School Librarians (a subdivision of the ALA), and the ALA's Library Education Division. She was elected president of the ALA in 1966. Many honors were bestowed on her for her contributions to school library development, for her training of librarians, and for her professional leadership by the New Jersey School Librarians' Association, Rutgers University, and the ALA.

The Herbert Putnam Honor Award of the ALA, which had been conferred only twice since its inception in 1939 and is considered one of the highest distinctions in librarianship, was presented to Gaver in July 1963. The accompanying citation called attention to her "significant contributions to the profession of librarianship in the areas of professional leadership in library development and organization, research, children's and school library work, library education and her professional and educational writing." (*Current Biographies*, 124) Gaver also received honorary LL.D. degrees from both C. W. Post College of Long Island University (1967) and Mount Holyoke College (1968).

Following her retirement from teaching at the Rutgers University Graduate School of Library Science in 1971, Gaver continued her work with Bro-Dart, Inc., as consultant for library and publisher relations. She was named a vice-president of the firm in 1973 and resigned from that position in 1980.

Gaver retired to Danville, VA, the town in which she had grown up. Although not a native of New Jersey, Gaver's outstanding professional accomplishments occurred during her 29 years of residence in the state and had significant impact on the school and public libraries of New Jersey.

Gaver's autobiography is *A Braided Cord: Memoirs of a School Librarian* (1988). Biographical sketches of Gaver appear in *Current Biography* (1966) and the *American Library Association Yearbook* (1977). Her letter to Lowell Martin is in the files of the School of Communication, Information and Library Studies, Rutgers University (New Brunswick, NJ). Her account of the Knapp Project appeared in "The Knapp School Libraries Project," *American Library Association Bulletin* 59 (1965):806–9.

*Katheryne C. McCormick*

## LILLIAN MOLLER GILBRETH, 1878–1972

Lillian (Moller) Gilbreth, pioneer woman in the fields of engineering and scientific management, was born on May 24, 1878, in Oakland, CA, the first surviving child of William and Annie (Delger) Moller. The comfortable home into which she was born—there would be eight children—revolved around her mother's perceived "frailty," which this matriarch sustained, together with her central position, into ripe old age. Considerable responsibility for constantly arriving babies was given to shy Lillian, thought too "sensitive" for school until she was nine. But once enrolled, the exceptional student decided that "since I couldn't be pretty, I had to be smart." (F. B. Gilbreth, *Time Out for Happiness*, 23)

Gilbreth wanted to pursue a strong interest in literature at college, but an otherwise loving father felt this un-

Lillian Moller Gilbreth at her Montclair home around 1921 with her husband and ten of their twelve children. As a pioneer in the fields of engineering and scientific management, Gilbreth applied the principles of motion study in her own home. *Courtesy, private collection.*

suitable for a young lady of her station. Although she initially complied with his wishes, she quietly persisted and one year later entered the nearby University of California, where she could both go her own way and comfort her parents by living at home. (Years later her respectful tact and nonconfrontational management style were to command profound respect from tough negotiators.) At college she excelled, not only in her studies, but unpredictably in drama, which led to her being chosen the university's first woman commencement speaker. After earning her B.Litt. (1900) she continued academic work at Columbia University in New York, but this first break from home was perhaps too abrupt and illness sent her back to California, where she completed a master's degree in English literature at Berkeley (1902) and promptly began doctoral studies there in literature and psychology.

In 1903 work and family life were interrupted for a European tour; en route she met Frank Bunker Gilbreth. At 35 he was one of Boston's leading building contractors

and fast achieving a national and international reputation for what was later called "motion study," an innovative system of technology and management. They married in Oakland on October 19, 1904, and began a partnership that was to produce a new business, a pioneering contribution to the nascent sciences of management and industrial psychology, numerous books and articles, and a dozen children. His quest for the "one best way" to do a job was to become theirs, as together they expanded the concept to include the "one best marriage." (Yost, *Frank and Lillian Gilbreth*, 119)

Although both were immensely talented, it is doubtful that either alone would have achieved what they did together. Gilbreth's husband introduced her to work with which she had no previous contact and continuously encouraged her exceptional gifts. In their early years she provided most of the formal education and writing skills for their many books, but later she successfully urged him to give up his lucrative construction business to devote both their energies to the developing fields of motion study and management. As early as 1908 she startled an otherwise all-male meeting of engineers by suggesting that the new and suspect science of psychology would be a necessary part of the yet newer science of management. To this end she switched her doctoral program and earned her Ph.D. at Brown University (1915); her dissertation, "The Psychology of Management," was published by her husband in 1921 and became a classic. Meanwhile, and in the midst of several projects besides study and publications, the family grew almost yearly toward the planned total of six daughters and six sons, a goal achieved and then frustrated by the early death of their second daughter. Frank's energetic and efficient mother had lived with the new family from the beginning. Whatever tensions this may have involved, these arrangements and the help of several servants gave Lillian some freedom from physical domestic responsibilities.

New York seemed the best location for promotion of scientific management, but they needed a great deal of space for the home-office-laboratory-school they were evolving. And so in 1919 they came to 68 Eagle Rock Way, Montclair, NJ, which was to become famous as the home of the "Gilbreth System." The overflowing household became an often uproarious testing ground for many of Gilbreth, Inc.'s efficiency studies. The whole family served as research subjects and seemed to revolve around the strenuous projects of an exuberant father, but as a son later wrote: "in the last analysis, the person responsible for making the system work was Mother." (F. B. Gilbreth, *Cheaper by the Dozen*, 18) Regardless of other demands, Gilbreth rose early to spend time with her children, helped with homework, and read to them every night. She made each one feel like an only child, for "when a child talked . . . she listened and listened, and made sure she understood. So that she knew what every one of her individual children wanted, needed, dreaded and dreamed about." (F. B. Gilbreth, *Time Out for Happiness*)

After Frank Gilbreth's sudden death in 1924, most of their consultant contracts were canceled by clients who did not think a woman could carry on the business alone. Determined to maintain the reputation of the Gilbreth System and the value of motion study, and to establish an independent reputation as a management consultant, Gilbreth sailed for Europe three days after her husband's death to deliver a scheduled speech. Deprived not only of a beloved partner but of the income that had made servants possible, she turned to her older children to share the physical and psychological responsibilities of rearing the rest. Once again the system worked, and according to family and friends, with zest, humor and "time out for happiness."

As businesses and home economists became interested in the housewife as economic unit, Gilbreth studied the application of management methods in the home, which led to two more books and articles in popular magazines. After 1926 she was consultant to university departments of home economics and had considerable impact on the development of courses. Here the principles of motion study were applied to the kitchen in particular. The carry-over from earlier work was that the "one best way" involved the least exertion, better health, greater happiness, and therefore increased productivity of the worker—ideas that were revolutionary when the Gilbreths developed them.

Meanwhile, Gilbreth set up a "Motion Study Institute" at her home to instruct executives in the detailed study of the work process. "Mother's College" (so-called by her children) lasted from 1926 to 1932, when engineering colleges began to offer such courses. Then she served as adviser to many of these schools as scientific management programs began to proliferate and she later became a full professor at Purdue University (1935), Newark College of Engineering (1941), and the University of Wisconsin (1955), as well as a visiting professor at other schools.

She took particular pride in her use of motion study to design special routines and equipment to make housework and a greater degree of independence possible for the disabled.

Despite a difficult beginning as a speaker—at least twice she was refused admittance to men's clubs at which she was to have been principal speaker—Gilbreth built a national reputation as publicist for the system. Resistance continued to her conviction that the most effective management emphasizes motion (the worker's comfort) rather than time (the employer's profit). But by 1931 motion study had become widely accepted and the first Gilbreth Medal (named for her husband) was awarded to Lillian Gilbreth by the Society of Industrial Engineers.

As her business improved and children grew up, she devoted more and more time to volunteer work: the Girl Scouts, organizations for the disabled, churches and libraries in Montclair. She also served six U.S. presidents on committees dealing with employment, civil defense, war production, rehabilitation of the disabled, and problems of aging.

A long list of honors includes honorary membership in the Society of Industrial Engineers in 1921 (which did not admit women at the time); the Gilbreth Medal; the Gantt Gold Medal, awarded to her and to her husband posthumously by the American Society of Mechanical Engineers (1944); and the Hoover Medal for distinguished public service (1966). (She was the first woman to receive this award.) Many other commendations and honorary degrees testified to the enduring value of her work.

Gilbreth continued working into her eighties and retired at 90. She died three years later, on January 2, 1972, from a stroke in Scottsdale, AZ.

Gilbreth's papers and memorabilia are available at Purdue University (Lafayette, IN). Books by her children describing life in the Gilbreth household are Frank B. Gilbreth, Jr., and Ernestine Gilbreth Carey, *Belles on Their Toes* (1950) and *Cheaper by the Dozen* (1949); and Frank B. Gilbreth, Jr., *Time Out for Happiness* (1970). An account of the partnership between the Gilbreths is Edna Yost, *Frank and Lillian Gilbreth: Partners for Life* (1949). Gilbreth's opinions about child rearing and career appear in her book *Living with Our Children* (1928). A sketch of her appears in *NAW-MP*. Her obituary appeared in the *New York Times*, Jan. 3, 1972.

*Donna Walling*
*Daryl Boylan*

## HETTY GOLDMAN, 1881–1972

Hetty Goldman, archaeologist and first woman professor at the Institute for Advanced Study in Princeton, was born in New York City on December 19, 1881, the daughter of Julius Goldman, a lawyer, and Sarah (Adler) Goldman, a homemaker, both of German Jewish descent. Her paternal grandfather, Marcus Goldman, a banker in New York City as early as 1869, was cofounder with Samuel Sachs of the investment banking firm Goldman, Sachs and Co.

Goldman's interest in classical antiquity and archaeology was fostered at an early age when she attended the School for Girls in New York, founded in 1891 by her uncle, Julius Sachs, an educator who was president of the American Philological Association (1891) and of the New York Society of the Archaeological Institute of America (1900–1903).

She majored in ancient Greek and English at Bryn Mawr College and received her B.A. in 1903. She continued studying ancient Greek in graduate courses at Columbia University (1903–4, 1906–7) and also worked as a reader of manuscripts for the Macmillan publishing company (1903–4). Convinced that a career in writing was not her interest, she turned to scholarship and completed her M.A. at Radcliffe College in 1910. Her first article, "The *Oresteia* of Aeschylus as Illustrated by Greek Vase Painting," was published in 1910, and that same year she became the first woman to be awarded Harvard's Charles Eliot Norton Fellowship to attend the American School of Classical Studies at Athens, Greece.

While at the school Goldman began her first fieldwork in 1911 at a small classical site in north Boeotia called Halae. The Balkan Wars interrupted her fieldwork in 1912 and 1913, but the terra-cotta finds from Halae's cemetery became the subject of her doctoral dissertation, with which she earned her Ph.D. from Radcliffe in 1916. More important, at Halae she found early traces of the Neolithic village culture and began to focus her studies on the prehistory of Greece.

The Balkan Wars and the upheaval of World War I revealed another facet of Goldman's character: her concern for the victims of war. She was a volunteer nurse in a Greek hospital, then left Greece in 1914 and worked for the Red Cross in New York on research in anticipation of the Versailles peace agreements. In 1918 she returned to the Balkans to report on the Jewish communities there for the American Jewish Joint Distribution Committee (JDC), organized in 1914 to assist refugees in Europe. She worked in the JDC's Paris office in 1920. This concern continued throughout her life, especially leading up to and during World War II, when she was active in sponsoring refugees fleeing the Nazis.

Her reconnaissance in Greece, the islands, and Asia Minor during 1921 resulted in the selection of Colophon (25 miles south of Izmir in Turkey) for a new excavation. With a permit secured through the auspices of the American School of Classical Studies at Athens, she directed (for the Fogg Museum of Harvard University) an extraordinary team of scholars who were to become leaders in the archaeological work of Greece and Rome: Carl Blegen (prehistory of Greece and Asia Minor), Leicester B. Holland (ancient architecture), Benjamin D. Meritt (Greek epigraphy), Franklin P. Johnson (founder of the magazine *Archaeology*), and Kenneth Scott (Roman archaeology). These excavations, which made possible the reconstruction of the first tangible picture of one of the oldest and most famous cities of ancient Ionia, were interrupted by the Greco-Turkish War in 1922.

Goldman's pioneering interest in the pre-Greek and earliest Greek peoples, in the Eastern contacts of mainland Greece, and in relationships among the peoples of the Aegean led her to excavate the site of Eutresis in Boeotia (1924–27) as director of the Fogg Museum excavations. The arts and crafts of Eutresis, an agricultural center during the bronze age, provided new insights into mainland Greek contacts with the outside world. Her 1931 publication on Eutresis's remains, with its well-preserved early houses, became a basic text for prehistorians.

Throughout Goldman's life, most of her work in training students occurred on site at her excavations, but in 1928 she became a visiting lecturer in archaeology at the Johns Hopkins University in Baltimore, MD. Soon she was back in the field, and after advisory work for the Fogg Museum in Yugoslavia (1932) and reconnaissance in Cilicia, Turkey, she began her fourth major excavation: the site of Tarsus on the southeast coast of Turkey. Bryn Mawr College, Harvard University, and the Archaeological Institute of America were joint sponsors. Tarsus was an ancient strategic city with ties to the peoples of the Greek world and of the lands around the Mediterranean.

In 1936 Goldman was appointed to the permanent faculty of the Institute for Advanced Study, School of Historical Studies, at Princeton, NJ. The institute became the base for her research and Princeton her home until her death.

The beginnings of World War II interrupted her fieldwork in 1939, and she did not return to Tarsus until 1947. It was in 1949 that she reached the deepest levels at Tarsus. In the fall of 1947 Goldman became professor emerita at the Institute for Advanced Study and devoted her time to publishing the Tarsus excavations in collaboration with her associates. The results are embodied in three large volumes (1950, 1956, 1963). The site, excavated to levels dating back to the sixth millennium B.C., produced important seals, seal impressions, and inscribed texts. The data in these volumes are invaluable additions to our knowledge of the early Eastern Mediterranean peoples, including their religious ideas and their commerce. In addition to the prehistoric period, the volumes encompass finds that reach down to the Roman period of our era.

Goldman's generosity in sharing her knowledge with her colleagues in archaeology was well known. Honors came to her from Radcliffe (the medal for Distinguished Achievement in 1953), from her colleagues (a volume of essays edited by the prominent prehistorian Saul S. Weinberg in honor of her 75th birthday in 1956), and from the Archaeological Institute of America (the Gold Medal Award for Distinguished Archaeological Achievement, its highest honor, in 1966).

Goldman's life as scholar, editor and writer, mentor of archaeologists, humanitarian, and amateur musician (violin and piano) came to an end on May 4, 1972, when, at age 91, she died in Princeton of pulmonary edema. She was buried in the Mount Pleasant Cemetery in Hawthorne, NY. Goldman, who remained single, reached the pinnacle of the academic world in her field at a time when women rarely received research appointments or directed full-scale excavations.

Goldman's publications are listed in Institute for Advanced Study, *Publications of Members, 1930–1954* (1955). A sketch of her appears in *NAW-MP*. Her obituary appeared in the *New York Times*, May 6, 1972.

*Anna S. Benjamin*

## ALBERTA GONZALEZ, 1914–

Alberta (O'Farrell) Gonzalez, migrant farmworker and labor leader, known respectfully as Doña Alberta, was born in Carolina, Puerto Rico, on July 12, 1914, and now lives in Penns Grove (Salem County), NJ. The oldest of eight surviving children, four boys and four girls, she is the daughter of Mariano and Maria (Hernandez) O'Farrell. Her father was the son of a French farmer in Puerto Rico; her mother was the daughter of a poor Spanish sugar refiner. Her grandparents were born in Puerto Rico and were very much influenced by the Spanish and Indian tradition of the Puerto Rican culture.

At the age of four Gonzalez was sent to a local town school to learn to read and write. She was influenced by Luisa Capetillo, a Puerto Rican woman who was her teacher and one of the leaders in the Puerto Rican labor movement. Gonzalez's mother was also influential, teaching her to be independent and encouraging her to finish high school (1928). Her mother hoped she would never have to depend on a man for support. But in spite of her mother's influence, Gonzalez's father expected her to follow the traditional Puerto Rican cultural pattern of marriage as a means of economic survival.

At age sixteen, Gonzalez was compelled to marry Perfecto Hernandez, a Puerto Rican chauffeur ten years her senior. Although Hernandez physically abused her, she stayed with him until he left her and their daughter, Carmen Iris Hernandez, who was then ten years old.

Gonzalez recalls having to struggle with Latino male chauvinism: "In Puerto Rico, the males usually have overall dominance in societal functions, with the general exception of running the household or raising children . . . the Latino male is given a high degree of freedom, whereas, females in the family are closely observed and chaperoned." (Interview, June 20, 1986)

In July 1950, with economic conditions in Puerto Rico deteriorating and no viable opportunity for single women in the work force, Gonzalez migrated to Mullica Hill, NJ, and moved in with her migrant farmworker sister. She was 36.

Upon arrival in Mullica Hill, she found a large farm that looked like a concentration camp. Conditions were worse than those she had left in Puerto Rico. Gonzalez realized there was no return to Puerto Rico, and so she accepted employment at the farm owned by Jim Lernner. Her schedule began at four each morning, when she prepared breakfast for 50 men and her sister. From four to six she cooked in the kitchen, and from six to eleven she worked in the farm's packing house. From 11:00 to 12:30 P.M. she cooked lunch for the men, and from 1:30 to 4:00 P.M. she worked in the fields. At 4:00 P.M. she ran to the camp to cook for the 50 men who returned for 6:00 P.M. dinner. From six to nine each evening Alberta cleaned, prepared clothes for camp members, and took care of other chores. Gonzalez followed this schedule for six months each year for 34 years. Her salary was 60 cents an hour, the same as the men.

She married Antonio Gonzalez, a migrant farmworker ten years her junior, in 1951. They were both hired by Jim Lernner's farm to supervise the 50 migrant farmworkers who traveled six months of the year from Puerto Rico, Florida, and Philadelphia to New Jersey.

Gonzalez's goal was to improve her life and that of the migrant farmworkers in New Jersey. She asked the Lernners for better water facilities, kitchen utensils, cooking stove, and a heater. She also asked for better living conditions for the men in the camp. The Lernners agreed to these requests as long as Gonzalez and her husband provided him with camp supervision and guaranteed him 50 men each summer season.

In the summer of 1954 Gonzalez became the first Puerto Rican woman crew leader to supervise a labor camp for migrant farmworkers in New Jersey. In addition, she negotiated with the Lernners for work in the packing house during the day while the men were in the field. During this period she raised her children: Anthony, Larry, and Berta Gonzalez. Firmly committed to education, she managed to send her children to school daily in spite of the farm and work schedule. She changed the name of the *campamento* (labor camp) to the "House to Feed and Shelter Puerto Rican Migrant Workers." Some farmworkers called it the "Kitchen Soup House," others called it an "Emergency Shelter for Workers." (Gonzalez, Interview, Mar. 23, 1986)

Gonzalez believed that male migrant farmworkers (Puerto Rican and Mexican) were exploited by farmers and vendors who came to the south Jersey camps and sold consumer goods at exorbitant prices. Most of these men worked long hours, from four each morning to six or seven each night, in spite of rain, heat, or cold. Gonzalez recalls that if migrant farmworkers became ill in the evening, she and her husband did not have a telephone to call the doctor, who lived miles away. She and her husband would make herb teas and remedies to ease the pain of workers. In addition, she wrote and read letters to the workers because none of them could read or write. She also provided shelter and emergency refuge for illegal Mexican farmworkers.

Gonzalez introduced the first informal savings bank for migrant farmworkers at the camp. Her husband and two other workers established an accounting system to insure that camp members saved money for their return to Puerto Rico. The money was kept in a safe. According to Gonzalez, most of the men left the camp with enough money to build homes in Puerto Rico.

The migrant farmworkers were grateful for Gonzalez's assistance, calling her *La Vieja* (the lady in charge). She recalls: "Every year farmworkers brought me *recao* (Puerto Rican seasoning), *gandules* (pigeon peas), tropical fruits, Mother's Day presents, and other gifts as tokens of appreciation. . . . Also, when things got really bad at the camp the men helped out with contributions." (Interview, Mar. 23, 1986)

For six months of the year, Gonzalez, her husband, and the children remained in the camp with its ten empty rooms. Their only source of economic survival for more than 34 years was personal savings from the seasonal work, plus individual donations received from the Puerto Rican

farmworkers. Gonzalez remembers having to stretch one large supply of groceries to feed her family for a period of six months. The Lernners permitted her family to remain if they maintained the camp and did repair work. The family was not eligible for welfare or unemployment compensation because, under New Jersey labor laws, they were classified as temporary workers. Gonzalez's husband, a proud man, would not accept government help.

In July 1979 Lernner retired and closed the farm. Gonzalez's farmhouse was also closed down and her men were transferred to another farm, along with her family. Here she was appalled at the oppression of the farmworkers, who paid $40 a week for meals, only to be forced to wait outside on line and be served through a window. They had to drink water from the outside well.

On August 13, 1980, Gonzalez and the workers staged the first Puerto Rican migrant workers strike in New Jersey. Shortly after the strike ended, she bought a house in Penns Grove where she still resides with her husband.

Gonzalez became the advocate, protector, doctor, counselor, teacher, mother, and organizer for many Puerto Rican migrant farmworkers in south Jersey. She has spent her life caring for farmworkers, many of whom write to her and call her the *abuela* (the grandmother) of their children.

Still strong and active, Gonzalez collects emergency food for migrant farmworkers and tends her garden. Her husband continues to work on the farms six months a year.

Interviews with Gonzalez on Mar. 23 and June 20, 1986, provided useful information. The Farmworkers Support Committee (Glassboro, NJ) maintains a collection of correspondence, clippings, and newsletters that details Gonzalez's work as a migrant farmworker organizer.

*Gloria Bonilla-Santiago*

## RUTH EVELYN GORDON, 1910–

Ruth Evelyn Gordon, a renowned bacterial taxonomist, was born in Richmondville, NY, on August 30, 1910, the oldest of four children of Jennie (Letts) and Julius Clinton Gordon. Her parents, of Scottish, German, and Dutch ancestry, were both schoolteachers who eventually went into farming. The pressure of work was tremendous and they had little time to spend with the children, who were soon providing labor on the farm as well.

Gordon's years as a child on the farm were mainly drudgery. Her high school was located five miles from the house and transportation was by horse and buggy until she was old enough to drive the family car. Upon graduation as valedictorian from the Cobleskill High School in 1928, Gordon was awarded a N.Y. state fellowship to attend Cornell University. Her brother, who inherited the family farm, and one of her sisters, who became a lawyer, were later to receive similar awards. Gordon majored in chemistry at Cornell and worked during the summers to supplement her income. She graduated with a B.A. in 1932 and stayed at Cornell to do graduate work in bacteriology, with a minor in biochemistry. The head of the department of bacteriology was James Sherman, whose work on the taxonomy of streptococci was of interest to Gordon. She was fascinated by the challenge of bacterial identification and soon knew that she wanted to be a bacterial taxonomist.

After receiving an M.A. in 1933 and a Ph.D. in 1934, Gordon went to work with William A. Hagan of the Cornell Veterinary School, where she was assigned the study of mycobacterial skin lesions of cattle. Thus she started her first line of specialization with the rapidly growing mycobacteria, which were easily isolated from soil. In the process, Gordon also discovered that some other pathogens, such as *Nocardia asteroides*, were also soil organisms. This piece of work became a classic and she broadened her expertise to include the soil actinomycetes.

In 1939 Gordon left Cornell for the Department of Agriculture in Washington, D.C. Her first post in Washington was with the Bureau of Home Economics but she soon transferred to Charles Thom's Division of Soil Microbiology, where she was associated with Nathan R. Smith. She collaborated with Smith in a monumental study of the aerobic endospore-forming bacteria (*Bacillus*), for which she became widely known. She coauthored a monograph on the subject (1946) that is considered a classic and that has been updated twice (1950, 1973).

A desire to contribute to the war effort took her to the Army Medical Center during World War II. At the center she worked on bacterial meningitis. She worked for the American Type Culture Collection from 1944 to 1950 and had reached the rank of curator of the whole collection when, upon the recommendation of Charles Thom, Selman A. Waksman hired her to supervise the microbial collection of the Department of Microbiology of the College of Agriculture of Rutgers University in New Jersey. When the Institute of Microbiology of Rutgers University opened in 1954, Gordon was associate professor. Without losing her expertise in the bacilli, she devoted most of her research time to the taxomony of the mycobacteria, the nocardiae, and the streptomycetes. In 1971 she was promoted to professor.

Upon her retirement in 1981, Gordon returned to the Washington area as a visiting investigator at the American Type Culture Collection, a position she still holds. A mine of information and a source of authenticated strains, Gordon has had an international influence in the fields of her expertise. She is a member of the U.S. Federation of Culture Collections, where she served on the Executive Committee from 1971 to 1976; the American Society for Microbiology; the Society for General Microbiology; the Canadian Society of Microbiologists; and numerous other

societies. She was a member of the group devoted to the genus *Bacillus* within the International Working Group on Mycobacterial Taxonomy. She was honorary president of International Symposia on the Biology of Actinomycetes at Merida, Venezuela, in 1974, and at Cologne, Germany, in 1979. In 1983 she received the J. Roger Porter Award of the U.S. Federation of Culture Collections.

An interview with Gordon provided biographical details. A brief entry for her appears in *American Men and Women of Science* (1986).

*Hubert A. Lechevalier*

*Spartan Boy,* a stone sculpture created in 1963 by Dorothea Schwarcz Greenbaum. Working out of her Princeton studio, Greenbaum was a prominent figure in New Jersey arts for over 30 years. *Courtesy, private collection.*

## DOROTHEA SCHWARCZ GREENBAUM, 1893–1986

Dorothea (Schwarcz) Greenbaum, painter, sculptor, and printmaker, was born June 17, 1893, in Brooklyn, NY, to Emma (Indig) and Maximilian Schwarcz, a Hungarian-born importer. She moved to Princeton (Mercer County), NJ, in 1953 and was a prominent figure in New Jersey arts from that time until her death in 1986. Her *Susannah* was the first sculpture by a New Jersey artist acquired for the new State Museum in 1965. An elected member of the National Institute of Arts and Letters, Greenbaum was a founder of both the Sculptors' Guild and the Artists' Equity Association and was one of two women on the National Board of the latter.

As a child, Greenbaum was sickly and did not attend school regularly. She and her father were very close, and with his encouragement, she began to study painting seriously at fifteen. When she was 22, her father, aboard the *Lusitania*, was drowned.

Greenbaum studied intermittently between 1908 and the 1920s with Kenneth Hayes Miller at the Art Students League in New York City and was a painter of Miller's Fourteenth Street School. She showed her paintings at the National Academy of Design and the Whitney Studio Club (later the Whitney Museum of American Art). It was not until after her marriage to an attorney, Edward S. Greenbaum, on October 20, 1920, and the birth of their two sons, David (b. 1923) and Daniel (b. 1926), that Greenbaum began to experiment with clay, the medium in which she made her name.

From then on she was a sculptor, not a painter, and largely self-taught. Her first efforts were exhibited by the Whitney Studio Club. By the late 1920s she had created a series of small sculptures cast in bronze. Greenbaum never tired of using new materials. She worked in terra cotta next, and her first work was exhibited in a one-woman show at the Weyhe Gallery in New York City. Her second solo show, also at the Weyhe, in 1939, included bronzes with political overtones such as *Tired Shopper* and *Fascist*, an oversized, brutal-looking head in which she tried to show the fascist mentality.

Early in her career Greenbaum became active in artists' organizations. During World War II, after she moved with her family to Washington, D.C., where her husband, a brigadier-general, was stationed, she helped found the Sculptors' Guild, a group of highly individualistic artists who had trouble agreeing or conforming to bureaucratic restrictions.

In Washington, Greenbaum began to carve in stone. These works, with titles ranging from *Little Angel* to *Snob*, give an idea of her humor and style. In 1941 the Pennsylvania Academy of Fine Arts in Philadelphia awarded her the George Widener Memorial Medal for *Tiny*.

When she returned to New York after the war Greenbaum worked for artists' rights and the improvement of their economic opportunities. One of the founding members of Artists' Equity in 1947, she later became one of two women on the organization's national board.

When the American Academy of Arts and Letters honored Greenbaum with a $1,000 grant in 1947, they did so "in recognition of sculpture of a high order replete with a warm and sensitive appreciation of the human spirit." In 1952 Greenbaum represented sculpture for the United States at a UNESCO International Conference of the Arts in Venice, Italy, where delegates discussed the world future of the arts.

Greenbaum and her family moved to Princeton, NJ, in 1953. She continued to work "all day, every day" in a converted carriage house at the rear of their three-story Victorian home. Greenbaum carved rocks she picked up on the beach on Martha's Vineyard and sculpted in hammered lead, a medium she found "alive and responsive," and in which she achieved particular renown. Sometimes she worked with other artists. In 1962 she and two other sculptors cast 500 pounds of plaster of paris in a larger-than-life family group for Frank Perry's film *David and Lisa*.

Greenbaum's sculpture, described as "classically styled" evokes "the warmth and often . . . the humor found in her subjects." (Princeton Gallery of Fine Art, press release) A small, crouched gorilla is entitled *Ancestor*. The bronze *Child with Bird* has been much photographed. Greenbaum's work can be seen in numerous private and public collections, including the Whitney Museum of American Art, the Smithsonian Institution, the Philadelphia Museum of Art, the Newark Museum, and the New Jersey State Museum. She had solo shows throughout the country and was featured at the New Jersey State Museum in Trenton in 1970 and 1980 and the Princeton Gallery of Fine Arts in 1970, 1973, and 1975.

Greenbaum was awarded the Medal of Honor from the National Association of Women Artists in 1953, and was included among those exhibiting in New Jersey's tercentennial pavilion at the New York World's Fair in 1964. She was elected a member of the National Institute of Arts and Letters in 1968.

After her husband died in 1970, Greenbaum continued to live and work in Princeton. Unable to pursue active sculpture because of her own ill health, she turned to intaglio printmaking. When she planned an exhibition for the American bicentennial in Princeton, she chose goldfinches, the New Jersey state bird, as her visual motif, expressing her love of the earth and its inhabitants.

Greenbaum died, at age 92, at her Princeton home on April 6, 1986, of progressive dementia. Her remains were cremated at the Ewing Crematory in Trenton.

Greenbaum's work is noted in Chris Petteys, *Dictionary of Women Artists* (1985), and in Charlotte Rubenstein, *American Women Artists* (1982). Her article "Elderly, Then Old" appeared in the *New York Times*, Dec. 11, 1981. A profile of her, "At 81, She Finds She Can't Hold to a 5 Day Week," appeared in the *New York Times*, July 14, 1974.

*Sally Shearer Swenson*
*Sheila Cowing*

## ANNA LOUISE SANDO MCGEE GROOME, 1923–

Anna Louise (Sando) McGee Groome, known later as Anne, a volunteer civic worker of notable accomplishment in New Jersey's fight against crime and drug abuse, was born in Newark (Essex County), NJ, on July 16, 1923. A tireless worker for the prevention of drug abuse in both Essex and Morris counties, she is the eldest of the three children of Marguerite (Fox) and Francis Sando. Groome's father (1898–1961) was born and raised in Scranton, PA, and graduated as a mechanical engineer from Cornell University. He worked for Esso Corporation, where he invented the Sando Condenser. Groome's paternal grandfather, Michael F. Sando, served as judge of the Lackawanna County Orphan's Court in Scranton for 40 years. Groome was named after her paternal grandmother, Anna Louise (Blair) Sando.

When Groome was nine years old, her parents separated. From then on the major influences in her life were her mother and her two grandfathers. Her mother had great strength of character and imbued her children, William Fox, Marguerite Mary, and Anne Louise with a deep faith in their Roman Catholic religion. She moved her family to her father's home on Greenwood Lake, NJ, where she kept house for her widowed father. In later years, Groome's mother became postmistress of the Hewitt, NJ, Post Office and achieved a degree of financial independence.

Groome attended Marywood College in Scranton, on whose Board of Trustees her paternal grandfather served. After her freshman year she got a summer job at Wright Aeronautics, and she was almost immediately promoted to an office supervisor. (She later attended Rutgers University in 1960–61.)

In November 1945 Groome married Eugene D. McGee, a first lieutenant and pilot in the U.S. 9th Air Force. When he was discharged from service in 1947, he went to work for Foley Chevrolet, then Central Cadillac of Newark, NJ. The couple settled in East Orange (Essex County), NJ.

In 1959 her son, Eugene David McGee, Jr., was born, and the family settled in Morris County. They became involved in the social and political life of the Morristown area. McGee died on February 17, 1967.

Groome married for the second time in June 1968 to Preston E. Groome, who was born in November 1904 in Petersburg, VA. He had two children from a previous marriage and was employed by AT&T as a manager in government communications. After he retired he became active as sales manager for COM DEV, a manufacturer of computer-based communications-related equipment.

In 1950 Groome joined the League of Women Voters and from 1951 to 1953 served as president of the East Orange chapter. She was then elected to a term on the State Board of Directors. It was during this period that she was called to serve on the Essex County Grand Jury. According to a March 1966 article in *Suburban Life* magazine: "When Anne McGee fulfilled a routine civic duty by serving on an Essex County grand jury, her eyes were suddenly opened to the shocking relationship between drugs and crime."

In 1956 she became legislative chair for the local Grand Jury Association and then for the New Jersey Grand Jury Association. There she worked toward the initiation of legislation to combat the drug problem and developed

cooperation between the association and the League of Women Voters and the New Jersey State Federation of Women's Clubs. Groome said: "A massive community and governmental effort is needed if the drug problem is to be brought under control." (Interview, Aug. 5, 1986)

In 1960 Groome and her family moved to Convent Station in Morris County, and she joined the Woman's Club of Morristown, becoming active immediately in its Civics Department. She was elected first vice-president of the Woman's Club in 1969 and president in 1971. During her two-year term as president, Groome worked with *Daily Record* reporter Enda Slack to establish a program for the needy at Christmas time called "Operation Holiday." Through this program, newspaper articles tell the stories of local people in need of help. Donations received at the Woman's Club from the public are then distributed. This program has received approximately $150,000 plus donations of material to benefit the poor in the Morristown area.

Groome's work in the field of drug abuse shows the degree of her commitment to the good of the community. In January 1964 she planned and acted as moderator for an open-to-the-public panel discussion on drug problems at the Woman's Club of Morristown. As a direct result of that presentation, the Committee for Narcotics Prevention of Morris County was formed and incorporated in September 1965, with Groome as chair.

The committee operated a booth at the Morris Regional Health Fair and sponsored public meetings with the Essex County Sheriff's Office, the Federal Bureau of Narcotics, the Morris County PTA Council, the schools of Morris County, and local clergy. The committee formed a speakers bureau and in 1966 prepared a research library, housed at the Morris County Library. The Woman's Club of Morristown received a prize in the Community Improvement Contest, sponsored by Sears Roebuck, for its work in the field of drug abuse by Groome and her assistants.

Governor Richard J. Hughes appointed Groome a member of the Narcotics Advisory Council, Department of Institutions and Agencies, on March 20, 1967. As chair of the Committee for Narcotics Prevention, Groome saw one of her plans come to fruition when Freeholder Everett Vreeland made an announcement at one of their all-day seminars that an after-care clinic would be established at All Souls Hospital in Morristown. It was the first one in the county and one of the first in the state. In 1967 alone the clinic treated 3,474 cases.

Groome was made a member of the N.J. Narcotic Enforcement Officers' Association in 1969. The Federated Women's Clubs honored her in 1972 as a "First Lady" and in 1976 for "outstanding service." The freeholders of Morris County presented her with an award for her "outstanding contribution to drug prevention."

Groome was recognized for her work to combat alcoholism when she was given the Paul H. Gallien Award. When the Morris County Drug Council ceased to exist, Groome helped found New Jersey Prevention, Inc. (nonprofit and private) and became its first chair. A year later its staff presented her with an award as a "driving force" in the prevention effort. She also received the 1986 Dedication of Personal Effort ("Dope Open") award for exceptional service to humanity, an award sponsored by Dope Open, Inc.

Groome's philosophy behind her civic drug work is "that until each individual recognizes the dangers inherent in the problem, it will continue to escalate and undermine the growth and future of our country. Treatment for addiction and control of supply has not been very successful. It comes down to an all-out effort of education and prevention." (Interview, August 5, 1986)

An interview with Groome on Aug. 5, 1986, provided useful information. Clipping files on Groome are available at NJ-MO and the *Morristown Daily Record*. Arden Melick, "A Career of Volunteering," *Suburban Life Magazine* 36 (Mar. 1966):41, 60–61, details her accomplishments.

*Ryta Doyle Sims*

## FLORENCE LILLIAN HAINES, 1869–1955

Florence Lillian Haines, music teacher, suffragist, and legislator, was born in Newark (Essex County), NJ, on December 26, 1869. The second of nine children (seven girls and two boys) of Jared Haines, a Newark attorney, and Julia Moore (Ross) Haines, a member of an old Colonial family, Florence Haines lived in Newark all her life.

Haines attended Newark public schools and graduated from the state normal school at Newark (now Kean College). Haines reminded her classmates in a senior essay of the many instances where the "so-called weaker vessel has stood first, steadfast and unshaken," and called upon them to accept the "awful responsibility of the work we have undertaken; . . . each word and deed may bear fruit for good or evil through unknown ages." (Haines family papers, Rutgers University Library)

Her first teaching job was at the Monmouth Street School in Newark. She was promoted to primary vice-principal at the Franklin School and less than a year later was named assistant music supervisor for the entire Newark school system. In about 1915, she became supervisor of music for all Newark's schools, a post she retained until her retirement in 1933.

During World War I Haines drove ambulances between camps and hospitals in New Jersey and New York for the National League for Women's Service motor corps,

and for these activities she was named an honorary member of the Melvin Spits Post, Disabled American Veterans.

She was active in the woman suffrage movement, joining the Women's Political Union (WPU), a small centralized organization of business and professional women founded in Newark in 1908. Haines became secretary of the WPU and was vice-chairman of its "Votes for Women Ball" at the Palace Ball Room in Newark in November 1914. She worked actively with the Newark unit to secure the vote for women until the 19th Amendment was ratified by the New Jersey State Legislature in 1920.

A charter member of the New Jersey League of Women Voters, Haines worked her way up through the Republican organization and in 1926 ran successfully for the New Jersey Assembly to represent Newark. Reelected to four consecutive one-year terms, she served on several committees concerned with education and the handicapped: the joint committees for the Home for Feeble-Minded Women, the Industrial School for Girls, and the State Library. She chaired the Assembly Education Committee (1929), was a member of the Assembly Appropriations Committee (1930–1931), and chaired the Joint Committee for the School for Feeble-Minded Children.

Noted for her interest in child welfare, she sponsored a law to extend the physical, educational, and vocational benefits of the state's Rehabilitation Commission to children under sixteen, and to regulate the manufacture and sale of fireworks. Her interest in the young extended to obtaining better educational opportunities for the children of migratory workers. For three years she fought to bar the employment of these children during the school year. Her efforts helped bring about the establishment of a legislative investigatory commission shortly after she left the assembly, and several years later a series of laws on the subject resulted from the commission's actions.

In 1932 Haines founded the Organized Women Legislators of New Jersey and became its first president. Known as OWLs, the group was limited to past and present women members of the state legislature. At round table discussions, veteran legislators acted as "big sisters" for the inexperienced and offered advice on ways to cope with the obstacles facing the newly elected. The OWLs' major purpose was to elect more women, obtain more appointments to public office, and help them function effectively once in office.

Six years later Haines responded to an invitation from the Connecticut Order of Women Legislators and journeyed to Washington, D.C., to join with women from more than a dozen states to establish the national Order of Women Legislators (OWL). At the national Order's first business meeting on April 21, 1938, its constitution and bylaws were unanimously adopted, and in elections later that day Haines was voted one of four vice-presidents. Like the New Jersey OWLs, the national Order aimed to bring together past, present, and future women legislators so that they might share information, learn from one another, and work together for the election or appointment of more women to public office.

Her financial resources depleted, Haines died of heart disease, at age 85, after a long and costly illness on August 7, 1955, at the Home for Incurables in Newark. She was buried at Mount Pleasant Cemetery in Newark. Until about a year before her death Haines had been cared for at home by Margaret Haines, her sister, also a former New Jersey assemblywoman. Florence and Margaret Haines were the first sisters to serve in the New Jersey State Legislature.

A collection of Haines family papers is at NJ-RU. Her role in the formation of the Organized Women Legislators of New Jersey is in Felice Gordon, *After Winning: The Legacy of the New Jersey Suffragists, 1920–1947* (1986). Obituaries appeared in the *Newark Evening News*, Aug. 8, 1955, and the *New York Times*, Aug. 9, 1955.

*Sally Dudley*

## JOY BRIGHT HANCOCK, 1898–1986

Joy (Bright) Hancock, the third and last director of the WAVES, the Women's Reserve of the U.S. Naval Reserve, was born in Wildwood (Cape May County), NJ, on May 4, 1898, the third of six children of William Henry and Priscilla (Buck) Bright. She was the third girl and, as she later recalled, "To offset my father's disappointment that I was not a boy I was named Joy." (Hancock, *Lady in the Navy*, 9) The next three children were boys, but Hancock continued to perform a number of what were at the time considered male chores, and she later became an excellent mechanic. Her mother, an accomplished "couturiere-seamstress" from a family of Pennsylvania German dairy farmers, encouraged all the children's ambitions and she and her husband worked actively in the woman suffrage movement.

Hancock's father, the son of English and Irish immigrants, left Philadelphia in 1882 and helped establish Wildwood, NJ, as a resort community. He started a real estate business, became a banker, and as a progressive Republican was elected sheriff of Cape May County in 1904 and served in the state legislature from 1918 to 1930, eventually becoming president of the senate. Like her siblings, Hancock attended the Episcopal church and local public schools, graduating from Wildwood High School in 1916.

During World War I Hancock completed the secretarial courses at the Pierce Business School in Philadelphia, and in 1918 she enlisted as one of the 11,275 women authorized for temporary duty in the wartime navy. As a "Yeoman (F)," the navy's temporary designation

Joy Bright Hancock of Cape May County was one of the first officers of the WAVES. She became head of the WAVES in 1946 and successfully lobbied to integrate women into the regular navy and the naval reserve. *Official U.S. Navy photograph.*

for its female yeomen, she worked as a courier in a Camden shipyard. Later, as a chief yeoman, she served at the Naval Air Station, Cape May, NJ. The navy mustered out all the women by the end of 1919.

While at Cape May in 1919, she met her first husband, Lieutenant Charles Gray Little, a Harvard graduate who had won the Navy Cross flying dirigibles in France. When he was assigned to England for additional training in rigid airships, Hancock joined him and they were married October 9, 1920, in Elloughton-Brough, Yorkshire. On August 24, 1921, her husband was killed in the explosion and crash of dirigible ZR-2 over the Humber River at Hull, England.

In March 1922 the young widow was accepted as a civilian clerical employee in the navy's embryo Bureau of Aeronautics in Washington, D.C. Because of her continuing interest in lighter-than-air ships, she requested transfer to the Naval Air Station at Lakehurst, NJ, arriving as a stenographer-clerk in December 1923. There she met Lieutenant Commander Lewis "John" Hancock, a U.S.

Naval Academy graduate from Texas, a submariner turned airship aviator. On June 3, 1924, after her resignation from the navy, they were married in her parents' home in Wildwood and established a residence at Lakehurst. A year later, on September 3, 1925, he was killed when the airship *Shenandoah* crashed during a storm near Ava, OH. Twice a widow by age 27, Hancock suffered physically as well as mentally. For nearly a year she was hospitalized while doctors sought to locate the cause of a paralysis that afflicted her. When she was finally discharged, she and her sister Eloise Bright took a six-month cruise of the Orient, then shared an apartment in Paris for two years, where they attended a branch of Parson's New York School of Fine and Applied Arts. Since women had been declared eligible for the U.S. Foreign Service in 1928, Hancock applied, but after spending two years at the Crawford Foreign Service School in Georgetown and passing two sets of written examinations, she was rejected by the State Department on the oral examination. It was, she recalled later, "a bitter blow to my pride." (Hancock, *Lady in the Navy*, 41)

She turned again to aviation and the navy. She took flying lessons and conquered her fear of the air and aircraft. She also applied for a civilian position in the navy's Bureau of Aeronautics. Rear Admiral William A. Moffett, bureau chief, was very supportive of her and in 1930 he appointed her his special assistant and civilian chief of the bureau's General Information Section. When, on April 4, 1933, Moffett was killed in the crash of the naval dirigible *Akron* off the New Jersey coast, Hancock was stunned. "Why is it that every time I fall in love with or become very fond of someone he gets killed?" her brother recalls her asking. (Captain Cooper B. Bright, USN-ret., Interview, Apr. 29, 1987) After another extended cruise to the Orient and temporary residence in Europe, she returned to the Bureau of Aeronautics in March 1934, where, until 1942 she was civilian chief of the renamed Editorial and Research Section with responsibility for the bureau's press relations. She also edited the bureau's weekly newsletter and authored articles in popular magazines. In 1938 she wrote a book, *Airplanes in Action*.

Women had been excluded from the naval reserve since the end of World War I, but with the defense buildup in the United States in 1941, the more unorthodox leaders of the Bureau of Aeronautics began making plans for the inclusion of women in the navy. Hancock went to Canada and reported on the successful use of women by the Royal Canadian Air Force. However, resistance among many senior admirals was overcome only by a campaign led by the naval aviators, the chief of naval operations, and their civilian allies. In July 1942 Congress finally authorized the WAVES (Women Accepted for Volunteer Emergency Service in the Navy), technically the Women's Reserve of the U.S. Naval Reserve. The first director was Mildred McAfee, president of Wellesley College. On October 23,

1942, Hancock became one of the first officers in the WAVES, a lieutenant. Most of the leaders of the WAVES were former civilian women educators, with Hancock the only member of the inner circle to have a long affiliation with the navy. Although her title was Women's Representative to the Chief of the Bureau of Aeronautics, Hancock really served as liaison between the old navy and the new WAVES. She was promoted to lieutenant commander on November 26, 1943, and to commander on March 5, 1945.

Many naval officers thought the WAVES should be used primarily as clerks and typists. Hancock helped convince the navy that women should be employed in a wide variety of duties. Thus, by the end of the war 86,000 WAVES were serving not simply as yeomen and storekeepers, but radio and telegraph operators, photographers, personnel supervisors, control tower operators, aviation gunnery instructors, and aviation machinists. "Women always had to prove themselves," Hancock reflected later, "but they overcame the initial hostility of a reluctant Navy and won admiration and respect." (Quoted in *Retired Officer*, Dec. 1982, 17)

With the end of the war, the WAVES were cut back to 2,000, and many admirals thought they should be eliminated entirely. Hancock, however, worked actively to convince civilian and naval authorities to give women a permanent place in the navy. When the first director of the WAVES, Captain McAfee, returned to academic life in February 1946, she was first replaced by her assistant, Captain Jean T. Palmer, and Hancock became assistant director of the WAVES. Then, on July 26, 1946, Hancock was promoted to captain and appointed the head of the WAVES. In that capacity, she lobbied actively to obtain authorization to integrate women into the regular navy and the naval reserve. When the House of Representatives tried to limit women's service to the reserves, she joined professional women and a number of naval officers to prevent it. The Women's Armed Services Integration Act of June 12, 1948, authorized women to serve among the regulars as well as the reserves.

When the WAVES entered the regular navy, Hancock became, on October 15, 1948, one of the first six women to receive a regular commission. As assistant chief of naval personnel for women, she served as "advisor on women's affairs." She was also a key figure, during the Korean War (1950–53), in expanding the WAVES to 9,000 members. When, on June 1, 1953, after seven years as head of the WAVES—and after 30 years of connections with the navy—she retired at the mandatory retirement age of 55, she was hailed within the service as the "First Lady of the Navy." (Hancock, *Lady of the Navy*, 261; also Fellows, "First Lady of the Navy," *All Hands*, July 1978, 33)

In retirement, Hancock renewed an old acquaintanceship with a former naval aviator, Vice Admiral Ralph A.

Ofstie, then deputy chief of naval operations. They were married in August 1954. In 1955, when Ofstie was appointed commander of the Sixth Fleet, Hancock accompanied her husband on his tour of duty in the Mediterranean. The following year he underwent surgery for cancer and died in November 1956. A widow for the third time, Hancock returned to Wildwood, NJ, attended to family business, and wrote her memoir, *Lady in the Navy: A Personal Reminiscence*, in 1972. She went back to the Washington area to live at a navy retirement home in McLean, VA. On August 20, 1986, she died at the Bethesdea Naval Medical Center of respiratory arrest at the age of 88. Burial was in Arlington National Cemetery.

Hancock was the recipient of many citations and awards. Among them were the Legion of Merit and the Navy Commendation Medal. On March 20, 1950, Governor Alfred E. Driscoll and the New Jersey Legislature honored her at a public ceremony at the State House for her "distinguished service in two wars." In her honor, in 1978 the navy dedicated the Joy Bright Hancock Elementary School, Murphy Canyon naval housing area, San Diego, CA.

Hancock's papers are kept in the Manuscript Division, Library, University of Georgia (Athens). Additional information is found in the Operational Archives at the Naval Historical Center (Washington, D.C.). Hancock's autobiography is *Lady in the Navy: A Personal Reminiscence* (1972). She was profiled in *Current Biography* (1949). Articles based on interviews with her are: Marjorie Donchey, "Navy Was Capt. Hancock's Life," *Atlantic City Press*, June 13, 1976; Catherine Fellows, "First Lady of the Navy," *All Hands* (July 1978):33–35; Susan Godson, "Capt. Joy Bright Hancock: Builder of the Co-ed Navy," *Retired Officer* (Dec. 1982):15–17; and Godson, "Capt. Joy Bright Hancock and the Role of Women in the U.S. Navy," *New Jersey History* (Spring/ Summer 1987):1–17. Personal interviews with Hancock's brother, Capt. Cooper B. Bright (USN-ret.), Cambridge, MD, in 1987 provided useful details. Obituaries appeared in the *Washington Post*, Aug. 22, 1986, and the *New York Times*, Aug. 25, 1986.

*John W. Chambers II*

## MARY BELLE HARRIS, 1874–1957

Mary Belle Harris was born on August 19, 1874, in Factoryville, PA, the first child of John Howard Harris and Mary Elizabeth (Mace) Harris. A pioneer in the prison reform movement, she was responsible in the quarter century preceding World War II for changing New Jersey penal institutions for women from places merely of confinement to ones that prepared prisoners for reentry into society.

Harris's mother died in 1880, leaving Harris and two younger brothers, Herbert and Reece. The family then lived in Factoryville, PA, where Harris's father had his first job as founder and principal of the Keystone Academy. He did not leave this post until 1899, when he became president of Bucknell University. John Harris was also ordained as a minister in 1872 and became pastor of the Baptist Church in Factoryville in 1881.

Within a year of his first wife's death, John Harris married her cousin, Lucy Adelaide (Bailey) Harris. They had six boys: George, Spenser, John, James, Walter, and Stanley. All nine Harris children graduated from Bucknell. Harris shared a close relationship with her father during her childhood, when they read and studied history and philosophy together. In later years, he was a great support during her career in prison management.

Harris graduated from the Keystone Academy in 1890 and entered Bucknell University, from which she received a music degree in 1893, an A.B. in 1894, and an A.M. in Latin and classics in 1895. In 1896 she enrolled in the doctoral program at the University of Chicago, where she received a Ph.D. in Sanskrit and Indo-European comparative philology in 1900. Her many interests included music, art, linguistics, and numismatics. She continued playing the organ throughout her years at the university, and afterward. She also composed and published music.

After she received her Ph.D., Harris taught in schools in Kentucky and Chicago and worked at Hull House in Chicago. Later, she went to Baltimore to study numismatics at Johns Hopkins University and to teach Latin at the Bryn Mawr School under the administration of Edith Hamilton. Harris visited Europe from 1912 to 1914 and traveled through Italy studying art and Roman coins. She spent the winter of 1913–14 at the Kaiser Friedrich Museum in Berlin writing a research paper, which was published in Berlin.

In May 1914, when Harris returned to the United States, she was met at the dock by a friend she had known at the University of Chicago, Dr. Katherine B. Davis, the first woman commissioner of corrections of New York City. Davis asked her to take on the temporary superintendency of the Women's Workhouse on Blackwell's Island in New York City. Harris accepted this challenging post even though she had no penology experience.

At the Women's Workhouse she found overcrowded, unclean living conditions with only 150 cells to house 600 to 700 prisoners. There were no mattresses or sheets provided in the crowded cells. There was frequent violence among the prisoners, and Harris quickly recognized idleness as the source of the problem. She procured bed linens, set up a dining room, and fenced in an outdoor yard so that inmates could leave their cells. She even allowed card games and provided a library for diversion.

In July 1914, when Harris began her work at Blackwell's Island, the Harrison Narcotic and Boylan Laws were passed, increasing the number of drug addicts sent to prison. Before Harris's arrival, drug addiction at the Women's Workhouse had been aggravated by a prison doctor later convicted of selling narcotics to the prisoners. Harris instituted several successful reforms to deal with the drug situation, instituting strict precautions to keep narcotics out of the building. A special ward was established for the addicts during withdrawal, when they were under the continuous supervision of nurses.

She also established a program to detect and treat venereal diseases in the prisoners, for Harris believed they should be treated and dealt with on an individual basis. Her friend Davis was one of the first to agitate for scientific individualized treatment of prisoners. In 1916, in conjunction with the policy of Davis, who was chairman of the new Parole Commission of New York City, Harris instituted pre-parole interviews with inmates. She also set up networks with other social agencies so that paroled women could live and work in protected environments after they left the workhouse.

In January 1917 Harris resigned from her position at Blackwell's Island when a new political party came into power in New York City. The next month she began work in a new position as superintendent of Clinton Farms, the New Jersey State Reformatory for Women.

Eight years before, the first superintendent of Clinton Farms had established a system of self-governance that received much publicity because of its success. In the interim between the first administration and Harris's arrival, however, the system had been abandoned. Harris reinstituted self-governance at Clinton Farms with such success that she developed similar systems in all other institutions where she took charge. The success of this system brought her nationwide recognition for the reform of women's penal institutions. In commenting on self-governance in prisons, she wrote: "I believe the educational value of inmate participation, the outlet it offers for initiative, and the superior preparation it affords for adjustment in the community amply compensate for all the attention and supervision it entails." (Harris, *I Knew Them in Prison*, 113).

Harris had been at Clinton Farms for only seven months when she was called to help the war effort. From September 1918 to April 1919, Harris traveled to Florida, South Carolina, Virginia, and Georgia to establish detention homes for women camp followers who had been arrested for misdemeanors. In 1919 Harris returned to Clinton Farms and shortly thereafter assumed the superintendency of the State Home for Girls at Trenton, NJ.

When Harris arrived at Trenton in May 1919, there was insubordination, vandalism, and continual breakouts. There was no schooling, outdoor work, or recreation for the girls and women, and staff and facilities were inadequate to maintain order. Harris arranged for transfer of the severely disturbed inmates to the State Mental Hospital for treatment. She established a program for the detection and treatment of venereal diseases. She had a new, larger laundry built and hired more staff to teach and supervise

farm work. To provide the girls with a sense of accomplishment, she inaugurated graduation ceremonies from school and encouraged the display of farm produce at state fairs. Harris brought national youth organizations into the home and allowed the girls to participate outside in local community activities. She also encouraged musical productions and classical music. She provided inmates with training in special skills to obtain work when they were ready for parole. At Trenton, Harris successfully established a system of self-government that culminated each year in Harvest Home, the one day of the year when the girls ran the institution themselves.

Harris remained at Trenton for five and a half years, leaving on January 1, 1925, to take a position as executive secretary of the International Policewomen's Association in Washington, D.C. Her stay in this position was brief as she was appointed superintendent of the first federal prison for women in the spring of 1925.

The Federal Industrial Institution for Women was to be built in Alderson, WV, and Harris was placed in charge of designing it and developing its policies. To help her plan, she visited some 30 penal institutions. She trained the new staff herself, bringing the philosophy of self-government, which she had first learned in New Jersey, to Alderson. In expressing her philosophy of prison management, she commented: "We govern with the consent of the governed, with their cooperation and affectionate loyalty. That is the basis, I believe, of real discipline." (Harris, *I Knew Them in Prison*, 305) Harris promoted education and achievements in vocational skills. Alderson, which became a model institution, where inmates were individually classified and treated, had an excellent record of rehabilitation, for among the 682 selected for parole from 1928 to 1935, only 2.4 percent failed.

Harris brought progressive ideas to prison management and was successful in reforming prison life by substituting humane care for the traditional harsh treatment. She was a dynamic administrator, and the amazing success record of her parolees was a tribute to her leadership.

At the end of her life Harris returned to Lewisburg, PA, where she became a trustee of Bucknell University and the Baptist Church. She toured Europe and North Africa for a year in 1953. Harris died of heart failure on February 22, 1957, at age 82, in Lewisburg, PA, where she is buried.

Harris's autobiography is *I Knew Them in Prison* (1936). Her biography of her father, *Thirty Years as President of Bucknell* (1926), details family background. In *The Pathway of Mattie Howard to and from Prison* (1937) she describes her prison work. A sketch of her appears in *NAW-MP*. Her obituary was in the *New York Times*, Feb. 23, 1957.

*Constance B. Schuyler*

## CORA LOUISE HARTSHORN, 1873–1958

Cora Louise Hartshorn, cofounder of the first New Jersey birth control clinic, was born on March 21, 1873, in Springfield (Union County), NJ. She was the oldest of three children born to Stewart and Joanna (Randall) Hartshorn. From Joanna Hartshorn's seven pregnancies, only three children survived, causing her much distress, a factor that led to her daughter's work in the birth control movement. A brother, Stewart, was born in 1876 and a sister, Joanna, in 1879.

Hartshorn knew wealth from the beginning of her life. Her father, Stewart Hartshorn, developed the Spring Shade Roller, for which he received a patent in 1864. A successful businessman, he acquired land in the Short Hills area and dedicated his life to the development of Short Hills. He is credited today as the founder of the community.

Hartshorn's mother, who was born in Nova Scotia, Canada, participated in community activities, especially the local Republican party. In 1930 the Woman's Club of Millburn "was dedicated to the memory of Mrs. Stewart Hartshorn, Sr., who did such splendid work along civic lines." (*Item*, Oct. 9, 1930) Hartshorn later wrote about her mother: "She was one of the early suffragists when suffrage for women was bitterly fought both by men and by many women. She was always about 20 years ahead of her time in her knowledge of social and political questions and took a distinctly constructive part in the life of the Community and the State." (*A Little History of Short Hills*, 23)

Hartshorn was educated at home until 1887, when her mother sailed for England with the three children. After a year in England, the family went to Paris, where the children attended Madame Yeatman's School. In 1893 the family returned to Short Hills. Hartshorn, who never attended college, and remained single throughout her life, became involved in the development of Short Hills along with her parents.

Hartshorn also pursued an interest in art both as a creator and a collector. While enrolled in an art course in New York City she came into contact with Margaret Sanger for the first time. Sanger, who was out on bail after her arrest for opening a birth control clinic in the Brownsville section of Brooklyn, NY, spoke at a large protest rally at Carnegie Hall in January 1917. The rally had been called to protest the closing of the clinic and the arrest of Sanger and her sister, Ethel Byrnes. Hartshorn, then 44 years old, went to the rally, and Sanger's speech made a lasting impression on her. In an interview almost 40 years later Hartshorn said: "I had known the devastating effect in families of the lack of contraceptive knowledge and was shocked that our civilized country could imprison people for trying to help these poor women." (*Item*, Jan. 6, 1956)

Sanger went on to win her battle for birth control

clinics and open the first permanent clinic in New York City in 1923. Anxious to have more clinics, Sanger asked her friend Henrietta Hart to explore the possibility in New Jersey. Hart knew Hartshorn and of her interest in the movement, so she appealed to her for help. In an interview many years later Hartshorn said: "It was a vital cause that all women should help, so when Margaret Sanger decided to open a clinic in Newark, I organized our Short Hills Birth Control Committee." (*Item*, Jan. 6, 1956)

Cora Hartshorn used her contacts and influence in Short Hills to enlist committee members. During 1926–27, she held "parlor parties" in her home to raise funds for the clinic. Sanger often spoke at these gatherings. The two women, so different in background, became lifelong friends and supporters.

As interest in the birth control movement spread in New Jersey, a statewide committee called the New Jersey Birth Control League was formed. The League opened the Newark Maternal Health Care Center, located at 41 New Street, in 1928. Funded entirely from private donations, the primary function of the clinic was the dissemination of birth control information to married women. The clinic staff included only a doctor and nurse-receptionist. Criteria for the early patients were that a woman had to be married, have at least five children, and be unable to afford a private physician.

Establishing the Newark clinic with Sanger marked only the beginning of Hartshorn's efforts on behalf of the birth control movement. She worked actively with the New Jersey Birth Control League and headed the Short Hills district. In 1934 she campaigned with Sanger for a national Birth Control Bill, which would legalize the dissemination of contraceptive information and supplies by physicians; the bill was never passed. In 1941 the New Jersey Birth Control League was renamed the New Jersey League for Planned Parenthood. Hartshorn was active in the organization, particularly the Essex County district, until her death in 1958.

Her work for the birth control movement was Hartshorn's most significant role in New Jersey history, but it did not represent her only contribution. In the 1920s she became actively involved in the development of a flower and bird reservation on a 16.45 acre plot of land. The property, located on Forest Drive near the train station in Short Hills, had been a gift from her father.

In 1931 she began the construction of Stone House, a large community building on the reservation property that was completed in 1933. When Hartshorn died, she bequeathed the entire reservation to Millburn Township, and it became known as the Cora Hartshorn Arboretum and Bird Sanctuary.

Although a shy person by nature, Hartshorn always helped those who were less fortunate than she was. She quietly financed the college education of several local students. She also gave support to promising young artists, buying their paintings long before they were recognized. In time she developed a substantial collection of early modern American paintings. Some of the collection is located today at the Newark Museum and includes works of Marsden Hartley and Georgia O'Keeffe. Although her liberal views often clashed with those of her more conservative family, Hartshorn participated actively in political causes, particularly through the League of Women Voters. Ernestine Hartshorn, her niece, recalls how "Aunt Cora" favored the rights of labor unions despite the fact that their interests did not always agree with those of the family business.

Cora Hartshorn died, at age 85, from heart failure, at her home in Millburn Township on October 17, 1958, and was cremated at Rosedale Crematory in Orange, NJ.

Hartshorn wrote *A Little History of Short Hills* (1946), describing her parents' involvement with the founding of the community. A useful source of information on Hartshorn's life and activities are issues of the *Item of Millburn & Short Hills* (Millburn, NJ). Marsha Morrison of the Verona (NJ) Planned Parenthood Association has a collection of Hartshorn's correspondence. Telephone interviews with Ernestine Hartshorn, her niece, of Short Hills; Janet Gale, a friend; and Liz Naughton, the director of the Cora Hartshorn Arboretum and Bird Sanctuary (Short Hills), provided useful information. Her father's obituary appeared in the *New York Times*, Jan. 12, 1937, and hers appeared on Oct. 19, 1958.

*Susan Hanna*

## ETHEL BROWNE HARVEY, 1885–1965

Ethel (Browne) Harvey, biologist and author, was born in Baltimore, MD, on December 14, 1885, the youngest of five children (two sons and three daughters) of Bennet B. and Jennie (Nicholson) Browne. Her father was a Baltimore obstetrician-gynecologist and professor of gynecology at the Women's Medical College of Baltimore. Both her maternal and paternal ancestors left England in the 17th century and came to America.

Her parents believed in the education of women and sent their daughters to the Bryn Mawr School in Baltimore, the first preparatory school for women in America, from which Harvey graduated in 1902. Mary and Jennie, her sisters, followed their father's profession and became physicians.

Harvey continued her education at the Woman's College of Baltimore (later Goucher College), graduating in 1906. After graduation she spent the summer at the Marine Biological Laboratory, Woods Hole, where she took a graduate course, and for the rest of her life she returned to the laboratories as an investigator for at least a part of each summer.

Harvey supported her further education with fellow-ships and temporary, untenured instructorships or laboratory assistantships from 1906 to 1913. She received an M.A. (1907) and a Ph.D. (1913) from Columbia University.

She met Edmund Newton Harvey during her graduate years, when he was taking a course at the Woods Hole laboratories. They were married after he became professor of zoology at Princeton in 1916. Harvey and her husband formed a successful team, sharing similar scientific interests throughout their lives but working independently of each other. Edmund Harvey became known for his work on bioluminescens, and Ethel Browne Harvey became best known for her experimental work on the development of the sea urchin. Although they traveled all over the world, their social and cultural lives centered around Princeton, NJ.

Harvey was an energetic person who excelled in basketball, swimming, and tennis. Her great physical energy was further demonstrated when she and her husband, while on their honeymoon in Japan, walked from Watsui (on the west coast of Japan), through the high mountains, on to Tokyo, and then on to the Marine Laboratory of the Imperial University at Misaki. (Johnson, "Edmund Newton Harvey," 1967)

Harvey bore two sons, Edmund Newton (b. 1916) and Richard Bennet (b. 1922), in the first six years of her marriage while continuing her laboratory research. During those early years, Harvey was able to function as a researcher and a mother with the support of a maid in Princeton and a mother's helper at Woods Hole. While her husband searched the world for luminous fishes, she took her children with her to l'Institut Oceanographique in Monaco (1920) and the Stazione Zoologyical in Naples, where she depended on governesses for help.

Harvey joined Princeton's biology department in 1931 as an honorary member and an independent worker. She was associated with the department until 1962 but received only the minimum of support for her research. She was never admitted to the Princeton faculty and never held a regular scientific appointment. The university gave her office space and allowed her to share her husband's laboratory. It also paid her summer fees at Woods Hole, where she was assigned a working space in her husband's research area. Her professional status came—as it did for so many women without formal appointments—from her work at Woods Hole.

Harvey became an internationally recognized researcher despite the lack of institutional and financial support for her work. She occupied the American Women's Table at the Naples Zoological Station in 1925–26. Ida Henrietta Hyde, a physiologist, had founded the Naples Table Association for Promoting Scientific Research by Women. The association had set up a small equipped laboratory (a table), enabling women to carry out their research in Naples where women had not previously been welcomed.

Harvey had become interested in the broad areas of descriptive and experimental cytology and embryology as a graduate student, and she was particularly interested in the role of the nucleus and cytoplasm in inheritance and development. She used the sea urchin egg as her experimental organism, and her first paper dealt with the effects of oxygen lack on its development (1927).

Harvey developed a technique of centrifuging sea urchin eggs at forces of 10,000 times that of gravity. This resulted in the eggs dividing into two parts (fractions or merogones); one part had a nucleus and the other did not. She learned how to stimulate the fractions and induced the nonnucleated merogones to divide further. The continued division of egg fragments containing no nucleus was unexpected, since biologists assumed that when egg fragments were devoid of either maternal or paternal chromosomes they lacked a directing force and could not divide.

Harvey's nuclei-free egg fragments divided into as many as 500 cells and lived for about four weeks. Her work drew popular attention to the fact that biologists had intervened in the life process, and on November 28, 1937, she made the front page of the *Sunday New York Times* with the headline "Life Is Created Without Parents." Her book *The American Arbacia and Other Sea Urchins* (1956) was the culmination of several years of research and study. It established her reputation as a scholar, which she further enhanced by publishing about 100 papers in scientific journals. Her scientific accomplishments were noted by English scientist J.B.S. Haldane in his book *What Is Life?* In the chapter "Women in Science" Haldane cited Harvey's sea urchin work, the only mention of an American woman's research in the book.

Harvey was elected a fellow of the American Association for the Advancement of Science, the New York Academy of Science, and l'Institut International d'Embryologie. She also became an honorary member of the Societa Italiana de Biologia Sperimentale. And in 1950 she was elected a trustee—the only female trustee—of the Marine Biological Laboratory at Woods Hole.

In 1956, 50 years after her graduation, Goucher College conferred an honorary D.Sc. degree on Harvey. In so doing, President Kraushaar said of Harvey's work: "Your fruitful career, combining dedication to the pursuit of truth with devotion to the tasks of motherhood and family is an illustrious example of the achievements of a complete woman." (Thomas, "An Alumna Sees Her Daughter Graduate," 8)

Harvey died on September 2, 1965, at age 79, in a nursing home in Falmouth, MA, where she had lived for the previous two years. The cause of death was peritonitis, following an attack of acute appendicitis. She is buried in the cemetery in Woods Hole, MA.

Insights into the Harvey family appear in Frank Johnson, "Edmund Newton Harvey, November 25, 1887–July 21, 1959," *Biographical Memoirs of the National Academy of Science* 39 (1967):192–239. Her work is cited in J.B.S. Haldane, *What Is Life?* (1947). The awarding of Harvey's honorary degree is described in Christine Thomas, "An Alumna Sees Her Daughter Graduate," *Goucher Alumnae Quarterly* 34 (Summer 1956):6–8. A sketch of Harvey appears in *NAW-MP*. Her obituary appeared in the *New York Times*, Sept. 3, 1965.

*Joy B. Phillips*

## ELIZABETH HAWES, 1903–1971

Elizabeth Hawes, fashion designer, union activist, writer, and critic of high fashion, was born in Ridgewood (Bergen County), NJ, on December 16, 1903, the second of four children (three daughters and a son) of John and Henrietta (Houston) Hawes.

Hawes's mother was, in many respects, unusual for her time. An 1891 graduate of Vassar College, Henrietta (Houston) Hawes functioned as a traditional middle-class wife, mother, and homemaker. However, she also contributed significantly to life outside the home as a founder of a local tuberculosis and health association, a licensed plumber and general contractor for the construction of several houses, and the first woman member of the local board of education, on which she served for eighteen years. During the Great Depression of the 1930s she was the salaried director of relief for Bergen County. Hawes wrote in 1938 that her mother had been "saving various situations all her life. Obviously I come naturally by a desire to save humanity." (Hawes, *Fashion Is Spinach*, 33)

Hawes's father was formally educated only through grade school. However, he pursued a career spanning nearly 50 years with the Southern Pacific Railroad, rising from shipping clerk to general freight agent.

Showing an early interest in fashion design and dressmaking, Hawes began to sew her own clothes at ten and made her first commercial sale at twelve. She was educated in the Ridgewood public grade and high schools and went to Vassar College, as did her mother and sisters. While at college she pursued her interest in fashion design during the summer.

In 1925, after graduating from Vassar with a bachelor's degree in economics, Hawes traveled to Paris to learn about fashion at its then-acknowledged source. She spent three seasons copying high-fashion designs for a Paris copy house and sketching for American buyers and manufacturers in Paris. Combining fashion and journalism, she became correspondent for an American fashion syndicate and Paris correspondent for the *New Yorker* magazine. She was also Paris stylist for two prestigious U.S. department stores, Macy's and Lord and Taylor.

Hawes left these jobs in 1928 for the opportunity to

design with the noted French couturiere Nicole Groult. To this experience may be traced her first strong sociopolitical awareness, which was to culminate more than a decade later in union activism. She began to realize that she was out of sympathy with the French leisure class and wished instead to design more practical clothes for American women.

She returned to the United States and on December 16, 1928, her 25th birthday, opened a made-to-order women's fashion shop in New York City with her friend and financial backer Rosemary Harden. The venture busily produced much well-received clothing, but lost money.

In 1930 Hawes married Ralph Jester, a sculptor, whom she credited with inspiring her to think of clothes architecturally. With an abiding appreciation for the value of publicity, she chose July 4, 1931, for an exhibition in Paris of her own American fashion, the first display in that city by an American designer. Two years later she took another step toward a working-class consciousness, joining a New York garment district firm to design modestly priced, ready-to-wear clothing. She soon left to open a new and larger business of her own. In 1935 she exhibited her clothes in the Soviet Union, the first exhibition by an American woman designer since the Russian Revolution.

By 1933 Hawes had separated from Ralph Jester and in 1935 they were divorced. Two years later she married film director Joseph Losey. Their son, Gavrik, was born in 1938 and was raised primarily by Hawes's mother.

That same year her best-selling first book, *Fashion Is Spinach*, was published. In it she argued against the whims of fashion, both French and American, and for a functional, classic, enduring style. In 1939 her next book, *Men Can Take It*, attacked the uncomfortable clothing worn by men and reiterated her advocacy of functional design.

Hawes closed her business in January 1940 for a combination of reasons, among them her belief that the day was over for made-to-order clothing. Later that year she began to write a regular column of practical advice on eating, dressing, and entertaining on a limited budget for the New York City newspaper *PM*.

Hawes continued to combine fashion with journalism until the advent of World War II, when she turned her attention to women's adjustment to wartime. She became an advocate in *PM* and elsewhere for comfort and freedom for women, in areas ranging from the wearing of pants to child care centers for working mothers.

For a brief time in 1943 Hawes worked the midnight shift at the Wright Aeronautical plant in Paterson, NJ, primarily to do research for a book addressing the concerns of working-class women. This experience led her to support unionizing efforts and to join a United Auto Workers (UAW) local. Her book *Why Women Cry*, published later that year, recounted her experiences at the war plant, defended women's need to be free of domestic routine, and

detailed the hardships of working women. In the book she stated her fear of the elimination of protective legislation for women workers. She, like many labor union women and their middle-class supporters, came to oppose the Equal Rights Amendment because she thought it might become a rationale for doing away with such legislation.

In 1944 Hawes and Joseph Losey were divorced. That same year she moved to Detroit, where she worked for some months in the education department of the UAW. Then, after another brief stint at her own fashion design business, she became dismayed by growing political conservatism in the United States and moved to the Virgin Islands in 1950.

In 1952 she moved again, this time to California, where neither her efforts at fashion design for a select few women nor her writing earned her much money. In her final book, *It's Still Spinach* (1954), Hawes reiterated her consistent plea for men and women to break away from the absurdities of fashion.

In the late 1960s she returned to New York City, where she was recognized by the Fashion Institute of Technology for her contribution as a trailblazer in American fashion. In 1967 the institute presented a retrospective show of her designs.

Hawes died on September 7, 1971, in New York City, at age 67, of a gastrointestinal hemorrhage resulting from "chronic ethanolism" (alcoholism).

During the 1930s her outspoken criticism of women's slavery to fashion, culminating in her 1938 book *Fashion Is Spinach*, was unique, preceding the revitalized feminist consciousness of the 1960s by a quarter century. Her concern for the problems facing working women, articulated in *Why Women Cry*, raised issues such as adequate child care, which are still relevant nearly a half century later.

Hawes's best-known work is *Fashion Is Spinach* (1938). She was profiled in *Current Biography* (1940) and *NAW-MP*. Interviews with her brother, John Hawes, and her sister-in-law, Judith Hawes, on Jan. 3, 1986, provided useful information. Her obituaries appeared in the *New York Times*, Sept. 7, 1971, and the *Ridgewood* (NJ) *Herald-News*, Sept. 9, 1971.

*Roberta C. Moore*

## CARYE-BELLE HENLE, 1895–1977

Carye-Belle (Henle) Connamacher Goldfus, New Jersey's first woman radiologist, was born in Greenville, MS, on December 5, 1895, the daughter of Estelle (Lyon) Henle of Mobile, AL, and John Henle, a German immigrant. Shortly after her birth, her family moved to New York City, where her father worked in retailing.

As a girl Henle attended annual summer camp in upstate New York, where she developed a lifelong love of swimming, boating, and the out-of-doors. When she graduated from Washington Irving High School in New York City she went to the Savage School for Physical Education to train as a physical education instructor. Following her graduation in 1917 she taught in New York City, but was discontented with her work. Since she especially enjoyed the medical classes that were part of her physical education studies, she decided to go into medicine despite her father's misgivings about its suitability as a field for women.

Henle began taking premed courses in 1919 at Columbia University and graduated with honors in 1921. Despite the difficulties women generally experienced in gaining admission to medical school at the time, she was accepted at the College of Physicians and Surgeons of Columbia University and completed her medical degree in 1925.

While in medical school Henle met and secretly married Harold Connamacher, who graduated with her in her medical school class. Following graduation they remarried publicly and interned together at Bellevue Hospital in New York City. Upon completion of their internships in 1926, she continued her studies and became the first woman resident (in radiology) at Mt. Sinai Hospital in New York City, while her husband established a general practice in Newark, NJ. As Mt. Sinai's first woman resident, she was a curiosity to the staff and was carefully scrutinized in her work. A soft-spoken and enthusiastic woman with a brilliant mind and quick grasp of radiology, Henle soon won over her critics.

After completing her residency in 1928, Henle joined her husband in his Newark practice and became an adjunct radiologist at Newark's Beth Israel Hospital. That same year her first child, Jane, was born. In 1929 her second daughter, Patricia, was born, and then in 1934 a son, Robert. By this time Henle had established her practice as a radiologist.

Early in the 1930s Henle became active in the New Jersey Medical Women's Association (NJMWA), an organization founded in 1924 that became an important social and professional network of New Jersey women physicians. In 1933 she and some colleagues founded the Clara Krans Research Fund to honor the first president of the NJMWA and to provide financial support for women medical students. Henle managed the fund her entire life.

In the late 1930s and early 1940s Henle was a member of the Committee for the Relief of Distressed Women Physicians, a group under the aegis of the American Medical Women's Association (AMWA) that worked through the years of World War II to aid and relocate to the United States women physicians in Austria and Germany who had been persecuted and deprived of their practices and property. (A colleague, RITA SAPIRO FINKLER, was also active in this cause.)

Later in her life Henle served as president of the NJMWA (1952–1953) and as recording secretary of the AMWA (1954–55). She was honored in 1963 as the NJMWA "Woman of the Year."

Henle became a volunteer associate radiologist at Newark City Hospital in 1939, and then as World War II developed she assumed more public work. She became a radiologist for the Health Department of Newark in 1941, holding that post until 1971. She was an associate at St. Michael's Hospital from 1942 to 1950. During the war, when hospitals were badly understaffed, Henle assisted at Newark City Hospital and single-handedly read X rays at St. Michael's and at St. Mary's Hospital in Orange, sometimes reading 250 X rays a day.

Henle's husband died in 1950 and in 1954 she remarried, to an optometrist, Maxwell Goldfus, whom she divorced a few years later. By this time she was well known in her field. In 1950 she began serving as radium consultant for West Hudson Hospital in Kearny and continued in this capacity until 1969. She was the only woman among the 80 members of the Radiological Society of New Jersey when she was elected president of the organization in 1956.

Henle continued to study and take courses to keep current in her field, studying nuclear medicine and mammography in particular. She was selected in the 1950s as project radiologist for the Radium Research Project, a major study by the New Jersey Department of Health under contract by the U.S. Atomic Energy Commission (AEC). The project was a ten-year medical study (November 1957–February 1967) of the long-term effects of radium on people who had worked as luminous watch, clock, and instrument dial painters in northern New Jersey in the 1920s. Radium dial workers such as KATHERINE SCHAUB had used radium paint and put the paintbrush tips in their mouths to point them. As a result of ingesting the radioactive material many workers had suffered severe damage to bones and organs from radiation. Henle and her colleagues identified 900 workers and studied 750, collecting valuable knowledge on the effects of atomic radiation. The final report of the project, *Epidemiological Follow-up of New Jersey Radium Cases*, was published in 1968 by the AEC. Henle's work on the project was a high point in her career.

In 1968 Henle was appointed clinical associate professor of radiology at the University of Medicine and Dentistry of New Jersey, becoming emeritus professor in July 1974.

After her retirement from practice in 1974, Henle moved her residence from Newark to a country house she owned in Kinnelon (Morris County). There she became active in environmental and civic affairs and continued her lifelong interest in swimming, camping, and hiking. She died in Kinnelon on July 14, 1977, at age 78. She had survived a severe heart attack in 1973 but died of leukemia. Her remains were cremated at the Cedar Lawn Crematory in Paterson.

Materials on Henle are available at NJ-UMDNJ. Articles about her are: "Male Tribute Pleases Woman Radiologist," *Newark Sunday News*, July 8, 1956; and "Woman of the Year No Idler," *Newark Evening News*, Mar. 14, 1963. Her obituary appeared in the *New York Times*, July 25, 1977.

*Christine Haycock*

## MARGARET SULLIVAN HERBERMANN, 1878–1963

Margaret (Sullivan) Herbermann, physician, surgeon, social reformer, and pioneer in public education for physically disabled children, was born on January 30, 1878, in Jersey City (Hudson County), NJ, the younger of two daughters of Daniel and Margaret (Noonan) Sullivan. Both her parents were born in County Kerry, Ireland. After emigrating to the United States, they settled in New York City, where her father sold produce in the Gansevoort farmers' market in lower Manhattan. A few years later, the Sullivans moved to Jersey City, where a daughter, Catherine, was born in 1874, and four years later Margaret was born.

Within a few years, Herbermann's father became a successful market dealer, hiring Irish immigrants like himself to work for him. Her mother was assertive, capable, and managed the family's various real estate properties. Although formally uneducated, her parents' industrious spirit and desire to succeed in a new country manifested itself in Herbermann's own determined, energetic character.

Herbermann received her education in Jersey City's public schools. The robust, good-natured young girl with golden brown hair and blue eyes had an intense love for learning and was admiringly described by her family as "book crazy." Thus, when she announced her desire to become a doctor upon graduation from Bay Street High School, her parents and family wholeheartedly supported her. But because Herbermann was a woman, entry into medical school was difficult.

In 1896 she first attended Pratt Institute in Brooklyn, a school that offered the preparatory science courses she needed. With perseverance and the help of teachers and family, she was finally accepted in 1904 to the Woman's College of Philadelphia, a medical school founded exclusively for the education of women physicians. After graduation in 1908, she went on to specialize in surgery. She served her internship at the College Hospital, Philadelphia, and took postgraduate courses at Columbia University and the Post Graduate Hospital, New York City.

Upon completion of her medical training, Herbermann went back to Jersey City to live and practice. During these early years as a physician (1908–16), she also worked on the staff of the New York Infirmary for Women and Children (today Beekman Hospital). As assistant attending physician and surgeon, she treated New York City's poor.

Besides offering medical help, she educated women about cleanliness, fresh air, sunlight, and healthy food to overcome tuberculosis, malnutrition, and high infant mortality.

The first woman surgeon to be appointed to the staff of Jersey City Hospital (1914)—a position for which she received no monetary compensation—Herbermann devoted herself to medicine and crusaded for better living conditions in Jersey City. As president of the Child Welfare Association, she supported the State Tenement Housing Commission when other officials discredited its work and tried to abolish it. She believed that "the proper supervision of the planning and building of homes, and especially the homes of poor people, is truly the foundation of welfare work," and that establishing a code of laws and enforcing it is vital to prevent overcrowding and disease. (*Jersey Journal*, Jan. 26, 1915)

Herbermann's leadership efforts in organizations such as the Child Welfare Association and the Mothers' Institute and her medical reputation brought her further recognition. In 1915 Mayor Mark Fagan publicly praised her ability and appointed Herbermann to the Jersey City Board of Education. She was committed to the cause of education during her fifteen years of office. Besides regularly attending board meetings and various school graduations, she helped select qualified teachers and principals and was responsible for obtaining higher teachers' salaries.

An accomplished speaker, Herbermann was also dedicated to educating women about their rights and urged them to take part in public affairs. "We are no longer counting votes by trousers," she declared in an address to members of the Union Democratic Woman's Club. (*Jersey Journal*, Feb. 4, 1921) With the newly won right to vote, women, she believed, should band together to make their organizations "not merely political ones but educational ones as well." She pointed out that although Jersey City had increased teachers' minimum salaries from $600 to $1,400 within her tenure on the Board of Education, women still had far to travel to achieve their "rightful place in the world's standing."

Although Herbermann had no children of her own, she was extremely fond of her many nieces and nephews and she loved children. A personal experience triggered her special interest in educating the disabled. While visiting a twelve-year-old polio victim who lived near her home, she became disturbed that the young boy could not read because illness had prevented him from attending school. Herbermann therefore devised a kind of home tutorial system for him. She arranged for older children in the neighborhood to take turns reading to him and eventually teaching him how to read.

Herbermann sympathized with the disabled and actively campaigned for the passage of three legislative bills. These landmark bills were passed by the New Jersey Legislature in 1919 and provided that "every municipality having fifteen or more crippled children must provide classes and transportation for them, the State to give to the city $100 for the education of each crippled child, adjacent municipalities to be allowed to cooperate." In an effort to understand the specialized needs of the disabled, Herbermann traveled abroad and researched methods and equipment used in schools there. Finally, due mainly to her work, the Clifton Place School for Crippled Children, hailed as the first of its kind in the United States, opened its doors in Jersey City to 53 disabled children on April 18, 1921. The school accepted children from all over Hudson County—Union City, Bayonne, Kearny, and Jersey City—and offered transportation, meals, special equipment, a rooftop enclosed sun room, gymnasium, and specialized medical staff.

The school grew rapidly, and a new, larger facility was built that eventually became known as the A. Harry Moore School for Crippled Children. Although Herbermann fought hard for passage of the legislation and played a dominant role in founding the school, Commissioner Moore (later elected governor) received public recognition for its establishment. Herbermann, according to others, became caught in the intricacies of politics. Because she refused to give in to pressure from Mayor Frank Hague to support certain choices of doctors for positions at the hospital, she believed that he denied her this recognition.

In 1929, two years after serving her last term on the Board of Education, she married Henry Herbermann, founder and owner of the American Export Steamship Lines and a native of Jersey City. They were married in a quiet ceremony (newspapers reported it as "secret") at a Jesuit retreat in Morristown, NJ, and lived in New York City. The marriage was brief but happy. Because of her husband's prominence and career, they traveled extensively, entertained, and shared an active social life until his sudden death caused by a stroke in 1935.

Lonely after by her husband's death, Herbermann returned to Jersey City where she resumed her practice. Reportedly, she rediscovered her interest in endocrinology and worked at Lenox Hill Hospital in New York on the uses of insulin and adrenaline.

Herbermann retired from private practice in 1960. In her later years she took up short-story writing and was devoted to her sister's family until her death. She died of arteriosclerosis at the age of 85 on March 24, 1963, and was buried in Holy Name Cemetery in Jersey City.

An interview with Herbermann's niece, Eileen Groeschel, provided material on her background. Material on Herbermann is available at NJ-JCPL and the Medical College of Pennsylvania (Philadelphia).

*Astrid S. Dadourian*

## EMILY GREGORY HICKMAN, 1880–1947

Emily Gregory Hickman, college professor and peace advocate, was born in Buffalo, NY, on July 12, 1880, the second of six children and the first of three daughters born to Alice (Gregory) and Arthur Washington Hickman, a prominent attorney and two-term Republican member of the New York Assembly. Graduating from Buffalo high school in 1897 and Cornell University in 1901, Hickman taught in Buffalo high schools for five years. After doing graduate work at Cornell and Yale, she received her Ph.D. in history from Cornell in 1911. That same year she was appointed to the history faculty at Wells College, a women's college in Aurora, NY, where she spent sixteen years teaching and performing administrative duties, ultimately as head of the history department and acting dean.

In 1927 Dean MABEL SMITH DOUGLASS hired Hickman as her assistant and as a full professor of history at the New Jersey College for Women (later Douglass College) in New Brunswick. Vigorous disagreements between the two women ended Hickman's administrative career at the college in 1929, but she continued to teach history there until her death. In addition, the popular teacher, a small, dynamic woman known for her picturesque hats, turned her energy to the cause of world peace.

Already distressed by America's failure to join the League of Nations, Hickman began her peace activities in 1925, when she became a member of the National Committee on the Cause and Cure of War (CCCW). Founded that year by Carrie Chapman Catt, the former suffragist leader, the CCCW enabled women to take leadership in educating public opinion in favor of a system of world law and an international structure for enduring peace. At both national and state levels, the CCCW served as a coordinating body of representatives from women's organizations such as the General Federation of Women's Clubs, the League of Women Voters, and the Young Women's Christian Association (YWCA). Within the peace movement, the CCCW offered a moderate alternative to more radical groups such as the Women's International League for Peace and Freedom.

Hickman later said that she continued to follow the advice Catt gave her at their first meeting, to "stick" to the peace movement. (*Current Biography, 1945,* 282) The history professor became state chair of the New Jersey CCCW in the early 1930s and later vice-chair of the national organization. In 1936 she was one of 20 American women delegates to the Universal Peace Conference in Brussels. An effective speaker, she made two lecture tours across the United States in 1938 and 1939 under the auspices of the Carnegie Endowment for International Peace.

During World War II Hickman was one of the original members of the Commission to Study the Organization of Peace (the "Shotwell Commission," formed by Prof. James

T. Shotwell of Columbia University in late 1939). She headed the Committee on Women in World Affairs from its inception in 1942. When women were excluded from the planning conference for the United Nations at Dumbarton Oaks, Washington, D.C., in 1944, she helped form the Committee for the Participation of Women in Postwar Planning, subsequently becoming its chair. With the CCCW's dissolution in 1943, Hickman joined the newly formed Women's Action Committee for Victory and Lasting Peace, chairing its education committee from 1946 to 1947. She also headed the National Peace Conference's commission on a world community. In New Jersey, she was state president of the United Nations Association and also headed the international relations committee of the state Federation of Business and Professional Women's Clubs.

She was an active member of the New Brunswick YWCA and, beginning in 1932, served on the national board. From 1938 to 1946 she served as chair of the YWCA's National Public Affairs Committee. Hickman had inherited an affiliation with the Republican party from her parents, but in 1936 she publicly switched to support the reelection of President Franklin D. Roosevelt. (*New York Times*, July 30, 1936) Thereafter, she continued to support the Roosevelt administration and was a personal acquaintance and admirer of Eleanor Roosevelt.

In 1945 Hickman was appointed to attend the United Nations' organizational conference in San Francisco. She was one of two women assisting the State Department's Division of Public Liaison as aides to the U.S. delegation. Nationally recognized for her work in support of the U.N. and world peace, Hickman received the Avon Award for the Women of Achievement of 1946 and was awarded an honorary degree of Doctor of Humane Letters from Russell Sage College in 1947.

She drowned in an automobile accident on June 12, 1947, when her car failed to make a turn and plunged into the Amawalk Reservoir near Lincolndale, NY. She was 66 years old. Burial was in the family plot in Buffalo, NY. Editorial writers praised her qualities of mind and spirit, which had "made a lasting impression on the opinion of her times." (*New York Herald Tribune*, June 14, 1947) In 1964 Douglass College dedicated its new liberal arts building as Emily Gregory Hickman Hall.

NJ-DC and NJ-RU maintain material on Hickman. A sketch of her appeared in *Current Biography* (1945). On Hickman's role at Douglass, a colleague, Margaret Judson, professor emerita of history, was interviewed August 3, 1987; see also George Schmidt, *Douglass College: A History* (1968). Obituaries of Hickman appeared in the *New York Times*, June 13, 1947, the *Home News* (New Brunswick, NJ) June 12, 1947, and the *New York Herald Tribune*, June 14, 1947.

*John W. Chambers II*
*Larayne J. Dallas*

## BEATRICE ALICE HICKS, 1919–1979

Beatrice Alice (Hickstein) Chipp (who was known as Beatrice Alice Hicks), engineer, head of a manufacturing company, inventor of a device that helped the United States achieve a moon landing, and cofounder of a national organization that advanced women in engineering, was born on January 2, 1919, in Orange (Essex County), NJ. Nicknamed "Noonie," she was the elder of two daughters of William Lux Hickstein, a chemical engineer, and Florence Benedict (Neben) Hickstein, a homemaker devoted to the Christian Science religion. Hick's only sibling, Margaret Lurene, ten years younger than she, was born mentally retarded and was institutionalized near Princeton, NJ.

Hicks was twelve when her father lost his job at Westinghouse during the Depression. The Hicksteins lost their house and had to pitch a tent in the fields of Livingston, NJ. While the family survived on hamburgers and dandelion greens, Hicks's father borrowed money to market a safety control he had designed that automatically cut off hot water in steam heating systems. He founded the Newark Controls Co., and on a $15-a-week salary he moved the family into a tenement in Orange, NJ. In 1936 Newark Controls moved to Bloomfield, NJ.

Educated in Orange public schools, Hicks showed great aptitude for mathematics, physics, chemistry, and mechanical drawing. She was awed by the Empire State Building and the George Washington Bridge, two engineering feats of her time, and vowed to become an engineer. Teachers tried to discourage her. Her parents, burdened with the cost of her sister's special care, encouraged her to study stenography instead, but Hicks resolved she would not "just be taking notes." (Kasso, Interview, July 12, 1986)

After graduating from Orange High School in 1935, Hicks entered Newark College of Engineering (now New Jersey Institute of Technology) and earned her tuition by working. She was one of two women in a class of 900. She received her B.S. in chemical engineering in 1939, and for three years worked as a research assistant at the college. Her research there on the history of the inventions of Edward Weston furnished material for a book, *A Measure for Greatness* (1949), by David O. Woodbury.

The need for engineers after the United States entered World War II opened up opportunities for women, and in 1942 Hicks was hired by Western Electric, the Kearny-based manufacturing arm of the Bell Telephone system. Initially the company gave Hicks, its first female engineer, the title of technician, and co-workers lacked confidence in her. "At first, some of the men acted as if I alone would sabotage the entire World War II effort then in progress," she later said. ("Outstanding Engineer, Manager, and Consultant Is Also a Woman," 137–38) But she quickly proved herself and was given the title and salary of an engineer. At Western Electric she designed telephone equipment for the first long-distance dial system and crystal oscillators to control radio frequencies in aircraft communication equipment. Meanwhile, she also took advanced courses in electrical engineering and studied library science at Columbia University.

In 1945 she left Western Electric, and for a short while was a private consultant. In June 1946 her father died, and the family-owned Newark Controls Co. was reorganized. Hicks became vice-president and engineering director, in which capacity she supervised a 22-man team that designed, developed, and manufactured electromechanical heat controls. She earned a master's in physics from Stevens Institute of Technology in 1949.

Despite her own success, Hicks was aware that schools were failing to encourage girls to enter engineering even though the nation was facing a critical shortage of engineers. She believed women were potentially the greatest source of additional engineering talent and tried to persuade the public that failing to tap that talent would pose risks to the nation's security. In 1951 Hicks cofounded and became first president of the Society of Women Engineers (SWE), which was dedicated to advancing girls and women in engineering. As president of SWE, Hicks supported changes in protective labor laws, originally passed to protect women and children from exploitation in factories; by the 1950s, Hicks contended, the restrictions on hours of work and working periods in these laws were holding back professional women. She applauded New Jersey's move to exempt professional women from those restrictions.

*Mademoiselle* magazine named Hicks one of ten outstanding "Young Women of the Year" in 1952. Her growing fame brought press interviews, which she used to correct the image girls and their parents had of engineering. "Women think that an engineer is a man in hip boots building a dam," she said. "They don't realize that 95 percent of engineering is done in a nice air-conditioned office." (*New York Herald Tribune*, Mar. 4, 1960) In frequent talks to schoolchildren Hicks pointed out that dress designers and slipcover makers have the same ability to see and think in three dimensions that is required in engineering. As far as gaining respect in what was generally regarded as a man's field, she maintained that in the sciences competence was what counted. However, women engineers did encounter discrimination, she claimed, when they tried for administrative posts.

In her work at Newark Controls, where she became president in 1955, Hicks designed, developed, and produced environmental sensors and controls. She invented a gas density switch, patented in 1962, that was considered an engineering breakthrough necessary for space travel. The device monitored the density of a sealed-in atmosphere and signaled when that atmosphere's density changed—for example, when there was a leak. The switch

was also used to activate controls, such as to open a valve or to start a pump. Hick's invention had many applications, especially on aircraft and missiles. It was used in antenna couplers on the Boeing 707 and in ignition systems on the Saturn V rockets that launched the Apollo moon missions, as well as to monitor nuclear weapons in storage. Other sensors Hicks developed could monitor pressure, fuel levels, or the rate of flow of liquids or gases. One sensor set off an alarm when a rocket, missile, or plane exceeded a speed that was structurally safe.

On August 12, 1948, Hicks married Rodney Duane Chipp in New York City, where he was director of engineering for the Du Mont TV network. Chipp, originally from New Rochelle, NY, had designed radar systems while in the navy during World War II. The couple lived in Montclair, NJ, until 1963, when they moved to Troy Towers in Bloomfield. They played badminton, bicycled, and skiied together. Hicks also relaxed by sculpting and playing an electric organ. She regarded both as private pastimes: she hid her sculptures in the attic and played the organ with earphones on.

Hicks, who received an honorary doctor of science degree from Hobart and William Smith colleges in 1958, used the name Dr. Beatrice A. Hicks professionally and Mrs. Rodney D. Chipp in private life. She had changed her maiden name Hickstein to Hicks to avoid what she perceived as anti-Semitism in situations such as trying to make airline reservations. She was Protestant.

In 1960, in the wake of Eugene Burdick and William Lederer's book *The Ugly American*, which had portrayed American engineers overseas as insensitive, the National Society of Professional Engineers chose Hicks and Chipp from 2,000 applicants to go on a goodwill and fact-finding tour of South America, called Project Ambassador. Both learned Spanish in preparation for the trip, on which they observed the problems of American engineers in foreign countries and formulated suggestions for training engineers for work overseas.

In 1961 Chipp founded his own communications-engineering consulting firm, Rodney D. Chipp and Associates, in Bloomfield at the same location as Newark Controls. Hicks and her husband worked closely in the ensuing years. She continued at Newark Controls but also consulted for Chipp's firm. Chipp, who supported his wife's work to advance women in engineering, died on December 28, 1966. Two years later Hicks established the Rodney D. Chipp Memorial Award at SWE to be given to a man or a company for advancing women engineers to executive or management positions.

After her husband's death, Hicks moved to the country near Dover, NJ, and later to New York City. She sold Newark Controls in order to run Chipp's firm. Among the projects she undertook was one to design a closed-circuit TV system to enable teaching hospitals to tape-record operations performed by experienced surgeons.

Hicks traveled to seven countries between 1954 and 1975 as a U.S delegate to international management congresses, to which she brought her experience as manager of a small business and her concern for the implications of technology in international management. She was made a fellow of the International Academy of Law and Sciences. She was a member of the Defense Advisory Commission on Women in the Services from 1960 to 1963, and director of the First International Conference on Women Engineers and Scientists in 1964.

The Society of Women Engineers gave Hicks their Achievement Award in 1963 with a citation that read "In recognition of her significant contributions to the theoretical study and analysis of sensing devices under extreme environmental conditions, and her substantial achievements in international technical understanding, professional guidance, and engineering education." (SWE files) In 1965 Hicks was the first woman ever awarded an honorary doctor of engineering degree by Rensselaer Polytechnic Institute. In 1978 she received honorary degrees from Stevens Institute of Technology and Worcester Polytechnic Institute. She was the sixth woman ever awarded membership in the National Academy of Engineering.

Hicks died of a heart attack on October 21, 1979, at age 60, in Princeton, NJ. She was buried next to her husband in Arlington National Cemetery, Arlington, VA.

The Society of Women Engineers (NYC) maintains a collection of speeches, articles, and letters by and about Hicks. Articles about her include: Marilyn Mercer, "Company President Is Professional Engineer," *New York Herald Tribune*, Mar. 4, 1960; "Outstanding Engineer, Manager, and Consultant Is Also a Woman," *Product Engineering* 39 (Apr. 8, 1968):137–38. An interview with Hicks's cousin, William O. Kasso, of New York City, on July 12, 1986, provided useful information. Hicks is profiled in *Current Biography* (1957).

Diane T. Masucci
Maggie Sullivan

## CELESTE HOLM, 1919–

Actress and singer Celeste Holm, winner of the 1947 Motion Picture Academy Award for Best Supporting Actress, was born in New York City on April 29, 1919, the only child of Theodor and Jean (Parke) Holm. Multilingual Theodor Holm, one of a Norwegian minister's eleven children, had emigrated to the United States in 1909; he worked until World War I as an importer, then as an insurance adjustor and later as director for Lloyd's of London in America. Jean (Parke) Holm, born in Minnesota to Goddard and Blanche Eugenie (Newell) Park, had at age sixteen left home to study art in Brooklyn. She added the *e* to her surname "to be her own woman." (Holm, Interview,

Apr. 3, 1986) She worked until about 1914 at D. W. Griffith's Biograph Studios in Fort Lee, NJ, and later became a recognized portrait painter.

Celeste Holm's attachment to New Jersey began in her early childhood, when her maternal grandmother and step-grandfather, Edmund Gale Jewett, bought 22 acres of farmland at the border of Morris and Warren counties, a property Holm calls "the only place I have roots." (Quoted in Schulze, "Celeste Holm Lauded," 40) On that land, "the family spent weekends and summer holidays in tents. Some of my fondest memories are of those days," says Holm. (Quoted in Kalman, "Jersey Casts Celeste Holm," I:28) As a child, Holm began acting at the farm in a theater her father built in the woods. Much later, in 1943, a Revolutionary-period house on the property was bought by Holm's father. It is now the weekend retreat of Holm and her fourth husband, actor (Robert) Wesley Addy.

Holm's formal education in childhood was acquired at some fourteen schools, because her father's business moved the family from New York to Chicago and her mother's painting exhibit took them briefly to France. Holm liked school but most enjoyed trips to the theater with her grandmother and frequent contact with theatrical and literary friends of her family. She believes that her career choice stemmed primarily from her childhood experience of Anna Pavlova's impact on audiences, and she recalls having learned very early to imitate various performers. In 1934 she graduated from Francis W. Parker High School in Chicago.

Promised four years of support by her father if she would study, young Holm left Chicago promptly after high school to stay with her grandparents in Brooklyn to start in the theater. Within three years, she was self-supporting. Her first jobs were in a summer tryout at Locust Valley, Long Island (1935), and summer stock at Deer Lake, PA (1936).

Her first Broadway break came with William Saroyan's hit *The Time of Your Life* (1939), when Holm, at 20, put up her hair and took off her makeup to play convincingly and poignantly a 35-year-old alcoholic, thus garnering her first attention from Broadway critics. Seven major roles on Broadway quickly followed. The plays proved short-lived, but Holm's performances in them earned critical praise. Meanwhile, Holm continued to study acting and voice and gained further experience through work in touring companies and nearby New Jersey and Connecticut playhouses. A second break came finally with the part of Ado Annie Carnes in *Oklahoma!* (1943), for which Holm says she auditioned because she needed musical employment to qualify her to sing at the Stage Door Canteen. Her enormous success as Ado Annie was followed by the lead role of Evelina in *Bloomer Girl* (1944); Holm was now well established as a Broadway star.

Twentieth Century-Fox signed Holm to a contract in

1944, and by 1950 she had made eleven films, including the three that put her in the Oscar league: *A Gentleman's Agreement* (1947, Best Supporting Actress Award for the role of Anne Detry), *Come to the Stable* (1949, Supporting Actress nomination), and *All About Eve* (1950, Supporting Actress nomination). In 1950, however, Holm disagreed with Fox studio head Darryl Zanuck, gained release from her contract, and returned to Broadway to star in the hit *Affairs of State* (1950–51), written by Louis Verneuil especially for her.

Since 1951 Holm's career has been a complex, fast-paced multimedia mix moving her from coast to coast. In the 1960s, for example, she did a radio show, "People at the United Nations," for three years. Singing engagements have been a long-term staple. Holm has played supporting roles in films such as *The Tender Trap, High Society, Bachelor Flat,* and *Bittersweet Love*. Her television appearances include guest spots on major prime-time variety shows and series, and a dozen parts in specials and playhouse productions. Most notably, Holm was the fairy godmother in the much replayed 1965 Rogers and Hammerstein "Cinderella," and she earned an Emmy Award nomination as Mrs. Harding in "Backstairs at the White House" (NBC, 1979). More recently, she played in "The Shady Hill Kidnapping" (PBS, 1983), six episodes of "Falcon Crest" (CBS, 1985), "Murder by the Book" (CBS, 1987), and an episode of "Magnum, P.I." (CBS, 1987).

Of greatest importance to Holm have been her diverse starring roles. Although she is probably best known for musical comedy, Holm has starred in works by Aeschylus, Chekhov, Ibsen, Shaw, Noel Coward, and Tennessee Williams. A three-year run in *Mame* (1967–69) was the basis for her 1969 Sarah Siddons Award. New Jersey productions starring Holm have included *Light Up the Sky* (1975, Paper Mill Playhouse), the one-woman show *Paris Was Yesterday* (1978, George Street Playhouse), and *Hay Fever* (1980, McCarter Theatre).

A twice-named "Performer of the Year" by Variety Clubs of America (1966 and 1971) and the 1986 winner of Public Television's New Jersey Broadcast Award, the energetic Holm shows no sign of quitting the tough "illusion" business. "What is my favorite part? My next one!" she exclaims. (Holm, Interview, Apr. 3, 1986) Her July 6, 1986, contribution to New Jersey's Liberty Weekend festivities yielded an example of her unflinching professionalism: with husband Wesley Addy as John Adams, Holm portrayed Abigail Adams—looking cool and serene in a heavy taffeta period costume, despite record-breaking heat and humidity, in an unairconditioned church seating 700 perspiring admirers.

Charitable and civic groups have showered Holm with honors and awards for her myriad public service activities in both New York and New Jersey. She currently chairs the New Jersey Motion Picture and Television Commis-

sion, of which she has been a gubernatorially appointed member since its 1978 inception. Most meaningful in her own eyes has been her work in mental health, both as a board member for the Welkind Hospital in Chester, NJ, and as president since 1977 of the pioneering Creative Arts Rehabilitation Center in New York City.

Holm was briefly married three times and bore two sons, Theodor Nelson (b. 1936) and Daniel Dunning (b. 1946), before she was 30. Her fourth marriage, to Wesley Addy, took place on May 22, 1966. Addy had been a friend of Holm ever since he, she, and her first husband, Ralph Nelson, were players in Leslie Howard's 1936–37 *Hamlet* national tour. Holm and Addy have worked together in many productions, and have periodically co-starred in their special show *With Love and Laughter*, a "collage" of material about relationships between men and women. Their free time is largely divided between their spacious Manhattan apartment and the New Jersey farm.

Despite her own professionally focused life, Holm feels annoyed with women who fret over careers; she asserts that marriage and children are the most important part of every woman's life. She is wary of the term feminist: "I believe that if a man does a job as well as a woman, he should be paid as much," she quips, but then seriously adds, "I consider myself a member of the human race—and that includes men." The "philosophy" behind a person's life, she believes, is far more important than the factual details of it: "I try to find scripts that make me proud to be human." (Holm, Interview, Apr. 3, 1986)

Holm was interviewed at her New York City apartment on Apr. 3, 1986. Additional sources include Michele A. Schulze, "Celeste Holm Lauded," *Newark Star-Ledger*, Oct. 15, 1985; Vic Kalman, "Jersey Casts Celeste Holm for Lead as Film Promoter," *Sunday Star-Ledger* (Newark), Sept. 18, 1983; and her sketch in *Current Biography* (1944). NJ-HS maintains a clipping file on Holm. Among other volumes, she is listed in *Who's Who in the Theatre* (1977), and in *Contemporary Theatre, Film, and Television* (1984).

*Sandra Lee Jackson*

## MILDRED BARRY HUGHES, 1902–

Mildred (Barry) Hughes, first woman elected to the New Jersey Senate (1965), was born on February 11, 1902, in Elizabethport, the Irish Catholic section of Elizabeth (Union County), NJ. She was the second child of William F. and Harriet V. (Gannon) Barry, whose first child, a son, had died shortly after birth. Hughes's mother died when she was five and her sister, Margaret, three. Her father's opportunities for schooling had been limited, but he read widely, educated himself, and advanced from a job as a letter carrier to be postmaster of the city of Elizabeth. Later he was corporate secretary and treasurer of the Elizabethtown Water Co.

Hughes's childhood years were unsettled. Her father remarried twice. Her first stepmother, Margaret Gaynor, died and a second, Kathryn Grall, later gave birth to a daughter, Kathryn. Family life was interrupted by several moves: Hughes attended four different elementary schools and two high schools. Nevertheless she did well in her studies and after graduating from Mount St. Mary's Academy in North Plainfield, NJ, in 1919, she enrolled at Georgian Court College, Lakewood, NJ, from which she graduated cum laude in 1923.

Hughes elected Latin as her major in college, even though history and English were her first loves. She reasoned that she would find more teaching opportunities if she chose a subject few liked. She realized her expectations, teaching Latin and English at Grover Cleveland High School in Elizabeth. She enjoyed her work there and gained a reputation among her pupils for being firm but fair.

In 1929 she married Peter L. Hughes, Jr., a young attorney, and stopped teaching to become a homemaker. Before their first child was born they leased "the Blue House," a rambling 18th-century landmark in Union in which she lived for 50 years. They had three sons, Peter L. III (b. 1931), William Barry (b. 1933), and David J. (b. 1941).

Over the years her role in community service grew. She was instrumental in introducing Catholic Youth Organization (CYO) activities to Immaculate Conception Parish, Elizabeth, NJ; every Friday night found her at a gym with the girls and afterward at a joint social held in the church. At home she found the time to design and make her own clothes.

In 1952 she was asked to join the Elizabeth League of Women Voters to become editor of their handbook, *This Is Elizabeth*, a 100-page survey of the town's history and character, its government and services. Her work on this book brought Hughes's abilities to the attention of persons active in politics and resulted in her being asked to run on the Democratic ticket for the New Jersey Assembly in 1955. Her husband and sons persuaded her to accept, even though to run as a Democrat in Union County was at that time virtual assurance of losing.

Her first step was to visit every newspaper editor to assure them personally that any press release issued over her name would be her own words and would report only meetings she had attended and speeches she had delivered. Then she began appearing at factory gates at 5:00 A.M., at morning coffees, and at luncheons, teas, dinners, and night meetings. Since she did not drive, her husband chauffeured her to many engagements; they would wind up having coffee together at 2:00 A.M. in a diner. "Campaigning was," she said later, "the most grueling thing I ever did."

Despite her all-out effort, that first campaign ended in defeat; but she had the consolation of getting the highest vote on the Democratic ticket. Two years later, in the next assembly race, she renewed her efforts but so taxed her energies that she contracted Asian flu, which developed into pneumonia, and was ill in bed when news of her victory came. To oblige newspaper photographers she got up, dressed, posed for pictures, and then went back to bed.

Victory was not Hughes's alone. A sudden, unexpected, and sweeping reversal had breached the Republicans' 46-year grip on Union County. All three Democratic candidates for assembly had been carried into office on the tide that helped Governor Robert B. Meyner trounce Malcolm Forbes and win a second term.

Assemblywoman Hughes was reelected in 1959, 1961, and 1963 even though Republicans regained much of the ground they had lost. After 1963 she was the lone Democrat among Union County's State House delegation. Hughes became the first woman to serve on the Assembly Conference Committee, on the Governor's Conference Committee, and as assistant majority leader. During her final assembly term, the Eagleton Institute of Politics cited her as the legislator who in one year had sponsored the most bills that passed both houses and were signed into law.

Legislative reapportionment, mandated by the courts, opened the way for Hughes to gain a New Jersey Senate seat in 1965. Although unable to topple Union's County powerful Republican senator, Nelson O. Stamler, she did capture her county's newly created second seat; her elation over being the first Democrat in 75 years to win a Senate seat in Union County was far greater than she felt at being the first woman senator. Union County had been electing women legislators for years. The first, Irene Griffin, won an assembly seat in 1944. FLORENCE DWYER served in the assembly from 1949 to 1956 and then went on to Congress. In 1965 both major parties nominated women for the Senate.

Hughes enjoyed a good working relationship in what, until then, had been New Jersey's most exclusive all-male club. Despite her diminutive four foot eleven height, she was not afraid to express her views, and when a point at issue was important to her she proved herself willing to stand alone. But accommodating differences was more her style. She spent eight years of her legislative career painstakingly ironing out differences to gain approval of a badly overdue revision of the Food and Drug Act. She championed New Jersey's first "Good Samaritan" act to protect those who render aid to accident victims; it had been suggested to her by two young delegates to Girls' State held at Douglass College. Hughes only once introduced a measure that she considered purely in the interest of women; it added fabric for home sewing to the list of sales tax exemptions.

Other bills she sponsored that became law dealt with

billboard control, the mentally retarded, state aid to schools of nursing, mental health, school elections, revisions to the Division of Aging, and establishing the Historic Sites Council, and the Interstate Compact on Drivers Licenses. She also sponsored bills every year to curtail the sale of liquor to teenagers and the use of obscenity in publications.

Hughes received considerable recognition for her legislative achievements. Georgian Court College presented her with a doctor of humane letters, honoris causa, in 1967. The New Jersey Association for Retarded Children cited her contributions to the welfare of the handicapped, as did the Union County Mental Health Association for her leadership. Honors also came from the Christian Communications Apostolate, the Knights of Columbus (for promoting high moral standards), the Fraternal Order of Eagles (for a Jobs After 40 program), and the Manhattan College Institute for Forensic Research.

Hughes's political career ended when permanent reapportionment lines drawn by the State Constitutional Convention of 1966 forced the entire legislature to run for election the following year. Every county except Mercer, Middlesex, and Hudson was engulfed in a Republican tide that November.

After serving ten years under three governors, Hughes made no further attempt to involve herself in politics, although she did serve as a public member on a state Obscenity Commission. Her husband's health had begun to fail at about this time and she nursed him until his death in 1971. Later, she became active in the national Order of Women Legislators (OWL), which strives for better government, particularly at the state level. In 1982 she was installed as national OWL president.

Hughes also turned to art, taking courses at Kean College of New Jersey. Her oil paintings, along with pictures of grandchildren and memorabilia, adorn her retirement apartment in Basking Ridge, NJ. Active and outgoing, she continues to busy herself with art courses, choral singing, and volunteer work and still finds pleasure in reading, music, opera, and sewing.

Personal interviews with Hughes on May 1, 1986, and March 25, 1987, together with a biographical resumé furnished by Hughes, supplemented biographical and election data drawn from the *Manual of the Legislature of New Jersey* (1956, 1958, 1960, 1962, 1964). It is the intention of Hughes that upon her death her papers will go to the national OWL.

*Jessie Havens*

## CARLEEN MALEY HUTCHINS, 1911–

Carleen (Maley) Hutchins, scientist, violin maker, author, lecturer, and scholar, is acclaimed as the creator of a new violin family of eight instruments. She is known for having one of the most systematic and scientific approaches to quality violin making. Hutchins, the only child of Grace (Fletcher) and Thomas William Maley, of English and Irish ancestry, respectively, was born in Springfield, MA, but grew up in Montclair (Essex County), NJ. Her father was an accountant and her mother a homemaker and assistant local director of the Girl Scouts.

Carleen Maley Hutchins making a violin, c. 1980. She is the creator of a new family of violins, known as the octet, which ranges from a giant seven-foot contrabass violin to a tiny eleven-inch treble violin. *Courtesy, Woodfin Camp.*

Hutchins's early interest in woodcrafting led her mother to challenge school tradition by requesting that the sixth grade all-male woodworking class admit her daughter. Hutchins entered the class and continued to take woodworking courses through Montclair High School, developing the skills that would later mold her career. Her musical skills were nurtured on the trumpet in high school and college.

Hutchins graduated from Cornell University (1933) with a B.A. in biology and from New York University

(1942) with an M.A. in education. She married Morton A. Hutchins, a Harvard-educated chemist, in 1943.

For fifteen years beginning in 1933 Hutchins was a science teacher in New York City, teaching mostly in private schools. Her curiosity about stringed instruments began in 1945 when, as a teacher at the Brearley School, she was invited to play the viola in an afternoon chamber music group. She purchased a cheap viola, taught herself to play, and within a month had joined the group. Frustrated with the viola's poor tone, she increasingly questioned the cause of its mediocrity. In 1947 she began constructing her own viola by studying a blueprint and a book. In two years the viola was completed. She was further encouraged by her husband, who thought it would be advantageous for her to have another interest since she was leaving teaching to raise a family.

Their son, William Aldrich, was born in 1947 and their daughter, Caroline, in 1950. After the birth of William the family moved from New York City to her parents' home in Montclair, where she and her husband still reside. Living with three generations under one roof wasn't easy, but the new situation gave Hutchins the degree of freedom she needed to pursue her viola making.

A turning point in her career came in 1949 when she met Frederick Saunders, the retired chairman of the Harvard physics department and a pioneer (in this country) of acoustical research on the violin. Hutchins offered to make experimental instruments on which to test his theories and identify the effects of structural changes on the acoustics of violins and violas. She built 45 experimental instruments for Saunders. Together, they tested hundreds of other violins and several Stradivarius instruments, as well as a Guarnerius owned by Jascha Heifetz.

Hutchins collaborated with Saunders in research and acoustical testing of violins for fourteen years, until his death in 1963. From the results of their joint research, Hutchins coauthored four major articles that appeared in professional journals.

For eight years during this period Hutchins studied classical violin making with Karl Berger and with Simone Sacconi, the renowned violin maker, restorer, and connoisseur of Stradivarius violins. Once a week, she traveled to New York for this training.

As a founding member and permanent secretary of the Catgut Acoustical Society (1958), Hutchins has been a catalyst in the growth of this group into an international organization of 900 members. The society, which promotes violin research, acoustics, and new technologies, also publishes its findings in a semiannual newsletter and in other technical journals. Hutchins has developed the society's material into archives that have become one of the leading worldwide collections of scientific and acoustical research on the violin.

The culmination of her work came with the creation of the new violin family, a consort of eight acoustically balanced instruments in graduated sizes and tunings. The concept was originally suggested to Hutchins by the composer Henry Brant. With her acoustical experience and classical violin making skills, Hutchins brought the idea to fruition within eight years.

The new violin family, known as the octet, ranges from a giant seven-foot contrabass violin to a tiny eleven-inch treble violin. Each instrument of the octet was mathematically scaled by John C. Schelleng, a retired research director of the Bell Telephone Laboratories and one of the original members of the Catgut Acoustical Society. The main challenge in constructing the octet was to project the power and resonance of the violin into the newly scaled instruments. Hutchins achieved this through techniques of acoustical tuning that she designed and perfected and that are acclaimed as among the most successful scientific methods of fine violin making. The instruments are intended not to preempt the present strings of the orchestra but to enrich them, and for use in ensembles or as solo instruments, as well as to blend and contrast with other instruments such as winds.

The first performances of the octet in New York City in 1965 and at the Harvard Music School in 1966 generated an enthusiastic response and hope of new music. With five sets of the octet in existence and a sixth in the making, the greatest problem at present is its scarcity. Two sets of the octet are in universities in Wales and Sweden; the other three sets are in California, Massachusetts, and New Jersey. As the octet gains recognition, much new music is being composed for it. Hutchins hopes that her octet will continue to grow in favor not only with the public but with composers and musicians, and become known in concert halls worldwide.

To help finance some of her early violin making, Hutchins authored three children's books and also sold many of her handmade instruments to defray expenses. In 1959 and 1961 she received two grants from the John Simon Guggenheim Memorial Foundation that enabled her to complete the octet. Three grants from the Martha Baird Rockefeller Fund helped her purchase electronic acoustical testing equipment. Hutchins also edited children's science books at Coward McCann, Inc., for fifteen years and was science consultant for the Girl Scouts of America for eight years.

Hutchins lectures extensively at universities and at worldwide acoustical conferences. In 1982 she spent a month in China at the invitation of the Acoustical Society of China. She also lectured in Japan and Hong Kong and has published extensively in professional and technical journals.

Her many awards include an honorary doctorate of engineering from the Stevens Institute of Technology (1977) and an honorary doctorate of fine arts from Hamilton College (1984). Hutchins, the first woman to receive the Acoustical Society of America's Silver Medal (1981), is a fellow of the Acoustical Society of America and serves on its Executive Council.

Never abandoning her original love of teaching, she continues to share her knowledge and depth of experience with students who come to a scientific violin making workshop in her home in Montclair, which she conducts on weekends from February to May. Hutchins has made nearly 300 instruments, each of which takes 200 hours to complete.

Hutchins attributes much of her success to her endlessly patient family, and particularly to the wholehearted support of her husband, who helps to maintain her home workshop and laboratory and who, in his retirement years, has worked on various aspects of research such as analysis of wood and chemical experiments on varnish.

Hutchins's distinguished contributions belie a modest and practical personality. Because of the breadth of her interest and the depth of her commitment, art and science have merged to create new horizons of music.

A personal interview with Hutchins on Nov. 22, 1985, in Montclair, NJ, supplied useful information about her life and work. Two of her articles appeared as cover stories in *Scientific American*: "The Physics of Violins," 207 (Nov. 1962):78–93, and "The Acoustics of Violin Plates," 254 (Oct. 1981):170–86. Biographical sketches of her are: "Mother of a New Family of Fiddles," *Life* 551 (Nov. 29, 1963):61–62; "Stradivariuses by the Dozen—Maybe," *New York Times*, Feb. 21, 1967; Bruce Frisch, "Violins of the Future," *Science Digest* 64 (Aug. 1968):54–61; and "Fiddling with the Future," *Discover* (Sept. 1987):58–66.

*Kathryn Lawrence Schmid*

## ESTHER HYMER, 1898–

Esther (Wanner) Hymer, representative of the International Federation of Business and Professional Women, a nongovernmental organization (NGO) of the United Nations with consultative status I, and chair (1972–1982) of the Committee for the International Women's Year and the Decade for Women, was born July 20, 1898, in Chicago, IL, to Andrew and Elizabeth (Kleitz) Wanner. Fourth in a family of five children, Hymer's siblings were Lillian, Frank, Arthur, and William, all of whom, along with Hymer, were college educated.

Hymer's father owned and operated a Chicago printing business that manufactured printing presses and was one of the few printing businesses to have survived the great Chicago fire. Hymer's mother was a homemaker and patron of the arts who was involved in community service locally and nationally. Both her parents were deeply committed to the work of the Methodist church, holding local,

state, and national offices and often inviting missionaries to stay in their home. It was through these visiting missionaries that Hymer was exposed at an early age to the desperate needs of the people of the world.

Graduated from Nicholas Senn High School in Chicago in 1916, Hymer was not only an accomplished athlete, winner of tennis, golf, and basketball championships, but had also spent her summers teaching Bible school in the worst neighborhoods of Chicago. There she met and worked with Jane Addams of Hull House and was influenced by Addams's philosophy, which opposed violence and advocated job training to build self-worth through increased economic opportunity.

After high school, Hymer graduated from the Walter Spry School of Music in Chicago before enrolling at the University of Wisconsin, from which she graduated with a B.A. in 1920. She went on to study at Northwestern University, Columbia University, and the Zimmern School of International Affairs in Geneva, Switzerland.

In 1922 she married Howard Hymer, a mining engineer and geologist who was a pioneer in the mining industry in Arizona. His career took the young couple and their son, William (b. 1924), to Europe and Africa as well as to several midwestern states. Their daughter, Elizabeth, was born in 1937. The next year they moved to New Jersey, and by 1941 the family had established permanent roots in Shrewsbury, NJ.

Throughout her early married life, Hymer gave countless hours to volunteer work. She contributed her talents to the YWCA and the Girl Scouts, served on the state and national boards of the American Association of University Women (AAUW), and became increasingly involved in supporting women's issues. From 1935 to 1940 Hymer served as a member of the AAUW National Committee on International Affairs. During the 1940s she was a member of the AAUW's Committee to Study the Basis for a Possible World Society. During the 1950s Hymer wrote on the Equal Rights Amendment for the National Federation of Business and Professional Women, which the group disseminated in support of "Operation Buttonhole." This project had as its goal the contacting and lobbying of congressmen on the issue of equality for women. Hymer recalls that this issue grew more controversial as it became apparent that equality was a total package and many women did not want to give up advantages such as an earlier retirement age for an equality that would profoundly change the way they lived.

In 1934 Hymer became active in the work of the National Committee on the Cause and Cure of War (NCCCW) as a representative from the AAUW. She chaired the Marathon Round Tables sponsored by the committee; beginning in 1938, Hymer organized Round Tables nationwide and it was her responsibility to write the materials for the discussion of such issues of foreign policy as the Neutrality

Act. When the CCCW became the Women's Action Committee for Victory and Lasting Peace in 1943, Hymer continued as a member.

It was while she was working in the peace movement that she began to focus more on women's issues. Hymer believed that if women had more power, there would be a more constructive foreign policy and a better chance for peaceful world relations. Her involvement in the work of the National Committee on Education for Lasting Peace led Hymer to the organizing conference for the founding of the United Nations (UN) in San Francisco in June 1945. There Hymer became aware of the potential value of the NGOs and has since served the International Federation of Business and Professional Women as technical adviser, UN chair, and representative to the UN. In this capacity Hymer eventually became a driving force behind the push for an International Women's Year, which later became the Decade for Women.

For nine years (1955–64) Hymer directed the World Relations program for Church Women United (CWU) and their World Community Day Observance, observed by churchwomen across the United States. She also served on the Board of Church World Service and committees of the National Council of Churches and World Council of Churches dealing with programs to improve opportunities for women and the conditions under which they lived and worked. In 1964 she began the CWU's UN program in the Church Center for the UN.

In 1972 Hymer was part of a small group of women who proposed the idea of an International Women's Year. They received the endorsement of the UN Commission on the Status of Women, then meeting in Geneva, and proceeded to promote the idea within their governments and among the delegates to the General Assembly. When the International Women's Year was set for 1975, Hymer organized and was elected chair of the Committee for the International Women's Year and the Decade for Women, a post she held from 1972 to 1982. She served on the planning committees of the NGO forums that met simultaneously with official conferences of government delegates (Mexico City, 1975; Copenhagen, 1980; and Nairobi, 1985), thus allowing women to meet to determine their own action agenda.

The committee organized seminars and workshops and issued "calls to action" to present the goals of first the International Women's Year and then the Decade for Women, and it urged members to influence their governments to write these goals into legislation.

Hymer, widowed in 1979, continues to work as an NGO delegate to the UN and recently received the Messenger of Peace Award for her work representing the International Federation of Business and Professional Women during the International Year of Peace, 1986. Over the course of her career, Hymer has been a prolific writer of pamphlets, articles, and study materials and has worked as a newspaper columnist and radio broadcaster and writer. She has served on a wide variety of committees, including the Advisory Committee for the U.S. Foreign Operations Administration (1953–55), and represented the United States at the First Population Conference in Rome in 1954. She chaired the Committee on Women as part of the first White House Conference on International Cooperation in 1965 and is on the Advisory Committee for the UN Development Fund for Women, which initiates community development projects in many countries.

She continues to travel widely and has visited 46 countries, attending conferences that seek to improve opportunities for women and meeting with groups of women. During her career, Hymer has been the recipient of numerous awards for her service to humanity—from the U.S. government, international women's groups, church groups, and CBS news, as well as from the UN. She is active in her local chapter of the AAUW and continues to serve the people of Shrewsbury, NJ, on the Planning Board and the Environmental Commission.

Papers related to Hymer's work with the Cause and Cure of War are available at M-SL. Papers on her work with the United Nations Commission on the Status of Women are available at the United Methodist Church, Church Center for the United Nations (New York City). Hymer was interviewed at her home in Shrewsbury, NJ, Oct. 24, and Nov. 1, 1987.

*Margaret Dooley Nitka*

## MARIA JERITZA, 1887–1982

Maria Jeritza, dramatic soprano, was born Mitzi Jedlicka (or Jedlitzka) in Brünn, Austria, on October 6, 1887, and was a distinguished resident of Newark, NJ, for the last 34 years of her life. Her love for music developed at an early age. She began voice training at age twelve under Professor Auspitz from the Brünn Conservatory and later sang in the chorus of the Brünn opera as an apprentice.

Often described as a shy girl, she was afraid to sing solo before audiences and would not audition at opera houses. It was during a rehearsal at her instructor's studio that the manager of the Olmütz Opera House hid behind the curtains to hear her sing. He was so impressed with her that he engaged her immediately for productions at the Olmütz, where she gained the self-confidence to overcome shyness and fear. In 1910, at age 23, she made her professional debut.

Jeritza's career developed rapidly until some of the world's most celebrated composers composed works especially for her. Puccini, Strauss, Korngold, and Janaček were some of the famous composers captivated by her voice.

When she went to audition at the Vienna Volksoper, she was interrupted after singing only a few measures of Micaela's aria from *Carmen* and told that she was hired. This led to two successful years at the Vienna Volksoper, where she served as understudy and built an impressive repertoire. Her portrayal of Elizabeth in *Tannhaüser* made such an impact on Rainer Simons, the director of the Vienna Volksoper, that he presented her in the world premier of *Der Kuhreigen*.

Her voice and beauty commanded the attention not only of musical directors but also of such members of the nobility as the Emperor Franz Josef. He first heard her when she performed in *Die Fledermaus* and was instrumental in having her transferred to the Vienna Hofsoper. In 1912, at age 25, she was honored by being asked to sing an original work written by Max von Oberleithner based on the novel *Aphrodite* by Pierre Louy. Jeritza's personality played an important part in his conception of the role of Aphrodite. Known for causing stirs, she created a commotion when she wore a nude-looking outfit as Aphrodite.

Her triumphs were numerous as she became a prima donna of the Vienna Imperial Opera. On October 25, 1912, she premiered in the role of Ariadne—a role that had been created for her—in Richard Strauss's *Ariadne auf Naxos* at the Stuttgart Royal Opera.

Jeritza, called the "most popular operatic star of Central Europe," toured Europe, appearing in Stockholm, Prague, Budapest, Berlin, Bremen, and Odessa. Her performances were described as "brilliant and dazzling." (She did not appear in London—in *Tosca* at Covent Garden on June 16, 1925—until after her success in the United States.) Reference was always made to her great beauty as

Maria Jeritza as the Egyptian courtesan Thaïs in the opera of the same name by Jules Massenet. *Courtesy, Music Division, New York Public Library at Lincoln Center, Astor, Lenox and Tilden Foundations.*

well as her outstanding voice. It was reported that every seat in the opera house was filled when she performed. Critics claimed that she was exceptional in her interpretation of every role that she portrayed.

In 1913 she was invited to perform at the Metropolitan Opera House in New York City, but the contract was not completed due to World War I, and it was not until 1921 that she made her debut at the Metropolitan. Meanwhile her career continued in Europe. In 1918 she created the title role in Janaček's *Jenufa*. On October 16, 1919, she performed in *Die Frau ohne Schatten* by Strauss. This was the first performance of the opera, with Jeritza creating the role of the empress. In Hamburg, Germany, on December 4, 1920, she performed what was deemed an impressive Marietta in Korngold's *Die Tote Stadt*. She later sang the premier of the opera at her Metropolitan debut on November 19, 1921.

Her career soared at the Metropolitan between 1921 and 1932. Critics such as Richard Aldrich of the *New York Times* wrote: "her blond piquancy [is] undeniable. She is an actress of native ability and represented the wayward and controlled nature of the dancing woman with spirit, vivacity, and full-blooded dramatic power." (Quoted in Ewen, *Musicians Since 1900*, 370) The same reviewer, however, had reservations about her voice during the performance.

Jeritza appeared in *Der Rosenkavalier, Jenufa, Tosca, Turandot,* and *Der Fleigende Holländer.* She was also known for her role as Elizabeth in *Tannenhäuser,* her interpretation of Elsa in *Lohengrin,* and that of Siegluode in *Die Walküre.* When the resident company of the Metropolitan revived *I Gioielli Della Madonna* in Italian, Jeritza was one of the lead singers. Her other roles were in Puccini's *The Girl of the Golden West,* Korngold's *Violanta,* Alfano's *Madonna Imperia,* and Strauss's *Die Aegyptische Helena.*

At the end of her eleven-year tenure with the Metropolitan Opera House she resigned and became a freelance concert performer. Her work took her to London and throughout Europe and America, and she served as guest artist with the Los Angeles and San Francisco opera companies. She also mastered light opera, performing in *Cavalleria Rusticana, Die Fledermaus, Faust, Carmen,* and *Music Hath Charm.*

Jeritza's popularity continued to grow and through the years she remained a popular performer in Vienna. From 1922 to 1949 she was the foremost soprano at the Vienna Staatsoper. Her last performance of *Tosca* was to a sold-out house at the Newark Symphony Hall in the mid-1960s.

Jeritza often brought sensational attention to her performances and her personal life. She was frequently in an Austrian court suing an author or a publishing company. She was also involved in incidents with other performers. In one, the tenor Beniamino Gigli was reported to have kicked her in the shins over priority during a curtain call.

Jeritza thereupon went onstage weeping and said to the Metropolitan audience, "Mr. Gigli is not nice to me." (Quoted in *New York Times*, July 11, 1982)

In 1919 Jeritza married the first of her three husbands, Baron Leopold Popper Von Podhragy. She divorced him in 1935. After receiving an annulment sanctioned by the Roman Catholic church, she married Winfield Sheehan, an American motion picture executive. Her marriage to Sheehan ended with his death in 1945. While married to Sheehan, she settled in Hollywood, CA, became a U.S. citizen, and made an unsuccessful attempt at a movie career. On April 19, 1948, in Newark, NJ, she married Irving P. Seery (known as Pat), a New Jersey businessman and lawyer. Seery was fascinated with grand opera and fell in love when he first saw Jeritza on the stage in 1910. It was said that he remained a bachelor for 38 years until he could marry her. In 1948 they moved into the Ballantine mansion, which she redecorated and where she held lavish parties, making the mansion the showplace of Newark.

After Seery died in 1966 Jeritza remained in her Newark home assisted by Liesel Hilfreich, her private secretary of many years. Although she had many houses—a castle in Salzburg, a ranch in California, a home in Rome, an apartment in New York City—she always thought of Newark as home.

Jeritza became one of New Jersey's distinguished citizens. She won the first Governor's Award, given by the New Jersey State Council on the Arts in 1971 for her outstanding contributions to the arts. She was a dedicated supporter of the New Jersey State Opera. In 1935 she was the recipient of the First Class of the Order for Meritorious Service in Austria. Jeritza, a devout Catholic, directed much of her philanthropy to churches and world charities. It is also said that many prisoners in Nazi concentration camps obtained their freedom through her efforts.

Jeritza did not wait until the end of her career to write her memoirs. Her autobiography, *Sunlight and Song,* was published in 1924. Many of Jeritza's friends gathered at her Newark estate to celebrate her 90th birthday. She made her last major appearance in New Jersey in 1978 as the guest of honor of the New Jersey State Ball at Newark International Airport.

Jeritza died of a stroke, at age 94, on July 10, 1982, at St. Mary's Hospital in Orange, NJ. After a funeral mass at St. Patrick's Cathedral in New York City, she was buried in Holy Cross Cemetery, North Arlington, NJ.

Jeritza's autobiography is *Sunlight and Song: A Singer's Life* (1924). See also Ernst Decsey, *Maria Jeritza* (1931); and David Ewen, *Musicians Since 1900* (1978). Obituaries appeared in the *New York Times* and the *Newark Star-Ledger,* July 11, 1982.

*Harriet Anderson Mayner*

## CORDELIA THOMAS GREENE JOHNSON, 1887–1957

Cordelia (Thomas) Greene Johnson, founder and president of the Modern Beautician Association, president of the National Beauty Culturist League, and president of the Jersey City chapter of the National Association for the Advancement of Colored People (NAACP), was born in Elkton, MD, on May 23, 1887, to ex-slaves, John and Margaret (Craig) Thomas, who themselves were born in Maryland. She was the eleventh daughter of fifteen children, all of whom were girls except the last. A great-grandniece, Elsie Emmons, describes Johnson's father, a laborer, as a quiet, introspective man and her mother, a laundress, as a mild, positive person who believed in the power of education and quietly ministered to those in her care. Neither could read or write.

Johnson received her early education in Elkton. Her educational background has been difficult to verify. Interviews with relatives and friends suggest that she arrived in Jersey City, NJ, with only an elementary school education. Others claim she may have completed high school in Baltimore or at Dickinson High night school in Jersey City and even may have taken courses at several colleges, including New York University and Columbia University.

As a youth Johnson was active in her church and Sunday school in Elkton. When President Theodore Roosevelt visited her church, Johnson was so impressed that she resolved to become active in civic and political affairs. She took an interest in the founding of a chapter of the Young Women's Christian Association by the churchpeople in her town. This interest was to remain throughout her career.

Johnson came to Jersey City about 1915, staying with her sister at first, and remained there. To support herself in those early years she took in washing, as her mother had before her. She was married twice. The date of her first marriage to Harry Green[e] is unknown; he died on October 24, 1917, from double lobar pneumonia. It was about this time that Johnson submerged herself in the life of the community.

She became a member of the New Jersey Women's Suffrage League and went about the state speaking on its behalf. She developed such a reputation as a speaker that Dr. George E. Cannon, the state Republican black political leader, asked her to join him in supporting Calvin Coolidge for president of the United States. They toured the county together, speaking in support of him. In the following presidential campaign she went around the county speaking in support of Herbert Hoover. As she traveled during these political campaigns she visited various beauty shops and saw the unsanitary and unsafe conditions in them.

Johnson attended the beauty school of Madam C. J. Walker, who became one of the first black millionaires in the country. The school gave her an appreciation for the proper methods and conditions of this trade. Although she received her training from the Walker school, she allied herself with the Apex system, a rival method of hair styling for black women. She opened her own beauty shop at 49A Kearney Avenue in Jersey City, and in 1929 she became president of the New Jersey Apex League. In 1934 she opened her own school at 57 Belmont Avenue. On November 24, 1934, she married her second husband, Albert T. Johnson, who had a daughter, Vivian.

During the early 1930s there was a clamor to license beauty shops, operators, and schools because of the health and safety problems in the business. It was not unusual to find women whose heads were scarred or injured by inexperienced hairdressers. Johnson joined with others, both black and white, in lobbying for standards in training, safer products, and better sanitary conditions in beauty shops. She was asked by New Jersey Assemblyman Mercer Burrell from Essex County to speak to the state legislature on a bill to regulate beauty shops and their operators. As a result, the word *straightening*, a method of using a hot steel comb to take tight curls out of hair, was written into the law. This was most important to black women, since it was a standard method used by them in styling their hair.

Johnson's lobbying efforts resulted in a strategy to ensure that blacks be considered in the writing of legislation on the profession and in the selection of a black for the five-member State Beauty Control Board, whose function was to oversee the law once enacted. The committee was the forerunner of the Modern Beautician Association, of which Johnson was the founder and the president. The thrust of this organization was to develop a unity among black beauticians in the state, to set standards of safety and professionalism in order to ensure the safety of its customers, to inform operators of new developments, and to train them in the art and skill necessary to meet the changing needs of customers. The association's main concern was to manage the business of operating the shops and industry in a professional manner. It also stressed education, encouraging many of the members to finish high school, college, and other professional schools.

Johnson led the Modern Beautician Association to affiliate itself with the national Beauty Culturist League, and in 1938 she became its president (until her death in 1957). The essential ingredient in building the state and national organization was "continuing education" in the skill and art of beauty culture and in the professional management of its shops. She organized a unit in the national organization known as the Institute of Cosmetology. This unit was open only to members who were interested in advanced beauty culture methods and techniques. She organized a sorority for those interested in more advanced techniques. The other elements in furthering the industry were to ensure that state governments developed laws consistent with the organization's goals. These efforts led to the unabated growth of the organization and its members.

In 1955 Johnson was elected president of the Jersey City branch of the NAACP. The branch was at its low point organizationally. Among other things, Johnson instituted a cotillion for the young people and a newsletter for its membership. These steps did much to invigorate the organization financially and structurally and they remained a tradition with the branch through the civil rights period of the 1960s.

Johnson ended her career working as an active member of the Church of Incarnation, a youth worker at Grace Episcopal Church, a Red Cross instructor, an observer with the United Nations, a member of the President's Advisory Board for the Small Business Administration, and an active board member of the Infantile Paralysis Foundation.

Johnson died of cancer at the age of 69 on January 19, 1957, at her home in Jersey City. She was buried in Rosemount Memorial Park in Newark, NJ.

Taped interviews with Johnson's friends and relatives are available at the Afro-American Historical and Cultural Society museum (Jersey City, NJ). Articles on Johnson appeared in the *New Jersey Herald News* (Newark, NJ), July 1, 1935, July 23, 1938, and Oct. 5, 1946; the *Newark Evening News*, Mar. 20, 1935; and the *Jersey Journal* (Jersey City, NJ), Jan. 17, 1957.

*Theodore Brunson*

## PAULA KASSELL, 1917–

Paula Sally Kassell, founder of the national feminist newspaper *New Directions for Women*, was born on December 5, 1917, in New York City, the younger of two daughters of Daniel and Bertha (Jaret) Kassell. Her parents were both native New Yorkers. Daniel Kassell, largely self-educated, was a stockbroker. He was also a self-taught musician who played the violin, the piano, and the mandolin and was an expert bridge player. Bertha (Jaret) Kassell was a homemaker who was active in community organizations. When Kassell was six, the family moved to Yonkers, NY, where she lived until she married in 1941.

Kassell attended public elementary school and Yonkers High School. As a child and teenager she often accompanied her mother to the Jewish Home for the Blind, a short distance from the family home. There she played with the blind children and later read to them and helped them with their homework. This experience awakened an interest in helping others that remained with her and resulted in a brief career in social work.

Daniel Kassell was ambitious for his daughters. At a time when relatively few women went to college, there was never any question that his two daughters would go. Both sisters went to Barnard College. Kassell graduated in 1939, with a major in psychology and sociology.

At college her feminist consciousness took root; according to Kassell, Barnard, under the leadership of Virginia Gildersleeve, was a heady place for a young woman. Students were imbued with ambition. It was also here that Kassell read and was greatly influenced by Margaret Mead's book *Sex and Temperament in Three Primitive Societies*, which introduced her to the thesis that society, not nature, determined sex roles and even temperament.

After college, Kassell worked briefly for the Yonkers, NY, Relief Department. On August 16, 1941, she married Gerson Friedman and moved to Dover (Morris County), NJ, where she has lived ever since. (Beatrice, her sister, married Gerson Friedman's brother.) A son, Daniel, was born in 1942, and in 1946 a daughter, Claire, was born. Of her marriage Kassell said, "There can be no such thing as an equal marriage in our society, but mine was certainly among the most feminist." Her husband not only helped raise the children, he contributed many hours of work to *New Directions for Women*. He died April 21, 1986.

After the birth of the children, Kassell worked in the social welfare field for a while, but then chose to stay home to raise her family. By the time she was ready to seek employment again in 1955, she had lost some of her interest in social work. With encouragement from her husband, she became a technical editor at a company that did research on rocket motors, and then at Bell Telephone Laboratories, where she stayed until 1970. When she reentered the job market she used her birth name at work and her husband's name socially. Gradually she used her own name more and more until she was using it exclusively.

In the early 1960s a new feminist voice began to make itself heard in American society. In 1966 the National Organization for Women (NOW) was formed. As soon as Kassell heard about it, early in 1967, she joined. NOW did not yet have local chapters. Kassell had already begun her feminist work as a member of the Women's Equity Action League. Her first project was to convince local newspapers to integrate help wanted ads. Previously, newspapers had published separate sections labeled "Help Wanted, Male" and "Help Wanted, Female."

In 1970 Kassell became dissatisfied with her job at Bell Laboratories because, "Essentially we were working for the military. This was not bettering the world." At the same time, Marge Wyngaarden, a New Jersey feminist leader, was trying to bring together feminists from all parts of the state. When Kassell heard of this effort she suggested that a conference be held that would bring out potential recruits to the movement. It was decided to hold the conference at Fairleigh Dickinson University in Madison. Thus Kassell became coordinator of New Jersey's first statewide feminist conference, held on May 1, 1971. Called "New

Directions for Women in New Jersey," it attracted 350 participants.

After the conference, the organizers decided to spend $240 in profits on a newsletter so that New Jersey women interested in feminism could stay in touch with each other. Kassell agreed to be editor. The first issue of *New Directions for Women in New Jersey*, a fourteen-page mimeographed bulletin, appeared on January 1, 1972. It was the first statewide feminist publication in the United States. The second issue, in November 1972, was an eight-page typeset tabloid. Enough advertising was sold to cover printing costs. In February 1973 it became a quarterly. That same year, Kassell and Marilyn Grant founded the Lakeland chapter of NOW, which later became the Morris County chapter.

In the spring of 1975 New Jersey was dropped from the title of the newspaper and *New Directions for Women* began to be distributed nationally. In 1980 it became a bimonthly with a circulation of 50,000. Set up as a nonprofit enterprise, it is written, edited, and managed by paid and volunteer personnel.

Since its inception, *New Directions for Women* has sought to cover the whole spectrum of feminist activity, focusing especially on stories not likely to be covered adequately by the mainstream press. In its news pages, *New Directions for Women* has covered the political, legal, economic, and social issues that affect women. Articles on health and the arts appear regularly. Since 1972, an extensive book review section has been a feature in every issue.

Kassell was editor-publisher until 1977, when she resigned because of back problems brought on by the long hours and responsibilities of running the paper. Her title became associate editor and, in 1987, senior editor (Kassell, letter, July 20, 1987), and she remained on the Board of Trustees and the Editorial Board. She also continued to write a column on employment, "Equal Pay," as well as occasional editorials and book reviews.

Although Kassell was freed from daily responsibility for the paper, she remained involved with women's media. She became United Nations representative for the Women's Institute for Freedom of the Press, a national association of media women and media-concerned women of which she is vice-president. She has also participated in the organization's efforts to set up a national and international women's news service, attending international conferences on women's media in Copenhagen, at the United Nations, and in Washington, D.C. She contributed a chapter on these efforts to *Communications at the Crossroads: The Gender Gap Connection* (1988).

In 1980 Kassell bought ten shares of stock in the New York Times Company; her investment was made with a purpose. She attended stockholder meetings, each time raising issues of interest to feminists, especially the advancement of women employees in all departments at the *Times*. At the April 30, 1986, meeting she brought up the use of the honorific "Ms." in the *Times'* pages. Long after most major newspapers had started to use Ms., the *Times* adamantly refused to do so, despite staff protests and letters to the editor from Kassell and others. At the meeting the publisher, Arthur Ochs Sulzberger, agreed to challenge the editorial staff to debate the issue. About a month later Kassell received a letter from Sulzberger stating "midst great cheers from the women (and many of the men) who serve as reporters and editors of *The New York Times*, the attached notice was posted on the bulletin board. . . . Beginning today (June 19, 1986), *The New York Times* will use Ms. as an honorific in its news columns." Eliminating sexist language from the media was a long-term issue on Kassell's agenda. Her effect on the *Times* was given widespread media attention.

Farsighted and idealistic, Kassell is soft spoken and conservative in appearance. Called ladylike and traditional as well as feminist to the core by her friends, she describes herself as very determined and persistent. Quick to give credit to others, one of her most frequently used phrases is "I wasn't the only one."

Dr. Donna Allen, president of the Women's Institute for Freedom of the Press in Washington, D.C., and a long-time colleague of Kassell, said of her: "She never attacks. She takes what is strong and good about people and ideas and ignores the rest. She's a builder. Perhaps her greatest strength has been her sense of where things are going and where they should go. She recognizes the time to act. She has been in the forefront of women's media."

A profile of Kassell appeared in *NOW-NJ Newsbreaks* (Trenton, NJ), Oct. 1985.

*Suzanne Messing*

## MARIE LOUISE HILSON KATZENBACH, 1882–1970

Throughout her life, Marie Louise (Hilson) Katzenbach worked to broaden access to education for the people of New Jersey. She was one of the first two women appointed to the State Board of Education, on which she served for 44 years, and its first woman president. Her efforts touched many—children, adults, the disabled, even soldiers at Fort Dix during World War II, to whom she furnished books. Born on December 8, 1882, in Trenton (Mercer County), NJ, she was the second in a family of six children, and the oldest girl.

Katzenbach's mother, Matilda (Hunt) Hilson, was of an old Trenton family, one of her forebears being Nicholas de Belleville, doctor to Napoleon Bonaparte's brother, Joseph, who had settled near Trenton around 1830. Her father, Henry Hilson, was from Charleston, SC. Katzenbach grew up in Trenton and went to high school at the Trenton Model School, which was an adjunct to the New Jersey State Normal School, now Trenton State College, the change thanks in part to Katzenbach's later efforts.

Upon graduation at eighteen, Katzenbach followed her mother onto the board of the Union Industrial Home, an institution for orphaned children from four to twelve years old. With the energy and foresight that was to characterize her long life of public service, Katzenbach identified the gravest problems in the orphanage and went about correcting them. The children were kept isolated on the grounds of the home; she pushed for educating them in public schools. When the children were sent to farms or foster homes, she inspected those places herself. Of that early effort, she said: "This gave me the incentive to work, to give children what they didn't have." (*Trentonian*, Jan. 15, 1965) Later, in 1913, when she joined the home's Board of Managers—a position in which she was to serve for over 50 years—she urged that psychiatric help and special education be made available to disabled and troubled children.

Although the family's means were not sufficient to send her to college, Katzenbach read extensively on her own. In an interview given in 1963 (quoted in the *Trenton Evening Times*, Feb. 4, 1970, 4), she said: "We always had books around us at home. My father was a businessman but a very bookish man, too, and very interested in education." It was natural, then, that in 1902 and under necessity of earning a living, Katzenbach should take a job at the Trenton Public Library. (Two of her sisters also went into library work.) She started at $30 a week as an apprentice assistant and worked her way up. In 1905 she went to the Chautauqua Library School for six weeks and was subsequently made head of the Catalogue Department. Despite her youth, she was a treasured staff member, and in 1909, at the age of 26, she was made acting librarian-in-chief for the summer. She took some courses at the University of Pennsylvania in connection with her job, but it is ironic and perhaps revealing that the woman who was often referred to as New Jersey's "first lady of education," and who worked so long to open higher education for others, did not herself have the privilege of earning a degree.

In 1911 she met and married Edward Lawrence Katzenbach, a highly regarded attorney and native of Trenton, who was then serving on the library's Board of Trustees as treasurer. He served as attorney-general of New Jersey from 1924 to 1929. In 1919 their first son, Edward L., Jr., was born, and in 1922 their second, Nicholas deB. (Both sons later distinguished themselves in public service.) In 1934 Edward Lawrence, Sr., died, leaving Katzenbach alone to bring up her young sons.

In 1921 Katzenbach accepted an appointment to the state Board of Education, on which she was to serve for 44 years, the last nine as president. Her accomplishments on the board must be seen in light of her broad goal, which

was to bring education to as many people as possible and thereby enable them to lead satisfying and productive lives. When she first took office, places in higher education were limited in New Jersey. She was instrumental in the formation of the state college system; during her tenure on the state board the three two-year normal schools were transformed into four-year state colleges, and three more state colleges were founded. She also pushed for the development of Rutgers into the State University in 1955, and sat on the State University Board of Trustees from 1932 to 1965. Her special interest was Douglass College for women, and in 1963 a college dormitory there was named for her. Through her efforts, major college course revisions were implemented and the county college program was begun.

Katzenbach's early experience on the board of the Union Industrial Home encouraged her major concern for educating disabled and emotionally disturbed children. From the time she joined its board in 1923, she had a long and close association with the State School for the Deaf (Trenton). For over 50 years she worked to guide its policy, helping to plan the Sullivan Way campus and the present buildings. In all those years she never missed a Christmas dinner there. In 1965 the school was renamed in her honor. Katzenbach also helped to found the Mercer County Child Guidance Center; from 1948 to 1965 she sat on its board, and from 1954 on was president.

She was also active on the boards of the New Jersey Jewish Family Association, the Mercer County Legal Aid Society, the Trenton YWCA, the Bordentown Training School, the Family Service Agency, the Housing Authority of Trenton, and other organizations. In 1934 Katzenbach moved to Princeton, where she was president of the Princeton Garden Club and active in the Episcopal church there. She was given many awards for her efforts, most notably the first annual Higher Education Service Award in 1960, as well as honorary doctorates from Douglass College in 1948 and from the Newark College of Engineering in 1957.

In 1947, as a delegate from Mercer County, she was elected vice-president of the State Constitutional Convention and was in large part responsible for women being designated as "persons" in the new New Jersey Constitution. Commenting on the results of that convention in an interview in the *Trentonian* (July 7, 1949, 84), Katzenbach stressed that there was no field of public activity in which a woman could not contribute. She also argued that a woman "limits herself mentally and spiritually if she is not aware of the limitation of opportunities for others, or their needs."

At 83, after a serious car accident in 1964, Katzenbach resigned the presidency of the state Board of Education, although at Governor Richard J. Hughes's request she stayed on as consultant. She died at her home in Princeton on February 4, 1970, at age 87, and was buried in Ewing

Church Cemetery. When a doctorate of humane letters from the Newark College of Engineering was conferred on Katzenbach, her citation noted her "unselfish service to her family, to education and to the welfare of her fellow citizens of the State of New Jersey." President Robert C. Clothier of Rutgers, in presenting his university's highest honor, spoke of her service in "building a future citizenry of intelligence and character." She characterized herself as "just an old-fashioned grandmother" (*Trentonian*, July 7, 1949, 84) and "New Jersey through and through." (*Newark News*, Jan. 12, 1965)

Information on Katzenbach appears in newspaper articles. See: *Trenton Evening Times, Feb. 4, 1970;* a feature on Katzenbach, *Trentonian* (Trenton, NJ), July 7, 1949; an interview by Judy Rizzello, *Trentonian*, Jan. 15, 1965; and an article on her retirement, *Newark News*, Jan. 12, 1965. Also helpful were telephone interviews with her son Nicholas deB. Katzenbach, Oct. 8, 1987; a nephew-in-law, Dr. Buckman Katzenbach, Oct. 8, 1987; Veronica Cary, former librarian, Trenton Public Library, Oct. 20, 1987; and Harold Thompson, director, Trenton Public Library, Oct. 21, 1987.

*Blair T. Birmelin*
*Daryl Boylan*
*Lumina Pacheco*

## MYRA LYLE SMITH KEARSE, 1899–1982

Myra Lyle (Smith) Kearse, physician and civil rights advocate, was born in Lynchburg, VA, on May 18, 1899. She was the only child of two African-American schoolteachers, Theodore Parker and Clara Roberta (Alexander) Smith. She came from a family of activists who believed in the value of education. In fact, in 1977 Kearse stated that "her determination and that of others like her was no doubt rooted in the intense race consciousness of the era in which she was born," a time characterized "by mounting racial oppression and white resistance to black achievements. Our parents knew the history of race," she explained. "The denials, the struggles. And we didn't hear anything else from the time we were born but get yourself ready to serve the race." (*New York Times*, Nov. 16, 1977)

Kearse's maternal grandparents, Royal and Amalie (Terry) Alexander, were former slaves who never went to school. But they craved knowledge, learned to read, and educated seven of their ten children who lived to adulthood. The Alexanders were married December 19, 1867, approximately four years after President Abraham Lincoln signed the Emancipation Proclamation. Royal Alexander had the misfortune of seeing his mother and brother sold by the slavemaster and was never to see or hear from them again.

Kearse earned her B.S. in 1921 from Howard University and was the only woman in the class of 1925 at Howard University Medical School. After interning at Freedman's Hospital in Washington, D.C., she moved in 1926 to Newark, where she practiced surgery at the former Kenney Memorial Hospital, a facility founded by John Kenney, a black physician. Kenney hoped to provide opportunities for other black physicians to practice in a hospital, but a state law prohibiting overnight patients in frame hospital buildings forced Kenney Hospital to close. Kearse started her private practice in the Vauxhall section of Union in about 1927. A general practitioner for approximately 42 years, Kearse took care of the medical needs of the sick and impoverished of Union.

She married Robert Francis Kearse in Orange on July 30, 1929. The couple had two children: a daughter, Amalya Lyle (b. 1937), and a son, Robert Alexander (b. 1943). Kearse's husband served as U.S. postmaster in Vauxhall for 32 years. There were, however, many trying episodes before he was finally appointed to that position. After taking the civil service examination twice and passing with the highest score each time, Robert Kearse's name was not submitted to President Franklin D. Roosevelt for appointment. Instead, both times a white man was made acting postmaster. He tried for many months to secure his position. Finally, Myra Kearse wrote a letter to Eleanor Roosevelt, and Robert Kearse was named Vauxhall's postmaster in 1936. He died in June 1968.

Asked by the *New York Times* to reflect on her early years as a doctor, Kearse commented in 1977 that "she found it more difficult to be a black doctor than a woman doctor. Because she was black it took her fifteen years to get on the staff of a hospital in Newark. In the interim she lost a great deal . . . in fees, work experience, and training. When World War II broke out and there was a shortage of white doctors and pressure from the NAACP, the hospitals in Newark and elsewhere started to open up." Kearse also served on the staff of St. Elizabeth Hospital in Elizabeth.

Kearse not only maintained her private medical practice but was also active in community service. She worked with the Committee for Desegregation of Schools of Union Township in 1962 to establish equal opportunity and open enrollment for black students. Under the sponsorship of the Alpha Kappa Alpha Sorority, Kearse researched African-American history in New Jersey. With her friend VERA BRANTLEY MCMILLON she broadcast several radio programs on African-American history and served as consultant and researcher for the New Jersey Library Association's 1967 reference publication *New Jersey and the Negro: A Bibliography, 1715–1966*.

After retiring from medical practice in 1967, Kearse continued working with community improvement organizations. In 1972 she helped organize the Family Health Center for low-income families in Vauxhall. She served as executive director of the Union County Anti-Poverty

Council in 1967, of the Union County Community Action Organization from 1970 to 1973, and of the Opportunities Industrialization Center of Union County from 1978 to 1981.

She was particularly interested in programs that taught clerical and office skills to young people. Kearse was also interested in the rights and needs of senior citizens. As a member of the Union Senior Residence Housing Corporation, she worked from 1974 to 1977 to gain access to public housing for elderly blacks. She was a commissioner of the Union County Cultural and Heritage Commission from 1971 to 1978.

Because of her many community involvements and contributions, Kearse was widely honored for her humanitarian work by civic, church, alumni, and professional organizations. The Dr. Myra Smith Kearse Center, a public multiservice facility in Union, is named in her honor.

Kearse's personal interests were broad and varied. She traveled widely to Africa, Asia, and Europe, enjoyed playing bridge, and was a fan of the Brooklyn Dodgers. She was the first woman to become a member of the vestry of her church, Epiphany Episcopal Church in Orange.

Kearse was active until February 14, 1982, when she died of cardiac arrest at her home in Vauxhall at age 82. She was cremated at the Rosedale Crematory in Orange.

Kearse was interviewed for the article "Black Women M.D.'s: Spiritual Endurance," *New York Times*, Nov. 16, 1977. An interview with her son, Robert Alexander Kearse, provided useful information. The NJ-UTPL maintains a clipping file on her. Additional biographical sketches appear in *Who's Who among Black Americans* (1980), *Who's Who of American Women* (1974), and *Who's Who in the East* (1975).

*Esther Vincent Lloyd*


## DOROTHY KIRSTEN, 1917–

Dorothy Adelle Kirsten, lyric soprano, star of radio, light opera, and grand opera, was born on July 6, 1917, in Montclair (Essex County), NJ, the third child of Margaret Irene (Beggs) and George William Kirsten, a building contractor. Her family often gathered around the piano to play and sing, her mother at the piano, her father with his mandolin, Kirsten and her two older sisters singing, and her younger brother playing his cornet. Kirsten's maternal grandfather, James J. Beggs, who lived with the family the last few years of his life, was a strong musical influence. "An elegant, colorful, and fascinating old gentleman" (Kirsten, *A Time to Sing*, 27), he had been in charge of all musical entertainment in New York City's parks, conducted Theodore Roosevelt's campaign bands and Buffalo Bill's Wild West Show band as well as his own.

After an indifferent high school career, Kirsten took a job with the New Jersey Bell Telephone Company. The work bored her, but she was able to help at home and put some money aside. Weekends were spent at the Jersey shore. One weekend a music-loving friend suggested a career on Broadway for her. Kirsten got the name of a voice teacher, quit her job, and moved to New York City.

She began to build a repertoire of show and operetta tunes. When her savings ran out, she did secretarial work and housekeeping for her teacher. At the voice studio, she met Eddie and Grace Albert, later famous on Broadway and in motion pictures, who were partners on a radio show called "The Honeymooners." They set up an audition for Kirsten at the radio station WINS. Within a few days Kirsten began her radio career.

At WINS she had a fifteen-minute spot, earning $5 per show. The show exposed her to many people who were to advance her career. Among these was J. E. Dinty Doyle, a columnist for the *New York Herald Tribune*, whose favorable notices led to engagements with radio groups such as the Ted Straeter Singers and to billing as top soprano on the "Kate Smith Show."

In the spring of 1938 Dinty Doyle introduced Kirsten to Grace Moore, an older, more experienced opera singer. This meeting was the beginning of a close mentor relationship and launched Kirsten's career in opera. Kirsten auditioned for Moore, who was so impressed that she arranged for Kirsten to study in Rome and Capri with maestro Astolfo Pescia.

The threat of imminent war interrupted Kirsten's Italian studies. At home she sang again for Moore, who, astonished at how much Kirsten's voice had grown, decided to bring Pescia to New York. Kirsten also began work on musical interpretation with Queena Mario and continued her Italian lessons.

During World War II Kirsten sang at army camps all over the country. At Fort Dix, in New Jersey, she renewed her friendship with a soldier, the engineer on her old WINS radio program, and in January 1943 she and Edward Oates were married. The marriage was short-lived. Kirsten was often away on the West Coast, busy with radio shows, concerts, and opera, and she and her husband had little in common.

Kirsten sang her first professional concert before 200 friends and opera luminaries invited by Grace Moore on August 8, 1940. Three months later, she sang her first operatic role, "Pousette" in Massenet's *Manon*, with the Chicago Opera Company. The following year she was assigned major roles in Chicago: "Musetta" in Puccini's *La Bohème*, and "Micaela" in Bizet's *Carmen*. She debuted in New York City, singing "Mimi" in Puccini's *La Bohème* with the San Carlo Opera. Her career as an opera singer was under way.

Kirsten believes that light opera was "the golden stairway to success as an opera singer." (Kirsten, *A Time to Sing*, 219) Her first operetta performance was in Franz Lehar's *The Merry Widow* at the Paper Mill Playhouse in Millburn, NJ, in 1942. After that she sang more than 500 performances of different operettas throughout the country.

The night of her debut with the New York City Center Opera, November 9, 1944, singing "Manon" in Puccini's *Manon Lescaut*, Kirsten was asked by Frederic C. Schang, Grace Moore's manager at Columbia Artists, to sign a contract, and her career took off. She signed contracts to sing with the San Francisco Opera Company and with the Metropolitan Opera in New York City. Schang introduced her to a renowned accompanist, Lester Hodges, who played for her at recitals and concerts. She began to sing with leading symphony orchestras. Schang guided her to outstanding radio programs on which she appeared regularly for many years, including the "Kraft Music Hall," the "Railroad Hour," the "Voice of Firestone," the "Standard Hour," the "Bell Telephone Hour," the "Bing Crosby Show," the "Jack Benny Show," the "Edgar Bergen Show," and "Light Up Time."

Late in 1945 Kirsten debuted with the San Francisco Opera and the Metropolitan Opera in New York City singing "Mimi" in Puccini's *La Bohème*. She sang with the San Francisco Opera for more than 25 years and with the Metropolitan Opera for 30 years. She was best known for Puccini roles—"Mimi" in *La Bohème*, "Manon" in *Manon Lescaut*, "Tosca" in *Tosca*, "Cio Cio San" in *Madame Butterfly*, and "Minnie" in *The Girl of the Golden West*—but she sang others as well: "Violetta" in Verdi's *La Traviata*, "Marguerite" in Gounod's *Faust*, "Musetta" in Bizet's *Carmen*, and "Louise" in Charpentier's *Louise*, for which she studied in Paris with the composer.

Kirsten performed with nearly every operatic tenor singing between 1940 and 1975 and partnered more than 60 in their American debuts. She was known as a musical "fireman," noted for stepping in at the last minute when illness or fits of temperament caused other stars to cancel.

In May 1951 Kirsten married Eugene Chapman, an obstetrician from San Antonio, TX, and they built a French provincial home, a favorite of Kirsten's. When Chapman was appointed assistant dean of the Medical School at the University of California at Los Angeles, they moved to California. Chapman became seriously ill and in January 1954 died of uremic disease complicated by malaria contracted in the South Pacific during World War II. On July 18, 1955, Kirsten married John French, a neurosurgeon and the first director of the Brain Research Institute at UCLA.

Despite a busy concert and opera schedule in the United States, Kirsten traveled widely, although she never had what she considered an international career. In 1945 and 1946 she sang in pre-Castro Havana, Cuba, and in Mexico City's Teatro de Bellas Artes. She performed with the

Stockholm, Sweden, opera in 1961 and also with the Stockholm Symphony Orchestra. In 1962 she sang several roles in the Soviet Union as part of a State Department cultural exchange program. The Russian people had seen Kirsten's starring performance as an American prima donna in the film *The Great Caruso*, with Mario Lanza and Ann Blyth. In Tbilisi, the audience chanted her name and hung out of the theater boxes calling, "We love you!" Later, in June 1975, the Metropolitan Opera flew Kirsten and the entire company of 300 with costumes and scenery to Japan for three performances.

Throughout her singing career Kirsten received many honors. In 1951 Ithaca College awarded her a doctor of music degree; and she was awarded a doctor of fine arts degree from Santa Clara University in 1971 and Pepperdine University in 1986. She received the keys to many cities. Italy awarded her its highest cultural award in 1977 in recognition of her contribution to U.S.-Italy relations.

As her singing career slowed, Kirsten began to paint and concentrated on golf, her hobby for many years. She taught master classes at several universities, including a two-week course in 1973 at UCLA, "Interpretive Techniques for the Musical Theatre." She collaborated with Lanfranco Rasponi to write her autobiography, *A Time to Sing* (1982). She and her husband divide their time between their home in Pauma Valley, CA, and an apartment on the island of Maui in Hawaii.

Kirsten's autobiography is *A Time to Sing* (1982). She is profiled in Lanfranco Rasponi, *The Last of the Prima Donnas* (1982).

*Sheila Cowing*
*Arthur Forman*

## ANN ROSENSWEIG KLEIN, 1923–1986

Ann (Rosensweig) Klein, politician, was born on July 23, 1923, in New York City. She was the second child of Hilda (Barnett) and Mack Rosensweig, a wealthy manufacturer and businessman. Though she was raised in affluence, young Klein showed heartfelt concern for those suffering the hardships of the Great Depression. This humane empathy remained with her and became the hallmark of her extensive government service, from her years as president of the New Jersey League of Women Voters, to her two campaigns for governor and her work as a member of Governor Brendan Byrne's cabinet.

Klein was a precocious student who entered Barnard College at age sixteen. When she graduated, barely 20, her father, a rather rigid traditionalist, refused to allow her to apply to law school. He told her that as a woman she could become either a teacher or a social worker, occupations he assumed she would abandon when she married. She chose social work and received a master's degree from the New

York School of Social Work (now a part of Columbia University) in 1945.

She married Robert Klein, an engineer, on September 11, 1943, and soon accepted her first job as a psychiatric social worker at the Child Guidance Clinic in Worcester, MA. In 1952 Klein and her husband moved to Morristown, NJ, where she was to make her home until her death in 1986. According to a *Daily Record* article of May 8, 1967, she once said: "I had never really put down roots any place, had never really identified with a town. Here I do." While raising two children, David (b. May 4, 1947) and Mara Jayne (b. July 3, 1944, and adopted at age twelve), Klein served as president of the local PTA and vehemently—but unsuccessfully—opposed the state's construction of Route 287 through the center of Morristown, contiguous to a large elementary school.

During these years she began active involvement with the League of Women Voters. She first served as president of the Morristown League and characterized herself as "kind of vinegary. . . . When the Morristown League asked me to be president, they made me one condition—I mustn't get carried away." (*Daily Record*, May 8, 1967) Klein eventually served as president of the New Jersey League of Women Voters from 1967 to 1971.

With enthusiastic support from the League of Women Voters, Klein successfully ran for the New Jersey Assembly in 1971. She became the first Democrat elected in Morris County in over 60 years. Klein deliberately chose politics because of her earlier frustrations as a social worker, for, as she once stated: "In dealing with the individual person I became very much aware of the lack of referrals for people. That got me interested in law and government and eventually I got out of social work and into the political arena." (*New York Times*, Mar. 17, 1973)

She remained a vibrant but controversial personality in politics for the rest of her life. An eloquent and forceful proponent of women's rights, Klein campaigned to encourage women to participate in government on any level. She decried what she termed the "slave psychology of women," stating that "when the slaves were freed, many just remained with their masters—they were brought up to be protected and cared for." (*Daily Record*, Jan. 10, 1974)

As an ardent supporter of a woman's right to abortion, Klein once angered Roman Catholics, who issued a bitter denunciation of her when she first ran for the State Assembly. Always self-assertive, she insisted on marching straight to a local convent to hold an open discussion with a group of nuns to distinguish her personal opposition to abortion from her support of other women's rights.

Klein resigned from the New Jersey Assembly in 1973 to become the first woman from the state to run as a major party candidate for governor. She was endorsed in the primary by the *New York Times*, which on June 6, 1973, called

her "outstanding . . . forthright and responsive to the state's problems." After a vigorous campaign, she placed second in the Democratic primary, losing to Brendan T. Byrne, who was elected governor in the general election.

Nevertheless, she was heartened that she had set a precedent for women in high office. This was a full decade before another woman ran as a Democratic candidate for vice-president of the United States. Klein proclaimed: "We have carved a doorway through the wall of blind prejudice. . . . Someday another woman will walk through that door. . . . We have expanded the horizons for every little girl in the United States." (*Daily Record*, June 7, 1973)

After her primary loss, Klein threw her support to Brendan Byrne and was appointed in 1974 to his cabinet, where she served for virtually his whole administration. She was first selected as Institutions and Agencies commissioner, an appointment "believed to be the most significant ever accorded to a woman in the state." (*New York Times*, Jan. 3, 1974)

From 1974 to 1981, during her years of service in Governor's Byrne's cabinet, Klein, tall and slim and dressed in her customary pants suit, remained continually before the public eye. Everyone agreed with the *New York Times* headline "Ann Klein Loves the Challenge of Her Nearly Impossible Job," but there was continual debate on whether she was "brusque and unfeminine or compassionate, warm and genial." (*New York Times*, May 5, 1974) Despite the controversy, she was elected Woman of the Year by the Women's Political Caucus of New Jersey in 1974.

In 1976, at Klein's urging, Governor Byrne split her Institutions and Agencies Department into a State Prisons Division and a Human Services Division, which oversaw social services that included Medicaid, welfare, and the state's mental hospitals. As director of the Department of Human Services she remained controversial, but identified herself as an adoptions advocate, a leader in the fight against child abuse, and a proponent of a more efficient Medicaid system. She devoted herself to improving the quality of life of any of the institutionalized, whether they were physically disabled, retarded, or mentally ill.

Klein's own motto was "Don't talk to the people until you've listened to the people." (*Daily Record*, May 1, 1974) Among her major accomplishments in the Department of Human Services—which she termed "no bed of roses"—were her closing of the archaic Glen Gardner home for tubercular patients, and its reopening as a model geriatric psychiatric nursing home. She also closed three children's units at psychiatric hospitals and opened other new ones.

Her intense personal commitment to her myriad tasks became legendary. When irritated with an incompetent colleague or the slow pace of change in government policy, she would spend a sleepless night spewing out her wrath in what she called a "midnight special," a vehement letter of outrage to the "guilty." Sometimes she mailed these; sometimes she thought better of it. She once so incensed a Republican official that he called on Governor Byrne to demand her resignation.

A more poignant anecdote of her personal commitment to those she served concerns a small girl, ten or twelve years old at the time, who was a severe hydrocephalic confined to a crib. From her first visit to Ancora, the psychiatric hospital where the girl resided, Klein was completely captivated by the bright, engaging child. After subsequent visits, Klein arranged for a prominent neurosurgeon to examine the child. In consultation with Klein and the devoted parents, the surgeon recommended a highly experimental and dangerous operation. Klein and the parents gave permission, but all three were heartbroken when the child died shortly after the operation. Those who knew her saw Klein go through an intense period of mourning, as though she were the mother of that child.

In 1981 she resigned as Human Services director to become a gubernatorial candidate for the second time. This time, however, she was not a front-runner and finished tenth in a field of thirteen Democratic candidates. In her last public office she served as an administrative law judge in Newark, NJ, from January 1982 until her resignation (due to illness) in May 1984.

Fulfilling a lifelong dream, Klein was accepted at Columbia University as a law student, though ill health prevented her from matriculating. She remained politically astute in the last year and a half of her life, despite serious illness. Klein died of cancer on Feb. 23, 1986, in Morristown, NJ. Only three days before, she had fired off a telegram of protest to President Ronald Reagan denouncing his handling of politics in the Philippines. Klein the politician indeed "etched an indelible mark upon the political landscape of New Jersey." (*Daily Record*, Feb. 25, 1986) She is buried in Woodbridge, NJ.

Interviews with Klein's daughter, Mara Miller of New York City, and her former personal assistant, Selma Rubin of Morristown, NJ, provided valuable information. The *New York Times* covered Klein's career from 1972 to 1981. Clipping files on her are available at the *Morristown Daily Record* and at the Center for American Women in Politics at the Eagleton Institute, Rutgers University (New Brunswick, NJ).

*Noel Robinson*

## HELEN JACKSON LEE, 1908–

Helen (Jackson) Lee, author and New Jersey civil servant, was born July 23, 1908, the fifth of seven children (four girls and three boys) of Charles Neason and Nannie (Brisby) Jackson of Richmond, VA. Her father was a building superintendent, and her mother was a teacher and homemaker. Lee's African-American maternal grandparents were Anne (Cumber) and William Henry Brisby. He was born free in New Kent County, VA, in 1831. A self-educated blacksmith, lawyer, sheep farmer, and landowner of (179 acres), he was an elected officeholder from 1865 to 1895. During his long career as a magistrate he tried members of both races. Lee's paternal grandparents were a white businessman and his black wife, Elizabeth Jackson.

Lee was reared in a middle-class family that sought to protect its children from racism and instill religious values. Yet in the state with the highest mulatto population in the country, where blacks measured social status by lightness of color, Lee recalls that "the Negro society aped the values of the FFV's" (First Families of Virginia). Still, blacks could not borrow books from the Richmond Public Library, and as young children, Lee and her brother were cursed and chased from the grounds of the governor's mansion while whites were allowed to stay.

Lee attended Virginia State University (VSU) from 1926 to 1930, graduating with a B.A. in French and English. She met her husband, Robert E. Lee of Trenton, NJ, while attending college. He was a student at Howard University's College of Pharmacy. They were secretly wed (during half time at the VSU homecoming football game) on November 1, 1930. The Lees' daughter, Barbara, was born in 1934 and their son, Robert, Jr., in 1935.

Unable to find a job as a pharmacist in either Trenton or Philadelphia, where they moved in 1933, Robert Lee did menial work. Helen Lee cared for their two children, did freelance writing for Philadelphia's black newspapers, and tried to make ends meet on her husband's wages as an elevator operator. Faced with hard times, the family returned to Trenton in February 1940. Four months later Robert Lee was killed in an automobile accident.

A widowed mother of two small children, Lee found a job with the WPA Writer's Project, but it was phased out after Pearl Harbor. Refusing to listen to the black Trenton physician who told her "you best go back South . . . because no nigger woman can make it in Trenton unless she teaches school or goes to work in some white woman's kitchen," Lee sought employment in state government.

*Nigger in the Window*, the autobiography Lee wrote after retiring from 31 years in state government at age 65, chronicles her quest for equity as a black state employee. Lee takes her reader from her first job with the N.J. Unemployment Compensation Commission (UCC), from 1942 to 1947, as "one of the dozen Negro employees set apart . . . from the others at UCC," through the civil service examinations that resulted in no jobs, the scores of less qualified employees who received the promotions she was due (over two decades as a senior clerk-stenographer with the N.J. Department of Institutions and Agencies), the harassment for being "too outspoken" during the McCarthy era, and all of the other realities of northern institutionalized racism.

This enlightening, witty, fast-paced, and historically illuminating book is at the same time a sobering work. *Nigger in the Window* stands alone among autobiographies written by black women, because its focus on middle-class northern urban life is unique. Based on 30 years of diaries and over 60 years of living, this work not only clarifies the workings of discrimination in state government, but explains how Lee's religious faith and fortitude allowed her to say at her retirement party in 1973, "Shed no tears for Helen Lee / The best is yet to be," while simultaneously raising her fist and shouting, "Power to the people. Right on!"

Lee's *Nigger in the Window* (1978), an interview with her at her Trenton, NJ, home on Jan. 15, 1986, and documents from her personal collection provided information for this article.

*Kathryn Daughtrey Brown*
*Gloria H. Dickinson*

## SOPHIE KRESCH LEVINE, 1905–1988

The birth of Sophie (Kresch) Levine, community volunteer, in Bayonne (Hudson County), NJ, to Anna (Krant) and A. Jacob Kresch, Austrian Jewish immigrants, was registered on August 8, 1905, but was celebrated on July 30. Her father, who was self-educated, started in this country as a factory worker. He was then able to go into business for himself, opening a grocery store and later expanding into real estate investing. He became a leader in the local Jewish community. Her mother, a homemaker, worked in the family store and in her middle years attended night school to obtain her high school diploma.

As a child, the two strongest values stressed in her home were education and charity. All of Levine's siblings, two sisters and five brothers, were college educated, and all learned to give to charity at the time of every significant event, positive or negative, in their lives. Levine's life followed this tradition of giving and caring, of working for the society in which she lived. She was nine years old when she first started giving speeches and promoting drives for charity. Filled with boundless energy for worthwhile causes, her dedication to her community was mixed with a strong sense of integrity and accountability.

As a teenager she was active in a Young Judea group called "Blossoms of Zion." They disbanded in 1928, leaving her in charge of their treasury of $49.68, to be donated to a Jewish community center, planned for construction. She kept watch over the money for almost 20 years, going to the bank and recording the interest four times a year. In 1947, when the building was finally nearing completion, she donated a $100 war bond in the name of the organization. War bonds were a focal point of her volunteer efforts.

Levine graduated from Public School No. 11 in Bayonne, Bayonne High School, and attended Columbia University, where she majored in commercial Spanish, literature, and poetry. She married Sol Levine, an accountant, on September 15, 1940.

In her youth, Levine had been the first president of the Junior Council of the National Council of Jewish Women (NCJW). She became an active member of NCJW for almost 60 years. The organization focuses on improving social services in Israel and within the Jewish community in the United States, as well as the entire community. The council identified community needs and helped to establish programs that were later absorbed by the local or state community. An example of this type of activity was the establishment in 1956 of the Occupational Center of Hudson County in Jersey City, which provided diagnostic and rehabilitative services that enabled trainees to hold jobs and be self-supporting. This project evolved from a joint effort of the Bayonne, Jersey City, and North Hudson County sections of the NCJW and the Association for Retarded Children. The council was involved in 1963 in establishing a preschool class of brain-injured children at the Bayonne Jewish Community Center, opening a day nursery in Bayonne in 1967, and obtaining from the New Jersey State Division of Community Mental Health Services the original $15,000 grant in 1972 that started a mental health center in Bayonne. As an active member and lifetime director of the council, Levine participated in many of these community efforts.

Her greatest personal contribution occurred during World War II, when she single-handedly sold almost a million dollars in war bonds. From the first War Loan Drive in 1941 until the seventh drive in 1945, Levine, acting as a committee of one, collected donations from friends, relatives, and townspeople. She used her own precious gas-rationing stamps when picking up monies and purchasing bonds. She kept detailed records in bank books and had the banks and post office send her letters recording the totals. These drives culminated in the purchase of a bomber that was named the "Spirit of Bayonne Council of Jewish Women." Levine received citations for this work from the mayor of Bayonne, the N.J. administrator of the War Finance Committee, the N.J. chair of War Bonds, and U.S. Secretary of the Treasury Henry Morgenthau, Jr.

She assisted in instituting the "Penny a Plane Club." People were urged to place a penny in a fruit jar for each Axis aircraft brought down by Allied forces. A daily score was published in the local paper, the *Bayonne Times*.

On January 25, 1977, Levine received the Hannah G. Solomon Award from the National Council of Jewish Women. In honoring her, the NCJW praised her lifetime of "commitment and enthusiasm," as evidenced by her commitment to the War Bond Drive, her activity in furnishing a recreation room for enlisted men at the Bayonne

Naval Base, her membership on the Bayonne Price Control Board, her organization of the National Council of Jewish Women Thrift Shop, and her chairing the Bayonne Community Concert series and the dedication of the Jewish Family Service Room at the Bayonne Jewish Community Center. She was also instrumental in the dedication of an auditorium in the National Council High School in Jerusalem. She served as treasurer of the Women's Auxiliary Board of the Bayonne Hospital. To preserve the history of the National Council of Jewish Women, in which she was so active, she authored the "50-year History of the Council" (1972) and, later, the "60-year History of the Bayonne Section of National Council of Jewish Women" (1982).

Levine died on May 17, 1988, at age 82, as the result of a stroke. She was buried in the Baron Hirsch Cemetery on Staten Island.

Levine was interviewed on Dec. 27, 1985. She maintained a collection of memorabilia. See also "Mrs. Sol Levine to Get Solomon Award," *Jersey Journal* (Jersey City, NJ), Jan. 20, 1977.

*Judith Witt Brodman*

## MINNIE STRULOVICI LIBERTI, 1898–1984

Minnie (Strulovici) Liberti, labor union activist and community leader, was born on October 28, 1898, in Austria-Hungary to Jewish landowning parents. She was the oldest of sixteen children of Chaie (Hudes) and Hersch Strulovici.

Liberti called herself a "tough lady" like her mother and enjoyed offering as proof the account of her own birth. Her mother was working in the garden when labor began, and she quickly gave birth to her first child. Liberti recounted: "She put me in her apron, and took me next door to the neighbor's and asked her to get the midwife. By the time the midwife came, she was back working in the garden. I think that's why I'm a tough lady like her." (*Record*, Sept. 14, 1976)

From her early childhood Liberti began a lifelong process of opposition to all forms of exploitation. A vivid memory of her childhood was the procedure of dividing the crops among the peasants and the Strulovici family at the end of each harvest season. Her father would divide the yield, with the peasants receiving one-third of the harvest, while her family kept two-thirds. When Liberti questioned the justice of this, she was severely punished by her mother. She resolved the situation by taking meat from her family's supply and bringing it to the peasants so they would have a little meat to eat along with their bread.

Liberti attended high school, but whether or not she graduated remains in doubt, for she left home in her early teens. She was fluent in German, Yiddish, and Slavic. She

left Europe for America in 1912 against her father's wishes but with her mother's approval. Her mother believed America to be a rich country, a place where her daughter could work and send money back home. Finally, her father bought her a ticket and gave her money, which her mother carefully sewed into her underwear to avoid theft. Liberti left her home and family to travel alone to America, where she found her way to family friends and relatives in New York City.

Liberti's first job in America was in a New York dress factory, where she worked twelve-hour days for $1.50 per week. She quickly became involved in union activity, which remained a major commitment for the rest of her life. She had been at work for one week when her shop went out on a strike, which lasted two weeks and resulted in a pay increase to $4.50 per week. This strike was the first of many for Liberti and was a crucial experience for her. The strike and the picket line became her strongest weapons against injustice, not only in the workplace, but in the civil rights struggle and the fight for world peace.

Her union activities introduced her to Frank Liberti, a founder of the International Ladies Garment Workers Union (ILGWU) and the organizer of the ILGWU's Local 145 in Passaic, NJ. Frank Liberti was born in Palermo, Sicily, in 1894 and emigrated to America when he was ten years old. He began his union career in 1910 when he helped lead a cloakmakers' strike. He became business manager of the ILGWU's New York Dress Joint Board in 1919 and was active as an organizer and business agent for the Passaic local from 1934 to 1955.

She and Frank Liberti met at a union meeting in New York City. They began living together in 1919 and stayed together for 46 years, until Frank Liberti's death in 1965. Liberti told an interviewer in 1980 that Frank was her best friend and would never leave her; therefore, marriage never became necessary. They had three children: Thomas (b. 1922), Dante (b. 1926), and Rosalia (b. 1930).

Throughout their lives together, the Libertis were partners at home and in public, where they worked for better lives for working people through the ILGWU, relief from discrimination for victims of various forms of bigotry, and better education for young people. They were members of the Congress on Racial Equality, the National Association for the Advancement of Colored People, and the New Jersey Council of Americans for Democratic Action.

Liberti preferred a less visible role than that of her husband. She summed up her position in a 1968 interview: "Ever since we've been married he attempted to bring about needed social changes and I've supported him. I would rather help than be directly involved." (Crane, "Minnie Liberti," 1984) However, she was not a woman who remained quietly behind the scenes. She enthusiastically joined him in the strikes and picket lines that were significant in New Jersey's textile industry. She especially liked to recall the 1926 strike when they were on a picket line in Lodi. Liberti was in the last weeks of her second pregnancy. This did not, however, prevent her from fighting with a scab who thought it improper for a pregnant woman to participate in such activity. As a result of the fight, Liberti entered the hospital and gave birth to her second son.

In 1965, when she was 67, Liberti suffered a severe blow in the death of Frank Liberti. However, she soon began a new career as a volunteer and an activist in her own right in the causes she and her husband had supported for so many years. She was an outspoken advocate of birth control and abortion rights, and was an early supporter of women's rights. Liberti devoted the years between her husband's death in 1965 and her own death in 1984 to her children and grandchildren, her many friends, and the causes she loved. Much of her activity was centered in Garfield, NJ, her home from 1928 until she died. She was involved as a volunteer with Garfield's Senior Citizens Housing and with that city's Meals on Wheels program, which was established in 1968. The Garfield Public Library was another favorite cause. After her husband's death, Liberti established the Frank Liberti Collection at the library. This collection has become a resource for those interested in African-American labor, and, women's history and is now called the Frank and Minnie Liberti Collection.

In her later years, Liberti's interests were not confined to Garfield; she was an active member of the Urban League, the Bergen County Community Action Program, Inc., the New Jersey Community Action Institute, New Jersey SANE, and the Democratic party.

Liberti was a small woman with a warm and ready smile. She loved music, books, and good food and claimed to make the best spaghetti and meatballs in the world. Her daughter, Rosalia Jacobs, said of her: "She was woman, sweetheart and partner to my father; teacher and protector to her children and their children. . . . She loved people and she loved just causes. She fought for human rights, civil rights, womens' rights, welfare rights and always the struggle for peace." (Letter to Mary K. Dykstra, May 1, 1986)

Liberti died of a heart attack at the age of 85 at her Garfield home on May 20, 1984, after attending a local political dinner. Her remains were cremated at the Cedar Lawn Crematory in Paterson, NJ. Her collection of books and pamphlets on labor history, human rights, the Russian Revolution, and radical political thought of the early 20th century was donated to the American Labor Museum/ Botto House National Landmark in Haledon by her children.

Information on Liberti was obtained through a letter from her daughter, Rosalia Liberti Jacobs, written May 1, 1986, and from a telephone interview with Helen Palubniak, May 10, 1986. Also useful were newspaper articles: Jim Dwyer, "Of Love, Justice, and Mrs. Liberti," *Record* (Hackensack, NJ), Sept. 14, 1976; and Jeff Crane, "Minnie Liberti, 85: Union, Civic Activist," *Record* (Hackensack, NJ), May 22, 1984.

*Mary K. Dykstra*

Anne Morrow Lindbergh, poet, author, and pilot, with Charles Lindbergh and an experimental Curtiss biplane in 1929, the year of their marriage. *Courtesy, Lindbergh Picture Collection, Yale University Library.*

## ANNE MORROW LINDBERGH, 1906–

Anne (Morrow) Lindbergh, poet, pilot, and writer, was born in her parents' rambling, clapboard home on Palisade Avenue in Englewood (Bergen County), NJ, on June 22, 1906. She was christened Anne Spencer Morrow, the second child and second daughter of Dwight Whitney Morrow, a lawyer, financier, and diplomat and Elizabeth Reeve (Cutter) Morrow, a poet and philanthropist devoted to education and social service.

Within a few years Lindbergh's younger brother and sister were born into the warm Morrow circle, which often grew with the visits of relatives who had shared her parents' staunch Presbyterian upbringing in the Midwest. The Englewood of Lindbergh's childhood was "a town, not a suburb, with generous backyard life and neighbors' children wearing paths through scraggly privet hedges." (Lindbergh, *Bring Me a Unicorn*, xiii) The wider world was suggested by summer pilgrimages to Cape Cod, later to the family estate in North Haven, ME, and by European tours organized to further the children's instruction as well as their father's work with J. P. Morgan. At home or abroad, there were encounters with accomplished and powerful people of the time.

The role of observer suited Lindbergh and nourished the perceptive spirit that inspired her writing even as a little girl. "I was shy," she said years later, "and couldn't talk in front of people. . . . So I wrote down in a diary what I couldn't say. Diary keeping is old-fashioned, but . . . a marvelous tool for a writer." (Lindbergh, "The Journey, Not the Arrival," 4) That tool would be both consolation and resource throughout her life. Her diaries and correspondence with family members was the raw material for at least seven of her thirteen books.

Lindbergh attended Englewood schools and went on to become president of her class at Miss Chapin's preparatory school in New York City. Graduating in 1924, she longed for Vassar, but entered Smith, her mother and older sister's college, in accordance with her family's wishes. In her senior year Smith awarded Lindbergh two prestigious literary prizes, for critical and creative writing, respectively; and her poem "Height," which had placed first in a competition, was published in *Scribner's* magazine. She graduated from Smith in June 1928.

The literary successes were remarkable, considering an even more momentous preoccupation of her senior year. Her father, recently named U.S. ambassador to Mexico, had invited Colonel Charles A. Lindbergh, hero of the preceding May's first nonstop solo flight across the Atlantic, for a Christmas goodwill visit to the embassy in Mexico City. Her diary describes Charles Lindbergh—keen, laconic, and totally impatient with superficiality—as a "bomb" dropped in the midst of the "college-bred, forever book-reading, introspective" Morrows.

Her engagement to Charles Lindbergh was announced from the embassy in Mexico City on February 13, 1929. "Don't wish me happiness," she wrote a friend. "I don't expect to be happy, but it's gotten beyond that, somehow. Wish me courage and strength and a sense of humor—I will need them all." (*Unicorn*, 228)

Throughout their engagement and even their honeymoon, they were hunted by the press, which had besieged Charles Lindbergh since his landing in Paris. Admonished by her fiancé to write nothing she wouldn't want to find on the front page of a newspaper, Lindbergh stopped writing in her diary for three years. They were married secretly in

the seclusion of "Next Day Hill," the new Morrow estate in Englewood, on May 27, 1929.

During her first year of marriage Lindbergh traveled with her husband constantly, planning the new Transcontinental Air Transport passenger route between New York and Los Angeles and inaugurating Pan American Airways routes to Central and South America. With one day's instruction, she became the first woman in the United States to receive a gliding pilot's license. Two months before her first child was born, she acted as navigator on the initial coast-to-coast flight of their new plane, which broke the transcontinental speed record.

In June 1930 Charles Augustus Lindbergh, the Lindberghs' first child, was born in Englewood. During the next year Lindbergh savored motherhood, studied radio theory and Morse code, learned to fly, and planned a new home on a wooded hill in the Sourland Mountains, near Princeton, NJ. She spent the summer and early fall of 1931 hedge-hopping across Canada, Alaska, Russia, Japan, and China with her husband on the survey trip she described in her first book, *North to the Orient*. They had been home for only five months when their baby was kidnapped from the supposed sanctuary of their new house in Hopewell on March 1, 1932. In May his body was found in the woods a few miles from home.

For Lindbergh, pregnant with her second child, the intervening ten weeks of investigation and negotiation were a nightmare of mingled hope and sorrow, complicated by intense and often bizarre public preoccupation with the case. The experience, she wrote, was "a complete wiping out of faith in the goodness and security of life." (Lindbergh, *Hour of Gold, Hour of Lead*, 254)

But she found consolation in a return to her diary; the birth of Jon, a second son, in August 1932; and preparations for another exploratory flight—around the Atlantic—accomplished between June and December of 1933. Her role as copilot and radio operator on the 40,000-mile venture earned her the Cross of Honor of the United Stated Flag Association in 1933; and in 1934 she received the National Geographic Society's Hubbard Gold Medal for achievement in exploration. Lindbergh's article on the Atlantic survey mission was published in September 1934 by *National Geographic*. In August 1935 *North to the Orient* was published; it became a best-seller.

Having lived in the longed-for Hopewell house for less than 100 days before taking refuge at the Morrow estate in Englewood, the Lindberghs explored the possibility of giving "Highfields" to the state of New Jersey (it eventually housed one of the country's few successful rehabilitation centers for teenagers with criminal records). The death of her father in 1931, her son in 1932, and her older sister in 1934 had left a cumulative sorrow. After a new blizzard of publicity surrounding the trial and conviction of the accused kidnapper, and threats against the safety of their living son, the Lindberghs sought seclusion in Europe in December 1935. Life resumed in the peaceful setting of a country house in Kent and on a wild island off the coast of Brittany. The Lindbergh's third son, Land, was born in London (1937), and Lindbergh wrote another book, *Listen! The Wind!*, her account of the Atlantic survey. She also traveled extensively with her husband at the invitation of American diplomats and intelligence officers seeking subtle assessments of European—especially Nazi Germany's—air power. She was torn between Morrow internationalism and her husband's isolationist convictions: faith in American self-sufficiency and concern that war would culminate in Russian domination of Eastern Europe. Her reflections in *The Wave of the Future* seemed an attempt to reconcile her own ambivalence.

After Hitler's annexation of Czechoslovakia in 1939, Lindbergh and her husband returned to the United States, still seeking a lasting home for their growing family. Committed to neutrality, Charles Lindbergh made widely reported speeches for the America First Committee and was branded "traitor," "Nazi," "fascist," "knight of the German eagle" by pro-interventionists. Under open attack from President Franklin D. Roosevelt, he resigned his Air Corps Reserve commission in the spring of 1941. "One tries to work without hate," Anne Lindbergh wrote, "but each morning's paper brings some . . . dreadful lies or calumny that one must fight down in one's heart." (Lindbergh, *War Within and Without*, 176) While her husband plunged into advisory work for civilian corporations that eventually led to his flying 50 combat missions in the South Pacific, she spent the war years making homes on Long Island and in Michigan, writing journals and a book about flying, *The Steep Ascent*, and bearing a daughter, Anne (b. 1940), and another son, Scott (b. 1942).

By 1945, when their younger daughter, Reeve, was born, the Lindberghs were settled in a wooded retreat on the Connecticut shore that became their primary residence, despite later acquisition of homes in Switzerland and eventually Hawaii. Morrow now became her husband's writing critic as he wrote his autobiography, returning the support he had provided during her early fits of insecurity.

Lindbergh's most famous and popular work, *Gift from the Sea*, was published in 1955. She described this book as a "meditation" to reconcile the dual roles of wife-mother and creative writer, and a comment on the nature of an enduring marriage. *Gift* won the first Book Award of the National Council of Women of the United States, and the Christopher Award for 1955.

The primary public concern of the Lindberghs' subsequent years together was the championing of conservation and "earth values," which is the central theme of *Earth Shine*, published in 1969. They were joint recipients—she for literature, he for conservation—of the gold medal of

the National Institute of Social Sciences in 1968.

After 45 years of marriage, Lindbergh's husband died of lymphatic cancer in August 1974. He was buried near their vacation home on the island of Maui. "I am at another stage of the journey," Lindbergh told Smith College students four years later; "I am a widow and . . . Like you, I must 'find my true center alone.'" ("The Journey, Not the Arrival," 7) In the years preceding and following her husband's death, Lindbergh prepared for publication the five volumes of her own diaries and letters, from school years and the most public years of their marriage.

Lindbergh holds honorary degrees from Smith and Amherst colleges and the University of Rochester. She became the first female director of Harcourt Brace Jovanovich in 1975. During a 1977 interview, reporter Alden Whitman found her "lithe and vibrant" at the age of 71, when one of her daughters told him, "Some people think my mother, all 90 pounds of her, is a fragile woman. She's about as fragile as a bar of steel." (*New York Times*, May 8, 1977, 17, 18)

Lindbergh's diaries and letters have been published in five volumes: *Bring Me a Unicorn* (1972), *Hour of Gold, Hour of Lead* (1973), *Locked Rooms and Open Doors* (1974), *The Flower and the Nettle* (1976), and *War Within and Without* (1980). Her lectures at Smith College appear in the *Smith Alumnae Quarterly*: "Earth Values" (Apr. 1970):15–18, and "The Journey, Not the Arrival" (Aug. 1978):3–7. Alden Whitman, "Anne Morrow Lindbergh: Reminiscences about Life with Lindy," *New York Times Magazine*, May 8, 1977; and Walter S. Ross, *The Last Hero: Charles A. Lindbergh* (1964), detail her married life. For perspectives on the Morrow family, see Harold George Nicolson, *Dwight Morrow* (1935). Lindbergh's manuscripts and family letters are at M-SC and her original diaries and correspondence from the late 1930s to the present are at C-YU.

*Frances Ward Weller*

## MIRIAM LEE EARLY LIPPINCOTT, 1877–1947

Miriam Lee (Early) Lippincott, educator and outspoken champion and defender of women's rights, was born in Hightstown (Mercer County), NJ, on March 10, 1877, to Harriet Whitmore (Ogborn) and Robert Morrison Early. There is no record of siblings.

Lippincott's lifelong love of elocution and dramatics was kindled at Pennington Seminary in New Jersey and at the Northwestern University School of Oratory in Evanston, IL. Her formal education finished by 1900, Lippincott returned to Pennington Seminary, where she taught elocution and physical culture, and then taught public speaking at Swarthmore College, Swarthmore, PA, until 1915. Living in Camden, NJ, during this time, she enjoyed her hobbies of tennis, walking, and driving, and was a member of the Philadelphia Art Alliance, a Philadelphia women's club, and several literary societies.

In 1913, at the age of 36, she became the second wife of 47-year-old widower Ahab Haines Lippincott, M.D., a prominent and respected Camden urologist and surgeon. They lived in Camden for the rest of their lives. Until his death on March 10, 1937, Ahab Lippincott was a proud supporter of his wife's endeavors. In her innovative and independent way, she did anything to help him. The Lippincotts' strong, close relationship helped them endure the tragic death of their only child, Barbara Lee, at three days old, in 1915.

Lippincott was reportedly unable to have any more children. For the rest of her life, with thoughts of her daughter, she devoted herself to causes she believed would strengthen family life. Well known in Camden as an elocution teacher, public speaker, dramatic reader, interpreter of literature, and director of plays for various groups, Lippincott was also active in the Little Theater movement. The plays she presented in a local church, taking all the parts herself, were very popular, and the admission receipts financed her many projects for the public welfare.

Lippincott expressed her belief in the equality of men and women through her work in the N.J. Woman Suffrage Association (NJWSA) and its successor when suffrage was achieved, the League of Women Voters of New Jersey (LWV). By 1914 she was a declared suffragist, serving the NJWSA first as a member-at-large from Camden, and later as a member of the Executive Committee.

The LWV's purpose was to educate women as voters, and Lippincott gave 20 years to this effort. Believing that women should become politically active, she served on the LWV's State Board of Officers and Directors, and as chair of the Department of Government and the Legal Status of Women for several years during the 1930s. Among the concerns of Lippincott's department in 1935 was the status of women on juries. A league survey that year revealed that some counties in New Jersey did not permit women to serve on juries. Lippincott's group met with judges and others in power, trying to persuade them to appoint women jurors. When women were finally selected for jury service on the U.S. District Court, District of New Jersey, in November 1936, Lippincott was in the first group of women jurors.

A Republican all her life, Lippincott was on the boards of the N.J. Women's Republican Club and its successor, the State Council of N.J. Republican Women. Elected to the Republican State Committee in 1920 and 1922, Lippincott also served as delegate-at-large from New Jersey to the 1924 Republican National Convention.

Like many woman suffragists, Lippincott was an ardent Prohibition advocate, supporting passage of the 18th Amendment. During the almost fifteen years of Prohibition, as a vocal leader of the futile fight to maintain the dry laws, she was chair of the N.J. Committee for Law Enforcement (NJCFLE) and a board member of the N.J. Anti-Saloon League (NJASL). As opposition to Prohibition grew, judiciary committees of both the U.S. Senate and the House of Representatives began hearing testimony supporting and attacking the 18th Amendment. In 1926 Lippincott appeared twice before the Senate, and in 1930 she witnessed before the House, representing both the NJCFLE and the NJASL. Deprived of its purpose by repeal on December 5, 1933, the NJCFLE was dissolved.

Always committed to education, especially of women, Lippincott began her 25-year affiliation with the New Jersey College for Women (now Douglass College) when she was elected to its Board of Managers in 1922. This board was replaced by the Rutgers University Board of Trustees Committee on the College for Women in 1932, when women were first permitted on the Rutgers board. Lippincott immediately became a trustee, serving short terms as a member or the chair of several committees, and serving fifteen years as a member of the Committee on the College for Women. For fifteen years Lippincott provided the Barbara Lee Lippincott Scholarship at the New Jersey College for Women, in memory of her daughter. Following Lippincott's death in 1947, the scholarship was funded for three years by her estate, her nephew's wife, and the Women's Club of Camden.

Lippincott belonged to the Woman's Club of Camden for more than 30 years, and was president from 1927 to 1930. The music building at the New Jersey College for Women was the gift of over 100 women's clubs in the state, and the Camden Club honored Lippincott by providing funds to dedicate a studio to the memory of her daughter. Lippincott also gave funds generously for this building. Lippincott's many contributions to the New Jersey College for Women and Rutgers were recognized in 1962, when a dormitory at Douglass was named for her.

The first woman appointed to the Camden City Board of Education, Lippincott served as board vice-president from 1924 to 1927. She was also a member of the Camden branch of the American Association of University Women from 1936 to her death.

Active in many social service groups, Lippincott was a 1938 charter member of the Goodwill Commission of New Jersey and was active in YWCA work. A promoter of good health and adequate medical care, Lippincott organized the Auxiliary to the N.J. State Medical Society and was its first president, from 1927 to 1928. She also organized county auxiliaries and later served as president of the Camden County Auxiliary, often holding meetings in her home. She served as director of the N.J. State Tuberculosis Association, national chairman of public relations of the National Auxiliary of the American Medical Association, and trustee of Jeanes Hospital in Philadelphia from 1940 to 1947.

As did many reform-minded women of her day, Lippincott became interested in the world peace movement through two major women's pacifist organizations, the Women's International League for Peace and Freedom and the Committee on the Cause and Cure of War (CCCW). She served on the state committee of the CCCW as a representative of the YWCA from 1931, while EMILY HICKMAN was chair, and was a delegate in 1935 from the CCCW to the World Peace Conference in Brussels, Belgium. Lippincott also served as the N.J. State Federation of Women's Clubs' committeewoman-at-large of the Department of International Relations, and as chair of the Camden County Council on International Relations. Shortly before World War II, as chair of United China Relief in New Jersey, Lippincott organized the sale of Chinese goods and returned the proceeds to China for relief purposes.

In 1937 Lippincott was named by the Soroptimist Club as Camden County's most outstanding woman for her service, leadership, citizenship, and womanhood.

Also in 1937, at the age of 60, Lippincott began a nine-year campaign for early cancer detection as the first N.J. field army commander of the American Society for the Control of Cancer, the forerunner of the American Cancer Society, N.J. Division. A gifted orator, her thousands of speeches before almost every organized group in New Jersey had mobilized residents of all 21 counties to form chapters of the society by January 1947.

Until the short illness preceding her death, Lippincott remained active, lecturing at colleges in the New England states, New York, New Jersey, and Pennsylvania.

At Camden's Cooper Hospital, on August 28, 1947, the 70-year-old Lippincott succumbed to a blood clot in her lung following a heart attack. Leaving only an aunt and a nephew, she was buried near her daughter and husband in the family plot at Harleigh Cemetery, Camden.

Lippincott's social and political activities are described in Felice Gordon, *After Winning: The Legacy of the New Jersey Suffragists, 1920–1947* (1986). Zula Casselman, "A True Civic Leader—Miriam Lee Early Lippincott," *New Jersey Clubwoman* 22 (Oct. 1947):10–12, is a detailed obituary written by a friend.

*Susan E. Powell*

## HELEN TRACY LOWE-PORTER, 1876–1963

Helen Tracy Lowe-Porter's literary reputation rests upon her English translations of almost all of Thomas Mann's major works, which include some of the most difficult novels of the 20th century.

She was born Helen Tracy Porter in Towanda, PA, on June 15, 1876, to Henry C. Porter, a pharmacist, and Clara (Holcombe) Porter. Her parents had moved to Towanda from Waterbury, CT. Although her family, which could trace a long English genealogy, belonged to the middle class, Lowe-Porter's politics verged on Fabian socialism throughout her life. A strike at Reading, PA, where she witnessed the brutality of security police hired by management, reinforced her deep political conviction. That conviction was part of a more general fervor that led one of her daughters to describe her as "beautiful, strong, and clear-minded, with an ardent, sometimes frightening idealism, but a certain basic shyness." (Thirlwall, *In Another Language*, ix) Later, a peculiar combination of ardor and self-effacement would allow her to insist that she was the best person to translate Mann and yet cripple her with deep anxieties about the ultimate quality of her translations.

The middle of three children, Lowe-Porter attended Towanda public schools and Wells College, in Aurora, NY. At Wells she was elected to Phi Beta Kappa and served as assistant editor on the *Chronicle*, the college literary magazine, which published her first articles and poems. (In 1964 Wells College instituted an annual translation award in her name.) After graduation in 1898 Lowe-Porter prepared folios of Shakespeare and Robert Browning with an aunt, Charlotte Endymion Porter, an eminent women's rights activist whose feminism profoundly influenced her niece.

Lowe-Porter spent the next few years in Europe, working as a guide for students at the American College of Classical Studies in Rome. While studying drama in Munich in 1906 she met Elias Avery Lowe, a Latin paleographer whom she married in Switzerland in 1911. Most of the couple's early married life, spent in Europe, was devoted to the establishment of Elias Lowe's distinguished career and to beginning a family of three daughters: Prudence Holcombe Lowe (b. 1912), Frances Beatrice Lowe (b. 1913), and Patricia Tracy Lowe (b. 1917).

In 1923, while the family was living in England, Lowe-Porter met Thomas Mann and took on the formidable job of translating his novel *Buddenbrooks* into English. She finished her translation in 1924. From the beginning, the novel had appealed to her because it wasn't sentimental—she "welcomed emotion cooled off and served in ice." (Thirlwall, 3) As would always be the case, Lowe-Porter worked in close collaboration with Mann, who pronounced her work "extraordinarily sensitive and accomplished." (Thirlwall, 4) But even in its early stages her relationship with Mann was made difficult by Lowe-Porter's insecurities about her own abilities and by Mann's misgivings about turning his best writing over to a woman—and to a female point of view that might in some way change or distort it. When Lowe-Porter asked to translate his next book, *The Magic Mountain*, he bluntly informed her that the "book with its deeply intellectual and symbolic character makes . . . demands on the translator—demands which I sometimes deem would be more readily met by a male rather than a female temperament." (Thirlwall, 9) Though

Lowe-Porter accepted Mann's lapse of confidence in her, she at last persuaded him to let her attempt a translation. *The Magic Mountain* won the Nobel Prize in 1929. From then on Lowe-Porter translated all of Mann's work, with the exceptions of *The Black Swan, Felix Krull*, and *Royal Highness*. During her long career, she also translated a number of minor German writers into English.

Although the recognition she received for her translations was considerable, the extent of these accomplishments can obscure her own achievements as a writer. She wrote a novel, *Sea Change* (completed in 1956 but never published); a collection of poetry published under the title *Casual Verses*; and *Abdication, or All Is True*, a play based on the abdication of Edward VIII, deeply influenced by Shakespeare's chronicle plays, and successfully produced at Dublin's Gate Theatre in 1948.

The problems and frustrations Lowe-Porter faced as a translator with a highly creative intelligence reflect the dilemmas of the women who were her contemporaries in a male-dominated culture that granted them only a secondary and provisional place. At the same time, however, Lowe-Porter found ways to use Mann's writing to express herself. The symbolic intensity of his writing, the complexity of his ideas, and the convolutions of his German prose style all made the job of casting his novels into a new language, while remaining faithful to his ideas, especially demanding and an artistic project in and of itself. "I cannot enter into the work of other writers unless their themes and techniques and general *Lebensauffassung* [conception of life] appeal to me as what I have been employing as original work," Lowe-Porter wrote in the essay "On Translating Thomas Mann." (Reprinted in Thirlwall, 188)

Ultimately, she found translating not at all a menial chore. On the contrary, she saw it as a way of "marrying word-cultures" and felt herself to be as powerful as Thomas Mann, her figurative spouse: "This great artist, of a controlled mental energy and scope so great it was like nothing I had ever imagined before, . . . was using my ideas and so I used him to give myself private satisfactions. What a tool!" (Thirlwall, 188–89)

Although the requirement that she use only ideas already formulated by someone else suggests that she had to give up personal creativity, it also allowed her considerable freedom to experiment with the boundaries of her own identity. She signed all her translations H. T. Lowe-Porter, not only leaving her gender in question but also inverting her married and family names. Her novel, *Sea Change*, likewise fantasizes the exchange of sexes between a boy and girl, suggesting a fanciful version of her own relation to the male writer whose personality she both put on and changed to suit herself.

After Elias Lowe's appointment to Princeton's Institute for Advanced Study in 1936, the Lowe family settled in New Jersey, where Lowe-Porter remained until her death.

In Princeton she counted among her many acquaintances Albert Einstein, whose papers and addresses she translated into English. She also wrote several essays about her work with Mann; these, however, have more to do with him as a personality, and with the thematic and stylistic intricacies of his work, than with her own experiences in translating his writings. Lowe-Porter began to decline mentally and physically as she completed Mann's *The Holy Scandal* in 1955. This was to be her last translation; she spent the rest of her life in Merwick, a nursing home of Princeton Hospital, where she died, at age 86, of arteriosclerosis on April 27, 1963.

Documents pertaining to Lowe-Porter are kept at C-YU. John C. Thirwall, *In Another Language* (1966), provides biographical information and details Lowe-Porter's relationship with Mann. A sketch of her appears in *NAW-MP*. Her obituary appeared in the *New York Times*, Apr. 23, 1963.

*Jayne E. Lewis*

## EDITH ELIZABETH LOWRY, 1897–1970

Edith Elizabeth Lowry, national leader in the expansion of ministry to migrant agricultural workers and pioneer in the unification of Protestant churchwomen, was born on March 23, 1897, in Plainfield (Union County), NJ, the only daughter and sole surviving child of Elizabeth (Darling) and Robert Hanson Lowry, a banker. Lowry's mother was thought to be descended from French and English settlers of Colonial America, and her father's family was of Scots-Irish descent. Her paternal grandfather, the Rev. Robert Lowry, composer of Christian hymns, became the first pastor of the newly constructed Park Avenue Baptist Church (later known as First Park Baptist Church) in Plainfield in 1876. Lowry's only sibling, Clarence Loxley Lowry, was born in 1891 and died in 1895.

Lowry enjoyed a comfortable middle-class childhood in Plainfield in the shadow of the Baptist church her grandfather had served and that the family still attended. She went to Stillman Elementary School in Plainfield and graduated from Plainfield High School in 1915. She attended Wellesley College, where she majored in languages, studied religion, and participated at Lake George in the annual conference of the Wellesley Christian Association. She was secretary of the Wellesley Class of 1920.

Following graduation with an A.B., Lowry served for more than a year as a volunteer with the Girl Reserves in the Plainfield Young Women's Christian Association and as a tutor and teacher. In 1922 she joined the staff of the Department of Education and Publicity of the Board of National Missions of the Presbyterian Church in the U.S.A. In 1927 Lowry became assistant to the executive secretary and assistant director of the work with agricultural migrants for the Council of Women for Home Missions, an agency sponsored by women's home missionary societies in a group of Protestant denominations. By 1929 Lowry was director of migrant work on the Council of Women for Home Missions, and in 1936 she was named its executive secretary, enlarging her responsibilities to include missionary activities with American Indians and sharecroppers. She continued to direct the program for migrants throughout the United States.

In 1940, when the Council of Women for Home Missions merged with the Home Missions Council to become the Home Missions Council of North America, Lowry became coexecutive secretary of the larger organization, a position she held until 1950, when the National Council of Churches of Christ (NCC) was formed. At that time Lowry became associate executive secretary of the Division of Home Missions and national director of the Migrant Ministry Program of the NCC. She remained in those positions through 1961.

In addition, Lowry served as a consultant for various departments of the NCC concerned with social and economic welfare. She was active in the General Department of United Church Women on committees that focused on social welfare and on several nonchurch groups that fostered social concerns.

Under Lowry's direction the ministry on behalf of migrant laborers expanded enormously. During the 1930s she oversaw ten projects supervised by a staff of three. By 1959 the ministry consisted of projects in 31 states involving a staff of 25 full-time workers, 500 summer employees (largely college and seminary students), and 7,000 volunteers.

Lowry encouraged cooperation among employers of migrants, community agencies, and local churches in order to provide services for people who fell between the cracks of state-sponsored relief and welfare agencies because they followed the crops, never staying in one area long enough to satisfy the residence requirements for receiving aid.

The migrant ministry established day-care centers for the laborers' children; supervised health, nutrition, recreation, and education of both adults and children; offered summer courses to children who had fallen behind in school; educated migrants about Social Security benefits; provided recreational and religious activities and counseling. During the 1950s the ministry sent station wagons called "Harvesters" equipped with sports supplies, films, record players, movie projectors, first-aid supplies, games, portable altars, and organs to remote migrant camps. Intimately involved in the ministry, Lowry personally visited migrant camps all over the United States.

In New Jersey Lowry worked closely with her friend ELIZABETH WHITE, owner of White's Bog and employer of migrant workers in her blueberry fields, to develop better living conditions for migrants involved in blueberry

cultivation and harvest. Under Lowry's direction, other New Jersey migrant worker centers were established for Italian cranberry and blueberry pickers, asparagus and strawberry harvesters, and potato pickers.

The 50th project in Lowry's nationwide program was the Shell Pile Social Center for black oyster shuckers working near Port Norris, NJ. Oyster shuckers were not, strictly speaking, migrant workers since they were members of a traditional industry located permanently in New Jersey. However, they had many needs similar to those of migrant workers. To meet these needs the center established a preschool nursery for workers' children and after-school education and recreation for older children in cooperation with local community groups.

To educate the public on the condition of the migrant labor force, Lowry produced books, articles, and bulletins, both church related and secular. Her work received national attention in a 1952 *Saturday Evening Post* article, "The Ladies Have the Answer," describing the work of the Home Mission Division of the NCC and Lowry's ministry to migrant workers.

Lowry participated in many national denominational conferences, and she spoke frequently before churchwomen, describing the work of the Home Missions Council and informing her listeners about the plight of migrants.

In August and September 1939 Lowry was the first woman to speak from a nationwide radio pulpit. Drawing on her experience as an interdenominational church executive who had worked for nearly two decades with churchwomen throughout the nation, her weekly NBC broadcasts focused on "Women in a Changing World." She described woman's role as pioneer, homemaker, educator, social worker, voter, citizen, molder of public opinion, and individual—all roles Lowry herself personified.

Although the term *homemaker* traditionally referred to a married woman who cared for her family and supervised house and family activities, Lowry, though unmarried, was indeed a homemaker, always returning from her travels to the Plainfield home she shared with her parents. After her mother died in 1937, Lowry continued to live in Plainfield with her father. When he became ill, she put a hospital bed in the dining room and hired a nurse to care for him during her frequent absences. Her father died in 1960, at age 95.

Lowry was a member of First Park Baptist Church (formed by a merger in 1929 of the Park Avenue and First Baptist churches) in Plainfield. She served on an advisory committee for the Plainfield Council of Church Women as they established a neighborhood house. She was a member of the College Club, which became the American Association of University Women.

After her retirement from the NCC in January 1962, Lowry continued her advocacy for migrants working part time for the National Council on Agriculture and Labor, a clearinghouse for 35 national private organizations interested in farm labor problems. She moved to Washington, D.C., the council's headquarters, in order to keep member organizations of the council alert to the progress of congressional bills involving migrants and to encourage council members to write letters of support for the bills to key members of Congress.

Friends described Lowry as outgoing, cooperative, and cheerful, yet down-to-earth and modest. Although she was a nationally recognized expert on migrant workers' problems, the people closest to her often had no idea of the extent of her leadership and expertise. Lowry's friends often visited in her home and accompanied her on her travels. Her hobbies included entertaining, gardening, reading, collecting antiques, and caring for pets. As a loyal Baptist, Lowry never drank alcoholic beverages. She showed continued interest in Wellesley connections, writing of her activities to the alumnae news and attending class reunions.

In 1965 Lowry sold her house in Plainfield and retired to a 65-acre farm near Wethersfield, VT, where she restored the farmhouse and pursued her avid interest in gardening. She developed the woodlands on her property in cooperation with a state conservation program.

Lowry, age 72, died in the Claremont, NH, General Hospital of arteriosclerotic heart disease on March 11, 1970. She was buried in Hillside Cemetery in Plainfield. In her memory, Wellesley College established the "Edith E. Lowry Memorial Scholarship Fund for Migrant Children" to honor the woman one biographer described as "the most conspicuous and best-informed leader in the ministry to migrants." (Handy, *NAW*, 4:429)

Lowry's two major books are *Migrants of the Crops* (1938) and *Tales of Americans on Trek* (1940). Her correspondence, speeches, and articles are available in the archives of the National Council of Churches, Presbyterian Historical Society (Philadelphia). The Wellesley College Alumnae Association (Wellesley, MA) and the NJ-PPL maintain clipping files on Lowry. Interview sources include Lowry's cousins, Mrs. C. Norman Gustafson and Arthur Taylor, Jr., both of Scotch Plains, NJ, and Lowry's longtime friends Marjorie B. Brown of San Jose, CA, and Mrs. Caryl Dunavan of Plainfield, NJ. Lowry is profiled in *NAW-MP* and her obituaries appeared in the *New York Times*, Mar. 14, 1970, and the *Courier-News* (Plainfield, NJ), Mar. 13, 1970.

*Alyce Mitchem Jenkins*

## LUCILLE MANNERS, 1911–

Lucille Manners, concert singer and radio star, was born on May 21, 1911, in her grandmother's modest frame house on South Sixth Street in Newark (Essex County), NJ. Named Marie Emily McClinchy, she was the only child of Emily (Raab) McClinchy, an accomplished amateur pianist, and Peter Joseph McClinchy, variously de-

scribed as a plumber, silversmith, and the manager of a men's hat store. Manners's maternal grandfather, Conrad Raab, known for his exceptional tenor voice, and her maternal grandmother, Maria Raab, emigrated from Germany. Her father's parents came from Ireland.

At the age of six or seven, Manners began to appear at amateur nights at the Liberty and City theaters in Irvington, where she lived. During her grammar school days at Coit Street School she sang in the choir of the Emanuel Evangelical Church. By the time she entered Irvington High School she was single-minded in her determination to become a professional singer. Directing all of her energies toward that goal, Manners left school and worked full time to pay for voice lessons.

From 1930 to 1932 she sang with the Opera Club of the Oranges. The musical director, Dutch-born Louis Dornay, and his wife, Betsy Culp, the club's official accompanist, both musicians of stature in Europe, were instrumental in helping launch Manners in her career. Dornay was an enthusiastic advocate of his young pupil's talent and secured her audition on the radio program that would make her a star.

Lucille Manners, concert singer and popular radio star of the 1930s and 1940s. *Courtesy, private collection.*

Manners's first big opportunity was a fifteen-minute spot on WOR's Woman's Club program. Each day at noon she would dash to the radio station from her office, sing, and race back to work, usually arriving late and breathless. This weekly transformation almost got her fired, and when she had a more secure and lucrative radio job, Manners quit.

Hired as a substitute on NBC's Friday night "Cities Service Concert" in 1935, Manners became the show's star by 1937. With a repertoire of light opera and semiclassical pieces, she was an immediate success on this prestigious program.

Dubbed the "Cinderella of the Airwaves" by the press, she captured the imagination of studio audiences and faithful listeners with her beauty, sweet temperament, and mellifluous voice. Although newspaper articles emphasized the fairy-tale quality of her meteoric rise from the typing pool to "one of the bright new stars in the radio firmament" (*Brooklyn Daily Eagle*, Feb. 4, 1937), her success was achieved by hard work and dedication to the highest levels of artistry. Lessons in singing, French, and Italian were part of her continuing education. She was unashamed to put her career first and advised aspiring singers to do the same.

In the late 1930s, at the height of radio popularity, she was "one of the highest paid singers on the air." Her success enabled her to buy two houses, the first a gracious manor house on Long Island, the second a Tudor-style mansion in Short Hills, NJ, where she lived for many years with her mother. Home ownership was important to Manners, and she selected many fine paintings and lovely antique pieces for both houses. Although she lived comfortably, she was extremely practical and responsible in monetary affairs. This trait enabled her to continue to live well after her career waned.

In addition to the Cities Service program, Manners concertized, appearing in 1938 with the National Symphony in Washington, D.C., and in 1939 in a recital at Town Hall in New York, singing selections by Scarlatti, Brahms, and Schubert. Music critics were enthusiastic and praised "her light lyric voice and dreamy, introspective approach" (*New York Times*, Mar. 23, 1939), as well as her range and polished style.

The City Center Opera Company in New York provided the vehicle for Manners to sing "Mimi" in *La Bohème*, "Marguerite" in *Faust*, and "Micaela" in *Carmen*. During this period, in the early 1940s, fans and professional colleagues admired her patriotism, which carried her around the country to sing at bond rallies. Accompanied by Charlotte Brinser, her best friend, who played at various free concerts for the military and high school wartime refugee aid, Manners became a regular on the Pullman routes. She also sang for servicemen at the Stage Door Canteen in New York City on Friday evenings after her Cities Service

broadcasts.

Manners appeared at the Millburn Paper Mill Playhouse in Desert Song in 1943. The following year, on January 6, 1944, in the historic Short Hills home she had purchased some years earlier, she married William Jackson Walker, an army officer from Cortland, NY. Their marriage ended in divorce in September 1948, shortly after the birth of their son, William Jackson Walker, Jr., in May 1947.

While her mother managed her household and helped raise her son, Manners continued performing but had to contend with declining opportunities as television replaced radio. Summer stock and touring sporadically during the 1950s seemed less appealing to her. Gratified by her achievements in the era of radio entertainment and satisfied with the level of musical artistry she had reached, Manners made an easy transition to the next stage of her life. With an appearance in Radio City Music Hall's "Stairway to the Stars" in 1957, she bid farewell to the glamorous New York performing world. After that, she continued to give concerts in New Jersey and sing as a paid soloist in church.

A resident of the retirement community of Leisure Village in Lakehurst, NJ, Lucille Manners sings in a church choir and gives occasional concerts. Her friend Charlotte Brinser lives nearby and is a vital reminder of her glamorous past as well as an important part of her everyday life. Still a beautiful and vibrant woman, Manners remains dedicated to the ideal of the consummate artist.

A personal interview with Manners provided useful information. The clipping files of NYPL-LC and NJ-IPL provide additional biographical details.

*Barbara Gilford*

## MARGHERITA FRANCES MARCHIONE, 1922–

Sister Margherita Marchione, a Roman Catholic nun and college professor for almost 50 years, was born on February 19, 1922, in Little Ferry (Bergen County), NJ, the youngest of eight children. Her parents, Crescenzo and Felicia (Schettino) Marchione, had left a small village near Salerno, Italy, in 1902 and settled on a farm in New Jersey. The dairy business they ran allowed them to live comfortably and raise a large family. Her mother, Sister Margherita recalls, was a religious woman, but not so her father, an honest and enterprising man.

Sister Margherita enjoyed a happy childhood and attended an elementary school taught by Benedictine nuns in Hackensack. From her early years she knew she would be a nun, but she was also aware that her parents would not approve. When she was thirteen her mind was set and she made the necessary arrangements with the superior of the

Sisters of Saint Lucy Filippini at Villa Walsh in Morristown, NJ. At the dinner table on Labor Day, 1935, she announced that she was leaving that same afternoon for the convent. She still remembers her parents' surprise and sorrow. But she was determined and, despite their objections, entered Villa Walsh High School, where she continued her education. At nineteen she became a nun.

Sister Margherita earned a B.A. from Georgian Court College in 1943 and began to teach in parochial and private high schools in Maryland and New Jersey. She also became an accomplished organist and directed church choirs. While teaching in Jersey City, she attended graduate school at Columbia University, earning her M.A. in 1949 and her Ph.D. in 1960.

At Columbia, Sister Margherita met Giuseppe Prezzolini, director of the Casa Italiana and professor of Italian literature, a well-known figure on the Italian cultural scene, who had a great influence on her future. He found a devoted student and friend in Sister Margherita. Years later he still recalled the two nuns who entered his Columbia class and did not demur when informed that they would be reading Machiavelli, whose work was sometimes irreverent toward the Catholic church.

"My love and interest in Italian literature and culture is the result of my study at Columbia," Sister Margherita says. Her friendship with Prezzolini was lifelong; she often visited him and his wife in Italy and in Lugano, Switzerland, where she sometimes nursed the elderly couple and managed their household. She accompanied Prezzolini to Rome when he was honored with an award by the president of the Italian Republic on his 100th birthday in 1982. Among the 30 volumes Sister Margherita published are several studies on Prezzolini, as well as two anthologies of his writings, used in Italian schools.

Prezzolini convinced Sister Margherita in 1956 to begin work toward a doctorate, with a dissertation on Italian poet Clemente Rebora. The following year she was named Columbia University's Garibaldi Scholar. In order to interview the terminally ill poet, she spent weeks at his bedside shortly before his death. Her work on Rebora resulted in the book *L'imagine tesa*, later introduced to the American public with an English adaptation, entitled *Clemente Rebora*, in the Twayne's World Author Series. Rebora was well known, and his conversion and ordination to the priesthood were of interest to the Vatican, so Sister Margherita presented the book to Pope Paul VI upon publication. During that 1966 audience, when she brought the pope regards from Prezzolini, a professed agnostic who also had visited him at the Vatican, the pope, with a twinkle in his eyes, said to her: "Teach him to pray." To which she replied: "Your Holiness, if you did not succeed, what can I do?"

While pursuing her studies, Sister Margherita had continued teaching Italian literature and language at Villa Walsh

Junior College, from 1949 to 1963, and at Seton Hall University, from 1963 to 1965. In 1965 she began her long career as the first nun to become a tenured professor at Fairleigh Dickinson University. This appointment lasted almost 20 years, until she retired as professor emerita in 1984. Among administrative positions, she has been provincial secretary and treasurer for the Religious Teachers Filippini. Although teaching was part of her life and she got deep satisfaction from interacting with students, Sister Margherita needed more time for another great interest in her life: the Philip Mazzei Project. This project began in 1974 when Peter Sammartino, chancellor of Fairleigh Dickinson, asked her to investigate a little-known patriot, Philip Mazzei, for the bicentennial of the Declaration of Independence. A native of Tuscany, Italy, Mazzei was colonial Virginia's agent in Europe and an active propagandist and participant in the American Revolution.

With a grant from the New Jersey Bicentennial Committee, Sister Margherita initiated her research, which took her to embassies and libraries in France, Italy, Poland, Austria, Switzerland, Spain, and Czechoslovakia. Financed by grants from other sources, she collected copies of all Mazzei's writings and correspondence. These have been edited and published and are now preserved at the Mazzei Center in Morristown, NJ, and at the American Philosophical Society library in Philadelphia. In addition, she was instrumental in obtaining both an Italian and a United States international airmail stamp of Mazzei. She was included as no. 144 of the Women's History series by the National Organization for Women. Sister Margherita is currently involved in a project for a movie and a television miniseries on Mazzei, "Eagles at Monticello."

Aside from a genuine interest in Mazzei, another purpose of Sister Margherita's research was to encourage pride among Italian-Americans in their heritage, which goes back to prerevolutionary Virginia. (*Sunday Star Ledger*, May 21, 1978)

Relentless in the pursuit of her causes, Sister Margherita has been called "a mixture of Catholicism and American independence" by Prezzolini. (*La Nazione*, July 28, 1957) She has earned many honors, including the Star of Solidarity of the Italian Republic Award, the UNICO National Rizzuto Award, the AMITA Award in Education, the National Italian American Foundation (NIAF) Award for Literature, and the George Washington Honor Medal for Excellence in the category of Individual Achievement from the Freedoms Foundation at Valley Forge.

A favorite anecdote about her acceptance of the NIAF Award in Washington, D.C., in 1984 concerns her remark in the presence of President Ronald Reagan: "The last woman to receive this award was Sophia Loren." She then paused, with a comic's timing, and said: "I'm happy to be following in her footsteps." (*Washington Post*, Sept. 17, 1984)

Sister Margherita is a member of many organizations, including the New Jersey Historical Commission and the American Italian Historical Association. A frequent lecturer in Europe and the United States, she has made numerous radio and television appearances. In addition, since 1983 she has been director of Corfinio College, a coeducational summer studies program associated with Thomas A. Edison State College in New Jersey, which combines classroom study and independent travel in various locations in Italy. Although retired, Sister Margherita is still treasurer of the Religious Teachers Filippini and has not only translated and adapted the life of Saint Lucy Filippini (*From the Land of the Etruscans*, 1986), but also published a short history of the founding of the Religious Teachers Filippini in the United States (*U.S. Catholic Historian* 6, no. 4, [1987]).

In 1987 Sister Margherita received the National Italian American Bar Association "Inspirational Award" as well as the Columbus Day "Woman of the Year" Award by the *Italian Tribune News*.

Personal interviews with Sister Margherita provided useful information. She is the subject of numerous newspaper and magazine articles: *La Nazione*, July 28, 1957; the *Sunday Star-Ledger* (Newark), May 21, 1978, Sept. 2, 1984, and Oct. 7, 1987; the *New York Times*, Jan. 27, 1984; the *Washington Post*, Sept. 17, 1984; the *Daily Record*, Oct. 11, 1987; and *"Selezione" dal Reader's Digest*, Nov. 1987. A biographical sketch listing her writings appears in *Contemporary Authors*, vols. 37–40 (1979). For a complete bibliography of her works, see *Books in Print* Database, R. R. Bowker Co.

*Simona Balzer*

## ANNE CLARK MARTINDELL, 1914–

Former U.S. ambassador to New Zealand, Anne (Clark) Martindell was born in New York City on July 18, 1914. Her parents, William Clark, third circuit federal judge, and Marjory Bruce (Blair) Clark, American Red Cross volunteer and homemaker, had three children; Martindell was their only daughter.

Martindell received her elementary education at Miss Fine's School in Princeton, NJ, and graduated from St. Timothy's Boarding School in Maryland. After graduation from St. Timothy's she applied and was accepted as a member of the class of 1936 at Smith College. She spent a year at Smith, but left to marry George C. Scott in 1934. Although she never returned to Smith to study, the school lists her as one of the outstanding members of her class.

Martindell and Scott had three children: Marjory, George, and David. The family was living in Montreal when Scott was called into active duty in World War II. During the war, Martindell joined with three women friends to run a small mountain hotel and ski lodge. She

did not earn much money, but it was her first work experience. During this time, she also enrolled for a semester of study at Sir George William College in Montreal.

Her marriage to Scott ended in divorce. She returned to New Jersey and married Jackson Martindell on August 12, 1948. He worked as an investment counselor and publisher, and she took care of her three children from her first marriage and her son, Roger, from her second marriage.

During the fifteen years between her second marriage and her employment as a teacher and reading supervisor at Miss Mason's School in Princeton in 1963 Martindell pursued volunteer work that prepared her for a political career. She regrets the current trend away from volunteer service, citing the essential political skills she learned through such involvement. (Interview, Apr. 6, 1986)

Martindell grew up with strong examples of volunteer service. Her mother devoted much time and energy to the American Red Cross, at one point running its Eastern Region Division. Marjory (Blair) Clark also actively campaigned for her husband when he ran for office. Martindell remembers how impressed she was as a small child, sitting beneath a cloth-covered podium, listening to her mother give a speech. (Interview, Apr. 6, 1986)

Martindell also had contact with her mother's friends, many of whom were active suffragists. Like so many women in the generation before her, Martindell's volunteer work reflects both political and service interests. Over the years, she served as a member of the Friends of the New Jersey State Museum and the New Jersey Historical Society, and she was an early commissioner of the New Jersey Public Broadcasting Authority. Her first appointment was to the Board of Managers of the New Jersey State Diagnostic Center; she later served as its vice president. She was a trustee of Mercer County Community College and president of the New Jersey Neuro-Psychiatric Institute Association. Her early political activity was as a member and, later, director of the Princeton League of Women Voters.

In 1967 she left her teaching position at Miss Mason's School and joined Senator Eugene McCarthy's presidential campaign for a year as New Jersey finance cochair. She attended the 1968 Democratic Convention as an observer and was an active progressive member of the party. This led to working in 1969 as state finance chair of the New Democratic Coalition and secretary of the State Commission on the Reform of the Democratic Party. From 1969 to 1973 she was vice-chair of the Democratic party of New Jersey, chair of the New Jersey delegation to the 1972 convention, and after the convention, national deputy director of the George McGovern presidential campaign.

In 1973 Martindell was elected New Jersey state senator from the Fourteenth Congressional District. She held that office until 1977 and during that time cochaired the committee that led a successful campaign against casino gambling in New Jersey. She was—and she remains—concerned about the "social costs" of gambling: the cost of curing compulsive gamblers, as well as the cost of maintaining police and investigative forces.

Senator Martindell was one of the first prominent New Jersey politicians to support actively President Jimmy Carter's 1976 campaign. Her support led to a presidential appointment to a 20-member advisory board that judged the qualifications of prospective U.S. ambassadors; in 1977 it led to her appointment as director of the Office of United States Foreign Disaster Assistance. In 1979 she began a two-year term as U.S. ambassador to New Zealand.

Ambassador Martindell became the subject of a *New York Times* article almost immediately after her appointment. The article noted her report that the "second thing" New Zealand Prime Minister Robert D. Muldoon said upon meeting her was "I don't like lady politicians." Martindell "felt he meant it." (*New York Times*, July 1, 1979)

She had encountered other men in her years in politics who tried to exclude women, overtly or covertly, from the process. Early in her career, when she was informed about an important New Jersey Democratic party meeting to discuss George McGovern's reform rules (which she had studied carefully), she asked to be included. She was told that the men wanted the meeting to themselves. She drove to the meeting anyway and, upon arrival, had to be announced at the gate. Though she could overhear the unhappy response of the men in charge, she made it to the front door. "Anne, all the boys like you," she recalls one of them saying, "but sometimes we like not having to worry if our language is offensive." Martindell replied, "I don't give a shit what language you use," and she sat down. (Interview, Apr. 6, 1986) It may have been uncharacteristic Martindell diction, but it was characteristic Martindell action. One of the "boys" in the room liked the story so much, he took it to the press. She believes it helped her win her bid for the state senate. (Interview, Apr. 6, 1986)

As director of the Office of United States Foreign Disaster Assistance, Martindell continued to rise to the challenges confronting a woman in a leading role. Once, at a reception in Nicaragua where she was guest of honor, she noticed that she was the only woman in the room. The other women had not only moved to a corner (a common practice), but to another room entirely. She joined them there for a time, despite the language barrier, and they "sat and smiled at each other." When men and women moved into separate groups at receptions during her years as ambassador, Martindell actively tried to bring both groups together. (Interview, Apr. 6, 1986)

Martindell encourages women to become involved in the political process not simply to represent themselves, but because she believes women as a whole are "more idealistic" than many men. (Interview, Apr. 6, 1986) Martin-

dell's decision to concentrate her energy on the peace movement after she completed her service as ambassador reflects her ideal of cooperation. She campaigned actively against the Vietnam War and in the 1980s worked for the New Jersey nuclear freeze movement. She was cochair of a N.J. campaign that resulted in the passage of a referendum calling for a nuclear freeze.

As one of the leaders of Women for a Meaningful Summit, Martindell met with the Soviet leader Mikhail Gorbachev for 40 minutes at the 1985 U.S.-Soviet Union summit in Geneva. Martindell, along with politician Bella Abzug and actress-activist Jane Alexander, took 1.5 million petitions to summit delegates, urging them to proclaim verifiable moratoriums on the testing of land and space weapons and to work with other nations toward global nuclear disarmament.

Martindell is currently chair of the Advisory Board of the Institute of Peace Studies and Conflict Resolution, funded by the New Jersey State Legislature. The institute will provide training for teachers and college students. She also headed a commission for the state legislature to determine whether a state chair in women's studies was needed. The commission said yes, and the Blanche, Edith and Irving Laurie New Jersey Chair in Women's Studies at Douglass College was established. In 1984 Rutgers awarded her an honorary doctor of laws degree.

Martindell continues to be active in foreign affairs, serving as vice-chair of the Speaker's Committee of the Foreign Policy Association and as a member of the Council of American Ambassadors. She founded and served as the first president of the United States-New Zealand Council, an organization devoted to the friendship between the United States and New Zealand. Now she is leading a campaign to interfere with conflict-making behavior—a fight she believes requires action "every day." (*Bernardsville News-Observer Tribune*, Dec. 12, 1985)

An interview with Martindell in Princeton, NJ, on Apr. 6, 1986, provided useful information. Articles in the *New York Times*, July 1, 1979, and the *Bernardsville News-Observer Tribune*, Dec. 12, 1985, provided additional details. Martindell is listed in *Who's Who in American Politics* (1987–88).

*Jill Fritz-Piggott*

## DOROTHY HOPE MARVIN, 1904–1986

Dorothy Hope Marvin, obstetrician and gynecologist, was born in Cleveland, OH, on February 12, 1904, the first child of Walter Taylor and Adelaide Camilla (Hoffman) Marvin, both natives of New York City. Marvin lived most of her life in New Brunswick, NJ, where her father was professor of philosophy and dean at Rutgers University. Her mother, a Barnard graduate and the driving force behind the development of a municipal recreation program, was a vigorous worker for the establishment of a college for women in New Jersey.

Following graduation from New Brunswick High School, Marvin attended Barnard College for two years and then finished at Vassar College, graduating in 1924. Although there were many obstacles for women who aspired to become physicians in the early part of the 20th century, Marvin encountered none of them. She even received encouragement from an uncle who had attended Columbia College of Physicians and Surgeons, the only medical school to which Marvin applied, and Columbia readily accepted her.

After her four years (1924–28) at Columbia, where she was elected to Alpha Omega Alpha (the medical honor society), Marvin obtained a two-year internship at Presbyterian Hospital in New York City, followed by a one-year residency in obstetrics and gynecology at Strong Memorial Hospital in Rochester, NY, where she completed formal training.

Marvin returned to New Brunswick to begin private practice as an obstetrician. There was only one other woman doctor in the city of New Brunswick at the time. Marvin soon gained a reputation among her patients as a dedicated, compassionate, and unassuming physician. In the course of her 47 years in practice, she delivered more than 3,000 babies and performed three therapeutic abortions.

A common practice at that time was the use of general anesthesia for cesarean deliveries. Distressed by the adverse effect of this practice on babies, Marvin chose to employ a local anesthetic (Novocain), resorting to a general anesthetic only when suturing the patient. By using this procedure, she found the infants' condition at delivery much improved.

The prenatal clinic at Middlesex General Hospital (now Robert Wood Johnson University Hospital) became her special interest. Since most patients did not come for treatment until the sixth or seventh month of pregnancy— or until some problem arose—and since she was a firm advocate of early prenatal care, Marvin worked to change this practice among clinic patients.

In 1936 a group of prominent women in the area asked her to set up a birth control clinic at the Middlesex General Hospital. A detailed survey made the previous year by trained social workers in New Brunswick had pointed up the need for this service. Although there were efforts a decade earlier to found such a clinic, community opposition was too strong. But with the onset of the Depression and mounting concern about welfare costs, conditions were now more favorable. Studies showed that relief families had 50 percent more children than families with breadwinners. Moreover, there was evidence of an appalling rise of illegal abortions.

Dr. Marvin recalled, "[I] was not a crusader, but when they asked me to head the clinic I was quite willing to do it." (Interview, Jan. 14, 1986) During her years of medical training in New York, she was well aware of the work of Margaret Sanger and remembered the times Sanger had been jailed. With this consideration in mind, the Maternal Health Committee set aside part of its funds for payment of any possible legal costs that might arise. There was some criticism of the clinic, but according to Marvin, "No one tried to lock me up." However, because of her involvement with the clinic, her staff privileges were discontinued at St. Peter's Hospital, a Catholic institution in New Brunswick.

The clinic, held the second Tuesday of each month, began operation on April 14, 1936. This was seven months before a federal court decision provided legal sanction for birth control, under medical direction, and allowed physicians to receive contraceptives and contraceptive literature through the mails. Marvin knew of no other birth control clinics in the state at that time. Officially, her unit was under the sponsorship of the Maternal Health Committee, which had raised the money to support the clinic that first year. After that time, the clinic was expected to be self-supporting.

Open to all married women residents of the county, patients were accepted upon recommendation of their private physician. Other patients could apply and were often accepted for justified social or physical reasons.

Most physicians had had no training or experience in fitting diaphragms, the favored contraceptive. Soon after opening her private practice Marvin felt the need to obtain such training, so she went to the Holland Rantos Company factory in New York to acquire the proper technique. That company had been established in 1925 and financed by J. Noah Slee, Margaret Sanger's husband, to eliminate the need to smuggle diaphragms into the U.S. from Germany.

For most of the birth control clinic's existence, it was operated solely by Marvin. In 1971 the Planned Parenthood League of Middlesex County opened its clinic at Middlesex General Hospital, replacing this facility.

In 1978, 50 years after completing medical school, friends and former patients of Marvin funded the establishment of the Dorothy H. Marvin Lectures in Obstetrics—the first ever for a living person—at the University of Medicine and Dentistry of New Jersey. That same year Marvin retired to her lifelong summer home in Woods Hole, MA. She died on October 18, 1986, at age 82 in Falmouth, MA, and was buried in the cemetery in Woods Hole, MA.

An interview with Marvin on Jan. 14, 1986, provided useful information. Material on Marvin, most notably clippings from the *Home News* (New Brunswick, NJ), are available at NJ-RU. Her obituary appeared in the *Home News* on Oct. 20, 1986.

*Katheryne C. McCormick*

## ERNEST MAE McCARROLL, ca. 1898–

Ernest Mae McCarroll, a retired physician, was born in Birmingham, AL, on November 29, 1898, the fourth of six children of Ernest Frank McCarroll, a letter carrier, and Mary (Prevard) McCarroll. For approximately 48 years McCarroll practiced general medicine and distinguished herself in the fields of medicine, public health publications, and community service.

At the turn of the century, when McCarroll was born, a black female could expect to lead a life circumscribed by social and career limitations. Whatever the obstacles, Mc-Carroll charted a straight course, beginning with her early education in the Birmingham public school system. She completed secondary school at the high school department of Talledega College in Alabama. In 1917 McCarroll received her A.B. from Talledega. Upon completion of courses in physics and chemistry at Fisk University, she entered the Women's Medical College in Philadelphia, PA, and graduated from medical school in 1925, one of the first black women physicians.

McCarroll did her internship at Kansas City General Hospital No. 2 and then entered general practice in Philadelphia, where she worked for two years. She married Leroy Baxter, a dentist, in 1929 and moved to Newark, NJ, where she had 44 years of successful medical practice.

McCarroll pioneered in attempting to eradicate venereal disease in Newark. Because of her dedication and hard work with patients suffering from sexually transmitted diseases, McCarroll was appointed a clinic physician in the Venereal Disease Division of the Newark Department of Health in 1934. Later she became assistant epidemiologist for the city of Newark. In 1939 McCarroll received her M.S. in public health from the College of Physicians of Columbia University and completed postgraduate studies at Harvard.

McCarroll's article "Standard Curative Treatment of Early and Late Syphilis" appeared in the *Journal of the National Medical Association* in July 1941. Despite the publication of this article and McCarroll's tireless work to acquire advanced qualifications for herself, and to seek to eliminate venereal diseases in the community, she was not appointed to the staff at Newark City Hospital until 1946, at which time she became the first African-American appointee ever named to the staff at Newark City Hospital. McCarroll's appointment was made during the national doctor shortage caused by World War II, which offered increased opportunities to qualified women and African-American physicians. With her long years of distinguished service finally recognized, McCarroll was appointed deputy health officer for the city of Newark and granted courtesy privileges at the Newark Beth Israel Medical Center.

She was a member of the Essex County Medical Society, the State Medical Association of New Jersey, the American Medical Association, the American Venereal Disease Association, and the American Public Health Association. McCarroll served as president of the North Jersey Medical Association and the New Jersey Medical Society while the medical organizations in the southern states and the District of Columbia were still barring membership of African-Americans.

The National Medical Association (NMA) was organized in 1895 by and for black physicians, with its official magazine, the *Journal of the National Medical Association*, first published in 1909. In 1929 McCarroll joined the NMA and took an active role in improving the quality of the *Journal*. She served on its Board of Trustees for sixteen years, from 1949 to 1955 and from 1963 to 1973. For 32 years McCarroll served as a member of the Publication Committee. From its inception in 1955 until 1968 McCarroll was chairperson of the Committee on General Practitioner of the Year Award. In addition, she performed many other services for the NMA, for which she was named "First Lady of the NMA."

McCarroll was the first female physician whose picture appeared on the cover of the *NMA Journal* (July 1963). The *Journal* usually featured only physicians who were retired or deceased on its cover, but an exception was made because of her dedicated service. On August 14, 1973, she was presented with a plaque: "In recognition of her dedicated involvement in the affairs of the National Medical Association—Its Publication Committee and Board of Trustees."

In addition to her work with medical organizations, McCarroll was a board member of the Newark branch of the NAACP, the Union League of Essex County, and the Fuld Neighborhood House. She organized the Neighborhood Guild and was also a member of the National Alliance of Postal Employees. Some of the other organizations and institutions in which McCarroll held membership were the Bethany Baptist Church, the League of Women Voters, the Daughters of Elks, and the Delta Sigma Theta Sorority. She also served as a field worker and member of the Planned Parenthood Association of New Jersey. In 1955 McCarroll was awarded a plaque from the North Jersey Medical Society as its first "General Practitioner of the Year." In recognition of her constant and dedicated service to the citizens of Newark, the city named a building for her; the Department of Health is now located in the Haskins/McCarroll Building.

McCarroll's 1929 marriage to Leroy Baxter ended in divorce in 1939. On August 16, 1958, she and Robert E. Hunter, a bank executive, were married, and that marriage ended when Hunter died.

McCarroll closed her medical practice in July 1973 and moved out of New Jersey. On December 4, 1983, she and Joseph L. Johnson, M.D., were married. They live in Washington, D.C., and Miami, FL.

A telephone interview with McCarroll on Nov. 5, 1985, provided useful information. Christine E. Haycock, "Women Physicians of New Jersey: The Early Era," *Journal of the Medical Society of New Jersey* 81 (1984):773–77, contains a brief entry on McCarroll. Articles on her appeared in issues of the *Journal of the National Medical Association*: 47 (1955):411; 55 (1963):367–68; 65 (1973):544–45. McCarroll's correspondence is available at the Moorland-Spingarn Research Center, Howard University (Washington, D.C.).

*Esther Vincent Lloyd*

## RACHEL K. McDOWELL, 1880–1949

Rachel K. McDowell was a devout woman whose entire adult life was devoted to reporting and editing religious news. Born in Newark (Essex County), NJ, on January 11, 1880, one of five children, she took pride in the fact that her great-grandfather, the Rev. Dr. William Anderson McDowell, and her great-granduncle, the Rev. Dr. John McDowell, had each served as moderator of the General Assembly of the Presbyterian Church. In her own way, she followed in their footsteps, attending Union Theological Seminary in New York, where she studied church history, and writing about the church for daily newspapers and religious journals.

McDowell's education was in Newark, where she attended Miss Robb's and Miss Stanley's private schools, Newark High School, and the Newark Normal and Training School. As a child, her literary achievements were noted: she won cash prizes for her contributions to both Newark and New York newspapers. By the time she was 22 she was a reporter for the *Newark Evening News*. Six years later, in 1908, she went to work as religious news editor of the *New York Herald*, a position she held until 1920, when she left for the *New York Times*.

During the summers McDowell used her vacations to attend Bible conferences and present lectures. She was well known at such places as Northfield, MA; Chautauqua, NY; and Silver Bay on Lake George, NY. One summer she made seventeen religious addresses while traveling on the West Coast.

Throughout her professional life she was a member of the Women's Press Club, taking a leading role in establishing high standards for her peers and personally encouraging young women to look upon reporting and editing as both challenging and rewarding.

McDowell was an ardent advocate of temperate language. She pressed her colleagues at both the *Herald* and the *Times* to avoid blasphemy and profanity of all forms,

organizing in both offices a Pure Language League. She wrote many articles and printed appeals on the subject, especially during the last week in each year. Her colleagues respected her for these efforts.

During the 28 years that her by-line appeared in the *Times*, she also wrote for many church periodicals and lectured frequently on religious topics. For several years she had her own radio program of religious news and for more than a quarter century she provided a weekly article for the *Presbyterian*. She was a regular contributor to the official monthly journal of the Moody Bible Conference and Schools. She was particularly proud of an essay called "Witnesses," which she wrote as a tribute to the life of her sister, Nora McDowell Culver, and was published in 1944 by the American Tract Society.

She provided the *Times* with scores of exclusive stories over the years, gathering news through her far-reaching network of contacts, which included leading pastors and church executives, many of whom were her personal friends. She referred to these clergy friends as "my sky pilots." The editors of the *Times* once commented: "No old-fashioned police reporter running down a clue to a murder could be more persistent than Miss McDowell trying to get at the heart of a story in the world of religion." Whenever she got a "scoop"—which happened frequently—she gloried in the achievement.

McDowell covered important church meetings in many countries and twice had audiences with Pope Paul XI, who both times sent her a signed apostolic benediction. After her first audience in 1935 she wrote a widely reprinted account, "My Audience with the Holy Father." As a result McDowell received 1,200 letters from various countries. She selected 115 of those letters, bound them in a book, and presented them to the pope when she saw him again in 1937.

That year she made a pilgrimage to the Holy Land, which she later described in her column. She regarded "the most thrilling moments of my life" to have been when she knelt in the Church of the Nativity in Bethlehem, in a church in Nazareth, and on the Mount of Olives, the Garden of Gethsemane, and in the Church of the Holy Sepulchre.

She tried, in her own words, "to be a friend to all." Ministers from many Protestant denominations, as well as Roman Catholic priests and Jewish rabbis, were the subjects of articles on her Saturday "church page." Monday's *Times* regularly featured her coverage of the sermons of prominent clergy. She was especially interested in interchurch and interfaith activities and often wrote about contributions to "brotherhood" and peace. Her career was appraised by two New York rabbis shortly after her retirement from the *Times* on December 31, 1948. Rabbi Joel M. Segal praised her spirit of goodwill to all religious groups and credited her with a major role in establishing the methods and style for modern religious reporting. "Today we take for granted the religious reporting that has become an institution in our metropolitan press," he said, adding, "it took such people as Rachel McDowell to set the patterns to give the religious columns permanence." Rabbi William F. Rosenblum said, "It is a pity that Pulitzer Prizes are not given out at the moment for fine religious reporting for the advancement of human relations through the newspaper page."

She was 68 when she retired, having lived for many years at the Hotel Times Square. That location, close to the newspaper office, made it possible for her frequently to entertain her colleagues and then return to her desk in the evening to work on a story that would appear the next morning or later in the week.

On May 24, 1949, she entered University Hospital and was unable to go to Valparaiso University in Indiana, where she was to have received an honorary doctor of laws. The degree was presented to her at the hospital and the hood placed over her shoulders by a member of the American Lutheran Publicity Bureau. The citation described her as an "eminent journalist, learned author, inspiring leader, devoted servant of the church."

McDowell had hoped to write her memoirs after regaining her health, but her condition declined steadily until her death on August 30, 1949. In an unusual gesture, the *Times* took note of her death on the editorial page. The editors acknowledged her religious devotion and her respect for "the spiritual element in human life wherever she found it." But these, they said, were accompanied "by a keen instinct for journalism." Using the superlatives of which news writers are cautious, the *Times* said, "There was no better newspaper woman anywhere around than Rachel K. McDowell."

It was a mark of their respect and affection that the *Times'* staffers turned out in force for McDowell's funeral service held at the Fifth Avenue Presbyterian Church. They were joined by many religious leaders. She was buried in the Fairmont Cemetery in Newark, NJ.

McDowell's values were evident in death, as they had been in life. Her estate, valued at a modest $12,500, was divided among the Missionary Training Institute in Nyack, NY; the Tract Society, to continue the distribution of the essays she had written; Newark's Lutheran Memorial Hospital; and the Newspaper Guild of New York, to be used for printing and distributing literature "protesting against blasphemy and profanity."

Articles about McDowell, including her obituary and eulogies, appeared in the *New York Times*, Jan. 1, Aug. 31, Sept. 3, and Oct. 26, 1949.

*J. Martin Bailey*

## VERA BRANTLEY McMILLON, 1909–1987

Vera (Brantley) McMillon, social worker and student of New Jersey's African-American history, was born on October 8, 1909, on her family's farm in Cedar Springs, GA, the youngest of nine children. Her father, John Bennett Brantley, one of eight children born to former slaves, raised cotton and sugarcane, as well as much of the family's food. One of McMillon's sharpest memories of her father was his ambition to make the thickest cane syrup, grow the best melons, and run a "two-horse farm" in an area where one horse was typical. As an adult she recalled following him around the farm, wearing his old boots and trying to match his long strides. She later credited him with teaching her self-reliance and "everything I know about loans— don't lend what you can't afford to lose." (McMillon, Interview, 1986) Besides farming, John Brantley also served as the local minister of the Good Hopes African Methodist Episcopal Church in Cedar Springs, fulfilling the functions of the traveling minister during his absence.

McMillon's mother, Hennie (Miller) Brantley, died in 1914, leaving eight children. Marie, the eldest, had already left home to attend a teacher training school, so the care of four-year-old McMillon fell to the next sister, Eva, who took over the housekeeping for about five years until their father married again, to Eula Choice.

Like many others, McMillon's family left the South after World War I to become part of the growing northern urban African-American population. In response to a recruiting agent's offer, two of her uncles migrated to Elizabeth, NJ, to work for the Singer Sewing Machine Company. In 1922 McMillon joined her oldest sister and her husband, who had moved to Newark. Following with his second wife, her father also moved north and took a job with the Singer company, but died soon afterward.

McMillon attended the Newark public schools and graduated from Barringer High School in February 1929, one of three African-Americans in her class of 120. The recipient of a grant raised in the Newark school system, she attended Howard University and received a B.A. cum laude in social science in 1932. In 1935 she earned an M.A. in economics from Howard. Concentrating on the field of labor, she wrote a thesis entitled "The Influence of Working Class Movements on Public Education from 1800 to 1860." Throughout her life she kept returning to school for further study. She was certified in elementary education at Newark State College in the late 1930s. She took courses in case writing and alcoholism at the New School for Social Research, New York City, in the 1950s, social work at Columbia and Rutgers universities in the 1960s, and American history at Rutgers in the 1970s.

In 1933 McMillon applied for a job with the Newark Department of Public Welfare. At first she was told, "If we ever need a colored worker, your application will be a very valuable addition to our files" (McMillon, Interview, 1986), but she was eventually hired by the department as a social investigator. Shortly thereafter, on August 8, 1936, she married Grady Allen McMillon, a 1931 graduate of Morgan State College in Baltimore and a health investigator for the Essex County Welfare Board. She and her husband lived for a time in north Newark but moved later to the Weequahic section. They had two sons, Grady Brantley (b. 1944) and Gilbert Allen (b. 1947). McMillon kept her job after her children were born, taking only short maternity leaves. Her older sister, Eva Brown, who had cared for her when their mother died, helped McMillon with her own children, enabling her to balance a full-time career with a family. Later in their lives (1975 on) McMillon and her husband lived in West Orange.

McMillon worked with the Department of Public Welfare in Newark for 37 years, moving from the positions of caseworker, family visitor, junior supervisor, and senior supervisor to supervisor of social caseworkers. She became convinced that most people on public assistance desired work and accepted welfare only for lack of alternatives. This belief led her to develop the Positive Approach to Welfare Program, a predecessor of the Welfare Incentive Program (WIN). From 1965 to 1966 she supervised a pilot project on Rehabilitation of the Hard Core Unemployed, a $3 million job-training program federally financed under the Economic Opportunity Act.

A participant throughout her career in black church, club, and college alumni affairs, McMillon became especially active in state and community affairs in the 1960s. In 1964 she was appointed to the New Jersey Commission on the Status of Women by Governor Richard Hughes. She served on both the New Jersey Committee Against Discrimination in Housing and the Advisory Committee for the Robert Bruce Halfway House in Newark. She was a founder of the Tri-City Citizens Union for Progress, a neighborhood organization serving Newark, Jersey City, and East Orange with programs in health, education, housing rehabilitation, and child care.

After her retirement in 1970, and until 1973, she was an instructor in the Arts and Sciences Department at Kean College in Union, teaching, supervising student teachers in the field, and helping to coordinate inner-city programs.

McMillon was perhaps most noted for her advocacy of the teaching of African-American history, an interest that started in college and continued throughout her life. Noticing the absence of information on blacks in an elementary school textbook on New Jersey history, she began in the early 1960s to search for ways of bringing to the public's attention what seemed to her a glaring omission. It was not, she noted later, that African-American history did not exist, but only that it existed "largely in people's closets." She added, "Real history takes into account the contributions made by all races, all professions, and all

people." (McMillon, Interview, 1986)

Inspired by a Howard professor, MARION THOMPSON WRIGHT, she and another Howard graduate, MYRA SMITH KEARSE, wrote and produced a weekly radio program on WLIB for several months in 1963 on contributions of blacks to New Jersey history. Then in 1964 McMillon was asked to address the annual professional conference of the New Jersey Historical Society. Her lecture sparked the formation of the Librarians' Committee on the Negro in New Jersey, and she and KEARSE served as consultants to the committee's subsequent work, *New Jersey and the Negro: A Bibliography, 1715–1966*, the first such compilation for New Jersey.

For the next 20 years McMillon pursued her own study of African-American history, becoming a frequent visitor at the Newark Public Library. She was appointed to the New Jersey Historical Society's Committee for the Study of Negro Life and History and then served as a society trustee. The North Jersey Chapter of Links, Inc., recognized her contributions to black history by awarding her the chapter's Bicentennial Award in 1976.

McMillon died after a long illness, at age 77, at St. Barnabas Medical Center in Livingston on February 20, 1987. Her husband had predeceased her in 1985. Her funeral was held at St. James African Methodist Episcopal Church in Newark, where she had been an active member since 1944. She was buried in Fairmount Cemetery in Newark.

Interviews with McMillon in Sept. and Oct. 1986 in West Orange, NJ, provided biographical information. Her obituary appeared in the *Sunday Star-Ledger* (Newark, NJ), Feb. 22, 1987.

*Ruth T. Penner*

## CHARLOTTE NICHOLS MONTGOMERY, 1904–

Charlotte (Nichols) Montgomery, writer, consumer issues journalist, advertising and consumer consultant, was born in Brooklyn, NY, on March 31, 1904. She was the middle child of three children (two daughters and a son) born to Roswell Nichols, a New York lawyer, and Margaret (Pellett) Nichols, a Vassar graduate and suffragist. Both parents' ancestors were farmers from upstate New York.

While Montgomery was very young, the family moved to New Jersey, first to Roselle for a few years, and then to Westfield, where the children grew to adulthood. Montgomery was raised in a gregarious, affluent, doting family that instilled her with confidence to fulfill her potential. She retained childhood memories of her mother's dedication to the struggle for women's voting rights.

After attending public elementary school, Montgomery was enrolled at Hartridge, a private high school for girls in Plainfield, NJ. Upon graduation, she chose Vassar, her mother's alma mater, where she concentrated her interests on English, history, and economics. Her flair for writing gained her the managing editorship of the college newspaper, and in 1927 she graduated Phi Beta Kappa with an A.B. She returned to Westfield and commuted to New York, where she worked for various advertising agencies.

On a blind date arranged through mutual friends she met advertising executive Harry M. Montgomery. Following their marriage on October 6, 1928, in New York City, the newlyweds rented an apartment in Manhattan, where Montgomery continued to work until the birth of Sarah, their first child, in 1930. Upon the birth of Harry, Jr., their second child, in 1932, the family moved to Westfield, where they raised their children.

During World War II Montgomery began a new phase of her career. While her husband joined the army and rose first to lieutenant-colonel and then to military governor of the city of Heilbronn in occupied Germany, Montgomery began writing copy in her husband's adverstising business. She credits Emma Watson, her committed live-in maid of 22 years, with supplying the necessary support to free her for her revitalized career. Always in the wings, as well, were her devoted widowed father and her unmarried sister, who lived nearby.

Shortly after World War II, when women were returning to the home, Montgomery ventured into male-dominated territory. She approached the editors of *Tide*, the advertising trade journal, and laid before them an innovative concept—a column expressing the views of the intelligent consumer. Technological advances during the war had generated myriad new products, and Montgomery anticipated the need to critique these proliferating "miracle" goods. The editors agreed to the experiment, and in the January 30, 1948, issue, Montgomery's column, "The Woman's Viewpoint," was launched. Montgomery was the sole woman on the staff of the magazine and the only writer given a by-line. The experiment lasted seven years.

Montgomery continued to contribute freelance articles, all dealing with consumer concerns, to various magazines—*Nation's Business*, *National Observer*, and *Redbook*, among others. Her articles attracted the attention of the editor-in-chief of *Good Housekeeping*, who requested she write a column for the magazine. The *Good Housekeeping* articles spawned Montgomery's series on "the woman and her car" in an era when women were assumed to lack the aptitude for understanding such complicated machinery. Additional columns for the magazine soon reflected other consumer issues.

After four years, *Good Housekeeping* acquired her column from *Tide* and made her a contributing editor. In June 1955 she began a general consumer column for the magazine. At first entitled "Strictly as a Customer," Montgom-

ery's adman husband suggested the change to "Speaker for the House." The column thrived for 27 years under Montgomery's by-line and remains a current feature of *Good Housekeeping*.

When asked what she wanted to be remembered for, Montgomery's answer was her preoccupation with and dedication to consumerism. A pioneer for consumer rights, she impelled manufacturers to become more consumer oriented and educated her readers to become better consumers. She proposed and popularized the idea of attaching care and content labels to garments.

Montgomery was one of the early advocates of what is today called market research. She understood the wisdom of gathering information at the source—from the potential buyers—to determine what it was they wanted in a product. She was hired as a consultant in this area by General Foods and other companies.

Other accomplishments included the publication of *Charlotte Montgomery's Handbook for Women Drivers*, sponsored by Cities Services Oil Company, which emphasized car maintenance, operation, and safe driving in its text and photos, instead of the stereotypical car ads using women as adornments to lure male consumers. Montgomery wrote articles in the automotive field, including Ford's "Buyers' Digest of New Car Facts" and "Fine Cars," its Lincoln-Mercury publication. Speaking engagements for Exxon and Phillips Petroleum were sandwiched into Montgomery's crowded schedule. She did most of her writing from home, where she maintained an office and employed Marjorie Stallings Pavelec as her secretary. For 35 years Pavelec helped her to respond to most of the several hundred letters a month received from her readers.

Throughout her career, Montgomery remained in demand as a speaker for clubs, consumer groups and forums, trade and business organizations, such as the Association of National Advertisers and the National Automobile Dealers' Association. Montgomery was accompanied by her husband on many of the trips to speaking engagements. His constant support and encouragement facilitated the pursuit of her career. He died in 1975.

Montgomery has achieved considerable recognition during her career. Among her coveted awards are Advertising Woman of the Year, awarded by the Advertising Federation of America (1953); Headliner of the Year (1973), by Women in Communications; and Distinguished Service to Consumers Award (1977), by the U.S. Council of Better Business Bureaus.

She has served as officer and board member of several national organizations and is an honorary member of Theta Sigma Phi, National Professional Society for Women in Journalism and Communications. A memorable experience, by her own account, was her appointment as voting delegate to the National Women's Conference in Houston in 1977.

Montgomery lives in Westfield in the home where she reared her children and wrote most of her columns. Friendly, gracious, and keenly interested in affairs of the day, she was slowed by a stroke in 1982. Recently, she commented that even at the pinnacle of her prolific career her compensation was not commensurate with that of her male colleagues; but in those days, she recalled, women did not "make waves" and risk the stigma of being known as aggressive. Montgomery contrasts her former philosophy with her current thinking: "When I was in my twenties, people said I thought like a man and I was flattered. Today I would rather be told that I think like a woman." (Montgomery, Interview, Dec. 1985)

Interviews with Montgomery and Marjorie Stallings Pavelec, her secretary, took place in December 1985. Montgomery maintains a collection of her diaries and correspondence. See also "Pioneer Consumerist Still Personalizes Advice," *Newark Star-Ledger*, Feb. 14, 1982.

*Marcia Kestenbaum*
*Lynn Wenzel*

## AMELIA BERNDT MOORFIELD, 1876–1950

Amelia (Berndt) Moorfield, suffragist and peace advocate, was born in Newport, KY, Unlike the Non April 17, 1876, the only child of Caroline (Marsh) and Gustave Berndt. Moorfield, whose parents moved to Newark, NJ, when she was a child, left no record of her formative and early adult years. She seems to have come into her own after her marriage to Frank Moorfield, a Newark watch case materials manufacturer. In 1909 when she was 33, Hannah, her only child, was born. The role of housewife and mother did not suffice for Moorfield, and she also worked as office manager in her husband's factory, her first sortie into the public sphere.

In 1914, Moorfield was recruited for the cause of woman suffrage by Mina Van Winkle, president of the Newark branch of the Women's Political Union (WPU), a woman suffrage group founded in 1908 in Newark as the Equity League of Self-Supporting Women. Unlike the New Jersey Woman's Suffrage Association (NJWSA) headed by LILLIAN FEICKERT, the WPU believed that the proper strategy for gaining suffrage was by an amendment to the U.S. Constitution rather than amendments to state constitutions. However, the NJWSA saw New Jersey as crucial in the effort for a suffrage breakthrough on the industrialized and ethnically diverse eastern seaboard. A referendum to add a woman suffrage amendment to the N.J. Constitution was set for October 1915.

Despite tactical differences, the WPU cooperated fully with the NJWSA to work for the New Jersey amendment. Moorfield had become financial secretary of the New Jersey branch of the WPU, and her young daughter was adopted as mascot of the group. Moorfield's main responsibility was fund raising, which she accomplished by sponsoring luncheons, dinners, and ballroom dances. She also collected material, both pro and con, on the suffrage issue to enable the suffragists to make informed responses to their opponents.

Moorfield later recalled that occasionally she would emerge from behind the scenes to tour the state with her fellow suffragists in a temperamental old car named Victor. On the road she expressed her own conservative viewpoint on feminism. She sought to allay men's fears that if women entered the male preserve of politics they would abandon family life and wear male attire. The antisuffrage literature Moorfield collected was filled with such charges and she was extremely sensitive to them. She abhorred the "dreadful picketings" and demonstrations that militant suffragists engaged in (see ALISON TURNBULL HOPKINS). Moorfield's fund-raising activities became more critical than ever as N.J. suffragists focused their energies on a federal constitutional amendment after the defeat of the amendment to the N.J. constitution in 1915. She continued to work with the WPU until the ratification of the 19th Amendment in 1920, after which the WPU merged with the newly formed League of Women Voters.

In the early 1920s Moorfield became involved in the international peace movement. Women had taken the lead in founding many liberal and radical peace organizations in the World War I era; Jane Addams had helped establish the Women's Peace Party in 1915 and its successor, the Women's International League for Peace and Freedom (WILPF), in 1919. In 1922 Moorfield joined the New Jersey branch of the WILPF. In 1923 her husband died and she began to devote herself completely to the cause of peace. Her daughter was recruited, and peace became a mother-daughter enterprise. The organizational skills Moorfield demonstrated in the suffrage movement prompted her rise to vice-chair and publicity chair, and in 1927 she was elected state chair. Under Moorfield's direction, the New Jersey WILPF was organized according to congressional districts and each district had a leader who organized letter-writing campaigns to put maximum pressure on congressional representatives.

The first priority of the WILPF was disarmament. In line with this policy, Moorfield proclaimed it a fallacy that huge arms appropriations were the key to the preservation of peace. In February 1928 Moorfield took charge of the New Jersey campaign to defeat the Vinson Bill, a proposal for $616 million for new naval programs, and organized a massive letter-writing campaign against the bill. The WILPF had a powerful ally in President Herbert Hoover and the Vinson Bill was defeated. When Senator Gerald Nye (Rep., ND) initiated an investigation into the munitions industry, he received strong support from the

WILPF, with the New Jersey affiliate extremely active.

Moorfield's daughter, Hannah Shannon, rose to be the WILPF's publicity chair, a vital post since it encompassed the educational efforts the WILPF fostered. Radio networks provided peace advocates with free air time and they used it to disseminate their ideas. Responding, in part, to the WILPF's urgent appeals, Princeton University was among the institutions that added courses in international relations to their curriculum.

Moorfield sought to associate the WILPF with holidays that had a peace motif, such as Mother's Day, Armistice Day, Interracial Sunday, Good Will Day, and Peace Sunday. In 1935 she added the 20th anniversary of the founding of the WILPF to the list. Moorfield put special emphasis on Kellogg Pact Day, commemorating annually the adoption of the Kellogg-Briand Pact of 1928, an agreement negotiated by American Secretary of State Frank B. Kellogg and French Foreign Minister Aristide Briand in which the two governments renounced war as an instrument of national policy. Eventually the treaty was signed by 65 countries, including Germany, Japan, and the USSR. Regardless of the different intentions of the signatories and the lack of any provision for enforcement, the pact was widely hailed as a significant step toward securing a peaceful world.

When the Japanese made a travesty of the Kellogg-Briand pact with their attack on China in 1932, the WILPF strategy was to keep the conflict localized. Moorfield added her voice to other peace advocates, urging the United States to cooperate with the League of Nations. Like her colleagues, she pressed for U.S. involvement in the World Court's peace efforts. Moorfield, a firm believer in *vox populi*, asked that letters be written commending those New Jersey congressmen who had voted in favor of cutting $60 million from a military appropriations bill; she also sought support for a congressional resolution calling for an amendment to the Constitution for a referendum before war could be declared. Peace advocates everywhere were heartened by Moorfield's slogan: "Do not give way to pessimism." She ended a memo on the Sino-Japanese conflict (1932) by saying, "Remember, during war everyone works day and night. This is the time to wage peace by working as hard to prevent war."

Mussolini's invasion of Ethiopia (1935) was a turning point for the WILPF, and thus for Moorfield. She had to confront the fact that there would be no peace so long as unappeasable aggressors were loose in the world. Moorfield's branch of the WILPF joined with the League Against War and Fascism and began to focus on picketing the consulates of offending countries. On October 20, 1935, she was involved in mass picketing against the Italian vice-consul, who had an office at the Federal Trust Building in Newark. Moorfield wrote of the event three days later to Dorothy Pennell, treasurer of the New Jersey

WILPF. Since Mussolini was recruiting among Italian-Americans, Moorfield felt the peace advocates' impact could be measured by the fact that Italian-Americans appeared at the demonstration protesting the aggressive policies of Mussolini.

After the outbreak of World War II, Moorfield continued to be active in public life. She became president of the New Jersey Women's Press Club, the Women's Press Club of New York, and a director of the National Opera Club. She died of heart disease on February 24, 1950, at age 73, in her daughter's home in Nutley, NJ. She is buried at Evergreen Cemetery in Elizabeth, NJ.

Moorfield's papers dealing with her suffrage work are available at the NJ-HS. Correspondence relating to her work with the New Jersey WILPF is available at P-SC. Her obituary appeared in the *New York Times*, Feb. 27, 1950.

*Sylvia Strauss*

## NELLE KATHARINE MORTON, 1905–1987

Nelle Katharine Morton, churchwoman and educator, advocate of racial and economic justice, and pioneer in feminist theology, was born in a mountain cabin in Sullivan County, TN, on January 7, 1905. She was the first of three daughters of hardworking and deeply religious Scottish-Irish parents, Mary Katharine (O'Dell) Morton, a teacher and graduate of a teacher's academy, and Jonathan Morrell Morton, a merchant with an elementary school education.

"Appalachian women have a reputation of being strong persons. My mother was a very strong woman and had deep commitments," Morton said, and added that one of the deepest was to educate her daughters. Morton explained that providing education equally to women and men was part of the inherited ethos of the Scottish-Irish Presbyterians who had settled that part of Appalachia. (Gallagher, rolls 3 and 4, 5) Morton received her A.B. in 1925 from Flora McDonald College. After graduation, she moved to New York City and enrolled in Biblical Seminary, where, in 1931, she received a masters in religious education. The journey that was to become a central fact of her life, as well as a shaping image for it, had begun.

Morton returned to the South, to Richmond, VA, where for seven years in the 1930s she functioned as the director of youth programs for her denomination, the Presbyterian Church in the U.S. Here she organized interracial youth camps that flouted the Jim Crow laws then prevalent in the South. She later went to work for the Fellowship of Southern Churchmen, an integrated group committed to racial and economic justice, where for five years in the late 1940s she held the post of general secretary. During this period Morton's life was a struggle against the tides of dominant opinion. A firestorm of religious fundamentalism was sweeping the South. Northern industrialists, moving south to avoid paying higher wages, sub-sidized evangelists to aid their cause, and the same re-ligious language pervaded the political arena. Morton described the times this way: "Politicians would ride buses with their New Testaments in their pockets and pull them out to prove . . . that the blacks were inferior or that the Jews had no place in that area and that labor organizing was a work of the devil." (Gallagher, rolls 3 and 4, 6) It took courage and involved significant risk for Morton to speak out as she did for a different view of Christian justice.

A severe health crisis brought this chapter of Morton's life to a close. As part of her work for the Fellowship of Southern Churchmen, Morton covered thirteen southern states. "I did not have my roots down anywhere," she said. (Gallagher, roll 5, 2) Ill and in need of rest, she decided to return home and stay with her father, who was by then a widower.

Back in Tennessee, Morton's work took a new and un-expected direction. Employed by the Tennessee and Vir-ginia boards of education, she spent more than two years developing curricula for disabled children. This work, which undoubtedly fed her vision that "every human being in the world is holy" (Gallagher, roll 28, 3), is described by Morton as "one of the richest experiences I ever had." (Gallagher, roll 5, 3)

In 1956 Morton accepted an invitation to join the fac-ulty of the Theological School of Drew University in Madison, NJ, to teach Christian education. Morton arrived when this Methodist seminary was a center for the study of German theology. Again she found herself battling against prevailing currents. While the majority of the faculty members were focused on the importance of words and of reason, Morton came to realize that "we live out of our images; not out of our concepts or ideas." (Morton, *The Journey Is Home*, 31) Work in Switzerland with the psychol-ogist Jean Piaget during a sabbatical leave in 1962–63 helped her understand the way in which children acquire the deep images that usually shape their lifelong view of the world. Religion, she realized, was the central store-house for such imagery. Painfully, she also came to see that contemporary Christian images were deeply flawed by rac-ism, classism, and sexism.

The Drew years crystallized Morton's dedication to the "woman movement" (phrasing she insisted on because she found it dynamic and nonparochial). On realizing the theo-logical implications of what was happening among femi-nists, "my whole life just fell open," Morton said. (Gal-lagher, rolls 3 and 4, 2) Separate life paths marked "women," "justice," and "theology" converged to form one road. In 1969 Morton offered at Drew what may well have been the first course given anywhere in "Theology, Lan-guage, and Women."

With her characteristic openness, Morton turned late in life to feminist spirituality, giving a careful hearing to women involved in the Goddess movement. In 1977 she concluded that "in a sexist culture and sexist religion the option for the Goddess may be the only, the only sane, redemptive move." (Morton, *The Journey Is Home*, 145) Yet, with an equally important emphasis on the need for religious imagery to remain dynamic, she said that the sig-nificance of the Goddess lay in her ability "to make herself dispensable." (Morton, *The Journey Is Home*, 144)

Morton retired from Drew in 1971, never having been promoted to full professor in spite of a national reputation as one of the leaders in women's theology. Recognition came later. In March 1984 she was awarded an honorary doctor of humane letters degree by Drew University on the occasion of the fifth annual Nelle Morton Lecture sponsored by the Women's Center of the Theological School.

In 1976 Morton journeyed to Claremont, CA, where she continued in her retirement years to counsel and en-courage women and men searching for ways to acknowl-edge and give expression to feminist theology and spir-ituality. On July 14, 1987, Nelle Morton died at age 82, after a long-term blood disorder. She is buried in Shipley's Cemetery, near Bristol, TN.

Throughout her life, Morton was committed to move-ment, to journey. At times the sense of rootlessness pained her. The work of her eighth decade was about dis-covering that "the journey is home," the title of a collec-tion of a decade's worth of writing and speaking, published in 1985. In the preface to this volume Morton wrote, "Home is a movement, a quality of relationship, a state where people seek to be 'their own,' and increasingly re-sponsible for the world."

An important collection of Morton's speeches and writings is *The Journey Is Home* (1985). Her letters and papers, copies of her pub-lished work and speeches, as well as audio and videotapes are available at the Historical Foundation of the Presbyterian and Re-formed Churches (Montreat, NC). A documentary film, *Nelle's Journey*, tells the story of her life. Tapes and films of Morton's classes and lectures are available at the Christian Resource Cen-ter, the Theological School, NJ-DU.

*Karen McCarthy Brown*

## MARY YAMASHITA NAGAO, 1920–1985

Mary Chiyoko (Yamashita) Nagao, advocate of mi-nority rights and leader in Japanese-American affairs, was born on December 2, 1920, in San Bernardino, CA, and named Chiyoko, the only child of Japanese immigrants, Moro(za)emon and Fuki (Mochizuki) Yamashita.

Her father had left home at an early age to go to sea, then worked on the railroads in the United States, before he began raising vegetables in East Los Angeles, CA. Her mother had been widowed and had left two daughters and two sons in Japan with relatives when she came to America to remarry. She had not known her husband personally before this, but was introduced by her brother and his family, who lived in Los Angeles.

Nagao's childhood was sheltered and happy despite increasingly overt discrimination against people of Japanese ancestry on the West Coast. Before starting at Riggin Avenue Grammar School in Los Angeles she spent a year with her mother in Japan. Known as Mary, she studied home economics and graduated from Garfield High School in 1938. Although she was a talented singer who had performed on the radio and achieved success in singing contests, she soon gave up a promising career for marriage and a family.

On March 19, 1939, she married Charles Toshimasa Nagao, an American-born but Japanese-educated sales clerk, and they moved in with her parents on their small truck farm. Pauline Nobumi and Irene Kiyomi, their twin daughters, were born on October 5 that year.

The Japanese bombing of Pearl Harbor on December 7, 1941, increased the extreme anti-Japanese sentiments already present on the West Coast. On February 19, 1942, Franklin D. Roosevelt signed Executive Order 9066, authorizing, on the grounds of "military necessity," the removal and relocation of 120,000 people of Japanese ancestry, most of whom were American citizens by birth. Although this was in direct and flagrant violation of their civil rights, most Japanese-Americans felt they could best help the war effort and prove their loyalty to America by cooperating fully with the government. That spring Nagao's family and her parents were sent to Manzanar Relocation Center in Owens Valley, CA, about 250 miles northeast of Los Angeles and just south of the small town of Independence.

The three generations of Nagao's family, identified as Family No. 3564, occupied a single room in Building No. 13 of Block 22 on the northern side of Manzanar, which housed 10,000 people in rows of drab, tar-paper-covered barracks. This "was an area of violent natural contrasts" with hot days and cold nights. "Nearby to the westward was Mt. Whitney, stabbing the sky at 14,495 feet, the highest mountain in the Continental United States. Not far to the southeast was Death Valley, and the lowest point in the nation—282 feet below sea level." (Bosworth, *America's Concentration Camps*, 143–44)

Life there was stressful and traumatic; but Nagao soon began work as a seamstress in the industrial division of the camp garment factory, which produced work clothing for evacuees. She was eager to help others more directly, so while her mother took care of the twins, she found a job using her linguistic abilities, lively energy, and friendliness as a social worker and liaison with camp authorities. Although the family, like most others, had suffered financial losses in the hasty, compulsory evacuation, the pay for all

jobs was minimal, far less than that paid in the outside world. Throughout the internment Nagao also kept busy with crafts and handiwork and delighted in surprising others with items she had made. She and her husband later felt justly proud that they managed to hold their family together in spite of the negative aspects of camp life.

Toward the end of the war, Nagao and her family relocated to New Jersey, where C. F. Seabrook's frozen foods company was expanding, although there were wartime labor shortages. A shrewd businessman, C. F. Seabrook was so impressed with the reliability and diligence of the first few Japanese-American workers he had hired that he arranged with the government to recruit workers from the various internment camps. When Nagao heard that they could relocate with other Japanese-Americans to work for Seabrook on a six-month contract with modest housing provided, she soon persuaded her very reluctant husband that they should seize this opportunity to make a new life for themselves in the East. In December 1944 the extended family arrived in Seabrook in Upper Deerfield Township (Cumberland County), NJ.

Mary Yamashita Nagao, c. 1955, arranging table flowers for the annual chow mein dinner of the Seabrook Chapter of the Japanese American Citizens League. *Courtesy, private collection.*

With zeal born of the determination to prove herself a good American citizen, Nagao plunged into community life. At Seabrook Farms she rose to the position of production forewoman and became a union representative for the Amalgamated Food and Meat Cutters' Union, Local No. 56, representing frozen food and cannery workers in southern New Jersey, many of whom were immigrants. She and her husband became active members of the Deerfield Presbyterian Church, where she sang in the choir, and joined the Women's Guild and the Ambassadors for Christ. First among the Japanese Americans in the area to own an automobile, Nagao and her husband willingly drove others to appointments, especially older people who needed help with English.

At 4 feet 9 inches tall, Nagao was outgoing, forthright, and outspoken, which was unusual for a Japanese-American woman. This was partly because, as an only child and a U.S. citizen, she was responsible for the care and welfare of her aged, noncitizen parents. However, because her parents lived with her until their deaths in the 1950s, she was freed of some household and child-care responsibilities. After many difficulties—but much to the family's delight—Charles Scott, a son, was born to Nagao and her husband on August 27, 1950. Nagao enjoyed a close relationship with her children, and although she always worked outside the home, she was involved in the Brownies, which she started at Seabrook for her daughters, and in the Cub Scouts.

In 1956 Nagao began work at the Cumberland County Clerk's Office in Bridgeton, about 20 miles away. A devoted and dedicated employee, she was supervisor of the microfilm section at the time of her retirement in 1981. Later she served on the Atlantic Electric Company Roundtable Committee.

She derived most satisfaction and enjoyment, however, from her work with senior citizens. She was president of the volunteer advisory group to the Cumberland County Office on Aging and on the Advisory Board of the Retired Senior Voluntary Program. On May 29, 1984, she received the Outstanding Senior Citizen Award from Governor Thomas Kean for her "leadership, guidance and efforts on behalf of the Elderly Population of New Jersey." On June 16, 1984, Nagao and her husband were presented with a citation by the Board of Chosen Freeholders praising them as "Outstanding Citizens of Cumberland County."

Nagao devoted countless hours to the Seabrook chapter of the Japanese American Citizens League (JACL). She held every office, including president (1976), and was awarded the national JACL Silver Pin in recognition of her contributions. In 1984 she was the program chairperson for the special Installation and Recognition Dinner marking the 40th anniversary of the arrival of Japanese-Americans in Seabrook. This involved research to produce a souvenir program, and Nagao later wrote a historical account, "Japanese Americans in Upper Deerfield" (1984), which is kept on file at the Municipal Building in Seabrook.

Despite debilitating rheumatoid arthritis, Nagao made numerous presentations at churches and schools on Japanese culture and history, participated in the Cultural Awareness Festival, and hosted foreign exchange students of different nationalities in her home. She supported her husband fully in his community activities and ensured that her children had a college education. A renowned cook, Nagao taught adult education classes in Oriental gourmet cooking and studied with a top culinary expert in 1972 when she visited Japan with her husband, by then an executive with Wheaton Industries in Millville, NJ. Always an efficient and thorough organizer, Nagao was often called to help with wedding arrangements for people of all races and religions.

Nagao's hobby was collecting jewelry and other objects depicting tortoises, for she admired their patience, perseverance, and determination. People likewise admired Nagao's determination to earn respect and guarantee rights for Japanese-Americans and all minorities, but they also responded to her vitality, warmth, and generosity. She always gave unstintingly of herself, fulfilling her pledge as a JACL member "to actively assume my duties and obligations as a citizen, cheerfully and without any reservations whatsoever, in the hope that I may become a better American in a greater America."

After a short illness Nagao died of cancer in Philadelphia, PA, at age 64, on May 14, 1985. She is buried in New Jersey in the Deerfield Presbyterian Church cemetery. A resolution paying "tribute to her outstanding record of dedicated service to the citizenry of this State" was introduced to the New Jersey State Assembly in Trenton after her death, and the most valuable scholarship awarded by the Seabrook chapter of the JACL has been named in her honor.

A brief biography of Nagao appears in *Women to Be Remembered* (1986), a project of the Bridgeton (NJ) Research Club. F. Alan Palmer, *This Place Called Home* (1985), includes material compiled by Nagao, and the chapter "The Japanese of Upper Deerfield" is dedicated to her. Allan Bosworth, *America's Concentration Camps* (1967), details life in the camps. Biographical information on Nagao was provided in interviews with her husband, Charles Nagao, and with F. Alan Palmer. Obituaries appeared in the *Bridgeton (NJ) Evening News*, and the *Vineland (NJ) Times Journal*, May 16, 1985.

*Kirsten Jensen Cais*

## ELLEN NOGUCHI NAKAMURA, 1919–

Ellen (Noguchi) Nakamura, journalist, was the first Japanese-American woman to settle in Seabrook (Cumberland County), NJ, two years after she and her parents and older brother, Mamoru, were sent to an internment camp in Jerome, AR. She was born on July 10, 1919, in Tulare, CA, the third child of Sato (Kunimoto) and Suyekichi Noguchi, successful farmers who emigrated to California from Kumamoto, Japan, after the turn of the century. Her father came to Tulare in 1905 to seek a more prosperous life and her mother followed in 1918. Her two brothers were born in Japan.

While growing up in Tulare, Nakamura helped her parents operate their fruit and vegetable farm and their roadside market. She graduated in 1939 from the College of the Sequoias in Visalia, CA, with an associate of arts degree in journalism. As a freelancer, she wrote feature articles for the *Rafu Shimpo*, a Japanese-American newspaper in Los Angeles, and the *Nichi Bei*, a San Francisco newspaper. Her stories were based on the people she met while operating her parents' roadside market.

Farming ended for Nakamura and her family when they were sent to the Fresno (CA) Assembly Center for five months (May-October 1942) during World War II, after President Franklin D. Roosevelt signed Executive Order No. 9066 on February 19, 1942. The fateful order gave the army the authority to move Americans of Japanese ancestry to ten remote internment camps. While at the Fresno center, the young journalist edited a newspaper called *Grapevine* and a booklet, *Vignette*, detailing the stories of life in an assembly center.

Like 120,000 other Japanese-Americans—both American-born Nisei and their parents, alien Issei—the Noguchis were sent to an internment camp with rude barracks surrounded by barbed wire and armed military guards. Nakamura recalls that their trip to Jerome, AR, was the loneliest journey of their lives: "We traveled for four days on a train. The land was desolate, but the only thing that reassured me, that gave me courage, was that the stars were the same ones that shone on us in California." (Nakamura, Interview, Jan. 13, 1987) An older brother, Suyeyoshi, had returned to Japan in 1940 to run the Noguchis' ancestral estate and farm. The rest of the family spent two years from October 1942 to June 1944 in the camp, where they lived in cramped quarters and suffered from their enforced idleness.

In April 1944 Nakamura was the only woman to serve on a three-person Relocation Planning Commission of the Jerome camp. Commission members were invited by Charles Franklin Seabrook to visit Seabrook Farms in southern New Jersey, then the largest farm and food-processing facility in the world, to study the possibility of family relocation.

The delegation spent several days examining working, housing, and educational opportunities. "When I saw south Jersey with its beautiful farms I knew this was the right place for us and that we would be happy to move there from Jerome," she recalls. (Nakamura, Interview, Jan. 13, 1987) Seabrook was providing food for the Allied forces and needed many laborers to work in his factory, which operated 24 hours a day. He believed that Japanese-Americans had the work ethic he required. Nakamura gave talks to hundreds of Japanese-Americans, describing Seabrook Farms and urging them to relocate there.

A few months later, on May 27, 1944, she married Kiyomi Nakamura, a native of Fowler, CA, whom she had known previously, and the young couple moved to Seabrook. Nakamura was the first woman to arrive in the area. "It took a lot of courage," she recalls. "My husband still had a farm in Fowler, and we had the opportunity to return to the part of the country we knew the best. Seabrook was an unknown and would be a tremendous challenge." (Nakamura, Interview, Jan. 13, 1987)

For the next three years Nakamura served as liaison between Seabrook Farms and the camp evacuees. Working closely with Charles Seabrook, Nakamura acted as interpreter for the elderly Issei who did not speak English and helped to provide housing, education, medical care, and recreation and responded to emergencies. "Mr. Seabrook was a man of substance," said Nakamura. "He made us all feel welcome and did everything possible to assist the 2,500 Japanese-Americans who moved to Cumberland County. He called me into his office for daily meetings. He relied on me." (Nakamura, Interview, Jan. 13, 1987)

Two years after they moved to south Jersey, the Nakamuras bought 73 acres in Elmer and started a vegetable and soybean farm. Their son, Kennon, was born in 1945, the first Japanese-American baby conceived in Seabrook. The couple were among the originators of the Seabrook Jodo Shin Buddhist Temple, and Nakamura was named one of the five outstanding Buddhist Sunday school teachers in 1975 and became a lay speaker in 1976.

She worked with the Seabrook Housing Corporation until her retirement in 1983. She was president of the Japanese American Citizens League (JACL) from 1972 to 1974 and during her tenure a weekly radio program, "The Fuji Hour," was launched on station WSNJ in Bridgeton in 1974 (it lasted until 1986). Nakamura was a recipient of the JACL silver pin and the sapphire pin, awarded for lifetime service (1984). Since 1982 she has served on the editorial board of the *Pacific Citizen*, as Eastern District representative for the national JACL publication.

Nakamura is the coordinator-narrator for the Seabrook Minyo (folk) Dancers. "Our group really put Seabrook on the map," she recalled. "We performed at the Smithsonian Folklife Festivals during 1975 and 1976. In 1977 we were first on the program for 'People's Inaugural' festivities for the Inauguration of President Jimmy Carter at the National Visitors Center and John F. Kennedy Center for the Performing Arts." (Nakamura, Interview, Jan. 13, 1987) The troupe was honored by Governor Thomas H. Kean of New Jersey for representing the state at the 1983 Festival of American Folklife on the National Mall in Washington, D.C. Many of its performances were televised and broadcast by satellite around the world.

Nakamura, now a widow (her husband died in 1986), continues to teach Sunday school and write articles for various publications. Since 1985 she has served on the Board of Directors of Elmer Community Hospital. She is a life member of Beta Sigma Phi International, an organization dedicated to the betterment of humanity through understanding and selfless giving. She is past president of the Preceptor Eta chapter in Elmer.

Nakamura derived much inspiration from her mother, whom she describes as both a "follower and a leader, with strong convictions of right and wrong." Her mother had worked hard on the family fruit farm and always regretted that she was unable to continue her education. "This burning desire she kept foremost in her mind in rearing her children." (Nakamura, Interview, Jan. 13 1987)

Despite the injustice of being sent to an internment camp during World War II, Nakamura is not bitter. Like her parents, she has a capacity for tolerance and understanding. "Despite the problems of readjustment to a new life, all the Japanese-Americans who settled in New Jersey thrived," Nakamura remembered. "I am proud to have been a part of the success story." (Nakamura, Interview, Jan. 13 1987)

An interview with Nakamura taped on Jan. 13, 1987, provided useful biographical information.

*Joan Babbage Ellsworth*

## HELEN JOSEPHINE NEAVE, 1911–

Helen Josephine Neave, dermatologist and horsewoman, was born in Glen Ridge (Essex County), NJ, on August 23, 1911, the only child of Pierson Mitchell and Helen Lindsay (Fairchild) Neave. Her father, a member of the Sons of the American Revolution, was an engineer; her mother was a teacher. Both were of Scottish-British descent.

Neave graduated from Mt. Holyoke College in 1933 with a B.A. and then became one of only eight women to earn a medical degree from Cornell University in 1937. After an internship at Baltimore City Hospital in 1937–38 and a residency at the New York Infirmary in 1938–39, she practiced medicine, specializing in dermatology, in New York City from 1939 until 1971. Her professional

life included postgraduate work at the New York Skin and Cancer Hospital and Columbia University, teaching in the dermatology department at New York University for fifteen years (1960–75) and providing leadership in medical and women's medical societies, notably the North American Clinical Dermatology Society as a Board of Governors member.

During these years of medical practice, Neave commuted to New York from her Glen Ridge home, where she was able to pursue an interest in horses that had started at summer camp when she was twelve years old. In 1952 she began showing American Saddlebred horses and finally purchased her own horse in 1963 from the Robin Hill Farm in Pittstown, NJ. As her interest and participation in the horse industry grew, Neave moved to Bedminster in 1963 to be in the country nearer her horses. She also became part owner of the Garden State Stables and the Garden State Stud Farm. In 1972 she retired from practice in New York City and in 1986 she moved to Quakertown, NJ, because of heavy land development in Bedminster.

Neave's success in her horse-showing career is apparent from the many ribbons and awards she has won. She has also served as secretary since 1975 of the New Jersey Horse Council, as a delegate to the Equine Advisory Board of the Department of Agriculture, and as secretary to the American Saddlebred Horse Association of New Jersey until 1985. In 1986 she received the American Horse Show Association Award for Zone 2. In 1987 Neave's four-year-old Fine Harness gelding won the Zone 2 Championship and also became Reserve Open Fine Harness horse of the nation. Her activities in civic affairs include twelve years as chairman of the Bedminster Board of Health.

Information for this article was based on an interview with Neave.

*Grace A. Aqualina*
*Sarah B. Pfaffenroth*

## ALICE NEEL, 1900–1984

Alice Hartley Neel, portrait painter of New York poets, writers, political organizers, artists, critics, and Hispanics and "quintessential bohemian," was the fourth of five children of George Washington and Alice Concross (Hartley) Neel. Born into a middle-class household in Merion Square, PA, on January 28, 1900, she was raised in Colwyn, PA, near Philadelphia, where the family moved shortly after her birth. In 1934 the family established a summer home on the Jersey shore, first in Belmar, then at Spring Lake, where Neel was to summer the rest of her life.

Neel's father was of Irish descent. A kind hardworking, refined, head clerk of the per diem department of the Pennsylvania Railroad, he had little formal education. Alice Neel's mother was of English lineage and could trace her family back to one of the signers of the Declaration of Independence. Although her mother was intelligent and cultured, she was lonely and unhappy, lording it over her husband. The young Neel reflected this in her own discontent with what she considered the boredom of her small-town upbringing with only her mother to stimulate her mind. She remembers being terrified and fascinated by people, attracted by the "morbid and excessive."

Neel had always wanted to be an artist, though her parents gave her little direct encouragement. Instead, they wanted her to take business courses in high school, which she did in her last two years. She then worked for three years in civil service jobs out of a sense of family obligation. She took some art courses at night, without telling anyone, and finally enrolled in the Philadelphia School of Design for Women (later Moore College of Art) in 1921, paying her own tuition. She chose this woman's school over the more distinguished Philadelphia Academy of Art partly to protect herself from her own budding sexuality. She also wanted more traditional training rather than the impressionist method being taught at the academy, since, as she said, "she wasn't happy like Renoir."

In 1924 she attended a summer session at the academy, where she met Carlos Enrique, a wealthy Cuban. Attracted by the unconventional, she married him the next year, and they moved to Havana, where they lived a sophisticated bohemian existence and "painted like mad." She had her first exhibition in Havana in 1927.

Then a series of events led her to a serious breakdown. She and Enrique moved to New York, where they both had to work while trying to paint. A first child, Santillana Enrique, was born in December 1926 and tragically died before age one of diphtheria. In her grief Neel painted *Requiem* (1928) and *Futility of Effort* (1930), which showed a signlike form of a dead child whose head had caught in the bedposts, a story she had read in the newspaper. In spite of her conflicts about motherhood versus art, she gave birth to another child, Isabella Lillian Enrique, in November 1928.

Times were difficult as the Depression eroded the support they received from Enrique's parents. Her husband returned to Cuba in 1930 for a visit, taking Isabella with him, and promising they would all go to Paris. Instead, he went on his own with what little money he could raise from friends, leaving Isabella in Cuba and effectively abandoning Neel. She painted frantically, then went into a state of nervous collapse, was hospitalized, and tried to commit suicide. Enrique returned, but too late to help. He went back to Paris to his new life and woman friend, while Neel fought for nine months to return to health.

Piecing her life together and beginning to paint again, she met Kenneth Doolittle, an intellectual sailor, with whom she moved to Greenwich Village in 1932. A portrait of Doolittle shows him in orange long underwear, leaning back in his chair, legs out front, a wily smirk on his face. Opposite in attraction was John Rothschild, a gentle, high-class travel agent, who had seen her work at the annual Washington Square exhibition and pursued her his entire life, often taking her to dinners at the Harvard Club and Longschamps.

As in her art, she was drawn to two distinct types of men. She said, "You know what I loved? I loved to hit the depths and then to eat at the Harvard Club. I always loved the most wretched and the working class, but then I also loved the most effete and elegant."

Through Doolittle she met Village intellectuals. Rothschild was also sympathetic to left-wing causes. It was a time of fervent socialist and communist idealism, which Neel also encountered among the artists of the Public Works of Art Project (later the WPA), in which she enrolled in 1933. Neel remained with the project, turning in one painting every six weeks for modest government support, until 1943, when it closed down. It gave her a modicum of security and freedom for years.

Her commitment to the Left, a result of her noncon-formist sympathy for the underdog and a genuine social concern, lasted throughout her life. Though meetings bored her, she picketed with members of the Artists' Union, organized neighbors for rent actions, helped others get on the WPA, had parties, and made posters. Her art embodied these concerns in forceful portraits of left-wing writers, organizers, and communists, such as Pat Whalen, union man; Kenneth Fearing, radical poet; and Sam Putnam, Latin American expert for the *Daily Worker*. She also painted social-comment scenes of the New York streets. Later, in the 1950s, she painted the writer Mike Gold and in 1981, Gus Hall, head of the Communist Party, USA. This latter portrait was probably intended for her exhibition in Moscow that same year at the Russian Artists' Union, where she was one of the few Americans ever to exhibit.

Other events of her life interacted with her social concern. After Kenneth Doolittle slashed hundreds of her paintings and watercolors in a jealous rage over her relationship with John Rothschild in 1934, she met José Santiago, a Puerto Rican nightclub singer (1935). She lived with him, moving to Spanish Harlem in 1938, where she remained for the next 24 years. Her neighbors became her art; images of *T. B. Harlem* (1940) and *Two Puerto Rican Boys* (1956), among others, showed her sympathy to their situation and character. She would stop people on the street or talk to those sitting next to her in the theater, or even ply the Fuller brush man who came to the door to pose for her. She wrote, "I decided to paint a human comedy—such as Balzac had done in literature. Like Chichikov I am a collector of souls. If I could make the world happy; the wretched faces in the subway, sad and full of troubles, worry me." (Berrigan, "The Portrait and Its Double," 30)

Though she greatly loved Spanish Harlem, Neel began to spend summers on the Jersey shore in order to get away from the foment and hardship of New York. She and her parents first rented a house in Belmar in 1934 and then in Spring Lake from 1935, where they eventually bought a home. Her daughter from Cuba came to visit in 1934 and 1939, after which Neel never saw her. Her daughter went back to live in Cuba (and much later Miami).

Neel had started a new family of her own. Richard Neel was born in September 1939 of José Santiago, who left her just a few months afterward for another woman. Neel then met a Russian known simply as Sam, a bright, charming, intensely difficult photographer who was in and out of her life for the next eighteen years. Hartley Stockton Neel was born of that relationship in September 1941. Neel did all the work in bringing up these children, and each summer they would go to Spring Lake to stay with her parents. Later, after her parents died, her sons returned to Spring Lake with their own wives and children. These summers served as a close family center for Neel throughout her life and gave her a place to paint thoughtful portraits of her children and grandchildren.

Family life was important to Neel. She supported her children with money from Sam and by giving private art lessons. All phases of family life became subjects for her individualistic and revealing portraits: children, couples, nudes, family groups, old age, and death.

The myth of Neel's neglect as an artist is not quite justified, though she was out of step with the dominant abstract generation of the 1940s and 1950s. She had an occasional show in a gallery (five between 1938 and 1954), yet she had not hit a firm stride and skill until she engaged herself more directly with the art world in the late 1950s, after her children were off to school. She began to attend meetings of the Club, an informal artists' organization, where the abstract expressionists argued with each other, and by the early 1960s, as a result of therapy, began to recognize her own block about getting work out into the world. She called Frank O'Hara of the Museum of Modern Art, who had said he was interested, and asked him to come pose. Two stunning portraits, in which she began to free herself for an expressionist brush and emotive exaggeration, were the result. As she met others in the art world and others sought her out over the next 20 years, she painted artists such as Milton Resnick and Pat Passlof, Andy Warhol, Duane Hanson, Isabel Bishop, and the Soyer brothers; critics John Perrault, Cindy Nemser (with her husband in the nude), Linda Nochlin, and Gregory Battcock (in his French underwear); and collectors such as

Arthur Bullowa. She rendered Village characters as well, such as transvestite Jackie Curtis, or notables such as civil rights activist James Farmer and scientist Linus Pauling.

In 1960 her O'Hara portrait was reproduced in *Art News*, and in 1962 critic Hubert Crehan asserted that her work showed that modern portraiture was not dead. She began to exhibit regularly at the Graham Gallery, was in group shows, won purchase awards, and by the 1970s—with the added boost of the women's movement—had an average of four to five shows a year plus major retrospectives at the Whitney Museum (1974) and the Georgia Museum of Art (1975). There were also shows in New Jersey at the Summit Art Center, Old Mill Gallery (Tintern Falls), and in Princeton. In 1971 her alma mater, now the Moore College of Art, awarded her an honorary doctorate; in 1976 she was elected to the American Academy and Institute of Arts and Letters. In fact, she became a minor art world celebrity because of her incisive portraits and her funny, sharp, and mordant tongue. She appeared on the Johnny Carson show twice in the last year of her life.

Neel spent her last productive decades, the 1960s and the 1970s, on the West Side of Manhattan and between 1970 and 1975 she allowed John Rothschild to live with her. She worked vigorously into her eighties, slowed by cancer only in her last nine months. She died of cancer on October 13, 1984, at age 84, in New York City, and was buried in Lamoille County, VT.

The major monograph on Neel and her work is Patricia Hills, *Alice Neel* (1983). An additional biographical account is Cindy Nemser, "Alice Neel: Portraits of Four Decades," *Ms.* 2 (Oct. 1973):48–53. A critique of her work is Ted Berrigan, "The Portrait and Its Double," *Art News* 64 (Jan. 1966):30–33. For an assessment of her painting in the context of women's art, see Ann Sutherland Harris and Linda Kochlin, *Women Artists: 1550–1950* (1976). A sketch of Neel appears in *Current Biography* (1976). Her obituary appeared in the *New York Times*, Oct. 14, 1984. An interview with Neel's daughter-in-law, Nancy Neel, provided useful information.

*Sara Henry*

## MARY TERESA NORTON, 1875–1959

Mary Teresa (Hopkins) Norton, a member of the U.S. House of Representatives for 25 years, was born in Jersey City (Hudson County), NJ, on March 7, 1875, the eldest daughter of Thomas Hopkins, a construction worker, and Maria (Shea) Hopkins, a homemaker and governess before her marriage. Both her parents, staunch Roman Catholics, were Irish immigrants. Her older brother, James (b. 1868), became principal of Jersey City (now Dickinson) High School and superintendent of schools in Jersey City; she also had two younger sisters, Anne (b. 1877) and Loretta (b. 1880).

As was common in immigrant Catholic families of the time, Norton's brother, James, was educated with the idea of entering the priesthood; but Norton herself did not complete elementary school, a fact not revealed during her lifetime. She left school when she was about twelve, to relieve the family of the financial burden of appropriate clothing and to cope with her self-consciousness about her early mature appearance. Like other young women without formal education, Norton apparently sharpened her reading and writing skills on her own.

Norton's mother died when she was seventeen, and from then she ran the household with the assistance of a housekeeper. When her father remarried four years later, Norton and her sisters moved to an apartment in New York City. They attended Packard Business College for secretarial training and worked in clerical positions to support themselves.

On April 21, 1909, she married Robert Francis Norton, a widower with two children who managed a cooperage firm in Jersey City. Robert Francis, Jr., their only son, died in infancy the following year, and Norton had to adjust to the fact that she could bear no more children.

In her grief and disappointment, she turned to public service and volunteer work. With the encouragement of a local pastor at St. Joseph's Church and other parish women, in 1912 she helped launch the Queen's Daughter's Day Nursery, a nonsectarian day-care center for the children of working women in Jersey City. Norton worked for the nursery for fifteen years, three as secretary and twelve as president. She also organized a Red Cross workroom for women in the parish hall basement during World War I.

Norton's fund-raising activities for the nursery brought her to the attention of Mayor Frank ("Boss") Hague of Jersey City. He responded to her request for money and introduced her to local politics. Norton had not been interested in politics before meeting Hague, nor was she active in the woman suffrage movement of the previous decade. Seeking to gain party support from newly enfranchised women, Hague asked Norton to represent Hudson County on the Democratic Committee of New Jersey in 1920. Norton organized women to participate actively in the Democratic party organization rather than in nonpartisan organizations such as the League of Women Voters.

With Hague's support, Norton progressed in her political career and became the first woman member of the Democratic State Committee, serving alternately as either chair or vice-chair between 1921 and 1944. She was elected to the Hudson County Board of Freeholders as the first Democratic woman freeholder in New Jersey in 1923. Her work on the board included securing board approval of the construction of a maternity hospital in Jersey City at county expense, a special project of Hague. With approval and money forthcoming, the Margaret Hague Maternity Hospital, named after the mayor's mother, was constructed.

In 1924, with Hague's backing, Norton became a candidate for the House of Representatives from the Twelfth Congressional District of New Jersey. Despite large Democratic losses nationally that year, Norton was elected and became not only the first Democratic woman elected to Congress without being preceded by her husband, but also the first woman elected from an eastern state.

As a member of Congress from March 4, 1925, to January 3, 1951 (thirteen successive terms), Norton was the first person in the history of the House of Representatives to chair three important standing committees: District of Columbia, World War Veterans' Legislation, and Labor. While serving on the Committee for the District of Columbia, she championed the principle of home rule for the District and became its "first woman mayor." As a member of the Veterans' Committee, she obtained funds for the construction of the first veterans' hospital in New Jersey. As chair of the Labor Committee, she guided the passage of the Fair Labor Standards Act of 1938. After leaving the Labor Committee in 1947, she was appointed to the House Administrative Committee, which she chaired from 1949 until her retirement in 1951. During World War II she sought federal funds for day-care centers through the passage of the Lanham Act. After the war, she lobbied unsuccessfully for the continuation of the provision. Norton regarded motherhood as women's highest service to God and country.

Norton's position on women's rights reflected her family background and local constituency. As a Roman Catholic, she opposed the birth control movement of Margaret Sanger in the 1920s and voted against the proposed Gillett Bill in Congress in 1931 for the use of federal funds to distribute birth control information. She refused to support the proposal for an Equal Rights Amendment to the U.S. Constitution because she feared it would mean the loss of protective legislation for women, legislation that she felt was the only available means of combating the general exploitation of women and of protecting nonunion women. In her writings and addresses, she not only identified but also adeptly analyzed such problems of working women as maternity leave, child care, the myth of "pin money," job-training programs, latchkey children, displaced homemakers, and equal pay for equal work.

Norton was a significant role model for women in politics. Once a male colleague in Congress condescendingly offered to "yield to the lady from New Jersey," to which Norton retorted, "I'm no lady. I'm a member of Congress, and I shall proceed accordingly." She advocated women's full political participation as voters, party members, and candidates for office and challenged patriarchy in American politics. She held that women should be involved in politics at all levels of government from volunteers at the ward level to cabinet positions and even the presidency.

For Norton, women's political activism was not an issue of women's rights but of women's rightful place in American democracy. She frequently claimed, "What is good for women of this country is good for the nation." (Radio interview, Jan. 3, 1948) Norton's husband died on June 17, 1934, and she was then a widow, a frequent assumption even before it became fact because of her husband's low public profile and continued residence in Jersey City during her congressional career.

A popular congressional leader, Norton received many honors. She was appointed by Governor A. Harry Moore to represent New Jersey on May 24, 1927, at the Woman's World's Fair in Chicago. She received honorary doctor of laws degrees from St. Elizabeth's, Convent Station, NJ (1930), and Rider College, Trenton, NJ (1937). At a baseball game at Roosevelt Stadium in Jersey City, where there were thousands in attendance, Mayor Hague proclaimed August 26, 1942, "Mary Norton Day." The dedication to her read, "For her loyalty to the president and to the people." During the 81st Congress she was the only Democratic representative from New Jersey, thus representing all New Jersey Democrats in the Congress and leading the state's congressional delegation. She served as delegate-at-large from New Jersey to every Democratic National Convention from 1924 to 1948, when she was chair of the Credentials Committee. She enjoyed the support of the American Federation of Labor and the Congress of Industrial Organization and was mentioned as a vice-presidential candidate from her party in 1932, 1940, and 1944.

Though not eager for the post, she headed a national campaign to secure the Democratic vice-presidential nomination for India Edwards (vice-chair of the Democratic National Committee) at the 1952 convention. She was considered as a gubernatorial candidate for New Jersey in 1943, but felt a woman was not yet acceptable for such a high-ranking elected office. Norton also received the "Woman of Achievement" award from the Women's National Press Club (1946) and the Siena Medal from the National Catholic University Women (Theta Phi Alpha) as the outstanding Catholic woman of the year (1947).

Norton's retirement from the House of Representatives at age 75 coincided with the end of the Hague regime in Hudson County in 1950. That same year, Secretary of Labor Maurice J. Tobin appointed her Womanpower Consultant to the Defense Manpower Administration, a post she held until September 1953. She lived the last three years of her life in Greenwich, CT, where she died of a heart attack, at age 84, on August 2, 1959. She was buried at Holy Name Cemetery in Jersey City, NJ.

Norton's papers, including her unpublished autobiography, are available at NJ-RU. For details of her political activities, see Gary Mitchell, "Women Standing for Women: The Early Political Career of Mary T. Norton," *New Jersey History* 96 (Spring-Summer 1979):27–42. Norton is profiled in *NAW-MP* and *Current Biography* (1944). Her obituary appeared in the *New York Times*, Aug. 3, 1959.

*Carmela Ascolese Karnoutsos*

## MARIAN STEPHENSON OLDEN, 1888–1981

Marian (Stephenson) Olden, leader of a movement that advocated sterilization of the unfit, was born Marion Stephenson on March 29, 1888, in Philadelphia. Her father, Arthur Stephenson, ran the family yarn business on Chestnut Street, but his real interest was in the single tax reform. He founded the Philadelphia Henry George Club and campaigned for the single tax so energetically in Delaware that he was arrested and spent a week in the Dover jail. Her father's death in 1902 left an emptiness in Olden's life. His commitment to principle became the model for her later crusade for human betterment.

Olden completed finishing school in 1905 and married James Henry, Jr., in 1907. Her only child, Dorothy, was born in 1909. Her first marriage lasted only a short time; in 1914 she married Billy deVictor. When she was 30 years old she was introduced to New Thought, a religious movement that affirmed both the Supreme One and the Indwelling Presence. Olden felt a great relief in giving up her agnosticism and surrendering to the will of God. Along with reliance upon God, New Thought pointed her toward an ideal of truth and urged upon her the necessity of being loyal to her understanding of it. "Justice, Truth, all sorts of ideas and principles," she wrote in 1948, "are things I am ready to fight and die for." (Letter to Dr. Wood, Jan. 4, 1948) It was many years before her idealism found an object. After Billy deVictor's death, about 1927, she attempted social work but could not agree with the policy that forbade giving birth-control information to poor women. In 1928 she married Paul R. Coleman-Norton, a professor of classics at Princeton. She attended the 1932 founding meeting of the Princeton chapter of the League of Women Voters and in 1933 was asked to chair the club's Social Hygiene Committee.

When she began her work in 1934, it was already apparent to Olden that she had found a cause worthy of her idealism. She led field trips to state institutions, arranged for speakers, and studied social and biological issues. As early as March of that year she formed a group to study sterilization of the unfit and convinced the league's Executive Committee to present a petition supporting a sterilization bill in the New Jersey State Legislature. Olden summarized the arguments for sterilization in a report of May 1934. She wrote that if the present rate of increase among the insane, retarded, blind, deaf, and epileptic continues, "in less than 100 years one-half of our population will be eligible for asylums." The solution was simple: "Sterilization of the male . . . is about as serious as pulling a tooth." The operation for females was more difficult but still safe. She concluded her report with a plea for action. "Is parenthood an inalienable right . . . ? Or is it a privilege society has a right to withhold from its defective members? If we do not . . . safeguard our racial future, then what is the use of our solving any less fundamental problems?"

Eugenic sterilization originated in the late 19th century as a means of eliminating what were then considered hereditary defects: insanity, retardation, blindness, and even criminality. Against such "festering sores in the life of society" as the mentally retarded, wrote an expert in 1904, "the only protection is that which the surgeon gives." (Barr, *Mental Defectives*, 190) The first eugenic sterilization took place in 1899, and by 1934 27 states had compulsory sterilization laws. By the 1930s, however, attitudes toward sterilization were shifting. In 1930 sociologist Stanley Powell Davies objected to sterilization for the mentally deficient both because of the weak scientific basis for the inheritance of mental defects and because it often proved ineffective or unnecessary. Although Olden was isolated from the male professionals who determined social policies, she was well read and highly intelligent. Once she committed herself to compulsory sterilization for the unfit, she never turned back.

By the end of 1935 the activities and attitudes that Olden carried throughout her crusade had been established. She wrote pamphlets for the League of Women Voters in support of sterilization, took exhibits to conventions on health and social work, and actively supported the sterilization bill before the New Jersey State Legislature. (New Jersey's sterilization law of 1911 had been declared unconstitutional by a New Jersey court in 1913.) When Roman Catholic opposition defeated the bill, Olden began to study the involvement of the Catholic church in politics. Her pamphlet *Sterilization and the Organized Opposition* was the first of many attacks she made on the political power of the Catholic church.

An organization devoted solely to eugenic sterilization appeared necessary to its supporters by the late 1930s. The League of Women Voters was becoming less hospitable to Olden's crusade, and she had begun to antagonize some of her coworkers. In 1937, at the urging of interested individuals throughout the state, she gathered people to form a statewide organization. The Sterilization League of New Jersey was formed on March 20, 1937, in Trenton. Olden, as the executive secretary, carried out the work of the league by arranging meetings, speaking to interested groups, writing pamphlets, recruiting members, and taking displays to conventions.

During 1938 she toured Europe with her husband. She made good use of the trip to study sterilization laws on the continent so she would be able to help draft a model law for New Jersey. "In the Scandinavian countries," she told the Montclair League of Women Voters after her return, "the quality of the population is becoming so superior that there are no slums and very few jails." (Marian Olden papers, 1938 file) She required a salary in 1939, after she separated from her husband that summer. She was divorced from Paul Coleman-Norton in 1940, and in 1941 she married Roger Olden, an engineer. Meanwhile, the work of the league continued to be the great challenge and motivation of her life.

By 1942 Olden faced a crisis. "All day in Trenton," she wrote in her diary on January 19. (She was there seeking support for a sterilization bill.) "Senator Hendrickson insulting. Mr. Everson didn't know me. Senator Lance put me off." On January 22 a supporter told her, "It is political suicide." Eugenic arguments had continued to erode during the 1930s, and by the 1940s they had too much resemblance to Nazi racial policies to be accepted. Conflict within the league was also taking its toll. Olden wanted to transform the New Jersey league into a national one. It became apparent, however, that the new association would be controlled by its Executive Committee. Rather than see her cause snatched from her control, Olden resigned.

Olden's commitment never faltered. During January 1943 friends and supporters convinced her to establish a national organization separate from the old one. By May 1943 Birthright, Inc. had been formed. Its goals, like those of the New Jersey Sterilization League, were to provide information and to work for state laws for compulsory sterilization. For more than five years Olden continued the work she had begun with the New Jersey league. By the late 1940s, however, her relationship with Birthright was deteriorating. Birthright's president, Dr. Emlen Wood, apparently envisioned a broad reorganization, including less emphasis on the compulsory aspect of sterilization and an end to attacks on the Roman Catholic church. Neither of these policies was acceptable to Olden, and she struggled to keep the organization on its original course. On June 14, 1948, she was dismissed from her position.

Olden's involvement with the organized promotion of sterilization was at an end. In 1952 she wrote an article on sterilization for the *Encyclopedia Americana*. In the 1960s and 1970s she occupied herself by writing the history of the New Jersey Sterilization League and successor organizations. She and her husband, Roger Olden, retired to Gwynedd, PA, in November 1967. Olden died there September 10, 1981, at age 93.

Olden's papers, including correspondence and her diary, are available at NJ-RU. Two of her pamphlets are: *Human Betterment Was Our Goal* (1969) and *History of the Development of the First National Organization for Sterilization* (1974). Biographical details were supplied in interviews with her husband, Roger Olden, and with Dorothy Frank, Aug. 20, 1987. For background information on the sterilization movement, see William Ray Van Essendelft, "A History of the Association for Voluntary Sterilization: 1935–1964" (Ph.D. diss., University of Minnesota, 1978); and Martin W. Barr, *Mental Defectives: Their History, Treatment and Training* (1904).

*John C. Spurlock*

## ESTELLA ELIZABETH PADGHAM, 1874–1952

Estella Elizabeth Padgham, Unitarian minister, was born on June 10, 1874, in Syracuse, NY, the youngest of three children born to English immigrants. Her father, Amos Padgham, was a mechanical engineer, though he retired when Padgham was a young child. Her mother, Emma Elizabeth (Holloway) Padgham, was apparently a homemaker. Both of Padgham's parents were Unitarians and were married by the Rev. Samuel J. May, the Unitarian abolitionist from Syracuse, NY. Padgham herself was raised in the May Memorial Church (Unitarian) in Syracuse, where her father served as clerk for many years.

Though originally intending a career in music, Padgham was influenced by two events to enter the ministry. First, she heard a woman preach in her home church, and second, Marie Hoffendahl Jenney Howe (1870–1944), an older friend from high school, became a minister.

Though her sister, Clara, disapproved of "college women" and her father felt she was not strong enough to leave home, Padgham attended Smith College and graduated in 1898. In 1899 she entered Meadville Theological School in Pennsylvania and received a B.D. in 1901. The same year she preached and worked with the Rev. Mary Augusta Safford (1851–1927) in Des Moines, IA. Safford was the leader of the Iowa Sisterhood, an unofficial group of women ministers who, beginning in 1880, stepped into many of the existing pulpits in Iowa, took over the Iowa Unitarian press, held leadership positions in the Iowa Unitarian Association, and created fifteen new church communities. In September 1901 Padgham traveled with Safford and Marie Jenney Howe to Syracuse for her ordination and then back to Iowa, where Padgham accepted the call to the Unity Church (Unitarian) of Perry, IA.

At the time of Padgham's ordination only a handful of denominations, including the Universalists, Unitarians, and Congregationalists, ordained women to the ministry as a matter of church policy. Olympia Brown (1835–1926), who was ordained in 1863 to the Universalist ministry, was the first woman ordained with full denominational authority.

Of the denominations ordaining women, the Unitarians had the most uniform standards required throughout the country. At the time of Padgham's ordination in 1901 just under 30 women were in the Unitarian ministry;

less than half of them were settled in parishes. The beginning of the 20th century was a high point for women in the Unitarian ministry. During the 20th century the number of Unitarian women ministers declined until the rise of the women's movement in the 1970s. Padgham's ministerial career spans this peak and decline of women's presence in the Unitarian ministry.

Padgham stayed in Perry, IA, for three years (1901–4), during which time the congregation grew, a Sunday school was established, building improvements were made and the mortgage was paid in full. During the summer of 1904 Padgham and her sister, Clara, attended a Unitarian conference at Star Island off the coast of New Hampshire. There Padgham was asked to preach at the Church of Our Father in Rutherford, NJ, before she returned to Iowa. Padgham accepted and filled the Rutherford church with her friends and alumnae of Smith College for the occasion. After her return to Iowa the Rutherford church asked Padgham to be its minister.

A call to a woman minister from a Unitarian church in the East was no small matter. An unidentified layperson of the Rutherford church wrote the president of the American Unitarian Association, "Now Miss Padgham is certainly an attractive woman . . . she shows herself a girl of exceptional good sense and sanity of mind. She has neither the gush nor the fatal tendency to over-conversation which so often has been the limitation of our women preachers. As a private member of the Rutherford parish, I should prefer her ministry to that of any of the men who have yet preached. But is it safe to encourage a movement to put a woman preacher in New Jersey?" (Samuel Atkins Eliot Collection, Andover Harvard Library)

A move from Iowa to New Jersey was a significant one. Among her Unitarian female colleagues, Padgham was noteworthy for having spent most of her ministerial career not on the western frontier, where opportunities for women clergy were greater, but on the eastern seaboard in Rutherford. Padgham also held the longest single pastorate known to Unitarian women clergy of the time, coming to New Jersey in 1905 and resigning 22 years later, in 1927.

During Padgham's first two years in Rutherford the church achieved enough financial security to increase the minister's salary and give up the aid it had been receiving annually through the American Unitarian Association. In the second year the church began raising funds for a new parish building, which it built several years later. The Sunday school enrollment grew to be the largest of the Unitarian churches in the East.

In Rutherford Padgham fostered relations among clergy. She organized and was the first president of the Rutherford Ministerial Association. In 1924 Padgham served as president of the New Jersey Ministers' Association. She was also the first woman chaplain to open the New Jersey State Legislature in prayer.

Padgham was a supporter of women's advancement. She marched with the woman suffragists despite the dismay of the Rutherford Unitarian Church's Women's Alliance that their minister would parade in such a way. She argued for women's equality with men. She also believed that certain advantages came with being a woman—and a woman minister. She thought men and women were more likely to confide in her because she was a woman. Apparently people from within her church and beyond came to her with their concerns. She referred to herself as a confidante-at-large.

Theologically, Padgham was a middle-of-the-road Unitarian for her era. With the optimism that often characterizes Unitarianism, Padgham described her tradition as a "well-spring of hope and trust and good cheer." (*Unitarianism: A Religion Good to Live By,* 1) Those aspects of Unitarian thought that most appealed to her were the ideas of continuous revelation and free will. She resolutely rejected the notion of predestination and institutional creedalism. A theist, she rejected religious humanism, a movement that was coming into its own during the second half of her career. "I believe in a personal God," Padgham wrote, "not a God shaped like a man, but a spiritual being whose spirit and life I share. Without such a source I cannot account for that which my experience teaches me." (*When Half-Gods Go,* 4)

Padgham and her sister, Clara, were close during adulthood, frequently visiting each other and traveling together to religious conferences. The sisters, neither of whom married, also took vacations together, often accompanied by their mother. When Padgham retired in 1927, she returned to Syracuse, where she and her sister cared for their ailing mother. She became an active member of May Memorial Church and its Sunday school. She also served as a director of the Mohawk Valley Conference of Unitarians and Religious Liberals.

A year after the fiftieth anniversary celebration of her ordination, Padgham died on December 4, 1952, at age 78, in her home in Syracuse. Memorial services were conducted at the May Memorial Church, the Unitarian congregation in which Padgham grew up.

The Unitarian Universalist Association (Boston, MA) contains Padgham material, including an autobiographical essay, photographs, clippings, and pamphlets, two of which are *Unitarianism: A Religion Good to Live By* (n.d.) and *When Half-Gods Go* (1929). Padgham's life and career are covered in Catherine F. Hitchings, *Universalist and Unitarian Women Ministers* (1985); and in an unpublished manuscript by Clara Cook Helvie, "Unitarian Women Ministers" (1928), available at the Andover-Harvard Theological Library (Cambridge, MA).

*Marta Morris Flanagan*

Nellie Morrow Parker with her father and brother, c. 1927. In the face of discrimination and great community opposition, Parker became the first African-American public school teacher in Bergen County and taught in the Hackensack school system for 42 years. *Courtesy, private collection.*

### NELLIE KATHERINE MORROW PARKER, 1902–

Nellie Katherine (Morrow) Parker was the first African-American public schoolteacher in Bergen County, NJ. To secure her post, she endured Ku Klux Klan threats and social ostracism, witnessed colleagues' resignations, and found little support in the local black community. Parker was born August 27, 1902, in Hackensack, NJ, the second child and only daughter of John Eugene and Mary Ann (Hayes) Morrow. Both Parker's parents could read and write—not common among African-Americans of their era. Her father, who was a Methodist minister, had taken a job as custodian of Johnson Public Library in Hackensack while he was a sexton, giving his children easy access to a world of books. Part of Parker's remarkable success is the direct result of the value her parents placed on religion and education. By her own account, Parker was born to be a teacher. But in high school she was encouraged to take sewing and home economics, so she could obtain work as a maid. Her father insisted, however, as he did with all his children, that she be allowed to follow a college preparatory curriculum. He did not want his daughter to end up cleaning white people's floors. Parker would go to college—no matter what the financial strains. As it turned out, monetary sacrifices were not the greatest obstacle she faced.

It was difficult to grow up black in Hackensack. New Jersey had been one of the last states in the Union to outlaw slavery, and Hackensack had had its share of slaves, so the specter of slavery remained. The city's YMCA—forbidden to African-Americans in Parker's childhood—had been the site of one of the largest plantations in the North, and the first lynching of a black in Bergen County took place on the site of the Hackensack courthouse.

The Morrow family lived on the outskirts of a white middle-class neighborhood, but in the early part of this century most of Hackensack's black children attended either the Union Street or the Broadway School. Parker's father fought to have his children admitted to the State Street School in their own district. Once admitted, the children braved jeers and taunts—and violence—each morning as they walked through the streets of the white neighborhood on their way to school.

Parker's childhood was lonely, for she was weak, studious, and often sick. Since the Morrows had to perform better than average in order to stay in their school, many blacks interpreted their diligence as haughty and superior, accusing them of "acting white." Whites didn't like them because they refused to "act black." But Parker and her brothers clung to their parents' belief that performance rather than rebellion was the route to success for blacks.

Fortunately, the Morrows had one another, and the family turned inward for comfort and social activity. Parker played piano, a talent she nurtured all her life, and other family members sang or played various instruments. There were often concerts at home and in the church. Frederick Morrow, Parker's brother, calls his sister the jewel in the family crown. Her humor and compassion helped buoy the family and give them courage.

After graduating from Hackensack High School, Parker entered Montclair Normal School (later Montclair Teacher's College) in 1920, receiving a teaching certificate in 1922. She attended a New Jersey college instead of a black school in the South because her father did not want to give whites—or blacks—the opportunity to claim that she was not properly educated to teach in New Jersey. Her goal was to teach in Hackensack, and Parker's father was untiring as he worked toward securing a position for his daughter.

The Hackensack Board of Education, though, was adamant: it did not want a black schoolteacher. Dr. William Stark, the superintendent of schools, was in no position to fight the board, even though Stark had given Parker a practice-teaching post during her last year of college. That appointment had caused an uproar in the community, which feared that such a position would lead to a permanent job. During this time, Parker's father appeared before the board many times, petitioning for her hiring.

But the failure of the town's African-American community to support her is what Parker remembers most during this period. They labeled her efforts "stuck-up" and "biggity." The head of the African-American delegation, addressing the Board of Education meeting in April 1922, said: "I regret to publicly have to publish the consensus of the Negro community. However, after due reflection and long consideration, we believe the appointment of a Negro teacher at this time would not be in the best interest of the race or the community. We feel our children would not respond or learn under a Negro teacher, and that her presence would only add to the many problems that already exist in the system." (Morrow, *Way Down South Up North*, 92)

But Parker's fate was not yet decided. Superintendent Stark was wrestling with his conscience. For various reasons, his relationship with the board was already tenuous. In a last, courageous move, he decided to give Parker a contract. According to Parker, the next day Stark stepped down as superintendent of schools in Hackensack—and Parker stepped up to a teaching position, on a three-year trial basis. Finally, she had a classroom of her own.

The community made life difficult for Parker during those initial three years when she was tormented, ridiculed, and isolated. There were town meetings, press disapproval, and hate mail. The family was criticized and rebuked by salesmen, friends, and strangers, and both the Daughters of the American Revolution and the Knights of Columbus expressed their fierce opposition to her appointment. An angry night parade organized by the KKK placed the Morrows' home, and their lives, in danger—yet Parker never considered quitting.

Every year the new superintendent would call Parker into his office to ask her to transfer to a segregated school in the South—where she would have more "opportunity." After three years of this, Parker looked him in the eye and said, "It's too bad if one little colored girl can be such a bother to you." (Parker, Interview, winter 1986)

Parker survived her trial period and remained in the Hackensack school system teaching fifth and sixth grade for 42 years. She began teaching at the First Street School, but when an integration plan was instituted in the district in 1953, she was transferred to the Beech Street School, where she stayed until retirement in 1964. During her teaching years, Parker focused on creating an atmosphere of love and helpfulness. She instilled a sense of self-respect in her students, as well as a sense of black pride and identity. She also shared her love of music with them by leading the school choir.

Parker continued her education and was active in the community throughout her teaching career. She earned a B.S. (1937) and an M.S. (1952) from Columbia University Teacher's College. She was a founding member of the Black Women's Business and Professional Organization and helped establish the Mary McLeod Bethune Scholarship Fund. A member of the Alpha Chapter of Phi Delta Kappa, a teacher's sorority, Parker has also led her church choir and served as organist for the Varick Memorial Church in Hackensack.

Parker's successful professional life stands in marked contrast to her marital one. In a sense, Parker's classroom was a haven, a place where she could put aside personal troubles. She married William Parker, an insurance agent originally from Virginia, in 1928. Their life together was unhappy, though they remained together for 25 years—until Parker's mother became ill.

In the early 1950s Parker left her husband and returned to the house on Berry Street in which she had grown up. She cared for her mother—raising her youngest brother at home—until Mary Ann Morrow died in 1954. Parker was never legally separated and her husband continued to live in the house on Railroad Avenue that they owned jointly.

The Board of Education renamed the Maple Hill School the Nellie K. Parker School in July 1981 when Parker was presented with a plaque for her years of service to Hackensack. She was hailed as "a pioneer in racial equality in education" by the 400 attendees at a ceremony on September 20, 1981. Today Parker lives in Baltimore, MD.

Interviews with Parker and her brother, Everett Frederick Morrow, provided useful information. For details of Hackensack and the Morrow family during the early 20th century, see Everett Frederick Morrow, *Way Down South Up North* (1973). For an account of the Nellie K. Parker School dedication ceremony, see "City School Renamed after Education Pioneer," *Central Bergen Reporter* (Hackensack, NJ), Sept. 23, 1981.

*Amy Gash*

## RUTH MARCUS PATT, 1919–

Ruth (Marcus) Patt, community leader and author, was born in New Brunswick (Middlesex County), NJ, on September 29, 1919. She was the fourth child and one of identical twins in a family of five daughters born to Joseph D. and Bessie (Laurie) Marcus. Both parents were of Russian Jewish ancestry and had immigrated to the United States in the late 1800s, arriving in the New Brunswick area by 1907. Her father was an active community leader who was in the scrap iron business. Her mother joined her husband in community service while raising their five children.

Educated in the New Brunswick public schools, Patt graduated from Douglass College in 1940 with a B.A. in sociology. After graduation she spent a year training as a psychiatric social worker at the State Hospital at Marlboro, where she lived and worked on the premises. When her training was completed she worked at the hospital for six months before leaving to marry Milton S. Patt, her childhood sweetheart, on March 22, 1942.

The Patts soon settled into a Brooklyn, NY, apartment to be near Milton Patt's military assignment. While her husband was fulfilling his World War II tour of duty, Patt volunteered her time to the American Women's Voluntary Services, working three days a week as Brooklyn chair of victory gardens. This job involved educating the public about the victory garden project and was the beginning of Patt's long and diverse career in secular and religious community service and volunteerism.

In 1946 Patt and her husband moved back to New Brunswick, where her son Richard was born that same year. Her son Steven was born in 1949. While Steven was still an infant, Patt joined Hadassah, a women's Zionist organization founded before the formation of the state of Israel in 1947, to serve Jews living in Palestine. She quickly rose through the ranks of the organization and became Hadassah group president in 1952 and then New Brunswick chapter president in 1954. From 1957 to 1972 she produced and edited the southern New Jersey regional Hadassah newsletter, teaching the skill of bulletin writing to local chapters. She also represented her region on several national Hadassah committees.

Patt took an active role in the Anshe Emeth Memorial Temple in New Brunswick and was president of its Sisterhood from 1962 to 1964. Her mother and two of her sisters had held this same office at other times. Patt was one of the first women elected to the Board of Trustees of the temple, and she wrote its monthly bulletin for eight years.

As her children grew, Patt continued her work in secular volunteer projects. She was active in both Boy Scouting and Girl Scouting and in the Livingston School Parent-Teacher Association, which she served as president in 1958. A staunch fund-raiser for the Alumnae Association of Douglass College, she wrote and prepared a slide-lecture, used by alumnae chapters worldwide, celebrating the 50th anniversary of the college in 1968. For her service to the college she received the Douglass Alumnae Recognition Award in 1974.

Patt's interest in writing and in her Jewish heritage took new directions in 1977 when she called together a group of local Jewish residents. Together, they formed the Jewish Historical Society of Raritan Valley, and she was named its first president. Her first book, *The Jewish Scene in New Jersey's Raritan Valley: 1698–1948*, was published by the society in 1978. She subsequently published three other books on the history of Jews in New Jersey. Under Patt's direction, the Jewish Historical Society of Raritan Valley grew to encompass a tri-county area. In 1982 it became the Jewish Historical Society of Central Jersey, establishing the Jewish Archives of Central Jersey the same year.

Patt's leadership in regional history led to her appointment in 1979 as general chair of the 1980 City of New Brunswick Tercentennial Celebration. Under her direction, the celebration involved 130 separate events and included diverse ethnic and religious groups. Patt was instrumental in inspiring the creation of written histories of the African-American and Hispanic communities of the city. The tercentennial celebration and its printed record, edited by Patt, became a model for similar historic celebrations. She was named Citizen of the Year in 1981 for her service to New Brunswick.

Over the years Patt has received numerous awards for her community service. In 1980 the New Jersey Historical Commission presented her with its Award of Recognition. In 1981 she received the Douglass Society Award for distinction in public service and the Rutgers University Medal, the highest honor conferred by Rutgers upon an individual for service to the university. She also received the Anshe Emeth Memorial Temple Leadership Award in 1981 and, with her husband, the Lehman Award for Service to the Jewish People.

Patt has a wide range of cultural interests. She continues to write and plays golf and tennis. She is director of the Jewish Archives of Central Jersey.

A taped interview with Patt provided useful information. The interview, as well as other Patt material, is available at the Jewish Archives of Central Jersey, housed at the Central New Jersey Jewish Home for the Aged (Somerset, NJ).

*Arlene Ferman*

## LOUISE PEARCE, 1885–1959

Louise Pearce was an eminent medical pathologist who was responsible for a number of medical discoveries, most notably the cure for African sleeping sickness. She was born in Winchester, MA, on March 5, 1885, the eldest child of Charles Ellis and Susan Elizabeth (Hoyt) Pearce. After the birth of her younger brother Ronald, Pearce's family moved to California, where she attended the Girl's Collegiate School in Los Angeles from 1900 to 1903.

Pearce entered Stanford University in 1903 and graduated in 1907 with an A.B. degree in physiology and histology. Eager to study at Johns Hopkins with the world-famous pathologist Dr. William Henry Welch, Pearce first attended Boston University School of Medicine for two years. She was then admitted to Johns Hopkins Medical School in 1909, with advanced standing, and graduated

with an M.D. in 1912. She served as the medical house officer there in 1913 and was recommended by Dr. Welch to the Rockefeller Institute in New York City as "a promising medical pathologist." She joined their staff in 1913 and became assistant to Dr. Simon Flexner, the first director of the Institute.

Pearce remained on the faculty of the Rockefeller Institute throughout her professional career, from 1913 to 1951. A frequent research associate of Dr. Wade Hampton Brown during much of her career, Pearce and he began by testing the arsenical drug tryparsamide to determine its biological action. According to Pearce, "The promising curative results obtained in various species of animals infected with pathogenic trypanosomiasis . . . led to the application of the drug to the treatment of human trypanosomiasis, or sleeping sickness, in the Belgian Congo in 1920." (Pearce in *Science*, Jan. 23, 1925, 91)

Pearce was sent by the Rockefeller Institute to the Belgian Congo for a series of field tests of the new drug on human subjects. She went alone in May 1920 to Leopoldville, where her first test subjects included 77 Africans in various stages of the disease. This experiment demonstrated that treatment with tryparsamide resulted in: "(1) a prompt disappearance of trypanosomes from the blood and lymph glands, (2) a rapid improvement of the abnormal cerebrospinal fluids of advanced patients which in the majority of cases amounted to a restoration to normal and (3) a marked improvement of both physical and mental states." (*Science*, Jan. 23, 1925, 91)

Through the cooperation of government officials and missionary doctors, tryparsamide was eventually tested in eight other African colonies. The Rockefeller Institute reported that "during the period lasting just 20 years from the first introduction of the drug by Dr. Pearce in Africa, over 500,000 Africans received treatment with tryparsamide." (*News from the Rockefeller Institute*, Aug. 10, 1959, 1)

For her efforts, the Belgian government decorated Pearce with the Order of the Crown in 1921 and, 34 years later, with the Royal Order of the Lion. She was also awarded the King Leopold II Prize of $10,000 in 1953 by King Baudouin of Belgium, in recognition of her work some 34 years earlier. In 1965 Rockefeller Institute's historian, Dr. George Corner, stated: "The development of a curative drug for African sleeping sickness was one of the two greatest achievements in medical practice made at the Rockefeller Institute." (Corner, *A History of the Rockefeller Institute*, 494)

After her trip to the Belgian Congo, Pearce continued to work with Brown. They experimented with treponema pallidum in rabbits to study the effects of syphilis on vital organs and to test the effects of arsenical drugs on the disease. Pearce used these drugs to treat syphilis in human subjects, finding a significant difference in the blood pictures of treated and untreated groups of syphilis patients.

Pearce and Brown also studied malignant tumors in rabbits, discovering that rabbit cancer could be transplanted into other rabbits. At the end of her life, this cancer—known as the Brown-Pearce carcinoma—was "still among the most widely studied tumors of animals in search for clues to the disease in humans." (*New York Times*, Aug. 11, 1959)

Appointed associate member of the Rockefeller Institute in 1923, Pearce continued experiments during the 1920s and 1930s. In this ten-year period Pearce and Brown conducted a series of experiments on an immense rabbit colony to investigate hereditary and constitutional factors in rabbits, to determine their susceptibility to infections and deterioration processes. In 1932, 1933, and 1935 outbreaks of rabbit pox threatened the colony, but they also stimulated Pearce to investigate the etiology of the pox and eventually discover the virus that caused it. Because of the danger of the infection spreading and the increasing scope of the experiments, Pearce and Brown's program was transferred to Princeton, NJ, in 1935. Soon after the Princeton move Brown's health deteriorated, forcing him to retire. Pearce continued studying the rabbit colony by herself, but had to reduce the scope of the program. By 1940 she had discovered more than 20 hereditary diseases and deformities in the rabbits. During the 1940s she published many articles on her findings about hereditary achondroplasia, osteopetrosis, and premature senescence in rabbits. Over the course of her professional career Pearce had more than 130 articles published about her research; several posthumous publications also appeared.

Pearce distinguished herself in the field of education as well. She was a visiting professor of medicine at Peiping Union Medical College in China in 1931 and 1932. In 1941 she became a member of the Board of Corporators of the Woman's Medical College of Pennsylvania, and from 1946 to 1952 she served as president of the college. A colleague once described her as "an energetic and enthusiastic member of the American Association of University Women" (Fay, *Journal of Pathology and Bacteriology*, 543); Pearce was a director of this organization from 1945 to 1951 and one of its leaders in international policies.

Pearce received many honors during her distinguished career, notably honorary degrees from five colleges. She was a member of Alpha Omega Alpha, Phi Beta Kappa, Phi Beta Phi, and Sigma Xi. The New York Infirmary for Women and Children presented her with the Elizabeth Blackwell Award in 1951, which honored her as "an active imaginative and creative force in medicine." (*News from the Rockefeller Institute*, 3) Pearce served in many medical and scientific organizations in this country and abroad. Her longest term of service was on the General Advisory Council of the American Social Hygiene Association, from 1925 to 1944. She was a trustee of the New York Infirm-

ary for Women and Children for ten years and also on the executive board of the American Medical Women's Association. In addition to membership in more than fifteen medical associations in this country, Pearce was also a member of medical societies in England, France, Ireland, and China.

After retiring in 1951, Pearce traveled and spent many summers abroad with her friend the novelist Ida Wylie. She lived with Wylie and Dr. Josephine Baker, onetime assistant commissioner of health of New York City, at Trevenna Farm in Skillman, NJ. A colleague described Pearce's home as "a most delightful and interesting place to live and study. Her shelves were crowded with many old editions of medical treasures, the latest scientific literature and the latest works on international questions. She had a wonderful collection of Chinese carvings and porcelains." (Baumann, *Journal of American Medical Women's Association*, 793) According to friends, Pearce was a charming host with wide interests and a delightful sense of humor.

While returning from a European voyage Pearce, then in her early seventies, fell ill. Upon reaching the United States she was taken to New York Hospital, where she died on August 10, 1959, at age 74. She bequeathed her extensive and valuable library collection on syphilis to Johns Hopkins Medical School.

A bibliography of Pearce's scientific writings from 1915 to 1960 and a biographical sketch appear in Marion Fay, "Louise Pearce," *Journal of Pathology and Bacteriology* 82 (1961):542–51. Pearce described her work with trypanosomiasis in "Tryparsamide Treatment of African Sleeping Sickness," *Science* 61 (1925):91–92. George Corner, *A History of the Rockefeller Institute* (1964), details her work at the institute, and an article in *News from the Rockefeller Institute* (Aug. 10, 1959):1–4, provides a profile of her. A sketch of her appears in *NAW-MP*. Obituaries appeared in the *New York Times*, Aug. 11, 1959; and in Frieda Baumann, "Memorial to Louise Pearce, M.D.," *Journal of the American Medical Women's Association* 15 (1960):793. Her correspondence can be found in the Flexner Papers at the Library of the American Philosophical Society (Philadelphia) and in the Archives of the Medical College of Pennsylvania (Philadelphia).

*Constance B. Schuyler*

## ELEANORE KENDALL PETTERSEN, 1916–

Eleanore Kendall Pettersen, architect and first New Jersey woman to open her own architectural office, was born on February 18, 1916, in Passaic (Passaic County), NJ. She was the second child and only daughter of Einar Arnolf Pettersen, a self-educated Norwegian who immigrated to the United States at age 21 and later started a successful lumber business in New Jersey, and Katherine Marie (Christopherson) Pettersen, artist, homemaker, and mother, born in Benson, MI, to Scandinavian parents who had become homesteaders.

Pettersen's decision to study architecture at age nineteen was unexpected, but in retrospect one can see how her parents, her life experiences, and her aptitude all strongly influenced her career choice. Since her father was a successful lumberman, the young Pettersen was constantly exposed to new construction as well as efficient business practices. A man who equated female attractiveness with intelligence, Pettersen's father was a strong influence on his only daughter's education and love of learning. Pettersen characterized her mother, an artist, as a "free spirit," and it was to art that Pettersen originally aspired. "I feel very lucky to have had the parents I had. It was the perfect combination for what I finally chose to do." (Pettersen, Interview, Feb. 4, 1987) The spacious Pettersen family house, which included the most innovative finishings and fixtures, was also a noteworthy influence on her early perceptions of custom-designed living space.

Pettersen attended the Passaic Collegiate Elementary School through the eighth grade. Anxious to leave home, she convinced her parents to send her to the National Park Seminary in Forest Glen, MD, a prestigious and innovative boarding school. The architecture of the school's buildings, the freedom she experienced, and the love for learning she developed all formed lasting impressions even after the loss of her family's fortune forced her to leave the school in her second year of college.

Simultaneously, she broke off an engagement because of her perception that "in those days [the 1930s] marriage was like being put in a closet. You were a possession. I wanted to be free, wanted to belong to myself. I knew that there was something in me that wanted to come out. There was something else that had to happen before I could get married." (Pettersen, Interview, Feb. 4, 1987) Though she had the opportunity several times during her life, Pettersen never married. "It was always the work that was the gyroscope in my life. I don't know who could have lived with me. As an architect you're absolutely devoured. A woman's cast in a lot of roles and a man isn't. I couldn't be an architect and be a wife and a mother." (Pettersen, Interview, Feb. 4, 1987)

Though bitter to have had to leave the school she so enjoyed, Pettersen began to view the situation as an opportunity. It was the time in her life when "the cage flew open and I could fly out." (Pettersen, Interview, Feb. 4, 1987) She moved to New York City and began supporting herself with a well-paying job in the automotive industry. In 1937 she began night school at Cooper Union with the intention of studying painting. "I had a long list of things I wanted to be and architect was at the bottom. Then I subsequently found out this was what I had the greatest ability for." (Pettersen, Interview, Feb. 4, 1987)

When she graduated from Cooper Union in 1941, with a Certificate in Architecture, Pettersen sought an opportunity to learn the construction trades and fortunately found it as an apprentice with Frank Lloyd Wright in Spring Green, WI. She became a good carpenter and gained extensive hands-on experience with masonry, plumbing, and electrical work. This early foundation later enabled her to work confidently with tradespeople while supervising her own projects. "If I had not gone to Wright's I am sure I would have lost the courage to go on. The enormity of the door I had opened to the architecture world would have overwhelmed me. Wright became my architectural father." (Pettersen, Interview, Feb. 4, 1987) Most significant were Wright's personal encouragement and support.

Pettersen completed her apprenticeship at Wright's in 1943, and fighting the temptation to stay on in the protected and architecturally stimulating environment, she sought work elsewhere. With World War II still in progress, she began to work with the National Defense Research Committee in Princeton, NJ. Working with the exceptional physicists of the day, her position involved analyzing enemy building structures for bombing purposes. In 1944 she worked for R. H. Macy and Co. in New York, designing shops and exhibits. In 1945 she accepted a design position with the Tennessee Valley Authority (TVA) in Knoxville, TN. The work entailed the design of a wide variety of government facilities, providing her with an exceptional opportunity to learn. She remained until 1948, when the TVA began to curtail its rate of building.

As a woman, Pettersen was unique in what was then a man's field. She felt that she was indeed often challenged to prove her capabilities, but did not find that being a woman interfered with securing employment.

Pettersen returned to New Jersey in 1948 for a short visit with her mother. The visit extended to a year, giving her time to study for and successfully pass the rigorous architectural licensing exams. In 1949 she accepted a position with Clifton, NJ, architect Arthur Rigolo, where she was responsible for designing two award-winning projects.

Dissatisfied with being under someone else's roof both at home and at work, in 1952 Pettersen purchased a barn in Saddle River for her residence and at the same time decided to open her own architectural practice. The barn was to accommodate both living and working quarters. In 1952 Pettersen was the only woman architect in New Jersey with her own office. Her professional expertise, acute business sense, and ability to relate well to clients were, and still remain, the cornerstones of her practice and have enabled her to become well respected in her field, as well as financially successful. The original barn has seen several additions since 1952, and as of 1986 nine people were employed in her Saddle River office.

Pettersen's sense of community responsibility led her to become actively involved in many civic and professional organizations. Her involvement in Altrusa International, a service organization for business and professional women, provided her with community ties and also contacts with many dynamic businesswomen. Pettersen was president of the Altrusa Club of Bergen County in 1968–70, and again in 1978–80, and she was governor of District Two, comprising six states and Ontario, in 1977–79.

She has served on numerous professional committees, most notably as the first woman president of the New Jersey State Board of Architects (1975–76) and as the first woman president of the New Jersey Society of Architects (1984–85). In her practice, Pettersen has designed and executed a wide range of projects both in scope and cost: private residences, including former President Richard Nixon's residence in Saddle River; nursing homes; industrial and office buildings; restaurants; and most recently, a prestigious 181-unit luxury town home complex in Park Ridge, NJ.

The key to Pettersen's success can most aptly be summed up by her own enthusiasm: "The most interesting thing in life is people. There's no architecture without [them]. That's why architecture is so fascinating to me . . . it's the clients, the contractors, the people!" (Pettersen, Interview, Feb. 4, 1987)

An interview with Pettersen taped on Feb. 4, 1987, in Saddle River, NJ, provided information for this article.

*June Shatken*

## JEANNETTE RIDLON PICCARD, 1895–1981

The Rev. Dr. Jeannette (Ridlon) Piccard, balloonist, scientist, activist, and first woman to be ordained a priest in the Episcopal church, was born in Chicago, IL, on January 5, 1895. A twin, she was the eighth child and sixth daughter of the nine children born to John and Emily (Robinson) Ridlon.

Piccard grew up in the comfortable, upper-middle-class home in Evanston, IL, provided by her father, a distinguished orthopedic surgeon and one of the founders of the American Orthopedic Association. Her mother presided over the home and children in accord with her strict Victorian values. She carefully monitored Piccard's books, friends, and activities.

Though the Ridlons encouraged their children to attend Sunday school in the Episcopal church, Emily (Robinson) Ridlon was not prepared for her daughter's career aspirations in 1906 when she was eleven. "My mother came into my room one night, sat down beside my bed and asked me what I wanted to be when I grew up," recalled Piccard. "When I said I wanted to be a priest, poor darling, she burst into tears and ran out of the room. That was the only time I saw my Victorian mother run." The priesthood at that time was a male vocation from which women were barred.

Piccard received her secondary education at the University School for Girls in Chicago and at Miss Shipley's School near Philadelphia. Though her mother was not pleased with Piccard's desire to attend college, her father reluctantly gave his support, and Piccard entered Bryn Mawr in 1914. She told M. Carey Thomas, Bryn Mawr's president, of her aspiration to become an Episcopal priest. Unlike others, who reminded Piccard that the priesthood was closed to women, Thomas encouraged her and suggested that she prepare by studying philosophy and psychology.

After receiving her A.B. from Bryn Mawr in 1918, Piccard entered the University of Chicago to pursue a master of science degree in organic chemistry. Shortly after receiving her degree, she married Jean Felix Piccard, a Swiss scientist and professor she had met at the university. The Piccards left for Lausanne, Switzerland, soon after their wedding on August 19, 1919.

Piccard bore three sons during the couple's seven years in Switzerland: John Augustus (b. 1920), Paul Jules (b. 1924), and Donald Louis (b. 1926). During this period and the eight years following their return to the United States, Piccard served as mother, homemaker, and wife.

Piccard experienced freedom in these roles because of the self-sufficiency of her husband and their sons. While the children were young, she went away to attend a week-long conference, leaving a well-ordered home stocked with prepared meals. When she returned, she was met by a radiantly happy husband and three joyful children. The house was a mess and the carefully prepared meals untouched. Jean and the boys had so enjoyed planning their own schedules and preparing their own meals that they had simply forgotten about the ones she had left for them. Piccard never again worried about their welfare in her absence.

After leaving Switzerland, the Piccards lived near Boston for three years before moving to the lower Berkshire valley of New Jersey, near Sparta, in 1927. Here Piccard became active at St. Mary's Episcopal Church. Years later, her son John indicated that the six years the family lived in New Jersey were a significant time in her spiritual development.

According to a letter written by Piccard on March 30, 1977, the New Jersey period was the launch pad of her 1934 record-making stratospheric balloon flight. She wrote, "Jean lost his job (research chemist with Hercules Powder Co.) in 1932. We couldn't get back into teaching. Job hunting is the most discouraging, humiliating business. We printed up a biographical resume and mailed it around without result. Basically, we made the stratosphere balloon flight because he didn't have a job. The upshot, of course, was that after the flight he was a successful aeronautical engineer and we got a job teaching in that field."

Jeannette Piccard piloted a balloon 57,579 feet over

Lake Erie on October 23, 1934, while Jean studied the effect of cosmic rays in the stratosphere. This flight made her the first woman to enter space, setting an altitude record that held until Soviet cosmonaut Valentina Tereshkova orbited the Earth in 1963. It was also the first successful stratospheric flight made through a layer of clouds, and the first in which the balloon remained under control for the entire flight. Piccard recalled, however, that it was difficult to get a sponsor for such a daring flight piloted by a wife and mother.

In 1936 the Piccards moved to Minneapolis, where Piccard earned her Ph.D. in education from the University of Minnesota in 1942. She also did volunteer work at St. Paul's Episcopal Church and was a housing advocate for the Red Cross. After Jean's death in 1963, Piccard served as a consultant for the National Aeronautics and Space Administration from 1964 to 1970.

In the 1970s Piccard was finally able to realize her dream of entering the Episcopal priesthood. She authored a motion, which in 1967 became Episcopal church law, that women be allowed to serve as lay readers in worship services on an equal basis with men. She commented, "Somebody had to do it," when the law finally passed.

After passing written and oral exams and medical and psychological tests, Piccard was ordained a deacon in the Episcopal church at age 76 on June 29, 1971. The next step, ordination as a priest (which would allow her to conduct the communion service and grant pardon from sin), was still closed to women. Nonetheless, Piccard began preparing for the priesthood by attending General Theological Seminary in New York in 1972.

On July 29, 1974, at the Church of the Advocate in Philadelphia, Piccard became the first woman ordained to the Episcopal priesthood. At 79 she was also the oldest of the eleven women ordained that day. Since this took place before the church allowed women to become priests, Piccard's ordination was not recognized by the Episcopal church until January 1977.

Piccard served as associate pastor of St. Phillip's Episcopal Church in St. Paul, which she had attended since 1965. She also encouraged women who entered the priesthood after her, lectured, and received many honorary degrees for her pioneering work in space travel and as a priest.

Piccard was a woman who soared, making history in stratospheric flight and in her pilgrimage to the Episcopal priesthood. When she died, at age 86, of ovarian cancer on May 17, 1981, in Minneapolis, her ashes, like those of her husband, were placed in Lake Vermillion, MN, where they had shared a summer home.

Collections of material on Piccard are available at the Smithsonian Institution (Washington, D.C.), the Minnesota Historical Society (St. Paul, MN), and Bryn Mawr College (Bryn Mawr, PA). She is profiled in Betsy C. Smith, *Women in Religion* (1978).

Her obituary appeared in the *New York Times*, May 19, 1981. Correspondence between the Rev. Katrina Swanson and Piccard and her granddaughter, the Rev. Kathryn Piccard, provided useful information, as did a June 1986 telephone interview with her son Paul Piccard.

*Esther Byle Bruland*

## OLIVE MAE BOND POLK, 1894–1979

Olive Mae (Bond) Polk, New Jersey "Mother of the Year" in 1967, was to her family and church and, later, to her town and state the model of how an educated woman could combine full-time commitment to home and children with a life of public service. For a black woman of her generation to see her achievements honored so widely beyond her own community was most unusual.

Born on May 4, 1894, in the small southern town of Enfield, NC, she was eldest of the three children of Eugenia Bond and Joseph Hewlin. The family was of mixed (black, white, and Indian) background, which, by law and custom, meant "Negro." Eugenia Bond worked as a domestic for a white family and Joseph Hewlin, officially, as a "white man's" barber. Forbidden to cut "Negro" hair in his shop, he served black customers at night in his home, according to family stories. The couple prospered sufficiently to own their own home and encourage their children to pursue education all the way to college. Polk attended Enfield public elementary schools and then, despite the seven-mile walk, the Joseph K. Bucks Industrial High School, operated by the American Missionary Association in Whittaker, NC. She graduated in 1916 and left for Washington, D.C., where she worked her way through Howard University. She had to leave after her first year to return to Enfield and work so that her brother, described by his niece as "a bit of a playboy," might begin college. He did not stay long in higher education, and the following year Polk returned to Howard, where she majored in sociology, with thoughts of a career in social work. Following graduation (A.B., 1921) she was offered a fellowship in the sociology department, but illness prevented acceptance.

Meanwhile, she had met Charles Carrington Polk, a Howard medical student from New Jersey, who received his M.D. in 1921. They were married in Brooklyn, NY, on October 1, 1923, and moved to Westfield, NJ, where he began his general practice. The following year they bought the house in Roselle, NJ, which was to be home, office, library, and center for their expanding family, circle of friends, colleagues, and anyone else passing by in need of a meal, book, job, place to live, or just good talk. In this house four daughters were born: Carolyn, Gene Ann, Barbara, and Josephine. This was not only a matter of home birth by choice. Until the 1940s, black doctors could not admit obstetrical patients to local hospitals except in unusually difficult cases and then as referrals to white doctors.

Polk managed her husband's office and, while caring for her own children, other young live-in relatives, and a constant parade of visitors, as well as doing the housework and cooking, became active in her church. She joined the Heard African Methodist Episcopal Church when she moved to Roselle and was a lifelong member, serving on the Stewardess Board and as church mother (1973). Her children characterized her as a "frustrated social worker," and it was through her church that she began what she considered her most important task—her work with young people. She organized two youth groups, the Silver Star and the Scotch Plaid. Later she began a Girl Scout troop and a long campaign to expand opportunities for African-American scouts. One activity from which they were then excluded was camping. She succeeded in making hers the first African-American troop in the state to be allowed to use a Girl Scout camp. The rationalization for exclusion rested in part on "cleanliness." Polk observed that her troop left the camp "cleaner than they found it."

Work with Girl Scouts, on whose board she was eventually to serve (the first African-American to do so), led to work with the YWCA in Elizabeth, NJ, and successful efforts to open their facilities more widely to blacks. She was interested in the services provided for foreign students far from home, to whom she extended much hospitality. A young German woman became a lifelong friend. Eventually Polk joined the Elizabeth YWCA's board and was a member of its Brotherhood Committee for 20 years.

Her daughters entered public school in a Roselle neighborhood better integrated racially then than now, but when Polk attempted to become active in the PTA, she was firmly discouraged. This was especially ironic, since she was better educated than most of the women in the organization. She dealt with this rebuff with her usual courteous, pleasant persistence and was eventually able to bring black speakers and musicians to programs at Roselle High School and a local auditorium. She initiated an eventually successful movement to have qualified blacks accepted as teachers in Roselle public schools and led a project to include books about and by blacks in the Roselle Public Library. She and her husband collected these books, especially those on African-American history, and donated generously to the library. She was finally asked to be the first African-American to serve on the state Board of Education, but refused because by then she had no children in the schools and believed that only parents who did should serve.

Despite these and many other commitments, she loved to cook for groups and found time to indulge her passion for music, particularly classical music and ballet. Her daughters cherish a memory of pulling up in high style to Newark's Symphony Hall in the 1932 family Buick only to see the car door come off in the doorman's hand.

She was a charter member of the New Jersey branch of the black National Association of College Women. She had joined the National Association for the Advancement of Colored People (NAACP) in college and was also a charter member of its New Jersey branch. Her husband became active in the black National Medical Association and she in its Women's Auxiliary. Other opportunities for service arose from her membership in the League of Women Voters, the Union County chapter of the United Nations, the New Jersey Division Against Discrimination in Housing, the Urban League, the Union County Board of Family and Children's Service, and the Howard University Alumnae Association.

Her selection in 1967 as New Jersey "Mother of the Year" brought her great pleasure, as did the attendance of her husband, daughters, grandchildren, and more than 300 relatives and friends at the dinner honoring her given by her sorority, Alpha Kappa Alpha.

She died at home on August 24, 1979, at age 85, of natural causes and her funeral took place at the Heard Church, where she had begun what the Urban League called, in its citation, her "valuable service and dedication."

An interview with members of the Polk family on July 9, 1987, provided biographical information. Also useful were scrapbooks in the private collection of the Polk family.

*Daryl Boylan*

## ELLEN CULVER POTTER, 1871–1958

Ellen Culver Potter, physician, scholar, and administrator, was a prominent leader for social reform in both the state and national arenas. She was born in New London, CT, on August 5, 1871, the elder child of Thomas Wells and Ellen (Culver) Potter. She had one younger sibling, Thomas W. Potter, Jr., who died in 1880 at age five. Her father was a grocer in New London and the family was active in the Third Baptist Church there. It was through this church that Potter developed her first interest in social welfare. She was active in the church's mission work and was invited by the state missionary society to visit other societies. As a youth she attended the Coit Street School and the Young Ladies High School in New London.

In her early twenties, Potter began studying art. From 1893 to 1894 she studied at the Art Student's League in New York City. Following this, she studied at the Academy of Art in Boston and at another art school in Norwich, CT. At the suggestion of a professor, who felt students would become better artists if exposed to the social conditions of the underprivileged, she began working at the Baptist Morning Star Mission in New York City. There she saw a great need for medical services to the poor and she decided to change her career from art to medicine.

Potter entered the Woman's Medical College of Pennsylvania in 1899 and graduated in 1903. While in medical school she continued to be active in public work. She was treasurer of the local YWCA and helped raise money to pay off its mortgage. After graduating from the medical college, Potter became chief resident physician at the college hospital in 1904. In 1905 she established a private practice in Philadelphia, specializing in obstetrics and gynecology.

During her years in private practice (1905–20) Potter taught on the faculty of the Woman's Medical College and also lectured on social hygiene at Bryn Mawr College. She continued her interest in social welfare as a public school medical inspector (1912–18) and as a state supervisor, in conjunction with the War Department, for reducing the incidence of venereal disease in military camps (1918–20).

Potter's administrative skills were recognized in 1920, when she was appointed head of the Division of Child Health in the Pennsylvania Department of Health. In eighteen months under her guidance more than 200 child health stations were set up. She organized the Bureau of Children in the Pennsylvania Department of Welfare in 1921 and guided the bureau in setting standards for the operation of child welfare institutions. In 1923 Potter was named secretary of welfare in Pennsylvania, becoming the first woman to hold a state cabinet post. Her administration was notable for its achievements in improving the quality of service in state-owned welfare institutions. She conducted research on state institutions and the laws governing them and used statistical data to point out the need for reforms. She was a capable writer and speaker and was adept at enlisting the help of community organizations to push through needed reforms for social welfare.

In 1927, with a political change in the state administration, Potter left her position in the Pennsylvania state cabinet. She accepted a position in New Jersey under the direction of William J. Ellis, the commissioner of the New Jersey Department of Charities and Corrections. Potter was appointed director of medicine of the New Jersey Department of Institutions and Agencies, but she also turned out to be "Ellis' life line to the world of social workers and welfare councils." (Leiby, *Charity and Corrections*, 212) She began her work by helping to develop the new North New Jersey Training School for Feeble Minded Females in Totowa and served as the medical director there for a year. In 1928, while continuing in her position in the New Jersey Department of Institutions and Agencies, she did a brief stint as acting superintendent of the State Reformatory for Women at Clinton and then proceeded to Trenton, where she headed the New Jersey State Home for Girls until 1930. In 1932 she was elected president of the Conference of Superintendents of Correctional Institutions for Women and Girls.

In New Jersey, Potter followed the same approach she had used in Pennsylvania, conducting research on conditions in state institutions in order to demonstrate the need for reforms. In her study of New Jersey correctional farms for women, she found that management usually justified conditions by "cost accounting rather than by . . . therapeutic value." (Leiby, 231) She continued to work with community organizations and the public to change the laws governing state institutions and social practices. She was instrumental in upgrading the state adoption laws, thus reducing the selling of babies in the black market. Her influence also led to the development of community mental health clinics.

Potter's success in Pennsylvania and New Jersey led to national recognition and she became involved in social welfare at the federal level. In 1932 she was instrumental in establishing the National Committee on Care of Transients and Homeless and became its chair in 1933. Through her influence with the Federal Emergency Relief Administration she helped develop the Federal Transient Service in 1933. She became an adviser to the Technical Committee of the President's Commission on Social Security in 1935. Other national committees on which she served included the Wickersham Commission on Prisons and Parole, the Pathfinding Committee on Governmental Relief Methods, the Advisory Committee on Children in War Times, the Advisory Committee for Day Care for Children of Working Mothers, and the Committee on Planning for the Chronically Ill. She was the chair of the last two committees. She was on the Steering Committee of the Social Work Conference on Federal Action, and in 1945 she was elected president of the National Conference of Social Workers. Her responsibilities at the national level notwithstanding, Potter continued to serve actively in the New Jersey Department of Institutions and Agencies and in 1946 was promoted to deputy commissioner. She remained in this position until her retirement in 1949.

Potter was also a dynamic figure in her profession and at the Woman's Medical College of Pennsylvania. In 1929 she was elected president of the American Medical Women's Association (AMWA) for a two-year term. She taught on the faculty of the Woman's Medical College, was medical director of its hospital (1918–20), served as acting president of the college (1941–43), and was a member of its Board of Corporations (1929–53).

Potter was also active at Rutgers, the State University of New Jersey. In 1949 she was appointed chair of the Planning Committee of the School of Social Work at Rutgers. She later served on the Advisory Council for the new school. In recognition of her efforts, the North and South New Jersey chapters of the American Association of Social Workers established the Ellen C. Potter Scholarship.

Potter received an honorary doctorate of law from Rutgers University in 1936 and an honorary doctorate of social science from Woman's Medical College of Pennsylvania in 1950. In 1948 she was the first winner of the W. S. Terry, Jr., Memorial Award from the American Public Welfare Association. She received the Elizabeth Blackwell Award in 1953 and was named "Medical Woman of the Year" in 1954 by the AMWA.

Potter, who remained single, continued her dedication to the improvement of social services throughout her life. Commissioner Ellis described her as feisty little woman who was an indefatigable worker. (Leiby, 231)

Potter died, at age 86, in Philadelphia on February 8, 1958. In a memorial she was noted for her great capacity for work, clear thinking, humor, and willingness to see both sides of a question: Potter "combined a wide vision of needs in the medical-social fields with the ability to execute the visioned plan." (Baumann, "Memorial," 297) She was buried with her parents and brother in the Cedar Grove Cemetery in New London, CT.

The archives of the Medical College of Pennsylvania (Philadelphia) contain Potter's papers and other memorabilia. Additional information, including her work in founding the Rutgers School of Social Work, is available at NJ-RU. Two of her works used for this article are: "Woman as a Social Force" (1952) and "Evolution in the Field of Medical Care," *Journal of the American Medical Women's Association* 7 (Jan. 1952):1–4. Insights into Potter's social work activities appear in James Leiby, *Charity and Correction in New Jersey* (1967). Potter is profiled in *DAB, Supp. 6* (1980). See also Margaret Steel Moss, "Ellen C. Potter, M.D., F.A.C.P.," *Public Administration Review* 1 (Summer 1941):351–62; and Frieda Baumann, "Memorial to Ellen Culver Potter, M.D.," *Journal of the American Medical Women's Association* 13 (July 1958):296–97. Her obituary appeared in the *New York Times*, Feb. 10, 1958.

*Constance B. Schuyler*
*Betty Hayes*

### JENNIE E. PRECKER, 1892–1981

Jennie E. Precker, founder of the nation's first women's bank, was born on December 5, 1892, in New York City. She was the third of four children (two sons and two daughters) born to Joseph and Regina Mary (Balmuth) Precker, both Austrian Jews. Her mother came to this country by herself when she was twelve to live with an uncle. Here she met and married Joseph Precker, a hatter.

Precker went to the Newark Normal School (now Kean College) and taught elementary school before she attended the New Jersey Law School (now Rutgers University Law School, Newark). She was awarded an LL.B. cum laude in 1922 and passed the bar exam in 1922 on the first attempt. While in law school she was first struck by the unfair status of women: "A professor explained that the dower or courtesy right of a wife in rents, profits and proceeds of a home jointly owned was one-third compared

with one-half for the husband." (*Sunday Star-Ledger*, Oct. 15, 1978)

Precker joined her brother Abram's Newark law firm as a partner after her graduation from law school and practiced mostly real estate law.

In 1923 Precker founded the Susan B. Anthony Building and Loan Association (SBA), 1186 Raymond Boulevard in Newark. Named after the suffragist Susan B. Anthony, whom Precker greatly admired, the SBA was formed to make it easier for women to develop thrift and to own homes. It was the first in the world whose officers, directors, counsel, and staff were all women. Precker felt strongly that women were superior to men as mortgage appraisers because they were more careful. Thirteen other women helped Precker in the organization of the bank.

In 1923 Jennie E. Precker founded the Susan B. Anthony Building and Loan Association, the nation's first women's bank, in Newark. This photograph of Precker was probably made around 1930. *Courtesy, private collection.*

The SBA sold $200 installment shares to its savings members at $1 a month, to mature in eleven years; later the shares were payable in $5, $10, and $25 increments. The SBA was open only one evening a month, the third Wednesday, to receive mortgage and shareholder payments, but Precker met with customers in her law office at other times. A slight, wiry woman, she was strict and scolded those who were late with their payments. Some recall her vitriolic tongue, while others recall her as a conscientious woman who "lived for that institution." (William B. Lewis, Interview, July 27, 1987)

The SBA remained strong during the Depression largely because of Precker's foresight in setting up reserves greater than those required by law at that time. In 1961 it became a savings and loan association, and in 1978 it was merged with Carteret Savings and Loan Association, Newark. At that time it had on deposit an estimated $300,000 in savings and $250,000 in outstanding home mortgages. The name was transferred to a new Carteret branch being opened in Livingston, where until after Precker's death women made up the entire staff. Precker was retained as counsel and as a member of the Advisory Board.

During the Depression, Precker went back to New Jersey Law School and earned a master of chancery in 1932. In 1951 she earned a master of law degree from New York University Graduate School of Law, where she was named to the "King's Bench," an academic honor.

She was a member of the federal, Essex County, and New Jersey bar associations, the National Association of Women Lawyers, and the Alumni Association of New York University. As counsel to the New Jersey Women's Republican Club, she joined a movement that was successful in gaining remedial legislation to equalize women's shares of marital property. In 1978 she stated publicly her support for the constitutional Equal Rights Amendment. She was active for 30 years as counsel for the Salvation Army, Newark, and she founded the Women's Auxiliary of New Jersey. Precker was awarded a citation for British War Relief, the Crest Award (for "dedicated service to mankind") from the Salvation Army in 1975, and the International Award from the Salvation Army that same year. She also served as counsel for the Humanity Baptist Church of New Jersey and the Tabernacle Baptist Church, and was made an honorary member of the Baptist Church. Precker lived in Newark before moving to South Munn Avenue, East Orange, in 1957.

Precker was active in Deborah, a Jewish organization funding medical projects to combat heart and lung diseases, and the Lawyers' Division of the United Jewish Appeal of Metropolitan New Jersey. She served as a member of the board of the Newark YM-YWHA. She was also active in the Rutgers Alumni Association. In 1975 she was awarded a bronze plaque for "service and devotion to the legal profession" from the New Jersey State Bar Associa-

tion.

Precker remained single. Her hobbies included arranging art exhibits, going to the theater, ballet, and opera. Her two nieces remember her as vivacious, devoted, and caring. In July 1980 she had surgery for stomach cancer. Then on March 12, 1981, at age 88, she died of chronic pernicious anemia. At the time of her death, Precker was in the Hartwick Nursing Home, East Orange. She was buried in the Talmud Torah Cemetery, in Newark.

Articles on Precker are: Alexander Milch, "Steely Jennie Proved Mettle in Banking," *Sunday Star-Ledger* (Newark, NJ), Oct. 15, 1978; and Joan Cook, "Women Successfully Run Small Savings Institutions," *New York Times*, Jan. 12, 1976. Interviews with Precker's nieces, Gertrude Isserman, Orange, NJ, Sept. 4, 1986, and Selma Rothseid, Boynton Beach, FL, Sept. 23, 1986, and with William B. Lewis, former NJ Deputy Commissioner of Banking, Nutley, NJ, July 27, 1987, and Dora P. Rothschild, Esq., Newark, NJ, July 27, 1987, provided useful information. Materials on Precker's bank are available in the files of the New Jersey Department of Banking (Trenton, NJ). Her obituary appeared in the *Jewish News* (Newark, NJ), Mar. 19, 1981.

*Phoebe Seham*
*Sherie Fox Schmauder*

## JESSIE D. READ, 1903–1978

Jessie D. (Blunt) Read, New Jersey gynecologist and obstetrician, was born on May 19, 1903, in Florence, CO, the third of five children of Joseph D. and Vina (Patterson) Blunt. Her father, a lawyer and district judge, was born in Jackson (Lanaconing County), MD, and her mother, a grade school teacher, was born in Ontario, Canada. Her father, formally educated only through the third grade, was taught by his wife and gained admission to the University of Michigan, where he earned a law degree in 1902. In addition to his judicial duties, Joseph Blunt ran a freight line up Phantom Canyon, near Florence, to Cripple Creek. Read's parents were among the first settlers of Fremont County, CO.

Read graduated from Florence High School in 1920. She attended the University of Colorado at Boulder for a year and then studied at the University of Denver when her family moved to that city. By 1925, when she received her B.A. from the University of Denver, she had already completed a year of medical school at the University of Colorado Medical School in Denver.

While in college Read met Chester Louis Read on a blind date. In 1925 she moved to New York City and the couple was married on August 8, 1925, in the Little Church Around the Corner in Manhattan. Read continued her medical training at Long Island College Medical School. During her summers she worked as a proofreader for the *American Journal of Biological Chemistry* and as a substitute intern at Bellevue Medical Center and the Eye, Ear, Nose and Throat Clinic. She received her M.D. in 1928. Chester Read received his Ph.D. in physical chemistry from Columbia University in 1930 and became a chemical engineer for ESSO. The couple had two children: Nancy (b. 1932) and Ruth (b. 1934).

Read began medical practice in New York hospitals but soon moved to New Jersey. From September 1928 to January 1929 she worked in the New York Infirmary for Women and Children, in obstetrics and gynecology. Following this she worked as an intern at Bellevue Hospital, in children's surgery and in adult surgery and medicine, and at Manhattan Maternity Hospital. In 1930 she became a resident obstetrician at Margaret Hague Maternity Hospital in Jersey City and her long practice in the state began. Read opened her own office in Jersey City in October 1931, but relocated to Westfield in 1934 while she continued working at Margaret Hague Hospital as a biochemist and pathologist.

Read felt strongly that one should have a doctor who could be confided in. Her office was in her home, and many of her patients were family friends. In order to manage the demands of her professional and private life, she had the support of several people. Her daughter Nancy was cared for by a nurse, and when her daughter Ruth was born, Chester Read's parents came to live with the family. With the help of live-in servants, her mother-in-law took on the responsibility of running the household and kitchen. Read and her husband divided other family responsibilities.

In 1943, when her daughters were in grade school, Read volunteered for the U.S. army, leaving her Westfield practice to be taken over by Dr. Martha Maurer. Read was one of only thirteen female Army physicians. She spent her first fifteen months at Fort Riley, Kansas, and Fort Oglethorpe, Georgia, where her daughters visited her during the summer. Read was then sent overseas to the European theater for seventeen months. After a brief inactive duty at Fort Dix, she was mustered out in April 1946 with the rank of major. Read felt the armed services had been overstaffed with physicians during the war, forcing many doctors to work as clerks; she herself, however, was kept busy as a doctor.

After her tour of military service Read returned to private practice and formed an obstetrics and gynecology partnership in Westfield with Dr. Daniel Jarvis and Dr. John McGeary, which lasted from 1948 to 1957. Read had been named a diplomate of the American Board of Obstetrics and Gynecology in 1939, and she became a fellow of the American College of Surgeons in 1948. She was a founding fellow of the American College of Obstetricians and Gynecology in 1952. She served as a consultant in obstetrics and gynecology at St. Barnabas Medical Center in Livingston and on the emeritus staff at Overlook Hospital in Summit.

Read was particularly interested in vaginal cytology as a diagnostic procedure and had been taking vaginal smears well before the use of the pap smear became routine. In March 1954 she coauthored a paper with Ray F. Chesley, "Vaginal Cytology as an Office Procedure: Report of a Six Year Survey," which was published in the *Bulletin of the Margaret Hague Maternity Hospital*.

In 1966 Read was named Woman of the Year in Medicine by the New Jersey Medical Women's Association. She was a member of the American Medical Association, the New Jersey Medical Society, the New Jersey Obstetrics and Gynecology Society, and the American Medical Women's Association.

In her spare time, Read liked to keep busy with handiwork. She made rugs, sewed, worked with stained glass, crocheted, knitted, and did needlepoint, which she gave as gifts.

Read died, at age 75, of a heart attack on December 29, 1978, while vacationing in Denver, CO.

Telephone interviews with Read's daughters, Ruth Ogden Russell of Tucson, AZ, and Nancy Zavitz of Arvada, CO, provided biographical details. Biographical records, including "The Blunt Book," a typewritten family genealogy, are in the possession of Russell. Read's article is "Vaginal Cytology as an Office Procedure," *Bulletin of the Margaret Hague Maternity Hospital* 7 (Mar. 1954):1–10. Her obituary appeared in the *New York Times*, Jan. 9, 1979.

*Penny Harter*

## MARY GINDHART HERBERT ROEBLING, 1905–

Mary (Gindhart) Herbert Roebling, banker, businesswoman, and philanthropist, was born July 29, 1905, in West Collingwood, NJ, the eldest of four children born to Isaac Dare Gindhart, Jr., and Mary (Simon) Gindhart of Philadelphia, whose ancestors dated back to Colonial America.

Roebling's childhood was comfortable and secure. She and her siblings, John, Floyd, and Margaret, enjoyed the financial comforts afforded through their father's position as president of the Keystone & Eastern Telephone Company. Roebling's mother, a pianist and vocalist who introduced sight reading of music to the public school system, flooded the large Gindhart home with music and the arts while her father brought the business world in the door. Even as a young girl, Roebling took her place at head tables, accompanying her father to civic and business functions when the demands of young children kept her mother at home. These years were good training for the young woman, who was influenced deeply by her father's business sense and was to spend the majority of life at head tables around the world. Educated in public schools, Roebling loved to dance and watch classical dance, but her overriding impression of those early years was her strong sense of family, which influenced her business methods and relationships later in life. "Every day my parents told me that they loved me," she said. "That is the most important thing in the world! You should tell a child you love him every day of his life." (Roebling, Interview, Nov. 17, 1985)

In 1921, at the age of sixteen, Roebling married Arthur Herbert, a young soldier and nephew of the great American composer-conductor Victor Herbert. Although the marriage produced a daughter, Elizabeth, in 1922, it was cut short by tragedy. Young Herbert had been mustard-gassed in the war and contracted an infection in his nose. "We didn't have penicillin in the twenties, you understand," Roebling explained, "and the infection developed into blood poisoning. One day we were having dinner together, and 24 hours later, he was dead." (Interview, Nov. 17, 1985)

A 20-year-old widow with an infant daughter, Roebling returned to the shelter of her parents' home and entered the business world. Working in a Philadelphia brokerage house, she spent her evenings studying merchandising and business administration at the University of Pennsylvania. It was during this time she met Siegfried Roebling, grandson of Colonel Washington Roebling, builder of the Brooklyn Bridge. The two were married in Morristown, NJ, in 1931 and had a son, Paul, in 1934. Siegfried Roebling died suddenly of a heart attack in 1936, leaving Roebling once again widowed, with two small children. This time Roebling's life took a dramatic turn that started her on the path of achievement and public service that has become the hallmark of the rest of her life. Roebling remembered how her career as a banker began: "Mr. John A. Roebling [Siegfried Roebling's father], my father, and the lawyers insisted that as executor of my husband's estate, I become president of the Trenton Trust [the Roebling family bank]. In those days you did what your parents told you to do. . . . I didn't have any choice. When I told them I didn't know anything about banking, John A. Roebling told me that I had the rarest commodity in the world—common sense—just use it." (Interview, Nov. 17, 1985) She ran the bank by day and rode the commuter train from Trenton to New York to take evening banking courses at New York University.

Roebling credited her parents' presence and care of her children during those years as the means by which she was able to dedicate the long hours to her career. She not only saved the Roebling bank during years of economic upheaval, but established innovative practices of public relations, merchandising, drive-in banking, and other services that many banks still copy. Through these innovations, she dramatically increased the Trenton Trust's $17 million in assets to more than $200 million, a proud achievement for

the first woman to serve as chairman of the board of a major commercial bank.

Although she was described repeatedly in newspapers and magazines as "attractive" and a "helluva good-looking woman," Roebling had no social life outside her work and community commitments. She felt that remarrying would have made it impossible to accomplish the community work and business innovations for which she was responsible. Instead, she channeled her energies into the banking business and civic concerns. "I did nothing but work. I made my work my hobby. I was lucky that way," Roebling said. "Mother and Daddy were always there and provided a home and family for me to go to at the end of the day." (Interview, Nov. 17, 1985) She made those who worked for her part of that family, taking an active interest in their health, families, and education.

In succeeding years Roebling was called upon to serve her country as well as private industry. President Franklin D. Roosevelt appointed her to the committee working on the China Relief Bill. President Harry S Truman made Roebling the only woman member of the Citizen's Advisory Committee on Armed Forces Installations. She successfully served in such diverse appointed roles as delegate to the Atlantic Congress for NATO and the White House Conference on Refugee Problems to chair of women's activities for the International Chamber of Commerce's 17th Congress and the Citizens Advisory Council to the Committee on the Status of Women. In 1958 Roebling was named the first woman governor of the American Stock Exchange and hailed as "America's first lady of finance" by the president of the exchange. In 1972, when the Trenton Trust Company was merged into the National State Bank, Roebling was elected board chair of the combined institutions. She helped found the Women's Bank of Denver in 1978, the nation's first chartered bank established by women.

Roebling was honored by many civic and government organizations as well as by many foreign countries. She received the Commendatore of the Order of the Star of Solidarity from the president of Italy, the highest award allowed a civilian, and the Israel Freedom Medal. Deeply committed to the U.S. military ("I think it began when I was ten years old and wrapped bandages at Fort Dix"), Roebling received the President's Medal from the U.S. Army, a Distinguished Service Award from the U.S. Marine Corps, and the Outstanding Civilian Service Medal. She also served as honorary colonel of the Jersey Blues. The founding president of the Army War College Foundation, Roebling maintained a steadfast belief in universal military training. "The military is a service that all citizens—men or women—should render to their country," she said.

Service is a byword for Roebling, a woman of great exuberance and warmth who, in her eighties, puts in eighteen-hour days and maintains that she still hasn't "done it all or given near enough." She was distinguished as the first woman to serve as economic ambassador of the state of New Jersey, director of the New Jersey Fire Insurance Company, Life Trustee of National Defense Transportation Association, and as a member of the Interstate Commission on the Delaware River Basin and of the New Jersey State Investment Council. Roebling has been awarded many honorary degrees, including doctor of commercial science, St. John's University; doctor of law, Ithaca College; and doctor of humanities, Wilberforce University.

An interview with Roebling in Nov. 1985 provided useful information, as did a biographical pamphlet prepared by her office for distribution in Sept. 1984. A sketch of Roebling appeared in *Current Biography* (1960).

*Denise V. Lang*

## IDA COHEN ROSENTHAL, 1886–1973

Ida (Cohen) Rosenthal, cofounder and president of Maidenform, Inc., was born January 9, 1886, in Rakov, Russia. She was the eldest of the seven children of Abraham and Sarah Kagonovich, who changed their surname to Cohen when the family emigrated to America.

During her early years, Rosenthal, who came from a Jewish family and whose father was a Hebrew scholar, helped her mother run a small grocery store, which supplemented the family income. At sixteen, she went to Warsaw, Poland, where she worked as a seamstress and began to develop her considerable skills as a dressmaker. During that period she used her spare time to her advantage by studying Russian and mathematics.

The years between 1904 and 1909 marked several changes in Rosenthal's life. Around 1904, when she was 18, she followed her sister Ethel's lead and emigrated to the United States, where she settled in Hoboken, NJ, and worked as a dressmaker. By 1906 she had met and married William Rosenthal, a young man who had fled to the United States to escape being drafted into the Russian army.

The newly married Rosenthals combined their skills as seamstress and merchant and continued to develop their dressmaking business. By 1909 the members of Rosenthal's family who had remained behind in Russia emigrated to the United States and settled in New York. There they, too, went into business and established A. Cohen & Sons, wholesalers of silverware, cut glass, and clocks.

During their years in Hoboken, the Rosenthals flourished both personally and professionally. Their son, Lewis, was born in 1907, followed by the birth of their daughter,

Beatrice, in 1916. (Lewis died in 1930, at the age of 23.) At the same time their dressmaking business was growing steadily, and by 1918 they employed about 20 workers. It was during the winter of that year that the Rosenthals moved to New York. The city of Hoboken required the Rosenthals to shovel the snow from the substantial sidewalk in front of their shop. Infuriated by the city's demands, they packed up and moved their family and growing business to Washington Heights, NY.

In the early 1920s Rosenthal and her friend Enid Bissett formed a partnership and opened a dress shop on W. 57th Street in Manhattan. The combined talents of the two women soon led to a fashion innovation—the design of a new type of undergarment. Because the dresses of the 1920s were very boyish, women bound their breasts tightly with a plain strip of cloth to achieve a flat-chested appearance. Rosenthal and Bissett transformed this brassiere into a more comfortable, natural garment by changing it from a simple band that hooked in the back to the bandeau. They cut the band in half and gathered it with tucks to form cups that gave support and uplift to a woman's breasts.

Rosenthal and Bissett's new bandeau might even be seen as a sign of the times for women. In 1920 women voted for the first time in a presidential election. During the Roaring Twenties women were relieved of much of the drudgery of household tasks by the new luxury of appliances, canned food, and ready-made dresses such as those made by Rosenthal and Bissett. These women of the 1920s welcomed the new brassiere. At first Rosenthal and Bissett gave them away free with their dresses. As women returned to buy the new bandeaus, Rosenthal and Bissett made them out of silk and sold them for a dollar.

As Rosenthal and Bissett's business expanded, it grew too large for the New York City factory. By 1924 the Maiden Form Brassiere Company factory moved to Bayonne, NJ. Rosenthal's brothers advised her not to develop the brassiere portion of her business but to manufacture only dresses. She did not follow their advice and her business sense proved prophetic when, in 1929, almost all of the dress houses failed and Rosenthal survived the financial disaster.

As the bandeau grew in popularity, dress styles changed as well to a softer, more feminine look. Sales increased steadily, and by 1938 Rosenthal and Bissett's Maiden Form Company had annual gross earnings of more than $4.5 million. Much of the success of Maiden Form can be credited to Rosenthal's vigorous, innovative style. A tiny, vivacious woman whose presence affected every aspect of her business, she was the company treasurer in charge of sales and finance. Her husband, William Rosenthal, company president, was in charge of design and production. He created brassiere sizes that evolved into A, B, C, and D cup bras and are still the industry standards today. The company was also known for innovative labor practices, creative design, and excellent management.

In 1940 Enid Bissett's poor health forced her early retirement and the Rosenthals continued as the principal managers of Maiden Form. As World War II raged and manufacturing companies vied for scarce raw materials, Rosenthal was able to convince the government that her business was vital to the American war effort. She claimed that WACs and Waves would be less fatigued if they wore her bras. Maiden Form also supplied soldiers with vests equipped with special pockets designed to hold carrier pigeons.

In the late 1940s Rosenthal began an aggressive ad campaign that was to be one of the most effective and well-known campaigns in advertising history. Print advertisements showed fashionable young women engaged in a variety of activities such as shopping, dining, and going to the theater—clothed above the waist only in their Maidenform bras. The ad copy read, for example, "I dreamed I went shopping in my Maidenform bra." This highly successful ad campaign ran for 20 years and made the Maiden Form Company famous. Annual gross earnings jumped from $4.5 million in 1938 to $40 million by 1964.

Upon the death of her husband in 1958, Rosenthal became president of Maiden Form and by the next year she also served as chairman of the board. In 1960 the Maiden Form Company changed its name to Maidenform, Inc., which is also the trade name of its products. During that decade, Rosenthal, who was in her seventies, traveled to over 100 countries to oversee the worldwide interests of Maidenform. This included a trip to her homeland, the USSR, as part of an international industrial study team. She continued in an active role in Maidenform into her eighties.

Rosenthal had many philanthropic interests. With her husband, she founded Camp Lewis, a Boy Scout camp named after their deceased son and located in Sussex, NJ. They also made contributions to the Albert Einstein College of Medicine of Yeshiva University and supported the activities of the Anti-Defamation League of B'nai B'rith.

On March 28, 1973, at age 87, Rosenthal died of pneumonia in New York City.

An interview with Beatrice Coleman, Rosenthal's daughter, on Nov. 1, 1985, provided biographical information. For magazine articles on Rosenthal, see "Maidenform's Mrs. R," *Fortune* 42 (July 1950):75–76, 130, 132; and "I Dreamed I Was a Tycoon in My . . . ," *Time* 76 (Oct. 24, 1960):92. Rosenthal is profiled in *NAW-MP*. Obituaries appeared in the *New York Times*, Mar. 30, 1973; *Time* and *Newsweek*, Apr. 9, 1973.

*Grace A. Aqualina*
*Margaret Dooley Nitka*

## ANNE RYAN, 1889–1954

Anne (Ryan) McFadden, artist, was born on July 20, 1889, into an upper-middle-class Irish Catholic family in Hoboken (Hudson County), NJ. Her maternal great-grandparents, Michael and Bessie (Eaton) Smith, arrived in America from Meath, Ireland, and settled in Hoboken in 1840. Her father, John Ryan, was a bank officer who wrote poetry in his spare time, and her mother, Elizabeth (Soran) Ryan, was a homemaker who painted and took occasional trips to Paris. Ryan, their eldest child, had three younger brothers. Both parents died when she was thirteen, and the next year (1903) she entered the Academy of St. Elizabeth Convent in Convent Station, NJ.

The Ryans spent the summers at their house in Asbury Park, where Ryan married her childhood playmate William Joseph McFadden in 1911, leaving college in her junior year. Her husband, from a wealthy New Brunswick, NJ, family, graduated from the Rutgers Law School and became a prominent lawyer in Newark. During her married life Ryan resided in the affluent section of Clinton Hill, Newark, summering in Belmar, NJ. The McFaddens were married for twelve years and had three children: twins, Elizabeth and William J., Jr. (b. 1912), and Thomas Soran (b. 1919). In 1923 Ryan was legally separated and resumed her family name.

In 1931 she decided to visit Europe and the exotic island of Mallorca, where her imagination was captivated by people, towns, and colors. In Paris she enjoyed the art exhibits and met many American artists and writers. She was inspired to write and tried her hand at different forms of literary expression: the short story, poetry, and the novel. But the rent she received from her house in Newark did not provide a sufficient financial base for her life abroad, and she had to return to the United States. Her comfortable life-style was at an end. She opened a bakeshop and a tearoom in Glen Ridge, NJ, to support herself and her younger son, Tom. In 1935, when Ryan was 46, she and her son moved to Greenwich Village in New York City, where she opened a restaurant, Hearthstone.

From this time on, Ryan focused her talents on the visual arts. In this field, as previously in literature, she tried different forms in search of the right medium. She began with painting, followed by etchings and engravings, completing about 100 woodcuts. Finally, six years before her death, she found her medium in collage.

In New York she became part of a community of American and emigré European artists that included Tony Smith, Hans Hofmann, Fritz Bultman, Barnett Newman, and Giorgio Cavallon. Encouraged by Hans Hofmann, she began painting in 1936 and had her first one-woman show in 1941 at the Pinacotheca, 777 Lexington Avenue. That same year she met Stanley William Hayter, joined his Atelier 17, and did a series of engravings entitled *Constellations*.

For Ryan, 1948 proved to be a critical year. She saw an exhibit of collages by Kurt Schwitters at the Rose Fried Gallery. His work fascinated her, and she immediately started to create in this medium. Within a year, she had her first solo exhibit in collage at the Marquie Gallery on 57th Street.

In six years Ryan created over 400 collages in a unique expressive style, work that established her as a leading American woman artist. The message in her work was entirely different from that of Kurt Schwitters. While Schwitters was making a comment on the outside world surrounding him, Ryan explored through collage the inner world of her own being. Schwitters was a journalist, Ryan a philosopher. In her collages she created that inner *Raum* in which to breathe and move, individual and introspective.

One can find in her style echoes of Klee, Kandinsky, Braque, Picasso, and Miró. Her collages are small: from four-by-five to eight-by-ten inches. Composition, texture, and color are varied and captivating. Most colors are pastels. Shapes overlap, run parallel, juxtapose, concentrate, and disperse. Her best works incorporate the rich textures of paper handmade by Douglass Howell. Fabrics of different quality and sometimes pieces of thread are included in her composition. Viewed from a distance, shapes become almost animate and organic. Her most distinguished works are from her "White" series, where shades of white are the basic elements. These compositions usually present an oval superimposed on a square or a rectangle. Although Ryan did not invent the collage, she was a pioneer in saturating it with intellectual quality.

After 1942 Ryan's daughter, Elizabeth McFadden, became her lifelong companion, her advocate and protagonist. In 1951 Ryan was forced to vacate her apartment, and her first impulse was to return to New Jersey. She persuaded her daughter to look for a house in Hoboken—her birthplace. Her daughter, however, realized that the artist, to succeed, had to be in constant contact with the art world. And the art world in those years did not extend beyond the Hudson. Ryan settled for an old house in Greenwich Village reminiscent of the Hoboken brownstone of her childhood residence. She remained there for the last three years of her life.

Ryan was not a traditional mother, yet she instilled in her children respect and devotion to her. They always congregated around Ryan, admiring her spirit, vivacity, and energy. After separating from her husband, Ryan relentlessly pursued her own interests and way of life. Her motto and philosophy, as stated by Elizabeth McFadden, was "Bound by no rules and for myself alone." (McFadden, Interview, Mar. 14, 1986)

McFadden believes that two people exerted the strongest determining influence on the formation of Ryan's character: her maternal grandmother, Anne Smith, and SISTER HELEN ANGELA DORETY at the Academy of St. Elizabeth

Convent. Her grandmother passed on to her the belief that a woman has a right to her life. SISTER HELEN ANGELA impressed on her the value of an inquiring and creative mind and a firm conviction that learning and creating are unending, lifelong processes.

Ryan lived in two worlds: the world of the "awkward everyday" and that of "the imagination." In 1949, in the art publication *Tiger's Eye*, she stated her outlook: "The rights of the imagination are greater than any other rights. In the secret country where the solitary mind exists, where it is possible for only one, the self, to enter, all colors, arcs, patterns, images, have steady room for themselves to move about and resolve at last under the fingers. The rights of the imagination have nothing to do with the awkward everyday, of the insistent, crooked wheel of the hour going over and over, but with creed, with the 'I believe' taken again and again to the center of purpose but still able to see as far as the furthest, distant rim. All faith, delight, and instinct is the atmosphere to breathe in." (Ryan, "The Ideas of Art," 55–56)

In the "awkward everyday" life, Ryan was a child who tragically lost both parents at thirteen and at fourteen drastically changed her life-style from one of leisure and comfort to the rigid routine of a convent school, who separated from her husband and took on different jobs to sustain her three children. On the surface Ryan was gregarious, vital, and friendly. In the world of the imagination she was exceptionally private, persistent, determined, and inexhaustible. Ryan was propelled all her life by a creative energy manifested by her writing and her art. She died in Morristown on April 18, 1954, at age 65, of complications from a stroke, and is buried in East Hanover, NJ.

The Archives of American Art (New York, NY) contain Ryan's correspondence, notebooks, exhibit catalogs, and manuscripts of her writings. A personal interview with her daughter, Elizabeth McFadden, of Warwick, NY, on Mar. 14, 1986, provided useful information. Ryan's personal artistic philosophy appears in "The Ideas of Art: 11 Graphic Artists Write," *Tiger's Eye* 1(1949):55–56. Exhibition catalogs provide details of her life and work; see Sarah Faunce, *Anne Ryan, Collages* (1974); Eric Gibson, *Anne Ryan: Collages 1948–1954* (1979); and Judith McCandless, *Anne Ryan Collages and Prints* (1979–80). Ryan is profiled in *NAW-MP*.

*Halina R. Rusak*

## MARGERY AUSTEN RYERSON, 1886–

Margery Austen Ryerson, an award-winning painter and printmaker known for her portrayals of children, was born in Morristown (Morris County), NJ, on September 15, 1886, the only child of Mary McIlvaine (Brown) Ryerson, a sculptor, and David Austen Ryerson, a Newark attorney. Her father was descended from early Dutch settlers, a family prominent in the Pompton Plains area of Passaic County, where they owned several ironworks. Her mother, born in Philadelphia, lived in Princeton, NJ, with her uncle, a Princeton professor and Presbyterian minister, after the death of her parents. Mary (Brown) Ryerson's father was a teacher, writer, and art collector.

Ryerson spent her early years in Newark, moving to Morristown when she was about three. Wherever she lived, art was an important part of her environment. Her mother, who had studied with prominent sculptors, including Augustus Saint-Gaudens, always reserved a room in their home for a studio. As a young child Ryerson spent many hours there modeling for her mother and learning to draw. Drawing was like playing for her, she said.

Ryerson went to school in Morristown, first to the Peck School and then to Miss Dana's Seminary for Young Ladies. At Miss Dana's, Ryerson's strong-minded determination to follow her own course surfaced when she decided to go to Vassar College. She had not been academically prepared for college at the finishing school, her teachers discouraged her, and there were family financial problems because of her father's poor health. But she overcame these obstacles and was accepted at Vassar "by the skin of my teeth," she recounted. (Interview, May 1986) She financed her education with family gifts, loans, scholarships, and by working at whatever jobs she could find. In 1909 she received her B.A. in mathematics.

For the next two years she taught school, but she gave it up because she didn't like teaching. In 1911 she enrolled as a graduate student at Columbia University, where she studied English and mathematics but never finished her M.A. She also worked for a year at Columbia Teachers' College writing mathematics textbooks.

In addition to teaching, studying at Columbia, and writing, she continued to follow her lifelong interest in art. During summers spent at Cape Cod, encouraged by her mother, she studied painting with Charles Hawthorne, founder of the Cape Cod School of Art. Hawthorne, a well-recognized painter, was impressed with Ryerson's talent and encouraged her to study at the Art Students' League in New York City with Robert Henri, a realist painter who was leader of the Ash Can School, an art movement dedicated to freedom of expression in the depiction of modern urban life. Sometime after the death of her father in May 1910, Ryerson and her mother moved to New York City so that she could more easily study art.

Between 1910 and 1915 Hawthorne and Henri were Ryerson's chief mentors in the development of her artistic style. They shared a similar approach to painting, that of working quickly and spontaneously in broad swatches of color with little or no drawing. Henri advised his students to compose a painting in "large masses" of color. "Don't do details, features until you get the large masses right," he cautioned. (Henri, *The Art Spirit*, 26) Ryerson recalled that Hawthorne emphasized "learning to see 'color notes' in nature" and noticing "how one color and value was related to another. . . . Don't see a barn; see a spot of red." (Movalli, "A Conversation with Margery Ryerson," 63) Ryerson based her own style of painting on these ideas of her teachers. She described how she painted a portrait: "I begin a painting with four spots of color: the hair, the background, and the face—two for the face: one for the light and one for the shadow. The flesh is what the painting is all about, and then comes whatever looks good against it." (Movalli, 59)

With her years of art apprenticeship behind her, about the time of World War I Ryerson began her long struggle to earn enough as an artist to support both herself and her widowed mother. Her teachers gave her no advice on how to succeed as a woman artist; but more important to her was the fact that they taught her what she considered was "the right way" to paint. Yet in spite of her recognized talent and training by competent teachers, it was almost impossible for her to get her work exhibited. Men organized the art shows, Ryerson recalled, and they did not ask women artists to exhibit with them.

Failing to get her paintings exhibited, she turned, with typical practicality and determination, to making prints and created for herself a unique niche in the art world. She found an inexpensive printmaking class. Using an old set of dental tools given to her by her dentist, instead of expensive engraving tools, she took her copper printmaking plates to Lower East Side settlement houses in Manhattan, where she sketched the children of poor immigrants. She worked directly on the plates with a few decisive lines, portraying children asleep during their naps and children on the move. Some of the most successful were her prints of the settlement house children during their free music lessons—a child playing the violin or piano, a child conducting—all totally absorbed in what they are doing.

Competent in many media, she also portrayed children in oils, watercolors, and pastels, but she first gained recognition with her prints. By 1922 her prints had been exhibited at the Chicago Art Institute, the Toledo Museum, and other places. An article praising her etchings appeared in *Art in America*, October 1922. In 1925 another article in the same journal described her as "one of the best known American interpreters of babyhood and childhood in pastels and drypoints" (Ely, "Margery Austen Ryerson," 283) and added that in depicting poor immigrant children "she practically has the field to herself." (Ely, 287) As her reputation grew she received commissions for oil portraits of children of the affluent. She painted landscapes and portraits of adults, but children remained her primary subject.

Ryerson's depictions of children are often less portraits than quick studies of children emphasizing body language rather than facial characterization. Her commissioned oil portraits, however, emphasize a more individualized characterization of the specific child, though she never was "especially interested in getting likenesses. . . . When that's the main concern, the work is usually pretty boring." (Movalli, 58)

Success brought her membership in and awards from many art societies, including election to the National Academy of Design in 1944. Her work in all media has been frequently exhibited and acquired by many museums and galleries here and abroad. Although she never married and was never a mother, she won a hard-earned place in a man's world with traditional woman's subject matter—children.

Writing and editing formed a second career for Ryerson. She is best known for compiling material from the art school lectures and writings of her teacher, Robert Henri, into a book called *The Art Spirit*. The book is a loose collection of Henri's views on how to paint and his philosophy of art and art appreciation. First published in 1923, it has become a classic in its field, read by many art students and reprinted many times. In the late 1930s the wife of Charles Hawthorne asked Ryerson to help her assemble a similar compilation of Hawthorne's ideas on art. This book, *Hawthorne on Painting*, was published in 1939. Ryerson's own writings include articles on other artists, advice on how to paint children, and book reviews.

Ryerson, alert and outspoken two days before her hundredth birthday in September 1986, appeared at the opening of a centennial exhibition of her work at Ringwood Manor, once the home of her great-grandparents and now part of Ringwood State Park in Passaic County, NJ. The manor is now the home of the Ringwood Manor Art Association, founded by Ryerson. The house contains family furniture that she donated. Displayed there is a landscape painted by her great-grandmother, Frouche Van Winkle Ryerson.

A telephone interview with Ryerson in May 1986 provided useful information. A collection of her papers and artworks are in the possession of Janet Le Clair (New York, NY). Ryerson assisted with the writing of two books: Robert Henri, *The Art Spirit* (1923); and Charles Webster Hawthorne, *Hawthorne on Painting* (1939). Articles on her work include Charles Movalli, "Conversation with Margery Ryerson," *American Artist* 40 (Nov. 1976):58–73; Catherine Beech Ely, "Margery Austen Ryerson," *Art in America* 13 (Aug. 1925):283–88; and "The Etchings of Miss Margery Ryerson," *Art in America* 10 (Oct. 1922):257–58. Ryerson appears in *Who Was Who in America* 7 (1981) and *Who's Who in American Art* (1980).

*Patricia D. Heath*

## WINIFRED LOEB SALTZMAN, 1912–

Winifred Rose Millicent (Loeb) Saltzman, a dedicated volunteer worker for the National Council of Jewish Women for almost half a century, helped formulate national policies for resettling Jewish refugees from the death camps of Europe after World War II. She was also instrumental in founding Passaic County Children's Shelter and in the development of family and mental health services in Passaic (Passaic County), NJ, where she was born on May 21, 1912, the first of two children (both daughters) of Harry and Dorothy (Weisman) Loeb.

Born in Vienna of Austrian and Russian Jewish parents, Saltzman's mother grew up in New York City, where she helped draft legislation for a state assemblyman and became an ardent woman suffragist, concerned with social justice issues. She stopped working outside the home after marrying Harry Loeb, a young attorney of German Jewish descent, born in Cincinnati, OH, and reared in Passaic, NJ, where the couple settled.

Until she was eight years old and her sister, Norma, was born, Saltzman was raised as an only child. She believes that as a young girl she was treated with special patience by her teachers because her father, one of the first Jewish lawyers to practice in Passaic, was a well-liked, respected member of the Passaic school board. Her father imbued Saltzman with a rigid sense of honesty and self-discipline.

Educated in Passaic's public schools, Saltzman graduated from Passaic High School in 1930. She attended Cornell University, graduating in 1934 with honors in English literature, and then sought work as a writer. Finding potential employers more interested in hiring a typist, she taught school, but did not enjoy it. Meanwhile, she had met J. (Jason) Bernard Saltzman, a native New Yorker who was practicing law in Passaic. After a civil marriage ceremony on August 5, 1935, the Saltzmans were married in a religious ceremony nine days later on board the SS *Manhattan*, on which they sailed for Europe.

Saltzman gave up her teaching career to concentrate on raising her son, Peter Ronald (b. 1939). She hired Kaethe Pezall, a Jewish war refugee, to help care for him. Pezall asked for assistance in finding the fiancé she had left behind when she fled Nazi Germany. This led Saltzman to increase her work as a volunteer for the National Council of Jewish Women (NCJW) since this organization had an active refugee assistance and search program. Pezall's fiancé was never located. However, Saltzman rose rapidly in NCJW's ranks because of her research and organizational skills. In 1943 Saltzman represented the regional division of NCJW on a coalition of 20 organizations seeking to improve sanitary conditions in New Jersey. That year she attended monthly meetings in Newark; then she spent four more years commuting to Trenton to lobby lawmakers on the issue. When the bill reorganizing the N.J. Department of Health was finally signed into law on May 22, 1947, Saltzman was among those invited by Governor Alfred E. Driscoll to witness the signing.

As president of the Passaic section of NCJW in 1947, Saltzman helped to arrange for funding, formulate operating guidelines, and hire personnel for the first nonvolunteer, professionally staffed Jewish social service agency of Passaic, Clifton, and the vicinity. She became president of the new agency's Board of Directors.

In 1949 Saltzman accepted the national vice-chairmanship of NCJW's Service to the Foreign Born Committee and was also elected to the Executive and Administrative committees of the United Service for New Americans (USNA). Her duties included traveling to other states to find suitable host families and to convince them to sponsor immigrants to the U.S. She also attended weekly meetings to set national policy for resettling Jewish refugees in this country. In 1951, as second vice-president of USNA, Saltzman chaired the committee that negotiated the merger between USNA and the Hebrew Sheltering and Immigrant Aid Society and Saltzman served as a director and Executive Committee member of the new agency, the Hebrew Immigrant Aid Society (HIAS), until 1956.

During this same period Saltzman was a director of the interracial Guidance Guild Nursery School in Passaic, set up and funded in part by the local NCJW. She was also an active member of the Citizens Committee on Temporary Shelter Care, a group intent on establishing a separate shelter for Passaic County's delinquent and abandoned children. Saltzman convinced Lloyd Marsh, the Republican county political leader and a political ally of Saltzman's husband, who was an assistant Passaic County prosecutor, of the need for the shelter. With Marsh's backing, the Passaic County Board of Chosen Freeholders authorized the use of county-owned land for the shelter and allocated funds to build it. On January 1, 1955, the freeholders appointed Saltzman to a three-year term on the shelter's first Board of Directors. She subsequently wrote to communities all over the country for models of bylaws for the new facility. Along with the other shelter directors, Saltzman also supervised the building, furnishing, and staffing of the shelter. In 1958 she was appointed to a second term on the shelter's board.

During her son's childhood, Saltzman was torn between her duties as a parent and her volunteer commitments. To ensure that Peter would be cared for whenever she was not at home, in 1942 she and her husband accepted her parents' offer to share their eleven-room house, where they stayed until Peter left for college in 1956.

In the 1960s and 1970s Saltzman chaired the NCJW committee responsible for negotiating employee wage agreements, supporting higher salaries and benefits for office workers. In 1961, after helping to establish the Mental Health Clinic of Passaic, she became its first president. She continued research in preparation of publications for NCJW on women's pension rights, censorship, U.S. domestic violence, and foreign policy in the 1980s.

Widowed in 1978, Saltzman continued to live in Passaic. At the Golden Anniversary Celebration of the Jewish Federation of Greater Clifton-Passaic in 1984, Saltzman was given an "In Appreciation of Leadership" award for her work as president of the Jewish Family Service in 1949–50. Also in 1984 she received the Hannah G. Solomon Award, the highest award given by NCJW. The award, named in honor of its founder, is given to a woman who has helped change and expand the role of other women in vital areas of community life, and whose leadership has resulted in progress and enlightenment in the community.

Taped interviews with Saltzman on Feb. 3 and 5, 1986, as well as Saltzman's personal papers and clippings, provide the major sources of information on her. Telephone interviews with Helen Powers, assistant executive director of the National Council of Jewish Women (New York), and Pat Bremer, of the Jewish Family Services of Clifton and Paterson, also provided useful details on her life. Saltzman narrated a part of the film *Living Testimony: The Story of National Council of Jewish Women Advocacy* (1985) dealing with refugee resettlement work after World War II; it is available from the National Council of Jewish Women (New York).

*Estelle Siegal Perry*

## KATHERINE SCHAUB, 1902–1933

Katherine Schaub, a watch dial painter and an early victim of radium poisoning, suffered from an occupationally caused disease throughout much of her short life, but continually fought for justice and for happiness. Born in Newark (Essex County), NJ, on March 10, 1902, she was the second child of William and Mary (Rudolph) Schaub. As a teenager, she lived with her grandfather and an orphaned cousin, in addition to her parents, brother, and two sisters. Like many working-class girls, she left school at the age of fifteen and went to work with her cousin Irene Rudolph, also a teenager.

Schaub and her cousin considered themselves fortunate enough to find work in a nearby "watch studio," where as many as 200 young women would gather to paint luminous numbers on watch faces. The studio was on the top floor of the U.S. Radium Corporation's plant in Orange, NJ. Light streamed in through an all-glass roof, illuminating the tedious but light work, and the room was quiet so the young workers, many of whom were friends and relatives, could socialize. A good worker like Schaub could paint about 200 watches a day and earn about $20 in a five-and-a-half-day week. This was considered good pay for women then. Schaub described the work as "interesting and of a far higher type than the usual factory job." (Schaub, "Radium," 138)

Schaub and Irene Rudolph worked steadily from 1917 to 1919, but by 1920 the work became sporadic, and the cousins left Orange by 1921. Schaub found a clerical position with another group of friendly women at an automobile roller bearing factory. In the fall of 1921 Schaub returned to dial painting, only to leave again in the spring of 1922. She then went to work as a parcel wrapper at Bamberger's, a large department store in Newark.

During the winter of 1921–22 Irene Rudolph became ill. Her jaw became infected after a problem with her teeth, and she suffered from anemia. After "a most terrible and mysterious illness" lasting one and a half years, Rudolph died. (Schaub, "Radium," 138) Her family suspected some connection between Rudolph's illness and her work as a dial painter. Schaub herself reported Rudolph's death, another similar death, and a third suspicious illness to New Jersey's Health and Labor departments, but no known dangerous compounds were found in the luminous paint, and the plant met all legal requirements. Despite one chemist's suspicions that radium might be at fault, and the discovery of several other suspicious cases by an Orange health officer, the U.S. Radium Company was given a clean bill of health by the state.

Schaub herself began to have some trouble with her teeth in November 1923, about six months after her cousin's death. Even though two teeth were removed, her jaw continued to pain her, and she became concerned. "I kept thinking about Irene," she wrote later, "and about the trouble she had with her jaw." (Schaub, "Radium," 138) She began to meet with other dial painters similarly afflicted, and with their doctors and dentists. They all believed that they were dealing with an occupational poisoning. During this time Schaub began to suffer from what she called "nervousness," and she was often depressed, "gloomy and morbid," an understandable reaction to her plight. (Schaub, "Radium," 139)

In 1924 a private organization, the New Jersey Consumers' League, a branch of the National Consumers' League, with the energetic Katherine Wiley as executive secretary, stepped in and began documenting the illnesses and deaths among the dial painters. Wiley interviewed Schaub, and Schaub explained the details of the dial-painting process. She had at times personally instructed new employees. As she later testified in court, "I instructed them to have a very good point on the brush. . . . I instructed them to put the brush in their mouth to get the best point on it." (Schaub trial testimony) Wiley was sure that radium was the cause of what was colloquially called "jaw rot." She interested several health professionals in her theories, including the county health examiner, and she urged Schaub to consult with him. Schaub then learned that radium ingested and inhaled at work was plated in her bones, causing the necroses, joint deteriorations, anemias, and eventual cancers from which she and other dial painters suffered.

New Jersey's workers' compensation program covered only those occupational poisonings listed specifically in the statute, and radium poisoning was not among them. To file liability claims, the dial painters needed to have acted within a two-year statute of limitations, counted from the last day of employment, unless the company had acted so as to prevent the dial painters from understanding the nature of their illnesses. Wiley and the Consumers' League helped some of the dial painters find a lawyer willing to take their case, and Schaub helped supply evidence that the company had acted fraudulently. Schaub testified that in December 1925, a few months after she had been diagnosed as radioactive, she was examined by a Dr. Frederick Flinn. He told her that none of her illnesses was attributable to radium. In December 1926 Flinn published his conclusion that "an industrial hazard does not exist in the painting of luminous dials." (Flinn, "Radioactive Material an Industrial Hazard?" 2081) The Consumers' League discovered that Flinn was employed by the U.S. Radium Corporation.

This and other evidence of a coverup by the corporation, as well as adverse publicity orchestrated by the Consumers' League, led the Radium Corporation to offer a generous out-of-court settlement to Katherine Schaub and four coworkers who had brought suit with her. They each received $10,000 immediately, a $600 annuity for as long as they suffered from radium poisoning, and full payment of all their medical bills.

Schaub had been informed that an early death was inevitable, but she helped allay her fears through religious faith. She spoke of wishing to visit Canadian shrines "with the faith and the hope that something can be done for me by prayer." (*Newark Sunday Call*, May 13, 1928) Shortly before she died, she wrote, "My great consolation has been my faith in an omnipotent God." (Schaub, "Radium," 141) But less ameliorable through faith was loneliness; Schaub wrote scornfully of friends who "won't own up. . . . They know it isn't rheumatism they've got. . . . God—what fools—pathetic fools! . . . Afraid of being ostracized!" But Schaub, at the age of 26, must have identified with their fear "of losing their boyfriends and the good times." (Schaub, unidentified newspaper clipping, Raymond Berry Papers)

Her first action after the settlement was to repay her parents for their years of support. She then invested some money, but used the balance to buy the fancy clothes she had always wanted, vowing, "For a year I would live like Cinderella as the princess at the ball." (Schaub, "Radium," 140) Despite a relapse that sent her to the hospital for four weeks in the early months of 1929, Schaub found that "seeking forgetfulness" granted her some relief from her anxiety, and her overall health improved a little. A year after the settlement, some newspapers suspiciously reported that the women "doomed to die" were still living, but Schaub struggled to avoid depression. She decided to continue her education and enrolled in a home study course through Columbia University. She studied college preparatory and writing courses and worked on an autobiography.

Her illness caught up with her in August 1930. The radium plated in her bones had weakened a leg so much that it spontaneously fractured. Osteogenic sarcoma was discovered, and doctors urged amputation by October 1932. Schaub refused.

By this time she had spent all of her $10,000, but she managed to subsist on medical coverage and her annuity. Schaub lived in a private sanitarium in Roseland, NJ, during the two years preceding her death. She took taxis wherever she wished to go and, despite the Radium Corporation's protests, continued to send them the bills for home and transportation as part of her medical expenses. Almost 31 at her death on February 18, 1933, Schaub was a woman who doctors found to be "a highly hysterical woman . . . too difficult to handle" but who herself celebrated, "I have been granted . . . [a] priceless gift—I have found happiness." (Schaub, "Radium," 141) She was buried in Holy Sepulcher Cemetery in Newark.

Most of Schaub's writings were destroyed by a sister, but a fragment was published: "Radium," *Survey Graphic* 68 (1932):138–41. The best primary source is a file on her at the Center for Human Radiobiology, Argonne National Laboratory, Argonne, IL. Based on data from this file, Dr. William Sharpe wrote "Radium Osteitis and Osteogenic Sarcoma: The Chronology and Natural History of a Fatal Case," *Bulletin of the New York Academy of Medicine* 47 (1971):1059–82. Additional primary sources are her lawyer's files (which include trial transcripts), known as the Raymond Berry Papers, also called the Records of the National Consumers' League, at DC-LC; also the papers of the National Consumers' League at DC-LC; and the papers of the Consumers' League of New Jersey at NJ-RU. Schaub also appears as a numbered case in various medical studies on dial painting. The article referred to by Frederick Flinn is "Radioactive Material an Industrial Hazard?" *Journal of the American Medical Association* 87 (1926):2080–81.

*Claudia Clark*

## VERA SCHECTMAN, 1890–1971

Vera (Schectman) Abrams, Newark physician, was born in Ananiev, Odessa, Russia, on April 18, 1890. She was the fourth of seven children (four girls and three boys) born to Benjamin and Bella (Miller) Schectman.

Little is known about Schectman's early life in Ananiev. The early 1900s in Russia was a time of unrest and peril for Jews, and this unrest may have led to the decision of Schectman's parents to emigrate to the United States with five of their children. Schectman and her sister Hannah, however, were left in the care of their grandparents, who

were financially secure landowners. She completed the *gymnasium* and at sixteen taught private pupils in the home she shared with her grandparents. Prompted by Schectman's desire to study medicine, and perhaps by recent pogroms in Kishinev, not far from Ananiev, her grandmother arranged for her and her sister to join their family in the United States.

In 1906 Schectman settled with her family in Newark, NJ, where her father owned a bicycle shop on Belmont Avenue. The Jewish community had proliferated and prospered in Newark and though she was thousands of miles from Ananiev, Schectman had the support of her family and community to smooth her adjustment. She took a job and also attended secretarial school, learning shorthand "that I might take down notes in shorthand at college classes." (Wingert, "Newark Doctor")

Schectman's dream of becoming a doctor began to come true in 1908 when, at the age of eighteen, she entered the Woman's Medical College of Pennsylvania. The financial burdens of her education were eased by a brother who had become a druggist and gave her $5 a week to help pay for her books and her wardrobe of two blouses and a skirt. Schectman later recalled that she studied her medical books with an open Russian dictionary and an open English dictionary at hand. In four years, on May 29, 1912, she graduated from the medical school with a class of 30 women.

Schectman never returned to Russia. She did, however, return to Newark in 1912, where she became the first woman intern at Newark's Beth Israel Hospital. There she earned a reputation as an active, conscientious, and hardworking doctor. In 1916, in addition to her work on the hospital staff, she became a member of the Committee of Public Health Education in Newark and traveled around the city giving talks on sex education to women's groups. She spoke Polish, Yiddish, German, French, and Italian, in addition to Russian and English, and was thus able to communicate effectively with many of the newly arrived immigrant women who needed the assurance of speaking with a doctor in their own tongue.

She married Maurice Abrams, a Russian-born milling engineer from Hightstown, NJ, in Newark on June 15, 1919. The marriage lasted until Abrams died in 1961. Their daughter, Sandra Pearl, was born in 1920. Schectman took pride in training her daughter and collected memorabilia she hoped would be "instrumental in making Pearl proud of her mother." (Wingert) The demands of motherhood and marriage, however, did not dull Schectman's dedication as a doctor. Confessing that her career demanded many sacrifices, she found great satisfaction in combining married and professional life. "It [medicine] has given me the opportunity of becoming a great friend to women and girls. They are usually not reticent in telling me all their troubles, and I am thus able to help them considerably." (Wingert)

By 1926 Schectman was serving on both the medical and the teaching staffs of the hospital. She was still the only woman on the hospital staff. Her private practice, which she started near the old Beth Israel Hospital on High Street, was by this time well established. In a 1926 newspaper interview she commented: "[I] have seen the sex prejudice against women physicians wear off to a great extent. Fourteen years ago the prejudice was very bad, and securing a practice was a hard, uphill climb." (Wingert)

Throughout her long professional life, Schectman dedicated her practice to inner-city residents, primarily women, charging modest fees or waiving fees altogether, paying for prescriptions herself if necessary, offering her own home for a mother in labor to save hospital costs. Her office was in her home and her patients were her friends. She practiced family medicine, delivered babies, and made house calls until the age of 70, when she developed a specialty in weight control. Having successfully treated an obese patient who wished to have a baby, Schectman found she was getting referrals of obese patients seeking weight-reduction therapy. The care of these patients increasingly dominated her practice. Not entirely satisfied with a practice devoted to "well" patients, she consulted one of the city agencies and started making house calls in inner-city minority neighborhoods whenever needed.

During her career Schectman served as physician and medical examiner for the Civil Service of New Jersey and as a substitute school physician. The last doctor in her community to make house calls, she was 80 when she retired, deeply disappointed because she could not find another doctor to take over her inner-city practice.

Schectman died in South Orange, at age 80, of heart disease on March 1, 1971, within a year of her retirement. She was buried in Beth Israel Cemetery in Woodbridge.

A brief biographical sketch of Schectman appears in the *Jewish Community Blue Book of Newark* (1924). An interview with her was written by Dorthea Wingert, "Newark Doctor Left Russia as a Girl to Fulfill Ambition," *Call* (Newark, NJ), Dec. 12, 1926. Correspondence with Schectman's daughter, Sandra Miles, on Nov. 11, 1985, provided biographical details. The archives of the Medical College of Pennsylvania (Philadelphia) contain Schectman memorabilia.

*Dolores Davis*

## ANTOINETTE QUINBY SCUDDER, 1888–1958

Antoinette Quinby Scudder, poet, painter, playwright, and cofounder of the Paper Mill Playhouse, the daughter of Wallace M. and Ida V. (Quinby) Scudder, was born on September 10, 1888, in Newark (Essex County), NJ. Her father, the son of a justice of the New Jersey Supreme

Court whose family had settled near Trenton before the Revolution, had founded the *Newark Evening News*, a successful liberal newspaper. Her mother, the daughter of a former mayor of Newark, came from a prominent manufacturing family of English descent.

Scudder and her brother, Edward, grew up as members of one of Newark's most influential families. Her father was a philanthropist and patron of the arts who was involved in many charitable activities and served on numerous boards. In 1903, when Scudder was fourteen, her mother died. Her father remarried in 1906, giving her a stepmother and later a stepbrother, Wallace M. Scudder, Jr.

The education Scudder received was typical of her social class at the turn of the century. She attended Miss Townsend's School in Newark, where she enjoyed acting in plays. Like many children, she acted out fairy tales at home with friends and "wrote" plays with her older brother. But by the age of fifteen it was apparent that Scudder had a penchant for the theater, and a talent as well. She wrote a five-act tragedy in verse before graduating from school. Since Scudder was expected to join in the usual round of debutante parties, it was not until 1915 that she enrolled at Columbia University to study literature and language. At the same time, she was studying at the Art Students' League with George Bridgeman. After World War I ended, Scudder worked overseas for Anne Morgan's Committee for Devastated France. She continued her painting while abroad.

When Scudder returned to the United States she continued studies in New York with George Bridgeman at the Art Students' League. She learned anatomy and line drawing from Bridgeman and subsequently received training from Martin Leach and Charles Hawthorne, also at the Art Students' League. During the mid-1920s she continued to write plays, travel abroad, and study painting at the Cape Cod School of Art. She became a member of the Summer Art Association of Provincetown, where she spent her summers and acted with the Wharf Theater.

Meanwhile, Scudder and her brother, Edward, became interested in founding a drama branch of the Newark Art Club. She contributed one-act plays to be performed. These amateur productions were staged in the auditoriums of the West Side High School and the School of Fine and Applied Arts, where facilities were far from ideal. In fact, many years later Scudder would recall Ibsen's *Lady from the Sea* being performed with a basketball game going full tilt in the adjoining room.

In 1928 Scudder wrote a play called *Prince Pentaur*, which was successfully produced in New York by a poetry group. Scudder was a member of this group. The play's success was instrumental in the founding of the Paper Mill Playhouse.

The lead in *Prince Pentaur* was played by Frank Carrington, a young actor who had recently arrived from the Pasadena Playhouse in California. Also performed in Newark that year, in the ballroom of the Dryden residence in Lincoln Park, *Prince Pentaur* was so well received that it led to the organization of the Newark Art Theater, with Scudder as president and Frank Carrington as director.

The group planned and produced such plays as Shaw's *Androcles and the Lion*, Sir James Barrie's *Quality Street* and G. Martinez Sierra's *Romantic Lady*. *The Bluebird*, a delicate fantasy, won the company a letter of appreciation from its author, Maurice Maeterlinck.

Despite the group's successes, Carrington discovered an unwillingness to support a community art theater in Newark; the Newark Art Theater was changed to the Essex Repertory Theater when the group found a regular following in Montclair. Then Carrington and Scudder decided to look for a permanent home for their theater.

In 1934 Scudder purchased a paper mill from the Diamond Paper Mill Company in Millburn. The property was near transportation, had colonial charm and possibilities for enlargement. With the help of Newark architect Henry D. Scudder, renovation—underwritten by Antoinette Scudder—began. Four years later the Paper Mill Playhouse, conceived by Scudder and Carrington as both theater and arts center, opened with its first dramatic performance: Sierra's *Kingdom of God*.

At first, the playhouse produced only plays. Works by Shaw, Galsworthy, Barrie, and Coward were performed by Broadway stars. But in 1940, when *The Mikado* was inserted into a vacant week of summer stock, Carrington and Scudder discovered the popularity of musicals, and the next season they scheduled nothing but operettas. During those early years Scudder was a jack-of-all-trades, a role she relished. She served as playwright, property woman, wardrobe mistress, and actor.

In addition to her involvement with the playhouse, Scudder continued her literary pursuits. Public recognition of her talents had come as early as 1930, when her play *The Second Generation* won a prize for best play written by a woman. By 1932 she had written 5 full-length plays and 24 shorter ones. Her awarding-winning plays had been produced in Massachusetts, Pennsylvania, and Maryland. Scudder was a poet as well as a playwright, and by 1932 had two published volumes: *The Maple's Bride* and *Out of Peony and Blade*. In 1934 she published *East End, West End*, a book of poems inspired by observations from her studio at Provincetown. Another collection of poems written over a period of three years was published in 1947. Many of her poems appeared in anthologies. In 1949 she published *World in a Matchbox*, drawn from what she considered the best of her one-act plays.

Meanwhile, Scudder continued painting. Her studio was in a room on the top floor of the Paper Mill Playhouse, where her paintings covered the walls and were stacked on the floor. An exhibition of some 30 of her paintings, ranging from decorative and symbolic subjects to landscapes and portraits, was held at the Academy of Arts in Newark in 1948. Although she lived in Newark, sharing a house in later years with a friend and nine cats, she preferred to work in her studio at the playhouse to keep in touch with Paper Mill affairs. The playhouse continued to thrive from the 1940s through mid-1950s, especially because of the popularity of the musicals it produced.

Scudder, physically trim and petite, was businesslike in manner. She had a direct way of speaking and a brisk way of handling problems. She has been described as the spiritual financial angel of the Paper Mill Playhouse, conceiving the idea of a community theater, and contributing more than $1 million to it before she died of a heart attack, at age 69, on January 27, 1958, at her home in Newark.

Biographical details of Scudder and her family appear in Moses Bigelow, *The Scudder Family of Trenton* (1948). She authored a collection of her plays, *The Cherry Tart and Other Plays* (1938), and her poems, *Italics for Life: The Collected Poems of Antoinette Scudder* (1947). An account of her founding of the Paper Mill Playhouse appears in her *World in a Matchbox* (1949). Articles describing her activities are "Influential Friends Help Realize Founding of Community Venture on Site of Old Mill," *Newark Star-Ledger*, Oct. 21, 1934; "Artist Explains Her Versatility," *Newark News*, Dec. 18, 1948; and "Antoinette Scudder Is Painter, Writer and Executive," *Newark Sunday Call*, Mar. 6, 1932. Her obituary appeared in the *New York Herald Tribune*, Jan. 27, 1958, and the *New York Times*, Jan. 28, 1958.

*Pamela A. Shaftel*

## LENORA SUSAN SLAUGHTER, 1906–

Lenora Susan (Slaughter) Frapart, for 32 years the executive director of the Miss America Pageant, one of Atlantic City's most notable events, was born on October 23, 1906, in Liveoak, FL, to Alpheus Byron and Susan Letitia (Johnson) Slaughter while they were on vacation from their home in Columbus, GA. She was the second of four children and the only daughter. Slaughter's father worked as a farmer in Georgia and Alabama and as a businessman in Virginia. She attended various schools as her family moved around the South, graduating from high school in Newport News, VA, in 1927. Shortly after her graduation her father moved the family to St. Petersburg, FL, where he joined the fire department.

Slaughter could not afford to attend college, so she went to work as a bookkeeper, first for a wholesale grocer in Virginia and then for the Chamber of Commerce in St.

Petersburg. There she discovered she had a talent for working with people. She described herself in an interview as a "born promoter."

In 1935 she was recruited for a six-week assignment to help reorganize the Miss America Pageant, a beauty contest that began in 1921 as an attraction to extend the tourist season in Atlantic City, NJ, beyond Labor Day. Over the succeeding years, the pageant's circumstances had varied, and it was discontinued in 1927. One attempt to revive it in 1933 met with only limited success, but in 1935, coincident with Slaughter's appointment, promoters were able successfully to reestablish the contest on a long-term basis.

What began as a six-week loan of her services to pageant officials turned into a lifetime's work for Slaughter. During her 32 years of association with the Miss America Pageant, she helped shape the once-faltering event into a popular American institution. Under her leadership, the pageant evolved from a bathing beauty contest into a display of young American womanhood that was part of an elaborate scholarship foundation that awarded over $37 million in financial aid to Miss America contestants between 1945 and 1985. She also succeeded in making over the pageant to promote the qualities she admired in American girls—youth, beauty, innocence, and a willingness to work hard to achieve a goal.

The name "Miss America" had been used by illustrators of the late 19th century to depict the ideal American woman as young and virginal, free to join the work force, athletic, and as reflecting the youthful outlook and vitality of a new, energetic country. Beauty contests, too, had a long tradition in America: in the late 19th century they were often held as attractions at carnivals, dime museums, city and state festivals, and as promotion devices by major metropolitan newspapers. The present Miss America Pageant retained features of the festival atmosphere; elaborate boardwalk parades and outdoor swimming exhibitions during the pageant's early years were later replaced by skits and acts performed by the contestants themselves.

Slaughter was initially hired to garner public support within Atlantic City for the pageant and to coordinate the civic activities surrounding the pageant. Central to her strategy was her conviction that the well-to-do in Atlantic City and throughout the nation would accept the pageant only if its seminude exposure of women was legitimated through devices designed to render it respectable. The festival setting helped, as did her success in 1935, the first year of her involvement, in persuading Atlantic City civic leaders to serve as chaperons for the young women. In 1948 she succeeded in having the winner crowned wearing an evening gown, not a bathing suit, a change that lent a greater respectability to the show. In 1949, when the Miss America of that year married during her reign, pageant officials required that the winner remain single until she

passed the crown on to her successor. Thus the association of the contest with the presumed sexual innocence of the unmarried woman was maintained.

Throughout her years as executive director, a post she assumed in 1941, Slaughter developed a national system of civic organizations, notably the Jaycees, that conducted local and state pageants that sent winners to the finals in Atlantic City. Slaughter said she relied on those organizations because they could reach the type of young woman she wanted to see compete: someone who was fresh and wholesome in appearance and who was sufficiently skilled to provide a pleasant musical or dramatic performance. For three decades Slaughter traveled extensively throughout the country, visiting and recruiting groups that franchised the local and state events.

Perhaps as much as any woman of her time Slaughter influenced millions of American girls who watched the Miss America winners and tried to copy their hairstyles, clothes, and poise. But the image of physical appearance the contest winners consistently presented was neither innovative nor unusual, and it is notable that most faded into obscurity once their reign ended. The Miss America Pageant was basically a conservative institution, reflecting the values of an America dedicated to purity for its young women and to a consumption ideal under which competition is a keen value. Slaughter's own ideas meshed well with these, and thus the popularity of the contest she promoted also attests to the strength of these values, even in times of seeming liberalization.

When she had the pageant "under control," she took time out to marry Bradford H. Frapart in August 1948. A native of Chattanooga, TN, he was in the hotel management business and served as business manager for the Miss America Pageant after their marriage. Slaughter and he owned a home in Northfield, NJ, where she enjoyed gardening during her rare hours off. They did not have children, but Slaughter had no regrets, considering the Miss America "alumnae" as her daughters.

Because of Slaughter's central role in running the pageant for over 30 years, when she retired in 1967 her title of executive director was retired also. Her successors are called executive secretaries. After her retirement, Slaughter and her husband moved to Scottsdale, AZ, where he died in 1972.

Telephone interviews with Slaughter in 1985 and 1986 provided biographical details. Information on the Miss America Pageant appears in Frank Deford, *There She Is: The Life and Times of Miss America* (1971); and Lois Banner, *American Beauty* (1983).

*Sheila Lacouture*
*Lois Banner*

## CORA PETERSON SMITH, 1884–1986

Cora Elizabeth (Peterson) Smith, foster parent to over 70 children, was born on November 26, 1884, on Hornblower Avenue in Belleville (Essex County), NJ, and lived all of her life in that community. Samuel Peterson, her father, was Swedish. Hannah (Sloan) Peterson, her mother, was partially of Cherokee descent and came from Flanders (now Hackettstown), NJ. Smith was the youngest of four children (two boys and two girls).

Smith attended Belleville Community School No. 1 (now the Belleville School Board office), which at that time housed grades one through twelve. After graduating from high school, Smith worked as a messenger with the Tiffany Company, whose glass manufacturing plant was in Newark, with offices and retail outlet in New York. On December 25, 1912, at the Thirteenth Avenue Presbyterian Church in Newark, she married Frank Smith, a trumpet player and leader of both a dance band and an orchestra that played for local church functions. Smith herself was an able musician and played both violin and piano.

Although Smith and her husband never had children of their own, over the years she was a mother to more than 70 children, starting with her sister's daughter, Cora Stout. Smith's care of her infant niece might have been temporary at the beginning, but it became permanent when Stout's father died, leaving his widow with twelve other children. Stout, who with her aunt's help became a professional violinist, continued to live with her aunt until the latter's death in 1986. In that era of larger families and more stable communities, such interfamilial caretaking arrangements were not uncommon; nor are they unusual today in close-knit communities where an aunt or a grandmother will often raise or help in raising a child.

In some cases Smith raised not only the child, but the children of that child. For instance, in 1939 Smith took in Marlene Delaney Talmadge, who was distantly related to her. A generation later she raised Talmadge's son. Smith was a foster parent to children of all races and backgrounds. Donna Miller, who was white, was brought to Smith when she was five days old. Years later, Smith raised Miller's daughter.

Cora Stout tells the story of a man who came at eleven o'clock one evening with his three children, aged eight, six, and three, and asked Smith to take them in temporarily. They ended by staying for several years, until their mother returned for them.

According to Stout, there were usually anywhere from five to eight children living with Smith. Some stayed only a few months, until their parents could take them back, or until they were permanently adopted by others; other children stayed on to be raised by Smith; and a few, like Cora Stout, stayed with Smith as adults.

After her husband's death in 1940, Smith started the Cora Smith Catering Service, which catered many civic, social, and service organizations in Belleville and neighboring towns. The income she earned from this enterprise augmented her late husband's Social Security benefits and made it possible for Smith to give her foster children extra luxuries, including music lessons for those who showed talent.

Most Belleville residents were unaware of the number of foster children Smith cared for over the years. Only in 1962, when she received the Mother of the Year award from American Legion Post 105 of Belleville, was the extent of her effort understood.

Smith was for many years the secretary of the Little Zion Church on Stephen Street in Belleville, which was founded in 1888 by Hannah Peterson, her mother, and William Henry Sloan, her uncle. Smith was also a member and secretary of the Belleville Colored Women's Welfare Club.

On Smith's hundredth birthday, November 26, 1984, the town of Belleville honored her outstanding commitment to children and community service by proclaiming Cora E. Peterson Smith Day. She died a year and a half later on July 12, 1986, at her home in Belleville at age 101, and was buried in Glendale Cemetery, Bloomfield, NJ.

Information for this article was obtained by telephone interviews with Smith's niece, Cora Stout, and with Joseph Grosch, retired Belleville school principal, in Mar. and Apr. 1987. Smith's obituary appeared in the *Newark Star-Ledger*, July 13, 1986.

*Blair T. Birmelin*

## FLORENCE TENNEY STARKEY, 1901–

Florence Gould (Tenney) Starkey, a pioneer industrial microbiologist, was born in Pawtucket, RI, on October 3, 1901. She was the oldest of four girls born to May Diantha (Gould) and Louis Burton Tenney. Her mother was a professional organist and pianist who performed at churches and taught music in Virginia, New York, and Connecticut, following the career moves of her husband, an architect and builder. The families were of Scots-Irish origin, established on the American continent since the 17th century. One ancestor on her mother's side, Oliver Wolcott, signed the Declaration of Independence.

After graduating in 1920 from the public high school of Ellenville, NY, Starkey was awarded a New York State scholarship that permitted her to attend Barnard College. She transferred to the Connecticut Agricultural College (later the University of Connecticut), where her father then worked and where she majored in chemistry and minored in microbiology. In 1925 Starkey received her B.S. from the Connecticut Agricultural College. Her science studies qualified her for a fellowship at the Rutgers College of Agriculture, where she worked with Selman A. Waksman. The future Nobel Prize winner was then involved in a basic study of the decomposition of organic matter in nature. Under his direction, Starkey received an M.S. in 1927 and a Ph.D. in 1928. These studies resulted in nine journal publications between 1925 and 1930 dealing with the decomposition of cellulose and lignin, two abundantly produced macromolecules.

While she was a graduate student with Waksman, Robert Lyman Starkey, a former student of Waksman, was enticed to leave the University of Minnesota by the offer of an associate professorship in Waksman's department. The Starkeys were married on September 8, 1928.

Starkey's professional ambitions were limited by the reluctance to hire women and by the general economic sluggishness of the Depression. She worked with Thomas J. Murray at Rutgers College from 1929 to 1930 on the analysis of microbial cells, a project sponsored by Johnson and Johnson.

When she applied for a position to teach microbiology at the New Jersey College for Women, she was told that the position would never go to a woman. In 1937–38, Robert Starkey conducted research in the laboratories of Albert J. Kluyver at the Technical University of Delft, Holland. Starkey accompanied her husband and served as his laboratory assistant.

Upon her return from Holland, Starkey was asked by the very person at the New Jersey College for Women who did not want to hire a woman to substitute for one year for the man who had been appointed in her place. With World War II, other opportunities developed. Dr. Johanes C. Hoogerheide, then at Squibb and Sons, asked Starkey to join the antibiotic development program. This position launched her career as an industrial microbiologist, which lasted from 1941 to 1965. Soon she was put in charge of the process quality control laboratories, which had both chemical and microbiological components, overseeing a staff of 50 to 60 persons. She remained in that post until retirement.

Starkey and her husband retired the same year and live in New Brunswick, NJ, in a house designed by Starkey's father. Her hobbies include traveling, photography, lapidary work, and gardening. Active in local affairs, Starkey is a former president of the New Jersey chapter of the American Association of University Women (AAUW) and of the Middlesex County chapter of the League of Women Voters. She also chaired a committee of the New Jersey AAUW devoted to the status of women in academia. Starkey is a past chairperson of the Unitarian Society of New Brunswick, NJ.

An interview with Starkey on Mar. 19, 1986, provided biographical details. She described her professional work on a videotape,

*Interview of Four Former Students of Selman A. Waksman*, Waksman Institute of Microbiology, Rutgers University (Piscataway, NJ), 1981.

*Hubert A. Lechevalier*

## MILDRED FAIRBANKS STONE, 1902–

Mildred Fairbanks Stone, the first woman officer of a major American life insurance company, was born in her parents' home on Clarendon Place in Bloomfield (Essex County), NJ, on May 21, 1902, the eldest of four children (two girls and twin boys fourteen years her junior) of Ida Louise (Garabrant) and Franklin A. Stone, both graduates of Bloomfield High School. Her father worked in the family's wholesale paper business in New York City. Interviewed in 1987, Stone remembered that her father had Bloomfield's first safety bicycle and the second automobile in town, built not in Detroit, but in Bloomfield by a neighbor.

Both Stone's mother and father were descended from families that had settled in the community several generations before. One of her ancestors, John Collins, emigrated from Ireland, fought in the American Revolution, and settled in Bloomfield. Another, David Cairns, the son of Scottish immigrants, became a successful merchant in New York and settled in New Jersey after his wife died in a cholera epidemic. Cairns was a founder in 1851 of the First Baptist Church in Bloomfield.

Stone was educated in the Bloomfield public schools and graduated from high school in 1920. She remembers the family car trips through New England and day trips to museums and stores in Manhattan she enjoyed as a child, and notes the broadening effect of these experiences. She traveled across the country with her grandfather to California and the Canadian Rockies while still in high school. Stone credits Ella Draper, the principal of Bloomfield High School, who had taught her parents and was a family friend, with encouraging her to continue her education. Upset with the idea that Stone did not intend to go to college, Draper urged her to persevere. Stone chose Vassar College, because it was not far from home. She was elected to Phi Beta Kappa and graduated with a B.A. in 1924.

After college Stone taught cooking part-time at Bloomfield High School for a year, but an acquaintance who was a young assistant vice-president of Mutual Benefit Life Insurance Company in nearby Newark urged her to take a position with that firm. Stone started with Mutual Benefit in April 1925 with the promise that she would stay two years. As it turned out, she made her career in the life insurance industry and worked for Mutual Benefit for 43 years.

At the time Stone joined the company, the life insurance industry was experiencing tremendous expansion. World War I had changed people's concept of adequate life insurance because wartime programs had set $10,000 as a standard for young men, a significant increase over earlier levels. After the war there was an influx of new energetic salespeople into the company, which before had enjoyed a staid and conservative reputation. As the fourth oldest life insurance company in the country, Mutual Benefit in the mid-1920s was suffering morale problems because of the significant gaps in age and outlook within its sales force.

Stone was assigned the job of agency personnel secretary, although she had no special training in employee relations, and was given a free hand in helping to solve the company's morale problems. "The first thing I did was to find out everyone's birthday and start writing birthday letters to roughly 1500 salesmen all over the United States." (Stone, Interview, Oct. 19, 1987) In various ways over the next 40 years she was responsible for maintaining positive employee relations within the company. In the process she developed hundreds of enduring and satisfying personal relations with Mutual Benefit employees. Although she never married, she came to be known affectionately as "the mother of the agents."

Stone was elected an officer, agency field secretary, of Mutual Benefit in 1934, the first woman to achieve such rank in a major life insurance company. In the 1920s and 1930s women were only slowly being accepted in the profession.

Stone's career as an insurance professional transcended her work with Mutual Benefit. In 1929 she was one of the first people in the nation to earn accreditation as a Chartered Life Underwriter (CLU). She remained active throughout her professional life as a promoter of the American College. She also became a historian of the life insurance industry, publishing in 1942 *A Short History of Life Insurance*. In 1960 she published a full-length biography of the educator who inspired the founders of the American College, Solomon S. Huebner of the University of Pennsylvania, and followed that in 1963 with a history of the organization. Her book *Since 1845: A History of the Mutual Benefit Life Insurance Company* (1957) represents her considerable expertise as archivist and chronicler of her own company. In 1979 she published *Extraordinary Ellen*, the biography of a notable woman life underwriter.

Stone has been active as a leader in diverse community organizations before and since her 1968 retirement. She traces some of her commitment to community affairs to the influence of GERTRUDE WARD, founder of the League for Friendly Service (now League for Family Service [LFS]). Stone became active in the LFS of Bloomfield-Glen Ridge in 1927 and served the organization for 37 years. Also in 1927 she became a charter member of the local chapter of the American Association of University Women.

In 1936 Stone was a founding member of the Friends of the Bloomfield Library, serving as president in 1936–38. She served as a trustee of Mountainside Hospital (1949–64), served on the Bloomfield Board of Education (1954–64), and was president of the Essex County chapter of Phi Beta Kappa (1955–56). Active in cultural affairs, she was a charter member in 1962 of the Historical Society of Bloomfield and served as its president (1984–86). In 1977 she was an original member of the Bloomfield Cultural Commission and served as a founding trustee (1981–83) of the Oakeside-Bloomfield Cultural Center.

Stone takes particular pride in a position she has held since 1974 on the Board of Governors of the Northeastern Bible College, in Essex Fells, NJ. Still active in the community and in her church, the Brookdale Baptist of Bloomfield, Stone lives in Bloomfield, as she has all her life.

An interview with Stone on Oct. 19, 1987, in Bloomfield, NJ, provided information. A biographical sketch of her is Nicole Gudowsky, "Mildred Stone Shares Inspiring Reflections of Her Years at Mutual Benefit Life," *Currents* 9 (July 1987):3.

*John E. O'Connor*

### RUTH CHENEY STREETER, 1895–

Ruth Cheney Streeter, first director of the U.S. Marine Corps Women's Reserve, is the middle child and only daughter of Charles Paine and Mary (Lyon) Cheney. She was born in Brookline, MA, on October 2, 1895, into a life of affluence and New England heritage on both sides of the family, although she lived most of her adult life in Morristown (Morris County), NJ. Her mother was an early graduate of Wellesley College. Her paternal grandfather, Benjamin Pierce Cheney, made a fortune in the railroad business and was a director of the Atcheson, Topeka, and Sante Fe Railroad.

When Streeter was two, her father, a Harvard graduate and banker, died of tuberculosis. Her mother remarried when Streeter was twelve, to William Henry Schofield, a professor of comparative literature at Harvard, and the family settled in Boston.

Streeter was educated at private day schools in Boston and at a finishing school in France. After a year as a debutante she became involved in volunteer work with the underprivileged, developing a commitment to social welfare causes.

A natural leader with a strong personality and eager for independence, Streeter enrolled at Bryn Mawr College in 1914. During her sophomore year she was elected class president, but she left school that year and returned to Boston. There she met Thomas Winthrop Streeter (1883–

1965), a graduate of Dartmouth College and Harvard Law School and an attorney with a Boston firm. They were married in May 1917.

During the final year of World War I Streeter and her husband lived in Washington, D.C., where their first child, Frank Sherwin, was born in 1918. After the war they moved to New York City, where Thomas Streeter went into banking. Two more sons, Henry Schofield and Thomas Winthrop, Jr., were born in 1920 and 1922. Later in 1922 the family moved to Morristown and made their permanent home there. A daughter, Lillian, was born in 1927.

Soon after moving to New Jersey, Streeter plunged into volunteer service. By 1923 she was president of the local Visiting Nurse Association and a member of the board of the Morris County Children's Home, which she reorganized from a residential institution to a foster home placement agency. She also organized the Junior League of Morristown. In 1930 she was appointed to the New Jersey Board of Children's Guardians. She was also a board member of the New Jersey Conference of Social Work and was active in the League of Women Voters of New Jersey and the New Jersey Women's Republican Club.

During the Depression Streeter was appointed to the State Relief Council and was in charge of distributing aid to needy families, mostly in the form of food. In 1935 she became the first woman president of the Morris County Welfare Board, serving until 1942.

As the United States came closer to entering World War II, Streeter, who had always been interested in aviation, bought a yellow single-engine airplane and began flying lessons at age 45. In 1941 she became the only woman member of the Committee on Aviation in the New Jersey Defense Council and by 1942 had received her commercial pilot's license. She wanted to join the Women's Airforce Service Pilots (the WASPs), an organization of women pilots who ferried army planes around the country, but was refused because she was twelve years overage.

Bitterly disappointed, and with all three of her sons in military service, she was anxious to make a wartime contribution. She tried to join the Civil Air Patrol (CAP), but was again turned down, this time because patrolling the New Jersey coast was considered too dangerous for a woman. "The men told me I could come down to the hangar and make coffee. I was absolutely furious. I was more qualified than they were. I said the hell with them." (Streeter, Interview, Sept. 1985) But she lent her plane to the CAP for coastal patrol missions.

Her chance to serve came when an influential friend, Basil O'Connor, recommended her to President Franklin D. Roosevelt as director of the newly formed Marine Corps Women's Reserve. An appointment followed and on February 13, 1943, she was sworn in as director of the new service unit with the rank of major. She was later pro-

moted to full colonel and after the war received the Legion of Merit. For nearly three years she lived in Washington, D.C., and saw her family on weekends. Her husband, who had retired from banking in 1939 to pursue his avocation as a collector of rare books and documents, took care of the home front, and her daughter, Lillian, went to boarding school in New York.

As director of the Women Marines, Streeter was responsible for approximately 19,000 enlisted women and 1,000 officers who served under the direct command of male Marine Corps officers at their various bases. Women Marines performed a variety of noncombat duties, from parachute rigging to clerical services, air traffic control, and food service. In 1943 the press described Streeter as tough, capable, and efficient, as well as sympathetic, tactful, charming, and gracious. "Stoutish and husky, with reddish brown hair . . . in her trim Marine uniform she looks as if she would tackle any problem and lick it." (Streeter, collected newspaper clippings, 1943)

When Streeter left the service on December 7, 1945, she turned her energies toward state and local civic projects. In 1947 she was elected a member of the New Jersey Constitutional Convention. She was named to the Electoral College for the 1948 presidential election and cast one vote for Republican candidate Thomas E. Dewey. Locally, she was head of the Morris Township Civil Defense and Disaster Control from 1952 to 1962.

In her later years Streeter became increasingly interested in historic preservation. Before her husband's death in 1965, the Streeters donated a strip of land to Patriot's Path, a linear park running through Morris Township. She was president of the National Society of Colonial Dames, an organization that restores historic sites. She also served on the Board of Trustees of the New Jersey Historical Society and of Macculloch Hall Historical Museum in Morristown. In the early 1970s Streeter provided the impetus and considerable funds for the creation of Speedwell Village in Morristown, a group of historic buildings that includes the home and barn of Alfred Vail, developer of the telegraph. She served on the Village's Board of Trustees and in 1972 received a medal from the American Scenic and Historical Preservation Society for her contributions to Speedwell Village.

Streeter was named grand marshal of the 50th Anniversary Parade of the Morristown National Park in 1981. A detachment of the U.S. Marine Corps Band played "March of the Women Marines," composed in her honor. Surrounded by honors, awards, and more than 60 direct descendants, she remarked, "Thank God for your friends, who make allowances for you, and for your enemies—their eye on you keeps your foot from slipping." Streeter continues to live in Morristown.

Two interviews with Streeter in Sept. 1985 provided biographical details. Also helpful was her privately printed memoir, *Tales of an*

*Ancient Marine* (n.d.); and Florence Newman Trefethen, "Profile: Ruth Cheney Streeter," *Bryn Mawr College Alumnae Bulletin* 18 (Spring 1985):20–21.

*Marian H. Mundy*

## MIRIAM VAN ARSDALE STUDLEY, 1899–1984

Miriam Van Arsdale Studley, one of New Jersey's leading local history librarians, was born in Amoy, China, on July 18, 1899, to the Rev. Hobart and Josephine Studley. Studley's father, first an Episcopal priest and later a clergyman in the Reformed Church, was rector to a Chinese congregation in Manila, the Philippines. Studley's mother was a native of Rutherford, NJ. Tales of rural New Jersey remained among Studley's earliest reminiscences, as were accounts of life in New Jersey nearly a century earlier told to her by her grandparents on her visits to the United States. As a young girl, Studley crossed the Pacific Ocean five times, finally settling in the United States at sixteen.

Studley received her early education in the Philippines. In 1922 she graduated from Vassar College with an A.B. She attended Columbia University from 1922 to 1923 and during summers from 1932 to 1936, receiving a B.S. in library science. From 1923 to 1926 she taught school in Dayton, OH. She worked at the New York Public Library from 1927 to 1931, serving as an assistant in children's work. Then she went to work at Newark Public Library, where she served as children's librarian until 1943. She became interested in local history while trying to answer children's questions about the bicentennial of George Washington's birth and during the Newark City charter centennial celebration in 1936.

Studley's contribution to New Jersey local history and the Newark Public Library grew out of the library's commitment to Newark, Essex County, and New Jersey collecting, which began in 1912. In the early days of the collection, the library's materials were scattered throughout the institution. In 1944 Studley was appointed senior reference librarian and placed in charge of the New Jersey material. In 1951, when the main library building was extensively renovated, a special New Jersey collections room was opened to house both historical and current information about the state.

While Studley was in charge of the New Jersey Division it grew into one of the state's leading collections of New Jerseyana, filled with books, newspaper clippings, documents, maps, illustrations, and a variety of valuable local history indexes and finding guides. Soon the name "Miss Studley" became associated with research excellence to scholar and student alike.

Studley helped many of the state's best-known writers, yet she was equally proud of her attempt to extend the collection beyond the range of typical historical collections. She and her colleagues Gertrude Cahalan and Syvella Copeland successfully incorporated current news clippings and New Jersey state and local documents into the traditional library files, an innovative practice at the time.

Studley shared her knowledge of the state in a variety of ways, notably through her publications. Her book *New Jersey Through Visitors' Eyes* was volume 18 in the state Historical Series in 1964 and included a selection of travel accounts of New Jersey by famous travelers. In 1949 she wrote a popular newspaper series for the *Newark Sunday News* entitled "When Newark Was Younger." This 30-part essay became one of the finest series ever written about Newark. In addition, she produced study guides, bibliographies, book reviews, book lists, and local history radio scripts.

Because of her many contributions to popularizing New Jersey history Studley received several honors and awards. She was made a fellow of the New Jersey Historical Society, given a citation from Governor Hughes for her historical efforts during 1964, and awarded an honorary doctorate from Kean College (Union, NJ).

During her professional life, Studley was active in a variety of organizations, including the Library Board of the New Jersey Historical Society, the New Jersey Historical Commission, the American Association of State and Local History, the American Library Association, and the state library association. She was also active in the New Jersey Folklore Society, the Interstate Hiking Club, and the League of Women Voters. In 1964 and 1966 she served as an adviser of the New Jersey and the Newark tercentenary commissions.

After retiring from the Newark Public Library in 1966, Studley decided to take some time off, but within a few months became editor of the prestigious Stevens Papers at the New Jersey Historical Society. After overseeing the filming of 40 microfilm reels of the papers, she finally retired to her home in Livingston, NJ. Studley died, at age 84, May 8, 1984, after a lifetime of working with information about a state she had first heard of as a young girl in China.

Biographical information on Studley appears in *Who's Who in Library Service* (1966).

*Charles F. Cummings*

## EDYTHE LOIS SYDNOR, 1920–

Edythe Lois Sydnor, social service administrator, political activist, and humanitarian, was born on December 24, 1920, in Newark (Essex County), NJ, the youngest of seven children of Samuel and Sarah (Guaffney) Sydnor.

Both her parents had migrated to Newark from their birthplace, Boydton, VA. After Sarah Sydnor died in 1924, the four girls and three boys were raised by their father, who died in 1940.

The Sydnor family was close-knit, with all working together for the household. Some chores were assigned to boys or to girls, while others were shared by all. Samuel Sydnor, the supervisor of a bank building in downtown Newark, was actively involved in his children's upbringing. He taught them how to perform their responsibilities, even those considered girls' jobs. He loved to fix things, and Sydnor often watched with fascination as he repaired household objects. The children joined their parents' church, the Bethany Baptist Church in Newark, in which Sydnor continues to maintain membership.

Sydnor attended Central High School in Newark, graduating in 1938 with commercial training. She later studied at the college level, taking courses at New York University in the early 1960s and at the Newark campus of Rutgers University during the 1970s.

During her senior year of high school, Sydnor took a U.S. Civil Service examination. Federal employment was then one of the most desirable job opportunities open to African-American women. While she waited for a position to become available, she worked in a lawyer's office. In 1940 she accepted a job in the Harborside Terminal in New Jersey, a U.S. government quartermaster's terminal.

Although more rewarding than private-sector alternatives, the job was a "dead end," one without potential for promotion. Thus, in 1942, Sydnor's interest was caught by a newspaper report of a campaign to train civilians for aviation ground crews. The shortage of human resources in the military was serious, and employment of civilians (regardless of race and sex) allowed the transfer of trained soldiers overseas. The day after completing a three-month training program at the Casey Jones School of Aeronautics in Newark, she traveled to the Rome, NY, air force base. With one other woman in the class, she graduated as a qualified airplane engine mechanic. By the time the war ended Sydnor was a crew chief of a racially and sexually integrated engine repair crew.

Sydnor returned to New Jersey in 1945, joining two of her siblings in Montclair. She was hired as executive secretary in the Montclair Neighborhood Center, which provided community services in a predominantly black area of the town. Supported with funds from the Council of Social Agencies, the center was housed in a small building owned by the Junior League. Sydnor's task was to run the center; she raised funds, developed programs, and led the ultimately successful drive to establish a federal credit union through the Neighborhood Center. She encouraged political activism, rather than limiting the center to activities such as sewing circles or cooking clubs. In particular, she was a leader in the successful fight against an urban re-

newal plan that would have resulted, according to its proponents, in the relocation of residents to alternative housing three to five miles from Montclair. The area targeted for change included a large proportion of the town's African-American residents. The center's involvement in this issue led to a withdrawal of funding, and Sydnor had to become a fund raiser "overnight." In 1953, feeling the need for a career change, she resigned from her position at the center.

Sydnor remained active in local politics through the 1950s and into the 1960s. She served in several nonpartisan voter registration drives, and in the 1956 and 1960 campaigns of candidates for local office. In 1962 Sydnor was the Montclair campaign manager for congressional candidate Robert Peacock. She sometimes worked with the regular Democratic organization and at other times with the "Good Government" Democrats, depending on the particular issue. Part of the growing movement for representation of the African-American community, Sydnor ran for Town Commission in 1964. Although unsuccessful, her campaign was of symbolic importance: she was the first black woman to run for local office and the first woman to run since 1936. Sydnor's campaign was part of a changing climate in a town that had a five-to-one ratio of Republicans to Democrats after World War II. Another black, Matthew Carter, did become a town commissioner. He won reelection in 1968 and became the first black mayor of Montclair.

Remaining politically active in Montclair, Sydnor went on to work in Newark, providing administrative support to organizers of the Textile Workers Union in a losing battle against the departure of jobs to the nonunionized South. In the mid-1950s she was office manager at the Northern Division Headquarters of the Salvation Army in Newark. She led modernization of the office, aiding in a record-breaking fund-raising campaign.

In 1959 Sydnor moved to the Essex County Division of Youth Services, from which she retired in 1983. She rose from secretary to supervisor of Administrative Services at the Children's Shelter in Belleville. The shelter, opened in 1958, grew to house and provide professional services to over 100 children, including infants. Sydnor helped lead the growth in size and scope. The shelter obtained grants that committed the county to providing the service after the external funding ended. She retired when the shelter was closed as part of a national trend toward deinstitutionalization.

Since her retirement, Sydnor has focused her activities on the community of Bungoma, Kenya. Introduced to the area by a Kenyan student she met in a course at Rutgers in 1978, Sydnor began making visits to Bungoma before her retirement. She has become a member of the community, where she has spent visits of increasing length. She assists by raising funds and encouraging locally appropriate development. Her first project raised funds for the construction of a new primary school. The next undertaking is the construction of a technical high school for the teaching of agriculture and animal husbandry.

Sydnor established a nonprofit corporation in August 1984 for educational and medical development in the Bungoma area. She has raised funds in the United States with activities ranging from her own handcrafted beadwork to large-audience entertainment and educational events. Her work for Bungoma benefits from her decades of experience as an administrator and fund raiser, and her commitment to the project reflects the values with which she was raised and that guided her earlier activities in New Jersey. In the mid-1980s Sydnor was honored by nomination for the Essence Magazine Award and for the Robert W. Pierce Award for Christian Service.

An interview with Sydnor on May 11, 1987, provided useful information. See also "Miss Sydnor Enters Race," *Montclair Times*, Apr. 2, 1964; "Edythe Sydnor—a Kenyan Odyssey," *Montclair Times*, July 2, 1985; and "Essex Woman 'Adopts' Needy Kenya Village," *Newark Star-Ledger*, Apr. 19, 1987.

*Laura Kramer*
*Kathryn Daughtrey Brown*

## TOSHIKO TAKAEZU, 1922–

Toshiko Takaezu, American ceramicist, weaver, and sculptor, was born in Pepeeko, HI, on June 17, 1922, of Japanese parents who had emigrated from Japan. The sixth of eleven children, she describes herself as "the navel of the family, right in the middle." (All quotations: Takaezu, Interview, May 18, 1986)

Although the family was poor, they were fortunate in that they experienced no major personal tragedy. "My mother raised all her children to their maturity. Eight of the eleven were educated and entered a variety of professions. My mother took pride in that." Her mother, an educated woman, helped guide the children. Her father, who had never had the same opportunity to learn, was a laborer in Hawaii, working in the sugarcane fields. But he loved music and at night often played the shamisen, a Japanese stringed instrument that is plucked like a guitar.

In 1948 Takaezu enrolled at the Honolulu School of Art with the intention of becoming a sculptor. Of that period she says, "When I realized the dedication and work that was needed to become a sculptor, I decided to work in clay, not realizing then that a ceramicist must have the same dedication. At the time ceramics seemed lighter. I thought less of a commitment was needed in this medium. However, the more I worked, the more I had to learn and the harder I had to strive." From 1949 to 1951 Takaezu

taught ceramics in Hawaii. In 1951 she traveled to the mainland to attend Cranbrook Academy of Art in Bloomfield, MI, for three years, where she studied with Maija Grotell. Takaezu's first teaching position was at the University of Wisconsin from 1954 to 1955.

Toshiko Takaezu, ceramicist and weaver, at her Quakertown farm-studio in 1987. *Courtesy, artist's collection.*

In 1955 she went to Japan to study with master potters for eight months, spending a short period in a Zen temple. Growing up a child of the East in a country of the West, Takaezu often felt vulnerable—pulled in two directions and unsure of where she fit. In Japan she was able to explore her own background and come to some spiritual integration; she was able to accept her own individuality as being both Eastern and Western and to draw from the best of both worlds.

As far as her religiosity, she says simply, "My work is my religion." In 1984 she began studying the tea ceremony with a master in New York City. "The ceremony is ritualized discipline," she said. "It forces one to do things very slowly, very deliberately. All the movements have to be controlled. One is forced to savor, not only the tea, but also the preparation of the tea, and even the utensils. One understands within the format of the ceremony that life itself is an art that must be slowly and carefully cultivated."

Takaezu returned from Japan in 1956 and taught at the Cleveland Institute of Art for eight years. In 1964 she moved to Clinton, NJ, where she had a large studio on the ground floor of a theater building with an apartment above her studio. In 1967 she began teaching in the Visual Arts Program at Princeton University, where she has been ever since.

Today Takaezu lives on what used to be a small chicken farm in Quakertown, NJ. She converted the farmhouse into a studio, gallery, and living quarters. She made her own rugs on a large loom in the corner of her living room. From her indoor kiln, large enough for a person to walk into, emerge large cylindrical shapes, pots the shape of moon rocks, and what she calls "trees," ceramic interpretations of upright shapes with intricate glazed patterns that give all her objects a surrealistic look. She uses a smaller, outdoor kiln for "raku" firing, a process of actually burning the glaze onto the clay.

From Takaezu's Eastern heritage comes her love of nature, her respect for living plants, and her sense of being in tune with an unspoken feeling, an implicit quality that cannot be defined. She works this into her pottery. She likes making pots "rounder than round and it is not round." Many of her pots assume the fluid shape of a moon. She displays them together with her "trees." They are representative of creative forces on which the whole universe depends. The groupings form their own world, have their own harmony, create their own quiet music.

Takaezu uses images of the womb when she talks of her students working together in a studio at Princeton University, all concentrating on what they are doing. "I have had a moment in my teaching," she said, "when it was quieter than quiet. It was a moment of supreme beauty for me. They were all there, intent, bent over, doing what had to be done, just as if they were in a womb."

Her house—studio, gallery, kiln, and living space—is a reflection of her philosophy toward life. What appears to have happened accidentally, casually, has been carefully thought out and planned.

Takaezu sees very little difference between gardening, cooking, teaching, or throwing pots on a wheel. Each activity requires a commitment from the whole person, an involvement from the inside with something on the outside. It is in that connection—spiritual, transcendent, mysterious—that meaning and beauty can be found, she says.

She speaks about her garden, a deliberate random arrangement, planned so that there are flowers blooming from April through October. "Growing things," she says, "is such a beautiful mystery. Plants know their time, when to come up, when to die."

Takaezu never married. "I did not find the appropriate father for the children I wanted," she says. Asked if she regrets now the course her life has taken, she says, "No. Art demands a kind of commitment that could not be diluted. If I had children, I could not have done what I have done. I have a freedom living alone, experiencing my own individuality. I am not lonely. Yet, sometimes, I feel sad."

Recently, she has returned to sculpting, making large bronze bells, which she casts at the Johnson Atelier. A number of her bells hang in her garden, calling the students to a task or providing time signals for firing their pieces.

Takaezu continues to work hard. In spite of her recognition and regular invitations to exhibit her work, she says, "I never had the sense of myself as an accomplished artist, and I always had to work three times as hard as anyone else to make my pieces as good as they could be. I am never completely satisfied. There always seems to be something just beyond my reach."

Biographical details come from an interview with Takaezu on May 18, 1986, at her home in Quakertown, NJ. For articles discussing her work, see Joseph Hurley, "Toshiko Takaezu: Ceramics of Serenity," *American Craft* 39 (Oct. 1979):2–9; "Toshiko Takaezu: A Thrown Form," *Ceramics Monthly* 23 (Nov. 1975):32–37; Susan Mayer, "The Pottery of Toshiko Takaezu," *American Artist* 33 (Feb. 1969):42–47; and Conrad Brown, "Toshiko Takaezu," *Craft Horizons* 19 (Mar. 1959):22–26.

*Gertrude W. Dubrovsky*

## CLARA MAE TAYLOR, 1898–1988

Clara Mae Taylor, nutrition scientist, educator, and author, was born in Vineland (Cumberland County), NJ, on March 15, 1898, the second of four children and only daughter of Alexander Miller and Minnie Florence (Stuart) Taylor. Her father was the son of a physician who established a drugstore in Vineland and farmed in South Vineland. Her mother was the daughter of a successful merchant. All four of her grandparents were of Scottish and English descent and were born in the eastern United States.

Taylor's interests and aspirations were greatly influenced by her family. Her father, a prosperous businessman in real estate and insurance, took her on his rural business trips so that she could see how other, less fortunate families lived. Her mother believed in the value of the home and the extended family and brought grandparents, uncles, and cousins to live in the immediate family at various times. Both parents were active in church and community affairs in Vineland and encouraged their children to participate. Taylor maintained her membership in the Presbyterian Church of Vineland for 50 years.

Taylor and her brothers were raised to value education; their grandfather and his brother, both physicians, had been educated at Princeton University and Pennsylvania Medical School. It seemed a natural choice for Taylor to seek further education, in home economics and later nutrition, after her graduation as an honor student from Vineland High School in 1916.

Taylor's academic degrees are from Teachers College, Columbia University, although she also studied at Rhode Island State College and at Oxford University, England. She received her B.S. in home economics in 1920 and her M.A. in education in 1923. In the 1920s she taught home economics at the Academy School in Bridgeton, NJ, and at Rhode Island State College.

During 1925 and 1926 Taylor did summer volunteer work in New York City as a community nutrition worker for the East Harlem Nursing and Health Demonstration. She accompanied nurses on home visits to study the living conditions and food habits of Italian immigrant families. During the summer of 1926 she traveled in France and Italy, where she visited hospitals in Naples and studied the background of Italian immigrants. It was at this time that her lifelong interest in community nutrition and public health began.

Another major influence on Taylor's career was her contact with Mary Swartz Rose, the first full-time staff member in nutrition at Teachers College, Columbia University. To specialize in nutrition had become Taylor's dream, and when she was offered an assistantship in 1926 she did not hesitate to accept this opportunity to study and work with Rose. Rose made it clear that she wanted Taylor to get her Ph.D. and be trained to carry on the nutrition program at Teachers College. Taylor speaks with pride and pleasure of her fourteen years' work with Rose and of the inspiration and guidance she received as a student, colleague and friend of this pioneer in nutrition.

Taylor continued on the faculty at Teachers College for the next 37 years. She received her Ph.D. from Columbia University in 1937, was appointed full professor in 1948, and became professor emeritus in 1963. She lived in New York City while she taught at Teachers College but kept close ties with her family in Vineland, spending her vacations there and in the Red Bank area.

Taylor was an outstanding research investigator and a painstaking compiler of reliable food composition tables. Her dissertation research was on energy metabolism and mechanical efficiency of young boys, and she continued investigations of energy expenditure in children and wom-

en for over fifteen years. She studied the role of ascorbic acid in the diet of guinea pigs and the effects of various human diets on the growth of experimental animals.

Teaching was Taylor's first responsibility at Teachers College. She taught nutrition courses to nutrition majors, home economists, nurses, and health educators and developed off-campus courses for schoolteachers. She was an inspiring and gifted teacher whose philosophy strongly influenced her students. She is fondly remembered by former students for her warmth of personality and for her expert use of scientific data and illustrative materials.

After Taylor became director of the nutrition program at Teachers College in 1944, she established two major programs, one in public health nutrition and the other a doctor of education degree in nutrition education. She coauthored revisions of Rose's classic textbooks, served as nutrition consultant for several agencies, and was an active member of many professional organizations. After she retired in 1963, her colleagues and students established the Clara Mae Taylor Fellowship Fund as a tribute to her years of service at Teachers College.

After her retirement from teaching, Taylor coauthored a bibliography of nutrition education and a biography of Mary Swartz Rose and published several articles in professional journals. In 1965 she bought a home in Red Bank, NJ. She kept in close touch with her family and with her many students from the United States and foreign countries, also maintaining active membership in professional, community, historical, photographic, and garden organizations.

On April 10, 1970, in the Presbyterian church in Red Bank, Taylor married Carl Olson, professor emeritus of education and former director of the Health and Physical Education Department at the University of Pittsburgh. Olson died in 1978 following an automobile accident. Taylor continued to live outside Pittsburgh in Monroeville, PA, until she died of congestive heart failure, at age 89, after a long illness on January 6, 1988.

Taylor's books, reprints of her articles, and an autobiographical sketch are available at the Milbank Memorial Library, Teachers College (New York, NY). Brief sketches of her appeared in *Who's Who of American Women* (1971) and *American Men and Women of Science* (1967). Her obituary appeared in the *New York Times*, Jan. 15, 1988.

*Juanita Archibald Eagles*

## MARY WOLFE THOMPSON, 1886–1970

Mary (Wolfe) Thompson, author of more than 20 junior historical novels and vocational books for girls, was born in Winsted, CT, on December 7, 1886, the second daughter and only surviving child of Gertrude (Franklin) and Dr. Theodore Frelinghuysen Wolfe. She received major literary recognition at age 82 by winning the 1969 Dorothy Canfield Fisher Memorial Children's Books Award, given by the Vermont Congress of Parents and Teachers, for *Two in the Wilderness*. The direction of her writing and her development as an author reflected her childhood in a small New Jersey town and the early influence of her parents.

Her family, by her own account, was "of good plain old stock, German, English and Scotch; families who have been in this country since colonial days." (*Current Biography*, 568) In 1887 she and her parents settled in her father's hometown, Succasunna, a tiny village located along the Morris Canal in Morris County, NJ. Her father, a retired physician whose medical career had been cut short by tuberculosis, was an austere, scholarly man who turned to research and writing. Her mother, witty, gay, pretty, and socially inclined, was a buffer between the redheaded impulsive child and her elderly father.

Thompson grew up in a literary household. Her father's work habits dominated family life. His meticulous note taking, technical discussions on the flow of prose, and fact-finding visits to New York and Boston fascinated the young girl. And she shared with local residents awe and pride in his publication of four best-selling literary guides. These were happy years: a mixture of orderly winters spent as a bright but inattentive student at the two-room schoolhouse her father had attended 50 years earlier and carefree summers at her family's lakeside log cabin in Connecticut.

Thompson's idyllic childhood ended sadly at age fourteen when her mother died in 1900, "and the sun went out of the sky for my father and me." (Thompson, *Theodore Frelinghuysen Wolfe*, 63) The Queen Anne-style house in Succasunna was closed, the little summer place in Connecticut sold, and Thompson went off to boarding school. Concerned for her future, her father insisted she train to be a teacher, an acceptable occupation for a young woman of that period. Grudgingly, she enrolled in the New Jersey State Normal School in Trenton. Companionable summer vacations were spent in Europe with her father, who considered travel part of her education.

In 1905 Thompson graduated, returned with her father to their home in Succasunna after a five-year absence, and reluctantly taught first grade for several years in the Roxbury Township public school system. Her teaching career ended when she became eligible for a $200 college tuition refund paid to every Trenton Normal School graduate who taught for two years. Many years later she laughingly recalled that she collected her bonus, bought a fur coat, and never taught another class.

In 1914 Thompson took a last trip to Scotland with her father, who died of tuberculosis shortly after returning home. On September 11, 1915, she married Charles D. Thompson, an electrical engineer who also lived in Roxbury Township. To their deep regret, the couple never had children. Her husband's work in the newly developing electrical industry was demanding and time-consuming, so Thompson revived her childhood ambition to become a writer and enrolled at Columbia University in 1920. Encouraged by her professors, her skill in handling words quickly surfaced. "I guess I just picked up the knack by osmosis," she later said in an interview with the *Bennington Banner*.

She began her career by writing short stories for adult magazines. "Old Diz" was her first success, published in April 1923 in the *Midland*, a national literary magazine. Several of her later stories were featured in the O'Brien *Best Short Stories* collections. In 1923 she also published her first book for children, *Farmhouse Tales*. This charming collection of short stories, as told by farm animals, showed her potential for juvenile writing. The book's publication surprised her; she whimsically inscribed her personal copy "to myself with great affection and best wishes for success." Her astonishment notwithstanding, the book launched a career that would span almost 50 years. Concentrating on writing for young children, Thompson published in rapid succession six fictional works. These books, delightfully simple and wholesome, drew on her rural childhood experiences.

Gradually Thompson turned to writing vocational fiction for young adults. In 1938 she published *Highways Past Her Door*, her first career book for older girls. The book's format became the model for her subsequent books in which she presented realistic job problems facing young people, always stressing that hard work and persistence insured success. Several of her career books published in the 1940s were included in the 1950 list of basic books for high schools, compiled by a joint committee of the American Library Association, the National Council of Teachers of English, and the National Education Association.

In 1951 Thompson and her husband left New Jersey and their farm in Ho-Ho-Kus, and retired to West Arlington, Vt. Claiming her output had slowed, she nevertheless published three more career books. *Snow Slopes* (1957), set in Vermont, became a Junior Literary Guild selection.

In Vermont, Thompson lived in a picturesque saltbox-style house located near a covered bridge on the scenic Battenkill River. She and her husband tended a large vegetable garden, sharing its abundance with friends. Typically thorough, Thompson had taken courses in fruit growing and market gardening at the New Jersey State Agricultural Station prior to their move. She became an active member of the Arlington Garden Club, a dignified, articulate, but serious presence. She and her husband, as members of the Battenkill Grange, valued their friendship with fellow member artist Norman Rockwell. Charles Thompson was his occasional model, and Rockwell counseled Thompson on literary matters.

After her husband's death in June 1954, Thompson temporarily drifted away from writing. Then in 1961 New Jersey friends brought her news that the Roxbury Women's Club planned to convert her childhood home to a town library. Fifty years earlier her father, a lover of books, had sought donations for a town library. In tribute to him and her happy childhood, she changed her will, making the proposed library her residuary legatee.

Buoyed by her renewed Succasunna ties, she resumed writing. A love of New Jersey history inspired *The Wag on the Wall*, an account of her childhood. The publication of this delightful book about turn-of-the- century small-town life from a child's point of view was followed by *Theodore Frelinghuysen Wolfe*, a short biography of her father, and *A Summer's Adventure on the Morris Canal*, a juvenile novel based on her personal experiences.

In 1963 ill health necessitated her move to the Prospect Nursing Home in North Bennington, VT. Undaunted after cancer surgery, she looked for a new writing challenge. Vermont local history appealed to her, and *Two in the Wilderness* (1967) won her the 1969 Dorothy Canfield Fisher award, based on popular vote by young Vermont students. Two sequels, continuing the saga of an early pioneer family, were published in 1968 and 1970. As a writer, Thompson was endlessly observant and a lifelong researcher dedicated to accuracy. In the *Wilderness* series she meticulously double-checked all details of 18th-century pioneer life, even consulting local farmer friends on crops and farming methods.

On Christmas afternoon, December 25, 1970, at age 84, Thompson died unexpectedly. She was buried beside her husband in Evergreen Cemetery, Burlington, VT. The Roxbury Township Library, whose existence she described as "still miraculous to me" (Mary Wolf Thompson Papers), received over $100,000 under the terms of her will. The bequest motivated the town to raise funds to replace the small, overcrowded quarters in her former home with a large modern facility where the entire collection of her books and original manuscripts are housed.

Thompson's papers and memorabilia are available at the Martha Canfield Memorial Free Library (Arlington, VT) and at the Roxbury Township Library (Succasunna, NJ). Thompson's *Wag on the Wall* (1962) and *Theodore Frelinghuysen Wolfe* (1964) contain autobiographical material. Accounts of her life and writings appear in *Current Biography* (1950) and *Contemporary Authors*, vol. 107 (1983). Her obituary appeared in the *Bennington* (VT) *Banner*, Dec. 27, 1970.

*Sharon Doremus*

## AGNES SLIGH TURNBULL, 1888–1982

For more than 60 years, best-selling author Agnes (Sligh) Turnbull wrote for three hours a day, longhand, producing seventeen novels, four juvenile books, one diary, one memoir, and numerous short stories.

Turnbull was born on October 14, 1888, in New Alexandria, PA, the second daughter (and last child) of Lucinda Hannah (McConnell), a descendant of Scots-Irish pioneers, and Alexander Halliday Sligh, a stonemason and country storekeeper who came originally from Berwick-on-Tweed, Scotland.

In the strong Scots-Irish Presbyterian tradition, it was the Sligh family's custom to pray together both morning and night. Indeed, life in the entire village revolved around the church. And although her family, like most in the village, had little money, Turnbull later commented that her childhood was a happy one filled with love, fun, and books.

Turnbull attended the village school in New Alexandria and enjoyed writing as a child. Since her village had no high school, she boarded at Washington Seminary in Pennsylvania. In 1910 she delivered the valedictory to her graduating class at Indiana Normal School, Indiana, PA, and then enrolled in graduate studies at the University of Chicago. She taught high school English for several years in Pennsylvania before marrying James Lyall Turnbull in 1918, at age 29.

When Turnbull's husband left for World War I soon after their marriage, she began writing short stories, which she steadily sold to such periodicals as the *American Magazine* and *Women's World* from 1920 to 1932. During that time she wrote fiction based on the biblical characters or incidents she had studied during her childhood.

Around 1920, Turnbull and her husband moved to Maplewood, NJ, where she lived for the rest of her life. When Turnbull was 39, in 1927, she and her husband adopted Martha (Pat) O'Hearn as their daughter. Turnbull clearly delighted in her husband's good-humored company and doted on her daughter, as can be seen in *Dear Me, Leaves from the Diary of Agnes Sligh Turnbull*, published in 1941. Turnbull maintained that her family was her greatest joy and always came first, but she also revealed the tension she felt juggling the work of a homemaker and an author. "It would be easier to be all Woman or all Author, I suppose." (*Dear Me*, 9) James Turnbull, an executive with a lighting fixture company, died in December 1955 from a heart condition. Throughout their married life Turnbull valued her husband's opinion of her works-in-progress.

*The Rolling Years* (1936), her first novel, is set in western Pennsylvania and draws upon her childhood background. Partially based on family stories, this novel of three generations of Scots-Presbyterian women was extremely successful: in 1971, 35 years after it was first published, it went into its 36th printing. For Turnbull's strong, self-reliant women characters, the family is their center, with the church offering another source of community and comfort.

While Turnbull's work generally reflects the traditional role of women, her thoughts must have been on the condition of women as she wrote *The Day Must Dawn* (1942). While writing this historical novel from a woman's point of view, she muses in her diary on women's place, past and contemporary. "Why in the long pattern of civilization should one woman live in a log hut in the wilderness . . . while another woman in a later age lives in comfort . . . and finds the hours . . . hanging heavy on her hands? . . . Was one woman chosen to suffer and the other to live in ease?" (*Dear Me*, 75)

Turnbull used her writing to convey her own deep religious commitment to a wide public audience. Two of her best-selling novels, *The Bishop's Mantle* (1947) and *Gown of Glory* (1952), deal with the sense of duty and ministry. Other famous titles include: *Remember the End* (1938), *The Golden Journey* (1955), and *The King's Orchard* (1963).

Turnbull's novels were sometimes criticized as overly optimistic, but she held true to her vision and contended it was just as realistic to write about good people as bad— and much more satisfying. The secret of her considerable popularity was that people were as eager to read inspiring stories about good people as she was to write them. She made traditional virtues seem both appropriate and admirable in a modern world. Her books were translated into several languages and went through many editions.

Her memoir, *Out of My Heart*, was published in 1958, when she was 70 years old and widowed. In it she tried to reconcile what she had seen of life's problems with her strong religious faith and to provide guidance for others. She spoke out about the importance of a woman's relationship with her children and advised mothers to enjoy their children's younger years. She saw childhood as a person's lifelong spring of "strength and happy security" and felt that to provide a happy, secure childhood is "the most important work in the world." "Enjoy them," she wrote about women's years with small children. "There will be plenty of time later on for you to write or paint or head committees, run women's clubs, or serve Great Causes." (*Out of My Heart*, 20–21)

Turnbull was a Maplewood resident for more than 60 years and served as a member of the Maplewood Library Board of Trustees from 1947 to 1953. She spoke fondly of the friendliness of Maplewood and took special pride that it was a "church-going community." (*Maplewood South-Orange News Record*, Oct. 10, 1957) Maplewood returned her goodwill by proclaiming her "Outstanding Citizen of Township" on October 31, 1963.

Widely honored during her lifetime, she was made an honorary doctor of literature by Westminster College (Pennsylvania) in 1945. Her alma mater, now known as Indiana University of Pennsylvania, named a woman's dormitory in her honor in 1963 and in 1974 made her an honorary doctor of letters.

She died from a heart infection on January 31, 1982, at age 93, at St. Barnabas Medical Center in Livingston, NJ. Turnbull was buried in her beloved New Alexandria, PA.

Turnbull's two autobiographical works are *Dear Me, Leaves from the Diary of Agnes Sligh Turnbull* (1941) and *Out of My Heart* (1958). *American Women Writers* 4 (1982) lists her work and criticizes her fiction; *Something about the Author* 14 (1978) provides an interview. Manuscripts of some of her works are available at the Mugar Memorial Library, Boston University (Boston, MA), along with a collection of her papers, awards, and clippings. The files of the NJ-MaPL and the NJ-MCL also contain many clippings on Turnbull. An interview with Turnbull's daughter, Pat O'Hearn of Spring Lake, NJ, provided useful information.

*Kathy Bieger Roche*

## CONCEPCIÓN VALDÉS-MUÑOZ, 1917–1980

Concepción Valdés-Muñoz, a lawyer who worked to help Cuban refugees, was born in Havana, Cuba, on December 25, 1917, into a middle-class family. She was the first of five children (one boy and four girls) born to Manuel de la Campa, a salesman for a pharmaceutical company, and América Garcia, who stayed home to take care of her children.

When Valdés-Muñoz started attending the University of Havana, her interests were in diplomatic law. She had been very influenced by an uncle in the same field. However, she finally decided not to specialize in that field.

Valdés-Muñoz's family went through rough financial times, as did many other Cuban families during the government of Gerardo Machado in the 1930s. The corruption and greed of this government, coupled with the ongoing worldwide depression, had a devastating effect on the Cuban economy. To make things worse, Valdés-Muñoz's father died during this period.

After her father's death, she decided to get a job while she continued to pursue her education. She wanted to help her mother and siblings financially. For some time she worked in a pharmacy owned by an uncle. Also, she opened a small private grammar school with one of her sisters. She graduated from the University of Havana in November 1945. At the university, she met Ernesto Valdés-Muñoz, whom she married in 1942. They had two children, Ernesto (b. 1948) and Lourdes (b. 1950).

Valdés-Muñoz was not a typical Cuban woman of her times. Most middle-class women in Cuba stayed home, even if they had earned a higher education degree, especially after marriage and the birth of children. Valdés-Muñoz, an independent woman, was active as a lawyer. Her husband, also a lawyer, began to resent his wife's dedication to her career. Social pressures, role conflicts, and perhaps even professional competition brought tension into the marriage, which finally ended in divorce in 1972.

After the Cuban revolution in 1959, Valdés-Muñoz and her family decided to leave the country for the United States. Their decision to leave Cuba was based on their disagreement with the new revolutionary government's policies. Valdés-Muñoz, her husband, and two children arrived and settled in West New York, NJ, in December 1961.

During the early years after the revolution, the majority of Cubans who emigrated to the United States were professionals and members of the upper and middle classes. Many emigrés from Cuba, especially medical doctors, participated in retraining programs in the United States and were able to continue in their professions. Lawyers, however, had particular difficulties in being retrained, because of the difference in the legal codes existing in the two countries. Many lawyers went into new careers, such as teaching and social work.

As is common among educated immigrants and refugees (in particular those coming from non-English-speaking countries), the great majority of Cubans experienced a downgrading of their socioeconomic status after migrating to the United States. Upon arrival in West New York, Valdés-Muñoz worked in a garment factory for a couple of years and took English lessons and courses in social work. In 1963 she began to work in the Cuban Program of the Hudson County Welfare Board. This was the local branch of the federally funded Cuban Program established by President John F. Kennedy in 1961 to assist Cuban refugees. Ten years later, she became director of the Cuban Program. In this role, she administered the resources allocated to provide emergency financial assistance, job training, employment opportunities, and other services to the refugees.

While studying, working, and taking care of a family, she became active in a group of Cuban lawyers in Hudson County, NJ, who helped the newly arrived to get jobs and to retrain in law or other more feasible fields. She became the only female member of this group's board of directors. A very religious woman, she also became involved in the Catholic church, particularly in programs helping recently arrived Cuban exiles.

Throughout her life, Valdés-Muñoz showed great determination to achieve the goals she set for herself. If she experienced self-doubt, her response was to try harder. The immigration experience was difficult. It required major adjustments in terms of both career and family, but she persevered.

The hardships of exile did not embitter Valdés-Muñoz. Instead, she turned her own difficulties into a learning experience to enable her to help others going through the same thing. She devoted most of her life in the United

States to serving a significant segment of the New Jersey community.

Valdés-Muñoz retired in January 1980, at age 62, three months before cancer ended her life on April 30. She was buried in Flower Hill Cemetery in North Bergen, NJ. She treated her job as a mission, and her dedication to the Cuban Program is remembered by many, especially the families and individuals she helped.

An interview with Lourdes Gil, Valdés-Muñoz's daughter, on Aug. 20, 1986, provided information for this article.

*Yolanda Prieto*

## MARJORIE SCHUYLER VAN NESS, 1914–

Marjorie (Schuyler) Van Ness, a leader in New Jersey horse associations, was born in Massapequa, NY, on July 23, 1914, one of two children of Philip Van Rensselaer and Jeannie Floyd-Jones (Carpender) Schuyler. When she was five she moved with her family to Plainfield, NJ, where an aunt introduced her to horses. Her riding skills and love for horses grew during these formative years.

At eighteen, she dropped out of high school to marry Eugene Van Ness on April 22, 1933. For the next 20 years she devoted her life to raising four children: Marjorie (b. 1934), William Peter (b. 1939, d. 1962 in a storm at sea), Philip Schuyler (b. 1941), and Joan (b. 1942). Her family responsibilities and a severe case of polio in 1949 kept her from riding during these years.

When Joan, her youngest child, learned to ride at camp, Van Ness's interest in horses was rekindled. A move in 1958 to Hope Farm in Blackwell's Mills near Princeton led to the purchase of two brood mares and two show horses. Both Van Ness and her daughter showed horses, and Joan conducted a riding school there and later at a family farm in Hunterdon County while Eugene Van Ness supervised the business aspects of the farm.

Through her involvement with showing and breeding, Van Ness has worked to build the horse industry in New Jersey. She was the first woman member of the State Board of Agriculture (1971–75), the first woman president of the New Jersey Agricultural Society, chair of both the Equine Advisory Board (1967–68) and the Horse Advisory Committee of the New Jersey Farm Bureau (1981–84), an Executive Committee member since 1975 for the American Horse Council, founder and past president of the American Saddle Horse Breeders and Owners Association of New Jersey (now the American Saddlebred Horse Association of New Jersey), and founder of the Hunterdon County Horse and Pony Association. In 1970 she won the National Pleasure Driving Horse Award from the American Saddlebred Horse Association. In 1977 she received the Distinguished Service Citation from the State

Board of Agriculture, and in 1983 she was the recipient of the Golden Medallion, the New Jersey Agriculture Society's highest award. In 1986 she was awarded the Hunterdon County Chamber of Commerce Award. Her numerous other civic and horse-related activities include serving as trustee for the Hunterdon County Medical Center and the Clinton Historical Museum and as fund-raising chair for the New Jersey Horse Park at Stone Tavern.

Articles on Van Ness appeared in the *Sunday Star-Ledger* (Newark, NJ), Sept. 22, 1985, and the *Hunterton County Democrat* (Flemington, NJ), Aug. 28, 1969. Interviews with Van Ness in Sept. 1985 provided additional biographical details.

*Grace A. Aqualina*
*Sarah B. Pfaffenroth*

## ASTRID VARNAY, 1918–

In one of the most remarkable debuts in the history of the Metropolitan Opera, Astrid Varnay stepped onto the stage on December 6, 1941, to sing the demanding role of Sieglinde in a broadcast performance of Wagner's *Die Walküre* conducted by Erich Leinsdorf. This was her first onstage appearance since she left high school in 1935. With one rehearsal after the notice of cancellation by Lotte Lehmann, this young soprano won ovations from the audience and praise from critics for her dramatic intensity and vocal strength. Six days later she replaced the indisposed Helen Traubel in the role of Brunnhilde in the same opera. The *New York Post* critic wrote, "For the second time in the space of a week Miss Varnay stole the show from a cast of seasoned Wagnerians." At age 23, Varnay had embarked upon an operatic career that would make her an acknowledged master of the German dramatic and lyric repertoire.

When Ibolyka Astrid Varnay was born on April 25, 1918, in Stockholm, Sweden, her parents were both active in the European opera world. Her mother, a Hungarian coloratura, was known professionally as Maria Javor; Alexander Varnay, her father, was a tenor of Hungarian ancestry. Together with the city's fathers, he formed Oslo's own first opera company. Besides singing he also directed opera performances.

In 1923 the Varnay family left Europe for a tour of South America and from there went to New York, where Alexander Varnay died soon after his arrival. Following his death, Varnay's mother resided briefly in Manhattan and Brooklyn before settling her family in Jersey City, NJ, where young Astrid attended PS No. 11 on Bergen Avenue and studied piano with Ralph Ganci of Jersey City at his New Jersey Musical College. Later, she enrolled in the commercial course at William L. Dickinson High School, a public school in Jersey City, where she was known as Violet Astrid Varnay.

During her high school years she performed in school plays, sang in the Glee Club, and wrote the words and music for a class song entitled "Summer Memories." Varnay's fellow graduates were among the first to recognize her talent, predicting the success of their classmate in the June 1935 yearbook. But even these early fans overestimated the required years of apprenticeship. They prophesied that her Metropolitan debut would not take place until 1950— nine years after the actual event. Despite the encouragement of the music faculty at Dickinson High School, Varnay believed that her musical future lay not with opera but with her piano studies. In 1935 the family returned to Manhattan, where the young graduate took piano lessons, worked as a typist at an export firm, and later as a bookstore clerk, using her facility with languages.

With the realization that she lacked the ability for a professional career as a pianist, Varnay gave up instrumental lessons and began studies with her mother, then a professional vocal coach. By 1939 both teacher and pupil knew that Varnay was ready for a more advanced instruction so, following the advice of Kirsten Flagstad, they approached Hermann O. Weigert, an assistant conductor and head of the German wing at the Metropolitan Opera who was a former conductor at the Berlin Staatsoper and a former professor at Berlin's Hochschule für Musik.

Weigert was so impressed with the young singer that he accepted her as his own pupil and then brought her to the attention of conductors George Szell and Erich Leinsdorf. Several years later, in 1944, Varnay and Weigert married and made their home on Riverside Drive in New York. Varnay also became an American citizen in 1944.

Under Weigert's tutelage, Varnay advanced to the point that Edward Johnson, general manager of the Metropolitan, auditioned her in May 1941. On the basis of this tryout, she was admitted to the 1941–42 season's roster. She remained with the company until 1956 and sang 129 performances in 20 roles, 14 of which were in Wagnerian operas. In fact, she was the first artist to sing all of Wagner's soprano heroines at the Metropolitan. She also sang some Italian parts, creating the role of Telea in the 1942 premiere of Gian Carlo Menotti's *The Island God*.

With increased travel possibilities at the end of World War II, Varnay sang with other companies, expanding her career by opening the 1946 season in Rio de Janiero as Isolde; and she continued performing with the San Francisco Opera Company, the Chicago Opera Company, the Cincinnati Opera Company, the Mexico City Opera Company, and Covent Garden in London during the late 1940s. During these years she added more Italian parts to her repertoire and scored a triumph in December 1949 in a concert performance of the title role in Strauss's *Elektra* with the New York Philharmonic.

When the first postwar season of Wagner's Festspiel-haus opened in Bayreuth, Germany, in 1951, Varnay was invited to perform by the composer's grandson, Wieland Wagner, artistic director for the opening season. Not since 1894 had an American dramatic soprano sung at Bayreuth, and no one from the United States had ever been selected to sing the three parts of Brunnhilde. Varnay thus became a symbol of America's musical maturity. She returned to Bayreuth regularly until 1967. During those years she appeared frequently at other major European houses, where she established an international reputation as a forceful singing actor.

In 1947 Weigert left his post with the Metropolitan to teach private students and to serve as accompanist to his wife. His death in New York in 1955, at age 64, affected Varnay deeply. The following year Varnay left the United States for Europe, where she made her home in Munich.

Varnay considers her 1964 *Elektra* under Herbert von Karajan in Salzburg one of the highlights of her career. Renowned for principal roles in the European houses, she later turned to character parts where her acting skills assured her success. Wieland Wagner, known for his stark abstract sets, has been quoted as commenting: "Why do I need real trees on my stage when I have an actress like Astrid Varnay?" (*New York Times*, Nov. 10, 1974, sec. 2, 21)

After an absence from the Metropolitan Opera stage of eighteen years Varnay returned to the United States in February 1974 for a Carnegie Hall concert version of Klytemnestra in *Elektra*, with the Cleveland Orchestra, conducted by Lorin Maazel. Harold Schonberg, music critic for the *New York Times*, wrote that "her low notes had become something spectacular." (*New York Times*, Feb. 6, 1974) Then, in December 1974, she returned to the Metropolitan to sing Kostelnicka in Janáček's *Jenufa*. Varnay closed her American career at the Metropolitan in Kurt Weill's *Mahagonny* on Dec. 22, 1979, but she continued to sing in European houses and performed in the made-for-television film of *Elektra* conducted by Karl Boehm in 1981.

The force of Astrid Varnay's personal conviction was apparent from the early days of her Jersey City youth, where her high school yearbook carried the personal motto "I can!" Indeed, at the conclusion of her musical career, the world-famous soprano could well say, "I did!"

Information on Varnay's Jersey City roots can be found in the New Jersey Room of the NJ-JCPL. Details of her professional career, including clippings, press releases, and photographs, are available at the NYPL-LC. *Current Biography* (1951) contains a profile of her, and additional information appears in David Ewen, *Musicians Since 1900* (1978).

*Joan F. Doherty Lovero*

## GRACE J. VOGT, 1873–1976

Grace J. Vogt, a reporter for the *Newark Evening News* from 1902 to 1967, helped break ground for women in New Jersey during her 64-year career as a newspaperwo-man, conquering social, sexist, and political barriers to get her stories into print. Born in Morristown (Morris County), NJ, on September 30, 1873, Vogt was the daughter of Louis A. Vogt, the editor of the *True Democratic Banner* in Morristown and a correspondent for the *Newark News*, New York papers, and wire services, and Mary Elizabeth (Day) Vogt of New Providence, NJ, whose ancestors reportedly came to America on the *Mayflower*. Vogt's sister, Anna (b. 1875), and brother, Frank (b. 1885), lived with her later in life.

Vogt's family was prominent among New Jersey settlers. Six ancestors arrived with Robert Treat in Newark, and Massachusetts relatives Richard Cutter and John Pike founded Woodbridge. Another ancestor, Elizabeth Swain, is honored in a mural in the Essex County Court House in Newark, and is said to be the first white woman to have set foot in Newark. Vogt was also the descendant of a long line of journalists, ten of whom held positions ranging from reporter to editor and publisher. Her paternal grandfather, Louis C. Vogt, born in Germany, came to New York, where he was a staff member with the *Commercial Advertiser* and the *Evening Post*.

Educated at Miss Dana's (private) School in Morristown, Vogt studied at the Art Students' League in New York before going to work on her father's newspaper as a reporter at the turn of the century. In 1902 Vogt walked into the Morristown office of the *Newark News* for her first day of work as a correspondent, but walked right out again when she found herself without a desk and a warning from a news editor that he did not want women working around him. Vogt returned home, wrote her stories and for the rest of her newspaper career entered the office only a handful of times.

For male reporters at the turn of the century obtaining news was difficult; for women it was almost impossible. Vogt said, "Those first days were difficult. No one wanted to give me any news." (*Newark Sunday News*, Oct. 23, 1966) She also told of being blocked from covering a political school sponsored by Morristown Republicans because she was "the poisonous Democratic lady. I told the Republicans I was assigned by the state editor of my newspaper to cover their meeting—that I was a reporter, not a spy. They refused to let me inside." (*Newark Sunday News*, Oct. 23, 1966) Finally, after hours of waiting, the speaker who directed the forum passed her sitting on the steps of the meeting hall and she was able to question him and find out what took place.

Vogt's coverage of the news expanded and became as wide as the events of the day—suffrage campaigns, local and state politics, local history, society events, and women's rights. During the suffrage campaign she interviewed hundreds of women and spent months covering in depth women's activities in the movement. Although she focused her stories on social and political events of interest to women, she also covered the careers and social events of the millionaires who made Morristown a society center during the Gilded Age (1890–1929). During her career, Vogt collected an impressive number of by-lines on news stories at a time when by-lines were rarely given.

Vogt scored a major statewide "scoop" while covering a speech by a prominent Republican state senator before a GOP women's club in Morristown. At the conclusion of his talk, a woman from the audience asked why the state legislature consistently turned down Governor Charles Edison's selections to fill the vacated commissioner of education post. "Oh, we're just giving the Democratic governor the run-around," the senator answered. (*Newark Sunday News*, Oct. 23, 1966) Vogt turned the senator's remarks into the lead story on the front page the following day.

Vogt is credited with the first story announcing the construction of a museum in Morristown National Historical Park (1934) and in 1958 the building of a replica of the hospital in the Jockey Hollow section of the National Park (now demolished) where General George Washington's troops recovered from smallpox.

Vogt was active in local and state civic women's and historical organizations. She was a member of the Morristown chapter of the Daughters of the American Revolution for 60 years. There were eleven members in the chapter when Vogt joined the organization on July 31, 1906. She was instrumental in the purchase of the historic Schuyler-Hamilton House in Morristown and its preservation and refurbishing. She also wrote the official history of the house, which is operated by the chapter. During her career she held the offices of registrar, curator, vice-regent, and first historian.

Vogt was a charter member of the Women's Town Improvement Committee, (1910), which later became the Woman's Club of Morristown. She designed the original gardens at the clubhouse and was instrumental in having the building named on the New Jersey Register of Historic Places (1971) and the National Register of Historic Places (1973). Vogt served as a trustee the first year the club was organized and was a member of its executive Board.

A charter member of the Home Garden Club (November 5, 1924), she won many blue ribbons for her arrangements of dried flowers and was a frequent judge at the New York Flower Show. In 1929 Vogt was the author of the official pamphlet for the 150th anniversary of the Continental Army in Morristown and was a consultant for the publication distributed at the rededication of the Morris County Court House in 1956. She was the recipient of a

30-year bar from the Morristown chapter of the American Red Cross, a member of the Advisory Board of the Morris Junior Museum (renamed the Morris Museum of Arts and Sciences in 1969) and the Morris County Historical Society, and a trustee of the Macculloch Hall Museum.

Vogt, who lived for 101 years at 51 Franklin Street in Morristown, died on July 7, 1976, at the Crestwood Nursing Home in Whippany, NJ, of cardiac arrest at age 102. She is buried in the family plot in Evergreen Cemetery in Morristown.

An interview in the *Newark Sunday News*, Oct. 23, 1966, provided information on Vogt's life and career. The clipping file of the NJ-MO contains material on Vogt. Her obituary appeared in the *Morristown Daily Record*, July 8, 1976.

*John W. Rae*

## FLORENCE EMELINE WALL, 1893–1988

Florence Emeline Wall, nationally recognized chemist and cosmetologist, was born on January 4, 1893, in Paterson (Passaic County), NJ, the first child of Stephen Augustine and Florence Therese (Corley) Wall. She had two siblings, a brother, Stephen, who died four days after birth, and a sister, Stephanie, who became a professional singer. Wall's father, also born in Paterson, was educated at Fordham University before beginning a career in real estate and insurance. Her mother, born in Montreal, Canada, was educated at a private academy. Her paternal grandfather was born in Ireland and married her grandmother in Paterson in 1845. Her maternal grandparents were of English-Irish descent and lived in Canada.

Wall graduated from the Academy of St. Elizabeth in 1909 and entered the College of St. Elizabeth, where she majored in chemistry and minored in English. She received both a B.A. and an education diploma in 1913. Wall completed an M.A. in health education at New York University in 1938 and the work for a Ph.D., except for a dissertation, in 1943. She was awarded an honorary LL.D. by the College of St. Elizabeth in 1980.

Wall's independence was established early when her father died during her first semester in college. Her mother died shortly after Wall finished college. Wall remained single and spent her life living and working primarily in New Jersey and New York. She began her career as a high school teacher, first as a science teacher in Camden, NY, and later as a science and English teacher in Suffern, NY. In 1917, however, she made the first of her many career moves and became an industrial chemist.

Her first industrial job was with the Radium Luminous Material Corp. in Orange, NJ. Initially, she analyzed the incoming ore, but within a short time, because she had taken a college course in radioactivity, she transferred to the electroscopic analysis of radium. The hours were long, often until 1:00 or 2:00 A.M., and the work was potentially dangerous; she left this job after six months. She was one of the first women, if not the first, to work in an industrial laboratory of this type.

In early 1918 she became an analyst at the Seydel Manufacturing Co. in Jersey City. The company had three plants in which textile chemicals, fur dyes, and benzoic acid were made and for which Wall ran the daily quality control tests. The fur dye, although primarily used for dying muskrat, was also used as a human hair dye. This was the first time Wall worked directly with a cosmetic. For the time being, however, her career moved in yet another direction.

At the suggestion of Seydel's owner, Wall began to synthesize as many derivatives of benzoic acid as she could from the supplies available to her at the company. Some of these derivatives proved to be valuable. While visiting the laboratory the chief chemist of Squibb recognized one of the compounds Wall was distilling and asked her for a sample. A week later Wall was asked to appear at the office of the Fellows Medical Manufacturing Co., where a representative of the U.S. Chemical Warfare Service asked her to take over the manufacture of two compounds needed for airplane wings. She was put in charge of manufacturing until the plant closed after the armistice.

In 1919 she joined the Ricketts Laboratory, located in a warehouse in lower Manhattan. Since the laboratory accepted almost anything for analysis, Wall's professional flexibility was, again, an asset. One of her projects was for a syndicate that was attempting to develop a process for improved gasoline yields. Because of the quality of her work, the syndicate asked her to join them as their chemist. Eventually, Wall told them that their project would not be profitable and, in the still prevailing postwar industrial depression, she found herself without a job.

Unable to find work in the chemical industry, Wall spent the next few years traveling, studying, teaching, and becoming involved with the fledgling American Institute of Chemists (AIC). After a year in Europe and two in Cuba, Wall returned to the United States and began attending the organizational meetings of the AIC. In September 1923 she joined the AIC as a fellow, one of the first women to join that organization. In 1930 and 1931 she was editor of the *Chemist*, the official publication of the AIC. In later years Wall was the AIC's official archivist. Throughout her life, she was a mainstay of the organization and was named an honorary full member in 1960. In addition to her accomplishments, her sense of humor and limitless energy distinguished her. At the January 1986 meeting of the New York chapter of the AIC, Wall was given a special award to recognize her long involvement.

In 1924 Wall returned to the chemical industry, but continued to teach, write, and further her own education. This was also the period in which Wall concentrated on her

work in cosmetology. First, she joined Inecto, Inc., of New York City, then the largest manufacturer of hair colorings. Shortly thereafter she established the first postgraduate school for specialists in hair coloring and wrote the first of her many textbooks. Although she left Inecto after a few years to do consulting work, she continued her efforts to establish what she felt was cosmetology's proper place in the higher levels of education. It was at this time that she completed her M.A. and the work for a Ph.D. Having thus armed herself with knowledge and credentials, she developed a curriculum for teachers of cosmetology at New York University, where she taught for the next seven years. Although the course most properly belonged in the health field, it was still considered a "woman's trade" and was, therefore, placed in the School of Home Economics.

During World War II Wall added yet another credit to an already varied career, that of technical editor. She worked for General Aniline and Film, Ralph Evans Associates, and the Chemical Publishing Co., the latter for six years. Again, her broad interests made her especially qualified for the job. In addition to her technical background and writing abilities, Wall was fluent in six languages, an invaluable asset in translating, editing, and writing technical material.

Over her lifetime, Wall taught at many colleges and universities, including Clemson, the University of Texas, Oklahoma State, Oregon State, and the University of Kansas. One summer she taught a group of dermatologists at the NYU Medical School.

Wall's books include *The Science of Beautistry* (1932) and *The Principles and Practice of Beauty Culture* (1941). Many articles by her appeared in the *Journal of Chemical Education* and *Southern Beauty Shop*. One of her most innovative, published in 1932, was on beautifying the human male, a concept considered ridiculous in the thirties and another example of Wall's foresight. Wall wrote on a wide range of subjects—biography, history of science, women in chemistry, and technology.

As part of her work in cosmetology, she collaborated with Senator Royal Copeland on establishing cosmetic standards for the revised Pure Food and Drug Law. She worked with the Bureau of Investigations of the American Medical Association on a study of hair dyes and also frequently assisted the New York City Board of Health. In 1956 Wall was the first woman to receive a medal from the Society of Cosmetic Chemists, and as a result of her contributions to cosmetology Wall was inducted into the Cosmetology Hall of Fame in 1965.

In addition to her involvement with the American Institute of Chemists, Wall was active in the American Chemical Society, gathering data on the history of chemistry and encouraging women to pursue careers in chemistry. She was also a member of the Cosmetic Career Women, the American Women in Science, the History of Science Society, and the Society of Medical Jurisprudence.

Although work and travel were her chief interests, Wall also collected rare books. In 1975 she gave her entire collection of old and rare books on chemistry, alchemy, and the history of science to the Mahoney Library at the College of St. Elizabeth. Wall lived in New York City until a stroke and subsequent coma occasioned her removal to a convalescent home in Fairfield, CT, where she died, at age 95, on October 2, 1988. She was buried in the Holy Sepulchre Cemetery in Totowa, NJ.

An interview with Wall provided details of her life and work. A 1985 videotape contains Wall's account of the beginning of the American Institute of Chemists (AIC) and is available from AIC (Washington, D.C.).

*Nina M. Roscher*
*Marlene Miller Thich*

## HARRIET WARE, ca. 1873–1962

Harriet (Ware) Krumbhaar, composer and pianist known professionally as Harriet Ware, was born August 26, sometime between 1870 and 1877 in Waupun, WI, the only child of Emily (Sperry) Ware and Silas Edward Ware. All four of Ware's grandparents were Western pioneers of New England ancestry. Her maternal grandparents, Charlotte and Willis Sperry, a manufacturer, owned land in Waupun, a property shared by the young Ware family.

Ware's childhood is obscure, but her memories of her mother singing lullabies and her father practicing with his quartet in the parlor evoke images of a musical home. When she was three, her father gave her a toy piano and she began picking out lullaby tunes, improvising, and composing. Over the next 80 years, she composed more than 100 art songs, cantatas, and operettas and was one of America's earliest recognized woman composers.

When Ware was twelve, the Ware/Sperry family moved to Owatonna, MN, and she entered the Pillsbury Academy, studying instrumental and vocal music and composition, in addition to academic courses. She made her debut at fifteen, playing the piano with an orchestra in St. Paul, MN. After graduation in 1891 she taught vocal music while continuing her studies. She then continued piano study for two years under William Mason and George Sweet in New York. At Mason's suggestion, she went to Paris, where she studied composition and piano under Sigismund Stojowski and voice under Mme. de la Grange and Juliani. Stojowski, recognizing her genius, persuaded her to devote her time to composing. She went to Berlin and studied composition under Mme. Grunewald and Hugo Kahn.

In 1906 Ware returned to New York, where her cre-

ative energies were unleashed. In October and November of that year she published the songs "Joy of the Morning," "The Cross," and "Moonlight." It was "The Boat Song," published in 1908, that brought her worldwide recognition, with more than a million copies sold. "The Boat Song" established a pattern she followed over the years: the song was a poem by a young friend, set to music by the composer.

Ware wrote music for the poems of many others, including New Jersey poet Joyce Kilmer and British poet Edwin Markham. Markham, whose poetry is known for its social consciousness and spirituality, was an inspiration to the young composer. The songs "Joy of the Morning" and "The Cross" are Markham poems. The tone poem "The Artisan" emphasizes Markham's line "Come let us live the poetry we sing!" Markham wrote the words for the tone poem "Undine" at Ware's request.

At the time Ware's songs were first being sung on the radio and at musical programs around the country, she lived in Garden City, NY, teaching music and helping her mother run a boardinghouse. Hugh Montgomery Krumbhaar, a young chemical engineer born in New Orleans in 1881, was one of the boarders. The couple were married in New York on December 8, 1913.

In 1917 Ware and her husband bought a 200-year-old farmhouse on Terrill Road in Plainfield, NJ. Called Lambkins Farm, it was a short train ride from Manhattan and provided an artist's climate of solitude, gardens, and animals. The couple bought other old buildings in the area and moved them to the farm. The restored buildings, each in its own setting of trees and gardens, gave the farm the appearance of a small colonial village. Here the artist was "in solitude and close to God, two things absolutely necessary for creative work." (*Newark Sunday Call*, Aug. 23, 1936)

A tiny, energetic woman, Ware is remembered by those who knew her at the farm as deeply spiritual with a magnetic personality. At the same time, she loved the movies and read movie magazines from cover to cover.

Ware and her husband dreamed of starting an artists' colony in Plainfield, and although the dream never materialized, family and friends came and stayed. Carrie Jacobs-Bond, a close friend famous for the song "I Love You Truly," was a frequent visitor. Ware held musical programs at the farm to which she invited Plainfield friends to hear New York artists and, occasionally, her own and her students' work. She also gave performances at the Monday Afternoon Club, the woman's club of Plainfield.

Ware's compositions were known and loved throughout the country at a time when there were almost no women composers. Her song "The Artisan" was performed by both the New York and Philadelphia Symphony orchestras. The tone poem "Undine," performed as a one-act opera, was so highly regarded that the Library of Congress requested the manuscript. "The Women's Triumphal March" was chosen the national song of the General Federation of Women's Clubs, and "The Rose Is Red," the national song of the American Mother's Association.

According to Ware, her popular "Mammy Song" was taken by Jerome Kern and turned upside down for "Old Man River." Other well-known Ware compositions include "Sir Olaf," a cantata for four-part chorus of women's voices; "Stars," set to a Joyce Kilmer poem; "This Day Is Mine," considered by some critics her finest song; and "The Greatest of These," a version of I Corinthians 13 set to music, which is her last published work.

G. Schirmer, Inc., published many of Ware's early works. The firm's records illustrate some of the composer's methods. "Stars" was published in April 1921 as a song for high or medium voice, in April 1922 as a song for low voice, in February 1927 as a part-song for chorus of mixed voices, and in March 1929 as a part-song for chorus of women's voices. Ware, in commenting on the creative process, reported that she wrote "The Boat Song" in just one day, whereas "The Greatest of These" took several years to complete. She started her own publishing firm, Harriet Ware, Inc., Publishers, in 1926, although Schirmer also continued to publish her work. One of Ware's dreams came true with the production of *The Love Wagon* at the Paper Mill Playhouse in Millburn in 1947. Three years in preparation, *The Love Wagon* was a completely New Jersey work, artistically, creatively, financially, and in terms of production. Creative credits included music by Ware; book by Frank Carrington, managing director of the Paper Mill; and lyrics by Agnes Morgan and ANTOINETTE QUINBY SCUDDER, Newark artist and patron of the arts. Although the play did not go on to Broadway, as Ware had hoped, it was well received by critics. Three years later, when *The Love Wagon* was revised and new melodies were added, it reopened at the Paper Mill as *Waltz for Three*.

Ware was interviewed at her home on Terrill Road, Plainfield, by a local radio station during a day-long celebration of her birthday, on August 26, 1936. During the interview she was asked to comment on the future of American music. She said: "America will express itself in music and will contribute a music of its own to the world. . . . Our music will have a buoyancy, a youth, a freshness and a high note of spirituality." (*Plainfield Courier*, Aug. 26, 1936) All these characteristics had been used by critics to describe Ware's own work.

Ware was a member of the American Society of Composers, Authors, and Publishers; the Music Committee of Paper Mill Playhouse; and the National Committee of the Fine Arts for the General Federation of Women's Clubs. After her husband's death, in 1950, of heart disease, Ware moved to New York City, where she died at her home on February 9, 1962, of natural causes, following several months of ill health after breaking a hip. She was buried in Greenfield Cemetery, Hempstead, NY.

Ware's works appear in Aaron Cohen, *International Encyclopedia of Women Composers* (1981). Biographical information and an annotated bibliography appear in Susan Stern, *Women Composers: A Handbook* (1978). A telephone interview with Jane Krumbhaar in Jan. 1986 provided additional information. The *Plainfield* (NJ) *Courier* maintains a clipping file on her. Her obituary appeared in the *New York Times*, Feb. 11, 1962.

*Joan Hylander*

## SARA SPENCER WASHINGTON, 1889–1953

Sara Spencer Washington, millionaire black businesswoman and founder of Apex News and Hair Company of Atlantic City, NJ, was born on June 6, 1889, in Beckley, VA, the daughter of Joshua and Ellen (Douglas) Phillips. It is not known when Washington assumed the surname she used professionally, but she became widely known as Madame Washington.

Washington attended public school in Beckley, a small village in Princess Anne County that is now part of the city of Virginia Beach. She was a graduate of Norfolk Mission College, Norfolk, VA, which despite its title was a secondary school with an elementary department. The school was founded after emancipation by the Board of Missions of the United Presbyterian Church. Courses offered in the academic department were traditional and included a Greek elective; the industrial department curriculum included cooking and sewing for girls and printing for boys. The courses of study reflected early 20th-century beliefs held by some educators that the recently freed African-Americans were better served by vocational training than liberal arts education.

Washington studied hairdressing in York, PA, and worked as a dressmaker in that city. By 1913 she had started a hairdressing business in Atlantic City, NJ. During this period Atlantic City was a large resort area with a sizable black population. This, coupled with its proximity to Philadelphia, made it an attractive area for Washington to settle in. Working days in her salon and teaching students her trade at the same time, she used her evenings to canvass the city with her products. She founded the Apex News and Hair Company in 1919, maintaining a laboratory and offices in Atlantic City as well as an office in New York City.

Washington started with a one-room beauty shop and by 1946 had created a business worth $500,000. "This is a predominantly white country but I can be black and successful," she declared. (Jasper, "Would She Have Lived Any Longer," 1) Her Apex Beauty College slogan was "Now is the time to plan for your future by learning a depression-proof business." Her beauty colleges were located in twelve cities in twelve states as well as Johannesburg, South Africa, and the Caribbean Islands. At its peak Apex graduated approximately 4,000 students a year.

Over 75 products were manufactured in her Atlantic City plant from raw materials purchased by the boxcar load. The finished products were sent on to her agents. Washington had her own delivery system using a fleet of company trucks and cars. Her company provided employment for over 215 men and women as chemists, lab technicians, office workers, teachers, sales representatives, and chauffeurs, as well as for 45,000 active Apex agents.

By 1946 some of her properties included the beauty schools, a drugstore in Atlantic City, Apex Farm, and Apex Rest. The Apex Farm, a 120-acre tract in Egg Harbor, NJ, was bought in 1934. Also in the 1930s she purchased a fifteen-room recreation center in Atlantic City, known as Apex Rest, a club primarily for her employees but available to the public. African-Americans had limited access to large meeting areas, so they welcomed the facility.

Washington also published a journal, the *Apex News*, a national magazine for Apex beauticians and agents. First issued in 1928, it was published regularly after 1935. It featured articles and pictures of local offices and staff members, news of beauty school activities, staff, and graduates, as well as news from the Atlantic City headquarters. Featured articles were of general interest to all in the beauty field. A separate feature on styling kept beauticians abreast of new trends.

Washington has been called one of the most important business executives in the black community. She had a reputation as a pioneer in promotional techniques and established a public relations department that worked with African-American organizations throughout the country to explain the importance of buying from blacks and supporting black businesses.

Washington was at times affiliated with Father Divine (born George Baker), the founder of a nonritualistic religious group known as the Peace Mission Cult and a flamboyant religious leader of the 1930s and 1940s. Father Divine was considered by his followers God incarnate on earth. During the Depression, his missions provided low-cost meals, known as banquets, with a service of songs and impromptu sermons. The Peace Mission had a reported membership of over one million.

Washington was often seen at banquets held at the missions in New York and Philadelphia. She received endorsement from Father Divine for her products, except for skin bleaches and hair straighteners. In so doing, Father Divine gave further support to the concept of racial solidarity for black business people. In 1944 Washington purchased the Hotel Brigantine on Brigantine Island, NJ, from Father Divine for the sum of $1 and agreed to assume the unpaid taxes of over $21,000. This property, leased by him to the U.S. government during World War II, had

been the subject of much controversy since its purchase in 1942 by a "white angel" (a follower of Father Divine) with $70,000 cash. The hotel became the site of the first integrated beachfront in the Atlantic City area.

Washington adopted her cousin, Joan Cross, as her daughter. Cross was educated at Palmer Memorial Institute, Sedalia, NC, a leading black college preparatory school, and went on to attend Howard University in Washington, D.C. As a result of Cross's attendance at Palmer, Washington was closely affiliated with Dr. Charlotte Hawkins Brown, a noted black educator. In 1944 Washington announced her marriage to Stumpert Logan, who later became secretary of her company.

Active in politics, Washington served as an Atlantic County committeewoman for several years. She also served as a delegate to the Republican national convention and was a staunch member of the Standpatters Republican Club.

In 1939 Washington was awarded a medallion at the New York World's Fair as one of the outstanding businesswomen of New York State. She also received a citation for meritorious service during World War II. She was the recipient of numerous awards from schools, organizations, and businesses nationwide.

Washington was a member of the Daughter Elks, president of the Northside Business and Professional Women's Club, and chair of the Industrial Department of the New Jersey State Federation of Colored Women's Clubs. During World War II she was secretary and treasurer of the New Jersey Welfare Commission on the Conditions of Urban Colored Population and assistant public director of Atlantic County Welfare Association.

Washington suffered a paralytic stroke in 1947 and retired from many of her activities. But she worked to regain her voice and walk without a cane. During this time she joined the Christian Science Movement. She died of heart disease at the age of 63 on March 23, 1953, after a brief illness. The bulk of her estate, valued at over $1 million, was left to her adopted daughter. She was buried in the Atlantic City Cemetery in Pleasantville, NJ.

A profile of Washington appears in Gladys Porter, *Three Negro Pioneers in Beauty Culture* (1966). A tribute to her appears in John Jasper, "Would She Have Lived Any Longer?" *African-American*, Apr. 11, 1953. Obituaries appeared in the *New York Amsterdam News*, Mar. 28, 1953, and *Jet* (Mar. 30, 1953):25.

*Barbara Polk Riley*

## VIOLA GERTRUDE WELLS, 1902–1984

Viola Gertrude (Wells) Evans, internationally acclaimed jazz, blues, and religious singer whose career spanned over six decades, was born on December 14, 1902, in Newark

(Essex County), NJ. The eldest child of Roberta Olivia (Simmons) and Earle Henry Wells, a laborer, Wells was soon joined by two sisters, Estelle and Isabelle, and a brother, Earle. The family lived in a small brick house at 21 Scott Street until 1906, when Roberta Wells died in childbirth. Wells, aged four, was sent to live with her maternal grandparents, the Rev. Morgan and Annie Simmons, of Surrey County, VA. It was in her grandparents' barn that Wells first recognized her vocation: organizing, singing, and dancing in family shows. "My grandmother just laughed, but I knew then that I wanted to be a singer." (*Newark Star-Ledger*, Nov. 1, 1982)

Wells began her training upon her return to Newark in 1910. At the age of nine she joined the Presbyterian church and sang in the choir for the next fourteen years. She attended the Central Avenue Elementary School and Cleveland Junior High School in Newark through the eighth grade. At twelve she joined the Salica Johnson Glee Club, touring New Jersey and nearby states. Encouraged by Ruth Reid, her voice and piano teacher, Wells learned early what a singing career entailed. "I had the voice as a child, but . . . voice alone won't capture an audience. You have to have personality and stage presence, something to bring you in contact with the audience." (*Newark*

Viola Gertrude Wells at a recording session with the Jay Cole Band, c. 1944. Known to jazz and blues fans as "Miss Rhapsody," Wells was a native of Newark. *Courtesy, Sheldon Harris Collection.*

*Star-Ledger*, July 27, 1973) Her father, a strict churchgoer, would not allow Wells to embark on a stage career. "Whatever social life I had revolved around the church." (*New York Times*, Feb. 14, 1982) Her first public appearances were limited to parties and impromptu gatherings.

Wells's professional career began in 1921, at age nineteen, the same year she married Howard Nicholas. A frequent winner at Newark's Orpheum Theater Amateur Hours, she was asked to take part in a traveling show playing at Minis Theater in Newark and soon began performing at the Orpheum Theater in Washington, D.C. Working theater dates in Washington and Atlantic City into the late 1920s, Wells's performance of two songs, "Rhapsody in Rhythm" and "Rhapsody in Song," won her the name "Miss Rhapsody" from a Chester, PA, columnist. She used the name professionally for the next 60 years.

Wells toured clubs, theaters, taverns, dances, and one-night tent shows throughout New Jersey and Pennsylvania well into the 1930s, singing more than once before her idol, Ethel Waters. Waters returned the admiration, capping off a Wells performance with the praise "That's my baby." (*Jazz*, Feb. 1965, 22) Wells's wide-ranging repertoire included blues, show tunes, popular songs, ballads, and gospel hymns.

After the birth of her only child, Yvonne, in 1934, Wells joined the Banjo Bernie Band as a singer and dancer, touring the length of the East Coast and into the Midwest during 1936–37. "I worked in clubs so exclusive that one had to die to get into them. But I also worked in towns as big as my hand." (*Jazz*, Feb. 1965, 22) In more than one location, Wells's group was the first African-American act ever to perform. "I especially remember the time I was playing the big Hotel Savannah with Banjo Bernie. The hotel was snow white. They didn't even have a colored porter in the place—we were the first to break in. I did *Brown Gal* [Wells's theme song] and when I looked up I was encircled. They were all standing around me and this beautiful woman, she told every man, 'Give her 10 dollars, give her 20 dollars, give her anything she named.'" (*Jazz*, Feb. 1965, 22) While producing a Scranton show at the Chinchilly Club, Wells discovered Pearl Bailey and gave her her chance before the public.

In 1937 Wells toured the black vaudeville circuit throughout the East and Midwest with famous blues shouter Ida Cox's Harlem Strutters, but was fired from the road show when her rave notices outshone her employer's. Far from home, she stopped in Kansas City and ended up staying sixteen months, headlining, emceeing, and producing shows at the Sunset Crystal Palace with her own group, working with the biggest names of the Swing Era, and discovering such major talent in the blues and jazz field as Walter Brown and Joe Turner.

Returning to Newark in 1938, Wells began the busiest and most successful period of her career. She worked local clubs with Johnny Jackson's Band, often played at New York's famed Apollo Theatre beginning in 1939 under the name Viola "Rhapsody" Underhill (Harold Underhill was her accompanist and close friend of many years), and filled New York night spots and theaters with major orchestra leaders. It was a measure of her popularity that she performed with the all-white Charlie Barnet and Bunny Berigan bands. In 1940 Wells fit into a tight performance schedule feature appearances for fourteen weeks on New York radio station WOR's "Sheep and Goat Club," a series that pitted gospel against secular music. She also appeared with the Count Basie Orchestra at President Franklin Roosevelt's Inaugural Ball in Washington, D.C., and worked military bases in Europe in a USO show with Willie Bryant's group. Touring the East Coast, Midwest, Canada, and Los Angeles in the 1940s, Wells kept Kelly's Stable, one of New York's major night clubs, as her home base. During this period she shared top billing as "Miss Rhapsody the Ebony Stick of Dynamite" with such jazz giants as Nat King Cole, Art Tatum, Benny Carter, and Coleman Hawkins and toured widely with her own group, the Three Sportsmen of Rhythm.

At this time Wells was approached by Decca to record race records. "Somebody thought that in order to write lyrics for a colored blues singer you must write in southern dialogue and broken language. I don't go for 'dis' and 'dat' and besides, it was a little too risqué to suit me. I've been a race woman all my life. All my life I've fought back by myself." Her first records were finally recorded under the Savoy label with the Jay Cole Band in 1944–45.

Retiring from music in 1947 to care for her family, Wells returned to Newark and worked at a variety of jobs to make ends meet, among them managing her own restaurant. "'What kind of mother are you?'" Wells recalled asking herself at the time. "I felt I should be with my daughter instead of traveling around." (*New York Times*, June 24, 1973) Though the details of her marriage are not known, Wells was no longer married to Nicholas by this time and had remarried, to Melvyn Evans. Following her husband's death, she was able to devote more time to her first love, singing in her local church, the New Eden Baptist Church, where she had been a longtime member. She was eventually nominated "Mother," or oldest member of the church, where she sang in the Senior Choir and was director of the Junior Choir. She was active in the Newark chapter of the National Council of Negro Women and also developed a talent for physiotherapy, "a natural one, not by schooling or teachin'" (*Jazz*, Feb. 1965, 26), helping the physically disabled, elderly, and troubled.

Starting in 1965, at age 62, Wells began a new singing career, working club and concert performances in the Newark–New York area; recording on the Saydisc/Matchbox label (1972), the 400 W 150 label (1973), and the Barron label (1975 and 1977); and making feature appearances on New York radio stations. In these recordings Wells's keen sense of phrasing, timing, and delivery are evident. Her rich and mellow alto voice, her vitality, and her vocal control in both blues and gospel songs "cannot be faulted and are worthy of a woman a fraction of her age." (Gaster, *Storyville*, Oct.–Nov. 1972) Using a cabaret-style approach to music, she could get her audience's attention with the tilt of her head, a smile, a wink.

In 1975, at age 73, Wells went international and finally received the public recognition she had been getting from performers in her field for decades. Her life and music were profiled in a six-part French TV documentary; she was a featured performer at the Oude Stijl Jazz Festival in Breda, Holland, and the Ghent Folk Festival in Belgium (1977); and she made seven European tours with the Harlem Blues and Jazz Band. She got star treatment from all her audiences.

Wells once said that in music "I can do anything I make up my mind to do." (*New York Times*, June 24, 1973) The same proved true with her life. In 1980, as a result of an overenthusiastic fan stepping on her toe, the diabetic Wells was faced with the necessity of a below-the-knee amputation of her left leg. Convalescing at the Theresa Grotta Nursing Home in West Orange, Wells so encouraged her fellow patients as a volunteer counselor and morale booster that she earned the 1982 "Woman of the Year Award for the Handicapped" and was presented with the 1983 Concerned Citizen of the Year Award. She received the keys to the city of Newark from Mayor Kenneth Gibson and was feted in 1982 on the occasion of her 60th anniversary in show business by a host of jazz and blues performers. The tribute, at which CONSTANCE WOODRUFF served as mistress of ceremonies, attracted more than 500 friends and fans. Her pleasure in the accolades she received was marred only by the death of her daughter in 1981.

Skillfully using an artificial leg, Wells resumed a full schedule of professional appearances at age 79, performing for over a year at the Ginger Man in New York (1981–82). Her final performance was December 8, 1984, at Sweet Basil's in Greenwich Village. Wells died on December 22, 1984, at age 82, in Belleville as a result of a heart attack and was buried at the Heavenly Rest Memorial Park in East Hanover, NJ.

Wells's life was marked by tragedy, hardship, and wearing years on road tours. She even witnessed the murder of her father, stabbed in a dispute over a past-due bill. She was to remember him as "the kindest man I ever knew, always helping someone." (Matchbox/Saydisc album liner notes) Like her father, she gave help and encouragement to everyone who needed her and was known as a strong, compassionate woman. "I always said you don't sing a blues without a soul. Blues seem to be a simple thing to handle," she remarked, "but it's one of the hardest things there is."

(*Jazz*, Feb. 1965)

Wells is profiled in Sheldon Harris, *Blues Who's Who* (1979). See also Sheldon Harris, "Miss Rhapsody," *Jazz* (Feb. 1965):22–23, 26; and Gilbert Gaster, "Miss Rhapsody," *Storyville* (Oct.-Nov. 1972):16–23. Newspaper articles on her appeared in the *New York Times*, June 24, 1973, and Feb. 14, 1982, and in the *Newark Star-Ledger*, July 27, 1973, and Nov. 1, 1982. See also Matchbox/Saydisc SDM 227 album liner notes by Sheldon Harris. A telephone interview with Harris on Feb. 24, 1988, provided personal insights on Wells. Obituaries appeared in the *Newark Star-Ledger*, Dec. 24, 1984, and in the *New York Times*, Jan. 7, 1985.

*Caroline Wheeler Jacobus*
*Sheldon Harris*

## CYNTHIA WESTCOTT, 1898–1983

Cynthia Westcott, a plant pathologist known as "the plant doctor," was born June 29, 1898, in North Attleboro, MA, one of two children (a boy and a girl) of Elizabeth (Tourtellot) Westcott, a teacher, and Frank Westcott, a civil engineer. Westcott had a proud ancestry whose maternal line could be traced back to Roger Williams and paternal line to Stanley Westcott, a companion of Roger Williams during the settling of Rhode Island in 1636. Her early interest in the outdoors and plants was enhanced by two farms owned by the family: one, their home in North Attleboro, and the other, a 300-acre site on Chopmist Ridge, 30 miles away in Scituate, RI. Westcott loved the Chopmist Ridge farm, where she would often lie for hours listening to the winds sighing through the pine trees.

After graduating from North Attleboro High School in 1916, Westcott planned to attend Wellesley College and major in German and Latin. Two sciences were required, and Phila Helt, her high school English teacher and a 1913 Wellesley graduate, encouraged Westcott to choose botany as one of these courses. She did so and was inspired by the teaching and guidance of Wellesley botany professor Margaret Ferguson. Westcott graduated in 1920 with a major in botany.

She wanted to continue in advanced botany studies at Cornell University because Ferguson had graduated from Cornell. But the university had few assistantships available at that time, so Westcott taught science for one year at Northboro High School in Massachusetts, while pursuing an assistantship at Cornell. She finally received an offer, not in botany as she had hoped, but in the department of plant pathology. She soon acquired enthusiasm for that field through the influence of H. H. Whetzel, head of Cornell's department of plant pathology, and Louis M. Massey, chair of her graduate committee. In 1921 Whetzel offered her a full-time job as a research assistant funded by the Heckscher Research Foundation.

Westcott, the only woman in a department of 40 men, was given tasks her male colleagues were not assigned, such as responsibility for the material room, preparing tea each afternoon, and packing picnic lunches for collecting trips. But Westcott used these experiences to her advantage.

Her responsibility for the material room required her to prepare microscope slides for Whetzel's course in plant pathology as well as dry, press, and preserve specimens. During the course each student chose fifteen diseases representing all types of plant pathogens for study. Because Westcott did the specimen preparations and mimeographed sheets on the life histories of organisms and the symptoms and control of the diseases they caused as part of her material room duties, she became familiar with many times that number.

While living at Sigma Delta Epsilon House, the graduate women's scientific sorority, she planted her first rose garden and first test garden for sprays and dusts. Skills she learned making tea and packing picnic lunches were incorporated into putting on an event Westcott called Rose Day, a time for both teaching and socializing she held each year.

While at Sigma Delta Epsilon, Westcott became a close friend of Irene Dobroscky, an entomologist. Dobroscky studied insects in bird nests, and the two women often climbed trees together to collect specimens for Dobroscky. Later they became business partners in plant doctoring.

Westcott was awarded a doctorate from Cornell University in 1932 after completing her dissertation on a cause of brand canker in roses. She soon learned that there were few jobs available for women in her field. She accepted a part-time assistantship as a bacteriologist with the New Jersey Experiment Station at Rutgers, taking further courses at Rutgers in her spare time. Whetzel, whom she highly respected, encouraged her to go into practical plant doctoring. Dobroscky did not have a permanent job either, and in 1933 the women decided to take Whetzel's advice and open a partnership as plant doctors in Glen Ridge, NJ. Their business was operated like a medical doctor's was at that time: Westcott made house calls to diagnose problems, treating roses and other ornamental plants in her clients' gardens. During winter months she wrote, lectured, and traveled.

By 1934 Dobroscky left the partnership for another job, but Westcott continued as a plant doctor for 30 years, giving nearly 1,000 lectures and traveling to every state in the union, collecting specimens along the way. She taught garden courses at Macy's, plant clinics at Bambergers, and special courses at the New York and Brooklyn Botanical Gardens. Her articles appeared in garden magazines and she wrote regular columns in the *New York Times* and *Home Garden*. She also contributed to a book, *Ten Thou-*

*sand Garden Questions Answered*, published by *Home Garden*. Westcott developed a large clientele, including actor Helen Hayes and playwright Maxwell Anderson. Friends and colleagues associated with experimental stations and universities often referred prospective clients to her.

In 1943 the U.S. Department of Agriculture asked Westcott to work temporarily in Mobile, AL, on a devastating disease of azaleas. The disease had adversely affected tourism throughout the South and Congress had allocated a special appropriation for Westcott's work. She was able to culture and identify the fungal pathogen, developing a chemical treatment that saved the blooms. She was one of the first plant pathologists to control a disease with the new class of fungicides now known worldwide as Zineb and Maneb.

Equally important, she communicated the procedures for control to the public. In a letter complimenting Westcott on her success in treating the azalea blight, her former professor H. H. Whetzel praised her combination of scientific skill and ability to teach others what she had discovered. He wrote: "It is with a good deal of pride that I learned that one of my old students and assistants had put it over the boys who have heretofore worked on azalea blight. The Cornell training does show up, doesn't it? Your personal experience as a practical plant pathologist has also greatly contributed to your success on this problem. It is not enough to solve a problem of this kind. You have the spirit and technique for getting your solution before the public; that is quite as important as the research work itself."

In a further effort to share her knowledge with the public, Westcott opened her home and office in Glen Ridge annually for Rose Day. This event, a continuation of the one held during her years at Cornell, endeared her to many visitors as they enjoyed her hospitality and learned more about gardening.

Articles about Westcott appeared in magazines and newspapers, including the *New Yorker*, which profiled her in 1952. J. G. Horsfall and E. B. Cowling honored her by dedicating volume 4 of their series *Plant Pathology: An Advanced Treatise* to her as "the prototype practitioner of plant pathology." Westcott herself wrote several books about plant care, including *The Gardener's Bug Book* and *The Plant Disease Handbook*.

Westcott was a member of numerous professional societies and organizations that recognized her outstanding contributions to the field of plant pathology. The Northeast Division of the American Phytopathological Society gave her its Award of Merit in 1969 and the American Phytopathological Society appointed her a fellow in 1973. Although Westcott worked with a broad range of plants, her greatest interest and love centered on roses, and in 1975 the American Rose Society honored her at its national convention with a presentation called "This Is Your Life, Dr. Cynthia Westcott." That same year the Jackson and Perkins Company named a hybrid tea rose "Cynthia" in her honor.

When Westcott retired in 1962, she moved to a retirement community near Croton-on-Hudson, NY. She died of a heart ailment, at age 84, on March 22, 1983, in North Tarrytown, NY.

Articles detailing Westcott's life and professional contributions are: E. Kinkead, "Physician in the Flowerbeds," *New Yorker* 28 (July 26, 1952):26–28; J. Houser-Shea, "Cynthia Westcott, the Plant Doctor," *Cornell Countryman* 77 (1980):10–11; and R. K. Horst, "Pioneer Leader in Plant Pathology: Cynthia Westcott, Plant Doctor," *Annual Review of Phytopathology* 22 (1984):21–26.

*R. Kenneth Horst*

## KATHARINE ELKUS WHITE, 1906–1985

Katharine (Elkus) White, U.S. ambassador to Denmark, politician, and quintessential public servant, was born November 25, 1906, in New York City, the third of four children born to Abram I. and Gertrude (Hess) Elkus. Her father, a lawyer, was appointed the U.S. ambassador to Turkey by President Woodrow Wilson and was later a judge in the New York Court of Appeals. Her mother, a woman concerned with political and social issues, was acclaimed as a gracious lady and accomplished hostess.

The Elkus family was active in politics. Albert Elkus, White's uncle, was the mayor of Sacramento, CA, from 1921 to 1925. Her father was the attorney who investigated the causes of the disastrous Triangle shirt factory fire in New York and was active in the Democratic party. Her mother was active in the woman suffrage movement in New York City and was later an alternate delegate to the 1928 Democratic Convention in Dallas. The family socialized with the prominent politicians of the time, including Jimmy Walker, Herbert Lehman, Alfred E. Smith, Franklin and Eleanor Roosevelt, and Woodrow and Ellen Wilson. Introduced to diplomacy as a child, White recalls peeking through the curtains to watch the receptions and all the important people her parents entertained at their summer home, "Elkridge," in Red Bank, NJ, site of such festivities as a surprise birthday party for Woodrow Wilson. Eleanor Roosevelt became a strong role model for White.

White credited Sarah Elkus, her aunt, with inspiring her to live a life of social service. Sarah Elkus founded a settlement house in New York City to teach English to immigrants, and White and her Aunt Sarah became very close as White watched Sarah "fight city hall" on many occasions.

White's early education was at the French school in Istanbul. Her family left Turkey when the United States broke off diplomatic relations with that country in 1917. Traveling from Turkey by train, they reached Paris just as General John J. Pershing arrived with the first American troops.

White then attended private high schools in New York City and received a degree in drama from Vassar in 1928. "It helped me later in politics," she explained, "because sometimes you have to put on a good act." She accompanied her mother to the 1928 Democratic Convention in Dallas. After the convention, at a political gathering held on the lawn of Elkridge, White was asked to read a telegram from Alfred E. Smith, presidential candidate and family friend. White's poise was such that she was thereafter called upon to make many speeches on Smith's behalf and she thus discovered her natural gift for extemporaneous speech. This youthful involvement marked the beginning of a life filled with political activism.

After the 1928 presidential election, the Elkus family took a six-month trip around the world. It was on this trip that she met Arthur J. White, a stockbroker from Boston traveling with his mother. They fell in love in Rome, became engaged in Malaya, and were married in Red Bank, NJ, on October 3, 1929. They lived for a time in New York City, where White acted briefly with a New York theater company, appearing in many of the productions and even playing the part of a nun just before the birth of Lawrence Elkus White, her first child, in 1931, in Red Bank.

White gave up her stage career when the family moved to Red Bank and established their lifelong home at Elkridge, in the expanded cottage that had once been White's childhood playhouse. Frances Elkus White, a daughter, was born in 1933 and from then on White put her theatrical talents to use as a speaker for family, political, and philanthropic ventures—pursuits that kept her closer to home.

While White was in the hospital recovering from the birth of Frances, she was nominated for the Red Bank Borough Council. She had to run against a "Let's Keep Katie in the Kitchen" campaign and lost by thirteen votes. In 1935 she lost an election for the Monmouth County Board of Freeholders. Undaunted by losses at the polls, she plunged into volunteer work.

During World War II White served as chair of the War Bond Drive in the greater Red Bank area. As vice-chair of the Women's Committee for the 1948 Democratic National Convention, White labored long and hard in the New York office. She eventually was rewarded for her political tenacity when she won a campaign for the unpaid position of mayor of Red Bank in 1950. She was the first woman to serve Red Bank as mayor and the first Democratic mayor in twenty years. Arthur White had become an official with the U.S. Department of Labor and the nonpartisan nature of his position often required him to leave the house when White hosted political gatherings.

White was pleased with her success. "Everything I had ever done paid off," recalled White in a 1978 interview. "During the Depression I ran a project at the River Street School, canning vegetables for distribution to people who needed food, and people remembered me. They said, 'You were the girl at the tomatoes.'"

"The girl at the tomatoes" served three terms as mayor of Red Bank, from 1951 to 1957. White was the first mayor to appoint African-Americans to city positions. Predictably, her special attention was focused on social services, but she also devoted a great deal of time to the Fire Department, updating old equipment and improving performance.

In 1954 White was appointed a commissioner of the New Jersey Highway Authority, which operated the Garden State Parkway. She was made chair of that agency in 1955, thus becoming the first woman in the United States to head a toll road authority. During this time White was introduced as "New Jersey's first woman highwayman." White served for nine years as chair and brought the parkway from the opening of the first tollbooth in 1954, through the completion of the New York Thruway connection in 1957, and to the opening of the Garden State Arts Center in 1964.

White was sustained by her role models, especially Eleanor Roosevelt. Referring to Roosevelt in a speech, White said, "All over the world she was regarded as a great woman. She held the torch so high that we, as the women of her generation, will have to work unceasingly to reach the torch and carry it on to greater heights." In White's quest to carry the torch to greater heights, she ran for the Third U.S. Congressional District seat in 1960. She was narrowly defeated and decided not to run again for the House of Representatives. She realized it meant campaigning every two years, which would limit her ability to work effectively as a legislator.

White served as acting treasurer for the state of New Jersey in 1961. This was her first paying job in over 30 years of public service. Her second job, as a consultant to the administration of Governor Richard J. Hughes, was also for the state of New Jersey. In that post she initiated and developed the New Jersey State Department of Community Affairs. President Lyndon Johnson appointed White chair of the Advisory Council of the President's Committee on Traffic Safety in 1963 and 1964.

While White was planning to run for the U.S. Senate in 1964, President Johnson appointed her U.S. ambassador to Denmark. She held this position until 1968. During her stay in Denmark, the Grand Cross of the Order of Dannebrog, one of Denmark's highest honors, was presented to her by the Danish royal family.

For almost a generation White *was* the Democratic party in Monmouth County, according to N.J. Representative James J. Howard. She served in almost every capacity, from delegate-at-large to the Democratic National Convention to chair of the state Democratic Woman's Advisory Council. And her activities were not confined to politics. She was also deeply involved with the Marlboro Psychiatric Hospital, the United Negro College Fund, the YMCA, the American Association of University Women, Monmouth County Organization for Social Service, and the Rutgers University Board of Governors. In 1967 she was awarded an honorary doctor of law degree from Douglass College, Rutgers University.

To many, especially those closest to her, White became a role model. She was considered a great lady who accepted both victories and defeats gracefully. Throughout her career White stressed the use of discretion and tact. She once said, "You don't always speak out on everything you happen to be thinking or believe in. When you speak for others you have to learn to speak more carefully."

White's husband died in 1979. She died peacefully in her sleep on April 24, 1985, in Red Bank, at age 78, and was buried at the family mausoleum in Beth Olom Cemetery in Brooklyn, NY. Many tributes were paid to her in the press, but the most moving read: "To Monmouth County, the name of Katharine Elkus White has stood for community and achievement and excellence for more than a half century. Her death has taken something from all of us, something we may not possess, but know we could possess. It has to do with Mrs. White's deep conviction that our social and political systems can work, and that each individual can make a difference for the greater good." (*Shrewsbury Register*, Apr. 26, 1985)

Interviews with White's daughter, Frances W. Cohen, Pittsburgh, PA; her son, Lawrence E. White, Red Bank, NJ; her former secretary, Lillian Murray, Fair Haven, NJ; and her close friend Cecile Norton, mayor of Sea Bright, NJ—all in Mar. and Apr. 1986—provided biographical details. White was profiled in *Current Biography* (1965). Obituaries appeared in the *Asbury Park* (NJ) *Press*, Apr. 26, 1985; *Shrewsbury* (NJ) *Register*, Apr. 26, 1985; and the *New York Times*, Apr. 27, 1985.

*Karen Geyer McGrain*

## PHYLLIS A. WHITNEY, 1903–

Phyllis Ayame Whitney, romantic suspense writer and best-selling author of 70 novels, was born on September 9, 1903, in Yokohama, Japan. Her mother, Mary Lillian Mandeville, and her father, Charles Joseph Whitney, had been engaged to marry when they were young in Cleveland, OH. A quarrel separated them, and when a well-known actor, Gus Heege, came to town with his own company, Mandeville married him and went on the stage, acting in the plays he wrote, here and abroad. Charlie Whitney went off to the Orient and lived for a time in Hawaii and then in Japan. When he learned through a mutual friend (some eighteen years later) that Mandeville's husband had died, he asked her to come out to Japan to marry him and sent her the steamer ticket. She accepted, and Phyllis Whitney, the couple's only child, was born in Japan.

Whitney, whose middle name is Japanese for "iris," spent the first fifteen years of her life in Japan, the Philippines, and China. In Japan her father worked for a shipping firm. In Manila and in Hankow, China, he was a hotel manager. She inherited her father's love for new places, and later this was to show up in her writing. She was close to both of her parents, and it was very hard for her when her father died in China in 1915, and her mother in San Antonio, TX, in 1918. After her mother's death she went to live with an aunt in Chicago, where she attended McKinley High School.

Earlier, while attending an American missionary school in Kuling, China, an English teacher encouraged her to write. She began writing stories when she was about twelve, though it was many years before she was ready for publication. She could not go to college, but went to work in bookstores and libraries—an experience she feels was good for her as a writer.

In 1925, in Chicago, Whitney married George A. Garner, whom she had known in high school. On December 19, 1934, her only child, Georgia Garner, was born in Chicago. Later, Whitney and Garner were divorced. Whitney met her second husband, Lovell Jahnke, a Mobil Oil executive, during World War II. She was working as children's book editor for the *Chicago Sun*. The paper sent her twice a year by train to New York to interview the editors of children's books at the big publishing companies. On this occasion she came to the line in a crowded dining car; her future husband was in line at the other end of the car, and the headwaiter put them at the same table. Whitney likes to think of this as one of the many "meaningful coincidences" in her life. In 1950, after she had moved to New York, she and Jahnke married.

The couple lived on Staten Island, NY, until Jahnke retired, when they moved to Sussex County, NJ, and later to Hope, NJ, where her husband died of cancer in 1973. Several of her books are set in New Jersey.

All this time Whitney was working at her writing. She sold her first short story to the *Chicago Daily News* and for several years wrote for pulp magazines. Her first book, *A Place for Ann*, was published in 1941. After that she wrote for teenagers for many years. Her fourth book was an adult mystery novel, *Red Is for Murder*. This was not a success at the time, but many years later was published in paperback as *The Red Carnelian* and sold very well. *The Quicksilver Pool* (1955) was her first novel in the romantic suspense field. After that she alternated between adult and juvenile novels for many years. Now she writes only in the adult field.

When she left Chicago, she became children's book editor for the *Philadelphia Inquirer* for a short time. She was also instructor in juvenile writing at New York University for eleven years. All these were free-lance jobs that she could do while working on her writing. Like most writers, she had to juggle several jobs in order to earn a living. Not until her novels began to sell in greater numbers was she able to give up the other work and concentrate on her adult novels.

In a June 1987 interview, Whitney said she had faced no particular problems as a woman writer in the juvenile field. There was never any difficulty about placing her adult books either, which quickly began to sell more copies than the standard tough-detective mystery novel, written mostly by men. She has always written because she "couldn't help it." Her goal today is still to learn and grow in her work, and she feels that she is doing better writing now than when she was younger.

Whitney usually takes a year to write each book, with several months spent in preparation, developing her characters and story after having first visited its setting. She writes and rewrites, spending much time on revision in order to "get it right." Her books have been translated into many languages. She likes to read in her own field, numbering among her favorite writers Barbara Michaels, Mary Higgins Clark, and Velda Johnston.

In 1986 Whitney built her own house in Virginia, in the foothills of the Blue Ridge mountains, southwest of Charlottesville. Her daughter and son-in-law built a house nearby for themselves. Whitney is now writing about Virginia.

Discussing the basics of story development, Whitney commented during an interview that the first requirement for her after setting is "a strong [woman] character and a strong problem." This main character must always struggle against high odds in the course of the story. When she writes about some distant place, Whitney uses the viewpoint of a stranger—which is her own viewpoint.

Asked about the main satisfaction she derives from her career, she said, "There are so many satisfactions. Seeing the story begin to come to life. Developing it into a book that I will one day hold in my hands. Receiving letters from readers whom I've made happy. It has been a long uphill journey, but decidedly worth it."

As well as her mystery novels, Whitney has written excellent textbooks for writers—*Writing Juvenile Fiction and Novels* and *Guide to Fiction Writing*, both published by the *Writer* in Boston, as well as many articles for the *Writer* magazine.

Her books and papers have been placed with the

Mugar Memorial Library at Boston University.

Whitney's papers and books are available at the Mugar Memorial Library, Boston University (Boston, MA). She was interviewed by telephone on June 11, 1987. Whitney has done an account of her life on tape available at the Patchogue-Medford Library, Patchogue, NY. Profiles of Whitney appear in *Current Biography* (1948) and in *American Women Writers* 4 (1982).

*Dina Morello*

## MADALINE WORTHY WILLIAMS, 1894–1968

After nearly a lifetime of community service with church, civic, and civil rights groups, Madaline (Worthy) Williams took the legislative oath of office in Trenton in January 1958 to become New Jersey's first black assemblywoman. Born in Brunswick, GA, on May 5, 1894, the daughter of Josephine Frances (Jenkins) and Ephraim Wilford Worthy, Williams had two sisters, Katherine and Renne, and a brother, George.

She attended an all-black public elementary school in Brunswick, which, she later recalled, did not afford her the same educational advantages and opportunities as those provided for the area's white children. Since there were no local facilities for further public education for black children, her parents sent her to Selden Normal School, sponsored by the Presbyterian Board of Missions for Freedmen. She went on to Atlanta University, studying there for one year.

In about 1917, when many southern blacks were migrating north for job opportunities, the Worthy family moved to Trenton, NJ. There Williams did substitute teaching, qualifying for a provisional certificate after her one year of college. During this time she attended the State Normal School at Trenton (later Trenton State College) as an extension student.

Williams taught in the one school for black elementary students in Trenton. She was especially helpful in communicating with newly arrived southern children, whose habits and speech were unfamiliar to northern teachers. Because of overcrowded and deteriorated conditions, the Board of Education finally decided to build a new school big enough to accommodate Trenton's black students from kindergarten through high school. The new school would keep black and white students from attending high school together as they had done in the past and the black teachers were asked to visit black homes and churches to encourage parents to send their children to the new all-black school. Williams and one other teacher refused to comply. They were dismissed, ending Williams's eight years as a Trenton teacher.

She soon met Samuel Williams, a Newark Post Office worker, and they were married in New York City on April 2, 1926. Samuel Alexander, their only child, born Febru-

ary 15, 1927, suffered a birth injury and was crippled and blind for the 23 years of his life.

After their son's birth, the Williams family moved to East Orange, where, although her son's care consumed much of her time, Williams became active in civic and church activities. She was the youth division adviser of both the local Oranges-Maplewood branch of the National Association for the Advancement of Colored People (NAACP) and the New Jersey State Conference of NAACP branches. Her division dealt with young people between the ages of twelve and 25, with a focus on vocational guidance, character building, and recreational programs that emphasized a sense of community fellowship and responsible citizenship. In addition, she was an Executive Board member of the Oranges-Maplewood branch. She shared this activity with her husband, who was a member of the National Board and was the New Jersey State president of the NAACP.

Williams became a den mother for the Cub Scouts of her church, the Union Baptist Church of Orange, and also served as a board trustee for the New Jersey Society for Crippled Children for six years. She was a volunteer at the YWCA of the Oranges and Maplewood for twelve years, serving at various times as vice-president and secretary of the Board of Directors, chairperson of the Building Maintenance Committee, and organizer and chairperson of the Public Affairs Committee.

One of the organizers of the East Orange League of Women Voters in 1947, she served as its vice-president and secretary and as chair of the Foreign Policy Committee. She was first vice-president of the Council of Negro Women of the Oranges and Maplewood, as well as a member of the Executive Board of the Council of Church Women of the Oranges and Maplewood, the Policy Committee of the United Community Services, the East Orange Friends of the Library, the Human Relations Conference of East Orange, and the East Orange Democratic Club.

In 1952 Governor Alfred Driscoll appointed Williams to the New Jersey Migrant Labor Board. Although an unsalaried position, this was her first public appointment. Five years later, Governor Driscoll reappointed her for a second five-year term. Years later she said, "I had nothing to do with it whatsoever except I was concerned about people and, all through the years, I had worked for the betterment of the community." (Dannett, *Profiles of Negro Womanhood*, 317)

Williams had many conferences with members of the New Jersey State Legislature because of her position on the Migrant Labor Board and met many people who expressed admiration for her keen interest in government procedure. When she was 62 Williams was approached by John McMahon, chairman of the Essex County Democratic Screening Committee, to run as a Democratic candidate for the New Jersey State Assembly in 1957. With the full cooperation of her husband and the young people with whom she worked, Williams ran and won the election. As an assemblywoman, her special interests were child welfare, child labor, juvenile delinquency, and migrant worker legislation.

Williams ran and was reelected to the legislature in 1959. In 1960, less than a year later, she was asked to run in the impending election for the office of Essex County Register of Deeds and Mortgages. After winning this election, she resigned from the assembly. As register, she was responsible for handling tax liens from the federal government and veterans' discharges in Essex County. She was reelected to a second five-year term in this post in November 1965.

Elected an alternate delegate to the 1960 Democratic National Convention, four years later she served as alternate delegate and vice-chair of the New Jersey delegation to the convention in Atlantic City.

Governor Robert Meyner established the New Jersey Civil War Commission in May 1959, following Congress's creation of the National Civil War Centennial Commission. Williams was one of two legislators selected to represent the New Jersey Assembly at the national conference. She became the focus of national attention in 1960 when she was denied accommodations at the Francis Marion Hotel in Charleston, SC, where the National Commission's Fourth National Assembly was to be held. After National Commission officials, the mayor of Charleston, and hotel officials refused to rescind the denial, the New Jersey Commission voted to boycott the celebration.

The National Commission remained firm in its denial of Williams's request, even after the intervention of New Jersey's U.S. Senator Clifford Case and Representative Hugh Addonizio. Finally, at the suggestion of President John F. Kennedy, a compromise was worked out and the assembly was held at the Charleston naval base. Williams accepted the adjustment with grace and good humor and later recalled her participation as a rewarding experience.

Following her election to the New Jersey Assembly in 1959, Williams was honored at a testimonial dinner sponsored by the Oranges-Maplewood branch of the NAACP. The testimonial acknowledged her distinguished contributions to civil rights and her superior public service without thought of gain. She was one of two Essex County women cited by the National Council of Church Women in Cleveland, OH, in 1955 for community Christian citizenship. And in 1957 she was presented with the Shafer Award for outstanding work in civic and community affairs.

Williams died of cancer in Montclair on December 14, 1968, at age 74, and was buried in Hollywood Cemetery in Union. She was eulogized by Governor Richard Hughes as an "outstanding public servant and citizen of New Jersey . . . a woman of grace, dignity and human compassion."

(*Evening News*, Dec. 15, 1968)

The NJ-NPL is the most lucrative source of information on Williams. A profile and interview with her appears in Sylvia Dannett, *Profiles of Negro Womanhood*, 2 vols. (1966). Her obituary appeared in the *Evening News* (Newark), Dec. 15, 1968.

*Mildred Lipscomb*

## THERESA LOUISE MARTENS WILSON, 1880–1975

Theresa Louise (Martens) Wilson, educator and peace activist, was born in New York City on January 2, 1880, the youngest of three children of Carl Martens, a maker of stringed instruments and a music publisher, and Josephine (Weeks) Martens, a Quaker from Chappaqua, NY, who in her later life was a school principal in College Point, NY.

Wilson lived with her family in lower Manhattan until 1888, when they moved to Hoboken and later, Rutherford, NJ. She was educated by private tutors, at private schools, and in the public school system of New York City. She studied the violin and piano for the concert stage, but decided to major in literature at Hunter College, from which she received a B.A. in 1901.

She married the Rev. Henry Blauvelt Wilson, an Episcopal priest, on October 24, 1901, in New York City. From 1901 to 1907 they lived in Jersey City, and then Brooklyn, where they adopted their daughter, Jane Mary (b. 1898). For health reasons, the Rev. Wilson was offered a position at St. John's Church in Boonton, NJ, and in December 1907 he accepted the offer.

Two years later the Wilsons began St. John's School in the rectory of the church. The school relocated four times to accommodate its students, finally settling in its present location on the Boulevard in Mountain Lakes, NJ. Boys and girls attended for the first six grades, and then girls only through high school.

Wilson took up a number of causes in addition to her duties as a minister's wife. In 1913–14 she served as second vice-president of the Boonton Equal Suffrage League. She marched in local demonstrations and worked in the league's tearoom. This group became a springboard for her activities in local civic and humanitarian groups.

When her husband died in March 1923, Wilson became headmistress of St. John's School. In addition to her administrative duties, she taught English composition and literature, French and German. She explored new theories of education and applied progressive education, which she explained to St. John's School as emphasizing the educator who is always a student. She introduced the progressive "Dalton Plan," in which the student moves at his or her own pace and chooses subjects to study. As part of her "One World" program she discontinued the flag salute and singing of the national anthem. Because these actions branded her a radical, the school's trustees withdrew their support and many parents withdrew their children. Consequently Wilson resigned as headmistress on November 18, 1927, and moved to New York City, where she became involved in the peace movement.

Wilson had joined the Fellowship of Reconciliation (FOR), a pacifist organization, sometime in the early 1920s and was elected to its council and Executive Committee in September 1927. Founded in England soon after the outbreak of World War I, the FOR's American branch was organized about a year later, in November 1915. The group appealed to Christians to renounce war under all circumstances and to find nonviolent means of resolving conflict among nations, within families, between races, and in industry. When Wilson was an Executive Committee member, in 1927, the FOR sent a mission to five Central American countries, including Nicaragua, where they tried unsuccessfully to negotiate an end to the conflict between the U.S. Marines and General Augusto Sandino, the Nicaraguan insurgent.

Wilson became associate secretary of the Committee on Militarism in Education (CME) in May 1928. This group, founded in 1925 by members of the FOR and located in the same building, sought to remove military training requirements (such as Reserve Officer Training Corps) from public schools and universities. During her two years with CME, Wilson spoke to a variety of organizations—mostly women's groups in New Jersey and New York—about militarism in education and related topics.

In Wilson's absence, St. John's School was beset with problems, both financial and philosophical, so in 1932 she returned as headmistress. She continued to work for peace, but did so through local organizations. Active in the Woman's Club of Mountain Lakes, she was their president from 1933 to 1935. Her inaugural speech, "Why a Women's Club in Mountain Lakes?" stressed that women should serve their community and the world, not just their families.

In 1941 she was elected president of the Mountain Lakes Branch of the College Club (now the American Association of University Women). Wilson used her public positions as forums to advocate progressive education, women's rights, and the need for global disarmament.

Wilson continued as headmistress of St. John's School until her retirement in 1959. During the early 1940s she was editor of the school edition of the *Atlantic Monthly*.

St. John's School was renamed the Wilson School in October 1965. In 1966 Wilson published a history of the school titled *The Idea of a School*. From then until her death Wilson continued in her role as the school's matriarch. She always believed in the value of educating women and held their schooling as essential to the well-being of the world.

In the 1960s, while in her eighties, Wilson led a weekly devotional group at St. Peter's Episcopal Church in Mountain Lakes. She died, at age 95, from cancer of the bladder on November 14, 1975, in Pine Brook, NJ.

Wilson's *Idea of a School* (1966) provides information on her early life and philosophy of education. The papers of the Committee on Militarism in Education, available at P-SC, contain correspondence from Wilson in her role as associate secretary. The archives of St. John's Church (Boonton, NJ) and the Wilson School (Boonton, NJ) contain useful information about her activities.

*Janet Gibbs-Albanesius*

## EVELYN MAISEL WITKIN, 1921–

Evelyn Ruth (Maisel) Witkin, a leading geneticist concerned with the mechanism of mutations, was born in New York City on March 9, 1921. She was the younger of two daughters of Mary (Levin) and Joseph Maisel. Both parents were born in Russia and emigrated to the United States under the pressure of tsarist anti-Semitism. Witkin's mother was trained as a nurse and her father as a pharmacist. Though conscious of their Jewish heritage, both embraced liberal ideals and were not inclined to religious practice.

When Witkin was born her father owned a pharmacy in Manhattan, but when she was three years old he died in an accident. Six years later, Mary (Levin) Maisel remarried, to another pharmacist, and the family moved to Forest Hills, NY, where Witkin's stepfather owned a drugstore. Both her mother and stepfather worked in the pharmacy, so the Maisel girls were encouraged to be self-sufficient and independent.

At the time there was no high school in Forest Hills, so Witkin commuted to Manhattan to attend the all-girl Washington Irving High School, from which she graduated in 1937. Her interests were literary, with a penchant for French. She became fluent in French but was also attracted to science, especially biology.

Witkin continued her studies at the Washington Square College of New York University, where she majored in biology, with minors in chemistry and French. She developed a strong interest in music and joined the college choir, which specialized in Bach cantatas.

Although Witkin graduated magna cum laude in 1941, her graduation was delayed and an offer for a graduate fellowship in biology at New York University was retracted because of her prominence as a leader in a protest against racial discrimination in athletics. This contretemps, however, had a beneficial effect on her career. Disenchanted with New York University, she did her graduate work at Columbia University, where she studied with Theodosius Dobzhansky. Witkin had been attracted to genetics in college by the theories of Trofim Lysenko on the effect of the environment on heredity. Columbia, with its informal but close association with the Carnegie Institution of Washington at Cold Spring Harbor, was an ideal location for a budding geneticist; Witkin was exposed to all the great minds in the field. Soon the falsity of Lysenko's ideas became apparent to her. Under the guidance of Dobzhansky and S. E. Luria, she was awarded an M.S. in 1943 and a Ph.D. in 1947 for studies of radiation-resistant mutants of *Escherichia coli* that she isolated.

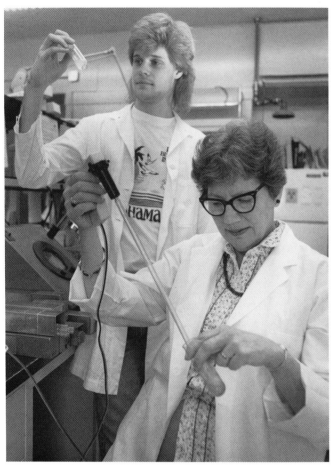

Evelyn Maisel Witkin, professor of genetics at Rutgers, the State University of New Jersey, with a student in her laboratory, 1986. Witkin is an expert in the field of gene mutation. *Courtesy, private collection.*

In 1943 she married Herman A. Witkin, an experimental psychologist specializing in cognition. The couple had two sons, Joseph (b. 1949) and Andrew (b. 1952).

Witkin held various positions in teaching and research. She was an instructor in biology at Hofstra College, Hempstead, NY (1942–43), and at Brooklyn College, Brooklyn, NY (1943–44); an assistant in zoology at Columbia University, (1944–45); and a research assistant, a postdoctoral fellow, and eventually a staffmember in the Department of Genetics at the Carnegie Institution of

Washington at Cold Spring Harbor (1949–55).

Witkin's children were born while she was working at Cold Spring Harbor. The Carnegie Institution was then under the enlightened directorship of Vannevar Bush, who asked Witkin what maternity leave arrangements she would like to make, and not only did she get what she wanted (a return to half-time work after a year's leave), but her salary was not reduced. Bush said that her salary remained the same because he knew that she would achieve full-time productivity. She continued to work on a part-time basis until her younger son completed high school.

Witkin accepted a position at the Downstate Medical Center of the State University of New York, when her husband obtained a position at the same institution. Between 1955 and 1971 she progressed from assistant professor to professor. In 1971 Witkin was named professor in the Department of Biological Sciences of Rutgers, the State University of New Jersey. She became Barbara McClintock Professor of Genetics at Rutgers in 1979, the year her husband died.

Working with her first discovery, a radiation-resistant mutant of the bacterium *Escherichia coli,* Witkin then concentrated on learning how radiations and cancer-causing chemicals affect deoxyribonucleic acid (DNA), the carrier of genetic information, and how these agents induce gene mutations. She showed that damage to DNA caused by ultraviolet light can be repaired by cells in several ways, and that one type of DNA repair is "error-prone," whereas others are accurate. Her work has led to the conclusion that radiation-induced mutations are mistakes made in a particular type of DNA repair mechanism known as "SOS" repair because it permits seriously damaged cells to survive.

Witkin has received numerous honors during her career, among them her election to the National Academy of Sciences in 1977 and an honorary doctor of science degree from New York Medical College. She received the New Jersey Women of Achievement Award in 1983.

During her career, Witkin has come in contact with many great figures in the field of genetics. While at Cold Spring Harbor her close association with Barbara McClintock, the future Nobel Prize winner, permitted her to follow the development of the concept of transposable genes. Witkin, however, is a loner in many ways. She is the sole author of the majority of her research publications because she did not have the opportunity to work with graduate students until she joined Rutgers University, and after 40 years of research activities she has not yet guided a postdoctoral fellow.

Witkin lives in Princeton, NJ; her interests outside her field of genetics are literature, especially Victorian poetry, and music.

An interview with Witkin on Apr. 2, 1986, provided details of her life and work. She is listed in *Who's Who of American Women* (1987–88).

*Hubert A. Lechevalier*

## DEBORAH CANNON PARTRIDGE WOLFE, 1916–

Deborah (Cannon) Partridge Wolfe, national leader in education and ordained Christian minister, was born in Cranford (Union County), NJ, on December 22, 1916, the third and youngest child of Gertrude (Moody) and the Rev. Dr. David Wadsworth Cannon, Sr. As an African-American woman coming of age in New Jersey in the 1930s, Wolfe's personal development and career path were strongly influenced by her deeply religious, well-educated, and community-minded parents. Both were social activists and role models for her. Wolfe's mother was a high school principal, social worker, and public servant. Although blocked from joining the exclusively male ministry of her times, her mother taught Sunday school, became a leader of religious organizations, and worked closely with church leaders. Wolfe's father instilled in his daughter pride of black heritage, love of God, and determination to combat segregation and discrimination. "My parents taught me the strength of self and gave me an appreciation of racial and religious roots," Wolfe commented. (Interview, Jan. 10, 1986)

Wolfe's family had placed a high value on education for the past four generations. "My grandparents were born in slavery in Virginia and North Carolina. Papa's parents could read and write, and all of their fifteen children were educated." (Wolfe, Interview, Jan. 10, 1986) Her mother and father had an insatiable need to learn. "They told us, 'You're not finished with your education until you wear a doctoral robe.'" (Wolfe, Interview, Jan. 10, 1986)

Influenced by her family's keen desire for education, Wolfe excelled as a scholar and athlete at Cranford High School, from which she graduated in 1933. At the age of sixteen she entered New Jersey State Teachers College in Jersey City (later Jersey City State College); she was the youngest student enrolled at the college. Her decision to major in education and minor in social studies and English was guided by the career paths of her parents and siblings.

While an undergraduate Wolfe worked summers, first as director of the community center of the First Baptist Church of Cranford in 1935, and the following two years as director of a community center for migrant workers in Hurlock, MD. Before receiving her B.S. in 1937 Wolfe taught her first classes through a Works Progress Administration (WPA) adult education project at Lincoln School in Cranford, which she later served as a supervising teacher and principal. In 1938, while involved in the WPA project, she earned an M.A. in education and sociology at Teachers College of Columbia University. The title of her thesis was "A Background Study and Teacher Training Program for the Education of Migrants."

At this point in her life Wolfe suffered blatant racial discrimination. Although her academic qualifications were superior to those of white applicants, she was flatly refused teaching jobs in Cranford and other towns in New Jersey. "I've seen discrimination in my lifetime. Until 1947 there was legal segregation in New Jersey. They talk about Dixie. I'm talking about my state that I love. It was discrimination detrimental to body and soul," she recalled. (Wolfe, Interview, Jan. 10, 1986)

Mabel Carney, a faculty mentor of Wolfe's at Columbia University, suggested she apply for a position at Tuskegee Institute, a black higher education institution in Alabama, since positions were closed in the north for the promising young educator. Wolfe was quickly hired by Tuskegee, where she served as a member of the faculty from 1938 to 1950. She performed so well that she became head of the department of elementary education and director of graduate studies. From 1938 to 1943 she also served as principal and teacher trainer of elementary and junior high school levels at Prairie Farms School in Tuskegee, and from 1943 to 1945 as principal and teacher trainer at Mitchell's Mill School in Tuskegee. "I'm glad I had these experiences in Alabama," she has commented. "I doubt I would have had the same opportunity at a white institution." (Wolfe, Interview, Jan. 10, 1986)

In June 1940 in Cranford, Wolfe married Henry Roy Partridge, a professor at Tuskegee Institute. Her only child, Henry Roy Partridge, Jr., was born in 1947. Four years later the marriage ended in divorce. In 1959 she married a teacher and insurance executive, Estemore Wolfe, in Roselle, NJ. As her career advanced, her marriage faltered, ending in divorce in 1966. She attributes both dissolved marriages to her strong professional commitments. "Work has had a very big place in my life. . . . It's very difficult for work and career not to get in the way of a lasting marriage. . . . I think men are especially insecure [about] women with doctoral degrees." (Wolfe, Interview, Jan. 10, 1986)

Wolfe's first husband had encouraged her to continue graduate studies while he served in the U.S. Army during World War II. In 1943 she received a two-year fellowship from the General Education Board, which enabled her to study at Vassar College in 1944 and to receive her Ed.D. degree from Columbia University in 1945. Extending her interests beyond scholarly pursuits, in 1941 she became a civilian pilot and one of three women to join the ranks of the Tuskegee Airmen. Wolfe accepted postdoctoral research work at the University of Pennsylvania from 1950 to 1951.

Wolfe then returned to Cranford and from that time on was based in New Jersey. She joined the faculty of Queens College, the City University of New York, in 1951 as coordinator of laboratory schools and associate professor of education. She was the institution's first African-American faculty member. Wolfe devoted her summers to teaching courses in education and human relations at colleges and universities across the nation, among them the University of Illinois, New York University, and Columbia University, while continuing postdoctoral studies (1952–54). In 1969 she started the first African study abroad programs in the United States for the City University of New York.

In 1958 the focus of Wolfe's career began to shift from the classroom to state, national, and international involvement in education and public service. She toured the United States, Asia, Africa, South America, and Europe from 1960 to 1961, delivering more than 100 lectures and visiting schools in the Soviet Union. Wolfe's professional reputation brought her invitations to serve on four White House conferences. In January 1962 Wolfe was appointed chief of education for the U.S. House of Representatives' Committee on Education and Labor; she was the first African-American to hold this position. As the committee's leading expert on education, she was responsible for all legislative matters affecting education and related subjects and served as liaison between the House and the Department of Health, Education and Welfare. During her three years as chief of education, 35 laws affecting education and labor were enacted, among them: the Elementary and Secondary Education Act, the Higher Education Assistance Act, the Vocational Education Act, and the War on Poverty Act. She was instrumental in the passage of legislation that originated financial aid, created community colleges, and revised vocational education for the first time since 1917.

In 1964 Wolfe was appointed a member of the New Jersey State Board of Education. When the state legislature created a New Jersey Board of Higher Education in 1967, Wolfe was named to serve on that board as well. She continues to serve on both boards. Wolfe was elected chair of the Board of Higher Education in July 1987. Her contributions to education have been recognized by public and private institutions, which have awarded Wolfe eight honorary degrees and named two buildings in her honor.

Wolfe retired from her professorship at Queens College in February 1986 after 35 years on the faculty, but continues to work as a consultant for publishing companies and educational organizations. Since 1970 she has been a member of the United Nations Committee of Non-Governmental Representatives. She currently chairs the group's Executive Committee and attends a weekly briefing at the United Nations.

Since retirement from her professorship, she has devoted most of her time to the ministry, a second career she began at age 54. Ordination was a long-standing goal for Wolfe, a short woman with a broad smile, a forceful voice, and bright eyes that radiate warmth, self-confidence, and

determination. Since childhood she had felt that women had been denied important positions in the church by a male hierarchy that refused to ordain women on the basis of gender. Her study at the Union Theological Seminary from 1951 to 1953 helped her overcome obstacles to reach the goal she had set early in life. In 1970 Wolfe became the first African-American woman minister to be ordained by the Baptist church, and in the years since has served as associate minister of the First Baptist Church of Cranford. Today she preaches, conducts services, directs religious education, and assists in all church activities. She proudly states, "I stand where Papa stood. I wear Papa's robe." (Wolfe, Interview, Jan. 10, 1986) Through her pastoral work Wolfe hopes to continue improving social conditions and human interrelations. "I [am] determined to fight to make things better. I hope I've had a great influence on women. . . . Through the ministry I want to influence [people] of all faiths and colors." (Wolfe, Interview, Jan. 10, 1986)

An interview with Wolfe on Jan. 10, 1986, provided useful biographical information. See also *Current Biography* (1962); *Who's Who Among Black Americans* (1981); *Who's Who of American Women* (1987); and *Who's Who in America* (1987).

*Ellen J. Wayman*

### EDITH ELMER WOOD, 1871–1945

The passionate concern of Edith (Elmer) Wood was attractive, healthful, low-cost public housing for low-income families. She saw substandard housing as a prime cause of juvenile delinquency, crime, disease, and high death rates. From her early forties until a serious illness at age 71, she devoted her energies to academic and public service work in the cause of housing for the unskilled worker's family.

Born in Portsmouth, NH, on September 24, 1871, to New Jerseyans Horace and Adele (Wiley) Elmer, Wood and her younger brother, Nixon Wiley, relocated often during their childhood because of their father's naval career.

The creative, cheerful, and self-willed girl was taught mathematics and foreign languages by her father and also educated by tutors and governesses. At fifteen she enrolled at Smith College, receiving her B.L. in 1890 after only three years. She was dubbed "the Prodigy" by her classmates.

Soon after graduation Wood served at a settlement house on New York's Lower East Side. Her mother, a suffragist and worker in charitable organizations, would not permit her daughter to live at the settlement house and criticized her style of social work. Wood's mother was accustomed to the "lady bountiful" style of providing alms for the needy, whereas her daughter reflected new attitudes that emphasized the provision of education, child care, and other self-help resources.

At the time of her marriage in 1893 to naval lieutenant Albert Norton Wood, Wood was a writer of romantic novels and short stories. She continued this work for seventeen years after she married. Her first novel, *Her Provincial Cousin* (1893), describes Breton peasant customs and shows a concern for the role of women and the conditions of the poor. During this period she had four sons, each of whom was given her maiden name as a middle name.

Wood's interest in social work continued after her marriage. She identified and tried to effect needed reforms wherever she went. During her husband's tour of duty (1898–99) in Japan, Korea, and China, where their oldest son died of spinal meningitis at age three, Wood prepared an analysis of infant health practices in the Orient. In 1906, in Puerto Rico, Wood discovered that their cook was desperately ill with tuberculosis. Finding no facilities for the treatment of working people, Wood organized the Anti-Tuberculosis League of Puerto Rico, which built a sanitorium for the poor and developed full-scale educational and preventive programs. She learned that although the tuberculosis bacillus died quickly in sunlight, it lives a very long time in dark rooms. The poor, dark, overcrowded hovels of San Juan were a perfect breeding ground for disease; consequently, she wrote San Juan's first housing code to further the cause of public health.

The connection of poor housing with disease was further emphasized by her survey (1913–15) of housing in Washington, D.C.'s notorious alleyways. Tuberculosis and crime were endemic in this area of shacks crowded behind dark tenements without water, heat, or sewers. Wood was distressed because although the authorities became interested in tearing down the slums, they made no plans for housing the displaced people.

By 1915, Wood had come to grips with her life project. Her last novel had been published in 1910; her husband (who died in 1933) had been recalled from retirement to active duty in World War I, obviating the possibility of settling down in their recently acquired home in Cape May Court House, NJ; her oldest son had completed secondary school; and she was becoming increasingly concerned with housing questions.

As she recalled years later: "I had arrived at two conclusions of personal importance. One was that . . . there simply wasn't time to run a house and a family, write fiction for the market and engage actively in the housing movement. . . . my unfortunate habit of saying what I thought and my complete unconsciousness of locally accepted taboos, kept pushing me into the firing line in a position of quasi-leadership. . . . So on both counts I decided to drop fiction and prepare myself for a professional career in housing by going back to school." ("Housing in My Time,"

*Shelter*, 1938, 28) In 1915, at age 44, she, with her two younger sons, settled for two years in New York to enroll at Columbia University's graduate school. She earned an M.A. (1917) and later a Ph.D. (1919) in social economy, as well as a diploma from the New York School of Social Work (1917). Her doctoral thesis was published under the title *The Housing of the Unskilled Wage Earner* (1919).

Wood was convinced that good housing was necessary if children were to grow up to be mentally, morally, and physically healthy. She insisted in a 1919 statement to the American Association of University Women (AAUW): "If we permit children to grow up in damp basements, in dark bedrooms, in tumble-down shacks, and indecently crowded tenements, we need not be surprised that hospitals, sanitoriums, prisons, reform schools, and institutions for the feeble-minded are filled to over-flowing." She publicized evidence that delinquency and crime were not racially linked; the correlation was to run-down neighborhoods rather than to racial or ethnic groups. Delinquency and crime rates charted by neighborhoods in many cities over a period of years showed that as immigrant groups followed one another into a high-crime neighborhood, the crime rate remained high in the deteriorated area, but the crime rate of the group itself decreased as the group's members moved to areas of adequate housing. (1935 speech at N.J. State Conference on Crime)

Wood's philosophy of housing was that "restrictive" legislation, which sets minimum standards for housing, was not enough. "Constructive" legislation, which gives financial support to the building of low-cost housing, was also needed. She recommended that such housing be financed through government-backed initiatives, such as the attractive government-financed housing projects she surveyed in Western Europe.

Wood headed the Housing Committee of the AAUW from 1917 to 1929. In 1921, as chair of the committee, she urged Secretary of Commerce Herbert Hoover to begin a home-building project to employ the unemployed and to house low-income families. Ten years later, in 1931, President Hoover called a National Housing Conference and initiated the Federal Home Loan Bank Act and the Reconstruction Finance Corporation. During the 1920s Wood also spearheaded a drive by the AAUW and the General Federation of Women's Clubs to get housing questions on state and national censuses.

Wood was concerned with both theoretical and practical aspects of the housing movement. Teaching at Columbia University Extension (1926–30) and Columbia Teachers' College summer sessions (1925, 1932, 1936, and 1937), she also served on the executive committee of the International Housing Association (1931–37) and was an officer and director of the National Public Housing Conference (1932–45). Wood was a consultant for the Public Works Administration (PWA) Housing Division and its successor, the United States Housing Authority (USHA), from 1933 to 1942, presenting statistics that supported constructive housing legislation.

In 1934, while Wood served as a commissioner of the New Jersey State Housing Authority (NJSHA), a New Jersey Real Property Inventory of 155 municipalities was made. The results showed that more than a quarter of multiple-family dwellings were in need of major repairs, many totally unfit for habitation. To Wood's disappointment, only two low-cost housing developments resulted from the survey: one for blacks in Atlantic City, and one for whites in Camden. Wood later said that the NJSHA "was smothered by politics, and I resigned in disgust." (Letter to Mrs. Mulford, Sept. 15, 1937)

The work Wood did is exemplified by her book *Slums and Blighted Areas in the United States* (1935), in which she reports the depressing results of the Department of Commerce's 1934 nationwide Real Property Inventory, which reported that inadequate housing for the poor prevailed everywhere. Her final public work was to assist the USHA in the determination of housing needs of relocated defense plant workers from 1940 to 1942. The next year, poor health forced her retirement.

In 1940 Wood was awarded an honorary LL.D. by Smith College, her alma mater. The degree citation praised her accomplishments as a "leading American housing expert, valiant fighter against slums and tenements; she has helped roof our world, and by her knowledge of the requirements for decent, comfortable living, she has given a new meaning to the word home."

Wood died on April 29, 1945, at age 73, at Greystone Park, NJ, and was buried at the United States Naval Academy Cemetery in Annapolis, MD.

Wood's papers, including letters, pamphlets, plans for housing surveys, speeches, drawing, and photographs, are housed at the Avery Architectural and Fine Arts Library, Columbia University (New York, NY). Sketches of her appear in *NAW* and *Who Was Who in America* 2 (1950). A dissertation by Eugenie L. Birch, "Edith Elmer Wood and the Genesis of Liberal Housing Thought, 1910–1942" (Columbia University, 1976), and her briefer article, "Woman-Made America," *Journal of the American Institute of Planners* 44 (1978):130–44, contain personal as well as professional information on Wood. A telephone interview with Albert Elmer Wood, her son, added additional details.

*Doris B. Armstrong*
*Wayne F. Armstrong*

## CONSTANCE ONEIDA WILLIAMS WOODRUFF, 1921–

Constance Oneida (Williams) Woodruff, journalist, labor leader, educator, political activist, and women's rights advocate, was born on October 24, 1921, in New Rochelle, NY, the eldest of three children of Frederick Isaac and Carolyn (Pines) Williams. Among her many accomplishments, she has served as president of the National Association of Commissions for Women, chairperson of the New Jersey Advisory Commission on the Status of Women from 1975 to 1988, and director of the International Ladies Garment Workers' Union (ILGWU) eastern region's Department of Community Relations for 20 years.

In Newark, NJ, where her parents operated a successful catering business, Woodruff attended Monmouth Street Elementary School and studied piano, hoping to become a concert artist, a dream she gave up after she graduated from South Side (now Shabazz) High School in 1939 and was unable to gain admission to the music school of her choice.

That same year Woodruff began work as a novice reporter for the now defunct *New Jersey Herald News* and, during her twelve years there, advanced to city editor. When hard drugs came to Newark, she wrote articles on drug abuse and the drug traffic, reflecting concern for victims and their families. She covered court trials, civic, social and religious events, gaining knowledge of her city. Her assignments brought her in close contact with leading political figures. Woodruff was already fascinated with politics, since her mother had been a Third Ward district political leader and a suffragist.

In 1958 Woodruff took a secretarial job with the ILGWU, later becoming educational director and political coordinator. Guided by Peter Defleffen, a trade unionist with 45 years experience, she learned to interpret and negotiate contracts, solve grievances, and organize political rallies. In her 20 years with the ILGWU, Woodruff initiated educational programs, served as buffer between management and workers in union shops, and developed such a strong political action committee that she helped make the ILGWU one of the most politically active unions in New Jersey. In 1967, when ILGWU officials established the Department of Community Relations in Newark, Woodruff was appointed director. The new department was later expanded to include affiliate locals coast-to-coast.

Woodruff's involvement with the personal problems of union members led her to join those who gathered in Newark streets after the 1967 riots to help calm residents in the face of New Jersey National Guard and State Police gunfire. She helped collect thousands of dollars worth of canned goods and clothes, which were distributed to needy city residents not only in Newark but also in other cities, such as Paterson and Jersey City, when they were shaken by rioting.

At this time Woodruff also wrote a column for the *New York Amsterdam News*. Occasionally she still wrote political columns for local periodicals, but by the early 1970s her interest shifted to a more active political role. Her work with the ILGWU brought her into many areas of New

Jersey's civic and political life and led to her first major appointment, by Chief Justice Richard J. Hughes, to the state supreme court's Advisory Committee on Judicial Conduct, a committee she served on from 1972 to 1974.

Woodruff served as a member of the Essex County Democratic Committee in Newark from 1962 to 1967. She also served on the executive boards of the Essex County Democratic Women's League and the Essex County chapter of the New Jersey Women's Political Caucus. In 1974 she became the first African-American to serve as secretary of the New Jersey State Democratic Committee, and in 1976 she cochaired the New Jersey delegation to the Democratic National Convention in New York City. For eight years, from 1975 to 1982, Woodruff served as Democratic national committeewoman.

In 1975 Governor Brendan Byrne appointed Woodruff to the first of four terms as chair of the New Jersey Advisory Commission on the Status of Women, an eleven-member board that recommends action on such issues as teenage pregnancy, mental health, and women's alcoholism. That year in Mexico City, and again in 1977 in Houston, TX, Woodruff represented the governor at the International Women's Year Conference. She has been an avid advocate of an international network for women through her efforts with the United Nations Commission on the Status of Women.

Despite her busy schedule, Woodruff returned to school, earning a bachelor's degree in labor education from Empire State College (SUNY) in 1971 and a master's degree in labor studies from Rutgers University in 1977.

In 1978 Woodruff joined the faculty at Essex County College as director of public relations and development. She also teaches courses in the Labor Studies Division. As adviser to A. Zachary Yamba, the college's president, Woodruff helped fund a Women's Center on campus.

In 1985, after serving on the national board of directors of the National Association of Commissions for Women (NACW) for seven years, Woodruff was elected president, the first New Jersey woman to hold this office. The NACW represents 200 state, county, and city commissions in 41 states. Woodruff's first accomplishment was to establish a national information and referral center in Washington, D.C.

Her studies, linked with her ILGWU work and her community involvement, enriched Woodruff, who thrives on activity. She is an inveterate joiner with a real interest in people. She is a member of more than 40 organizations, serving as a volunteer or board member for many, including the National Association of Negro Business and Professional Woman's Clubs, the National Organization for Women (NOW), and the YM-YWCA of Newark. Among the more than 100 honors and awards she has received are the Outstanding Citizen Award from the Newark City Council in 1975 and the A. Philip Randolph Institute Award for Achievement in Labor Relations in 1971. On March 30, 1984, Peter Rodino, U.S. Representative from New Jersey, read a tribute to Woodruff into the *Congressional Record* to accompany a testimonial dinner at which she was declared Woman of the Year. In 1985 she was honored as one of America's top 100 black professional women by the magazine *Dollars & Sense*.

Woodruff and her husband, William, an engineer and former superintendent of the Passaic Valley Sewage Commission, live in West Orange. They have been married since 1955, and throughout her professional life, Woodruff has enjoyed her husband's complete support as she worked toward personal and professional goals.

Possessed of a trenchant wit, Woodruff is much in demand on the lecture circuit, speaking at ceremonies and college campuses all over the country. She is a former radio talk show host and now appears frequently on radio, network, and cable television in the New York City area.

A natural leader, Woodruff is a person whose presence in a room leaves little doubt that she is in command. She admits that her greatest failing is the inability to say no to a cry for help. She is "one of those rare individuals who works 24 hours a day, seven days a week," said Essex County College president A. Zachary Yamba. "Calls come from all sectors . . . and somehow she always finds the time to respond." Woodruff is "a crusader for social change," wrote Representative Peter Rodino, "an ardent and articulate champion of human and individual rights."

An interview with Woodruff on Mar. 1, 1986, provided biographical details. See also Peter Rodino, Jr., "Tribute to Connie Woodruff," *Congressional Record*, Mar. 30, 1984; Robert Queen, "Connie Grew Up in Newark," *New Jersey African-American* (Newark, NJ), Apr. 5, 1984; and Charles Finley, "Frankness Wins Admirers for Women's Leader," *Newark Star-Ledger*, June 17, 1984.

*Arlene Hampton*
*Sheila Cowing*

## REGINA JONES WOODY, 1894–1983

Regina (Jones) Woody, dancer and author of children's literature, is remembered for her contribution to American culture and her dedication to the youth of America. Born to Lewis Lewellyn and Regina (Lichenstein) Jones on January 4, 1894, Woody was raised in an atmosphere of culture and wealth. She spent her childhood in a rambling house in Chestnut Hill, MA.

Bright, imaginative, and irrepressible, she had a natural penchant for dancing. She attended Dana Hall, a preparatory school for Wellesley College, where she played a minor role in *A Midsummer Night's Dream*. Following the performance, Henry Savage, a theatrical producer, called out to her, "See you in tights. You belong behind the footlights, not on the lawn of a girl's school." (Woody, *Dancing for Joy*, 12) The school faculty was not amused by a lovely sophomore stealing the limelight at a senior play. She was unrepentant and her mother would not proffer an apology or promise reformation on her daughter's behalf. Woody did not return to Dana Hall.

Instead, her parents decided to spend part of a legacy to further Woody's dance studies. Chaperoned by her mother, Woody left for London in 1911. Anxious to pursue her dance career, she braved a London fog to reach the Gaiety Theater and impresario Leslie Stuart. She won Stuart over with her dancing and a hard-luck story of an orphan in search of a scholarship. Through him, she secured introductions to two famous dance teachers of the time, Monsieur D'Auban and Madame Zanfretta.

Only seventeen, Woody absorbed all that her teachers offered her, surpassing other dancers, incurring first their envy, then their admiration. She studied Pavlova's movements, watching the great ballerina almost nightly at the Gaiety. She eventually danced her way to success via garden parties, church bazaars, aristocratic mansions, and with London's street entertainers, known as buskers.

When she moved to Paris, Woody studied under Monsieur Leo Staats and Madame Stichel. Soon she made her debut at a gala hosted by a well-known Parisian party giver. She later recalled, "I was announced as La Petite Danseuse Americaine vouée au Bleu. My name was changed to Nila Devi, meaning the Blue Goddess. My dance was called L'Idole Turquoise, and opened with me standing in a replica of a golden frame of the god Siva in the Musée Guimet." (Woody, *Dancing for Joy*, 157) Woody was dressed in blue with an elaborate jeweled costume, fitted by a craftsman with a pair of pliers, matched to her blue wig, and her skin dyed blue for the occasion.

As Nila Devi she auditioned at the Étoile Palace before Paul Franck, who was in search of original talent. The 300 dancers who auditioned were instructed to perform as if they were "accused of adultery." (Fenton, *Daily Journal*, Oct. 29, 1978) Woody was the 124th dancer to be auditioned. As soon as she finished, Franck stopped further auditions, made her sign a contract, and started rehearsals immediately. Hours later, the theater was swarming with gendarmes, summoned by an anxious mother who was convinced that her daughter had been kidnapped.

In 1913, at the age of nineteen, Woody was the Danseuse Étoile at the Folies Bergère. Opening night was a tremendous success, but she was upset by the prolonged hissing from the audience, unaware that it was merely a form of French appreciation. Once established as a star, Woody soon began to perform at the Moulin Rouge, Concert Mayol, and the Alhambra. Gifts and adulation came from all sides; one such admirer, Mata Hari, advised her: "I am giving your Mama good advise to keep you innocent in the midst of the cynical world of the Theater." (Woody, *Dancing for Joy*, 216)

Nila Devi decided to appear in Algiers at a time when French influence there was at its height. Anxious to see genuine Bedouin dances, mother and daughter traveled several hundred miles across hot desert sands to the oases of Bon Saarde. She danced before a hundred or more Bedouin tribesmen while girls giggled from behind a harem grill.

Woody gave performances in key European cities, including Constantinople and Budapest, shortly before the assassination of Archduke Franz Ferdinand of Austria-Hungary. The threat of war brought daughter and mother back to the United States, where the Blue Goddess danced at exclusive private clubs.

Lee Shubert, at that time a talent scout, lured Woody to dance at the Winter Garden in New York in 1915. Here she met Martin Beck and Eva Gautier, a Canadian operatic singer, from whom she learned Oriental dancing. Striking out on the vaudeville circuit for 52 weeks, Woody and Gautier traveled all over the United States and Canada. Reminiscing years later on this period of her life, Woody said: "I came back to the U.S. and found what I thought was a glorious act, which I spelled with a capital A, was spelled quite differently. It was spelled S.E.X." (*Elizabeth Daily Journal*, Jan. 1981)

During the winter of 1916 she did something unthinkable for a dancer in training: she went ice skating, and tore a ligament in her leg. Her dancing career ended abruptly.

During World War I Woody contributed to the war effort by donating all earnings from dancing, private lessons, fitness classes, and private parties. Woody also became an ambulance driver during the war with the Women's Volunteer Motor Corps of Boston. She tackled the duties of motor maintenance with extraordinary grace, whether sprawling over the mud guard, straddling the hood, or cranking the starter. As an ambulance driver, Woody needed to learn first aid. The class she attended was taught by an assistant dean at Harvard Medical School, and at the end of the fourteenth week Dr. McIver Woody, the instructor, asked her for a date. They were married on May 1, 1918.

The couple moved to Memphis, TN, when McIver Woody was made dean of the Tennessee College of Medicine. He later became Dean of Baylor College. In 1928 he became the first industrial physician in the United States when he accepted a position with Standard Oil in Linden, NJ. He became medical director of Esso until his death in 1970.

After her marriage Woody took up writing, which came easily for her. She had once remarked she wanted to dance like Pavlova and write like Hans Christian Anderson. She had entered a children's writing contest in Boston when she was seven and won first prize. In Paris, dissatisfied with the publicity her troupe was receiving, Woody had written her own press releases. Later she created her own librettos.

In the early years of her marriage, Woody contributed articles to *Hygeia* and *Parents* magazine. "I studied up on alcoholism, mental health, dance therapy, smoking, and thanks to my husband's interest and guidance, produced books of fiction with answers to the characters given by experts in the field, complete with heroines with whom the young readers could identify, and thus learn to deal with their own problems." (Fuller, *More Junior Authors*, 264)

Her first book was *The Stars Came Down*. Seventeen books followed, most of them with an autobiographical tinge. She was editor of a section for young dancers in *Dance* magazine and gave a series of lectures on children's literature at New York University from 1947 to 1957.

When they settled in New Jersey in 1928, the Woodys lived in Elizabeth, not far from the present PS No. 23 (Nicholas Butler School). Students would visit the Woody home, sit on the floor of the living room, and ask questions of the author, whose books they had read.

Woody was a member of the First Presbyterian Church in Elizabeth. She was also a member of the Daughters of the American Revolution and of the Descendants of the Colonial Clergy. Woody worked closely with Hazel Elks of the Elizabeth Public Library to interest children in books and reading. She donated many of her lecture notes, galley sheets, and scrapbooks to the Elizabeth Public Library. For her contribution to the cultural life and activities of Elizabeth, Mayor Thomas Dunn presented her with the key to the city, as Elizabeth's Distinguished Citizen.

After her husband died in 1970, Woody shared a house with her longtime friend Julia Knapp, also a widow.

Woody entered a retirement community in Columbus, OH, on December 15, 1980, where she battled with chronic lymphocytic leukemia for some time. Shortly before her death, she was working with one of the community's activity therapists to develop a program of exercise for wheelchair-bound residents. She died on September 2, 1983, at age 89, and was buried in Evergreen Cemetery in Brighton, MA.

Woody's autobiography, *Dancing for Joy* (1959), was written for young readers. Biographical sketches of her appear in Muriel Fuller, *More Junior Authors* (1963); and in *Something about the Author*, vol. 3 (1972). Memorabilia, including manuscripts, photographs, clippings, scrapbooks, and an interview with Woody taped in 1977, are available at NJ-EPL.

*Lumina Pacheco*

Marion Thompson Wright, scholar and teacher of sociology and the history of African-American education. *Courtesy, Prints and Photographs Department, Moorland-Springarn Research Center, Howard University.*

## MARION MANOLA THOMPSON WRIGHT, 1902–1962

Marion Manola (Thompson) Wright, scholar and teacher of the sociology and history of African-American education, was the first woman to become a leader in this field. She was born in East Orange (Essex County), NJ, on September 13, 1902, the youngest of four children. She had twin older sisters and a brother who died young. Both her parents were African-American. Her mother, Minnie (Holmes) Thompson, who separated from her father, Moses R. Thompson, worked as a servant in a white household. She was devoted and energetic in her support of her youngest daughter's education and career.

Little is known of Wright's childhood, except that she attended Barringer High School in Newark. At age sixteen she married William H. Moss, and two children Thelma (b. 1919) and James (b. 1920) were born before the young couple separated. Upon the urging of a counselor, and at her mother's insistence, Wright returned to high school. She graduated in 1923 at the head of her class, with grades unsurpassed by any student, white or black. She enrolled as a freshman at Howard University under her maiden name, while the children were in the custody of their father, a foreman in an industrial plant. She was forced to conceal the fact of her marriage, motherhood, and 1925 divorce because under Howard University's rules divorced women and even married women could not be accepted as students.

Wright majored in sociology at Howard and earned her bachelor's degree in 1927, magna cum laude. She showed leadership as an undergraduate on the student council, debate team, and a conference on world peace. She was active in the women's personnel division under Dean of Women Lucy Diggs Slowe, who became her friend and colleague in the peace movement and in developing guidance facilities for women students. Wright completed a master's degree in education at Howard in 1928 and was an instructor in education there from 1928 to 1930.

Wright's second marriage, in the spring of 1931, brought her back to the Newark, NJ, area. (This marriage, to postal worker Arthur M. Wright, also ended in divorce.) She had already begun studies toward a doctorate at Teachers College, Columbia University, but interrupted them to work for the Newark Department of Public Welfare and later for the New Jersey Emergency Relief Administration (ERA; 1933–36). Under the ERA, she became a case supervisor, a substantial achievement for a young black woman at that time. She studied for and earned a diploma from the New York School of Social Work (1938). She lived with her husband and mother in a house jointly owned by her and her mother in Montclair, NJ, a home she maintained throughout her life. Wright helped her daughter, Thelma, with college and postgraduate training by permitting her to live in the Montclair home while studying.

Wright again took up her work at Teachers College under the guidance of Merle Curti, the only white historian at that time who considered African-American history a serious field of research. Spurred by a topic suggested by Howard University's Charles H. Thompson, head of the Education Department, Wright completed her dissertation, "The Education of Negroes in New Jersey," which Teachers College honored by publishing in book form (1941). She was the first black historian to receive a Ph.D. from Columbia University.

Wright dedicated the book to her strongest motivator and supporter, her mother. It is a history from slavery to the 1930s documenting the lack of good schooling for African-Americans, as well as the instances of excellence

that gave cause for hope. Wright's conclusion notes that New Jersey had had a law since 1881 "prohibiting the exclusion of any child from any school because of nationality, religion, or color." (Wright, *Education of Negroes*, 198) Yet she saw that New Jersey schools circumvented this law in various ways. She called for a comparison of the achievements and social attitudes of white students and blacks, in both integrated and segregated schools, in order to discover what conditions were helpful in overcoming prejudice, achieving educational goals, and sustaining a healthy democracy. She called for "planned programs of social engineering . . . [for] democratic living" (203), and emphasized that prejudice harms the dominant group as well as the subordinate one.

In 1940 Charles Thompson asked Wright to return to Howard as assistant professor of education. During the 22 years that followed she was book review editor of the *Journal of Negro Education* (founded and edited by Thompson) and wrote a column for it called "Notes from Recent Books." She was director of student teaching in the Department of Education (1940–46), attained the rank of full professor (1950), and was acting head of the department (1952–53).

Recognizing an unmet need, Wright proposed that Howard University create a student counseling service and in 1946 served as acting director during its first year, and part-time counselor thereafter. In 1954 she independently studied guidance and personnel at Columbia University and brought her findings to bear when she coordinated Howard's Volunteer Program for Extending Remedial and Counseling Services.

Wright was active in organizations involved with women's concerns and with guidance: the National Association of College Women, the American Association of University Women, American Personnel and Guidance Association, and her sorority, Delta Sigma Theta. She served on the Board of Directors of two institutions in Washington, D.C.: the Iona Whipper Home for unwed mothers, and the Adams-Morgan project, a center for recreation, education, child care, and counseling.

Students often came to her Washington apartment with their work to ask for her criticism and help. She insisted on correctness of detail at the same time that she nurtured and supported them. She was unstinting in the number of hours she would give to her students.

Wright felt that the rank of full professor was slow in coming to her. She was the only woman in the Education Department who had a Ph.D., but she did not become a full professor until 1950, after ten years in the department.

Wright published regularly in the *Journal of Negro History*, addressing issues of New Jersey history in such articles as "New Jersey Laws and the Negro" (1943), "Negro Suffrage in New Jersey, 1776–1875" (1948), and "Extending Civil Rights in New Jersey" (1953). "Racial Integration in Schools in New Jersey" (1954) described her hopes and criticisms of New Jersey schools. In other journals she published "New Jersey Leads in the Struggle for Educational Integration" (*Journal of Educational Sociology*, 1953) and "Quakers as Social Workers among Negroes in New Jersey from 1763 to 1804." (*Bulletin of the Friends' Historical Association*, 1941)

During the early 1950s Wright served as researcher for the National Association for the Advancement of Colored People (NAACP), compiling evidence for the public school desegregation cases decided by the Supreme Court in 1954. The methods of research she used to gather data on New Jersey were applied to a study of the United States as a whole, showing injurious patterns of discrimination throughout the nation.

In 1961 Wright received a fellowship from the *Washington Evening Star* to write a biography of her old friend and colleague Lucy Diggs Slowe, who had changed the position of dean of women from that of mere matron to one of specialist in the education of women. Wright's short biography of Slowe in *Notable American Women* (1971) was only a sketch of the book she intended to write. She completed the necessary research and interviewing, but did not finish the project.

Wright did not acknowledge, even to those closest to her, that she had had an early marriage and two children. Indeed, she distanced herself from her children until the last years of her life, when there was a reconciliation. Some who knew her felt that she was lonely, even though she had a warm circle of friends.

Wright was 60 years old when her body was found in her car in her garage on October 26, 1962. According to her death certificate, she died of cardiopulmonary failure. A funeral service was held at the Andrew Rankin Memorial Chapel at Howard University, and she was buried in Rosedale Cemetery, Orange, NJ.

Wright's dissertation was published as a book, *The Education of Negroes in New Jersey* (1941). A memorial to Wright is Walter G. Daniel, "A Tribute to Marion Thompson Wright," *Journal of Negro Education* 32(1963):308–10. Her papers are in the possession of Carroll Miller, Howard University (Washington, D.C.); Clement Price, Rutgers University; and her son, Dr. James A. Moss, Adelphi University (Garden City, NY).

*Margaret E. Hayes*
*Doris B. Armstrong*

## FLORENCE LYDIA MCENALLY ZUCK, 1912–

Born February 5, 1912, on a 100-acre farm known as "Elmsford" in Chesterfield County, VA, Florence Lydia (McEnally) Zuck, conservationist and teacher, was the ninth of ten children of William Wolcott and Dollie Craven (McFaul) McEnally. Because of the failing health of Zuck's paternal grandfather, Charles, three generations of the McEnally family had arrived in Virginia from Michigan in 1904, seeking a warmer climate.

Although not formally trained as an agriculturalist, Zuck's father had taken botany courses at the University of Michigan and from principles learned was able to transform fallow land into lush, productive land. "He was the first person to open my eyes to the beauty of plants," remembers Zuck. "I followed my father around on the farm instead of learning the things little girls learned." (Easton and Picker, "Struggle to Preserve Open Spaces," 15) Her mother was a passionate gardener as well. In addition to keeping her children well fed, clothed, and instructed in Christian principles, she expressed her love of flowers by creating vast beds of roses, pansies, and hollyhocks in which Zuck played. "I grew up as a child of nature," Zuck says. "My earliest conscious reaction to being alive was the feeling that the natural world was created for me to enjoy and explore and that it was big and beautiful, full of flowers, trees, birds, and loving people." (Interview, Apr. 1986)

In 1931, after schooling in Virginia, Cleveland, and Chicago, Zuck headed for the Oberlin Kindergarten-Primary Training School in Oberlin, OH. She was an honor student and president of her senior class. After her graduation in 1933 she was encouraged to enter Oberlin College to work for an A.B. in botany. Art and classics were also strong interests, and it was while enrolled in a pencil-sketching class at Oberlin that she met Robert Karl Zuck, who also shared her enthusiasm for botany and art. When Florence Zuck graduated in 1936, joining the staff of the University of Chicago Settlement House, the two maintained a correspondence until they were married on August 21, 1938.

Their first home together was in Knoxville, TN, where Zuck turned her interests to organizing a day nursery for children whose parents worked in the textile mills, while her husband completed his M.S. in botany. When Robert Zuck was accepted into the Ph.D. program at the University of Chicago, the two returned to Illinois in 1941. In 1943 they moved to Evansville, IN, where he taught botany at Evansville College. After a brief stint in Beltsville, MD, where Robert Zuck had been invited to do war-related research on fungal problems related to fiber deterioration, an invitation came for him in 1946 from Drew University in Madison, NJ, to develop a program in botany. Two years later Zuck joined the Drew faculty, at first teaching part time and then full time. Then the couple began a teaching collaboration that was to last 32 years. Students of theirs have gone on to achieve prominence as researchers, professors, and environmentalists. One has even named a tree after them: discovered in New Guinea, it's known as *Timonius Zuckianus*.

Zuck's career has always been important to her, but "it's my family—my husband, my children, and grand-children," she says, "that I care about most of all." (Interview, Apr. 1986) Julia Margaret (b. 1942), a daughter, was her first child. Three sons followed: David William (b. 1944), Robert McEnally (b. 1949), and Michael George (b. 1951).

Home for the Zucks is a carriage house, located adjacent to the Drew campus, which they have painstakingly renovated by themselves. Their gardens, created over a span of 32 years, now attract national attention. (Frey, "A Very Personal Garden")

Although Zuck's main concern has been her teaching, which has ranged from university level to adult education classes, both the community and the state have reaped the benefits from her efforts to protect the environment. The Reeves-Reed Arboretum in Summit and the Frelinghuysen Arboretum in Morristown are only two of the many horticultural centers she has helped create.

In the mid-1950s the Zucks became involved in the most crucial environmental issue ever to face the state of New Jersey when plans were revealed to transform the Great Swamp, an area of approximately 10,000 acres, into one of the largest jetports in the world. As members of the original committee of conservationists, the Zucks worked intensively for years to save the area. Since proof was needed to show the ecological value of the Great Swamp as a natural habitat for plants and animals, an herbarium was assembled under Zuck's guidance to show the floristic significance of the area. Victory came in 1964 with the establishment of the Great Swamp National Wildlife Refuge; in 1968 part of the land was designated by act of Congress as a National Wilderness Area, the first such area in the eastern United States.

Upon their retirement from Drew University in 1980, the Zucks were honored by the designation of the Florence and Robert Zuck Arboretum on the campus. Located in a forested area the Zucks had been instrumental in saving, the arboretum includes two natural glacial ponds as well as a variety of native and exotic trees and plants.

Over a 33-year period, Zuck has conducted hundreds of botanical field trips, freely sharing her love and knowledge of the natural world and teaching, by example, the value of preserving open lands. In addition to volunteer activities ranging from garden restorations to the granting of scholarships for students interested in pursuing degrees in botany, she continues her work with the Madison Shade Tree Authority and the Morris County Park Commission. In 1982 she helped write and illustrate the Madison Environmental Commission's *Environmental Resources Inventory*, a manual—dedicated to her—that assists local government in land-use decisions. As a trustee of the Great Swamp Watershed Association, a citizen's organization founded to protect this important wetland, she continues

her cataloging of local flora. "The rate of extinction of plants throughout the world per year," she says, "is frightening." (Frey, 76) Keeping an eye on developers who would cut a swath through the area's remaining forested land is another activity she can't relinquish. "I'm busier today in retirement," she says, "than when I was teaching. I keep saying I'm going to stay home and just read a book, but there's always something to be done." (Interview, Apr. 1986)

Interviews with Zuck at her home in Madison, NJ, took place on Apr. 13, 14, and 15, 1986. For details of her environmental work, see Susan Frey, "A Very Personal Garden," *Garden Design* 4 (Summer 1985):74–81; and Louise Easton and Ida Picker, "Struggle to Preserve Open Spaces," *Madison* (NJ) *Eagle*, Sept. 20, 1984.

*Kristen McLaughlin*

## SUSANNA WEARE PEIRCE ZWEMER, 1895–

Susanna Weare (Peirce) Zwemer, professional librarian, college professor, and president for fifteen years of the Consumers' League of New Jersey, was born in Sioux City, IA, on March 9, 1895, the second of three children and only daughter of Howard Gilpin Peirce, a livestock commission merchant whose English ancestors came to America in the 17th century, and Mary Ely (Weare) Peirce, descended from Swiss and English immigrants.

Education was important to the Peirce family, and young "Susanne," as she was called, graduated from Sioux City's Central High School in June 1913; and capped that with a year at St. Margaret's School, a preparatory school in Waterbury, CT. She then spent three years at Smith College, where she specialized in political science.

World War I interrupted her college career, and on November 24, 1917, she married Richard Adrian Zwemer in New York City. The newlyweds were separated when her husband went overseas. Zwemer, an atypical bride, completed her senior year as an undergraduate at Barnard College, where she received her bachelor's degree in 1919.

The postwar years were busy. Richard Zwemer practiced law. A son, Howard Adrian, was born on September 19, 1923. While living in Evanston, IL, Zwemer received a master's degree in international relations from Northwestern University in June 1928. Then on July 18, 1929, Richard A. Zwemer died.

Packing up her possessions and taking her five-year-old son by the hand, Zwemer returned to her hometown, where she obtained employment at Morningside College. Between 1930 and 1934 she was an assistant professor of political science; she also taught history. Financial problems brought on by the Great Depression, along with the death of her mother, combined to propel Zwemer to New Jersey, to join forces there with her brother, a chemical engineer.

At her arrival in Westfield, NJ, in 1934, Zwemer was introduced to activists in the League of Women Voters and, later, the Consumers' League. Her mentor was Marion Douglas, who was then the president of the Westfield chapter of the League of Women Voters (LWV) and on the board of the Consumers' League of New Jersey. Many of the pioneers in both groups were still active in the organizations when Zwemer joined, and she rejoiced in her new-found activities and associates.

Zwemer succeeded Marion Douglas to the presidency of the Westfield LWV and soon found herself on the state board. She was active in Mrs. Edward Bebout's Government in Operations Department. Bebout's son John, a professor at Rutgers, was drawing the league into an emerging effort to revise the state constitution, which had been virtually unchanged since 1844. Soon the league formed the Committee on Revision of the Constitution, and Zwemer served as its secretary.

When the constitution rewriting idea caught on, the New Jersey Constitution Foundation was organized, and Zwemer became its field representative for south Jersey. Work geared up in 1940 and lasted until 1947, when the new state constitution went into effect. Zwemer helped prepare educational material in the Newark headquarters and participated actively in field work. Her south Jersey responsibility meant considerable travel to the area. On a typical trip, March 29 to April 17, 1943, she visited Gloucester, Camden, and Atlantic counties and addressed a ministerial association, the DAR, and the State Conference on Legislation of the State Federation of Women's Clubs.

Meanwhile, Zwemer had become a participating member of the Consumers' League of New Jersey and this group became a primary focus for her, surpassing her LWV involvement. The Consumers' League revived an earlier interest of hers in promoting social action through legislation and education. As a student at Barnard, she had taken a course on women in factory work with Dr. Emilie Hutchinson. As part of the course, the class did volunteer social work and Zwemer found herself reporting to Chelsea House, a New York City settlement house. Zwemer soon learned about other aspects of the settlement movement, including Lillian Wald's Henry Street Settlement and Florence Kelley's work as general secretary of the National Consumers' League.

The Consumers' League of New Jersey drew her in, especially, through its work for migrant farm workers, milk pricing and quality, and wages and hours. Zwemer saw it all as a continuing effort to aid workers.

Zwemer became president of the league, serving from 1940 to 1947 and, again, from 1963 to 1971. As New Jersey president she became a member of the board of the National Consumers' League, whose headquarters were in New York City. Her association with the national group later claimed a considerable portion of her time.

Meanwhile, an important early effort on the state level was the minimum wage law. Although the Consumers' League had secured minimum-wage laws for women in a number of states, their constitutionality was challenged. Zwemer found herself drawn into a dispute over wages for laundry workers. Based on the landmark Oregon minimum-wage law argued by Louis D. Brandeis years before, Zwemer and Roger Hinds, the Consumers' League's counsel, were able to gain overtime pay at time and a half the regular hourly wage, instead of a rate one and a half times the minimum wage.

Through information dissemination, especially through its *Newsletter*, which Zwemer edited, the Consumers' League aided the fluoridation campaign (1971–74), payment for radiation exposure (1968–79), and improvement of credit practices. Zwemer also found herself serving on governmental committees on both state and national levels. She was on the Advisory Committee to the state milk director in the 1940s; the Governor's Task Force on Farm Labor (1964–66), for which she received a letter of commendation from Governor Richard Hughes in 1966; and was appointed by Secretary of Health, Education and Welfare Wilbur J. Cohen to the Medical Assistance Advisory Council, or Medicaid (1968–71).

During World War II Zwemer's son, Howard, became a fighter pilot, and Zwemer went back to school. After she received a degree from the Columbia University School of Library Science (1944), she worked at the libraries of Newark and Elizabeth; later, she served as librarian at Union Junior College, Cranford (1947–58). Understandably, the National Consumers' League asked her to prepare its archives for the Library of Congress. This five-year task was completed during her service as recording secretary (1940–59). She also served a two-year term (1959–61) as chair of the National Consumers' League Board in Washington. Zwemer later classified the archives of the New Jersey Consumers' League for Rutgers University.

When Zwemer became more deeply involved with the Consumers' League, she put aside her work with the Public Affairs Committee of the National YWCA. Active on the national level from 1938 to 1942, she had already served the Westfield YWCA beginning in 1934. The Public Affairs Committee was concerned with civil rights questions; when the United States entered World War II, Zwemer became a member of its Speakers Bureau.

Other Zwemer activities included service on the Christian Social Relations Board of the Episcopal Diocese of New Jersey (1955–83); a directorship on the National Consumers' Committee for Research and Education

(1953–86), and trustee and secretary of the Consumer Education Foundation, Inc. (1971–79). As late as March 1982, Zwemer was asked by Joy Williams of the New Jersey Division, United Nations Association of the U.S.A., to serve on its board of directors.

The Consumers' League of New Jersey presented Zwemer with the Mary L. Dyckman Award, a distinguished service award, on April 30, 1985, for her 51 years of "leadership to improve the lives of consumers, workers, and citizens of New Jersey." This citation succinctly stated the essence of her life.

Zwemer has retired to Silver Spring, MD, in order to be near the National Archives and Library of Congress, where she is working on her family genealogy.

An interview with Zwemer provided biographical information. Material on her association with the League of Women voters is available at NJ-RU; papers on her work with the Consumers' League of New Jersey and other organizations are available at NJ-HS. For details of her years with the Consumers' League of New Jersey see their *Fiftieth Anniversary Booklet* (1950).

*Ella Handen*

# LIST OF BIOGRAPHEES

## 1600–1807

Mary Spratt Provoost Alexander
Sarah Livingston Alexander
Catharine Anderson
Elizabeth Ray Clark Bodly
Rachel Bradford Boudinot
Esther Edwards Burr
Hannah Ogden Caldwell
Elizabeth Carteret
Hannah Dent Cooper
Elizabeth Crook
Elizabeth Davis Brick Worthington Dunlap
Theodosia Johnes Ford
Elizabeth Downes Franklin
Elizabeth Haddon
Jemima Condict Harrison
Eunice Foster Horton
Sarah Van Brugh Livingston Jay
Sarah Kiersted
Mary Lewis Kinnan
Lenape Women
Sybilla Righton Masters
Mary Ludwig Hays McCauley
Margaret Hill Morris
Cornelia Bell Paterson
Annetje Van Wagenen Plume
Annis Boudinot Stockton
Margaret Vliet Warne
Rachel Lovell Wells
Ann Cooper Whitall
Temperance Wick
Patience Lovell Wright

## 1808–1865

Agnes Morgan Reeves Appleton
Clara Barton
Sarah Staats Bayles

Antoinette Louisa Brown Blackwell
Charlotte Bonaparte
Elizabeth Mulford Crane
Bridget Dergan
Dorothea Lynde Dix
Silvia Dubois
Elizabeth Sutliff Dulfer
Abigail Goodwin
Sarah Moore Grimké
Angelina Grimké Weld
Cornelia Hancock
Hannah Hoyt
Anne Hyde de Neuville
Elizabeth Miller Keasbey
Elizabeth Clementine Dodge Stedman Kinney
Jarena Lee
Louisa Sanderson Macculloch
Mary Paul
Martha Austin Reeves
Lilly Martin Spencer
Rebecca Buffum Spring
Charity Still
Betsey Stockton
Lucy Stone
Susan Catherine Moore Waters

## 1866–1920

Elizabeth Almira Allen
Sarah Byrd Askew
Caroline Cheever Peddle Ball
Margaret Bancroft
Mary Katharine Jones Bennett
Maria Botto
Cornelia Foster Bradford
Stella Stevens Bradford
Charlotte Emerson Brown
Emma Coleman
Ann Hora Connelly
Margaret Anna Cusack

Juliet Clannon Cushing
Mary Fenn Robinson Davis
Rebecca Harding Davis
Mary Mapes Dodge
Amanda Minnie Douglas
Mabel Smith Douglass
Minnie Radcliffe Douglass
Sarah Jane Corson Downs
Florence Peshine Eagleton
Emma Ward Edwards
Lillian Ford Feickert
Grace Baxter Fenderson
Susan Pecker Fowler
Mary E. Wilkins Freeman
Caroline Bamberger Frank Fuld
Lucy McKim Garrison
Mary Exton Gaston
Hetty Howland Robinson Green
Emilie Koehler Greenough
Phebe Ann Coffin Hanaford
Lydia Young Hayes
Christine Terhune Herrick
Jennie Tuttle Hobart
Alison Low Turnbull Hopkins
Martha Brookes Hutcheson
Jewish Farm Women
Julia Hart Beers Kempson
Elizabeth Sarah Kite
Alice Lakey
Ella Condie Lamb
Marie Louise Lefort
Anna Lindner
Clara Louise Maass
Mary Williamson Macfadden
Abbie Eliza Magee
Mother Mary Xavier Mehegan
Alice Duer Miller
Elisabeth "Bessie" Holmes Moore
Mary Nimmo Moran
Mary Stanahan Hart Pattison
Alice Stokes Paul
Mary Philbrook
Dorothea Miller Post
Sophia Presley
Alice Huyler Ramsey
Florence Spearing Randolph
Restelle Elizabeth Richardson Revey
Ruth St. Denis
Mary Buell Sayles
Hannah Silverman
Erminnie Adele Platt Smith
Elizabeth Cady Stanton
Mary Mercer Steele
Mary Virginia Hawes Terhune

Mary E. Tillotson
Mary Lua Adelia Davis Treat
Frances Bartlett Tyson
Jennie Carolyn Van Ness
Gertrude Potter Ward
Carolyn Wells
Charlotte Fowler Wells
Alma Bridwell White
Elizabeth Coleman White
Pearl White
Emily Hornblower Williamson
Beatrice Winser
Caroline Stevens Alexander Wittpenn
Marietta Huntoon Crane Woodruff
Margaret Tufts Swan Yardley

## 1921–Present

Harriet Stratemeyer Adams
Virginia Apgar
Anna Mahala Field Atchison
Mary Crapelli Augusto
Catherine Hayes Bailey
Sylvia Woodbridge Beach
Enid Bell
Maria de Castro Blake
Helen Francesca Franzolin Boehm
Margaret Bourke-White
Elizabeth Rock Brackett
Louise Delling Branthwaite
Eva Topkins Brodkin
Margaret Christina Brown
Bernarda Bryson
Mary Allison Beasley Burch
Jane Grey Burgio
May Margaret Carty
Jeanette Lake Cascone
Gladys St. John Churchman
Dorothy Allen Conley
Emma Loehwing Conlon
Elizabeth Cooper
Marianna Fidone Costa
Margaret Creswell
Dorothy Cross
Marguerite Lofft de Angeli
Geraldine Owen Delaney
Adèle de Leeuw
Lini de Vries
Geraldine Rockefeller Dodge
Nell Doremus
Sister Helen Angela Dorety
Elsie Driggs

Florence Price Dwyer
Mary Ann Rowley Eager
Lena Frances Edwards
Eleanor Egg
Dorothy Daggett Eldridge
Anne Elstner
Dorothy Harrison Eustis
Madge Evans
Jessie Redmon Fauset
Millicent Hammond Fenwick
Rita Sapiro Finkler
E. Alma Flagg
Grace Margaret Freeman
Wanda Hazel Gág
Kathryn Elizabeth Gamble
Muriel Morris Gardiner
Mary Virginia Gaver
Lillian Moller Gilbreth
Hetty Goldman
Alberta Gonzalez
Ruth Evelyn Gordon
Dorothea Schwarcz Greenbaum
Anna Louise Sando McGee Groome
Florence Lillian Haines
Joy Bright Hancock
Mary Belle Harris
Cora Louise Hartshorn
Ethel Browne Harvey
Elizabeth Hawes
Carye-Belle Henle
Margaret Sullivan Herbermann
Emily Gregory Hickman
Beatrice Alice Hicks
Celeste Holm
Mildred Barry Hughes
Carleen Maley Hutchins
Esther Hymer
Maria Jeritza
Cordelia Thomas Greene Johnson
Paula Kassell
Marie Louise Hilson Katzenbach
Myra Lyle Smith Kearse
Dorothy Kirsten
Ann Rosensweig Klein
Helen Jackson Lee
Sophie Kresch Levine
Minnie Strulovici Liberti
Anne Morrow Lindbergh
Miriam Lee Early Lippincott
Helen Tracy Lowe-Porter
Edith Elizabeth Lowry
Lucille Manners
Margherita Frances Marchione
Anne Clark Martindell

Dorothy Hope Marvin
Ernest Mae McCarroll
Rachel K. McDowell
Vera Brantley McMillon
Charlotte Nichols Montgomery
Amelia Berndt Moorfield
Nelle Katharine Morton
Mary Yamashita Nagao
Ellen Noguchi Nakamura
Helen Josephine Neave
Alice Neel
Mary Teresa Norton
Marian Stephenson Olden
Estella Elizabeth Padgham
Nellie Katherine Morrow Parker
Ruth Marcus Patt
Louise Pearce
Eleanore Kendall Pettersen
Jeannette Ridlon Piccard
Olive Mae Bond Polk
Ellen Culver Potter
Jennie E. Precker
Jessie D. Read
Mary Gindhart Herbert Roebling
Ida Cohen Rosenthal
Anne Ryan
Margery Austen Ryerson
Winifred Loeb Saltzman
Katherine Schaub
Vera Schectman
Antoinette Quinby Scudder
Lenora Susan Slaughter
Cora Peterson Smith
Florence Tenney Starkey
Mildred Fairbanks Stone
Ruth Cheney Streeter
Miriam Van Arsdale Studley
Edythe Lois Sydnor
Toshiko Takaezu
Clara Mae Taylor
Mary Wolfe Thompson
Agnes Sligh Turnbull
Concepción Valdés-Muñoz
Marjorie Schuyler Van Ness
Astrid Varnay
Grace J. Vogt
Florence Emeline Wall
Harriet Ware
Sara Spencer Washington
Viola Gertrude Wells
Cynthia Westcott
Katharine Elkus White
Phyllis A. Whitney
Madaline Worthy Williams

Theresa Louise Martens Wilson
Evelyn Maisel Witkin
Deborah Cannon Partridge Wolfe
Edith Elmer Wood
Constance Oneida Williams Woodruff
Regina Jones Woody
Marion Manola Thompson Wright
Florence Lydia McEnally Zuck
Susanna Weare Peirce Zwemer

*Abbreviated Biographies*

Elizabeth Harker Elmer
Irene Taylor Fallon
Sarah E. La Salle Jones
Annie Oakley
Sarah E. Strickland

# INDEX

This is both a subject index and an index of persons' names, geographic locations, institutions and organizations. In general, a reference is indexed only if it leads the reader to substantive information on a woman in the volume. Casual references to people, places, institutions, or organizations are not indexed.

Entries for geographic locations, institutions, and organizations focus specifically on those within New Jersey. Entries for institutions and organizations refer to founders, executive officers, and those with a more substantive involvement than membership alone.

Entries relating to career fields refer to women who devoted a significant portion of their working lives to that field. Not indexed, due to their large number, are references to homemaking, child care, and home nursing which nearly every woman performed in addition to her other achievements. The name of a woman appears in the listing of more than one career field when her working life was varied.

Entries relating to religious affiliation contain references only to women with a substantive involvement with a denomination. Entries relating to ethnicity refer to immigrants, daughters of immigrants and those whose lives were explicitly involved with their ethnic affiliation.

Page references for photographs are printed in italics.